The Science of Romantic Relationships

Why do people fall in love? Does passion fade with time? What makes for a happy, healthy relationship? This introduction to relationship science follows the lifecycle of a relationship – from attraction and initiation, to the hard work of relationship maintenance, to dissolution and ways to strengthen a relationship. Designed for advanced undergraduates studying psychology, communication, or family studies, this textbook presents a fresh, diversity-infused approach to relationship science. It includes real-world examples and critical-thinking questions, callout boxes that challenge students to make connections, and researcher interviews that showcase the many career paths of relationship scientists. Article Spotlights reveal cutting-edge methods, while Diversity and Inclusion boxes celebrate the variety found in human love and connection. Throughout the book, students see the application of theory and come to recognize universal themes in relationships as well as the nuances of many findings. Instructors can access lecture slides, an instructor manual, and test banks.

Theresa DiDonato is a professor of psychology at Loyola University Maryland, where she has served as the Director of the Undergraduate Program in Psychology. She volunteers on the Teaching Committee of the International Association of Relationship Research (IARR) and is a long-time member of SPSP. Her research focuses on humor, attraction, and self-authenticity in relationships, and she is the author of the Psychology Today blog, "Meet, Catch, and Keep," which has accrued over 30 million views.

Brett Jakubiak is an associate professor of psychology at Syracuse University and won the Syracuse University Meredith Early Performance Award for exemplary teaching. Brett also maintains an active program of research focused on the interpersonal support processes that regulate stress, encourage autonomous goal pursuit, and enhance relationship quality across the lifespan. This research has been funded by the National Science Foundation and the National Institutes of Health.

"What is really fabulous about this book are the many real-world examples of people's lives that help us situate these concepts into diverse contexts. Didonato and Jakubiak give us a textbook that expertly explains the foundational theories of relationship science while providing critical updates in line with contemporary thinking. It is a book that multidisciplinary learners, as well as established experts, will truly find valuable for their lives and work."

Joan K. Monin, Yale University

"In addition to being a thorough examination of the literature, *The Science of Romantic Relationships* is an engaging and enjoyable-to-read textbook that will connect with students. I particularly liked the thought-provoking questions that open each chapter, the spotlights on empirical articles that emphasize the importance of research, and the focus on diversity and inclusion."

Kevin P. McIntyre, Trinity University

"DiDonato and Jakubiak have produced a truly remarkable resource for relationship scientists. The centerpiece of this masterful text is its careful and methodical approach to understanding diversity, equity, and inclusion. This book will be a game changer for the field!"

Brian G. Ogolsky, University of Illinois at Urbana-Champaign

"This textbook breathes new life into relationship research by providing a diverse array of fresh perspectives on everything from romantic attraction and relationship initiation to relationship maintenance and dissolution. Their commitment to diversity and inclusion is especially laudable. In addition to covering all aspects of modern relationship science, the authors provide a strong chapter on state-of-the-art research methods. This is an ideal textbook for students or anyone seeking an up-to-date, comprehensive overview of scientific research on relationships and the theories that guide it."

Gregory D. Webster, University of Florida

The Science of Romantic Relationships

THERESA DIDONATO
Loyola University Maryland

BRETT JAKUBIAK
Syracuse University

CAMBRIDGE
UNIVERSITY PRESS

Shaftesbury Road, Cambridge CB2 8EA, United Kingdom

One Liberty Plaza, 20th Floor, New York, NY 10006, USA

477 Williamstown Road, Port Melbourne, VIC 3207, Australia

314–321, 3rd Floor, Plot 3, Splendor Forum, Jasola District Centre, New Delhi – 110025, India

103 Penang Road, #05–06/07, Visioncrest Commercial, Singapore 238467

Cambridge University Press is part of Cambridge University Press & Assessment,
a department of the University of Cambridge.

We share the University's mission to contribute to society through the pursuit of
education, learning and research at the highest international levels of excellence.

www.cambridge.org
Information on this title: www.cambridge.org/highereducation/isbn/9781108841603

DOI: 10.1017/9781108894388

First published 2024

A catalogue record for this publication is available from the British Library.

Library of Congress Cataloging-in-Publication Data
Names: DiDonato, Theresa, 1979– author. | Jakubiak, Brett, 1988- author.
Title: The science of romantic relationships / Theresa DiDonato, Loyola University, Maryland, Brett Jakubiak,
    Syracuse University.
Description: Cambridge, United Kingdom ; New York, NY : Cambridge University Press, 2024. | Includes
    bibliographical references and index.
Identifiers: LCCN 2022060658 (print) | LCCN 2022060659 (ebook) | ISBN 9781108841603 (hardback) |
    ISBN 9781108794961 (paperback) | ISBN 9781108894388 (epub)
Subjects: LCSH: Man-woman relationships. | Interpersonal relations. | Social psychology.
Classification: LCC HQ801 .D5343 2024 (print) | LCC HQ801 (ebook) | DDC 306.7–dc23/eng/20230119
LC record available at https://lccn.loc.gov/2022060658
LC ebook record available at https://lccn.loc.gov/2022060659

ISBN 978-1-108-84160-3 Hardback
ISBN 978-1-108-79496-1 Paperback

Additional resources for this publication at www.cambridge.org/romantic-relationships

For Patrick

For Emily

BRIEF CONTENTS

DETAILED CONTENTS

ABOUT THIS BOOK: FOR INSTRUCTORS

In this book, we use students' curiosity as a springboard to provide a fresh and focused introduction to the guiding theories, key concepts, and recent findings that shape the interdisciplinary field of relationship science. We frame the textbook by first introducing foundational relationship concepts, highlighting prominent relationship theories, and reviewing research methods particular to relationship science. We then proceed step by step through the life course of a relationship. This intuitive organization provides a natural progression to your course syllabus over a semester. Throughout the text, we use relatable language, vivid examples, and thought-provoking questions so that students can acknowledge their current beliefs and see them anew given the current evidence. We pay attention to diverse representations of relationships and infuse modern topics and trends throughout (e.g., the role of technology in building, sustaining, and undermining relationships). By addressing contemporary topics and questions while emphasizing critical thinking, this textbook encourages sustained engagement with the material, which translates into more interesting classroom discussions, more compelling term paper topic proposals, and more insightful questions asked during lectures.

Who Is This Book for?

This book is appropriate for advanced undergraduate students. We ask little of our reader, other than a basic understanding of psychology (experience with research methods is a bonus). The book engages generalists in thinking about relationships, while providing sufficient rigor and depth for those students who are seeking specialized expertise in romantic relationships. We accomplish this goal by inserting engaging pedagogical features throughout the book (see list below), as well as appropriate scaffolding for students' first exploration into relationship science. By meeting students where they are, this textbook teaches students more than knowledge about relationship science: it gives students the tools to think critically about relationship information relayed to them in the news, media, online, or in their social circles.

Guiding Teaching Philosophy

From its first pages until the end, this book energizes students' critical thinking about relationships. Students progress away from the idea that love is mysterious and toward the notion that relationships are predictable (if complex), logical, and capable of being understood through the lens of science. In writing this textbook, we drew on years of experience teaching the science of romantic relationships, our contagious passion for relationship science, and a pedagogical philosophy grounded on these four principles:
1. Students are innately curious about relationships and variations in the human experience.

2. Students retain knowledge when they connect the material they are learning to their own lives.

3. Students develop sophisticated habits of thinking when they are challenged to question simple answers to complex questions.

4. Students become life-long learners when they discover the value of research and gain skills in critically evaluating research.

Chapter Organization and Content Highlights

This book supports student learning through its overarching organization and the key ideas that it highlights throughout the text.

- **Intuitive Organization.** We often form, maintain, and dissolve relationships: why not have a book that follows this trajectory? As shown in Figure P.1, we organized this book along the life course of a relationship. Our students love this organization because they have a ready framework on which to map their growing knowledge. As instructors, we value having an intuitive organization for a semester-long syllabus on relationships.

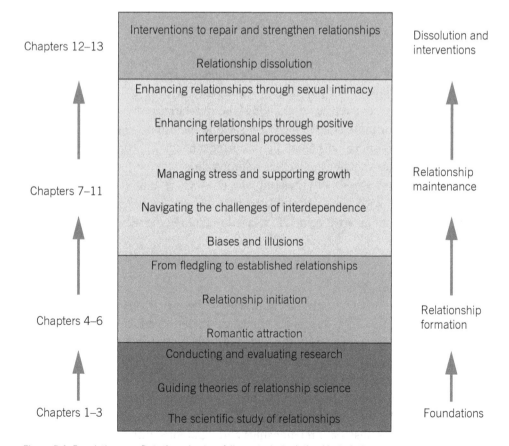

Figure P.1 Foundations are first, then chapters follow a typical relationship trajectory.

- **Honoring Human Diversity.** We embed human diversity throughout this book, featuring discussions of gender, sexual orientation, race, and culture in each chapter. This celebrates the natural variety in relationship representations and experiences.
- **Emphasizing Context.** Contextual factors can come in many forms, including culture, socioeconomic status, and social networks (e.g., friends, family), and these factors contribute to relationship experiences in profound ways. As much as we attend to person and relationship factors, this book also highlights the role of context in shaping our relationships – a quiet force that is easy to overlook, but one that students benefit from attending to as they think about relationships.
- **Noting Contemporary Issues.** This textbook grapples with the most pressing issues facing modern-day relationships and relationship scientists. To mention a few, we discuss consensually non-monogamous relationships, singlehood as an alternative to partnering, changing marriage and divorce rates, and ways the Internet continues to affect dating (e.g., technoference, catfishing). Along with many other current topics, we also provide a contemporary consideration of the science of relationships, including consideration of questionable research practices and the benefits of Open Science.
- **Valuing Social Support**. All relationship textbooks touch upon social support, but ours provides a special emphasis on the topic, dedicating Chapter 9 to developing students' understanding of support.
- **Paying Attention to Relationship Transitions.** Typically, students – who are often in a period of heightened transition – love to think about turning points and pivotal moments in a relationship's trajectory. We do, too. Accordingly, this book discusses significant relationship transitions (e.g., cohabitation, marriage, parenthood), and how transitions alter interdependence.
- **Highlighting Self-Concept Change.** How relationships shape the self-concept, and how the self-concept shapes relationships, is gaining attention in the field for good reason: so much of who we are is tied to our relationship experiences. In discussing how relationships form, persist, or end, this textbook elevates the interplay between self and relationships. Doing so is appreciated by our students, many of whom are deeply engaged in identity development.

Key Features

We include a set of pedagogical features to enhance engagement, connect relationship science with students' experience, and offer paths for furthering knowledge on specific topics.

- **Opening Vignettes**. Each chapter begins with a compelling story about a person or relationship designed to prime students' interest in the chapter's focus. These vignettes represent people with different backgrounds, relationships structures, goals, and sociocultural contexts, showing diversity in how relationships are experienced.
- **Guiding Questions and Major Take-Aways**. We capture and focus students' curiosity at the beginning of each chapter with a set of focal questions. These questions represent learning aims for the students; a successful read of the chapter yields sophisticated

answers to these questions. At the end of each chapter, brief statements summarize important lessons covered. These serve as important learning checks for students.

- **Diversity and Inclusion Boxes.** These segments foster awareness and critical thinking by directing students' attention to research on under-studied populations, minority relationship structures, and/or issues related to the generalizability of specific findings. Examples include:
  - the need to apply an intersectional lens in the study of relationships (Chapter 1);
  - the problem of White supremacist beauty ideals and the negative effects of colorism (Chapter 4);
  - mental health and positive relationship illusions (Chapter 7); and
  - asexuality and living-apart-together relationships (Chapters 11 and 6).
- **Researcher Spotlights.** How does someone end up studying relationships as their profession? In these boxes, students can read first-hand accounts of the diverse career paths of several of today's influential relationship researchers. Researchers from varied disciplines and in various stages of their careers share their perspective on the field, explain why they study romantic relationships, and discuss the inspirations and challenges they encounter as researchers.
- **In-the-News Boxes.** Helping students make connections is a key goal of this textbook. Accordingly, we include callout boxes that reinforce specific concepts through discussion of real-world events (e.g., COVID-19, #MeToo). Students see the relevance of relationship science through these highlights and gain skills in using relationship science to understand current events.
- **Article Spotlights.** Each spotlight focuses on one research study carefully selected because it both (1) extends students' understanding of an aspect of relationships and (2) showcases an interesting method, design, or analytic procedure. This value-added feature provides helpful depth to our introduction of relationship science and promotes skill development by supporting research literacy.
- **"Is This True for You?"** In each chapter, we present current research and invite students to reflect on whether the results match their intuition or experiences. When they do not, students can consider explanations for why their individual experiences might differ.
- **Further Readings.** We offer a curated list of accessible review and empirical papers at the end of each chapter. Each article can serve as a jumping-off point for independent research into specific topics, and we offer an "If you are interested in . . ." guide to help students pursue their curiosities.

Instructor Resources

There is no one "right" way to teach a course on relationships. Accordingly, we provide a set of tools that can be flexibly applied to meet the diverse needs of our instructors.

- **Lecture slides**. These PowerPoint slides will accompany and extend the material from the textbook, serving as a wonderful resource for novice and experienced instructors alike. They correspond with each chapter's material, while also offering discussion points, classroom activity opportunities, and conversation starters.

- **Instructor Manual**. Instructors can customize their relationship course using the high-impact practices and experiential learning opportunities presented in this Instructor Manual. In addition to classroom activities and discussion ideas, this manual provides instructors with an expanded outline that maps to the lecture slides to facilitate lecture presentations. It also contains essay questions for each chapter, as well as assignment ideas and paper writing prompts.
- **Sample syllabus**. Instructors step into teaching from this book with all they might need to hit the ground running. A sample syllabus offers a plan for a typical semester, which includes pacing as well as assigned reading, assignments, and assessments.
- **Test bank**. We offer instructors a carefully developed test bank that includes auto-graded multiple-choice questions – an MCQ test bank. These tests will be available as LMS-ready cartridges. Emphasis is on assessing students' concept understanding, critical thinking, and concept application.

Why do people fall in love? Is passion only for new relationships, or can it last? What, in fact, makes for a happy, healthy relationship? If you have ever pondered these, or similar, questions, then you're in the right place, and we're glad you're here. Welcome to the exciting world of relationship science!

Relationship science is an interdisciplinary field that submits our beliefs and questions about relationships to rigorous empirical scrutiny. It is a field that relies on theory-driven hypothesis testing, systematic data collection, and careful analysis in order to build a reliable body of evidence that we can use as our basis for understanding relationships. Study after study, relationship scientists are at the frontlines: observing marital conflicts and measuring physiological reactivity, analyzing flirting behavior on Tinder, querying volunteers about their feelings toward their ex-partners ... the list goes on and on. An initial study might provide tentative insight, but when multiple studies point to a consistent view of relationship factors or dynamics, the findings warrant attention. Knowledge grows, allowing scholars to ask new, more nuanced questions. This cycle keeps relationship science moving forward, and we gain an increasingly more complete and accurate understanding of relationships.

This Book Will Help You Rely on Science to Understand Relationships

As scholars and scientists, we – your authors – are passionate about the research process underlying relationship science. Accordingly, we designed this book to highlight the field's scientific foundations and many of its cutting-edge frontiers. We lean on meta-analyses, well-powered studies, well-established (i.e., reproduced) findings, and research using diverse samples, to do so. At the same time, as much as we are scientists, we – like you – are also ordinary people living our daily lives in our own romantic relationships, with friends and loved ones doing the same. From this perspective, we know it can be challenging to suspend intuition when it runs counter to empirical findings. This text will meet you where you are and help you grow in your appreciation for the importance of basing relationship knowledge on scientific evidence.

You Will Discover How Critical Diversity and Context Are for Relationships

Relationship science is concerned with all types of relationships, but this book focuses specifically on romantic relationships, which are generally regarded as our closest and most influential relationships. Romantic relationships often play a critical role in our health and well-being, shape our decisions and emotions, and tie into our sense of self. These typical features of romantic relationships emerge even as each relationship is beautifully original, emerging from unique partners and their unique partnership. Indeed, diversity is a key feature of romantic relationships. Asking when particular theories and findings do and do not apply is a critical task for a relationship scientist (even a novice relationship scientist). We encourage this questioning and point out known boundaries to existing findings whenever possible. We also recognize that every relationship occurs within a specific context that can either support or inhibit the relationship. Accordingly, this textbook introduces romantic relationships by emphasizing human diversity and context (which often go hand in hand). We infuse diversity and contextual factors throughout each chapter so that these considerations stay at the forefront as you learn.

The Journey Begins

A college course on relationships is your chance to gain insight into what many people think is a mysterious phenomenon. You will discover that relationships are not so much mysterious as just complex outcomes of situational, personal, and relational factors, which in turn play a major role in shaping our lives. As your companion on this journey, this textbook offers the theoretical tools and empirical insights to form a nuanced understanding of a fundamental component of the human experience. Some of what you will learn will confirm your intuitions, and other material may challenge long-held ideas about attraction, attachment, or why relationships end. We ask that you approach this book with an open mind. Get ready for some fun!

ACKNOWLEDGEMENTS

My work on this book would not have been possible without the support, sacrifices, and good humor of my amazing husband Patrick. Thank you, Pat; I love you! A heartfelt thank you also to my trusty sidekick Braeden for his encouragement ("You can do it, Mommy!") and motivation ("Are you done with that book yet?").

I am deeply indebted to my mom and dad for a lifetime of love; to Alicia, Dwane, Mike, and Jen for cheering me on; and to my family-in-law – Eileen and John – for being part of this book-writing journey.

Friends make life easier when you're tackling big goals. Many thanks to my book club (a dozen years and counting!); my Stoneham sisters; Karen and Aaron; Andrea; my Loyola colleagues-turned-friends; and my friends-turned-family here in the mid-Atlantic (you know who you are!). Thank you for being there for me in a million different ways during this process.

I know I would not be in a position to write a book, a process that I have loved deeply, if it were not for Steven Schiavo of Wellesley College and Joachim Krueger of Brown University. Thank you both for your mentorship and for giving me the freedom to discover my academic passions. I also wish to thank my students for inspiring me, for teaching me, and for test-driving this book. Lastly, and with the greatest enthusiasm, thank you to Brett, for (against your better judgment) taking my phone calls.

Theresa

They say, "if you can read this, thank a teacher," so imagine how many teachers an author needs to thank. I am grateful to my mom, my first teacher, for stoking my passion for learning and for sharing what I've learned with others. I am grateful to Theresa (my college professor turned friend turned co-author) for introducing me to relationships research and changing my career trajectory. I am grateful to my doctorate advisor, Brooke Feeney, for providing rigorous research training and balancing it with a healthy dose of encouragement. And I am grateful to my students, who have proven to be some of my most important teachers.

I am also immensely grateful to my parents, whose sacrifices made my path easier and made this book possible. Thank you to my Grammy for dreaming big for me. You said one day we'd rent a cabin in Maine while I wrote my great novel . . . this isn't a novel, but writing in snowy Syracuse felt an awful lot like Maine. Thank you to my Loyola crew for your steady friendship and to my Syracuse friends for helping me feel at home in a new town. And finally, thank you to my wife, Emily, who has shown me the enormous blessing of having a loving partnership and has inspired me to learn (and then write about) every possible way to maintain it.

Brett

Projects like these do not happen without behind-the-scenes support. Thank you Maureen Dormer, Grace DeTommaso, and Audrey O'Neill for helping with the glossary and Mike and

Jen DiDonato for reading early drafts. We gratefully acknowledge our editor Janka Romero, for taking a chance on us. We also thank Jane Adams, Emily Watton, and Rachel Norridge who managed our many questions as novice authors and helped to bring this book to fruition. We're so grateful to the team at Cambridge University Press for the immense amount of work that made this book possible.

Theresa and Brett

PART I

FOUNDATIONAL IDEAS OF RELATIONSHIP SCIENCE

1 THE SCIENTIFIC STUDY OF RELATIONSHIPS

The Uniqueness and Universality of Relationships

Reginald ("Reg") Kenneth Dwight, born in Pinner, England in 1947, suffered a lonely and difficult childhood. As he later wrote, "My dad was strict and remote and had a terrible temper; my mum was argumentative and prone to dark moods. When they were together, all I can remember are icy silences or screaming rows" (John, 2019). To escape this stressful home life, Reg found refuge playing his grandmother's piano, and his musical genius emerged quickly. As his parents' marriage fell apart (they divorced when he was 13), Reg's future in music began to take shape. Soon, Reg – the man we now know as Elton John – hit the world scene. With popular songs and a reputation for brilliant, wildly theatrical perform-ances, Elton John was singing, playing, and hand-standing his way toward mega-star status. His love life, however, was on unsolid ground. Elton John's relationships, be they with women or men, never lasted, despite his desire for a long-term commitment.

Hoping to change his relationship patterns, Elton John proposed to Renate Blauel, the woman who would become his wife on Valentine's Day in 1984. Despite an auspicious date for a wedding, this marriage had a rocky run, not made easier by Elton John's alcohol and drug addiction. After four years together, the couple divorced. Later, in 1993, the now sober Elton John met Canadian-born David Furnish, an advertising executive fifteen years his junior, and felt an immediate attraction to David's maturity and independence. Observers noted how David embraced Elton John's lifestyle, fame, and public image in a way that previous partners had not. After twelve years together, Elton John and David Furnish affirmed their commitment in a Civil Partnership Ceremony on December 21, 2005, the day Great Britain recognized same-sex couples as having many of the same rights as married different-sex couples. Since then, they have welcomed two children into their family (see Figure 1.1). "Our love has grown stronger and stronger," Elton John stated in a public interview, adding, "you have to work at it" (Kimble, 2017).

Elton John's romantic relationship experiences are at once both unique and universal. They are unique because they reflect the specifics of his personality and personal history intersecting with those of his chosen partners, and they exist within the specific sociocultural context of his international fame in England in the late 1900s. Yet, Elton John's motivation to find love, and the highs and lows on that journey, are also quite universal. Even though relationship experiences are idiosyncratic, we can see consistent patterns in how they form, how their dynamics take shape, and how these relationship dynamics affect the partners' well-being. In other words, all relationships share critical commonalities and predictable differences that make them a rich topic to study empirically.

(a) (b)

Figure 1.1 Elton John and Renate Blauel celebrating their 1984 Valentine's Day wedding (a); David Furnish and Elton John with their two children (b). Why do some relationships flourish while others do not? (Photo: Patrick Riviere / Hulton Archive / Getty Images [a] and Michael Kovac / Getty Images Entertainment [b])

This chapter will introduce you to the exciting world of relationship science. You will learn about the human drive for belonging, how we define and categorize relationships, and why relationships are critically important. Your goal in this chapter is to gain appreciation for aspects of relationships that are common across people and the diverse ways that people can experience their relationships.

 GUIDING QUESTIONS

Consider these questions as you read this chapter:
- What is relationship science?
- What is a romantic relationship?
- Why do people need relationships?
- How do relationships contribute to psychological and physical health?

Relationship Science

What questions come to mind when you think about Elton John's relationships? What questions do you have about your own relationships? Relationships are central to our lives, yet we often feel they are mysterious, random, or impossible to predict. Quite on the contrary. As you will see, although early relationship scientists encountered considerable skepticism, the science of relationships today is a flourishing field that has produced extraordinary and important insights into all aspects of human relationships. Let's start at the beginning.

Early Attempts to Study Relationships Scientifically

Rigorous scientific inquiry takes resources. You need lab space, equipment, and technology; education, training, and expertise; and participants willing to offer their time, trust, and information. Plus, when scientists focus on one question, they do so at the expense of investigating other questions; funding that supports one line of inquiry deprives a different line of inquiry. Any research endeavor, therefore, should be worth all the investment. Are relationships worth it? Should we commit resources to the theoretical and empirical study of relationships?

Historically, not everyone has thought so. Take, for example, William Proxmire, a former US Senator from Wisconsin. Senator Proxmire created the notorious Golden Fleece Awards, ironic honors he bestowed to government agencies when they engaged in what he judged as wasteful spending of taxpayer money. In March 1975, Senator Proxmire presented his inaugural Golden Fleece Award to the National Science Foundation (NSF) for giving $84,000 of grant money to support one of the first scientific investigations of love. Research on love, he argued, was an obvious waste of money.

The fallout from Proxmire's "award" was swift and consequential for the pioneering scientists studying relationships. Elaine Hatfield, the principal investigator of the awarded NSF grant, became the main target (Hatfield, 2006). The press derided her work, and she received threatening mail by the bagful. While some people stood steadily in her corner, the majority seemed ready to relegate the study of love permanently to poets and philosophers. A magazine took an informal poll and only 12.5 percent of readers were in favor of applying the scientific method to a study of romantic love (Hatfield, 2006). The Golden Fleece Award also shined its unwelcomed spotlight on Ellen Berscheid, who joined Hatfield as a polarizing figure, but a visionary scientist whose research and writings were laying the groundwork for decades of future research (Reis et al., 2013). The Golden Fleece Award proved to be a serious setback for the scientific study of love and relationships, but on account of Berscheid's and Hatfield's work, which gained increasing traction in the 1980s and 1990s, relationship research would nevertheless soon coalesce into what we now recognize as **relationship science**.

 RESEARCHER SPOTLIGHT: Elaine Hatfield, PhD

How did you become a relationship scientist?
In 1962, I realized that, in the daytime, all my pals, who were working with Gordon Bower, worked with rats in a runway, constructing math models, but in the evening, we complained about our romantic lives. When I suggested we might conduct research on love, I received mockery. When I suggested the same thing to Leon Festinger's research group, they were equally mocking. But, of course, I went ahead. Today, thousands of researchers work on this topic.

How did you stay motivated during your career and what did you enjoy?
One of the ways I stayed motivated was to always work on several topics at once, so when one failed I was optimistic about others. As for what I enjoyed, I very much enjoyed working with colleagues and with students, and I love research.

Figure 1.2 Dr. Elaine Hatfield is a professor of Psychology at the University of Hawai'i. (Photo courtesy of Elaine Hatfield, PhD.)

What makes for a good relationship scientist and what's next for the field?
To me, curiosity is a quality that makes for a great relationship scientist. In the future, I would love to see the field of relationship science expand to include more cross-cultural research.

Relationship Science Today

Relationship science today is a vibrant, thriving academic discipline. The last decade alone saw 1.5 million publications relating to romantic relationships (Sharkey et al., 2022); clearly, what Hatfield (2006) once termed, "l'affaire Proxmire" is history. Today, relationship science is an interdisciplinary field devoted to understanding all aspects of human relationships. Its central goals are to (1) describe relationship dynamics (i.e., relationship-relevant thoughts, emotions, and behaviors) and (2) identify the precursors and predict the consequences of these relationship dynamics. Regarding the second goal, being able to see what leads to, and results from, certain dynamics gives us a chance to differentiate the healthy processes from those that are less adaptive. Research into these questions can reveal how joining, participating, or leaving a relationship affects individuals, their broader social network, and society at large. In addition to basic research goals, that is, gaining knowledge about relationships for the sake of understanding, some relationship scientists also conduct applied research, which is designed to inform interventions to improve relationship dynamics.

Relationship researchers have the challenging job of demystifying complex interpersonal dynamics. Dyadic relationships – those relationships between two people – contain several sources of information and influence. Each individual brings their own personality, history, and goals into the relationship. Through these factors, dyad-members influence each other bidirectionally. For example, Elton John's touring lifestyle impacted each of his partners, and his partners' unique personalities similarly impacted Elton John's experiences. An additional, albeit invisible, player that influences and is influenced by each partner is the relationship itself. Every relationship develops its own identity and is therefore greater than the sum of its parts (i.e., the partners). In relationships defined by more than two partners, the same principles apply, but in a triadic, quadratic, or other (you get the picture) structure. Further, as we will discuss in a moment, each relationship is situated in a broader context that has a role in shaping partners and the relationship. This complexity is one reason that relationship science is so interesting and offers so many opportunities to explore meaningful questions.

Since the early work of Berscheid and Hatfield, relationship science has flourished, profiting from its multidisciplinary nature. Fields like the biomedical sciences, anthropology, communication, gerontology, philosophy, education, and economics join the more dominant voices of psychology (e.g., social, personality, evolutionary, clinical/counseling, cognitive), behavioral neuroscience, human development, and family sciences to round out what we currently know about human relationships. These multiple voices make a difference. A study of passionate love within romantic relationships, for example, can be advanced by knowing the neurochemical underpinnings of emotion, by examining cultural differences in expressions of love, by considering love as an adaptation that promotes bonding, and by documenting how passion changes over the life course. Each discipline offers important insights that help reveal more about human relationships.

(a)   (b)

Figure 1.3 The importance of recognizing the significance of context and diversity is abundantly clear when we think about commitment-related rituals that occur cross-culturally. Every sociocultural context, for example, provides constraints and opportunities that influence the way in which people express their romantic interests, form relationships, and live out their relationships. (Photo: PeopleImages / iStock / Getty Images Plus [a] and Rawpixel / iStock / Getty Images Plus [b])

Current Directions in Relationship Science

Having accumulated a basic understanding of how relationships are built, experienced, and broken, the field of relationship science is now digging deeper. Its questions are becoming more nuanced and specialized. For example, relationship scientists are now identifying boundary conditions for established effects (e.g., when is a friend's support no longer beneficial?) and revealing intermediary factors that explain relationship outcomes (e.g., is support beneficial *because* it communicates affection?). They are asking directional questions to differentiate causal forces from outcomes, and they are zeroing in on differences between laboratory-established patterns and how people experience relationship events in real life (e.g., do people actually choose romantic partners who have the traits that they say they want?). New ways to access data (e.g., Big Data) and advanced analytic methods (e.g., machine learning) are further energizing the field.

Relationship scientists are also moving the field toward a greater focus on context and diversity. Context refers to the setting, framework, or environment in which something occurs. It is both difficult to notice and incredibly influential, and while context is not a new focus, it has new energy today (Schoebi & Campos, 2019). After all, imagine what Elton John's relationship with his husband would be like if they fell in love in another culture (e.g., Russia, Nigeria) or during another time (e.g., 100 years ago, 50 years from now)? Relationships are clearly fundamentally tethered to their contexts. They are also inherently diverse. On account of its increasing attention to relationship diversity, relationship science is on the verge of an inclusion revolution. We will return to this important idea in detail, later in this chapter.

The Need to Belong

Could you imagine a life with zero social relationships? No one to look at; no one to think about; no one to talk to you; no one to touch you. Prolonged aloneness is such a strange and terrifying idea that it regularly captures screenwriters' attention (e.g., *The Martian, Cast Away*, and *Gravity*), but we do not need to go to outer space or a remote desert island to realize how critical social interactions are to our well-being. Consider what happens to your thoughts and emotions when you accidentally offend a friend; when your romantic partner will not hold your hand; or when someone you care about does not text you back.

The Damaging Effects of Social Isolation and Exclusion

As humans, we are deeply social creatures. From infancy to old age, the profoundly negative psychological, emotional, cognitive, behavioral, and physical outcomes of neglect or a lack of social connection underscores how much we need other people (Cornwell & Waite, 2009; Hildyard & Wolfe, 2002). The consequences of isolation are even more dire when people are subjected to social exclusion, a state of emotional or physical separation from others which is perceived as intentional and punitive (Wesselmann et al., 2016). Consider solitary confinement, a form of social exclusion used in the prison system and widely judged as a form of torture. Solitary confinement typically involves separating an inmate from the general prison population for 22 to 24 hours a day for at least fifteen consecutive days (Resnik et al., 2018). As shown in Figure 1.4, some solitary confinement sentences span months, even years. National survey data show that over 60,000 inmates in the United States, a number equivalent to approximately every resident in Santa Cruz, California, or every resident of Grand Junction, Colorado, are living their day-to-day life in solitary confinement. This group has over-representation of Black men and Black women, relative to their proportion in the general prison population.

As you might expect, the psychological toll of solitary confinement is considerable. Quantitative and qualitative data show higher rates of depression and anxiety in solitary confinement prisoners compared with the general inmate population, and substantial numbers of people in solitary confinement report significant psychological distress, serious mental illness, self-harm attempts, and suicide attempts (Reiter et al., 2020). These associations do not demonstrate that solitary confinement *causes* these outcomes, as mental health

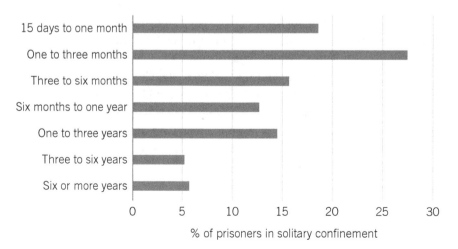

Figure 1.4 The percentage of inmates in solitary confinement by duration of confinement in thirty-three jurisdictions, inclusive of over 31,000 inmates. (Source: Adapted with permission from Bertsch et al. [2020])

issues or psychopathology may factor into receiving solitary confinement sentences, yet individuals in solitary confinement experience it as unnatural and psychologically challenging. Said one inmate, "It's dehumanizing. No human contact. As [a] human being, I feel like we're meant to socialize, and it [has] an effect on your mentality while you're sitting in the cell" (Reiter et al., 2020, p. 559).

Are we "meant to socialize" like this inmate suggests? Yes. According to the **belongingness hypothesis**, people have an innate, fundamental motivation to form, maintain, and keep close interpersonal connections (Baumeister & Leary, 1995). This motivation is presumed to drive all people, regardless of gender, sexual orientation, culture, or other differentiating factors. It suggests that in the same way humans require sleep, food, and water, they also have a basic requirement for satisfying relationships on which their thriving, and indeed their survival, depends.

  IN THE NEWS

Social Distancing and COVID-19

What was it like for you when, in 2020, your daily social interactions experienced an abrupt change? Recall how COVID-19 ("Coronavirus"), a highly contagious and potentially deadly respiratory virus, threatened to overwhelm healthcare systems, leading governments to require that people practice *social distancing*. Social distancing involves physically spacing oneself from others (e.g., by six feet). Overnight, businesses closed their offices and shifted to tele-communication, students transitioned to online learning, people stopped traveling, and, in many areas, gatherings of more than ten people were prohibited. People accustomed to interacting with dozens of people over the course of a day were now engaging in very few in-person conversations, if any at all (Figure 1.5).

As you might expect from the belongingness hypothesis, many people found this new reality incredibly difficult, with some failing to resist the urge to gather and others finding refuge in virtual communication. Public service announcements emphasized that social distancing need not result in social disconnection, but widespread difficulties with social isolation led public health campaigns to focus on preventing loneliness, fostering relationships, and maintaining psychological health. The heavy burden of navigating months of constrained social interactions highlights how ingrained the need to belong is in human psychology.

Figure 1.5 In what ways do virtual conversations help fulfill your belonging needs and how do they fall short? (Photo: Oscar Wong / Moment / Getty Images)

Locating belonging as a fundamental need implies that it is a universal human feature, one that is etched into the very basic biological and psychological systems that define being human. As such, the need to belong likely reflects an evolutionary past in which being with other people conferred critical advantages for reproduction and survival. Think about it: children who formed attachments with their parents (and their parents with them) may have enjoyed better odds of survival; people motivated to stay with their sexual partners may have shepherded more children safely toward adulthood; people compelled to live in groups (e.g., families, communities) may have benefited from greater safety, cooperative problem solving, and resource sharing, not to mention having others around to care for them when they were sick or injured. The motivation to be with other people likely provided our ancestors with such an impressive array of benefits that it ultimately became a dominating characteristic of those who survived and reproduced. Over time, the need to belong was thus engineered as a core human drive.

The Importance of Social Acceptance

Aloneness is appealing at times, but healthy and well-adjusted people tend to immensely value their relationships. Relationships provide people with the feeling of **social acceptance**, which helps fulfill their belongingness needs (Leary, 2010). Social acceptance is inherently rewarding and much more desired than its painful counterpoint, social exclusion (DeWall & Bushman, 2011). Consider Figure 1.6. Recall that social exclusion

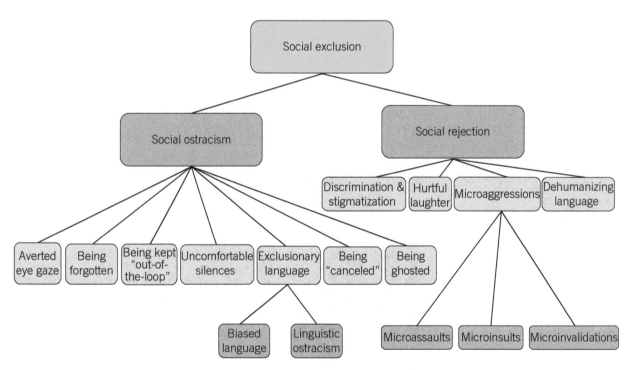

Figure 1.6 A taxonomy of social exclusion. Which types of social exclusion have you experienced or enacted against others? (Source: Drawn based on data in part from Wesselmann et al. [2016])

is an experience of feeling separated from others. Social exclusion can occur through social rejection, when people direct negative attention (e.g., insults, microaggressions, or hurtful laughter) toward a specific person, or through social ostracism, when people actively or passively ignore someone (Wesselmann et al., 2016). Social rejection and social ostracism, like social acceptance, can be dramatic or subtle; but unlike social acceptance, they are highly aversive and unpleasant. Their bitter taste (DeWall & Bushman, 2011) may be part of an ingrained system that keeps us sensitive to any potential signs that our connections are shaky or in danger, and keeps us oriented toward re-establishing social connections.

The belongingness hypothesis allows for some fascinating predictions. If, in fact, belonging evolved to be a fundamental need, we should see a cascade of adverse consequences across all areas of human psychology when this need is not met. In the same way that sleep-deprived people suffer cognitively, emotionally, and behaviorally, so too should socially deprived individuals. This is, indeed, what scientists have observed. As shown in Figure 1.7, after social rejection, people think less clearly, perform worse on tasks, and suffer pain, distress, sorrow, and anger. Further, just as our brains crave restorative REM (rapid eye movement) sleep after sleep deprivation, the belongingness hypothesis contends that we should yearn for relationships and enact behaviors to re-establish human connection when deprived. Indeed, when belongingness needs are threatened, people are especially motivated to affiliate, that is, to be near and to interact with others.

A growing body of research supports the predictions of the belongingness hypothesis, as shown in Table 1.1, furthering the notion that the need to belong is a basic motivation. One highlight from this research is that self-esteem, or people's general feeling of self-worth, often serves as an index of how well their belonging needs are being met (Leary & Baumeister, 2000). Sociometer theory anchors self-esteem to interpersonal relationships, suggesting that people perceive themselves positively when they are socially connected and negatively when they lack sufficient social connection. To tie such a fundamental judgment as one's own worth to feeling connected underscores the critical importance of belonging.

The belongingness hypothesis contends that we direct a great deal of energy toward our relationships because belonging is a core component of being human. Specifically, the belongingness hypothesis proposes that: (1) people require a minimum number of generally positive (or at least not predominantly negative) social interactions; and (2) these social interactions should occur within an ongoing interpersonal context marked by (ideally mutual) care and concern.

Regarding this first proposition: how many social interactions do you need to satisfy your belonging needs? Like all basic needs, people show some variability in how much they require to feel satiated. This is a familiar idea: we all need sleep, but some people feel well rested after 6 hours and others require 10. Some evidence suggests individuals have good awareness of the intensity of their own belongingness need. A validated single-item measure of the Need to Belong simply asks people to indicate

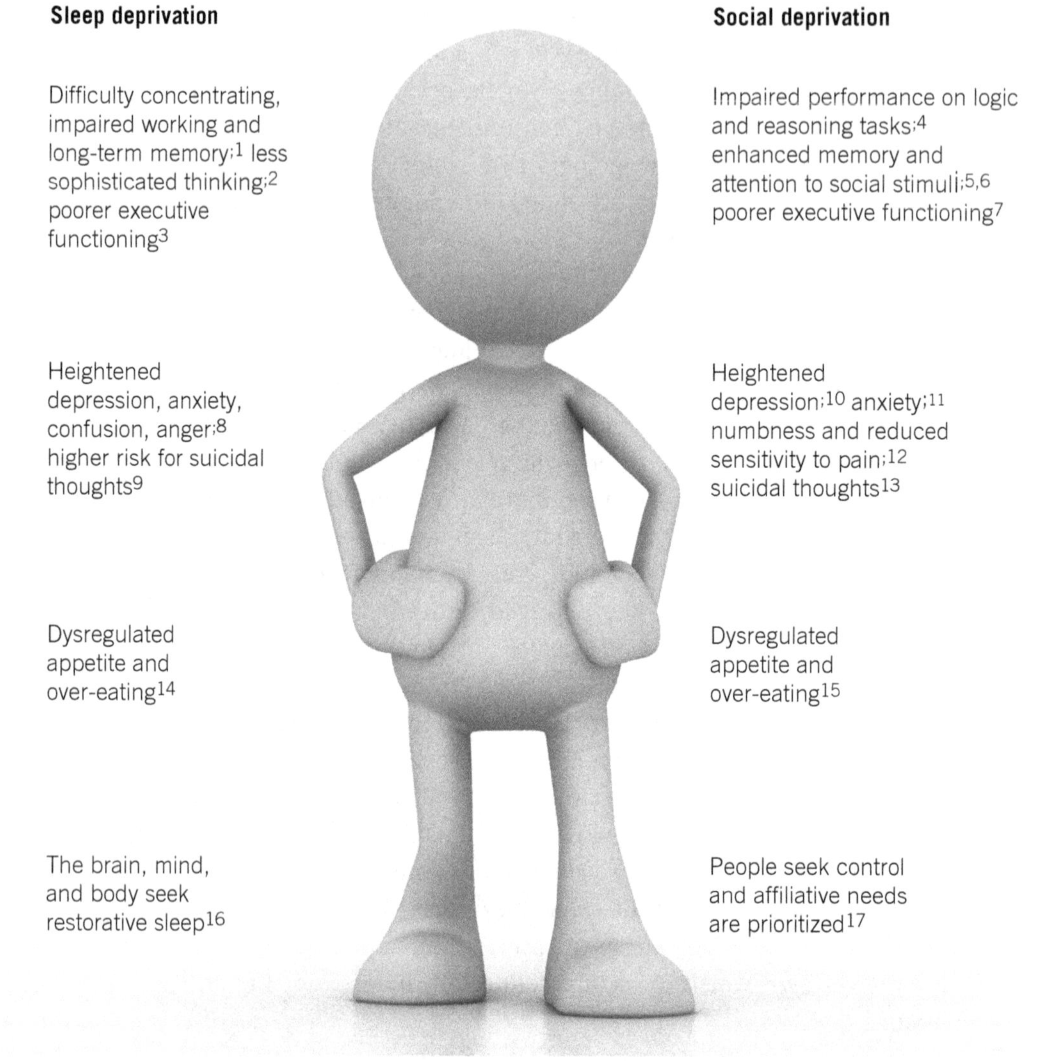

Sleep deprivation

Difficulty concentrating, impaired working and long-term memory;[1] less sophisticated thinking;[2] poorer executive functioning[3]

Heightened depression, anxiety, confusion, anger;[8] higher risk for suicidal thoughts[9]

Dysregulated appetite and over-eating[14]

The brain, mind, and body seek restorative sleep[16]

Social deprivation

Impaired performance on logic and reasoning tasks;[4] enhanced memory and attention to social stimuli;[5,6] poorer executive functioning[7]

Heightened depression;[10] anxiety;[11] numbness and reduced sensitivity to pain;[12] suicidal thoughts[13]

Dysregulated appetite and over-eating[15]

People seek control and affiliative needs are prioritized[17]

Figure 1.7 How does social deprivation compare to sleep deprivation? (Photo: CGinspiration / E+ / Getty Images)
1. Alhola & Polo-Kantola, 2007; 2. Killgore et al., 2008; 3. Nilsson et al., 2005; 4. Baumeister & Twenge, 2002; 5. Gardner et al., 2000; 6. Dewall et al., 2009; 7. Cacioppo & Hawkley, 2009; 8. Short & Louca, 2015; 9. Littlewood et al., 2018; 10. Slavich et al., 2010; 11. Baumeister & Tice, 1990; 12. Dewall & Baumeister, 2006; 13. Chen et al., 2020; 14. Spaeth et al., 2013; 15. Jaremka et al., 2018; 16. Borbely et al., 1981; 17. Gerber & Wheeler, 2009; Maner, Dewall et al., 2007.

their agreement, using a 1 (strongly disagree) to 5 (strongly agree) scale, to the statement, "I have a strong need to belong" (Nichols & Webster, 2013). Where do you fall on this question?

Table 1.1 Evidence supporting the idea that belonging is a fundamental human need

Domain		Predictions *When belonging needs are not met . . .*	Evidence
Cognition	Attention and memory	People will prioritize socially relevant information	When belonging needs are threatened: • people are more accurate at reading social cues (e.g., vocal tone, reading others' emotions)[1] • people show selective memory for socially relevant events[2] • people are better able to distinguish between real and fake smiles[3]
	Performance	People will become preoccupied with social connections	Threats to belonging reduce performance on other demanding cognitive tasks, such as intelligence tests[4]
Emotion	Mood	People's moods will be adversely affected	Social rejection reduces positive mood[5]
	Pain	People experiencing "social pain" will feel real, physical pain	• Cross-culturally, people talk about social pain using language similar to physical pain[6] • Social pain and physical pain may share a neural pathway[7] • Physical pain relievers (e.g., acetaminophen) can reduce social pain after social exclusion[8]
	Negative feelings	People will experience negative feelings	Social rejection elicits anger and sadness,[9] as well as shame and humiliation[10]
Behavior	Attempts to affiliate	People will try to re-establish social connections	• When belonging needs are not met, people often engage in antisocial behaviors to regain control and, if those control needs are met, engage in prosocial behaviors to promote reaffiliation[11] • People try to affiliate with unoffending others after social rejection[12] • People conform to group norms and change their self-concepts to be more similar to others to promote connection after social exclusion[13, 14]

1. Pickett et al., 2004; 2. Gardner et al., 2000; 3. Bernstein et al., 2008; 4. Baumeister & Twenge, 2002; 5. Blackhart et al., 2009; 6. Macdonald & Leary, 2005; 7. Eisenberger, 2012, 2015; Ferris et al., 2019; 8. DeWall et al., 2010; 9. Chow et al., 2007; 10. Dickerson, 2011; 11. Gerber & Wheeler, 2009; 12. Maner, Dewall et al., 2007; 13. Richman et al., 2015; 14. Williams et al., 2000.

IS THIS TRUE FOR YOU?

Seeking a Social Surrogate: A Creative Way to Satisfy Your Belonging Need

Sometimes it's hard to find a friend. Whether you just moved to a new city, broke up with a romantic partner, or are simply having trouble affiliating with other people, feeling lonely is a common challenge. What do you do to manage your need to belong?

Without even realizing it, you could be transforming activities that have no actual human interaction into psychologically social experiences (Gabriel et al., 2016). Playing with your dog, spending time with some fictional "F · R · I · E · N · D · S" on TV, or tuning in to a football game are all activities you can do with no other people around. Yet, they are oddly social. As such, they help satisfy a desire for social connection.

Have you ever relied on non-human companionship to feel connected? Scientists refer to the substitutes that people use for actual human interaction partners as **social surrogates**. Think about how you interact with your Alexa Smart Speaker (shown in Figure 1.8) or your dog, or how a child engages with their stuffed animal. According to the social surrogacy hypothesis (Derrick et al., 2009), when belonging needs are threatened, people unknowingly lean on their non-human connections to restore their sense of belonging.

Social surrogates tend to fall into three categories (Gabriel et al., 2016). The first category includes objects that remind people of relationships, such as photos on Instagram or social media, a loved one's sweatshirt, or family comfort foods (Troisi & Gabriel, 2011). The second category includes fictional social worlds in which people can immerse themselves, such as through television or music (Schäfer & Eerola, 2017). Indeed, viewing a favorite show can reduce loneliness and enhance belonging (Derrick et al., 2009). The final social surrogacy category focuses on parasocial relationships. **Parasocial relationships** include one-sided relationships with non-humans, fictional characters, or celebrities, and imagined relationships with others (be they Elton John or your crush). The one-sidedness of parasocial relationships makes them particularly safe: celebrities or fictional characters are unlikely to fight with you, insult or offend you, or in other ways reject you.

Figure 1.8 People can feel connection with non-human objects, such as a Smart Speaker, a manifestation of our deep psychological need for social interaction. Do you have any parasocial relationships or feel connected to certain objects or fictional worlds? If yes, when are these relationships more or less intense? If not, why might that be? (Photo: RossHelen / iStock / Getty Images Plus)

The **social affiliation model** suggests that people regulate their need for social contact, attempting to optimize their degree of social interaction over the course of each day (Hall, 2017; O'Connor & Rosenblood, 1996). Too much alone time? People will initiate behaviors to be with others. Too much time with people? People will seek ways to be alone. The balance point, or point of **social homeostasis**, varies for any given individual, but at the heart of the model is the idea that people are compelled to make adjustments in order to meet their own affiliation needs.

The belongingness hypothesis also suggests that not all social interactions satisfy our need to belong to the same degree. A day of conversing with strangers might affect us differently than spending that time with family, friends, or a romantic partner. But in what ways, and why? To understand differences in social interaction, we need to determine what is and what is not a relationship.

How Scientists Define a Relationship

The term *relationship* is surprisingly difficult to define. Think about all the relationships you have experienced in your life: how do you whittle down their variety to an essential core? Beginning with a wide lens, most **relationships** refer to a mutually recognized interpersonal context in which two (or more) people engage in ongoing social interactions; these interactions are shaped by previous interactions and affect future interactions (Hinde, 1979). By this definition, we have relationships with coffee baristas who know our order, college professors who greet us by name, and neighbors who greet us with friendly waves. Under this definition, we also have relationships with our best friend, parents, and romantic partners. Yet, this latter set of relationships feels markedly different from the previous set. Can you imagine asking your coffee barista to help you move? Would you invite your professor to your Super Bowl party? How upset would you be if you never saw your friendly neighbor again? Now ask these questions about your brother or sister, your best friend, or your romantic partner.

Relationships clearly vary in their importance to us. **Close relationships**, on which the majority of relationship science has focused, play a uniquely vital role in our lives. These relationships – sometimes called intimate or personal relationships – shape the very nature of who we are. Consider Elton John and his relationship with his parents: how would he differ had his parents been consistently supportive, affectionate, and encouraging? How would his life today change if his marriage fell apart? Three features help us differentiate close relationships from casual relationships. The first is interdependence.

Close Relationships Involve Interdependence

Interdependence refers to mutual influence: in a dyadic context, any changes experienced by one person (e.g., in thoughts, emotions, or behaviors) affect the other person, and likewise, any changes experienced by the latter person affect the former person. In relationships with multiple partners, the influence occurs among and between partners. Suppose Elizabeth and Aaron are a married couple. If Aaron decides to train for a Tough Mudder, Elizabeth will be impacted by this decision: she might develop a more (or less!) favorable view of these races, she might suddenly see Aaron as "driven," "adventurous," or "athletic,"

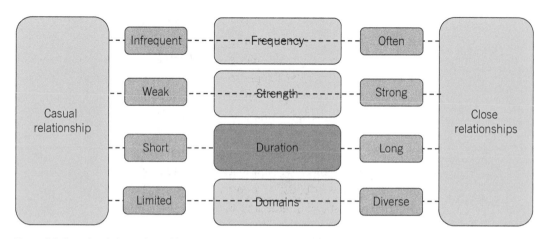

Figure 1.9 Casual and close relationships can be distinguished, in part, by the frequency, strength, duration, and domains of mutual influence. How would you characterize the relationships you have with the people you've encountered today?

and she might spend more time thinking about mud, workout clothes, and trail mix. Meanwhile, how effectively Aaron pursues his Tough Mudder dream depends in part on Elizabeth; she could either facilitate or inhibit this goal through the influence that she exerts on him. A high degree of interdependence is a defining characteristic of close relationships. To understand how interdependence works, we should consider its four key dimensions: frequency, strength, duration, and diversity, shown in Figure 1.9.

Frequency of Interdependence

First, how frequent is another person's influence? People in close relationships exert their influence on each other more regularly than those in less close relationships. As a married couple, if Elizabeth and Aaron see each other every day, text when they are apart, and make everyday decisions with the other person in mind, then their influence is frequent. Meanwhile, if their good friend Alex calls, texts, and visits periodically but not every week, Alex's influence on Elizabeth and Aaron (and theirs on him) will be less frequent. Frequency differentiates Elizabeth and Aaron's relationship as closer than theirs with Alex.

Strength of Interdependence

Another dimension of interdependence that differentiates close from casual relationships is how strongly partners influence each other. Strong influence evokes significant response; partners change their emotions, thoughts, or behaviors in meaningful ways because of each other. Influence strength, be it symmetrical or asymmetrical, can be seen in how couples navigate the little and big decisions they make over the course of the day. The decisions that Elizabeth and Aaron make, for example, are not independent: they are influenced by the other's point of view, any costs the other might incur, and any benefits the other might reap.

Duration of Interdependence

Another important dimension of interdependence is simply time. How long have people been influencing each other? The kind of interdependence that characterizes close relationships, like Elizabeth and Aaron's, typically takes a great deal of time to build. Knowing the length of a relationship can give important meaning to strong and frequent influence.

Defining the length of a close relationship is sometimes straightforward (e.g., "It was love at first sight!"), but is often more nuanced. Generally, close relationships begin when partners start to exert influence on each other; that is, they experience mutual, bidirectional influence, even if it is somewhat asymmetric. This moment might be hard to pinpoint, especially given that many relationships (e.g., off-again, on-again) do not progress steadily toward greater interdependence.

Domains of Influence

Finally, close relationship partners influence each other in diverse ways and in diverse contexts, a point that cannot be overstated. We do not relegate the influence of our close relationship partners to only one domain of our lives; instead, their influence (and ours on them!) extends across situations and environments. For instance, suppose Elizabeth is lucky enough to have a personal trainer. When Elizabeth and her personal trainer are actively working out together, they are influencing each other's feelings and thoughts. When those 60 minutes are done, however, Elizabeth heads to the showers and her trainer turns her attention to her next victim. The extent of their mutual influence is largely limited to their sessions together. This context-dependent influence is true for many casual relationships, but not our close relationships. Close relationship partners actively shape us across multiple contexts. Consider how Aaron affects a wide range of domains in Elizabeth's life, from which jobs she pursues, to which candidates she votes for, to when she seeks medical attention, and to when (and if) she becomes a parent. Likewise, Elizabeth's influence touches on many of the spheres in Aaron's life, similarly shaping who he is and who he will become. If a relationship is truly a close relationship, partners influence multiple areas of our lives.

Close Relationships Involve Intimate Knowledge

How well do you know your dentist? A reasonable question, given that you probably spend more face-to-face time with your dentist than some of your favorite relatives. During your periodic one-on-one sessions together, you give your dentist your best attention. You focus and listen: The start of a cavity, yikes. Keep up the flossing, OK. Meanwhile, your dentist picks and prods at your teeth and gum line, studying and making concerning "hmm . . ." sounds. When it comes to intimate knowledge, no one on this planet knows the inside of your mouth better than your dentist (Figure 1.10).

But does this knowledge lay the groundwork for relational closeness? Along with interdependence, intimate knowledge is a defining feature of close relationships (Gable, 2019). **Intimate knowledge** refers to the personal details that people know about one another which strangers or mere acquaintances might not know. Unfortunately for your dentist, intimate knowledge about teeth is not (usually) the basis for a close relationship. The intimate knowledge that compels close relationships tends to be more

Figure 1.10 Your dentist might have better knowledge of your teeth and gums than anyone on the planet, but is that enough to make this a close relationship? (Photo: Andersen Ross Photography Inc. / DigitalVision / Getty Images)

psychologically meaningful and self-defining. It might include background information, like where someone grew up, what their childhood was like, and where they went to school; hobbies and interests, like favorite sports teams or a passion for crocheting; and basic likes (gelato!) and dislikes (tuna!). Part of the job of being in a close relationship is learning and remembering relevant details of our partners.

Imagine, for example, that you had this thought, "I love banana bread." Or this thought, "I just cheated on my romantic partner." Or this one, "My mother's new partner is a better parent to me than my mom." With whom would you share these thoughts, if with anyone at all? **Self-disclosure** refers to the intentional sharing of personal information with other people and can involve basic facts or more personal feelings, preferences, motivations, and goals. People discriminate among the members of their social networks by self-disclosing the less intimate factual and descriptive information broadly, but reserving the intimate, emotional disclosures for a select few (Derlega et al., 2008). Simply the process of sharing important details can deepen a relationship's closeness. The act of self-disclosure – so long as the person listening is responsive – promotes feelings of intimacy and liking (Collins & Miller, 1994; Laurenceau et al., 1998).

Intimate knowledge in close relationships is a two-way street. A therapist, hairdresser/barber, or physician can get to know you well if you decide to self-disclose. But, when the disclosure is not occurring in both directions, it is not a close relationship. Similarly, disclosure needs to match the closeness of a relationship. Your discomfort when an acquaintance over-discloses ("TMI, bruh") reveals a mismatch between the degree of disclosure and your current relational closeness. Close relationships are defined by *mutual* self-disclosure that leads to *mutual* intimate knowledge.

Close Relationships Involve Commitment

A final feature that distinguishes close relationships from casual relationships is commitment. **Commitment** refers to an intention – be it spoken or unspoken – to remain in the relationship now and into the future. Many relationships in our lives operate with an understanding of commitment. Our friendships, for example, have no expiration date ("Sorry Jackson, we can only be friends until April, then well, it's over"), parent–child relationships are structured to continue perpetually, and romantic relationships are often maintained under explicit expectations of permanent commitment. Close relationships, therefore, have a future orientation: we see these people as part of our lives today and tomorrow. Perhaps this is one of the reasons why losing a close friend or partner is so difficult: we grieve the many future conversations and interactions we would have had, the many untold ways in which they would have shaped our future selves.

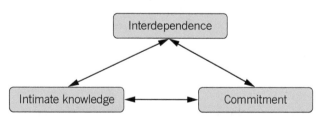

Figure 1.11 Potential pathways of influence among the key features of a close relationship.

Thinking about commitment helps us understand interdependence and intimate knowledge in relationships. All three of these aspects are linked in defining relational closeness, as shown in Figure 1.11. Less close relationships might feature only one or two of these characteristics (e.g., **arranged marriages** tend to be high in commitment, but lower in intimate knowledge and interdependence, at least initially [Ingersoll-Dayton et al., 1996]). In general, relationships high in commitment are typically high in interdependence (Agnew et al., 1998; Sabatelli & Cecil-Pigo, 1985). Further, commitment and intimate knowledge are linked, in that we tend to selectively disclose to individuals with whom we share more committed relationships; likewise, we might feel more committed to the relationship after a self-disclosure (Sprecher & Hendrick, 2004).

Casual Relationships

Although close relationships impact us most, casual relationships can also help us satisfy our belongingness need. These weak ties tend to be characterized by minimal intimacy, low emotional involvement, and irregular or infrequent interaction (Sandstrom & Dunn, 2014b). Converging evidence suggests that, on a day-to-day basis, people who interact more frequently with casual acquaintances report greater belonging and happiness, particularly on days when they interact less with their closest relationships, or strong ties (Sandstrom & Dunn, 2014a, 2014b).

The power of casual interactions tells us there is more than one way to fulfill a sense of belonging. Indeed, scholars have identified at least four paths toward satisfying the human need for connection (Hirsch & Clark, 2019): the minor-sociability path (having brief interactions with others, such as weak ties), the general-approbation path (achieving status, admiration, or recognition by others), the group membership path (being part of a group, collective, or community), and the communal-relationship path (maintaining close relationships that provide security and support). Each of these paths has potential for renewing, enhancing, or maintaining people's sense of belonging.

Focusing on Romantic Relationships

All close relationships share the features we've just discussed – interdependence, intimate knowledge, and commitment – but the broad category of "close relationships" includes considerable diversity. Friendships, parent–child relationships, sibling relationships, romantic relationships ... each of these has its own unique features and each tells us something important about the human experience. Relationship scientists are interested in all close relationships; however, the majority of research has focused on romantic relationships, a bias that some scholars feel is problematic (DePaulo & Morris, 2005). The field's emphasis on romantic relationships (and this book's!) can be criticized for: (1) neglecting the relationship experiences of single individuals; (2) unintentionally implying that any romantic relationship – regardless of quality – is better than no romantic relationship (not so!); and (3) inadvertently reinforcing negative stereotypes about singlehood ... even as many unpartnered individuals want to be single and are enjoying thriving, satisfying lives (MacDonald & Park, 2022; Park et al., 2022). Indeed, single people celebrate many advantages of singlehood, including having more time for themselves, more opportunity to focus on their goals, and freedom to choose what they want to do (Apostolou & Christoforou, 2022). Perhaps the field's bias reflects the fact that romantic relationships are an advantageous context for exploring relationship dynamics and processes, many of which are relevant to other types of close relationships as well. Romantic relationships are close relationships that include a sexual aspect and some degree of relational commitment. When adults maintain a romantic relationship, it is typically their closest relationship, and as such, it is generally characterized by more interdependence, intimate knowledge, and commitment than their other relationships. We devote a disproportional amount of time and attention to finding romantic relationships, and, when we have them, they often reside at the center of our lives, with our thoughts, emotions, and behaviors inextricably tethered to those of our partner(s). For these reasons, romantic relationships provide an opportune relational context on which to concentrate as we try to understand how humans form, maintain, and end relationships.

Need Fulfillment Within Romantic Relationships

In Western culture, romantic relationships are distinct from other relationships with regard to the expectations placed on each partner to meet the needs of the other partner(s) (Finkel et al., 2014). In Western culture, romantic relationship partners are generally viewed as a primary source for intimacy, companionship, security, emotional, self-enhancement and sexual needs (Drigotas & Rusbult, 1992), with some romantic partners also expecting partners to help cultivate their personal growth and self-expressive needs (Finkel et al., 2014).

Let's begin with intimacy needs. Intimacy needs refer to individuals' desires for closeness and connection. These needs can be met through self-disclosure and shared experiences. People often turn to their romantic partners to share their feelings about their work, their friends, or the latest Netflix release; they share secrets, fears, and dreams with their romantic partners. If you are thinking, "Well, I'm not in a relationship and my best friend Tonya fulfills those needs for me," then you have tapped into some of the overlap between romantic relationships and friendship (see Table 1.2). Romantic relationships do not hold a monopoly on intimacy-need satisfaction. Good romantic relationship partners, however, are tuned into supporting each other's intimacy needs.

Likewise, romantic partners provide companionship. They delight in spending time together and seem to take great pleasure in being near each other. They have fun together! By fulfilling companionship needs, romantic partners can support each other's basic need for belonging. Indeed, Western cultural norms often reinforce the idea that romantic partners fulfill each other's companionship needs and subtly suggest that without a romantic partner, an individual's companionship needs cannot be fully satisfied. This is particularly true in cultures structured to support couple living ("Table for two? Oh. I see. You're eating alone."), potentially at the expense of single individuals' comfort (DePaulo & Morris, 2005). Friendships, however, can also satisfy people's companionship needs, with need fulfillment by friends helping to predict people's happiness (Demir & Özdemir, 2010).

Table 1.2 **Primary rules of friendship**

1.   Friends tell each other about their successes.
2.   Friends offer each other emotional support.
3.   Friends help each other when help is needed.
4.   Friends try to make each other happy.
5.   Friends trust each other and confide in each other.
6.   Friends are loyal; they stick up for each other.

Which rules of friendship might also serve as "rules for romantic relationships"? What rules are specific to romantic relationships?

Source: Argyle & Henderson (1984).

Romantic relationships also help satisfy security and self-enhancement needs. Security refers to interpersonal safety; having a dependable and trustworthy person in your life. Feelings of safety are considered primary psychological needs (Maslow, 1943), and romantic partners can be a reliable source of this type of psychological support, serving as mental sanctuaries. When your partner "has your back," and you know they want you around, your security needs might be well met. When this relationship also bolsters your self-image, for example, your partner admires and appreciates you for you, then your self-enhancement needs are also supported through the relationship. For single individuals, security and safety needs are often satisfied by siblings and friends, whereas people in romantic relationships tend to turn to their romantic partners (Schachner et al., 2008).

Romantic relationships help address people's emotional needs as well. In times of distress, partners provide support, and in times of joy, they cheer us on and celebrate with us (Collins & Feeney, 2000; Gable et al., 2006). Romantic relationships also provide a unique context for expressions of certain feelings, like love, desire, and passion. While people love their parents, children, and friends, the emotional and physiological experiences of romantic love help differentiate romantic relationships from these other relationships.

Finally, in addition to the above needs, romantic relationships help people satisfy their sexual needs. This feature differentiates romantic relationships from most other relationships, which might likewise be characterized by love and affection. Romantic partners who are motivated to fulfill each other's sexual needs tend to have more rewarding relationships (Muise & Impett, 2015), underscoring the importance of sexual need fulfillment in these relationships. Of course, romantic relationships are not the only contexts that support sexual need fulfillment. Uncommitted relational contexts (e.g., friends-with-benefits, one-night stands) can provide an important setting for single individuals to meet their sexual needs (Schachner et al., 2008). The commitment inherent in a romantic relationship differentiates it from these other contexts that support sexual need fulfillment.

Need Fulfillment Outside of Romantic Relationships

Romantic relationships tend to function better when they support partners' fundamental needs and tend to be less stable when partners meet their needs elsewhere (Machia & Proulx, 2020). Satisfying needs extradyadically (outside of the relationship) is linked to relationship instability, in part because people who meet their needs extradyadically perceive more desirable alternatives to their romantic relationships. Some romantic relationships, however, termed consensually non-monogamous relationships, are structured such that partners intentionally fulfill their sexual (and perhaps other) needs with more than one partner. How well people's needs are being met within or outside of these relationships is still important for relationship functioning (Muise, Laughton et al., 2019): for example, men (but not women) who report better sexual fulfillment outside of their primary relationship tend to be more satisfied in general with their primary relationships.

The Biological Basis for Relationships

The pervasiveness and potency of our need to be with other people suggests we are not in relationships because we have learned to be, but rather, we are in relationships because we are *compelled* to be. This compulsion could be ingrained in our biology. As a multidisciplinary field, relationship science draws on the expertise of biological anthropologists, neurobiologists, and social neuroscientists among others to explore the biological underpinnings of relationships. To do this work, these scientists often study the behaviors and biology of non-human animals and make tentative extrapolations to the human experience. Much of this work targets the potential biological foundations for romantic attachments and sexual relationships in humans, but many of the mechanisms implicated may also extend more generally to a story of connection pursuit, including through friendships and family relationships.

The Biological Basis for Relationships in Non-Human Animals

Are you familiar with prairie voles? They look a lot like mice but are a little fluffier and much more loyal. Unlike mice and unlike their distant cousin the meadow vole, prairie voles form lifelong attachments (i.e., pair-bonds). They are, in fact, monogamous, a discovery that prompted some investigation ... what happens if you take a promiscuous meadow vole (the "Don Juan" of voles) and modify one of its genes to resemble that of its cousin, the faithful prairie vole? Quite readily, that promiscuous meadow vole will show signs of selective preference for one partner (Young et al., 1998). Does this hint at a biological basis for monogamy?

In non-human relationships, monogamy typically refers to a male and a female that selectively affiliate or bond with each other, and this bond is maintained throughout life. Monogamy is surprisingly rare in mammals, with only 3 to 5 percent of species practicing monogamy (Lukas & Clutton-Brock, 2013), but prairie voles exhibit classic signs of monogamy after mating. They prefer to spend their time with one partner, and the male prairie vole will aggressively defend their territory, his female companion, and their offspring. You might think monogamy implies sexual exclusivity, but pair-bonding does not universally preclude multiple sexual partners. Female prairie voles might have offspring fathered by more than one male prairie vole, but they still hang with their best male buddy. The focus is thus on social monogamy rather than sexual exclusivity. When it comes to human relationships, monogamy refers to an orientation toward one partner at any given time. That partnership might not work out and you might find another partner, or indeed, you might have multiple partners all in sequence (i.e., serial monogamy), but the idea is that if you are oriented toward monogamy, you will focus on, protect, and devote resources to only one romantic partner at any given time.

Because prairie voles demonstrate all the primary features of monogamy, they provide an excellent non-human animal model for pair-bonding in humans. The neurobiological mechanisms at play in their mating and bonding experiences may translate to the human experience. Some of these neurobiological mechanisms include the vasopressin gene (Va1R), arginine vasopressin (AVP), and oxytocin (OT), each of which has received considerable attention as a neuropeptide implicated in non-human pair-bonding, attachment, and love. Both vasopressin and oxytocin are produced by the hypothalamus and released by the pituitary gland during sex, birth, and breast-feeding (Zeki, 2007). Vasopressin appears essential for the aggressive protective behavior of pair-bonded voles and is of particular importance for male prairie vole partner preference. Oxytocin has strong links with the affiliative drive that promotes proximity and closeness behaviors in voles and is critical to the female prairie vole bonding experience.

The Biological Basis for Relationships in Humans

While it's fun to think about prairie voles, can we extend these findings to humans? Maybe. Painting a clear picture of the biological foundations for human relationships is difficult in part because of the methodological challenges of examining the neurochemistry of humans. This area of research, however, easily attracts the general public's attention, such as when oxytocin was dubbed "the cuddle hormone." Shortly thereafter, a market emerged for oxytocin-laced nasal spray as a means of promoting trust. Sounds intriguing, doesn't it? People embraced the idea that oxytocin might be the key driver of interpersonal bonding and that it might uniformly produce positive effects on prosocial behavior and social cognition.

Table 1.3 Biological changes in hormones/neuropeptides tied to relationship formation

Hormones and/or neuropeptides	Hypothesized role in human relationship development and function	Evidence supporting proposed role in human relationships
Vasopressin	Implicated in aggressive relationship-protective behaviors	Lack of evidence at this time
Oxytocin	May facilitate trust, pair-bonding, and affiliation	Some evidence links pair-bonding and affiliation; trust evidence is weak[1]
Dopamine	Part of a reward system that supports the drive for romantic love, sex, and affiliation	Implicated in sexual motivation and arousal; experiencing intense romantic love or viewing romantic partners produces heightened activity in regions of the dopaminergic system[2]
Testosterone	The challenge hypothesis suggests that higher testosterone supports mate-seeking behaviors and lower levels may support parenting and caregiving	Meta-analytic work shows small effect size connecting low testosterone to marital status (i.e., being married), parenting status (i.e., having children), and higher-quality parenting in men[3]
Cortisol	A stress-related hormone that may be involved in romantic attraction	Tentative evidence points to a link between cortisol and individuals' attractiveness as romantic partners; cortisol increases when encountering potential partners[4]
Serotonin	A neurotransmitter implicated in sex drive and emotion regulation	The use of SSRI anti-depressants (which increase serotonin) is associated with reduced sex drive and emotional blunting[5]

[1] Lane et al., 2016; Mierop et al., 2020; [2] Fisher et al., 2005; Hull et al., 2004; Melis & Argiolas, 1995; Takahashi et al., 2015; [3] Grebe et al., 2019; Meijer et al., 2019; [4] van der Meij et al., 2010; van der Meij et al., 2019; [5] Fisher & Thomson, 2007; Shih et al., 2022.

Empirical findings, however, are mixed, making such a sweeping evaluation of oxytocin inappropriate. The original study that showed oxytocin enhances trust when navigating a social dilemma (Kosfeld et al., 2005) has not replicated well, and this area of research appears to suffer from a file-drawer effect, where non-significant findings were never published (Lane et al., 2016).

Although oxytocin may not reliably promote pro-sociality, its ability to facilitate bonding and affiliation may be on surer footing. Some research measuring oxytocin in the blood, for example, has shown that oxytocin levels predict self-reported relationship quality in married couples (Holt-Lunstad et al., 2015) and predict whether or not dating couples are likely to still be together six months later (Schneiderman et al., 2012). While much additional research needs to be done, these results point to the possible role of oxytocin in supporting human pair-bonding. As such, it complements a much stronger body of literature pointing to a link between oxytocin, the maternal infant–child relationship, and parenting (Feldman & Bakermans-Kranenburg, 2017; Galbally et al., 2011). By leaps and bounds, oxytocin research has outpaced vasopressin research, with both areas requiring critical attention in order to build a more cohesive story of the neuroendocrinology of human relationships (see Table 1.3).

In both prairie voles and humans, vasopressin receptors and oxytocin receptors are located in the brain's dopaminergic reward system. This reward system centers on the activation of dopamine, a neurotransmitter, which – for both prairie voles and humans – is generally viewed as responsible for life's rewarding "highs." Why does it feel so good to nosh on a luscious piece of chocolate, win a big gamble, or make an online purchase? These behaviors, among others (e.g., exercise, cocaine use), activate the dopaminergic reward system. The release of dopamine creates the rewarding experience of, say, eating chocolate, which makes us *want* chocolate: the dopaminergic reward system is thus responsible for the motivation that drives certain behaviors. When it comes to relationships, dopamine may underlie both our drive for sex and our drive for romantic love (Melis & Argiolas, 1995). This makes sense: if reproduction is a primary evolutionary drive, both the act of sex and the bond that keeps parents together (i.e., romantic love) should be rewarding.

What Makes Each Romantic Relationship Unique?

Although romantic relationships share some critical properties (e.g., interdependence, intimate knowledge, commitment) and are supported by a biological basis common to all humans, the world is rich with variation when it comes to romantic relationship experiences. As shown in Table 1.4, romantic relationships differ in their structure, composition, duration, and motives, among other features. Some of these relationship characteristics can vary across time within a given relationship (e.g., a couple that periodically shifts from monogamous to polyamorous), while other dimensions tend to be stable within couples, but capture important differences between couples (e.g., same-race versus interracial relationship, personality traits). Variations in the way relationships are configured are important if and when they shape the dynamics of the relationship, particularly when these dynamics are tied to the relationship's quality and trajectory. For example, specific types of relationships may have

Table 1.4 Types and dimensions of diversity in romantic relationships

Structure	Physical arrangement (e.g., geographically proximal or geographically distant); in-person or internet-based; cohabitating or not cohabitating
Exclusivity	Number of people involved and their relation to one another (e.g., monogamous versus non-monogamous, primary versus secondary partner)
Composition	Individual differences variables (e.g., demographic characteristics, personality, personal history) contributed by each member of the relationship
Duration	Length of the relationship
Motives	Reasons for having the relationships (e.g., short-term/sexual versus long-term partner; approach versus avoidance motive)
Commitment	Degree of commitment (e.g., dating casually, married)
Consistency	Whether the relationship dynamics (i.e., interdependence, commitment) have been constant or fluctuating over time (e.g., on-again/off-again relationships)

Romantic relationships can vary in different ways. Can you think of any others?

unique challenges (e.g., long-distance relationship partners aiming to maintain intimacy), unique experiences (e.g., navigating meeting the parents in an interracial relationship), or unique opportunities (e.g., consensually non-monogamous partners finding need fulfillment in multiple relationships). In other words, to form a comprehensive understanding of how relationships work, we need to pay attention to differences in relationships to evaluate if and how these differences give rise to unique relationship processes.

Demographic Variables

Diversity in romantic relationships emerges in part because people themselves are unique, and they bring their uniqueness into their relationships. Recall Elton John's story and the importance of *him* in his relationships. Who he is – particularly his demographic characteristics, his personality, and his personal history – is critical to his relationship experiences, just like who you are shapes your relationship experiences. Along with personality and personal history, relationship science has emphasized four individual difference variables that can be influential in the study of romantic relationships: gender and biological sex, sexual orientation, race, and socioeconomic status (SES).

Gender and Biological Sex

Relationship researchers have long been interested in both gender, the psychological experience and expression of masculinity and femininity, and biological sex, a designation assigned to individuals based on their physical bodies, specifically their genitals and reproductive organs. Attention to these two constructs dates back to some of the earliest work on relationship formation and maintenance; interest over time has generated copious insights into their roles in relationship functioning. Take gender, for example. We have documented gender differences in marital conflict styles, partner preferences, self-disclosure habits,

Figure 1.12 Gender and biological sex often play an important role in who people desire as romantic partners and how those relationships function. (Photo: Fabio Formaggio / EyeEm / Getty Images)

relationship beliefs, and attitudes toward sex, to name a few. Attending to gender has allowed researchers to have a more nuanced understanding of relationship dynamics than would otherwise be possible (Figure 1.12); to ignore gender would be to obscure important variability in how people perceive and experience their relationships. Although evaluating gender differences can provide key insights, the predominance of evidence points to more similarity across genders than differences between them (Helgeson & Mascatelli, 2018).

Notably, however, scientists have typically conceptualized gender in binary terms (men and women), a critique that is gaining attention. We do not yet know how the experiences of gender minority individuals – those people whose gender identification does not fall into traditional men/women categories (e.g., non-binary individuals) – might compare to those who identify as men or women. Further, scholars have typically focused on the experiences of individuals who are cisgender, meaning that they experience a match between their biological sex and psychological gender (i.e., male – men, female – women). Little research examines the specific relationship experiences of individuals who are transgender, that is, who identify as a gender different from their assigned biological sex. In many of the same ways that cisgender individuals benefit from romantic relationships, so too do transgender individuals, particularly when relationship partners are gender affirming (Meier et al., 2013; Pulice-Farrow et al., 2019). Throughout this textbook, we will discuss the emerging research on how non-binary, non-binary transgender, and binary transgender individuals experience romantic relationships when possible, noting that these are psychological meaningful distinctions in gender identity (Bradford & Catalpa, 2019).

Biological sex, while often examined in concert with gender, has its own important role in relationship science. Scholars using an evolutionary perspective to derive hypotheses about attraction, infidelity, or jealousy, for example, have revealed fascinating sex-differentiated effects. These differences are anchored to the idea that evolution has exerted different pressures on females than males because of their different biologically based roles in reproduction (Trivers, 2017), and accordingly, we can now witness sex-differentiated patterns in how people approach their relationships (Kenrick et al., 1990). Work on hormonal changes across the menstrual cycle that correspond with aspects of romantic attraction is also strongly grounded in aspects of people's biological sex (Gildersleeve et al., 2014a; Jones et al., 2019). As with gender, biological sex has been conceptualized predominantly in binary terms (i.e., male – female), yet today's contemporary view of biological sex represents sex along a spectrum (Ainsworth, 2015). Challenges in relationship research include considering biological sex as separate and distinct from gender and viewing sex and gender as separate from sexual orientation.

Sexual Orientation

Are same-sex relationships alike or different from different-sex relationships? And if different, how? This question rose to the forefront of American conversation in 2015 when the Supreme

Court's ruling on the landmark *Obergefell* v. *Hodges* case legalized same-sex marriage. Simultaneously, the United States witnessed a dramatic shift in American attitudes toward same-sex relationships. As late as 1996, Gallup Polls reported that only 27 percent of Americans were in support of same-sex marriage; a more-recent 2019 survey suggests that 67 percent support same-sex marriage (Pew Research Center, 2019). Remarkably, this change is not driven by one specific cohort (e.g., youth): the observed shift represents changes in attitudes across all age cohorts, among people of different races, religions, and educational backgrounds, and within different regions of the United States over the last few decades (Twenge & Blake, 2021).

Although it was "same-sex" relationships that were formally legalized, this terminology falls short, given the differentiation of biological sex and gender described in the previous section. The term "same-sex relationship" prioritizes biological sex and ignores individuals who are non-binary or transgender. Accordingly, relationship researchers have increasingly shifted from merely assessing a dyad's (or triad's, etc.) biological sex composition (e.g., female-female must mean both partners identify as lesbian or bisexual) to more nuanced consideration of partners' biological sex, gender identity, and sexual orientation (the direction of individuals' romantic and sexual interests toward individuals of a particular gender or set of genders). Nonetheless, terminology shifts slowly, and nearly all research and public discourse prior to 2020 conflates the terms "sex" and "gender," meaning that the term "same-sex relationship" served as a catch-all for same-sex and same-gender relationships (or gender was ignored completely). In this book, we use the terms "same-sex relationship" and "different-sex relationship" to match the published work upon which we draw; however, we urge readers to consider that this terminology misses the nuance of sexual and gender minority relationships.

Relationship science has recently worked to overcome its over-representation of heterosexual individuals and different-sex relationships in research and has accumulated initial insights into how the relationships of sexual minorities are developed, experienced, and dissolved, often in comparison to heterosexual individuals. Some of the earliest sexuality research, including the shocking "Kinsey Reports" of the mid-1900s (Kinsey et al., 1948), challenged the traditional binary view of sexual orientation. Indeed, heterosexuality (attraction to a different gender) and homosexuality (attraction to the same gender) do not sufficiently represent the diversity people exhibit in their sexuality. Other forms of sexual orientation, including bisexuality (attraction to both men and women), pansexuality (attraction to all genders), and asexuality (no sexual attraction), capture meaningful differences in how people live out their relationship experiences, yet are understudied. Like gender and biological sex, scholars support the idea of representing sexual orientation along a spectrum (Savin-Williams, 2016), noting too that sexual orientation is fluid and can change over time (Diamond, 2008; Diamond & Butterworth, 2008).

Importantly, labels of sexual orientation do not always correspond with behaviors or romantic interests. Individuals can engage in sexual acts with members of their same gender and/or report romantic and sexual attraction to members of the same gender, yet still identify as heterosexual. As shown in Figure 1.13, a multinational study showed that the proportion of the population who self-identifies as heterosexual, lesbian, gay, and bisexual, as well as the proportion who self-report sexual attraction to same or different genders, are quite similar

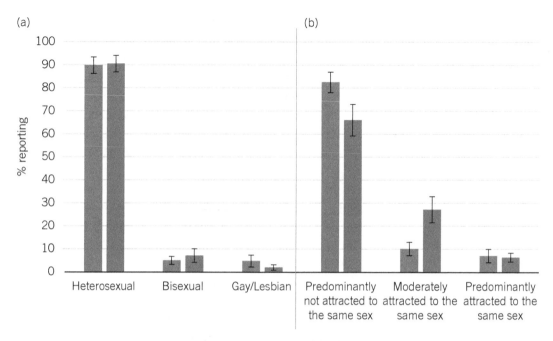

Figure 1.13 Average prevalence rates of reported sexual orientation (a) and self-reported sexual attraction (b) across twenty-eight countries. Red refers to reports by self-identifying men; green indicates reports by self-identifying women. Terminology presented ("same sex") is consistent with data collected. (Source: Drawn based on data from Rahman et al. [2020])

cross-culturally (Rahman et al., 2020), underscoring the strong biological origin to sexual orientation. The idea that one might identify as heterosexual and also experience at least some sexual attraction to their same gender, and that one might identify as gay or lesbian but also feel attraction to a different gender, provides the backdrop for the terms, "mostly heterosexual" and "mostly gay/lesbian" – terms that further challenge the notion of sexual orientation as a dichotomy (Vrangalova & Savin-Williams, 2012).

Race

In 1958, Richard Loving and Mildred Jetter were married in Washington, DC. Soon thereafter, they returned to their home state of Virginia only to be arrested, in the middle of the night, for violating Virginia's Racial Integrity Act, a law that sanctioned marriages only between people of the same race. The "problem"? Richard was a White man, of European descent; his wife, Mildred, was a Black woman who identified as a Native American of the Rappahannock tribe. At the time, interracial marriages were outlawed in most states, with only 3 percent of new marriages in 1967 occurring between people of different racial identification. After pleading guilty, Richard and Mildred avoided a year in prison by moving back to Washington, DC (where interracial marriages were legal). Later, however, they decided they wanted to raise their children in Virginia. They launched a lawsuit and, in 1967, the Supreme Court ruled on the *Loving* v. *Virginia* case, and legalized interracial marriages across the nation. Social norms shifted accordingly; a national survey conducted fifty years after the ruling showed that 89 percent of Americans approve of **interracial marriages** (marriages between individuals who identify as different races), and nearly one in six new marriages in the United States are between people of different races (Livingston & Brown, 2017).

Race contributes to individuals' romantic relationship experiences. Because race is a social construction, individuals can vary in their racial identification, either over time or across contexts. While some people's racial identity is fairly static, others, particularly those who appear racially ambiguous to perceivers, experience race more fluidly (Davenport, 2020; Liebler et al., 2017). In the United States, the historic privilege afforded to people who appear White and the historical marginalization of people of color, including Black Americans and other racial minority and ethnic minority groups, has created forces that make forming and maintaining relationships easier for some people, and harder for others. Insufficient research has focused on the unique ways in which racial minorities and those in interethnic relationships might experience their relationships (Gaines et al., 2015; Marks et al., 2006), although there is reason to suggest the need for focused attention. Compared to White couples or Mexican American couples, Black couples tend to report lower marital quality and are at greater risk of relationship dissolution (Bulanda & Brown, 2007). Interracial marriages are also characterized by more instability than same-race marriages (Bratter & King, 2008). The information that relationship scientists have acquired about relationships, when based exclusively on White couples, likely have limits in the extent to which they can help us understand the relationships of racial (and sexual) minorities; this underscores the notion that relationship experiences are tethered to their unique context (Gabb & Singh, 2015). Research focused on Black Americans, for example, identifies racial factors (e.g., racial discrimination, financial strain, and minority status) that are important in predicting marital outcomes (e.g., quality, stability) and that are either irrelevant to the privileged racial majority or disproportionally factoring into the relationships of Black Americans relative to White Americans (Bryant et al., 2010). Minority stress, which will be discussed in more detail in Chapter 9, refers to the specific challenges that individuals experience *because* of their identification with a minority group (Meyer, 2003; Rostosky & Riggle, 2017), an important focus if attempting to understand variation in relationship experiences.

Socioeconomic Status

The role of race in individuals' relationship experiences must be considered alongside of socioeconomic standing, even as these social categories make independent contributions to relationship functioning. Socioeconomic status (SES) refers to an individual's social power, wealth, and educational opportunities, as well as perceptions of their social class. The historic and continued marginalization of racial and ethnic minorities means that, today, race and SES are highly striated: with race and ethnicity often serving as markers for SES, and SES serving as a critical context for the relationships of racial minorities. A growing economic inequality across the globe, including within the United States, which boasts one of the sharpest disparities in wealth (OECD, 2020), highlights the need to consider the divergent or compounding ways in which both race and SES might facilitate or impede relationships. Copious data, for example, show the deleterious effects of economic distress on couple well-being. Economic distress is linked to marital instability and marital quality, including heightened negative behaviors, such as hostility and anger, particularly within more vulnerable couples (Conger et al., 1990; Masarik et al., 2016). Research taking an intersectional approach, one that considers individuals' experiences in light of their membership to multiple meaningful social categories, is only yet emerging in relationship science.

DIVERSITY AND INCLUSION

Applying an Intersectional Lens to Romantic Relationships

Applying an intersectionality framework to the study of people's romantic relationships reflects the lived experiences of understudied populations. Rather than focusing on only one dimension of people's identities (e.g., race), to take an **intersectionality** approach involves considering multiple dimensions of people's identities (e.g., race, sexual orientation, gender) and their related social consequences of oppression or privilege (e.g., racism, homophobia, sexism) simultaneously and in light of system-level forces (Crenshaw, 1989). The many dimensions of people's identities, those that garner privilege and those that incur oppression, are interrelated and mutually influential, so they need to be considered together (Figure 1.14).

Intersectionality emphasizes relationality, power, social inequality, social context, and social justice (Collins & Bilge, 2016) and could prove exceptionally helpful in relationship science. Recent work argues for the use of an intersectional lens to understand the experiences of intercultural queer partners, who navigate multiple forms of marginalization (Chan & Erby, 2018). Intercultural relationships are those that have partners of different ethnic or racial backgrounds; queer relationships are those in which at least one member belongs to a sexual or gender minority. The benefits of examining intercultural queer partners through intersectionality theory include a much richer understanding of how these specific forms of minority status work together to shape people's relationship goals, dynamics, and outcomes.

Figure 1.14 We can understand people's relationships better when we apply an intersectional lens. How do your many identities work together to affect your relationship experiences? (Photo: Westend61 / Getty Images)

Personality

Are you gregarious or reserved? Critical or agreeable? Traditional or open-minded? **Personality** refers to an array of individual difference variables ("no two personalities are alike!") that describes typical patterns in thought, emotion, and behavior that endure over time (Allport, 1937). Personalities give insight into how people approach new situations and navigate their social worlds, including their romantic relationships. Romantic relationships, however, are not solo performances in which one aspect of personality dominates; relationships are a glorious symphony of personality in which each facet of each partner's personality plays its own little tune. One person's neuroticism reverberates with another's agreeableness and vice versa. In the highly interdependent context of romantic relationships, people's personalities are shaping and being shaped by their partner's personality, and the interplay between personalities has consequences for the relationship's functioning (or dysfunctioning).

The Big Five Personality Traits

Relationship researchers often conceptualize personality using the Five Factor Model (McCrae & Costa, 1997), which is comprised of the "Big Five" traits: extraversion (e.g., gregarious, sociable), conscientiousness (e.g., reliable, thoughtful), neuroticism (e.g., irritable, easily upset), openness to new experiences (e.g., imaginative, non-conforming), and agreeableness (e.g., good natured, cooperative). Scholars have accrued substantial data evaluating the ways in which the Big Five personality traits predict aspects of relationship functioning (McNulty, 2013; Winterhead & Simpson, 2018). Neuroticism appears to have the most stable link to relationship quality and stability, consistently predicting worse relationship experiences (e.g., more conflict, less satisfaction) and outcomes (e.g., greater likelihood of divorce). Agreeableness, on the other hand, tends to predict more adaptive relationship dynamics and quality. As for the other factors (conscientiousness, openness, and extraversion), findings are inconsistent. This inconsistency may be a function of research methodology that often isolates one person's personality instead of considering it within the context of an interdependent relationship, or it may have to do with the broad and general nature of these personality traits.

The Dark Triad

Along with the "Big Five," scholars have devoted a fair amount of attention to the Dark Triad as a predictor of relationship dynamics and outcomes. The Dark Triad refers to a personality defined by high levels of narcissism (an inflated sense of self, entitlement, exploitative of others), psychopathy (e.g., impulsivity, low empathy, thrill-seeking), and Machiavellianism (e.g., a tendency to manipulate others). Individuals high on any or all Dark Triad traits tend to prefer short-term relationships characterized by low commitment rather than long-term committed relationships (Jonason, Li, & Cason, 2009; Jonason, Li, Webster et al., 2009; Koladich & Atkinson, 2016; Paulhus & Williams, 2002). Of the Dark Triad traits, narcissism has likely garnered the most empirical attention (Foster & Brunell, 2018). As you will see in later chapters, people high in narcissism initially attract others with their charisma and confidence, but they tend to enact a variety of maladaptive relationship behaviors, use their relationship partners for game playing, power, or status gains, and are not averse to adopting self-serving exit strategies (e.g., ghosting; Jonason et al., 2010; Jonason et al., 2012; Jonason et al., 2021).

Culture

Who should choose your life-long partner: you, or your family? In a romantic spat, are you inclined to prioritize harmony or "fight fire with fire"? If unhappily married, would you consider divorce? How we navigate relationships tends to reflect our cultural upbringings.

Culture is a primary contextual factor and refers to the vast and dynamic set of norms, practices, institutions, and artifacts that surround us and respond to us (Markus & Kitayama, 2010). If we, as individuals, develop default patterns of thinking and behaving that reflect our cultural context (i.e., "modes of being," Markus & Kitayama, 2003), these basic ways of operating will likely play out in our relationship experiences. This possibility has led relationship researchers to examine how culturally driven independent versus interdependent orientations (Markus & Kitayama, 1991) might predict variations in relationship experiences. Individuals in Western cultures (e.g., American, European) tend to move through the world with an independent or individualistic orientation that prioritizes separateness, self-reliance, uniqueness in comparison to others, and standing up for oneself. In contrast, people in Eastern cultures (e.g., Japanese; Korean, Venezuelan) generally take an interdependent or collectivist orientation, valuing group harmony, connection, reliance on others, and fitting in. How these two sociality styles affect relationship dynamics is not the only question put forth by cross-cultural relationship researchers, but studying them has helped clarify the generalizability of key relationship theories and principles.

Other Key Individual Differences

By now, you should have a sense that relationships are unique, reflecting the uniqueness of each of us. Studying individual differences and how they predict relationship dynamics and outcomes respects the diversity of relationships and the diversity of the people in them. The above discussion highlights central individual difference variables that appear important in forecasting relationship outcomes, but there are other dimensions of diversity that the field has not made as much progress exploring. Relationships among or with individuals who have mental health disorders (e.g., bipolar disorder, depression), intellectual or social disabilities (e.g., autism), or chronic illness, for example, represent a small subset of the breadth of diversity that the field could learn more about, and in doing so, better understand people's relationship experiences and what makes them work well.

Why We Study Romantic Relationships

Love is a many-splendored thing, but that is not enough reason to study it. The field of relationship science is energized to study romantic relationships because, as our closest relationships, they play a critical role in shaping who we are, how we feel, and how we live. Who would Elton John be if he were married to home-making legend Martha Stewart, rather than David Furnish? It might be hard to anticipate which aspects of John would be different, but it is clear he would not be identical to the person he is today, nor would his day-to-day life be experienced in the same way.

Consequences for the Self-Concept

Romantic relationships play a vital role in shaping who we are. The self-concept (or simply, "the self") refers to a dynamic set of traits, attitudes, beliefs, and behaviors that comprise our identity. The self is inherently social – constructed and altered through interactions with others.

In adulthood, people tend to view their partners as part of themselves, not necessarily consciously, but implicitly. We see this anecdotally, when romantic partners take pride in each other's achievements, feel offended when the other is slighted, and approach the world as a "we" rather than two solitary "I"s. We see this empirically, when we study how people's self-concepts expand to include aspects of their partner as they fall in love, as shown in Figure 1.15 (Aron et al., 1995). Models of the self that emphasize its interpersonal dimensions, like a relational self (one that emerges from assimilating with close others; e.g., Brewer & Gardner, 1996), underscore the idea that our romantic partners become part of us. We can think about relationship-induced self-change as a manifestation of pair-bonding (Branand et al., 2019).

Figure 1.15 As these new romantic partners spend time with each other, they assume aspects of their partner as their own. This integration of self and other is important to pair-bonding. What might the consequences be for the self-concept should they later break up? (Photo: Luis Alvarez / DigitalVision / Getty Images)

Consequences for Psychological Well-Being and Physical Health

How's your mood today? How about your physical health? To evaluate everyday factors that contribute to your overall well-being, we might ask about your nutrition, stress, and exercise and sleep habits, but an equally useful question is: how socially connected are you feeling today? It may sound surprising, but both your psychological well-being and your physical health are tied to the health of your social relationships. Here we review how people's relationship status, relationship quality, and their social integration each relate to their health and well-being.

Relationship Status

Because romantic relationships tend to be prominent sources of social connection in adulthood, some scholars focus on relationship status when exploring the link between relationships and health. **Relationship status** is a designation of whether someone is in a romantic relationship, and if they *are* in a relationship, which type of relationship they are in, a proxy for commitment (e.g., dating casually, dating seriously, cohabiting). Are people in highly committed relationships (e.g., married) happier and healthier than people who are single or in less committed relationships?

The **marriage effect** suggests yes: married people fare better than others on myriad indices of health and well-being, with marriage possibly providing a protective benefit against psychological distress and physical disease. Married people have lower mortality rates than unmarried people (Holt-Lunstad et al., 2010; Sbarra, Bourassa, & Manvelian, 2019; Shor et al., 2012), and they are more likely to survive health threats than unmarried people (King & Reis, 2012). Married individuals also boast better subjective well-being compared to individuals in other structured relationships (e.g., cohabiting, dating) and relative to single individuals (Kamp Dush & Amato, 2005). Longitudinal research shows that new changes in relationship status (i.e., from single to married or to cohabiting) are associated with lower levels of depression and greater happiness (Musick & Bumpass, 2012). These findings are buttressed by cross-cultural research, which controlled for sociodemographic factors and found that "marrieds" reported more happiness than "unmarrieds" in sixteen of the seventeen studied industrialized countries (Stack & Eshleman, 1998). Being married is also associated with lower psychological distress for Latino men and women than any other relationship status (e.g., cohabitating, single, separated, divorced; Darghouth et al., 2015).

Consistent with this idea, legally married same-sex couples report lower psychological distress and fewer depressive symptoms than same-sex couples in relationships that are not legally recognized (Kornblith et al., 2016; Wight et al., 2013). Likewise, college students in committed dating relationships tend to have better mental health and engage in fewer risk behaviors than their single counterparts (Braithwaite et al., 2010). For older (heterosexual) adults, however, the effects seem to weaken. Older married men experience similar well-being to older cohabitating men, and both groups report better well-being than single men; meanwhile, older women experienced no status-based differences in psychological well-being (Smith et al., 1999).

Might relationship-status-based distinctions emerge because of a selection effect (i.e., maybe happy/healthy people are more likely to be married)? Psychologically healthier people do seem to both enter marriage and stay in their marriages at higher rates than those who are more psychologically distressed (DeMaris, 2018; Wilson & Oswald, 2005). Yet, the marriage effect *still persists* above and beyond the self-selection into (and out of) marriage. Indeed, research controlling for pre-marital psychological health also shows that married people are more satisfied in life than those who are unmarried (Grover & Helliwell, 2019). So, the marriage effect may have some weight to it. We cannot easily test whether marriage drives these effects: good ethical judgment prevents us from randomly assigning individuals to be married or not, and then see what happens; so we must instead rely on accumulating evidence, especially longitudinal work, to try to discern the role of marriage in personal well-being.

Perhaps, instead, relationship-based distinctions obscure important heterogeneity among single individuals (i.e., what about the happy/healthy single people?). Long-term single people are indeed a diverse group: some are single because they choose to be; others experience singlehood because of challenges in forming relationships (Pepping et al., 2018). Research that has not differentiated single-by-choice individuals from other types of single parties, or research that does not include divorced individuals among those who have chosen marriage, might make the true nature of the marriage effect harder to see.

Relationship Quality

If you're thinking that relationship *quality* (not just status) might matter here, you're right. **Relationship quality** refers to a subjective overall judgment about one's relationship, with high relationship quality typically indicating high levels of desirable relationship characteristics, such as satisfaction, trust, intimacy, love, passion, and commitment (Fletcher et al., 2000). Relying on relationship status in predicting well-being might assume happy marital relationships, when we know not all marriages are happy (Figure 1.16). Some partners are affectionate, loving, and supportive; other partners are dismissive, callous, and manipulating. It makes intuitive sense that personal well-being outcomes would vary for people in these qualitatively different relationships. So, if evidence shows that married people on average experience greater health and well-being, perhaps the observed benefits over-represent happy couples. Consistent with this idea, the protective health benefits of marriage are more pronounced in people with satisfying compared to unsatisfying marriages (Lawrence et al., 2019).

One study on survival fifteen years after a coronary-artery grafting procedure showed both the marriage effect (i.e., 60 percent of married women were still alive compared to 26.3 percent of unmarried women) and the importance of relationship quality (King & Reis, 2012). The women in satisfying marriages were over three times (!) more likely to be alive fifteen years after the procedure (83 percent survived) compared to married women with unsatisfying marriages (28.6 percent survived).

Figure 1.16 They may be smiling here, but Scarlett Johansson and Adam Driver's portrayal of a divorcing couple in *The Marriage Story* showed the significant psychological distress of a break-up. Is staying married but in an unhappy marriage better or worse for psychological health than leaving and being alone? (Photo: Alberto Pizzoli / AF / Getty Images)

A meta-analysis of 126 studies similarly suggests that better-quality marital relationships predict better physical health, including better cardiovascular functioning during marital conflict and lower risk of death in general in both men and women (Robles et al., 2014).

Meanwhile, maintaining a lower-quality relationship predicts a host of problems. A meta-analysis of ninety-three studies, for example, showed that lower marital quality is associated with higher levels of stress, depressive symptoms, and substance use, and it also predicts the onset of psychiatric disorders (Proulx et al., 2007). The link between lower relationship quality and poorer personal outcomes (anxiety, depression, substance use) is also evidenced in sexual and gender minorities, including sexual minority women, transgender men, gender-diverse individuals, and male and female same-sex couples (Sarno et al., 2022; Whitton & Kuryluk, 2014). One study showed that suicide vulnerability is highest for individuals who are in low-quality relationships (higher than for single individuals) and lowest for people in happy relationships (Till et al., 2017).

Although happy relationships seem to produce happy people, happy people may be prone to entering especially happy marriages, in part because they are more likely to stay single than enter an unhappy marriage (Chapman & Guven, 2016). Further, happy people bring their cheery disposition into their relationships. Compared to less happy people, happier people perceive their partners as more supportive, important to them, and helpful, while viewing their relationship as more satisfying; they may create a positive interpersonal space that benefits both their own and their partner's relationship outcomes (Moore & Diener, 2019).

Relationship Loss

For many of us, the psychological importance of close relationships is never felt so intensely as when we lose a highly interdependent relationship. The death of a spouse and divorce, for instance, are considered the two most stressful possible life events, requiring the most social and psychological adjustment (Scully et al., 2000). In response to romantic break-ups, even as we might experience some relief, people enter an intense period of sadness, anger, and emotional volatility (Rhoades et al., 2011; Sbarra & Emery, 2005). As such, the aftermath of a break-up is a period of heightened risk for a first onset of major depressive disorder for adolescents (Monroe et al., 1999). In the long run, most people who experience break-ups or divorce readjust and have positive outcomes; the minority of individuals who suffer poor outcomes may have pre-existing vulnerabilities, such as previous challenges with anxiety (Sbarra et al., 2015).

Losing one's relationship may be harmful in part because it reduces one's social network. In addition to severing the romantic tie, individuals who break up may lose shared friends or access to their in-law family. This is no minor problem: our non-romantic relationships (e.g., friendships, family relationships) are also integral to health and well-being.

Social Integration, Health, and Well-Being

An abundance of evidence suggests our health depends on having a strong social network comprised of various relationships – called social integration. Social integration is a protective factor against infectious disease and depression, is associated with better cardiovascular health and lower risk of stroke, and supports less cognitive decline that might accompany aging (for review, see Cohen & Janicki-Deverts, 2009). The impact of social integration was first demonstrated in a landmark study showing that people who were socially integrated were more likely to survive over time than people who were less socially integrated (but otherwise similarly healthy; House et al., 1988). Today, a robust body of research shows the protective benefits of close relationships and the risk associated with social disconnection. One study, for example, focused on Romanian orphans who were institutionalized prior to adoption. While at the orphanage, these children were provided with food, but no sustained social contact. Children who were institutionalized for over six months (and therefore experienced sustained social deprivation) showed clear cognitive, emotional, and social impairments fifteen years later (Rutter et al., 2012). This was despite sufficient nutrition, supporting the idea that we do not thrive on food, water, and sleep alone. Indeed, unusually high mortality rates of custodial-care orphans later in life bear witness to the fact that humans need social connection (UNICEF, 1997).

Other research in this area is simply startling. For instance, a meta-analytic review of 148 studies revealed that odds of survival were *50 percent better* over a seven-and-a-half year time period for people with stronger social relationships, results that controlled for initial health, age, and gender (Holt-Lunstad et al., 2010). When it comes to mortality risk, *not* having strong relationships is as dangerous as smoking up to fifteen cigarettes a day and more dangerous than widely recognized health risks like obesity, leading a sedentary life, or engaging in alcohol abuse (Holt-Lunstad, 2018). This is not a story about having or not having a romantic partner; this is a story about the dangers of lacking *any* close relationships. So hazardous is the absence of strong relationships that some researchers are calling out pervasive social *dis*connection as a public health crisis (Holt-Lunstad et al., 2017).

Loneliness, Health, and Well-Being

We all know what it feels like to experience occasional loneliness – an unpleasant, distressing feeling tied to a perceived deficit in the quality or quantity of one's social connections

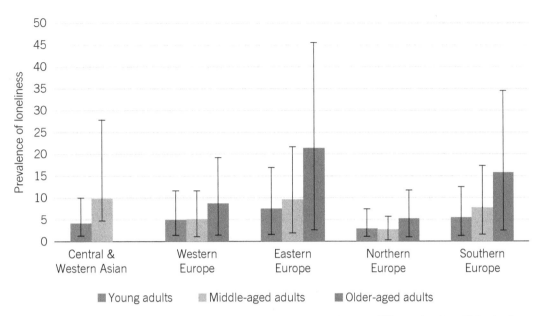

Figure 1.17 Meta-analysis of studies using nationally representative samples from over 100 countries shows higher loneliness prevalence with age, but social context matters, too. Eastern Europe shows comparatively higher loneliness than other European regions. Error bars represent 95 percent confidence intervals. Data were not available for older adults in Asia. (Source: Drawn based on data from Surkalim et al. [2022])

(Cacioppo et al., 2009; Perlman & Peplau, 1981). What makes loneliness so interesting is that it is based on a subjective judgment that one's belonging needs are not being met. As such, people can (and do) experience loneliness while in the company of other people. Rates of loneliness are strikingly high: by some estimates, 35 percent of American adults 45 or older report being lonely once a week or more, a number that includes 51 percent of never-married individuals and 31 percent of people currently married (Anderson, 2010). Cross-cultural research supports the notion that loneliness is a universal experience, even as it is tied to sociocultural context. As shown in Figure 1.17, loneliness is more common among older adults in Asia and Europe compared to younger adults, with region also playing a role in loneliness (Surkalim et al., 2022). The prevalence of loneliness is alarming since we know that experiences of social disconnection predict poorer health and longevity.

  ARTICLE SPOTLIGHT

Does Technology Make the iGen Lonely?

If you were born between 1997 and 2015, you are part of Gen Z, a generational cohort also called the iGen (Twenge, 2017). This designation (a quippy take on the iPhone) highlights the unique role that technology and digital media have played in the upbringing of this generation. It was not so long ago (circa 2011) when less than a quarter of adolescents had a smartphone at their disposal. By 2018, this number was up to a whopping 95 percent, with 45 percent of survey respondents saying they are online "constantly" (Anderson & Jiang, 2018).

If iGen'ers use texting and social media more than any previous generation, is this at a cost to real-time, face-to-face social interaction? A cross-generational comparison – that is, at the cohort level – would help figure this out. Such analysis would involve comparing Boomers, XGen'ers, Millennials, and iGen'ers at the same developmental stage (e.g., when they were all adolescents). Differences in social interaction at the cohort level would support a *time displacement hypothesis*: we only have so much time, so if we are on digital technology, it must be at the expense of in-person interaction. Alternatively, we could investigate this question at the individual level. For some people (e.g., extroverts) and not others (e.g., introverts), digital technology might complement face-to-face socializing rather than replace it. This *complementarity hypothesis* suggests technology enhances opportunities for social connection for some people.

Twenge, Spitzberg, and Campbell (2019) showed the benefits of looking at data from these two perspectives (cohort level and individual level) to learn how technology is linked to in-person interaction and loneliness. Their analyses focused on two nationally representative surveys that provided self-reported information on the loneliness, leisure time, and face-to-face peer interactions (e.g., hanging with friends, dating) of approximately 8.2 million adolescents. Because their data spanned decades, beginning in the 1970s, they could test for differences in technology use, loneliness, and social interaction between cohorts, while also examining links among variables at the individual levels.

Cohort-level results supported the time displacement hypothesis: iGen'ers use more digital media and also spend markedly less time with their friends than previous cohorts did when they were adolescents. iGen'ers also report more loneliness than any other generations of the past (see Figure 1.18a). But don't throw your phone out

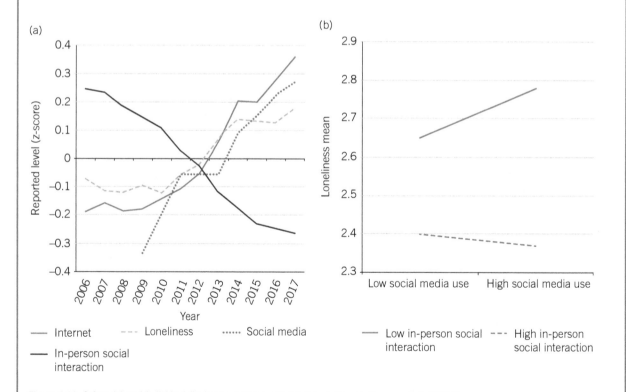

Figure 1.18 Cohort (a) and individual (b) level correlates with loneliness (Source: Twenge et al. [2019])

yet. Analyses at the individual level supported the complementarity hypothesis; many individual iGen'ers who spent a lot of time on social media also enjoyed many in-person interactions (see Figure 1.18b). At risk for loneliness were a subgroup of iGen'ers who relied heavily on social media without also having in-person interactions. These results show that phone use is not uniformly problematic, but has collectively decreased social interaction for iGen'ers. The overall drop in social interaction, even with its varied individual-level effects, motivates the need for greater inquiry into the long-term consequences of the displacement of real face-to-face interaction with social media.

Loneliness is also tied to individual differences variables, such as minority status, gender, and personality, although a close look at these links is warranted. Racial minority identification, for example, predicts loneliness, but this link can be explained by the association between minority racial identification and lower income and lower socioeconomic status, which likely drive loneliness (Hawkley et al., 2008). Similarly, minority stress and lack of connection to an LGB community likely explains the link between sexual orientation and loneliness (Kuyper & Fokkema, 2010). Women often report more loneliness than men, and while women's loneliness appears to steadily increase with age, some evidence suggests men's appears to be highest around age 40 and then again around 80, with a dip occurring in mid-life (Pinquart & Sörensen, 2001; von Soest et al., 2020). Meta-analytic research also identifies a personality link with loneliness. Higher levels of extraversion, as well as agreeableness, conscientiousness, and openness, tend to predict lower levels of loneliness, while more neuroticism is linked to greater loneliness (Buecker et al., 2020).

Consequences for Families and Society

The importance of social connection for mental and physical health was anticipated by a French sociologist named Émile Durkheim over 120 years ago (1951). Durkheim argued that social integration, and a stable set of norms that support social connection, is essential for well-being. He observed rates of suicide to be higher among those who were less integrated, which in his time meant unmarried and without solid links to church or the broader community. Consistent with these ideas, recent data suggest that divorced or separated individuals have an 88 percent higher likelihood of dying by suicide compared to married people (Kposowa et al., 2020). Today, thwarted belonging is well recognized as a key factor predicting death by suicide (Joiner, 2007; Van Orden et al., 2010). Even recalling experiences of ostracism, imagining ostracism, or experiencing brief social exclusion in an online ball-tossing game increases suicidal thoughts (Chen et al., 2020). The link between belonging and suicide underscores the importance of a societal structure that encourages sustained relationships. It highlights how a lack of social connection can threaten family-level and societal-level well-being: one person's suicide or suicidal ideation can create ripples of despair that spread through the family and society. We study relationships because relationships have consequences for individuals (the self, psychological and physical health) and because the quality of one's relationships has broader impacts on family and society.

Consider how one person's loneliness can impact society broadly. There is a common belief – echoed by the media – that people who carry out school shootings were bullied, rejected, or isolated. Although there are many reasons that people make the terrible decision to enact violence, social rejection is common among those who go on to become "school-shooters" (Leary et al., 2003), and lab work shows that social exclusion increases aggressive behavior and a terrorist mindset (Pfundmair, 2019; Twenge et al., 2001) The ability for people to form and maintain close relationships matters for individual well-being and the peaceful functioning of society.

The health of any given close relationship is of concern not only for its members, but for the surrounding family, social network, and society more broadly. Think, for example, about how parents' relationships affect their children. Parental relationship transitions (e.g., divorce, remarriage) are associated with poorer social, emotional, and behavioral outcomes for many (though not all) children (Cavanagh & Fomby, 2019; Raley & Sweeney, 2020). Parental discord alone, without divorce, is similarly detrimental. Children experience more cognitive, emotional, and behavioral problems, as well as heightened physiological reactions, when their family dynamics are marked by interparental conflict (Rhoades, 2008). Children with parents who are abusive or violent to each other are in a particularly vulnerable position; meta-analytic research documents a strong overall association between exposure to domestic violence and trauma symptoms (Evans et al., 2008; Wolfe et al., 2003). Friends, too, are affected by one another's relationship decisions. For example, adult couples whose friends get divorced are more likely themselves to get divorced (McDermott et al., 2013). Such expanding relationship instability suggests that friends can model how to leave unhappy or unhealthy relationships; it also suggests that supporting friends' romantic relationships (when they are worth saving) might in turn help your own, and potentially society more broadly. This is particularly notable given the significant psychological, financial, and social costs of divorce.

Conclusion

Elton John's story highlights the intersection of person, partner(s), and context in shaping relationship experiences. With multiple forces of influence, relationships are both unique and universal, and despite their mystique, we now know a great deal about relationships because of the multidisciplinary field of relationship science. We also still have much to learn. Relationship scientists are on a continuing mission to understand the factors, behaviors, and processes that support stable, high-quality relationships. Thankfully, this mission is well supported by the strong set of productive theories that we can use to generate new questions and frame new findings. We turn to the dominant theories in relationship science in Chapter 2.

Major Take-Aways

- Relationship science is an emerging interdisciplinary field devoted to all aspects of relationship experiences.
- Romantic relationships are a type of close relationship, which are typically described by high interdependence

(which includes frequent, long-term, strong influence across multiple domains), high intimate knowledge, and high commitment.

- People are biologically driven toward relationships; their need to belong is

- strong and pervasive, and people suffer when they do not have sustained connections.
- Relationships are diverse in structure, exclusivity, composition, duration, motives, commitment, and consistency, to name a few key dimensions.

- Relationships support psychological and physical health, and affect not only the relationship partners, but their families, communities, and society more broadly.

Further Readings

If you're interested in ...

... a summative description of people's pervasive motivation to have strong, meaningful connections, read:
Baumeister, R. F., & Leary, M. R. (1995). The need to belong: Desire for interpersonal attachments as a fundamental human motivation. *Psychological Bulletin, 117,* 497–529.

... how your phone may interfere with the quality of your social interactions, read:
Dwyer, R. J., Kushlev, K., & Dunn, E. W. (2018). Smartphone use undermines enjoyment of face-to-face social interactions. *Journal of Experimental Social Psychology, 78,* 233–239.

... sexual minorities and the unique factors that shape relationship quality for lesbian women, read:

Kimberly, C., & Williams, A. (2017). Decade review of research on lesbian romantic relationship satisfaction. *Journal of LGBT Issues in Counseling, 11,* 119–135.

... how modern-day marriages are rendered more, or less, vulnerable, read:
Robles, T. F. (2014). Marital quality and health: Implications for marriage in the 21st century. *Current Directions in Psychological Science, 23,* 427–432.

... social *dis*connection and the factors that extend and shorten the damaging effects of ostracism and exclusion, read:
Williams, K. D., & Nida, S. A. (2022). Ostracism and social exclusion: Implications for separation, social isolation, and loss. *Current Opinion in Psychology, 47,* 101353.

2 GUIDING THEORIES OF RELATIONSHIP SCIENCE

Why Do We Love the Way We Do?

Emmy-award-winning actor Samira Wiley and her wife, accomplished screen writer and producer Lauren Morelli, are a dynamic and devoted pair. They first met on the set of *Orange Is the New Black*, and although Morelli (who was married at the time) later confessed that she "immediately had a crush" on Wiley, their relationship began with a close, confiding friendship (Lamphier, 2016). Only after Morelli separated from her husband did their relationship transition to romantic. Married since 2017, they confess to sharing a beautiful kind of love, one defined by the type of intimacy that many people long for and struggle to find. Says Wiley of Morelli, "she could see all these parts of me and still want to be with me, and I could see all these parts of her and still want to be with her" (Lamphier, 2016). Now mothers to their daughter, George Elizabeth, born in 2021, Wiley and Morelli (Figure 2.1) juggle careers, fame, family, and their romantic relationship. As Wiley has said, "life is now about navigating it together" (Juneau, 2021).

Figure 2.1 Samira Wiley (known for her roles in *Orange Is the New Black* and *A Handmaiden's Tale*) smiles with her wife, Lauren Morelli (writer and producer). Why do some relationships progress smoothly and others not? (Photo: Jason LaVeris / FilmMagic / Getty Images)

Wiley and Morelli's relationship, like many relationships, is marked by a push and pull of each person's unique motives, personality, and needs, as well as a steady orientation toward the other. Their relationship is tantamount to an invisible tether: a "we" that binds the "I" and "you." Wiley and Morelli not only appear to desire this tether, but they seem to rely on it for comfort, use it to pursue their goals, and nurture it diligently. Relationship scientists are driven to understand why some romantic relationships are healthy, like this one, where others are decidedly not. To understand what makes this – or any – relationship function, we need a cohesive story of human relationships, or a theory, that provides a logical explanation for *why* we might expect specific relationship patterns. Theories provide context that gives meaning to individual research findings; they bind different studies together to help create a more complete story of human relationships.

The current chapter focuses on the frameworks, or theories, that relationship scientists use to guide their study of romantic relationships. You will learn why theory is important and why having differing theoretical perspectives is a critical advantage to a burgeoning field. You will be introduced to the "big three" theoretical approaches in relationship science: evolutionary theories, attachment theory, and interdependence theory. We will also highlight the importance of context by introducing you to social ecological models. Your goal in reading this chapter is to become familiar with prominent perspectives in relationship science, so that you will move through the remainder of this book well-equipped with the tools to interpret what we currently know about relationships.

 GUIDING QUESTIONS

Consider these questions as you read this chapter:
- What are the problems that each major theory in relationship science aims to address?
- What assumptions guide evolutionary theories, attachment theory, and interdependence theory?
- What critiques can you offer of each guiding theory?
- What are the connections among different theories in relationship science?

The Three Main Theories in Relationship Science

Two questions for you: (1) Why do people have romantic relationships? and (2) What explains relationship thoughts, feelings, behaviors, and success? These are big questions, and if you're like most relationship scientists, you'll quickly see that no one answer suffices, even as you recognize the need for some "big ideas" around which to frame your understanding. These "big ideas" are theories. Formally defined, theories are logical statements that explain how and why a set of two or more constructs are related. In the relationship context, this means that theories give us insight into why people form relationships, why they cheat, why they feel lonely, and why any and all relationship experiences happen, including why some relationships work well and others struggle. Three "big ideas" guide contemporary relationship science: evolutionary theories, attachment theory, and interdependence theory. Each views relationships (and specific experiences and behaviors in relationships) as solving a different fundamental problem.

Consider infidelity. From an evolutionary perspective, cheating on a partner might serve the purpose of acquiring more desirable genes for offspring, without sacrificing the resources provided by a steady partner. This is because evolutionary theories view modern relationship behaviors as *solving sex-specific survival and reproduction problems*. Meanwhile, from an attachment perspective, an affair might deliver support and fulfill needs when a primary partner falls short. Attachment theory contends that people's relationship behaviors *solve the specific evolutionary problem of how to maintain support from close others*. Finally, interdependence theory might explain an affair as a person's attempt to maximize their benefits in their romantic relationship. Interdependence theory views relationship behaviors as *solving problems emerging from the relationship's situation*, which refers to the underlying dependency structure of a relationship (e.g., how one partner's behaviors affect the other).

The idea that the relationship behaviors can be understood in different ways might seem intimidating: what is the real answer if different theories postulate different explanations? Here we say: evaluate the assumptions, look at the empirical evidence, and be open to the idea that multiple theories can be useful to explain the same phenomenon.

Evolutionary Theories: Solving Problems of Survival and Reproduction

Wiley and Morelli are both beautiful, intelligent, charismatic women. How might their physical attractiveness and personal characteristics have affected their initial attraction? And more importantly, why? The appeal of certain faces and certain characteristics is so ingrained in how we live our lives that rarely do we pause to wonder why we judge some physical and internal traits more favorably than others. Evolutionary theories, which have historically focused on explaining different-sex relationships, can help. These theories provide productive lenses by which we can think about attraction, short-term affairs, long-term love, infidelity, and more, even as we consider their shortcomings. Let's turn now to the basics of evolutionary theories.

Evolutionary Theories: The Basics

Evolutionary theories assume that the modern-day mind is the latest version of generations upon generations of ancestral struggle to survive and reproduce in the face of environmental pressures. In other words, evolutionary theories offer survival and reproduction goals as explanations for *why* humans are as they are (**ultimate explanations**) and delineate *how* psychological mechanisms work to achieve these goals (**proximate explanations**). When applied to relationship science, evolutionary approaches are particularly helpful in explaining partner preferences and relationship initiation tactics; identifying the roles of hormones and pheromones in modern relationships; revealing benefits of negative relational behaviors (e.g., jealousy; infidelity); and exposing how behaviors that make sense for people in our contemporary world (e.g., taking birth control) might have surprising consequences (Eastwick, 2016; Perlman et al., 2018). To understand evolutionary approaches, we need to review their basic underlying premises.

Darwin's (1859) theory of evolution rests on the idea that whatever helps a species survive and reproduce becomes standard within that species. To see how this **natural selection** process works, first consider that when animals have offspring, the offspring are many and varied. If you share biological parents with a sibling or two, then you know what we mean: you share DNA with your siblings, but you are not clones. One of you might be taller, faster, or have a lower resting heart rate. If any given variation proves especially advantageous, it could (over successive generations) become a fixture within a given species.

For example, suppose the only available food for a species of sharks is a tough-skinned fish. If one shark happens to be born with exceptionally sharp teeth (Figure 2.2), then this random mutation increases its likelihood to secure food, survive, and reproduce, at the disadvantage of the dull-teethed sharks. This **competition for resources** is a key generator for evolutionary change. Sharp-teethed sharks will eat, survive, and reproduce when other sharks cannot (**survival of the fittest**). Eventually, what started as a lucky break (sharp teeth) will become standard in this species of shark, yielding **population change**. The same is true for humans: physical and psychological adaptations that promote reproduction and survival become universal standards.

Figure 2.2 Why is this shark smiling with such intimidating chompers? Sharp teeth likely evolved in environmental conditions that gave them a key advantage. (Photo: wildestanimal / Moment / Getty Images)

Sexual Selection Theory

Relationship scientists are particularly interested in Darwin's (1859, 1871) **sexual selection theory**, a look at the mating game through an evolutionary lens. Sexual selection theory explains the seemingly unnecessary extravagance in male adornment (think dramatic peacock plumes or awkward deer antlers; Figure 2.3). These ornaments are stunning, but they confer no survival benefit. If anything, they attract predators: Here I am! Come eat me for lunch! So why do they exist? Sexual selection theory suggests extravagant features are retained over generations not because they help with survival (they do not), but because they help with reproductive success through **intrasexual selection** or **intersexual selection**.

(a)   (b)

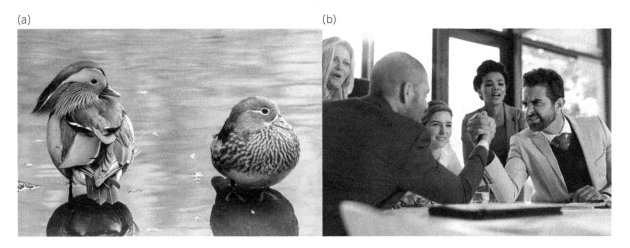

Figure 2.3 Male Mandarin ducks flaunt their striking feathers to attract females (a), and human males show their dominance by status and strength competitions (b). What else do humans display to attract partners? (Photo: Edwin Godinho / EyeEm / Getty Images [a] and PeopleImages / iStock / Getty Images Plus [b])

*Intra*sexual (within sex) selection begins when a trait helps animals out-shine, out-wit, out-maneuver, or otherwise out-compete their rivals for access to sexual partners. Over time, these features are metaphorically "selected" by evolution and become more typical of that sex. *Inter*sexual (between sexes) selection elevates certain traits because the other sex preferentially chooses partners with those traits again and again. If female Mandarin ducks find vibrantly colored plumage wildly exciting, then the dowdy males will not enjoy as much action. Less action, less offspring. The competitive pressures exerted by members of the same sex and the selection pressures imposed by the opposite sex can alter the presence of certain characteristics over successive generations.

Do modern-day humans show signs of an evolutionary past shaped by intrasexual and intersexual pressures? You bet (Puts, 2016). Contemporary mating efforts continue to be explained to some extent by sexual selection theory. Saturday night at the club, you'll see various ways men and women try to stand out and appeal to the partner(s) they desire. Key tactics of intrasexual competition include self-promotion (bragging or boasting), rival derogation (insults! rumors!), competitor manipulation (lying to shift rivals' attention away from your partner of interest), and mate manipulation (strategically directing a desired partner's attention only to you; Fisher & Cox, 2011). Of course, human courtship is not as simple as "winning" access to "mates" by besting same-sex competitors, but the parallels are clear.

 IS THIS TRUE FOR YOU?

Flaunting Your Feathers: Do You Engage in Intrasexual Competition?

From overt aggression to vicious rumors, people can go to great lengths to stand out among perceived rivals. Is this true for you? To what extent do you engage in intrasexual competition (Figure 2.4)?

(a)   (b)

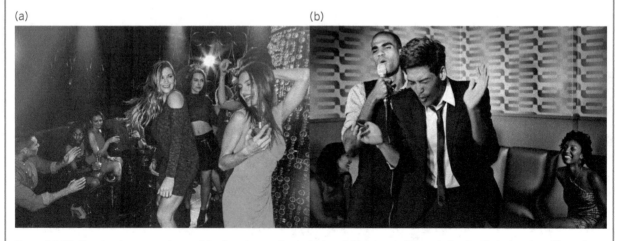

Figure 2.4 Whether dancing, conversing, or doing karaoke, people can try to outshine one another and attract a desired partner. What other examples of intrasexual competition have you seen? (Photo: gradyreese / E+ / Getty Images [a] and Blend Images / Jill Giardino / Tetra Images / Getty Images [b])

Scholars measure this drive using the Intrasexual Competition Scale (Buunk & Fisher, 2009), which includes statements like, "I can't stand it when I meet another man/woman who is more attractive than I am," and "I tend to look for negative characteristics in attractive men/women." While some people strongly agree with these sentences, others might say, eh . . . not really. This variation could point to factors (such as culture or relationship status) that dampen or amplify biological predispositions toward intrasexual competition. Personality, for instance, appears linked to intrasexual competitiveness: more neurotic men and women engage in greater intrasexual competition, and more agreeable women tend to engage in less (Buunk & Fisher, 2009).

Recall, however, that evolved drives generally operate outside of conscious awareness. Might you compete without realizing it? Gossiping, for example, might not feel like a mating strategy, but it can elevate your social status relative to others' damaged reputations. Further, the topics that men (achievement) and women (physical appearance and social information) gossip about tend to align with traits generally desired by the other sex. This reinforces the idea that gossiping about members of the same sex may elevate one's position in the mating hierarchy, even if that was not its consciously intended goal (Davis et al., 2018). Perhaps this explains why women tend to gossip most about women who pose a threat; they often pass along damaging social information about physically attractive, flirtatious, or provocatively dressed women (Reynolds et al., 2018).

People can also use social media to inadvertently engage in intrasexual competition. Posting workout stats or fitness updates, for example, can subtly signal your health and vitality (desired traits in a partner), and give you a competitive advantage over other people vying for partners (Vandenbroele et al., 2020). Other behaviors, like posting attractive images of yourself, can also be interpreted through this lens. Does this provide a plausible explanation for some of your social media behaviors? If not, what other explanations are there for self-promotion?

Intersexual pressures may be especially important in human courtship. Think about the ways people show off, if subtly, in the attempt to attract a partner. Costly signaling theory helps explain seemingly extravagant, wasteful, or high-cost displays put on by humans and animals alike by drawing on the *handicap principle* (Zahavi, 1975). If you run a marathon or pick up the tab at the end of the night, doing so incurs costs or a handicap. Presumably, if you are making these grand gestures you can afford these costs, which could make you more attractive (Hennighausen et al., 2016; Nelissen & Meijers, 2011; Sundie et al., 2011). Status and resources (at least in the long term), just like intelligence, youth, kindness, and health, are hard to fake. Behaviors that require effort or sacrifice (i.e., costly signals) are therefore often reliable cues for underlying partner qualities.

Parental Investment Theory

Both intrasexual selection pressures and intersexual selection pressures tend to alter characteristics of the sex that is *less* involved in raising children, the sex that has less parental investment. Parental investment refers to a parent's commitment of energy, resources, time, etc. to one offspring, which limits their ability to invest in other offspring (Bateman, 1948; Trivers, 1972). Across species (including humans), males tend to invest less than females. This presents a puzzle: if males and females both pass on their genes most effectively when their offspring survive, why don't males and females invest the same amount?

The answer to this question is a central premise to parental investment theory (Bateman, 1948; Trivers, 1972), and it all begins with basic biology. Let's think specifically about human evolution: what is the bare minimum investment our ancestors must have made in order to reproduce successfully and have a child who survives into their reproductive years (Kenrick et al., 1990). At minimum, our female ancestors endured an extensive gestation period, engaged in a risky birthing process, and provided vital nutrition to babies by breast feeding for multiple years. They then typically cared for each child to the point of independence. One child, therefore, was a hefty investment for our female ancestors. Our male ancestors, meanwhile, had a minimum required investment of healthy sperm and the time it might take to deposit said sperm. A scant sacrifice in comparison to the years of commitment demanded of females. This dramatic sex-based asymmetry in minimum parental investment is termed **differential parental investment**.

Other biological factors accentuate these differences: males are fertile throughout their adult lives, have endless sperm to offer, and can produce sperm when they wish; females have a restricted age-range of fertility, a limited lifetime supply of viable eggs, and ovulation occurs only about once a month, at an exact time-point that eludes easy detection. So not only do females invest more in any given child relative to males, but they also have far fewer opportunities to pass along their genes. Under optimal conditions, females usually max out at around twelve offspring over the course of their lives, a number that far exceeds the modern-day norm of around two to three children globally. Cross-culturally, men (with a less rigid upper-limit) tend to have more children than women, even today (Schoumaker, 2019).

Differential parental investment, along with asymmetries in fertility, have important downstream consequences (Bjorklund & Shackelford, 1999). For example, different strategies become most effective at promoting each sex's reproductive success. A quantity-over-quality approach, or short-term strategy, becomes adaptive for males, who face the challenge of identifying fertile women. They can increase their reproductive success by throwing more darts at the dartboard and hoping a few land well. Meanwhile, a quality-over-quantity approach, or long-term strategy, is most effective for women, who face the challenge of identifying resource-providing partners with good genes. They have only a few darts to toss so they must line up their shot carefully. Relatedly, differential parental investment and fertility asymmetries result in females becoming the choosier sex (they need to be careful with their limited darts), while males become rivals for their attention (Trivers, 1972).

Parental investment theory is based specifically on *minimum* biologically required investments, without consideration of context, culture, or individual choice. In modern relationships, several shifts have changed the nature of minimum investments. Paths toward parenthood vary dramatically today, with children entering families through adoption, surrogacy, and in-vitro fertilization (sometimes after years of painful fertility treatments); further, formula provides a sex-neutral alternative to breast feeding and many men are extremely invested in their children, whether they are serving as their primary caretakers or not. Critically, ancestral minimums do not determine modern individuals' intended or actual parental investment (Kenrick et al., 1990).

Sexual Strategies Theory

Sexual strategies theory (Buss & Schmitt, 1993, 2019) proposes that modern men and women navigate the sex-specific challenges put in place by differential parental investment by drawing on an evolved set of psychological adaptations and mating strategies. Among these psychological adaptations are emotions, like love and jealousy, as well as **mate preferences**, which are psychological tools for discriminating among partners. **Mating strategies** include tactics (i.e., actions or behaviors) used to solve problems tied to mate acquisition and retention. Even though mating strategies are, well, strategic, they operate outside of awareness. They are a gut-level reflection of a psychological inheritance that made our ancestors successful at reproducing. And they were successful: otherwise, we wouldn't be here!

Sexual strategies theory contends that people have a remarkably extensive repertoire of mating strategies that they can use to pursue reproductive success. Depending on the situation, optimal mating strategies can include short-term mating (sexual activity without commitment), long-term mating (high commitment), serial monogamy (maintaining only one sexual relationship at a time), mate poaching (stealing other people's partners), mate guarding (protecting your own partner), and infidelity (social monogamy with extradyadic affairs). Wiley and Morelli's marriage, for example, reflects a long-term strategy that prioritizes monogamy and mutual investment in their child. Humans' diverse set of mating strategies allows them to respond flexibly to different environmental contexts.

Strategic pluralism theory (Gangestad & Simpson, 2000) emphasizes this diversity. While differential parental investment suggests men prefer short-term strategies and women long-term strategies, people do not uniformly adhere to this pattern. We're too clever to rely on only one approach, and instead we consider aspects of our situation, such as our attractiveness, what the competition looks like, and what resources we need. Then, there's some math. According to strategic pluralism theory, heterosexual men calculate their potential payoff of pursuing short-term partners versus offering long-term parental investment, and heterosexual women calculate their potential payoff of selecting a good-genes guy versus a resource-providing man (who might not be the same). Whichever approach produces the best outcome (highest payoff), strategic pluralism theory suggests that's the approach people take.

 RESEARCHER SPOTLIGHT: Norman Li, MBA, PhD

How did you come to be a social-personality psychologist?
I started my career in business and, while working as an investment consultant, I took an evening introductory psychology course at Northwestern University (NU). I loved it! After taking a few more courses and working on a research project, I became increasingly interested in psychology and sought out advice from Dr. Michael Bailey, a professor at NU. He mentored me and helped turn my research project into what eventually became my first paper. Eventually, I left finance to pursue psychology.

What, to you, are the most compelling features of evolutionary approaches?
Evolutionary approaches provide the most satisfying answers! An evolutionary perspective is directly connected to all the major sciences and provides the ultimate reasons for thoughts, feelings, and behaviors. As with all living things, humans have moved through millions of years of evolution and, thus, all of our physical and mental mechanisms tie back to survival or

Figure 2.5 Dr. Norman Li is a professor of Psychology in the School of Social Sciences at Singapore Management University. (Photo courtesy of Norman Li, MBA, PhD.)

reproductive functions. At the same time, we now have increasingly more unsolvable issues because of evolutionary mismatch: technology has made our environment vastly different from the one in which we evolved and, thus, for which our psychology is adapted.

Where do you find research inspiration and what do you like most about your work?
One major source of inspiration for me is when I repeatedly encounter a consistent bias that people have or some behavior I don't understand (and nobody else seems to really know either). I feel compelled to understand why. It's exciting to find answers to otherwise puzzling questions. I also enjoy explaining things to other people not only via publications and talks, but also through classes, and, best yet – personal conversations!

What qualities make for a great relationship scientist?
Being open-minded, persistent, and a good communicator are all relevant!

Life History Theory

The idea that people pursue reproductive success differently on account of their situations is highlighted in life history theory, which considers how the environments in which people are raised – be they chaotic or predictable – shape romantic relationships. A relative newcomer to the set of evolutionary theories, life history theory suggests that people, like all organisms, have limited energy, resources, and time and that they try to best maximize their reproductive fitness, that is, survival and reproduction (Del Guidice et al., 2016; Kaplan & Gangestad, 2005).

Spending energy, resources, and time on one activity precludes spending them on other activities, so allocation decisions are essentially trade-offs. Three key trade-offs anchor life history theory: (1) reproducing now or later; (2) having higher-quality offspring or a greater quantity of offspring; and (3) investing in mating goals or parenting. The ways individuals navigate these trade-offs become their *life history strategies*, variation in which can be captured on a slow-to-fast continuum (Ellis et al., 2009; Nettle, 2010). As shown in Table 2.1, slow strategies are associated with a host of "big picture" perspectives and long-term gains; fast strategies optimize immediate gain at the expense of future outcomes (Griskevicius et al., 2013).

An important consideration in life history theories is that each strategy (fast or slow) emerges as a rational response to one's environment. Environments can be tainted by different kinds of stressors, specifically harshness, which refers to a scarcity of resources and a lower life expectancy (often captured by SES), and unpredictability, which refers to erratic changes to the family environment, such as moving, divorces, remarriages, and parents' job changes (Ellis et al., 2009). If you grew up knowing poverty and hunger (a harsh environment), or if you grew up in a chaotic household marked by uncertainty (an unpredictable environment), "fast" strategies become adaptive responses (Griskevicius et al., 2013; Simpson, 2019). Life history theory provides a useful tool for understanding how different personal histories might lend themselves to different strategies to achieve optimal reproductive fitness.

Table 2.1 Allocating resources toward fast or slow strategies

		Early-life environment	
		Unpredictable / harsh (resource scarce, dangerous)	Predictable / gentle (resource abundant, safe)
		Fast strategies	Slow strategies
Mating	When will you start having sex?	Younger	Older
	How many sexual partners will you have?	More	Fewer
	What kind of relationship are you looking for?	Casual	Committed
Parenting	When will you start having kids?	Younger	Older
	How many children will you have?	More	Fewer
	How much will you invest in any given child?	Low	High
Reward orientation	What perspective helps you the most?	Short-term	Long-term
	Is acting impulsively beneficial?	Yes	No
	Is it worth taking a high-risk approach?	Yes	No

Life history theory suggests that the predictability and harshness of early experiences lead people to allocate resources toward fast or slow strategies.

Source: Based on data from Griskevicius (2013).

Critiques of Evolutionary Theories

Evolutionary theories (summarized in Table 2.2) remind us that we are biological beings with basic motivations, and that our romantic relationship experiences may not always result from conscious decision-making. But who is this "we"? How well do evolutionary theories explain Wiley and Morelli's same-sex relationship, for example? A key critique of evolutionary theories is that they privilege a binary conceptualization of sex and gender (male/men, female/women) and are based on heterosexual mating and reproduction. Evolutionary theories struggle to provide insight into same-sex attraction and love. David Buss, an eminent evolutionary theorist, has said that variation in sexual orientation is "a mystery of human mating and an empirical enigma for evolutionary theory" (Buss, 2016). A growth edge for this perspective,

Table 2.2 Selected evolutionary theories relevant to relationship science

Theory	Main assumptions	Key theorists
Sexual selection theory	Sex differences can be explained by intrasexual competition and intersexual selection pressures	Darwin
Parental investment	Sex differences in minimal required investments in offspring have widespread implications for human behavior	Bateman, Trivers, Kenrick, Shackelford
Sexual strategies theory	Humans use diverse goal-directed mating strategies to maximize reproductive success	Buss, Schmitt
Life history theory	Harsh or unpredictable childhood environments make fast reproductive paths (short-term gains) more adaptive than slow reproductive paths (long-term gains)	Kaplan, Gangestad, Ellis

then, is determining how and when evolutionary frameworks can help us understand diverse sexual orientations and the relationship experiences of LGBTQ+ individuals.

Two other key critiques are worth highlighting. First, we cannot directly test evolutionary theory's premises because we cannot observe evolution in action (it takes millions of years). Assumed causal pathways (e.g., sexual selection pressures *caused* men to prioritize short-term relationships) cannot be submitted to empirical scrutiny, which scholars recognize as a major conceptual limitation (Jonason & Schmitt, 2016). Second, evolutionary theories' emphasis on biologically based universals may undervalue the role of social and cultural forces in shaping relationship experiences. Take mate preferences, for example. Although evolutionary theories posit that humans evolved to prioritize specific mate preferences, mate preferences actually vary between cultures in ways that highlight the importance of sociocultural context (Zentner & Eagly, 2015). Considering evolutionary perspectives along with social and cultural forces may provide a much fuller picture. Stay tuned over the next few years as evolutionary theories continue to develop and be refined, both within relationship science and in the field of psychology more broadly (Buss, 2020; Zagaria et al., 2020).

Attachment Theory: Solving the Problem of Support Availability

Imagine you've planned a romantic weekend getaway. You're packed and ready to go. Your partner, however, *always* early and prepared, is fumbling around, clearly not ready. Do they not want to go? Are they mad you planned this trip? How would you react? Partners regularly do (or say or text) ambiguous or seemingly hurtful things to each other. How the other responds – what they think, feel, and do – can give insight into how they view both themselves and their relationship. Incidentally, this scene unfolded for Wiley and Morelli. Whereas some people might have interpreted Morelli's odd procrastination as immediately concerning ("does she want to break up?"), Wiley was only "confused." Turns out, Morelli's uncharacteristic behavior was actually a prelude to a surprise proposal (Silman, 2017). No break-up here. One useful framework for understanding why people react differently to ambiguous partner behaviors is attachment theory, originally developed by John Bowlby and elaborated by Mary Ainsworth. With origins in developmental psychology, attachment theory is a favorite of relationship scholars, who apply its ideas to adult relationships, especially romantic relationships (Hazan & Shaver, 1987; Mikulincer & Shaver, 2018). This perspective sheds light on universal, or *normative*, ways in which people have evolved to seek proximity – or closeness – to responsive others. It also explains the origins and consequences of individual differences in proximity seeking, variations that shape our relationship experiences from "cradle to the grave" (Bowlby, 1982, p. 208).

Normative Processes of Attachment

At the core of attachment theory is an evolutionary story in which little humans are much more likely to survive (and then later, reproduce) if they stay near an adult, a person capable of helping them. Think about the staggering vulnerability of infancy and early childhood: young people need food, comfort, protection, and a million forms of caregiving. Enacting behaviors that promote proximity to an adult who is "stronger and wiser" (Bowlby, 1973) confers a clear evolutionary advantage relative to going it alone. On account of this advantage, Bowlby (1973, 1980, 1982) argued that the human brain evolved an **attachment behavioral system**. This system includes all the actions that govern how people naturally approach their primary relationships in order to achieve a "set goal" of **felt security**, a state of well-being that results from feeling safe, protected, and loved (Sroufe & Waters, 1977). At its core, the attachment behavior system is oriented toward seeking and maintaining proximity to at least one supportive person.

 IN THE NEWS

Parent–Child Separations at the Mexican–American Border

The Mexican–American border captured the world's attention in 2018, when new policies were put into action by the United States' then-President Donald Trump. Intended to discourage border crossings, the Trump administration's "zero tolerance" policy required an unprecedented level of law enforcement. Undocumented immigrants, with no exceptions for asylum seekers or immigrants accompanied by minors, were all to be subjected to criminal prosecution. According to US law, undocumented immigrants must be detained in a federal detention center prior to prosecution; yet, no children are permitted in these centers (CRS, 2019). This meant that, by necessity, in order to execute the new policy, children were being separated from their parents (Figure 2.6). Upon separation, these children were deemed "unaccompanied alien children" and placed in the custody of the Department of Health and Human Services (DHHS). The exact number of separated families is unknown, with some presumed low estimates suggesting about 3,000 separations between the launch of the policy on May 7, 2018 and the June 20 reversal brought about by national outcry about the policy.

DHHS was given fourteen days to reunite the more-than 100 children aged 5 or younger with their parent(s) and thirty days were allowed for older children; however, no efficient procedures were in place to support reunification. Proof of parenthood was required, but not easily obtained; children lingered indefinitely in DHHS's foster care or impersonal shelters with no mechanisms for managing their distress. Said one detained teenager of his peers, "they would cry sometimes, alone, or they would hit themselves against the wall" (NBCnews, 2019). The Society for Research and Child Development (SRCD), an international organization dedicated to developmental science and promoting human welfare, quickly denounced the "zero tolerance" policy. The SRCD condemned parental separations as a "toxic stressor," citing long-term adverse effects of parental separations for children of all ages, especially young children, even with subsequent reunification (Bouza et al., 2018).

The SRCD's conclusion aligns with attachment theory's predictions (Bowlby, 1973, 1982) in which caregiver separation, deprivation, and loss are considered primary causes for ill-health and poor psychological well-being. Today, we know that the trauma of losing an **attachment figure** early in life can initiate neurobiological changes that increase risk for psychopathology, such as depression and anxiety (Heim & Nemeroff, 2001). Such profound early-life stress places too high of a demand on the hypothalamic–pituitary–adrenal (HPA) axis, which modulates people's stress responses, creating lifelong problems in the stress-response system (Maniam et al., 2014). Indeed, separating children from their parents is a toxic stress that can change brain structure and function, impair memory, interfere with mood regulation and impulse control, increase disease susceptibility, increase likelihood of unhealthy lifestyles, and predict engagement in high-risk behaviors (e.g., drinking, drugs; Shonkoff et al., 2012). Being able to access attachment figures is critical for health and well-being, yet government policies that separate children from their families occur all over the world, with this example being particularly damning. The issue is far from resolved. Not only have reports suggested that children continued to be separated from their parents after the end of the policy, but children who suffered the trauma of separation will carry the effects with them throughout their lives.

Figure 2.6 Attachment theory can be used to explain the distress of this 2-year-old child, as she watches officers detain and search her mother. Young children separated from their families suffer irreparable damage to their psychological health and well-being. (Photo: John Moore / Getty Images News)

(a)   (b)

Figure 2.7 Close relationships across the lifespan share features that suggest humans have an enduring attachment behavioral system. How do your behaviors demonstrate close emotional bonds? (Photo: Jose Luis Pelaez Inc. / Digital Vision / Getty Images [a] and Hinterhaus Productions / Stone / Getty Images [b])

The merits of an attachment behavioral system are obvious for infants and young children, who are especially dependent on others. A little baby is scared by a loud sound (i.e., a threat), cries out (i.e., a proximity-seeking behavior), and a parent responds by soothing the child, which restores felt security. Indeed, cross-cultural evidence supports the notion of an evolved universal attachment system, in which hard-wired proximity-promoting behaviors kick in when children are stressed, drawing them closer to caregivers (Mesman et al., 2016). Yet, this attachment system does not dissipate with age, but instead persists, conferring evolutionary benefits across the lifespan. As shown in Figure 2.7, we can see parallels in the form and functions of attachment relationships over time, as well as some notable differences.

Attachment Figures

Who do you turn to when you're stressed, afraid, or upset? Following from attachment theory, when we feel threatened, we seek closeness with our attachment figure(s) (Table 2.3). As you might imagine, a child's attachment figure is typically the caregiver (often a parent) who has built an emotional bond with the child through responsiveness to the child's repeated bids for proximity. This work pays off. The caregiver becomes the sun of the child's little solar system, representing all four special features of what Bowlby (1982) termed the "attachment bond" (Ainsworth, 1993; Hazan & Shaver, 1994; Mikulincer & Shaver, 2016). Namely, this attachment figure: (1) receives the child's proximity bids; (2) serves as a safe haven (an interpersonal space of refuge, relief, and protection); (3) provides a secure base for exploration by offering support while respecting and promoting the child's autonomy (Bretherton, 1987; Posada et al., 2013); and (4) serves as the focal point for the child's separation distress. As the child ages, however, the caregiver gradually loses their

Table 2.3 An adaptation of the six-item measure of attachment needs

Who is/are your attachment figure(s)?	
Answer each question by writing down the name(s) of the person(s) who fulfill(s) these attachment roles.	
Proximity-seeking and separation	Who is the person you most like to spend time with?
	Who is the person you don't like to be away from?
Safe haven	Who is the person you want to be with when you are feeling upset or down?
	Who is the person you would count on for advice?
Secure base	Who is the person you would want to tell first if you achieved something good?
	Who is the person you can always count on?
Scoring: Assign a "3" to anyone who is named for either or both proximity-seeking/separation questions, safe-haven questions, and secure-base questions (i.e., full-blown attachment). Assign a "2" to anyone named for either or both proximity-seeking/separation questions and safe-haven questions. Assign a "1" to anyone named for either or both proximity-seeking/separation questions. Higher numbers indicate greater fulfillment of attachment needs.	

Source: Adapted from Fraley & Davis (1997); reproduced with permission from John Wiley & Sons, Inc.

coveted spot as "top dog" in the attachment hierarchy, and attachments shift to friends and, when applicable, romantic partners (Fraley & Davis, 1997; Hazan & Zeifman, 1994).

For adults in romantic relationships, romantic partners generally serve as "full-blown" attachment figures fulfilling proximity, safe haven, and secure base needs, with their absence associated with distress (Hazan & Shaver, 1987; Shaver et al., 1988). Indeed, romantic partners tend to be the strongest attachment figures for adults in monogamous relationships and adults in consensual non-monogamous relationships (Doherty & Feeney, 2004; Mitchell et al., 2014; Moors et al., 2019). From an evolutionary perspective, an attachment behavioral system that promotes strong adult romantic bonds makes sense in terms of the evolutionary advantages it confers. Proximity seeking, for example, can increase chances for reproduction in different-sex couples, and support offspring survival through co-parenting.

If not romantic partners, adults tend to orient their attachment needs around their adult children (particularly older adults), friends or siblings (especially unpartnered adults), or mothers or fathers (Doherty & Feeney, 2004). Further, even if one person holds the "number 1" attachment spot, people typically have more than one important attachment figure (Doherty & Feeney, 2004), with emerging adults often maintaining about five attachment figures (Trinke & Bartholomew, 1997). Moms tend to be high on the list, even for emerging adults with romantic partners (Carli et al., 2019; Doherty & Feeney, 2004). In the face of challenges and life changes, people can pursue different attachment figures for support, such as shifting from a now-ex-romantic partner to friends after a break-up (Umemura et al., 2018), or shifting to rely more heavily on a parent when expecting a first baby (Carli et al., 2019). Thus, while evidence generally (not universally; Freeman & Simons, 2018) supports a hierarchical model that prioritizes a principal attachment figure, how adults organize their closest relationships might be better represented as a network of attachment figures, given potential shifts tied to individuals' needs (Fraley, 2019).

Note too that people also target non-humans to meet their attachment needs, an idea that might sound odd at first, but think about your social world with a broad lens. We feel comforted by many sources, like pets, places, and even inert objects (e.g., a favorite sweater, a stuffed animal). People also report strong attachments to God and to deceased partners (Cicirelli, 2010; Van Assche et al., 2013). In the same way that prototypical attachment figures provide a safe haven, people regularly experience boosts in felt security through mental representations or interactions with non-human entities (Keefer et al., 2014).

 DIVERSITY AND INCLUSION

How Does Attachment Work in Consensually Non-Monogamous Relationships?

Consensual non-monogamy poses some intriguing puzzles for attachment theory, which has long operated on an implicit assumption (derived from Western cultural norms) that people maintain one primary attachment figure. Even as adults are recognized to maintain multiple attachments across different social domains (a partner, friends, parents), they are still presumed to have one person to fulfill their attachment needs. Consensual non-monogamy challenges these ideas.

An umbrella term, consensual non-monogamy (CNM), refers to a general romantic relationship structure in which two or more partners agree that they each can have romantic and/or sexual relationships with other people (Figure 2.8). Three popular variants of CNM include **polyamory** (maintaining ongoing romantic and sexual relationships with multiple partners), **open relationships** (engaging in primarily sexual, not usually romantic, relationships with people other than one's primary partner), and **swinging** (engaging in sexual relationships as partners with other partners). This is not atypical or deviant behavior; about one in five people (20 to 25 percent of the population) have had experiences in CNM (Haupert et al., 2017). This is as common as cat ownership (Moors & Matsick, 2018).

Figure 2.8 Will Smith once said of his and Jada Pinkett Smith's long marriage, "In our marriage vows, we didn't say 'forsaking all others . . . The vow that we made was that you will never hear that I did something after the fact' (Simpson, 2005). Jada in turn has commented, "The man that Will is, is a man of integrity. So he's got all the freedom in the world . . . So as long as Will can look at himself in the mirror and be OK? I'm good." (Daily Mail Online, 2015). (Photo: Axelle / Bauer-Griffin / FilmMagic / Getty Images)

CNM exposes some of the cultural biases within classic conceptualizations of attachment theory while at the same time helping us better understand the full nature of romantic attachment. For instance, despite stigma and stereotypes that might suggest otherwise (Conley et al., 2013), people in CNM relationships tend to report more comfort with closeness than people in monogamous relationships (Moors et al., 2015). Plenty of people with healthy support-seeking skills and positive world views maintain CNM relationships, benefiting from the need fulfillment enabled by multiple partnerships (Moors et al., 2017). Indeed, individuals in polyamorous relationships tend to both feel securely attached to multiple partners and report high need fulfillment by multiple partners (Mitchell et al., 2014; Moors et al., 2019), which differs from the one primary attachment figure perspective.

Attachment Behaviors

So, if you know who you want to turn to when you're stressed, afraid, or upset (your attachment figure!): how do you make this happen? According to attachment theory, perceiving a threat causes your attachment behavioral system to initiate an array of proximity-seeking behaviors (Collins & Feeney, 2000; Mikulincer & Shaver, 2009). Children scream, wail, cling, and cry some more to solicit support from their attachment figures. Adults typically have more developed support-seeking skills and can draw upon a broad, flexible, and nuanced repertoire of support-seeking behaviors to connect with their attachment figures (Campa et al., 2009; Dewitte et al., 2008; Mikulincer & Shaver, 2016). Unlike children's support-seeking strategies, adult proximity-seeking attempts are also generally context sensitive ("I can wait until my partner finishes her video conference before asking for a hug"), and adept at eliciting favorable responses (I can say, "I could really use a hug" instead of poking my partner until she turns around). Adults can even conjure up mental representations of their partners, and that alone is often enough to soothe and support (Mikulincer et al., 2002; Mikulincer & Shaver, 2004).

At the same time, the ways in which adults orient toward each other are remarkably parallel to the behaviors used by children: non-verbal expressions, eye contact, smiling, touching, holding hands, etc. Indeed, if you have an astute eye, you can easily notice that many of the same proximity-seeking behaviors exhibited by children at a daycare drop-off are exhibited by adults preceding their romantic separations. Next time you find yourself waiting at a train station or an airport, conduct an informal replication of Fraley and Shaver's (1998) naturalistic observational study on adult proximity seeking. In that study, couples preparing to head off in different directions looked at and touched each other (among other proximity-seeking behaviors) more than couples who were boarding the same plane or otherwise headed in the same direction (Figure 2.9).

Figure 2.9 Departures signal the onset of separation, triggering functions of the attachment behavioral system like proximity seeking. How do you seek proximity with your attachment figure(s)? (Photo: Hill Street Studios / DigitalVision / Getty Images)

As much as people seek support from their attachment figure(s) and rely on them to serve as a safe haven in times of threat, they also lean on their attachment figures as a secure base for exploration (e.g., ventures away from the attachment figures in childhood, and specific goal strivings in adulthood). Paradoxically, being able to depend on an attachment figure is what promotes healthy independence across the lifespan (Feeney, 2007).

The Attachment System in Concert with Other Behavioral Systems

The attachment system works with other behavioral systems to promote caregiving, care-receiving, and felt security (Feeney & Collins, 2019). Consider Figure 2.10, which depicts a normative attachment cycle. When all is calm (felt security, bottom of figure), people engage with the world. Their exploratory behavioral system activates, fueling an innate motivation to pursue curiosities, to work, and to discover. This system is easier to turn on and keep on when attachment needs are met and an attachment figure is accessible. If – while exploring – a person encounters a threat, this threat will activate their attachment behavioral system along with all its associated goal-directed behaviors. To restore felt security, they will make a bid for proximity (an adult calls their girlfriend; a child wails for their parent) which will then activate the attachment figure's caregiving behavioral system.

The caregiving behavioral system contains a universal drive to protect and support others (Bowlby, 1982; Shaver & Mikulincer, 2019). Whereas in the child–caregiver relationship, the adult's caregiving system is oriented to the child's attachment needs, in romantic relationships, partners' caregiving systems are oriented toward each other's attachment needs, reflecting mutuality (rather than asymmetry) in caregiving.

As shown in Figure 2.10, for adults, the attachment system also interfaces with the sexual behavioral system, the behavioral system that promotes intercourse and reproduction (Birnbaum, 2015). This provides another key distinction in attachment between child-caregivers and romantic partners: the physical touch (e.g., caressing, kissing, cuddling) that occurs within child–caregiver relationships is driven by attachment or caregiving systems, whereas physical touch in adult romantic relationships may also reflect the sexual system's needs. Each of these systems activates in response to one's own needs, one's partner's needs, and the relationship's needs. Laid out in this way, the attachment behavioral system, working in concert with the caregiving and sexual systems, seems beautifully equipped to help us manage stress and find support, but if this is a universal attachment system, why do people have such varied reactions to relationship events?

Individual Differences in Attachment

Think about flower seeds for a moment. If you take the same flower seeds and plant them in different locations, through no fault of their own, they become exposed to differing levels of sunlight, water, fertilizer, pollinators, and vermin. The results are predictably diverse. Beautiful blooms, mediocre blossoms, persistent attempts to bud that are cut short by hungry deer . . . the seed's programming reacts to its environment, trying to obtain the best possible outcomes. Seeds lucky enough to be nurtured by green thumbs will thrive, others will make the most of less hospitable environments. Similarly, people's attachment systems operate within different interpersonal contexts yielding different results. Proximity bids are met with varied degrees of responsiveness and sensitivity; safe havens feel steady or fleeting; secure bases are trustworthy

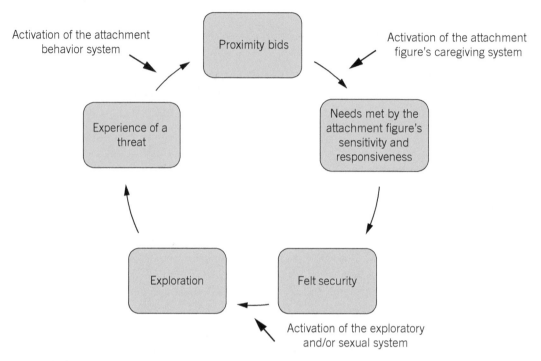

Figure 2.10 The exploratory behavioral system, the attachment behavioral system, and the caregiving behavioral system all work together in attachment relationships.

or unreliable. Starting in infancy, the machinery of the attachment system adapts, rationally and flexibly, to its environment. Over time, early caregiver relationships can create entrenched patterns that resist modification, particularly as we gravitate preferentially toward people who match our expectations. In order to appreciate how individual differences in attachment play out in romantic relationships, let's briefly visit the child–caregiver relationship and its potential to guide attachment systems in specific directions.

Working Models of Attachment

A sleeping toddler is startled awake by a crack of thunder. What happens next? According to Bowlby (1973), the child's next move is strategic, driven by an attachment system that is learning from and adapting to chronic patterns of responses by caregivers. The child quickly computes an interpersonal equation: what should I do to feel safe? Based on previous successes or failures, the child develops expectations regarding how their proximity bids would be met, expectations captured in mental scripts. The child may, for example, develop a secure base script, "If I cry out, even quietly, my dad will come quickly. I'll feel safe." Having had different, less satisfying past experiences, the child might have developed an alternative script: "If I cry out, my dad will not come right away, but if I keep crying like a raging hyena, he might come," or "If I cry out, nothing will come of it, so I'll just tough it out myself."

The idea here is that children notice how reliably caregivers meet their attachment needs, and these relationship-specific observations provide the bases for more abstract mental representations of both themselves and others (Bretherton, 1985; Collins et al., 1996). These mental representations of self and other, which Bowlby (1982) termed internal working models, are built on past interactions and allow for predictions of future relationship interactions. A child whose proximity bids are regularly met by a caregiver's attention and responsiveness develops a working model of: (1) the self as loveable, worthy, and valuable; (2) the caregiver as trustworthy, reliable, and loving; and (3) the world as a safe place. When proximity bids are met with inconsistent attention, insensitivity, rejection, or other unsatisfying responses, the child's working model of self may contain doubts or downright disbelief about their own self-worth. Under such circumstances, working models of caregivers might be colored by uncertainty, distrust, and wariness, and the child might view the world as an unreliable, unsafe place.

Jumping forward in time, toddlers become adults, and these adults enter romantic relationships (and other relationships) with pre-formed working models of self and other (referring to close others in general), built over years of social interactions. Their default or "chronically accessible" working model tends to reflect how well their caregiver met their attachment needs. In other words, what began as a context-specific pattern of caregiver–child interactions becomes a guiding framework for adult relationships. The stronger the pattern in childhood, the more entrenched an adult's working model. Still, these are *working* models; they can be updated and revised through new relationships or new relationship experiences. Nonetheless, adults are not "blank slates" when they start new relationships; rather, they bring with them working models of self and other that actively shape their social experiences.

This helps explain why different people can experience the same relationship events quite differently. Every aspect of our interpersonal life is filtered through our working models, usually reinforcing, though sometimes challenging, pre-existing ideas about self and other. These working models lay the foundation for individual differences in attachment.

Attachment Styles and Dimensions of Attachment

Take a look at Table 2.4. Which paragraph best characterizes you? Make a note of your selection before you continue (we'll refer back to this table in a moment).

Table 2.4 Hazan and Shaver's (1987) Attachment Styles

Which of the following paragraphs best describes your feelings?
Option A: "I am somewhat uncomfortable being close to others. I find it difficult to trust them completely, difficult to allow myself to depend on them. I am nervous when anyone gets too close and often, love partners want me to be more intimate than I feel comfortable being."
Option B: "I find it relatively easy to get close to others and am comfortable depending on them and having them depend on me. I don't often worry about being abandoned or about someone getting too close to me."
Option C: "I find that others are reluctant to get as close as I would like. I often worry that my partner doesn't really love me or won't want to stay with me. I want to merge completely with another person, and this desire sometimes scares people away."

Source: Copyright © 1987 by American Psychological Association. Reproduced with permission. Hazan, C. & Shaver, P. (1987). Romantic love conceptualized as an attachment process. *Journal of Personality and Social Psychology, 52*(3), 511–524.

Had you lived in Denver in 1986, you might have seen these three paragraphs (Table 2.4) in the *Rocky Mountain News*. If interested, you could have cut out the survey, completed it, and been one of the 1,200 people to mail your responses to the researchers (life before online data collection!). By doing so, you would have been participating in groundbreaking research, the first significant application of attachment theory to adult romantic love (Hazan & Shaver, 1987). While multiple scholars (e.g., Bowlby, Ainsworth, Weiss) viewed attachment as a lifelong process and noted parallels between child–caregiver relationships and romantic partners, it was Hazan and Shaver's (1987) empirical work that ignited a new wave of attachment research focused on romantic love.

Hazan and Shaver's (1987) goal was to translate childhood attachment styles focused on child–caregiver interactions into mature adult styles of approaching romantic relationships. Remember the different working models we discussed a moment ago? Attachment styles are chronic patterns of thought, emotion, and behavior that reflect those underlying working models of self and other; they are derived from individuals' attachment history. By the 1980s, led by Bowlby's theory and Mary Ainsworth's insights and empirical methods (Ainsworth, 1967; Ainsworth et al., 1978), the field recognized a distinct set of attachment styles in young children, linked to the caregiver's sensitivity and the quality of the child–caregiver interaction. If children's ideas about attachment take root, perhaps they enact the patterns they learned as children in their later relationships. Hazan and Shaver (1987) tested this idea: can adults be sorted into different attachment styles that mirror those observed among children?

Yes. When the data came from their *Rocky Mountain News* survey (Table 2.4), Hazan and Shaver discovered that 56 percent of their adult community sample self-sorted into secure attachment (option B above). This corresponded with 60 percent of children in an earlier study by Ainsworth (Ainsworth et al., 1978); the children exhibited behaviors (e.g., happy reunions with their caregivers, a readiness to explore) that, like the adults who chose option B, suggested they viewed the self as valued and their attachment figures as available, reliable, and trustworthy. Secure attachments may reflect a learned idea that attachment figures are responsive and sensitive. If not self-sorted as secure, adults indicated their thoughts and behaviors as consistent with one of the two insecure attachments. One-quarter of adults (25 percent) categorized themselves as having an avoidant attachment (option A), a style reflecting negative, untrusting views of close others. This prevalence aligns with Ainsworth's observation that 20 percent of children showed distancing behaviors from their attachment figure when stressed; they appeared stoic and unemotional, despite their underlying distress. This deactivation of the attachment system may have emerged as an adaptive response to rigid, rejecting caregivers. An additional one-fifth (19 percent) of adults self-sorted as having an anxious attachment (option C), corresponding nicely to Ainsworth's finding that 20 percent of children exhibited this style. For these children, reunions with caregivers were charged with intense, often conflicting, emotions; this hyperactivation (an extreme ramping up) of their attachment system – similar to what we see in adults – likely developed in the face of a caregiver's inconsistent responsiveness (Ainsworth et al., 1978; Hazan & Shaver, 1987). Overall, the prevalence rates observed by Hazan and Shaver (1987) in their adult sample were quite similar to Ainsworth's rates in children. These rates have since been replicated in a larger, nationally representative sample of adults in the United States (Mickelson et al., 1997), cross-culturally (van Ijzendoorn & Bakermans-Kranenburg, 2010), and across sexual orientations (Ridge & Feeney, 1998).

The match between childhood and adult rates of attachment suggests potential continuity over time: that secure kids become secure adults and insecure kids become insecure adults. This is further supported by retrospective reports in which securely attached adults describe their childhood families as warm and supportive (Hazan & Shaver, 1987) and longitudinal work linking 18-year-olds' attachment security with years of documented supportive parenting, family stability, and friendship quality (Fraley et al., 2013). While a growing body of evidence points to associations between early childhood experiences and adult relationships (e.g., Chopik, Moors, & Edelstein, 2014; Fraley, 2002; Pinquart et al., 2013), these associations are sometimes weaker than might be expected. This hits a key point: childhood influences, but does not determine, adult attachment styles (Fraley, 2019). As Fraley and Roisman (2019) put it, "foundations are not fate."

Contemporary research on romantic attachment extends beyond Hazan and Shaver's (1987) initial three-category model in important ways. First, researchers improved upon the measurement technique, turning to more precise multi-item attachment scales rather than asking people to select a representative paragraph (Collins & Read, 1990; Simpson, 1990). Second, theorists shifted the focus from attachment categories to attachment dimensions, or continuums (Brennan et al., 1998; Feeney & Noller, 1990). Two dimensions of attachment gained headway and are primary in how we think about attachment today: attachment anxiety and attachment avoidance. High attachment anxiety reflects pervasive concerns about not being loved and fears about being abandoned, whereas high attachment avoidance focuses on discomfort with intimacy and a preference for independence.

Attachment anxiety and avoidance can also be thought of as pertaining to working models of self and other, respectively, as shown in Figure 2.11 (Bartholomew, 1990; Bartholomew & Horowitz, 1991). Attachment anxiety tells us how people think about themselves: people with low anxiety maintain positive self-images, and people with high anxiety maintain negative self-images (e.g., see themselves as unworthy of love). Attachment avoidance, meanwhile, reveals how people think about others: people with low avoidance hold a positive image of others, and

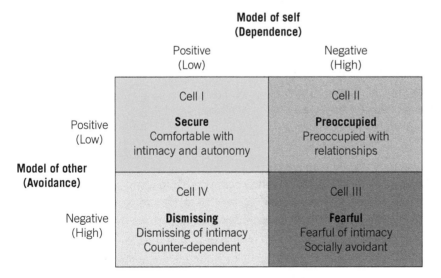

Figure 2.11 Four attachment styles derived from models of self (anxiety) crossed with models of others (avoidance). (Source: Copyright © 1991 by American Psychological Association. Reproduced with permission. Bartholomew, K., & Horowitz, L. M. [1991]. Attachment styles among young adults: a test of a four-category model. *Journal of Personality and Social Psychology, 6*[12], 226–44.)

people with high avoidance hold a negative image of others (e.g., view others as unavailable and unresponsive). To combine attachment anxiety and avoidance (as shown in Figure 2.11) reveals not three, but four distinct attachment styles. Essentially, this updated model integrates one's sense of worthiness and lovability (or unworthiness and unlovability) with one's general beliefs about other people as trustworthy and accepting (or untrustworthy and rejecting). Note that, even as these are depicted categorically in Figure 2.11, attachment anxiety and avoidance are dimensions: people vary by degree of attachment anxiety (from low to high) and by degree of attachment avoidance (from low to high).

Attachment Styles in Action

Imagine you were just in a car accident. You're okay but really shaken up. What do you do? Just like a thunderstorm kickstarts a child's attachment behavioral system, a stressful event activates an adult's attachment behavioral system. Critically, attachment styles bias the normative system to adapt to the (perhaps outdated) social environment. To see how this works, consider the illustration in Figure 2.12, which is based on Mikulincer and Shaver's (2002, 2003, 2016) control-system model. The model depicts the conditional outcomes of: (1) interpreting the presence or absence of a threat; (2) believing that there is or is not an available and responsive attachment figure; and, if not, (3) believing proximity seeking will or will not achieve security goals. Any path that you take through this "yes" or "no" maze becomes a more likely path next time around. In other words, while your attachment style might influence which path you take, your experiences shape your attachment style, which can then lead you down the same path the next time a threat arises.

Securely attached individuals find success relying on *primary attachment strategies*. They anticipate helpful responses from available attachment figures, act accordingly, and receive support, again and again. This leads to a wellspring of core positive emotions, builds resiliency and emotional stability, and allows mental resources to be devoted to other systems (e.g., caregiving) and other tasks, like exploring the world, being creative, enjoying life, and growing one's skills and perspectives (Mikulincer & Shaver, 2016; 2020). This cycle allows secure individuals to feel calm, content, and happy for extensive periods of time, benefiting psychological health and well-being.

Individuals with insecure attachment styles have a profoundly different experience. Based on prior experiences, they expect to navigate stressful experiences feeling alone and unsupported, so they unconsciously adapt to use *secondary attachment strategies*. Which secondary strategy they take depends on their past experiences (Mikulincer et al., 2003). If previous support-seeking attempts were met with rejection or punishment, then pursuing proximity is not only unhelpful, but also possibly dangerous. Instead, people defensively and protectively engage in a deactivation of the attachment system. This strategy minimizes future pain: better to deal with the issue alone or ignore it than expose oneself to a cold, rejecting, or even violent attachment figure. Avoidant attachment styles orient people toward deactivation strategies, and deactivating strategies reinforce avoidant attachment orientations.

Alternatively, if previous attachment figures were inconsistent in their support (sometimes supportive and other times rejecting), people might be compelled to lean in with intensity and keep trying proximity bids on the chance it might work. This is called hyperactivation, a secondary attachment strategy designed to rev up primary attachment strategies. Hyperactivation that elicits support is reinforced, potentially reinforcing attachment anxiety.

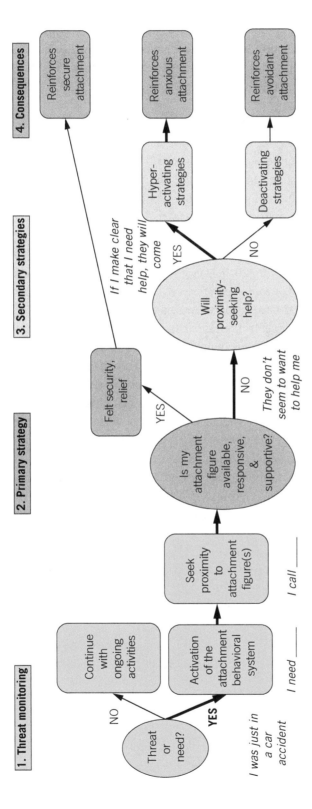

Figure 2.12 An adaptation of Mikulincer and Shaver's (2016) control-system model of how the adult attachment system operates. The example situation, presented in italics, follows one particular path in which a car accident is deemed a threat and activates the attachment behavioral system (stage 1). Continuing to follow the bold lines through the model, we see that the primary attachment strategy is not sufficient to produce relief (stage 2), so the individual uses a hyperactivating strategy (stage 3), which reinforces attachment anxiety (stage 4). This example demonstrates how a path can become "grooved" and easier to follow in the future. (Source: Used with permission of Guilford Publications, Inc., from Mikulincer and Shaver [2016]; permission conveyed through Copyright Clearance Center, Inc.)

Mikulincer and Shaver's (2016) model shows how pre-existing beliefs can bias the attachment process. A little nothing becomes a total crisis; a legitimate threat is downplayed to nothing. For instance, a partner being uncharacteristically unprepared for a romantic getaway, like Morelli before proposing to Wiley, might have led some people (anxiously attached partners) to hear alarm bells or others (avoidantly attached partners) to shut down and pull back. Secure people make **attributions** as well, also aligned with their expectations, but in their case, their attributions are unthreatening.

Critiques of Attachment Theory

Attachment theory emerged within a specific Western sociohistorical context, and as a result, its principal tenets are grounded on some culturally specific assumptions, despite its intention as a universal explanation for relationship dynamics. For instance, the primacy of one attachment figure (i.e., the mother) reflects a common family structure in mid-twentieth-century Western culture, particularly among middle- and upper-class nuclear families, wherein mothers generally served as primary and sometimes sole caregivers to their children. Only recently have researchers attempted to correct for the general neglect of the role of fathers as caregivers (Bretherton, 2010; Van Ijzendoorn & De Wolff, 1997). Same-sex parents and consensually non-monogamous parents were also neglected in classic attachment work. Further, much of the world raises children within the context of multiple caregivers, an idea that rocks the notion of one central primary caregiver. How the attachment system operates within diverse arrangements of caregiving requires careful attention (Keller, 2016).

The "cultural blindness" in attachment theory goes beyond assumptions of dyadic, different-sex parenting spearheaded by mothers. Key tenets of attachment are called to question when you move outside of Western society, including aspects of caregiver sensitivity and ideal dependency between children and caregivers (Boiger, 2019; Mesman et al., 2016; Rothbaum et al., 2000). For instance, the anticipation of children's needs and symbiotic relationship typical of Japanese mothers and children would be seen by American standards as over-involved. Further, foundational descriptions of healthy attachments stipulated in attachment theory often reflect Western values and ideology. People from cultures with strong interdependent orientations, for example, define healthy attachment with more features of attachment avoidance than do Americans (Wang & Mallinckrodt, 2006).

Still, the universality of the normative attachment system may exist despite cultural-specific features; emotional bonds play an important role in relationship functioning cross-culturally. What we need is more evidence and less reliance on Western samples. Energizing research on relationships in countries and cultures under-represented in the current body of attachment research will help. So too will finding the theory's growth edges by looking at attachment processes in romantic relationships of different arrangements (e.g., polyamory) and under different situations (e.g., socioeconomic stress).

Interdependence Theory: Solving Situation-Based Problems

What does Wiley personally gain from being married to Morelli, and vice versa? Is this an unromantic question? A tactless question? For some scholars, this is *the* question. Think about it: just by being in a relationship, you reap rewards and suffer costs; your decisions change; how you set and pursue goals changes. When people transition from a solo to a duet (triad, quartet, etc.), they do so because they hope the newfound interdependence will enhance their experiences. Unlike evolutionary theories and attachment theory, the theories to which we now turn do not view relationships as solving a fundamental evolved motivational problem (e.g., reproductive success, support). Instead, these theories assume people have a broad array of goals and needs (Rusbult & Van Lange, 2003), and that relationship behaviors are strategic solutions to problems in present-moment situations.

Social Exchange Theory

The crass question of "what do you get" out of a relationship takes center stage in social exchange theory, the situation-based theory we present first because of its sweeping influence. According to social exchange theory, social interactions amount to a calculated give-and-take, a reciprocal exchange of tangible and intangible offerings, which vary in their benefits and costs (Blau, 1964; Homans, 1961). The benefits that people reap from relationships – also called rewards – are aspects of a relationship that add positive value, and can include material gains (e.g., money, a place to live), emotional gains (e.g., intimacy, happier mood), and social gains (e.g., status). Costs, meanwhile, are the toll of participating in the relationship: you might lose privacy, time, or money, or you might experience worry, stress, or loneliness. Any "con" or aspect that adds negative value is considered a cost, which might yet be endured if the rewards are sufficient. Indeed, social exchange theory is economic in orientation, emphasizing that people anticipate rewards or costs and then make self-interested decisions. Its assumptions include (Burns, 1973): (1) all social behavior can be viewed as a kind of reward or cost; (2) people are rational so they try to maximize rewards and minimize costs; (3) other people control some rewards (which we can obtain by offering them something they want); and (4) people expect reciprocity (if we receive a reward from someone, they expect to receive a reward). These assumptions suggest that a reward exchange underlies all sustained interactions.

The importance of rewards relative to costs is captured in this equation, which flexibly defines one's overall outcome or experience in the relationship as a function of rewards and costs:

Outcome = Rewards of interaction – Costs of interaction

In this simple model, outcomes are a direct result of how much we profit from the relationship. As such, it suggests relationships, including whether people stay together or break up, can be understood by counting rewards and costs; yet, we know life is not this simple. People surprise us by staying in miserable relationships and they surprise us by leaving pretty good ones.

To help with this issue, we can consider the personal standards that individuals use to evaluate their relationships (Thibaut & Kelley, 1959). Comparison level (CL) refers to the outcomes people *expect* to experience in close relationships, on account of their personal histories. Take this hypothetical: if Wiley thinks being married means never doing laundry, she will be profoundly dissatisfied when she finds herself doing laundry three times a week. However, if Wiley's expectations for marriage include daily laundry, she will be highly satisfied with her marriage when Morelli offers to split the work. In this way, comparison levels affect satisfaction:

$$\text{Satisfaction} = \text{Outcomes} - \text{CL}$$

This equation suggests that whenever a person's experienced outcomes exceed what they expect, they will be satisfied. The more a person's outcomes exceed their expectations, the more satisfied they will be.

Social exchange theory also offers a standard that helps to explain dependency: the extent to which we rely on, and therefore need to stay in, a relationship. Dependency is separate from satisfaction; people who are satisfied may or may not also be reliant on their relationship. Like satisfaction, dependency includes a subjective comparison. In this case, comparison level of alternatives (CL_{alt}) factors into dependency by defining the appeal of people's alternatives to the current relationship (e.g., dating your flirtatious neighbor, being single).

$$\text{Dependency} = \text{Outcomes} - \text{CL}_{alt}$$

This equation demonstrates that a person will be dependent on (i.e., be motivated to stay in) their relationship whenever their current outcomes are better than their alternatives, but not the reverse. CL_{alt} recognizes that the relationship occurs within a broader social context.

Thus, social exchange theory helps us understand relationship dependency and satisfaction by highlighting the calculated comparisons of one's current situation to personal standards and available alternatives. Putting it all together: If outcomes are better than expected (CL) and alternatives are poor relative to one's current outcomes, relationships are satisfying, stable, and sturdy (i.e., dependent). It's "see you later" when outcomes fail to meet standards and alternatives offer better outcomes, or if alternatives are so appealing they outweigh a reasonably satisfying relationship. Even more interesting, this perspective helps us understand why people persist in unhappy relationships: their outcomes might be worse than their expectations, but they judge their available alternatives (including being single) as *even worse*.

Interdependence Theory

Imagine a hypothetical Wednesday evening in the Wiley-Morelli household. Wiley has an audition to prep for, and Morelli is up against a writing deadline. They also have a child asking for dinner and a bedtime story. What do they do? And importantly, how do they make the decision?

Romantic partners regularly experience scenarios like this one, similar in structure if not in content. Indeed, to be in a relationship is to experience the repeated collision of each partner's goals, needs, and preferences. Sometimes in sync, sometimes partially aligned, and other times in direct opposition, the motives and needs of one partner and those of the other partner(s) produce complex social interactions. From seemingly inconsequential interactions (like deciding which movie to see or where to go for dinner), to major life events (where to live, how to manage children's education, or when to retire), any given social interaction has *a lot* going on.

One of the most useful ways to examine social interactions is through the lens of interdependence theory (Kelley & Thibaut, 1978; Thibaut & Kelley, 1959), which has close theoretical ties to social exchange theory. It is the structure of interdependence (how people influence one another) underlying an interpersonal situation that is the focus of interdependence theory. As Caryl Rusbult and Paul Van Lange (2008) noted, "analogous to contemporary physics – where the relationships between particles are as meaningful as the particles themselves – in interdependence theory, between-person relations are as meaningful as the individuals themselves" (p. 2050). With a strong emphasis on the structure of social situations, interdependence theory is very much a study of relationship *dynamics*.

The Problem of Dependence

Imagine Wiley and Morelli are deciding who will work and who will manage dinner and bedtime. In this conversation, they each have motives that are short-term (I need to get work done tonight) and long-term (I want a strong career and a happy marriage); they each have needs that are concrete (I need time to do work) and symbolic (I want to feel loved and respected); and they each have thoughts that are self-oriented (I have a lot to do) and prosocial (I feel empathy for my partner). Drawing on their history together, they each also bring expectations about how the interaction will transpire. They even bring thoughts about the other person's thoughts, and thoughts about what the other person thinks they themselves are thinking. You get the picture: a rich set of psychological processes are at play. We can map this interaction using the SABI model (Holmes, 2002; Kelley et al., 2003) shown in Figure 2.13, a useful equation that defines the key elements of any given social interaction. Try reading it left to right, following the labels.

The SABI model highlights that even if you knew everything about Wiley (Person A) and Morelli (Person B), these individual inputs are not enough to determine how they will experience an interaction. To predict the interaction's outcomes, you need to analyze the structure of the interdependence *between* people, that is, the situation. How much does Person A's behavior influence Person B? Who has more power and who is more dependent? Each type of situation will bring to life different emotions, thoughts, and needs for each person. Therefore, the nature of the situation – called the interdependence structure – is a critical starting point for an interaction-based analysis.

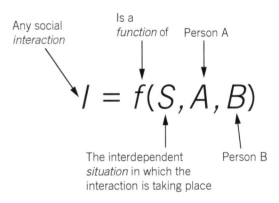

Figure 2.13 The SABI model: any given social interaction is a function of Person A, Person B, and the situation underlying the interaction – that is, their interdependent relationship.

Interdependence Structure

If you find logic inherently satisfying, as we do, you will likely enjoy interdependence theory's outcome matrices. An outcome matrix is a conceptual (not literal) representation of dependency structures underlying social interactions (Kelley et al., 2003; Kelley & Thibaut, 1978). It uses numbers – or payoffs – to depict the positive or negative outcomes made possible by an interdependence structure. Outcome matrices are typically framed around two people, although the model can be extended to accommodate multi-person

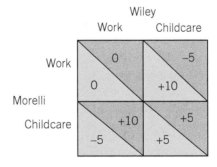

Figure 2.14 Interdependence theory emphasizes that interactions can be understood by analyzing their underlying dependency structures. Wiley's outcomes are shown in green, and Morelli's outcomes are shown in orange.

relationships. Figure 2.14 shows a matrix plotting the dependencies within Wiley and Morelli's example conflict (who works tonight and who cares for their child). This example uses a simple 2 × 2 outcome matrix: each of the two partners chooses one of two different actions and each partner's choice affects the other's outcomes to varying degrees.

Outcome matrices reveal conflicting interests in differing payoffs. Let's assume both Wiley and Morelli find their work gratifying and pleasurable. If Wiley works while Morelli cares for their child, Wiley has a highly favorable outcome (+ 10), while Morelli must manage the evening childcare rituals alone (dinner, clean-up, bath time, bedtime). Depending on their daughter's mood, this outcome is possibly unpleasant for Morelli (–5). Likewise, Morelli would enjoy a productive evening (+ 10) if Wiley were to manage their daughter, which could have a less favorable outcome for her (–5). If both Morelli and Wiley attend to their daughter, they can enjoy time together as a family, a pleasurable outcome, but neither of them finishes any work (+ 5, + 5). The decision to both work results in a moderately poor outcome for each of them (0, 0): they would have to spend money on a babysitter and worry their child might distract them from productive work.

Outcome matrices can take many different forms. Sometimes partners' individual outcomes result entirely from their own behaviors (termed: bilateral actor control), whereas other times, partners' individual outcomes rest fully on their partner's behaviors (mutual partner control). This latter case beautifully captures social exchange, an "I scratch your back, you scratch mine" scenario (Kelley et al., 2003). Still other times, outcomes are based on both one's own and one's partner's behaviors (mutual joint control), such as when coordination leads to better outcomes (corresponding mutual joint control) or in "zero-sum games" when what benefits one partner harms the other (conflicting mutual joint control). Bilateral actor control, mutual partner control, and mutual joint control (corresponding and conflicting) are considered the four basic interdependence structures that can be modified to capture a wide variety of interpersonal problems.

Take another look at Wiley and Morelli's work conflict. The dependency structure (which you may recognize as the classic Prisoner's Dilemma) reflects a combination of bilateral actor control and mutual partner control: choosing the self-oriented option (working) is most beneficial, but only if the other person behaves prosocially (stays home). Scholars have charted twenty-one distinct structures (including *Twist of Fate*, *Hero*, *Chicken*, and more; Kelley et al., 2003) that pull back the curtain on social interactions to reveal their underlying dependency structures. Think about a recent social interaction that you have had: can you map the outcomes along a matrix?

Straightforward structures, like the structure underlying Wiley and Morelli's work conflict, sometimes, but not always, reflect reality. Sometimes the quantity of options differs between actors: one person might have five options, someone else two. Sometimes the "payoffs" are not symmetrical: one person might benefit more from one option than the other. Most importantly, social interactions do not occur in isolation: any social interaction is simply one in a stream of social interactions, affected by previous social interactions and affecting what is likely to happen in the future. Wiley and Morelli's decision tonight, for instance, will likely affect how tomorrow evening is negotiated. Because one lone matrix does not attend to the temporal sequence of Person A and Person B's behaviors, scholars might supplement a matrix with other illustrations (e.g., transition lists) to show how interdependence structures

Table 2.5 How does interdependence work?

Properties	Functions	Motives or individual differences in ...
1. Level of dependence	Determines dependence on partner, relative to self	Comfort with dependence and independence
2. Mutuality of dependence	Determines degree of bilateral dependence	Holding power and being vulnerable
3. Basis of dependence	Leads to control through exchange or coordination	Being dominant vs. submissive, and assertive vs. passive
4. Covariation of interests	Promotes prosocial or self-interested goals; promotes trust or distrust	Comfort with cooperation or competition; orientations toward trust or distrust of partner
5. Temporal structure	Encourages immediate or delayed goal pursuits	Tendencies toward being dependable vs. unreliable; loyal vs. disloyal
6. Information availability	Requires coping with uncertainty and incomplete information	Comfort with uncertainty vs. openness; optimism vs. pessimism

Source: Adapted from Holmes (2002) and Rusbult and Van Lange (2008). Used with permission of Blackwell Publishing, John Wiley & Sons, Inc.; permission conveyed through Copyright Clearance Center, Inc.)

change or morph into their next interdependent situation (Kelley, 1984). Outcome matrices reveal key properties of interdependence, as shown in Table 2.5 (Kelley & Thibaut, 1978). These properties include the extent to which partners' outcomes depend on one another's actions (*level of dependence*), whether power is symmetric or asymmetric (*mutuality of dependence*), the extent to which partners need to work together to achieve favorable outcomes (*basis of dependence*), and whether partners' outcomes correspond versus conflict (*covariation of interests*). Another key property of interdependence is a situation's *temporal structure* (Kelley et al., 2003): is this going to be a one-shot or ongoing interaction? "Extended situations" emphasize dependability and loyalty, and hurt the short-sighted player. Finally, *information availability* underscores how some interpersonal situations have inherently more risk than others. How certain are you about your partner's motives, the consequences of either of your decisions, or what future opportunities will be available on account of your current behaviors? Do both partners have the same information? These questions define the structure of any social interaction.

Interdependent Processes

What do you think: will Wiley head toward the door and say, "I'm off to study lines! See ya, Lauren!"? Probably not! Romantic partners rarely approach social interactions guided solely by self-interest and immediate outcomes. Instead, being in a relationship leads partners to experience a psychological transformation of motivation that orients them toward the "effective" situation. In the effective situation, it's not all about me; preferences reflect partner concern, long-term goals and strategies, and other broader considerations.

Along with transformation, the concept of adaptation helps us understand interdependent relationships. Individuals develop habitual responses to certain interdependent structures (Rusbult & Van Lange, 2003). Likewise, whereas new partners are still figuring it out, established couples have default styles of interacting with each other. In addition to personal adaptations and relationship adaptations, people's interactions adapt to the norms of their broader social context: politeness, apologies, and anger, for example, reflect adaptations to cultural norms.

The Investment Model of Commitment

Wouldn't it be nice if you could predict whether romantic partners will stay together or break up? This golden egg of relationship science became more accessible with the introduction of the investment model of commitment (Rusbult, 1980). Note that this "investment" model is distinct from the theory of parental "investment" posited as part of evolutionary theory. This investment model (Rusbult et al., 1998) extends social exchange theories by suggesting that (along with dependency and satisfaction) people also factor their investment (how much they would lose if the relationship ended) into whether they will stay in or leave a relationship. Let's review this model in more detail.

As shown in Figure 2.15 (Impett et al., 2001; see also Rusbult et al., 1998), the investment model contends that relationship stability is most directly predicted by commitment. The more strongly someone *intends* to maintain their relationship, the more likely they actually maintain it. The model further explains that commitment results from high satisfaction, low quality of alternatives, and high investment (Rusbult et al., 1998). In other words, people are committed to maintain their relationships when: (1) their relationship outcomes (rewards minus costs) meet or exceed their expectations; (2) their relationship is better than available alternatives (e.g., alternate partners, singlehood); and (3) when they stand to lose a lot if their relationship ends (e.g., shared possessions, a way of life, years of devoted time, money, and/or emotional energy).

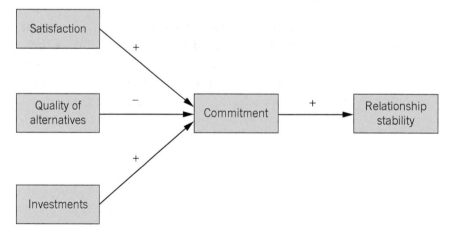

Figure 2.15 Why do you stay in a relationship? The investment model suggests greater satisfaction and investments predict greater commitment, whereas greater quality of alternatives predicts less commitment. Commitment, then, contributes to the probability the relationship will persist, that is, relationship stability. (Source: Used with permission of Springer Nature BV from Impett et al. [2001]; permission conveyed through Copyright Clearance Center, Inc.)

This investment model of commitment is widely supported; satisfaction, alternatives, and investment independently (separately) predict commitment in romantic relationships and friendships, in marital and non-marital relationships, in same-sex and different-sex romantic relationships, in monogamous and consensually non-monogamous relationships, in early-stage and long-term relationships, in young adults and older adults, and all around the globe (Tran et al., 2019). As useful as this model is in explaining stability in diverse relationships, its form and emphasis may yet be fine-tuned toward the privileged group on which it was constructed (Western, White, different-sex, intra-racial, economically advantaged, monogamous couples). Indeed, the model tells us the most about commitment for these relationships. Measuring other factors, such as minority stress, prejudice and discrimination, and weak institutional support, may be necessary to more fully understand commitment in marginalized relationships (Beals et al., 2002; Greene & Britton, 2015). Further, individuals in marginalized relationships (i.e., same-sex, age-gap, interracial couples) report strong commitment, but they invest less in their relationships than individuals in non-marginalized relationships, possibly on account of societal disapproval (Lehmiller & Agnew, 2006; Tran et al., 2019). Investments may thus factor into commitment differently in marginalized versus non-marginalized relationships, or possibly, the types of investments (e.g., tangible vs. intangible) that predict commitment may differ between marginalized and non-marginalized partners (Lehmiller, 2010). These questions warrant additional empirical attention. In general, of the three predictors, satisfaction typically predicts commitment most strongly across diverse relationships (Tran et al., 2019). One notable counter example is relationships with interpersonal violence. People often remain committed to abusive relationships when they lack quality alternatives or have invested heavily in the relationship, regardless of their satisfaction (Rusbult & Martz, 1995).

 ARTICLE SPOTLIGHT

Staying Together for You, Not for Me: A Theory Extension

You've just been introduced to the investment model: what immediate critiques can you offer? Maybe you noticed that the investment model is primarily self-focused. The model focuses on *your* satisfaction, *your* investment, and *your* perception of available alternatives predicting *your* commitment, and thus the relationship's stability. But recall the concept of transformation of motivation:

Figure 2.16 Even amid the pain of a break-up contemplation, people still think about their partners. (Photo: Nick Dolding / DigitalVision / Getty Images)

people's behaviors often reflect broader considerations, not just their own outcomes (Figure 2.16). Might people make stay/leave decisions for the sake of their partners?

This question formed the basis for Joel, Impett, Spielmann, and MacDonald's (2018) investigation of partner considerations during relationship stay or leave decision-making. They theorized that self-focused reasons are not sufficient to explain relationship stability. Even when someone wants out, prosocial motivations can compel them to think about their partner's interests and needs. How bad would this break-up be for my partner? If we judge our partners to be highly dependent upon the relationship, we might be less inclined to call it quits, even if we have ample self-focused reasons to end things.

To test this idea, Joel and colleagues (2018) conducted two studies, each of which used a prospective design (i.e., gathered data from couples prior to their breaking up). Study 1 ($N =$ 1,281) queried participants about their own relationship dependence (i.e., the investment model components) and their partners' relationship dependence (judgments of the partner's commitment and potential distress were they to break up). The researchers also measured participants' communal strength (i.e., other-orientation). Over the study's ten-week period, people were more likely to continue their relationships if they knew breaking up would be especially hard on their partners, regardless of their own investment. Further, communally oriented people were particularly inclined to consider their partners' dependency when making stay/leave decisions.

Study 2, pre-registered with the Open Science Framework (a "good research practice" discussed in Chapter 3), sampled 500 participants who felt uncertain of their relationship's future and assessed whether they broke up two months later. In addition to Study 1's questions, the researchers added nuanced measures of both partner-focused and self-focused reasons to continue the relationship. For instance, "staying together would make my partner [me] happy" and "My partner [I] couldn't handle a break-up right now." They also measured anticipated feelings of guilt, fear of partner retaliation, and concerns about negative judgments by others (friends, family) on the chance these explain why people stay in relationships they might otherwise leave. Results again showed that people are more likely to stay with their partners when they felt staying together benefited their partner. Guilt, retaliation fear, and concerns about negative social judgments did not explain these relations: people stay in their relationships out of genuine concern for their partners. Again, communal strength played an important role; this time, only individuals high in communal strength based their break-up decisions on their partners' dependency. Prosocial motives may thus be key in orienting people toward their partners' needs during break-up decisions.

As this study reveals, break-up decisions afford a unique opportunity to see transformation motivations at work, and many questions remain. Is staying in a relationship for your partner's sake satisfying? Do people also consider the needs of people outside their relationship (e.g., children, parents, friends) when deciding to stay or leave? This research reminds us that even established models can benefit from tweaks and extensions.

Critiques of Interdependence Theory

Social exchange theory, interdependence theory, and the investment model of commitment each highlight that underlying dependency structures play a critical role in shaping how people behave and experience their relationships (Rusbult & Van Lange, 2008). As functional theories, they suggest we gravitate toward those relationships that give us good outcomes, and we distance ourselves from relationships that provide poor outcomes. This is perhaps why these interdependence theories are often critiqued for prioritizing selfishness (Wallach & Wallach, 1983); however, the broader considerations that define transformation of motivations leave ample room for prosociality, care for the other, and even altruism (Rusbult & Van Lange, 1996). In fact, an advantage of interdependence theory is that it separates the structure of a situation from the construal (i.e., interpretation) of a situation; construal is reflected in the transformation motivations. Of note, however, if someone deviates from expected "rational" outcomes, the nature of the transformation at play is yet a mystery. It could be habit, care for partner . . . any possible motive. Interdependence theory does not give insight into figuring out *why* people engage in behaviors contrary to obvious outcomes. It does, however, allow a place for metacognition, a rarity in relationship theories.

Social Context and Relationships

Interdependence theory defines situations as dependency structures underlying social interactions, but situations can also refer to a relationship's context, the social and culture environment in which it resides. In the same way that a ship sailing the ocean is only as stable as the water and winds that support it, relationships thrive or falter in response to their surrounding circumstances. Thankfully, we have theoretical tools for thinking about how a relationship's external context shapes its development, quality, and stability.

Social Ecological Theories

Social ecological theories attend to the person–environment interaction. For example, Bronfenbrenner's ecological systems theory, a well-known social ecological theory, posits that people (and their relationships) operate within nested layers of environmental influence (Bronfenbrenner, 1977; 1979; Bronfenbrenner et al., 1986). From this viewpoint, a relationship's success depends not only on the interactions between partners, but also on how partners interplay with forces in their social and environmental context. As shown in Figure 2.17, people's relationships are influenced by their immediate environments (their microsystem; e.g., Are family supportive? Is their neighborhood safe?). Relationships are further shaped by the interrelations among their immediate environments (the mesosystem), as well as the specific structures and institutions in which these environments reside (the exosystem). For example, people's work obligations can affect how they meet romantic partners; available social services can impact conflict; and religious organizations can impact cohabitation and reproductive decisions (Lehrer, 1996, 2000). Even further along the Russian nesting doll of social influence (Bronfenbrenner, 1977), overarching cultural ideologies shape relationships (the macrosystem). For example, cultural priorities guide governmental policies that impact who can legally marry, who has children (e.g., the affordability of reproductive assistance, the option for abortion, China's former one-child policy), and parenting options (e.g., the availability of childcare subsidies). Finally, underlying the ebb and flow of each system's influence, as well as the historical context in which a relationship occurs, is the notion of time (the chronosystem; Bronfenbrenner & Morris, 1998). Critically, people – and

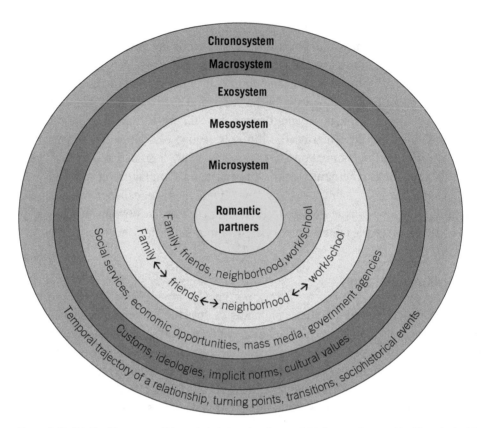

Figure 2.17 Relationships occur within nested circles of environmental influence. Can you identify ecological forces affecting your own or your friends' romantic relationships? (Source: Based on Bronfenbrenner [1977]; Bronfenbrenner & Morris [1998])

relationship partners – interface actively and dynamically with each level of their social ecology.

Social ecological models spotlight the role of stressful environments in determining a relationship's trajectory. Belonging to historically marginalized groups, experiencing low socioeconomic status, and navigating local, national, or global emergencies – like a pandemic or a war– are all examples of external stressors that create toxic contexts for relationship health and well-being (Karney, 2021; Karney & Bradbury, 2005; Neff & Karney, 2017; Pietromonaco & Overall, 2020). External stressors exert their deleterious effects by introducing new problems to a relationship (triggering tension and conflict), and by diverting partners' energy away from relationship-promoting activities. Social ecological models remind us to recognize relationship partners as socialized people navigating the constraints and affordances of their particular privileges and oppressions given to them by their cultural experiences.

Vulnerability-Stress-Adaptation Model

Another prominent perspective that highlights the role of context, specifically external stress, in relationship well-being is the **vulnerability-stress-adaptation model** (VSA model; Karney, 2010; Karney & Bradbury, 1995), shown in Figure 2.18. This model (perhaps best understood

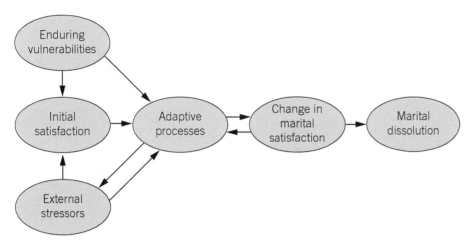

Figure 2.18 How do your relationships fare during stress? The vulnerability-stress-adaptation model suggests relationship health depends on how well partners cope in light of their initial satisfaction and enduring vulnerabilities. (Source: Copyright © 2010 by American Psychological Association, reproduced and adapted with permission. The official citation that should be used in referencing this material is Karney, B. R. [Feb. 2010]. Keeping marriages healthy, and why it's so difficult. *Psychological Science Agenda*, 1–3. www.apa.org/science/about/psa/2010/02/sci-brief. No further reproduction or distribution is permitted without written permission from the American Psychological Association.)

from right to left) describes relationship outcomes as a function of adaptive processes (e.g., responsiveness, support, collaborative problem solving) that can make – or if absent, break – a relationship. Working further left in the model, the VSA model identifies three broad factors that facilitate or interfere with adaptive processes: (1) initial satisfaction; (2) enduring vulnerabilities (e.g., pre-existing personal traits and contextual factors); and (3) external stressors imposed on a relationship. External stressors are theorized to hinder adaptive processes, a situation made worse by pre-existing personal or contextual vulnerabilities that can exacerbate interpretations of and reactions to stressors. In other words, heightened stressors can have a particularly deleterious effect when compounded by enduring vulnerabilities. Consider the COVID-19 pandemic's impact on relationships (Pietromonaco & Overall, 2020). For some partners, the pandemic introduced extraordinary stressors, such as family deaths, job loss, forced separations (e.g., if one partner was in a hospital or nursing home), health risks at work, social isolation, and no childcare. With unknown duration and high uncertainty, pandemic stressors were particularly difficult to manage, especially within the context of existing vulnerabilities. Socioeconomic status, race, parenting status, and age, as well as mental health and attachment style, may have been critical in amplifying or reducing the impact of COVID-19 on relationship health (Pietromonaco & Overall, 2020). The vulnerability-stress-adaptation model reveals the importance of context in shaping relationship well-being.

Conclusion

The guiding theories in relationship science might operate on different premises and view relationship processes through different lenses, but they are not in competition. Rather, they

Figure 2.19 What questions do you have about your relationships? Theories offer helpful, explanatory frameworks. Besides the "big three" theories, relationship science celebrates a strong set of narrower, yet highly influential, theoretical perspectives, including those presented in this figure. (Photo: Adapted from Rumi Fujishima / DigitalVision Vectors / Getty Images)

each contribute unique and important insights that only together can produce a holistic understanding of human relationships. As a field, we are much better equipped to solve any relationship question with a diverse set of theoretical tools (see Figure 2.19 for additional prominent theories in relationship science). This does not mean scholars refrain from having theoretical leanings; some questions lend themselves to particular theories more than others. The challenge is to stay open minded, and maybe even see ways to connect different perspectives.

Consider the culinary metaphor proposed by Eli Finkel, Jeffry Simpson, and Paul Eastwick (2017) wherein they compare relationship theories to different dishes (e.g., beef lo mein, lasagna), derived from a common set of core ingredients (e.g., vegetables, proteins, carbs). The fourteen core ingredients, or principles, that appear frequently in diverse relationship theories reveal their common ground (see Table 2.6). Consider Principle #5, responsiveness, for example. We could view responsiveness as a way to promote sexual faithfulness from an evolutionary perspective, as a means to foster security in attachment theory, or as a behavior that maximizes outcomes through the lens of interdependence theory. These principles remind us that theories in relationship science appear to be built on a set of shared principles. The next question becomes: what are the best ways to test hypotheses derived from theories? In other words: it is time to learn about research methods in relationship science.

Table 2.6 Fourteen principles guiding relationship theories organized by the major theoretical questions they address

What is a relationship?	How do relationships operate?	What do people bring to relationships?	How does context affect relationships?
1. **Uniqueness** – Relationships are the outcomes of unique people who, when they interact, create unique patterns	4. **Evaluation** – Relationships involve people judging their partners and their relationships	8. **Predisposition** – People bring personalities and personal histories	11. **Diagnosticity** – Contexts vary in the extent to which they reveal partners' motives
2. **Integration** – Relationships are the outcomes of interdependence, which leads to a merging of self and other	5. **Responsiveness** – Relationships include responsiveness which benefits self, partner, and relationship	9. **Instrumentality** – People bring goals and needs; relationships affect goal achievement and need fulfillment	12. **Alternatives** – Contexts vary in the extent to which they include attractive alternatives to the relationship, which threatens its stability
3. **Trajectory** – Relationships change over time as people's self, partner, and relationship judgments change over time	6. **Resolution** – Relationships involve partners managing relationship events, and their effectiveness at this task has consequences	10. **Standards** – People bring idiosyncratic standards and compare their relationships with these standards	13. **Stress** – Contexts vary in the extent to which they include external stressors and demands that can strain relationship stability
	7. **Maintenance** – Relationships can include commitment which promotes behaviors that help sustain relationships		14. **Culture** – The cultural context of relationships influences all aspects of the relationship

Relationship theories answer many of the same questions, drawing on key principles.
Source: Based on data from Finkel et al. (2017).

Major Take-Aways

- Relationship-related thoughts, emotions, and behaviors are viewed as solutions to problems along the path toward reproductive success (evolutionary theory), problems maintaining proximity to supportive others (attachment theory), and problems anchored to the situation (interdependence theory).

- Evolutionary theory assumes that modern relationships reflect ingrained sex-specific adaptations to challenges

derived from differential parental investment and affecting reproductive success.

- Attachment theory contends that humans have an evolved attachment behavioral system that activates under threat and keeps people close to caring others; the child–caregiver relationship can bias this attachment system, creating individual differences that persist into adulthood.

- Interdependence theory suggests people rationally attempt to maximize their outcomes. Underlying structures of dependence, however, must be viewed in light of transformation of motivations to understand relationship behaviors.

- In relationship science, theories share foundational building blocks; rather than competing, they work together to reveal insight into human relationships.

Further Readings

If you're interested in ...

... the building blocks of diverse theoretical perspectives of relationship science, read:
Finkel, E. J., Simpson, J. A., & Eastwick, P. W. (2017). The psychology of close relationships: Fourteen core principles. *Annual Review of Psychology*, *68*, 383–411.

... early work linking childhood attachment styles to how adults experience romantic relationships, read:
Hazan, C., & Shaver, P. (1987). Romantic love conceptualized as an attachment process. *Journal of Personality and Social Psychology*, *52*, 511–524.

... how attachment might function in consensual non-monogamous relationships, read:
Moors, A. C., Ryan, W., & Chopik, W. J. (2019). Multiple loves: The effects of attachment with multiple concurrent romantic partners on relational functioning. *Personality and Individual Differences, 147,* 102–110.

... the unique contributions of interdependence theory to relationship science, with its interpersonal emphasis and its focus on the situational structures underlying social interactions, read:
Rusbult, C. E., & Van Lange, P. A. (2008). Why we need interdependence theory. *Social and Personality Psychology Compass, 2,* 2049–2070.

... evolutionary theory, and how childhood might predict different attachment orientations, potentially explaining why people choose different reproductive strategies, read:
Szepsenwol, O., & Simpson, J. A. (2019). Attachment within life history theory: An evolutionary perspective on individual differences in attachment. *Current Opinion in Psychology, 25,* 65–70.

Love in the Time of Technology

Have you checked your phone lately? Browsed? Scrolled? Texted? Better yet, are you reading this chapter *on* your phone? Whether you're a phone-checker, browser, scroller, texter, or reader (or all of the above), you are surely familiar with the (ding!) staccato of (ding!) technological interruptions (ding!) that routinely attempt (ding!) to hijack your attention when it drifts away from your phone. A WhatsApp message, a Facebook notification, an alert that a friend is "going live" on Instagram . . . it's exciting to stay connected and also quite a lot to manage when you're trying to engage in some real-world living. You can thank (blame?) Mark Zuckerberg, the founder, chairman, and CEO of Facebook (the company that also owns Instagram and WhatsApp) for his role in helping to create technology-based connections and disruptions (Figure 3.1).

Although we (as textbook authors) are somewhat concerned about technology interfering with your textbook reading, we are much more concerned (as relationship scientists) about "**technoference**," the experience of technology interrupting or altering the quality of face-to-face interpersonal interactions (McDaniel & Coyne, 2016). Romantic partners have experienced interruptions during their interactions throughout all of history (e.g., "A saber-toothed tiger got into the cave! Run!"), yet the frequency and intensity of these interruptions has almost certainly increased with the advent of new technologies designed to fuel the attention economy.

Figure 3.1 Since its launch in 2004, Facebook and its associated social media apps have become pervasive. (Photo: Teera Konakan / Moment / Getty Images)

Even Zuckerberg is not immune to the potent force he created. The photograph in Figure 3.2 shows him **phubbing** (a word created by smashing the words 'phone' and 'snubbing' together) his wife, Priscilla Chan, as he talks on his cell phone on a walk. Given concerns about technoference, Zuckerberg (as CEO), and Zuckerberg and Chan (as parents of three adorable children), have worked to establish limits on technology. Zuckerberg introduced features called "time well spent" in 2018 to help

(a)   (b)

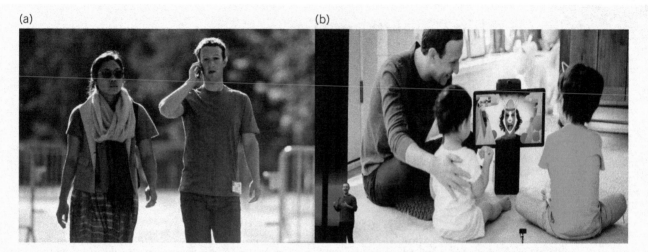

Figure 3.2 Mark Zuckerberg "phubs" his wife, Priscilla Chan, but also uses technology to help his older children maintain connections with distant family. (Photo: Bloomberg / Getty Images [a] and Justin Sullivan / Getty Images News [b])

people monitor (and consciously limit) their social media use, and Zuckerberg and Chan limit their daughters' time on technology as well (Farr, 2018; Wagner, 2018). Although they limit screen time, Zuckerberg lets his kids use Portal (a video-chat product produced by, you guessed it, Facebook) "so they can stay in touch with their grandparents easily [and] their aunts who live across the country" (Juneau, 2019).

Clearly technology brings us together, though perhaps it also (ding!) interrupts our interactions and pulls us apart. Are we more or less satisfied with our relationships as a result of available technology? How can we know?

In this chapter, you will learn how relationship scientists conduct research to answer technoference questions and many, many other questions about relationships. You will learn about the research process, including how hypotheses are derived from theory, which study designs best suit specific questions, how scientists can measure or manipulate variables, and what scientists consider when recruiting a sample to participate in research. You will also get a glimpse into the cutting-edge techniques that relationship researchers are using today both inside and outside of the laboratory. Additionally, we will discuss how researchers approach questions about boundary conditions (when general trends do not apply), mechanisms (the processes underlying their findings), and best practices for conducting ethical and reproducible research. Finally, we offer a guide for how to read and evaluate empirical research articles. Your goal in reading this chapter is to learn what you need to consider when designing your own research and when critically evaluating others' research.

GUIDING QUESTIONS

Consider these questions as you read this chapter:
- What do correlational and experimental studies contribute to our understanding of relationships?
- How do scientists measure or manipulate relationship-relevant variables?
- Who participates in relationships research, and why does the sample matter?
- How do we assess boundary conditions (when general trends do not apply) and mechanisms (the process underlying research findings)?
- What ethical issues do relationship researchers need to consider?

Asking Questions and Finding Answers with Research

Intuition, personal experience, what your grandma told you ... these are all sources of information (and may at times be accurate), but they are woefully incomplete and wholly unscientific. To answer questions about relationships, we must take out our meta-phorical microscopes and observe relationships under the lens. It may seem unnecessary to rely on scientific techniques to study close relationships – a topic we are so intimately familiar with in our own lives. However, if you ask 100 people what makes a relationship work, you might get 100 unique and conflicting answers. The best way to know about the world – including the world of relationships – is to rely on empiricism, making many careful observations and integrating these observations to understand general trends. Let's see how this is done.

Most research begins with a theory (which is why this chapter follows what you just learned in Chapter 2). Although theories can be broad (like the "big three" theories), we often act as lay person theorists in our everyday lives. We connect disparate observations into coherent statements about how we think the world works. For example, the statement "I think using technology in the presence of a partner (or friend or close family member) reduces relationship satisfaction" is a lay person theory, an informally generated explanation for how technology use (i.e., an aspect that can vary ... hence variable) and relationship satisfaction (another variable) are connected. Critically, scientific theories must be testable, meaning evidence can be gathered to show support (or not) for these theories. To test theories, researchers rely on the research process: a series of steps to obtain and interpret this evidence (see Figure 3.3).

Research process

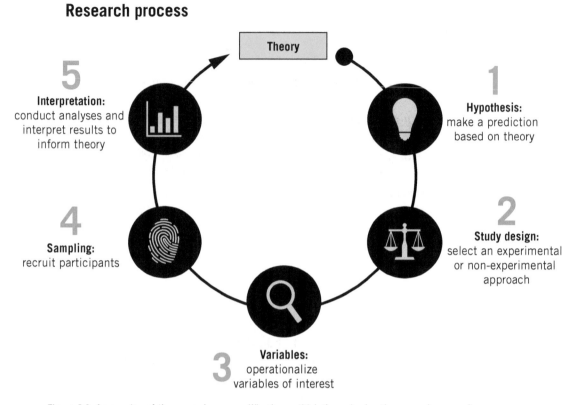

Figure 3.3 An overview of the research process. Why do you think theory begins the research process?

  IS THIS TRUE FOR YOU?

Are Phones a Problem in Your Relationships?

Our lay person theory that technology use reduces relationship satisfaction is actually consistent with a perspective called **evolutionary-mismatch theory** (Sbarra et al., 2019). Evolutionary-mismatch theory assumes that humans evolved to prioritize social bonding and are therefore motivated to self-disclose (share personal information with others) and to react to others' disclosures. Whereas many moons ago, self-disclosure and responsiveness necessarily involved face-to-face interaction, today, smartphones allow us to self-disclose and respond to others on a much larger scale. We can give "status updates" to everyone we know at once and can "like" others' posts en masse . . . all the while unintentionally ignoring the real people right next to us. The "evolutionary mismatch" between our basic drives and our current "tech-heavy" world explains why technology use might undermine relationship satisfaction. Simply put, we are trying so hard to connect online that we miss opportunities to connect in person (Figure 3.4).

The idea of an evolutionary mismatch between how we evolved to maintain close relationships and how we use smartphones is intriguing, but are the adverse effects personally true for you? Theories often need to be revised to include boundary conditions – the cases where the theory does not apply. Perhaps this evolutionary-mismatch theory does not apply to all kinds of people or to all kinds of close relationships. If it doesn't feel

Figure 3.4 A group of friends spending time with their cell phones . . . and one another. (Photo: Franek Strzeszewski / Image Source / Getty Images)

true for you, how might you or your relationships differ from others? Maybe technoference hurts relationships when couples have limited quality time together, but has little impact when couples have an abundance of quality alone time; maybe phubbing reduces relationship satisfaction only when someone is already questioning their partner's commitment, but has no effect for stable, secure couples. These are potential boundary conditions that the theory would need to take into account. In your own relationships, when does phubbing bother you most, and when is it less troublesome?

The first step in the research process is to develop a specific **hypothesis**, a prediction that follows logically from the theory being tested. In other words, *if* the theory is true, *then* what should we be able to observe? For our example, *if* using technology in the presence of a partner reduces relationship satisfaction, *then* people who experience more technoference will have lower relationship satisfaction than people who experience less technoference. This prediction is **directional**: it describes the direction that we expect the observed association to take. A hypothesis should be clear enough that someone else could sketch the expected pattern. Figure 3.5 provides a sketch of our directional hypothesis.

In order to test a hypothesis, researchers need to make a series of important decisions: what type of study design to use, how to measure the variables of interest, and who to recruit to participate in the study. Together, these decisions impact the inferences that we can draw from the research. Each decision

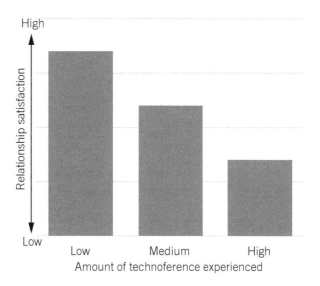

Figure 3.5 A sketch of the directional hypothesis that people who experience more technoference will have lower relationship satisfaction than people who experience less technoference. Why do you think it helps researchers to sketch their expectations?

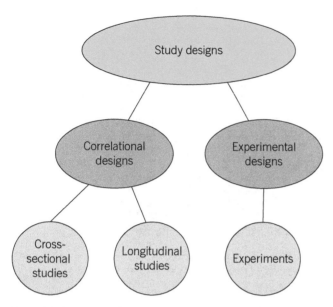

Figure 3.6 An overview of common study designs. Why is it critical to use diverse methods to examine one question?

involves trade-offs because each approach has strengths and weaknesses. Researchers – and readers of research – need to be aware of these decisions and their implications so that they can understand what a research study can (and cannot!) tell us. Ultimately, the evidence we obtain from research studies is used to evaluate a theory, making theory the alpha and omega (beginning and end) of empirical research.

Selecting a Study Design

With your hypothesis set, the first major challenge in the research process is selecting an appropriate study design. This decision follows directly from your research question: what do you want to be able to infer from your data? The biggest distinction in study design is between non-experimental and experimental designs (see Figure 3.6). **Non-experimental designs** involve observing naturally occurring patterns in the world to assess whether there are associations, or connections, between variables. The most common non-experimental design used by relationship scientists is the **correlational design**, a design in which researchers measure two variables and test for their association. **Experimental designs** instead involve manipulating one or more variables to assess whether changing one variable causes corresponding changes in another variable (Mashek et al., 2018). Correlational and experimental designs are both used commonly in relationship science, for different purposes. A correlational study, for example, could tell you whether partners who experience more technoference tend to have low relationship satisfaction, but only an experiment can tell you whether technoference *causes* relationship satisfaction to decline.

Correlational Designs

Correlational studies are an excellent way to describe naturally occurring patterns in the world. For example, correlational studies can test how relationship quality is related to specific relationship characteristics or personal characteristics and answer questions such as:

- Do couples who spend more time apart tend to have less conflict?
- Is introversion associated with a preference for monogamy?

Perhaps most informatively, some correlational designs also allow researchers to predict how relationships change over time. For example, researchers can ask:

- Does the frequency of expressing affection predict the extent that relationship satisfaction declines over time?
- Is experiencing a relationship conflict associated with a higher subsequent likelihood of getting sick?

We could also test our technoference hypothesis with a correlational design, reframing it as: *the more technoference people experience, the lower their relationship satisfaction will tend to be*. Let's see how two types of correlational studies – cross-sectional correlational studies and longitudinal correlational studies – could provide data to test this hypothesis. Because study design is closely tied to data analysis and interpretation, this section will also review typical analysis strategies for each design and the inferences each strategy allows us to make.

Cross-Sectional Studies: A Snapshot in Time

In order to assess whether technoference and relationship satisfaction are linked, we could conduct a cross-sectional study, a study in which researchers collect descriptive data at one moment in time, as though they were taking a quick snapshot of a sample of people's experiences. As long as technoference and satisfaction are measured only once, it is a cross-sectional study design. Once we have our snapshot – a measure of each variable for each participant – we can test the hypothesis by assessing the covariation between technoference and relationship satisfaction.

Covariation means that, across people, values in one variable correspond in a consistent way with values in another variable. Figure 3.7 shows three scatterplots illustrating patterns of linear covariation that we could potentially observe. In these scatterplots, the location of a dot indicates a participant's technoference score and their relationship satisfaction score. Panel A shows strong covariation (across participants, technoference scores are closely linked to relationship satisfaction); panel B shows weak covariation (technoference is weakly linked to relationship satisfaction); and panel C shows no covariation (technoference is unrelated to relationship satisfaction).

Relationship scientists typically measure covariation between two variables with a Pearson correlation coefficient (r). Correlations can range from –1.00 to +1.00. Positive correlations describe a pattern in which a high score on one variable corresponds with a high score on another variable (e.g., the *more* technoference, the *more* conflict), and negative correlations describe a pattern in which a high score on one variable corresponds with a low score on another variable (e.g., the *more* technoference, the *less* relationship satisfaction). Stronger correlations are indicated by r-values closer to –1.00 or +1.00, and weaker correlations are indicated by r-values closer to 0.00. In Figure 3.7, panel A depicts a

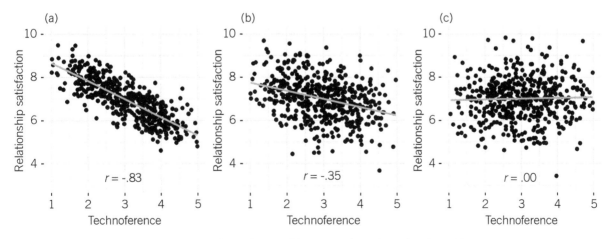

Figure 3.7 Simulated (made-up) scatterplots depicting three possible patterns of covariation (correlations) between technoference and relationship satisfaction.

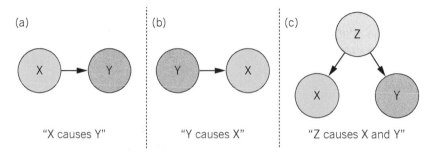

Figure 3.8 Possible causal explanations of a correlation between two variables (X and Y). Why is it critical to remember that correlations do not tell us about causation?

correlation of –0.83 (a strong negative correlation), whereas panel B depicts a correlation of –0.35 (a weaker negative correlation). What's the difference? When a correlation is stronger, the variables are more closely linked, so knowing a participant's score on one variable provides more accurate information about the other variable.

Cross-sectional studies can be a great source of information about close relationships, but they have a significant limitation. They have low internal validity; that is, they cannot tell us anything about causation. When we observe a correlation between two variables (like technoference and relationship satisfaction), there are three possible causal explanations. A negative correlation between technoference (X) and relationship satisfaction (Y) *could* mean that technoference causes people to be less satisfied with their relationships (Figure 3.8, panel A). However, two other possibilities cannot be ruled out.

First, we could have uncovered a reverse-causal relationship: low relationship satisfaction causes greater technoference (see Figure 3.8, panel B). In other words, to the extent that people are less satisfied with their relationships, they spend more time on their phones when they are with their partners. Plausible, right? Second, technoference and relationship satisfaction may not cause each other in either direction. Instead, their correlation could be due to a third variable, some other variable (Z) that we have not measured, but simultaneously causes high technoference and low relationship satisfaction (see Figure 3.8, panel C). For example, maybe this whole story is really about age (Z). Perhaps younger people engage in more technoference than older people because they are part of the tech-savvy iGeneration (Z➔X), and younger people also happen to have lower relationship satisfaction than older people because their relationships tend to be relatively newer and still in an adjustment phase (Z➔Y). Thus, age could drive both technoference and relationship satisfaction. As we will see, only experiments can support one of these causal interpretations. However, collecting data over time can provide some insight into the direction of observed links.

Longitudinal Studies: Film Reels over Time
Researchers often want to do more than describe the state of variables at a particular moment: they want to observe how variables change over time and they want to predict those changes. To observe how variables change over time, researchers can use a longitudinal study – a study in which variables are measured more than once. If a cross-sectional study is like a snapshot, a longitudinal study is like a film reel with several still images played in sequence to create the illusion of motion. A flip book, if you will. Each assessment

provides information that, when combined, can reveal how relationship processes play out over time. Longitudinal studies allow researchers to determine temporal order – which variables precede others in time – to support one causal process and rule out the reverse causal link.

To test whether technoference predicts changes in relationship satisfaction over time (and to rule out the reverse), we could assess technoference and relationship satisfaction several times, perhaps over the course of a year. With a longitudinal design, we can revise our hypothesis to: *people who experience more technoference will subsequently report greater decreases in relationship satisfaction than people who experience less technoference.* In other words, we can hypothesize that technoference precedes (not causes!) decreases in relationship satisfaction.

With a longitudinal design, we could collect data any number of times, but let's walk through an example with three assessments. Imagine we gathered a sample of participants and assessed their technoference and relationship satisfaction when they first enrolled in the study (i.e., baseline), six months after this baseline, and twelve months after baseline, as shown in Figure 3.9.

Participants would likely have some stability in their reports across time (e.g., people with high technoference at baseline probably also report high technoference six months later), as shown by the solid black arrows. Our primary interest, however, is in the red arrows – the association between technoference at one time-point and relationship satisfaction at the next time-point. This line represents our testable hypothesis: do people who experience higher technoference at one time-point report greater decreases in relationship satisfaction from that time-point to the next? If we observe these predicted changes, we have evidence that high technoference precedes decreases in relationship satisfaction. As a happy bonus, this design also allows us to test for the reverse-causal explanation by examining whether relationship satisfaction at one time-point predicts a subsequent change in technoference (this pathway is depicted in the dotted arrows). If technoference predicts decreases in relationship satisfaction, but relationship satisfaction does not predict changes in technoference, then we have determined the temporal order of these variables.

Experience sampling is an intensive type of longitudinal study in which participants complete many assessments throughout their daily lives (Bolger & Laurenceau, 2012). Participants may be instructed to complete questionnaires after a set period of time

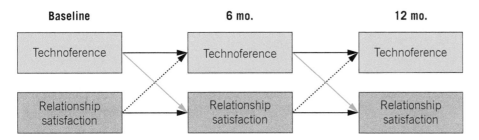

Figure 3.9 Longitudinal data collected at three time-points over one year. How does this improve on cross-sectional approaches? Solid black arrows depict the stability in technoference and relationship satisfaction over time; dotted black arrows depict the association between relationship satisfaction and subsequent technoference; and red arrows depict the association between technoference and subsequent relationship satisfaction.

(interval-contingent), whenever they receive a signal from the experimenter (signal-contingent), or whenever an event occurs (event-contingent; Reis et al., 2014). The **daily-diary method** is particularly common in relationship research. This is an interval-contingent approach where participants complete assessments once per day. Were we to assess techno-ference and relationship satisfaction using a daily-diary method for a period of time, we could test:

1. whether *people* who experience technoference report lower relationship satisfaction compared to *people* who experience less technoference (between-person); and
2. whether any individual person reports lower relationship satisfaction on *days* when they experience more technoference compared to the *days* when they experience less technoference (within-person).

To understand how these two questions differ, take a look at Figure 3.10. This figure depicts how technoference scores vary over the course of a week (a seven-day daily diary) for two participants, Serena and Venus. As you can see in the figure, Venus reported higher overall technoference than Serena throughout the week, so there is a between-person difference in technoference. With this information, we can test whether *people* like Serena (who have lower technoference overall) report higher relationship satisfaction than *people* like Venus (who have higher technoference), as one test of our hypothesis. Additionally, we can see from Figure 3.10 that both Serena and Venus reported varying levels of technoference throughout the week, evidence of within-person differences in technoference over time. If we also measure relation-ship satisfaction on each day, we could test whether any person (e.g., Serena) reports higher relationship satisfaction *on days* when she reports lower technoference than *on days* when she reports higher technoference. This within-person association can provide additional evidence that technoference is linked with relationship satisfaction. Experience sampling is a powerful method because it allows researchers to study relationship processes in the real world.

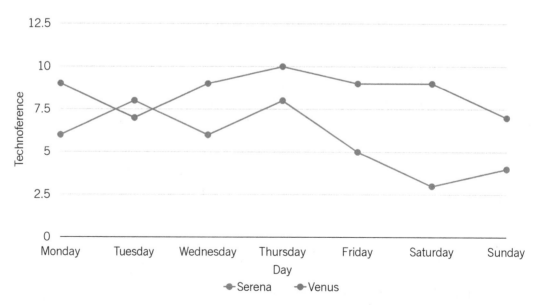

Figure 3.10 Between-person and within-person differences in technoference. Each line shows the within-person variation in technoference from day to day. If you compare the two lines, can you see between-person variation in technoference throughout the week?

Longitudinal studies provide more information than cross-sectional studies, but they require more resources (time and financial) and an additional challenge for researchers: participant retention. The longer participants are asked to stay involved in a study, the more attrition – loss of participants – will occur. Attrition can limit a study, especially if its occurrence is not random – that is, if some people are more likely to drop out of the study than others. For example, people with lower socioeconomic status drop out of studies at higher rates than people with higher SES (Ahern & Le Brocque, 2005). Ultimately, attrition can lead to a sample of participants that systematically leaves out some types of people. To design longitudinal studies that limit attrition, researchers must find ways to motivate or incentivize sustained participation.

In our example, longitudinal designs can help to rule out reverse causation – that relationship dissatisfaction drives technoference, but these designs still cannot tell us that technoference caused relationship satisfaction to decrease over time or day to day. This is because longitudinal designs cannot rule out third variables. For example, even if technoference at an early time-point predicts a decrease in relationship satisfaction at a later time-point, we cannot be sure that technoference is what caused satisfaction to decrease. Participants who experience a lot of technoference may be different from participants who experience low levels of technoference in numerous other ways, and any of those other differentiating factors (third variables, also called confounds) could be the real cause of declining relationship satisfaction. For instance, perhaps people in the throes of a bad mood experience more technoference than those in a less-bad mood because partners withdraw into their phones to avoid their ire. So then, if crankiness varies systematically with technoference across time, we cannot separate the two. It could be that technoference causes declining satisfaction, or it could be that crankiness causes both technoference and declining satisfaction. And worse still, *any* variable that covaries with technoference could be the actual cause of relationship satisfaction decline, even variables we are not considering. To rule out confounds, we need a hero to save the day … not a bird, not a plane, not even Superman … we need the mighty and powerful experiment.

Experimental Designs

Experiments have two defining features that enable them to determine causality. In experimental designs, researchers: (1) manipulate the predictor variable – called the independent variable (IV) – while holding everything else constant; and (2) randomly assign participants to conditions (more on this soon). If researchers include these two features in their design, they can test whether the independent variable really does, in fact, *cause* changes in the outcome variable, the dependent variable (DV). Together, manipulation and random assignment allow for tentative causal inference because they take steps to ensure that any link between the predictor and outcome could be caused only by the predictor. Score one huge point in favor of experiments.

Returning to our original question of whether experiencing technoference (IV) *causes* poorer relationship satisfaction (DV), we now see that this causal question requires an experimental design. In order to test the presumed direction of effect, we need to find a way to manipulate technoference. In other words, as the researchers, we need to tinker with the situation to make some participants experience partner phubbing and other participants experience no (or at least less) partner phubbing. These two experimental conditions could be referred to as the *phubbing condition* and the *control (no phubbing) condition* and they must be distinct: one sideways glance at a phone during a 30-minute interaction does not a phubbing condition make! A good design requires a strong manipulation of the independent variable coupled with a **control condition**, which serves as a comparison or reference point. In an experiment, our question becomes: "Are participants who experience phubbing subsequently *less* satisfied with their relationships *than* participants in the control condition, who don't experience phubbing?"

We could manipulate technoference in many ways. We could, for example, invite participants to the laboratory with their romantic partners and have their partners serve as confederates to help with the manipulation. **Confederates** are typically members of the research staff who act as though they are participants or bystanders, but their true goal is to behave in predetermined ways toward the real study participants. How they behave is scripted to be consistent with the participants' assigned experimental condition. Romantic partners could serve as confederates if they agree to behave in a particular way toward their partners, a.k.a. the target (or real) participants during the study. For target participants in the phubbing condition, we could secretly instruct partners to take out their phones and stay on them during an activity, whereas we could secretly instruct partners of those in the control condition to keep their phones away during the same activity. The exact activity does not matter too much as long as the activity (and everything else) is the same in both conditions. Holding everything constant between the conditions (except the independent variable) allows researchers to isolate the manipulated independent variable (phubbing) as the only potential cause of any subsequent differences. Participants should complete the conditions in the same place, they should be treated in the same way by the research staff, they should participate at the same times of day ... and so on. When you design an experiment, you might pretend you are being sworn in as a witness in research court: "I swear to manipulate the independent variable, the whole independent variable, *and nothing but the independent variable*, so help me God."

With sufficient control in place and partner-confederates doing their part, we are ready to get our hands dirty with some data. All participants could complete a measure of relationship satisfaction after their assigned phubbing condition. Figure 3.11 shows a bar plot of example data from 100 participants (simulated to show a group difference). The bar plot depicts the average relationship satisfaction in the phubbing group (6.99) and in the control group (8.52), and it has error bars to show how individual participants' scores cluster around these averages.

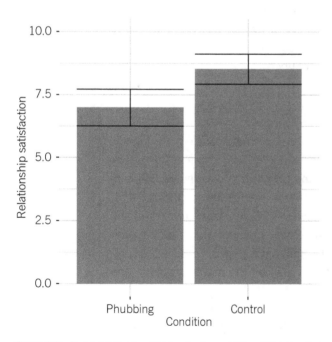

Figure 3.11 Simulated (made-up) data showing condition differences in relationship satisfaction. Error bars indicate one standard deviation above and below the group means.

We could use a number of approaches to analyze these data, with null hypothesis statistical testing (NHST), a popular (if often critiqued; Cumming, 2014) approach. In this simple study with two conditions, the most common NHST choice would be a *t*-test. This approach assesses whether the observed difference between conditions is large enough that obtaining such a difference would be highly unlikely if, in reality, technoference had no effect on relationship satisfaction. Even when we observe differences so extreme that they are unlikely to be due to chance (i.e., a statistically significant effect), we have not *proved* the presence of the effect; we simply say, "hey, it would be really unusual to obtain our data if the effect were not there." We can also quantify the effect size, the magnitude of the difference between conditions to estimate the extent of the effect. A significant effect can be extremely small or extremely large in magnitude, which underscores the importance of reporting effect size and considering it when interpreting others' findings. Suppose we observed a "statistically significant" medium-sized condition difference in our example data. This means we can tentatively infer that the technoference manipulation caused group differences in relationship satisfaction. Why? The only difference between participants in the phubbing condition and the control condition is that partners were phubbing in the phubbing condition, so phubbing must be the cause of group differences in satisfaction.

An astute reader may be questioning this logic and wondering: "Couldn't participants in the phubbing condition have just been less satisfied with their relationships to begin with?" Well, possibly, but it's unlikely because of the second defining feature of experiments, random assignment. When participants are randomly assigned to conditions, any individual differences between participants are equally distributed between the groups, ensuring that groups do not differ at the outset. Of course, some participants enter the study less satisfied with their relationships and some begin the study more satisfied with their relationships (not to mention, some enter the study as extroverts, optimists – you name it). When we randomly assign everyone to a condition, the consequence is an even distribution of all individual differences: the highly satisfied participants are equally distributed among the phubbing and control conditions, and the unsatisfied participants are as well (and the extroverts, optimists ... etc.). On account of random assignment, on average, the groups will be the same in every way. This is the magic of experimental design! There is one caveat: random assignment can only function effectively if a sufficient number of participants (perhaps at least fifty, though the more the better) are recruited for the study. This is because random assignment relies on chance to disperse individual differences: the larger the sample size, the more unlikely it is to have any individual difference accumulate in one condition.

The previous example describes a between-subjects experimental design, a design in which participants are assigned to experience only one of the conditions (i.e., some participants experience the phubbing manipulation and others experience the control condition). An alternative approach is a within-subjects experimental design, a design in which every participant experiences all conditions. For instance, all participants could report their relationship satisfaction twice, once immediately after experiencing partner phubbing *and* once immediately after experiencing no phubbing. In this design, individual differences are held constant between conditions because each person essentially serves as their own control. It is the difference between their own scores across conditions (e.g., each participant's score in condition A minus their own score in condition B) that helps answer our research question.

One limitation for within-subject designs is that experiencing one condition may impact participants' subsequent experiences in another condition (**counterbalancing** can sometimes help, by randomly assigning participants to experience the conditions in different orders).

Because experiments, both between-subject and within-subject, allow researchers to make causal inference, they are celebrated for their high internal validity. But like correlational research, experiments too have a potential downside. Remember: *Research decisions always entail trade-offs*. Let this be your mantra. By creating a controlled experimental environment, researchers boost internal validity, but may threaten external validity: how well the study results generalize (apply) to other situations. The controlled experimental setting (e.g., quiet, clean, emotionally neutral) likely differs substantially from the settings where couples actually interact (e.g., Thanksgiving with the in-laws and a broken oven, in traffic on the Long Island Expressway). Further, experiments can only be used when researchers can ethically manipulate the independent variable of interest. Some variables cannot be manipulated (e.g., relationship length), and others would be unethical to manipulate (e.g., long-term social isolation). To maximize internal validity and external validity, relationship scientists often conduct a series of studies, each with a different methodology to balance internal and external validity concerns (Tashakkori et al., 2012).

RESEARCHER SPOTLIGHT: Sarah Stanton, PhD

Figure 3.12 Dr. Sarah Stanton is a senior lecturer (equivalent to associate professor) of Psychology at the University of Edinburgh, Scotland. (Photo courtesy of Sarah Stanton, PhD.)

How did you come to be a relationship scientist?

I fell in love with relationship research (pun intended) during the third year of my undergraduate degree. Initially, I had planned to pursue clinical psychology, but after taking several clinical courses I realized I was more interested in (and, frankly, better suited to) other careers. After taking research methods, I found myself passionate about the idea of using research to help people improve their lives. I became a research assistant, did an honours thesis, and from there, I went on to graduate school, a postdoc, and the rest is history!

What's most exciting about designing experimental interventions?

The most exciting part to me is knowing that the intervention (i.e., the manipulation) could make an important difference for people in their day-to-day lives. It's also fun to figure out *why* an intervention works. Finally, I love collaborating with other passionate researchers. It takes a strong team to design and implement an intervention effectively!

What are the biggest methodological challenges facing relationship scientists today?

I think different research fields could do a better job of talking to one another. We would benefit from looking into and incorporating methods and paradigms that other disciplines use when advancing our science. On a more practical level, in relationship science and other fields, it is challenging to create ecologically valid non-questionnaire measures when designing online or lab studies.

What unexpected challenges have you experienced when designing relationship interventions?
Striking the right balance between what you would ideally like to do with what is feasible to do is surprisingly difficult! There are always trade-offs when designing relationship interventions, as well as a vital need for flexibility on the part of the researcher. For instance, the global outbreak of COVID-19 required that I completely revamp a planned in-person intervention to a fully online format, which took months. As unexpected as this challenge was, I learned that in-person interventions can often be adjusted for online formats without sacrificing rigor or depth. Having to make unexpected trade-offs and dealing with other surprises might introduce challenges, but we can often learn exciting things in the process.

Measuring Variables

After you choose your design, the next step in the research process is deciding how to operationalize (i.e., measure or observe) the variables of interest. For an experiment, you would operationalize your independent variable(s) through effective manipulation and operationalize your dependent variable(s) through effective measurement. To showcase the rigor and creativity involved in measurement, let's focus on a correlational design, which would require measurement of both technoference and relationship satisfaction. How would you precisely measure these constructs? We have no ruler we can whip out to measure technoference and no biological specimen we can draw to measure particles of relationship satisfaction. Instead, researchers rely on self-report, implicit, observational, and physiological measures.

Self-Report Measures

One straightforward way to assess relationship-relevant variables is to ask people directly. This type of approach is called self-report because, just as it sounds, people report on their own experiences. Self-report measures involve a standard set of questions (a questionnaire or scale) intended to measure the relevant aspects of a variable. For example, to assess the extent to which people experience technoference in their relationships, Roberts and David (2016) developed items – specific statements for people to respond to – that capture different aspects of technoference. Take a look at Table 3.1 to try it for yourself. For each statement, circle the number that is true for you in your own romantic relationship or close friendship.

To estimate the level of technoference in someone's relationship, we compute an average of their responses: we add all of the circled numbers together and divide by the total number of items (nine). You can try this for yourself based on your own responses. Because of the response scale used in this measure, the lowest possible average – or mean – is 1, and the highest possible mean is 5. Note that item 7 requires reverse-scoring, because it is worded oppositely of the other items. Whereas an "all of the time" response to most items indicates high technoference, responding "never" indicates high technoference for item 7. Using reverse-scored items helps ensure that participants are reading the individual items carefully.

After deciding how to measure technoference, the next task is to determine how to measure relationship satisfaction. We could again consider administering a self-report measure, such as the Couples Satisfaction Index (CSI; Funk & Rogge, 2007). Try it for yourself. For

Table 3.1 Self-report measure of partner phubbing

Partner phubbing scale	Never	Rarely	Sometimes	Usually	All the time
1. During a typical mealtime that my partner and I spend together, my partner pulls out and checks his/her cell phone.	1	2	3	4	5
2. My partner places his or her cell phone where they can see it when we are together.	1	2	3	4	5
3. My partner keeps his or her cell phone in their hand when he/she is with me.	1	2	3	4	5
4. When my partner's cell phone rings or beeps, he/she pulls it out even if we are in the middle of a conversation.	1	2	3	4	5
5. My partner glances at his/her cell phone when talking to me.	1	2	3	4	5
6. During leisure time that my partner and I are able to spend together, my partner uses his/her cell phone.	1	2	3	4	5
7. My partner does not use his/her phone when we are talking (R).	5	4	3	2	1
8. My partner uses his/her cell phone when we are out together.	1	2	3	4	5
9. If there is a lull in our conversation, my partner will check his/her cell phone.	1	2	3	4	5

Note that item 7 requires reverse-scoring ("R"), because it is worded oppositely of the other items.
Source: Reprinted from Roberts, J. A., & David, M. E. (2016). My life has become a major distraction from my cell phone: Partner phubbing and relationship satisfaction among romantic partners. *Computers in Human Behavior, 54*, 134–141. Copyright 2016, with permission from Elsevier.

each statement in Table 3.2, think about your relationship with your partner or the same close friend you considered when completing the technoference scale, and circle the number that applies to you.

You can then calculate your own self-reported relationship satisfaction by computing the mean of your responses. If a sample of people were to complete these self-report measures of technoference and relationship satisfaction, we could test our hypothesis that more technoference is related to lower relationship satisfaction.

Table 3.2 Self-report measure of relationship satisfaction

Four-item Couples Satisfaction Index (modified to apply to close friends)						
1. Please indicate the degree of happiness, all things considered, of your relationship.						
Extremely unhappy	Fairly unhappy	A little unhappy	Happy	Very happy	Extremely happy	Perfect
0	1	2	3	4	5	6
2. I have a warm and comfortable relationship with my partner/friend.						
Not at all true	A little true	Somewhat true	Mostly true	Almost completely true	Completely true	
0	1	2	3	4	5	
3. How rewarding is this relationship?						
Not at all	A little	Somewhat	Mostly	Almost completely	Completely	
0	1	2	3	4	5	
4. In general, how satisfied are you with this relationship?						
Not at all	A little	Somewhat	Mostly	Almost completely	Completely	
0	1	2	3	4	5	

Source: Copyright © 2007 by American Psychological Association, reproduced and adapted with permission. The official citation that should be used in referencing this material is Funk, J. L., & Rogge, R. D. (2007). Testing the ruler with item response theory: Increasing precision of measurement for relationship satisfaction with the couples satisfaction index. *Journal of Family Psychology, 21*(4), 572–583. No further reproduction or distribution is permitted without written permission from the American Psychological Association.

Implicit Measures

Unlike self-reports, which assess attitudes directly, **implicit measures** assess attitudes indirectly, by observing reaction time or task accuracy. One common implicit measure used across disciplines is the Go/No-Go Association Task (GNAT; Nosek & Banaji, 2001). For this task, words appear on a computer screen one at a time and in rapid succession. The participant's job is to either press the spacebar ("Go") or do nothing ("No-Go") when they see each word, based on specific task instructions. In the classic GNAT, intended to measure participants' positive and negative attitudes toward bugs, participants complete one round (the *bugs + good* round) where they are instructed to "go" when they see a word that is either good (e.g., pleasure, likeable) or related to bugs (e.g., spider, mosquito). Then, in another round (the *bugs + bad* round), the same participants are instructed to "go" when they see a word that is either bad (e.g., nasty, dislike) or related to bugs. The words appear very quickly so participants do not have time to think; they just react.

Here is the most important part: participants will be more accurate (they will "go" and "no-go" at more of the right times) when the two response categories are more strongly linked in their minds. For example, if a participant has a negative attitude toward bugs, the *bugs + bad* round should be relatively easy for them because they essentially have only one category to remember (bad things!). Instead, a participant with an affinity for bugs would make more mistakes on the *bugs + bad* round because that participant would have to remember to "go" when they see something bad and when they see a bug, something not bad in their view. Researchers assess participants' *good + bugs* association and their *bad + bugs* association to evaluate implicit positive attitudes and implicit negative attitudes toward bugs, respectively.

"What's all of this talk about bugs?" you might be wondering. "I thought we were supposed to be learning about relationships." Well, yes. A nice feature of the GNAT is that it can be adapted for other topics, like relationships. Lee, Rogge, and Reis (2010) developed a version of the GNAT that they called the Partner-GNAT in which the good and bad categories are paired with a category related to one's romantic partner rather than bugs. In one round, participants are instructed to "go" whenever they see a name for their partner or a good word, like "understanding" or "accepting" (the *partner + good* round), and in another round, they are instructed to "go" whenever they see a name for their partner or a bad word, like "nagging" or "criticizing" (the *partner + bad* round). Accuracy on the *partner + good* round provides a measure of the strength of the association between one's partner and good stuff – one's implicit positive attitude toward one's partner – and accuracy on the *partner + bad* round provides a measure of the strength of the association between one's partner and bad stuff – one's implicit negative attitude toward one's partner. Lower accuracy on the *partner + good* round and higher accuracy on the *partner + bad* round each predict a greater likelihood that participants will break up with their partner within the next year (Lee et al., 2010). Some evidence even suggests that implicit measures predict future declines in relationship satisfaction better than the self-reports (McNulty et al., 2013).

Observational Measures

Another way to operationalize relationship-related variables is to observe couple-members' interactions and quantify behaviors of interest (Figure 3.13). **Observational measures** – measures that involve observing behaviors – can be thought of as careful, systematic people-watching. Researchers observe couples interacting out in the world or (more typically) they recruit couples to come to the laboratory and record their interactions there. Then, neutral third-party observers, called **observational coders**, quantify behaviors of interest based on a coding system (Sillars & Overall, 2017). Observational measures provide an objective (fact-based) measure of relationship behavior, in contrast to the subjective (opinion-based) reports produced by self-report measures. Both objective and subjective reports provide useful information because both the facts of the situation and people's feelings and opinions about the situation can influence relationships.

For example, we could assess the extent to which someone experiences technoference in their relationship by observing a typical relationship interaction and having a neutral third party (i.e., an observational coder) rate the extent to which the interaction was interrupted by technology. To quantify technoference, we could create a coding system like the example

(a)   (b)

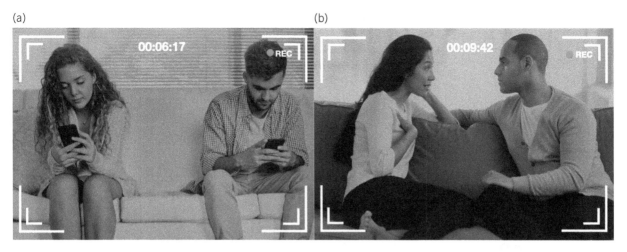

Figure 3.13 Video-recordings of couples in a research lab. If you were an observational coder, what might you be able to code from each of these recordings? (Photo: Adapted from Charday Penn / E+ / Getty Images [a] and Tetra Images / Getty Images [b])

shown in Figure 3.14 to measure the amount of time a participant spent on their phone and the degree to which phone use interrupted the interaction.

We created this brief observational measure of technoference because, to our knowledge, no observational measure of technoference already exists. For many relationship-related constructs, however, validated observational coding systems already exist for you to borrow (and borrow you should! Science is cumulative, and researchers often build on one another's contributions when making their own). For example, the Rapid Marital Interaction Coding System (RMICS) is commonly used to code problem-solving and communication behavior during a variety of interactions, such as problem-solving discussions (like planning a vacation) and social-support discussions (conversations about current stresses; Heyman, 2004). For each speaker-turn, raters assign a particular behavior code such as hostility ("all angry or irritated behavior"), withdrawal ("pulling back from the interaction"), self-disclosure ("statements about the speakers' feelings, wishes or beliefs"), or constructive problem discussion ("all constructive approaches to discussing or solving problems"; Heyman, 2004). Using this strategy,

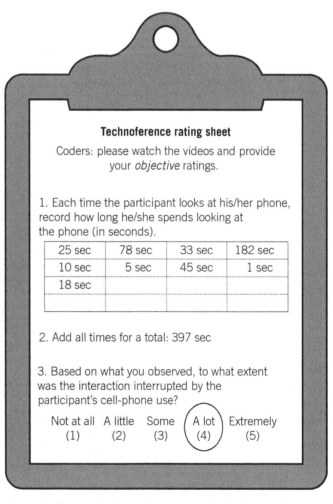

Technoference rating sheet

Coders: please watch the videos and provide your *objective* ratings.

1. Each time the participant looks at his/her phone, record how long he/she spends looking at the phone (in seconds).

25 sec	78 sec	33 sec	182 sec
10 sec	5 sec	45 sec	1 sec
18 sec			

2. Add all times for a total: 397 sec

3. Based on what you observed, to what extent was the interaction interrupted by the participant's cell-phone use?

Not at all	A little	Some	A lot	Extremely
(1)	(2)	(3)	(4)	(5)

Figure 3.14 An example observational measure of technoference. What would you add to this if you were conducting your own study?

researchers can obtain a metric of how often a couple behaves in each way. Observational measures provide a quantitative (numerical) representation of behavior and can be useful for relationship scientists who want to understand what actually occurred rather than partners' perceptions of what occurred.

Physiological Measures

One additional class of measures commonly used by relationship scientists is physiological measures (Figure 3.15). **Physiological measures** assess bodily function (e.g., heart rate, sweating) and therefore can provide another objective tool for measuring aspects of relationship interactions. Researchers often turn to physiological measures to assess stress-related outcomes, because the body's physiological response to stress is readily observable. For instance, researchers can measure salivary cortisol, the primary output of the hypothalamic-pituitary-adrenocortical (HPA) axis (Kemeny, 2011; Nicolson, 2008) to infer variation in stress responses. Acute stressors reliably activate the HPA axis and increase cortisol in the short term; and chronic stressors dysregulate cortisol's normal daily rhythm (Ockenfels et al., 1995). Salivary alpha-amylase is another salivary marker of sympathetic nervous system activity, and like cortisol, it can be measured by a salivary swab (Granger et al., 2008). Stress is also – and more commonly – assessed with physiological measures of heart rate and blood pressure. These measures can be assessed at intervals (e.g., before, during, and after a stressful task) or continuously using an electrocardiogram (ECG) and a continuous beat-to-beat blood pressure cuff to provide an objective measure of stress (Gerin et al., 2008; Goyal et al., 2008).

One additional, and increasingly common, physiological measurement technique is **neuroimaging**, recording images of the brain. Techniques like functional magnetic resonance imaging (fMRI) are particularly useful for relationship researchers because they reveal the function, rather than the structure, of the brain. Relationship scientists measure brain activity in certain regions of the brain to infer individuals' mental states. For example, the dorsal anterior cingulate cortex (dACC) and the anterior insula (AI) are two brain regions that are

(a)   (b)

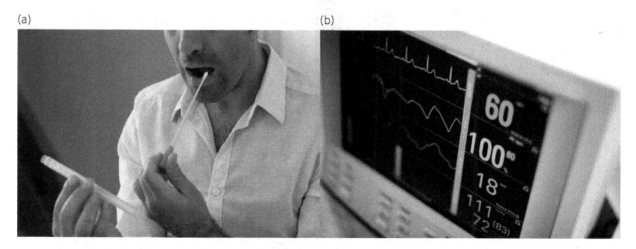

Figure 3.15 Physiological measures often include salivary (a) or cardiovascular assessments (b). Can you think of other physiological measures useful in relationship science? (Photo: BSIP / Collection Mix: Subjects / Getty Images [a] and Eyecrave Productions / E+ / Getty Images [b])

active when people experience physical pain (e.g., a burn or a cut) and when people experience social pain (e.g., social exclusion). That link, in itself, fascinates researchers because it suggests that social exclusion is experienced in the same way as a physical injury; it literally "hurts" to be left out (Eisenberger et al., 2003; Kross et al., 2011). Researchers also use fMRI to measure people's pain without having to rely on self-reports. For example, researchers found that looking at pictures of an ex-partner and recalling the break-up generally activates the dACC and AI, suggesting that recalling break-ups is painful (Fisher et al., 2010). Like any measure, researchers can consider variation in this brain activation to assess who has the strongest and weakest pain reactions and how these reactions relate to differences in break-up.

Comparing Measurement Strategies

With so many options, how should you operationalize any given variable? There is no one "right" operationalization; each measurement strategy has strengths and weaknesses (as shown in Figure 3.16). Just keep repeating the mantra: *Research decisions always entail trade-offs*.

Even with no "right" answer, researchers still have a few general considerations when they select a measurement strategy. First, measures differ in practical ways such as ease of

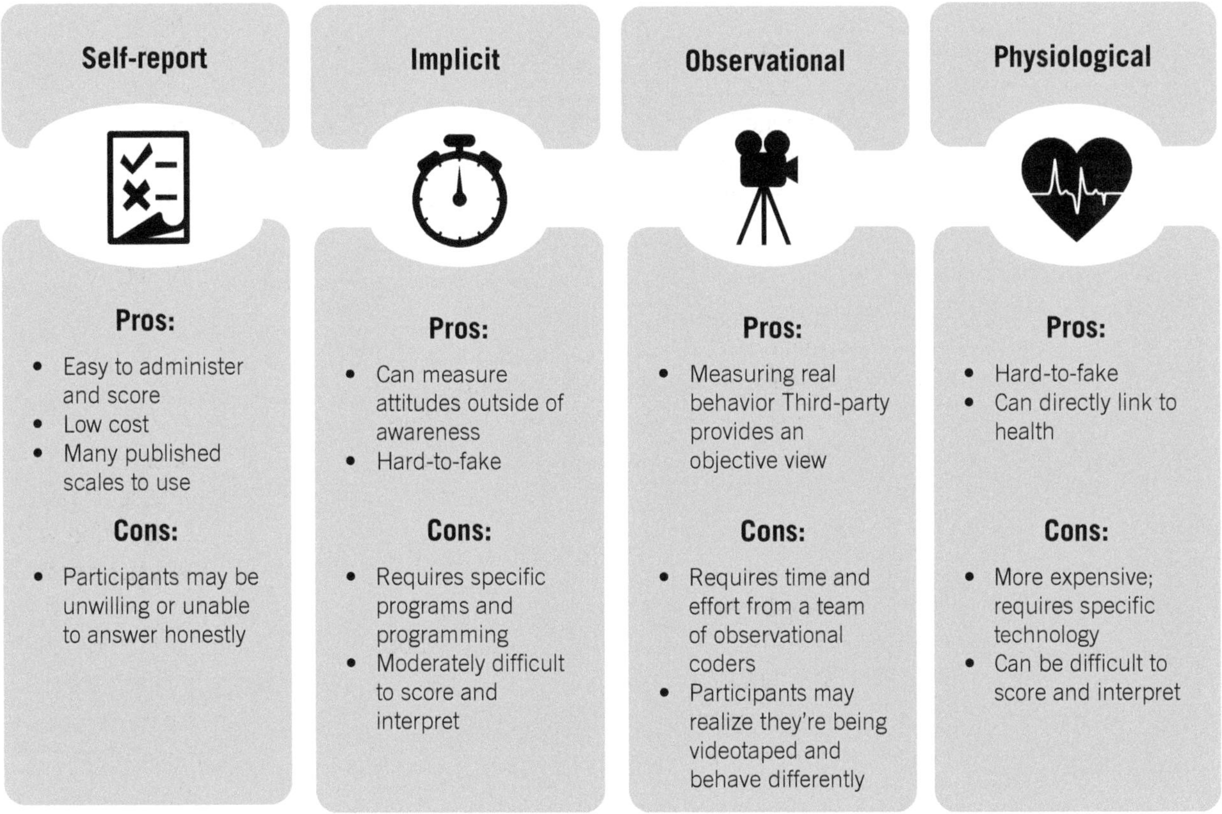

Self-report	Implicit	Observational	Physiological
Pros:	**Pros:**	**Pros:**	**Pros:**
• Easy to administer and score • Low cost • Many published scales to use	• Can measure attitudes outside of awareness • Hard-to-fake	• Measuring real behavior Third-party provides an objective view	• Hard-to-fake • Can directly link to health
Cons:	**Cons:**	**Cons:**	**Cons:**
• Participants may be unwilling or unable to answer honestly	• Requires specific programs and programming • Moderately difficult to score and interpret	• Requires time and effort from a team of observational coders • Participants may realize they're being videotaped and behave differently	• More expensive; requires specific technology • Can be difficult to score and interpret

Figure 3.16 Pros and cons of various measurement strategies. How do you decide what to use? (Source: Adapted from FingerMedium / DigitalVision Vectors / Getty Images; amtitus / DigitalVision Vectors / Getty Images; Yevhen Borysov / Moment / Getty Images; and bubaone / DigitalVision Vectors / Getty Images, from left to right, respectively)

use and cost (including time-costs and financial-costs). Researchers often prefer self-report measures because they are cheap (all you need is paper and pencil or an online survey platform), quick to administer and score, and readily available to use. Implicit measures are also quick to administer, but require specific programs (which can be expensive) and up-front time to program tasks. They can also be difficult to score and interpret. Observational and physiological measures are the most time- and resource-intensive, so they are selected despite – rather than because of – difficulty and cost. Observational measures, for example, typically require video- and audio-recording equipment, and they require people to do the meticulous work of coding these recordings. Physiological measures typically require the most expensive equipment, including hardware to record physiology and software to view and analyze physiological data.

Another critical consideration for researchers as they choose their measurement approach is whether they believe participants will provide accurate information. Participants may not self-report honestly because they want to present themselves and their relationships in a positive light (referred to as socially desirable responding) or because they are motivated to see their relationship positively. Implicit and physiological measures can avoid these issues because people do not have control over the accuracy or latency (reaction time) of their responses to implicit tasks, and they typically cannot control their physiological reactions. For example, people may want others to believe they are unphased by relationship conflict, but their physiology may show that the seemingly cool cucumber is pickling on the inside. Research has revealed this exact pattern in people with high levels of attachment avoidance: they tend to self-report low levels of stress during relationship conflicts, but physiological measures show heightened reactivity (Laurent & Powers, 2007; Pietromonaco & Barrett, 1997; Powers et al., 2006). Observational measures can also avoid socially desirable respond-ing in some cases, especially when participants are unaware that their behavior is being observed. Sometimes researchers refrain from telling participants that they are being video-taped in order to observe participants' natural interaction patterns (we will return to the ethics of this later in the chapter).

A final key issue that researchers consider (and one that we should keep in mind when we read published research) is a measure's construct validity: whether the measurement strategy actually captures the construct the researchers are intending to measure. For instance, if a researcher intends to measure relationship satisfaction, does their assessment strategy actually detect relationship satisfaction, or is it capturing something else? Imagine you are reading a paper and the researchers say they measured relationship satisfaction with one self-report question: *To what extent do you experience disagreements in your relation-ship?* The researchers infer that participants who report frequent disagreements are dissatis-fied with their relationship (low relationship satisfaction). Does this measure have high construct validity? Probably not. A person could disagree with their partner often and still be very satisfied with their relationship. Maybe rigorously debating with their partner is what makes their relationship satisfying! Other measurement strategies can similarly run into construct validity problems when they pick up on something other than the construct of interest. For example, heart rate is sometimes used as a physiological measure of stress, but it may also increase when people are excited or engaged in a task, which makes it a bit muddy and hard to interpret (Blascovich & Tomaka, 1996). When it comes to construct validity, the onus is on the researcher to justify their measurement choices so that readers of research, who are by nature a critical audience, agree that the variable intended to be measured was, in fact, measured.

Sampling

With the study design selected and variables operationalized, the last major hurdle in the research process is recruiting participants. This is a critical step in the research process because what you learn depends entirely on who you ask (or fail to ask). For example, let's say we want to understand the pervasiveness of technoference in the United States. Ideally, we would measure technoference in all people who live in the United States ("Yoo-hoo! Everyone! Please take a few minutes to complete my brief survey!"), but that is impossible. From a practical standpoint, the best we can do is sample some members of the population and use the information they provide to make a reasonable guess about the whole population. But how should we determine whom to sample?

One option is to use convenience sampling, an approach in which researchers recruit participants who are easy to access and readily available to participate. For instance, researchers might recruit young adults who are taking university courses or older adults at a local retirement center. Unfortunately, neither of these samples is representative of (similar to) the US population as a whole, so neither of these convenience samples would provide a reasonable estimate about technoference in the United States overall. Because young adults use technology more than older adults, the young adult sample would likely provide an overestimate of technoference, whereas the older adults sample would likely provide an underestimate.

Data from the Pew Research Center – a major US research organization – demonstrates this idea. In 2015, researchers at the Pew Research Center surveyed people from all around the United States about how they used their cell phones during their most recent social gathering (Raine & Zickuhr, 2015). As shown in Figure 3.17, young adults (red bars) reported using their phones much more than older adults (green bars), and neither age group was representative of the sample as a whole. Convenience sampling is, well, convenient, but results may not generalize to the overall population of interest.

In order to obtain results that *do* generalize, researchers need to recruit a representative sample, a sample that is roughly similar to that population of interest in meaningful ways. For example, researchers who are interested in how new parents navigate the transition to parenthood ideally want their results to generalize to all new parents (the population of interest). What happens if the researchers recruit a sample that is comprised primarily of women? Men and women can have quite different experiences during the transition to parenthood, so results will generalize primarily to women and may not apply to men. What if, instead, the researchers recruit a sample that is comprised primarily of new parents in Syracuse, New York? Whether these data would generalize to people outside of New York depends on whether people in Syracuse transition to parenthood differently than people in other places? Perhaps not (though this is arguable). A sample is generalizable if it is roughly similar to the population of interest in *meaningful* ways. Studies that generalize broadly are considered to have high external validity, whereas studies that can only generalize to a

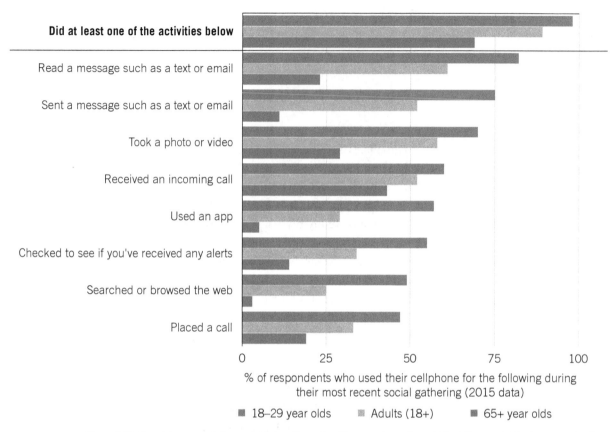

Figure 3.17 Smartphone use during social interactions. Consider your day so far: which of these activities have you done? (Source: Pew Research Center American TrendsPanel survey, May 30–June 30, 2014; drawn based on data from Raine & Zickuhr [2015])

specific group of people are limited by low external validity. Again, a study's external validity is critical because what you learn depends entirely on who you ask (or fail to ask).

 DIVERSITY AND INCLUSION

Who's Sampled and Who Isn't

Participants in social and behavioral science research tend to be recruited from Western, Educated, Industrialized, Rich, and Democratic nations; put that together and you get WEIRD, a suitable acronym considering that these (largely American) participants are quite unique from people in other parts of the world (Arnett, 2008; Henrich et al., 2010). Unfortunately, relationship science is not immune to these sampling biases. A review of relationship research published between 2014 and 2018 (Williamson et al., 2022) revealed that a large majority of studies sampled participants from the United States (73 percent), other English-speaking countries (the United Kingdom, Canada, Australia, New Zealand – 12 percent), or Europe (10 percent). By comparison, very few studies recruited their participants from Asia (3 percent), Latin America (<1 percent), Africa (<1 percent), or the Middle East (<1 percent). These samples were also likely to be primarily white (Williamson et al., 2022).

Systemic racial injustice, as well as stigmatization and discrimination of some identities and relationship types, further contributes to non-representative samples: historically marginalized groups are under-sampled and privileged majority members are over-sampled. Although this external validity problem is not unique to relationship science (Medin, 2017), it certainly has limited the scope of our knowledge about relationships. Consider how problematic it is to assume that information about college students' long-term relationships tells us something meaningful about couples who have been married for forty-five years. This might sound absurd, but it is actually quite common: over a quarter of samples used in relationships research papers between 2014 and 2018 were samples of undergraduate students (Williamson et al., 2022). Sure, college students have much in common with the general population, but they are also different in important ways. Recently, relationship scientists have been working to rectify this problem by harnessing the wide reach of the Internet to access larger and more diverse samples.

"Research, Meet the Internet"

Social scientists have increasingly moved their research studies from in-person to online (fully remote) in order to recruit larger and more diverse participant samples. Consider who is willing to transport themselves to a research laboratory (typically located on a college campus) to complete an in-person study: probably people who live on-campus or near campus, have reliable transportation, and have a bit of time to spare. That's certainly not most people! Now consider who is willing to complete online studies from the comfort of their own home: not everyone (e.g., some people lack internet access), but certainly a greater proportion of the overall population.

Researchers connect with eligible volunteers online through crowdsourcing websites, such as Amazon's Mechanical Turk (MTurk), Prolific Academic, and CrowdFlower, where they advertise their online research studies to people around the globe (Chandler & Shapiro, 2016; Peer et al., 2017). Eligible volunteers can then participate remotely through online data-collection platforms that enable researchers to post surveys and even set up online experiments (Gosling & Mason, 2015). Although internet samples are still not perfectly representative, they are typically more representative of the US population than in-person samples with regard to gender, socioeconomic status, and age (Berinsky et al., 2012; Gosling et al., 2004). Internet samples also have the advantage of **anonymity** – participants do not need to reveal their identities to researchers in order to participate – so people with stigmatized identities may be more willing to participate and report potentially embarrassing information.

Although online studies have strengths, they also have potential downsides (another research trade-off). For instance, participants might split their attention between an online research study and watching a television show, or they might complete a research study while simultaneously having an argument with their partner about whose turn it is to fold the laundry. Depending on the nature of the study, these interruptions could threaten data quality. Researchers can take steps to ensure that they are collecting high-quality data by including **attention checks**, items that participants are instructed to answer in a particular way to demonstrate that they are reading carefully (Berinsky et al., 2014).

"Data, You've Gotten So Big"

Relationship scientists have also found creative ways to use "big data" to access large, generalizable samples (Kosinski, 2019). **Big data** refers to massive datasets (often containing millions or billions of raw datapoints), typically pulled from websites (such as social media sites), apps (such as online dating apps), and mobile sensors (such as wearable devices). All of these digital records can provide rich data about actual human behavior and can do so on a large scale (Harari et al., 2016). Consider how much researchers could learn about attraction by accessing Tinder swipes, or what researchers could learn about ongoing relationships by accessing GPS data from couple-members' cell phones and physiological data from their wearables. Believe it or not, this kind of research is already underway in the proof-of-concept phase and will likely provide insights for relationship science over the next several years (Timmons et al., 2017).

Individual Samples Versus Dyadic Samples

Relationship scientists have an additional sampling decision to make: whether to recruit a sample of individual people (e.g., Serena, Barack) or a sample of dyads (e.g., Serena & Alexis, Barack & Michelle). When they can afford the additional participant cost, researchers typically prefer dyadic samples because having information from both partners allows researchers to assess links (interdependence) between partners. Relationship scientists commonly use the Actor-Partner Interdependence Model, or APIM, to test how one partner's characteristics influence *their own* relationship experiences as well as *their partner's* relationship experiences (Kenny et al., 2006). For example, Figure 3.18 shows an Actor-Partner Interdependence Model focusing on heterosexual couples and testing whether a person's (i.e., an actor's) level of anxiety predicts their own relationship satisfaction (actor paths, A1 and A2,) as well as whether a person's level of anxiety predicts their partner's relationship satisfaction (partner paths, P1 and P2). These partner paths can uniquely demonstrate dyadic influence (i.e., interdependence).

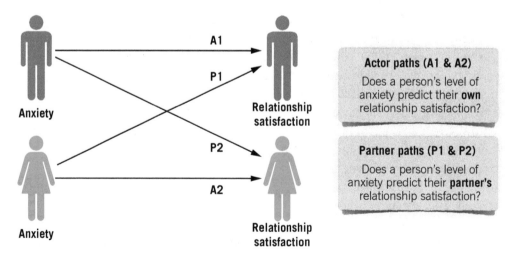

Figure 3.18 An example Actor-Partner Interdependence Model to test how a person's anxiety predicts their own relationship satisfaction and their partner's relationship satisfaction, separately for men and women. What other questions might APIM help answer?

The model shown in Figure 3.18 estimates actor and partner paths separately for men and women and therefore provides four estimates:

A1: the extent to which men's anxiety predicts their own satisfaction;
A2: the extent to which women's anxiety predicts their own satisfaction;
P1: the extent to which women's anxiety predicts their partner's satisfaction; and
P2: the extent to which men's anxiety predicts their partner's satisfaction.

Distinguishing partners based on their sex can be useful in samples of different-sex couples because it allows researchers to test for sex differences in either actor and partner effects (e.g., is the link between a person's anxiety and their own relationship satisfaction stronger for men [A1] than women [A2]?). The APIM model can be adapted to compare couple-members based on other distinguishing factors as well, such as the majority (i.e., White) partner and the minority (e.g., Black) partner in a biracial couple or chemotherapy patients and their caregiver spouses. Finally, the APIM can be used when couple-members are "indistinguishable" by just estimating one actor path (how any person's anxiety predicts their own satisfaction) and one partner path (how any person's anxiety predicts their partner's satisfaction). In that case, paths A1 and A2 would be set to be equal, and paths P1 and P2 would be set to be equal in the model. This dyadic version of the APIM can also be extended to consider polyamorous relationships by applying a one-with-many design in which individuals are linked to a group of others, who may or may not be linked to one another (Kenny et al., 2006).

Hopefully you can see how the Actor-Partner Interdependence Model is a flexible analysis technique that allows researchers to model interdependence between partners. Let's apply this model to our technoference and relationship satisfaction question. Imagine we recruited both members of 200 couples and had them report their own phubbing behavior and their own relationship satisfaction. Further, imagine that we collected data from different-sex and same-sex couples to make sure our data are generalizable to both types of relationships. Before reading on, take a second to think about how we could use the APIM to model these data. Once you have thought through it, take a look at Figure 3.19.

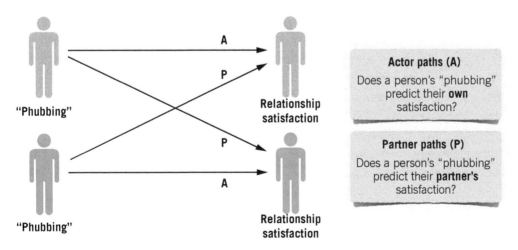

Figure 3.19 An Actor-Partner Interdependence Model (APIM) testing links between phubbing and relationship satisfaction for opposite-sex and same-sex couples.

In this case, we would link each person's self-reported "phubbing" behavior to their own relationship satisfaction and their partner's relationship satisfaction. And since our couple-members are indistinguishable based on sex (some couples are same-sex) and have no other obvious distinguishing feature, we would estimate only one actor path and one partner path.

 ARTICLE SPOTLIGHT

In Defense of Individual Samples

Relationship scientists have typically favored dyadic sampling because of the additional information that dyadic samples can provide. But remember our mantra: *Research decisions always entail trade-offs*. Might dyadic samples have a downside? One recent paper suggests this possibility.

Barton, Lavner, Stanley, Johnson, and Rhoades (2020) conducted a research study to empirically test differences between individual and dyadic samples. They had a hunch that people who volunteer to complete a research study with their partner (a dyadic sample) might be less representative of all people in relationships than people who volunteer to complete a research study on their own (an individual sample). Specifically, they expected dyadic samples to have a greater proportion of couples with high relationship quality than individual samples.

Imagine Rashad spots an advertisement on the bus: *Seeking volunteers for a relationships research study. Earn up to $50 for completing questionnaires! Email relationshipsresearch@any.edu for more information.* Rashad is interested, so he fires off an email to the research team. The reply informs him that to be eligible to participate, both he and his partner need to participate together. Rashad thinks about bringing up the study to his partner. He can imagine her mocking, "Sure, let's show the researchers how not to have a relationship, you cheating jerk." Not worth it ... delete. Although Rashad would have participated on his own, he was unwilling to participate with his partner.

Barton and colleagues wanted to test the hypothesis that dyadic sampling *causes* less representative samples than individual sampling, so naturally they used an experimental design. As shown in Figure 3.20, the researchers started with a nationally representative sample of people in serious, exclusive romantic relationships ("all participants"). Half of these participants were randomly assigned to invite their partners to participate with them, and the other half of the participants were assigned to participate on their own. Of the participants who were instructed to invite their partners to participate, some of their partners actually participated, and others did not. Maybe participants never invited their partners or maybe partners were invited, but declined. Regardless, the researchers were able to compare the characteristics of people who were assigned to participate *and* their partners participated (green box – a typical dyadic sample) to people who were not instructed to invite their partners (pink box – a typical individual sample).

As expected, participants who were assigned to invite their partners and their partners participated (green box) had significantly higher relationship quality (higher relationship satisfaction, higher commitment, lower self-reported likelihood of break-up) than participants who were invited to invite their partners and their partners did not participate (yellow box).

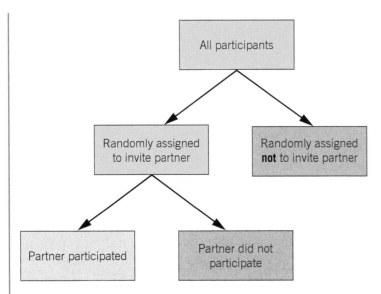

Figure 3.20 Schematic showing comparison groups. Why is this type of analysis so important for the field of relationship science?

This finding suggests that dyadic recruiting systematically over-represents couples with higher relationship quality and systematically under-represents couples with lower relationship quality. The participants who were randomly assigned to participate alone (pink box) had intermediate levels of relationship quality – not as high as participants in the green box and not as low as participants in the yellow box. In other words, participants who participated on their own (the individual sample) were more representative of all people in relationships than participants who participated with their partners (the dyadic sample). With these results in mind, a case can be made to recruit a dyadic sample – to assess how couple-members impact one another – or to recruit an individual sample – to ensure greater generalizability. *Ommmm. Research decisions always entail trade-offs. Ommmm.*

Analysis and Interpretation

The final step in the research process – analysis and interpretation – is perhaps the most straightforward. Like other steps in the research process, analyses follow from research questions: research questions require particular designs, and particular design decisions lend themselves to particular analytic approaches. Further, the inferences researchers can make depend entirely on their study design and sampling approach. Rather than reiterating these ideas here, we will highlight two analytic approaches that relationship scientists often use to dig deeper into their data: moderation and mediation.

Moderation: "It Depends on ..."

Let's imagine that we conducted a series of studies and found that: (1) people who report greater technoference report poorer relationship quality (correlational); and (2) people who are assigned to experience partner phubbing in the laboratory report poorer relationship quality than participants who are assigned to a no "phubbing" control group (experimental).

We'd probably be patting ourselves on the back, brushing our shoulders off, and high-fiving our furry friends. But soon, we would share our exciting finding with a colleague who would say something like, "Do you think that technoference is always problematic? Maybe technoference is problematic for new couples but not problematic for couples who have been together for a long time and are used to being together but doing things separately." What our colleague is suggesting is a moderating factor, or a **moderator**: a variable that changes the pattern of the results. In general, when the existence or strength of a relation depends on the level of a different variable, we have moderation. Moderation reveals the boundaries of a general pattern: it tells us when and for whom a relation appears, and when and for whom a relation is stronger or weaker. To address our colleague's question, we can test whether phubbing's link with relationship satisfaction *depends on* relationship length.

As shown in the simulated data in Figure 3.21, we can plot our data separately for people in short-term and long-term relationships to see the pattern of results for these two groups. The simulated data presented in Figure 3.21 depict moderation both in a scatterplot of correlational data (panel A) and a bar plot of experimental data (panel B). These simulated data show that technoference is associated with/causes less relationship satisfaction for couples in short-term relationships (green), but is unrelated to satisfaction for couples in long-term relationships (red). Moderation can be confirmed with appropriate statistical analyses (Hayes, 2018).

Again, moderation exists any time an effect or association depends on another factor (a moderator). The nature of the moderation can take one of three forms. First, as shown in Figure 3.21, the effect/association can exist for one level of the moderator and disappear for the other level of the moderator (e.g., technoference is associated with lower relationship satisfaction for people in short-term relationships, but there is *no association* between technoference and relationship satisfaction for people in long-term relationships). Second,

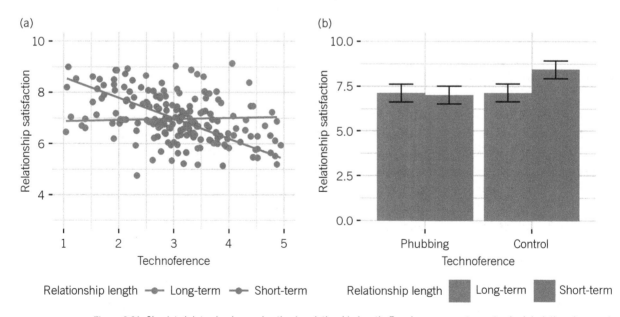

Figure 3.21 Simulated data showing moderation by relationship length. Error bars represent one standard deviation above and below the mean. What other variables might moderate this relation?

the effect/association can be stronger for one level of the moderator than the other (e.g., partner phubbing causes a *greater* decrease in relationship satisfaction for people in short-term than long-term relationships). Or third, the effect can reverse for one level of the moderator compared to the other (e.g., technoference is associated with *lower* relationship satisfaction for people in short-term relationships, but it is associated with *higher* relationship satisfaction for people in long-term relationships). Because people and relationships and situations differ in innumerable ways, relationship scientists often test moderation hypotheses to refine their findings. You will see examples of moderation throughout this book. When you see moderation, just remember, "it depends on."

Mediation: "It's Because of ..."

Again, imagine we conducted a correlational study and an experiment and found that technoference is associated with (and may even cause) lower relationship satisfaction ... pat on the back ... brush the shoulders off ... high-five the pets. This time, when we share our finding with our clever colleague, she instead raises a different question: "Hmm, I wonder why technoference reduces relationship satisfaction. Do you think technoference reduces satisfaction because it creates conflict? Or maybe technoference reduces intimacy to make people less satisfied?" Another great point! Identifying patterns in the relational world is great, but it is even better when we can understand the mechanisms underlying these patterns. To understand why technoference reduces relationship satisfaction, researchers rely on testing **mediation**, or indirect effects through intervening variables (Hayes, 2009). In other words, the reason why technoference reduces relationship satisfaction is *because of* some mediator or mediators.

For example, the link between partner phubbing and relationship satisfaction may be explained by the two potential intervening variables suggested by your shrewd colleague: more phone-related conflicts and less intimacy. A model depicting mediation by these two variables is shown in Figure 3.22. You can understand the model by attending to the direction of each path (+ or –). The first path indicates that partner phubbing leads to greater phone-related conflicts (positive link), and greater phone-related conflicts lead to less relationship satisfaction (negative link). Additionally, partner phubbing leads to less intimacy (negative link), and less intimacy leads to less relationship satisfaction (positive link).

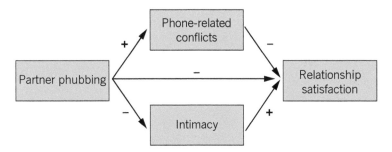

Figure 3.22 Mediation of the link between technoference and relationship satisfaction. Are there other constructs that could explain partner phubbing's link to relationship satisfaction? (Source: Drawn based on data from Halpern & Katz [2017])

Halpern and Katz (2017) actually tested this model and found support for it in a nationally representative sample of Chilean adults involved in romantic relationships. So, we can tell our colleague she has some evidence on her side: greater phone-related conflicts and lower intimacy may explain the link between partner-phubbing and poor relationship quality. Throughout this book, we will see many examples of mediation to explain the mechanisms that underlie relationship processes. When you see mediation, just remember, "it's because of."

Research Ethics

When researchers put on their white lab coats (literally or figuratively), they assume a position of relative power. They transform into authority figures to whom participants will readily defer; they collect information – sometimes very personal information – about research participants; and they publish research findings that can form the basis for public policy. With this power comes an ethical responsibility to protect research participants' well-being, to safeguard their personal information, and to conduct research in a way that results are likely to be accurate and unbiased.

Ethics of Conducting Research with Human Subjects (and Their Human Partners)

As in all research with human subjects, relationship researchers are required to: (1) provide enough information about the study ahead of time so that participants can choose whether or not they wish to participate; (2) allow participants to stop participating in the research at any time without penalty; (3) maintain participants' confidentiality by ensuring that their responses cannot later be linked back to them; (4) protect participants from physical or psychological harm; and (5) fully debrief participants after the study has concluded. Researchers submit their plans to an Institutional Review Board (IRB) made up of other researchers, administrators, and community-members who review the research plan and ensure that it is ethical prior to data collection.

Relationship research in particular raises a few additional ethical questions. Let's address some potential ethical questions that are common in research with couples with a quick Q&A session:

Q: I'm designing a study to test which personality traits predict hostility during relationship conflict. I'm planning to measure hostility observationally, so I need to record conflict discussions to code them. I'm afraid that if I tell participants they'll be videotaped, they will not behave naturally. Do I need to tell participants that they'll be recorded?

A: Participants have the right to know what data will be collected from them and how it will be used, so participants have to consent before you can view the recordings. However, researchers sometimes wait to inform participants about recordings until the end of the study so that participants can behave naturally while they are recorded. This compromise maintains the purity of the observational data and still allows participants to decide whether and how their data will be used. Ultimately, the IRB will evaluate what information participants need to have up-front and what information can be saved for the end of the study based on a costs/benefits ratio.

Q: I'm designing a study to assess predictors of break-up, so I want to have participants complete a measure about the likelihood that they will break up over the next year. Is asking participants to think about breaking up with their partners ethical? What if I inadvertently cause a couple to break up?

A: Researchers are required to protect participants from physical and psychological harm, but that does not mean we need to place participants in physical/psychological safety-bubbles. Researchers should make participants aware of what their participation entails and any potential risks so that the participants can decide for themselves whether they are willing to participate. In your example, participants should be informed that the study involves thinking about and reporting on their relationship and that participating may lead to some discomfort. Participants should also be made aware that they are free to skip any parts of the study and that they can stop participating at any time. Yes, a couple may break up after participating in your research study, but as long as your study did not unduly harm the relationship, the study is ethical. (Of course, always get IRB approval!).

Reproducibility

Like all scientists, relationship researchers worry about the three Rs: not "reduce, reuse, recycle" (although we're concerned about those Rs, too), but "repeatability, replicability, reproducibility" (Plesser, 2018). Relationship scientists work hard to generate true and accurate insights about close relationships, so we want our research findings to be **repeatable** (able to be obtained again by the same researchers using the same study design), **replicable** (able to be obtained again by different researchers using the same study design), and ultimately **reproducible** (able to be obtained again by different researchers using a different study design).

 IN THE NEWS

Are Most Scientific Research Findings False?

In 2005, a physician and researcher named John Ioannidis wrote that "most current published research findings are false" (Ioannidis, 2005, p. 696). Predictably, this provocative statement caused a stir in the scientific community and led teams of researchers to attempt to replicate past findings to confirm their veracity. In 2015, the journal *Science* published a paper summarizing the results of 100 studies attempting to replicate past findings from the field of psychology. Only thirty-nine of the studies replicated. Although many researchers argued that this high-profile failure-to-replicate did not represent the state of the field (citing issues with the replication studies themselves), psychology nonetheless took center-stage in the reproducibility crisis. Newspaper headlines reflected the ongoing debate in the field: "Psychology Is Not in Crisis," "Psychology Is in Crisis Over Whether It's in Crisis," and, finally, "Does Social Science Have a Replication Crisis?" (Feldman Barrett, 2015; Palmer, 2016; Tucker, 2016). Researchers across disciplines – including relationship scientists – began taking inventory of their research practices to identify the methods that are responsible for false-positive results. Today, the headlines have changed. In 2019, the Associated Press published an article entitled, "The replication crisis is good for science" (Loken, 2019). The article states, "… it's not really a scientific crisis, because the awareness is bringing improvements in research practice, new understandings about statistical inference and an appreciation that isolated findings must be interpreted as part of a larger pattern" (Loken, 2019). Indeed, by pointing out past failures to replicate, researchers have embraced new practices that increase the likelihood of producing reproducible research and are better scientists for it.

The result of the "replication crisis" and subsequent self-reflection has been the advent and broad adoption of "open science" research practices that promote reproducibility. Today, open science is quickly becoming the norm in relationship research (Finkel, Eastwick, & Reis, 2015).

Open Science

In general, open science practices entail being transparent about all aspects of the research process and all decisions researchers make in designing their studies, recruiting participants, and collecting and analyzing data. Two cornerstones of open science are pre-registration and making materials and data available to other researchers.

A **pre-registration** is a clear and comprehensive ahead-of-time plan for a research study. It includes information related to all aspects of the research process (see Table 3.3), and it is saved in a permanent, inalterable format where it is accessible to others.

Table 3.3 Pre-registration questions for each aspect of the research process

Aspect of the research process	Pre-registration planning questions
Research questions/ hypotheses	• What are the planned hypotheses?
Variable operationalization	• How will variables be measured? • What summary scores will be computed (e.g., mean, sum)?
Study design	• What is the design of the study? • If the research is experimental, how will the independent variable be manipulated, and what is/are the control condition(s)?
Sampling participants	• How many participants will be sampled? • How will participants be recruited? • Who is eligible to participate?
Analysis/interpretation	• What participants (if any) will be excluded from analyses? • What analysis approach will be used to test the planned hypotheses? • Are there other analyses that will be conducted in an exploratory fashion?

This type of plan encourages researchers to distinguish confirmatory analyses (analyses used to test planned hypotheses) from exploratory analyses (after-the-fact exploration of the data for any interesting patterns). Exploratory analyses are more likely to capitalize on chance and produce irreproducible results; therefore, pre-registration "keeps researchers honest" with themselves and others about which findings are exploratory and should be retested in a confirmatory way before we can be confident about their legitimacy. Additionally, pre-registration plans prevent researchers from making decisions that can increase the likelihood of irreproducible results, such as continuing to recruit participants until they find a significant effect or measuring a variable in several ways and reporting on the measures that show interesting results.

In addition to pre-registration, researchers increasingly make their data and materials – including their full measures and the analysis code they used to analyze the data – available for others. Having the data and materials available allows other researchers to more easily replicate findings using the same approach and/or attempt to reproduce the findings using other measures or research designs. Because researchers need to maintain participant confidentiality, only data that allow participants to remain anonymous can be made available. This can be a particular challenge for relationship researchers because participants themselves could feasibly access the data, identify their own responses (based on demographics or open-ended responses), and find their partner's linked responses. This would be a lot of work to find out whether your partner reported that she is "somewhat committed" or "completely committed" to you, but it is possible, and people have done more for love! To avoid this issue, researchers need to remove pieces of information that could collectively allow participants to be identified by others or by themselves. There are many sites, including the popular Open Science Framework (www.osf.io), that provide free accounts for pre-registration and storage of open materials and data.

Meta-Analysis

Despite these safeguards, the unfortunate reality is that the results of any one study could be due to chance. Although our statistical approaches are intended to minimize false-positives, we have no way to eliminate them. This is why it is appropriate to say we can *tentatively* infer causality from experimental results; from one study, we cannot draw firm conclusions. Given this fact, researchers need to think about individual studies in the context of related studies (Cumming, 2014). Do several studies all show the same trend?

Meta-analysis, an approach that quantitatively integrates results of multiple studies to estimate the overall effect across studies, is perfectly suited to this high-level perspective. For instance, a researcher who wants to understand the consequence of technoference for relationship quality could conduct a meta-analysis of the effect across the studies they conducted or could even track down others' research (published and unpublished) to estimate the effect across all relevant studies. Because meta-analyses integrate many disparate research studies (each with their own unique set of participants and intricacies), researchers can estimate an overall effect with greater certainty. Meta-analysis is an extremely powerful approach, and we will rely on it throughout this book to draw conclusions about relationships.

How to Read Empirical Articles

Many of us get our science news from our favorite news sources: *The New York Times*, *The Wall Street Journal*, and even *Buzzfeed News* all have science sections. If you are interested in learning about technology's role in close relationships, you may read a news article like "Your smartphone may be powering down your relationship," which was originally published by CNN in 2013 (Kerner, 2013). This article states, "Researchers from the University of Essex found that people who engaged in personal discussions when a cell phone was nearby – even if neither was actually using it – reported lower relationship quality and less trust for their partner." As you can see from the quote, news articles are second-hand retellings of research, and like any second-hand retelling, they may lack key detail.

To get the full story, we need to go to the source; we need to read the original empirical article where the researchers present their theory, describe their studies, and interpret their findings. Empirical articles can appear intimidating at first, but like a textbook, a novel, or a recipe, empirical articles have a structure. Once you learn the structure, you can approach the article confidently and find the information you most need to understand and evaluate the research. Table 3.4 breaks down the sections of an empirical article and highlights what information you should be looking for in each section. As you approach your first (or 500th) research article, answer each of the questions presented in the table.

If we dig into the original article that led to the catchy headline ("powering down your relationship"), we can better understand what was actually learned from the research. The original paper contained two experiments (Przybylski & Weinstein, 2013). In the first experiment, researchers randomly assigned strangers to become acquainted in groups of two, either with a cell phone in the room (phone condition) or with a pocket notebook in the room (control condition). Seventy-four people participated in this study, and the average age of participants was 22 years old. After getting to know each other for 10 minutes, all participants self-reported their closeness to and the quality of the relationship with their new acquaintance. The key findings were that people who met with a cell phone in the room reported less closeness and lower relationship quality than people who met without a phone in the room. Now that we have the full story (at least a very shortened summary of the full story – for the full story, look up the article and read it in its entirety!), we know that the researchers did obtain evidence that the presence of the phone *caused* participants to report lower closeness and relationship satisfaction. Next, we might turn to generalizability: can these results generalize to older people and to people who are interacting with others they already know rather than strangers?

In the second study, the authors tested whether the consequences of having a mobile phone present *depend on* the type of conversation people are having. In other words, they tested moderation. In Experiment 2, sixty-seven participants were randomly assigned to talk with a stranger with a phone or other object present, as before, but now the researchers also manipulated the type of conversation participants had together. Participants were either assigned to discuss their thoughts and feelings about plastic holiday trees (casual conversation condition) or to discuss the most meaningful events of the past year (meaningful conversation condition). Afterward, they reported their relationship quality with their assigned partner, their trust toward the partner, and their perception of their partner's

Table 3.4 Sections of an empirical article

Section	Purpose	What you should look for in this section
Title & abstract	Brief overview of research	• Basically, what is this paper about? • Is this a paper I want to read?
Introduction	What question did the researchers aim to test, and why?	• What is the broad problem that motivates this research? • What do we already know about this topic from past research, and what new questions will this study address? • What are the authors' specific hypotheses, and why do they expect these results?
Method	How did the researchers test their question?	• What is the study design? (cross-sectional, longitudinal, experimental) • Who were the participants that the researchers sampled? Are there any concerns about this research generalizing? • How did the authors measure the outcome variable(s)? • If the research is experimental, how was the independent variable manipulated, and what is the control condition? • What exactly did participants do, step-by-step?
Results	What did the researchers find?	• For each hypothesis, did the results support the hypothesis? • What is the key information the researchers are trying to present in each table and figure?
Discussion	What did we learn from this research, and what questions remain?	• What are the main take-aways and implications? • In what ways is this research limited or weak? • What are the next steps in this line of research?

empathy (understanding of them). The results here showed that the impact of the phone on relationship outcomes depended on the type of conversation. When participants were assigned to have a meaningful conversation, the presence of a phone caused them to report lower relationship quality, trust, and perceived empathy after the discussion. However, if the dyad was assigned to have a casual conversation, the presence or absence of the phone had no effect. Again, the empirical article provided a great deal more information than the news summary.

By reading the original source, we can obtain a more comprehensive and accurate understanding of the research and develop ideas for future research. Remember, *research decisions always entail trade-offs*. It's our job, as the consumer of research, to evaluate the merits of each researcher decision. By evaluating their specific trade-offs, we can determine whether we are convinced by their findings and think about how we might extend their research to improve upon it.

Conclusion

Although we are all experts on our own relationships, the only way to know about relationships in general is to conduct (and read) empirical research. By observing many people and systematically integrating these observations, relationship scientists are able to test theories about how relationships form and what factors contribute to satisfying relationships. As they design their studies, researchers make trade-offs and accept that every method has strengths as well as limitations. The unavoidable limitations of any individual study motivate researchers to provide converging evidence using a variety of study designs and to conduct meta-analyses to estimate effects across several studies. Published research studies – upon which our science, and this textbook, are based – are vetted for methodological rigor by other researchers with relevant expertise as part of the peer-review publication process. That means that we can have confidence in the collective findings produced by relationship scientists. However, the power of studying relationships scientifically is that additional research can always challenge, extend, or confirm existing findings. As relationship scientists work to recruit more generalizable samples and learn about diverse types of close relationships, some findings will be confirmed more broadly, and others will be revised to account for human variation. Behold science.

Major Take-Aways

- Correlational research designs reveal associations between variables at one time-point (cross-sectional) or over time (longitudinal), whereas experimental studies provide evidence of causal relations between variables.
- Relationship scientists operationalize variables of interest using self-report, implicit, observational, and physiological measures, each of which has associated strengths and weaknesses.
- Researchers sample a subset of individuals or dyads from the overall population of interest to learn about relationships. Findings based on representative samples generalize

broadly, whereas findings based on restricted samples do not.
- Evidence of moderation reveals that a pattern of results differs based on a characteristic of the person, situation, or relationship (i.e., a finding *depends on* some other variable). Evidence of mediation instead reveals the mechanistic process underlying a particular research finding (i.e., a finding is *because of* something else).
- Relationship researchers must behave ethically, both in their interactions with research participants (e.g., by protecting them from harm) and in their efforts to generate reproducible research findings (e.g., by pre-registering hypotheses).

Further Readings

If you're interested in ...

... how digital traces such as texting logs can be used to understand how relationships develop, read:
Brinberg, M., Vanderbilt, R. R., Solomon, D. H., Brinberg, D., & Ram, N. (2021). Using technology to unobtrusively observe relationship development. *Journal of Social and Personal Relationships*, *38*(12), 3429–3450.

... how relationship scientists can optimize their research practices so that they limit false-positives and false-negatives, read:
Finkel, E. J., Eastwick, P. W., & Reis, H. T. (2015). Best research practices in psychology: Illustrating epistemological and pragmatic considerations with the case of relationship science. *Journal of Personality and Social Psychology*, *108*(2), 275–297.

... an accessible introduction to the art of critically reading an empirical paper, read:
Jordan, C. H., & Zanna, M. (1999). How to read a journal article in social psychology. In R. F. Baumeister (Ed.), *The self in social psychology* (pp. 461–470). Philadelphia, PA: Psychology Press.

... how implicit and explicit relationship satisfaction differ and the different ways in which they change over time, read:
Larson, G. M., Faure, R., Righetti, F., & Hofmann, W. (2022). How do implicit and explicit partner evaluations update in daily life? Evidence from the lab and the field. *Journal of Experimental Psychology: General*, 151(10), 2511–2533.

... representation within close relationships research, the current state of the field, and how we can do better, read:
Williamson, H. C., Bornstein, J. X., Cantu, V., Ciftci, O., Farnish, K. A., & Schouweiler, M. T. (2022). How diverse are the samples used to study intimate relationships? A systematic review. *Journal of Social and Personal Relationships*, *39*(4), 1087–1109.

PART II

RELATIONSHIP FORMATION

4 ROMANTIC ATTRACTION

Is Attraction Predictable?

When he first locked eyes with now-wife Sabrina, British actor Idris Elba knew he had found "the one": "there she was, and the rest was history" (Walters et al., 1997–present). In that seemingly magical moment, two people's lives pivoted toward each other, like magnets reorienting to a predestined position. The couple, shown in Figure 4.1, is not alone in experiencing love at first sight: Ricky Martin and Jwan Yosef, John Krasinski and Emily Blunt, Ellen DeGeneres and Portia de Rossi ... the list goes on and on. For many people, love at first sight seems mystifying and miraculous, fodder for romance novels and fairytales. But is this type of attraction actually predictable? As you will see, relationship scientists strongly contend that, yes, we can study and understand how attraction works and why we like some people more than others.

Figure 4.1 Idris Elba, famous for his roles in *Luther* and *The Wire*, said it was love at first sight when he met Sabrina Dhowre. Does love at first sight really exist? (Photo: Gareth Fuller / AFP / Getty Images)

In this chapter, you will learn about interpersonal attraction, one of the earliest points of inquiry in the field of relationship science. Interpersonal attraction refers to the subjective appeal of another person, a positive evaluation that can be accompanied by a desire for greater closeness to that person (Berscheid & Hatfield, 1969; Finkel & Baumeister, 2019). In this sense, it involves a mental judgment, an emotional reaction, and an affiliative motivation (Montoya & Horton, 2020). Romantic attraction in particular generates an "all-systems go" response and is often described as a "dizzyingly intoxicating" experience (Farley, 2014; Fisher, 1998, 2000). From an evolutionary perspective, the body's heightened physiological arousal and the mind's fixation reflect a keenly designed emotional attraction system, one that effectively recruits and directs resources to the all-important task of high-quality partner selection. Whether we're speaking of romantic attraction or interpersonal attraction in general, the people whom we find attractive have the potential to help us meet important needs. Your goal for this chapter is to learn not only what we find attractive, but also *why*. So, let's start with the first question: what do you find attractive?

GUIDING QUESTIONS

Consider these questions as you read this chapter:
- What are the broad motivations that drive romantic attraction?
- What do people look for in a partner, and why?
- How do a person's sex and their relationship goals affect partner preferences?
- When do hypothetical partner preferences predict attraction?
- What situational factors promote attraction and why?
- What contextual factors promote attraction and why?

Partner Preferences as a Means to an End

About ten years ago, Elena Murzello published a self-help book called, *The Love List: A Guide to Getting Who You Want*. The premise was simple (if unscientific): just like you need a shopping list to visit a grocery store, Murzello argued that you should have a "yay" and "nay" list of traits you want (and don't want) in a romantic partner before playing the dating game. The romantic partners we choose have important bearing on our day-to-day happiness, our achievements and economic status, whether or not we have children (and, often, the genes those children have), and even how long we live (Fitzsimons & Finkel, 2018; Lawrence et al., 2019; Moore & Diener, 2019). So, if ever there were a time for good decision-making, this would be it. Like Murzello, relationship scientists are interested in people's partner preferences, and how these preferences might guide romantic interest. Unlike Murzello, relationship scientists approach this question by drawing on well-formed theories and applying empirical methods.

Ideal partner preferences refer to the traits and characteristics that comprise people's mental representations of a hypothetical, hoped-for romantic partner. These preferences are the presumed cardinal points on our attraction compass, and they serve as standards by which we evaluate actual partners (Fletcher et al., 2000; Simpson et al., 2001). Two findings make partner preferences so fascinating. First, although it counters logic, people's ideal partners are not a "perfect 10," someone who is superlative on every possible desirable trait (Fletcher et al., 1999). Perhaps recognizing that perfect 10s are extraordinarily rare (if they exist at all) and realizing their own potential limits in attracting such a perfect partner (more on this later), people tend to be more realistic in their ideal partner preferences.

The other intriguing finding is that partner preferences differ. Some people value a prospect's intelligence more than their physical appeal; others readily sacrifice brains for good looks. Why? Dozens of studies show that some of this variation is tied systematically to gender, culture, and relationship types (short-term versus long-term), even as certain preferences appear to be idiosyncratic and others near universal. Take a few minutes to complete Table 4.1: what do *you* want in your ideal romantic partner?

Table 4.1 What do you look for in your ideal partner?

Using a scale of 1 (not at all) to 7 (extremely), indicate how important each trait is in your ideal partner.		
Column 1	Column 2	Column 3
_____ Adventurous	_____ Good job	_____ Understanding
_____ Nice body	_____ Financially secure	_____ Supportive
_____ Outgoing	_____ Nice house or apartment	_____ Considerate
_____ Sexy	_____ Successful	_____ Kind
_____ Attractive	_____ Dresses well	_____ Good listener
_____ Good lover		_____ Sensitive

Which column of traits is most important to you for a long-term partner? _____

Which column of traits is most important to you for a short-term partner? _____

Identify and rank your top 3 "must have" traits:	Identify and rank your top 3 "dealbreakers"
1. _____	1. _____
2. _____	2. _____
3. _____	3. _____

Finally, consider the following questions:

How important is it that your partner lives close to you? (not at all) 1 – 2 – 3 – 4 – 5 – 6 – 7 (very much)

How similar do you want your partner to be to you? (not at all) 1 – 2 – 3 – 4 – 5 – 6 – 7 (very much)

These traits help us understand common dimensions of attraction. What other traits do you desire in a romantic partner (e.g., witty, charming, musical, loyal)?

Source: Copyright © 1999 by American Psychological Association, reproduced and adapted with permission. The official citation that should be used in referencing this material is Fletcher, G. J. O., Simpson, J. A., Thomas, G., & Giles, L. (1999). Ideals in intimate relationships. *Journal of Personality and Social Psychology*, *76*(1), 72–89. https://doi.org/10.1037/0022-3514.76.1.72. No further reproduction or distribution is permitted without written permission from the American Psychological Association.

Goal-Directed Models of Attraction

Was it challenging to identify your preferences? Even if it requires a bit of hemming and hawing about the relative importance of different traits, people typically know what they want. What is the utility of these preferences? Finding love would be much easier if we were happy partnering with anyone!

Recall from Chapter 1 that people pursue relationships as a means of achieving needs and goals. People want to belong, to feel safe and secure, to experience pleasure, and to feel good about themselves. Satisfying these deeply entrenched, if general, goals is highly rewarding.

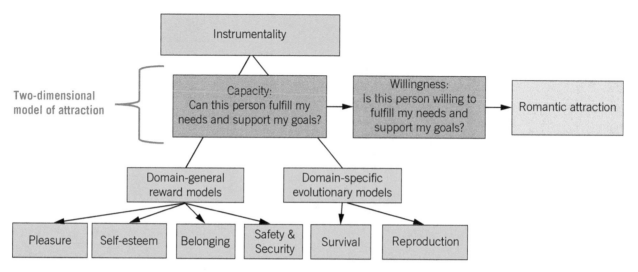

Figure 4.2 Romantic attraction is not arbitrary: it reflects fundamental goals and our hope of achieving them. Can you map your own attraction experiences onto this model? (Source: Drawn based on data from Montoya and Horton [2014] and Finkel and Baumeister [2019])

People are also, as we know, compelled by the specific goals of survival and reproduction. Thus, people have two clusters of primary motives: one general set centered on experiencing rewards; and one specific set centered on evolutionary needs. Accordingly, partner preferences, and indeed all aspects of romantic attraction, tend to be tied to the former, domain-general rewards, or the latter, domain-specific evolutionary goals. In other words, we deem attractive that which helps us make progress toward important goals, a concept subsumed in the idea of instrumentality (Finkel & Eastwick, 2015). Romantic attraction is neither arbitrary nor mysterious: we gravitate toward those whom we believe can help us satisfy fundamental human goals.

Highlighting the instrumentality of romantic attraction helps coalesce the many disparate studies of attraction (Finkel & Baumeister, 2019). Along these lines, the two-dimensional model of attraction (Montoya & Horton, 2014) suggests we are attracted to people whom we evaluate as being (1) *able* to support our goals and needs, and (2) *willing* to do so. This model and the idea of instrumentality are both shown in Figure 4.2. These models would explain Idris's instant attraction to Sabrina, and indeed any person's love-at-first-sight experience, as the favorable outcome of one person's initial evaluation of another person's ability and willingness to support their important general and/or specific needs.

Traits as Indicators

Returning to Table 4.1, why now do you think you selected the traits you did? The concept of instrumentality and the two-dimensional model suggest that the traits you desire constitute a person's ability or willingness to produce rewards and promote evolutionary goals. Some of these desired traits are directly observable. For example, if you find being around extroverted people rewarding (many people do), observing someone's enthusiastic and gregarious style is probably enough to know, hey: that person is extroverted. Other times, however, the exact trait that would most help us achieve our goals is not readily observable. An interest in having children with an intelligent partner, for example, poses a problem because we cannot directly observe fertility or intelligence. So, what do we do? We rely on other traits that might suggest those qualities (e.g., youth, humor).

External traits cue us into internal qualities only if the traits are *reliable* indicators of the underlying qualities that we want. If you are looking for an intelligent partner, height or socioeconomic status would be poor cues (they are unrelated to intelligence), as would a potential partner's own statement of his or her "braininess" (they might be motivated to fib). If you are looking for an intelligent partner, you need a truly reliable, honest signal of intelligence, such as their use of witty humor (Greengross & Miller, 2011). Humor is considered a reliable indicator of intelligence because it is hard to fake. In other words, being able to produce one-liners and quick-witted quips requires intelligence, so this type of behavior can only be produced by someone who is intelligent (DiDonato & Jakubiak, 2016a). When observable behaviors exist only with the presence of an underlying quality, they reliably indicate that quality and they become important in attraction. As you will see, we regularly make behavior-based and trait-based inferences that then inform romantic attraction.

Although people consider a wide range of traits when imagining their ideal partners, many of these traits can be organized into overarching categories. Look at Table 4.1 again: do the traits in each column seem similar? These columns represent an influential model of partner ideals, which organizes preferred traits along the dimensions of *physical attractiveness–vitality* (column 1), *social status–resources* (column 2), and *warmth–trustworthiness* (column 3; Fletcher et al., 1999). Let's dig deeper, beginning with attractiveness.

 IS THIS TRUE FOR YOU?

The Pull of Fatal Attractions

What first attracted you to your most recent ex-romantic partner? Was it their ambition, easygoingness, or life-of-the-party attitude? And why did your relationship end?

Sometimes the traits that draw us initially toward a romantic partner become the very traits that undermine our relationships. These **fatal attractions** tend to share certain features (Felmlee, 1995, 1998). First, they tend to be traits characteristic of the partner, but not the self. In other words, the allure of someone's ambition or spontaneity might draw you in, but eventually create conflict when paired with your work-life balance or planful style. Second, fatal attractions tend to be extreme or unique traits. Moderate ambition or spontaneity, for example, are less likely to become fatal attractions than extreme ambition or extreme spontaneity. Finally, fatal attractions tend to counter normative expectations, such as being gender atypical: a women's encyclopedic knowledge of football or a man's love for Zumba might at first seem endearing, but later become annoying (again, this is when the self does not share these interests). Before they precipitate the end of a relationship, fatal attractions are observed in ongoing relationships (Felmlee, 2001), suggesting they are not an effect of post-break-up distorted recollection, but rather an outcome of disenchantment, or the dropping of illusions that may have colored initial romantic intuition.

Look again at the traits that you want in a partner – are any potential fatal attractions?

Physical Attractiveness and Vitality

What drew Idris to Sabrina on the night they met? No doubt her former-Miss-Vancouver beauty played a role. Indeed, people fall in "love at first sight" more often with highly physically attractive people than with less attractive people (Zsok et al., 2017). This pattern reflects a dominating finding in relationship science, that physical attractiveness breeds liking. **Physical attractiveness** refers to the aesthetic appeal of a person's outward appearance, especially their face and body. Song artists like Jimmy Soul may urge you to marry only ugly people (he insists your happiness depends on it!), but most listeners won't take his advice. People want attractive partners. This is no casual desire: it is, cross-culturally, an oft-cited *essential* feature in a hoped-for romantic partner (Buss, 1989; Li et al., 2002; Lippa, 2007a; Walter et al., 2020).

How important is physical attractiveness? Consider the "Mother of All Blind Dates," a seminal research study conducted in the late 1960s at the University of Minnesota that involved inviting first-year students to attend a "Computer Dance" (Walster et al., 1966). The event was wildly popular, and with tickets purchased ($1.00) participants completed pre-dance questionnaires, including personality, intelligence, popularity, and self-esteem measures. Unbeknown to them, research assistants surreptitiously also rated their physical attractiveness. On the night of the big dance, students were allegedly matched with someone of "the same expressed interests," yet in reality the pairs were randomly assigned. They later rated their "date," and researchers used these ratings, along with their pre-dance question-naires, to assess which factors best predicted attraction. The winner? Physical attractiveness. Indeed, it was the *only* factor that determined attraction. Physical attractiveness is now well established as a primary factor that breeds liking in face-to-face encounters (Luo & Zhang, 2009; Selterman et al., 2015). In American culture, having a physically attractive partner may even be more important today than it was seventy plus years ago (Buss et al., 2001).

Why is physical attractiveness so strongly linked to attraction? Consider instrumentality: which fundamental goals might a physically attractive partner help us to meet?

Physical Attractiveness: Signaling Domain-General Rewards

Being with a physically attractive person may confer domain-general rewards. People take great pleasure in being with attractive people. Indeed, simply viewing images of beautiful people activates known reward centers of the brain and it may be a quite basic trigger of pleasure, given that babies stare at attractive faces longer than unattractive faces (Aharon et al., 2001; Chuan-Peng et al., 2020; Cloutier et al., 2008; Langlois et al., 1987). Further, we ascribe a plethora of positive attributes to beautiful people, attributes that are not necessarily connected to physical appearance, yet bring us pleasure or status or belonging – an idea captured in the **what is beautiful is good** maxim (Dion et al., 1972; Eagly et al., 1991). Westerners tend to think that beautiful people have desirable personalities, are socially competent, and live successful lives. They expect beautiful people to be more sexually warm, more intelligent, more dominant, and more mentally healthy than less attractive others (Feingold, 1992). Evidence from Korea, a more interdependent (less individualistic) culture, supports the idea of a universal what-is-beautiful-is-good stereotype, but defines it differently, with people judging beautiful people not as more dominant, but as having greater integrity and concern for others (Wheeler & Kim, 1997).

The beautiful-is-good effect extends to strangers and known others alike, and even shapes our behaviors: we *treat* attractive people better than less attractive others (Langlois et al., 2000). This biased treatment then elicits favorable responses (Snyder et al., 1977), perhaps explaining why some positive perceptions of attractive people, like seeing them as especially socially competent, are grounded in reality. Enjoying a lifetime of such positive treatment affords attractive people with ample opportunity to develop an array of social skills. Even in online dating, people with more beautiful profile photos benefit from strangers' more invested attempts to solicit responses (Guéguen et al., 2009). Our orientation toward beautiful people suggests physical attractiveness confers significant domain-general rewards.

 DIVERSITY AND INCLUSION

Love Is Not Blind: Colorism in Romantic Attraction

Racism permeates American culture, systems, and institutions, and accordingly, it affects romantic relationships from desire to dissolution. One way it prejudices attraction is through colorism. **Colorism** is the use of skin tone to differentiate among people of color, privileging lighter-skinned individuals over darker-skinned individuals (Hunter, 2007, 2013). Colorism occurs within an American context that promotes racialized standards of beauty and links Whiteness with attractiveness (e.g., in movies, advertisements, fashion; Figure 4.3). This is harmful to people of color, especially darker-skinned individuals. Internalized racist ideas of beauty adversely impact self-worth and self-perceived attractiveness, with many darker-skinned Black women judging themselves as less beautiful than lighter-skinned Black women (Hill, 2002; Silvestrini, 2020). A fallout of colorism, darker-skinned women in many areas of the world are encouraged to use bleach and skin-lightening creams to enhance their attractiveness, even as these methods can be toxic (Hunter, 2007).

Colorism operates within a cultural context in which Black women are especially likely to date and marry within race (Yancey, 2009). This same-race preference appears for Black women even as they experience a documented scarcity of desirable Black partners, a trend attributed to the disproportionally high incarceration, unemployment, and substance abuse rates among Black men as a result of systemic racism (Hamilton et al., 2009). Available and

Figure 4.3 Following from culturally entrenched White supremacist ideas of what is beautiful, Black men in the United States often overlook darker-skinned Black women in favor of lighter-skinned Black women. In what other ways are ideas of beauty anchored to culture, rather than to more universally desired characteristics? (Photo: FG Trade / E+ / Getty Images)

desirable Black men can therefore enact preferences for a higher-status partner, and in doing so, often select Black women with lighter skin to be their partners. On account of colorism, and the link between status and skin tone, lighter-skinned Black women are more likely to marry and marry earlier than darker-skinned Black women (Edwards et al., 2004).

Because "beautiful is good," American culture's distortion of beauty ideals toward Western, European standards (Akinro & Mbunyuza-Memani, 2019) has serious negative consequences for people of color, particularly those with darker skin tones. The effect is now recognized as **skin-tone trauma** (Landor & Smith, 2019). Skin-tone trauma impacts psychological, physical, and behavioral health, and underscores the importance of efforts to change racist and colorist ideas about beauty, such as the Black is Beautiful Movement. Launched in the 1960s, the Black is Beautiful Movement highlights the fact that Black women and Black men are inherently beautiful, dark skin is *not* undesirable, and Black people should not pursue White supremacist notions of beauty. Full representation of Black, Indigenous, and people of color (BIPOC) in positions of power, media, movies, and other arenas will play an important role in dismantling the narrow White supremacist notions of beauty and help prevent the damaging internalization of racist ideas of beauty in the next generation.

Physical Attractiveness: Signaling Good Genes and Good Partner Traits

According to evolutionary theories, the features we now call "physically attractive" are preferred cross-culturally because, throughout our ancestral history, copulating with people with these characteristics provided better odds that (1) an offspring would result, (2) the offspring would be healthy and have desirable genes, and (3) the offspring would survive. For example, if women with fewer wrinkles and more youthful bodies were generally healthier and more fertile, men's evolving of a preference for those features would make adaptive sense: it would advance their reproductive success. Likewise, if physical strength enabled men to secure more resources and offer better protection (and thus be a better partner), women's evolving of a preference for muscular men would prove advantageous. Said in another way, some features may be physically attractive because they suggest someone has "good genes" (those linked to reproductive success or desirable inheritable characteristics), and other features may be attractive because they suggest "good partner" traits (the qualities we want in a companion or co-parent).

What Makes for an Attractive Face?

When it comes to attractiveness, scholars regularly focus their attention on four facial features. First on the list: **facial symmetry**. Imagine you were to draw a line from the center of the top of your forehead down to your chin. The bilateral symmetry – or match between each side of your face – is unlikely to be perfect (sorry!), but it could be close. Facial symmetry is cross-culturally linked to attractiveness, possibly because it indicates development occurring with limited environmental stress (Fink et al., 2006; Little et al., 2007; Thornhill & Møller, 1997; Scheib et al., 1999). Additionally, facial symmetry could suggest resistance to pathogens or toxins, a clue to more immunocompetent partners (Ainsworth & Maner, 2019; Møller & Thornhill, 1998). Identifying healthy partners supports evolutionary goals by increasing the odds for a healthy offspring.

Next is facial sexual dimorphism, the perceived femininity of female faces and masculinity of male faces. Meta-analyses show that people judge sex-typical faces as highly attractive (Rhodes, 2006), possibly because, like facial symmetry, facial sexual dimorphism also signals health. Even today, these evolved preferences are amplified when they serve a strong purpose. For example, women exhibit stronger preferences for masculine faces in countries where poorer health has a more direct link to longevity and survival (Debruine, Jones, & Crawford, 2010). Masculine male faces (those with strong jawlines and pronounced eyebrow ridges) result from exposure to testosterone, which itself is an immunosuppressant, so their presence – like a costly signal – suggests a man has the "good genes" that can withstand such stress (Foo et al., 2020; Rhodes et al., 2003). Why people prefer feminine faces is less clear; there is no parallel story for estrogen. We do know that appealing feminine facial features appear to fall into two categories. On one hand, people judge big eyes, petite noses, and small chins (often called neonate features) as attractive; on the other hand, features characteristic of maturity, such as slender cheeks and pronounced cheekbones, are desired (Cunningham, 1986). These different feminine features may serve different goals. Neonate features may elicit protective responses from others, supporting women's evolutionary goals of survival, and mature features could suggest status, which can be rewarding for potential partners.

Another feature, facial averageness, is also typically considered attractive. We might think distinctive, stand-out faces capture our interest, but evidence suggests people prefer typical, average faces, an effect observed cross-culturally (Langlois & Roggman, 1990; Rhodes, 2006; Rhodes et al., 2001; Trujillo et al., 2014). Scientists can manipulate averageness using computer-generated composite faces. Take a look at Figure 4.4. Can you see the appeal of these composites? Average faces may be preferred because they seem familiar, and familiarity suggests safety, supporting survival goals from an evolutionary standpoint.

Facial symmetry, facial sexual dimorphism, and facial averageness are regularly highlighted as basic features defining attractiveness, yet the evidence is not conclusive. Unanswered questions and inconsistencies persist, especially with regard to how these features relate to actual health outcomes (Weeden & Sabini, 2005). One late arriver to the

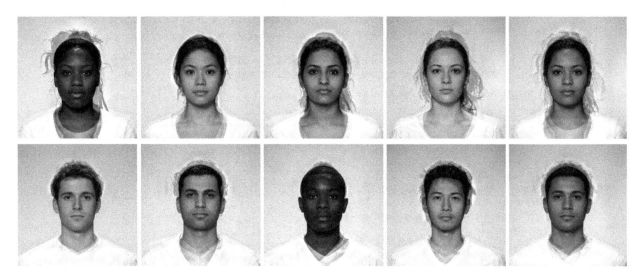

Figure 4.4 People tend to perceive more average faces as more attractive. (Photo: DeBruine, 2016)

"what predicts attractiveness" party is **facial adiposity** – the perceived weight in a person's face – and unlike its bedfellows, facial adiposity has consistent and robust support. People reliably see lower facial adiposity as more attractive and judge faces with lower facial adiposity as healthier. Not only do people accurately estimate body mass index (BMI) from facial adiposity, but facial adiposity reliably signals diverse aspects of health, including poorer cardiovascular health, higher blood pressure, and greater risk of disease and infection (Coetzee et al., 2014; Coetzee et al., 2009; de Jager et al., 2018; Rantala et al., 2013). For these reasons, an evolutionary explanation for the visual appeal of facial adiposity is persuasive.

Many other physical features associated with the face have also been linked to attractiveness. For example, men often show a preference for long hair on women, perhaps because women can maintain long hair only if they are healthy. In this sense, long hair may be a costly signal that indicates "good genes" (Bereczkei & Mesko, 2006; Mesko & Bereczkei, 2004). Relatedly, longer eyelashes on women, especially older women, increases their perceived attractiveness (Adam, 2021; Pazhoohi & Kingstone, 2020). Eyelash length and whitening are tied to age (a marker for fertility), so darker and longer eyelashes provide a cue of fertility. This evolutionarily linked preference may help to explain the cosmetic trends of applying mascara and semi-permanent false eyelashes that darken and extend lashes.

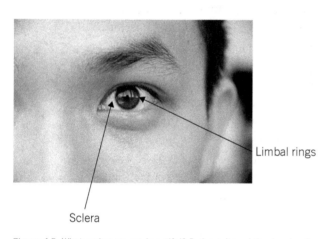

Aspects of the eyes themselves are also implicated in attractiveness. Specifically, the whiteness of the sclera (the eyeball part of your eye) is a good marker for health, with disease and older age associated with yellowing or reddening of the sclera. Not surprisingly, then, whiter sclera are perceived as more attractive (Russell et al., 2014). Another feature of the eye which may also be a cue for health and age is **limbal rings**, the dark outline surrounding the iris of the eye (see Figure 4.5). Not only does a dark limbal ring create a contrast between the iris and sclera that accentuates the whiteness of the sclera, but the ring itself appears linked to physical health. Accordingly, limbal rings enhance perceived attractiveness, especially for women evaluating men's faces when seeking short-term relationships, a context in which they may be especially attuned to maximizing "good genes" (Brown & Sacco, 2018; Brown et al., 2019; Peshek et al., 2011).

Figure 4.5 What makes an eye beautiful? Perhaps its subtle signals of health. (Photo: Yumiko Sakurai / EyeEm / Getty Images)

IN THE NEWS

The Golden Ratio and Beauty

Can mathematicians, with a little help from artists, objectively define the most beautiful faces? Proponents of the **golden ratio** believe so. The golden ratio, which may have helped Renaissance artists create aesthetically pleasing faces, focuses on the geometric layout of the face and facial structures (Prokopakis et al., 2013). According to this notion, the closer the proportions of the face (e.g., length-to-width of the face, width-to-height of the lips, etc.)

are to Phi, or the number 1.618, the more beautiful the face will be perceived to be. One plastic surgeon from London, Dr. Julian De Silva, uses a series of facial measurements to assess how well people's faces match the golden ratio's definition of "perfection." In a 2022 Instagram post, Dr. De Silva identified Jodie Comer as the "most beautiful woman in the world," with a 94.52 percent match with Phi, followed by Zendaya (94.37 percent) and Bella Hadid (94.35 percent; Figure 4.6a). News sources also picked up Dr. De Silva's 2023 Instagram crowning of Bridgerton star Regé-Jean Page (Figure 4.6b) as the "most beautiful man," with a 93.65 percent match to the golden ratio's specifications. Incidentally, Idris Elba came in at number 8 in Dr. De Silva's (2019) rankings, with an 88.01 percent and a "near perfect" chin.

(a)   (b)

Figure 4.6 Bella Hadid and Regé-Jean Page have been recognized for nearly perfect faces. Are they particularly attractive to you? (Photo: SAVIKO / Gamma-Rapho / Getty Images [a] and Jeff Spicer / Stringer / Getty Images Entertainment [b])

Empirical evidence, however, fails to align the golden ratio with perceived attractiveness (Harrar et al., 2018; Stieger & Swami, 2015). In other words, people do not judge faces as more beautiful to the extent that they adhere proportionally to Phi. Attempts to use the golden ratio to map an ideal face are also criticized for their Eurocentric emphasis, as the proportions are particularly ill-fit with faces of people of East Asian and sub-Saharan African descent and seem to be best matched with a highly masculinized White woman's face (Holland, 2008; Mantelakis et al., 2018). Faces can be plotted and assessed for their match with the golden proportion, but this information is merely descriptive, not predicting perceived beauty. As it was most eloquently stated, "the golden ratio is attractively simple and beguiling as a theory, but ultimately incomplete" (Singh et al., 2019, p. NP5). The parts do not seem to equal the whole, suggesting that subjectivity is a critically important – and extraordinarily difficult – factor to measure in assessments of attractiveness.

What Makes for an Attractive Body?

Just like facial features, people judge bodily features as attractive because they support their goals. For instance, when it comes to men's bodies, heterosexual women tend to prefer upper body muscularity, broad shoulders, and height (taller than themselves; Li & Kenrick, 2006). Muscularity suggests successful endurance of testosterone's immune system handicap and therefore is considered a reliable "good genes" indicator (Thornhill & Gangestad, 1999). Even in contemporary society, women select for muscularity and strength: more muscular men have more mating and reproductive success than less muscular men (Lidborg et al., 2022). Not only might muscularity signal heritable immunocompetence, but it also suggests competitive strength, which might lead to better success in acquiring resources, a useful "good partner" trait. The appeal of muscularity in initial attraction may give way once a relationship is well-established, when the dad bod (a soft, not-overweight-but-not-particularly-fit common body type among middle-aged married [American] men) might reign supreme. Observers infer more positive parenting (e.g., nurturance, caring, protection) from men with dad bods, and more negative parenting (e.g., hostile, dislike of kids) from high-muscle, low-fat men (Sacco et al., 2020). In other words, the uptick in BMI that men typically experience when entering fatherhood (Garfield et al., 2016) may signal they are "off the market" and devoted to their partner, not seeking a new mate.

When it comes to evaluating women's bodies, men tend to consider their breasts, as well as the contour of their buttocks (Li & Kenrick, 2006). Breast size is estrogen-linked, making it a reasonable candidate as a signal of fecundity (a woman's future capacity or potential to reproduce), but men tend to opt for breast firmness more than size across cultures, perhaps because it indicates youth, which is an indirect fecundity cue (Havlíček et al., 2017; Kościński, 2019).

Men also tend to prefer women with a thinner waist and wider hips, a waist-to-hip ratio (WHR) approximating 0.70 (Furnham et al., 1997; Singh, 1993; Singh et al., 2010; Singh & Young, 1995). Scholars have speculated that WHR might be a sign of health or fertility, but these hypotheses have not been well supported (Bovet, 2019; Lassek & Gaulin, 2018). Instead, WHR appears to be a reliable indicator of (1) whether a woman is currently pregnant (as shown in Figure 4.7) and her nubility, signs that she is sexually mature but has not previously given birth. Women who are or have been pregnant tend to have higher WHR (Lassek & Gaulin, 2019). On account of this, men's adaptation to prefer low WHR would have reproductive advantages. Men gain no reproductive benefit from copulating with an already-pregnant woman, and women who have already had children may have fewer in the future. Perhaps this is why men cross-culturally show a preference for women's bodies with a lower WHR (Furnham et al., 1997; Singh et al., 2010).

Figure 4.7 Low waist-to-hip ratios (WHR) are attractive, yet WHR often increases after a woman gives birth. For modern-day mothers, what types of pressures might this create, if they wish to be viewed as attractive? (Photo: Westend61 / Getty Images)

Sex Differences in Desiring Physical Attractiveness

While most anyone seems pleased with the idea of an attractive partner, men tend to emphasize the importance of a physically attractive long-term partner more than women. This sex-linked difference has been well substantiated in cross-cultural samples and in samples with participants of diverse sexual orientations (Ha et al., 2012; Lippa, 2007a; Walter et al., 2020). The magnitude of this sex difference tends to dissipate when shifting from long-term to short-term contexts: both men and women – but especially men – highlight the need for a good-looking partner when it comes to a short-term affair (Buss & Schmitt, 1993; Fletcher et al., 2004; Li & Kenrick, 2006; Regan et al., 2000, 2001).

The premium that heterosexual men place on women's physical attractiveness is often understood through an evolutionary lens. Men, more than women, need to concern themselves with the fertility of opposite-sex partners because female fertility declines over time more than male fertility. With attractiveness linked to health and youth – and therefore women's fertility – men's persistent interest in physical attractiveness for both short- and long-term contexts makes sense. Women, however, might enjoy the "good genes" that come with a short-term affair with an attractive partner, but their primary challenges are anchored to securing a partner's resources, not anchored to identifying fertile men. The relative emphasis that men place on physical attractiveness and women place on resources echoes the idea of instrumentality: we want what we need.

 ARTICLE SPOTLIGHT

Measuring Attraction: Explicitly Versus Implicitly

On a scale of 1(*not at all*) to 9 (*extremely*), how physically attractive is your ideal partner? As you might recall from completing your partner preferences in Table 4.1, answering this kind of question involves conscious deliberation. This *explicit* method for measuring partner preferences provides the cornerstone of attraction research; yet we know unconscious, spontaneous reactions can also drive relationship-related decisions and behaviors, including romantic attraction. Accordingly, Eastwick, Eagly, Finkel, and Johnson (2011) developed an *implicit* measure of romantic preferences for physical attractiveness. They wondered if the strength of these implicit preferences might predict explicit preferences, and further, they were curious what these implicit preferences might reveal about romantic liking. Explicit preferences consistently predict liking in imaginary, hypothetical situations; might implicit preferences triumph when it comes to attraction in live, in-person interactions?

In order to implicitly measure preferences for physically attractive partners, the researchers employed a like/dislike rendition of the classic go/no-go association task (GNAT; Nosek & Banaji, 2001; see Chapter 3). This involved comparing reaction times to "go" words about physical attractiveness and ideal partner traits with "go" words about physical attractiveness and non-ideal partner traits. The researchers also measured explicit preference for physically attractive partners by simply asking participants the extent to which traits (e.g., good looking, sexy, attractive) described their ideal partner. Finally, because the researchers wanted to know how explicit preferences and implicit preferences might predict attraction in different contexts, they assessed romantic interest to photographs of attractive and unattractive people, attraction in a speed-dating scenario, and romantic interest toward a confederate (i.e., research assistant).

Clear evidence emerged that: (1) people do implicitly prefer physically attractive others; and (2) these implicit preferences reveal different information than explicit preferences. Indeed, the correlation between implicit and explicit preferences averaged $r = 0.00$ across multiple studies, underscoring how they are distinct. Implicit preferences are spontaneous and emotional, whereas explicit preferences are deliberate and calculated, and while they both may play a role in attraction, their influence may depend on context. Indeed, explicit preferences for physical attractiveness nicely predicted romantic interest toward photographs of attractive versus unattractive people, but did not fare well in predicting romantic interest toward confederates or toward strangers in a speed-dating context. Implicit preferences, however, nicely predicted romantic interest in actual interactions with people of varying attractiveness. To say this a different way, the researchers found evidence of a *double dissociation*: explicit preferences for physical attractiveness predicted interest in people in photographs but not real-life attraction, whereas implicit preferences predicted real-life attraction but not interest in people in photographs. This occurred even when the primary outcome measures across contexts (photographs, speed-dating, interactions with confederates) were explicit self-reports of romantic interest.

Implicit measures are often the subject of critique (especially the Implicit Associations Task [IAT]; see Schimmack, 2021), but if measured well, underlying implicit preferences (Sripada, 2022) may provide fascinating insight into attraction. New ways of approaching implicit measurement may benefit relationship science. For instance, the GNAT used by Eastwick and colleagues could be revised to include images rather than words, and perhaps provide an even-more sensitive assessment of implicit preferences (Meltzer & McNulty, 2019). Not all questions require implicit measures and not all implicit measures have good support, but pursuing the role of implicit preferences in close relationships may be fertile ground for future research (Faure et al., 2020).

Physical Attraction in Everyday Life

Did Idris Elba deserve *People Magazine*'s 2018 designation, "Sexiest Man Alive"? Most people would offer a resounding "yes!" This is because, as you now know, people share a set of fundamental human needs (domain-general or evolutionarily specific), and when certain physical features address those needs, people commonly judge those features as attractive. Our shared tastes help explain how, in a sea of nearly 8 billion people, we often have consensus on who is (Idris Elba!), or is not, attractive. At the same time, however, if you and your best friend were to sit on a park bench and rate the physical attractiveness of passersby, would you always agree? Even with evolved shared tastes, you would differ at times in your judgments. The idea that "beauty is in the eye of the beholder" reflects the potential subjective or idiosyncratic nature of perceived attractiveness. People's personal tastes can vary, with their own personal histories affecting their notion of what is, and what is not, attractive (Germine et al., 2015; Hönekopp, 2006).

Other factors also influence attractiveness judgments. These include the perceiver's own attractiveness, their openness to sex outside of a committed relationship, and their behaviors, such as drinking alcohol (have you heard of "beer goggles"? Bowdring & Sayette, 2018; Montoya, 2008; Provost et al., 2006). The subjectivity of physical attractiveness judgments is never clearer than when those judgments can be manipulated by new information. Indeed, perceivers readily revise how attractive they perceive someone to be when presented with personality information, judging people with more desirable personalities as more physically attractive (Lewandowski et al., 2007; Swami et al., 2010).

The key to remember is that everything we judge as attractive, we do so for a reason: it either helps us meet basic needs (like esteem, security, and belonging), promotes our evolutionary goals, or suggests a willingness to help us toward these goals. Our human needs are basic, coloring whom and what we find attractive.

Social Status, Education, and Intelligence

Partner preferences extend beyond external appearance to include qualities that address practical and social concerns. Remember, the appeal of these qualities is not arbitrary; these qualities are attractive because of their instrumentality. The three social features often highlighted in attraction research – social status, education, and intelligence – are excellent examples of the appeal of a person who can support domain-general and specific evolutionary goals.

Social Status

Are you looking for a partner with money (or power or prestige)? You're not alone. People often desire partners with high social status, which refers to a person's relative standing on socially valued traits like wealth, athletics, or power. By seeking and securing a partner of high social status, individuals benefit from otherwise inaccessible resources, opportunities, and influence, and they assume a prestige through their relationship that they might not otherwise have. Social status is therefore appealing because it suggests someone's *capacity* to meet one's needs. Review column 2 in Table 4.1: how highly do you rank social status relative to other characteristics in a potential partner?

Sex Differences in Desiring Status

One of the earliest documented gender differences in partner preferences, a pattern observed cross-culturally, is that women tend to emphasize the importance of their ideal partner's financial prospects more than men (Buss, 1989; Walter et al., 2020). This fits with the evolutionary idea that women, burdened with a high minimal parental investment (e.g., extended pregnancy, breast feeding), benefit from partners who have the resources to provide for and protect both them and their offspring (Kenrick et al., 1990; Trivers, 1972). Indeed, cross-culturally women have indicated that status and resources are a necessity, not merely a luxury, when describing their ideal partner (Li et al., 2002, 2011). The decision to pursue partners with high status may come at a trade-off for mutual love (Shackelford, Schmitt, & Buss, 2005), though the two need not be mutually exclusive (Figure 4.8).

Figure 4.8 Men tend to emphasize physical attractiveness in their partners, while women more often emphasize social status and resources. How might this explain trends in which beautiful women pair with difficult, less-beautiful men? (Photo: Jeffrey Mayer / WireImage / Getty Images)

Women's interest in high-status partners may have its roots in evolution, but a sociocultural framework offers a different take. This social-roles perspective suggests that people adapt their partner preferences to the needs created for them by the cultures in which they live. When women are systematically oppressed by a patriarchal system that limits their rights and/or access to status and power, to desire high-status partners is a rational social adaptation. Consistent with this view, women who live in societies with greater gender inequality tend to emphasize status-related characteristics in their ideal partner (Eagly & Wood, 1999; Zentner & Eagly, 2015). This same emphasis occurs in countries that limit women's access to education and prevent their reproductive freedom (Gangestad et al., 2006; Kasser & Sharma, 1999; Zentner & Eagly, 2015). While some evidence contradicts this social roles theory (Schmitt, 2015), a likely possibility is that sociocultural factors explain *some* variability in partner preferences even as, cross-culturally, sex-based differences in men and women's preferences remain strongly anchored to inherited preferences (Conroy-Beam et al., 2015). The notion that partner preferences might begin from an evolved starting point, but shift given people's context, is captured in research that looks beyond biology and culture to consider people's environmental circumstances. Initial evidence shows that men and women shift their preferences toward prioritizing wealth and dominance, for instance, in scenarios marked by poverty or violence, such as a post-nuclear scenario (Marzoli et al., 2013).

Desiring Intelligence and Education

Sometimes related to status, intelligence and education are gaining increasing attention as unique and important dimensions of partner preferences in and of their own right (Csajbók & Berkics, 2017; Shackelford, Schmitt, & Buss, 2005). Across cultures and sexual orientations, people consistently report wanting intelligent, educated partners (Atari et al., 2020; Li et al., 2002; Lippa, 2007a; Regan et al., 2000; Walter et al., 2020). This makes sense when you consider the benefits of being with an intelligent partner: intelligent people solve problems, make accurate predictions, and can take others' perspectives; from an evolutionary standpoint, intelligence favors resource acquisition and co-parenting abilities. No wonder people want smart long-term partners (Csajbók & Berkics, 2017; Walter et al., 2020).

The story becomes more precise when we consider intelligence and education not in the general sense, but relative to the seeker. In the long-term context, men and women most prefer partners of equal or higher intelligence than themselves, and of equivalent education; whereas, in the short-term context, women maintain these preferences, but men do not. Men lower their standards for intelligence with less relationship involvement (Buunk et al., 2002). Indeed, men are comfortable having short-term affairs with women who are less intelligent or less educated than themselves, potentially judging these women as "easy targets" (Jonason et al., 2019; Jonason & Antoon, 2019). Men do not ignore highly intelligent women for short-term affairs: intelligence is simply not a primary consideration for men seeking short-term relationships.

Women may place a premium on intelligence regardless of context because in all cases they risk pregnancy and they want "good genes" for their potential offspring. The heritability of intelligence and the broad scope of its benefits highlights the need for reliable, observable indicators of this somewhat hidden capacity. Along with education, other attributes – such as artistic ability, creativity, humor, and musical skill – may have evolved to serve as "honest" signals of intelligence (Miller, 2000).

As a final note, there does seem to be a threshold after which any more intelligence is too much intelligence, which is different from most other traits. Exceptionally kind partners and exceptionally beautiful partners might be exceptionally desirable, but not so with intelligence. Intelligence in the 99th percentile is *less* rather than *more* attractive than intelligence around the 90th percentile (Gignac & Starbuck, 2019). Why this is remains unclear, although people might draw on stereotypes and assume extreme intelligence comes at the cost of social skills; alternatively, the idea of forming a romantic relationship with an extremely intelligent person may be less appealing because interactions are unlikely to boost esteem regarding one's own intellect.

Warmth, Kindness, and Trustworthiness

Is it a surprise that people prefer warm, caring, and trustworthy partners over cold, mean, deceptive partners? Probably not. Domain-general reward models remind us that experiencing kindness gives us pleasure and, as suggested by interdependence theory, can help us achieve favorable outcomes. Warmth, kindness, and trustworthiness are also cues that a partner is willing to use their resources and skills to benefit us. As we know (Montoya & Horton, 2014), a capacity to fulfill needs along with a willingness to do so is a tough combination to beat.

While a preference for warmth, kindness, and trustworthiness is not surprising, what is remarkable is the consistency with which people rank these traits as priorities for long-term partners across studies conducted with diverse populations. Early research found that men and women desired "kindness and understanding" in their partners above all other traits (Buss & Barnes, 1986), and this preference persisted in a study of over 10,000 people sampled from across thirty-seven different countries (Buss, 1989). A recent replication of this research, which included over 14,000 people from forty-five different countries, showed that kindness continues to be a top preferred trait in romantic partners, cross-culturally for both men and women (Walter et al., 2020). These findings are consistent with research in the Muslim-majority countries of Iran, Pakistan, and Turkey, wherein "kindness/dependability" are preferred above partner status, attractiveness, education, and religiosity (Atari et al., 2020). People view kindness as a necessity in a long-term partner, rather than a luxury, a pattern observed in Western samples (Li et al., 2002; March et al., 2018) and in large international samples (Thomas et al., 2020). The general desire for kind partners persists across sexual orientations as well (Lippa, 2007a), and the limited research on transgender individuals shows a similar emphasis on mutual love, dependability, pleasantness, and sociability above all other traits (Arístegui et al., 2018). The broad appeal of warmth, kindness, and trustworthiness highlights how effectively these qualities support need fulfillment.

Sex Differences in Desiring Warmth/Kindness

Even as warm traits appear to be universal "must-haves," when a gender difference is documented, women emphasize the importance of these traits more than men (Atari et al., 2020; Fletcher et al., 1999; Sprecher & Regan, 2002; Walter et al., 2020). Both heterosexual and lesbian women stress the need for kind partners more than heterosexual and gay men (Lippa, 2007a). Both the broad appeal of warmth-related traits and women's emphasis on these traits make sense from an evolutionary standpoint. Recall differential parental investment (Kenrick et al., 1990; Trivers, 1972) and sexual selection theory (Buss & Schmitt, 1993), which together suggest that women's hefty minimum parental investment for any given child (e.g., pregnancy, labor, nursing) makes them highly selective in their partners. Partners willing to share resources, offer protection, and co-parent increase the likelihood of offspring survival, thus explaining women's particular preference for warm/trustworthy partners.

Women's preference might be stronger, but desiring warm/trustworthy partners also supports a long-term strategy for men. It helps men address a key challenge that they face: paternity uncertainty. Whereas all pregnant women give birth to a child who is genetically theirs (traditionally; modern methods like in vitro fertilization introduce uncertainty, and egg donation alters this equation), men face the potential risk that they will unwittingly invest for years in a child who is not biologically their own. To prefer partners who are honest, loyal, and faithful (all subsumed in this warmth-trustworthy category) is to protect one's own reproductive success. Thus, along with wanting a good partner and a good parent, men may value warmth/trustworthiness because it supports their paternity certainty.

Altruism and Heroism

Akin to the traits of warmth, kindness, and trustworthiness are other highly desirable prosocial traits, like altruism and heroism (Miller, 2007). Altruistic and heroic acts are costly signals, that is, difficult-to-fake behaviors that require sacrifice. As such, they are reliable cues to enduring "good parent" and "good partner" personal qualities (Bhogal et al., 2020). Accordingly, both men and women find altruism highly appealing and both men and women (women especially) desire heroic partners particularly for long-term relationships (Barclay, 2010; Bhogal & Bartlett, 2021; Farrelly, 2013; Moore et al., 2013). The appeal of potential partners who engage in altruistic and heroic behaviors is amplified when these do-gooders are also physically attractive (Ehlebracht et al., 2018; Farrelly et al., 2016; Margana et al., 2019). Maybe this explains why Idris Elba became all the more dreamy when he rushed to the rescue of a stranger having seizures, after which the Epilepsy Society deemed him a super-hero (Society, 2019). Heroism combined with physical attractiveness is exceptionally sexy because they together suggest an abundance of good genes and good partner/parent qualities.

(a)   (b)

Figure 4.9 On screen, Thor captures people's hearts through his heroic acts; off screen, actor Chris Hemsworth impresses with public philanthropic acts, including his $1 million 2020 donation to Australian Fire Relief Fund. How does instrumentality explain why heroic and altruistic acts have romantic appeal? (Photo: Simon James / FilmMagic / Getty Images [a] and Mark Metcalfe / Stringer / Getty Images Entertainment [b])

Do We Always Prioritize Warm and Kind Traits?

Our focus thus far has been on *long-term* partner preferences; however, as we know, not all romantic relationships are intended to be long-term. In the unemotional, no commitment, purely sexual space of short-term relationships (e.g., hookups, one-night stands), people's preferences tend to shift away from internal traits and toward external qualities, particularly physical attractiveness (Kenrick et al., 1990; Li & Kenrick, 2006). This shift in preferences occurs regardless of sexual orientation (Lucas et al., 2011; Regan et al., 2001). Consider booty-call relationships, which are primarily sexual but include an ongoing emotional component, a hybrid of short- and long-term relationships (Jonason et al., 2011). Men tend to view booty-calls as low-commitment sexual encounters, whereas women are more apt to see booty-calls as a potential starting point for a long-term relationship (Jonason, Lee, & Cason, 2009). Accordingly, men do not prioritize kindness in their booty-call partners, but women do (March et al., 2018). Ask women specifically about purely casual short-term encounters, however, and they readily trade kindness for other desirable traits (e.g., physical attractiveness). Men and women sometimes go as far as indicating that kindness is a luxury and unnecessary in short-term partners, though this is not a consistent finding (Li & Kenrick, 2006; March et al., 2018).

Why do people modulate their interest in kindness in the short-term context? For women, evolutionarily speaking, flexible selection criteria make sense. Forgoing "good partner" traits for "good genes" could be an adaptive solution in the short-term context in case a child is conceived (Gangestad & Simpson, 2000). A similar story explains this shift for men: rather than needing a "good partner" as they do in a long-term context, in the short-term context, men's reproductive success hinges on sexual encounters that produce offspring, so partners' fecundity is a must. When qualities offer advantages within specific relational contexts, those qualities become especially attractive.

Other Key Partner Preferences

Although the categories of physical attractiveness, status, and warmth capture much of what is considered desirable in a partner, we would be remiss to ignore several other key factors.

Desiring a Partner of a Particular Gender

When people say they want kind, sexy, funny, or ambitious partners, they are often thinking of partners of a specific gender and/or biological sex. The direction of their desire – toward a person of the same and/or different gender – is captured in the concept of sexual orientation (introduced in Chapter 1). How people identify in terms of their sexual orientation (e.g., heterosexual, gay, lesbian) often reveals their preferred partners; however, individuals can identify one way (e.g., heterosexual) and engage in sexual activity with people other than those anticipated by their sexual orientation (Reback & Larkins, 2010). Designations like "mostly heterosexual" help clarify the extent to which a preference for a given sex prevails across different situations (Savin-Williams & Vrangalova, 2013). Some evidence suggests individuals with bisexual patterns of attraction often have a preferred gender for their partners, and relative to individuals who are predominantly attracted to one gender, show more fluctuations in their attraction toward their less-preferred gender (Diamond et al., 2017).

Today's changing cultural attitudes may support more fluidity in partner preferences and more openness to same-sex encounters (recall from Chapter 1 that, although "same-sex" is the standard term, it does not reflect the complexity of identity or partner preference). The last thirty or so years have seen an increase in same-sex sexual experiences, especially for women, possibly aligned with cultural attitude changes or possibly the rise of hookup culture (Twenge et al., 2016). At the same time, we still see strong preferences for cisgender partners. Initial evidence suggests that 87.5 percent of people would not consider dating transgender individuals, and this preference is particularly strong for cisgender heterosexual men and women (Blair & Hoskin, 2019). As you have likely noticed, the field's understanding of partner preferences and attraction is based largely on different-sex monogamous relationships between cisgender individuals, and the dominant domain-specific explanatory approaches (e.g., evolutionary theories) are grounded in male–female relationships. Because of this disproportional attention to privileged identities and relationship structures, the field has failed many of the readers of this book. Attraction, in reality, emerges between and among people of all genders and sexualities and we expect to see more inclusive theories and more representative research moving forward.

Desiring a Partner of an Ideal Age

People often overlook age when they start listing their partner preferences, but if you ask, most people have an opinion or "range" that they would find acceptable in a partner.

They might even call on the layperson's "half your age + 7 rule," to define the minimum appropriate age of a dating partner. For example, according to this rule, at age 50, Idris Elba can date women who are 32 or older (as it happens, Idris and Sabrina are eighteen years apart in age). This rule has the concrete "yes or no" appeal of an equation, but it generally amounts to more leniency compared to what most people actually judge as socially acceptable for romantic couples (Buunk et al., 2001).

Would Idris and Sabrina's relationship spark controversy if Sabrina were the one who was eighteen years older? Possibly: it would certainly buck the norm. Cross-culturally, women tend to prefer men who are slightly older than themselves; men, meanwhile, tend to prefer women who are increasingly younger than themselves, the exception being teenage boys, who tend to prefer slightly older women (Buss, 1989; Conroy-Beam & Buss, 2018; Kenrick & Keefe, 1992; Walter et al., 2020). We see these age-preference patterns in surveys of ideal partners, in analyses of personal ads, in marital records that document couples' ages, in money spent on prostitutes (more on younger prostitutes), and money spent on pre-marital customs (more when brides are younger). These age preferences appear sex-based and hold across sexual orientation. The ages of preferred and actual partners is similar between heterosexual men and gay men, and between heterosexual women and lesbian women; indeed, initial evidence suggests bisexual individuals' preferences adhere to their sex as well (Antfolk, 2017).

Relationship context (short-term versus long-term) can play a role in age preferences. Men, for example, tend to desire short-term affairs and engage in sexual fantasies about women in their 20s, even when they themselves are much older (Figure 4.10; Buunk et al., 2001). This makes sense from an evolutionary perspective: men's fertility extends into older adulthood, so men desiring women at peak fertility for sexual encounters could help these men pass along their genes. Women, meanwhile, tend to orient toward older men across most relational contexts, perhaps because older men have more time to acquire wealth and status, and women in short-term or long-term contexts can benefit from resource acquisition. That said, in the unique context of sperm donation – defined by an absence of possible resource acquisition – women tend to prioritize sperm donated by younger men, perhaps equating youth with health (and thus, more viable sperm; Whyte et al., 2016). For long-term relationships, men and women's age preferences are less divergent from their own ages. Men tend to desire long-term partners who are about 3 years their junior, whereas women seek partners who are 3.5 years older than themselves (Conroy-Beam & Buss, 2018).

While an evolutionary-based explanation helps us understand the near universal pattern of partner's age preferences, a sociocultural framework has garnered good support as well for explaining cross-cultural variability in preferred ages. People living in countries with greater gender equity tend to report interest in partners closer to their own age than people living in less equitable countries (Eastwick et al., 2006; Walter et al., 2020; Zentner & Eagly, 2015). In other words, specific ages become desirable because, just like other factors promoting attraction, they suggest how well someone might help you achieve either domain-general or specific evolutionary goals.

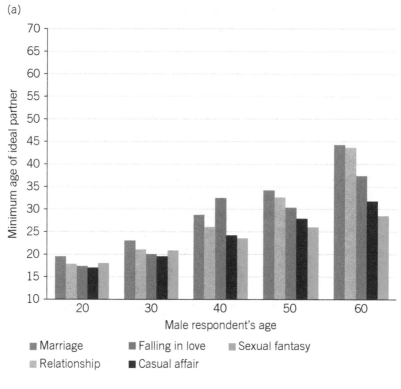

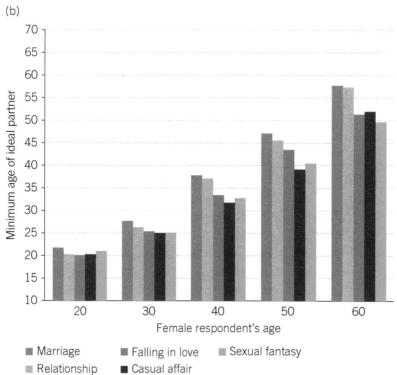

Figure 4.10 Preferred minimum partner age depends on gender and relational context (e.g., marriage versus sexual fantasy). How might culture reinforce or constrain evolved preferences? (Source: Reprinted from Buunk et al. [2001], with permission from Elsevier)

RESEARCHER SPOTLIGHT: Peter (PK) Jonason, PhD

How did you come to be a social-personality psychologist?
As an undergraduate, psychology was uninteresting to me. It was not until
I was exposed to evolutionary psychology as a fourth-year student that
I found myself wanting to move from law to psychology. I was originally
interested in mating psychology, but I was offered the opportunity to teach
personality psychology and this content just fit me so well, I ended up
making a career out of it.

How did you decide to study mating strategies?
The reasons we reject people seemed to be important and understudied.
We thought we could document why people reject others and we ended up
revealing more interesting patterns of decision-making. We studied this and
other mating strategies (like playing hard-to-get) because, in part, the field
is so saturated that one must find more specific aspects of relationships to
study than what is more commonly studied – simple mate preferences. That
is, to carve out my own niche in this area, I had to focus on unanswered and
even unasked questions.

Figure 4.11 Dr. Peter (PK) Jonason is a social-personality psychologist in the Department of General Psychology at the University of Padua, Italy. (Photo: Javier Schejtman.)

Where do you find inspiration for your research questions?
I can't even lie. I find inspiration in my life, in the lives of others, and even in TV shows and movies. There
are real-world phenomena that ivory tower academics can often miss with their heads in the clouds or
books.

In your relationships work, what have you enjoyed thinking about the most?
I enjoy being provocative in the sense that I enjoy challenging people's cherished beliefs. I enjoy designed
studies and revealing truths that often do not sit well with people's default or desired assumptions about
the world.

What's next in attraction research?
The future is likely big data and machine learning, where we can determine people's choices and preferences
in a multidimensional way with multicultural data to provide evidence that is increasingly harder for nay-sayers
to dismiss.

Knowing What We Don't Want in a Partner

By now, you probably have a good sense of people's partner preferences, but what about
partner aversions? Overlooked until recently, the emerging study of **dealbreakers** suggests
that the traits that people avoid in their romantic partners play an important role in shaping
people's evaluations of potential partners (Jonason et al., 2015; White et al., 2021). Indeed,
dealbreakers (i.e., the "ick") have a stronger negative effect on partner evaluations than

desired preferences had a positive effect, suggesting knowing someone's dealbreakers is more informative than knowing their preferences (Jonason, White et al., 2020). Even if a potential partner possesses other desirable traits, the added presence of a dealbreaker can remove them from the running (Boysen et al., 2019).

So what do people *not* want? Dealbreakers run the gamut and can include appearance-related and health-related problems (e.g., unclean, smells bad, has an STD), undesirable personality traits (e.g., lazy, racist, abusive, stubborn), mismatched values (e.g., different religion), different family plans (e.g., does not want kids, has kids), undesired habits (e.g., too much TV/video games, too athletic/not athletic), and concerns regarding availability (e.g., already in a relationship) and intimacy (e.g., bad sex, low sex drive; Jonason et al., 2015). People report more dealbreakers for long-term than short-term relationships, and women list more dealbreakers than men, but across contexts and genders, people are generally repulsed by poor health and aversive personality traits. Experimental evidence also suggests people's interest drops also when they learn about a person's mental illness (Boysen et al., 2019). This highlights how people with mental illness often endure stigma even within their most intimate relationship experiences.

From Hypothetical Preferences to the Real World

A conversation about partner preferences is, in many ways, a hypothetical conversation: what do you *think* you want in a partner? The rubber hits the road when we evaluate what happens in *actual* face-to-face interactions: do people's preferences drive their romantic interest and, further, are situational factors also at play? Attraction is a complex process. Sometimes we are attracted to people for reasons we readily recognize; other times we do not realize the reasons for our attraction, even as this attraction is predictable from a scientific standpoint. Let's begin with the tension between stated preferences, like those you reported in Table 4.1, and actual liking in real face-to-face interactions.

Figure 4.12 A couple on a speed-date. How do your initial impressions of someone coincide with your preferences? (Photo: Fuse / Corbis / Getty Images)

Preferences in Face-to-Face Attraction

Back in the aughts (early 2000s), speed-dating was the craze; your roommate, your cousin, your best friend, everyone was signing up to attend speed-dating events, held at restaurants, bars, clubs, you name it (Figure 4.12). At speed-dating events, people who are "single-and-looking" go on a series of 4-minute "dates" (hence, speed-dates) with ten to twenty-five people who are also single-and-looking (Finkel & Eastwick, 2008; Finkel et al., 2007). At the end of each date, potential partners rate whether they are interested in going out with one another again, and at the end of the event, couples who matched (both said "yes" to a future meet-up) are given one another's contact information. People might join speed-dating events to expedite the drudgery of dating, but relationship scientists saw an opportunity to study *attraction in action*. They recreated speed-dating in the laboratory. By running speed-dating events themselves rather than observing speed-dating events elsewhere, researchers could observe attraction in real-life and further, they could, if needed, manipulate aspects of the speed-dates to test predictors of attraction experimentally. It's the best of both worlds from a research standpoint: real-life meets lab meets real-life!

Speed-dating allowed for direct testing of the question of how well people's stated, hypothetical preferences predict actual attraction (Eastwick & Finkel, 2008b). Looking only at the stated preferences, researchers first observed the traditional sex-linked pattern (i.e., men emphasized physical attractiveness in a partner more than women, and women emphasized earning prospects in a partner more than men). No surprise there. In the face-to-face meetings made possible in speed-dating, however, both men and women desired the highly physically attractive people and those with good earning potential. There were no gender differences in real-life liking. Further, individuals' own stated preferences were not helpful in predicting the partners they actually liked, said they would date, or with whom they experienced "chemistry." This study raised questions about the usefulness of stated partner preferences, preferences that had been assumed to guide people in choosing their partners.

Subsequent studies have replicated the imprecise match between stated preferences and real-time liking between strangers and on blind dates (Selterman et al., 2015; Sparks et al., 2020). Even for friendships, desired friendship traits predict the friends people select in profiles, but in real interactive contexts those preferences shed no light on actual friendship interest (Huang et al., 2020). Although some evidence points to the role of partner preferences in speed-dating contexts (Li et al., 2013; Valentine et al., 2020), meta-analysis has summatively questioned the functional utility of partner preferences in determining real-life attraction (Eastwick et al., 2014).

The possibility that preferences guide liking may find more support as we transition beyond initial meetings and into more stable relationship contexts. Indeed, just because a relationship is initiated does not mean it will last (Li & Meltzer, 2015). In support for the usefulness of partner preferences for ongoing relationships, a large-scale pre-registered study showed that preferences were good predictors of with whom a sample of single individuals paired during the study's five-month duration (Gerlach et al., 2019). Other work also demonstrates a link between preferences and partner characteristics in established couples, suggesting that preferences drive partner selection, rather than alternative explanations, such as preferences changing as a function of the partner (Conroy-Beam & Buss, 2016).

Dating in a preference-consistent way may be challenging from a practical standpoint, which would explain weaker-than-expected associations between ideals and real-partner characteristics. We are constrained by who is available, persuaded by other traits they might offer, limited by our own attractiveness, and may at times lower our standards simply to be in a relationship (Jonason et al., 2019; Li & Meltzer, 2015; Spielmann et al., 2013). Clear evidence suggests that partner preferences can fail to predict attraction, yet scholars puzzle over why partner preferences would be so pervasive if they did not have purpose (Fletcher et al., 2014). We can expect to gain clarity as scholars refine their methods, analytic strategies, and use of moderators to explore this question.

Social and Situational Factors

The link between trait preferences and actual attraction may also be modulated at times by other factors that influence liking. These social and situational factors (i.e., proximity, familiarity, similarity, and reciprocity) remind us that attraction happens within an influential context. Still, as you will see, the principles that guide our attraction remain the same as those that shape our trait preferences. We have needs – some general and some evolutionarily specific – and attraction amounts to a positive appraisal that someone has both the capacity and the willingness to help us achieve our goals. In other words, each of these social and situational factors can be understood for their instrumentality.

Proximity: You're Accessible to Me, So I Like You

Proximity, sometimes called propinquity, refers to the simple geographic nearness between people. This situational factor plays a major role in attraction. To a degree, this is obvious. Idris Elba, for instance, would not have met Sabrina if they were never in the same physical (or virtual) place. The role of proximity in attraction, however, becomes interesting when we consider the expansiveness of its effect. For example, some of the earliest work on proximity (from the mid-1900s) showed that about one-third of people ended up marrying someone who lived within *blocks* of them and rates of marriage decreased as distance increased between residences prior to marriage (Bossard, 1932; Davie & Reeves, 1939; Marches & Turbeville, 1953). Why might this be? In the mid-1900s, people married younger than they do today and often stayed closer to home until marriage. Further, the predominant trend in American culture in the mid-1900s (and that which continues today) was not arranged marriages, but love matches, and in order for two people to fall in love and agree to marry, at some point, they need to meet (Figure 4.13). People are much more likely to meet if they live near each other and frequent the same local places (and this was especially true before the Internet).

Proximity's role in attraction changed when online dating became a possibility. These days, people can log on and quickly gain access to other people looking for relationships, changing the nature of what it means to be "proximate." Online dating apps connect people who would not otherwise meet, allowing more people to reap the affiliative benefits of proximity, albeit virtual proximity (Finkel et al., 2012). A subset of online dating apps even use geolocation to connect people who are already in the same place. In these cases, old-fashioned physical proximity is still a key factor, but technology reduces barriers ("Um, hi, are you here alone?") that might otherwise prevent individuals from interacting.

Proximity may also predict attraction because people who live near one another or frequent the

Figure 4.13 How does where you live affect who you meet? The proximity-breeds-attraction hypothesis suggests that diverse neighborhoods, schools, colleges, and universities promote relationships among people with different racial, ethnic, religious, and socioeconomic backgrounds simply by offering them a chance to get to know one another. (Photo: Westend61 / Getty Images)

same spaces see one another more frequently, and research shows that simply seeing someone frequently may itself initiate a positive impression. Consider the classic study in which English-speaking Americans were asked to rate the positivity of Chinese ideographs (Zajonc, 1968, 2001). Participants saw some ideographs only once and others multiple times, and, surprisingly, participants rated the frequent ideographs more favorably than the infrequent ones. Turns out there is more allure to repetition than novelty. Repeatedly seeing some images created an affinity for these images, perhaps because of their relative salience compared to the other images (Mrkva & Van Boven, 2020). This mere-repeated-exposure effect is not limited to objects or images; it works for people as well (Moreland & Beach, 1992; Moreland & Zajonc, 1982). The more frequently we see people, the more we tend to like them. This effect occurs outside of our consciousness, meaning we do not necessarily recognize these people as people we know, and while robust, it operates with an important caveat: we must have an initially neutral or positive first impression (Ebbesen et al., 1976). Repeatedly seeing someone you do not like may make you like them less.

Why does repeated exposure promote liking? The effect is likely tied to our evolutionary need to survive, which requires heightened attention to novel stimuli, including strangers. A history of neutral or positive interactions with a person makes them less threatening. Indeed, if they haven't attacked you in your last ten encounters, they are unlikely to attack when you meet for the eleventh time. Thus, the mere-repeated exposure effect, brought about through proximity, increases a person's attractiveness because recognition, implicit or conscious, is linked to safety. Further, people we recognize are easier to cognitively process; this cognitive ease is rewarding and pleasurable. Ultimately, mere exposure promotes familiarity.

Familiarity: I Know You, So I Like You

Familiarity refers to how well someone knows another person, and scholars debate about familiarity's role in attraction (Norton et al., 2007; Reis et al., 2011). Divergent views reconcile when we consider familiarity under specific conditions. In the pre-relationship stages of acquaintance, familiarity breeds attraction when: (1) initial impressions are positive or neutral; (2) people are not in a competitive situation; (3) new information that increases familiarity reinforces initial impressions; and (4) new information that increases familiarity does not create boredom or disgust (Finkel, Norton et al., 2015). Quite a few social interactions fall under these conditions, such as the friendly chats you enjoy with people you see regularly. These strangers might begin on the fringes of our social worlds and stay there, or they might become more important characters in our lives. One way in which scientists have assessed the role of familiarity in sparking attraction is through "get acquainted" studies. These studies invite strangers to speak with each other, asking pre-determined questions, such as, "What are your hobbies?" (Reis et al., 2011). Naturalistic studies like these support the familiarity-breeds-attraction hypothesis, showing that the more people get to know each other, the more they tend to like each other.

How exactly does familiarity produce attraction? Consider instrumentality. Evolutionarily, the familiar is known and therefore safe and less threatening. Familiar stimuli are also processed more easily, a type of cognitive fluency that can be pleasurable, supporting domain-general needs. Moreover, familiarity may support fundamental needs of belonging. Beyond mere information exchange ("I like pizza"), familiarity is built through the exchange of contextualized information ("I like the pizza my dad makes using his wood-pellet oven") and involves responsiveness on the part of the listener ("oh, that sounds amazing!"). Familiarity creates attraction to the extent that people learn more about each other, feel comfortable, and experience responsiveness (Reis, Maniaci et al., 2011). Thus, familiarity may be appealing because it helps us feel safe, is pleasurable, and helps us meet belonging-ness needs.

Similarity: You're Like Me, So I Like You

The free spirit and the planner; the Red Sox fan and the Yankees fan: do opposites attract? The idea has a certain intrigue, one captured in the notion of complementarity. Perhaps we are attracted to people who have strengths where we have weaknesses, have deficits where we have skills, or have ideas that will broaden our perspectives. Despite the logic tied to complementarity and the common adage that "opposites attract," a vast body of literature insists that it is similarity, not difference, that attracts us in most circumstances (Byrne, 1961; Newcomb, 1961). There are a couple of exceptions. For that hot summer fling, that study-abroad romance, or that short-term affair, people are apt to express more attraction to someone who is different from them compared to someone who is similar (Amodio & Showers, 2005). Spending time with someone different can be thrilling and help us grow in exciting new ways (a domain-general need). The appeal, however, will be short lived. When we are in it for the long haul, we much prefer similar others. Even when meeting new people, we like them more when we are strongly similar, when our similarities are highlighted, and when we are similar along aspects that are centrally important to us (Montoya & Horton, 2013). On this latter point, discovering a shared interest, such as playing chess, could be nice or could be *everything*, depending on how important that interest is to a person.

Similarity is regularly documented in established romantic couples, an effect we would expect if similarity breeds liking (for review, see: Luo, 2017). Married couples tend to be of similar age and, within American culture, of increasingly similar educational background and socioeconomic status. They also tend to be of the same race, ethnicity, and religion, although this pattern is declining. Romantic partners also tend to be similar in abilities and intelligence, including emotional intelligence, and to favor the same hobbies and habits (e.g., exercise, degree of coffee, tea, and alcohol consumption). While personality dimensions often differ, couples tend to resemble each other along attitudes, values, and religiosity (Gonzaga et al., 2010), underscoring the idea that attraction is far from a random process. The process that leads to these pairings is often called assortative mating, wherein people connect with others who are like them on a host of traits, behavioral tendencies, attitudes, and demographics.

Assortative mating refers to any dimension on which people organize themselves, and it forms the basis for the matching hypothesis, the idea that people "match" with others along dimensions of social desirability. The popular jocks date the popular jocks; the nerds date the nerds; the concept is easy to grasp. Despite originally referring to a host of socially desirable traits (Walster et al., 1966), the matching hypothesis today is often used to refer exclusively to appearance-based matching: that people match with similarly physically attractive others. In its purest form, the matching hypothesis contends that people not only pair off, but they *seek* partners who are similar in physical attractiveness as themselves. A surprising dearth of evidence supports this idea, despite its broad appeal. Highly attractive participants might seek attractive partners, but so does everyone else; less attractive people simply connect with whomever remains (i.e., the less-attractive people) after the highly attractive people are taken (Berscheid et al., 1971). The minimal evidence for the matching hypothesis along the dimension of physical attractiveness (it does apply for popularity; Shaw Taylor et al., 2011) calls to question its emphasis in many textbooks.

Similarity may breed liking because of people's need for self-esteem, an idea consistent with the domain-general rewards models of attraction (Byrne, 1961; Finkel & Eastwick, 2015; Newcomb, 1961). It feels good to be around others who share our world view. Indeed, proposed explanations for why similarity breeds liking include validation, or the affirmation of each other's attitudes and beliefs, which may increase positive affect and trust (Hampton et al., 2019; Singh et al., 2017; Sprecher, Treger et al., 2013). Perceived similarity may also generate attraction because it produces more certainty that we ourselves might be liked (a highly appealing idea), presents an opportunity for self-expansion, or simply suggests the possibility for fun, enjoyable times interacting together (Hampton et al., 2019; Sprecher, Treger et al., 2013). Of note, most of this work has been conducted within Western cultures. While other sources of attraction, like familiarity, persist cross-culturally, the similarity-attraction link is considerably stronger in Western, American culture than it is in Eastern, Japanese culture (Heine et al., 2009). This makes sense considering how individualistic Western cultures tend to prioritize the self. If self-enhancing motivations underlie the similarity-attraction link, we would expect this effect would be strongest among those who place special importance on the self.

Of critical importance in the similarity-attraction research is the distinction between *actual* similarity and *perceived* similarity. Actual similarity refers to real sameness: people really do share traits, attitudes, hobbies, passions, or the like. Perceived similarity is simply the *belief* that you share these attributes. Perceived similarity can be anchored to reality, or it can deviate, motivating the question: which more strongly promotes attraction, actual or perceived similarity? Perceived similarity appears to take the cake. The degree to which people think they are similar to another person predicts their attraction, especially in the general sense (rather than on specific traits) and even if they are, in fact, not really similar (Sprecher, 2014; Tidwell et al., 2013). While actual similarity may influence attraction between strangers, perceived similarity is also important in these contexts and also drives attraction between acquainted individuals (Montoya et al., 2008). The thoughts a person holds about another, in this case, appear more important than reality in predicting attraction.

Reciprocity: You Like Me, So I Like You

How does it feel when someone likes you? That warm fuzzy feeling of being liked is intrinsically rewarding and has an interesting effect: it makes us like the person who likes us. This reciprocity effect of attraction, the tendency for expressed attraction to breed attraction, emerged early in attraction science and has received considerable empirical backing (Aronson & Worchel, 1966; Backman & Secord, 1959). Today, we can anchor our understanding of the reciprocity effect to a multifaceted response (Montoya & Insko, 2008). First, people have a positive emotional reaction to the experience of being liked; they also infer that the person expressing liking will be kind and helpful, that is, that the person is trustworthy (Montoya & Horton, 2012). This critical prosocial inference, which suggests a person's willingness to give, support, or in other ways benefit the self, is (as you know) a key factor in the two-dimensional model of attraction (Montoya & Horton, 2014). Inferring someone's willingness to help us meet our varied goals thus heightens our feelings of attraction and leads us to behave in ways that demonstrate our own attraction. Hence, we feel and express attraction to those who feel and express attraction toward us.

Do we ever feel *less* attracted to people on account of them liking us? Here's where we can make a critical distinction between dyadic liking (when a person likes one other person) and generalized liking (when a person likes many people). Speed-dating research suggests that dyadic liking generates attraction (Eastwick et al., 2007); we return people's romantic desire when they uniquely identify us as the target of their interest. However, this reciprocity effect appears to have its limits and does not extend to generalized liking. Liking everyone does not produce universal liking in return; instead, the people who non-discriminately express attraction to everyone are apt to be disliked. This is a sad story when you consider how it could be the most desperate and overeager of us who are willing to like everyone, yet these are the people for whom belongingness needs will not be fulfilled. People like to be liked, but only when it makes them feel special – a boost to self-esteem.

Do we ever feel attracted to people specifically because they do *not* appear to like us? At first blush, this might seem strange, but consider all the romantic comedies based on this very premise. People sometimes play hard-to-get, and it can work. **Playing hard-to-get** is a strategic attempt to increase one's own desirability by creating the impression of unavailability (Jonason & Li, 2013). Women tend to use this strategy more than men. They make themselves appear busy and inaccessible, they express interest and then back off, they seek attention but then ignore it, and these game-playing behaviors can increase their perceived value as a partner. Another way to consider playing hard-to-get is to break down its effects into liking, the emotional component, and wanting, the motivational component (Dai et al., 2014). Evidence suggests that easy-to-get tactics, such as smiling and being open, tend to elicit more liking than hard-to-get tactics, but if people are already committed to pursuing a person's affections, then hard-to-get tactics generate more wanting than easy-to-get tactics. More wanting, but not more liking.

Another potential caveat to the reciprocity effect could be the allure of uncertainty. Uncertainty can sustain good moods and is surprisingly pleasurable (Kurtz et al., 2007; Wilson et al., 2005), but could it increase liking? Some evidence suggests women prefer men whose interest is uncertain (either a lot or an average amount) to those who clearly state their liking when these women are reviewing profiles of different attractive strangers (Whitchurch et al., 2011). The idea here is that women spend more time thinking about the men whose interest is uncertain as they try to resolve the uncertainty, and the time spent thinking about these men actually enhances liking for them.

Overall, the pendulum swings in favor of the reciprocity effect: that we express more attraction to those who clearly like us. A growing body of research shows that people like and experience more romantic interest to those whose feelings toward them are certain, compared to uncertain, in both new and established relationships (Birnbaum et al., 2018; Montoya et al., 2015). From this vantage point, undoing uncertainty is a relationship-enhancing mechanism, consistent with risk-regulation models of relationships (Murray et al., 2006). The reciprocity effect thus stands: people like those who express liking toward them, more than those who express disinterest, dislike, or mixed messages.

Attraction in Context

Romantic attraction occurs within a context defined by broad sources of influence, such as those highlighted by sociocultural frameworks, and by specific sources of influence, such as the immediate situational forces. Regarding the immediate situation, had a few arbitrary details of their evening been different, like if Sabrina approached Idris instead of the other way around, would Idris have still experienced "love at first sight"? Research suggests that approaching an attractive stranger prompts more romantic interest than being approached (Finkel & Eastwick, 2009). This minor detail affects first meetings and casts a surprising, context explanation for women's greater selectivity in heterosexual attraction. At least in Western cultures, traditional gender norms proscribe that men be the approachers, a cultural norm that provides a situational, rather than evolutionary, explanation for why women tend to be choosier than men.

Another compelling situational factor that predicts heterosexual women's interest is the extent to which *other* women appear to like a given man (Anderson & Surbey, 2018; Rodeheffer et al., 2016). Termed **mate-copying**, women preferentially desire men who have already won the attention of other women (Anderson & Surbey, 2018; Gouda-Vossos et al., 2018; Pruett-Jones, 1992). Good old Mike might seem like a decent guy, but now that he has an attractive girlfriend he becomes even more attractive: if he secures her interest, he's probably a keeper! The opposite effect tends to happen when men evaluate women: they see a woman as less attractive when she is surrounded by men (Hill & Buss, 2008). As another important example of context, people's own relationship status affects their judgments of others. Indeed, people in relationships judge strangers as *less* attractive than single people, an effect observed in both explicit judgments and implicit measures of attention (Maner et al., 2009; Simpson & Gangestad, 1990).

Attraction in the Context of Physiological Arousal

The importance of context is readily evident when we consider the role of situationally based arousal and romantic interest. In a now famous study, an attractive female research assistant approached men walking alone across a long narrow suspension bridge over Capilano Canyon, shown in Figure 4.14 (Dutton & Aron, 1974). The bridge had alarmingly low handrails, swayed in the wind, and hung above an impressive 230-foot drop. In the middle of the bridge, the research assistant invited men to complete a psychology experiment, which unbeknown to them included the projective Thematic Apperception Test (TAT) to assess sexual arousal.

Figure 4.14 Crossing the Capilano Canyon or any such shaky bridge can be an exhilarating experience, one that people can misattribute as romantic interest to a nearby attractive stranger. Does this mean a well-selected first date (e.g., an amusement park, hiking or rock climbing, watching a scary movie) can help someone fall in love with you? (Photo: Gunter Marx Photography / Corbis Documentary / Getty Images)

At the end of the study, she thanked the men, handed them her number, and invited them to call her to learn more details about the experiment. The complete procedure was also carried out on a stable wooden bridge, 10 feet above the water with high handrails. The men in the shaky bridge condition responded with higher sexual imagery scores on the TAT and 65 percent of the participants who accepted her number called her, versus 30 percent in the steady bridge condition. An anxiety-sexual attraction link was proposed: physiological arousal, caused in this case by a frighteningly high and shaky bridge, can be misattributed as attraction toward a nearby attractive stranger.

Although not the most romantic notion, misattribution theory does provide a fascinating explanation for attraction. It draws from Schachter's two-factor theory of emotion which suggests that emotions are labels that people ascribe to physiological arousal (Schachter, 1964; Schachter & Singer, 1962). In the case of **misattribution theory** (Dutton & Aron, 1974), when people feel physiologically aroused, particularly for reasons they do not clearly know, they can (mis)label this arousal as romantic interest toward a nearby person. Meta-analytic work shows that the arousal–attraction link is reliable, but specific to physically attractive potential partners (Foster et al., 1998). An attraction-reducing effect appears for unattractive partners. Further, people do not need to be ignorant of the source of their arousal; even in cases in which the true source is quite obvious, people can still misattribute it to romantic attraction (Foster et al., 1998). This suggests a surprising situation-based reason for why we like whom we like: sometimes, we think we like them because we are feeling heightened physiological arousal.

Attraction within the Context of Women's Reproductive Cycles

Romantic attraction by women or toward women occurs within the context of their reproductive cycles. Unlike the females of many other species, women do not rotate through monthly or seasonal phases in which they are "in heat." Rather, women can want sex at any point in their typically twenty-eight-ish-day reproductive cycle. They also experience **concealed ovulation**; the exact moment of ovulation (release of an egg) is not directly obvious, even to the woman herself. For sex to produce an offspring, which is a primary evolutionary goal, the timing of that sex needs to occur before or near the time of ovulation, that is, during the woman's *fertile window*. This presents an obvious puzzle for the attraction system. How can we optimize reproductive fitness if we cannot detect peak fertility?

The Ovulatory-Shift Hypothesis

One possibility is that women's partner preferences shift across their reproductive cycle. This intriguing idea is at the heart of the **ovulatory-shift hypothesis**, which contends that women would have an adaptive advantage if they experienced heightened desire for short-term relationships with "good genes" men when their likelihood of pregnancy is high (during peak fertility) and prioritized "good partner" men when pregnancy is less likely (Gangestad & Thornhill, 1998; Gangestad & Haselton, 2015). For over two decades, researchers have pursued this compelling question. The task has not been easy, as methods for assessing ovulation are diverse and vary in their precision (Gangestad et al., 2016). Today, a substantial body of evidence demonstrates that women experience an ovulation-based shift in partner preferences, with heightened interest in masculinity during peak fertility, evidence synthesized in meta-analytic work (DeBruine, Jones, Frederick et al., 2010; Gangestad & Thornhill, 2008; Gildersleeve et al., 2014a; Jones et al., 2008). The robustness of these findings has been questioned and rebutted (Gildersleeve et al., 2014b; Harris et al., 2014; Wood, Kressel et al., 2014), with recent large-scaled work using a within-participant (rather than between-participant) design showing no evidence for a cycle-based effect on partner preferences (Jones et al., 2019; Jones et al., 2018). The need for additional research in this important area of work is readily apparent, and while the effects may be less robust than originally conjectured, the possibility remains that women have phase-dependent shifts in partner preferences.

A consideration of reproductive cycles as a context in which attraction takes place begs the question: What do older women and older men, who also experience a decline (if not so obvious) in their fertility, want in a partner? Some online dating evidence suggests that even in late adulthood, men preferentially desire physically attractive partners, while women continue to seek status more than men, and continue to be more selective than men (Alterovitz & Mendelsohn, 2009). This same study found that around age 75, women start looking for younger (rather than older) men. The preferences held by older adults may be weaker compared to those held by emerging adults; even within a truncated age range (18–40), older young people tend to be less selective (Fales et al., 2016; Sprecher et al., 2019). Also documented is a cross-cultural link between age and the prioritizing of communal traits, like sensitivity and smiling (Brumbaugh & Wood, 2013). Perhaps as we age, we maintain some of our evolved desires, but broaden our ideas of whom we might like, orienting especially toward the benevolent.

Attractiveness During Ovulation

Women might experience concealed ovulation, but are they somehow perceived as more attractive during peak fertility? Such a finding would make sense if the attraction system is designed to optimize reproduction and advance us toward evolutionary goals. One creative study tackled this question in a naturalistic investigation of professional lap dancers' menstrual cycles and the variability in their earnings over the course of two months (Miller et al., 2007). While all women earned less when menstruating, only normally cycling women (i.e., women not on birth control) made substantially more money per hour during peak fertility than at any other time in their cycle. Women on birth control do not ovulate, suggesting this peak could be tied to ovulation.

The money-making powers of ovulating lap dancers could be linked to fertility-related changes in how women sound, move, smell, and appear (Haselton & Gildersleeve, 2016; Jones et al., 2019). During peak fertility, women may dress in more revealing clothes and select sexier clothing to wear relative to low-fertility days (Durante et al., 2008; Haselton et al., 2007; Schwarz & Hassebrauck, 2008). While a pre-registered study using over 25,000 diary entries did not find evidence for clothing-related changes, it did robustly suggest that women see themselves as more desirable during ovulation and that they experience more sexual desire (Arslan et al., 2018). This is consistent with an ovulatory-shift hypothesis in which sexual desire, particularly extradyadic sexual desire, increases near ovulation (Shimoda et al., 2018).

Conclusion

We started this chapter with the intriguing idea that attraction, including love at first sight, like that which Idris Elba says he experienced, is predictable. Now that you have a full sense of what is attractive and how attraction works, what do you think? Remember that people desire those who can meet their needs. Love at first sight toward people whom we judge as potentially able to meet our needs might lead to forever love and make for the kind of stories that celebrity fans and grandchildren love hearing. Or, sadly, love at first sight might fizzle into repulsion at second glance, especially if new information reveals profound dissimilarity, dealbreakers, or failed reciprocity of liking. Ultimately, the name "love at first sight" is a misnomer: love is a complex emotional and cognitive experience. Love at first sight might be more aptly named "*attraction* at first sight," the kind of interest that comes with an openness to see what might be next. What follows is the subject of the next chapter: How does initial attraction turn into a relationship?

Major Take-Aways

- We are attracted to people who have traits and qualities that offer domain-general rewards or advance us toward specific evolutionary goals.
- People's desire for partners who have a high physical attractiveness; status, education, intelligence; and warmth/kindness can be explained from an evolutionary perspective as signaling "good genes" or "good partner" traits.
- Because men and women face different reproductive challenges, they tend to prioritize the qualities in a partner that best respond to those challenges.

- Hypothetical preferences do not always predict actual in-person attraction.
- Proximity, familiarity, similarity, and reciprocity breed attraction because they help support domain-general and specific evolutionary goals.
- Sociocultural factors, aspects of the immediate situation including experiences that induce physiological arousal, women's reproductive cycles, and the broader relationship trajectories all provide context for understanding romantic attraction.

Further Readings

If you're interested in ...
... evidence showing a mismatch between stated partner preferences and real-life initial attraction, read:
Eastwick, P. W., & Finkel, E. J. (2008). Sex differences in mate preferences revisited: Do people know what they initially desire in a romantic partner? *Journal*
of Personality and Social Psychology, 94(2), 245–264.

... the role of body odor in romantic appeal, read:
Hofer, M. K., Chen, F. S., & Schaller, M. (2020). What your nose knows: Affective, cognitive, and behavioral responses to the

scent of another person. *Current Directions in Psychological Science, 29*(6), 617–623.

... the problem of sexual racism and the role of racial stereotypes on romantic attraction, read:
Silvestrini, M. (2020). "It's not something I can shake": The effect of racial stereotypes, beauty standards, and sexual racism on interracial attraction. *Sexuality & Culture, 24*(1), 305–325.

... evidence showing an alignment between stated partner preferences and ongoing relationships, read:

Valentine, K. A., Li, N. P., Meltzer, A. L., & Tsai, M. H. (2020). Mate preferences for warmth-trustworthiness predict romantic attraction in the early stages of mate selection and satisfaction in ongoing relationships. *Personality and Social Psychology Bulletin, 46*(2), 298–311.

... how repeated exposure can induce liking, read:
Zajonc, R. B. (2001). Mere exposure: A gateway to the subliminal. *Current Directions in Psychological Science, 10*(6), 224–228.

5 RELATIONSHIP INITIATION

How Do Relationships Begin?

When Rose Tico first meets Finn in *Star Wars: The Last Jedi*, she babbles in awe, having come face-to-face with a "Resistance Hero." After a few early missteps (Rose stuns Finn with a shock prod to prevent him from stealing an escape pod), they take on a shared mission, become friends, and then (in what could be their moment!) she kisses him right after nearly risking her life to save him. Despite Rose's romantic gesture, their relationship remains in the "friendzone" (Figure 5.1), and they act as though the kiss never happened.

While Rose pines for Finn, fans can't help but notice romantic tension between Finn and three other lead characters: Rey Skywalker, Jannah, and Poe Dameron. Rey captures Finn's attention quickly, but as smitten as he seems, he never makes a clear "move." They remain friends. A potential romance between Finn and Jannah has a strong start in *The Rise of Skywalker*, given their shared history as stormtrooper defectors (similarity breeds liking!), but this too ends with unrealized chemistry. As for a Finn and Poe relationship, *Star Wars* fans and actor Oscar Isaac, the actor who played Poe, were all for it. Isaac said, "Personally, I kind of hoped and wished that maybe that would've been taken further in the other films . . . it seemed like a natural progression." And yet, this relationship also stalls at friendship (albeit an intimate "we-battled-the-First-Order-together" friendship).

Figure 5.1 Actors Kelly Tran and John Boyega fought the First Order together as Rose and Finn, but the transition to a romantic relationship never quite happened. Why? (Photo: Gerardo Mora / Stringer / Getty Images)

How do romantic relationships begin? Finn's almost-but-not-quite relationships reflect many of our realities. Perhaps you know the pangs of unrequited love, the careful resisting of another's subtle signs of interest, or the uncertainty of an unspoken energy that has no resolution. The space between two people must be bridged for a romantic relationship to start, and this requires an act, gesture, or "move" that renders a favorable response. This isn't easy; by some estimates, 30 to 40 percent of people find it difficult to initiate a relationship (Apostolou et al., 2018). As you will see, the challenge of relationship initiation begins before people even identify a potential partner and continues from there. A move, like when Rose kisses Finn, might lead to nowhere and never be spoken of again; or, it could be the start of something beautiful (can we re-write *Star Wars*?).

This chapter will introduce you to the earliest moments of relationship initiation, the process by which people come to mutually identify themselves as in a relationship. Relationship initiation describes the beginnings of any close relationship (e.g., friendships, mentorships), but this chapter will focus specifically on the beginnings of romantic relationships. This is an often overlooked topic, despite being a necessary, and therefore commonly experienced, stage in relationship development. As you read this chapter, your goals are to learn how relationship motivations shape relationship beginnings, to gain a sense of the challenges we experience in the pursuit of love, and to learn the methods that work (and don't work) to start a romantic relationship.

?	**GUIDING QUESTIONS**

Consider these questions as you read this chapter:
- How do relationship readiness and romantic motives affect relationship initiation?
- What are the key barriers to relationship initiation?
- How do people come to build rapport with an attractive stranger?
- What types of diverse paths can lead to relationships?
- How do other people influence relationship initiation?
- When do relationships fail to begin?

Why People Initiate: Timing and Romantic Motivations

Before we fall in love, before a first date, even before the first moments of romantic attraction, people differ in their relationship readiness and relationship goals. Think about it: are you open to starting a relationship? What are your motivations for doing so? Differences in openness and romantic motivations often shape people's future relationship potential. As we consider the early determinants of the path toward "in a relationship" status, we will emphasize the experience for single individuals (as the field does), yet keep in mind most aspects of relationship initiation are equally relevant to people already in relationships who are considering extradyadic partnerships and/or expanding their consensually non-monogamous relationships.

Relationship Readiness

If Finn were a friend of yours, and you repeatedly witnessed his romantic tensions fail to amount to romance, might you wonder if he's simply *not ready* for a relationship? Relationship readiness can be considered a precursor to actively pursuing partners and openly responding to others' overtures. Not every person who is single is ready for a relationship, and people can experience different degrees of readiness over the course of their lives. If a previous relationship just ended, if they're focusing on themselves or their work, or if life circumstances simply make the timing non-ideal, people may pass on the chance to start even a desirable relationship.

This is a central tenet of **relationship receptivity theory**, which suggests that timing is a critical contextual factor in relationship formation (Agnew et al., 2019, 2020; Hadden et al., 2018). For example, single people differ in their **commitment readiness** – how comfortable they are with the notion of entering a long-term relationship. Commitment readiness is not partner-specific, but rather a holistic sense that someone is prepared for the experience of linking themselves with another person (Hadden & Agnew, 2020; Hadden et al., 2018). Those single individuals with more commitment readiness tend to desire to date, want more closeness with an eventual partner, and engage in more behaviors linked to relationship initiation (e.g., dress to impress, flirt more; Hadden et al., 2018). Over time, they enter relationships more than single individuals with low commitment readiness, and they tend to be more satisfied and more invested in the relationships they enter.

These findings touch on an important difference among single individuals: not every person who is single is ready for or wants to be in a relationship. For some single individuals, the timing isn't right, so they are not currently pursuing partners. Many young people, for example, prioritize school or work with plans to find a partner after they are more established (Manning et al., 2010). For other people who are single, timing is not the issue at all; a paradigm shift emphasizing *single readiness* would be more apt. For these individuals, singlehood is a desired, stable, and secure choice (Pepping et al., 2018). Their readiness to enter a committed relationship is low and may be stably low.

Romantic Motivations

Why did Rose kiss Finn? Recall that we have domain-general needs (e.g., security, self-esteem, pleasure) and specific evolved needs (e.g., survival, reproduction). We pursue relationships with people whom we think can help us meet our needs, and our most salient needs shape the types of relationships we pursue and *how* we attempt to start relationships. Did Rose kiss Finn to initiate a no-strings-attached hookup or to initiate a long-term partnership?

Evolutionary theories describe **mating motives** – goals regarding the type of relationships people desire – on a spectrum with short-term sexual liaisons on one end, and long-term relationships on the other. People can adopt mating strategies aligned with their goals to direct their reproductive efforts. Recall that men tend to be more oriented toward short-term relationships, and women toward long-term relationships, yet both men and women can prioritize either type of relationship (Gangestad & Simpson, 2000). In fact, most people (regardless of their gender) do not pursue exclusively short-term or exclusively long-term relationships. For instance, a large-scale study of over 6,000 Greek adults showed that most people (68.7 percent of men and 67.6 percent of women) ideally want to pursue a mix of short- and long-term relationships (Apostolou, 2021b). The most popular of the mixed strategies is, over the life course, to first focus on either casual relationships or a series of long-term relationships and then find and secure a "forever" long-term relationship (with no extra-dyadic relationships). Exclusively heterosexual individuals, gay men, and lesbian women evince similar proportional preferences for long-term, mixed, and short-term strategies, with some suggestion that bisexual women and heterosexual women who also experience same-sex attraction are more likely to prefer short-term and mixed strategies relative to heterosexual women (Apostolou, 2021b).

While mating motives shape mating strategies, mating strategies determine mating tactics, or what people do to initiate relationships (Allen & Bailey, 2007). Our strategies and tactics are nimble, adjusting to align with our goals, and this adjustment happens largely outside of awareness. Endowed with a mating psychology attuned to what might best optimize our success, as you will see, we often attempt to initiate relationships by offering solutions to the adaptive problems facing our potential partner(s). Give them what they want, and they may just want you.

In Pursuit of Short-Term Relationships

Let's take an example in which a man is seeking a short-term relationship with a woman, a common starting point in evolutionary psychology (which tends to prioritize gender binary, different-sex relationships). As discussed in Chapter 4, for short-term relationships, women tend to prioritize the "good genes" that are cued by physical appearance, status, and dominance. Accordingly, it makes sense for men to show off these aspects as a short-term mating strategy. Indeed, tactics like enhancing one's appearance, acting macho, and down-playing rival men's strength (or better yet, competing and winning against those rivals) are effective for men pursuing short-term partners (Schmitt & Buss, 1996). A little conspicuous consumption is often part of men's repertoire as well (Griskevicius et al., 2007); men are particularly apt to engage in showy spending ("This round is on me") when looking for short-term partners (Sundie et al., 2011). Women tend to accurately interpret conspicuous consumption as an indicator of men's short-term interest, even as it increases women's interest in these men (again, for short-term, not long-term, relationships). Men also strategically pursue short-term relationships by suggesting they are open to a more invested relationship. This deceptive strategy responds to women's typical preference for long-term relationships. Implying love or commitment, inviting her to a private place, or making her dinner are all viewed as effective methods for promoting a sexual encounter (Greer & Buss, 1994).

Women who want to initiate a short-term relationship with a man take a different approach. From an evolutionary perspective, one challenge for men is identifying and accessing available sexual partners. Women who showcase their availability solve this problem, making it an effective short-term mating strategy (Schmitt & Buss, 1996). Enhancing and sexualizing their appearance, showing spontaneity, or acting seductively are all judged to be effective toward short-term goals. Women can also be direct: they can make propositions or simply ask a man if he wants to sleep with her; taking this direct approach is a highly effective method for women (but not men) to start a sexual encounter (Greer & Buss, 1994). Indeed, women might be more effective at starting short-term affairs than men: women's tactics (e.g., direct invitations, guiding his hands to her body, undressing herself, undressing him) are generally perceived as more effective than men's best attempts (Greer & Buss, 1994). This is perhaps because men tend to be more open to short-term relationships (Buss & Schmitt, 1993), meaning, less effort is necessary by women to secure short-term liaisons (or, conversely, women tend to be less open, meaning more effort is necessary). Beyond persuasive techniques focused on self-promotion, women seeking short-term relationships can also advance their goal by making other attractive women less appealing. They can, for example, derogate rivals' attractiveness or hygiene, or drop hints of their being sexually unavailable (Schmitt & Buss, 1996).

Some short-term mating tactics are similarly effective for both men and women. These include increasing non-sexual touching, creating a romantic atmosphere, showing attention, getting help from friends to spend time with this person, and dancing, especially a little bit closer than you would otherwise (Greer & Buss, 1994). Although research lags behind in this area, given the broad appeal of these tactics, there is reason to suspect they could be effective to initiate same-sex short-term relationships as well.

In Pursuit of Long-Term Relationships

If you're a man looking for long-term love with a woman, evolutionary theories suggest you might do well to solve women's adaptive problem of identifying men who will stay, share their resources, and co-parent. Indeed, displaying "good partner/parent traits" is an effective long-term mating strategy for men (even as it might be deceptively used to pursue short-term relationships). The big winner here is conveying benevolence, a dispositional orientation toward kindness, generosity, and goodwill. Remember how attractive kindness is in long-term relationships? Men who showcase their honesty and sensitivity reveal their suitability for a long-term relationship (Schmitt & Buss, 1996).

Another way to attract long-term interest is to engage in prosocial or altruistic acts, which demonstrate "good partner/parent" qualities (Bhogal et al., 2020; Norman & Fleming, 2019). Enacting prosocial behaviors increases people's odds of entering a stable relationship over the next year, an association that holds when controlling for personality and social involvement (Stavrova & Ehlebracht, 2015). Prosociality can go a long way in espousing one's worth as a potential long-term partner, but careful that you don't go overboard. Suggesting that more is not always better, women judge moderate altruism as more attractive than high levels of altruism (Bhogal et al., 2020), possibly because moderate altruism signals benevolence, but not excessive generosity. Moderately altruistic men give while also providing for themselves (and, presumably, a partner if they had one).

Men can also signal their benevolence through their preferences and decisions. Suppose you're talking to an attractive stranger and a waiter asks if they want a paper or plastic straw. Think about how annoying paper straws are, and yet they are *so much better* for the environment than plastic straws. Men opting for paper straws signal a willingness to sacrifice luxury for an eco-friendly option that benefits everyone. The willingness and ability to endure costs for the benefit of others is a form of generosity which women tend to find attractive (DiDonato & Jakubiak, 2016b; Palomo-Vélez et al., 2021). This does not apply to straws alone: following from costly signaling theory, men who engage in conspicuous conservation elevate their perceived status (Griskevicius et al., 2010). Caring about the environment is just one way to indicate traits desired in long-term relationships, and it works so well that "going green" is seen as a reliable signal of commitment (Borau et al., 2021).

Finally, let's consider how men's character strengths and moral standing could be displayed to increase their appeal as long-term partners. Soon after meeting Finn, Rey asks if he's in the Resistance, to which he quickly replies, "Yes I am. I'm with the Resistance," a statement that sings of virtue and a moral compass backed by action. Turns out, other than the lying part, this is not a bad plan if he's interested in initiating a long-term relationship with Rey. Women prefer long-term partners who have a strong sense of "right" and "wrong" (Brown & Sacco, 2019). Perhaps men who showcase their right/wrong morality become appealing as long-term partners because they are signaling their ability to follow rules (needed for monogamy). Initial evidence also suggests that a lightsaber swing against the First Order in the name of justice and rooted in moral outrage could help Finn, were he to pursue a long-term relationship with Rey. Men who engage in actions that suggest strong moral outrage (e.g., they participate in activism, work against injustices) are desired more as long-term partners than short-term partners (Brown, Keefer et al., 2021). Expressing moral outrage appears to be another tool in men's long-term initiation kit, provided their expressions of outrage are backed by actual effort to intervene and right the wrong.

Women motivated to form long-term relationships with men can also take a problem-solving approach and emphasize traits that suggest their faithfulness to resolve men's adaptive problem of paternity uncertainty. They might, for instance, showcase their commitment, honesty, and sexual exclusivity (while highlighting other women's promiscuity or unfaithfulness; Schmitt & Buss, 1996). Further, just as people use long-term tactics to secure short-term relationships, people (particularly women) use short-term tactics to initiate long-term relationships. For example, while both men and women are motivated to engage in hookups as a pathway to relationship (Garcia & Reiber, 2008), women adopt this goal more than men (Thorpe & Kuperberg, 2021; Weitbrecht & Whitton, 2020). Curious for more ideas? See Table 5.1 for highly rated relationship initiation tactics for men and women pursuing short- and long-term relationships.

Table 5.1 Top five tactics judged as most effective for relationship initiation

Enacted by women		Enacted by men	
Short-term	**Long-term**	**Short-term**	**Long-term**
1. Accept their sexual offer. 2. Suggest you spend time together alone. 3. Flirt. 4. Make subtle physical contact. 5. Make them think of having sex with you.	1. Show special loving devotion. 2. Avoid sex with other people. 3. Remain faithful. 4. Fall in love. 5. Date for a long time.	1. Accept their sexual offer. 2. Make yourself look good. 3. Make a good first impression. 4. Show that you're attracted to them. 5. Shower often.	1. Be understanding of their problems. 2. Remain faithful. 3. Find common interests. 4. Show special loving devotion. 5. Fall in love.

These tactics are recognized as highly effective in starting short- or long-term relationships. The original research's binary approach to gender follows from an evolutionary perspective that also emphasizes different-sex relationships. Which tactics might work for non-binary individuals pursuing short- or long-term relationships? How well might these tactics translate to same-sex relationships?

Sociosexuality

Have you ever noticed that some people are comfortable with casual sex, whereas other people reserve sexual activity for high-commitment relationships? Sociosexuality refers to how much relationship investment individuals require before engaging in sexual activity with another person (Gangestad & Simpson, 1990). On one end of the spectrum, individuals with unrestricted sociosexual orientations have low thresholds for physical intimacy, maintaining little or no relationship prerequisites prior to engaging in sexual behaviors. They might prefer to be in a stable long-term relationship (differentiating sociosexuality from promiscuity), but unrestricted individuals are open to purely sexual encounters and often adopt short-term mating strategies (Simpson & Gangestad, 1991). At the other end of the sociosexuality continuum, individuals with restricted sociosexual orientations maintain high thresholds for physical intimacy: they require closeness, time, and commitment before sexual activity. They tend to have a stronger motivation to form committed relationships than unrestricted individuals (Jones, 1998). Restricted individuals are solidly oriented toward long-term mating strategies.

Who has unrestricted versus restricted sociosexual orientations? Consistent with sexual selection theory and differential parental investment, men tend to have more unrestricted sociosexuality and women tend to have more restricted sociosexuality. This makes sense given the reproductive benefits of having multiple partners (men) and being highly selective (women). Both heterosexual and gay men tend to exhibit more unrestricted sociosexuality than women; among women, bisexual women tend to be the most unrestricted, followed by lesbian women and straight women, the latter two groups not consistently different (Howard & Perilloux, 2017; Semenyna et al., 2017). Linking biology to sociosexuality, preliminary evidence suggests that transgender individuals tend to have a sociosexual orientation aligned with their biological sex assigned at birth, rather than their gender (de Menezes Gomes et al., 2021). Preliminary work also suggests that women favoring monogamy and women favoring polyamory both tend to report similar (restricted) sociosexuality, whereas polyamorous men tend to be more unrestricted than monogamous men, who, again, tend to be more unrestricted than women (Morrison et al., 2013).

While these gender differences stand, within-sex variation on sociosexuality tends to be greater than between-sex variation (Simpson & Gangestad, 1991). This propels sociosexuality to its status as a fascinating construct. Both women and men may have an evolved underlying system that assumes restricted or unrestricted sociosexual orientations contingent upon their specific circumstances. Consider sexual pluralism theory (Gangestad & Simpson, 2000), which argues that people evaluate their own resources and situation (e.g., their own attractiveness, status) relative to that of their competitors, and unconsciously adopt strategies to optimize their reproductive success. An individual's sociosexual orientations may reflect an outcome of this calculation. Also consider sociosexuality through the lens of life history theory (introduced in Chapter 2; Del Guidice et al., 2016; Kaplan & Gangestad, 2005), which proposes that the harshness and/or unpredictability of a person's childhood can lead them to pursue fast or slow strategies (the former of which aligns with unrestricted sociosexuality; the latter with restricted sociosexuality). Consistent with this idea, people who have predictable early childhoods tend to develop more restricted sociosexuality as adolescents (Simpson et al., 2017; Szepsenwol et al., 2017).

Where do you fall on the restricted-unrestricted continuum? Try the questions in Table 5.2 to see how relationship scientists assess this characteristic. As reflected in the scoring

Table 5.2 Sociosexuality – three facets: behavioral, attitudinal, desire

Sociosexuality
Three facets: behavioral, attitudinal, desire

Behavioral sociosexuality

1. With how many different partners have you had sex in the past twelve months?	0 1 2 3 4 5–6 7–9 10–19 20+ *Score as:* 1 2 3 4 5 6 7 8 9
2. With how many different partners have you had sexual intercourse on *one and only one* occasion?	0 1 2 3 4 5–6 7–9 10–19 20+ *Score as:* 1 2 3 4 5 6 7 8 9
3. With how many different partners have you had sexual intercourse without having an interest in a long-term commitment relationship with this person?	0 1 2 3 4 5–6 7–9 10–19 20+ *Score as:* 1 2 3 4 5 6 7 8 9

Sociosexual attitudes

4. Sex without love is OK	Strongly disagree Strongly agree 1 2 3 4 5 6 7
5. I can imagine myself being comfortable and enjoying "casual" sex with different partners.	Strongly disagree Strongly agree 1 2 3 4 5 6 7
6. I do *not* want to have sex with a person until I am sure that we will have a long-term, serious relationship.	Strongly disagree Strongly agree 1 2 3 4 5 6 7 *This item is reverse scored:* 7 6 5 4 3 2 1

Sociosexual desire

7. How often do you have fantasies about having sex with someone with whom you do *not* have a committed romantic relationship?	1 – never 2 – very seldom 3 – about once every two or three months 4 – about once a month 5 – about once every two weeks 6 – about once a week 7 – several times per week 8 – nearly every day 9 – at least once a day
8. How often do you experience sexual arousal when you are in contact with someone with whom you do *not* have a committed romantic relationship?	1 – never 2 – very seldom 3 – about once every two or three months 4 – about once a month

Table 5.2 (*cont.*)

Sociosexuality Three facets: behavioral, attitudinal, desire	
	5 – about once every two weeks
	6 – about once a week
	7 – several times per week
	8 – nearly every day
	9 – at least once a day
9. In everyday life, how often do you have spontaneous fantasies about having sex with someone you have just met?	1 – never
	2 – very seldom
	3 – about once every two or three months
	4 – about once a month
	5 – about once every two weeks
	6 – about once a week
	7 – several times per week
	8 – nearly every day
	9 – at least once a day

Compute average scores for each facet of sociosexuality. Higher scores indicate greater *un*restricted sociosexuality.

Source: Copyright © 2008 by American Psychological Association, reproduced and adapted with permission. The official citation that should be used in referencing this material is Penke, L., & Asendorpf, J. B. (2008). Beyond global sociosexual orientations: a more differentiated look at sociosexuality and its effects on courtship and romantic relationships. *Journal of Personality and Social Psychology*, *95*(5), 1113–1135. https://doi.org/10.1037/0022-3514.95.5.1113. No further reproduction or distribution is permitted without written permission from the American Psychological Association.

procedure for this measure, sociosexuality can be segmented into three facets (Penke & Asendorpf, 2008): **sociosexual behaviors**, which refer to a personal history of engaging in sex outside of a committed relationship; **sociosexual attitudes**, how people evaluate casual sex; and **sociosexual desire**, the degree to which people are motivated to pursue uncommitted sex. Considered a personality dimension, sociosexuality aligns with people's relationship histories; unrestricted individuals tend to have more short-term casual relationships and relationships characterized by less interdependence, investment, and commitment relative to restricted individuals (Simpson & Gangestad, 1991).

Sociosexuality plays a fascinating role in relationship initiation, capturing important variation in short-term or long-term motives, strategies, and tactics. For example, to start a relationship, unrestricted men tend to assert their superiority; whereas restricted men, in the same situation, tend to showcase their "nice guy" qualities (Simpson et al., 1999). The extent to which women report unrestricted sociosexuality predicts their drinking during the first semester of college, potentially because drinking can be an intentional tactic for securing desired casual hookups (Testa & Hone, 2019). Unrestricted men and women, compared to restricted individuals, are also more inclined to use apps like Tinder and Snapchat specifically to hook up or gain access to casual sex (Moran et al., 2018; Sevi et al., 2018). Interest in online dating for casual sex versus long-term love is explained by sociosexuality better than it is by gender (Hallam et al., 2018). Despite these differences, unrestricted and restricted individuals alike often face various obstacles in pursuing a partner, a problem we turn to now.

Barriers to Relationship Initiation

Suppose Finn wanted to start a relationship: what pragmatic and psychological challenges would he encounter? Indeed, what obstacles do any of us face when we are looking for love?

Accessing Partners

The first barrier is purely logistical. Where do you go to meet someone? Naturally, some physical settings inspire an opportunity to start a relationship more than others. Cultural norms imbue certain settings with social, even romantic, expectations, such as wedding receptions, nightclubs, or parties; whereas initiating a relationship in other settings, like a funeral, a court proceeding, or a business meeting, would be bad form. In general, people are moderately optimistic about meeting a compatible romantic partner simply by going through their everyday activities (e.g., work, school, grocery shopping) or through their social network (friends, family), an optimism that tends to decline with age and does not typically extend to online forums (Sprecher, 2019).

Online Dating

Even if people aren't optimistic about online dating, established couples are increasingly likely to report that they met their current partner online. This contrasts how dating happened prior to the Internet, when people tended to meet their partners through friends, family, or in school. For different-sex partners, the move toward online has been fairly steady since the mid-1990s, with about 20 percent reporting they met their partner online in 2010, and increasingly since that time (see Figure 5.2). Online dating may be potentially displacing the social network's (friends, family) role in initiating romantic connection (Rosenfeld et al., 2019). The shift toward meeting online occurred even earlier and more dramatically in same-sex couples; by 2010, more than half of same-sex couples reported meeting online (Rosenfeld & Thomas, 2010).

Online dating solves the problem of access to potential partners, an obstacle to relationship initiation for everyone, but a problem that has historically been particularly pronounced among sexual minorities. Sexual minorities by definition are in the numeric minority, limiting the pool of potential partners. Online dating not only extends the geographical range of possible partners, but provides good certainty that the potential partners are of a compatible sexual orientation (Custer et al., 2008). The risk of mistaking someone's sexual orientation in an in-person relationship initiation attempt is greater for sexual minorities, and so reducing such stress is an added appeal of the access offered by online dating.

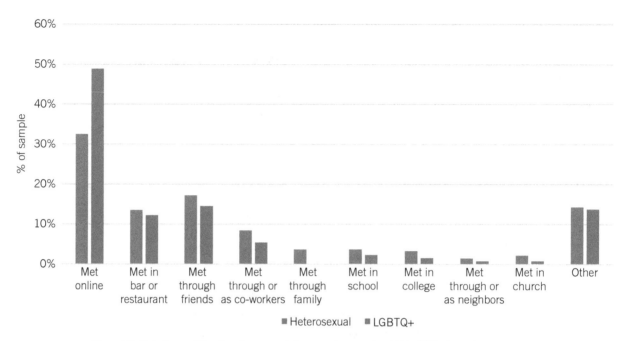

Figure 5.2 Data from a US nationally representative sample, spanning 2013–2017, show where people are meeting their different-sex partners ($N = 274$) and same-sex partners ($N = 131$). How might your dating experiences differ from those of your parents or your grandparents? (Source: Based on data from Rosenfeld et al. [2019])

A PEW Research Center survey of a representative sample of 4,680 adults in the United States documented the popularity of online dating in 2019 (Anderson et al., 2020). As shown in Figure 5.3, one in three adults have tried online dating, with use varying considerably by age and sexual orientation: younger adults and lesbian, gay, and bisexual adults use online dating apps and websites more than older adults or heterosexual adults. Of course, trying online dating does not mean you'll meet anyone, but about a quarter of American adults (23 percent) in this same study reported having gone on a date with someone whom they met online. Meta-analysis suggests that men and women use online dating differently, with men viewing more profiles and initiating contact more often than women (Abramova et al., 2016). Women, however, are more likely to receive responses when they send a message.

Partner Shortages and Partner Surpluses
Online dating apps and websites increase the size of people's **dating pool**, the accessible individuals who could be potential romantic partners. This is especially important when, in the course of their daily lives, people experience a **partner shortage**: little opportunity to access or interact with potential partners. Social habits (e.g., staying at home) or situational context (e.g., type of work, work hours, living arrangements) can produce such a partner shortage. Consider the experience of Black college women who are looking to date within their race, for example; they tend to face a shortage of similarly educated, financially secure Black men, on account of systemic discrimination and the under-representation of Black men in higher education (Boyd et al., 2020).

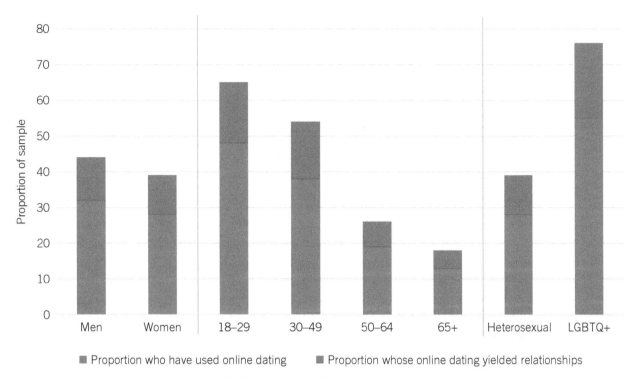

Figure 5.3 The percentage of people who have used online dating divided by men/women, age groups, and sexual orientation. Some online dating turns into relationships, as shown by the green subset of each group. (Source: Pew Research Center Survey of US adults conducted October 16–18, 2019; drawn based on data from Anderson et al. [2020])

In the face of a partner shortage, people adopt compensatory mating tactics. They can, for instance, abstain from dating if they have trouble meeting people or feel unable to find "the one," a tactic preferred by people seeking long-term relationships (Apostolou, 2017; Apostolou et al., 2020; Jonason, Betes et al., 2020). Some bisexual individuals report abstaining from same-sex dating and engaging in different-sex dating simply because of a same-sex partner shortage (Wu, Marks et al., 2020): percentage-wise, there are more potential different-sex partners. People can also lower their standards, a tactic more often in play for short-term than long-term relationships, and more readily adopted by individuals who fear being single (Jonason et al., 2019; Spielmann et al., 2013). Alternatively, some people facing a partner shortage decide to change their situational context by traveling farther in pursuit of desirable partners. For these individuals, incurring the costs associated with traveling saves them from lowering their standards or abstaining from dating. Men and women are more interested in traveling in response to a partner shortage when seeking a long-term relationship (Jonason, Betes, & Li, 2020).

Online dating solves the problem of a mate shortage, providing instead, a **partner surplus**: a veritable cornucopia of possible romantic partners, all at the tips of your fingers. Never in the history of ever have people had more opportunity to be connected, quickly, to such a vast pool of potential partners. In 2021, Tinder reports having orchestrated 60 billion matches since its inception in 2012; eharmony reports that people find love through their website every 14 minutes; OKCupid is responsible for over 50,000 dates every week. These are impressive statistics. You open the app and start swiping (or log on and start scrolling) and boom! Potential partners, ready, available, and "matched" with you. What is the consequence of such an abundance of potential partners? As discussed in the *Is This True for You?* box, having more options does not necessarily improve the relationship initiation experience.

IS THIS TRUE FOR YOU?

Can There Be Too Many Fish in the Sea?

Have you ever visited a restaurant that has a huge menu? Tacos, bibimbap, grilled salmon . . . so many good options! Deciding can be hard, a bit overwhelming in fact. The waiter comes, you order pasta pomodoro, and when it arrives it's predictably delicious . . . but, you can't help thinking: would the avocado bacon burger have been better?

Online dating offers unprecedented access to romantic partners, and such access might seem, at first, like a pathway toward a better romantic match. With more options, you can optimize your partner search, pairing with a better partner, right? "Best out of a billion" seems better than "best out of the seven age-appropriate single people in your neighborhood." Surprisingly, however, more options do not translate to better, more satisfying decisions. Instead, we experience the **paradox of choice**, where more options make for a worse rather than a better experience (Figure 5.4). Classic work on the paradox of choice shows that a larger set of options can trigger decision paralysis and render people less satisfied with their final selections (Iyengar & Lepper, 2000; Schwartz, 2004).

Figure 5.4 The ups and downs of online dating: is it a better way of meeting people? (Photo: Enes Evren / E+ / Getty Images)

Unfortunately, then, the very appeal of online dating (more possible partners!) can add discontent to an already difficult process. People can look, look, and keep looking, always wondering if they might uncover any even better partner. When people engage in this type of excessive searching in online dating platforms, they become overwhelmed, ultimately reducing the quality of their selection (Wu & Chiou, 2009).

Believe it or not, people are happier with their selected partners when they make their choice from a smaller versus larger pool of options, and are the least satisfied when they choose from a larger set and have the option to change their minds (D'Angelo & Toma, 2017).

Have you tried online dating? Did it make you feel pessimistic and overwhelmed? If not, perhaps you differ in your approach. Some people adopt a "satisficing" strategy: they go with the first "good enough" match, whereas others are "maximizers" who aim to find the absolute best partner. This latter group is more likely to engage in excessive searching and, paradoxically, end up with less optimal results (Yang & Chiou, 2009). What other moderating variables might help distinguish between those who enjoy online dating and those who do not?

Traditional Gender Roles

In the *Star Wars* universe, when two people are romantically interested in each other, who makes the first move? This might depend on whether you're a human, Wookie, or Ewok, and whether you're on the planet Tatooine, Coruscant, or Naboo. In other words, both biological and sociocultural forces may shape how people behave during relationship initiation. Here on Earth, and more specifically, in Western cultures that support love matches, scholars have noted that humans tend to adhere to gender roles in romantic initiation (Cameron & Curry, 2020; Rose & Frieze, 1989, 1993). Gender roles present a barrier to relationship initiation because they can impose hard-to-meet expectations and constrain "who does what," adding pressure and limiting freedom during what is already a high-stakes game. Those who deviate from gender stereotypic behaviors can earn the scorn of observers, who sanction their non-conformity by judging them as less competent, less warm, and less appropriate (McCarty & Kelly, 2015).

Gender roles are embedded in people's dating scripts, their mental representations of the sequence of events and expectations characterizing early relationship experiences. Both men and women maintain dating scripts that are similar not only in the behaviors involved in relationship initiation, but also in the gender-based expectations tied to those behaviors (Bartoli & Clark, 2006; Laner & Ventrone, 2000). Dating scripts are culturally bound and can change over time, yet even as they appear to be somewhat more egalitarian today than a few decades ago, relationship initiation is still strongly colored by gendered roles (Cameron & Curry, 2020). Indeed, cultural differences in self-disclosure, the sharing of information that helps build intimacy in relationships, are better understood as a function of variation in gender role traditionalism, rather than individualistic or collectivist orientation (Marshall, 2008).

Different-Sex Relationships

What men and women typically do in relationship initiation is well-defined and well-known, fueled by an abundance of cultural messages conveyed in the media, in families, and among friends. In these different-sex dyadic relationships, dating scripts earmark men as active initiators and women as passive receivers, traditional gender roles that both men and women typically endorse and perceive positively (McCarty & Kelly, 2015; Ömür & Büyükşahin-Sunal, 2015). Consistent with these scripts, men are more likely to initiate a relationship and women are more likely to rely on their partner to be the initiator (Clark et al., 1999; Rose & Frieze, 1993). This pattern holds for both long-term and short-term relationship initiation. For instance, people generally expect men to initiate a hookup and women report receiving more booty-calls than men (Eaton et al., 2016; Jonason, Li, & Cason, 2009). Most men and women also agree that men are more likely to ask someone out on a date, make independent plans for the date, drive or pick up the other person, open doors, pay the bill, and make any affectionate or sexual advances (Laner & Ventrone, 2000). This same research suggests women, meanwhile, are the ones who wait in the first-date game: they wait to be asked, wait for their date to arrive, and wait to see if their partner makes a move.

Of course, these group trends obscure individual variability. Women (more than men) and people with less sexist attitudes tend to favor more egalitarian dating scripts, and men with more relationship anxiety are more in favor of women using direct strategies (Cameron & Curry, 2020; Ömür & Büyükşahin-Sunal, 2015). Underscoring the sociocultural nature of gender norms, when women experience a boost in their sense of personal control, they shift in their willingness to initiate relationships and are willing to adopt direct strategies to the same extent as men (MacGregor & Cavallo, 2011). Showing a change in times perhaps, the question of "who pays" no longer elicits a simple "he does" answer. Although most men and women report that men still pay, almost two-thirds of men think women should contribute at times, and over 40 percent of men report that if a woman never paid that would be a dealbreaker for them (Lever et al., 2015).

Same-Sex Relationships

Early research into the dating scripts of gay men and lesbian women noted their parallels with different-sex dating, with some gendered behaviors appearing with added emphasis, such as an accentuation of sexual behavior and emotional intimacy in gay men's scripts and lesbian women's scripts respectively (Klinkenberg & Rose, 1994). More recent evidence, however, suggests that members of the LGBTQ + community may actively reject the gendered dating scripts endorsed by different-sex couples and celebrate a non-gendered script that involves communication, reciprocity, and negotiations (Lamont, 2017). Think about the "who pays" question. Whereas men in different-sex relationships might feel guilty accepting women's money (Lever et al., 2015), splitting the check or alternating who pays tends to be a comfortable experience in same-sex relationships (Lamont, 2017). Not having to adhere to specific gender roles is considered a unique benefit of being in a lesbian relationship (Rose & Zand, 2002).

Uncertainty in Relationship Initiation

Another key barrier to relationship initiation is uncertainty, the experience of being unsure or unable to predict the outcome of a given social interaction (Berger & Bradac, 1982). During romantic initiation, people might not know or might not be confident about their own and/or others' attitudes (cognitive uncertainty); they might also wonder how they should act and what their interaction partner will do next (behavioral uncertainty). While uncertainty can characterize relationship interactions well beyond initial meetings (Knobloch & Solomon, 2002), it is often particularly high during early interactions. Both uncertainty reduction theory and predicted outcome value theory provide insight into how people navigate the inherent ambiguity of relationship initiation (Knobloch & Miller, 2008).

Uncertainty Reduction Theory

Imagine you're speaking with an attractive stranger on an airplane. What might you say? Finn, snagging a chance to talk to Rey on the Millennium Falcon, slyly asks Rey if she wants to return to her home planet because of a boyfriend, using their conversation to try to gauge his romantic chances. Uncertainty reduction theory tells us that a primary purpose of communication in ambiguous situations is to add clarity, confidence, and predictability (Berger & Bradac, 1982; Berger & Calabrese, 1975). Because, at first, relationships typically have high uncertainty, the conversations tend toward casual, less-intimate topics (e.g., "How do you like this weather?"), include a good deal of reciprocity ("I'm a fan of rainy days, too!"), and prioritize seeking information (e.g., "How do you like to spend a rainy day?"). Reducing uncertainty can increase how much we like an interaction partner, heighten how sexually appealing we find them, and buffer against declines in initiation effort (Birnbaum et al., 2018). In essence, we like predictable interactions and pursue them, though it can take some work to arrive at a point of predictability.

So, how do people reduce uncertainty? Three strategies stand out (Berger, 1997; Berger & Bradac, 1982), as shown in Figure 5.5. First, people can engage in goal-oriented planning. Relying on previous experience in similarly ambiguous situations, they can devise a plan that will help them navigate a complex interaction. Second, people can hedge in various ways as they communicate, trying to learn about their interaction partner, figure out their romantic interest, and determine their own potential interest, without assuming too much. For instance, people might hedge by saying, "I'm hoping to try that new taco bar that just opened up," or "What do you have lined up for the weekend?" instead of diving right in with, "Do you want to go out for tacos on Saturday?"

A third uncertainty reduction strategy is information seeking, which people accomplish through a variety of approaches. The most obvious is by adopting interactive strategies, communicating directly with a person of interest (Berger & Bradac, 1982; Knobloch & Miller, 2008). People might ask questions, self-disclose with the hope of reciprocity, and try to relax their interaction partner in a way that makes them comfortable and talkative. Interactive strategies are

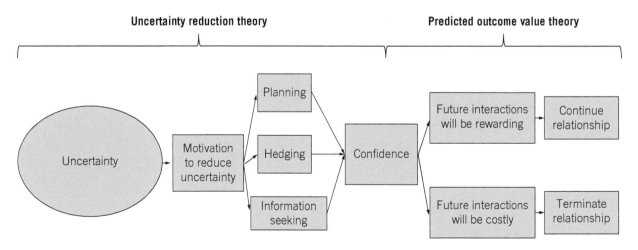

Figure 5.5 Uncertainty colors early interactions with potential romantic partners. Which forms of uncertainty reduction do you tend to use? (Source: Drawn based on content in Knobloch and Miller [2008] and Sunnafrank [1990])

not limited to face-to-face meetings. Computer-mediated conversations, like texting, chatting, or emailing, often include more question asking and more self-disclosure than traditional face-to-face interactions, allowing for uncertainty reduction (Tidwell & Walther, 2002).

People also adopt active strategies to gather information and reduce uncertainty. Active strategies can involve setting up the environment in a certain way and observing how a desired partner behaves ("come and meet my friends!") or gathering information about a desired partner from other people in your social network: you talk to your friend who is married to the cousin of your desired partner; information passes from ear to ear and helps you fill in the gaps.

Secret spy work is another way people gather information to reduce uncertainty. What do you do on the way home from meeting a new romantic interest? If you hop on Google, Instagram, or other online sources to learn more, you are probably information seeking to reduce uncertainty. When people adopt extractive strategies, which are specifically Internet-based, they use online searches to conduct "background checks" on potential partners (Ramirez et al., 2002). These searches can reveal quite a bit of information, increasing people's feelings of certainty (Carr & Walther, 2014). People also take advantage of social media as a passive strategy for gathering information (Fox & Anderegg, 2014). Scrolling through pictures and timelines inevitably produces personal information, including people's relationship status and sexual orientation.

Predicted Outcome Value Theory

Uncertainty reduction might be the root driver for how people manage ambiguous social interactions, but an alternative perspective, predicted outcome value theory, suggests uncertainty reduction is merely a mechanism to accomplish a different larger goal: rewarding social interactions. Recall from interdependence theory that dependency structures underlie social interactions (Kelley & Thibaut, 1978; Thibaut & Kelley, 1959); when you meet someone new, you simply do not yet know the structure of your interpersonal payoff matrix. Predicted outcome value theory suggests that people engage in uncertainty reduction behaviors to help them better predict future costs and rewards tied to a specific relationship (Sunnafrank, 1986, 1990). When initial conversations with a stranger yield projections of future positive outcomes, or when information seeking suggests rewards will outweigh costs, people like their interaction partners more, feel more similarity with them, and have more intimate conversations (Sunnafrank, 1988). As shown in Figure 5.5, positive first impressions engender the desire for future interactions; but if early-stage interactions create negative forecasts for the future, people are often ready to end those barely begun relationships. Unfortunately, some negative future forecasts are mismatched with the quality of the interaction itself. For example, even when an initial conversation is progressing quite nicely, people with low self-esteem often underestimate their partner's interest, perceiving fewer signals of acceptance (e.g., smiling; Cameron et al., 2010). This reminds us that individual difference variables impinge upon each step of relationship initiation.

Shyness and Social Anxiety

Interacting with a romantic interest, though necessary to initiate a relationship, often presents an intimidating barrier on the path toward a relationship. Although most people find relationship initiation anxiety-inducing (McNamara & Grossman, 1991), some people have more extreme reactions. **Shyness**, for example, can color how people think, feel, and behave during relationship initiation (Guerrero & Andersen, 2000). Individuals who are high in shyness suffer considerable inhibition in the presence of people they do not know well, feeling awkward, uncomfortable, or tense in these interactions (Cheek & Buss, 1981). People with social anxiety are also at a disadvantage during early initiation interactions. Social anxiety includes an intense concern about others' impressions and a strong fear of negative evaluation (Leary & Jongman-Sereno, 2014; Wenzel & Kashdan, 2008).

Critically, shyness and social anxiety both translate to poorer performance during relationship initiation. Shy people often exhibit poor social skills, including trouble starting and structuring conversations, a lack of composure during interactions, difficulty articulating thoughts, and an inability to detect if someone else is interested. Likewise, socially anxious people are prone to enact problematic behaviors during social encounters, such as fidgeting, not reciprocating smiles, or excessive reassurance seeking (Duran & Kelly, 1989; Heerey & Kring, 2007; Miller, 1995; Pilkonis, 1977). At the heart of it, both shyness and social anxiety appear to constrain individuals' ability to smoothly and effortlessly coordinate an interaction with a person they don't know well. They may, in fact, have the underlying social competence, and yet their in-the-moment performance suffers from internal physiological arousal, heightened sensitivity to even the possibility of rejection, and self-focus that renders negative judgments about how the interaction is going (Wenzel & Kashdan, 2008). Unfortunately, these difficulties have adverse effects on how others perceive them. People higher in social anxiety, for example, are generally less liked during attempts at romantic relationship initiation than those with lower social anxiety (Tissera et al., 2021). Problems during the early moments of a relationship may explain why shy people tend to enter relationships later than less shy people, and socially anxious people are less likely to be in romantic relationships than less socially anxious people (Asendorpf, 2000; Starr & Davila, 2015).

Online dating can help shy individuals overcome some of the psychological barriers between them and a relationship. When people date online, they have time to craft and re-draft messages and they need not simultaneously manage in-person non-verbals. The challenges that shy people experience engaging in self-disclosure and initiating relationships offline often disappear in the online context (Stritzke et al., 2004). Perhaps the advantages associated with online communication are why shy people and those with social anxiety are more likely to try online dating (Lenton-Brym et al., 2020; Whitty & Buchanan, 2009).

 DIVERSITY AND INCLUSION

Initiating Romantic Relationships and Autism Spectrum Disorder

Autism Spectrum Disorder (ASD) is a neurodevelopmental disorder that reflects deficits in social-emotional abilities and heightened rigidity, which might appear as repetitive behaviors, sensitivity to sensory input, or preferences for routines and sameness (American Psychological Association, 2013). The challenges associated with ASD often include interpersonal communication problems, which can impede individuals' ability to initiate romantic relationships (Girardi et al., 2020). When people with ASD engage in awkward or unusual behaviors, like poor eye contact or inappropriate smiling, others might assume that they are unmotivated to form social connections, but such assumptions are not necessarily accurate. The majority of high-functioning people with ASD desire to form romantic relationships (Jaswal & Akhtar, 2018; Strunz et al., 2017; Figure 5.6). Despite this motivation, people with ASD tend to report fewer opportunities to meet potential romantic partners and worry more than neurotypical adults that they may not find a future partner (Hancock et al., 2020).

Figure 5.6 A strong desire for love and companionship can motivate individuals with ASD to enter the confusing world of dating, a world made all the more intimidating by the challenges that come with ASD. To what extent can we apply models of relationship initiation based on neurotypical adults to the experiences of individuals with ASD? (Photo: Westend61 / Getty Images)

Both the desire for a romantic relationship and the struggle to find a partner emerge as themes in the Netflix television series, *Love on the Spectrum*. This original documentary captures the sometimes unique – and often universal – challenges that young adults with ASD encounter as they enter the dating world looking for love. We see the show's participants speak candidly of their relationship worries, their hopes, and their personal perspectives on what it is like to navigate early relationship development. Viewers witness tender first dates, uncertainties as relationships unfold, and unwavering devotion to the pursuit of love. From Michael's attempts to discern his compatibility with potential partners to Jayden's reflections on the challenges of decoding others' "hidden communication," much of *Love on the Spectrum* is familiar to anyone who has struggled with the confusion that is often inherent in dating. As reflected on the show, relationship initiation tends to progress more easily for individuals with ASD to the extent that they show more social and communication skill, and love is more apt to take flight when partners with ASD experience mutual liking, can provide support, and can meet each other's needs (Yew et al., 2021).

The Relationship Initiation Process

Now that we know key barriers that can inhibit people from initiating relationships, what is the typical process of moving from strangers – or friends – to romantic partners? Assuming there is a typical process, early theorists proposed stage models designed to break down the complexity of relationship formation into a neat sequence of presumed universal steps. These models simplify a fascinating interpersonal process, drawing our attention to critical psychological and behavioral elements. Consider social penetration theory (Altman & Taylor, 1973), for example. This approach begins with an orientation get-to-know-you phase, then moves to an information exchange phase, a negotiation of differences phase, and, finally, stable connection. Social disclosure is critical in this model, helping people become progressively more intimate; peeling off the layers of an onion, if you will. A different approach, the dual staircase model (Knapp, 1978; Knapp et al., 2013), builds off of social penetration theory, but maps out how relationships can escalate from "initiation" and "experimenting" (i.e., information seeking and testing compatibility) toward "integration" of self and partner, and "bonding" to form a couple identity (and also maps out how relationships de-escalate during breakup). As a final example of an early model, the premarital dyadic formation model (Lewis, 1972, 1973) highlights the social and situational forces that might encourage or discourage relationship formation. It suggests that partners first discover similarities, then develop rapport, engage in self-disclosure, assume roles, and, finally, form a partner identity.

As different as they are, each of these early models begins with strangers meeting and progresses toward intimacy. Each perspective also includes space for attraction, requires a back-and-forth process that emphasizes the interpersonal nature of relationship formation, and relies on communication for uncertainty reduction and building intimacy. A more modern stage model, developed by Bredow and colleagues (2008) and shown in Figure 5.7, describes these overarching steps. Let's consider these major steps in relationship initiation each in turn.

Stage 1: Appraisal of Initial Attraction

As described earlier in this chapter, relationship initiation begins even before attraction, with individuals' relationship motives coloring the attraction process (stage 1). These motives, and whether people act on these motives, are further shaped by culture, personality, demographics, and other background factors, such as situational context (Cunningham & Barbee, 2008). A college student, for instance, might desire casual hookups when they judge their peers as having good hookup experiences; and a married person might try not to notice attractive people and use self-control to resist initiation (e.g., Maner et al., 2009). In some cultures, individuals yield to family decisions in determining their romantic partners, removing their own motives or initial attraction from the equation (see discussion later in this chapter). When individuals themselves appraise initial attraction, their selectivity (i.e., whom they decide is sufficiently attractive) may derive not only from their motives, but also reflect aspects of self and situation, including those that we have mentioned previously, such as their sociosexuality, or fear of being single (e.g., Simpson & Gangestad, 1991; Spielmann et al., 2013). Thus, we cannot take for granted the importance of all that people bring with them and are experiencing in the lead up to relationship initiation: relationships never operate in a bubble and their start is no exception.

Stage 2: Decision to Make an Overture

Noticing and feeling attraction toward someone is generally considered a catalyst for deciding whether to make an overture (Bredow et al., 2008). Accordingly, this decision process marks stage 2 in Bredow's model. Whether a person decides to offer an overture is generally considered a joint effect of attraction and their expectation of acceptance, an effect that can be written out like this:

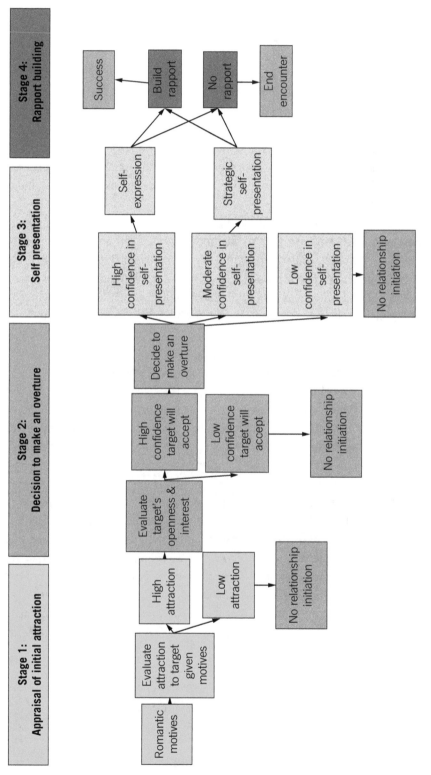

Figure 5.7 This four-stage model maps pathways to relationship initiation success and points where potential relationships are cut short. Where might shyness or social anxiety fit into this model? (Source: Used with permission of Taylor & Francis Group, LLC – Books, from Bredow et al. [2008], permission conveyed through Copyright Clearance Center, Inc.)

$$\mathbf{O} = f(\mathbf{A} \times \mathbf{P})$$

where O = making an overture, A = attraction, and P = probability of acceptance (Bredow et al., 2008). According to this equation, if rejection fear runs high, people might opt not to approach, even with strong romantic appeal; likewise, if a "yes" is a guarantee, this model contends that an overture will happen only if someone feels attraction. A meta-analysis of over 300 studies and over 5,000 participants supports the "A" in this equation: feeling attraction does in fact predict the use of direct initiation behaviors (attempts to initiate contact; e.g., talking, standing close), and, to a lesser extent, indirect initiation behaviors (attempts to be noticed; e.g., eye gaze, smiling; Montoya et al., 2018). Akin to the "P" in the above equation, situational and personal factors, such as anticipating rejection (i.e., judging a low probability of acceptance), shyness, and perceived social norms, can weaken the link between attraction and direct action (Montoya et al., 2018; Montoya & Sloat, 2019). Interestingly, however, meta-analysis suggests anticipating rejection does not dampen the link between attraction and indirect initiation behaviors (Montoya et al., 2018). In other words, if a person expects a tough audience, they might not approach, but instead might look, smile, and laugh, behaviors that signal interest without making oneself vulnerable to rejection. Perhaps this reflects a fundamental pro-relationship bias underlying our relationship-related decisions (Joel & MacDonald, 2021). As much as rejection concerns might have an inhibiting effect on initiation attempts, other strong motivators (e.g., the need to belong, the desire for intimacy) are compelling people toward relationships. Even in the face of likely rejection, we may yet take the chance.

Direct Overtures

Suppose someone decides to take a direct approach to initiate a relationship. The boldest of the bold might simply ask, outright, for a date or for sex. If such directness seems absurd, consider the seminal field studies on direct overtures conducted in the late 1970s, early 1980s, and 1990s (Clark, 1990; Clark & Hatfield, 1989). Moderately attractive research assistants approached unsuspecting strangers on campus and asked them to "go out tonight," to "come over to my apartment," or to "go to bed with me." As shown in Figure 5.8 (Panel A), men were generally agreeable to these offers, and over 70 percent were game for sex. Women were less agreeable to men's solicitations, and a whopping zero accepted the invitation for sex. Zero! This pattern replicated in the context of a party, suggesting the campus environment did not drive the findings (Baranowski & Hecht, 2015). From an evolutionary perspective, direct romantic or sexual overtures solve a key adaptive problem for men (e.g., access to partners), but for women, their problems (e.g., need for resources) persist and the costs of casual sex with moderately attractive strangers are considerable. This framework does a nice job of capturing why direct overtures work for women, but not for men.

A more recent online replication included men and women of different sexual orientations (though the sample still favored heterosexually identified individuals) and manipulated the attractiveness of the proposer (Edlund et al., 2021). The same biological sex-linked pattern emerged (see Figure 5.8, Panel B). Men responded more favorably to a stranger's direct request to go on a date, visit their apartment, or have sex, compared to women. Note that nearly a third of women in this study accepted a direct invitation for sex. This high rate of

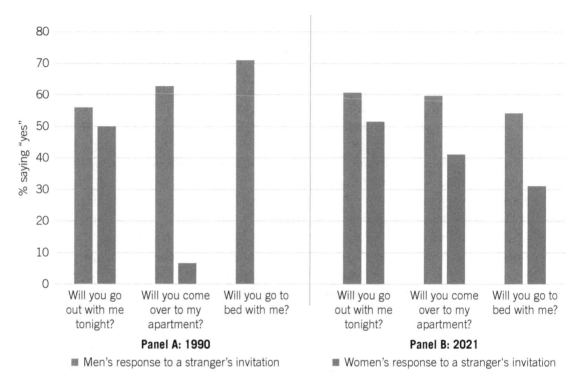

Figure 5.8 Seminal research on receptivity to direct sexual offers suggests women are (much!) less receptive than men (Panel A); but more recent research shows a less dramatic gender difference (Panel B). How would you respond if a stranger solicited you? On what would your answer depend? (Source: Drawn based on data from Clark [1990]; Clark & Hatfield [1989] [Panel A]; and Edlund et al. [2021] [Panel B])

acceptance may have been observed because data were collected online or perhaps because of a high number of highly attractive proposers. Consistent with a previous replication (Schützwohl et al., 2009), the physical attractiveness of the proposer was linked to women's agreement, a nod to the "good genes" that women might prioritize for short-term affairs. Also, and unsurprisingly, unrestricted sociosexuality was associated with greater receptivity to direct offers for sex (Edlund et al., 2021). A look at sexual minorities' acceptance or rejection of direct offers for sex supports an evolutionary story of biological sex-based variability, but with some interesting nuance (Matsick et al., 2021). Gay men tend to be more receptive of casual sex offers from other gay men than lesbian women are from other lesbian women, with both gay men and lesbian women reporting similar rates of receptivity to bisexual proposers.

If explicitly asking a stranger for a date or for sex is not your go-to plan, what other direct overtures might work? Here, we turn to pick-up lines. Pick-up lines, sometimes called **opening gambits**, generally fall into one of three categories: direct lines (not as direct as asking for sex; e.g., "Talk to me. I'd like to get to know you"), innocuous lines (e.g., "Hi there. How's it going?"), and flippant lines (e.g., "Are your legs tired? Because you've been running through my dreams all night"; Kleinke et al., 1986). In different-sex relationship initiation, men tend to favor women's direct lines, such as when women ask men out, give out their phone number, or suggest a date (Wade et al., 2009). Men prefer this directness to both innocuous lines and flippant lines (Fisher et al., 2020). Women also prefer directness, ranking approaches like using third-party introductions ("Meet my buddy Mike!"), friendly "hi-my-name-is" introductions, and direct compliments as more effective and more appropriate than flippant pick-up lines

(Weber et al., 2010). In general, women tend to judge flippant lines as ineffective and inappropriate (Cunningham, 1989; Kleinke et al., 1986; Weber et al., 2010).

Perhaps flippant lines fail because flippant humor gives the impression of low intelligence and low trustworthiness (Senko & Fyffe, 2010). When people use humor that signals desirable partner traits (e.g., intelligence and warmth), they have better luck. For example, people tend to judge attractive strangers using affiliative (i.e., warm, witty) humor as more favorable long-term partners than those who use negative (i.e., sarcastic, mean) humor (DiDonato et al., 2013). Likewise, men telling sexist jokes or people whose opening gambits include "dirty" humor are seen as less desirable long-term partners relative to those using benign or clean humor (Betz & DiDonato, 2020; Medlin et al., 2018). Contemporary relationship science suffers from a noticeable dearth in research on the opening gambits that might work or misfire in same-sex relationships, but if the existing findings generalize, direct lines and high-quality humor may support same-sex relationship building as well (this is an open empirical question).

Indirect Overtures

Instead of bravely introducing yourself to an attractive stranger or candidly saying you want "something more" to a friend, people may choose to play it cool, and make indirect overtures. Indirect overtures, with their subtlety and ambiguity, involve less risk than bold moves. They can be ignored with no embarrassment and are reasonably deniable ("I wasn't winking at her, I had a bug in my eye!"). In different-sex relationship initiation, men typically make the first *direct* overture, but usually only after women signal their interest first *indirectly*; indeed, women's non-verbal solicitation behaviors play an important first step in the relationship initiation (Moore, 2010).

Women indirectly communicate interest by using their eyes to make short darting glances and to make sweeping glances of the room; they fixate their gaze on targets of interest; they toss their heads and flip their hair; they smile and laugh; and if the context affords the opportunity, they perform solitary dances (Moore, 1985). Critically, the frequency with which women enact these pre-contact indirect overtures predicts the likelihood that a desired target will approach them, underscoring their important role in the earliest moments of initiation. More recent research suggests women are adept at offering a distinctive facial expression to deliberately express their romantic interest (and men perceive it as such) comprised of a turned head angled downward, a slight smile, and direct eye gaze (Haj-Mohamadi et al., 2021), such as shown in Figure 5.9. Men, in turn, might respond with their own pre-contact non-verbal behaviors, which can enhance their ability of being accepted. Men who engage in more short and direct glances and use non-verbal behaviors that show their social dominance (maintain an open posture, giving non-reciprocated touches to other) tend to have more success when they do eventually offer a direct overture (Renninger et al., 2004).

Figure 5.9 A downward-turned slightly tilted head, along with direct gaze and a smile, can suggest romantic interest. What other non-verbal behaviors encourage flirting? (Photo: quavondo / iStock / Getty Images Plus)

Stage 3: Self-Presentation

Once an overture has been made and received, the next key task is self-presentation, the art of impression management (Bredow et al., 2008). Leading up to this moment, people may have already engaged in strategic self-presentation through their dress, make-up, or hair styles, potentially signaling their romantic motives (Durante et al., 2008; Hendrie et al., 2020); but at this juncture of first interaction, people have a new opportunity to shape impressions and convey interest. As shown in Figure 5.7, different levels of confidence might lead people to adopt a more authentic representation of self or a more strategic one. The latter is purposefully designed to persuade someone of one's own desirable and attractive qualities (Bredow et al., 2008).

When people engage in strategic self-presentation, they intentionally emphasize and de-emphasize some aspects of themselves based on what they think the other might value (e.g., Goffman, 1959). Any intentional act with an underlying message, from costly signaling to casually mentioning that you hit the gym regularly, is designed to highlight what you have to offer. Presenting a "best self" is different from weaving lies; indeed, staying close to the truth is particularly important for people pursuing long-term relationships. As any fan of romantic comedies knows, if lies told to initiate a relationship are later uncovered, they can compromise trust and threaten a relationship's development. Individuals with short-term sexual goals, however, may be willing to manipulate their self-presentation with lies or deceit in order to move the relationship forward (Birnbaum, Iluz, & Reis, 2020). Tinder users, for instance, report engaging in more authentic self-presentation when looking for long-term relationships compared to those who are seeking sexual encounters (e.g., hooking-up) who adopt more deceptive means of attracting a partner (Ranzini & Lutz, 2017). Thus, whether people present themselves authentically, strategically, or utterly deceptively may reflect underlying goals. Visit the *In the News* box to see how frequently, and in what ways, people present themselves inaccurately when online dating.

 IN THE NEWS

Online Deception: The Harmless and the Harmful

Can you trust what you read in an online dating profile or in the online communication that follows? Yes and no. Deception occurs with surprising frequency in online dating, with some evidence suggesting eight out of every ten people knowingly present at least one piece of false information; however, these lies tend to be merely mild deviations from the truth (Toma et al., 2008). People might slightly misrepresent their weight or height, trying to present a desirable view of themselves while also anticipating an eventual in-person meeting.

On the extreme end of deception, **catfishing** refers to the insidious act of creating a false identity or impersonating someone else and then initiating an exclusively online relationship with an unsuspecting person (Campbell & Parker, 2022; Paat & Markham, 2021). While most catfishing likely ends with the act of deception (and the psychological aftermath for the victim), some people catfish with the goal of stealing personal information and/or money. In

2021, the local *ABC* news station in Houston, Texas, reported an instance of significant criminal catfishing. One of their residents was arrested for impersonating superstar Bruno Mars on Instagram and courting a 63-year-old woman who was looking for companionship. She believed he was really Bruno Mars (shown in Figure 5.10) and that they were in a relationship. When he eventually asked for some help covering tour expenses, she wrote out checks for $100,000. This type of dramatic catfishing may not occur frequently, but it underscores the power of deception in the vulnerable context of relationship initiation.

The risk of catfishing, along with other risks such as persistent unwanted communication, unwelcomed explicit photos, name calling, and threats (risks particularly commonly experienced by women and sexual minorities; Anderson et al., 2020), perhaps explains why nearly half of US individuals (46 percent) say that online dating is "not too safe" or "not at all safe."

Figure 5.10 Bruno Mars earns high marks on attractive qualities. Might some people who are seeking relationships be more susceptible to deception than others? Why? (Photo: Ethan Miller / Getty Images Entertainment)

Stage 4: Rapport Building

Self-presentation in face-to-face interactions is part of a more fundamental task: rapport building. **Rapport** reflects a satisfying harmony and easy synchrony within a social interaction, the kind we see from Finn and Poe almost immediately in *Star Wars: The Force Awakens*. Rapport is grounded in mutual attentiveness, coordination, and positivity (Tickle-Degnen & Rosenthal, 1990). As shown in Bredow et al.'s (2008) model, the successful building of rapport is not an automatic outcome of relationship initiation attempts, but people often enter these early interactions primed for rapport. If people feel attracted to someone, they tend to engage in warmer, more sociable, and more open behaviors, which then elicit positive interpersonal behaviors from their interaction partner and increase their liking (Curtis & Miller, 1986; Snyder et al., 1977). In other words, attraction begets liking which begets attraction. This reciprocal process is anchored to self-disclosure, the sharing of personal information to a responsive listener (Reis & Shaver, 1988). Self-disclosure is a key mechanism for generating rapport. For a variety of reasons (e.g., disinterest, shyness, traditional gender role orientation, avoidant attachment), people might differ in their degree of self-disclosure during a first meeting, but people also differ in their proficiency at eliciting others' self-disclosures. You know that person who seems to hear people's entire life story whenever they're on an airplane? When people meet someone new, some people are **high openers** who bring out others' disclosures by displaying attentiveness and by asking

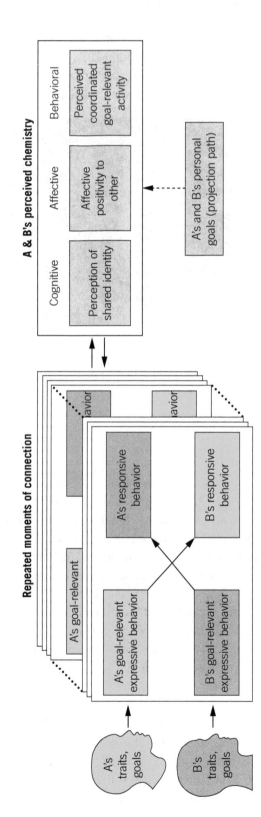

Figure 5.11 The interpersonal model of chemistry describes a special dynamic that can emerge between people. When Person A and Person B express personal information (as they are motivated to based on their own trait and goals) and that disclosure is met with responsive behavior from the other, perceived chemistry results. Projecting one's own goals, beliefs, or thoughts, though not necessary, can further encourage this process. When was the last time you felt chemistry with someone? (Source: Reis, Regan, & Lyubomirsky [2022])

questions (Miller et al., 1983). Thus, rapport is a function of individual differences as well as interpersonal processes.

The experience of rapport is akin to chemistry, which describes a unique relationship-level connection that can emerge between people and cannot be predicted by individual characteristics alone (Reis, Regan, & Lyubomirsky, 2022). Chemistry feels special and singular, and is more apt to happen when you believe that your interaction partner's interests are narrowly focused only on you (Eastwick et al., 2007). Some people recognize chemistry as an instant connection that comes with mutual enjoyment and attraction, love, reciprocal candor, and similarity; people also often say chemistry has an indescribable component to it (Campbell et al., 2018). Certainly, some people, like Finn with both Poe and Jannah, experience chemistry from the first moment they meet, but in most cases, chemistry likely unfolds over time through repeated interactions.

Consider the interpersonal chemistry model, shown in Figure 5.11 (Reis, Regan, & Lyubomirsky, 2022). This model suggests that chemistry develops when social interactions take on a pleasurable and coordinated dynamic in which openness is repeatedly met with responsiveness. One partner discloses personal details or feelings (like when Jannah reveals she was a stormtrooper) and the other responds with understanding, appreciation, and support (like when Finn jumps up to face her, leans forward, and with strong eye contact nods and shows he understands). This dynamic feels validating, promotes intimacy, and can increase sexual desire (Birnbaum & Reis, 2012; Laurenceau et al., 1998; Reis et al., 2004). The expression of mutual feelings and similar experiences (like when Finn discloses his own history as a stormtrooper) also generate interpersonal chemistry. From this perspective, interpersonal chemistry includes: (1) perceptions of similarity, complementarity, and shared goals; (2) positive emotions that support sustained attraction; and (3) coordinated behaviors that promote a feeling of "us."

Flirting

Flirtation – the art of displaying your own desirable qualities while subtly assessing the interest of the target of your flirtation – is an excellent strategy for developing rapport. Flirtation at this juncture can include some of the non-verbal behaviors that we discussed in the pre-contact stage (e.g., smiling, eye gaze), as well as additional flirtatious behavior. While some religious cultures do not permit this type of romantic or sexually suggestive interaction, in many cultures, flirtation is a normative part of relationship initiation. How well people navigate the back-and-forth of a flirtatious encounter might seem like a "natural" ability, but it is better represented as a skill. People even engage in practice flirting, where they flirt for fun, with no romantic motives, to strengthen their skills (Henningsen, 2004). This may be worth the effort: stronger flirting skills is linked to greater relationship initiation success and people who are involuntarily single often report a self-perceived lack of flirting skills (Apostolou, 2021a; Apostolou, Papadopoulou, Christofi, & Vrontis, 2019).

Within Western cultures, not all flirting is the same in its effectiveness. In different-sex conversations, men tend to find women's flirtatious behaviors most effective when they are sexually suggestive, whereas women see men's flirtation attempts as most effective when they convey commitment, caring, and exclusivity (Wade & Feldman, 2016; Wade & Slemp, 2015). Five flirting styles, shown in Table 5.3, have emerged in contemporary relationship science (Hall et al., 2010). Which best describes yours?

Table 5.3 Common flirting styles

Flirting style	Description
Physical style	Being comfortable using behaviors to show interest, expressing sexual interest confidently
Sincere style	Engaging in intimacy building; feeling comfortable approaching others and initiating conversation
Playful style	Focusing on having fun and creating enjoyment
Traditional style	Follows gender-based courtship norms, for example, men initiate
Polite style	Prioritizes civility and rules

People take different approaches to flirting. Of these listed, physical, sincere, and playful styles tend to predict the most relationship initiation success.

Source: Contents based on information in Hall et al. (2010).

Skillful flirts also tend to reveal their intelligence as they flirt, are cheerful and respectful, and show strong romantic interest (Apostolou & Christoforou, 2020; Li et al., 2020). Confidence and courage, physical attractiveness, and a bit of mystery also tend to support effective flirtation. As this suggests, flirting is a complex behavior. Indeed, in the evaluative context of relationship initiation, skillful flirts juggle self-promotion goals all-the-while trying to evaluate the person they're speaking to, an impressive feat. Happily, the lesser skilled of us have other paths to support our relationship-building attempts (see the "Relationship Initiation in Context" section, below).

RESEARCHER SPOTLIGHT: T. Joel Wade, PhD

Figure 5.12 Dr. Wade is a Professor of Psychology and Affiliated Faculty of Black Critical Studies at Bucknell University. (Photo courtesy of T. Joel Wade, PhD.)

How did you come to be a research psychologist?

I started out with an intended undergraduate major in Theatre. But, I decided very soon after taking an introductory psychology course that I wanted to major in Psychology. I ended up falling in love with Social Psychology. My undergraduate training at University of North Carolina (UNC) at Chapel Hill led to a love of implementing research. When it came time for graduation, I discussed the possibility of pursuing graduate study with my oldest brother, who was beginning his academic career as a Philosophy Professor. I decided to apply for graduate study in Social Psychology, and UNC-Chapel Hill accepted me. In graduate school, I was also able to receive extensive training in statistical analysis via the Quantitative Psychology program.

How did you come to study romantic relationships, particularly relationship initiation?

One of the first research projects I completed as a graduate student was a project examining how members of interracial couples who possessed varying levels of attractiveness and status were perceived. The findings from that study led to additional research on attraction. While doing background reading regarding attraction and relationships, I discovered that there was a dearth of research focused on aspects of relationship initiation, such as flirting, pick-up lines, etc., and I set out to try to help reduce that dearth.

What do you love about what you do?

One of the things I love about what I do is that I get to make initial discoveries, and on some occasions those discoveries influence other researchers to do additional research. I also love that I get to collaborate with other scientists who have similar interests.

On which areas of relationship initiation would you like to see more empirical attention?

I would love to see more empirical attention focusing on relationship initiation among people who are non-heterosexual, among non-White populations, among sexually fluid individuals, and across cultures. Some of that is occurring at present. I hope it will continue and expand.

Interpersonal Coordination

So, what does flirting look like to the nosy observer? If you were at a party and spying on two people from afar, would you be able to tell if it's "on," as they say? A major clue for your detective work could be found in their synchrony or matching of their behaviors. Consider the couple in Figure 5.13: both are leaning against the wall, heads turned, both have one hand relaxed and the other engaged, and both are smiling. They look like they like each other, and they probably do (Grahe & Bernieri, 1999). Interpersonal coordination refers to the behavioral, physiological, emotional, or cognitive harmony that occurs between two interaction partners (Bernieri & Rosenthal, 1991; Mayo & Gordon, 2020). As shown in meta-analytic work, interpersonal coordination has well-established positive downstream consequences, such as enhancing prosociality (Vicaria & Dickens, 2016).

A broad concept, interpersonal coordination can be subdivided into interpersonal synchrony, which focuses on coordinated timing of similar or complementary behaviors, and mimicry, which reflects a non-conscious mirroring of behavior, language, emotion, or facial expression (and is less focused on timing; Chartrand & van Baaren, 2009; Duffy & Chartrand, 2015). Both interpersonal synchrony and mimicry are natural and ubiquitous parts of human social interaction. Interpersonal synchrony is linked to social bonding and feelings of affiliation (Hove & Risen, 2009; Mogan et al., 2017), and mimicry is likewise part of the way we show rather than tell

Figure 5.13 Do the two people in this picture like each other? How do you know? (Photo: Thomas Barwick)

someone how we feel about interacting with them. We mirror their body posture, gestures, and mannerisms non-verbally; and we reflect back, repeat, and echo words used verbally.

Single people unwittingly mirror the behaviors of attractive potential love interests, and this mimicry is dampened for people already in committed relationships (Farley, 2014; Karremans & Verwijmeren, 2008). This reflects a key pattern: we mimic people we like and with whom we have rapport, and in turn, mimicry helps to build rapport and chemistry (Chartrand & Bargh, 1999; Reis, Regan, & Lyubomirsky, 2022; Stel & Van Knippenberg, 2008). Simply having an affiliation goal, such as we might see in a romantic initiation scenario, is sufficient to launch a cascade of unconscious non-verbal mimicry, which can help promote a desired person's interest (Lakin & Chartrand, 2003). Language matching seems to have a similar link to positive social perceptions. A speed-dating study revealed that dyads who exhibited similarity in language style (e.g., aligned use of personal pronouns, conjunctions, prepositions, negations, etc.) were more interested in seeing each other again than those couples who did not match on this nuanced measure of conversational style (Ireland et al., 2011).

Critiques of Stage Models

Stage models, like the contemporary model offered by Bredow and colleagues (2008), help us understand relationship initiation by pointing our attention to key elements that often shape the earliest moments of relationship development. This reductionist approach makes stage theories intuitively appealing, yet, they have important limitations, including a lack of empirical support and a want for specificity (Baxter & Montgomery, 1996; Mongeau, 2008). Stage models also typically assume relationships unfold linearly, when not all relationships follow an easy stepwise progression. On-again, off-again relationships, for instance, are a clear example of a common type of relationship with a non-linear trajectory.

Additionally, stage models have typically focused on the formation of different-sex monogamous relationships within Western culture. These models may yet provide insight into the unfolding of same-sex, polyamorous, and non-Western relationships, but this is a point of inquiry that still requires empirical substantiation. Unique relationships may have unique stages. For instance, transgender individuals, and people with stigmatized conditions (e.g., mental illness, sexually transmitted diseases), may experience a self-disclosure stage; people initiating non-monogamous relationships may experience a dialogue step involving discussion among existing partners; and relationship initiation in cultures where families play a more prominent role may feature a partner approval stage. Lastly, the narrow framework of stage models is also critiqued for not doing justice to the diverse ways relationships develop in the real world. For instance, these models typically begin with strangers meeting and can presume marriage goals (e.g., Lewis, 1972, 1973), which reflect outdated norms. In reality, there are multiple common paths to relationships, as described in the next section.

Divergent Paths to Relationships

How many romantic relationships do you know that did not begin between perfect strangers? People often share a relational history prior to beginning a romantic relationship. Friends, colleagues, ex-lovers, people pretending they are "just friends," and everyone in between regularly transition into and out of committed relationships or casual, primarily sexual relationships. Unlike the "two-strangers-meet" scenario emphasized in stage models, authentic relationship initiation is dizzyingly complex: relationships emerge from a host of social relations and no one path captures everyone's story.

From Friendships to Committed Relationships

Although research often overlooks friendship as the starting point for romantic relationships, recent meta-analysis suggests most relationships (two-thirds) spring from friendships and that friendship is regularly nominated as the ideal way to begin love (Stinson et al., 2022). Friendship-first relationships are especially common among same-sex partners and represent a common courtship script for lesbian women (Rose & Zand, 2002; Rose et al., 1993). Although research over-represents heterosexual partnerships in its study of love sprung from friendships, its key themes translate well: when friends could be partners, how do they navigate attraction, desire, and uncertainty in their relationship?

Defining the nature of their emotional bond and managing sexual attraction are two primary challenges for friends who could be, but are not currently, romantically involved with each other (Halatsis & Christakis, 2009; O'Meara, 1989). Typically, the primary bond between friends is feeling connected and close, yet, friends can also feel romantic and sexual attraction to each other, either mutually or asymmetrically (Bleske-Rechek et al., 2012). Possibly because it is a low-risk strategy of gauging another's potential interest, people flirt with friends with whom they desire a romantic relationship, and they also invest more in the friendship, giving more energy and seeking more time alone with that person (Guerrero & Chavez, 2005; Weger & Emmett, 2009). Friendships can often survive one friend's unreciprocated attempt to express love or attraction, but sometimes attempts to leave the "friendzone" can irreparably alter the nature of the friendship and even end it (Halatsis & Christakis, 2009). Accordingly, bids to escalate a relationship are risky. When the bold make their move, their friends are more likely to respond favorably toward shifting to a long-term relationship if they also feel attraction, are single, see more rewards than costs to the idea of becoming partners, and judge the friendship to be of a high quality (Akbulut & Weger, 2016).

An underlying assumption in the above discussion is that friends are available to date, but people can also harbor romantic feelings for friends who are already in relationships (regardless of their own relationship status). As such, friendships can be a strategic springboard for people with **mate poaching** goals (Mogilski & Wade, 2013). Mate poaching is the elegant art of stealing someone away from an existing relationship for a long-term relationship or a sexual liaison; in its strictest form, the poacher knows very clearly that yes, their target is already in a committed relationship (Davies et al., 2007, 2019; Schmitt & Buss, 2001). Mate poaching might seem like an insidious starting point to love, but it is actually quite common: cross-cultural data culled from fifty-three nations shows that a large percentage of both men (57.1 percent across nations) and women (43.6 percent) have made mate-poaching attempts in pursuit of long-term relationships and short-term relationships (56.9 and 34.9 percent, respectively; Schmitt, 2004). Mate poaching tactics are fantastically devious. While strangers or acquaintances can poach, becoming friends with an ulterior motive can help someone successfully weasel their way into an unsuspecting target's affections, sidestepping some of the risks (Mogilski & Wade, 2013).

Poachers disguising themselves as friends might strategically occupy their target's time, and strategically denigrate their target's partner (Schmitt & Buss, 2001). Such effort has an effect; poachers' targets can experience a decline in their commitment to their existing partner as they start to feel more desire for the poacher (Lemay & Wolf, 2016). Friendships, therefore, can launch long-term (or short-term) relationships even when the friends are not themselves single.

From Friendships to Sexual Relationships

Leaving mate poaching aside, many friends simply begin engaging in sexual activity with each other while maintaining that "we're not in a relationship." Friends are not only convenient sexual partners, but we trust them and feel comfortable with them (Bisson & Levine, 2009), making them potentially more desirable sexual partners than strangers (who are our partners in the classic definition of a hookup). One study found that approximately half of college students have engaged in sexual activity with at least one friend (Afifi & Faulkner, 2000). In fact, some people may unwittingly pursue and maintain certain friendships as an evolved response to reproductive challenges. Consistent with evolutionary perspectives, heterosexual men, more than heterosexual women, value different-sex friendships, particularly with physically attractive women, for their possible relationship opportunities (Lewis et al., 2011).

People (especially men) are more open to accepting a friends-with-benefits (FWB) overture if they feel physical attraction to their friend, they see the benefits of a FWB arrangement, judge the friendship as slightly lower in quality, and are more sexually permissive (Akbulut & Weger, 2016). Accepting a booty-call is likewise most strongly based on physical attraction, good timing for the call, interest in and availability for sex, and whether people have a prior relationship with the person (Jonason, Li, & Cason, 2009). Transitioning from a platonic friendship to an uncommitted sexual relationship introduces questions and new uncertainty into an existing relationship, though people rarely talk through these concerns (Bisson & Levine, 2009). Instead, people may work to keep the relationship low commitment through their actions, such as carefully controlling how often they communicate with their FWB partner or leaving after sex in a booty-call relationship (Collins & Horn, 2019; Jonason et al., 2011). Regulating commitment in these relationships is important because even as people might want emotional connection, people who pursue FWB relationships are primarily looking for sex and typically want to keep the relationship simple (Stein et al., 2019).

From Primarily Sexual to Long-Term Relationships

Recall from earlier in this chapter that people often start casual sexual relationships, like hookups, wanting them to become committed long-term relationships (Thorpe & Kuperberg, 2021; Weitbrecht & Whitton, 2020). Even as some people work to avoid "catching feelings" or having an emotional response to a hookup partner (Paul, 2013), sometimes these relationships beget love. About 20 percent of hookups and 20 percent of sexual encounters between friends transition into romantic relationships (Afifi & Faulkner, 2000; Weitbrecht & Whitton, 2017). When attempts to transition from friends-with-benefits (or booty-call buddies) to committed partners fail, they typically fail because the other partner is only looking for sex, doesn't want a long-term relationship, or sees better partner options elsewhere (Jonason, Li, & Cason, 2009).

Relationship Initiation in Context

The coming together of romantic partners is rarely a story about only the romantic partners themselves. Rather, how our relationships begin is shaped by the people around us, sometimes unconsciously, sometimes informally, and other times quite explicitly. Qualitative data, for example, show how young African American women's close friends help socialize them on notions of who, when, and how to date (Harper et al., 2004). At the other end of the lifespan, mid- and late-life adults often take the online dating leap only after being encouraged by friends, co-workers, and others in their social networks (McWilliams & Barrett, 2014). Thus, friends create mental maps for us on what is appropriate for relationship initiation and what we can or (in their view) should do in pursuit of relationships. They teach us the "rules" of relationship initiation through advice, letting us observe their own experiences, gossiping about others, and even direct sanctions at times (Baxter et al., 2001). For instance, friends might shape our views on who is an ineligible partner and caution against too much sexual or emotional commitment too soon. Women, particularly attractive women, place a premium on the romantic advice they receive from gay men, whose counsel they value because they can assume it comes with no ulterior motives of sexual interest or intrasexual competition (Russell et al., 2017, 2018). Social network approval, as will be discussed further in the next chapter, plays an ongoing important role in a relationship's development.

Our social networks are instrumental in connecting us with partners, an idea that is readily apparent in families who practice arranged marriages. Yet, even when people self-select partners, third parties play a more prominent role in our relationship initiations than typically noticed (Clark et al., 1999). In first-meeting recollections, 30 percent of different-sex couples and 20 percent of same-sex couples report being introduced by a third party, such as a friend or family member (Custer et al., 2008). Friends help us strategically navigate the sometimes stressful challenge of approaching people we like and avoiding people we don't, tasks subsumed under the umbrella of cooperative courtship (Ackerman & Kenrick, 2009). If you're familiar with the term "wingman," then you already know a bit about cooperate courtship. Friends readily and strategically help each other gain access to new partners, and (equally critically) help each other avoid undesirable potential partners. Courtship is thus not a solitary endeavor. This is consistent with the idea that we consider friends' opinions when judging potential partners. The opinions of parents (a little bit) and friends (a lot, particularly for individuals considering same-sex partners) can influence our early dating decisions (Blair & Pukall, 2015; Wright & Sinclair, 2012). With whom we progress to have a relationship may, therefore, be a function of our own interest, as well as the ever-present influence of others.

Failure to Launch: Initiation Gone Wrong

To move from initial attraction to an established relationship typically means traveling through a fragile, tenuous period of time peppered with opportunities for initiation derailment. As we know, many people emerge from this uncertain space into established relationships, but one study (see the Article Spotlight) that followed the changing romantic interests of single individuals over time suggests that the majority of could-be relationships (62 percent) never materialize (Eastwick et al., 2022). Why not? Perhaps the initiator never made a "move" or did so poorly, maybe interest waned, or perhaps the initiation attempt was rejected.

ARTICLE SPOTLIGHT

How Often Are Relationships Successfully Initiated?

One of the best ways to learn about a temporally bound process, such as relationship initiation, is to observe it unfold over time. Eastwick, Joel, Carswell, Molden, Finkel, and Blozis (2022) did just that when they assessed relationship attraction in real time to determine how often "could-be" relationships become actual relationships. Their sample of 208 first-year college students completed an initial battery of questionnaires and then, every three weeks for a total of seven months, these participants nominated two people with whom they wanted to form a romantic relationship. Participants could keep or change their nominees at any time, and answered a variety of questions about all nominees, including how much romantic interest they felt toward those individuals. Participants only rarely became sexual partners with the individuals they nominated, and they became romantic partners even less often (see Figure 5.14). Sixty-seven percent of participants reported some physical contact (i.e., kissing or other sexual activities) with a nominee over the seven months, whereas only 38 percent reported having formed a dating relationship.

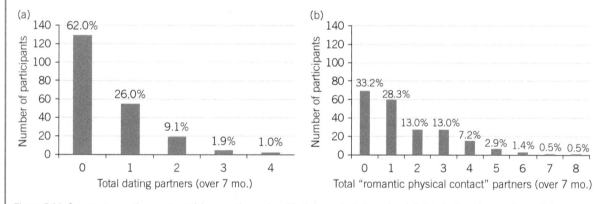

Figure 5.14 Over seven months, most people's romantic sparks with their nominated crushes failed to ignite: 62 percent reported zero dating partners and 33 percent reported no romantic physical-contact partners. You're not alone if your romantic interests lead nowhere. (Source: Eastwick et al. [2022])

Further, Eastwick and colleagues analyzed their data using machine learning – a "big data" approach focused on predictive accuracy, that is, determining the strongest and most reliable predictors of a particular outcome. Machine learning achieves this goal by using one data set to generate a statistical model (like a recipe that seems to work) and then using a new data set to test its model's accuracy (trying to reproduce the recipe). Eastwick and colleagues specifically used random forest modeling, an approach that involves sequentially segmenting data into branches using randomly selected predictors and a series of binary if-then decisions to produce decision trees. Data might be segmented by relationship status (single, not single), then by attachment style (secure, not secure), then by physical attractiveness measured on a 1 to 7 scale (below 5, 5 or above). As observations move through the decision trees, the algorithm "learns" which branches and leaves are most effective, resulting in an optimized model of the data. For example, a machine-learning algorithm using the random forest approach may identify the unique combination of one person's lightsaber skills plus another person's Jedi mindset to produce the greatest likelihood of a relationship forming or relationship attraction increasing.

In the actual study, results revealed that partner traits and the participant–partner dynamic explained 36 percent of variability in romantic interest. Participants' own traits, like sociosexuality, were somewhat less predictive (12 percent) of romantic interest and added little predictive help (between 0 and 3.5 percent) beyond that accounted for by the partner constructs. People were not uniquely pulled toward individuals who fit their stated partner preferences, reminiscent of a growing body of research showing that romantic interest is difficult to predict from prior-stated ideal partner preferences (Eastwick et al., 2022; Joel et al., 2017; Sparks et al., 2020). Additionally, findings indicated that neither partner characteristics, the participant–partner dynamic, nor one's own characteristics had any ability to explain change in romantic interest over time. When attraction grows versus fades is currently unpredictable, suggesting a need for additional research in this area.

Rejection

Rejecting some initiation attempts is often necessary to maximize your relational outcomes, but it is not easy. Rejecters balance the goals of unambiguously communicating "no," while also managing how they appear to others and protecting the initiator's self-image (Dillard, 2013; Tong & Walther, 2011). They consider cultural norms (what's appropriate here?), aspects of their immediate situation (are friends watching?), and whether they wish to preserve their current relationship with the initiator (if they have one). Unlike being the "rejectee," rejecters lack a clear cultural script on how to behave (e.g., "Do I need to be aloof or should I be friendly?"; Baumeister & Dhavale, 2012). Not an easy task!

Thankfully, kindness reigns in rejection. People might say they would readily reject undesirable partners, but in actual interactions, they feel other-oriented concern and care, and they are more willing to tolerate offers by unattractive or incompatible partners than they expect (Joel et al., 2014). When rejecters do reject, they often hide their real reasons and instead offer explanations that are impersonal, uncontrollable, and unstable (Folkes, 1982), such as the classic rebuff, "So sorry, I'm working this weekend." This refusal helps the rejecter maintain a positive self-presentation and lets the initiator "save face." Along with kind explanations, rejecters often bolster their refusals with politeness both in person and online. They offer apologies ("I'm so sorry"), appreciation ("I'm so flattered . . ."), concern ("Are you ok?"), encouragement ("You're such a good guy!") and statements that show interest in future interactions ("We can still hang out"; Tong & Walther, 2011). Of course, kindness can be misinterpreted as offering hope, which is not the rejecter's goal. Rejecters want to be kind, but they do not want to "lead someone on," or encourage affections they have no intent of returning (Baumeister et al., 1993). So, while rejecters might begin with gentle attempts, if the message is not received, they might resort to increasingly obvious and direct methods of rejection, such as walking way, avoiding, or ignoring unwanted suitors (Ackerman & Kenrick, 2009; De Becker, 1997; Goodboy & Brann, 2010; Moore, 1998).

People might also engage in deceptive rejection strategies like giving out fake numbers, saying they are already in a relationship, or pretending they need to answer their phone (Goodboy & Brann, 2010). In different-sex courtship, women may use deceptive rejection strategies, thinking that they will be less offending to men than direct statements; however, men often characterize deceptive rejections as affronts to their masculinity (Stratmoen et al.,

2020). This is a compelling point because rejecters are motivated to limit offending initiators, not only out of empathy, but to pre-empt adverse behavioral reactions to a rejection. Men, particularly those with strong masculine honor beliefs and/or social dominance orientation, are more likely to react with hostility to romantic rejection compared to women (Andrighetto et al., 2019; Kelly et al., 2015; Stratmoen et al., 2018). If you can imagine an aggressive, "You think I'm not good enough for you? Is that it?" type of response to a rejection (Stratmoen et al., 2018), then you can see how unwanted initiation attempts can place the rejecter in a vulnerable and potentially dangerous position.

Unrequited Love

Does Rose pine for Finn after her kiss fails to start a relationship? Of the many relationships that fail to begin, **unrequited love** (i.e., loving someone who does not return your affection) is especially poignant. Consider Figure 5.15, which shows a woman engaging in warm, affectionate touch, with seeming confidence and hope. But, what if her friend just wants to be friends?

Figure 5.15 Friendships are not the only context in which unrequited love can occur, but they may be particularly painful: this young woman can easily imagine a relationship with her friend, knows he's single, and thinks they would be great together. Can you maintain a friendship when one person is in love? (Photo: martin-dm / E+ / Getty Images)

People experience unrequited love for celebrities and strangers, acquaintances, friends, and ex-partners, even current partners who do not return their level of affection (Bringle et al., 2013). Each of these types of unrequited love are more frequent and less emotionally intense than mutual love relationships, but they do evoke strong emotions. A study focused on Filipino gay men, for example, suggests that unrequited love includes both strong negative and positive emotions, as well as fantasies about the desired partner. For many, unrequited love is prompted by uncertainty about the desired partner's sexual orientation, or (worse) falling in love with someone who is not attracted to one's own gender or biological sex (Diliman, 2011). In the earliest stages of relationship development, wanting a relationship with a specific person induces **partner-specific attachment anxiety** (Eastwick & Finkel, 2008a). This is a normal part of transitioning a fledgling relationship into an established relationship regardless of individuals' dispositional attachment styles. If a relationship begins, great! The attachment system can recalibrate around the new partner and chronic attachment dispositions can take over. If, however, a relationship does not begin, an unmet attachment drive nicely explains the agonizing experience of unrequited love as a form of protest and despair.

Ultimately, unrequited love is a crummy, aversive, "no win" situation for everyone. No one likes to be rejected and no one likes to deal with someone's persistent undesired romantic feelings. Pursuers feel the torture of rejection, and rejecters feel guilty, uncertain, and annoyed (Baumeister et al., 1993). Perpetuating the problem, rejecters and pursuers tend to perceive many of their interactions quite differently. Rejecters feel like they have clearly communicated their rejection and blame pursuers for persisting beyond a desirable degree. Pursuers, meanwhile, judge the rejecter as having been inconsistent and at times encouraging their interest. They do not see their own behavior as inappropriate (Baumeister et al., 1993).

Preferring Singlehood to a Relationship

Sometimes rejecters reject romantic overtures because they are, and want to be, single. Singlehood is a preferred relationship status for somewhere between 9 and 15 percent of single people (Apostolou, Papadopoulou, & Georgiadou, 2019; Lehmann et al., 2015). This might be a small subset of single individuals, but their satisfaction with their singlehood is an important reminder that not everyone desires or benefits from a relationship. From an attachment perspective, secure individuals' satisfaction with singlehood may indicate that they are meeting their attachment needs through other relationships (Pepping & MacDonald, 2019; Pepping et al., 2018). For many people, singlehood provides valuable freedom (Apostolou et al., 2020). Single individuals can channel the time, resources, and emotional energy they might otherwise spend on a romantic relationship to their careers, friends, and family, or be freely available for sexual encounters that they might desire. For these reasons, beginning a relationship – even with a potentially desirable partner – may be less appealing than maintaining status as a single person.

Conclusion

The *Star Wars* series keeps Finn single, despite quite a few opportunities to connect him with desirable partners. Perhaps what we witness, in his interactions with Rose, Poe, or Jannah, is relationship initiation as it often actually plays out: messily, over time, with hedges and pauses, hopes and doubts, bids and tests. Once people are talking and rapport is building, the leap into relationship territory is still not guaranteed. In this tenuous, often overlooked space between initiation and a relationship (Eastwick et al., 2022), we might act like Finn and show vague signs of interest or engage in more noticeable exploration of the possibility of a relationship. This is a delicate dance along the blurred line between a relationship and no relationship. We pick up with this fuzzy moment between meeting and whatever might lie ahead in the next chapter.

Major Take-Aways

- Timing matters in relationship initiation, and not every single person is interested in a relationship. People with short-term motives may differ in the strategies they use to initiate relationships compared to people with long-term motives.
- Access to partners is a major barrier to relationship initiation, as are traditional gender norms, uncertainty, and individual differences, including shyness and self-esteem.
- Romantic partners can begin as strangers, as is often emphasized in stage models, but they often originate from existing relationships.

- The people around us have a surprisingly influential role in our judgments about potential partners and potential relationships and in initiation itself.

- Most "could-be" relationships do not become relationships and the reasons "why" include failures on behalf of the initiator and rejection.

Further Readings

If you are interested in …

… the personal precursor of "readiness" to forming a new romantic relationship, read:
Agnew, C. R., Hadden, B. W., & Tan, K. (2019). It's about time: Readiness, commitment, and stability in close relationships. *Social Psychological and Personality Science*, *10*(8), 1046–1055.

… how researchers study flirting, and whether it "works," read:
Apostolou, M., & Christoforou, C. (2020). The art of flirting: What are the traits that make it effective?. *Personality and Individual Differences*, *158*(1), 109866.

… a modern-day version of Clark and Hatfield (1989) "Will you go to bed with me?" receptivity study, read:
Edlund, J. E., Clark, D. Q., Kalmus, A. M., & Sausville, A. (2021). Receptivity to casual sexual requests. *Journal of Social Psychology*, *161*(6), 779–784.

… dating as an older adult, and how older adults use online profiles to find partners, read:
Griffin, E. M., & Fingerman, K. L. (2018). Online dating profile content of older adults seeking same- and cross-sex relationships. *Journal of GLBT Family Studies*, *14*(5), 446–466.

… romantic relationships that begin as friendships, read:
Stinson, D. A., Cameron, J. J., & Hoplock, L. B. (2022). The friends-to-lovers pathway to romance: Prevalent, preferred, and overlooked by science. *Social Psychological and Personality Science*, *13*(2), 562–571.

6 FROM FLEDGLING TO ESTABLISHED RELATIONSHIPS

How Do Relationships Become *Relationships*?

When you're a world-class athlete, the public tends to pay attention to your dating life. For some people, this curiosity serves an ego-inflating purpose; for Dutee Chand, it is a platform for advocacy. Chand is an internationally medaled sprinter specializing in the 100-meter, who hails from the deeply rural, financially impoverished village of Gopalpur in Odisha, India (Abraham, 2019). Her Cinderella story from barefooted running to gold medals shows she is no stranger to adversity. So too does her 2014 experience of being banned from competitions because of her naturally elevated testosterone levels; Chand later appealed and won a landmark case that lifted her suspension (Banerjee, 2020; Macur, 2017). A few years later, on the heels of India's 2018 decriminalization of same-sex relationships, Chand publicly announced that she is in a long-term relationship with another woman from her village (BBC, 2019). This announcement made Chand, shown in Figure 6.1, the first openly gay professional athlete from India.

Chand's coming out has garnered her global admiration, but earned her mixed support at home. This is not surprising: many people in socially marginalized relationships face problems tied to others' expectations and disapproval as they solidify, and then later maintain, their relationships. Chand's traditional village is largely unsupportive of her relationship, and though her family has sometimes supported her, at other times they have threatened to disown her (Banerjee, 2020; Dhillon, 2019). Concealing her relationship, however, would not have been a healthy solution; holding such a secret is linked to worse mental and physical well-being (Lehmiller, 2009). Chand, however, is proud of her relationship and advocacy work, and she encourages others to follow their hearts: "One may fall in love anytime and with anyone. One does not decide that based on caste, religion or gender" (Press Trust of India, 2020).

Figure 6.1 While some relationships coalesce as fast at Chand sprints across the finish line, other relationships only slowly transition from separate people to "us." What factors support and inhibit the ease of this transition? (Photo: Lintao Zhang / Getty Images Sport)

In this chapter, we will examine how early relationships become established relationships, which (as in Chand's case) can include navigating social disapproval. We will consider relationship trajectories, how people approach building love, intimacy, and commitment, and how relationships change the self. We will then provide an overview of common major transitions (cohabitation, marriage, parenthood) and some key challenges therein, providing necessary contextual background for addressing relationship maintenance in future chapters. Your goal in reading this chapter is to recognize the critical role of context in shaping how relationships transition from fledgling to established.

 GUIDING QUESTIONS

Consider these questions as you read this chapter:
- How do we describe a relationship's trajectory?
- What is love and what happens when we fall in love?
- How do partners build intimacy?
- How do partners build commitment?
- How do cohabitation, marriage, and parenthood affect relationships?

Relationship Trajectories

Like many couples, Dutee Chand and her partner knew each other for quite a while before they began their relationship (Koshi, 2019). For a period of time, they lingered in that fragile space of "what ifs" that many of us know well. "I did start to like her a lot," confessed Chand in an interview, "But I was not sure what her feelings for me were" (Koshi, 2019). Only after her partner confessed her feelings and received her parents' permission did their committed relationship begin.

While many relationships fizzle out before they start, the ones that do begin can become the most important relationships in our lives. Can people identify the precise moment when their early relationship moved from "something" to "everything"? Maybe! Some people recall **turning points** in the development of their relationships, distinct moments that changed their relationship, such as the first time they were alone together, a first kiss, or a sudden realization that they were in love (Baxter & Bullis, 1986; Solomon & Roloff, 2018). For others, the task of identifying a precise moment is tricky. Maybe they can recognize a series of intensifying moments or, maybe their relationship unfolded so slowly, with almost imperceptible gains in intimacy, that to identify when it became a "full-fledged" relationship would require consideration of months or years.

Plotting Romantic Evaluations over Time

We can capture this variation on a **relationship trajectory**, which is an arc, or path, that plots how romantic evaluations change over time. As you might expect, no one trajectory fits all relationships, highlighting the fundamental diversity in our relationship experiences. Still, we

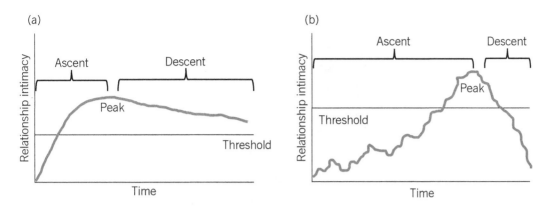

Figure 6.2 Relationship trajectories capture how relationships change over time. Panel (a) shows a relationship in which intimacy developed quickly and steadily (ascent) to a moderate level (peak) and then declined only minimally, but steadily, over time (descent). Panel (b) shows a relationship with a slow, volatile ascent to a high intimacy peak, followed by a rapid, steep descent, ending well below a break-up threshold. How would you describe your own or your friends' relationships? (Source: Drawn based on data from Eastwick et al. [2019])

can see patterns among people's trajectories that help us understand the effects of, for example, a first kiss, an affair, or the transition to parenthood.

Like any good love story, relationship trajectories have a beginning, a middle, and an end. The **relationship trajectories framework**, a meta-theoretical approach to structuring how relationships change over time (Eastwick et al., 2019), redefines these features as the relationship's *ascent*, *peak*, and *descent*. These features apply to various relationship judgments such as intimacy, commitment, even love. The *ascent* begins when people first meet and captures the escalation in romantic judgments over time. As shown in Figure 6.2, ascents reflect considerable diversity: some people move quickly into romantic feelings (e.g., Panel [a]), others move slowly (e.g., Panel [b]), and others fall somewhere in between. The ascent of any romantic evaluation ends at its *peak*, that is, its highest sustained level (Eastwick et al., 2019). As shown in Figure 6.2, some relationships have higher peaks in romantic evaluations than others; in Panel (b), intimacy peaks at a higher level than in Panel (a). Note that there is no predetermined time-point for when any relationship judgment peaks: a peak might occur right away or forty years into a relationship.

From there, evaluations have a *descent*, which can range in form from barely noticeable (e.g., Figure 6.2, Panel [a]) to extremely steep (e.g., Panel [b]). Descents that are nearly imperceptible could reflect a highly satisfying relationship (nearly stable high peak) or a consistently miserable one (nearly stable low peak). Likewise, steep declines reflect different experiences: they could lead to a break-up or not, depending on a person's break-up *threshold*. Because break-up thresholds vary, the person in Figure 6.2 Panel (b) would need to maintain a higher level of intimacy to avoid break-up than the person in Panel (a). People vary in the thresholds they maintain not only for break-ups, but also for a first kiss, sharing of personal history, sexual intimacy, marriage, and other relationship events. Relationships also vary in the fluctuations of their romantic evaluations, with some relationships characterized by steady romantic evaluations (e.g., Panel [a]) and others by high volatility (e.g., Panel [b]).

(a)   (b)

Figure 6.3 Ben Affleck and Jennifer Lopez dated from 2002 until 2004, separated, reunited seventeen years later in 2021, and married in 2022. How would you sketch their love trajectory? (Photo: James Devaney / WireImage / Getty Images [a] and Steve Granitz/ FilmMagic / Getty Images [b])

Trajectories as Insight into Relationships and Relationship Diversity

If you were to plot the trajectories for a set of romantic relationships you know, how would they differ? Early work on romantic trajectories (Surra, 1985) identified four typical patterns of increasing commitment for partners moving from dating to marriage. Some partners exhibit an **accelerated trajectory**, with a steep and steady ascent in interdependence (similar to Figure 6.2a); others move through an **accelerated-arrested trajectory** that starts strong but stalls; others follow an **intermediate trajectory** that progresses less intensely than the accelerated type; and, finally, some partners move through a **prolonged trajectory** with an extended, lengthy courtship. This early work forecasted the heterogeneity that scholars have since noted in early relationship formation for all types of relationships. Consider the commitment trajectories for **on-again/off-again relationships**, which take on a wavy ebb-and-flow pattern as partners commit, separate, and commit again (Dailey et al., 2013). These trajectories, such as that of Ben Affleck and Jennifer Lopez (Figure 6.3), may seem unusual, but not when we recognize that there is no one way to start a relationship.

When relationships begin, their ascents may tell us surprisingly little about whether they will ultimately be short-term or long-term. The **relationship coordination and strategic timing (RECAST) model** (Eastwick et al., 2018) suggests that short-term relationships could be long-term relationships that end prematurely, or long-term relationships could be short-term relationships that last; only in hindsight do we make these distinctions. Accordingly, the slopes of romantic judgments in these different relationships are indistinguishable initially; only later do they diverge as evaluations in long-term relationships continue and/or rise, and those of short-term relationships descend toward the relationship's end (Eastwick et al., 2018).

Trajectories also provide a temporal context that can help us understand a given romantic evaluation at one moment in time. A measurement of moderate love, for example, takes on different meaning if it is occurring on its ascent versus its descent. Stretching the timeline further, and recognizing that people may move through multiple relationship trajectories over their lifetimes (Eastwick et al., 2019), a moderate level of love could be the highest love a person has ever experienced, or it could pale in comparison to previous relationships.

 ARTICLE SPOTLIGHT

Are You Texting Your Way to Love? New Ways to Study Trajectories

That cute person you met last weekend just texted you. How quickly will you respond? How many texts will you send back-and-forth today? How many will you send between now and when you officially become "in a relationship"?

Recent research by Brinberg, Vanderbilt, Solomon, Brinberg, and Ram (2021) points to the potential of **mobile data donations** (participants voluntarily sharing their mobile data, such as texting logs) for advancing our understanding of early relationship development. Think about the challenge of studying the unfolding of a new relationship in real time: it requires gathering data from partners before they even know they will be partners. This is a tricky logistical task. Even if you could connect with pre-partners and track them as they move forward in time (classic longitudinal designs), such work is typically expensive and requires considerable resources. Texting logs not only provide easy access to partners' communications before and after they become partners, but the volume of information within these communications allows for precise and detailed analysis. Texting logs include a complete set of real, personal communications that actually happened, and include a record of when and what was said. This is incredibly valuable information that is much more accurate than relying on participants to accurately recall past behavior and much less resource-intensive than hoping to stumble across the start of a relationship in a longitudinal design.

In their initial work using mobile data donations, Brinberg and colleagues (2021) analyzed over 1 million text messages culled from the texting logs of forty-one college-aged couples and spanning from 30 to about 500 days. On any given day that partners texted each other, they sent an average of 162 texts, but this number varied considerably, as did participants' response times and the length of their responses. The texting logs of fifteen couples included their first messages exchanged, which made it possible for the researchers to tentatively consider texting trajectories before and after partners declared themselves "together." Figure 6.4 shows hypothetical data illustrating some of the themes noticed by Brinberg and colleagues. First, some trajectories showed a quick path from first text to relationship (A, C), whereas others' texting frequency suggested partners knew each other for longer prior to becoming a couple (B, D). Prior to establishing their relationship, some partners' texting

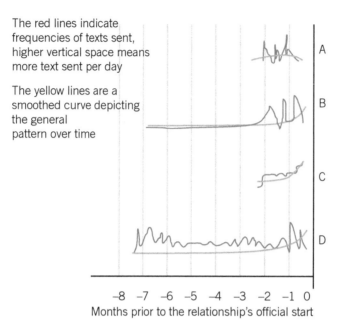

The red lines indicate frequencies of texts sent, higher vertical space means more text sent per day

The yellow lines are a smoothed curve depicting the general pattern over time

A

B

C

D

−8 −7 −6 −5 −4 −3 −2 −1 0

Months prior to the relationship's official start

Figure 6.4 Texting trajectories can reveal differences in communication leading up to the establishment of a relationship (the X axis depicts months until relationship establishment ["0"]). These hypothetical cases illustrate some of the trends apparent in Brinberg and colleagues' (2021) work. What would your texting trajectory look like? (Source: Drawn based on data from Brinberg et al. [2021])

frequency fluctuated considerably (A, D), whereas others had weeks or months of relatively steady texting (B, C). Finally, partners differed by whether the general pattern of their texting frequency intensified right before relationship establishment (B, C, D) or decreased (A), as illustrated by the yellow-line overlay.

Texting and other virtual communication play a critical role in early relationship development today, a point made all the more poignant when you consider the growing rates of different-sex and same-sex relationships that begin online where partners experience their first communications virtually (Rosenfeld et al., 2019). Mobile data donation is an unobtrusive, cutting-edge method that has enormous potential to harness readily available, ecologically valid data to describe relationship change over time and test relationship theories. For instance, down the road, mobile data donation could help us learn which texting trajectories characterize short-term versus long-term committed relationships; we might see that texting trajectories are tied to transitions (e.g., parenthood, getting engaged) in ways anticipated by theory; we might even be able to differentiate paths leading to highly satisfying versus unsatisfying relationships. With appropriate privacy considerations in place, the ethical use of mobile data donation may provide a treasure trove of insight into the day-to-day experiences of people in relationships.

Building Love

To ascend into a romantic relationship, particularly one that will continue into a long-term relationship, often means falling in **love**. Oh, to be in love! Love is a cross-culturally universal experience that compels people to be with each other (Aron & Aron, 1991; Jankowiak & Fischer, 1992; Reis & Aron, 2008). Around the globe, people recognize love between romantic partners as sharing a set of core features (de Munck et al., 2011; Nelson & Yon, 2019); namely: sexual attraction, altruistic self-sacrifice (e.g., "I'd do anything for you"), preoccupying and intrusive thoughts, partner well-being ("My love makes my partner a better person"), and strong feelings of happiness. The fact that diverse cultures share a common understanding of love highlights its universality and underscores its importance in the human experience. Love's pervasiveness also supports an evolutionary perspective that explains love as an adaptation designed to advance reproductive success (Bode & Kushnick, 2021; Buss, 1988a, 2019; Fletcher et al., 2015). In other words, love serves a purpose. It can signal sexual availability, faithfulness, and willingness to share tangible and intangible (e.g., emotional support) resources. Additionally, love can orient people's attention toward their partner(s) and suppress their interest in alternative partners, ultimately serving as a "commitment device" that helps sustain a relationship (Buss, 1988a; Fletcher et al., 2015; Gonzaga et al., 2008).

Differentiating and Defining Love

Think about how varied representations of love are in everyday conversations. People love tacos, vacation, sports, celebrities, new friends, and partners of seventy-five years. These loves are not the same. To pursue a clear understanding of love, even restricted to the close relational context, requires identifying what, exactly, we are referring to when we speak of love.

Our understanding of love today rests on early work that suggested love comes in two primary forms: passionate love, which includes intense feelings of longing; and companionate love, which reflects affection toward close others (Berscheid & Walster, 1978). Of these two forms, passionate love has since garnered the lion's share of empirical attention. Passionate love – often called romantic love – is an exciting, physically arousing experience that people cross-culturally tend to associate with sexual desire, despite unique biological underpinnings of passionate love and sexual lust (Diamond, 2004; Feybesse & Hatfield, 2019; Hatfield & Sprecher, 1986; Sprecher & Regan, 1998). Passionate love and companionate love nicely represent two key ways laypeople tend to talk about love, both as an experience within romantic or sexual relationships, and as an affectionate feeling within friendships and family relationships (Fehr, 1994). Consider Table 6.1, which includes items to assess passionate and companionate love.

The distinction between passionate love and companionate love is echoed in the triangular theory of love, a schematic that partitions love into three components: passion, intimacy, and commitment (Sternberg, 1986). Passion in this model reflects the "hot" element of love, associated with romance and longing. Intimacy, the "warm" component, captures the emotional bond (closeness and connection) between people. The last element, commitment, reflects the "cold" cognitive decision to be in a relationship. As much as passion or intimacy might move individuals toward a relationship, ultimately a decision to enter (or avoid) and then to maintain (or end) a relationship determines its stability. A large-scale study that included twenty-five countries and used the model's associated measure, Sternberg's *Triangular Love Scale,* found support for the model's three-factor structure, suggesting it appropriately captures a universal representation of love (Sorokowski et al., 2021).

Table 6.1 Passionate and companionate love scales

	Not at all true			Moderately true			Definitely true		
A 10-item short-form of the passionate love scale									
Sometimes I feel I can't control my thoughts; they are obsessively on _____.	1	2	3	4	5	6	7	8	9
I would feel deep despair if _____ left me.	1	2	3	4	5	6	7	8	9
I would rather be with _____ than with anyone else.	1	2	3	4	5	6	7	8	9
I'd get jealous if I thought _____ were falling in love with someone else.	1	2	3	4	5	6	7	8	9
I want _____ physically, emotionally, mentally.	1	2	3	4	5	6	7	8	9
I have an endless appetite for affection from _____ .	1	2	3	4	5	6	7	8	9
_____ always seems to be on my mind.	1	2	3	4	5	6	7	8	9
I eagerly look for signs indicating _____'s desire for me.	1	2	3	4	5	6	7	8	9
I possess a powerful attraction for _____.	1	2	3	4	5	6	7	8	9
I get extremely depressed when things don't go right in my relationship with _____.	1	2	3	4	5	6	7	8	9
The 7-item companionate love scale									
I feel that I can confide in _____ about virtually everything.	1	2	3	4	5	6	7	8	9
I find it easy to ignore _____ 's faults.	1	2	3	4	5	6	7	8	9
I would do almost anything for _____ .	1	2	3	4	5	6	7	8	9
I would forgive _____ for practically anything.	1	2	3	4	5	6	7	8	9
I would greatly enjoy being confided in by _____.	1	2	3	4	5	6	7	8	9
I care about _____.	1	2	3	4	5	6	7	8	9
I feel that I can trust _____ completely.	1	2	3	4	5	6	7	8	9

Love takes varied forms: passionate love and companionate love may, but do not have to, correspond. What implications for relationship quality might you conjecture from different combinations of passionate and companionate love?
Source: Used with permission of Blackwell Publishing, John Wiley & Sons, from Sprecher, S., & Regan, P. C. (1988). Passionate and companionate love in courting and young married couples. *Sociological Inquiry*, *68*(2); permission conveyed through Copyright Clearance Center, Inc.

As shown in Figure 6.5, different combinations of passion, intimacy, and commitment describe the different types of love experienced in a wide range of relationships (e.g., friendships, parent–child relationships, romantic relationships). We see the love-at-first-sight love of *infatuation*; the whirlwind Hollywood marriages depicting *fatuous love*; the peaceful

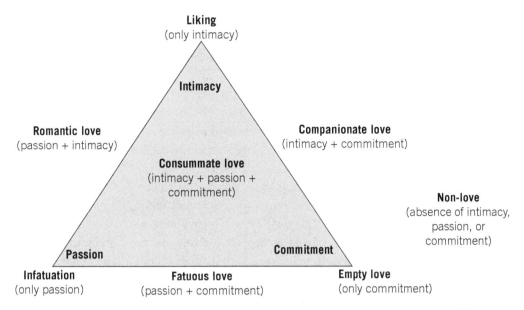

Figure 6.5 Using Sternberg's triangular theory of love, how would you describe your own or others' relationships that you have observed? (Source: Sternberg [1988], adapted and printed with permission)

love of *companionate love*. At the center of the triangle emerges *consummate love*: an ideal, complete love that might be difficult to sustain, but might serve as an ever-present striving. Different places on a triangle might capture different stages of a relationship as it moves along its trajectory, and two relationships captured by one descriptor might look very different. For instance, a once joyful but now unhappy marriage might be described by *empty love* (commitment in the absence of intimacy or passion). *Empty love*, however, might also capture the first stage of an arranged marriage, where individuals are committed to each other without having yet developed intimacy or passion. Thus, the triangular theory of love allows for an appreciation that relationships might change in intimacy, passion, or commitment, which may alter their development or stability.

Maybe, however, love is best differentiated into four types. The recent quadrumvirate model of love (Berscheid, 2010) adds attachment love and compassionate love to the previously established types of passionate (or romantic) love and companionate love (Berscheid, 2010). Attachment love and compassionate love appear to reflect distinct, if understudied, ways in which love manifests. Attachment love reflects the bond between people that compels them toward each other for support seeking, safety, and security, fulfilling the attachment functions described previously (Berscheid, 2010; Hazan & Shaver, 1987; Mikulincer & Shaver, 2016). Compassionate love, or altruistic love, refers to a tender concern for another person marked by selfless acts of sacrifice and support (Berscheid, 2006; Sprecher & Fehr, 2005; Underwood, 2002, 2009). Compassionate love occurs when someone deeply values another person, is open and receptive to the other, extends their concern in a context of free choice, and gives generously and empathetically from the self (Underwood, 2009). In other words, a cornerstone of compassionate love is "extending beneficence to another" (Fehr et al., 2014, p. 580). A nascent area of study, compassionate love appears linked to personal well-being and relationship functioning (e.g., social support), and appears among couples across the life span, especially those who are "in love" (Fehr et al., 2014; Neto

& Wilks, 2017; Sprecher & Fehr, 2005). The implications for psychological and relational well-being suggest that compassionate love warrants additional empirical attention.

How do we reconcile such varied ideas about love? Perhaps they highlight different dimensions of what may yet be an overall concept of "love." For example, meta-analytic work including over eighty studies and nearly 20,000 participants showed that the constructs of liking, passion, intimacy, and commitment all linked to an overarching construct that could be called "love," one that was different than obsessive love or friendship love (Graham, 2011). Other work has also suggested that love is a general construct (like intelligence), with passionate love, intimacy, and commitment as factors, rather than different types of love (Merino & Privado, 2020). Love may thus be a broad concept, with components that overlap even as they touch on different experiences and are associated with different relationship dynamics, behaviors, and outcomes. Critically, as we think about what love is, note that these theoretical models emerged relying either exclusively or predominantly on the responses of different-sex couples and including an implicit assumption that, when asked, participants were thinking about romantic love within a monogamous relationship. Different-sex dyads are only one type of relationship, and while these ideas about love may apply to other relationships, it may be necessary to correct for an overreliance on one type of romantic relationship (Thorne et al., 2019). Love can flourish with partners of any gender or sexual identity, within any variant of monogamy or non-monogamy, and an inclusive development of our understanding of love is an important next step for relationship scientists.

 IS THIS TRUE FOR YOU?

Does Passion Fade, or Can It Be Sustained?

Picture the romantic energy between two people in the early stages of love. Do you expect to see this same romantic energy between partners celebrating their fortieth anniversary? Will passionate love fade for you?

Most people assume that passionate love peaks during early relationship development and inevitably fades. Data often support this pattern (Hatfield & Rapson, 2008; Sorokowski et al., 2021; Sprecher & Regan, 1998), with some estimates suggesting that passionate love expires between six and eighteen months after a relationship begins (Fisher, 2000; Marazziti et al., 1999). The novelty wears off, the day-to-day drudgery kicks in, and access to habits chips away at infatuation. After all, can you really feel passionate love for someone when you're intimately acquainted with their personal hygiene needs?

Indeed, passion may relate to intimate knowledge, such that passion is high when intimacy grows, but low once you know someone (Baumeister & Bratslavsky, 1999). This would explain why people in new relationships, which are characterized by dramatic increases in intimacy, experience strong feelings of passion. Once intimacy stabilizes, logic follows that passion declines to a stable "low." Similarly, perhaps we feel strong emotions, like passion, primarily in contexts of uncertainty or when social interactions deviate from our expectations (Berscheid, 2010). Along these lines, passion may dominate in the newness of a developing relationship and fade with time because, in established relationships, we have more certainty and fewer surprises. Taking a stronger evolutionary lens, passionate love must fade after serving its purpose, that is, bringing people together, to give way to an attachment system guided by different priorities (Fisher, 2000).

If passion's inevitable decline doesn't ring true with your observations, you are in good company. A growing body of research rejects the idea that passionate love has an expiration date. Obsession?

Figure 6.6 Although passion declines for some, a large minority of people report passion long into their relationships. How might they do it? (Photo: Nitat Termmee / Moment / Getty Images)

That might end. However, the engrossing, emotionally intense, sexually charged side of passionate love can endure and predicts long-term relationship satisfaction (Acevedo & Aron, 2009). Consider data from a nationally representative sample of American different-sex couples married more than ten years in which 46 percent of women and 49 percent of men professed to be "very intensely in love" (O'Leary et al., 2012). The same research, looking at a randomly selected set of New Yorkers, found lower percentages, 19 percent of wives and 29 percent of husbands, and more recent work using a community sample in Madrid, Spain, found 17 and 18 percent, respectively (Cuenca-Montesino et al., 2015); these data all support the critical point: for a substantial portion of the population, passionate love does not end (as shown in Figure 6.6). See Chapter 10 for insight in how some partners "keep the spark alive."

Falling in Love

What does it mean to fall in love? From a scholarly perspective, **falling in love** is a transitional period, a move from a state of "not in love" to a state of "in love" (Aron et al., 2008). Thinking about love as an intense attachment bond, adults can fall in love with anyone of any gender, independent of their sexual desires (in the same way that the caregiver–infant attachment system is gender blind; Diamond, 2003, 2004, 2019). Sometimes, the intense emotional bond of love can spill over into sexual desire, for example, within a special same-sex friendship between heterosexual individuals. In other words, sexual orientation does not "orient" romantic love; rather, our attachment/romantic system and our sexual system are separate (if highly integrated) systems. While in many cases we might expect sexual desire to precede romantic love, romantic love (even with the "wrong" person) can also compel sexual desire. All this is to say, falling in love can happen just as Dutee Chand suggested, "any time with anyone" (Press Trust of India, 2020).

To fall in love is often an intense experience. Why else would we use the word "fall"? When people fall down or fall over, they lose control and have no choice but to give in to gravity; to fall in love is similarly to lose control as new emotions, thoughts, and desires oriented around a beloved partner emerge. When people are falling in love, they are mentally and emotionally absorbed by their partner; they have intrusive, obsessive thoughts about their partner; they are energized, might have disrupted sleep, and can lose their appetite; they feel euphoric, anxious, vigorous, and sometimes overwhelmed by what to do with these new emotions (Marazziti & Baroni, 2012; Tennov, 1978; Tomlinson et al., 2018). The emotions and behaviors of people falling in love reveal it to be a stressful experience, consistent with evidence showing that people newly falling in love exhibit higher levels of cortisol (Marazziti & Canale, 2004). Falling in love is akin to awakening a motivational system that attracts someone toward their partner, and neurological underpinnings make clear its powerful effect (Fisher, 2005). Functional magnetic resonance imagining (fMRI) of the brains of self-professed "in love" people has revealed that when lovers look at pictures of their partners versus acquaintances, the dopamine-rich caudate nuclei and ventral tegmental areas (VTA) of their brains light up (Aron, Fisher et al., 2005). These findings, observed cross-culturally and among people in love with same-sex and different-sex partners (Xu et al., 2011; Zeki & Romaya, 2010), reveal a connection between feeling love and activation of the brain's reward system. Indeed, the brain perpetuates early stage love by producing a powerful neurochemical high, making it as though people become "addicted" to their partners (Fisher et al., 2016; Frascella et al., 2010).

Building Closeness

To say that two people are becoming "close" often means their relationship is progressing to a state of greater intensity. For the development of romantic relationships, building closeness is a critical task, one that we will explore first by thinking about intimacy building and then by considering self-concept change.

Intimacy

Intimacy, a specific form of relational closeness, is an experience of "feeling understood, validated, and cared for" – not just in general or on superficial matters, but with regard to core aspects of the self (Reis & Patrick, 1996, p. 536). Intimacy is not simply the act of being vulnerable and sharing information about one's self; it is a fundamentally interpersonal phenomenon. How partners react to each other is essential for intimacy building. As you might imagine, intimacy building is not a one-time event; instead, partners must engage in ongoing efforts to create and sustain intimacy. So how does this intimacy building occur?

One path toward intimacy begins with a surprisingly ordinary interaction: having a conversation with your partner. This idea forms the basis of a highly influential framework for thinking about human bonding: the **interpersonal process model of intimacy** (IPM; Reis & Patrick, 1996; Reis & Shaver, 1988). The IPM conceptualizes intimacy as resulting from a dynamic process in which one partner offers a self-disclosure and the other, in turn, offers responsiveness. These two acts, self-disclosure and partner responsiveness, take an ordinary

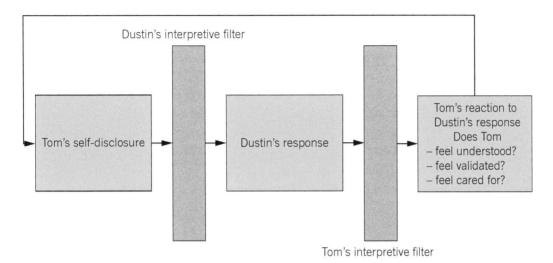

Figure 6.7 Like most couples, Tom and Dustin must navigate pathways to intimacy. If Tom self-discloses, intimacy is not guaranteed, even if Dustin offers validation and caring. Why? What can go wrong on the path to intimacy? (Source: Used with permission of John Wiley & Sons from Reis, H. T., & Shaver, P. [1988], Intimacy as an interpersonal process, in S. W. Duck (Ed.), *Handbook of Personal Relationships*; permission conveyed through Copyright Clearance Center, Inc.)

conversation and turn it into an interpersonal springboard for intimacy. Let's look a bit more closely at how this happens.

Self-Disclosure

As shown in Figure 6.7, the IPM begins with one partner, in this case, Olympic diver Tom, making a self-disclosure to his husband Dustin. Self-disclosures convey *self-relevant*, or personal, information and some types have more potential to promote intimacy than others (Reis & Patrick, 1996). For example, Tom might say to Dustin, "I learned a new dive today" or he might say, "I was super nervous trying out a new dive today."[1] The former, a descriptive or *factual self-disclosure*, has less consequence for intimacy building than the latter, an evaluative or *emotional self-disclosure*. Emotional self-disclosures involve vulnerability and, as such, create an opportunity for a partner to gain knowledge about core aspects of the self and respond supportively; emotional disclosures are thus primed to promote intimacy.

After Tom shares, what will Dustin do? Dustin's response will reflect a startlingly wide range of situational, motivational, and dispositional factors. Dustin might be tired, stressed, or intoxicated, situational factors that can influence Dustin's readiness to encourage additional disclosures or shut down the conversation. These situational factors interplay with Dustin's relational and personal goals. Dustin may personally aspire to be a supportive partner, to be in control, or to have a healthy relationship. Consider also the role of dispositional factors – such as attachment orientation or personality – in shaping Dustin's response. Dustin's comfort with intimate conversations or his agreeableness might factor into his response. As shown in Figure 6.7, from the very first moment that Tom's disclosure arrives in Dustin's consciousness, Dustin views it through a clouded lens, or a filter. He might see

[1] Please note that the quotes in this section are entirely fictional and used for illustrative purposes only.

Tom's self-disclosure as a genuine bid for support or a whiny plea for attention, depending on Dustin's pre-existing expectations, needs, goals, and fears.

So, when Dustin does respond, what kind of response promotes intimacy? Dustin could keep looking at his phone, snort, and say an undermining, "You take diving way too seriously," or Dustin could stop what he's doing, make good eye contact, and say, "Oh Tom! I bet that was so nerve-racking – this is such big deal – how did it go?" It doesn't take a PhD in relationship science to recognize that the latter response is more likely to promote intimacy. Why? Unlike the dismissing, insensitive first response, the latter reaction reflects *partner responsiveness*, actions that demonstrate attention, understanding, and concern (Miller & Berg, 1984).

Perceived Partner Responsiveness

As impressive as all this sounds, responsiveness falls flat if it is not recognized as such. Just as Dustin experiences Tom's self-disclosure through his own lens of expectations, needs, goals, and fears, Tom interprets Dustin's response through a similar filter. Dustin might be well-intended, but if Tom views his response as coddling or condescending, nobody wins. Similarly, Dustin could offer a backhanded response, but if Tom feels validated, bingo: Tom might experience feelings of (unintended) intimacy with Dustin. These extremes are illustrative, but generally speaking, people see a blend of their partners' actual responsiveness (reality) and their own motivated construction (bias) of their partner's response (Reis et al., 2004). Let's focus a bit more on Tom's interpretation of Dustin's response; this *perceived* **partner responsiveness** is the critical piece that enhances intimacy.

Perceived partner responsiveness is that wonderful belief that your partner really "sees" you, the most important aspects of you, and cares for you because of (or despite) who you truly are. To build intimacy, perceived partner responsiveness includes three essential psychological experiences: (1) feeling understood; (2) feeling validated; and (3) feeling cared for (Reis & Patrick, 1996; Reis & Shaver, 1988). Recall from Chapter 1 that "intimate knowledge" is a key component of a close, romantic relationship. To feel understood after offering a self-disclosure is to believe your partner paid attention, knows *you* and the emotions and details you have shared, and accurately grasps the significance of your disclosure. Understanding provides the foundation for validation, the heart of intimacy building. Validation is affirmation of the self; a belief that your partner not only acknowledges core aspects of you, but sees them as important, values you, and appreciates you. As you can see, understanding is a necessary prerequisite of validation. The final component, feeling cared for, reflects a belief that your partner holds a stake in your welfare, wants the best for you, and has affection for you. Together, feeling understood, validated, and cared for translates to intimacy.

Building Intimacy in Context

Empirical evidence supports the idea that intimacy follows from emotional self-disclosures when those disclosures are met by perceived partner responsiveness (Laurenceau et al., 1998, 2005). Note, however, the strong potential for contextual factors to interfere with this process. Partners bereft of the resources to disclose openly or to respond responsively, because of stress or external demands, may experience less intimacy and potentially a slower building of their relationship, than those couples who have the mental energy and time to devote to their partners (Karney, 2021; Neff & Karney, 2017). Low SES, for instance, can impose health, food, or housing concerns along with financial stress, all of which can deplete resources. These constraints make responding in ways that will be interpreted as understanding, validating, and caring all the more challenging (Figure 6.8). Drawing on the vulnerability-stress adaptation model (Karney & Bradbury, 1995), belonging to socially marginalized and oppressed groups adds another layer of intimacy-building challenge, as do pre-existing individual vulnerabilities like mental health disorders or neurological differences such as autism spectrum disorder.

Figure 6.8 This couple shares an intimacy-building exchange over coffee: but such relationship building takes time, effort, and (in this case) money. Some partners face obstacles that constrain their capacity to support their goal of building intimacy, even if they are fully willing to do so. (Photo: LordHenriVoton / E+ / Getty Images)

IN THE NEWS

Thirty-Six Questions to Fall in Love

The idea that self-disclosure can promote intimacy caught the American public's attention in 2015, when *The New York Times* published an article entitled, "To fall in love with anyone, do this," by Mandy Len Catron. Describing her own experiences with this social experiment, Catron offered a step-by-step guide to intimacy building, closely following the experimental protocol of a 1997 psychology study. In the original study, unacquainted strangers were paired together and invited to work through a set of thirty-six "get to know you" questions over a 45-minute time period (Aron et al., 1997). In Catron's "experiment," she and a friend moved through the questions and witnessed what happened. As you can see in Table 6.2, some of these questions are modestly personal, others quite intimate. The researchers organized the presentation of the thirty-six questions such that they become increasingly personal as the task progressed, a progression that Catron and her friend followed.

What do you think it would be like to ask and answer these questions, shown in Table 6.2, with someone you only casually know? What about sharing these questions with a new romantic partner? How might that feel?

In the original study (Aron et al., 1997), strangers who broached the personal questions reported significantly more closeness compared to participant pairs who talked for the same amount of time, but about "small-talk" subjects (e.g., "Do you prefer digital watches and clocks, or the kind with hands? Why?" or "What are the advantages and disadvantages of artificial Christmas trees?"). More recent research has supported the intimacy-building

Table 6.2 A sample of the thirty-six questions to fall in love

One person reads, and both partners respond to each question
Given the choice of anyone in the world, whom would you want as a dinner guest?
What would constitute a "perfect" day for you?
When did you last sing to yourself? To someone else?
Do you have a secret hunch about how you will die?
Name three things you and your partner appear to have in common.
Is there something that you've dreamed of doing for a long time? Why haven't you done it?
What is the greatest accomplishment of your life?
What do you value most in a friendship?
What is your most terrible memory?
Alternate sharing something you consider a positive characteristic of your partner. Share a total of five items.
How close and warm is your family? Do you feel your childhood was happier than most other people's?
Make three true "we" statements each. For instance, "We are both in this room feeling …"
If you were going to become a close friend with your partner, please share what would be important for him or her to know.
Tell your partner what you like about them; be very honest this time, saying things that you might not say to someone you've just met.
When did you last cry in front of another person? By yourself?
Share a personal problem and ask your partner's advice on how they might handle it. Also, ask your partner to reflect back to you how you seem to be feeling about the problem you have chosen.

Try these questions, a sample from the original Aron et al. (1997) study, with a romantic partner or friend and see how close you feel after your conversation.

Source: Aron et al. (1997), reprinted with permission: Aron, A., Melinat, E., Aron, E. N., Vallone, R. D., & Bator, R. J. (1997). The experimental generation of interpersonal closeness: A procedure and some preliminary findings. *Personality and Social Psychology Bulletin, 23*(4), 363–377. https://doi.org/10.1177/0146167297234003.

potential of asking personal questions, engaging in self-disclosure, and offering responsiveness. For example, strangers who engaged in a back-and-forth of personal questions in either a structured or unstructured format reported feeling closer to their partner, liking their partner more, and enjoying the interaction more than those in a small-talk condition (Sprecher, 2021). This pattern emerged regardless of whether the strangers were speaking face-to-face or interacting virtually (via Skype). Results showed a non-significant trend favoring the structured questions over the unstructured "get to know you" conversations, but in either case, the take-home message is clear: self-disclosure to a responsive partner is a strong pathway toward intimacy and liking (Collins & Miller, 1994; Laurenceau et al., 1998).

Did Catron and her question partner fall in love? Yes. And yes, intimacy building through these questions may have been an important contributor; however, Catron admits they were not strangers when they started the questions, and an initial attraction likely prompted their willingness to give them a try. Still, the experience of feeling understood, validated, and cared for is a powerful intimacy builder, addressing core psychological needs. For partners already experiencing romantic attraction, intimacy building through Aron et al.'s questions might be the tipping point toward love. Try it out and let us know.

Self-Concept Change in New Relationships

Closeness between romantic partners also emerges through the dramatic and exciting changes that happen to partners' self-concepts as their new relationship develops. People falling in love often undergo an intense period of rapid self-concept growth and diversification as they take on aspects of their new partner as their own (Aron et al., 1995). Partners start to see themselves as possessing new abilities, identities, skills, and resources (Aron & Aron, 1986; Aron et al., 2013) and experience a heightened sense of self-efficacy and enhanced self-esteem (Aron et al., 1995; Mattingly & Lewandowski, 2013). The way we weave our partners into our own sense of self reveals the depth of closeness that characterizes romantic relationships. It's not superficial, it's self-definitional.

Self-Expansion: A Fundamental Motivation

Why do our self-concepts change when we enter new relationships? Self-expansion theory, grounded in interdependence theory, provides a compelling explanation (Aron et al., 2013; Aron & Aron, 1986). Its two key principles, the *motivation principle* and the *inclusion-of-other-in-the-self principle*, suggest that: first, people are intrinsically motivated to expand their capacity to pursue goals; and, second, that they can do this by entering relationships and incorporating aspects of relationship partners into their own self-concepts. The more recent term *cognitive reorganization of the self-concept* captures this process more liberally, recognizing that through relationships, people can acquire new self-aspects and also enhance existing ones (Mattingly, Tomlinson, & McIntyre et al., 2020).

The self-concept change that happens in relationships generally occurs without awareness. Merely the desire to connect with a partner can be enough to compel an unconscious integration of partner aspects into one's own self-concept (Slotter & Gardner, 2009). Maybe you've seen this in action: your best friend suddenly becomes politically engaged, an expert in foreign films, and a craft beer critic just like their new beau: all examples of the unconscious positive self-growth that can accompany falling in love. Because self-expansion meets a fundamental need (according to the motivation principle), it should be no surprise that self-expansion is accompanied by personal and relational well-being. For instance, self-expansion predicts greater forgiveness, willingness to sacrifice, and commitment (Mattingly et al., 2014; McIntyre et al., 2015).

Self-expansion may be a fundamental motive, but people experience it to different degrees, which has implications for well-being. If you "enjoy doing familiar activities" and "find comfort in maintaining things the way they are," you might be less oriented toward self-expansion than people who readily endorse such statements as, "I am happiest when engaging in new skills" and "I like situations that challenge me to think differently about myself" (Hughes et al., 2020). As anticipated by self-expansion theory, those individuals who are motivated to self-expand tend to report greater life satisfaction, less stress, and better mental and physical health (Hughes et al., 2020).

Self-Expansion: Inclusion of Other in Self

As the relationship develops, partners begin to see themselves less as separate people and more as "partners." Partners experience each other's successes, humiliations, and joys as their own. While this integration reflects closeness, it also reflects a unique form of interdependence. Cognitive interdependence captures the collective sense of self that includes one's partner and emerges as people trade "I" for "we" (Agnew et al., 1998). On account of this merging of self and other, people confuse aspects of themselves with aspects of their partner (Aron et al., 1991; Mashek et al., 2003). They might struggle differentiating their partner's traits, memories, or attitudes from their own and vice versa, a rather alarming and fascinating outcome of blurring the lines between mental representations of self and other (Aron, Mashek et al., 2005; Smith et al., 1999). We can even see this at the level of the brain. Areas of the brain known to be associated with self-representation also activate, discriminately so, when people think of their romantic partners and close others (Courtney & Meyer, 2020; Ortigue et al., 2007). While cognitive interdependence stands out for its bi-directional link with commitment (Agnew et al., 1998), it also provides a map for the closeness that emerges as relationships develop.

Take a look at Figure 6.9, the one-item Inclusion of Other in Self scale (IOS; Aron et al., 1992; Gächter et al., 2015). This popular measure of closeness shows various pictorial representations of self and other (in this case, one's partner) and invites individuals to indicate which best depicts their relationship. Designed with dyadic relationships in mind, the Venn diagram structure of the IOS could easily be modified to depict the self's relationship with each partner, multiple partners, or relationships among partners.

In your ideal relationship, how much self-other overlap would you want with your partner (s)? This question may have important implications for relationship development, because how nicely a relationship's perceived closeness lines up with people's ideal closeness (both measured using the IOS) predicts relationship quality and stability (Frost & Forrester, 2013). In other words, it is the correspondence between actual and desired closeness, not the closeness itself, that seems critical in predicting relationship outcomes.

But what if you crave closeness and no matter how close your relationship might be, it is never close enough? A signature feature of anxious attachment is an intense motivation for connection and emotional intimacy. Anxiously attached individuals often struggle regulating closeness during relationship formation, pursuing too much closeness, too soon, which can

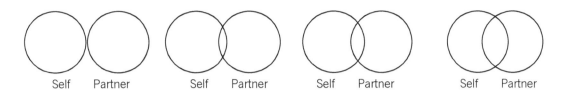

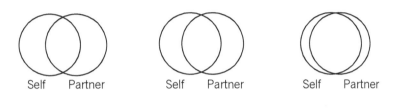

Least integration

Most integration

Figure 6.9 Consider a current or past relationship, or a relationship that you might wish to have: which circles would represent the degree of self-other-overlap that you have, and which represents that which you would most prefer? (Source: Copyright © 1992 by American Psychological Association, reproduced and adapted with permission. The official citation that should be used in referencing this material is Aron, A., Aron, E. N., & Smollan, D. (1992). Inclusion of Other in the Self Scale and the structure of interpersonal closeness. *Journal of Personality and Social Psychology, 63*(4), 596–612. https://doi .org/10.1037/0022-3514.63.4.596. No further reproduction or distribution is permitted without written permission from the American Psychological Association.)

be a turn-off (see Figure 6.10; Pistole, 1994). Later, as their relationships unfold, anxiously attached individuals are rarely satisfied, perpetually wanting more closeness than they have (Mikulincer & Erev, 1991). Perhaps in a reflection of their intense desire for closeness,

anxiously attached individuals exhibit a ready willingness to change their self to be more like their partner (Slotter & Gardner, 2012b). Self-change and inclusion of self in other are important in building interdependence, but readily sacrificing the self can leave someone feeling unsure about who they are and highly vulnerable, should the relationship break up. In contrast, avoidantly attached individuals work to protect their separateness and prioritize independence. The stronger people's avoidant attachment, the less likely they are to use "we" pronouns when discussing their relationships (Dunlop et al., 2020).

Figure 6.10 Wanting closeness is a natural and important part of relationship building; but finding the balance between independence and dependence can be challenging, especially for individuals with insecure attachment. Like the woman in this image, we debate: should we call? Text? Wait? (Photo: RapidEye / E+ / Getty Images)

The Many Forms of Self-Concept Change

Developing a new relationship can mean adding some fabulous new content to who we are, but it

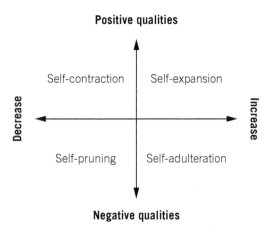

Figure 6.11 The two-dimensional model of self-change reveals how relationship participation can grow or shrink individuals' self-concept, either in positive, desired ways or negative, undesired ways. Think about five ways that you may have changed in your most recent relationship or that a friend has changed in theirs. (Source: Used with permission of Blackwell Publishing Inc., John Wiley & Sons, from Mattingly, B., Lewandowski, G., & McIntyre, K., [2014], "You make me a better/worse person": A two-dimensional model of relationship self-change, *Personal Relationships, 21*[1], 176–190; permission conveyed through Copyright Clearance Center, Inc.)

can also involve taking on some unhealthy habits, dropping some bad ones, or losing some of what we like about ourselves. The **two-dimensional model of self-change** (Mattingly et al., 2014) helps us appreciate these diverse possible changes. As shown in Figure 6.11, people's self-concepts can either grow or shrink on account of being in a relationship, and they can do so in subjectively positive or negative ways. **Self-expansion**, illustrated in the upper right-hand quadrant of the model, reflects an increase in positive qualities. Jump to the bottom right-hand quadrant and see how people's self-concepts can also increase in negative ways, a form of self-growth captured by **self-adulteration**. Under your partner's influence, you might start eating less healthily, you might take on undesirable social habits (e.g., feeling superior, gossiping), or you might become more aggressive. This may seem like a perverse way to build closeness, but, just like adding positive attributes, adding negative attributes accomplishes a key goal: it builds similarity and connection. People who have strong romantic motivation along with low self-esteem are particularly susceptible to taking on their partner's negative attributes; people with strong romantic motivation and high self-esteem are more inclined to engage in self-expansion (Slotter & Gardner, 2012a; Slotter & Kolarova, 2020).

As shown in Figure 6.11, the self can also shrink, or constrict, because of relationship involvement (Mattingly et al., 2014). If this happens through **self-contraction**, shown in the upper left-hand quadrant of the model, individuals lose positive qualities. Their relationships render their self-concepts smaller or less diverse: they become less capable, less resource-laden, or otherwise less equipped to achieve their goals. Maybe being with a romantic partner somehow means giving up seeing friends, dancing, or playing in your garage band. These losses can translate into less relationship satisfaction and lower commitment (Mattingly et al., 2014). A smaller self, however, can sometimes be a desired outcome. Indeed, relationship-facilitated **self-pruning** (lower left-hand quadrant of Figure 6.11) is a form of self-change that involves losing undesired aspects of the self, rendering a more ideal self. For instance, in the unconscious (or perhaps deliberate) pursuit of relational closeness, an individual might quit smoking or stop biting their nails. Self-pruning is associated with self-expansion, and like self-expansion predicts positive relationship processes, positive romantic evaluations, and a reduced propensity to think about leaving a relationship (Mattingly et al., 2014; McIntyre et al., 2015). From this vantage point, self-pruning and self-expansion are both forms of self-improvement, whereas self-contraction and self-adulteration are forms of self-degradation. In established couples, self-degradation appears to have an opposing role in relationships compared to self-improvement, with the former associated with dissolution thoughts, less willingness to engage in pro-relationship behaviors (e.g., sacrifice, **accommodation**), and more willingness to engage in destructive relationship processes (e.g., attention to alternative partners, revenge; McIntyre et al., 2015).

Building Commitment

Many of today's relationship structures explicitly rebuff commitment. Friends-with-benefits, booty-call relationships and hookups … these and other undefined situationships all have the signature feature of low, or no, romantic commitment; yet, some turn into committed relationships. Even relationships that have long-term potential right from the outset must, at some point, leap from "casually dating" to "in a serious relationship." How does this happen?

Commitment is an individual's psychological attachment to their relationship and their intention to maintain the relationship, not only now, but into the future (Arriaga & Agnew, 2001). When partners have a bad day or a rough year, commitment is the tether that allows their relationship to endure. We can conceptualize this tether as *personal dedication*, a desire to continue a relationship and to work to help it thrive, and as *constraints*, the ties that make leaving a relationship costly (Stanley & Markman, 1992). Both of these commitment facets play a unique role in relationship dynamics.

Contemplating and Communicating Commitment

When earnest lovers make a bid for greater seriousness, they lay their hearts on the line. At the whim of their partners, this vulnerability can be rewarded or scorned in a searing rejection. So, how do people decide to escalate their relationship's seriousness? The risk regulation model (Murray et al., 2006) suggests that people appraise their partner's judgments about them, and if they feel confident that their partner values and cares for them, they then pursue closeness and commitment. If, however, their appraisal has them questioning their partner's regard for them, the risk regulation model suggests people will prioritize self-protection goals over connection goals. Of course, any time we appraise our partner's feelings about us, our appraisals might be inaccurate or biased. Nonetheless, the risk regulation model articulates how these appraisals may lead to decisions to intensify a relationship.

One way people communicate commitment is to say, "I love you." This makes sense. The very purpose of love, from an evolutionary perspective, may be to serve as a commitment device (Bode & Kushnick, 2021; Fletcher et al., 2015; Gonzaga et al., 2008). Further, from an attachment perspective, commitment is a natural outcome of an activated attachment system in which love pulls us toward attachment figures (Morgan & Shaver, 1999). Although people tend to assume women take the lead in professing their love, such is not the case. In different-sex relationships, men are the ones who typically say "I love you" first, and this finding is robust cross-culturally (Ackerman et al., 2011; Watkins et al., 2022). Saying "I love you" is considered a critical relationship turning point and, like the decision to be exclusive, is associated with higher perceived commitment (Baxter & Bullis, 1986). People also view meeting someone's family (or introducing them to your own) as an important ritual necessary to obtain "relationship" status, an act that serves as an especially salient cue for Black versus White young adults (Jackson et al., 2011). Partners also report talking about their relationship, a meta-conversation called relationship talk, when they experience commitment changes in their relationship (Baxter & Bullis, 1986; Bullis et al., 1993). The very act of relationship talk is sometimes viewed as an intensifying turning point.

Relationship talk, however, can be challenging during transitions. A relationship transition is a period of instability when current modes of operating no longer work and adjustments must be made (Solomon et al., 2016; Solomon & Roloff, 2018). The relational turbulence model and relational turbulence theory (Solomon et al., 2016; Solomon & Knobloch, 2001, 2004) articulate that major transitions create new challenges for relationship partners by 1) introducing uncertainty and 2) causing disruptions in existing patterns of interdependence. Think about this latter point. What changes would need to happen for you to fully integrate a new partner into your day-to-day life, social network, and future goals? Maybe your new partner makes life easier ("Thanks for picking up pizza!"), which we call *partner facilitation*, but they can also get in the way ("You fed my dog pizza? Why would you do that?"), a problem termed *partner interference* (Solomon et al., 2010). Swinging from jubilation to irritation and having questions about your involvement in a relationship is expected under the relational turbulence model. The model explains that greater perceived partner interference, when coupled with uncertainty, leads to negative emotions and poor communication (Solomon & Theiss, 2011; Theiss & Nagy, 2012).

Meta-analytic review has provided both empirical and theoretical support for the relational turbulence model, showing the links between uncertainty, partner interference, and negative emotions (depressive symptoms), as well as avoidance (Goodboy et al., 2020). Indeed, topic avoidance appears especially high in contexts of relational uncertainty (Knobloch & Theiss, 2011). As much as some topics can become taboo during a transition, if people do engage in relationship talk, they tend to experience uncertainty for less time, suggesting that relationship talk may help people move beyond a transition and land on more steady ground. When young couples engage in "defining the relationship" talks, they often do so in order to resolve confusion and plan for the future, and they tend to experience greater intimacy, clarity, and commitment after these conversations (Knopp et al., 2020).

Commitment and the Social Network Effect

Before Dutee Chand announced her relationship publicly, she spoke with her family. "I asked my mother if she is 'ok' with it. ... [she] told me it is your choice and I won't stand in the way ... Now, my mother does not seem to be supporting me" (Koshi, 2019). Chand's experience is as singular as it is common: people across the globe struggle when their family or friends fail to, or inconsistently, support their relationships. This makes sense from a social network perspective, which reminds us that relationships occur within a web of constantly evolving interpersonal connections (Felmlee & Sinclair, 2018). Table 6.3 outlines principles from a social network perspective which are especially relevant for relationship science.

Table 6.3 Key ideas guiding a social network perspective on romantic relationships

Rather than background features, partners' social ties can be informative, focal points of study
How partners behave, think, and feel is interdependent with the experiences of their social networks
The structure and characteristics of a social network affect partners in their relationships
Partners' social networks have their influence via the exchange of support, disapproval, information, and resources

Who are your family, your friends, your friends' friends? If you were to draw each with a circle (a node) and use lines to represent interconnections, what would this web look like?

Source: Table based on information sourced from Felmee and Sinclair (2018).

As early relationships transition into more committed relationships, social networks rarely sit idly by. Instead, they exert influence aligned with their approval or disapproval of the relationship, and their meddling can shape a relationship's trajectory (Keneski & Loving, 2014; Sprecher, 2011). Often called the social network effect, relationships benefit in myriad ways from their social network's approval (Etcheverry et al., 2008; Sinclair et al., 2015; Sprecher & Felmlee, 1992). Having support makes a relationship easier: friends want to hang out with you and your partner(s), spending time with each other's family is (dare we say it) fun, and if you need help, you've got it. With friends' ringing endorsements dancing merrily in your mind, you are apt to feel more positive about your partner and experience greater intimacy and commitment.

In contrast, a lack of support for your relationship predicts lower relationship quality, lower feelings of security within the relationship, and worse mental and physical health (Blair & Holmberg, 2008; Lemay & Razzak, 2016). Experiencing relationship stigmatization from friends, for example, is associated with more depressive symptoms and an accompanying worse overall physical health (Rosenthal et al., 2019). Many times friends' support is primary, superseding the influence of parental support, particularly among adults (vs. young adults) who are less dependent on parents (Blair et al., 2018). For widowed or widowered individuals, dating can strain relationships with children who tend to be less accepting when their parent begins dating soon after their partner's death or if they remarry after a short courtship (Carr & Boerner, 2013; Engblom-Deglmann & Brimhall, 2016).

Individuals in non-traditional relationships (i.e., varying from different-sex, similar-demographics dyads who adopt culturally privileged behaviors, habits) are especially likely to be marginalized (i.e., to experience social disapproval because of the relationship; Lehmiller & Agnew, 2006). Consider the experiences of interracial partners. If their social networks include individuals who identify as one race, then their social networks likely show a bias toward same-race relationships, and often a strong bias against interracial relationships (Chuang et al., 2021; Skinner & Rae, 2019; Yancey, 2009). Multiracial individuals are more comfortable with and accepting of interracial relationships than their monoracial counterparts (Bonam & Shih, 2009; Skinner & Rae, 2019). People are also less likely to date outside their own race if their family disapproves (Miller et al., 2022). Consider the experience of Harry and Meghan (Markle) Windsor, shown in Figure 6.12, who relinquished their royal duties and moved across the Atlantic in the aftermath of perceived family disapproval. In their 2021 interview with Oprah Winfrey, Meghan confessed suicidal thoughts and strong concerns over their child's safety and security, saying, "I thought about [my biracial identity] because they made me think about it." Meanwhile, Harry said, "For us, for this union and the specifics around her race, there was an opportunity – many opportunities – for my family to show some public support ... Yet no one from my family ever said anything. That hurts." (Harpo Productions, 2021).

Figure 6.12 Meghan and Harry Windsor's experience illustrates how family support affects belonging, feelings of safety, and mental health. What could have been done differently? (Photo: Michele Sparatari / AFP / Getty Images)

Same-sex partners also experience marginalization, reporting less support from family than those in different-sex relationships (Holmberg & Blair, 2016). LGBTQ + individuals often must navigate the same identity-related stressors that they experience at an individual level (e.g., stigma, concealment, discrimination, and internalized homophobia) at the relationship level as well (Leblanc et al., 2015; Meyer, 2003). A woman's family may know she is bisexual, for example, but she may yet conceal her relationship with a woman, or if she reveals it, experience additional discrimination on account of the relationship. People are more apt to conceal their relationship when they anticipate social rejection (Baxter & Widenmann, 1993), and relationship concealment is associated with poorer health, lower self-esteem, and less relational commitment (Lehmiller, 2009).

Relationship-based stigma and perceived social network disapproval also predict heightened psychological distress among transgender women and their cisgender male partners (Gamarel et al., 2019), less commitment and lower relationship stability among age-gap partners (Lehmiller & Agnew, 2006, 2007), less integration of self and couple identity for individuals in intercultural relationships (Yampolsky et al., 2020), concealing behaviors among long-distance partners (Johnson & Hall, 2021), and secrecy about one's partners, particularly secondary partners, for individuals in polyamorous relationships (Balzarini et al., 2017). In sum, having a disapproving social network is strongly linked to poorer relationship well-being.

So how does the social network effect jive with Dutee Chand's strong relationship despite social opposition? Can others' disapproval ever fuel the fire of love? Coined the **Romeo and Juliet effect**, the idea that family interference can intensify (not dampen) love and commitment initially received empirical support (Driscoll et al., 1972). The star-crossed lovers and romantics among us nodded in hopeful agreement, but the finding does not stand. The vast majority of studies, including a contemporary replication of the original study, find little evidence that love flourishes in the face of social network disapproval (Sinclair & Ellithorpe, 2014; Sinclair et al., 2014). That said, people who react to their family's interference by asserting their independence, versus becoming oppositional and defiant, tend to maintain their relationships with little adverse effects from their family's disapproval (Sinclair et al., 2015). This does not support the Romeo and Juliet effect, however; instead, it suggests only that these individuals' relationships thrive in spite of, not because of, others' opposition (Sinclair & Ellithorpe, 2014). By and large, social approval fuels love better than social disapproval. Indeed, all signs suggest that Romeo and Juliet's love would have been all the grander (and perhaps they would had lived to enjoy it), had they had their social network's support.

Common Transitions in Established Relationships

The shift from a fledgling relationship to an established relationship is a major transition, but it is not the last for most partners. Long-term relationship trajectories are typically speckled with major life-altering decisions and experiences. Many of these are considered positive life events that can escalate commitment and interdependence, even as they introduce temporary turbulence that provides the backdrop for the partners' day-to-day experiences. Of course, partners also experience de-escalating transitions (e.g., infidelity, break-ups), but for now, we will focus on three key escalating transitions: cohabitation, marriage, and parenthood.

Cohabitation

Did your great-grandparents cohabitate (i.e., live together without marriage)? Why or why not? Moving in together marks a major relationship transition for most couples. Partners weave each other into their daily routines, they sign leases together and adopt puppies, they share grocery bills and buy couches, and most partners today first experience this family-like structure without the legal and emotional bind of marriage. Transitioning from dating to cohabitating escalates commitment and alters the interdependence within a relationship (Stanley et al., 2006), making it a fascinating temporary or permanent arrangement.

Cohabitation is increasingly common for different-sex partners and in some places is now even more common than marriage. Indeed, a 2019 survey found that 59 percent of American heterosexual adults, ages 18 to 44, have at one time cohabitated, which for the first time exceeded the percentage of people (50 percent) who have, at one time, been married (Horowitz et al., 2019). Today, nearly 70 percent of first marriages were first cohabiting relationships, a number that has risen dramatically since the 1970s (see Figure 6.13; Horowitz et al., 2019; Kuperberg, 2019). Women's access to education, entrance into the workforce, the "sexual revolution," and the availability of birth control pills in the 1960s and 1970s are some of the factors that may have contributed to increasing cohabitation rates (Kuperberg, 2019). In Europe, rates of currently cohabiting different-sex partners tend to be high in Nordic countries like Sweden (about 20 percent), moderate in the United Kingdom (about 12 percent), and low in Poland and Greece (about 2 percent; OECD, 2016). Once labeled a "Western idiosyncrasy" (Coleman, 2004), demographers today note that

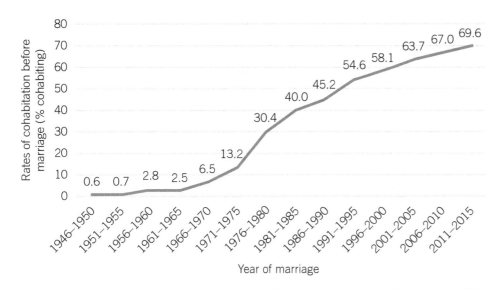

Figure 6.13 Rates of cohabitation before marriage in the United States have risen dramatically since the 1950s. What does cohabitation mean for a relationship today compared to seventy-five years ago? (Source: Kuperberg, A. (2019). Premarital cohabitation and direct marriage in the United States: 1956–2015. *Marriage & Family Review*, *55*(5), 447–475; Taylor & Francis Ltd, www.tandfonline.com, reproduced with permission)

cohabitation is on the rise not only within European and North American countries, but in Latin America, Asia, and East Asia (Lesthaeghe, 2020). In countries like India, where Dutee Chand lives, cultural and religious norms have historically prohibited cohabitation and emphasized women's pre-marital virginity; even so, a growing proportion of young people, particularly in urban areas, are cohabitating, potentially reflecting more individualized and fewer family-arranged marriages (Chakravorty et al., 2021).

Today, approximately 70 percent of Americans approve of partners cohabitating without plans for marriage, with an additional 16 percent approving if partners plan to marry (Horowitz et al., 2019). As shown in Figure 6.14, openness to cohabitation regardless of marriage intent varies systematically by age, race, religion, and political leaning. About half of young single women expect they will cohabitate, and this number jumps to about two-thirds among single women who plan to marry (Manning et al., 2019). While not everyone approves of cohabitation, many people now see cohabitation as a typical step in a relationship's development.

Cohabitators are a diverse group. The stereotypical cohabitator might be a childless young adult, but in reality, approximately half of cohabitators live with children (either theirs or of one of the partners) and, these days, older adults (over 50) are as likely to establish new cohabitating arrangements as get married (Brown et al., 2012; Horowitz et al., 2019; Smock, 2000). Cohabitation in the United States has historically varied by both race (with lower rates among White and Hispanic women than Black women) and educational attainment (higher

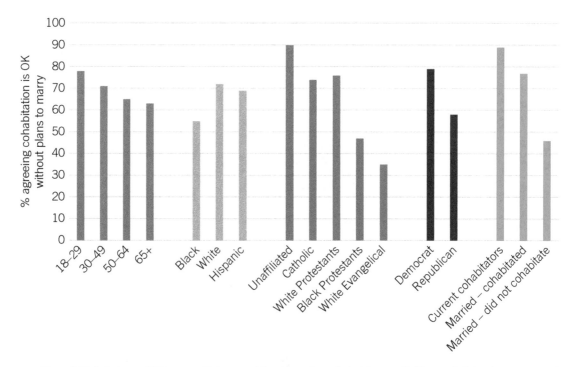

Figure 6.14 Data from a 2019 survey of heterosexual Americans shows that while, overall, 69 percent of Americans approve of cohabitation with no plans for marriage, not everyone feels this way. Labels on the bottom of the chart represent respondent characteristics. How might you explain this observed variation? (Source: Drawn based on data from Horowitz et al. [2019])

rates among less-educated women), but the most recent evidence suggests cohabitation rates are converging across race and educational attainment (Manning, 2020).

People's motivations for cohabitating range from the social and emotional (e.g., love, wanting to spend more time together), to the practical (e.g., financial, pregnancy), to the political (rejecting the institute of marriage; Horowitz et al., 2019; Rhoades et al., 2009b; Sassler, 2004). If dating partners are spending nearly every night with each other, cohabitation can solve the nuisance of driving back-and-forth and splitting clothes, toiletries, and other necessities between two places (Sassler, 2004; Sassler & Miller, 2011). This "mere convenience" motivation to live together is cited more frequently by individuals with higher SES than individuals with lower SES (Sassler & Miller, 2011). Likewise, individuals with higher SES are more apt to cite "economic rationality" than individuals with lower SES, who might reference (though it is not common) "economic necessity" as a reason for cohabitation. While people of varying SES can view cohabitation as a practical solution to housing problems, it tends to mean moving in together more quickly for partners with low SES than individuals with higher SES, perhaps because the latter group can afford the luxury of delay (Sassler & Miller, 2011; Sassler et al., 2018).

RESEARCHER SPOTLIGHT: Fenaba Addo, PhD

How did you come to be a social demographer (someone who studies social and cultural forces within population composition and change)?

I have always been interested in economic and social inequality. Growing up in NYC exposes you from an early age to extreme poverty and excessive displays of wealth. These childhood experiences undoubtedly inform my research and the questions I pursue. I also believe families are important contextual and determining factors of individual well-being. My desire to unpack these relationships and an interest in studying how economic resource deprivation contributes to inequitable health and wealth outcomes led me to graduate study. During my second year of my public policy PhD program, I became the research assistant for a family demographer on a project exploring relationship transitions and health outcomes. I noticed that the dataset contained questions related to how finances were arranged in the relationship and asked if I could run some models on relationship quality. This work would become one of my first publications! And as they say, the rest is history.

Figure 6.15 Dr. Fenaba Addo is Associate Professor of Public Policy at University of North Carolina – Chapel Hill. (Photo courtesy of Fenaba R. Addo, PhD.)

In your view, what contemporary questions are critically important for scholars to pursue right now (in the social demography of relationships)?

Our society is experiencing growing income and wealth inequality and unprecedented social and legal changes in family structure that continue to redefine our society. I believe that it is critically important to explore themes related to how economic resources influence the timing and likelihood of union transitions, and the quality of those relationships. Financial insecurity, like student loan debt, for example, is associated with remaining single or cohabiting among Millennials.

I'm also interested in how young adult couples integrate their finances and how this might link to individual and couple identity and the expected costs of relationship dissolution. People who cohabit vary on many dimensions, not just by how rapidly they move in together and whether they plan to marry. They also differ in how they invest in relationship-specific capital, such as pooling financial resources.

Looking ahead, I also think examining the institution of marriage and its role in contributing to wealth inequality is important. Fewer people today marry in young adulthood, and wealth is concentrated among a small share of married households, who are more likely to be White and socioeconomically advantaged. This work reaffirms the role that debt and wealth disparities serve in stratifying family formation by race and ethnicity among Millennials.

Cohabitation as Dating and as a Permanent Arrangement

For some people, cohabitation is essentially an *extension of dating*, albeit an intense form, where moving in together does not require especially high levels of commitment, but perhaps solves some practical issues (Sassler & Miller, 2017). This aligns with the fact that most cohabitators are not engaged to be married when they begin to live together and is consistent with the rising trend of serial cohabitation, the practice of sequentially living with dating partners (Lichter et al., 2010; Sassler & Miller, 2017). Today, nearly one in four Millennials who have cohabitated have done so with more than one partner, and, after one cohabitating relationship ends, they tend to move quickly (within about two years) into their next cohabitating relationship (Eickmeyer & Manning, 2018). Serial cohabitation suggests that, for some people, living together is not a pathway to marriage, but rather is one way to be in an exclusive dating relationship.

For another group of cohabitators, cohabitation represents a permanent *alternative to marriage or singlehood*; they are highly committed to their partner yet cannot, or do not want to, marry or live alone (Hatch, 2017). For a wide variety of reasons (e.g., not divorced from a previous partner), people who otherwise might marry cannot, so they cohabitate instead. Prior to the legalization of same-sex marriage, for example, cohabitation was a "marriage-like" relationship for many long-term same-sex couples. A different (and increasingly sizeable) group of permanent cohabitators *choose* cohabitation with no interest in marriage (Di Giulio et al., 2019). Partners might actively reject the marriage institution, think it unnecessary, or feel minimal incentive to marry (Hatch, 2017). Among these cohabitators-by-choice are people who want to resist what being married might mean for them (e.g., gender roles), who worry about divorce, or who have concerns about the potential effects of marriage on their relationship.

Cohabitation as a Pre-marital Arrangement

Cohabitors who plan to marry tend to fall into one of two groups: those who view cohabitation as a *trial marriage* and those who see cohabitation as a *prelude to marriage*. Marriage "testers" tend to be uncertain about their relationship, so they cohabitate as an information-gathering experiment, a chance to gain hands-on evidence of their compatibility (Harris, 2020; Rhoades et al., 2009b). While not a common reason for cohabitating, when individuals live with a partner to test their relationship, they tend to report more attachment insecurity, depression, and anxiety, and lower relationship quality (Rhoades et al., 2009b).

Other pre-marital cohabitators approach living together explicitly as a prelude to marriage, a next step in relationship progression. These partners are highly committed, differentiating them from the "testers" (Harris, 2020), yet they vary as well. Partners who enter cohabitation already engaged, for example, tend to report more confidence about their relationship, higher-quality dynamics, and more satisfaction with their relationship than those who become engaged later (Kline et al., 2004; Rhoades et al., 2009a). Among engaged partners, those who share a similar vision for when they will marry tend to enjoy higher relationship quality and fewer disagreements than partners who have conflicting or uncertain plans (Willoughby et al., 2012).

For some outside observers, highly committed partners who plan to marry but instead cohabitate present a bit of a conundrum. Why not just get married? Emerging evidence suggests that marriage might feel unreachable to some couples (Gibson-Davis et al., 2018; Harris, 2020). For example, interviews with unmarried, low-income, ethnically diverse parents, who had earlier planned to marry after their child's birth, suggest that people often delay marriage because they do not yet meet what they judge as marriage prerequisites, such as having their finances in order, a solid bank account, and job stability (Gibson-Davis et al., 2005). Credit card debt, and educational debt for women, are unique predictors of initial cohabitation versus marriage (Addo, 2014). People with higher SES are likewise raising the marriage bar, and expecting more (e.g., home ownership, career achievements) prior to walking down the aisle. Getting married may also be delayed, sometimes indefinitely, when partners want to save for a particular kind of wedding ceremony and reception. The average American wedding with engagement ring costs $34,000 excluding pre-wedding events (e.g., engagement parties, bachelor/bachelorette parties), and a honeymoon adds $5,000, on average, with some costing far more (The Knot Research & Insights Team, 2021). Thus, cohabitation may serve as a placeholder for couples of varied SES who are not questioning "if," but are questioning "when" they might marry.

The Cohabitation Effect

Does cohabitation support marriage success? Most young people believe that living together before marriage protects couples against divorce, based on the belief that a trial marriage allows them to weed out an incompatible partner before saying any vows (Bagley et al., 2020; Smock, 2000); however, the evidence points to the opposite pattern. The cohabitation effect describes a historical trend linking pre-marital cohabitation to long-term marital instability, low relationship quality, and higher likelihood of divorce (Brown et al., 2017; Dush et al., 2003; Rosenfeld & Roesler, 2019).

Two explanations have emerged for the cohabitation effect: selection and experience (Smock, 2000). The *selection hypothesis* focuses on demographic variables (e.g., liberal-conservative, SES) that differentiate cohabitators from non-cohabitators. This hypothesis suggests that the people who would choose to cohabitate are also more willing to consider divorce if their relationship sours; those who would not cohabitate are the same as those who would not consider divorce. Cohabitation's link with divorce might thus simply reflect a selection bias reflecting two different kinds of people. This selection argument was more persuasive when cohabitation was less prevalent.

An alternative perspective, the *experience hypothesis*, suggests that cohabitation itself increases a relationship's vulnerability. Cohabitating couples can experience, for example, an inertia effect, such that they "slide" rather than "decide" into marriage (Rhoades et al., 2009a; Stanley et al., 2006). Think about how cohabitation inadvertently elevates people's commitment constraints (e.g., shared address, joint purchases, etc.). This can make breaking up harder to do for cohabitators than partners living separately, and so cohabitators might ride their relationship inertia into marriage, when they otherwise would not have married. Another take on the experience hypothesis focuses on how practicing serial cohabitation might communicate that relationships are impermanent, and commitment is casual (Axinn & Thornton, 1992; Teachman, 2003). Having more past cohabitating partners and more previous sexual partners tends to predict worse future relationship stability and relationship quality (Busby et al., 2013, 2019). Critically, general pre-marital cohabitation may be more of the risk factor for divorce than pre-marital cohabitation with one's future spouse (Teachman, 2003). Recent meta-analytic findings suggest that the cohabitating effect does not hold when specifically considering cohabitating with one's future spouse (Jose et al., 2010; Manning et al., 2021).

Marriage

Getting married is a major event in a relationship's trajectory, whether it occurs after cohabitation or directly (without cohabitation). Within American culture, couples typically enter into an agreement to marry through an engagement ritual, centered around the culturally charged question, "will you marry me?" In different-sex relationships, the timing of this engagement is typically under men's control; women desiring to be married might try to persuade or maneuver their partner to propose, but they typically wait; if they do propose, their proposals are often repeated by their partner before their engagement is official (Baker & Elizabeth, 2013; Lamont, 2014).

Although called a "proposal," typically partners have already decided to marry and the proposal itself is a performance that, for different-sex partners, is done for the benefit of the woman and the couple's social network (Schweingruber et al., 2004). Indeed, couples' friends and family often make judgments about a relationship based on how well the proposal adheres to tradition norms (Schweingruber et al., 2008). Unmarried college-aged men and women strongly endorse the traditional different-sex proposal script, including who should propose and how (Robnett & Leaper, 2013). This script involves the man kneeling, presenting a ring, and asking the woman to marry him (Schweingruber et al., 2004). In addition, men are expected to arrange the proposal as a surprise, sometimes asking the woman's father or parents in advance for permission or their blessing. While men may feel pressure to seamlessly execute a creative, romantic, and magical proposal, usually women are working in the background, making direct requests or dropping hints, to ensure that the proposal has the features and style that they want (Schweingruber et al., 2008). Once engaged, revealing an engagement story is part of the pre-marriage ritual, yet couples can experience a tension between wanting to share their story and desiring to hold private this intimate moment (Moore et al., 2015).

Partners who take the non-traditional, if normative, route of cohabitating prior to engagement often feel the pull of traditional proposal rituals even as they value equality and partnership (Moore et al., 2015). Proposals among same-sex couples also often include the traditional elements in different-sex proposals (e.g., surprise, a ring, kneeling), with the person who assumes the role of proposer reflecting the dynamic of the couple (Jowett & Peel, 2019). More conventional same-sex proposals typically occur in the context of shifting a civil partnership into a marriage or beginning with marriage. Among those who began a civil partnership, they typically did so with no distinct proposal, but rather a discussed, negotiated, practical agreement.

As much as cohabitation is on the rise and fewer cohabitating relationships are transitioning to marriage, marriage today remains a highly desired arrangement for many people in Western culture. A vast majority of young heterosexual single women in the United States today think they will "definitely" (65 percent) or probably (28 percent) get married (Manning et al., 2019). Despite this continued desire, the median age of first marriage has risen dramatically since the mid-1950s, as shown in Figure 6.16, now standing at 30.5 years for men and 28.1 years for women (Census.gov, 2020). When people do marry, their reasons are diverse, including for love, companionship, for current or planned children, and for the formal commitment that marriage provides (Horowitz et al., 2019).

In areas of Asia, Africa, and the Middle East, marriages are predominantly arranged marriages, unions orchestrated by a third party, often parents (Anukriti & Dasgupta, 2017). Increases in urbanization and education, less focus on agriculture, and women working out of the home are associated with worldwide decreases in arranged marriages (Rubio, 2014), yet recent estimates suggest over half (approximately 53 percent) of current marriages across the world were arranged (Statistics Brain, 2018). Contrary to stereotypes, young people who do enter arranged marriages are not necessarily forced to do so. They enter these marriages

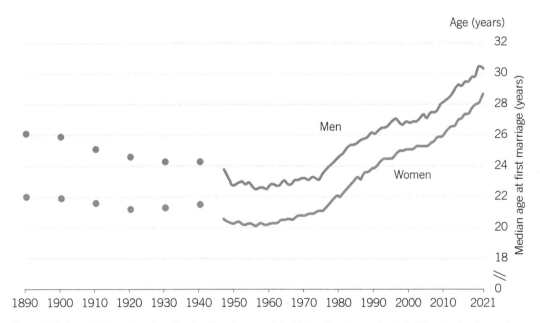

Figure 6.16 Age of first marriage is on the rise. How do you explain this trend? Note: Starting in 2019, estimates for marriages now include same-sex married couples. (Source: US Census Bureau, Decennial Censuses, 1890–1940, and Current Population Survey, Annual Social and Economic Supplements, 1947–2021)

for varied reasons, including wanting an objectively good match, and trusting their family to select wisely, unbiased by emotion (Bowman & Dollahite, 2013). For families, arranged marriages support economic stability and social security, often involve a bride price or dowry, and are the traditional and therefore appropriate way to create families (Anukriti & Dasgupta, 2017; Rubio, 2014). Women from cultures that practice arranged marriages, yet who are raised in Western culture, must negotiate different views on why and how people marry (Zaidi & Shuraydi, 2002). They sometimes reject their family's tradition of arranged marriages, other times accept it conditionally (e.g., if they can know their partner first), and more rarely, openly proceed with a traditional arranged marriage. Arranged different-sex marriages present a uniquely poignant problem for gay men or lesbian women, who might try to sidestep marriage or seek ways to cope with this "no-win" situation, even as it threatens their identity and imposes psychological harm (Jaspal, 2014).

 DIVERSITY AND INCLUSION

Living Apart Together

We often assume that long-term adult romantic partners live together, either as married or unmarried cohabiting partners, but this is not always the case. Indeed, many romantic partners intentionally do not live in the same residence, an arrangement that is gaining more visibility and scholarly attention (Levin, 2004). Often called non-residential partnerships or non-residential unions, people in **living apart together (LAT)** relationships maintain separate residences but generally live within an easy drive from each other (Duncan et al., 2014). These features distinguish LAT relationships from commuting partners (who live apart for work but otherwise share a primary residence), military partners (who reunite in the same residence post-deployment), and long-distance partners (though some LAT partners are, in fact, long-distance).

LAT partners often like the autonomy and freedom that comes with separate residences, enjoy being able to focus on friends and their careers, and feel their arrangement does not compromise their closeness nor pose a risk for the future of their relationship (Duncan, 2015; Duncan et al., 2014). To be in a LAT relationship is fairly uncommon, representing less than 10 percent (ranges from 1.5 to 9.6 percent) of Europeans in different-sex relationships, approximately 7 to 13 percent of Americans in different-sex relationships, and about 15 percent of lesbian women and 17 percent of gay men (Liefbroer et al., 2015; Strohm et al., 2009).

Of interest in the emerging study of LAT relationships is the question of whether LAT best reflects a transitional phase within courtship or a permanent alternative to cohabitation and marriage. Consistent with the notion that LAT represents a courtship phase, people in LAT relationships tend to be young and highly educated, and this young subset of LAT partners generally sees their current arrangement as temporary (Ayuso, 2019; Levin & Trost, 1999; Liefbroer et al., 2015; Strohm et al., 2009). They might simply not be "ready" to live together, or they might live apart because of practical constraints, such as educational pursuits or career goals, even as they expect to eventually live together. In contrast, about a quarter of

LAT partners plan to continue their relationship living in separate residences (Ayuso, 2019). Older adults are particularly inclined to see their LAT arrangement as stable, desirable, and permanent and both older women and individuals who were previously divorced tend to especially value the independence that comes with LAT (Ayuso, 2019; Lewin, 2018; Liefbroer et al., 2015; Wu & Brown, 2021).

People also keep separate households when they feel a responsibility to other people. Imagine a divorced mother of two, for instance, who might – were she not parenting – have already moved in with her new partner. Likewise, an older widow might appreciate her LAT arrangement because it requires no explanation to her adult children. LAT arrangements might be especially beneficial to individuals in marginalized relationships (e.g., same-sex relationships) who wish to keep their relationships private (Strohm et al., 2009). Thus, while LAT may describe a temporary courtship phase for many adults, for a critical subgroup, LAT offers an alternative way to structure a high-commitment relationship.

Parenthood

Why become a parent? Given its life-altering responsibilities, many parents make the decision to have children with a great deal of self-reflection and careful deliberation. Conscious decision-making is perhaps especially common among partners who take non-traditional means to build their families (e.g., surrogacy, adoption), as the hurdles to enter parenthood provide a series of decision points. For others, becoming a parent is an assumed, culturally approved path. Indeed, rarely do strangers say, "Oh, you have kids? Huh. That's an interesting choice." Instead, it is childless-by-choice, or **childfree**, couples who are burdened with justifying their decision of why they *don't* have children, having taken a "deviant" life path subject to social sanctions and stigma (Blackstone & Stewart, 2012).

Childfree partners are distinct from individuals who are involuntarily childless because of fertility challenges; they cite a variety of motivations to not have children (Blackstone & Stewart, 2012; Carmichael & Whittaker, 2007). They might be averse to the lifestyle changes that would be required to parent, have no interest in assuming parenting responsibilities, want to preserve their freedom and time, or desire other opportunities (e.g., career, traveling). They might also feel mismatched or ill-equipped to take on parenting. Intentions to be childfree might form early or develop over time, they might be solid or uncertain, and they might be shared early by both partners, emerge as shared intentions over time, or reflect one partner's reconciliation of their desire to remain in the relationship even if it means not having children (Lee & Zvonkovic, 2014). Research suggests that childfree older adults experience little regret from their decision (Stegen et al., 2020).

Pathways to Parenthood

For individuals who do enter parenthood, some do so joyfully, celebrating the much-anticipated arrival of a deeply longed-for baby. Others enter parenthood reluctantly, with a mistimed or unintended baby (e.g., accidental conception). These parenting intentions have a bearing on mental health and relationship well-being: unintended births are associated with maternal perinatal depression, and family functioning suffers more when a new baby is desired only by mothers than when the baby is desired by both parents but is mistimed (Abajobir et al., 2016; Li et al., 2019). Nearly half of all pregnancies in the United States are unintended, and these unplanned pregnancies are disproportionally accounted for by women with low SES and women who are cohabitating (Finer & Zolna, 2016). Cohabitating different-sex couples often wish to defer parenthood, and were they to unexpectedly conceive, most say they would (unhappily) have the child, some would choose to terminate the pregnancy, and others are not sure what they would do (Sassler, Miller, & Favinger, 2009). Timing and readiness are thus key considerations when we consider how partners transition to parenthood.

People also enter parenthood at different life stages. In the United States, teenage (ages 15 to 19) birth rates have dropped more than 70 percent since the early 1990s. Some young women today – more often Native American, Black, Hispanic, and Pacific Islander than White people – still give birth before they are 20 years old, some before age 14 (Martin et al., 2021), but the mean age for a first birth is now age 27 for American women. This number continues to rise in the United States and other developed countries, with more women than ever having their first child when they are of *advanced maternal age* (over 35). Fathers, too, are having their first child later in life (see Figure 6.17). Education and SES (including access to birth control) contribute to delayed entry into parenthood, which helps explain the older age of first-time mothers in cities and the coasts versus rural areas and in the South or Great Plains (Bui & Miller, 2018).

People's experiences transiting into parenthood are further diversified by the varied relational contexts in which parenthood occurs. Was your great-grandmother married when she had her first child? Did that matter? Sociocultural context underlies all facets of the transition to parenthood, including whether mothers are likely to be married at the time of birth. Today, about 40 percent of US babies are born to unmarried women compared to 28 percent in 1990 (Martin et al., 2021), a number that has been on the rise across all ethnic groups, but accounts for more births among Black women (69 percent) compared to Hispanic women (52 percent) and White women (28 percent; Wildsmith et al., 2018). The percentage of babies born to unmarried women is also rising across all educational attainment levels even as educational disparities persist. For example, in 2019, 62 percent (compared to 46 percent in 1990) of births to mothers with less than a high-school education occurred outside of marriage compared to 10 percent of births to mothers with a college education (up from 5 percent in 1990).

To be unmarried, however, does not mean to be unpartnered. Over half of unmarried women giving birth in the United States today are in a cohabitating relationship, which accounts for about one-fifth of

Figure 6.17 Human rights lawyer, Amal Clooney, became a mother at age 39, which she has labeled "quite late" (Galloway, 2017). Her husband, actor George Clooney, was 56 at the time. The average age people become parents is increasing for both women and men, particularly among highly educated individuals and people with high SES. (Photo: Duncan McGlynn / Stringer / Getty Images Entertainment)

all US births (Lichter et al., 2014). Cohabitation is thus a critical relational context for entering parenthood. Cohabitating relationships are notably less stable than married relationships, but when cohabitating couples transition to marriage before or after a baby's born, their separation risks mirror those of married partners (Musick & Michelmore, 2015). Pregnancy is often an impetus for union transitions (Lichter et al., 2014); thus, cohabitating partners might marry upon discovering they are expecting a baby. This is especially true for people who have been cohabitating for a short time; those who have been cohabitating for longer are less likely to transition to marriage when a baby comes (Thorsen, 2019). Pregnancy also often spurs unmarried non-cohabitating partners into cohabitation or direct marriage, either by the couple's own initiative or when families insist, that is, a "shotgun wedding." Reflecting strong racial and SES inequities, pregnancies rarely move Black unmarried or low SES women into cohabitation or marriage, whereas, among the highly educated, pregnancy is a strong engine for cohabitation and marriage.

People (particularly mothers) also enter parenthood as single parents, though the contexts in which they make this transition are quite diverse. Some pregnancies occur from sexual encounters with strangers, and others happen within casual relationships that subsequently end. People can also enter parenthood grieving the death of a partner or as they move beyond a divorce or break-up of a committed relationship. People also choose to become single parents (a group referred to as "single parents by choice"). Typically, single parents by choice are women in their late 30s or early 40s who are unpartnered, who want to parent, and who reach a point, sometimes out of biological necessity, when they decide it is time to start their family (Hertz, 2006). Single fathers by choice likewise reach a point when the timing feels right, having navigated concerns about single parenthood and moved past waiting for the "right" partner (Carone et al., 2017). Single parents by choice can enter solo parenthood via diverse ways, including artificial insemination, casual sex with the goal of conception, surrogacy, and adoption. While they experience the same transitional challenges in becoming parents as partnered parents, single parents by choice navigate their decisions by themselves (with support from friends and family); but, unlike most other single parents, they do so with greater preparation (Van Gasse & Mortelmans, 2020).

Experiencing New Parenthood

Transitions, as we know, are turbulent periods fraught with uncertainty, which require people to change existing routines, perspectives, and habits (Goodboy et al., 2020). New parenthood presents one of the most dramatic life transitions, demanding considerable adjustment. New parents are confronted with novel challenges (how exactly do you calm a crying baby at 3am?), novel worries (is the baby sick or is this normal?), and novel changes (will we ever have a date night again?). Along with an initial decline in leisure time, new parents must reconstruct their sense of self and identity as partners, negotiate shared child caretaking, and manage own and others' expectations and judgments about their parenting (Claxton & Perry-Jenkins, 2008; Lévesque et al., 2020). These challenges help define entering parenthood as a key transition, both for individuals and partners that are co-parenting.

The summative effect of parenthood on individual well-being is hotly debated. Some scholars align with the idea that, "people are better off not having children" (Hansen, 2012, p. 52), whereas others argue that parents are happier, experience more positive emotions, and perceive more meaning in life than their childless peers (Nelson et al., 2013). Rather than one outcome for all parents, a demands-rewards perspective recognizes that parenthood is a mixed bag: it comes with a dramatic increase in demands for parents' resources (e.g., financial, time; mental, emotional, and physical energy), but it also comes with an influx of rewards, including self-growth and progress toward life goals (Nomaguchi & Milkie, 2003, 2020).

Whether the rewards of parenting offset the demands can reflect parents' varied situations, social contexts, and personal characteristics. For example, parenting is especially demanding when parents have: a child with special needs; little control over their work schedule, considerable work interference, or career–parent conflict; worry about childcare arrangements; and concerns about children's encounters with racial biases (for review, see Nomaguchi & Milkie, 2020). Parenting is also especially demanding for low SES parents who have financial strain and limited resources, even as they tend to infer more meaning from parenting than high SES parents. Another key factor for parents' well-being is social support, which is often harder to come by for some parents, including LGBTQIA + parents (Reczek, 2020). In two-parent different-sex families, fathers tend to be especially happy and satisfied as parents, with mothers reporting more stress, more fatigue (from child-related sleep deprivation), and less happiness when caretaking (Musick et al., 2016; Nelson-Coffey et al., 2019). Evidence suggests that while having children may, in and of itself, have an enduring positive impact on people's sense of meaning and purpose, when parenthood is accompanied by considerable costs (especially financial strain for fathers and time and work costs for mothers), parents might not feel the benefits (Pollmann-Schult, 2014).

For partnered parents, the transition to parenthood can shape the trajectory of romantic evaluations. On average, having a baby produces a sudden modest decline in relationship satisfaction that persists for at least four years (Doss & Rhoades, 2017; Doss et al., 2009a). Even as parents' and non-parents' relationship satisfaction converges over time, new parents report less relationship satisfaction than non-parents, perhaps on account of sudden limitations to parents' freedom and work–parent-related conflicts, and this is especially true for high SES mothers and mothers of infants (Mitnick et al., 2009; Twenge et al., 2003). An uptick in conflict and relationship ambivalence, and a decrease in felt romantic love, appears similarly for both same-sex partners and different-sex partners alike when they bring home an adopted baby (Goldberg et al., 2010).

Of course, not all partners suffer when they enter parenthood. As shown in Figure 6.18, general trends may obscure important variability. A sizeable subgroup of parents remains highly satisfied with their relationship over the first year of parenthood, and a vast majority (83 percent) stay strongly committed to their relationship as they become parents; only a minority experience dramatic declines in either satisfaction or commitment (Leonhardt et al., 2022; ter Kuile et al., 2021). Poor communication skills between parents and low social support, as well as less time together before becoming parents, may make new parents particularly vulnerable to declines in relationship satisfaction (Bäckström et al., 2018; Trillingsgaard et al., 2014). Romantic partners can feel a strain on their relationship, but also experience new depths of connection, as they find a way to integrate an all-consuming new baby into their dynamic while navigating new ways of communicating and at least short-term changes in sexual intimacy (Delicate et al., 2018).

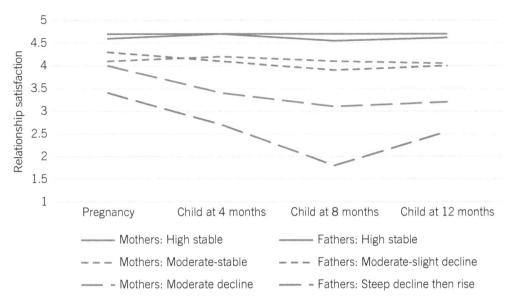

Figure 6.18 The transition to parenting need not harm relationship satisfaction: its effects tend to be heterogeneous. Red lines represent three trajectories mothers might experience, and green lines represent three trajectories fathers might experience. What might drive these diverse trajectories? (Source: Used with permission of Blackwell Publishing, John Wiley & Sons, from ter Kuile et al. [2021]; permission conveyed through Copyright Clearance Center, Inc.)

Conclusion

Whether we're thinking about Dutee Chand's relationship or any of our own, how people become partners is a fascinating process. In this chapter, you learned the importance of relationship trajectories in revealing diverse pathways to relationships, and the ways in which people build love, closeness, and commitment. We discussed how transitions may require heightened effort from partners, but the work of nurturing a relationship does not end once partners are "established" and major transitions are behind us. As you will soon see in Chapter 7, relationships require attention and consistent work in order to thrive, whether moving through ordinary events or facing acute relationship threats. As Dutee Chand would appreciate, a relationship once formed continues to operate within its social context, and this context, as you will see, continues to shape relationship experiences even after the relationship is established.

Major Take-Aways

- Relationship trajectories capture how romantic evaluations change over time.
- Love can be defined in different ways, including as companionate love, passionate or romantic love, compassionate love, attachment love, and through the triangular theory of love.

- The interpersonal process model shows how self-disclosure and perceived partner responsiveness build intimacy.
- People's self-concepts change when they enter relationships.
- The social context surrounding a relationship can facilitate or hinder the

experience of building relationship commitment.

- Cohabitation is becoming increasingly common and differs from marriage, which continues to be a desired relationship status.

- People take different pathways to parenthood, which has diverse effects on parents as individuals and romantic partners.

Further Readings

If you're interested in …

… current thinking about the possible sources for romantic passion, read:
Carswell, K. L., & Impett, E. A. (2021). What fuels passion? An integrative review of competing theories of romantic passion. *Social and Personality Psychology Compass*, *15*(8), e12629.

… trends in cohabitation and who is more likely to engage in serial cohabitation, read:
Eickmeyer, K. J., & Manning, W. D. (2018). Serial cohabitation in young adulthood: Baby boomers to millennials. *Journal of Marriage and Family*, *80*, 826–840.

… the challenge of transitioning to parenthood and the role of partners' social network, read:
Leal, D., Gato, J., Coimbra, S., Freitas, D., & Tasker, F. (2021). Social support in the transition to parenthood among lesbian, gay, and bisexual persons: A systematic

review. *Sexuality Research and Social Policy*, *18*, 1165–1179.

… the costs of *not* disclosing a romantic relationship, often endured by individuals who identify as sexual and gender minorities, read:
Lehmiller, J. J. (2009). Secret romantic relationships: Consequences for personal and relational well-being. *Personality and Social Psychology Bulletin*, *35*(11), 1452–1466.

… what people talk about when they want to shift their situationship into a relationship, and what having these conversations predicts, read:
Knopp, K., Rhoades, G. K., Stanley, S. M., & Markman, H. J. (2020). "Defining the relationship" in adolescent and young adult romantic relationships. *Journal of Social and Personal Relationships*, *37*(7), 2078–2097.

PART III

RELATIONSHIP MAINTENANCE

BIASES AND ILLUSIONS

What Does She See in Him?

A persistent love story in the Marvel universe is that between Tony Stark (a.k.a. Iron Man; Figure 7.1) and his assistant-turned-girlfriend-turned-wife, Pepper Potts. Although having Iron Man as a partner might sound dreamy (he's brilliant, wealthy, handsome, and heroic), the day-to-day reality of maintaining a relationship with Tony Stark is a bit nightmarish. So what does Pepper Potts see in Tony Stark that allows her to maintain her commitment to him? Or perhaps a better question is, what does she *not* see?

For those readers who have not ventured into the Marvel universe, here's a bit of backstory on Tony Stark. Tony is an attractive, wealthy, and powerful man. The world knows him first as the CEO of Stark Industries, and people recognize that he has few equals for passion, tenacity, or intellect. Eventually, his genius allows him to singlehandedly develop a technology that elevates him to superhero status: his Iron Man suit. His standout qualities help explain Pepper's initial attraction to Tony. However, Tony is also an arrogant and self-absorbed workaholic whose primary passions – re-designing Iron Man suits and antagonizing super-villains – occupy his full attention. While Tony spends his days and nights in his workshop tinkering obsessively on new designs, Pepper is alone. Despite her readiness to offer support, Tony perpetually chooses his robot assistant, J.A.R.V.I.S., to be his primary confidant. Worse, Tony's egotism repeatedly puts Pepper in danger, like when he provoked the Mandarin (his nemesis in Iron Man 3) by broadcasting their home address on live television. This taunting predictably led to the destruction of their beautiful home and Pepper's near death. Self-centered narcissism, an extraordinary lack of attentiveness, a disregard for safety ... as flashy and heroic as Iron Man might be, Tony has a lengthy list of undesirable partner qualities.

Objectively, Pepper's relationship with Tony does not provide her with the companionship or

Figure 7.1 Tony Stark (a.k.a. Iron Man) is a super-hero but a less-than-super boyfriend. What does Pepper Potts see in him? (Photo: Kevin Winter / Getty Images Entertainment)

security that most people seek in their relationships. *Objectively*, Pepper would be better served by seeking an alternative partner, and she would certainly have desirable alternatives if she sought them. In Iron Man 3, Pepper is pursued by a wealthy and powerful business-man, Aldrich Killian, who seems like an *objectively* desirable alternative (Pepper doesn't return his affections). *Objectively, objectively, objectively* ... and yet, luckily for Tony, people in committed relationships employ biases and have illusions that enable them to maintain their commitment. In other words, people in relationships often do not see their partners, their relationships, or their alternatives *objectively*.

This is not to say that people in relationships are oblivious to their relational experiences. Pepper is surely aware that Tony is standing her up (yet again) when he busies himself in his workshop. However, she may interpret that behavior differently than an objective observer would. Rather than thinking of Tony's preoccupation with his work as a shortcoming, she may find his dedication to be admirable. These kinds of biased interpretations serve to maintain commitment, for better or for worse.

In this chapter, you will learn about motivated cognition in relationships, the tendency for people to think in ways that are consistent with their goals (in Pepper's case, the goal to maintain her current relationship). We will start by situating motivated cognition among the assortment of strategies that people use to maintain their close relationships. Then, we will explicate the specific biases and illusions that people tend to have about their partners and their relationships, and we will consider the implications of this motivated inaccuracy for perceivers and their partners. Additionally, we'll consider how biased perceptions extend to people outside of the relationship: one's potential alternatives and even one's partner's potential alternatives. Of course, the extent to which people engage in motivated cognition and the consequences of motivated cognition depend on contextual factors, which we will describe to explain how normative processes differ in specific circumstances.

 GUIDING QUESTIONS

Consider these questions as you read this chapter:
- To what extent are people accurate versus biased in their perceptions of their partners' attributes?
- Do partners prefer to be idealized or to be seen accurately?
- In what ways are memory for past experiences and expectations for the future of the relationship biased?
- How does being in a relationship alter perceptions of attractive alternatives (one's own alternatives and one's partner's alternatives)?
- What individual and relational characteristics alter general motivated cognition processes?

Motivated Cognition as a Relationship Maintenance Strategy

So far, we've explored the roots of romantic attraction (Chapter 4), the process of initiating a relationship (Chapter 5), and how people begin to build love, intimacy, and commitment as they transition into established relationships (Chapter 6). We now turn to arguably the most important topic: the day-to-day work (and pleasure) of sustaining a relationship over time. This relationship maintenance represents the bulk of the experience of close relationships and refers to the various strategies individuals and partners use to preserve their relationships.

The need for relationship maintenance strategies is indisputable, as romantic relationships are notoriously difficult to maintain. Estimates suggest that the likelihood today that a first marriage will end in divorce is an alarming 43 to 46 percent, and that the likelihood that a *re*marriage will dissolve is higher still (Copen et al., 2012; Smock & Schwartz, 2020).

Not only do many established relationships break up or end in divorce, but the trajectory of relationship satisfaction over time is often downward, with a critical subset of people becoming less satisfied with their relationships over time (Birditt et al., 2012; Proulx et al., 2017; Van Laningham et al., 2001; Williamson & Lavner, 2020). Fortunately, this trend is neither universal nor inevitable. In one study that followed different-sex couples over their first sixteen years of marriage, 30 percent of wives and 31 percent of husbands experienced only slight declines in happiness over time (Birditt et al., 2012), demonstrating that sustained satisfaction is possible. How do some partners do it? Similarly, alternative partners are never entirely avoidable, but some people manage to ignore them while others' eyes wander. Why? Critically, like other phenomena in close relationships, the trajectory of a given relationship is predictable. Whether a couple ultimately maintains or dissolves their relationship can be explained, in part, by whether and how partners employ relationship maintenance strategies.

Relationship Maintenance Strategies: An Overview

People use countless active (purposeful) and passive (automatic) relationship maintenance strategies to maintain their commitment. Think of the lasting couples you know – what do they do to sustain their relationships? How do they think about each other, manage disagreements, spend their leisure time, and react to each other's successes, stressors, and opportunities?

Long-term couples, when asked what advice they would give to younger couples, said the following (HelloGiggles Team, 2019; Lim, 2020):

- "Look at the good of your partner, rather than their weaknesses."
- "You must always, always, be forgiving . . . Be prepared to forgive and forget."
- "Develop intimacy beyond sex. Figure out how to connect and have those special moments – it can be as simple as holding hands."
- "Find time to celebrate what you've accomplished together. Value and encourage each other in small ways and in big ways."

Figure 7.2 What does it take to be like this couple, who have been married for sixty-five years? (Photo: Tom Sperduto / Aurora Open / Getty Images)

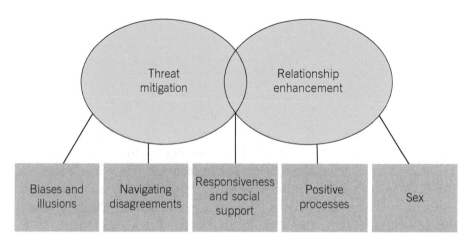

Figure 7.3 Relationship maintenance processes serve to mitigate threat, enhance the relationship, or both (Source: Drawn based on data from Ogolsky et al. [2017])

As you can see, partners have robust tools to maintain their relationships. They (1) sustain the status quo by *managing threats* (e.g., attending to the partner's strengths rather than weaknesses, forgiving bad behavior) and (2) improve the status quo by *enhancing* their connection (e.g., developing intimacy, celebrating accomplishments). This key distinction between maintenance behaviors that mitigate threats and those that enhance the relationship is highlighted in the integrative model of relationship maintenance (Ogolsky et al., 2017), shown in Figure 7.3.

On the threat mitigation side, people can build defenses against the inevitable experiences that could jeopardize a relationship's stability, such as getting to know a partner's less favorable traits, meeting desirable alternative partners, experiencing disagreements, and facing external stresses. These defenses include cognitive biases that enable partners to maintain positive perceptions of each other and behavioral strategies that help them convey understanding and facilitate conflict resolution. In addition, successful partners engage in relationship-enhancing behaviors to improve their relationships (think offense rather than defense here). Relationship-enhancing behaviors include expressing affection and gratitude, supporting each other's individual growth, and being sexually intimate. As any Avenger knows, strong defense plus strong offense is a winning combination, and so we must understand both forms of relationship maintenance. We begin, in this chapter, by focusing on motivated cognition – the biases and illusions that enable persistence by strategically mitigating threats to the relationship.

Rose-Colored Glasses: Truth and Bias

A key tenet of social psychology broadly is that people's perceptions are always subjective rather than objective; their own biases and goals impact what they notice, the interpretations they make, and what they remember later (Hamilton & Carlston, 2013; Higgins & Bargh, 1987). Two complementary forces drive subjective perception: the truth (the objective reality) and bias (a goal-driven misperception; West & Kenny, 2011). In other words, people perceive reality, but they perceive a version of reality that is colored by their own motivations (see Figure 7.4).

Motivated cognition, or subjective (mis)perception, of course applies to close relationships as well (Fitzsimons & Anderson, 2013). Meta-analysis integrating results from over 100 studies assessed the extent of accuracy and bias in various relational perceptions (Fletcher & Kerr, 2010). As shown in Figure 7.5, perceivers are consistently and substantially accurate *and* consistently and substantially biased (remember, an effect size of zero would indicate no effect).

How can people be accurate *and* biased? Remember the idea of tinted lenses; people see what is in front of them, but they see through a lens of illusion. For example, Pepper Potts can clearly see Tony Stark's egotism, but – motivated by love and a desire to maintain the relationship – she may view Tony as "somewhat" rather than "extremely" egotistical. Consider the biases and illusions we discuss throughout this chapter as lenses that make the view of one's relationship rosier (i.e., "rose-colored glasses") rather than as willful obliviousness. Indeed, Fletcher and Kerr (2010) found that the extent of accuracy is stronger than the extent of bias across all judgment types (see Figure 7.5).

Now that you have a sense of accuracy and bias, let's get a bit more technical. The meta-analysis described above actually assessed a particular form of accuracy called **tracking accuracy** and a particular form of bias called **mean-level bias**. To introduce these concepts, we'll rely on the example (made-up) data presented in Figure 7.6. This figure depicts the kindness of three Marvel Universe players: T'Challa (The Black Panther), Iron Man,

Figure 7.4 People see objective reality through the tinted lens of their own biases and illusions. Does this give new meaning to the adage "love is blind"? (Photo: Jesús Argentó Raset / EyeEm / Getty Images)

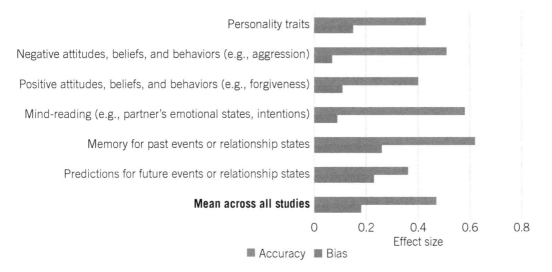

Figure 7.5 The effect sizes for tracking accuracy and mean-level bias in relationship judgments (Source: Drawn based on data from Fletcher & Kerr [2010])

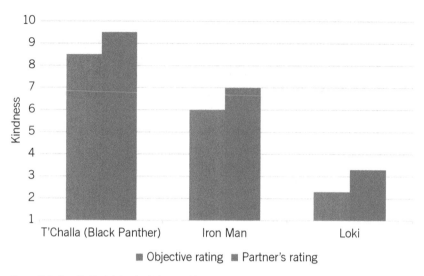

Figure 7.6 Hypothetical data depicting tracking accuracy and mean-level bias. High kindness is indicated by higher scores. Why might partners' ratings exceed objective ratings?

and Loki (a villain). As shown in red, T'Challa is objectively the kindest, followed by Iron Man, and then Loki (he's downright nasty). The green bars show how their romantic partners might rate their kindness.

We can note two critical patterns in this plot. First, partners' perceptions are close to the truth and "track" with the objective kindness ratings. In other words, T'Challa (the objectively kindest character) received the highest kindness rating from his partner, higher than Pepper Potts rated Iron Man, and higher than the rating Loki (the objectively least kind character) received from his partner. This is tracking accuracy. Technically, tracking accuracy reflects a correlation between objective ratings and partner ratings. Second, in every case, partners are rating these superheroes as kinder than the objective truth warrants; the partners of T'Challa, Iron Man, and Loki all perceive them one point kinder than the objective rating. This is mean-level bias, a tendency to over-perceive (or under-perceive) a particular trait. Why might people hold such inflated views? Critically, these misperceptions are not arbitrary or accidental. They serve a purpose. As we shall see, perceptual and interpretive biases play an essential role in protecting relationships against potential threats to their stability.

Staying Committed through Biased Perceptions of the Partner

How intelligent are you compared to the average college student? Less intelligent? More intelligent? Exactly average? Decades of research on the better-than-average effect suggests that the majority of readers will rate themselves as more intelligent than average (Alicke & Govorun, 2005). In fact, a large majority of college students rate themselves as better than average on most attributes, despite the mathematical impossibility of more than half of students being, in fact, better than average (Zell et al., 2020). This tendency to see ourselves unrealistically positively is part of a broader self-enhancement tendency. People are typically motivated to see themselves as kind, intelligent, attractive, and so on (Leary, 2007).

Now think about your romantic partner or closest friend. How would you rate them compared to the average college student (or relevant benchmark for them)? Less intelligent? More intelligent? Exactly average? As we will see throughout this section, people are not only motivated to *self*-enhance, they also are motivated to engage in *partner*-enhancement, viewing their partners unrealistically positively as well. Chances are, you rated your romantic partner or friends as more intelligent than average, at least if intelligence is something you value in a partner or friend. Perceiving your partner positively not only enables you to feel great about yourself ("Wow, I attracted quite a catch!"), it serves an adaptive function of facilitating continued commitment to the relationship. People who see their partners positively are able to reduce uncertainty about whether they have selected the right person, enabling them to stay satisfied with, and thus committed to, their partner (Murray, 1999).

To be clear, both self-enhancement and partner-enhancement refer to protective biases and thus are defensive threat-mitigating maintenance strategies. Despite the overlap in terminology, these self-enhancement and partner-enhancement tendencies are not relationship-enhancing behaviors, the offensive relationship maintenance strategies to be discussed in later chapters. For now, let's stay on the defense and review several ways in which perceptions of partners are biased (i.e., enhanced) to make imperfect partners seem a bit more perfect.

Positive Illusions

Which attributes will people be motivated to see – or to not see – in their partners? If you remember back to the chapter on attraction (Chapter 4), people typically seek long-term partners who are physically attractive and possess "good partner traits." Therefore, it would be advantageous for people to over-perceive these attributes in their partners. Spoiler alert: they do.

Physical Attractiveness

Tony Stark might see himself as handsome, but chances are, Pepper Potts has an even more positive impression of his good looks. In one study, people rated their partners as having greater facial attractiveness (e.g., nose, lips) and bodily attractiveness (e.g., waist, arms) than partners rated themselves (Barelds & Dijkstra, 2009). Notice in Figure 7.7 that this effect occurred for both men and women. Other research shows that partner idealization of physical attractiveness occurs in both early-stage romantic relationships (Barelds et al., 2011; Solomon & Vazire, 2014) and long-term marital relationships (Barelds & Dijkstra, 2009).

To evaluate the extent to which people have positive illusions about their partners, we need a "reality" benchmark for comparison (Barelds et al., 2011; Barelds & Dijkstra, 2009). In the example above, the researchers used individuals' own self-ratings as that reality benchmark. But remember the pervasive self-enhancement motive? Comparing partner ratings to self-ratings may actually underestimate the extent of partner idealization because people's self-views are likely already inflated. If we were to instead compare partner perceptions to a more objective benchmark, the extent of positive illusion should be larger. Indeed, follow-up research showed that people rated their partners as more physically attractive (overall attractiveness and facial attractiveness) than their partner's own self-ratings, and their partner's own self-ratings were also positively biased compared to more objective ratings from neutral, third-party observers who viewed their photographs (Barelds et al., 2011; Solomon & Vazire, 2014). In other words, people think they themselves are more physically

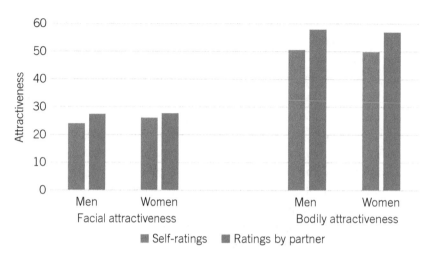

Figure 7.7 Partners' ratings of physical attractiveness are higher than individuals' own self-ratings. The maximum score for facial attractiveness was 35, whereas the maximum score for bodily attractiveness was 75. (Source: Drawn based on data from Barelds & Dijkstra [2009])

attractive than they really are, and their partners' perceptions of them are more biased still. Interestingly, partners are aware that they possess this positivity bias; they report that their perceptions of their partner's physical attractiveness are superior to their partner's own self-views (Boyes & Fletcher, 2007; Solomon & Vazire, 2014). These findings therefore provide evidence for both accuracy and bias in partner perceptions of physical attractiveness; people overestimate their partner's attractiveness, but are aware that they do so.

Physical attractiveness is one of the most desirable characteristics in a romantic partner, so a charitable evaluation on this trait may be uniquely important to maintaining commitment over time. Physical appearance also has the potential to change – perhaps more than other traits – over the course of a long-term relationship, so maintaining a positively biased perception may prevent declines in satisfaction as one's partner ages. Consistent with the idea that physical attractiveness is a key target for positive illusions, people actually *prefer* that their partners idealize them most with regard to physical attractiveness, compared to other traits (Swann et al., 2002).

"Good Partner" Traits

Unlike physical attractiveness – which is easily observable – perceiving another person's personality traits is rather complex and therefore provides additional opportunities for positive bias to infiltrate perceptions. According to the **realistic accuracy model** of person perception, accurately perceiving another person's personality traits entails four steps (Funder, 1995; Letzring & Funder, 2019). Specifically, the person being perceived (i.e., the target) must exhibit behaviors that are *relevant* to the trait being assessed, and that behavior must be *available* to the observer (i.e., the perceiver). For example, to assess your partner's agreeableness, your partner would need to exhibit behaviors consistent with agreeableness (e.g., helping a neighbor carry groceries) or inconsistent with agreeableness (e.g., hurling insults at a delivery person). Next – and here's where the magic of perceiver illusions can come in – you would need to both *detect* the behavior and *utilize* the information to inform your judgment of your partner's agreeableness. We're not talking detective work here, just paying attention and reflecting enough on the behavior to form a perception. In an objective world, you would notice your partner's agreeable or disagreeable behavior and update your judgment of their agreeableness accordingly.

Despite the simplicity of this process, people consistently rate their partners as higher in agreeableness than their partner's behaviors actually warrant (Miller et al., 2006). Interestingly, these same people do *detect* their partner's disagreeable behavior (they can enumerate a list of instances), but they do not *utilize* the unfavorable observations to inform their judgments. Some partner behaviors, like hostility or aggression, present such a threat to commitment that some people fail to even *detect* them when they occur (Capozzi et al., 2020). People who highly value their relationships are the most motivated to ignore or strategically misinterpret a partner's bad behavior when it occurs (e.g., Finkenauer et al., 2010). After a fight, for example, they might vastly under-perceive their partner's destructive conflict behaviors (Venaglia & Lemay, 2019). Interestingly, people who only minimally value their relationships actually over-perceive their partner's destructive behaviors (Venaglia & Lemay, 2019), a reminder that illusions in relationships need not always be positive. Motivated cognition is thinking in line with our goals, and people who do not value their relationships may have the goal of finding evidence to support the decision to break up.

Projecting One's Ideal and One's Self

One critical point to know about positive illusions is that people do not necessarily need to ascribe *every* positive trait to their partners. Instead, they can ascribe the attributes that are *most important* to them to maintain their commitment to the relationship. This idea was originally proposed by Murray and her colleagues, as part of the initial theorizing about the role of positive illusions in close relationships (Murray, 1999; Murray et al., 1996a, 1996b). In the now-classic research on this topic, Murray and her colleagues had a sample of married couples and a sample of dating couples rate the extent to which twenty-one interpersonal traits were characteristic of themselves, their partners, their hypothetical ideal partner, and the average partner (Murray et al., 1996a). Take a minute to consider the traits in Table 7.1. How would you rate yourself, your partner (or best friend), your ideal partner (or best friend), and an average partner (or best friend)?

Participants' reports of their partners were to some extent "accurate"; that is, they corresponded with their partner's own self-reports (which as we know are themselves biased). In addition to this presumed "accuracy," there was also evidence of partner bias, such that people projected their *ideal* partner's attributes onto their evaluations of their *actual* partners. For example, if Pepper Potts rated her ideal partner as extremely self-assured (9), and her actual partner (Tony Stark) rated himself as moderately self-assured (7), Pepper might have rated Tony as highly self-assured (8), with her perception of him influenced by both his *actual* attributes (truth) and her *ideal* (positive bias).

These partner ratings included another form of bias as well: a projection of one's *own* characteristics (Murray et al., 1996a). That is, people rated their partners as having attributes they possessed themselves. Why would people be motivated to project their own attributes onto their partner? Again, think back to the attraction chapter; people tend to prefer partners who are similar to themselves. By projecting their own attributes onto their partner, they view their partners as similar to themselves, a motivated perception that should facilitate commitment. People are so motivated to perceive similarity that perceiving dissimilarity in

Table 7.1 Accuracy and illusion in partner perception

Trait	Ratings			
	Self	Partner (or best friend)	Ideal partner (or best friend)	Average partner (or best friend)
Kind and affectionate				
Patient				
Understanding				
Responsive to my needs				
Critical and judgmental				
Lazy				
Emotional				
Moody				
Thoughtless				
Distant				
Complaining				
Self-assured				
Sociable or extroverted				
Intelligent				
Witty				

Rating your own, your partner's, and/or your best friend's traits: be a mock participant in classic research on positive illusions and rate each of these traits for how characteristic it is for yourself, your partner (or best friend), your ideal partner (or best friend), and the average partner (or best friend) on a 9-point scale from 1 (*not at all characteristic*) to 9 (*extremely characteristic*).

Source: Based on data from Murray et al. (1996a).

one domain (e.g., values) automatically triggers partner enhancement in other domains (e.g., interests), in order to protect the relationship (Auger et al., 2016).

The contribution of each of these three factors – accuracy, projection of one's ideal, and projection of one's self – to the perception of one's partner's attributes is shown in Figure 7.8, again using the example of Pepper's ratings of Tony. The numbers shown are ranges of standardized regression coefficients so they can be compared to one another to determine their relative strength (with higher numbers indicating a stronger relation). As shown,

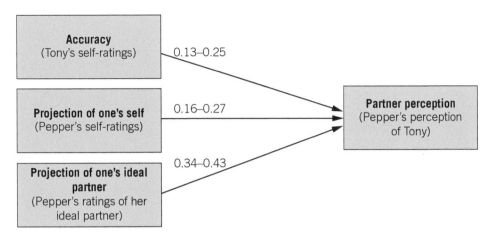

Figure 7.8 The relative strength of accuracy, projection of one's self, and projection of one's ideal partner on perceptions of one's actual partner. The original study assessed these associations at three time-points, so the range of the associations is presented for each path. (Source: Drawn based on data from Murray et al. [1996b])

partner perceptions are based much more heavily on projection of one's ideal partner than on reality or projections of oneself (Murray et al., 1996b). In short, according to Murray's research, we would expect Pepper to see Tony primarily the way she wants him to be. In this way, Pepper is experiencing a form of "augmented reality" in which she sees her ideal partner's attributes overlaid on the image of her real partner.

 RESEARCHER SPOTLIGHT: Sandra Murray, PhD

How did you come to be a research psychologist?
When I started college, I wanted to be an English major, but I found it really frustrating that there did not seem to be a way to objectively decide between two different interpretations of a text. Fortunately, I also took Mark Zanna's *Introduction to Social Psychology* class in my first year and that ignited my interest in social psychology and in research more broadly. When I took my first research methods class, it opened my eyes to a way of thinking about the world that made intuitive sense to me … it also gave me a way to decide between two different explanations.

How did you decide to study motivated cognition and idealization?
I had always been interested in understanding how people were able to convince themselves to believe things that seemed fantastical. As an undergraduate, I took John Holmes's interpersonal relations and research methods courses. He gave me Philip Brickman's book on commitment and introduced me to positive illusions. Hours and hours of conversations with John about the ideas in the Brickman book set me on this path.

Figure 7.9 Dr. Sandra Murray is a professor in the Department of Psychology at University at Buffalo. (Photo courtesy of Sandra Murray, PhD.)

What part of researching relationships is most energizing for you?
I really enjoy the struggle of trying to build an argument in written form and the back and forth of trying to construct the clearest argument possible. When I become frustrated or demoralized by the review process, I try to focus on what a luxury it is to be able to write and craft arguments to advance our own particular perspective on how relationships work.

What's next in motivated cognition?
I think it is critical to understand how relationship motivations operate in a broader motivational context. Broader motivations, like seeing the world as sensible or meaningful or protecting ourselves, shape how we think about our relationships and vice versa. Relationships don't operate in a motivational vacuum.

The Consequences of Seeing through Rose-Colored Glasses

We've hinted at times that perceiving a partner in biased ways may allow people to overlook the unflattering aspects of their partners to maintain satisfaction, and thus, sustain commitment. Does this actually happen, or might maintaining positive illusions prove costly? Consider the possible role of positive illusions in undermining satisfaction: it's a steep fall when people become disillusioned with their less-than-ideal partners (Niehuis et al., 2011). And what are the consequences of *being seen* through rose-colored glasses? Do people enjoy being idealized or does being put on a pedestal cause discomfort?

The Benefits of Positive Illusions

Starting with physical attractiveness, people who perceive their partners as more attractive than "reality" benchmarks do, in fact, generally report greater relationship quality than people who are less biased (Barelds et al., 2011; Barelds & Dijkstra, 2009). Because physical attractiveness is a highly valued trait in a partner, over-perceiving a partner's physical attractiveness may help to support a perceived match between one's partner and one's ideal partner. The benefits associated with over-perceiving a partner's physical attractiveness are especially strong for older adults compared to younger adults (Barelds & Dijkstra, 2009), perhaps because age-related changes threaten relationship quality in the absence of ongoing positive illusions. Interestingly, partners who are the target of positive illusions also report higher relationship quality (Barelds & Dijkstra, 2009), consistent with research indicating that people *prefer* to have their physical attractiveness over-perceived by their partners (Swann et al., 2002).

Empirical research also typically shows benefits of positive illusions for other attributes (Barelds & Dijkstra, 2011; Lackenbauer et al., 2010; Miller et al., 2006; Murray et al., 1996a, 1996b, 2002, 2011). For instance, Murray and colleagues (1996a) found that idealizing a partner on the twenty-one traits in Table 7.1 was associated with higher relationship satisfaction for both the person doing the idealizing and the person being idealized (Murray et al., 1996a). This pattern of results was evident in both samples of dating couples and married couples (Murray et al., 1996a, 1996b) as well as in different-sex and same-sex couples (Conley et al., 2009). Further, dating couples are more likely to stay together over the course of a year when they idealize each other to a greater extent, and this exciting finding is mediated by partners' greater satisfaction (Murray et al., 1996b). That is, partners who hold more positive illusions about each other's attributes stay together *because* they remain more satisfied. These couples are also most able to avoid conflicts and tend to report a decrease in conflicts over time, unlike couples who hold less positive biases (Murray et al., 1996b). In fact, meta-analysis suggests positive illusions may be the strongest predictor of relationship stability, eclipsing other predictors like love, trust, and closeness (Le et al., 2010).

The link between positive illusions and relationship satisfaction is critical, given how, for many couples, relationship satisfaction declines precipitously after marriage. As shown in Figure 7.10, a person's initial tendency to idealize their partner (a) and their partner's initial tendency to idealize them back (b) each predicted less steep declines in relationship satisfaction over time (Murray et al., 2011). This general pattern of results has also been observed over thirteen years of marriage in a study where both one's own and one's partner's idealization (with regard to agreeableness, in particular) predicted somewhat less steep declines in love (Miller et al., 2006).

Beyond general positive illusions, perceiving unrealistic similarity with one's partner also predicts higher relationship satisfaction, consistent with the idea that people desire similar partners (Murray et al., 2002). Those who over-perceive similarity report feeling more understood by their partners, which contributes to better relational experiences. Critically, people who project more of their own attributes and values onto their partners are less likely to report breakups with their partners over the next twelve to eighteen months (Murray et al., 2002).

Although positive illusions tend to produce relationship benefits, extreme idealization predicts poorer relationship outcomes than idealization grounded in reality (Tomlinson et al., 2014). In one experiment, people who were led to perceive that their partners viewed them with a strong positive bias *and* a high level of accuracy rated their relationships more

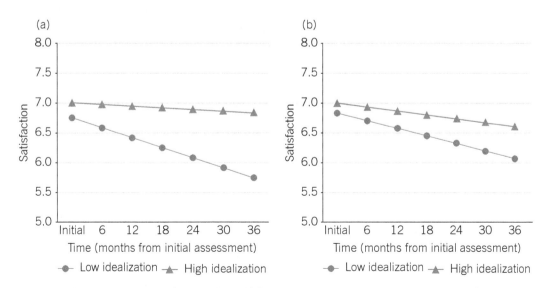

Figure 7.10 Can you see the power of positive illusions? Relationship satisfaction declines less steeply over the first thirty-six months of marriage for people who idealize their partner more (a) and for people who are idealized by their partner more (b). (Source: Murray et al. [2011], reprinted with permission from Sage Publications)

positively than people who were led to believe that their partners were solely accurate, solely biased, or both inaccurate and lacking a positive bias (yikes!).

The Importance of Being Seen Accurately

Idealization can also have a downside, at least for the person being idealized. Let's take the perspective of Tony Stark. Tony, like all people, is complex; he has multiple motives operating at once. Yes, Tony wants to feel good about himself (self-enhancement motive), but he also wants to be understood by the people close to him – he

Figure 7.11 Relationships benefit when partners idealize each other and when they see each other accurately. When is accuracy most important, and why? (Photo: monkeybusinessimages / iStock / Getty Images Plus)

wants to be seen accurately (Reis et al., 2017). If Pepper idealizes Tony, he may feel misunderstood and his relationship with Pepper may suffer. Although Pepper's positive illusions may meet Tony's self-enhancement motive, they conflict with his self-verification motive – his motive to be seen by others the way that he sees himself (Swann, 2011).

Supporting the idea that accuracy can at times be more beneficial than idealization, people tend to report greater intimacy in their relationships when their partners view their social skills accurately (the way they themselves view their social skills) compared to when their partners view them as more or less socially skilled than they view themselves (De La Ronde & Swann, 1998). A partner's accurate evaluation may be beneficial because it shows that the partner has paid enough attention to form an accurate impression and because accuracy may prevent awkward interactions (e.g., "Hey, I've told everyone you'll give a toast tonight because you're so socially skilled. I hope you don't mind." Yikes!).

To recap, people tend to experience better relationship outcomes when their partners idealize them *and* people tend to experience better relationship outcomes when their partners see them accurately (Figure 7.11). How do we reconcile these seemingly contradictory findings? Whether people prioritize self-enhancement or self-verification motives (and whether they therefore benefit from being idealized or being seen accurately) depends on the type of relationship and the type of trait or ability being considered (Kwang & Swann, 2010), as described next.

Accuracy and Idealization in Dating Versus Marital Relationships

Recall that relationships operate along trajectories, and a lot can change between the early stages of a relationship and its golden anniversary. One key shift is a decrease in the extent to which people make evaluations about their partners, as time goes on. Early in relationships, people scrutinize their partners to evaluate whether their partner is a good fit; by the time a couple is married (unless spurred to re-evaluate), they are generally done with the decision about the suitability of the partner and active evaluation wanes. People may not only evaluate their partners more when dating than when committed to each other, but these evaluations may be more high stake. A negative evaluation could be a dealbreaker in a new relationship sparking a self/partner-enhancement motive, whereas in marital relationships, people may be comfortable with being viewed accurately (self-verification motive). Indeed, negative spousal evaluations are not much of a threat in a context of relationship stability and might provide opportunities for self-improvement. Research has supported these ideas. Whereas people in dating relationships report greater intimacy in their relationships when their partners view them positively (regardless of their self-views), people in married relationships report the greatest intimacy when their partners view them not too positively, not too negatively, but just right – similarly positively to their own self-views (Swann et al., 1994). A meta-analysis of several studies supports this pattern of results, as does experimental investigation; being viewed positively (enhancement) offers benefits in dating relationships, whereas being viewed accurately (verification) offers benefits in marital relationships (Campbell et al., 2006; Kwang & Swann, 2010).

Accuracy and Idealization of Concrete Abilities Versus Abstract Traits

The other key moderator that helps to explain when idealization or accuracy is more beneficial is the type of trait or ability itself. Consider the many impressions we make about the people in our lives. Is your best friend a good cook? Are they kind? These two judgments vary in an important way: in their level of abstraction. Being a good cook is a concrete ability; either your best friend can whip up a delicious meal or they cannot. Alternatively, being kind is a more abstract trait, so you could point to many different behaviors as evidence that your friend is kind (e.g., they tell light-hearted jokes, they listen attentively). Because evidence for abstract traits can be varied, abstract traits are more amenable to positive illusions without sacrificing accuracy than are concrete abilities. For instance, you can accurately report that your best friend is kind even if they are occasionally unkind; on the whole, they're kind. However, to say your best friend is a great cook when instant ramen is their only specialty is just untrue.

Indeed, people do exhibit greater positive bias for abstract evaluations (e.g., "My spouse has a number of good qualities") compared to concrete abilities (e.g., a spouse's social skills, athletic ability, or tidiness; Neff & Karney, 2002; Swann et al., 1994). Critically, greater accuracy on *specific* concrete abilities predicts a lower likelihood of divorce over the first four years of marriage, suggesting that seeing accurately – and being seen accurately – with regard to tangible traits is advantageous (Neff & Karney, 2002, 2005).

To integrate what we've learned, accuracy and bias both play a role in relationship maintenance. Accurately assessing a partner's abilities allows the partner to feel seen and understood, whereas idealizing a partner (particularly on abstract traits) protects the perceiver and the partner from experiencing declines in relationship satisfaction. Of note, people tend to rate positive abstract evaluations as more important for a successful relationship than positive concrete evaluations; a "wonderful" partner (abstract evaluation) is essential, but an organized partner (concrete evaluation) typically is not (Neff & Karney, 2002). Therefore, accurate perceptions of a partner's concrete traits and abilities is not a threat for the perceiver, even if some of the perceptions are negative. Finally, accurate perceptions or a positive bias are both better than the alternative: seeing a partner more negatively than they see themselves. People who see their partners more negatively than partners see themselves experience the worst overall and daily relationship satisfaction, a finding that has been replicated cross-culturally (Seidman, 2012; Wu, Chen et al., 2020).

DIVERSITY AND INCLUSION

Mental Health and Self-Verification in Relationships

Consider the relationship implications of self-verification theory for those with negatively distorted self-views, specifically people with **depression**. Symptoms of depression include feeling sad or empty, a decreased ability to experience pleasure, a decreased interest in usually enjoyable activities, and, most notably, feelings of worthlessness, inadequacy, and self-disgust (Zahn et al., 2015). Self-verification theory, then, would suggest that people who are depressed would prefer to interact with those who see them as worthless and inadequate (Swann, Wenzlaff, & Krull, 1992a; Swann, Wenzlaff, & Tafarodi, 1992b), not the types of perceptions we generally attribute to healthy relationships.

Indeed, people who are depressed do seek negative self-verifying feedback (e.g., Giesler et al., 1996; Wakeling et al., 2020). In one set of studies, depressed people (unlike non-depressed people) reported greater desire to interact with a person who they believed viewed them unfavorably than a person they believed viewed them favorably (Swann, Wenzlaff, & Krull, 1992a; Swann, Wenzlaff, & Tafarodi, 1992b). For a depressed person, favorable evaluations or receiving positive feedback from another person is so contradictory to their own negative self-views that it can be an unsettling, or perhaps even disorienting, experience (e.g., Ashokkumar & Swann, 2020). A meta-analysis also found support for a moderately strong link between depression and more negative feedback-seeking in over 100 studies (Wakeling et al., 2020). This link was weaker (though still significant) in romantic relationships than in other relationship types, perhaps because people are more willing to receive non-verifying feedback if they trust their partner's perceptions (e.g., Weinstock & Whisman, 2004).

As much as negative feedback might be consistent with their world views, seeking and receiving self-confirming negative feedback can be maladaptive for people experiencing depression, resulting in increases in depressive symptoms (Borelli & Prinstein, 2006; Joiner, 1995, 2000; Pettit & Joiner, 2001). When someone experiencing depression prioritizes interacting with people who view them negatively, they risk feeling rejected and receiving (expected) negative feedback (Figure 7.12). This feedback, in turn, reinforces their view of

themselves as worthless and inadequate, ultimately reinforcing their depression (see Hames et al., 2013, for a review of the interpersonal processes that maintain depression).

Figure 7.12 When you are feeling bad about yourself, spending time with others who also view you negatively may provide the comfort of predictability, but may reinforce negative perceptions and exacerbate depression. (Photo: South_agency / E+ / Getty Images)

Dealing with Unfortunate Truths

The distinction between abstract and concrete traits helps to clarify how people can maintain positive perceptions of their partners even as relationships progress and people have more opportunities to observe unappealing information about their partners. With more time spent together, more annoyances are sure to arise, creating more opportunities for a partner to transform from a cool Bruce Banner to the hot-headed "Hulk." Cohabitation, for instance, can bring to light new types of information that have the potential to spark conflict; think household tasks, cleanliness (or lack thereof), and annoying habits (Rhoades, Stanley, & Markman, 2012a). The transition to parenthood, in all its sleep-deprived glory, can further reveal undesirable traits or bad habits, as partners take on the 24-hour job of childcare and renegotiate responsibilities (Doss & Rhoades, 2017). Despite this, about half of people in relationships endorse at least one idealistic statement such as "Every new thing I have learned about my partner has pleased me" (Fowers et al., 2002; Fowers & Olson, 1993). Wow! Every new thing? Really? That statement is not just idealistic; it's almost certainly unrealistic.

Even if people do not endorse the idea that *every* new aspect of their partner appeals to them, illusions still tend to be strong and enduring. How do people maintain positive perceptions when they inevitably encounter unfortunate truths about their partners? One strategy is to restrict negative perceptions of a spouse to concrete (rather than abstract) attributes. Awareness of undesirable concrete attributes is not particularly threatening. Consistent with this idea, people tend to use concrete descriptors when asked to list a partner's negative traits ("He has a poor sense of direction"), whereas they use more abstract descriptors when they describe their partner's positive traits ("He's just wonderful"), a strategy that helps to maintain an overall positive perception of the partner (Neff & Karney, 2002). Another strategy is to reframe potentially negative attributes as desirable because they contribute to positive outcomes or can be considered in a positive light. For example, a person might say: "My partner is picky which can be a bit irritating, but his pickiness makes him extremely tidy." This strategy neutralizes negative qualities by linking them with related positive qualities to preserve an overall positive evaluation (Murray & Holmes, 1999). People also protect relationships by using a "yes, but" approach that acknowledges a partner's faults while simultaneously highlighting an unrelated redeeming quality. "Yeah, she's not a great listener, but it's so sweet that she volunteers at the nursing home." Here, an unrelated positive trait offsets a negative trait to maintain satisfaction (Murray & Holmes, 1999).

Look at all this motivated cognition; at every turn, we find ways to see our partners as we want to, and still, there's more. Flip back to Table 7.1 and read through the list of attributes again. This time, think about which of the attributes you believe are *most important* for a romantic partner (or best friend) to have. Maybe they should be patient? Witty? Self-assured? It's up to you. Now, think about your actual romantic partner(s) (or best friend). Which attributes *actually describe* them most strongly?

Do you notice any overlap in the traits you see as important for a partner (or best friend) and the traits that you see in your actual partner(s) (or best friend)? Research shows that some people strategically shift the qualities they perceive as *most* important to align with their partners' (and friends') actual qualities (Fletcher et al., 2000; Neff & Karney, 2003). These **flexible ideal standards** provide a way to maintain satisfaction by "moving the goalposts." In other words, if your partner or best friend is witty, being witty *becomes* a trait

Figure 7.13 A man waits for his partner with a bouquet of red roses. What attributions will he make for their lateness? What attributions will the partner make for the gift of roses? (Photo: dima_sidelnikov / iStock /Getty Images Plus)

that you believe is important in an ideal partner or best friend. This works in the reverse as well. Let's say that you originally thought that being sociable is critical in a partner or best friend, but then you met yours and they are undeniably unsociable. You might then strategically view sociability as a less important trait, which allows you to maintain your belief that your partner (or best friend) is perfectly perfect.

Finally, people can strategically maintain positive perceptions of their partners by making attributions – interpretations of the partner's behavior – that preserve a positive view of the partner. Consider the man photographed in Figure 7.13. As he sits waiting for his partner, how does he explain their lateness? Are they late because they're thoughtless and self-centered? Or perhaps they're late because, despite leaving early, they got caught in a traffic jam? Clearly, these two attributions have differing implications for relationship maintenance.

People make attributions for the *cause* of a partner's negative behaviors along several dimensions, including its locus (whether it is internal or external), scope (whether it is global or specific), and stability (whether it is stable or unstable; Bradbury & Fincham, 1990). An attribution that a partner is late because they're thoughtless and self-centered places the locus internal to the partner (it's something about them); these broad trait-based explanations may also suggest that the partner's lateness is global (impacting other aspects of the relationship) and stable across time (unlikely to change). Alternatively, the traffic explanation places the locus external to the partner (it's something about the situation), and the cause is perhaps specific to this situation and more unstable. As you might expect, the extent to which people make external (rather than internal), specific (rather than global), and unstable (rather than stable) causal attributions for negative behaviors tends to predict better marital satisfaction (Fincham & Bradbury, 1992).

Researchers assess people's typical causal attributions, along with attributions for accountability – responsibility and blame – using the Relationship Attribution Measure (Fincham & Bradbury, 1992). Participants imagine their partner doing several negative behaviors (e.g., criticizing something they say, not paying attention to what they are saying, being cool and distant), and report their beliefs about the cause of the behavior and the extent to which their partner is responsible and blameworthy for the behavior. Table 7.2 shows a portion of the measure in which participants would make attributions regarding a partner's (in this example, a husband's) criticism. Responsibility and blame attributions presuppose that the cause of the negative behavior is internal (Davey et al., 2001).

In marital relationships, responsibility attributions tend to be particularly crucial for relationship functioning (Davey et al., 2001). People who attribute intentionality, selfish motivation, and blameworthiness to their partners tend to subsequently behave less warmly and with more hostility (two years into the marriage); these behaviors in turn lead them and their partners to experience declines in relationship quality over the first four years of

Table 7.2 Assessing measurement attributions

Relationship Attribution Measure	Dimension assessed
Your husband criticizes something you say:	
Cause	
1. My husband's behavior was due to something about him (e.g., the type of person he is, the mood he was in).	Locus (internal)
2. The reason my husband criticized me is *not* likely to change.	Stability (stable)
3. The reason my husband criticized me is something that affects other areas of our marriage.	Globality (global)
Responsibility – blame	
4. My husband criticized me on purpose rather than unintentionally.	Intentionality (intentional)
5. My husband's behavior was motivated by selfish rather than *un*selfish concerns.	Motivation (selfish)
6. My husband deserves to be blamed for criticizing me.	Blame (blameworthy)

Most partners will criticize each other at some point, and how we interpret such criticism can vary: how do you make sense of such critiques? Criticizing is an example behavior from the Relationship Attribution Measure that assesses several attributions for a negative partner behavior on a scale from 1 (disagree strongly) to 6 (agree strongly). While items here focus on husbands, they could be used for wives, spouses, or dating partners.

Source: Copyright © 1992 by American Psychological Association, reproduced with permission; Fincham, F. D., & Bradbury, T. N. (1992). Assessing attributions in marriage: The Relationship Attribution Measure. *Journal of Personality and Social Psychology, 62*(3), 457–468.

marriage (Durtschi et al., 2011). Let that sink in. The attributions you make today may impact your behavior in the future, which ultimately impacts your own and your partner's relationship quality further down the road. Fortunately, this means that "adaptive" attributions, those that direct responsibility away from the partner, have the potential to protect your own and your partner's relationship quality over time. The positive consequences of "adaptive" attributions have been observed in diverse samples, including couples of Indian participants, Chinese participants, French Canadian participants, and cohabiting gay men (Bell et al., 2018; Houts & Horne, 2008; Sabourin et al., 1991; Stander et al., 2001).

Think back to the unfortunate man sitting alone with the bouquet of flowers. When his partner finally shows up, what attributions might this partner make for the gift of flowers? Just as partners interpret each other's negative behaviors, they also interpret each other's positive behaviors, and they do so using the same types of attributions: people judge causality and responsibility. In the case of positive behaviors, however, attributions to internal (rather than external), global (rather than specific), and stable (rather than unstable) causes offer the greatest benefit for the relationship. These attributions lead to the inference that the partner deserves to be appreciated for a kind (and intentional) gesture.

People in relationships possess an arsenal of strategies that allow them to establish and maintain positive perceptions of their partners. These positive partner perceptions are one key component needed to maintain relationship satisfaction, and thus commitment to the relationship (e.g., Rusbult et al., 1998; Tran et al., 2019). Another key component is satisfaction with (i.e., positive perceptions of) the relationship itself. As we'll see next, motivated cognition is at work here as well.

Staying Committed through Biased Perceptions of the Relationship

When people evaluate their relationships (i.e., their interpersonal dynamics rather than the characteristics of their partner), they consider the relationship's past, present, and future. Specifically, they consider whether the relationship's trajectory (from past to present) has improved or worsened; they assess how their relationship compares to others' relationships in the present; and they consider their expectations for the future of the relationship. Before reading on, consider your own relationship with a romantic partner or close friend, and answer the questions in Table 7.3.

Table 7.3 Consider your own relationship with a romantic partner or best friend

Past
1. Look at the blank graph below. Think back to each of the times indicated, and for each time, mark the point on the graph that represents how happy you were with your relationship at that time. (0 = extremely unhappy; 100 = extremely happy)

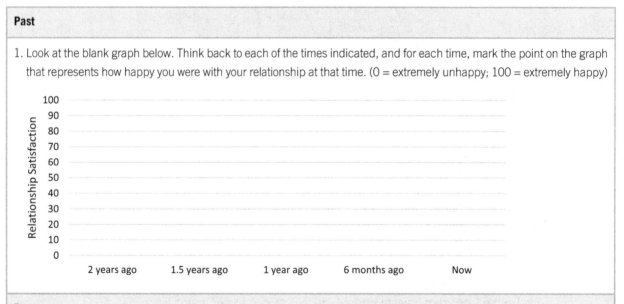

Present
2. List features of relationships that you think of as **good and desirable**. If you think that a feature is more typical of *your relationship than of others'*, begin the sentence with "My relationship ..."; if you think that a feature is more typical of *others' relationships than yours*, begin the sentence with "Other people's relationships ..." For example: - "My relationship is one of complete trust." - "Other people's relationships are exciting."

Table 7.3 (*cont.*)

3. List features of relationships that you think of as **bad and undesirable**. If you think that a feature is more typical of *your relationship than of others'*, begin the sentence with "My relationship ...", if you think that a feature is more typical of *others' relationships than yours*, begin the sentence with "Other people's relationships ..." For example:
   - "My relationship doesn't have much intellectual stimulation."
   - "Other people's relationships are emotionally distant."

Future

4. Over the next four years, do you expect that your overall feelings about your relationship will become ... (select one):
   Much worse – A little worse – Stable – A little better – Much better

Source: Copyright © 2002 by American Psychological Association, reproduced with permission; Frye, N. E., & Karney, B. R. (2002). Being better or getting better? Social and temporal comparisons as coping mechanisms in close relationships. *Personality and Social Psychology Bulletin, 28*(9), 1287–1299 (Question 1); Copyright © 1995 by American Psychological Association; reproduced with permission; Van Lange, P. A. M. & Rusbult, C. E. (1995). My relationship is better than – and not as bad – as yours is: The perception of superiority in close relationships. *Personality and Social Psychology Bulletin, 21*(1), 32–44 (Questions 2 and 3); and Lavner et al. (2013); reproduced with permission from Sage Publications [Question 4].

Biased Memory of the Past

Marvel fans know that Steve Rogers was a notably petite and scrawny man who was continually told he was unfit to serve in the military. That is, until he received a "super-soldier serum" that transformed him into bulky and hunky Captain America. Movie makeovers like this one are so compelling, in part, because looking back at a less desirable version of a person makes the present version seem *even more* appealing. Looking back on a less desirable version of one's relationship can make the present version seem more appealing as well.

To make their current relationships seem strong, people tend to denigrate past versions of their relationships (Frye & Karney, 2002, 2004; Karney & Coombs, 2000; Karney & Frye, 2002; Sprecher, 1999). In one set of studies, married different-sex couples were recruited in their first year of marriage and were contacted to report their marital satisfaction every six months for four years (Karney & Frye, 2002). At the final assessment, participants were also asked to think back on how their marital satisfaction had changed over the past four years and to estimate their marital satisfaction at each of the previous assessment points. This retrospective reporting of the trajectory of a relationship is what we asked you to do in the "Past" section of Table 7.3. Results were consistent with the idea that people mis-remember their past relationship satisfaction in order to perceive a positive trajectory over time.

As shown in Figure 7.14a, participants' concurrent (in the moment) reports of their marital satisfaction showed a slight downward trend, and this was true for wives and husbands in two samples. However, when people later looked back over the four years, they remembered a different, more favorable, trajectory (Figure 7.14b). They remembered an initial downward trend followed by an increase in marital satisfaction, an increase that did not actually occur. The researchers interpreted this pattern of results to indicate that participants believe (or want to believe) that "we've been getting better lately." Who doesn't want to feel like they're on the up-swing? Even if relationship satisfaction has declined, a recent upward pattern suggests that the future is bright (stay tuned for more on future expectations).

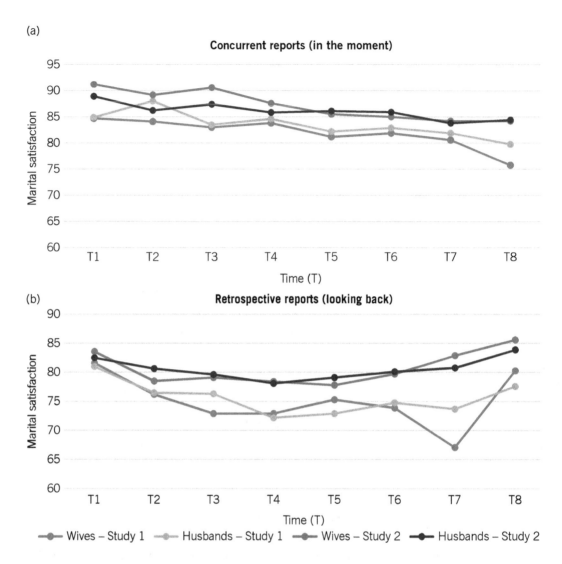

Figure 7.14 How well do these diagrams parallel your sense of your own relationship's trajectory? These figures show actual (a) and remembered (b) trajectories of marital satisfaction over time. In two studies, participants reported their current marital satisfaction every six months for four years (sample means at each time-point are plotted in Panel [a]). Then, at the final assessment (T8), participants reported (to the best of their memory) their marital satisfaction at each of the previous assessment points over the past four years. Scores could range from 15 (lowest marital satisfaction) to 105 (highest marital satisfaction). (Source: Drawn based on data from Karney & Frye [2002])

Biased Perceptions of the Present

Remember that better-than-average effect? Fascinatingly, people typically extend this positive bias to their relationships as well. This idea is captured by **perceived relationship superiority**: the tendency to view one's own relationship as better than others' relationships (e.g., Buunk, 2001; Buunk & van der Eijnden, 1997; Rusbult et al., 2000; Van Lange & Rusbult, 1995). Researchers assess perceived superiority by having people complete a "thought-listing" procedure in which they list features of good relationships and features of bad relationships for 5 minutes each. For each feature they list, participants indicate whether the feature is more typical of their own relationship or others' relationships. This should sound familiar; it's the same measure you completed in the "Present" section of Table 7.3. Evidencing perceived superiority, people generally list a greater number of positive features that are more typical of their own relationship than others' relationships, whereas they generally come up with a greater number of negative features that are more typical of others' relationships than their own (Rusbult et al., 2000; Van Lange & Rusbult, 1995). Interestingly, when people are reminded that relationships sometimes end (a threat), they engage in this protective motivated cognition to an even greater extent. Consistent with the idea that perceived superiority is a maintenance strategy, greater perceived superiority predicts increases in relationship quality over time (Rusbult et al., 2000).

Do we really think our relationships are better than our friends' and family members' relationships? Well, yes and no. The perceived superiority effect was originally demonstrated by asking people to think of "others' relationships." Who exactly are "others"? People in line behind you at the post office? Neighbors in the apartment next door? Your best friend or sibling? It turns out that when researchers replicated the perceived superiority effect and specifically asked people to indicate whether the positive and negative features were more common in their own relationship or in their closest friend's relationship, the perceived superiority effect was dramatically weakened (Reis et al., 2011). People still perceived more positive traits and fewer negative traits in their own relationship than their close friends' relationships, but the *degree* of perceived superiority shrank substantially. It seems that people are willing to denigrate the elusive "others'" relationships as a relationship-maintenance strategy, but are reticent to denigrate friends' relationships. Perhaps we are altruistic when it comes to our close friends; perhaps we have more information about their relationships, so we find it harder to obscure the truth; or perhaps seeing our friends positively is just another self-enhancement strategy (I'm great; my relationship is great; and even my friends' relationships are great. I sure know how to pick 'em.)

Perceived superiority, then, is a form of motivated social comparison. To maintain their relationships, people in relationships *strategically* bring to mind "others" who are worse off than themselves (making a downward social comparison). By doing so, they can give themselves an evidence-based evaluation of their own relationships as more favorable than "others." Additionally, people complete the thought-listing procedure by bringing to mind the attributes of good or bad relationships that are salient to them. Just like people flexibly shift their ideal standards to align with their partners' actual attributes, as described above (Fletcher et al., 2000; Neff & Karney, 2003), people can focus on the positive attributes that are true in their own relationships and the negative attributes that are not characteristic of their own relationships in order to protect their positive relationship perceptions.

 IN THE NEWS

Are #CoupleGoals Damaging Your Relationship?

Have you checked Instagram or Twitter today? If so, you probably scrolled past at least one post or news story that was tagged with the #CoupleGoals hashtag, a signifier that the relationship depicted or described is enviable and aspiration-worthy. Social media gives us access to literally innumerable envy-inducing photos of celebrities, friends, and "frenemies" with their partners laughing, kissing, and having seemingly perfect times. Although news sources routinely publish stories of A-list lovebirds' flawless relationships (Figure 7.15), some media outlets have begun to question whether we benefit from making these (likely inaccurate) upward social comparisons (March, 2020). Perhaps seeing successful couples encourages us to improve our own romantic relationships, or perhaps the upward social comparisons result in negative interpretations ("My relationship is lacking") and only motivates ending the current relationship.

Figure 7.15 Sue Bird (WNBA player, left) and Megan Rapinoe (US Soccer player, right) have been described as #CoupleGoals by ENews and EliteDaily (Grossbart, 2021; Wynne, 2019). How does looking up toward their satisfying relationship shape our own relationship perceptions? (Photo: Ethan Miller / Getty Images Sport)

Relationships research has supported this latter perspective. When we compare our own relationship with others' seemingly better relationships, we feel less relationship satisfaction and less commitment; we also become more oriented toward destructive relationship behaviors, like neglecting our relationship or thinking of leaving (Morry et al., 2018, 2019; Morry & Sucharyna, 2016, 2019). Online information about friends' relationships, like the kind we regularly see in social media, can make us feel less close to our partner and make us more interested in alternative partners (Morry et al., 2018).

Having others' fancy photos appear before our eyes may, however, only be a problem for couples who are not actively safeguarding their views of their own relationship. Compared to people who are only moderately committed to their relationships, those with strong commitment have more positive reactions to friends' superior relationships (Thai et al., 2020). They view them as less threatening and subsequently feel more optimistic about their own relationship. Thus, when encountering others' relationships, which we cannot avoid, motivated cognition can step in and help us keep our strong relationships strong. Strategic and protective relationship comparisons may be all the more important today, in our virtual #CoupleGoals world, because we are abruptly confronted with other people's seemingly amazing relationships ad nauseam. Beyond commitment, what other relational or situational factors might shape how we react to relationship social comparisons?

Biased Expectations for the Future

Another manifestation of the better-than-average relationship effect is that people routinely expect the future of their relationships to be better-than-average; they rate the likelihood of their own marriages failing considerably lower than the actual likelihood based on population averages (Fowers et al., 1996, 2001; Heaton & Albrecht, 1991). For example, in one study, people estimated a 10 percent likelihood that they would get divorced, on average, whereas the actual likelihood at the time was approximately 43 percent (Fowers et al., 2001). The modal (most common) participant response was 0 percent; in other words, most participants expected that there was no possibility they would divorce. Could participants have just been unaware of the actual divorce rate? A follow-up study ruled out this possibility (Fowers et al., 2001). Even when participants were told that approximately half of marriages end in divorce, they still rated their *own* likelihood of divorce at a mere 22.6 percent, on average. This under-estimation of the likelihood of divorce is likely a result of participants' perceived relationship superiority. Sure, 50 percent of *couples* divorce, but *we're* not an average couple; we're a better-than-average couple!

Another unrealistically optimistic future perception that people hold is the expectation that their romantic relationships will improve in the days, months, and years to come (Lavner et al., 2013). Just as people (mis)remember their relationship history to believe that they are on a positive trajectory, people typically expect future improvements as well. Even newlyweds, with their very high honeymooners' relationship satisfaction, predominantly expect their relationships to stay stable or improve (Lavner et al., 2013). Strikingly, over 80 percent of men and women expect their relationship satisfaction to increase over the first four years of marriage (see Figure 7.16) when they complete the same measure you completed in the "Future" section of Table 7.3. Despite these expectations, people typically report declines in relationship satisfaction over the next four years.

Although most people report positive expectations for the future of their relationships, people do not *always* hold positive expectations (Lemay & Venaglia, 2016). People tend to

Figure 7.16 What will your romantic relationship look like five years from now? Over 80 percent of men and women expected their relationship satisfaction to increase over the first four years of marriage. (Source: Drawn based on data from Lavner et al. [2013])

base their relationship predictions on their current experiences. Accordingly, when their relationships are currently going well, people tend to have overly positive future expectations; and when their relationships are currently going poorly, they tend to have overly negative expectations (Lemay et al., 2015). Because most people have a bias to view their relationships positively in the present, most people also tend to view the future of their relationships positively.

Critically, positive future expectations do serve a relationship-maintenance function (e.g., Baker et al., 2017). Even though relationship satisfaction tends to decline, on average, people with more positive relationship expectations tend to experience better quality relationships (e.g., greater trust, less conflict) than people with less positive expectations (e.g., Murray & Holmes, 1997). Positive relationship expectations may predict better relationship outcomes because they serve as self-fulfilling prophesies. In other words, when people believe that their relationships will succeed and their satisfaction will improve, people may behave in ways that make that expectation a reality (Lemay et al., 2015; Plamondon & Lachance-Grzela, 2018). For example, when people expect to be satisfied with their relationships in the future, they engage in more constructive problem solving and are more likely to forgive their partners' transgressions (Baker et al., 2017; Lemay & Venaglia, 2016), behaviors that actually enhance relationships.

Staying Committed through Biased Perceptions of Alternatives

Relationships operate within a lively social world, so naturally, partners interact with many other people over the course of any given day: co-workers, friends, neighbors, the milkman. Some of these people are available, attractive, and interesting ... and sometimes interested. What do we do to safeguard our relationships when other relationships are possible, and possibly appealing? We have seen how motivated cognitions can infiltrate people's perceptions of their partner and their relationship: they can also shape people's judgments of potential alternative partners. Recall that people tend to be more committed to their relationships when they perceive their relationship alternatives to be less desirable. Stated differently, the availability of desirable alternatives to one's relationship is a threat to relationship stability (Johnson & Rusbult, 1989; Maner et al., 2008). Given the threat they can present, how might people in relationships use motivated cognition to protect their relationships from alternative partners?

Take a careful look at the photographs in Figure 7.17. For each person, ask yourself: How attractive do you find this person? Would you be interested in meeting this person if you had the opportunity?

Now ask yourself: how long did you spend taking your careful look; did you glance and look away or spend several seconds poring over the photographs? Keep your experience in mind as we review the research on motivated perceptions of alternatives.

Inattention to Attractive Alternatives

Imagine you have a new goal to eat less processed food. What might you do? Perhaps you would move the Doritos and Captain Crunch to the barely reachable top shelf of the pantry or give away all your delicious processed food. Ahh, the age-old adage: "out of sight, out of

(a)   (b)

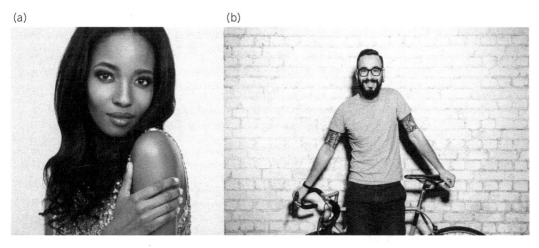

Figure 7.17 Potential "alternative" partners are attended to and perceived differently depending on one's commitment. Do you think these people are attractive? (Photo: PeopleImages / iStock / Getty Images Plus [a] and Hinterhaus Productions / Stone / Getty Images [b])

mind." Now imagine that you have a goal to maintain your relationship, and this goal includes avoiding infidelity and avoiding the dissatisfaction that could come from fantasizing about a "greener pasture." Now what might you do? Although you cannot move all of your attractive friends and co-workers to the top shelf, you can put them out of mind by directing your attention elsewhere.

This is very much what people do: they adopt a relationship-protective bias to avoid attractive alternatives. When their relationship feels threatened or when they think about their love for their partner, people in relationships look away from attractive faces more quickly than people who are single (Maner et al., 2008, 2009; Miller, 1997; Zhang et al., 2017). Fascinatingly, this looking away occurs automatically; it happens at early stages of visual processing that are not under conscious control. Just like staring at attractive faces is an automatic response, diverting attention from attractive faces is an automatic response for some people (e.g., Maner, Gailliot et al. 2007; Maner et al., 2003). Going beyond visual attention, researchers have also used fMRI (a measure of brain activation) to assess the extent to which people devote cognitive resources to attractive alternatives (Tsapelas et al., 2020). Using this technique, researchers discovered that people show less attention to attractive opposite-sex faces after recalling ways that their own romantic relationship allows for self-expansion (i.e., ways their relationship is exciting, novel, and challenging) compared to a control condition. Thinking of one's relationship as self-expanding diminishes attention to attractive alternatives even more than recalling times of feeling strong love for a partner. These findings are all consistent with *motivated* cognition; when people are particularly motivated to protect their relationships – either because they are aware of a threat, thinking of their love for their partner, or thinking of how their relationship enables self-expansion – they literally put attractive alternatives out of *sight* and out of *mind*.

Of course, not everyone in a committed relationship is equally motivated to disengage their attention from attractive alternatives. One factor that predicts the degree of disengagement is relationship identification, or how much a person has internalized their partner and relationship as part of their self (Linardatos & Lydon, 2011; Tsapelas et al., 2020). People who consider their partner and relationship as part of who they are automatically look away from attractive alternatives more than people who have not incorporated their partner and relationship into their identity (or do so to a less degree; Linardatos & Lydon, 2011). Similarly, people who report greater inclusion of their partners into their self-concepts also have more diminished neural responses to attractive opposite-sex faces compared to people who report less partner inclusion into the self (Tsapelas et al., 2020).

Although inattention to attractive alternatives was originally demonstrated in US samples, this phenomenon has recently been replicated in Chinese samples as well (Ma et al., 2015, 2019a, 2019b). Like Americans, Chinese individuals in committed relationships look away from attractive alternatives more quickly than those who are single. Interestingly, Chinese individuals tend to disengage from attractive alternatives when they think of their love for their partner *and* in control conditions, without being prompted to think of love or any relationship threat. Chinese participants' ability to disengage from attractive alternatives in neutral contexts may result from unique cultural norms that emphasize women's faithfulness and the importance of social and family harmony (Ma et al., 2015, 2019a, 2019b). We hesitate to draw any firm conclusion on the basis of a few studies, but this possibility is intriguing and should be explored further.

Devaluation of Attractive Alternatives

Sometimes looking away from attractive alternatives is not an option. Maybe your boss is a former Miss America pageant winner, or maybe you are assigned to complete a group project with someone who resembles T'Challa or his revenge-seeking cousin Erik Killmonger. What then? When people in committed relationships cannot avoid attractive alternatives, they can still engage in motivated person perception. Recall how people engage in motivated partner-enhancement to see their partners unrealistically positively; people in committed relationships can employ a similar strategy of alternative-devaluation to see potential alternative partners unrealistically negatively. Returning to the faces you evaluated in Figure 7.17, research suggests that your attractiveness ratings will depend on your own relationship status and sexual orientation. Specifically, people who are involved in monogamous, committed relationships will tend to devalue people of their preferred sex and will therefore tend to rate them as less physically attractive than single people do (e.g., Simpson et al., 1990).

Devaluation of alternatives occurs with regard to their perceived physical attractiveness, sexual attractiveness, intelligence, and even sense of humor (Johnson & Rusbult, 1989). People also devalue alternatives that they interact with by subsequently remembering more negative and less positive information about them (Visserman & Karremans, 2014). Consistent with the idea that devaluation occurs in response to relationship threat, the degree of devaluation is particularly strong when the alternative is either available (single) or shows romantic interest, both characteristics that make them particularly threatening to the current relationship (e.g., Bazzini & Shaffer, 1999; Cole et al., 2016; Lydon et al., 1999). Critically, the difference between single people's reports of alternatives and those of committed people have been shown to be due to committed people devaluing alternatives rather than single people enhancing their perceptions of alternatives (Lydon et al., 1999, 2003). Even on implicit measures, participants in committed relationships show a tendency to see attractive alternatives as less attractive than they are objectively (Cole et al., 2016) and to remember attractive alternatives as less attractive later on (Karremans et al., 2011). These findings suggest that people truly devalue attractive alternatives rather than merely report devaluation.

A consistent finding in the literature is that the extent to which people in committed relationships devalue attractive alternatives is predicted by their self-control. Accordingly, people do not always devalue alternatives to protect their relationships; they do so if they have higher self-control (Pronk et al., 2011). For example, men in committed heterosexual relationships flirted less with an attractive female confederate if they had higher self-control, and heterosexual men and women with greater self-control expressed less desire to meet an attractive opposite-sex person than people with poorer self-control (Pronk et al., 2011). In another study, compared to single heterosexual participants, heterosexual participants in romantic relationships rated attractive opposite-sex people as less desirable ... unless they had just completed a task that required self-regulation (Ritter et al., 2010). Participants who had just worked to suppress their emotions during emotionally evocative videos had their self-control resources depleted: they then rated attractive opposite-sex people as equally desirable as single participants. While it doesn't take super-human strength to devalue attractive alternatives, it does seem to require some self-control.

Consequences of Biased Perceptions of One's Alternatives

Having negatively biased perceptions of alternatives is considered a relationship maintenance strategy because it should presumably protect commitment. Research supports this idea. For example, people who indicate that they pay less attention to alternatives (a measure that correlates positively with actual attention to attractive models in the laboratory) are less likely to break up with their partner over the next two months (Miller, 1997). Other work shows that people who maintain their dating relationships over four years without infidelity are less attentive to alternatives at baseline and actually become less attentive to alternatives over time (Ritchie et al., 2021). Additionally, newlyweds who look away from attractive alternatives more quickly are less likely to divorce or separate two years later, and newlyweds who devalue attractive alternatives to a greater extent maintain higher relationship satisfaction over time (McNulty et al., 2018). The *Article Spotlight* provides more on these findings, including a mechanism to explain *why* biased perceptions of alternatives are protective.

 ARTICLE SPOTLIGHT

Why Do Biased Perceptions of Alternatives Protect Relationships?

It is often unsatisfying to know only *that* an association exists; we want to know *why* the association exists. Specifically, why do automatic inattention toward attractive alternatives and motivated devaluation of attractive alternatives protect relationships over time? McNulty, Metzer, Makhanova, and Maner (2018) tested this question in two samples of newlywed couples. Specifically, they tested the hypothesis that perceptions of alternatives decrease the likelihood of infidelity, which then explains greater relationship stability and relationship quality. First, participants completed background questionnaires, a measure of visual attention to alternatives, and a picture-rating measure to assess devaluation of attractive alternatives. Then, at baseline and over the next three to three and a half years, participants reported whether any infidelity had occurred, their relationship satisfaction, relationship commitment, and relationship status (i.e., whether the relationship was intact or dissolved). Over the follow-up period, 37 percent of individuals were unfaithful and 12 percent of couples dissolved their relationships.

Results revealed that participants who diverted their attention from the attractive alternatives more quickly were less likely to be unfaithful over the time they were involved in the study. In fact, looking away 100 ms quicker was associated with 50 percent lower odds of infidelity. Similarly, participants who devalued alternatives to a great extent were also less likely to engage in infidelity over the next several years; rating the attractive alternatives just 2 points lower on the rating scale (1 = not at all attractive; 10 = extremely attractive) was associated with 50 percent lower odds of infidelity as well. The researchers also found that the consequence of devaluing alternatives depended on the relationship's trajectory over the study period. People who reported minimal declines in satisfaction over the study period were unlikely to engage in infidelity regardless of their evaluations of attractive alternatives; however, people who reported greater declines in satisfaction were more susceptible to infidelity if they rated alternatives as attractive at the beginning of the study.

Finally, the researchers tested their hypothesized mediation process: that a lower likelihood of infidelity explains the association between biased perceptions of attractive alternatives and relationship stability. They found support for each of the models shown in Figure 7.18. Inattention to attractive alternatives and devaluation of attractive alternatives each predicted a lower likelihood of infidelity, and infidelity was negatively associated with relationship stability (i.e., people who committed infidelity were less likely to maintain their relationships). In sum, people who had biased perceptions of attractive alternatives maintained stable relationships *because* they avoided infidelity.

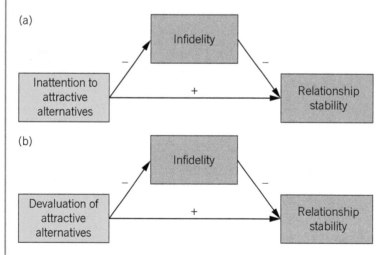

Figure 7.18 Newlyweds who were more inattentive to attractive alternatives were less likely to engage in infidelity and were therefore more likely to maintain their relationships (a). Newlyweds who devalued attractive alternatives to a greater extent were also less likely to engage in infidelity and were therefore more likely to maintain their relationships (b). (Source: Drawn based on data from McNulty et al. [2018])

The relationship consequences when people *do* notice attractive alternatives also vary, including as a function of self-control. For example, romantically involved people who report that they tend to notice attractive alternatives are more likely to register for a dating app and to express interest in alternatives through the app after having their self-regulation depleted (Brady et al., 2020). Newlywed couples are also most likely to be unfaithful to their partners over the next two years if they pay relatively high attention to alternatives and are relatively low in self-control (Brady et al., 2020). People who pay little attention to alternatives tend to have low rates of infidelity (near 10 percent) regardless of their level of self-control, whereas people who pay greater attention to alternatives have comparably low rates of infidelity if they have high self-control (near 10 percent) and dramatically higher rates of infidelity if they have low self-control (near 65 percent).

Biased Perceptions of One's Partner's Alternatives

In relationships, there are (at least) two people to consider, and each person has potential alternatives to the relationship that could undermine their commitment. Therefore, a person can protect their relationship from threats not only by modulating their attention away from their own alternatives, but also by modulating their attention toward their partner's alternatives. Marvel fans might remember some sparks between Spiderman's Aunt May and Tony Stark; might Pepper Potts pay some special attention to Aunt May if given the chance? A bias to preferentially attend to romantic rivals may protect the relationship by helping to defend against these rivals. Keep your friends close, but your enemies (romantic rivals) closer, as they say.

Romantic jealousy – the emotional, cognitive, and behavioral response to the presence of a potential rival – is considered an evolved relationship maintenance adaptation (e.g., Buss & Haselton, 2005; Maner & Shackelford, 2008). When people encounter a rival that could threaten their relationship, they often feel distressed and upset, especially when they perceive their relationship as close and satisfying (Attridge, 2013; Chung & Harris, 2018; DeSteno et al., 2006). Additionally, people may engage in relationship-guarding behaviors such as snooping, actively derogating rivals in front of the partner (e.g., pointing out flaws), and staying hyper-vigilant (e.g., Buss, 1988b; Buss et al., 2008; Buss & Shackelford, 1997; Shackelford, Goetz, & Buss, 2005). Jealousy can be considered an adaptive perceptional bias, much like the other biases we have reviewed in this chapter, though taken to the extreme, it can have negative relationship consequences (Andersen et al., 1995). If Pepper Potts had been in the room when the beautiful Aunt May met Tony Stark, might she have quickly registered the energy, experienced some jealousy, and zeroed her attention on Aunt May?

Probably! Evidence does indeed suggest that people automatically attend to potential romantic rivals, especially if those rivals are physically attractive (Ma et al., 2015; Ma, Xue, Zhao et al., 2019; Maner, Gailliot et al., 2007, 2009; Pollet & Saxton, 2020; Figure 7.19). In particular, people who tend to

Figure 7.19 Three's a crowd in dyadic relationships. What are some ways that jealousy protects relationships from rivals? (Photo: EduLeite / iStock / Getty Images Plus)

be chronically jealous show biased attention toward attractive same-sex "rivals," especially after first thinking of their partner flirting with someone else (Maner, Gailliot et al., 2007) or recalling a time they were concerned about infidelity (Maner et al., 2009). Consistent with biased processing of rivals, people who are chronically jealous also have better memory for attractive rivals and implicitly evaluate potential rivals in more negative ways (Maner et al., 2009). Watch out, Aunt May.

Of course, people vary in the extent to which they perceive their partner's attractive alternatives as threats to their relationships. For example, people with greater attachment anxiety tend to be particularly jealous and perceive a greater risk of infidelity; accordingly, they also engage in greater relationship-guarding behaviors (e.g., Barbaro et al., 2019; Kim, Feeney, & Jakubiak, 2018). Interestingly, people who themselves are interested in pursuing their alternatives tend to be more concerned about their partner's alternatives; they seem to project their own interest in an extra-dyadic relationship onto their partners (Neal & Lemay, 2019).

 IS THIS TRUE FOR YOU?

Partner Surveillance, Monitoring, and Snooping

Does your partner's phone vibrating cause you to buzz with curiosity? If so, you may be one of many people who engage in partner surveillance, monitoring, or even snooping. Almost two-thirds of the college students surveyed admitted to snooping on their partner in some way – seeking new information about their partners through covert means (Derby et al., 2012). More recently, slightly over one-third of participants in a community (non-college student) sample, aged 18 to 64, reported that they checked up on their partner by reading their text messages and checking their partner's browser history (Hertlein & van Dyck, 2020). People also report monitoring their partner's social media, especially when they feel particularly jealous (Muise et al., 2014), and especially if they are high in attachment anxiety (e.g., Fox & Warber, 2014; Marshall, Bejanyan, Castro et al., 2013; Muise et al., 2014; Reed et al., 2015).

Despite its common occurrence, snooping is typically related to relationship problems (e.g., Goodboy & Bolkan, 2011). People react negatively when they find out their partners have snooped (Klettner et al., 2020), and partner snooping predicts relationship conflict and desire to break up (Arikewuyo et al., 2021). Interestingly, people high in attachment avoidance report being particularly upset by a partner's snooping, whereas people high in attachment anxiety tend to report only positive reactions to a partner's snooping, perhaps because they interpret snooping as reassurance that their partners are invested in the relationship (Klettner et al., 2020).

Snooping and monitoring behaviors are reinforced and maintained by a positive feedback loop (Muise et al., 2009; Spottswood & Carpenter, 2020). When people snoop, they are likely to uncover ambiguous information that they over-perceive as threatening. As a result, they are motivated to engage in additional snooping, which turns up additional ambiguous information. Do you snoop? How would you react if you found out that a partner was snooping on you?

Perceived Alternatives in Non-monogamous Relationships

The extent to which alternatives threaten a relationship may depend on the nature of one's romantic relationship(s). In consensually non-monogamous relationships (particularly polyamorous relationships), romantic alternatives are not necessarily a threat because several relationships can be maintained simultaneously. Therefore, at least theoretically, people in polyamorous relationships need not avoid their own attractive alternatives or to experience jealousy toward a partner's attractive alternatives. In reality, people in polyamorous relationships do report jealousy, not because attractive alternatives pose a threat to exclusivity, but because they threaten the strength of a particular relationship (e.g., Rubinsky, 2018, 2019). For example, alternative partners can still threaten relationships when they fulfill important needs or when they disrupt the current relationship hierarchy (i.e., the role of one person as the primary partner).

People involved in consensually non-monogamous relationships also become jealous and distressed when they perceive that their partners (especially their primary partners) are cheating by crossing boundaries they have set for the relationship (Mogilski et al., 2019). People involved in consensually non-monogamous relationships do, therefore, engage in relationship-guarding behaviors, though they tend to engage in less relationship-guarding than those in monogamous relationships (Mogilski et al., 2017). Further, people involved in non-monogamous relationships tend to guard their relationships with their primary partners to a greater extent than their secondary relationships (Mogilski et al., 2019). Like people in monogamous relationships, those in consensually non-monogamous relationships perceive alternatives in ways that protect their relationships. The quality of their alternatives also predicts their commitment to their relationships (especially for their secondary partners; e.g., Balzarini et al., 2017), so biased perception is a relationship maintenance strategy.

Bias and Illusion in Context

Like most relational phenomena, contextual factors impact the extent to which people employ bias and illusion to maintain their relationships. Moreover, contextual factors impact whether engaging in bias and illusion offers benefits or is a detriment. In this section, we will explore who engages in biased cognition and who benefits from biased cognition.

Who Engages in Biased Cognition?

Several factors help shape the extent to which a person will engage in motivated cognition to protect their relationship from threat. Recall the risk regulation perspective (Murray et al., 2006), which recognizes that close relationships can be a source of both immense joy and immense pain. People regulate these risks and benefits by increasing their dependence in the relationship when they trust their partners to be responsive and avoiding or minimizing dependence when they trust their partners less fully (Murray et al., 2006). Critically, engaging in motivated cognition is itself a risk; idealizing one's partner and relationship and derogating relationship alternatives can artificially increase dependence in the relationship. Accordingly, people should be most willing to engage in such motivated cognition when they trust their partners (i.e., the risks of rejection or abuse are low). Indeed, the more people trust their partners, the more relationship-enhancing attributions they make (Miller & Rempel, 2004). Moreover, people who are confident that their partners love them idealize their partners to a greater extent than people who perceive less love (Murray et al., 2000, 2001). Similarly, whether people avert their attention away from a partner's negative traits (a cognitive bias that would protect the relationship) depends on their self-esteem (Lamarche & Murray, 2014). People with high self-esteem tend to perceive greater regard from their partners and accordingly are more willing to risk idealizing their partners than those with low self-esteem.

Another individual difference factor that shapes the extent to which people engage in motivated cognition is attachment orientation. Attachment orientation can also be thought of like a lens that people use to interpret relational experiences, and people with insecure models of attachment (high attachment anxiety, in particular) view their partners and relationships through lenses that are a little less rose-colored than securely attached people. People with high attachment anxiety have less idealized views of their partners, tend to make more negative attributions for their partner's negative behaviors, and show better memory for negative information about their partners than people with low attachment anxiety (e.g., Busby et al., 2017; Collins, 1996; Collins et al., 2006; Gallo & Smith, 2001; Pereg & Mikulincer, 2004; Sümer & Cozzarelli, 2004). Attachment avoidance also plays a role in motivated cognition. People who are in committed relationships and high in attachment avoidance do not automatically look away from attractive alternatives, report greater interest in meeting attractive alternatives, and have a greater likelihood of engaging in emotional and sexual infidelity (DeWall et al., 2011).

Finally, as described above, whether a person engages in motivated cognition is also a function of their cognitive resources. People who have high trait self-regulation (or have high self-regulation in the moment) are better able to avoid attractive alternatives (Pronk et al., 2011; Ritter et al., 2010), and time pressure undermines this ability as well (Ritter et al., 2010). Greater self-control also predicts an ability to avoid retaliating in response to negative partner behaviors (Finkel & Campbell, 2001).

Who Benefits from Biased Cognition?

Consider the implications of the biased cognitions we have reviewed. Could these biased cognitions ever have *negative* personal and relationship consequences? What if one's partner was Loki, Thanos, or another Marvel-ous villain? The most extreme example of a context in which positively biased cognitions could have negative consequences is the context of an abusive relationship (McNulty & Fincham, 2012). If a person in an abusive relationship downplays their partner's negative behaviors, makes relationship-promoting attributions for the abuse, unrealistically expects the relationship to improve, or falsely perceives that they have no alternatives to the relationship, the consequences could be dire. Even in non-abusive relationships, research suggests that positive biases can be problematic when one's relationship is unhealthy in some way (e.g., McNulty, 2010).

For example, whether benevolent attributions predict increases or decreases in relationship satisfaction over time depends on whether one's relationship is characterized by minor or major problems. Consistent with this idea, the greatest decreases in marital satisfaction are observed for people who initially make positive attributions and yet are involved in relationships characterized by particularly severe problems and particularly negative partner behaviors (McNulty et al., 2008). People who make negative attributions in these tough situations experience decreases in relationship satisfaction, but their declines are less severe, perhaps because people who make more negative attributions opt to address the problems with their spouses (McNulty et al., 2008). Removing the rose-colored glasses and seeing reality for what it is allows people to address problems or possibly terminate their relationships as necessary.

Positive expectations for the future can also be a liability when couples passively wait for their relationships to improve rather than behaving in relationship-promoting ways that could directly foster improvements (McNulty & Karney, 2004). People who have more positive expectations for their relationships engage in less constructive problem-solving behaviors when they experience severe relationship problems and subsequently experience greater decreases in relationship satisfaction over time, compared to people with less positive expectations (e.g., Lavner et al., 2013; Neff & Geers, 2013). Thus, the consequences of biased cognitions depend on the quality of one's relationship. In the next few chapters, we'll also see that the consequences of other relationship maintenance behaviors depend on the relationship context.

Conclusion

Pepper Potts and Tony Stark, just like non-superhero couples, must work every day to maintain their relationship. As we explored in this chapter, Pepper and Tony – like all of us – have a savvy set of skills ready to go to distort objective reality. These distortions allow people to (1) maintain biased perceptions of both their partners and relationships and (2) avoid the threat of potential relationship alternatives. Although these motivated cognitive processes are typically adaptive, we also considered situations in which accurate perceptions may be more advantageous than biased perceptions. This chapter is the first of several to detail relationship maintenance processes. In the next chapter, we review another way that people manage relationship threats: responding constructively to conflicts that arise from interdependence.

Major Take-Aways

- People typically view their romantic partners through a lens of positive illusion; they see their partners somewhat accurately, but employ distortions to view their partners more like their ideal partners and more like themselves.
- Positive illusions are generally associated with relationship benefits, but are most advantageous when grounded in reality and constrained to abstract traits.

- People tend to view their relationships as better than others' and improving over time, and these perceptions mitigate relationship threats.
- People who maintain their relationships tend to be good at disengaging their attention from attractive alternatives, in part because ignoring alternatives helps to prevent infidelity.

- Bias and illusions can be costly in poorer-quality relationships because seeing accurately can motivate people to intervene to improve their relationships or end dysfunctional relationships.

Further Readings

If you're interested in ...

... how people develop expectations about the future of their relationships and how these expectations influence commitment, read:

Baker, L. R., McNulty, J. K., & VanderDrift, L. E. (2017). Expectations for future relationship satisfaction: Unique sources and critical implications for commitment. *Journal of Experimental Psychology General*, *146*, 700–721.

... how self-control helps people maintain their relationships, read:

Brady, A., Baker, L. R., & Miller, R. S. (2020). Look but don't touch? Self-regulation determines whether noticing attractive alternatives increases infidelity. *Journal of Family Psychology*, *34*, 135–144.

... how current relationship quality predicts the extent to which people have biased perceptions of the past and biased forecasting of the future, read:

Peetz, J., Shimizu, J. P., & Royle, C. (2022). Projecting current feelings into the past and future: Better current relationship quality reduces negative retrospective bias and increases positive forecasting bias. *Journal of Social and Personal Relationships*, *39*, 2595–2616.

... the classic research revealing benefits associated with positive illusions, read:

Murray, S. L., Holmes, J. G., & Griffin, D. W. (1996). The self-fulfilling nature of positive illusions in romantic relationships: Love is not blind, but prescient. *Journal of Personality and Social Psychology*, *71*, 1155–1180.

... how stress can interfere with perceptual biases in relationships, read:

Neff, L. A., & Buck, A. A. (2022). When rose-colored glasses turn cloudy: Stressful life circumstances and perceptions of partner behavior in newlywed marriage. *Social Psychological and Personality Science*. Advance online publication.

8 NAVIGATING THE CHALLENGES OF INTERDEPENDENCE

Even the Smoothest Roads Have Some Bumps

The American version of *The Office*, a documentary-style sitcom, chronicled the nine-to-five grind of office workers in Scranton, Pennsylvania. Rife with awkward moments, and known for its humorous exaggeration of workplace protocols, *The Office* kept viewers tuning in to follow its central romance. Jim, a paper salesman, and Pam, a receptionist, spent three seasons in the "will-they-won't-they" drama that sitcoms thrive on before eventually initiating one of the most satisfying television relationships to date (Figure 8.1). From air high-fives and light-hearted pranks to thoughtful gifts and loving support, Jim and Pam had what many fans judged to be a near-ideal couple dynamic. Viewers watched as they spent the next several seasons enjoying their relationship without any real hiccups. They dated, got engaged, moved in together, married, and had two children, all while maintaining an easy affection and a playful relationship. As their relationship progressed, Jim and Pam became increasingly interdependent, relying on each other, meeting each other's needs, and sharing their time and resources.

(a) (b)

Figure 8.1 Actors John Krasinski as Jim Halpert and Jenna Fischer as Pam Beasley develop an easy, loving relationship that anchors *The Office*. (Photo: PictureLux / The Hollywood Archive / Alamy Stock Photo [a] and Reuters / Alamy Stock Photo [b])

But even the smoothest roads have some bumps, and the bumps for Jim and Pam came in Season 9, the show's final season. Pam's #CoupleGoals relationship transformed into a relationship characterized by #CoupleConflict when Jim decided to pursue an exciting career opportunity, pulling him away from Pam and the kids multiple days a week. While Jim struggled to launch a sports marketing company in Philadelphia, Pam struggled to manage extra childcare and home responsibilities back in Scranton. Jim's absence wore on them both, and the couple decided that the distance was not sustainable. Pam and the children would simply move to join Jim in Philadelphia. Problem solved! At least that was what Jim expected. Pam, on the other hand, agreed that the distance was not sustainable; all Jim had to do was return to Scranton full time. And there's the speed bump.

Even the most compatible people will eventually experience **conflicts** like this one which can threaten the relationship if a resolution cannot be found. Without malice or a diminishment in their love for each other, Jim and Pam experienced a serious disagreement because their perfectly reasonable individual goals conflicted. They eventually resolved their dilemma, but it required Jim to forego his career opportunity and return to Scranton. Something had to give for the relationship to continue, and in this case, Jim gave in. If even the smoothest relationships have bumps, consider how tumultuous other relationships can be. Interdependence inevitably results in conflict and often leads people to behave in ways that intentionally or unintentionally hurt each other (i.e., relational **transgressions**). These challenges can doom a relationship or provide opportunities to resolve incompatibilities and deepen connection, depending on how they are managed.

In this chapter, you will learn about the challenges of interdependence. We will review the ways in which goals and desires conflict to produce disagreements between romantic partners, and we will explore typical conflicts (conflict topics, how conflicts are experienced, their frequency) over the course of a relationship. You will then learn how people manage interpersonal conflicts to protect their relationships. We will highlight specific conflict behaviors that are typically destructive and specific conflict behaviors that are typically constructive, and we will investigate how the adaptiveness of conflict behaviors is situation specific. Finally, we will review how people can recover from conflicts and relational transgressions. Your goal in reading this chapter is to recognize how the near inevitability of conflict does not mean that breakup is also inevitable: much of how we move through and beyond conflicts can lead to stronger relationships.

 GUIDING QUESTIONS

Consider these questions as you read this chapter:

- Why does interdependence necessarily create conflicts?
- How do conflict topics and the frequency of conflicts change over the course of a relationship?
- What behaviors are constructive versus destructive during conflict, and how does the context influence which behaviors are beneficial?
- How do people recover from conflicts and partner transgressions to maintain satisfying relationships?

The Challenge of Interdependence

The idea of *interdependence* was introduced in Chapter 1 as one of the defining features of a close relationship. Recall that interdependence means mutual influence; any changes experienced by one person (e.g., in thoughts, emotions, or behaviors) affect the other person, and vice versa. As intimacy increases in a relationship, the individuals in the relationship begin to influence each other more frequently, more strongly, and in more areas of life (e.g., Knobloch & Solomon, 2004). For example, if one partner (Jim) decides to pursue a new work opportunity, the other partner (Pam) will be impacted in various ways. Jim's career change could (1) provide greater income and lead to a change in Pam's lifestyle choices, (2) introduce Pam to a new industry and new people, (3) increase Pam's caregiving responsibilities to compensate for Jim's reduced caregiving role, (4) create for her new feelings of pride, loneliness, hopefulness, or resentment, and so on. The impacts can be large, affect multiple life domains, influence feelings, thoughts, and behaviors, and be diverse in quality (some negative, some positive). On the positive side, as interdependence increases in a relationship, partners can enhance each other's daily activities; however, on the negative side, increased interdependence can mean more interference with (or more inhibition of) each other's daily activities (e.g., Knobloch & Solomon, 2004).

Can we predict whether the impacts of increased interdependence will be positive or negative in a given situation? According to interdependence theory (for review, see Chapter 2), we can look to a situation's unique structure for such insight. Recall how the SABI model proposes that the specific **S**ituation, the characteristics and behaviors of Person **A**, and the characteristics and behaviors of Person **B** jointly determine the quality of any **I**nteraction (Holmes, 2002; Kelley et al., 2003). In order to anticipate outcomes of increased interdependence, we can attend to a situation's covariation of interests, the extent to which the best outcomes for each person align (e.g., Rusbult & Van Lange, 2003). Interests covary when a given choice results in the greatest satisfaction for both Partner A and Partner B (a "win-win"). For example, fans of *The Office* know that both Jim and Pam can be very satisfied if they play a harmless prank on their co-worker, Dwight. Their interests are aligned; they both enjoy pranking Dwight and benefit from the same course of action. In fact, they may benefit even more from their interdependence when their interests are aligned (compared to pranking alone) because they can combine their skills and resources to be more effective pranksters. This possibility is explained in the theory of transactive goal dynamics (Fitzsimons et al., 2015); when people are interdependent, share common goals, and are able to coordinate their efforts effectively toward their goals, each person's experience is improved drastically (you + me = magic).

When, instead, interests do not covary, the situation can be described as a conflict of interest (Arriaga, 2013; Van Lange & Balliet, 2015). Now, one person's best outcome corresponds to a non-optimal outcome for another person (a necessary "win-lose"). In conflict-of-interest situations, both people cannot be fully satisfied at the same time. Conflicts of interest can range from minor, inconsequential disagreements to major, relationship-threatening disputes. A minor disagreement could be as simple as one partner desiring Mexican food for dinner, and the other partner preferring Italian. In such a situation, only one person can be completely satisfied with the meal choice, not both. Meanwhile, a

(a)   (b)

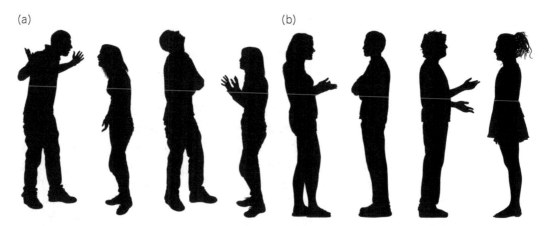

Figure 8.2 What was the nature of your last conflict with a partner or friend? Although the word "conflict" may bring to mind a fight, quarrel, or argument (a), a conflict is simply a disagreement and does not need to entail hostility (b). (Photo: 4×6 / DigitalVision Vectors / Getty Images [a] and Leontura / DigitalVision Vectors / Getty Images [b])

major disagreement is a situation in which pursuing the best outcome for one partner would entail a *substantial* cost for the other partner. Either Jim is happy because the whole family moves to Philadelphia, or Pam is happy because Jim returns to Scranton, but each person's desired outcome necessarily produces a major cost for the other. Moreover, in close relationships, both people's outcomes are also contingent (to some extent) on their partner's happiness. Winning does not feel much like winning if it results in a loved one's unhappiness. If Pam were to move to Philadelphia but the move makes her miserable, both Jim and Pam would experience poor outcomes (a lose-lose). Each person's possible outcomes are constrained by the other person's behavior and reaction to the situation.

This is the challenge of interdependence. Being linked to another person means necessarily experiencing situations when one cannot – or cannot easily – have their way (Figure 8.2). Interdependent relationships provide closeness, companionship, and other benefits, but they also inevitably produce conflict: interactions in which people have opposing interests, incompatible goals, or disparate views (Whitton, James-Kangal et al., 2018). This definition is perhaps different from our image of conflicts as fights, arguments, or shouting matches. Conflicts (i.e., conflicts of interest) are merely disagreements and do not need to include hurt feelings, anger, or power plays, whereas a fight is a particular type of conflict characterized by hostile behavior.

Conflicts as Diagnostic Situations

To understand the consequences of specific interdependent situations, interdependence theory directs us to consider each person's outcomes. Typically, we think first of the concrete outcomes, or the immediate satisfying or dissatisfying experience of the situation, for each person. For example, Jim's ultimate decision to return to Scranton means that his concrete outcomes are somewhat poor or dissatisfying. He did not get his way and he gave up a career opportunity. Jim did, however, maintain his relationship and resolve a source of conflict, so he experiences pleasure along with displeasure in his new situation. Pam's concrete outcomes are more positive, but still somewhat negative as well. On the one hand, she can enjoy Scranton and with Jim alongside her, as she wanted. On the other hand, Pam's pleasure is tinged with displeasure because she knows that Jim – whom she cares deeply about – is not perfectly satisfied with the decision.

In addition to these concrete outcomes, interactions also produce symbolic outcomes, positive or negative consequences of the situation based on the situation's broader implications (Van Lange & Rusbult, 2012). In the example of Jim and Pam's Philly versus Scranton dilemma, each couple-member might also experience pleasure or displeasure as they learn something broader about their relationship or partner through the conflict. For instance, Pam's recognition that Jim forfeited a major career goal to prioritize their relationship produces symbolic pleasure because she can bask in Jim's care for her and commitment to their relationship. If Pam appreciates Jim's decision and Jim recognizes Pam's gratitude, he can also experience symbolic pleasure as he sees that his partner acknowledged his efforts.

Because of these symbolic outcomes, conflicts are considered diagnostic situations, situations in which one's partner's underlying thoughts and motivations are made evident (Rusbult & Van Lange, 2003). Sure, situations with corresponding interests are more enjoyable, but they do not provide much useful "intel" about the partner's hidden feelings. For example, Jim might prank Dwight with Pam because he enjoys it or because he knows Pam will enjoy it. In conflicts of interest situations, a partner's behavior is actually telling. Jim's decision to move to Scranton unequivocally demonstrates his motivation to protect the relationship and to prioritize Pam's wishes because this behavior benefits Pam more than Jim. Thus, this situation provides new diagnostic information about Jim and the relationship. Diagnostic situations are a bit like costly signals from the evolutionary theory perspective. Willingness to experience a major cost for one's partner is a reliable cue for underlying partner qualities. Conflicts can, therefore, be an opportunity to reify the importance of the relationship and communicate one's love and commitment. However, repeated conflicts of interest may push the relationship to a breakpoint in which partners are no longer willing to endure costs to maintain the relationship. Conflicts, after all, are necessarily costly (a "win-lose"). Even when partners compromise to find a solution, both partners forfeit something desirable (Wieselquist et al., 1999). Who forfeits what, how often, and with what symbolic or concrete outcomes may help define for partners how much conflict is "too much."

What Topics Do Couples Disagree About?

Although every romantic relationship is different and will have some unique interdependence challenges, partners often disagree about similar topics, including those listed in Table 8.1. Disagreement topics have been shown to be similar in same-sex and different-sex relationships (Kurdek, 1994a), in American, British, Chinese, Russian, and Turkish cultures (Dillon et al., 2015), in interracial and same-race relationships (MacNiel-Kelly, 2020), and in Black and White couples (Oggins, 2003), though these findings are based on limited research and should be further investigated. There is some initial evidence that conflict about sex/intimacy, in particular, may differ based on the type of relationship (Rubinsky, 2021). LGBTQIA+ couples and couples engaged in consensual non-monogamy report many of the same sexual conflicts as monogamous different-sex couples (i.e., different sex drives, scheduling issues, lack of time), but people in LGBTQIA+ relationships also report some additional challenges related to transitioning genders, and people in non-monogamous relationships reported unique conflicts related to sexual jealousy.

In a nationally representative sample of adults from the United States (i.e., a sample with demographics that roughly match the demographics of the country in terms of race, age, sex, sexual orientation, and income), the most commonly reported conflict topics were

Table 8.1 Common topics of disagreement

Disagreement topic	Example
Money	Disagreeing about how money should be spent or how much money should be saved
Communication	Disagreements about the style, mode, or extent of communication
Habits, partner behaviors	Disliking a partner's habit, such as smoking or leaving dishes in the sink
Children, parenting	Disagreeing about how to discipline or how to spend time with children
Leisure, joint recreational activities	Disagreeing about how to spend leisure time or how much time to spend in leisure
Work, career	Disagreements about a partner's line of work or time spent at work
Relatives, in-laws	Disagreements about the involvement of in-laws or a partner's relationship with extended family
Friends	Disagreements about the choice of a partner's friends or time spent with friends
Intimacy, sex	Disagreements about the frequency of sexual activity or the ways that intimacy is displayed
Division of labor, household chores	Disagreements about how family and household responsibilities should be divided
Trust and jealousy	Disagreements about how much a partner can be trusted or about how a partner expresses jealousy
Ideology	Disagreements about social, political, or religious issues
Screen time	Disagreements about appropriate use of technology

What do you and your partner(s) disagree about? Consider these common sources of conflict in romantic relationships.

Source: Based on data from Bevan et al. (2014); Dillon et al. (2015); Kurdek (1994a); Meyer & Sledge (2022); Oggins (2003); Papp (2018); Papp, Cummings et al. (2009); Reese-Weber et al. (2015); Righetti et al. (2016); Stanley et al. (2002).

communication (reported by 50 percent of respondents), annoying habits (43 percent), household chores (42 percent), finances (40 percent), and parenting (reported by 34 percent of all respondents, but by 52 percent of parents; Meyer & Sledge, 2022).

Evidence suggests that the prevalence of particular conflict topics shifts depending on life stage and relationship stage. For example, unmarried young adults (early 20s) tend to experience the most disagreement with their partners around topics of *joint recreational activities*, *time spent together, and chores* (Righetti et al., 2016). This makes sense. In relationships with relatively less interdependence (i.e., typically no shared finances and no shared children), shared recreation may be the primary domain in which partners need to accommodate each other's interests. Household chores is likely most relevant to the subset of young adults who cohabitate.

Moving into a later life stage (late 30s), the most common conflict topics include *children*, *chores*, *communication*, *leisure*, and *money*, in that order (Papp, Cummings, & Goeke et al., 2009). Child-related conflicts dominate here (over one-third of reported conflicts), and although money tends not to be the most common conflict topic, conflicts about money are nonetheless common (implicated in about 20 percent of disagreements), particularly intense, and especially persistent and unresolved over time (Papp, 2018; Papp, Cummings, & Goeke-Morey, 2009).

Older adults (mid-50s) often disagree about *communication*, *chores*, *habits*, *leisure*, and *children*, in that order (Papp, 2018). Interestingly, people continue to disagree about parenting even after children have left the home, though the frequency of those disagreements decreases. Additionally, habits become a more predominant source of conflict later in life and later in relationships, perhaps because partners have more time together to pay attention to each other's (annoying) habits. Although this evidence could indicate shifts in conflict topics as people age, it could also reflect cohort effects instead. For instance, the things your grandparents argue about may be different from the things you argue about with your partner, not because of your different ages, but because of the different time periods in which you have lived. A more rigorous assessment of how conflict changes over the lifespan would need to follow the same people over time using a longitudinal design approach.

What conflicts tend to be fights? A nationwide (US) sample of married and engaged people who had never been divorced most commonly identified *money* as the "number one argument starter" in their relationships, regardless of their relationship stage (Stanley et al., 2002). As shown in Figure 8.3, conflicts about children were also frequently reported as the key argument starter, particularly for people married nine to twenty-five years. Conflicts of interests do not need to be arguments, but conflicts about money (and, to some extent, children) seem to go in that direction.

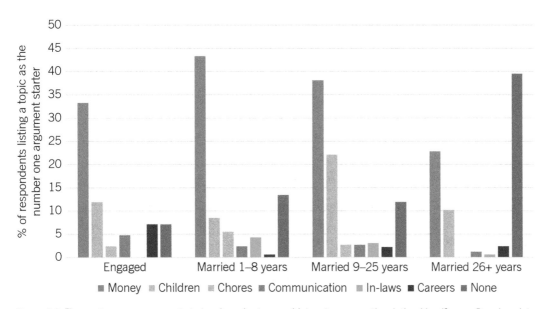

Figure 8.3 The most common argument starters in early-stage and later-stage romantic relationships (Source: Based on data from Stanley et al. [2002])

RESEARCHER SPOTLIGHT: Lauren Papp, PhD

Figure 8.4 Dr. Lauren Papp is the Jane Rafferty Thiele Professor in Human Ecology at the University of Wisconsin-Madison. (Photo: Andy Manis)

How did you come to be a relationship researcher?

As an undergraduate research assistant in a psychology lab, I was responsible for coding the emotional and behavioral expressions of new parents. These new parents were discussing how much of the childcare responsibilities and household tasks they each completed during this busy time in their family life. I was fascinated by the range of communication and conflict styles partners expressed in these discussions.

My undergraduate research experience led to a graduate program where I had the good fortune to join a new project investigating similar questions regarding couple conflict and its implications for parents and children. We developed and implemented a parent-reported diary method for assessing constructive and destructive marital conflict that occurred in families' homes. This experience demonstrated the importance of high-quality assessment when studying personal and sensitive experiences in daily life, and it shaped how I approach my work.

What do you love about your work?

Over the course of my career, I am continually struck by how students use their life experiences to identify valuable research questions, and then, in turn, they incorporate evidence from relationship science into their own personal and professional paths. Being a part of this positive cycle has been the most meaningful aspect of my career. I remain incredibly fortunate to study topics such as relationship conflict and health and how they are interconnected, which are highly applicable for students and the broader field alike.

What's next in research on conflicts in relationships?

The field faces pressing questions regarding close relationships and health. Both have been fundamentally altered by the COVID-19 pandemic and the changing landscape of daily life in this new era. Our previous understanding of the interdependence in partners' health behaviors has been challenged and needs to be re-examined in this acute pandemic era to remain relevant to couples, their families, and those who support them.

How Do People Typically Experience Relationship Conflicts?

Broadening beyond the interdependence theory account of conflict, we can also think about conflicts from an attachment theory perspective to understand how people *experience* conflicts in their relationships (Feeney & Karantzas, 2017; Pietromonaco et al., 2004; Simpson et al., 1996). According to attachment theory, people are motivated to maintain close relationships with their attachment figures (typically their romantic partners, in adulthood). A conflict of interest represents a potential threat to the stability of that relationship, and as such, it should activate the attachment system, resulting in distress (e.g., sadness, anxiety, stress), protest (e.g., crying), and proximity-seeking (e.g., clinging). Major conflicts (e.g., an incompatible preference about the future of the relationship) should activate the attachment system more strongly than minor conflicts (e.g., a disagreement about what color to paint a wall) and should therefore be particularly distressing.

Indeed, evidence suggests that experiencing conflict tends to be distressing: People report more stress, more sadness, more anger, more disgust, and less happiness in situations that are characterized by greater conflict compared to situations with less conflict (Gerpott et al., 2018; Righetti et al., 2016). In a study in which people were randomly assigned to discuss either a major problem or a minor problem, those who discussed the major problem experienced significantly more distress during the discussion than people who discussed the minor problem (Simpson et al., 1996). People also respond to conflicts physiologically (in their bodies). When couples discuss areas of disagreement in their relationships, they tend to experience increases in blood pressure (the force exerted by the blood on the arteries), heart rate (the frequency of heart beats), and cardiac output (the amount of blood the heart pumps through the circulatory system; e.g., Smith et al., 2020; Wright & Loving, 2011). Each of these outcomes indicates that the cardiovascular system is responding to a perceived demand in the environment to work harder and faster (termed cardiovascular reactivity). These physiological responses to conflict are indistinguishable in same-sex and different-sex relationships (Roisman et al., 2008), and they point to the strong distress response people have when experiencing conflict.

Conflict – especially severe conflict – also influences the endocrine (hormone-producing) and immune systems (Malarkey et al., 1994). Conflict causes the release of cortisol, a stress hormone, which can contribute to wear and tear on the body when it is consistently elevated, and bitter conflicts have been shown to suppress immune functioning (e.g., Kiecolt-Glaser et al., 1993; Kiecolt-Glaser & Wilson, 2017). In one particularly fascinating (and vile) study, researchers demonstrated that antagonistic conflict slows wound healing, a visible indicator of immune functioning (Kiecolt-Glaser et al., 2005). The researchers – with ethical board approval and consent from participants, of course – used a suction system to produce eight small blisters on each participant's forearm. These wounds healed more slowly following hostile conflict discussions compared to less hostile discussions.

As much as conflicts generally burden the mind and body, some people have stronger reactions to conflict than others. People who are high in attachment anxiety – those who are persistently concerned about rejection, abandonment, and their own worthiness of love and care – are especially reactive to conflicts, in part because they are most concerned about the negative implications of a disagreement. Is this the beginning of the end? Is this relationship over? People with higher attachment anxiety not only report greater distress during conflicts, but they also tend to visibly show more signs of anxiety than people with lower attachment anxiety (Overall et al., 2009). Along the same lines, people with higher attachment anxiety also experience stronger physiological reactions to conflict than people with lower attachment anxiety (Feeney & Karantzas, 2017; Powers et al., 2006). What about attachment avoidance? People with high attachment avoidance also tend to be especially reactive to conflicts, but for different reasons. These individuals want to maintain independence, so having their goals impeded by their partner or being asked to change is particularly frustrating. People with high attachment avoidance tend to downplay the importance of conflicts,

Estimates of frequency of conflicts

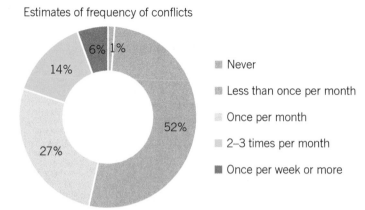

Figure 8.5 Estimates of the frequency of relationship conflicts, assessed retrospectively (Source: Based on data from McGonagle et al. [1992])

but also tend to experience more anger and greater physiological reactivity during conflict discussions than people with lower attachment avoidance (Feeney & Karantzas, 2017; Overall et al., 2013; Powers et al., 2006).

How Prevalent Are Conflicts?

Just how common are conflicts in real romantic relationships? When participants are prompted to report their relational experiences throughout the day, they report being in situations with corresponding interests more often than situations with conflicting interests. Conflicts of interest are actually relatively rare, reported in less than 10 percent of all situations people report in daily life (Columbus et al., 2021). This estimate aligns with other research suggesting that conflicts occur regularly, but infrequently (McGonagle et al., 1992). As shown in Figure 8.5, over 75 percent of married people report that they typically have conflicts with their spouse once per month or less, and only 6 percent of married people report experiencing conflicts once per week or more.

Although these studies reveal a somewhat low frequency of conflicts, the occurrence of conflicts will likely vary based on characteristics of the relationship, each partner, and the situation. For example, since conflicts of interest result from a divergence of interests, partners who are more similar should have fewer conflicts than dissimilar couples because their interests and goals will be aligned more often. Consider a hypothetical example of Extroverted Eddie and his romantic relationships with Extroverted Erin and Introverted Isla. In his past relationship with Extroverted Erin, they hardly ever had disagreements about how to spend a Friday night. Clubs – yes! Concerts – yes! Rowdy stadiums – yes! However, in his current relationship with Introverted Isla, disagreements are as common as Friday nights. Each week, Eddie wants to be with a crowd, whereas Isla prefers a quiet night in. In this example, similarity (or dissimilarity) in the personality characteristic of extroversion contributes to the frequency of conflict. Research indeed shows that couples with greater similarity report fewer disagreements than dissimilar couples (Surra & Longstreth, 1990).

Individual personality characteristics have also been linked to conflict frequency. For instance, people who are higher in agreeableness, extroversion, conscientiousness, and openness to experience all tend to report less conflict than people who score lower on these personality traits (Gerpott et al., 2018). Agreeable people like to get along with others, so they may have the goal of getting along rather than getting their way. People high in conscientiousness may have fewer disagreements with their partners because their ability to follow through on their duties may keep them from impeding their partner's goals or aggravating their partner.

The prevalence of conflict in a given relationship may also fluctuate as a function of relationship duration (Hatch & Bulcroft, 2004; McGonagle et al., 1992). Theoretically, conflicts should be more common earlier in relationships than later in relationships because partners are adjusting to each other's preferences. Over time (at least in relationships that are maintained), partners will settle into a routine so that conflicts are less common and more easily resolved (Arriaga, 2013). For example, Extroverted Eddie and Introverted Isla may initially disagree every Friday about how to spend the weekend, but ten years into their relationship, they will have established a predictable rhythm. Perhaps they alternate Fridays at home and Fridays on the town, or perhaps they have found subdued social activities that meet both of their needs (spending time with a small group of close friends, perhaps?). Early in relationships, partners also have to navigate how to divide household responsibilities which can result in conflict; ten years into the relationship, a couple may have a well-established routine that one partner folds the laundry while the other empties the dishwasher. These patterns and routines eventually require little effort, coordination, or compromise.

Research does, in fact, suggest that people in longer-term relationships report less frequent conflicts than people in shorter-term relationships (Hatch & Bulcroft, 2004; McGonagle et al., 1992). But, picture a couple who has been in a relationship for a relatively short time (let's say less than ten years), and then picture a couple who has been together for a relatively long time (more than thirty years). Are there notable differences between these couples other than their relationship length? To be together for thirty, fifty, or seventy (!) years requires some age as well, and so it makes sense that partners in longer-term relationships tend to be older and often (not always) in a different life stage than people whose committed relationships are less long-lasting. Many a newer relationship is among younger people in their 20s or 30s, whereas people who have been married over thirty years are more likely to be in their 60s or 70s. Indeed, data from a large national survey in the United States (The National Survey of Families and Households) support the idea that conflict is less a function of relationship length, and more a function of age (Hatch & Bulcroft, 2004). As shown in Figure 8.6, younger adults reported greater conflict frequency than mid-life adults, who themselves reported more frequent conflicts than older adults, regardless of relationship length. This finding suggests that age (or life stage), rather than relationship length, is the reason why people in longer relationships have fewer disagreements.

Although we might theoretically expect conflict to decrease as partners adapt to each other, longitudinal studies that follow couples over time also show no evidence that conflict decreases as a function of relationship length. Instead, conflict either tends to be stable over long periods of time (Kamp Dush & Taylor, 2012) or to increase over time, with partners reporting more tension, resentment, and irritation as time passes (e.g., Birditt et al., 2017). Why doesn't conflict decrease linearly over time? One reason is, perhaps, that relationships do not unfold linearly. Sometimes partners resolve problems in their relationships, but only temporarily, and the same problem needs be worked through again as the situation changes. Consider a long-term couple transitioning to parenthood. Suddenly, the practiced, well-oiled machine of their mutual lives is thrown into disarray by the unpredictable and exhausting demands of an infant. In the space of one heartbeat, many previously arranged compromises need to be renegotiated. A couple who had previously settled on a reasonable schedule to ensure time for work, personal leisure, and couple-time will have to re-enter negotiations

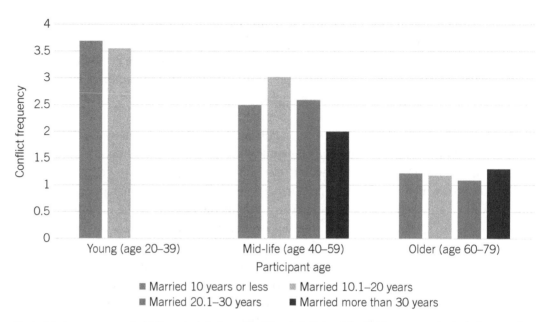

Figure 8.6 Are younger people feistier or just dealing with different challenges? Conflict frequency varies by both age and marital durations, but age seems to be the driver. In this figure, higher scores on conflict frequency indicate greater reported frequency. (Source: Hatch & Bulcroft [2004]; reprinted with permission from Sage Publications)

when a child upends their schedule. New disagreements will crop up as well: Who is responsible for coordinating pediatrician appointments? Who will sing the middle-of-the-night lullabies?

Consistent with these ideas, new parents do report more disagreements than non-parents, and new parents report more disagreements than they did prior to becoming parents (Chen et al., 2006; Crohan, 1996; Doss et al., 2009a; Kluwer & Johnson, 2007). This pattern of results is observed for both mothers and fathers, White and African American new parents, and within cross-cultural samples (Crohan, 1996; Huss & Pollmann-Schult, 2020; Kluwer & Johnson, 2007). Having a child in the home (versus not having a child) strongly predicts conflict frequency (Hatch & Bulcroft, 2004). Children, it seems, are adorable, squishy, sweet, little conflict-making machines.

Other transitional stages can similarly produce increases in conflict. Moving, changing jobs, the loss of a member of one's support network – any disruption can require readjustment, and readjustment can lead to a rehashing of old conflicts and the emergence of new conflicts. Next, we consider how conflict frequency is associated with relationship outcomes.

    IS THIS TRUE FOR YOU?

Power in Relationship Conflicts

People do not always negotiate conflicts on an even playing field. In many cases, one partner has more **power** than the other. Power is high when one has the ability to control or influence another person's outcome, and it is constrained when one is dependent on the actions of another person (Overall & Cross, 2019). A boss has power over their employees; a professor has power over their students; and in interdependent dyadic relationships, both partners have power over each other. Power in romantic relationships results from a partner's ability to influence the other (e.g., Jim can influence's Pam's outcomes by moving to Philadelphia). However, power is also constrained in close relationships because each person's outcomes also depend on their partner's behaviors (e.g., Pam's preferences can coax Jim right back to Scranton).

The balance of power – who has more power – is usually in favor of the partner who is less committed to the relationship, an idea called the **principle of least interest** (Kelley & Thibaut, 1978). The less committed partner holds the position of power because they have the ever-present option of leaving the relationship, so they do not need to be constrained by their partner's preferences or actions. Imagine if Jim said, "It's Philly or bust, Pam. Join me, or I'll start preparing the divorce papers." Such a powerful bargaining position is only feasible if Jim is willing to dissolve the relationship (or believes that Pam is unwilling to end the relationship and will comply). Consider your own close relationships. In what relationships do you have power, and in what relationships are you relatively less powerful? Do you feel that you have more power in relationships when you are less committed to maintaining the relationship than your friend or partner?

The pursuit of power in relationships can have dark implications. When people perceive low power in their relationships, they sometimes become aggressive in an attempt to restore their power (Cross et al., 2019; Fast & Chen, 2009; Overall et al., 2016). For instance, men who perceive low power in their romantic relationships (e.g., perceive that they do not have the ability to influence their partners' behavior, believe that they cannot get their own way, and do not feel that they get to make the decisions in the relationship) are more likely to threaten, belittle, or insult their partners during conflict discussions than men who perceive more power in their relationships (Cross et al., 2019). Men who desire greater power in their relationships also report greater verbal and physical aggression toward their partners than men who desire less power (Cross et al., 2019). This focus on men is not accidental. Research suggests that men are particularly concerned with maintaining power in different-sex relationships, especially if they have the attitude that women are trying to control men, an attitude termed **hostile sexism** (Glick & Fiske, 1996). Men who endorse attitudes consistent with hostile sexism (e.g., "Once a woman gets a man to commit to her she usually tries to put him on a tight leash"; Glick & Fiske, 1996) are more likely to perceive low power in their romantic relationships and are more desirous of high power, both of which contribute to relationship aggression in an effort to increase power (Cross et al., 2019).

Having the short end of the power stick has different implications for women (Pietromonaco et al., 2021). Women who perceive that they have low power tend to behave more submissively during their conflicts than women who perceive more power; that is, they tend to disengage, hold back, and be less open and honest. Men do this to some extent as well, but in different-sex relationships, the finding is stronger for women, especially if women hold more traditional beliefs about gender roles (e.g., men are the providers, women are the caregivers). Consider your own behavior when you feel that you lack power. Do you behave in line with these gendered predictions?

What Are the Consequences of Having Frequent Conflicts?

In general, dating and married couples with more frequent conflicts tend to report greater dissatisfaction concurrently and over time (Caughlin et al., 2013; Johnson et al., 2018). For example, people who report greater conflict frequency at one time-point report more dramatic decreases in relationship satisfaction one year later than people who report less frequent conflict. Does this mean having more frequent conflicts translates to poorer relationships? Maybe, but not necessarily. First, we have to consider how conflict frequency is measured. Researchers might ask: "How often do you and your partner disagree and quarrel?" or "How often are you and your partner annoyed or angry with each other?" (Johnson et al., 2018, p. 447). These questions measure conflict frequency, but they also measure the way that people perceive their conflicts and how they handle them. A quarrel, after all, is akin to an argument, so when answering such questions, people may focus on the frequency of *adverse* conflicts, in particular, rather than benign disagreements ("Who's driving tonight?"). Similarly, being annoyed or angry is not a necessary consequence of a conflict of interest; it is the consequence of only some, more destructive conflicts. Adverse conflicts lead to dissatisfaction in relationships, but benign conflicts may not.

The link between conflict frequency and relationship (dis)satisfaction becomes even more interesting when we consider the role of commitment. Contrary to expectations, conflict frequency *decreases* after people report that they are considering separation or divorce (Johnson et al., 2018). Before that time, people might be literally *fighting for their relationships*, quarrelling only because they believe their relationships are *worth the fight*. When the tide turns and commitment wanes, motivation to engage in conflicts might also wane. This suggests a possible inverted U-shaped curve linking conflict frequency and relationship outcomes. As shown in Figure 8.7, relationship quality may be highest at a sweet spot defined by moderately frequent conflict. When people report that they have no conflicts, relationship quality may actually be quite poor. Partners might be ignoring underlying incompatibilities and leaving festering issues unresolved. A great many conflicts may likewise indicate poor relationship quality. As anyone in such a situation knows, managing endless conflicts is draining and may lead people to wonder whether they would be better off in a different, less friction-filled relationship. Conflict frequency clearly contributes to relationship functioning and shapes people's everyday experiences in relationships, but a full appreciation for how conflict plays out in relationships demands a deeper look. After all, two relationships with equivalent frequencies of conflict can be dramatically different in quality. How conflicts are managed can tell us more about relationship well-being than conflict frequency (e.g., Whitton, James-Kangal et al., 2018). In particular, how partners discuss their conflicts, how they resolve their conflicts, and how they recover from conflicts, are critical, as described in the next section.

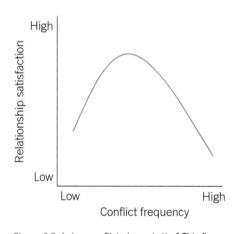

Figure 8.7 Is less conflict always better? This figure shows a possible inverted U-shaped curve linking conflict frequency and relationship satisfaction.

Managing Relational Conflict

Conflicts of interest pose a *potential* threat to a relationship, but only become an actual threat when they remain unresolved or poorly resolved. Conflicts generally harm relationships when they are avoided or discussed in such a way that partners experience negative concrete or symbolic outcomes that detract from relationship quality. Thus, finding ways to smoothly navigate conflicts is another critical relationship maintenance strategy (Ogolsky et al., 2017). Like the biases and illusions reviewed in Chapter 7, strategies for navigating disagreements allow partners to manage threats and maintain the status quo. Conflicts can even enhance a relationship when partners discuss their conflicts in ways that communicate commitment or care (recall that conflict is a diagnostic situation). Given the importance of managing conflicts effectively, a longstanding goal in the field of relationship science has been to identify behaviors that are particularly constructive (likely to produce positive personal and relationship consequences) and behaviors that are particularly destructive (likely to produce negative personal and relationship consequences) during conflict discussions.

To identify constructive and destructive behaviors, researchers commonly use longitudinal prospective research designs (e.g., Birditt et al., 2010; Heavey et al., 1995; Huston et al., 2001; Johnson et al., 2018; Markman, Rhodes et al., 2010; Sullivan et al., 2010). In prospective research, partners' conflict discussions are observed when they are satisfied with the relationship, and researchers isolate how specific conflict behaviors at the beginning of a relationship predict subsequent changes in the relationship over time.

Characterizing Conflict Discussion Behaviors

Research in this area typically relies on a paradigm in which couples are instructed to discuss their most severe unresolved relationship issue or disagreement for 8 to 15 minutes while their conversations are unobtrusively recorded (Crenshaw et al., 2021; Gottman & Notarius, 2000). Later, observational coders use specially designed coding systems to quantify the behaviors that partners exhibit during their conflict discussions. John Gottman's Specific Affect Coding System (SPAFF; Coan & Gottman, 2007; Gottman et al., 1995) is one such system. Gottman and his team rate the extent to which each partner in a couple exhibits specific positive and negative affective (emotional) behaviors during their discussions. Some of the specific behaviors that are measured by the SPAFF are defined with examples in Table 8.2.

The SPAFF's conflict codes can predict later relationship outcomes (e.g., Carrère & Gottman, 1999; Driver & Gottman, 2004; Gottman & Levenson, 1992; Gottman et al., 1998), including whether couples will remain together or go on to divorce (Carrère & Gottman, 1999). Its ability to predict relationship stability is tied to how the SPAFF allows positive and negative behaviors to be weighted based on their supposed relative impact (e.g., contempt, for example, can be weighted more strongly than defensiveness given its particular insidiousness). Work with the SPAFF reveals that partners who stay together exhibit more positive than negative behaviors during their discussions (a ratio favoring positivity) whereas couples who go on to divorce exhibit more negative than positive affective behaviors (a ratio favoring negativity). Both stable and unstable couples tend to behave in some positive and some negative ways; it is the relative extent of these behaviors that predict the relationship's future (Carrère & Gottman, 1999).

Table 8.2 Example codes from the Specific Affect Coding System

Code	Definition	Examples
Negative affective behaviors		
Anger	An expression of displeasure in response to a violation of the speaker's autonomy or respect	• "I'm so frustrated right now!" • Pursed lips, clenched jaw, tight neck
Contempt	A behavior that is intended to belittle, hurt, or humiliate another	• "Oh sure, that sounds *perfectly* reasonable," said sarcastically • Using a strange voice to imitate the partner
Criticism	An attack on someone's character or personality	• "You *never* refill the gas tank." • "You *always* ignore me."
Defensiveness	Deflecting responsibility or blame by arguing that something is not one's fault or counter-attacking	• "I couldn't have taken out the trash, it was raining!" • "Maybe I forget sometimes, but YOU always forget."
Stonewalling	Communicating an unwillingness to listen or respond	• Looking away or turning away to avoid contact • Avoiding normal head nods or behaviors that indicate attention
Positive affective behaviors		
Affection	Communicating care and concern, or offering comfort	• "I love you" • Offering a hug
Enthusiasm	Expressing passionate interest in a person or activity	• Smiling • Asking questions to show excitement
Validation	Communicating sincere understanding and acceptance of the partner's opinion	• Head nodding • "That's a really good point."

Source: Based on data from Coan & Gottman (2007).

 IN THE NEWS

The "Four Horsemen of the Apocalypse" and the "Magic Ratio"

John Gottman's work using the SPAFF has drawn the attention of major news outlets including *The Atlantic*, BBC News, *The New York Times*, and *Time Magazine*. In particular, Gottman has two findings that have captured audiences' attention: his "**four horsemen of the apocalypse**" and his "**magic ratio**." The four horsemen of the apocalypse are the four conflict behaviors that Gottman has identified as most destructive for relationships. These behaviors are (1) contempt, (2) criticism, (3) defensiveness, and (4) stonewalling.

As shown in Table 8.2, the SPAFF defines **contempt** as purposeful attempts to belittle, hurt, or humiliate the partner. Picture sarcasm, eye-rolling, mocking, and other purposeful "digs." These behaviors are intentionally cruel, and they are uncomfortable to witness. **Criticism** is defined as an attack on someone's character, though unlike contempt, it is not necessarily intended to be malicious. A criticism describes a problem behavior as characteristic of the person and often includes the words "never" or "always." A statement like "You never pay attention when I'm talking" is a criticism because it implicates and condemns the *person* rather than the specific behavior. Unlike critiques that are intended to resolve a problem ("hey, you forgot to put gas in the car this week"), a criticism implicitly communicates a character flaw ("you *never* refill the gas tank"). **Defensiveness** often occurs in response to criticism; after a person perceives an attack, they may respond by presenting their defense ("it's not my fault; the gas station is out of my way and closed any time I could go") or mounting a counter-attack ("why should I refill the gas tank if *you* never refill the gas tank?"). Defensiveness means not taking responsibility for any part of the problem and can make resolving disagreements impossible . Finally, **stonewalling** is the purposeful lack of engagement in the conflict. It is like becoming a stone statue: unresponsive, un-listening, there but not there. Although partners are doing nothing while stonewalling, they are communicating a great deal. Their silence says, "I'm not interested in this conversation. I refuse to discuss this with you" and maybe even "I don't care about you." According to Gottman, people can protect their relationships by showing appreciation (instead of contempt), using **"I" statements** like "I feel ..." or "I need ..." (instead of criticism), taking responsibility for some part of the problem (instead of defensiveness), and taking a break as needed (instead of stonewalling).

Importantly, relationships are not necessarily doomed by the four horsemen. This is where the "magic ratio" comes in. Based on his observations, Gottman identified 5 to 1 as the ratio of positive to negative conflict interactions that protects a relationship. In other words, partners who thrive tend to have at least five positive interactions for every negative interaction. This does not necessarily mean that you can make up for a contemptuous comment with five validating or affectionate behaviors, and it does not necessarily mean that maintaining a 5 to 1 ratio will guarantee your relationship's success. Although Gottman and his team have touted that they can predict which couples will divorce with 90 percent accuracy (a number that has been reported in numerous news stories), the actual ability of SPAFF behaviors to predict divorce seems to be much lower, closer to 45 percent accuracy (Heyman & Slep, 2001; Stanley et al., 2000). Like many research findings that end up in the news, the four horsemen of the apocalypse and the magic ratio have empirical support, *but* critical nuance, which the news stories might miss, has important bearings on the conclusions we can accurately draw.

While Gottman and his team conducted several studies using the SPAFF (Gottman & Notarius, 2000), other research teams have developed other coding manuals in an effort to identify destructive and constructive conflict behaviors, resulting in an array of overlapping findings with distinct terminology (Sillars & Overall, 2017). For example, the Marital

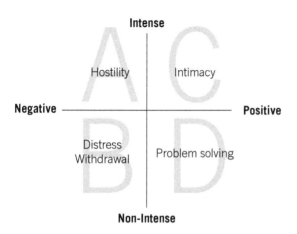

Figure 8.8 Where do your behaviors tend to fall in this two-dimensional way to categorize conflict behaviors? The horizontal axis represents the affective valence of the behavior, and the vertical axis represents the intensity of the behavior. Labels A through D define particular combinations of affective valence and intensity. (Source: Drawn based on data from Woodin [2011])

Interaction Coding Scheme (MICS; Heyman et al., 1995) has a code named "Blame," which includes criticizing and putting down the partner. This code clearly overlaps with criticism and contempt in the SPAFF. Other coding scales introduced new codes such as "Communicates Clearly (expresses oneself in a way that is easy to understand)" and "Negotiates (suggests solutions and compromises)" (Heavey et al., 1993; Sillars & Overall, 2017). Fortunately for us, relationship researchers have done the hard work of organizing all of these disparate conflict behaviors into a few clear categories or dimensions (e.g., van de Vliert & Euwema, 1994; Woodin, 2011).

As shown in Figure 8.8, researchers have concluded that conflict behaviors vary along two important dimensions (e.g., Woodin, 2011). First, they differ in **affective valence**, meaning that some behaviors express positive emotion (think kind, warm, cooperative behaviors), whereas other behaviors express negative emotion (think angry, cruel, or disagreeable behaviors). This distinction is perfectly in line with the SPAFF's classification of positive and negative affective codes. Sometimes this dimension is explained as cooperative versus competitive behaviors or simply as positive versus negative behaviors (e.g., Caughlin et al., 2013; Matthews et al., 1996). Second, behaviors differ in **intensity**; some behaviors are more active and forceful, whereas others are more passive and gentle (Woodin, 2011). This two-dimensional classification results in four combinations, as shown in the four labeled quadrants of Figure 8.8. Although each quadrant includes several specific behaviors, Woodin (2011) identified **meta-labels**, or overarching descriptions, that apply to all or many of the conflict behaviors in that quadrant. While forming meta-categories is not essential, doing so helps organize the findings and allows for us to more easily draw conclusions from the abundant research findings in this area.

The conflict behaviors in quadrant A are all affectively (emotionally) negative behaviors that are displayed with a high level of energy: these were given the meta-label of **hostility**. Hostile behaviors demonstrate harsh negative emotions and are considered active unconstructive forms of communication. Hostility includes specific conflict behaviors such as showing anger, verbally attacking, and criticism. Research suggests that women, more than men, tend to display hostility during conflicts (Woodin, 2011), that the use of hostility does not differ between gay, lesbian, and different-sex couples (Kurdek, 1994b; Roisman et al., 2008), and that hostility tends to be more common among Black than White American partners (Birditt et al., 2010; Orbuch et al., 2002). Chinese and Chinese American couples also express greater hostility during conflicts than couples from other cultures (e.g., Hiew et al., 2015; Schoebi et al., 2010; Tsai et al., 2006; Williamson et al., 2012). Among Asian cultures, hostility is common in mainland China, Taiwan, and Hong Kong, but not in Korea or Japan (Lee et al., 2013), suggesting important variation among Asian cultures.

Like the behaviors in quadrant A, the behaviors in quadrant B are also affectively negative, but they are enacted with less "umph." Meta-categories that fall into this quadrant are (1) distress – quieter negative emotions (e.g., anxiety, sadness) and milder negative behaviors (e.g., whining) – and (2) withdrawal – disengagement from the discussion (e.g., stonewalling, avoiding eye contact). Withdrawal is particularly low intensity; people who are engaging in withdrawal are often literally doing nothing; see Figure 8.9). Distress characterizes women's conflict behaviors more than men's, whereas men enact withdrawal more than women (Woodin, 2011). Black Americans also exhibit greater withdrawal than White Americans (Birditt et al., 2010).

Turning to quadrant C, intimacy is a meta-category that describes the positive, high-intensity behaviors people can engage in to manage conflict. These behaviors communicate affection, understanding, or positive affect (e.g., validation, humor, curiosity). They differ from the positive problem solving behaviors in quadrant D: construct-

Figure 8.9 Partners withdraw from their conflict discussion, physically and emotionally distancing themselves from each other. Although the partners are saying nothing, what does their silence seem to say? (Photo: fizkes / iStock / Getty Images Plus)

ive forms of communication that are more matter of fact, and thus, lower in intensity (e.g., offering solutions, asking clarification questions) than intimacy behavior. No gender differences have been observed in either the use of intimacy or problem-solving conflict behaviors; however, lesbian couples tend to behave particularly "harmoniously" during conflict discussions, compared to gay male couples and different-sex couples (Roisman et al., 2008). Further, same-sex couples (both male and female) report more positive problem solving than different-sex couples (Gottman et al., 2003; Kurdek, 1994b). No differences in affectively positive conflict behaviors have been observed between White and Black American couples (Birditt et al., 2010), and evidence that Chinese couples behave with less positivity than other ethnic groups is inconsistent (Tsai et al., 2006; Williamson et al., 2012).

Are conflict meta-behaviors associated with relationship satisfaction? Meta-analytic work suggests yes. Figure 8.10 shows how people who display more hostility, more distress, or more withdrawal during conflict tend to be less satisfied with their relationships than people who display less of these behaviors. Remember, these cross-sectional associations include bidirectional causality, so these associations reflect not only an effect of negatively valenced behaviors on dissatisfaction, but also the influence of dissatisfaction on negatively valenced behaviors. Likewise, people who display more intimacy or problem solving during their conflicts tend to be more satisfied than people who display less of these behaviors, both because satisfied people behave more constructively and because constructive conflict behaviors help to maintain satisfaction. While intimacy and problem-solving behaviors are similarly linked to relationship well-being, among negative behaviors, hostility stands out as especially strong in its link to poorer relationship satisfaction.

Consequences of Hostility

As suggested in Figure 8.10, hostility during conflict discussions is uniquely damaging. When *either* partner uses hostile conflict behaviors (e.g., shouting) at the start of a marriage, the

Figure 8.10 Are conflicts benign? Consider the direction and strength of the associations between each conflict meta-behavior and relationship satisfaction, based on meta-analysis. More extreme associations (farther from zero) represent stronger associations. Hostility, distress, and withdrawal are all negatively associated with relationship satisfaction, whereas intimacy and problem solving are positively associated with relationship satisfaction. (Source: Drawn based on data from Woodin [2011])

likelihood that the relationship will end in divorce increases (Birditt et al., 2010). Similarly, when newlyweds exhibit greater hostility during conflict, they tend to report lower relationship satisfaction over the next ten years of marriage (Sullivan et al., 2010). We can even observe conflict behaviors *prior to* marriage for a stronger test of whether hostility predicts the emergence of relationship dissatisfaction (Markman, Rhoades et al., 2010). After all, couples in the earliest stages of marriage may already be distressed (approximately 20 percent of couples divorce in the first five years of marriage; Raley & Bumpass, 2003), so relationship satisfaction or dissatisfaction could cause hostile conflict behaviors rather than the reverse. Consistent with the idea that hostility adversely affects relationships, couples who exhibit more hostility prior to marriage report lower relationship quality over the first five years of marriage (Markman, Rhoades et al. 2010).

Surprisingly, the link between hostility and distress is not as consistent as these studies would make it seem. Several other well-designed research studies have shown that greater hostility actually predicts *improvements* in relationship quality over time (e.g., Heavey et al., 1993; Overall et al., 2009). These discrepant findings have generated a fair amount of head scratching among researchers. Fortunately, a recent line of research has helped to clarify these findings by identifying contextual factors (i.e., moderators) that influence the direction of the association between hostile conflict behaviors and relationship outcomes (Overall, 2018, 2020; Overall et al., 2009; Overall & McNulty, 2017).

Think about the consequences of hostile behaviors. Imagine that you become so frustrated with your partner's messy habits that you angrily yell, "You are such a slob! I'd rather live by myself than in this pigsty with you. You're infuriating. Argh!" What consequences might result from this angry, critical outburst?

A. Your partner will defensively reply, "It's not *my* fault this place is messy. *You* are messy too!"
B. Your partner will feel stressed, sad, and/or anxious.
C. Your partner will tidy the pigsty (I mean, home) and think twice before they let it get that messy again.
D. All of the above.

The answer seems to be "D. All of the above." Hostile conflict behaviors can trigger reciprocal negativity (negative begets negative) and lead to hurt feelings, but hostile conflict behaviors also get the point across. *Clean up or pack up, pal!* Unlike passive negative behaviors (i.e., showing distress, withdrawing) or positive behaviors (i.e., calm problem solving or intimacy), hostility clearly indicates that there is a problem and communicates the intensity of one's displeasure. The first step in resolving a problem or conflict is recognizing that the problem exists (Baker & McNulty, 2020), so hostile conflict behaviors may promote resolution of conflicts by clearly conveying the existence of a problem. Even the distress resulting from hostile conflict behaviors can be useful in motivating change. Negative emotions help people to become aware of threats (in this case, a threat to the relationship) and behave in ways that mitigate threats (Baker & McNulty, 2020). Thus, hostile conflict behaviors may be more likely to catalyze a change in the partner's behavior than a "constructive" conflict behavior. If the partner changes, the problem is resolved, and the relationship is no longer threatened. Consistent with this logic, longitudinal work reveals that when partners engage in more hostility during conflict discussions, they tend to experience a decrease in the severity of the discussed problem over the following twelve months (Overall et al., 2009). Hostility: it gets the job done.

Before you put down your book and go yell at your partner or roommate, remember – this cannot be the whole story. Recall that a preponderance of research shows that hostility is associated with poorer relationship outcomes (review Figure 8.10). Yes, hostility can sometimes help to *resolve* relationship problems, but hostility can also *contribute to* relationship problems. What gives? The key factor differentiating beneficial versus costly hostility may be the severity of the problem. When a conflict is major, hostility predicts a decrease in problem severity (the problem resolves) and an increase in relationship satisfaction. However, when a conflict is minor, hostility predicts an increase in problem severity and a decrease in relationship satisfaction (McNulty & Russell, 2010). The consequence of hostility depends on whether the situation demands a direct and negative response to communicate the existence of a problem and to motivate a change or whether hostile conflict behavior constitutes an overreaction to a minor issue. Conflict behaviors must be proportionate to the problem they are addressing.

Consider again the messy pigsty example from before, and imagine expressing hostility toward your partner in order to change their behavior. In this case, your partner was the *target* of the desired change. Now imagine that you instead expressed hostility when your partner was requesting a change of you, when you were the target of the desired change. Your partner asks (with hostility or not) for you to clean up your mess and you yell, "Stop bothering me, you nag! You're always on my case. Let me live!" What consequences might result from this angry outburst?

A. Your partner will lovingly clean up your mess for you.

B. Admiring your confidence, your partner will become more satisfied with the relationship.

C. Your partner will perceive you to be uncommitted to maintaining the relationship.

D. All of the above.

Here, research suggests that the answer is "C: Your partner will perceive you to be uncommitted ..." The nuance of hostile conflict behavior continues (Overall, 2018). Not only does the consequence of hostility depend on the severity of the disagreement, but the consequence of hostility also depends on the *role* of the person behaving with hostility. In other words, hostility lands differently when it is used by the agent of the desired change (the person requesting a change) versus the target of the desired change (the person being asked to change). This distinction is illustrated in Figure 8.11. The upper panel (a) shows hostility on the part of the agent of change, whereas the lower panel (b) shows hostility on the part of the target of change.

The thought bubbles on the top right and bottom right of Figure 8.11 depict partners' responses to hostility coming from an agent of change and the target of change, respectively (Overall, 2018). When *agents* behave with greater hostility, their partners perceive them to

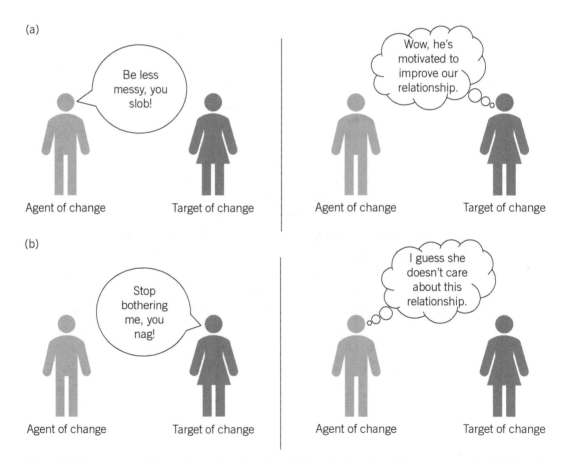

Figure 8.11 Are you an agent (requesting a change) or a target (being asked to change) when you express hostility? Agents' hostility leads their partners to perceive greater commitment (a), whereas targets' hostility leads their partners to perceive less commitment (b). (Source: Drawn based on Overall [2018])

be more committed to maintaining the relationship (*you're angry, so you must really care about improving our relationship*). Recall that conflict behaviors have symbolic outcomes because conflict behaviors are considered diagnostic of true feelings. Although a hostile reproach from an agent of change may feel upsetting in the moment, it also indicates that one's partner cares enough to "fight for" the relationship and therefore communicates their commitment. Over time, people who are asked to change perceive greater commitment and therefore stay more satisfied with their relationships when their partners used hostility in their request for change (Overall, 2018).

Alternatively, hostile conflict behavior from the *target* of change has the opposite consequence. When *targets* behave with hostility while being asked to change, their partners perceive them to be less committed to maintaining the relationship (Overall, 2018). As a result, partners of *targets* who behave with greater hostility go on to experience lower relationship quality themselves over time. Hostile behavior from a *target* of change communicates an unwillingness to compromise or adapt to protect the relationship. If you're considering behaving with hostility in an upcoming conflict, consider your role in the conflict first.

Hostile conflict behaviors are thus destructive only in certain contexts, and further, variability in the use of hostile conflict behaviors is better for relationship outcomes than persistent hostility (Overall, 2020). Variable hostility may indicate that hostile behaviors are used in appropriate contexts rather than in all contexts. All in all, hostile behavior is risky. It can be motivating and help to resolve problems or communicate commitment in the right contexts, but it can also prove destructive. Hostility: use sparingly and with great caution.

Consequences of Intimacy and Problem Solving

Unlike hostility, the research on positive affective behaviors (i.e., intimacy and problem solving) tends to be more consistent. Prospective studies have shown that greater observed humor, affection, and interest as newlyweds predicts greater relationship satisfaction over the next ten years (Lee et al., 2013), and greater positive communication (e.g., problem solving, validation) prior to marriage predicts higher relationship quality over the first five years of marriage (Markman, Rhoades et al., 2010). Unlike hostility, the consequences of intimacy/problem solving do not vary according to the partner's role in the discussion (agent of change versus target of change; Overall, 2018). Partners who exhibit greater intimacy/ problem solving (either while requesting a change or responding to a change) are perceived to be more committed, and intimacy/problem solving contributes to higher relationship quality over the following year.

Despite the relative consistency of these findings, we can still consider some key nuances. For instance, long-term longitudinal work shows that greater use of intimacy/problem solving at the start of the marriage (e.g., listening, discussing calmly, using humor) predicts a lower likelihood of divorce over time, but only if *both* partners engage in intimacy/problem solving (Birditt et al., 2010). At the same time, recall that hostility from *either* partner predicts a greater likelihood of divorce. To make sense of this, consider the interdependence inherent in these interactions (Arriaga, 2013). Each person's behavior influences their partner's outcomes. Problem solving and intimacy on the part of both partners may be necessary to produce cooperation and problem resolution, whereas hostility from either partner may be sufficient to produce problematic outcomes. One person's attempts to solve the problem may lead them to feel frustrated by their partner's unwillingness to do the same, or the partner prioritizing intimacy may be taken advantage of by a partner who uses hostility to force their goals (Rusbult & Arriaga, 2000).

All told, intimacy and problem-solving behaviors are largely beneficial. Behaving in constructive ways during conflict may be challenging, but partners who can do so benefit. Intimacy and problem solving: use regularly, don't hold back!

Consequences of Withdrawal

Withdrawal – the negative, low intensity meta-behavior – damages relationships when taken to the extreme (e.g., stonewalling), so it is typically considered a destructive conflict behavior. Indeed, greater withdrawal early in the marriage has been linked to a greater likelihood of divorce later on (Gottman et al., 1998). However, there are various types of withdrawal which may each have unique consequences (Holley et al., 2013; Roberts, 2000). Withdrawal can entail a stony silence or averted gaze in which one person actively ignores their partner (**angry withdrawal**), or withdrawal can entail avoiding the conflict by changing the subject, joking around, or finding a distraction (**conflict avoidance**). Angry withdrawal is more uniformly problematic for relationships than conflict avoidance because it communicates disdain and an unwillingness to engage (consider the symbolic outcomes here; Roberts, 2000). Indeed, when withdrawal is measured in such a way that it captures angry withdrawal (e.g., "I refuse to talk about the subject"), greater withdrawal is associated with poorer subsequent relationship satisfaction (Johnson et al., 2018). Alternatively, conflict avoidance has divergent outcomes. It can be destructive if it leaves disagreements unresolved or it can be adaptive if it keeps conflicts from becoming too intense; it might allow couples to refocus on their goals and return to the discussion prepared to behave constructively (Holley et al., 2013; Roberts, 2000). The consequences of withdrawal are thus context specific.

Much of what we know about withdrawal comes from the study of a specific dyadic interaction pattern called the **demand-withdraw pattern**. In this pattern, one partner makes demands (i.e., complaining, criticizing, and/or nagging), prompting the other person to withdraw. This type of withdrawal, in the context of a demand-withdraw pattern, is more strongly associated with relationship dysfunction than withdrawal on its own (Holley et al., 2013). Like the association between conflict behavior and relationship functioning, the association between demand and withdrawal is another bidirectional causal process in which the pattern plays out cyclically. Nagging leads to withdrawal, which leads to more extreme nagging, which leads to more extreme withdrawal, and so on. To see how this pattern plays out, read through the demand-withdraw dialogue of a hypothetical couple, shown in Figure 8.12.

In this dialogue, Dave withdraws in response to Ashira's request (which he may have perceived as demanding). Initially, his minimal response and focus on his phone demonstrates disinterest. In response to Dave's mild withdrawal, Ashira becomes more demanding. In response to Ashira's increasing demands, Dave withdraws further, leaving the room to demonstrate his unwillingness to continue the conversation. By the end of the brief conversation, both partners are convinced that the other is the problem. Ashira thinks, "If only you would stop withdrawing, I could stop demanding," whereas Dave thinks, "If only you would stop demanding, I could stop withdrawing." In reality, both partners contribute to the

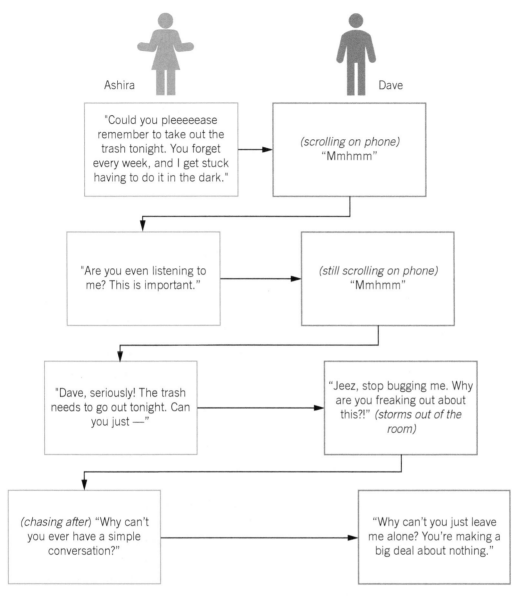

Figure 8.12 Is this type of demand-withdrawal dialogue familiar? As Ashira becomes more demanding, Dave withdraws more. As Dave withdraws more, Ashira becomes more demanding.

destructive cycle. As the conversation progresses, each person's behavior pushes the other more into demanding-mode or withdrawing-mode, and the pattern intensifies (Baucom, Dickinson et al., 2015).

Consistent with the example, demand-withdraw tends to be a gendered pattern in different-sex dyads. We're more likely to see a female-demander and male-withdrawer pattern than the opposite pattern (Eldridge et al., 2007). Consider, however, one exception to this trend: when the conflict discussion centers on a desired change in one partner, the partner requesting the change tends to enter the demander role, whereas the person being asked to change tends to occupy the withdrawer role (Eldridge et al., 2007; Papp, Kouros et al., 2009). In any case, the demand-withdraw pattern is associated with poor concurrent relationship quality (greater likelihood of divorce, poorer relationship satisfaction), poor concurrent personal well-being (i.e., greater anxiety, depression, physical health symptoms; Schrodt et al., 2014), and decreases in relationship quality over time (Heavey et al., 1995; Sasaki & Overall, 2021). Although demand-withdraw interactions do tend to include other destructive conflict behaviors (Papp, Kouros et al., 2009), links between demand-withdraw and relationship outcomes are not simply due to demand-withdraw interactions being more hostile or negative; something about the demand-withdraw pattern itself (which is not yet fully known) proves problematic (Caughlin & Huston, 2002).

 ARTICLE SPOTLIGHT

The Demand-Withdraw Pattern in High and Low SES Contexts

The demand-withdraw pattern helps us to put the consequences of withdrawal in context; however, the consequences of the demand-withdraw conflict pattern need to be put in context as well. Social ecological models (see Chapter 2) remind us that relationships exist in unique environmental contexts, and one critical environmental factor is the couple's socioeconomic status (SES; Ross et al., 2019). A recent paper by Ross, Karney, Nguyen, and Bradbury (2019) suggests that the consequences of demand-withdraw differ for relatively affluent and relatively disadvantaged couples.

Ross and her colleagues (2019) observed that the existing research linking the demand-withdraw pattern to poor relationship outcomes was focused on people with higher SES and may not generalize to those with lower SES. They hypothesized that the demand-withdraw pattern may be costly for people with greater economic resources because withdraw communicates disinterest or an unwillingness to acknowledge a partner's demands (i.e., to solve a solvable problem), but they expected demand-withdraw to have different consequences for people with low SES. Specifically, they predicted that demand-withdraw may be less costly (or perhaps even beneficial) for people with fewer economic resources: withdrawing from demands may be adaptive for people without sufficient resources to address the demands. In this context, withdraw (in response to demands) may constitute an adaptive recognition that the problem may not be resolvable.

Ross and her colleagues tested this hypothesis in two samples that included nearly 1,000 married couples in total. In the first study, participant couples who had been married for various lengths of time were observed having a discussion about a relationship disagreement and discussions about something each partner wanted to change about themselves (21 minutes of discussions in total). Couples' demand-withdraw behavior was observationally coded from these discussions, and participants reported their relationship satisfaction at the time of the discussions and eighteen months later. SES was assessed with a measure of sociodemographic risk that captured education, income, employment, and reliance on public assistance. Results revealed the classic demand-withdraw effects for couples with high SES: wife demanding and husband withdrawing predicted a decrease in wives' relationship satisfaction over eighteen months (see panel (a) of Figure 8.13). However, for couples with low SES, wives' relationship satisfaction decreased most strongly when they

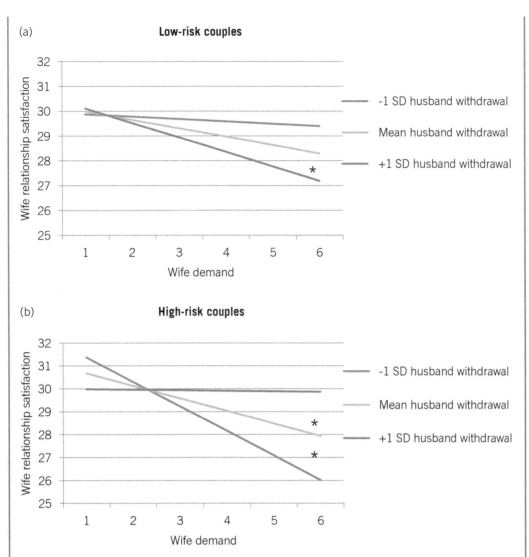

Figure 8.13 Low-risk couples (those with high SES) report the lowest relationship satisfaction when there is high wife demand and high husband withdrawal (a). Alternatively, high-risk couples (those with low SES) maintain their relationship satisfaction in response to wife demands when the husband withdraws (b). (Source: Copyright © 2019, American Psychological Association; reprinted with permission; Ross, J. M., Karney, B. R., Nguyen, T. P., & Bradbury, T. N. (2019). Communication that is maladaptive for middle-class couples is adaptive for socioeconomically disadvantaged couples. *Journal of Personality and Social Psychology, 116*(4), 582–597, https://doi.org/10.1037/pspi0000158) SD = soioeconomically disadvantaged; −SD = low SES; +SD = high SES.

demanded and their husbands *failed to* withdraw. In other words, withdraw in response to demands seemed to have a stabilizing role for low SES couples (see panel (b) of Figure 8.13).

The second study replicated the pattern of results in a sample of newlywed couples who were followed for over two years. In this study, the researchers assessed SES at baseline, and they measured conflict behavior and relationship satisfaction four times: baseline (T1), nine months (T2), eighteen months (T3), and twenty-seven months (T4) after baseline. With multiple observation points, Ross and her colleagues were able to test how demand-withdraw at a particular time-point predicted subsequent changes in relationship satisfaction. Unlike

Study 1, where demand-withdraw behavior was assumed to characterize the couple's typical way of behaving, Study 2 focused on a couple's demand-withdraw behavior at a given time-point relative to their demand-withdraw behavior at other observation time-points. Think of it this way: Study 1 is akin to testing whether *people* who drink more caffeine have a harder time falling asleep than *people* who drink less coffee (comparing *people* to one another; between-person), whereas Study 2 is akin to asking whether a person has more trouble falling asleep *on days* when they drank more caffeine than they usually do (comparing a person *on one day* to the same person on another day; within-person).

Again, the wife-demand/husband-withdraw pattern was associated with relationship satisfaction differently for those with low and high SES. For people with high SES, greater wife demand and husband withdrawal than usual predicted decreases in wives' relationship satisfaction. For people with low SES, greater wife demands than usual was problematic when husbands failed to withdraw, but greater wife demands than usual was beneficial when husbands withdrew.

This study reminds us to attend to the couple's context when we consider the consequences of particular relationship behaviors. It also reminds us that traditional approaches to sampling may obscure important variability. Demand-withdraw tends to be unhealthy in the types of samples that are easy to attain (people with moderate to high SES), but less costly for people with lower socioeconomic resources. For relatively more disadvantaged couples, withdrawal may be a useful strategy to protect the relationship when it is untenable to address demands head-on.

Even if people discuss their conflicts in ways that do not harm the relationship (and perhaps even enhance the relationship), more than a constructive discussion is required to manage a conflict or resolve a disagreement. Think back to the example of Jim and Pam's Scranton versus Philadelphia disagreement. Jim and Pam could discuss this disagreement without hostility (no name calling or anger); they could each stay engaged in the discussion (no withdrawal or stonewalling); and they could even validate each other's point of view and discuss solutions calmly, but still the disagreement would remain. Recovering from a conflict ultimately requires someone – or perhaps both people – to forego their own best interests for the best interests of the partner or the relationship. Someone needs to make a **sacrifice**.

Sacrifice

In a situation with conflicting interests, the only way to end a stalemate is for someone to sacrifice their own best interests for the best interests of their partner or the relationship (Van Lange et al., 1997). People sacrifice for many different reasons, as shown in Table 8.3. Some sacrifices are based on **approach motives**, meaning that a partner sacrifices in order to *obtain* a benefit. In this case, a person may decide to sacrifice because they anticipate that they will feel good, that their partner will be satisfied, or that the relationship will improve from the sacrifice. Alternatively, some sacrifices are based on **avoidance motives**: a partner sacrifices to *avoid* a negative consequence. When sacrificing for avoidance motives, people focus on the potential guilt, conflict, or even relationship dissolution that they can sidestep by making a sacrifice (Impett & Gordon, 2010; Righetti & Impett, 2017).

Critically, the reason why someone sacrifices predicts the consequence of the sacrifice for both the person making the sacrifice and their partner (the receiver of the sacrifice). When

Table 8.3 Motives for sacrifice

	Approach motive	Avoidance motive
Self-focused	• To feel good about myself • To gain my partner's appreciation	• To avoid feeling guilty • To prevent my partner from getting angry at me
Partner-focused	• To make my partner happy • To enhance intimacy in my relationship	• To avoid conflict in my relationship • To prevent my partner from becoming upset

Consider these examples of approach-based and avoidance-based motives for sacrifice, separated by whether they are self-focused or partner-focused. Why do you make sacrifices in your relationship?

Source: Based on data from Impett & Gordon (2010).

people sacrifice to obtain a benefit (either a self-focused or partner-focused benefit), they experience more positive emotions, greater happiness, and more positive relationship perceptions. In contrast, when people sacrifice to avoid a negative consequence (self-focused or partner-focused), they report more negative emotions, less happiness, and fewer positive relationship perceptions (Impett, Peplau, & Gable, 2005; Impett et al., 2014; Righetti & Impett, 2017). The receiver of the sacrifice also experiences more positive emotions and an increase in relationship quality when their partner sacrifices for an approach-based reason, but the same benefits are not accrued when partners sacrifice for an avoidance-based reason (Impett et al., 2014; Righetti & Impett, 2017). In fact, a partner's avoidance-based sacrifice may lead to a decrease in relationship quality over time (Impett et al., 2014). Returning to our example, we can infer that both Jim and Pam would benefit if Jim sacrificed his job to receive Pam's appreciation or to enhance their relationship, whereas Jim's sacrifice would prove costly to both Jim and Pam if he sacrificed to avoid feeling selfish or to prevent future conflicts.

This dichotomy of approach-based and avoidance-based sacrifices is neat and tidy, but the research is less straightforward. People are often motivated to sacrifice for both approach-based and avoidance-based reasons simultaneously (I will give up my job opportunity to make you happy *and* to avoid fighting). As a result, reactions to sacrifice are not typically positive *or* negative. Instead, sacrifice generally leads to ambivalence – simultaneous positive and negative feelings – for both the person enacting the sacrifice and their partner (Righetti et al., 2020). The sacrificing partners can experience ambivalence because they are giving up something they desire, which can lead to unhappiness or feelings of resentment, even if they are simultaneously relieved to have resolved the disagreement. The ambivalence felt by partners receiving the sacrifice may arise from feeling guilty or feeling pressure to reciprocate the sacrifice in the future; this can taint their satisfaction at having "won" their desired outcome.

Recovery Following Conflict

In the aftermath of a partner's sacrifice, an unresolved conflict, or a difficult conflict discussion, the strain of a conflict can linger (Prager et al., 2015, 2019). Partners report poorer moods and lower relationship satisfaction on days that they experience conflict, and these negative experiences can carry over into the following day. People with insecure attachment orientations themselves or people whose partners have insecure attachment orientations are especially likely to have continued negative moods and relationship perceptions following conflicts

(Prager et al., 2015; Salvatore et al., 2011). How they behave when in this post-conflict space can sustain their distress or serve a repair function. Spending quality time together (e.g., a date night) or showing affection (e.g., saying "I love you" or kissing), for example, serve as recovery strategies that help restore the status quo. Withdrawal strategies (e.g., sulking, keeping distance) end up maintaining negative affect and preventing positive exchanges from returning (Parsons et al., 2020; Prager et al., 2019; Salvatore et al., 2011). If partners "drop" the conflict (i.e., agree to disagree), they create a "ceasefire" (protecting relationship satisfaction), but the unresolved conflict lingers (contributing to ongoing negative emotions; Parsons et al., 2020). Still, "dropping" the conflict is better than harping on the conflict. Couples effectively sabotage conflict recovery when they perseverate on the conflict or bring up new disagreements as a conflict is winding down. They report lower relationship satisfaction one year later than couples who do not extend conflicts in this way (Haydon et al., 2017).

What about apologizing and forgiving? These commonly used behaviors are appropriate and relationship-protective in response to destructive partner behaviors during conflict, such as a biting comment or a hurtful silence (Parsons et al., 2020). They can also help in response to transgressions, which we turn to next.

Recovery from Partner Transgressions

Unfortunately, we hurt the ones we love. The people we are most interdependent with are the same people we have the most opportunities to wrong. We say insensitive words; we fail to follow through on our promises; we mercy kill each other's cats. Okay, that last one is a bit unusual, though it did happen on *The Office* (Figure 8.14). This particular transgression occurred when feline-fanatic, Angela, asked her boyfriend, Dwight, to give medications to

(a)   (b)

Figure 8.14 Have you ever had a relationship end because of a transgression? *The Office* romance between Dwight (actor Rainn Wilson; panel a) and Angela (actor Angela Kinsey; panel b) ends abruptly after Dwight puts Angela's cat, Sparkles, out of her misery. (Photo: Allstar Picture Library Ltd / Alamy Stock Photo [a] and PictureLux / The Hollywood Archive / Alamy Stock Photo [b])

her sick cat, Sparkles. As Angela listed Sparkles' medical ailments, Dwight looked appalled ... and determined. In the next scene, Dwight returned to announce that Sparkles was dead. If you've seen *The Office*, you know that Dwight is a principled man – a man willing to skirt convention (i.e., not killing a partner's cat under any circumstances) to do what he feels is right (i.e., putting an aged cat out of its misery). When Angela confronts Dwight, he explains, "When a farmer sees an animal that is in pain, that has no quality of life, that has no utility, a farmer does what city-folk don't have the stomach to do" (Daniels et al., 2007). Sensible? Perhaps. Justified? Maybe. A relational transgression? Absolutely. Although Dwight did not intend to hurt Angela, Angela ends the relationship.

Fortunately, most relational transgressions do not involve euthanasia. A list of common transgressions is shown in Figure 8.15, with negative communication and teasing topping the list. Unlike Angela and Dwight's situation, most relational transgressions also do not result in relationship dissolution. When minor transgressions occur (e.g., behaving with hostility during a conflict discussion, briefly giving the cold shoulder, making an offensive joke),

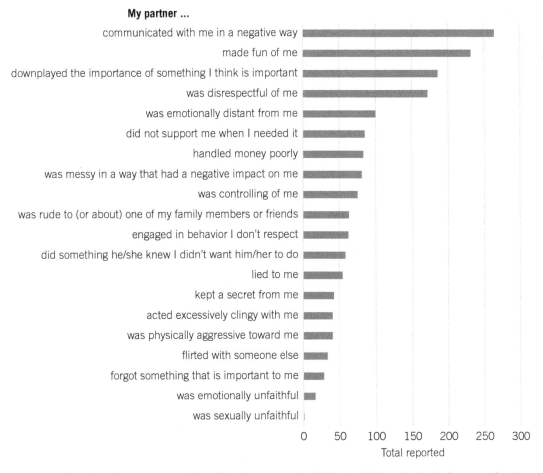

Figure 8.15 How do you hurt your partner(s), and how does your partner(s) hurt you? Shown here is the frequency of each of twenty partner transgressions assessed over a five-month period in 104 different-sex couples. On average, participants reported about nine transgressions each over the five-month period. (Source: Drawn based on data from Luchies et al. [2019])

partners often work to protect the relationship, despite their hurt feelings, by inhibiting their urge to retaliate and, instead, engaging in a more constructive behavior.

Responses to Partner Transgressions

When one person acts badly, their partner's initial, gut-level impulse is often to respond in kind (Kelley & Thibaut, 1978; Rusbult et al., 1991; Yovetich & Rusbult, 1994). If you snap at me, I'll snap at you, bucko. Such destructive responses to partner transgressions can be active (e.g., yelling at the partner) or passive (e.g., avoiding the partner, distancing from the partner) and tend to weaken a relationship. Happily, initial impulses to return fire with fire do not necessarily determine enacted behavior. In committed relationships, partners often transform their self-protective retaliatory motivation into a relationship-protective accommodation motivation. In other words, people in committed relationships choose to inhibit their initial destructive impulses and respond to partner transgressions in constructive ways (Yovetich & Rusbult, 1994). Like their destructive counterparts, constructive responses to relationship transgressions can be active (e.g., suggesting a solution, discussing the problem) or passive (hoping that the relationship will improve, praying for a solution).

Behaving constructively in response to a partner's transgression requires effort (i.e., cognitive resources), so people are most able to accommodate if they have greater self-control and if they are not under a time pressure (Finkel & Campbell, 2001; Yovetich & Rusbult, 1994). Indeed, people who accommodate tend to first consider destructive responses, think better of it, and engage in constructive responses instead (Yovetich & Rusbult, 1994). This process takes time and effort, at least for most people. People who are more agreeable and those who are lower in attachment avoidance accommodate without much effort, suggesting that accommodation may be their default response (Perunovic & Holmes, 2008).

Apologies and Forgiveness

One final response to a perceived wrong is forgiveness, often in response to an apology. An apology represents an attempt to repair the damage of one's transgression by admitting responsibility, conveying remorse, and communicating an intention not to transgress in the same way again (Lewis et al., 2015). Forgiveness, like accommodation, is a constructive response to a partner's transgression, but forgiveness is a more specific motivational and affective change that occurs in the mind of the "wronged" party. Forgiveness entails a shifting away from revenge-seeking or avoiding the transgressor and toward an abatement of the negative feelings (e.g., resentment, anger) that resulted from the transgression (Fincham, 2010). Forgiveness can be expressed, as in saying "I forgive you," but it is an intrapersonal process (occurring within an individual rather than between individuals). Forgiveness is an effective strategy to put transgressions in the past, and it accordingly leads to improved mood and relationship quality (e.g., Fehr et al., 2010; Fincham et al., 2006; Fincham & Beach, 2013). For example, forgiveness allows people to repair their closeness and commitment following a transgression (Tsang et al., 2006). Of course, it also is a motivated strategy aimed at preserving a relationship, so people are more likely to forgive when they are already more committed to their relationships (Donovan & Priester, 2017; Finkel et al., 2002).

DIVERSITY AND INCLUSION

Forgiveness and Religiosity

For many individuals, forgiveness calls to mind religion, and for good reason: in many of the world's religions, practitioners are encouraged to forgive those who have wronged them. The Qur'an states, "Those who spend (freely), whether in prosperity or in adversity, who restrain anger, and forgive (the offences of) people – for God loves those who do good" (Surah, 3:134). A similar instruction to forgive is conveyed in the Christian Bible. When Peter asked Jesus whether he needs to forgive as many as seven times, Jesus replied, "I do not say to you seven times, but seventy-seven times" (Matthew, 18:21–22). The Torah also provides a powerful example of forgiveness when Joseph forgives his brothers for selling him into slavery (if you have not read the Torah, perhaps you remember this story from the hit play *Joseph and the Amazing Technicolor Dreamcoat*).

Indeed, meta-analysis shows that greater religiosity is linked to greater forgiveness (Riek & Mania, 2012). To put the strength of this association in perspective, religiosity predicts forgiveness more strongly than self-esteem and conscientiousness, but less strongly than relational commitment or agreeableness. Further, the link between religiosity and forgiveness is stronger in hypothetical scenarios than in actual transgressions. Religious people may feel more motivated to forgive, but these motivations do not always translate into actual forgiveness. Interestingly, forgiveness may help explain the link between religiosity and personal well-being (Abu-Raiya & Ayten, 2020). Greater religious involvement appears to predict greater forgiveness, which then in turn predicts greater life satisfaction.

Do religious people forgive in order to be forgiven by God (i.e., divine forgiveness)? Generally, no. The link between perceiving God as merciful and engaging in interpersonal forgiveness appears to have other roots: people forgive because they perceive that *they themselves have been forgiven* (Fincham & May, 2021). Although religiosity predicts the likelihood of forgiveness, non-religious people also forgive. Across religious and non-religious people, meta-analysis shows that the strongest predictor of forgiveness is **empathy**, being able to feel what another person is feeling (Riek & Mania, 2012). Religious, agnostic, and atheist people tend to be inclined to forgive when they can empathize with the transgressor.

We tend to assume forgiveness is uniformly beneficial, but such is not the case. Forgiveness can have negative implications in certain circumstances. When transgressions are frequent or severe, for example, forgiveness is associated with an increase in problem severity and a decrease in relationship quality over time (McNulty, 2008a). Forgiveness may carry these costs because it serves as permission to reoffend, resulting in additional transgressions. Further, offenders who are low in agreeableness can interpret forgiveness as permission to continue behaving badly (McNulty & Russell, 2016). When highly agreeable people are forgiven, they tend not to transgress again; however, people lower in agreeableness are especially likely to re-offend. Finally, forgiving a partner who has not made amends makes people feel worse than forgiving someone who is genuinely sorry and is working to repair the harm (Luchies et al., 2010). Personal well-being is especially low after forgiving a partner who has not made amends for a severe transgression, in particular (Luchies et al., 2019). Forgiveness tends to be advantageous, but perhaps we should be thoughtful before we forgive seventy-seven times after all.

Conclusion

Jim and Pam's conflict of interest produced difficult conversations, hurt feelings, and, ultimately, sacrifice. Like most partners, they employed strategies to manage and resolve the disagreements that emerged from their underlying conflict. As we learned in this chapter, the existence of conflicts is not problematic, it is the way in which couples resolve conflicts that matters. Although specific conflict strategies tend to be more and less constructive, as you saw in this chapter, context shapes which strategy is more appropriate. People who navigate their conflicts successfully are able to mitigate threats to maintain their relationships, and we can imagine a hypothetical world in which Jim and Pam remain happily married. Conflict management, however, is not the only way in which people support relationship success. In the next chapter, we review how responsiveness and social support enable people to mitigate threats and to enhance their relationships in the absence of threat.

Major Take-Aways

- Conflict in interdependent relationships is inevitable, but tends to occur infrequently. The topics couples argue about change over time, but frequency of conflict does not decline.
- Hostility (negative valence, high intensity) is associated with poorer relationship quality concurrently. However, hostility predicts increases in relationship quality when problems are severe.
- Intimacy (positive valence, high intensity) and problem solving (positive valence, low intensity) are both associated with positive relationship outcomes.
- Withdrawal (negative valence, low intensity) can be costly, especially as part of a demand-withdraw cycle. However, demand-withdraw may be less harmful for couples with low SES.
- Resolving a conflict may require sacrifice, and sacrifice offers benefits for both partners if it is enacted to attain benefits (rather than to avoid costs).
- Partner transgressions – during conflicts or in other contexts – can produce a desire to retaliate. Interdependent couples often accommodate rather than retaliating. Forgiveness is an especially powerful response to a transgression, though it can have negative consequences if the transgressor continues to offend.

Further Readings

If you're interested in ...

... the link between marital conflict behavior and future divorce risk, read:

Birditt, K. S., Brown, E., Orbuch, T. L., & McIlvane, J. M. (2010). Marital conflict behaviors and implications for divorce over 16 years. *Journal of Marriage and Family*, *72*(5), 1188–1204.

... the consequences associated with stable versus variable negative-direct conflict behavior, read:

Overall, N. C. (2020). Behavioral variability reduces the harmful longitudinal effects of partners' negative-direct behavior on relationship problems. *Journal of Personality and Social Psychology*, *119*(5), 1057–1085.

... conflicts about finances, read:

Papp, L. M., Cummings, E. M., & Goeke-Morey, M. C. (2009). For richer, for poorer: Money as a topic of marital conflict in the home. *Family Relations*, *58*(1), 91–103.

... the positive and negative consequences associated with relational sacrifice, read:

Righetti, F., Schneider, I., Ferrier, D., Spiridonova, T., Xiang, R., & Impett, E. A. (2020). The bittersweet taste of sacrifice: Consequences for ambivalence and mixed reactions. *Journal of Experimental Psychology: General*, *149*(10), 1950–1968.

... meta-coding of specific conflict behaviors, read:

Woodin, E. M. (2011). A two-dimensional approach to relationship conflict: Meta-analytic findings. *Journal of Family Psychology*, *25*(3), 325–335.

MANAGING STRESS AND SUPPORTING GROWTH

A Social Support Double Play

Between 2001 and 2019, CC Sabathia made a mark on American Major League Baseball as a phenomenal left-handed pitcher. His legacy, however, extends beyond the field. As fans will know, Sabathia experienced a public struggle with alcoholism that nearly cost him his ability to play baseball competitively. In 2015, he made the difficult decision to enter rehab during a playoff run, worked toward recovery, and subsequently re-emerged as a stronger baseball player and person. His inspiring story of resilience speaks to his character, yet CC credits his wife, Amber (they married in 2003), with helping him to overcome and rebound from his addiction (Figure 9.1). As he wrote in the *Player's Tribune* in 2016, "I've been blessed to get support from those around me. There aren't any words to describe how amazing my wife, Amber, has been throughout this process" (Sabathia, 2016).

Amber, too, has benefited from her close and supportive relationship with CC. In 2021, she decided to pursue a career as a baseball agent, a goal CC encouraged and helped to bring to fruition with his support. Amber recalls how CC would encourage her saying, 'You know, you would make a great agent ... seriously, you've been my agent the past seven years" (Wagner, 2021). When Amber announced that she accepted a job as a sports agent, CC tweeted, "If you need me, I'll be in full-time dad mode," presumably taking on more parenting responsibility to free Amber's time to focus on career goals.

Amber's and CC's support for each other helps them to thrive as individuals and helps them sustain what appears to be a thriving relationship. Their experiences illustrate a key idea in relationship science: whether managing adversity or striving for personal growth, people desire and benefit from support. As you will see, receiving support in these two contexts contributes to satisfying and sustainable relationships.

Figure 9.1 CC Sabathia, and his wife, Amber Sabathia, lean on each other on and off the field to thrive as individuals and as a couple. How does support from close others enable thriving? (Photo: fizkes / iStock / Getty Images Plus)

In this chapter, you will learn about the importance of social support for relationship maintenance and individual functioning. Specifically, we will explore the consequences of social support for relational and personal well-being (1) in adverse or stressful contexts and (2) in the absence of stress or threats. First, we will review common stressors (e.g., life events, contextual factors) and their accompanying personal and relational costs. We will then consider the consequences of both perceived and actual support during stress. We will next highlight the role of supportive relationships to facilitate personal goal pursuit and desired self-change in non-adverse contexts. Finally, we will explore social support from the perspective of the support-provider and consider how caregiving can be both rewarding and costly. Your goal in reading this chapter is to explore the bidirectional nature of individual and relationship functioning: relationships enable individuals' resilience and growth, and people are more satisfied and committed to relationships that foster thriving in these ways.

 GUIDING QUESTIONS

Consider these questions as you read this chapter:
- How do environmental stressors influence individual and relationship functioning?
- How does social support protect and enhance individual well-being and relationship quality?
- What are the potential costs of receiving support during adversity?
- Why do supportive relationships enable personal growth, and what behaviors can partners enact to facilitate growth?
- What are the consequences of support provision for support-providers themselves?

Social Support and Responsiveness

Why do people want to maintain their relationships, given the work involved to mitigate threats and manage conflicts? Perhaps people recognize their need for social support. From an attachment theory perspective, adult romantic relationships serve two important functions: helping people to navigate threats (i.e., safe haven function) and helping people to approach personal endeavors with confidence (i.e., secure base function). When a romantic partner serves as an effective safe haven in adverse contexts and an effective secure base in non-adverse contexts, they are not only promoting individual outcomes; they are also contributing to the maintenance of the relationship (e.g., Jakubiak & Tomlinson, 2020; Randall & Messerschmitt-Coen, 2019). Partners' repertoires of supportive behaviors can include encouraging, reassuring, assisting, advising, or communicating esteem (e.g., Feeney & Collins, 2018; Lakey, 2013; Taylor, 2012). These common support behaviors can be classified into a few broad (though non-exhaustive) support types, as shown in Table 9.1.

Table 9.1 Broad support classifications

Support type	Definition	Examples
Emotional support (also called esteem support)	Expressions of caring, solidarity, encouragement, valuing, and/or a belief in the other's competence and ability	• "We can get through this together." • "I know you'll figure it out; you've solved problems like this before." • "That race sounds like a fun challenge. You should try it."
Instrumental support (also called practical or tangible support)	Provision of tangible assistance and/or specific resources	• "Your toilet was running so I replaced the fill valve. It's as good as new." • "I will take care of the housework this week so you can focus on studying." • "Here's $500 to help you out. Pay me back whenever you can."
Informational support	Advice and factual information that helps to define and/or understand the situation	• "I read about a loan forgiveness program. I'll send you the website." • "If you're serious about medical school, I think you should pay for MCAT classes." • "It seems like the best way to solve this is to tell her how you feel directly."

Source: Based on Cohen & Wills (1985); Cutrona et al. (2005); Taylor (2012).

Although support behaviors are typically intended to be helpful, any of these behaviors can be perfect strikes or wild pitches (totally off the mark) depending on the situation. Imagine that Layla tells her boyfriend Eric that she underperformed on an important exam, hoping for some reassurance, and Eric says something like, "You should try studying more next time. I have blank flashcards if you want them." Or perhaps Eric calls Layla because his car won't start, hoping she'll offer to bring jumper cables and assist, but she says, "That's horrible. You must be so stressed. I love you. Hope you get home soon. [click]" In both examples, support was provided, but the support-providers missed the mark on what was needed (or perhaps you could argue that the support-recipients failed to communicate what was needed). The support recipients did not leave the support exchanges feeling *understood* (that their needs, desires, or goals were accurately recognized), *validated* (that their point of view was valued and respected), or *cared for* (that the support-provider was warm and affectionate) and likely did not benefit from the support.

Perhaps these italicized words sound familiar; feeling understood, validated, and cared for are the three components of perceived partner responsiveness, one of the most important constructs in the science of close relationships (Finkel et al., 2017; Reis et al., 2004; Reis, 2012). We originally learned about perceived partner responsiveness in Chapter 5 because perceiving that a partner is responsive to one's self-disclosure allows intimacy to develop. In this chapter, we will see that perceiving partner responsiveness during support transactions

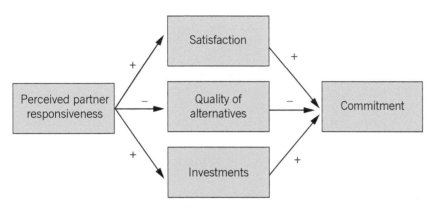

Figure 9.2 How important is perceived partner responsiveness? On weeks when a person perceives greater partner responsiveness, they tend to be more satisfied with their relationship, perceive poorer alternatives to the relationship, and perceive their investments to be higher, each of which contribute to greater commitment. (Source: Adapted from Segal & Fraley [2016], reprinted with permission from Sage Publications)

is also critical for relationships to persist and flourish (Crasta et al., 2021; Dooley et al., 2018; Gadassi et al., 2016; Jolink et al., 2021; Maisel & Gable, 2009; Segal & Fraley, 2016; Selcuk & Ong, 2013). When people receive support and feel understood, valued, and cared for, they can develop the general perception that their partners are responsive, certainly a boon for relationship maintenance. Indeed, as shown in Figure 9.2, perceived partner responsiveness predicts each component of the investment model of commitment and is therefore considered a contributing factor to relationship commitment and stability (Segal & Fraley, 2016).

As we move into the next sections of this chapter, we will investigate the contexts in which support is needed, the personal and relational consequences of support exchanges, and the many nuances inherent in providing (and receiving) responsive support that communicates understanding, validation, and caring.

Managing Stress and Adversity

Overcoming adversity – difficulties, setbacks, threats – is a theme in sports and beyond. Comeback stories capture our collective attention as we root for our heroes-turned-underdogs to return to greatness. For instance, the world watched (and talked and tweeted) as Simone Biles, a seasoned American gymnast, experienced very public adversity during the 2020 Olympic Games in Tokyo, Japan, and recovered just as publicly. While attempting to perform, she was overcome with an ailment referred to as "the twisties," a disorienting phenomenon in which a gymnast "literally cannot tell up from down," according to Biles (Austin, 2021). Fearing for her safety and unwilling to risk her teammates' chance to earn a medal, Biles withdrew mid-competition. After several days off, she returned to compete in the individual balance beam competition and won bronze (see Figure 9.3). Biles's resilient comeback illustrates how people can keep their stress in check during adversity and perhaps even become stronger through life's challenges.

Figure 9.3 Simone Biles's withdrawal from competition and subsequent comeback to win a bronze medal was the top story of the 2020 Olympic Games. What role might close others have played in her ability to manage the adversity she experienced and make a successful comeback just days later? (Photo: Jamie Squire / Getty Images Sport)

Although most of us have not experienced the "twisties," everyone faces adverse life experiences that are disruptive to daily functioning (i.e., require adaptation to a new situation) or are emotionally arousing. These experiences are referred to as **objective stressors** (Cohen et al., 1997; Cohen & Wills, 1985; Wethington, 2016). Recall that objective means *not* influenced by personal judgments, so these situations are presumed to be impactful for everyone. Objective stressors can be negative (e.g., being fired from work, legal trouble) or positive (e.g., marriage, moving to a new home) because both positive and negative experiences can be disruptive (Monroe & Slavich, 2020). Stressors can also be acute events that last a relatively short time (e.g., a breakup, a vacation, traffic, slow internet) or chronic, lasting a month or more (e.g., ongoing medical problems, retirement from work, experiences of discrimination; Muscatell et al., 2009).

Researchers quantify a person's **stress exposure**, the extent of objective stressors a person has experienced, by assessing the disruptive and demanding life events a person has faced and by assessing the extent to which a person has experienced **daily hassles**, smaller – though perhaps no less impactful – everyday difficulties (e.g., Epel et al., 2018; Wethington, 2016; Wright et al., 2020). Read through the list of disruptive life events (i.e., stressors) in Table 9.2, and circle any that you experienced during the previous year. This inventory estimates the relative impact of each life event, with 100 representing the greatest estimated impact. Note the impact of the events you circled as well as the relative impact of these stressors (i.e., the death of a spouse is presumed to be more objectively stressful than being fired). In addition, try to identify other disruptive or demanding life events you experienced in the last year that were not included in the checklist, and estimate their relative impact at the bottom of the scale.

The life events checklist assesses disruptive life events in one's physical and social environment (i.e., objective stressors), but does it actually assess the experience of **psychological stress** as we typically think of it? When we say a person is "stressed," we do not simply mean that they are in a disruptive or demanding situation; we mean that they are overwhelmed, anxious, and agitated. Unlike stressors, psychological stress has a subjective component. Stress is a consequence of both the objective stressors a person faces and a person's unique feelings and beliefs about those stressors.

Consider Jenelle and Javier, two students who transferred to a new college this semester. That objective stressor (i.e., the disruption of adjusting to a new school and perhaps also changing residences) could be perceived as stressful by one student and not the other. Perhaps Jenelle feels prepared for the new coursework and has a group of friends already on campus, whereas Javier is worried about the workload and is concerned about fitting in socially. You guessed it: in this example, Javier is more likely than Jenelle to *feel* stressed by

Table 9.2 Life events checklist

	Event	Impact (life change units)
1	Death of a spouse	100
2	Divorce	73
3	Marital separation	65
4	Detention in jail or other institution	63
5	Death of a close family member	63
6	Major personal injury or illness	53
7	Marriage	50
8	Being fired at work	47
9	Marital reconciliation	45
10	Retirement from work	45
11	Major change in the health or behavior of a family member	44
12	Pregnancy	40
13	Sexual difficulties	39
14	Gaining a new family member (i.e., birth, adoption, older adult moving in, etc.)	39
15	Major business readjustment	39
16	Major change in financial state (i.e., a lot worse or better off than usual)	38
17	Death of a close friend	37
18	Changing to a different line of work	36
19	Major change in the number of arguments with spouse	35
20	Taking on a mortgage	31
21	Foreclosure on a mortgage or loan	30
22	Major change in responsibilities at work (i.e., promotion, demotion)	29
23	Son or daughter leaving home	29
24	In-law troubles	29
25	Outstanding personal achievement	28

Table 9.2 (*cont.*)

	Event	Impact (life change units)
26	Spouse beginning or ceasing work outside the home	26
27	Beginning or ceasing formal schooling	26
28	Major change in living condition (i.e., new home, remodeling, deterioration)	25
29	Revision of personal habits (i.e., dress, associations, quit smoking)	24
30	Troubles with the boss	23
31	Major changes in working hours or conditions	20
32	Changes in residence	20
33	Changing to a new school	20
34	Major change in usual type and/or amount of recreation	19
35	Major change in religious activity	19
36	Major change in social activities	18
37	Taking on a loan (i.e., car)	17
38	Major change in sleeping habits	16
39	Major change in number of family get-togethers	15
40	Major change in eating habits	15
41	Vacation	13
42	Major holidays	12
43	Minor violations of the law (i.e., traffic tickets)	11
—	_____	_____
—	_____	_____
—	_____	_____

Circle any event you have experienced over the past year, and sum their impact to obtain your score. Add other stressful life events that you experienced but were not included in the checklist at the bottom of the scale, and estimate their relative impact. Higher scores indicate a greater likelihood of experiencing a stress-induced health problem.

Source: Copyright © 1967, Elsevier, reprinted with permission; Holmes, T. H., & Rahe, R. H. (1967). The social readjustment rating scale. *Journal of Psychosomatic Research*, *11*(2), 213–218.

the change. Javier's and Jenelle's distinct transfer experiences can be explained by how they each appraise the objective stressor, as described in the Transactional Stress Model (Lazarus & Folkman, 1984).

According to this model, people first make a primary appraisal; they assess the demand a stressor imposes and the extent of harm or disruption a stressor can cause (Folkman et al., 1986; Lazarus & Folkman, 1984). Critically, people also make a secondary appraisal in which they evaluate the extent to which they have the ability and resources to cope with the stressor (Folkman et al., 1986; Lazarus & Folkman, 1984). People experience psychological stress when they perceive that the *demands of a stressor exceed their ability and resources to cope with it*. Returning to Javier and Jenelle, Javier may be more stressed by transferring than Jenelle because he either perceives the transfer process to be more arduous (primary appraisal) or because he perceives that he has less ability and fewer resources to adjust (secondary appraisal).

Table 9.3 Perceived Stress Scale

In the last month, how often have you:	Never	Almost never	Sometimes	Fairly often	Very often
. . . been upset because of something that happened unexpectedly?	0	1	2	3	4
. . . felt that you were unable to control the important things in life?	0	1	2	3	4
. . . felt nervous and stressed?	0	1	2	3	4
. . . felt confident about your ability to handle your personal problems?	4	3	2	1	0
. . . felt that things were going your way?	4	3	2	1	0
. . . found that you could not cope with all the things that you had to do?	0	1	2	3	4
. . . been able to control irritations in your life?	4	3	2	1	0
. . . felt that you were on top of things?	4	3	2	1	0
. . . been angered because of things that happened that were outside of your control?	0	1	2	3	4
. . . felt difficulties were piling up so high that you could not overcome them?	0	1	2	3	4

Circle one number to indicate your agreement with each of the statements above. Then, sum your responses to determine your overall psychological stress. Higher scores indicate greater stress.

Source: Cohen et al. (1983), reprinted with permission from Sage Publications.

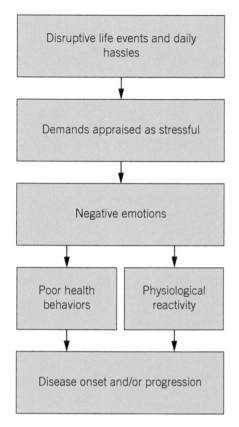

Figure 9.4 A simplified model of the pathways linking objective environmental stressors to disease onset and progression. At what stages might this process be halted or attenuated, and how? (Source: Adapted from Cohen et al. [2016], reprinted with permission from Sage Publications)

Given its subjective components, psychological stress can be assessed more precisely using measures that require participants to reflect on how they perceive the disruptions and demands in their environment rather than using measures that focus on stress exposure. Try completing the Perceived Stress Scale, shown in Table 9.3, and notice the difference between what it measures and what is measured by the life events scale (Table 9.2).

Consequences of Stress for Individuals

In order to appreciate the vital role of social support in shaping individuals' experiences with adversity, let's first briefly review the deleterious impact of stress on well-being. As you may know, repeated or chronic exposure to stressors is a major risk factor for poor psychological and physical health. People who experience greater stress exposure are at risk for developing or worsening of major depressive disorder, cardiovascular disease, infectious disease, cancer, asthma, autoimmune diseases, and HIV/AIDS, to name a few (Cohen et al., 2007, 2019; Miller et al., 2009). Critically, not all people who are exposed to stressful, or even traumatic, life events get sick (Cohen et al., 2019). Resilience in the face of objective stressors suggests that the mechanisms linking objective stress and health may be complicated, and importantly, modifiable.

Only when objective "stressors" are perceived as stressful do they undermine health and well-being (e.g., Carver, 2007; Cohen et al., 2007, 2016; Turner et al., 2020). Figure 9.4 depicts a simplified model of the pathways linking stress and poor health, and it starts with this appraisal. If, indeed, a stressor is appraised as stressful (perceived to overwhelm available resources), a person will experience negative emotions, such as anxiety and fear. These negative emotions can then (1) fuel poor health behaviors (e.g., smoking, substance abuse, neglecting physical activity) and (2) activate a physiological **stress response**, each of which directly increases one's risk for disease onset or progression (Cohen et al., 2016).

Have you heard of the stress response before? The stress response is a coordinated physiological reaction by which a body automatically readies itself for action (Cohen et al., 2016; Thiel & Dretsch, 2011). This response is orchestrated by two systems: the **Sympathetic-Adreno-Medullar (SAM) system** and the **Hypothalamus-Pituitary-Adrenal (HPA) axis** (Fink, 2017; Godoy et al., 2018; Thiel & Dretsch, 2011). When a threat is detected, the SAM system fires up first and produces the body's fast-acting stress response, whereas the HPA axis produces a somewhat slower and longer-lasting stress response. Both systems mobilize energy quickly to enable the body to either fight or flee (hence the fact that the stress response is often called the fight-or-flight response).

The primary output of the SAM system is adrenaline, and adrenaline (1) increases heart rate (to push blood to the muscles and enable fighting or fleeing), (2) increases respiration rate (to provide more oxygen to fuel exertion), (3) prompts the body to release glucose (to have energy ready to keep on fighting or running), (4) constricts blood vessels (so any wounds bleed less severely), and (5) dilates the pupils (to enhance the ability to detect danger). The slower-acting HPA axis's activation results in the release of cortisol, a hormone that sustains energy by facilitating the release of stored glucose. As you can see, the SAM system and the HPA axis are survival-oriented systems that evolved in response to specific survival-relevant threats (e.g., a hungry saber-tooth tiger, a hostile stranger wielding a spear).

Today, this same cascade of physiological reactions is activated in response to a "Please see me" email from your boss or a case of the late-night "What ifs" (e.g., What if I forgot to turn off the oven? What if there is a natural disaster?), situations that do not require immediate fighting or fleeing. Humans are uniquely able to imagine future scenarios, so they are uniquely able to anticipate disaster and experience stress in the absence of any current threat. Other common acute stressors in the modern age include public speaking, important exams, and interpersonal interactions that might elicit rejection (e.g., dating, job interviews). None of these situations is well-matched with a system designed to fight or to flee.

Unfortunately, though the stress response effectively equips us to survive occasional life-or-death threats, chronic stress activation can produce significant wear-and-tear on the body. For instance, a chronically high level of cortisol suppresses the immune system (e.g., Godoy et al., 2018), putting health at risk. Exaggerated responses to stress are also meta-analytically linked to poorer health and well-being over time; people who have more extreme stress reactions are more likely to experience cardiovascular disease and mortality than people with more regulated stress reactions (Turner et al., 2020). People are not all equally likely to experience stressors or to have the resources to adequately cope with stressors, so disparities in stress across racial and ethnic groups help to explain health disparities between groups as well (American Psychological Association, 2017). Further, although stress mobilizes energy, the energy can be counterproductive depending on the nature of the stressor. Adrenaline will help you to fight or run from an attacker, but it may not help you study. A moderate amount of stress may enhance attention and motivation, but an extreme stress response typically undermines performance by inducing panic, tunnel vision, and an inability to think logically.

Consequences of Stress for Close Relationships

Stress is not only problematic for individuals; it also impacts their close relationships. Recall the social ecological models of relationships (described in Chapter 2) and, in particular, the vulnerability-stress-adaptation (VSA) model. The VSA highlights the role of stressors outside of the relationship to shape relationship dynamics and outcomes. Empirical evidence supports the idea that external stressors affect people's relationships (e.g., Falconier et al., 2015; Hilpert et al., 2018; McNulty et al., 2021; Neff & Karney, 2004; Randall & Bodenmann, 2009). Couples who experience major life events and minor daily hassles report poorer relationship quality and greater decreases in relationship quality over time than couples who experience less stress. Let's consider how both individual stressors and a shared stressful context can adversely affect relationship well-being.

Individual Stressors

Some stressors – such as work-related demands, health problems, and interpersonal conflicts with someone other than a partner – primarily affect one individual in a relationship.

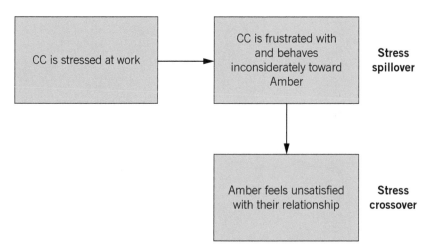

Figure 9.5 Can you distinguish stress spillover and stress crossover using this hypothetical illustration? Imagine how CC's work stress could impact both his own and his partner's (Amber's) relationship experiences. (Source: Drawn based on data from Karney & Neff [2013])

However, even when a stressor seemingly "belongs to" one partner, both partners and the relationship are impacted. In other words, when it comes to individual stress in interdependent relationships, research suggests that what's mine is yours. As shown in Figure 9.5, one partner's external stress can **spillover** into the relationship (Randall & Bodenmann, 2009) because experiencing stress in one domain (e.g., work) can lead a person to think or behave more negatively in another domain (e.g., in their romantic relationship). For example, if CC Sabathia is like the rest of us, he may perceive more severe problems in his relationship and behave more destructively when he is under a lot of stress (playoffs, perhaps). Further, in their interdependent relationship, we would expect CC's behaviors (and to some extent his thoughts) to influence Amber's behaviors and thoughts. Accordingly, one partner's external stress can **crossover** to influence their partner's relationship perceptions (e.g., Cooper et al., 2020; Larson & Almeida, 1999; Neff & Karney, 2007). Figure 9.5 shows how this works using a hypothetical scenario. When CC is stressed, Amber may feel unsatisfied with their relationship because CC's stress spillover means that Amber is experiencing an unpleasant and uncooperative partner.

Consistent with stress spillover, individuals who are under greater-than-normal stress evaluate their relationships more negatively, behave more destructively, and make more negative attributions for their partners' behaviors (e.g., Neff & Karney, 2004; Repetti, 1989). Consistent with stress crossover, men in different-sex relationships tend to report lower relationship quality when their wives experience greater personal stress (Neff & Karney, 2007). Women are also impacted by their spouse's personal stress, but only if they are also under simultaneous stress. Stress crossover is most pronounced in couples with a more negative communication style, supporting the perspective that negative communication is part of the process through which one person's stress impacts another person's relationship quality (Neff & Karney, 2007). This same pattern of results has been replicated and extended beyond different-sex couples (e.g., Cooper et al., 2020; Falconier et al., 2015; Totenhagen et al., 2017). For instance, men and women in same-sex relationships also report lower

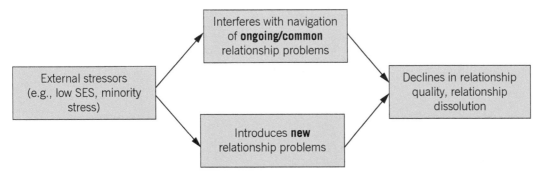

Figure 9.6 Can you see the varied ways external stressors influence your relationships? This model shows how external stressors can make it harder to navigate common relationship problems (e.g., conflict) and can introduce new problems (e.g., less time for intimacy and leisure). (Source: Drawn based on data from Neff & Karney [2017])

relationship quality on days when they (spillover) or their partners (crossover) experience greater-than-normal personal stress (Cooper et al., 2020; Totenhagen et al., 2017).

According to the VSA model, external stress influences relationship outcomes primarily through partners' behavior (i.e., adaptive processes; Karney & Bradbury, 1995). Theorists have recently elaborated this idea, positing that stressors contribute to declines in relationship quality through two behavior-based pathways, depicted in Figure 9.6. Specifically, external stressors (1) worsen interpersonal behavior in typical, ongoing relationship situations (e.g., daily life, ongoing conflicts) and (2) add new challenges to navigate (e.g., new conflicts), with new opportunities to behave destructively or neglect constructive behaviors (Neff & Karney, 2017).

As the first pathway suggests, external stressors reduce people's ability to manage typical relationship challenges, which can then reduce relationship quality. Common relationship challenges like managing conflict, problem solving, and forgiveness all require focus, effort, and self-control to respond constructively (rather than destructively), and wouldn't you know it, these resources are depleted by stress (e.g., Burnette et al., 2014; Finkel & Campbell, 2001). Consistent with this idea, people report greater self-regulatory depletion (e.g., feeling tired, relying heavily on willpower) on days when they are stressed, and that depletion leads them to behave more destructively (e.g., greater criticism and impatience) and less constructively (e.g., less affection and comforting) on the same day (Buck & Neff, 2012). In the context of high stress, these behaviors also take on particular weight; people under high levels of stress are particularly likely to adjust their overall relationship evaluations in response to their partner's negative behaviors (Nguyen et al., 2020). Also consistent with this first pathway, people who are under a great deal of personal stress experience normal relationship situations (e.g., differences in attitudes, partner habits) as particularly upsetting, which undermines their relationship satisfaction (Falconier et al., 2015). In other words, the context of stress depletes partners' ability to manage normal relationship problems with equanimity.

Evidence also supports the latter pathway, that individual stress adds new problems to a relationship. For instance, individuals who experience greater-than-usual work stress during the day are more distant and withdrawn from their partners in the evening; this disconnection constitutes a new relationship problem that must be managed (Repetti et al., 2009).

Figure 9.7 Stressful contexts, such as financial difficulties, simultaneously undermine effective problem-solving strategies and introduce new problems that need to be resolved. What stressful contexts do you experience in your relationships? (Photo: Gregory Byerline / Design Pics / Getty Images)

Further, people who are under personal stress can experience disruptions to their typical sexual functioning and, accordingly, lower sexual satisfaction, another new problem to manage (Bodenmann, Ledermann et al., 2007). External stress can also interfere with positive processes to the extent that one or more partners is compelled to use their time to resolve a stressor rather than to invest in the relationship (Neff & Karney, 2017).

Shared Stressful Contexts

Given the interdependence inherent in close relationships, many stressors impact partners simultaneously. Partners may move in together, become parents together (or face fertility challenges together), navigate tough relationships with shared friends or family together, and manage the daily hassles of maintaining a shared home together. *Your leaky faucet is my leaky faucet, as long as we both shall live.* In fact, many of the relationship transitions discussed in previous chapters (i.e., moving in together, getting married) are stressors that impact partners simultaneously (see Figure 9.7).

All partners will experience some shared stressors that have the potential to disrupt the relationship's steady functioning; but some partners unfortunately face continual stressors, putting their relationships at greater risk. Consider this finding: college-educated women are up to 40 percent less likely to divorce than women without a college degree, and this disparity is increasing over time (Copen et al., 2012; Karney, 2021; Lundberg et al., 2016). Or how about this fact: the likelihood of divorce is higher among people with greater financial problems than those with more financial security (e.g., Barton & Bryant, 2016; Gudmunson et al., 2007). Hmm, education and financial resources – that might sound familiar. These two characteristics make up the ever-impactful variable of socioeconomic status (SES), and SES is perhaps unsurprisingly linked to poorer relationship quality all around the world (Karney, 2021).

Having low socioeconomic status is thought to be a risk factor for relationship problems because low SES puts people at risk of experiencing a bevy of unique stressors and hassles (e.g., Karney, 2021; Trail & Karney, 2012). Relative to people with higher SES, people with lower SES are (1) more likely to live in neighborhoods impacted by violence and other crime, (2) less likely to have access to healthcare because their jobs are less likely to provide health benefits, (3) more likely to work jobs with non-standard hours and inflexible schedules, and (4) more likely to have debt or inadequate finances to meet their needs. Perhaps as a consequence of one or all of these differences, individuals with low SES are also at greater risk of experiencing health problems (e.g., cancer, cardiovascular disease) and are more likely to experience other objective stressors (like those we assessed in Table 9.2) than people with high SES (Karney, 2021).

As you recall from discussing individual stress, external stressors harm relationships in part because they deplete partners of the energy they need to successfully navigate the relationship challenges that are common to all relationships. Even some of the relatively automatic perceptual biases that benefit relationships (discussed in Chapter 7) require self-control, suggesting that chronic stressors associated with low SES could shape the extent to which people are able to protect their relationships with motivated cognition (Brady et al., 2020; Pronk et al., 2011; Ritter et al., 2010). Our rose-colored glasses may be a bit less rosy in high-stress contexts.

Couples who are financially strained behave less constructively during conflict and problem-solving discussions than financially secure couples, consistent with the perspective that stressors make it harder to navigate common relationship challenges (Barton et al., 2015, 2018; Conger et al., 1990; Cutrona et al., 2003; Masarik et al., 2016; Williamson et al., 2013). For example, couples under financial strain have been shown to behave less warmly and affectionately toward each other and to engage in more hostile behaviors instead. In fact, financial strain is a *primary* factor that interferes with effective communication; having trouble paying the bills and experiencing stressful life events (e.g., losing one's job, having a close friend or family member deported) are even more strongly associated with negative communication (e.g., hostility) than other important variables like relationship satisfaction (Williamson et al., 2013). When people are facing chronic stressors associated with low SES, their requisite resources that enable cooperation are depleted.

Stressful contexts, like individual stressors, also harm relationships because they introduce additional problems, over and above the challenges all couples face. Partners with low SES, for example, not only have more trouble managing conflicts than people with high SES, but they also have more conflicts to manage. In particular, couples living in low-income communities commonly report money management as a salient and severe marital problem (Dew & Stewart, 2012; Karney, 2021). When money is scarce, deciding how to spend it is especially challenging because it may require sacrificing important needs (e.g., transportation) for other important needs (e.g., housing). Partners with low SES also have less opportunity for shared leisure time than couples with high SES because they are more likely to have non-standard work hours (e.g., weekends, nights) and non-overlapping time off (Craig & Brown, 2014). With less time for leisure, low SES couples miss out on all the positive relationship processes that couples can engage in to enhance their relationships, such as affection and play (see Chapter 10 for more on these positive processes).

Another external stressor that – like low SES – can contribute to poorer relationship functioning is minority stress, the stress that results specifically from the stigma, prejudice, and discrimination that people face *because of* their identification with a minority group (Frost et al., 2017; LeBlanc et al., 2015; Rostosky & Riggle, 2017). Several types of relationships are commonly stigmatized (de-valued and perceived negatively by others), such as same-sex relationships, interracial relationships, consensually non-monogamous (CNM) relationships, and relationships characterized by a large age-gap (Conley et al., 2013; Lehmiller & Agnew, 2006). People in stigmatized relationships can experience stress as a result of governmental policies that fail to recognize their partnerships and create financial and legal hassles (e.g., lack of access to hospital visitation, challenges to parental rights). Additionally, people in stigmatized relationships can experience stress due to everyday situations in which people purposefully or inadvertently fail to recognize that they are partners or actively discriminate against them because of their relationship (Rostosky & Riggle, 2017). Indeed, over 75 percent of same-sex female couples and nearly two-thirds of same-sex male couples report experiencing rejection, devaluation, and discrimination based on their relationship (Frost et al., 2017). The experience of prejudice and discrimination because of one's relationship is associated with psychological and physical health problems (Hatzenbuehler et al., 2009; Lick et al., 2013). Accordingly, policies that protect people from discrimination protect well-being. For example, the prevalence of psychiatric disorders is lower among lesbian, gay, and bisexual individuals who live in states with policies protecting them from discrimination based on their sexual orientation than in states without these protections (Hatzenbuehler et al., 2013).

Research on stigmatized groups has accelerated in recent years, allowing us to see the consequences of stigmatization not only on individuals, but on relationship functioning as well. Emerging evidence is consistent with the idea that stigma is an external stressor that interferes with relationship functioning. Meta-analysis demonstrates that people who experience greater social stigma report poorer relationship functioning (e.g., lower relationship satisfaction and lower commitment; Doyle & Molix, 2015). Importantly, stigmatization does not originate only outside the relationship. People who are in stigmatized relationships can internalize societal attitudes and experience negative consequences related to their own internalized stigma. Internalized stigma is more strongly associated with poor relationship functioning than perceived external stigma, and people with greater internalized stigma report greater decreases in relationship satisfaction over time (Mohr & Daly, 2008). Internalizing stigma in a way that produces personal discomfort with CNM, for instance, predicts lower relationship satisfaction and commitment among individuals in CNM relationships (Moors et al., 2021). Another meta-analysis focused specifically on minority stress in same-sex couples similarly showed that minority stress (and particularly internalized homophobia) predicts poorer relationship functioning (Cao et al., 2017).

Like stress resulting from low SES, minority stress also likely influences relationship quality by reducing the energy couples have to manage typical relationship challenges and by adding new relationship challenges. Stigmatized couples who are chronically worried about being rejected or misperceived may have fewer cognitive resources to manage conflicts constructively and to problem-solve effectively. Further, stigmatized couples face additional challenges that can undermine their relationships (e.g., decisions about when or whether to self-disclose), and they may have fewer opportunities for relationship-enhancing behaviors, such as physical intimacy. Indeed, same-sex couples who report greater minority stress limit their displays of affection in public, reducing their opportunities for intimacy (Balzarini et al., 2018; Hocker et al., 2021).

Although research consistently emphasizes stress's potential to threaten relationship functioning, and rightly so, some stress early in relationships may be surprisingly healthy for relationships (Neff & Broady, 2011). A moderate amount of stress, early in a relationship, may provide partners with an opportunity to practice their coping skills prior to a major stressor, just like a vaccine, with its small dose of a pathogen, allows the body to practice mounting an immune response prior to a full-blown infection. Empirical findings support this **stress inoculating hypothesis**, but only for partners who had initial strengths (i.e., they discussed conflicts constructively, they sought support effectively). For these couples, stress early in the relationship predicted less stress spillover later in the relationship and predicted more stable relationship quality during the stressful transition to parenthood, each of which demonstrate resilience to external stress (Neff & Broady, 2011). As this research highlights, stress is not uniformly problematic for relationships or for individual functioning. Indeed, one critical determinant of stress's consequence is the social support people perceive and receive when they face stressors.

The Role of Social Support During Adversity

Before we delve into the research on how the damaging effects of stress can be mitigated by social support, we should clarify that social support commonly (and confusingly) has three distinct definitions (e.g., Cohen, 2004; Lakey, 2013; Uchino, 2009a, 2009b). First, social support may mean enacted/received support, the supportive actions (i.e., emotional, instrumental, and informational support types) that were introduced earlier in the chapter. However, social support may also mean social integration or it might mean perceived support availability, two additional and distinct social support subconstructs. The definitions for all three meanings of social support are provided in Table 9.4, along with concrete measurement items demonstrating how each is assessed.

Social Integration and Perceived Support

The power of social support is anchored to the idea that humans are fundamentally social, driven to form and maintain lasting bonds (Baumeister & Leary, 1995). According to social

Table 9.4 Subconstructs under the umbrella of social support

Social support subconstructs	Definition	Example measurement items
Social integration	Participation in a broad range of social relationships (i.e., having numerous and diverse social roles)	• How many close friends do you have? • How many colleagues do you talk to at least once every two weeks?[1]
Perceived support (or perceived support availability)	Subjective belief that others (e.g., family, friends) would provide appropriate assistance if needed	• There is at least one person I can turn to for advice. • If I needed help with household tasks, there is someone I could ask.[2]
Enacted (or received) support	Supportive actions that others (e.g., family, friends) provide with the intention of benefiting an individual's ability to cope with stress	• Someone comforted me by offering a hug or another form of physical affection today. • Someone gave me advice today. • Someone helped me with a task today.[3]

Source: Based on data from (1) Cohen (1991); (2) Cohen et al. (1985); (3) Barrera et al. (1981).

baseline theory, the human brain is so adapted to social living that its default expectation is social integration and this assumption shapes how humans evaluate and respond to the environment. People who are socially integrated can be less vigilant for and reactive to threats because they believe network members will share the load of managing any threats that arise. This idea is captured by perceived support (also called perceived support availability), a person's subjective assessment of whether someone would provide aid if needed. Critically, any violation of that baseline expectation (a lack of social integration or perceived support availability) heightens vigilance for threats and reactivity to external stressors (Beckes & Coan, 2015; Beckes & Sbarra, 2022; Coan & Sbarra, 2015). Alone, a threat is more dire. Best to be on high alert.

A key consequence of social integration, then, is perceiving the world as less risky, less challenging, and easier to manage (Bar-Kalifa & Rafaeli, 2014). In one elegant experimental demonstration of this idea, people who had a friend with them perceived a hill as less steep than people who stood facing the hill alone (Schnall et al., 2008). Having social relationships literally makes the obstacles around us seem more surmountable. The presence of close others also downregulates physiological and neurological reactions to threat. For instance, people experience lower physiological stress during parts of the day when their partners are physically with them than parts of the day when their partners are not present (Han et al., 2021). Viewing a picture of one's romantic partner or bringing one's partner to mind similarly reduces self-reported pain and physiological reactivity to stressors (e.g., Eisenberger et al., 2011; Master et al., 2009; Smith et al., 2004).

In another seminal demonstration of social baseline theory and the benefits of social proximity, researchers found that women who were randomly assigned to hold their partner's hand during threat of shock (they were literally waiting to be zapped) had less activation in areas of the brain that respond during threat (e.g., the ventral anterior cingulate cortex, anterior insula, caudate) than women who held a stranger's hand or no hand (Coan et al., 2006). A follow-up to this study demonstrated that partner handholding was more effective to reduce neurological threat for people who more strongly perceived that they had support available if they needed it (see Figure 9.8; Coan et al., 2017). In other words, social proximity is most beneficial when people perceive that support is available in those relationships.

Perceiving that support is available if you need it is hugely beneficial for health, well-being, and resilience in the face of stressors (e.g., Cohen & Wills, 1985; Uchino, 2009b; Uchino & Garvey, 1997; Wethington & Kessler, 1986). For instance, people who have closer ties to their social networks self-report better health and emotional well-being (Ermer & Proulx, 2020). One of the most powerful demonstrations of this idea came in the 1970s in a now-classic study linking lifestyle and mortality risk (Berkman & Syme, 1979). In this study, healthy men and women (aged 30 to 69) completed various

Figure 9.8 Handholding provides a psychological and physical sense of safety. What kinds of situations make you want to seek physical contact? (Photo: Westend61 / Getty Images)

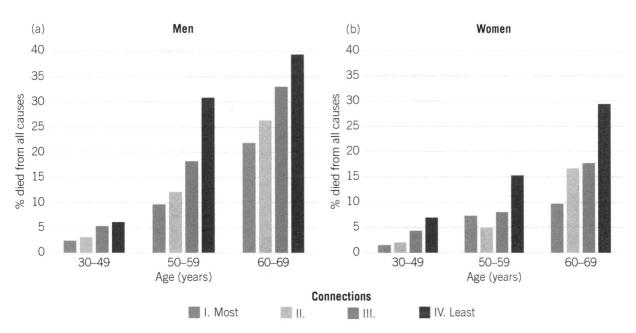

Figure 9.9 The all-cause mortality rate (number of people who die for any reason out of 100 people) is higher for those with less social contact than those with more social contact. (Source: Copyright © 1979 Oxford University Press; reprinted with permission from Oxford University Press; Berkman, L. F., & Syme, S. S. [1979]. Social networks, host resistance, and mortality: A nine-year follow-up study of Alameda County residents. *American Journal of Epidemiology, 109*(2), 186–204)

questionnaires assessing their lifestyle behaviors and social connections, and the researchers simply evaluated death records to determine who survived (versus who passed away) in the following nine years. As expected, lifestyle behaviors, such as avoiding smoking, exercising, and maintaining a healthy body weight, each predicted a lower likelihood of mortality; critically, the researchers also discovered that people who were more socially integrated (i.e., had more social contact, especially close social contact) were more likely to survive than people who were less socially integrated (see Figure 9.9).

Meta-analysis similarly shows that being socially integrated is associated with decreased mortality risk, providing a protective benefit superior to many other touted health behaviors, such as not smoking, abstaining from alcohol, getting a flu vaccine, and maintaining a low body mass index (BMI; Holt-Lunstad et al., 2010). Even an extremely simplistic indicator of social integration and support availability – marital status – is linked with mortality risk and well-being. People who are married (versus never married, divorced, or widowed) have a lower risk of mortality and better physical health and psychological well-being (Johnson et al., 2000; Rendall et al., 2011; Robles & Kiecolt-Glaser, 2003), though the benefits of being married are stronger in higher-quality marriages, are stronger for men than women, and have weakened over time (Braithwaite & Holt-Lunstad, 2017; Kiecolt-Glaser & Newton, 2001; Liu & Umberson, 2008; Proulx et al., 2007; Robles et al., 2014; Umberson et al., 2006).

Enacted (Received) Support

Interestingly, though research consistently shows that believing support is available buffers stress and protects health and well-being, actually receiving support has variable

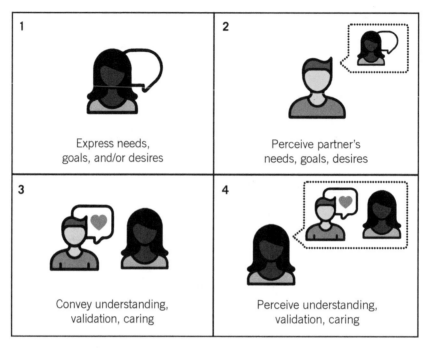

Figure 9.10 For Layla to perceive Eric's support behavior as responsive, Layla needs to express her needs, goals, or desires in such a way that Eric is able to accurately perceive them (top row). Then, Eric needs to offer support that conveys understanding, validation, and caring, and Layla needs to perceive it (bottom row). How might even well-intentioned partners strike out? (Photo: Adapted from rambo182 / DigitalVision Vectors / Getty Images)

consequences. Sometimes enacted support reduces stress (Allen et al., 1991; Ditzen et al., 2007; Feeney & Kirkpatrick, 1996; Kamarck et al., 1990; Kane et al., 2012; Lepore et al., 1993), and other times enacted support actually amplifies stress (Biehle & Mickelson, 2012; Bolger & Amarel, 2007; Gleason et al., 2008; Maisel & Gable, 2009; McClure et al., 2014; Taylor et al., 2010). Why might this be? Can you recall any times when someone tried to offer you support, but you ended up feeling worse? What went wrong?

Whether a support behavior reduces distress and enhances a relationship or adds additional stress ultimately depends on whether the support-recipient perceives that the enacted support behavior was *responsive*. In other words, enacted support is effective when it demonstrates to the support-recipient that the support-provider is *understanding* their needs, *validating* them, and *caring* for them (e.g., Dooley et al., 2018; Maisel & Gable, 2009). Remember Layla and Eric's unsuccessful support exchanges from the start of the chapter? Review Figure 9.10 for a reminder of the process of perceiving partner responsiveness in a dyadic interaction. Then, we will consider the many junctures at which this process can be derailed, leading support-recipients to perceive enacted support as unresponsive.

As shown in Figure 9.10, support can be unresponsive and ineffective if the support-provider (e.g., Eric) does not accurately perceive the support-recipient's (Layla's) needs, goals, and desires (box 2) and therefore cannot provide support that shows he understands and values her needs (box 3). This may happen more often than you think. To behave responsively, a support-provider needs to accurately perceive: (1) that the support-recipient is in need and requires support (*Is Layla in need right now?*); (2) the support-recipient's particular emotional experience (*Is Layla sad, angry, or overwhelmed?*); and (3) the support-recipient's desired response (*Does Layla want encouragement, help, or something else?*). A support-provider can fail to accurately perceive the support-recipient's needs and desires for many reasons, and these failures undermine the effectiveness of enacted support (e.g., Bodenmann et al., 2015; Don et al., 2013, 2019; Neff et al., 2021; Verhofstadt et al., 2008). The support-provider, for instance, could be stressed himself, and people who are stressed are less able to detect others' support needs (Neff et al., 2021). Additionally, people vary in their ability to accurately detect others' emotional experiences, that is, their empathic accuracy (Ickes, 1993; Ickes & Hodges, 2013), which may affect their ability to provide support (Verhofstadt et al., 2008, 2010). Finally, a support-provider can fail to accurately perceive a support-recipient's needs if the support-recipient does not express their needs or seeks support only indirectly (Armstrong & Kammrath, 2015; Cavallo & Hirniak, 2019; Don et al., 2019; Simpson et al., 1992; Zaki et al., 2008).

Accurately assessing a support-recipient's needs, goals, and desires is critical because, according to the optimal matching model of stress and social support (also called the "matching hypothesis"), enacted support is most beneficial when it matches the needs of the support-recipient (Cohen & Wills, 1985; Cutrona, 1990; Cutrona et al., 1990, 2007; Cutrona & Russell, 1990). Receiving either the wrong *type* of support ("I needed someone to talk to, not a check for $100) or the wrong *intensity* of support ("Why are you swooping in to try to save me? I was just a little overwhelmed") can prove costly, whereas receiving "matched" support reduces stress and enhances the relationship between the support-provider and support-recipient (Cutrona et al., 1990, 2007; Williamson, Oliger et al., 2019). The optimal matching model also proposes that specific types of support will generally be best matched to particular contexts (Cutrona, 1990). In contexts where a stressor is uncontrollable and no assistance can mitigate it (e.g., the death of a loved one, a failed exam), emotional support is theorized to be preferred and optimally beneficial. In contrast, when a stressor is controllable and information or assistance could help to resolve it (e.g., a broken-down car), informational and instrumental support are theorized to be preferred and optimally beneficial.

 IS THIS TRUE FOR YOU?

Do You Seek Support When You Are Stressed?

When people are stressed, they tend to seek support from their attachment figures – parents, romantic partners, and best friends – as well as from other people to whom they feel particularly close (Kammrath et al., 2020). However, not everyone seeks support, and support-seeking attempts vary (Forest et al., 2021). Recall a recent experience where you were particularly overwhelmed. Who (if anyone) did you turn to? What (if anything) did you do to solicit support?

Research shows that people differ in their willingness to seek support based on their culture, age, and attachment orientation (e.g., Jiang et al., 2018; Kim et al., 2008; Ognibene & Collins, 1998). People from individualistic cultures (e.g., European Americans), for example, tend to perceive it appropriate to ask close others to meet their individual needs,

Figure 9.11 When you seek support, who do you ask, and how do you ask? When you don't ask for help, why not? (Photo: CareyHope / E+ / Getty Images)

whereas people from collectivistic cultures (e.g., Asians, Asian Americans) tend to be focused on collective goals and therefore perceive support-seeking as inappropriate (Kim et al., 2008). Accordingly, Asian and Asian American individuals tend to seek less support from close others than European American individuals (e.g., Benjamin et al., 2021; Kim et al., 2006, 2008; Taylor et al., 2004; Taylor & Welch, 2007),

often because they do not want to make others stressed about their problems and are embarrassed to share their problems (Taylor et al., 2004). Older adults also report seeking less help from family and friends than younger adults because they are attuned to the potential costs that support provision will have for others (Jiang et al., 2018). Instead, individuals from collectivist cultures and older adults often seek **implicit support**; they pursue opportunities to spend time with others without sharing the stressor or divulging their distress (e.g., Jiang et al., 2018; Taylor & Welch, 2007). People who are avoidantly attached also tend to seek less support than people who report lower attachment avoidance (e.g., Collins & Feeney, 2000; Ognibene & Collins, 1998; Simpson et al., 1992), though the difference seems to be more related to breadth (seeking support from fewer people) rather than depth (seeking a lesser degree of support; Armstrong & Kammrath, 2015).

When you sought support most recently, what did you say or do (Figure 9.11)? Did you directly ask for help and give details of the problem (a direct verbal strategy)? Did you cry or show your distress in another way (a direct non-verbal strategy)? Perhaps instead you sought support indirectly by hinting or complaining about the problem without directly requesting help (an indirect verbal strategy) or by signing, sulking, or fidgeting (an indirect non-verbal strategy)? Whether you sought support directly or indirectly likely impacted the quality of support you received because direct support seeking tends to elicit more effective support than indirect support seeking (e.g., Collins & Feeney, 2000; Don et al., 2013, 2019). Unfortunately, people with lower self-esteem tend to seek support indirectly and therefore tend to receive poorer quality support, such as criticizing, **blaming**, and disapproval (Don et al., 2019). Over time, indirect support seeking (and the resulting poor quality support) predicts lower relationship quality as well (Don et al., 2013). Sexual minorities who perceive that their relationships are stigmatized are also especially likely to engage in indirect support seeking when they are seeking support from friends and family regarding their romantic relationships (Williams et al., 2016). Consistent with other research on indirect support seeking, this indirect approach tends to yield more unsupportive responses. Alternatively, people who perceive their partners as responsive tend to express their emotions (such as anxiety) directly

(Ruan et al., 2020), which results in higher-quality support provision and greater resulting relationship quality (e.g., Collins & Feeney, 2000). Perhaps consider these ideas the next time you need some help.

Even if a support-provider perceives another's need, they may still be unwilling, unmotivated, or unable to respond responsively due to their own characteristics or characteristics of the situation (Figure 9.10, box 3; e.g., Francis et al., 2019; Iida et al., 2008; Winczewski et al., 2016). For instance, more insecurely attached support-providers (high attachment anxiety and/or high attachment avoidance) tend to provide poorer quality support than support-providers with secure attachment orientations (e.g., Collins et al., 2009; Collins & Ford, 2010; Feeney & Collins, 2001). Insecurely attached people's own rocky support histories and their relationship concerns may interfere with their ability to offer effective support. Additionally, insecurely attached people tend to offer poorer-quality support because their motives for support provision tend to be more egoistic (i.e., based on obligation, a desire to avoid negative consequences, and a hope to get something in return) than those of securely attached people (Feeney & Collins, 2003). Research shows that people who are currently or chronically stressed also tend to provide poorer-quality support than people who are not stressed (Bodenmann et al., 2015; Brock & Lawrence, 2014; Clavél et al., 2017). Just as being stressed can interfere with a support-provider's ability to detect a support need, being stressed can also explain why some people fail to behave responsively in response to a support need that they notice.

So what do people do when they are unresponsive to support needs? They can either fail to act or engage in behaviors that are unsupportive (also called providing "negative support"). The innumerable ways of behaving unsupportively include such tactics as distancing, bumbling, minimizing, and blaming (Ingram et al., 2001; Lincoln, 2000). Table 9.5 includes definitions and examples of these negative support behaviors.

Finally, support exchanges can be ineffective or costly not because of the support-provider, but because of the support-recipient's interpretation of the support they receive (Figure 9.10, box 4). Layla's perception of Eric's responsiveness is the result of both Eric's objective support behaviors (i.e., Eric's communication content, tone, and style) *and* Layla's own subjective interpretation (i.e., Layla's construal, motivated reasoning) about those behaviors. On the one hand, this means that objectively unresponsive behaviors can occasionally prove beneficial if they are perceived favorably; on the other hand, even seemingly supportive behaviors can be unhelpful or stress-enhancing if they are construed negatively (see Figure 9.12; Bolger & Amarel, 2007; McClure et al., 2014; Rafaeli & Gleason, 2009). For example, attachment orientations bias perceptions in line

Figure 9.12 Have you ever been told to "just get over it" or been criticized for feeling overwhelmed? Support attempts can miss the mark, making enacted support hit-or-miss. (Photo: martin-dm / E+ / Getty Images)

Table 9.5 Selected items from an inventory of unsupportive (negative support) behaviors

Distancing: *Behavioral or emotional disengagement*
• Did not seem to want to hear about it
• Changed the subject before I wanted to
• Discouraged me from expressing feelings such as anger, hurt, or sadness
Bumbling*: Awkward, uncomfortable, or intrusive behaviors*
• Did not seem to know what to say, or seemed afraid of saying or doing the "wrong" thing
• From voice tone, expression, or body language, I got the feeling he or she was uncomfortable talking about it
• Did things for me that I wanted to do and could have done for myself
Minimizing: *Forcing optimism or downplaying concerns*
• Felt that I should stop worrying about the event and just forget about it
• Told me to be strong, keep my chin up, or that I should not let it bother me
• Said I should look on the bright side
Blaming: *Criticism or implying fault*
• Told me that I had gotten myself into the situation in the first place, and now must deal with the consequences
• Said "I told you so" or a similar comment
• Asked "why" questions about my role in the event

Source: Copyright © 2001, Guilford Publications, reprinted with permission from Guilford Publications; Ingram, K. M., Betz, N. E., Mindes, E. J., Schmitt, M. M., & Smith, N. G. (2001). Unsupportive responses from others concerning a stressful life event: Development of the Unsupportive Social Interactions Inventory. *Journal of Social and Clinical Psychology, 20*(2), 173–207.

with one's existing schemas of relationships. Therefore, people with insecure attachment orientations are biased toward perceiving ambiguous support attempts as unsupportive, in line with their perceptions that they are unworthy of responsive support and/or that others tend to be unavailable and uncaring (Collins & Feeney, 2004, 2010).

Receiving support (particularly instrumental or informational support) can also be costly if the support-recipient thinks the support-provider believes they lack efficacy or competence ("I guess he thought I couldn't handle this myself"). People need to feel capable, so support perceived to undermine their self-efficacy or competence can increase rather than reduce distress (e.g., Bolger et al., 2000; Bolger & Amarel, 2007; Crockett et al., 2017). Enacted support can also backfire when a support-recipient feels indebted to the support-provider or over-benefited in the relationship ("He helps me so much more than I'm able to help him; I'm a slouch"). When receiving support creates inequity in this way, it can enhance rather than reduce distress (e.g., Bar-Kalifa et al., 2017; Gleason et al., 2003; Ryon & Gleason, 2018).

Given these potential costs, some researchers see the benefits of invisible support, support that is either not noticed by the support-recipient or is noticed but not interpreted as help (e.g., Bolger et al., 2000; Zee & Bolger, 2019). To provide invisible support, the support-provider might de-emphasize their helping role (e.g., avoid saying, "Let *me* help you") or use examples to provide support indirectly (e.g.," My sister had a similar problem and tried ..." or "When that has happened to me, I felt better when I ..."; Howland & Simpson, 2010). In these ways, the support transaction feels more like a friendly conversation than a provision of assistance from a stronger or more knowledgeable person to a weaker or less knowledgeable person. Affectionate touch (e.g., a warm hug) can also provide "under-the-radar" support because affectionate touch effectively buffers stress without directly communicating that support (rather than affection or love) is being provided (Ditzen et al., 2007; Jakubiak & Feeney, 2016c, 2018).

Consistent with the relative benefits of invisible support over visible (noticed) support, people who receive invisible support experience less distress than people who are aware of support receipt (e.g., Bolger & Amarel, 2007; Girme et al., 2013, 2018; Howland & Simpson, 2010; Jakubiak et al., 2020). Of course, context still matters. Invisible support is more advantageous when the support-recipient is minimally upset (rather than extremely distressed; Girme et al., 2013), is motivated to evaluate their standing (rather than to take action; Zee et al., 2018), and is receiving help during stressful contexts (rather than everyday life or goal contexts; Jakubiak et al., 2020).

We have shown a variety of ways that enacted/received support can misfire (and you can probably think of some more!), yet support that receivers perceive as responsive is a critical asset to individuals and their relationships (Dooley et al., 2018; Maisel & Gable, 2009; Selcuk et al., 2017; Selcuk & Ong, 2013). Responsive support during stress helps people feel safer and less stressed, report better mood, and experience greater connectedness and more intimacy in their relationships (Collins & Feeney, 2000; Kane et al., 2012; Maisel & Gable, 2009). Partners who offer responsive support during stress serve as effective "safe havens" and therefore meet a key function of close relationships. Unsurprisingly, then, responsive support receipt also predicts greater overall relationship quality and a greater likelihood of relationship stability over time (Feeney & Collins, 2001). People want to maintain relationships with responsive support-providers.

Receiving and perceiving social support as responsive also mitigates the personal and relational costs of individual and shared stressors. For instance, among individuals in same-sex relationships (people who are presumably experiencing some degree of minority stress), greater social support receipt is a primary predictor of greater commitment, satisfaction, closeness, and resilience (Haas & Lannutti, 2021). Greater support receipt also mitigates the links between individual stress and relationship quality in daily life (Hilpert et al., 2018). Consistent with relational costs of stress, people who report more intense personal stress generally report lower relationship satisfaction (a spillover effect). However, the longitudinal link between stress and relationship satisfaction is weaker for individuals who believe their partners "show empathy and understanding toward me" and "listen to me and give me an opportunity to communicate what really bothers me" (Hilpert et al., 2018). In other words, stress may have less of a negative impact on relationship satisfaction for people whose partners offer responsive support.

Although scholars tend to focus on social support's potential to mitigate stress's negative consequences, receiving social support during stress can foster growth, beyond simply a return to baseline (Feeney & Collins, 2015b). In other words, supportive partners may thrive through adversity rather than merely cope. Such thriving can occur when partners not only offer responsive support, but also help each other view a stressor as an opportunity for positive change. Baseball fans will recognize that, in the same way a losing streak can spur the development of new skills, partners can use stressors as an opportunity to encourage growth.

 IN THE NEWS

Emotional Support Animals

Romantic partners, friends, and family may provide essential social support during stressful times, but what about pets (see Figure 9.13)? Airplanes, apartment complexes, restaurants, and universities are among the institutions that have debated whether to allow dogs, cats, hamsters, reptiles, and other non-human companions in their spaces to help owners manage stress and anxiety (e.g., Carrasco, 2021). While

Figure 9.13 Research shows that "man's best friend" provides support more effectively than actual human friends. What makes pet support so effective? (Photo: Ling Jin / Moment / Getty Images)

airplanes have ruled "no," many other places have opted to permit pets. Many university campuses even offer "pet therapy," opportunities to de-stress in the company of friendly animals (Castellano, 2021). As much as they make a good news story, do pets actually help us to cope with stress?

The research seems to suggest, "yes!" For instance, people who complete stressful tasks (e.g., an ice-bucket-challenge-like pain task) with a pet in the room (their own or someone else's) have been shown to have lower heart rate increases, lower cortisol, and lower blood pressure increases during the task than people who complete such tasks alone or with a friend in the room (Allen, 2002; Polheber & Matchock, 2014). Having a pet in the room after experiencing the stress of social exclusion may likewise buffer adverse effects (Aydin et al., 2012). Even just thinking about one's pet can reduce blood pressure during a stressful task (Zilcha-Mano et al., 2012). The stress-reducing benefits of spending time with pets point to myriad benefits of pet ownership, including greater self-esteem, greater overall well-being, and greater resilience to rejection.

Unlike our human friends, animals may be better stress-buffers because (1) they are non-evaluative (e.g., Fido is not judging you when you make mistakes) and (2) they allow for comfortable touch, a potent stress-reducing behavior (Ditzen et al., 2007; Jakubiak & Feeney, 2017, 2018; Vormbrock & Grossberg, 1988). Touch is a soothing and stress-relieving behavior across the lifespan, but between people its appropriateness is generally restricted to specific close relationships, such as romantic relationships (e.g., Feldman et al., 2010; Field, 2010; Jakubiak & Feeney, 2017). Dogs and other animals can be excellent sources for "contact comfort" because touch with these sorts of pets is natural and comforting and avoids the risks of giving offense or being rejected. Although emotional support animals can no longer fly on planes with us, the evidence supports the use of emotional support animals in safer (and legal) spaces.

Exploring, Growing, and Developing

In many marriage ceremonies, people vow to support each other "in good times and in bad." So far in this chapter, we have seen that we need support during bad times and that we view our relationships favorably when our partners serve as effective safe havens. But what about the good times? How do partners provide responsive support in the absence of threat? What kind of support is needed?

Motivated to Explore

During periods of relative calm, in the absence of immediate stressors or threats, people are innately motivated to explore the physical and social world, to pursue goals, to take on challenges, and to grow and develop as individuals (Bowlby, 1982, 1988). From an attachment theory perspective, feelings of safety allow people the opportunity to explore away from their attachment figures and prioritize adventure and personal growth. All people are presumed to be motivated toward personal growth because developing competence is considered a fundamental human need (Deci & Ryan, 2000; Ryan & Deci, 2000; White, 1959). Picture a toddler screeching "I do it!" as they struggle to put on their own clothes for the first time; it is the drive for competence and personal growth that compels them to repeatedly try shoving their right arm into their left pantleg. Think also of an adult who completes a 5k race only to set their sights on conquering an intense obstacle course run next; a continued and lifelong drive for self-development pushes them further, faster, harder. Even as individuals are motivated to explore and pursue personal growth (see Figure 9.14), as we shall see, close others are instrumental in facilitating or inhibiting exploratory urges.

(a)   (b)

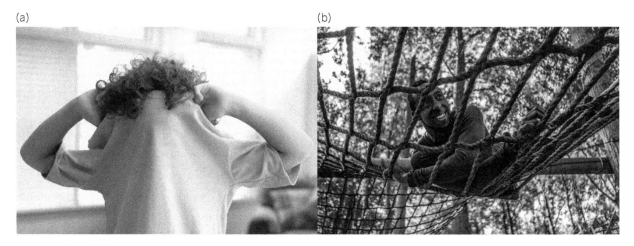

Figure 9.14 Developing competence and skills is a life-long motivation. How are you challenging yourself to grow and achieve this year? (Photo: Jose Luis Paleaz Inc. / DigitalVision / Getty Images [a] and Lorado / E+ / Getty Images [b])

ARTICLE SPOTLIGHT

Supportive Relationships Promote Personal Growth Cross-Culturally

Personal growth (e.g., learning, achieving, improving as a person) sure sounds like a *personal* phenomenon, doesn't it? Individual effort, motivation, skills, and planning are indeed required for a person to grow. Rarely, however, do award recipients say, "I worked hard and did this on my own." No! Individual success and personal growth are often credited to *interpersonal* factors, especially the supportive relationships that initiate, nurture, and maintain personal growth. ("I'd like to thank the academy, but mostly my mom, who encouraged me every step of the way.") Lee, Ybarra, Gonzalez, and Ellsworth (2018) termed this interpersonal process of personal growth the "I-through-we" perspective. In other words, *I* am able to grow because *we* have a close and supportive relationship. Lee and colleagues hypothesized that having supportive relationships enables growth because people who know they can rely on close others for support have higher self-confidence; they perceive that they have the skills, ability, or resources to be successful when they pursue opportunities. To assess this "I-through-we" theory, Lee and colleagues conducted three studies.

First, they recruited a sample of over 200 adults through Amazon's Mechanical Turk to complete an online experiment. Participants were randomly assigned to write about a person with whom they had (1) a supportive relationship or (2) an unsupportive relationship, or (3) a person they did not know well. Following this manipulation and a filler task (to obscure the purpose of the study), participants selected between two hypothetical jobs. The job at Company A offered decent pay and required only familiar work. The job at Company B offered a slightly lower salary but provided an opportunity for growth, that is, long-term career development through skill acquisition. Consistent with hypotheses, participants who were randomly assigned to think of a supportive relationship tended to prioritize an opportunity for growth by selecting Company B (Figure 9.15). Participants who were randomly assigned to think of an unsupportive relationship were least likely to select Company B.

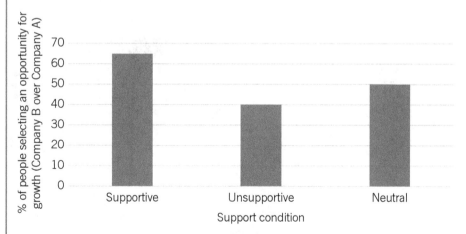

Figure 9.15 People who thought about a supportive relationship were most likely to prioritize an opportunity for growth in a hypothetical job choice. When have your supportive relationships encouraged you to take on a challenge? (Source: Adapted from Lee et al. [2018], reproduced with permission from Sage Publications)

Why did thinking of a supportive (or unsupportive relationship) have this effect? Lee and colleagues had two raters review participants' written descriptions of their supportive, unsupportive, or neutral relationship. These raters quantified the extent to which participants described this relationship as enhancing their self-confidence. For example, a response like, "CC makes me feel as if I can accomplish anything" would be rated high in self-confidence, whereas a response like, "CC makes me feel like I'm not good enough" would be rated low in self-confidence. Using this approach, Lee and colleagues showed that people who thought of supportive relationships wrote more about feeling self-confident and consequently were most likely to select the opportunity for growth (Company B). In other words, supportive relationships enable people to prioritize personal growth, in part, because they nurture self-confidence (see Figure 9.16).

In two additional studies, Lee and colleagues (2018) aimed to replicate this pattern of results and show that these results generalize across cultures. In one study, the researchers used data from a survey called Midlife Development in the United States (MIDUS), in which nearly 5,000 American adults ranging in age (28 to 84 years old) reported various

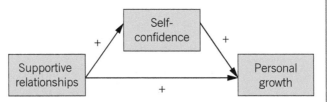

Figure 9.16 In three studies, Lee and colleagues (2018) found support for this model. When people had more supportive relationships, they reported higher self-confidence, which partially explained why they also were more motivated to pursue opportunities for personal growth. How have you grown because of your relationships? (Source: Drawn based on data from Lee et al. [2018])

personal and relational experiences. In the other study, the researchers used data from a survey called Survey of Midlife Development in Japan (MIDJA), in which over 1,000 Japanese adults (30 to 79 years old) completed the same questionnaires from the MIDUS study.

The MIDUS and MIDJA included questions about whether participants perceive that their family and friends really care about them and whether they can open up to their family and friends if they need to talk (i.e., supportive relationships). These surveys asked whether participants "think it is important to have new experiences that challenge how you think about the world" and whether participants are interested in "activities that will expand [their] horizons" (i.e., personal growth). Finally, participants rated whether they feel "confident and positive about [themselves]" and whether the word "self-confident" describes them, which Lee and colleagues used as a measure of participants' self-confidence.

Using mediation analyses, Lee and colleagues (2018) found consistent support for their "I-through-we" perspective in both samples. American and Japanese adults with more supportive relationships reported greater self-confidence, which indirectly contributed to greater motivation for personal growth. This cross-cultural replication is particularly notable because it demonstrates that supportive relationships are associated with personal growth in an individualistic culture that emphasizes personal achievements (United States) and in a collectivistic culture that prioritizes group achievements (Japan).

This study effectively demonstrates the interpersonal nature of personal growth using a variety of methodological approaches, but its primary strength may be in raising even more questions. How does having supportive relationships promote self-confidence to enable growth? In other words, what do partners and friends do to convey that they care, and how does supportiveness translate into the perception that one has the skills, ability, and resources to achieve? We hope more on this is to come.

Responsive Support for Exploration

Adults explore by learning, accepting challenges, and pursuing goals related to work and education, leisure, and social relationships (Carnelley & Ruscher, 2000; Elliot & Reis, 2003; Feeney et al., 2017; Green & Campbell, 2000; Hazan & Shaver, 1990; Jakubiak & Feeney, 2016b). These personal, self-driven explorations away from the safety of "the nest" and the security of routine are some of the most meaningful life experiences people can have (see Figure 9.17). Engaging in exploration, however, introduces the possibility of failure, embarrassment, and pain. What the nest lacks in adventure, it makes up for in coziness and predictability. This tension between adventure and safety is what supportive partners and friends can resolve by offering responsive support. What might responsive support look like in the context of exploration?

In his original writings, John Bowlby described close others' role in supporting exploration in this way:

> In essence this role is one of being available, ready to respond when called upon to encourage and perhaps assist, but to intervene actively only when clearly necessary. In these respects, it is a role similar to that of the officer commanding a military base from which an expeditionary force sets out and to which it can retreat, should it meet with a setback. Much of the time the role of the base is a waiting one but it is none the less vital for that. For it is only when the officer commanding the expeditionary force is confident his base is secure that he dare press forward and take risks.(Bowlby, 1988, p. 11)

It is from this description that the term "secure base" originated. In order to be motivated to explore, people need confidence that they have a secure base to whom they can return or from whom they can seek support if they encounter a threat. This "waiting" role means that the best way to provide responsive support for exploration may be to do less, to simply stand off to the side. Empirical research has supported and extended this theoretical depiction of a secure base by demonstrating that people are more likely to accept challenges, achieve goals, and persist through setbacks when their attachment figure (e.g., partner) is (1) encouraging, (2) available, and (3) non-interfering (Feeney, 2004; Feeney et al., 2017; Feeney & Thrush, 2010).

Let's review how responsive support works during exploration by imagining Amber Sabathia's decision to pursue a career as a sports agent. On the one hand, launching a sports agent career has clear "pros," including opportunities for respect, financial gain, accolades, and helping others. On the "cons" side, such a venture includes the possibility of public failure, embarrassment, or not being respected as a female in the male-dominated sports world. To be willing to take on the challenge, Amber needs to perceive that the opportunity is worthwhile

Figure 9.17 What makes some people (and birds) leave the safety of their routines (and nests) to explore the world? How do our friends (or bird-buddies) facilitate or undermine our exploratory urges? (Photo: Stan Tekiela / Moment / Getty Images)

and that she has a reasonable likelihood of success (e.g., Feeney, 2004; Feeney & Collins, 2015a; Feeney & Thrush, 2010). Encouragement from CC and others could tip the balance. Encouragement entails conveying excitement and enthusiasm about an opportunity or goal ("Imagine how cool this would be!") and expressing confidence that an exploration will be successful ("You could totally do that!").

After deciding to explore (i.e., take the job), Amber would still need support. Specifically, Amber would explore most effectively (with enthusiasm rather than continual risk monitoring) if CC and other members of her support network are physically available (located nearby) and/or psychologically available (attentive) during exploration (e.g., Feeney, 2007; Feeney & Thrush, 2010). CC could demonstrate his availability by stating his readiness and willingness to help (e.g., "I'll be here all day if you need anything") or by checking in during the exploration (e.g., texting "How's it going?"). Critically, availability is most effective when accompanied by non-interference, the passive waiting role that Bowlby described (e.g., Feeney, 2004; Feeney & Thrush, 2010). Interference, such as persistent advice or well-meaning practical support ("Amber, I called in a favor and got you your first client!"), transforms a personal undertaking into a team effort. Teamwork is lovely, but it undermines the goal of exploration and personal growth. Interference can also communicate a belief that the "explorer" needs help, which could undermine their self-efficacy.

Consistent with Bowlby's original theorizing, when people receive secure base support, they are more likely to accept a challenging opportunity, they make greater daily progress on their personal goals, and they are more likely to achieve their goals over time (Feeney et al., 2017; Jakubiak & Feeney, 2016b; Overall et al., 2010; Tomlinson et al., 2015). A meta-analysis also showed that partner support predicts goal outcomes and does so nearly as strongly as having a strong intention to achieve a goal (Vowels & Carnelley, 2022). People who receive secure base support also report better mood, greater self-esteem and self-efficacy, and greater perceived self-growth and learning over time (Feeney, 2004; Feeney et al., 2017; Feeney & Thrush, 2010; Tomlinson et al., 2015). These findings support a counterintuitive idea termed the dependency paradox: for people to be truly independent, they must be able to depend on others (Feeney, 2007). Not surprisingly, because growth is a primary human need, people evaluate their relationships favorably when their partners support their personal goals. Indeed, when people perceive that their partners are responsive in exploration contexts, they also report increases in relationship quality over time (e.g., Fivecoat et al., 2015; Jakubiak & Feeney, 2016b; Overall et al., 2010). Thus, responsive support contributes to relationship maintenance by enhancing the quality of the relationship and motivating people to want to maintain their relationships.

Partners can also be key forces in shaping personal growth more broadly, through a process called the Michelangelo phenomenon (e.g., DiDonato, 2020; Drigotas et al., 1999; Rusbult et al., 2009). Like Michelangelo chipping away at a slab of marble to "reveal the ideal form slumbering within" (Figure 9.18), our partners act

Figure 9.18 Like Michelangelo with his mallet and chisels coaxing a form out of a slab of marble, close others can behave in ways that bring out our ideal and authentic selves. How have your partners and friends supported you to be a "truer" you? (Photo: UniversalImagesGroup / Getty Images)

toward us in ways that bring forth the selves we most wish to become, the truest and most genuine versions of ourselves (Rusbult et al., 2009, p. 305). Partners "sculpt" us through two forms of affirmation: perceptual affirmation and behavioral affirmation. Perceptual affirmation refers to the partner perceiving us in ways that are consistent with our ideal self. For example, if Haley's ideal self is spontaneous, Annie's perception of her as a person who is spontaneous (at least to some extent) constitutes perceptual affirmation. This perceptual affirmation is important because it sets the stage for behavioral affirmation, the elicitation of behaviors that are congruent with one's ideal self (e.g., DiDonato & Krueger, 2010). For instance, Annie can engage in behavioral affirmation by providing opportunities for Haley to behave spontaneously, bringing out her spontaneity and actually helping to sculpt Haley toward her ideal self. The Michelangelo phenomenon, like enacted support more broadly, requires responsiveness to be effective. Annie cannot effectively use perceptual and behavior affirmation to bring about Haley's ideal self without accurately understanding Haley's ideal self, validating it, and caring for Haley enough to be motivated to contribute to her growth.

RESEARCHER SPOTLIGHT: Yuthika Girme, PhD

Figure 9.19 Dr. Yuthika Girme is an assistant professor in the Department of Psychology at Simon Fraser University (SFU). (Photo courtesy of Robyn Humphreys, SFU Faculty of Arts and Social Sciences.)

How did you come to be a research psychologist?

Like many psychology majors, I wanted to be a clinical psychologist. In my final year, however, I took a Close Relationships course and fell in love! I was fascinated with how close relationships can be the absolute best thing for us ... but also the absolute worst! I switched focus and pursued a doctoral degree in Psychology. What first drew me to relationship psychology is still what excites me about relationship research. To this day, my research program aims to uncover when and for whom relationships and singlehood are beneficial versus costly.

Why do you study social support, in particular?

The support literature is marked with an interesting paradox. Perceiving close others as supportive has important health and relationship benefits, but providing good support is challenging. Well-intended support can backfire. Given how central social support is to health and well-being, I felt it was important to understand when and for whom social support is most beneficial, and when social support might exacerbate recipients' distress.

What's next in social support research?

An important message emerging across the social support literature is that "one support does not fit all." If relationship scientists are to "crack the code" on when social support is most beneficial, we'll learn how people can provide support that is tailored to recipients' *changing* needs across social contexts and across time. Of course, this adds another layer of complexity, so it is also important to consider how to encourage tailored support in a way that does not burden support-providers.

Being Responsive: The Support-Provider's Perspective

In adversity and in periods of relative calm, individuals benefit from responsive partner support, but how does the partner fare when providing support? According to attachment theory, people are innately motivated to provide support (i.e., to serve as safe havens and secure bases for their close others) because people each possess a caregiving behavioral system. Just as the attachment system motivates people to seek proximity during threat and the exploration system motivates people to seek adventure during calm, the caregiving behavioral system naturally motivates people to respond to others' needs (e.g., Collins et al., 2009; Collins & Ford, 2010; Feeney & Collins, 2001, 2003). In other words, both CC and Amber may benefit not only from receiving each other's support, but by offering that support as well.

Consistent with the idea that caregiving is an innately motivated process, people report personal and relational benefits of providing support to close others (e.g., Feeney & Collins, 2018; Gosnell & Gable, 2015; Inagaki & Eisenberger, 2012, 2016; Inagaki & Orehek, 2017). For instance, people who naturally provide greater support as well as those who are randomly assigned to provide support to a loved one report feeling happy and connected and exhibit increased activation in "reward" regions of the brain (e.g., Inagaki & Eisenberger, 2012; Inagaki & Orehek, 2017; Nelson et al., 2016). Providing support also reduces stress on the part of the support-provider (e.g., Inagaki et al., 2016; Inagaki & Eisenberger, 2016; Poulin et al., 2013). These findings are in line with the idea that caregiving is naturally rewarding.

Despite these benefits, support provision has its costs. Providing support can be exhausting and depleting, reducing support-providers' self-control for other tasks (Gosnell & Gable, 2015, 2017). Support-providers can also be concerned (quite rightly) about their ability to meet their partners' needs. After all, no one wants to say the "wrong thing." Support provision attempts can backfire, leading to (1) stress about the possibility of providing support and/or (2) a lack of motivation to provide support at all. Critically, not all forms of support are perceived as equally costly by support-providers. Support-providers who imagine providing touch support (to hold their partner until they feel better) expect to fare better than support-providers who imagine providing verbal support (to say something to their partner until they feel better) or no support (Jakubiak, 2021). Touch support avoids some of the costs of support provision because support-providers expect it to be less difficult to provide and less likely to have unintended negative consequences than verbal support. Remember those fears about saying the "wrong thing"? Touch behaviors are more standard (a hug is a hug is a hug) and require less tailoring to each situation, lowering their difficulty and likelihood of being unresponsive. Further, support-providers expect to benefit personally from touch support provision (to feel more secure themselves), perhaps because touch tends to be bidirectional. To give a supportive touch is typically to receive a supportive touch as well.

 DIVERSITY AND INCLUSION

Support for Chronic Illness

For some people, support provision is more than an occasional and rewarding task. In cases of long-term illness, disability, or even normal aging, partners, family members, or friends can become caregivers tasked with coordinating and supervising daily routines (eating, dressing, bathing), managing doctor visits and treatment protocols, and handling finances (Schulz et al., 2020). Approximately 3 million US adults provide intensive "activities of daily living" care and approximately 43 million US adults provide at least some unpaid care to an adult relative (e.g., helping with household chores; Schulz et al., 2020). Informal caregiving can be extremely stressful because caregivers are typically untrained and are typically managing caregiving responsibilities on top of existing personal and work-related responsibilities. Perhaps it is no surprise, then, that caregiving can have serious psychological costs. Caregivers report significantly higher psychological distress than non-caregivers, and distress increases as people enter the caregiving role and as their caregiving responsibilities increase (e.g., Dunkle et al., 2014; Hirst, 2005). At least some caregivers also experience physical health consequences resulting from caregiving. Caregivers are most at risk for physical and psychological consequences if they are providing a high level of care (more than 100 hours per month; administering medical procedures), if they feel obligated to provide care, if they have limited social support themselves, and if they are the spouse of the care recipient, female, and have lower SES (Schulz et al., 2020).

In exploration contexts, support-providers can have an added challenge that undermines their ability to benefit from support-provision: **goal conflict**. Specifically, a partner's goal may be incompatible with one's own goals, meaning that to support a partner requires personal sacrifice. Recall Amber Sabathia's personal goal of becoming a sports agent. How might Amber's goal conflict with CC's own personal goals or their goals for their relationship? Maybe CC's plans to become a better golfer have to be put on hold as he takes on additional responsibilities to facilitate Amber's goal pursuit. Or perhaps Amber's goal requires her to meet clients in the evenings, interfering with Sabathia's relationship goal of spending regular time together as a family. Goal conflict contributes to worsening relationship quality and undermines personal well-being as well, though couple-members tend to avoid goal conflict by adjusting their goals to accommodate each other (Gere & Impett, 2018; Gere & Schimmack, 2013). Sacrificing one's own personal goals to support a partner's goals can be beneficial for the relationship or can prove costly, depending on how people frame the sacrifice (Righetti & Impett, 2017). When people sacrifice to approach a desired outcome (e.g., to make their partner happy, to feel good about themselves), the sacrifice tends to be more rewarding than when people sacrifice to avoid a feared outcome (e.g., upsetting the partner, breaking up, or personal guilt; Impett, Gable et al., 2005, Impett et al., 2014; Impett & Gordon, 2010; Righetti & Impett, 2017). Although sacrifice requires giving something up, research shows that people tend to under-perceive the costs of the sacrifice for themselves and over-perceive the benefits of the sacrifice for their romantic partners, which reduces a sacrifice's perceived burden (Visserman et al., 2021).

Although support provision has benefits as well as costs (varying in relative strength based on the context and type of support requested), some theorists speculate that costs of support provision in romantic relationships are steeper now than they have been in the past. In their "suffocation of marriage" model, Finkel and colleagues (2014) argue that marriages are increasingly burdened by support provision because expectations for romantic partners' support provision role have changed over time. Specifically, people tend to have fewer confidants and close friends aside from their partner than they did in the past, so they rely on their romantic partners to meet more of their personal needs, including support needs (for review, see Finkel et al., 2014). Additionally, whereas people traditionally expected romantic relationships to meet their basic needs (food, shelter, childcare), people now expect their partners to meet higher-level needs, such as needs for companionship, self-esteem, and personal growth (Finkel et al., 2014). A focus on higher-level needs means that relationships have the potential to be better and more fulfilling today than at any time in the past; however, it also means that there is greater opportunity to fall short of the rising expectations. This suffocation model is not without skeptics and critics. For instance, other theorists argue that the premise that higher-level needs are harder to meet than basic needs is unfounded (Feeney & Collins, 2014). What do you think? Is it more difficult to provide food, shelter, and safety or to help someone to strive to meet their personal goals and progress toward becoming their ideal self? Would *receiving* one of these forms of support motivate you to maintain your relationship more than the other form?

Conclusion

Throughout this chapter, we explored how supportive relationships enhance individuals' stress resilience and inspire growth. Relationships are a key resource for personal well-being and personal development because the security afforded by close relationships provides both a safe haven to weather life's rain delays and a secure base to lead off of and return to if a threat arises. Because supportive relationships serve these essential functions, people are satisfied with and committed to maintaining relationships with responsive support-providers and typically aim to be responsive support-providers themselves. Social support is part threat-mitigation (recovering from stressors) and part relationship-enhancement (enabling growth). In the next chapter, we will transition to other positive processes that enhance the relationship and foster relationship maintenance.

Major Take-Aways

- When people encounter objective stressors and perceive that the demands of the stressor outweigh their coping abilities, they experience psychological stress. In addition to interfering with personal well-being, stress undermines relational well-being by making it harder to navigate everyday problems and by introducing new problems.
- Social integration, perceived support availability, and *responsive* enacted support can minimize psychological

stress and foster resilience in response to objective stressors. Enacted support can, at times, enhance stress if the support-provider fails to understand the support-recipient's need, if the support-provider is unwilling, unmotivated, or unable to respond to the need, or if the support-recipient does not interpret the support as validating and caring.

- People are most willing to engage in exploration when they know they have support available if exploration becomes risky or threatening. Partners can enable exploration by offering encouragement and showing their availability, and by not interfering.

- Support-providers tend to find support provision rewarding, but also depleting.

Support provision is particularly costly when there is goal conflict or when support-providers fear that their support attempt will be ineffective.

Further Readings

If you're interested in ...

... how perceiving a partner's responsiveness shapes the experience of waiting for uncertain news, read:
Dooley, M. K., Sweeny, K., Howell, J. L., & Reynolds, C. A. (2018). Perceptions of romantic partners' responsiveness during a period of stressful uncertainty. *Journal of Personality and Social Psychology*, 115(4), 677–687.

... how support-providers and support-recipients differ in their evaluations of support exchanges, read:
Dungan, J. A., Gomez, D. M. M., & Epley, N. (2022). Too reluctant to reach out: Receiving social support is more positive than expressers expect. *Psychological Science*, 33(8), 1300–1312.

... the reasons why support during stressful experiences and during opportunities for exploration can promote thriving, read:

Feeney, B. C., & Collins, N. L. (2015). A new look at social support: A theoretical perspective on thriving through relationships. *Personality and Social Psychology Review*, 19(2), 113–147.

... the consequences of support to buffer stress and protect relationship well-being, read:
Hilpert, P., Xu, F., Milek, A., Atkins, D. C., Bodenmann, G., & Bradbury, T. N. (2018). Couples coping with stress: Between-person differences and within-person processes. *Journal of Family Psychology*, 32(3), 366–374.

... the benefits of support provision, read:
Inagaki, T. K., & Orehek, E. (2017). On the benefits of giving social support: When, why, and how support providers gain by caring for others. *Current Directions in Psychological Science*, 26(2), 109–113.

10 ENHANCING RELATIONSHIPS THROUGH POSITIVE INTERPERSONAL PROCESSES

The Good Stuff

The hit drama *This Is Us* chronicles the lives of triplets (two biological siblings and one adopted sibling) as they navigate made-for-TV tear-jerker moments, together, but also with their own romantic partners. The triplets – Randall, Kevin, and Kate – each face and overcome relationship challenges throughout the series, but it is perhaps their positive relationship moments that continually draw viewers back. Randall and his wife Beth (arguably the show's most enviable power-couple) warmly celebrate and relish each other's successes, make grand gestures and offer routine kisses to show their love, and intentionally take time to enjoy each other's company. These and other positive relationship behaviors serve as investments in their relationship and keep viewers invested in their storyline.

As the show progresses, Randall and Beth increasingly face competition for the *This Is Us* fan-favorite couple from Kate and her boyfriend-then-husband, Toby. Viewers take to Kate and Toby's relationship in part because of Toby's lighthearted and playful personality. Toby brings persistent fun and humor into their relationship, and this infusion of play and shared laughter helps to make their relationship highly rewarding. Whereas positivity abounds in Kate and Toby's relationship, and Randall and Beth display support and affection, Kevin's relationships are largely short-lived (spoiler: until the end!). Like us, he witnesses his siblings' relationship strengths and the ongoing dynamics they create.

Finally, all three triplets idolize their parents' – Jack and Rebecca's – relationship, which viewers observe through flashbacks and memories. Jack and Rebecca's relationship was by no means perfect, but the good certainly outweighed (and cushioned) the bad. In particular, their experience of raising the triplets brought constant novelty and excitement into their lives. As we shall see, such novelty and fun can support a relationship's continual growth and prevent relationship boredom and stagnation. Jack and Rebecca's relationship may have thrived in part because of the many engaging possibilities afforded to them by parenting the triplets (see Figure 10.1).

(a) (b) (c)

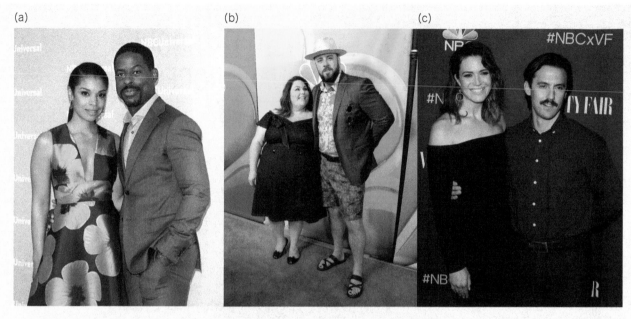

Figure 10.1 The couples featured in *This Is Us* (Beth and Randall [a], Kate and Toby [b], Rebecca, and Jack [c]) teach a master course on positive relationship behaviors. From physical affection to lighthearted play, these couples teach us how it's done. What relationship-enhancing behaviors have you learned from television power-couples? (Photos: Jim Spellman / WireImage / Getty Images [a], Gregg DeGuire / WireImage / Getty Images [b], and JB Lacroix / WireImage / Getty Images [c])

In this chapter, you will learn about positive interpersonal processes: interactions between people that actively enhance their close relationships. We will start by describing the field's shift toward studying positive processes and highlight the utility of considering positive phenomena as unique from negative phenomena. Then, we will review the specific interpersonal behaviors that have been shown to enhance relationships, including (1) spending time together (particularly spending time on novel and exciting activities), (2) co-experiencing positive emotions, and (3) communicating affection.

 GUIDING QUESTIONS

Consider these questions as you read this chapter:
- Why are positive interpersonal processes important? What functions do they serve?
- How much time do partners spend together, and what are the consequences of shared time for relationship-functioning generally?
- Why do novel and exciting activities help partners to make the most of their shared leisure time?
- What experiences enable partners to get in sync – to co-experience positive affect and behavioral and physiological synchrony – and why are these experiences relationship-enhancing?
- How do people express affection, who expresses affection, and what are the consequences of affectionate communication?

The Shift toward Positive Processes

Have you heard the common adage that "bad is stronger than good"? Indeed, negative events are more emotionally, cognitively, and physiologically impactful than positive events (Taylor, 1991), which is likely why the science of relationships started as a science of what *not* to do. Proscriptions to avoid harmful behaviors (e.g., don't criticize, avoid stonewalling) do make a difference in relationship success (e.g., Johnson et al., 2018; Markman, Rhoades et al., 2010), but so too do prescriptions to enact salutatory behaviors. Focusing on "the good stuff" is a goal increasingly advanced by researchers and theorists who have incorporated humanistic traditions and positive psychology into relationship science (e.g., Algoe, 2019; Feeney & Collins, 2015a; Gable & Gosnell, 2011; Reis & Gable, 2003). Stepping away from the field's initial negativity bias, we learn that the "good stuff," the positive experiences in relationships, is essential for relationship success.

The Uniqueness of Positive and Negative Experiences

Maybe you're wondering whether positive processes are merely the flipside or inverse of negative processes. For instance, is "not criticizing" an example of what we mean by a positive interpersonal behavior? Actually, no. "Not criticizing" is the absence of a negative behavior, but it is not the enactment of a positive behavior. This distinction may seem pedantic, but it is consistent with an abundance of research demonstrating that what we judge as positive and what we judge as negative are on separate dimensions (Cacioppo et al., 1997; Rogge et al., 2017; Watson et al., 1999). In other words, the "good stuff" (positive relationship processes) and the "bad stuff" (negative relationship processes) are not two opposite poles of the same continuum, but are unique dimensions of experience (see Figure 10.2).

To help wrap our heads around the idea that positives and negatives are best represented by two separate dimensions, consider this: positive and negative experiences can and do co-occur in relationships. For instance, people rate their partners as both helpful and upsetting, sometimes in the same contexts ("my partner is both helpful and upsetting when I need advice"), and sometimes in different contexts ("my partner is helpful when I need advice and upsetting when I need favors or assistance"; Cazzell et al., 2022). Does this seem counterintuitive? Simplistic conceptions of relationships encourage the idea that people have either strictly satisfying relationships (with a great deal of positivity and absent negativity) or strictly dissatisfying relationships (with a great deal of negativity and absent positivity).

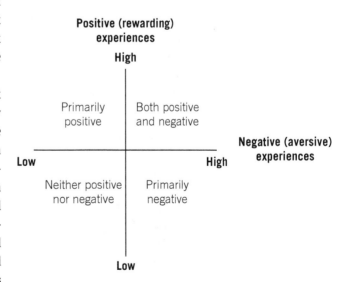

Figure 10.2 Positives and negatives are best represented by two separate dimensions rather than as opposing poles on the same dimension. This means that people can experience primarily positive experiences, primarily negative experiences, low levels of both positive and negative experiences, or high levels of both positive and negative experiences. Can you think of situations in which you have strong positive and negative experiences simultaneously?

But in reality, relationships are more complicated; most relationships include positive *and* negative interactions. Sometimes the relationship itself is evaluated with ambivalence: a co-occurrence of strong positivity and strong negativity ("My relationship is really enjoyable and fun, and it is also really unpleasant and miserable"; Rogge et al., 2017). Despite the presence of positivity, ambivalent relationships are associated with worse health consequences than strictly dissatisfying relationships; people cannot as easily ignore negative interactions in ambivalent relationships as they can in purely negative relationships, making the impact of negative experiences all the stronger (Birmingham et al., 2019; Holt-Lunstad & Uchino, 2019).

By respecting that positive experiences are unique and separate from negative experiences (not the opposite), we can attend to the roles of both in sustaining relationships. Critically, people cannot achieve high-quality close relationships by merely avoiding aversive relationship experiences; rather, partners must enjoy positive experiences as well for a relationship to thrive (Algoe, 2019; Gable, 2006). These dual requirements for relationship thriving are consistent with descriptions of human motivation more broadly. People possess both an **inhibitory system** that compels them to avoid aversive experiences (e.g., pain, embarrassment, conflict) and an **appetitive system** that compels them to seek rewarding experiences (e.g., pleasure, intimacy; Elliot & Church, 1997; Gable, 2006; Gable & Impett, 2012; Higgins, 1998). Well-being results from satisfying both inhibitory and appetitive drives. Accordingly, the positive interpersonal processes described in this chapter are critical components of high-quality relationships and are paramount for relationship maintenance.

The Interplay of Positive and Negative Experiences

Remember how we just said that positive processes are unique from negative experiences and important to understand in their own right? This does not mean positive processes are completely independent from negative processes. In fact, positive interpersonal experiences in relationships can mitigate the negative consequences of aversive relationship experiences, making positive and negative experiences quite intertwined (Cazzell et al., 2022; Driver & Gottman, 2004; Feeney & Lemay, 2012; Walsh et al., 2017; Walsh & Neff, 2020). In other words, the positive interpersonal processes we will review in this chapter (1) directly promote relationship well-being and (2) indirectly promote relationship well-being by providing a cushion to weaken the harmful impact of negative relationship experiences.

To appreciate this idea of "cushioning," picture a piggy bank. But unlike the typical piggy bank that accrues financial capital (i.e., assorted coins and folded dollars), this piggy bank collects **emotional capital**, the positive moments a person experiences in a particular relationship (see Figure 10.3). Emotional capital – just like financial capital – is a resource that can be accessed when something goes wrong, a relationship's "rainy day" fund. When an

Figure 10.3 Positive relational experiences serve as deposits into a relationship's emotional bank account. What do you do to invest in your close relationships? (Photo: Kittisak Jirasittichai / EyeEm / Getty Images)

appliance breaks in your home, you can crack open your piggy bank to pay to have the appliance repaired or replaced. Without that financial capital on hand, you have a much more serious problem. Similarly, when a difficulty or transgression occurs in your romantic relationship (or other close relationship), you can metaphorically crack open your relational piggy bank and withdraw your accrued "relationship wealth" to avoid serious relationship consequences (Feeney & Lemay, 2012, p. 1004).

This idea is more than a fun analogy; it is an important and empirically supported relationship maintenance process. When one partner (Jack) behaves unresponsively or negatively in daily life, the other partner's (Rebecca's) reaction depends on whether they (Jack and Rebecca) have accrued emotional capital in the relationship. People who report more positive relational experiences over time (i.e., they keep filling the piggy bank) continue to report high relationship satisfaction through turbulent times, whereas people who report fewer positive relational experiences report decreases in relationship satisfaction when the relationship hits inevitable bumps (Feeney & Lemay, 2012; Walsh et al., 2017). Emotional capital has this "cushioning" effect, in part, because people with more positive relational experiences are more forgiving of and make more constructive attributions for their partners' negative behaviors (Walsh & Neff, 2020). *I know you couldn't have meant to hurt me because you're typically so considerate and affectionate. I forgive you; let's move on.*

You must be wondering by now, what exactly are these positive relational experiences that function like money in the bank? In the studies just reviewed, the researchers assessed a wide range of positive interpersonal processes, including various behaviors a partner could do (e.g., "held my hand," "made me laugh," "complimented me"), and various activities partners could do together (e.g., "we spent time together," "we did something fun together"; Feeney & Lemay, 2012; Walsh et al., 2017). As you might imagine, there are innumerable positive, shared relational experiences that improve and protect relationships. In the following sections, we will explore several of these positive interpersonal processes that have been shown to enhance relationships and cushion relationship threats.

Spending and Leveraging Time Together

Time and attention are among the greatest gifts we can give to another person. Perhaps unsurprisingly, then, partners who prioritize spending time together tend to have more satisfying relationships than partners who share less time (e.g., Johnson et al., 2006; Johnson & Anderson, 2013; Lakey & Orehek, 2011; McDaniel, Galovan et al., 2021; Milek et al., 2015). Certainly, partners that are more satisfied with their relationships might choose to spend more time together than partners who are dissatisfied; however, greater shared time also predicts increases in relationship satisfaction over time, suggesting that shared time contributes to relationship improvements (Johnson & Anderson, 2013). The importance of shared time is highlighted in *This Is Us* when we see Kate and Toby's relationship deteriorate after Toby moves to another city for his career. The sudden lack of shared time quickly undermines what was a vibrant and rewarding relationship. The importance of shared time is also evident in the struggles of military couples during deployment or for partners who transition to long-distance.

According to relational regulation theory, spending time with close others enhances relationships (and provides personal benefits) because engaging in "ordinary yet affectively consequential social interactions" allows people to experience companionship and develop the belief that support is available should they need it (Lakey, 2013; Lakey & Orehek, 2011; Rivers & Sanford, 2020). In other words, when people engage in ordinary interactions with their partners (e.g., discussing work, laughing together, going to the movies together), they solidify their interpersonal bond and develop an expectation that they have someone to rely on in bad times (as well as good). Thus, shared time fosters perceived support availability and its myriad positive consequences (for a refresher, see Chapter 9).

Partners also report greater personal well-being (e.g., greater positive affect, lower negative affect) when they spend time together compared to time apart, with this personal benefit most pronounced for people in satisfying relationships (Flood & Genadek, 2016; Hudson et al., 2020). Emotions are regulated in the context of close, satisfying relationships, meaning that people who are with their partners are less concerned with risks or threats in the environment (e.g., Beckes & Coan, 2011; Beckes & Sbarra, 2022) and they have a greater ability to manage challenging emotions that arise (Butler & Randall, 2013; Milek et al., 2015). When relationships provide this regulatory function, people come to associate their partners with feeling calm and regulated, which can enhance their positive evaluation of the relationship and motivate them to prioritize interacting with their partner in the future.

Prevalence of Shared Time in Close Relationships

Just how much time do partners spend together? Estimates from the American Time Use Survey, a representative survey of over 45,000 married Americans (from 2003 to 2010), suggest that people spend approximately 3 hours and 20 minutes on weekdays, and about 7 hours on weekend days, awake with their spouses (Flood & Genadek, 2016). These estimates include time spent with the spouse alone and in the presence of others; estimates for time spent only with the spouse are lower, about 2 hours on weekdays and a little over 3 hours on weekend days (Flood & Genadek, 2016). These estimates make it sound like partners spend a lot of time together, but most people still report that they do not spend enough time with their partners (e.g., Roxburgh, 2006). After all, how many hours per day do you average on your phone?

The amount of time partners spend together varies according to several contextual and relational factors. One such factor is whether or not partners are parents: parents spend less time alone with their partners than non-parents, with parents of young children reporting the least exclusive spousal time (e.g., Bittman & Wajcman, 2000; Flood & Genadek, 2016; Genadek et al., 2016; Voorpostel et al., 2009). To illustrate the magnitude of this difference, consider a study in which non-parents reported spending approximately 4.5 hours together per day – approximately 3.5 hours of which was exclusive spousal time – whereas parents reported spending a little over 4 hours together per day, with only 75 minutes of exclusive spousal time (Genadek et al., 2016).

The gender composition of a particular couple also matters. As shown in Figure 10.4, female same-sex couples report more overall shared time and more exclusive time than male same-sex couples or different-sex couples (Genadek et al., 2020). Among parents, female

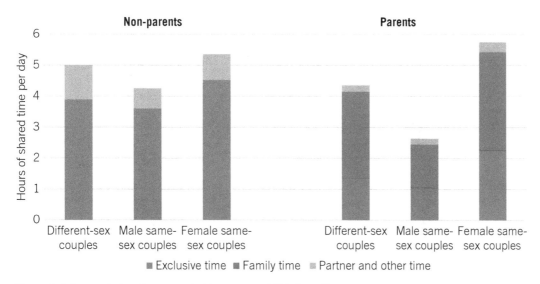

Figure 10.4 How much time do you spend with your partner? This figure illustrates shared time among married and cohabiting partners in the United States, from 2003 to 2016. Data are based on a large nationally representative sample, including 85,789 different-sex couples, 275 male same-sex couples, and 356 female same-sex couples. "Exclusive time" includes time spent with only the partner; "family time" includes time spent with the partner and one or more children; and "partner and other time" includes time spent with the partner in the presence of people other than children (e.g., friends, other family). (Source: Drawn based on data from Genadek et al. [2020])

same-sex couples also report more family time (time spent with one's spouse and children) than male same-sex couples or different-sex couples (Genadek et al., 2020).

Two other factors – work demands and culture – also predict partners' shared time. People with non-standard work hours spend less time with their partners than people with nine-to-five jobs, and people spend less time with their partners on days that they work than on days that they do not work (e.g., Dew, 2009; Flood & Genadek, 2016; Wight et al., 2008). Additionally, cross-cultural research shows that spouses sampled from Spain spend more time together (total shared time, exclusive spousal time, and family time) than spouses sampled from the United States or from France (see Figure 10.5; Roman et al., 2017). These differences seem to be driven by cultural norms rather than by differences in work demands between countries; spouses in Spain report greater shared time than spouses in France or the United States even on weekends, when most people in the samples were not working.

The amount of time that spouses spend together has also changed over time. Available data show a general trend of increases in shared time from 1965 to 1975 and then decreases in shared time through 2012 (Dew, 2009; Genadek et al., 2016). Non-parents spent increasingly more time together from 1965 to 1975, and they maintained an increase in exclusive spousal time through 2012. Parents show a similar but slightly different pattern. For parents, family time increased by about 60 minutes from 1965 through 2012, but total time increased by only about 30 minutes. In other words, American spouses traded some of their exclusive spousal time for family time from 1965 to 2012 (Genadek et al., 2016). Family time rose similarly from 1990 to 2010 in Sweden, but unlike in the United States, partners in Sweden did not experience decreases in spousal time (Neilson & Stanfors, 2018). These differences

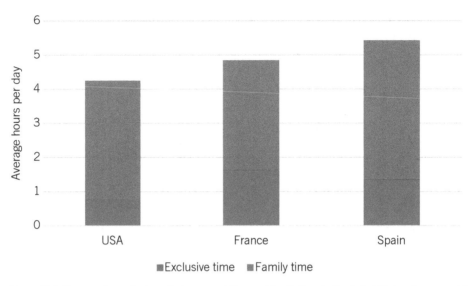

Figure 10.5 Time spent per day in exclusive spousal time and family time in the United States, France, and Spain from 2009 to 2010. How does this figure inform the challenge of transitioning to parenthood? (Source: Drawn based on data from Roman et al. [2017])

highlight the role of culture in how romantic partners navigate time together when they also wish to enjoy family time.

How Partners Spend Shared Time

When partners do spend time together, how are they spending that time? Figure 10.6 shows estimates of the proportion of overall shared time that parents and non-parents spend together engaging in several common activities: meals, leisure, television-watching, housework, travel, and childcare. Across all groups (parents and non-parents, same-sex and different-sex pairs), television-watching represents the largest proportion of shared time (about a quarter to a third of all shared time). This reflects a sociocultural shift since the twentieth century: spouses have cut their shared mealtime down by about half (from about an hour to a half hour) and spend increasingly more of their time together watching television (Genadek et al., 2016). **Shared leisure** – defined here as time spent playing games, exercising, socializing, or attending events together – accounts for the next highest amount of time, with partners spending approximately a quarter of their shared time engaging in these leisure activities.

Research strongly suggests that partners who enjoy more shared leisure time also enjoy more relationship benefits (e.g., Berg et al., 2001; Hill, 1988; Johnson et al., 2006). Note that the definition of "shared leisure" used by researchers varies and often includes all recreational activities that partners might do together. Partners might go out together to eat a meal, see a movie, or take a trip (Girme et al., 2014; Moore & Henderson, 2018). Such shared leisure activities tend to require financial resources and transportation, making them less accessible for partners with lower socioeconomic status than those with higher SES (Moore & Henderson, 2018). If these were the only types of activities studied, the link between shared leisure and relationship benefits might better reflect a SES difference than a benefit of shared

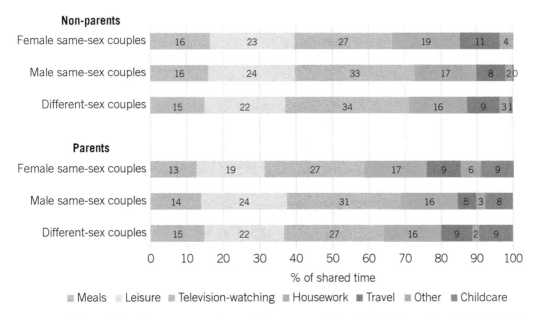

Figure 10.6 Estimated shared time spent on various activities among married and cohabiting partners in the United States, from 2003 to 2016. These data are based on a large nationally representative sample, including 85,789 different-sex couples, 275 male same-sex couples, and 356 female same-sex couples. Meals include any meals eaten together; leisure includes recreational activities such as playing games, exercising, or attending events together; television-watching involves watching the television simultaneously in the same location; housework includes activities such as cleaning, home repairs, and meal preparation; travel includes activities such as driving or taking public transportation together. (Source: Drawn based on data from Genadek et al. [2020])

leisure. A broad definition of shared leisure, however, also includes at-home activities done together, such as playing boardgames or videogames, watching television or movies, eating, exercising, or even completing enjoyable household tasks (e.g., cooking, yardwork; Girme et al., 2014; Moore & Henderson, 2018; Sackett-Fox et al., 2021). Lower SES couples report engaging in shared leisure by prioritizing these and other low-cost activities (Moore & Henderson, 2018); shared activities need not be resource-demanding to predict relationship benefits. Nearly any shared time in Figure 10.6 could be categorized as shared leisure if partners view it as recreation.

Of course, how partners engage with each other during their shared leisure time matters. For example, feeling close to one's partner during shared leisure predicts relational benefits, whereas technoference during shared leisure undermines its benefits (Girme et al., 2014; McDaniel, Galovan et al., 2021). Having other people present during shared leisure also weakens the positive associations between shared leisure and relationship benefits, at least among a sample of primarily young adults without children (Dobson & Ogolsky, 2022). Engaging in leisure activities that are desired by one partner and disliked by the other also confers costs rather than benefits (Crawford et al., 2002).

Like shared time generally, most people today engage in more shared leisure time with their romantic partners than previous generations (Genadek et al., 2016; Sevilla et al., 2012; Voorpostel et al., 2009, 2010). Shared leisure time varies based on the same factors that shape shared time generally, including the gender-makeup of the couple (female same-sex couples

(a)   (b)

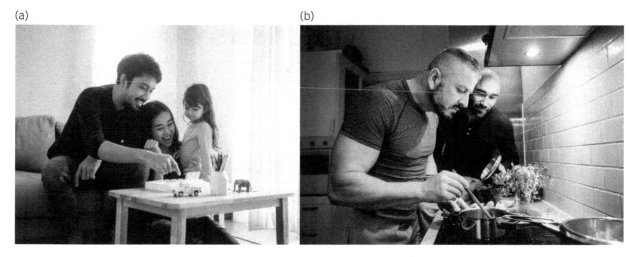

Figure 10.7 Shared leisure time, with or without children present, is associated with relational benefits. How might attachment theory, evolutionary theories, or interdependence theory explain this association? (Photo: staticnak1983 / E+ / Getty Images [a] and fotografixx / E+ / Getty Images [b])

spend more time in shared leisure than male same-sex couples or opposite-sex couples) and parental status (non-parents spend more time in shared leisure than parents; e.g., Flood & Genadek, 2016; Genadek et al., 2016, 2020; Figure 10.7). Parents experience a drop in shared leisure (as well as independent leisure) during the transition to parenthood, and although leisure levels eventually rebound, parents continue to spend less exclusive leisure time together as their children develop (Claxton & Perry-Jenkins, 2008). These changes are not necessarily problematic though; parents report enjoying family leisure time (leisure activities with both parents and children present) even more than exclusive (parents only) leisure time (Flood et al., 2020).

Leveraging Shared Time with Self-Expanding Activities

When partners spend leisure time together, are any activities particularly beneficial? To answer this question, we need to consider the functions of shared leisure in ongoing relationships. As you may recall, people are fundamentally motivated to expand their sense of self (self-expansion motivation), which they do automatically and easily in the early stages of their close relationships (e.g., Agnew et al., 1998; Aron et al., 2013; Mashek et al., 2003). Early in a relationship, nearly every interaction that people have with their partners constitutes a new and exciting experience that can result in learning knowledge or skills and gaining new perspectives, which is in part why people experience intense passion in the beginning of their relationships (Carswell & Impett, 2021; O'Leary et al., 2012; Sheets, 2014). Consider all that you could learn and experience by visiting a new partner's hometown for the first time. Over the course of a relationship, opportunities for automatic self-expansion diminish (there's a lot less excitement and learning during the fifteenth visit to a partner's hometown), which can contribute to personal stagnation and relational boredom (Aron et al., 2013; Aron & Aron, 1996; Sheets, 2014). Fortunately, some shared leisure activities provide opportunities for ongoing self-expansion and reignite passion in long-term relationships (e.g., Muise, Harasymchuk et al., 2019; Sheets, 2014). Complete Table 10.1 to assess the extent to which

Table 10.1 Brief daily self-expansion questionnaire

For each statement, circle one number to describe how you felt TODAY.	Not at All					Very much	
How much did being with your partner result in you having new experiences?	1	2	3	4	5	6	7
Did you feel a greater awareness of things because of your partner?	1	2	3	4	5	6	7
How much did being with your partner expand your sense of the kind of person you are?	1	2	3	4	5	6	7
How much did your partner provide you with a source of excitement?	1	2	3	4	5	6	7
How much did you feel you gained a larger perspective on things because of your partner?	1	2	3	4	5	6	7
How much did your partner increase your knowledge?	1	2	3	4	5	6	7

Higher summed scores indicate greater self-expansion in the context of the relationship. Early-stage relationships are rife with opportunities for self-expansion. What types of interactions would facilitate self-expansion in ongoing close relationships?

(Source: Copyright © 2019, American Psychological Association; reproduced with permission; Muise, A., Harasymchuk, C. Day, L. C., Bacev-Giles, C., Gere, J., & Impett, E. A. (2019). Broadening your horizons: Self-expanding activities promote desire and satisfaction in established relationships. *Journal of Personality and Social Psychology, 116*[2], 237–258)

you experienced self-expansion in a particular close relationship today (you can think of a romantic partner, friend, or family member). Then, read back over the questions in Table 10.1 and consider which types of interactions would lead a person to answer "very much" to the questions listed; in other words, what kinds of activities are self-expanding activities?

An impressive and still expanding (pun intended) body of research has shown that self-expanding activities are those shared leisure activities that are novel, exciting, and fun (e.g., Aron et al., 2000, 2013; Coulter & Malouff, 2013; Reissman et al., 1993; Tomlinson et al., 2019). People list a wide array of shared leisure activities as self-expanding, including outings (e.g., date nights or specific events), household activities (e.g., completing household tasks), disclosive conversations (e.g., sharing thoughts and feelings, discussing plans for the future), physical intimacy (e.g., having sex, cuddling), support provision, and support receipt (Muise, Harasymchuk et al., 2019). Regardless of the specifics, any activity is a self-expanding activity when it provides a sense of excitement, produces greater awareness of oneself or the world around oneself, and is perceived as novel and fun (Lewandowski & Aron, 2002; Muise, Harasymchuk et al., 2019).

Consistent with theorized benefits, partners who engage in more self-expanding activities tend to report higher relationship satisfaction (e.g., Aron et al., 2000; Coulter & Malouff,

2013; Graham, 2009; Harasymchuk et al., 2020; Muise, Harasymchuk et al., 2019). We see this link in between-partner comparisons (i.e., partners who engage in more self-expanding activities report greater relationship satisfaction than couples who engage in less of these activities) and within the same partners over time (i.e., partners experience greater relationship satisfaction at times when they engage in more versus fewer self-expanding activities). Interventions that enhance novel and fun activities also point to the relational benefits of self-expanding leisure activities (Aron et al., 2000; Coulter & Malouff, 2013; Muise, Harasymchuk et al., 2019; Reissman et al., 1993). Imagine signing up for a research study that invites you and your partner to crawl and climb through an obstacle course while tethered to each other: not something you probably do every day! Laboratory research on self-expansion as an intervention, using clever methods like these, has shown that partners who are randomly assigned to engage in novel and exciting leisure activities experience greater relationship well-being benefits than partners assigned to complete mundane or even pleasant leisure activities (Aron et al., 2000; Coulter & Malouff, 2013; Muise, Harasymchuk et al., 2019; Reissman et al., 1993). Couples who spend time getting to know another couple – an activity that is novel, potentially exciting, and encourages self-disclosure – also experience a relational benefit (they feel closer to each other; Slatcher, 2010).

Participating in novel and exciting activities with a partner offers relational benefits, in part, because these activities reignite passion and can enhance sexual desire (Harasymchuk et al., 2020; Muise, Harasymchuk et al., 2019; Raposo et al., 2020). For instance, people who received instructions to increase their self-expanding (i.e., "novel and exciting") activities with their partner over three days reported greater sexual desire than people who were assigned to increase "familiar and comfortable" activities (Muise, Harasymchuk et al., 2019). People also report greater sexual desire and are more likely to have sex with their partner on days that they perceive greater self-expansion through the relationship (Muise, Harasymchuk et al., 2019; Raposo et al., 2020). Participating in novel and exciting activities also offers relational benefits because these activities enhance security. They make people feel safe, cared for, and solid in their relationship (Cortes et al., 2020). Novel and exciting activities may have this security-enhancing benefit because they often require coordination, and provide an opportunity for support provision, responsiveness, and trust-building.

Self-expanding activities are closely related to **play** behavior (Figure 10.8), activities that are enjoyable, approached in a non-serious or lighthearted way, interactive, and enacted for the purpose of amusement or fun rather than a particular end-goal (Van Vleet & Feeney, 2015a, 2015b). Playing with one's partner is theorized to provide immediate and long-term relationship benefits because play may foster self-expansion (hence, the overlap with self-expanding activities), cooperation, perceived compatibility, intimacy, and shared positive affect (the

Figure 10.8 Partners can enhance their relationships by playing and by engaging in novel and exciting activities that provide opportunities for self-expansion. What activities do you do to self-expand with close others? (Photo: HEX / Getty Images)

topic of the next section of this chapter; Van Vleet & Feeney, 2015a, 2015b). Playfulness – a personality trait describing a propensity toward play – is also positively associated with relationship outcomes, further suggesting a positive role of play in relationships (for review, see Brauer et al., 2021).

IN THE NEWS

The Gift of Time Apart

Spending and leveraging time together can enhance a relationship, but can there be too much of a good thing? Might there also be benefits to having time apart? Cohabiting partners around the globe were faced with these questions during the COVID-19 pandemic's initial lockdowns and subsequent changes to daily life. Partners who previously spent the majority of their waking hours apart (e.g., working, commuting, after-work happy hours, yoga classes) were suddenly working from home, commuting to a shared home-office or the kitchen table, and attending social events and exercise classes over Zoom, with their partner either participating alongside or hiding out of sight of the webcam. With shared time pushed to the extreme, people began to recognize the value of time apart – time to socialize with other people or time to simply be alone – as reported in *The New York Times* (Dunn, 2021).

The benefits of a healthy balance of time together and time apart for optimal relationship functioning is supported by relationship literature as well (Carswell et al., 2021; Piechota et al., 2022). Time apart provides opportunities for partners to have separate experiences that they can later share with each other to spark novel, exciting, and even passionate conversation. Does this remind you of "self-expansion"? Indeed, the opportunity to self-expand is one reason time apart is so valuable. Greater **personal self-expansion** (i.e., learning, growth, and excitement that a person experiences independently or with other individuals as opposed to with a partner) on a given day is associated with greater reports of passion in the relationship on the same day (Carswell et al., 2021). When people have time apart for their own self-expansion, they can amass experiences that can translate into a more passionate relationship. ("You won't believe what I learned today. I've been dying to tell you about it." [Exciting and passionate conversation ensues.]) However, before you overdo it on the alone time, the benefits of daily personal self-expansion are tempered by the costs of sustained personal self-expansion (Carswell et al., 2021). People who self-expand outside of their relationships more overall (not just on a particular day) report lower passion than people who engage in less overall personal self-expansion. In sum, time apart (just like shared time) is relationship-enhancing until taken to the extreme.

Co-experiencing Positive Emotions

The role of emotion in relationships cannot be overstated. When you think of emotions, you may think of the big old negative ones – sadness, fear, anger – and forget about the positive emotions – joy, amusement, excitement (remember negativity bias?). Positive emotions, however, are essential for relationship well-being. A rich body of research at the intersection of relationship science and affective (emotion) science shows that partners who simultaneously experience positive affect benefit relationally (Brown & Fredrickson, 2021; Fredrickson, 2016). For instance, Randall and Beth may co-experience positive affect while they watch their daughter, Tess, take her first steps. In this moment, they may both shout "Go Tess!" smile at each other, and high-five after Tess's success. Randall and Beth could also co-experience positive affect when watching a comedian or while eating a delicious meal so long as they are truly experiencing the situation together (e.g., seeing each other smile, hearing each other laugh, mutually reveling in a fantastic barbecue). Experiencing the same emotion simultaneously but in isolation (without any real-time interaction) does not count as co-experienced positive affect (e.g., Brown & Fredrickson, 2021).

Co-experienced positive affect augments the positive emotional experience for each individual, leading to higher and more sustained "highs" (Brown & Fredrickson, 2021). Co-experienced positive affect also facilitates behavioral and physiological synchrony (e.g., Mogan et al., 2017). **Behavioral synchrony** includes coordinated movements and gestures such as nodding simultaneously or leaning toward each other in unison (e.g., Otero et al., 2020; Wells et al., 2022). **Physiological synchrony** includes a fascinating linkage in people's biological responses, such as their autonomic nervous system's physiological activity (e.g., heart rates might align between partners; Chen et al., 2021; Wells et al., 2022). Greater co-experienced positive emotion predicts greater physiological linkage during interaction tasks in the laboratory (i.e., conflict discussions), and shared positive affect is more strongly linked to physiological synchrony than shared negative affect or unshared affect (Chen et al., 2021). In other words, sharing specifically positive emotions, not just any emotions, links people together.

The co-experience and/or co-expression of positive affect is considered part of the manifestation and experience of "**love-the-emotion**." In other words, people *experience* their love and affection for each other in moments when their emotions, behaviors, and physiology are synchronized (Fredrickson, 2016). (They may also decide to *express* their love and affection for each other, as described in the next section of this chapter.) In these moments, positive affective states "resonate and reverberate between and among individuals," amplifying each person's positive affect and strengthening the social bonds between them (Figure 10.9; Brown & Fredrickson, 2021, p. 60). Experiences of shared positive affect may enhance relationship functioning by generating a feeling of oneness and self–other overlap, key foundations for interpersonal closeness.

Figure 10.9 When people simultaneously experience the same positive emotion, their positive emotion is amplified and their social bond is strengthened. What situations elicit shared laughter, shared joy, or shared feelings of awe for you and your friends? (Photo: Dean Mitchell / E+ / Getty Images)

Indeed, shared positive affect appears to uniquely differentiate satisfying from less satisfying relationships. Partners with greater co-experienced positive affect during neutral interactions (i.e., discussing events of the day), negative interactions (i.e., discussing an ongoing conflict), and pleasant interactions (e.g., discussing how they first met) experience greater relationship quality both immediately and over time (e.g., Brown, Chen et al., 2021; Kurtz & Algoe, 2015, 2017; Otero et al., 2020). Laughter works similarly (see *Article Spotlight*). Partners who engage in greater shared laughter during discussions report greater relationship quality, closeness, and perceived similarity (Kurtz & Algoe, 2015, 2017). Further, in most cases, co-experienced positive affect is more closely related to relationship quality than co-experienced negative affect or simply co-experienced affect (combined positive and negative affect). This suggests that co-experiencing positive emotions uniquely enhances relationship functioning. Further, beyond relational well-being, greater **positivity resonance** during interpersonal interactions (i.e., co-experienced positive affect, behavioral synchrony, and physiological synchrony) predicts better personal health trajectories and a reduced risk of mortality over thirteen years (Wells et al., 2022). These benefits point to the importance of finding ways to create positive emotions in relationships.

 ARTICLE SPOTLIGHT

Sharing a Laugh

How might shared laughter affect a relationship? Let's turn to the work of Kurtz and Algoe (2015, 2017), who used creative methods to investigate the role of laughter – spontaneous and manufactured – in relationship well-being.

First, in a correlational study, Kurtz and Algoe (2015) video-recorded romantic partners ($N = 77$) discussing how they met. Research assistants then watched these 5-minute conversations and coded second-by-second when partners laughed simultaneously (shared laughter), laughed alone (unshared laughter), and did not laugh (no laughter). Kurtz and Algoe correlated the proportion of time spent in shared laughter with self-report measures of relationship quality. As expected, greater shared laughter was associated with greater closeness and greater perceived social support, as well as with greater satisfaction, commitment, and passion for men (but not for women). These results emerged above and beyond other laughter that occurred during these conversations, suggesting that shared laughter independently contributes to relationship well-being outcomes.

To build on these correlational findings, Kurtz and Algoe (2017) tested whether manipulating shared laughter (versus unshared laughter) helps to foster a relationship between unacquainted strangers using strategic deception. To understand their approach, imagine participating in their study, ostensibly a study about computer-mediated communication and first impressions. You learn that you will be video-chatting with another participant while watching a slideshow of GIFs (i.e., computer images). The experimenter tells you: "While you're watching the GIFs, don't communicate with the other participant . . . For now, you should both just pay attention to the slideshow. Of course, you can look at each other, but refrain from talking or trying to communicate with each other in any way." The slideshow ends up being a 3-minute-long series of GIFs. Some of them are hilarious and you laugh aloud; others are not funny, so you don't laugh. When you glance at the other participant, you notice that they are laughing at almost all the same GIFs as you! Abracadabra – shared laughter! How did the researchers make this happen?

What you didn't know as a participant is that all GIFs used in this study were pre-tested and selected only if at least 50 percent of participants in the pre-test (i.e., pilot study) indicated the GIFs could reasonably be assumed to evoke laughter. Half of these potentially funny GIFs were "high laugh stimuli," having caused 60 percent of pilot participants to laugh aloud, and half were "low laugh stimuli," having caused fewer than 30 percent of pilot participants to laugh. Also, remember the "other participant"? They were actually a prerecorded video of a research assistant (i.e., a confederate) laughing on command. In the shared laughter condition, participants (like you) saw the "other participant" laughing as they viewed all of the high laugh stimuli. Odds are that these high laugh stimuli also elicited a laugh from you. Hence, shared laugher. Had you been assigned to the unshared laughter condition, you would have seen the same GIFs (half high laugh stimuli, half low laugh stimuli), but now the "other participant" would have laughed as you viewed the low laugh stimuli. Odds are, these GIFs did not make you yourself laugh. Hence, unshared laughter. Finally, the researchers assigned a subset of participants to a "no laughter" control condition that included only neutral stimuli and a smiling, but not laughing, confederate.

Kurtz and Algoe's (2017) clever manipulation worked. Participants in the shared laughter condition perceived greater shared laughter than participants in the unshared laughter condition or the control condition. Further (as intended), the amount of overall laughter in the shared laughter and unshared laughter conditions was the same; any differences between these conditions could therefore be explained by *shared* laughter, in particular.

And they did observe differences! Participants in the shared laughter condition liked the confederate more and wanted to establish a friendship with the confederate more than participants in the unshared laughter or control conditions. Explaining this relationship-enhancing effect, participants perceived themselves as more similar to the confederate in the shared laughter condition ("we laughed at the same things!") relative to the other conditions. In other words, sharing some laughs led people to perceive themselves as more similar to the confederate; they therefore liked the confederate more and were more motivated to befriend them. Together these findings suggest that a good laugh between strangers, friends, or lovers is more than simply pleasurable: it may help build and sustain connections.

Sharing Good News

One way to initiate shared positive emotion is through capitalization, a situation in which one person shares (i.e., retells) their own personal good news with another person (Gable et al., 2004; Langston, 1994). In sharing the good news, the discloser's positive emotion is amplified (Gable et al., 2004; Lambert et al., 2013; Reis et al., 2010) and the recipient also has the opportunity to co-experience the positive emotion (Conoley et al., 2015; Hicks & Diamond, 2008; Monfort et al., 2014). In other words, sharing news of a positive event provides an opportunity for the partner who shares ("the capitalizer") to re-experience and savor the positive experience and for the partner who receives ("the responder") to join in the celebration.

Capitalization attempts are common; on average, people share with their romantic partner the best part of their day between 60 and 80 percent of the time (Gable et al., 2004; Reis et al., 2010). Willingness to share positive news, however, can vary with culture and other aspects of self. For example, East Asians tend to make fewer capitalization attempts than European Americans (Choi et al., 2019). This difference may reflect East Asians' greater concerns (relative to European Americans) that sharing positive news might disrupt their relationships or make responders envious (Choi et al., 2019). Along similar lines, people also hesitate to disclose their accomplishments to others whom they perceive to have low self-esteem, perhaps because they anticipate that their success would upset or threaten these individuals (MacGregor et al., 2013).

Although sharing good news may feel uncomfortable for some people (e.g., they may feel that they are bragging), opting not to share positive news to protect others from feeling envious or threatened actually backfires when the others learn the news another way (Chan et al., 2021). Imagine that your best friend won an impressive scholarship and you heard about it through someone else. How would you feel? How would you imagine your friend feels about you? Although your friend may think they're just being humble, their withholding could make you believe they don't feel close enough to you or trust you enough to share their good news. In other words, people overestimate how much sharing good news will come off as bragging and underestimate how devalued others will feel when they find out a personal success was not shared with them (Chan et al., 2021). Sharing, in this case, is very much caring.

In general, sharing positive news (ranging from the most important successes to seemingly mundane positive experiences) is associated with an array of positive outcomes. These include personal benefits (e.g., increased self-esteem, positive mood, life satisfaction) and relationship benefits (e.g., increased connection, security, relationship satisfaction, relationship stability), for both the capitalizer and for the responder (Gable et al., 2004, 2006, 2012; Le et al., 2022; Pagani et al., 2015; Reis et al., 2010; for reviews, see Gable & Reis, 2010; Peters et al., 2018). Critically, however, the benefits of sharing good news depend on the partner's response (perhaps you're finding this to be a theme throughout this book). For instance, gay men report less negative affect on days that they share a positive event related to their sexual orientation (e.g., holding hands with someone in public, attending an event organized by an LGBT organization) with another person, but only if that other person responds enthusiastically and supportively (Feinstein et al., 2020). Figure 10.10 shows four hypothetical responses to a capitalization attempt; they vary in whether the response is active versus passive and whether the response is constructive versus destructive (e.g., Gable et al., 2004).

When partners respond in ways that are active (engaged) and constructive (encouraging, celebratory), capitalization attempts produce the best personal and relational outcomes (Donato et al., 2014; Gable et al., 2006, 2012; Logan & Cobb, 2013; Pagani et al., 2020; Reis, Li et al., 2022; Reis et al., 2010). Active-constructive responses to capitalization attempts (quadrant B) are those in which responders pay attention and convey enthusiasm and excitement by celebrating, asking follow-up questions, or highlighting additional positive consequences of the positive event. Passive-constructive responses (quadrant D) are similarly positively toned, but differ in their energy; a passive-constructive response is quicker and quieter than an active-constructive response and lacks elaboration that might amplify

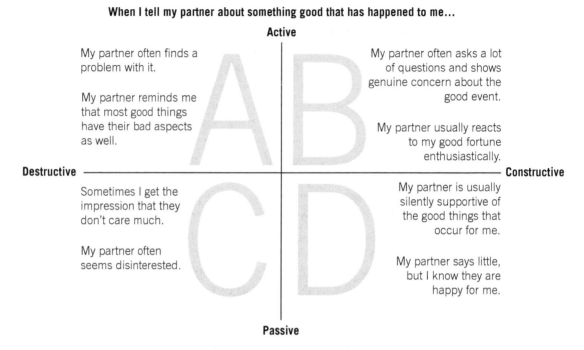

When I tell my partner about something good that has happened to me...

Active

My partner often finds a problem with it.

My partner reminds me that most good things have their bad aspects as well.

My partner often asks a lot of questions and shows genuine concern about the good event.

My partner usually reacts to my good fortune enthusiastically.

Destructive ——————————————————— **Constructive**

Sometimes I get the impression that they don't care much.

My partner often seems disinterested.

My partner is usually silently supportive of the good things that occur for me.

My partner says little, but I know they are happy for me.

Passive

Figure 10.10 Responses to capitalization attempts vary in whether they are active versus passive and whether they are constructive versus destructive. The items shown here measure each of the four combinations of responses. Active-constructive responses (top right) are associated with the best personal and relational outcomes. (Source: Copyright © 2004 by American Psychological Association; reproduced and adapted with permission. The official citation that should be used in referencing this material is Gable, S. L., Reis, H. T., Impett, E. A., & Asher, E. R. (2004). What do you do when things go right? The intrapersonal and interpersonal benefits of sharing positive events. *Journal of Personality and Social Psychology, 87*(2), 228–245. No further reproduction or distribution is permitted without written permission from the American Psychological Association.)

excitement or underscore the event's importance. **Active-destructive responses** (quadrant A) – like active-constructive responses – involve energy and elaboration, but here the elaboration involves pointing out the downsides of a positive event, undercutting the event's importance, and downgrading its worthiness for celebration. Finally, **passive-destructive responses** (quadrant C) are those responses that convey disinterest (low engagement) and minimal or no acknowledgement of the positive event.

Sharing good news and receiving an active-constructive response generates personal and relational benefits for a few key reasons. First, active-constructive responses validate the importance of a positive event and make the event more memorable over time than events that are unshared or shared but met with one of the other response types (Gable et al., 2004; Reis et al., 2010). More importantly, when people receive an active-constructive response to a capitalization attempt, they also perceive that they have available support in the relationship should a negative event occur. In other words, people perceive that those who celebrate their "highs" will also be there for them during their "lows" (e.g., Gable et al., 2012; Logan & Cobb, 2013). Sharing positive events and receiving an active-constructive response also enhances the relationship because capitalizers feel closer to and more trusting of others who provide active-constructive responses to capitalization attempts (Pagani et al., 2020; Reis et al., 2010). Further, as suggested previously, capitalization interactions can be one way for partners to co-experience positive affect and experience "love-the-emotion" (Brown & Fredrickson, 2021).

The benefits of sharing positive events and receiving an active-constructive response have been observed in early-stage relationships (e.g., Gable et al., 2004; Reis et al., 2010), in long-term established relationships lasting decades (e.g., Donato et al., 2014), and during particular relationship transitions, such as the transition to parenthood (Le et al., 2022), though capitalization may be associated with greater benefits earlier in relationships (Logan & Cobb, 2013). Of course, not everyone benefits from capitalization interactions equally; people with greater attachment avoidance tend to under-perceive their partners' active-constructive responses to their capitalization attempts, relative to trained coders who rate the interactions. Individuals with high attachment avoidance also have less active-constructive responses to their partners' capitalization attempts, especially if their partners are high in attachment anxiety (Gosnell & Gable, 2013; Shallcross et al., 2011). Cross-cultural work further suggests interesting context-dependent differences. In North American samples and cultures exposed to Western ideals (e.g., Taiwan), passive-constructive responses tend to have less positive consequences than active-constructive responses, but passive-constructive responses are as beneficial as active-constructive responses in Mainland China, where lower intensity emotions are considered culturally appropriate (Reis, Li et al., 2022).

Expressing Gratitude

People can share their good news; they can also share their gratitude. Gratitude is a positive emotion that someone feels toward another (i.e., a partner, friend, God) when they recognize that the other's actions have benefited them (Emmons, 2004). People can feel gratitude ("I feel appreciative that Jess helped me with the laundry"), express gratitude ("Hey Jess, thanks for helping me with the laundry"), and perceive another's gratitude ("Oh, that makes me feel so appreciated. Thanks for noticing!"), each of which produce relationship-enhancing benefits in early-stage and long-established relationships (e.g., Algoe et al., 2008; Algoe & Zhaoyang, 2016; Gordon et al., 2011). Feelings and expressions of gratitude can produce co-experienced positive emotion because people are more appreciative *of* their partners when they feel more appreciated *by* their partners (Gordon et al., 2012) and because expressing gratitude can lead to reciprocated expressions of gratitude ("No no thank *you*!). Conversations in which partners express gratitude also typically produce positive emotions (and reduce negative affect), which suggests that expressing gratitude could produce the co-experience of positive emotions beyond gratitude as well (Algoe & Zhaoyang, 2016).

In general, feelings of gratitude in ongoing close relationships result from perceived partner responsiveness, that is, believing a partner has behaved in a caring, understanding, or validating way (e.g., Algoe, 2012; Kubacka et al., 2011). These feelings of gratitude work to enhance a relationship by leading the expresser to focus their attention on positive aspects of both their partner and their relationship and by motivating the expresser to meet their partner's needs (Algoe & Haidt, 2009; Brady et al., 2021). Indeed, feeling grateful toward one's partner is associated with broad relationship benefits, such as greater relationship satisfaction, greater enactment of relationship maintenance behaviors, greater motivation to meet a partner's sexual needs, and greater relationship stability over time (Algoe et al., 2010; Brady et al., 2020; Gordon et al., 2012; Kubacka et al., 2011).

Expressing gratitude is sometimes called a relationship "booster shot" (Algoe et al., 2010) because it can directly enhance relationship well-being. Expressing gratitude motivates the expresser to behave in ways that benefit their partner and protect the relationship (Lambert et al., 2010; Lambert & Fincham, 2011). It can also lead a partner (the benefactor of this expression) to not only feel appreciated, understood, and cared for, but to also behave more responsively themselves as a result (Algoe et al., 2013; Gordon et al., 2012). People report greater feelings of connection and relationship satisfaction after their partners express gratitude toward them in daily life, and interventions that increase both partners' expressions of gratitude enhance their relationship satisfaction and boost their positive emotions (Algoe et al., 2010; Algoe & Zhaoyang, 2016). Perceiving a partner's gratitude also buffers negative links between attachment insecurity (particularly attachment avoidance) and relationship satisfaction, and buffers the harmful relational consequences of destructive conflict behavior and perceiving an unequal division of household labor (Barton et al., 2015; Gordon et al., 2022; Park et al., 2019). Expressions of gratitude, however, generate benefits only when they are perceived to be sincere and when they do, in fact, make benefactors feel understood, validated, and cared for (Algoe et al., 2013; Algoe & Zhaoyang, 2016; Leong et al., 2020). Unsurprisingly, people differ in their experience and expressions of gratitude. People with high attachment avoidance experience less gratitude toward their partners than people with lower attachment avoidance, and expressions of gratitude are more common from people in lower positions toward people in higher positions of power than vice versa (Anicich et al., 2021; Vollmann et al., 2019).

Communicating Affection

How do you show someone you love them? In *This Is Us*, Jack (the show's patriarch) tells Rebecca, "I love you as much as a human heart can love"; Beth (Randall's partner) declares, "When I look in your eyes, I see my home. I see eternity"; and Toby (Kate's partner) confesses, "The one thing I cannot live without is you" (Sprankles, 2021). These statements are examples of **affectionate communication**, the words, gestures, or other expressions we use to convey our feelings of love, closeness, and fondness for others (Floyd & Morman, 1998). According to **affection exchange theory**, all people have an inborn need and capacity to express and receive affection because affectionate communication is evolutionarily adaptive (Floyd, 2006, 2019). More specifically, adults who engage in affectionate communication are more likely to survive and reproduce because affectionate communication (1) enhances pair-bonds (i.e., fosters meaningful connection between people to improve or maintain relationship quality), (2) demonstrates parenting potential ("they're so affectionate with me – they'll make a great parent"), and (3) regulates physiological and psychological processes that mitigate stress and improve personal well-being (Floyd, 2019; Jakubiak & Feeney, 2017). Thus, aligning with evolutionary and attachment perspectives, affectionate communication is a means by which we can promote both personal and relational benefits (for reviews, see Denes, Bennett et al., 2017; Floyd, 2019; Hesse, Floyd et al., 2021; Jakubiak & Feeney, 2017). What exactly can people do to engage in affectionate communication?

RESEARCHER SPOTLIGHT: Kory Floyd, PhD

How did you come to be a communication researcher?

I have always been interested in how people make sense of each other and come together to form relationships. Unfortunately, I didn't discover the academic discipline of communication until after my undergraduate experience, but once I did, I realized that's what I wanted to do for my career.

What led you to develop affection exchange theory?

As a younger person, I was always perplexed about why some people were open to giving and receiving affection and others weren't. Most close relationships rely on the exchange of affection to some degree, yet there's a lot of variation in how affection is given and what it means. When I started to study affectionate communication, I saw the need for a theory that addressed *why* people communicate affection, rather than simply *how* they do so, and affection exchange theory was the result.

Figure 10.11 Dr. Kory Floyd is a professor in the Department of Communication at the University of Arizona. (Source: Photo by Michael Chansley)

What aspects of affection exchange theory do you think are most applicable to students' lives?

To me, the most important lesson in the theory is that we benefit from affection – and not just when we receive it. We benefit when we give it. That's useful to remember, because when we feel overwhelmed or stressed, we don't have to wait for others to come to our rescue. We can help our bodies and minds recover by offering affection to the people we care about.

What are some of the frontiers in research on positive processes, affection, and/or communication that you see as critical for studying in the future?

One provocative question is where our tendency to be affectionate comes from. We certainly learn how and when to communicate affection through our socialization processes, but I believe we also inherit a tendency to be more affectionate or less affectionate from our parents genetically. Some research bears this out, but much more is left to be learned.

How We Communicate Affection

Did you express affection for anyone in the past 24 hours? If so, to whom, and what exactly did you do? When a nationally representative sample of American adults were asked these questions, a large majority (84 percent) reported yes, they expressed affection in the last 24 hours (Floyd et al., 2021). Among the people who reported expressing affection, they indicated having engaged in approximately six unique expressions of affection in that time, on average. Although the extent to which people express affection varies (as we will review below), expressing affection is ubiquitous in close relationships around the world

Figure 10.12 People will go to great lengths (and great heights) to express their affection for one another. How do you express your affection for loved ones? (Photo: Image Source / DigitalVision / Getty Images)

(Caldwell-Harris et al., 2013; Floyd, 2019; Sorokowska et al., 2021). In the American sample (Floyd et al., 2021), people most commonly reported expressing affection in the past day to their romantic partners (43 percent of reports of expressed affection), children (22 percent), and friends (9 percent). Less common – though also present – were expressions of affection for other relatives (e.g., parents, siblings), casual acquaintances, co-workers, and even strangers. This pattern is consistent cross-culturally as well (Sorokowska et al., 2021). When over 14,000 participants from forty-five countries were asked whether they had expressed physical affection (i.e., embraced, stroked, hugged, or kissed) to close others in the past week, the prevalence of affectionate touch provision (the percent of people who said yes) was higher toward romantic partners (93 percent) and children (91 percent) than toward female friends (80 percent) and male friends (63 percent).

Perhaps even more interesting are the various ways in which people report expressing affection (Figure 10.12). According to the **tripartite model of affectionate communication**, people typically express their affection for one another in three common ways (Floyd & Morman, 1998). First, people commonly express affection verbally (i.e., **verbal affection**), by speaking or writing statements that convey their affectionate feelings. The phrase, "I love you," is a prototypical example of verbal affection, but compliments and expressions of appreciation can also be part of this category. Second, people show (rather than tell) their affection by providing various forms of **non-verbal affection**. **Affectionate touch** behaviors, such as kissing, hugging, caressing, cuddling, and even giving high-fives and fist bumps (Gallace & Spence, 2010; Jakubiak & Feeney, 2017), are perhaps the most obvious and salient examples of non-verbal affection. However, this category also includes close physical proximity (e.g., sitting close), smiling, laughing, eye contact, and attentive listening (Coduto & Eveland Jr, 2022; Hesse, Floyd et al., 2021; Twardosz et al., 1979).

Finally, people can communicate their affection indirectly by offering **supportive affection**, behaviors such as offering social support (e.g., helping with problems, providing encouragement), acknowledging accomplishments, and/or celebrating special occasions (e.g., a birthday; Floyd, 2019; Floyd & Morman, 1998). These behaviors are considered forms of affectionate communication if they are enacted with the purpose of conveying closeness, care, or fondness (Hesse, Floyd et al., 2021). People sometimes provide supportive affection when they are unsure whether affectionate communication is appropriate (e.g., whether affectionate feelings are reciprocated) and they want to maintain plausible deniability if their affection is rejected (e.g., "I was just being nice. It didn't mean anything. I would do that for anyone.").

Remember the sample of American adults who were asked if they expressed affection in the past 24 hours? In their responses, these same adults spontaneously reported using each of

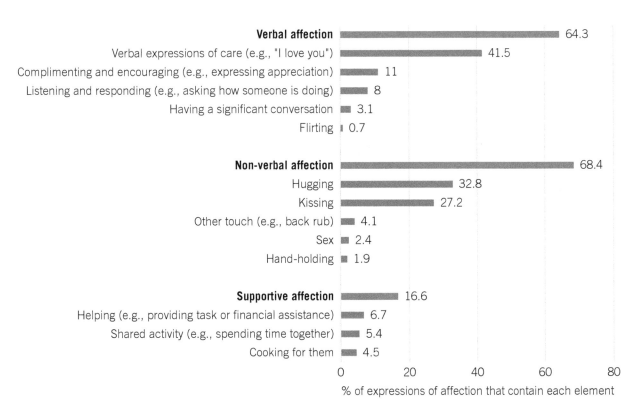

Figure 10.13 How do Americans express affection? Participants described each time they expressed affection to someone in the past 24 hours, and the content of their responses was coded and categorized. The red bars show the percent of expressions of affection that were categorized broadly as verbal affection, non-verbal affection, and supportive affection (note that one expression of affection could be categorized in more than one category). The green bars show the percent of expressions of affection that included each specific behavior. (Source: Drawn based on data from Floyd et al. [2021])

these three forms of affectionate communication (verbal, non-verbal, and supportive), lending support for this tripartite model (Floyd et al., 2021). As shown in Figure 10.13, Americans' recent expressions of affection typically include verbal affection (64 percent) and/or non-verbal affection (68 percent), with supportive affection occurring also, but at a lower rate (17 percent). The most common affectionate behaviors appear to be verbal expressions of care, such as "I love you" (42 percent), hugs (33 percent), and kisses (27 percent).

Although the tripartite model of affectionate communication has received empirical support, it was developed and has been tested primarily in American samples that are predominantly Caucasian and middle-class (Floyd, 2019). The specific ways that people express affection likely varies in other populations, an important avenue for future research.

 IS THIS TRUE FOR YOU?

Do You Have a "Love Language"?

Do you typically say, "I love you," or plan a date to show that you care? Do you feel more loved when someone offers a warm embrace or a homemade cookie? Is there another way that you prefer to provide and receive affection? According to Gary Chapman, author of the bestselling book, *The Five Love Languages: How to Express Heartfelt Commitment to Your Mate* (Chapman, 2009), people use five unique "languages" to communicate their love and affection for their romantic partners: words of affirmation, physical touch, acts, or service, quality time, and gifts (see Table 10.2 for examples). These love languages include many of the same behaviors described in the tripartite model of affectionate communication, but the categories are parsed somewhat differently.

Table 10.2 The five proposed "love languages"

Love language	Example behaviors (from Egbert & Polk's (2006) Love Language Scale)
Words of affirmation	• Complimenting my partner • Telling my partner that I appreciate them
Physical touch	• Hugging my partner • Holding my partner's hand
Acts of service	• Running errands for my partner • Finishing a chore for my partner when they don't have time to do it
Quality time	• Spending time doing something we both like • Having a quality conversation
Gifts	• Giving my partner a surprise present when there's no special occasion • Picking up a greeting card for my partner

Source: Based on data from Chapman (2009).

Chapman (2009) argues that each person has a primary love language, one way that they prefer to use to give and receive affection. Further, he suggests that the alignment between partners' love languages (whether they "speak" the same or different love languages) impacts their relationship quality. Imagine the frustration if someone prioritizes spending the day with their partner (their own love language) only to be criticized for never showing they care (by being physically affectionate, their partner's apparent love language). Can you recall times when your attempts to express affection were unappreciated or misunderstood?

Despite the popular appeal of this "love language" perspective of affectionate communication, it currently lacks empirical support (e.g., Bunt & Hazelwood, 2017; Surijah et al., 2021). Available evidence does not support the claim that people are primarily mono-lingual with regard to communicating affection. Instead, the extent to which people endorse using one love language to communicate affection correlates strongly with the extent to which they use other love languages as well (Egbert & Polk, 2006). Further, when people are forced to choose just one primary love language, their selection does not reliably predict their endorsement of particular affectionate communication strategies (i.e., a person who self-identifies as preferring gifts may be just as likely to engage in acts of service as someone who self-identifies as preferring acts of service; Polk, 2013).

Empirical research has also failed to support Chapman's (2009) claim that couples who share the same love language (i.e., those who are aligned) report higher relationship quality than those who are misaligned (Bunt & Hazelwood, 2017). Most people (over 75 percent) may be able to accurately report their partner's preferred love language, but this knowledge fails to predict relationship quality. It may be that couples communicate affection in multiple ways or that couples interpret their partners' behaviors as affectionate, even when they're speaking in a non-preferred love language. The good news then is that giving effective affectionate communication, and perceiving a partner's affection, may not be as difficult as the love languages perspective would suggest.

Who Expresses Affection?

Although affectionate communication is pervasive, people vary considerably in the extent to which they express affection. Would you consider yourself to be an "affectionate" person, or do you tend to keep your affection for others to yourself? Note that we are focused on *expressing* affection, which does not necessarily equate to *experiencing* affection; people can (and do) experience affection without choosing to express it. Try completing the Trait Affection Scale, shown in Table 10.3, to evaluate your own trait affection level, the extent to which you easily and comfortably express affection to other people.

Table 10.3 Items from Trait Affection Given Scale

For each statement, circle one number to indicate your agreement or disagreement.	Strongly disagree						Strongly agree
I consider myself to be a very affectionate person.	1	2	3	4	5	6	7
I am always telling my loved ones how much I care about them.	1	2	3	4	5	6	7
When I feel affection for someone, I usually express it.	1	2	3	4	5	6	7
I have a hard time telling people that I love them or care about them.	7	6	5	4	3	2	1
I am not very good at expressing affection.	7	6	5	4	3	2	1
I love giving people hugs or putting my arms around them.	1	2	3	4	5	6	7
Expressing affection to other people makes me uncomfortable.	7	6	5	4	3	2	1

Sum your responses to assess the extent to which you tend to express affection in general. Higher scores indicate greater affection provision. Do you provide affection easily and often, or are you more reserved when it comes to showing your care?

Source: Copyright © 2002, Eastern Communication Association, reprinted by permission of Taylor & Francis Ltd, http://www.tandfonline.com on behalf of Eastern Communication Association; Floyd, K. (2002). Human affection exchange: V. Attributes of the highly affectionate. *Communication Quarterly, 50*(2), 135–152.

As the name of the scale implies, the degree to which people communicate affection is considered to be somewhat stable and trait-like. However, the extent to which someone expresses affection can also vary over time ("I was very affectionate when we were first married, but not anymore"), across relationship types ("I frequently hug my mom, but I rarely hug my friends"), and across forms of affection ("I avoid direct expressions of affection such as saying 'I love you' or giving hugs, but I often give gifts to show people I care"). Several factors contribute to whether people express affection. As we shall see, some of these factors can help us understand differences between people who express more or less affection, and some can help us to understand variations within people over time or across relationships.

To start, whether you are more or less affectionate may depend, in part, on your cultural context. The prevalence of affectionate communication varies cross-culturally (Mansson et al., 2016; Mansson & Sigurðardóttir, 2017; Seki et al., 2002; Sorokowska et al., 2021; Zhang & Wills, 2016), with people in individualistic cultures tending to rate themselves as more affectionate than people in collectivistic cultures (Mansson et al., 2016; Mansson & Sigurðardóttir, 2017). For instance, people in the United States – a country that is highly individualistic – report greater trait affection expression than people in Russia, Slovakia, Denmark, Iceland, Poland – all countries that are relatively more collectivistic (Mansson et al., 2016; Mansson & Sigurðardóttir, 2017). Specific forms of affection also vary cross-culturally. For instance, some evidence suggests Germans express less verbal affection than Americans and that American students see more value in saying "I love you" than Chinese students (Caldwell-Harris et al., 2013).

One recent study on affectionate touch, in particular, demonstrates both the cross-cultural prevalence of and cross-cultural variation in affectionate communication (Sorokowska et al., 2021). In this study, people reported whether they had (1) embraced, (2) stroked, (3) hugged, and/or (4) kissed their romantic partner over the past week. Figure 10.14 shows

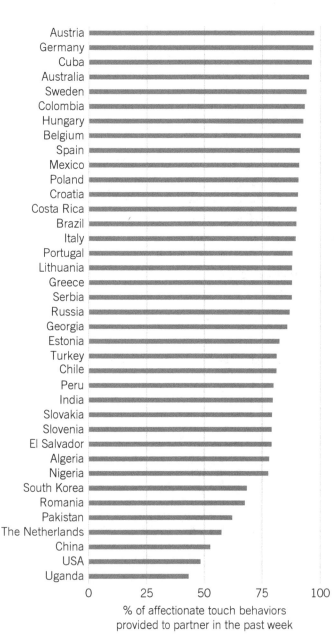

Figure 10.14 When over 14,000 participants from forty-five countries were asked whether they had embraced, stroked, hugged, or kissed their partner in the past week, participants in most countries endorsed at least three (75 percent) of the behaviors. Variability across cultures can help us to understand who is socialized to be physically affectionate. How does your culture compare to others? (Source: Drawn based on data from Sorokowska et al. [2021])

the percent of affection expression (0 percent = none of the behaviors, 100 percent = all of these behaviors) people reported on average, separated by country. In most countries, people reported providing three or more of the four affectionate behaviors to their partners in the past week, demonstrating a high prevalence of affectionate expression cross-culturally. However, the data show clear variability in how much people provide affectionate touch, with people expressing more affectionate touch in countries that are less conservative and less religious than in more conservative and religious countries (Sorokowska et al., 2021). People also reported expressing more affectionate touch in warmer climates, consistent with research that has classified countries closer to the equator (Mediterranean countries, countries in Central and South America) as "high-contact" cultures relative to the "low-contact" cultures located further from the equator (countries in Northern Asia, North America, and Northern Europe; e.g., Andersen, 2011; Dibiase & Gunnoe, 2004; Gallace & Spence, 2010; Remland et al., 1995). Other research has also revealed cultural differences in affectionate touch within countries. For instance, within the United States, Mexican Americans report more personal comfort with affectionate touch than European Americans (Burleson et al., 2019).

Your comfort expressing affection may also be related to your gender identity. Numerous studies have shown that women express more affection than men (e.g., Floyd, 2019; Floyd et al., 2021; Sorokowska et al., 2021). Women also report greater desire for affectionate communication (affectionate touch, in this study) than men in their dating and marital relationships (Jakubiak, Fuentes et al., 2021). Both cultural and gender differences in affectionate communication lend support to socio-cultural perspectives of affectionate communication, which suggest that people learn whether to communicate affection for others through socialization (Floyd, 2019). Specifically, people learn what is considered appropriate and acceptable behavior for a member of their gender and a member of their cultural group and display affection accordingly. Although socialization is surely part of the story, twin studies also show that approximately 45 percent of the variance in trait affectionate communication is heritable, revealing a genetic basis for affection expression as well (Floyd, York et al., 2020).

Attachment orientation also plays a role in whether people communicate affection. People who are securely attached (low on attachment anxiety and avoidance) report greater trait affectionate communication than people with high attachment anxiety, high attachment avoidance, or both (Floyd, 2002; Hesse & Trask, 2014). Greater attachment anxiety and attachment avoidance are also each associated with lower reported affectionate behavior (e.g., cuddling, having intimate conversation) following a sexual encounter (Bennett et al., 2019). Consistent with findings for affectionate communication broadly, greater attachment avoidance is associated with lower engagement in, initiation of, desire for, enjoyment of, and importance of affectionate touch in romantic relationships as well (e.g., Brennan, Clark et al., 1998; Carmichael et al., 2021; Jakubiak, Fuentes et al., 2021). People with high attachment avoidance also report less positive feelings toward cuddling with their partners and their children (Chopik, Edelstein et al., 2014). Conversely, greater attachment anxiety is associated with greater engagement in, initiation of, desire for, enjoyment of, and importance of affectionate touch in romantic relationships (Carmichael et al., 2021; Jakubiak, Fuentes et al., 2021).

Expressing affection for someone puts the expresser in a somewhat vulnerable position where they might be rejected or where the affection may not be reciprocated (Floyd & Pauley, 2011). Accordingly, some people opt to withhold their affection (express less affection than they feel) in order to avoid rejection or to avoid being seen as "clingy" or undesirable (Carton & Horan, 2014). People with lower self-esteem are especially sensitive to the perceived risks of expressing affection. Accordingly, people with low self-esteem tend to report less comfort expressing affection, give their partners fewer compliments (a form of verbal affection), and give compliments in a more half-hearted way than people with higher self-esteem (Luerssen et al., 2017). People also withhold affection in friends-with-benefits relationships and in cross-sex friendships more than in romantic relationships, perhaps because expressing affection in "casual" contexts threatens the status quo and may put the relationship at risk (Trask et al., 2020).

 DIVERSITY AND INCLUSION

Expressing Affection in Stigmatized Relationships

Expressing affection toward a partner is particularly risky (and therefore less common) for people in stigmatized relationships, who may face rejection or discrimination from people outside of the relationship when they express affection publicly (Formby, 2022; Kent & El-Alayli, 2011; Stammwitz & Wessler, 2021). Undergraduate students report that they are less comfortable with public displays of affection (PDA) from same-sex couples than opposite-sex couples and are least comfortable with PDA involving transgender individuals (Buck et al., 2019). In turn, LGBT+ people report that they avoid PDA, such as holding hands or kissing in public, to avoid making people uncomfortable and to prevent experiences of discrimination or hostility (Formby, 2022). For instance, women in same-sex relationships express less affection in public than people in different-sex relationships, a finding that is explained by greater perceived social disapproval (Kent & El-Alayli, 2011).

Other research shows that people in same-sex relationships express less affection in public particularly if they are experiencing high levels of minority stress (stress experienced due to sexual orientation), though this association appears to hold only for people with lower commitment to the relationship (Hocker et al., 2021). Participants with higher commitment report engaging in PDA regardless of the minority stress they experience (see Figure 10.15). This finding may seem to suggest that commitment might enhance affectionate communication; however, expressing affection despite minority stress may undermine the experience of expressing affection. Indeed, gender-diverse and sexually diverse individuals report that expressing affection in unsupportive contexts is less enjoyable than expressing affection in supportive

Figure 10.15 Same-sex partners, and other partners with stigmatized identities or relationship structures, may hesitate to express affection, especially in public. What do you think are the consequences of limiting affection in public? (Photo: MoMo Productions / DigitalVision / Getty Images)

contexts (Stammwitz & Wessler, 2021). Concerns about social disapproval or hostile reactions may also prevent people in other stigmatized relationships from expressing affection, especially in public. In a nationally representative sample of adolescent couples, interracial couples were less likely to engage in public and private displays of affection (e.g., holding hands) than intra-racial couples, but they were no less likely to kiss or have sexual intercourse in private (Vaquera & Kao, 2005).

Just as people can experience affection without expressing it (withheld affection), people can also express affection without feeling it (intensified affection). People express ingenuine affection to obtain favors ("You're my favorite lunch buddy! Hey, by the way, can you help me move next weekend?"), to avoid conflict or awkwardness ("I love you too …"), and to initiate sexual activity ("I want to take this relationship to the next level because I care so much about you"), among other motives (Bennett & Denes, 2019; Horan & Booth-Butterfield, 2019). Deceptive affection (withheld and/or intensified affection) during sexual activity is associated with lower sexual satisfaction as well as lower relationship satisfaction, suggesting that deceptive affection lacks the benefits that result from genuine expressions of affection. What are the benefits of communicating love and affection anyway? We review that next.

Consequences of Affectionate Communication

Put simply, available evidence suggests that communicating affection (both providing and receiving affection) in close relationships feels good, enhances relationship quality, and protects individual health and well-being. Before we go into greater detail on these benefits, pause and be sure to note that these benefits are observed *in the context of close relationships*, where affection is mutual (see Figure 10.16). These benefits do not generalize to affectionate

(a)   (b)

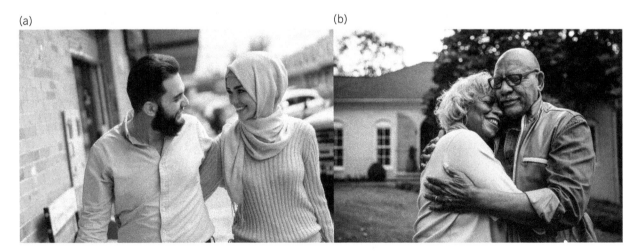

Figure 10.16 Both expressing affection for close others and receiving expressions of affection from close others promote relationship and personal well-being. How do you feel when you engage in affectionate communication? Does affectionate communication lead you to view your partner or relationship differently? (Photo: andresr / E+ / Getty Images [a] and MoMo Productions / DigitalVision / Getty Images [b])

communication in other contexts, such as with strangers, with casual acquaintances, or in relationships with complicated power structures like in the workplace. Unwanted affection – including unwanted physical contact, eye contact, statements such as "I love you," over-disclosure, and gifts – is perceived negatively and associated with stress and anxiety for the recipient (Van Raalte, Floyd, Kloeber et al., 2021). Providing unwanted affection can also be costly, as unwanted affection is often met with outright rejection or avoidance of future interactions (Van Raalte, Floyd, Kloeber et al., 2021). With these caveats in mind, what are the consequences of affectionate communication in close relationships?

Consistent with relational benefits of affectionate communication, romantic relationships that involve greater affectionate communication tend to be characterized by greater close-ness, intimacy, relationship satisfaction, sexual satisfaction, and perceived partner respon-siveness than those that involve less affectionate communication (Brennan, Wu et al., 1998; Debrot et al., 2017; Gulledge et al., 2003; Hesse & Tian, 2020; Jolink et al., 2021; Mackey et al., 2000; Muise et al., 2014; Van Raalte & Floyd, 2022). Contrastingly, **affection depriv-ation** (receiving less affection that one desires) is associated with poorer relationship satis-faction and greater relationship uncertainty (Floyd, 2014; Hesse & Mikkelson, 2017; Hesse & Tian, 2020). We see the link between affectionate communication and relationship satisfac-tion in different-sex romantic relationships, in romantic relationships involving LGBTQ + people (Haas & Lannutti, 2021), and in other close relationships, including friendships, sibling relationships, parent–child relationships, and grandparent–grandchild relationships (e.g., Floyd & Morman, 1998; Floyd & Morr, 2003; Mansson et al., 2017; Morman & Floyd, 1999; Russell, 1997).

Longitudinal and experimental findings provide more rigorous evidence that affectionate communication confers relational benefits. For instance, receiving or expressing affection at one time predicts subsequent increases in intimacy and relationship quality in romantic relationships (Debrot et al., 2013; Jakubiak, Debrot et al., 2021; Jakubiak & Feeney, 2018). Receiving affectionate touch in daily life is also associated with same-day increases in closeness, relationship quality, and perceived partner responsiveness – relational benefits that are observed even among people with high attachment avoidance, who report relatively low desire for and enjoyment of affectionate touch (Carmichael et al., 2021). Finally, couples who are instructed to increase their affectionate communication by kissing more frequently or cuddling more often report significant increases in relationship satisfaction (Floyd et al., 2009; Van Raalte, Floyd, & Mongeau, 2021). Affectionate communication thus not only occurs more often in happier relationships, but may directly improve relationship well-being.

Why might affectionate communication improve relationships? Several explanations have garnered empirical support. First, people who receive affection experience greater state security in the moment (i.e., they feel safe, loved, and cared for; Jakubiak, 2022; Jakubiak & Feeney, 2016a), which fosters relationship-enhancing perceptions and behaviors (e.g., Mikulincer et al., 2013; Mikulincer & Shaver, 2007, 2013, 2020). For instance, laboratory work shows that couples who are randomly assigned to touch affectionately while discussing ongoing conflicts communicate more constructively (e.g., greater cooperation, problem solving, accepting responsibility) than couples who are not assigned to express affection (Conradi et al., 2020; Jakubiak & Feeney, 2019). Partners are also more likely to prioritize shared activities and view their shared activities positively after engaging in affectionate behavior (Jakubiak et al., 2022). Spending shared time in this way contributes to relationship well-being broadly (see next section). Additionally, affectionate touch in daily life is associated with same-day increases in willingness to accommodate and sacrifice for one's partner (Carmichael et al., 2021). Affectionate communication may also improve relationship well-being by improving a couple's sexual relationship. For instance, people who report kissing their partner more frequently over the past year report better experiences in their most recent sexual encounter (e.g., greater arousal, greater sexual satisfaction, and a greater likelihood of experiencing orgasm), which contributes indirectly to greater overall sexual satisfaction and relationship satisfaction (Busby et al., 2020).

Finally, affectionate communication may have positive relationship consequences, in part, because affectionate communication confers personal benefits, which enable people to perceive their relationships more positively or behave more effectively in their relationships. One important personal consequence of affectionate communication is better stress regulation and recovery from stress (Floyd, Woo et al., 2020; Jakubiak & Feeney, 2017, 2018, 2019). For instance, people who express and/or receive more affection report less stress than people who express and/or receive less affection (e.g., Floyd, 2002; Jakubiak & Feeney, 2018). Further, daily fluctuations in affectionate touch behavior receipt coincide with daily fluctuations in stress and positive mood (e.g., Burleson et al., 2007; Debrot et al., 2020; Kolodziejczak et al., 2022). Intervention studies also show that people who are instructed to increase their affectionate behavior in daily life self-report lower stress and have lower alpha-amylase (a physiological marker of stress) than people who are not instructed to increase their affectionate communication (Floyd et al., 2009; Holt-Lunstad et al., 2008). Although affectionate communication is generally an effective stress buster, it works best in satisfying relationships; affectionate communication regulates stress less effectively in poorer quality relationships (Jakubiak, 2022; Van Raalte & Floyd, 2022).

The benefits of affectionate communication in close relationships is not limited to relationships; it extends to individuals. People who engage in more affectionate touch report better psychological well-being than those who give and receive less affection, and like the relational benefits of affectionate touch reported above, these personal benefits are observed even for people with high attachment avoidance, who report less desire for and enjoyment of affectionate touch (Debrot et al., 2020). Affectionate communication is also health-protective; a meta-analysis of forty-four empirical studies (and over 6,000 participants) showed that people who engage in greater affectionate communication report better physical and mental health outcomes, such as lower depression, anxiety, and stress reactivity, as well as better cardiovascular health and sleep quality (Hesse, Floyd et al., 2021). These links did not differ based on participants' sex or based on the form of affectionate communication (e.g., verbal versus non-verbal). Consistent with benefits of affectionate communication, self-reported affection deprivation is instead associated with poorer health, poorer sleep quality, and greater pain, depression, and loneliness (Floyd, 2014, 2016; Floyd & Hesse, 2017; Hesse, Mikkelson et al., 2021; Hesse & Mikkelson, 2017; Hesse & Tian, 2020). Affectionate communication even seems to boost immunity: people who receive more frequent hugs are less likely to become sick when they are exposed to a virus than people who receive fewer hugs (Cohen et al., 2015). Perhaps we should all consider adding a "hug a day" to our "apple a day" regimen to keep the doctor away.

Although affectionate communication in close relationships typically benefits both the relationships and individual functioning, could there be too much of a good thing? Affection exchange theory proposes that people have an "optimal tolerance" for affectionate behavior, meaning that they have both a minimal acceptable amount of affection that they need and a maximum amount that they desire (Floyd, 2019; Hesse & Mikkelson, 2021; Hesse & Tian, 2020). Based on this theory, both affection deprivation (discussed above) and excessive affection (receiving more affection than is desired) should predict poorer relationship outcomes. Consistent with this theory, children receiving more affection than desired from their parents tend to report poorer relationship satisfaction, life satisfaction, and self-esteem (Hesse et al., 2018). Excessive affection is similarly costly in romantic relationships, corresponding with lower relationship satisfaction and commitment, as well as greater stress and loneliness (Hesse & Mikkelson, 2021). Surprisingly, excessive affection in romantic relationships still predicts greater life satisfaction, suggesting that some benefits of affectionate communication may persist even when affection is perceived as excessive (Hesse & Mikkelson, 2021). All in all, affective communication is rife with potential to support relational and personal well-being, provided people respect its contextual boundaries and strive for optimal levels.

The Role of Approach Motivation

Positive interpersonal processes clearly improve relationships . . . but you need motivation to enact them. As described at the beginning of the chapter, people have both an appetitive system that motivates them to seek rewarding experiences (e.g., pleasure, intimacy) and an inhibitory system that motivates them to avoid aversive experiences (e.g., pain, embarrassment, conflict). Further, the extent to which people are motivated by the appetitive and inhibitory systems varies. People with high approach relationship goals are strongly motivated to achieve positive outcomes, such as growth and intimacy, in their relationships. In contrast, people with high avoidance relationship goals are strongly motivated to avoid negative outcomes – such as rejection or conflict – in their relationships (Gable & Impett, 2012). Which describes your motivational tendencies in relationships? Review Table 10.4 to gauge your approach and avoidance relationship goals in the domain of friendship.

Research suggests that the extent to which people endorse approach relationship goals is of particular relevance to whether and how they experience positive interpersonal processes. First, having stronger approach relationship goals increases the likelihood that people will engage in positive interpersonal processes (e.g., Elliot et al., 2006; Gable, 2006). For instance, greater social approach motivation is associated with a greater likelihood of engaging in self-expanding activities (Harasymchuk et al., 2020, 2021; Mattingly et al., 2012). People who are motivated to achieve positive relationship outcomes plan dates that are more exciting and more self-expanding than people with less approach motivation (Harasymchuk et al., 2021). Additionally, people (regardless of their typical approach relationship goals) are also more likely to engage in self-expanding activities, and experience the associated relational benefits, on days when they personally have greater approach motivation to achieve positive relationship outcomes (Harasymchuk et al., 2020).

Table 10.4 Approach and avoidance social goals in friendships

For each statement, circle one number to indicate your agreement or disagreement.	Not at all true of me					Very true of me	
Approach							
I am trying to deepen my relationship with my friends this semester.	1	2	3	4	5	6	7
I am trying to move toward growth and development in my friendships this semester.	1	2	3	4	5	6	7
I am trying to enhance the bonding and intimacy in my close relationships this semester.	1	2	3	4	5	6	7
I am trying to share many fun and meaningful experiences with my friends this semester.	1	2	3	4	5	6	7
Avoidance							
I am trying to avoid disagreements and conflicts with my friends this semester.	1	2	3	4	5	6	7
I am trying to stay away from situations that could harm my friendships this semester.	1	2	3	4	5	6	7
I am trying to avoid getting embarrassed, betrayed, or hurt by any of my friends this semester.	1	2	3	4	5	6	7
I am trying to make sure that nothing bad happens to my close relationships this semester.	1	2	3	4	5	6	7

Evaluate the extent to which you are approach and avoidance motivated in your own friendships.

Source: Elliot et al. (2006), reproduced with permission from Sage Publications.

Second, having stronger approach relationship goals amplifies the impact of positive interpersonal interactions when they do occur (Don et al., 2020; Jakubiak, Debrot et al., 2021). For instance, gratitude and capitalization interactions are more impactful for people with stronger (versus weaker) approach relationship goals. For these people, gratitude and capitalization especially facilitate positive emotions and perceived partner responsiveness. Affectionate behavior is also especially impactful when enacted for approach-motivated reasons (Jakubiak, Debrot et al., 2021). People who touch affectionately to achieve positive outcomes for themselves (to feel good, to feel taken care of) and their partners (to make their partners feel good, to show their partners they are there for them) experience greater daily relationship satisfaction than people who touch affectionately without or with less approach motivation (Jakubiak, Debrot et al., 2021). These findings suggest that efforts to develop interventions that incorporate positive interpersonal processes (e.g., a gratitude enhancement intervention, an affectionate communication intervention) may need to target not only behavior, but also motivation to enhance relationship well-being.

Conclusion

In this chapter, you learned about the positive interpersonal processes that enhance close relationships to promote relationship maintenance. We reviewed positive and negative interpersonal processes as separate processes and acknowledged how positive interactions can soften the impact of negative interactions. We also discussed how partners can leverage shared time by engaging in self-expanding activities, how partners can co-experience positive emotions (love-the-emotion) through shared laughter, capitalization, and expressing gratitude, and how partners can communicate love and affection in verbal and non-verbal ways to enhance their relationships. In the next chapter, we turn our attention toward another behavior with relationship-enhancing effects, but one that has so much complexity and variability that it requires its own chapter. How does sexuality shape relationship experiences?

Major Take-Aways

- Positive and negative interactions are not two opposite poles on the same dimension; they are best understood as separate, but related, relationship components. As such, avoiding negative interactions is insufficient; people want and benefit from positive interpersonal processes.
- Shared time is associated with improvements in relationship well-being, but not all shared time is created equal. Activities that provide opportunities for ongoing self-expansion (i.e., novel and exciting activities) enable partners to maintain passion, stave off boredom, and enhance their relationships over the long term.

- Experiencing positive emotions is good, and co-experiencing positive emotions is better. Partners who share and celebrate good news, laugh together, and feel and express gratitude for each other can enhance their relationships by providing opportunities for positive emotion to resonate and reverberate between them.
- Expressing love and affection is a common and effective strategy to enhance relationships. When people say, "I love you," embrace, or provide support to demonstrate their affection, they and their partners benefit. Strong approach relationship goals support the expression of affectionate communication and other positive interpersonal processes.

Further Readings

If you're interested in ...
... the predictors and consequences of affectionate touch, read:
Carmichael, C. L., Goldberg, M. H., & Coyle, M. A. (2021). Security-based differences in touch behavior and its relational benefits. *Social*

Psychological and Personality Science, 12(4), 550–560.

... how approach motives enhance the impact of positive relationship experiences, read:
Don, B. P., Fredrickson, B. L., & Algoe, S. B. (2022). Enjoying the sweet moments: Does

approach motivation upwardly enhance reactivity to positive interpersonal processes? *Journal of Personality and Social Psychology, 122*(6), 1022–1055.

... how partners in same-sex and different-sex relationships spend their time together, read:

Genadek, K. R., Flood, S. M., & Roman, J. G. (2020). Same-sex couples' shared time in the United States. *Demography, 57*(2), 475–500.

... the relational consequences of engaging in novel and exciting behaviors with a partner, read:

Muise, A., Harasymchuk, C., Day, L. C., Bacev-giles, C., Gere, J., & Impett, E. A. (2019). Broadening your horizons: Self-expanding activities promote desire and satisfaction in established romantic relationships. *Journal of Personality and Social Psychology, 116*(2), 237–258.

... why capitalization offers relational benefits, read:

Walsh, C. M., & Neff, L. A. (2020). The importance of investing in your relationship: Emotional capital and responses to partner transgressions. *Journal of Social and Personal Relationships, 37*(2), 581–601.

11 ENHANCING RELATIONSHIPS THROUGH SEXUAL INTIMACY

What Makes for a Satisfying Sex Life?

Figure 11.1 Willow Smith is polyamorous not because it might offer new ways to fulfill her sexual needs, but rather because the relationship structure feels right to her. What (mis)conceptions do you hold about who has sex, how frequently, and why? (Photo: Jerritt Clark / Getty Images Entertainment)

The complete recipe may yet be allusive, but many people have strong ideas about what promotes and impedes a thriving sex life. One such idea is that monogamy fosters the best sex life (e.g., most exciting, satisfying) relative to other relationship structures (Conley et al., 2013). This perspective, however, garners little empirical support. Yes, many monogamous partners relish in the pleasure of a satisfying sex life, but on average, consensually non-monogamous (CNM) partners report that they are happier with their sex lives than monogamous partners (Conley et al., 2018; Cox, Fleckenstein et al., 2021). People also hold misconceptions about the uniformity of sex within particular relationship structures. For example, though CNM partners tend to have more sex than the general population *on average*, CNM partners actually differ a great deal in how often they have sex (Conley et al., 2018; Cox, Fleckenstein et al., 2021). Willow Smith (Figure 11.1), an American artist and child of celebrities Will and Jada Smith, has spoken publicly about practicing polyamory and has pointedly asserted that she has the "least sex" of her friends, all of whom practice monogamy (Beck, 2021). For Smith, the benefits of consensual non-monogamy center on the "freedom to be able to create a relationship style that works for you," not the access to multiple sexual partners (Newsbeat, 2021).

Willow's self-disclosure is an important reminder that people navigate sex and sexual intimacy in varied ways, and not always in ways we might predict. Some people with a strong desire for sex have not had sex in years, while others, who have little desire for sex, are regularly sexually active (Bogaert, 2015; de Oliveira et al., 2021). Single individuals may or may not be having sex; people in committed relationships may or may not be having sex. When people do engage in sex, they begin at different ages, they have sex for varied reasons, and they might accumulate hundreds or only one partner over their lifetime. How do we make sense of such diversity? Happily, relationship scholars are inspired by variation in the ifs, whens, hows, and whys of people's sexual desires, beliefs, and behaviors. Relationship scientists strive not only to describe how people pursue, enact, and manage sexual intimacy in their relationships, but to identify the precursors and outcomes of different approaches to sex. As you read this chapter, your goal is to gain a greater understanding of human sexual intimacy and its role in relationship well-being.

 GUIDING QUESTIONS

Consider these questions as you read this chapter:
- To what extent is there commonality and diversity in people's sexual desires, sexual attitudes, motives for sex, and sexual behaviors?
- How often do people have sex and what are the implications of more, or less, frequent sex?
- How do people maintain satisfying sex lives, and how is sexual satisfaction related to relationship well-being more broadly?
- How do people initiate sex in casual contexts and in the contexts of ongoing relationships?

Dimensions of and Variations in Sexuality

Sex, or the broader term, sexuality, is a profoundly important relationship experience. Not to be dramatic, but the literal survival of our species is largely dependent on sex. Accordingly, humans have evolved a sexual behavioral system that generates sexual desire and sparks romantic and sexual behavior, with the primary purpose of enabling reproduction. This sexual behavioral system is distinct from the attachment behavioral system (Diamond, 2013; Fisher et al., 2002). In other words, by design, people can "mate without bonding" and they can "bond without mating" (Diamond, 2003). However, the fact that they *can* does not mean that they *do*. These separate systems often work together, meaning that casual sex does not always turn out to be casual.

Indeed, another evolved purpose of the sexual behavior system is to promote emotional connection and fuel enduring attachments (Figure 11.2), each of which could be reproductively advantageous, evolutionarily speaking (Fletcher et al., 2015). The built-in capacity for sex to facilitate attachment may explain why people "catch feelings" in sexual encounters that they had intended to enjoy without emotions involved, and why sex with an ex-partner is pursued more by people with lingering attachments (Paul, 2013; Spielmann et al., 2019). Sex as an attachment mechanism also helps explain why people have sex when it cannot lead

Figure 11.2 The sexual system and the attachment system are separate, yet they work together. In what ways might sex support emotional connection? (Photo: MoMo Productions / DigitalVision / Getty Images)

to reproduction, which – if these were separate systems – would not occur. Older adults, partners who cannot conceive (or are already pregnant), and same-sex partners regularly engage in sex, but not for reproductive purposes. As we will see, people have sex for many reasons, but love and connection are often high on the list, a nod to the strong link between the sexual system and the attachment system (J. R. Wood et al., 2014; Wyverkens et al., 2018).

An increasing body of research suggests that how people experience sex over the course of their lives is linked to their life satisfaction, mood, sense of meaning, and overall well-being (Kashdan et al., 2018; Park, Impett, & MacDonald, 2021; Schmiedeberg et al., 2017; Stephenson & Meston, 2015). Despite this, many of us know a lot more about how we should manage our sleep, nutrition, fitness, work projects, and household chores than we do about optimizing our sex lives. Whether you are single, in a committed relationship, or somewhere in between, understanding the sexual side of your life experience begins with understanding all its facets. Sexuality is multidimensional (Sprecher et al., 2018). It includes, for instance, people's desire or drive for sex, their attitudes and beliefs about sex, the physical behaviors that constitute a sexual experience, and their motives for engaging in sexual activity. To say that sexuality involves a wide range of relationship-relevant constructs is thus no understatement.

Sexual Desire

Wanting sex and thinking about sex are a natural part of being human. We can see considerable variation between people (e.g., see the *Diversity and Inclusion* box) and we can expect an ebb and flow within any given person's life course, yet yearning for and thinking about sex are meaningful features of the human experience. These motivational aspects of sexuality are subsumed in the term **sexual desire** (Diamond, 2004). Sexual desire is often referred to as sex drive, but is slightly broader, inclusive of all that propels individuals toward engaging in sexual activity. As such, sexual desire captures variation in the intensities of people's sexual pursuits, their perceived sexual needs, and their ideals for engaging in sexual activity.

Biological Bases for Sexual Desire

From a biological standpoint, human sexual desire reflects the complex workings of a sophisticated excitatory and inhibitory system (Pfaus, 2009). The field's increasing understanding of the neuroanatomy of sexual desire points to the roles of multiple brain structures, many of which are part of the limbic system (i.e., the hippocampus, amygdala, hypothalamus, and thalamus), and to a collection of hormones, neuropeptides, and neurotransmitters (e.g., testosterone, oxytocin, norepinephrine) that also play a role in modulating sexual desire (Calabrò et al., 2019). One primary driver in facilitating sex appears to be the dopaminergic system. In the excitatory phase, dopamine supports sexual arousal, which includes (1) a physiological response that helps prepare people for sex (e.g., an erection; vaginal lubrication) and (2) heightened thoughts and motivations toward sex (Alley & Diamond, 2020; Calabrò et al., 2019; Pfaus, 2009). A critical counterpoint to sexual excitation is sexual inhibition. Along with other substances (e.g., natural opioids), serotonin levels may play a key role in the lowering or inhibition of sexual desire (Olivier et al., 2019).

As robust as human sexual desire is (there are, after all, nearly 8 billion people on Earth), the sequence of biological responses required to promote sex is delicate, susceptible to interference. Alcohol, for instance, can lower sexual inhibitions but decrease sexual function, and antidepressants, such as those that alter serotonin levels, can profoundly dampen sexual desire and arousal (Peugh & Belenko, 2001; Serretti & Chiesa, 2009). Similarly, as much as marijuana may have an enhancing effect on the subjective experience of sex for women and men, it can, at higher doses, negatively affect men's sexual function (Lynn et al., 2019; Rajanahally et al., 2019). Sex is not affected only by substances. Critically, sexual desire and sexual arousal are connected to systems that control attention, interpret stimuli, and make decisions. The thoughts people have as they move through time toward the possibility of sex are essential to determining whether and when sex happens. A biological underpinning might provide the possibility for sex (in the absence of dysfunction), but sex and sexual desire are profoundly psychological (Brotto et al., 2016).

Variability in Sexual Desire

What kinds of variability do we see in sexual desire? This question usually begins with a consideration of gender, typically from a binary perspective: do men or women have stronger sexual desire? If you guessed "men!" your response has good empirical backing. Men, for instance, tend to think about sex more frequently than women, they engage in more sexual fantasies, they masturbate more, and they imagine having sex with other people more often than women do (Archer, 2019; Baumeister et al., 2001; Hicks & Leitenberg, 2001). In cross-cultural work sampling from ten world regions, men consistently desire more sexual partners over both the short term and long term than women, a finding that stands regardless of sexual orientation and relationship status (Schmitt et al., 2003). Other cross-cultural research, as shown in Figure 11.3, adds to the preponderance of data that suggest men have stronger sexual desire than women (Lippa, 2009).

Some scholars, however, question the strength and stability of this gender difference (Conley et al., 2011; Dawson & Chivers, 2014). Men, for example, have been shown to inflate their self-reported sexual interests and activities to adhere with perceived norms, and, while men may think about sex more than women, they also think about other needs (e.g., food, sleep) more than women (Alexander & Fisher, 2003; T. D. Fisher et al., 2012). Other research reminds us not to assume a biological origin of lower sex drive among women. Entrenched gender inequities that include disproportional household/childcare work, multiple roles, and objectification, for example, may induce stress, among other consequences, that make sex less desirable for women (van Anders et al., 2021). Applying a critical eye is appropriate. Even as most research still points to a gender difference in sexual desire, the magnitude of this gender difference may be smaller than people tend to assume. This is consistent with

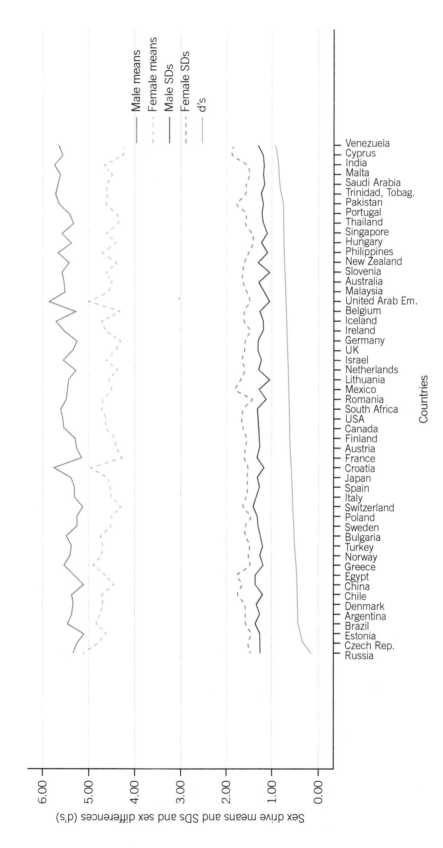

Figure 11.3 If gender differences in sexual desire exist, how would you explain them? The wave of these parallel lines shows cultural variability, even as men tend to report stronger sexual desires across all fifty-three surveyed countries. (Source: Adapted by permission from: Lippa, R. A. [2009], Sex differences in sex drive, sociosexuality, and height across 53 nations: Testing evolutionary and social structural theories, *Archives of Sexual Behavior*, 38, 631–651; with permission of Springer Nature)

meta-analytic work suggesting that *within* gender differences are larger than *between* gender differences when it comes to sexuality (Petersen & Hyde, 2010).

Variability in sexual desire may also be linked to personality. Some research suggests that extroverts have more sexual desire than introverts, and that the more open, less neurotic, less conscientious, and less agreeable people are, the stronger their sexual desire tends to be (Allen & Walter, 2018). Dark Triad traits also predict higher sexual desire, and this association is especially strong for individuals higher in psychopathy, whose sexual fantasies also cover a particularly broad scope of themes (Baughman et al., 2014). The low commitment sexual relationships to which people higher in Dark Triad traits gravitate bear witness to their strong sexual desire: higher levels of each of the Dark Triad traits are associated with stronger preferences for one-night stands, booty-calls, and friends-with-benefits (Jonason et al., 2012; Koladich & Atkinson, 2016).

In addition to personality, scholars have identified age and relationship length as predictors of sexual desire. As you might imagine, older adults tend to report lower sexual desire than younger adults (but not all older adults!). In one study, only 5 percent of 45 to 49 year old adults reported low sexual desire, but this number climbed to over 59 percent among 80- to 83-year-old adults (DeLamater & Sill, 2005). These findings still suggest that a solid proportion of older adults report high sex drives. People (especially women) may also experience an age-related "peak" in their sexual desires. For many women, this sexual peak may occur between 30 and 34, possibly to support reproductive goals within established relationships (Schmitt et al., 2002). In general, compared to men's sexual desire, women's sexual desire may fluctuate more, be more sensitive to sociocultural forces, and show less stability in response to relationship-related events (Baumeister, 2000; Lippa, 2009). As committed relationships mature, for example, women's sexual desire tends to decrease, whereas the sexual desire of their male partners stays more consistent (Klusmann, 2002; McNulty et al., 2019).

These declines in sexual desire are neither inevitable nor universal (Impett, Strachman et al., 2008), and the magnitude of change can also show diversity, yet these declines in sexual desire are worth noting – particularly in light of relationship transitions. Consider the major relationship transition of entering parenthood (Figure 11.4).

A study of different-sex parents showed that new mothers' sexual desire declines on average from mid-pregnancy through the transition into parenthood, beginning to rebound after three months post-partum (Rosen et al., 2021). Some mothers, however, begin pregnancy with relatively higher sexual desire and never decline to moderate or low sexual desire, others stay within a moderate level, and still others report clinically low sexual desire at all time-points, even as each group's sexual desires dips during their transition. In other words, declines are drops, but not necessarily deficits. Consistent with the idea that men's sexual desires experience less relationship-related fluctuations, men tend to show consistent sexual desire through the transition to parenthood (Rosen et al., 2021).

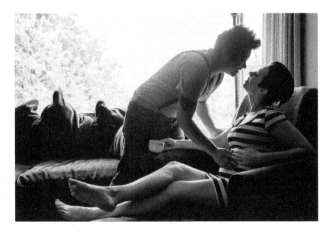

Figure 11.4 How sexual desire changes through transitions is studied predominantly in different-sex partners. What predictions might you make about sexual desire as same-gender partners enter parenthood? (Photo: Inti St Clair / Tetra Images / Getty Images)

DIVERSITY AND INCLUSION

Asexuality and Romantic Relationships

Can you have a strong, intimate romantic relationship in the absence of sexual attraction? If your immediate thought is "no," then your first impression aligns with a dominating view in relationship science, that sexual attraction is a critical component of a romantic relationship. This view, however, is based on research that has predominantly sampled individuals who, at baseline, report being sexually attracted to one or multiple sexes. What if your baseline is the absence of other-oriented sexual attraction?

Estimates suggest that approximately 1 percent of the general British population and between 0.5 percent (men) and 0.9 percent (women) of Americans identify as asexual, that is, they experience little or no sexual attraction to others (Bogaert, 2004; Fu et al., 2019). Asexual individuals are a heterogeneous group, but they tend to report little interest in having sexual partners, they are more likely than non-asexual individuals to report never having fantasized about sex, and they often report low sexual excitation and low subjective arousal (Bogaert, 2015; Prause & Graham, 2007; Yule et al., 2017). Asexuality is not a behavior-based identity. Even as asexual individuals typically have less sex than others, someone can identify as asexual and regularly engage in sexual activity, just as people who do not identify as asexual can be abstinent (Brotto & Yule, 2017). A small-sample estimate suggests that half of self-identified asexual individuals have engaged in sexual activity with a partner in the last six months (Fu et al., 2019; Rothblum et al., 2020). This may reflect the fact that sex can occur in the absence of strong desires for sex.

Although low sexual desire is common among asexual individuals, to be asexual does not preclude having sexual urges or desires (Bogaert, 2015). If present, these desires simply tend not to be other-oriented. Indeed, some evidence suggests asexual individuals report similar interest in masturbation as non-asexual individuals (Prause & Graham, 2007), with other work indicating that while asexual men masturbate at a similar rate as non-asexual men (90 percent in the last month), fewer asexual women (70 percent) masturbate compared to non-asexual women (Yule et al., 2017). Asexual individuals report a variety of motivations to masturbate, but they are significantly less likely to masturbate for sexual pleasure than their non-asexual counterparts (Yule et al., 2017).

Figure 11.5 How might asexual individuals' relationships be the same and different from relationships among non-asexual individuals? (Photo: Morsa Images / DigitalVision / Getty Images)

Critically, asexual individuals are just as likely to be in a committed, intimate relationship as other sexual minorities (Rothblum et al., 2020). Recall that sexual desire is distinct from romantic desire (Diamond, 2004, 2013), supporting the possibility for a deeply romantic and close relationship without sexual attraction. While some asexual individuals are also aromantic (experiencing no romantic interest in others), many asexual individuals are romantically attracted to others (Figure 11.5). For the former, an ideal intimate relationship might be quite like a friendship, whereas for the latter group, cuddling and other non-sexual affectionate behaviors are part of an ideal intimate relationship (Scherrer, 2008). Given these ideals, the kinds of behaviors that fuel relationship well-being among non-asexual individuals might look different for asexual individuals. Indeed, when people do not want sex, *not having sex* supports a rewarding sex life. As one asexual White male asserted, "The fact that I don't have sex and my partner accepts this is very satisfying" (Lindley et al., 2021).

Sexual Attitudes

Is it okay, or perhaps even preferable, to engage in sex casually, outside of a committed relationship? Or should sex be reserved for established (and perhaps only legally or religiously sanctioned) relationships? The answers to these questions constitute a few of many possible **sexual attitudes**, people's beliefs, perspectives, and values pertaining to sex. Consider your sexual attitudes by responding to the items in Table 11.1.

Table 11.1 What attitudes do you hold about sex?

Permissiveness[1]	Strongly disagree (1) to strongly agree (5)				
The best sex is with no strings attached	1	2	3	4	5
Casual sex is acceptable	1	2	3	4	5
It is okay to have ongoing sexual relationships with more than one person at a time	1	2	3	4	5
I do not need to be committed to a person to have sex with them	1	2	3	4	5

Pre-marital sex[2]	Always wrong (4) to Never wrong (1)			
Pre-marital sex is ...	1	2	3	4

[1] Sample items reproduced from the permissiveness subscale of the Brief Sexual Attitudes Scale.

[2] Item reproduced from the General Social Survey.

Source: 1. Hendrick, C., Hendrick, S. S., & Reich, D. A. (2006). The Brief Sexual Attitudes Scale. *Journal of Sex Research*, *43*(1), 76–86; © 2006 The Society for the Scientific Study of Sexuality, reprinted by permission of Taylor & Francis Ltd, www.tandfonline.com on behalf of 2006 The Society for the Scientific Study of Sexuality. 2. Davern et al. (2021).

Attitudes Toward Casual Sex

Permissiveness, a free and casual approach to sex, is generally more common in men compared to women (Hendrick et al., 2006; Petersen & Hyde, 2010). Parental investment theory offers a ready explanation for this gendered pattern: whereas men benefit from a permissive attitude that helps them spread their genes, women benefit from a more conservative and selective approach that mitigates potential costs (Kenrick et al., 1990). Recall from Chapter 6, and consistent with these attitude differences, that men are more willing than women to accept invitations for casual sex from strangers (Clark & Hatfield, 1989; Edlund et al., 2021). Likewise, men, more than women, report using the dating app Tinder specifically to pursue casual sex (Sevi et al., 2018). Across genders and sexual orientations, maintaining more permissive, liberal attitudes toward sex is associated with having more casual sex partners (Leri & DelPriore, 2021; Lyons et al., 2013; Townsend & Wasserman, 2011). At the same time, simply the experience of casual sex may alter views on sex: having had casual sex predicts more permissive attitudes in the future, as well as more future casual sexual experiences (Katz & Schneider, 2013).

Permissive attitudes toward sex, not surprisingly, align with sociosexuality, people's willingness to engage in uncommitted sex (Simpson & Gangestad, 1991). Across genders, unrestricted sociosexuality is associated with engaging in various sexual behaviors (e.g., masturbation, oral sex, sexual intercourse) at a younger age, engaging in more sexual activity, and having more lifetime partners (Yost & Zurbriggen, 2006). In general, people with more avoidant attachment styles report more permissiveness and unrestricted sociosexuality, a finding observed across cultures and across sexual orientations (Schmitt & Jonason, 2015; Starks & Parsons, 2014). People with permissive attitudes toward sex face a (hetero)sexual double standard: People judge women less favorably for engaging in frequent, casual sex relative to men, who are judged more positively for similar behavior (Endendijk et al., 2020). However, evidence also shows that more gender-equitable countries exhibit less of this traditional double standard, which suggests the possibility of a sociocultural component to how people think about permissiveness.

Attitudes toward Pre-marital Sex

Probably the most prototypical "sexual attitude" is how people think about pre-marital sex. Is it OK to have pre-marital sex? Never? Always? This question has a strong heteronormative bent and assumes a specific trajectory (i.e., marriage), but nonetheless, it can give us a sense of how liberally or conservatively people view sex. These views are not necessarily stable. They can change at the cultural level, developmentally as people age (after 30, people tend to become more conservative), or with specific generational cohorts (Harding & Jencks, 2003). Consider how beliefs toward pre-marital sex have changed within Western society in the last half a century or so. Analysis of the General Social Survey, for example, shows sharp increases in the percentage of people indicating favorable attitudes toward pre-marital sex from the 1960s to the mid-1970s across all age cohorts, with moderate increases continuing into the 1980s, holding steady, and then rising again after 2000 (Harding & Jencks, 2003; Twenge et al., 2015). Figure 11.6 shows how American attitudes toward pre-marital sex have become increasingly favorable since the 1970s.

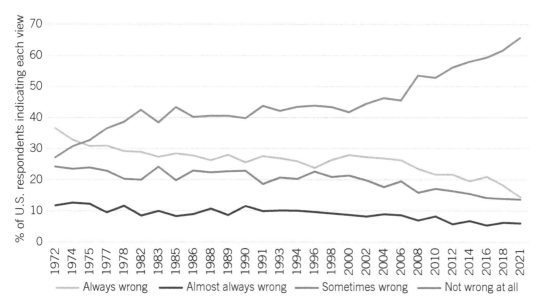

Figure 11.6 How might your grandparents or great grandparents have viewed pre-marital sex? How do you? Using a scale of 1 ("always wrong") to 4 ("not wrong at all"), US participants in the nationally representative General Social Survey have shown increasingly more favorable attitudes toward pre-marital sex. (Based on data sourced from: Davern, Michael; Bautista, Rene; Freese, Jeremy; Morgan, Stephen L., and Smith, Tom W., General Social Surveys, 1972–2021 Cross-section [machine-readable data file, 68,846 cases]. Principal Investigator, Michael Davern; Co-Principal Investigators, Rene Bautista, Jeremy Freese, Stephen L. Morgan, and Tom W. Smith; sponsored by National Science Foundation. – NORC ed. – Chicago: NORC, 2021: NORC at the University of Chicago [producer and distributor]. Data accessed from the GSS Data Explorer website at gssdataexplorer.norc.org.)

Sexual Motives

Sexual attitudes might reveal how people think and feel about sex, but why do people have sex? In other words, what are some common **sexual motivations**, or "conscious and subjective reasons" (Tang et al., 2012) that explain why people engage in sexual activity?

Give it a try: I think people have sex for _____, for _____, and for _____. If you went for some variation of, "for pleasure, for love, and for reproduction," then bravo! You landed on the "big three," reasons sometimes assumed to satisfy the question of why people participate in sexual activity (Hatfield et al., 2012). These reasons do play a role, but as a complete set, they fall short. People's sexual motives are wildly diverse. Consider how in one study (Meston & Buss, 2007), researchers received 237 distinct responses to the question of why people have sex; in a different study (Cooper et al., 1998), researchers received 335! Some of this diversity likely captures differences in context: people have random hookup sex, date night sex, post-baby sex, goodbye/hello sex, make-up sex, rebound sex, revenge sex . . . the list goes on. Even within specific contexts, however, people engage in sexual activity for different reasons (Kenney et al., 2014; Thorpe & Kuperberg, 2021). Consider the reasons listed in Figure 11.7: are these why you might engage in sexual activity? Motivations are as diverse as the people, partner combinations, and relationship contexts involved in the sexual activity.

Differentiating the Specific Content of Sexual Motives

Efforts to consolidate the hundreds of sexual motives by content have generated several taxonomies (Cooper et al., 1998; Hill & Preston, 1996; Meston et al., 2020; Meston & Buss,

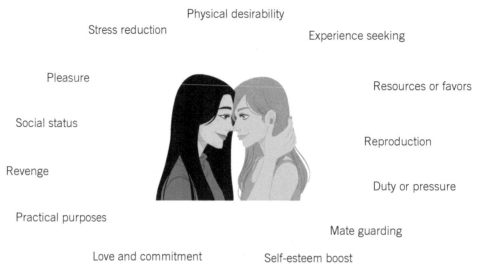

Physical desirability

Stress reduction

Experience seeking

Pleasure

Resources or favors

Social status

Reproduction

Revenge

Duty or pressure

Practical purposes

Mate guarding

Love and commitment   Self-esteem boost

Expression

Figure 11.7 Why do people engage in sexual activity? The reasons listed here are based on the original and updated YSex? measures of sexual motives, and they highlight the diverse reasons for sex. Can you think of reasons not listed here? (Source: Drawn based on data from Meston et al. [2020]; Meston & Buss [2007]; image: Rumi Fujishima / DigitalVision Vectors / Getty Images)

2007). Across these works, four primary themes tend to emerge. Specifically, people engage in sexual activity (1) for pleasure, (2) to achieve specific goals, (3) for emotional reasons (feeling valued, intimacy, love), and 4) to manage insecurity, cope, or respond to pressure. These specific motives and their consequences are described next.

For Pleasure

Sex can be fun and feel good; these are top reasons why adults across the lifespan engage in sexual activity (Wyverkens et al., 2018). When college students reflect on why they hookup, for example, they often cite the physical pleasure of sex as their motivation, an idea that corresponds with the view that hooking up can be an exciting solution to boredom (Kenney et al., 2014; Thorpe & Kuperberg, 2021). Similarly, some people are motivated to engage in sex because it can provide a pleasurable stress release or because they feel aroused by the attractiveness of a specific partner. Men tend to cite these kinds of physical reasons for sex more than women (Browning et al., 2000; Wyverkens et al., 2018); however, physical pleasure still represents a substantial subset of the "top 10 reasons" why women have sex, whether these women are younger (18 to 22) or a bit older (31 to 45; Meston et al., 2009). Lesbian, bisexual, queer, and questioning women endorse pleasure as the number one reason for having sex, with the physical attractiveness of a partner also high on the list (J. R. Wood et al., 2014).

To Achieve Specific Goals

A common reason people have sex is in pursuit of specific, and extremely variable, goals (Meston et al., 2020; Meston & Buss, 2007). These goals might be abstract, like engaging in sex to boost one's own social status, or quite concrete, like engaging in sexual activity for money, drugs, opportunities, or favors. While these latter resource-related goals are not strongly endorsed in general, initial evidence suggests they might motivate sexual activity within non-exclusive multi-partnered relationships more than in monogamous or non-exclusive single partner relationships (Mitchell et al., 2020). CNM partners may also pursue sex to seek out new experiences more than people engaging in sex with one partner (Kelberga & Martinsone, 2021), though curiosity is a general motive. Indeed, people often pursue sex because they are curious and want to understand what sex is, because they are looking for insight into their sexual identity, or as a means to affirm their sexual identity (Gillespie et al., 2021). The goals underlying sexual motivations can be relational. For instance, a portion of college students engaging in hookups – by some estimates a third to a half of them – often do so with the goal of starting a new relationship, particularly men (Garcia & Reiber, 2008; Kenney et al., 2014; Thorpe & Kuperberg, 2021; Weitbrecht & Whitton, 2020). Some achieve this goal: tentative evidence suggests hooking up may be a common pathway to a relationship, factoring into possibly two-thirds of college relationship beginnings (England et al., 2008). The idea that men pursue hookups for relationships more than women is counter-stereotypical, but also reflected in research on hookups between men. One study observed that 90 percent of their sample of 274 young men engaged in same-sex hookups hoping for additional relationship opportunities (Barrios & Lundquist, 2012).

Once in a relationship, people may engage in sex to help the relationship progress or move forward (Gillespie et al., 2021), or as a mate-guarding strategy (Meston et al., 2020; Meston & Buss, 2007). Sex might be a means by which people try to keep a partner's attention, prevent a breakup, or otherwise enhance the stability of their relationship. Other relational goals for having sex are spiteful. People engage in "revenge sex" in order to make an ex-partner jealous, to show them what they are missing, or "even the score" (Barber & Cooper, 2014; Meston et al., 2020).

Some people engage in sexual activity with the goal of gaining experience (Meston et al., 2020), which may be an especially important task for individuals who perceive themselves as inexperienced. In the United States, people historically valued chastity in potential partners, but this preference has decreased dramatically over time, for both men and women (Buss et al., 2001). This cultural shift provides the backdrop for a new kind of stigma, one related to sexual inexperience. People who perceive themselves as less sexually experienced than age-related peers report feeling odd or abnormal and that others treat them differently on account of their inexperience (Gesselman et al., 2017). They might be reluctant to disclose their inexperience, but so too, sexually experienced individuals may lie or hesitate to reveal their experience, depending on the audience (Barnett et al., 2021). Today, people sometimes perceive sexually inexperienced people as slightly less desirable partners, a bias more pronounced for individuals who themselves have more unrestricted sociosexuality (Gesselman et al., 2017). The general preference for sexual experience over none, however, is only to a point, as shown in Figure 11.8. Even if some experience is desired, people tend to prefer prospective partners who have no experience more than "too much" experience (Stewart-Williams et al., 2017).

People also have sex for reproduction goals (i.e., to conceive), a motive logically endorsed more frequently by people in different-sex than same-sex relationships (Hill & Preston, 1996; Leigh, 1989). People can pursue sex for reproductive goals in committed relationships as well

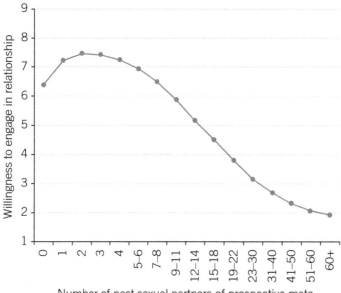

Figure 11.8 Might sexual inexperience motivate you to have sex? People's sexual histories may make them more (or less) desirable as potential partners. (Source: Stewart-Williams, S., Butler, C. A., & Thomas, A. G. (2017). Sexual history and present attractiveness: People want a mate with a bit of a past, but not too much. *Journal of Sex Research, 54*(9), 1097–1105. © 2017 The Society for the Scientific Study of Sexuality, reprinted by permission of Taylor & Francis Ltd, www.tandfonline.com on behalf of 2017 The Society for the Scientific Study of Sexuality)

as in casual encounters, though the latter is perhaps less common. For example, women pursuing single-motherhood by choice and men who want to be fathers sometimes seek out short-term partners to help them conceive (Carone et al., 2017; Jadva et al., 2009). How trying to conceive shapes people's sexual experiences is still a burgeoning area of research, but some evidence suggests having sex in order to conceive is linked to judgments of more satisfying sex lives among partners with lower relationship quality, and less satisfying sex lives among partners with higher relationship quality (Shreffler et al., 2021). As you might imagine, reproductive goals are more common among young-to-mid-life adults than older adults, whose sexual behaviors might stem from other goals, including "to feel young again" (Gewirtz-Meydan & Ayalon, 2019).

For Emotional Reasons

Remember how the sexual behavioral system can work in concert with the attachment system? The link between sex and attachment is exceptionally clear when we consider emotional reasons for pursuing sex in committed relationships. Here, sex is often a means of expressing love, feeling loved, and enhancing closeness. Indeed, in ongoing relationships, intimacy motives are regularly endorsed (Impett, Peplau, & Gable, 2005), whereas these motives are less apt to inspire sex in casual contexts. For instance, emotional motives do not make the top twenty reasons women have casual sex, but they dominate the top reasons women have sex in committed relationships with men or with women (Armstrong & Reissing, 2015). Indeed, in committed contexts, both men and women often explain their sexual activity as stemming from an emotional place (Davis et al., 2004; Meston et al., 2020), suggesting that sex helps them express love or supports intimacy building.

What about attachment? A healthy body of evidence suggests that people higher in attachment anxiety are especially apt to pursue sexual activity to experience intense closeness, and to feel loved (Davis et al., 2004; Schachner & Shaver, 2004; Tracy et al., 2003). Intimacy motives are favored by individuals higher in attachment anxiety even in a casual context (Snapp et al., 2014). This makes sense, given that desires for intimacy are key characteristics of attachment anxiety (Mikulincer & Shaver, 2016). Also nicely aligned with theory, individuals higher in avoidant attachment are less inclined to pursue sex to experience or express intimacy (Cooper et al., 2006; Impett, Gordon et al., 2008; Schachner & Shaver, 2004; Tracy et al., 2003).

For Insecurity Reasons

Do you think having sex would make you feel better about yourself or your relationship? Would it help you cope with personal issues, satisfy a perceived obligation, or manage peer pressure? For many people, these insecurity-based motives are precisely why they participate in sexual activity (Meston et al., 2020; Meston & Buss, 2007). In general, insecurity motivations tend not to be as prominent as pleasure or emotional motives, yet they still help account for people's sexual behaviors. Among college students, stress is associated with turning to hookups for coping (Kenney et al., 2014), but so too are individual differences. Attachment avoidance, for example, is positively associated with having sex in order to fit in and manage insecurities, the latter of which is also characteristic of attachment anxiety (Schachner & Shaver, 2004). Higher attachment anxiety is linked to heightened motivation to engage in sex to please a partner or to keep a partner's interest (Dixon et al., 2022). Wanting to hookup in order to cope is more common among less secure individuals, but similarly common among men and women (Snapp et al., 2014). Narcissism is also associated with turning to sex as a way to manage loneliness, to experience a self-esteem boost, and to seek affirmation of one's self-imagine, such as their attractiveness (Gewirtz-Meydan, 2017; Meston et al., 2020).

Differentiating the High-Level Structure of Sexual Motives

Beyond content, relationship scientists have also consolidated the diverse motives that people cite for their sexual activities by considering high-level structure of the motives. For instance, researchers differentiate approach motives, when people engage in sex in pursuit of rewards, from avoidance motives, when people engage in sex to avoid possible costs. These rewards and costs can vary in content, as described above. For instance, approach motives could entail having sex to pursue pleasure, closeness, or any particular goal. Approach motives for sex not only predict greater personal and relational well-being, but they can boost sexual desire and improve people's satisfaction with their sex lives (Impett, Peplau, & Gable, et al., 2005; Impett, Strachman et al., 2008; Muise et al., 2013; Muise, Boudreau et al., 2017). Avoidance motives for sex, such as not wanting to be seen negatively or to disappoint a partner, are instead associated with worse individual and relational well-being, and are linked to fewer affectionate behaviors and less satisfying sex lives (Cooper et al., 2015; Impett, Peplau, & Gable, et al., 2005).

Taking another "high-level" look at sexual motives, scholars have recognized that people can pursue sexual activity to benefit the self or to benefit a partner. As such, sexual motivations can be divided into self-oriented motivations and other-oriented motivations (Cooper et al., 1998, 2011). In other words, is someone participating in sexual activity in an attempt to satisfy their own needs, or in response to the needs of their partner? When people take the latter approach, their sexual behaviors can reflect communal sexual motives (Muise & Impett, 2016). Communal sexual motives describe individuals' efforts in the realm of sex and sexual activity to respond to and try to meet the needs of their partner. People with stronger communal sexual motivations tend to negotiate sexual decisions in ways that predict satisfying sex lives and relationship well-being for both themselves and their partners (provided individuals also recognize their own needs; Day et al., 2015). Indeed, meta-analysis suggests that stronger communal sexual motives predict greater personal well-being and higher relationship satisfaction for both the self and the partner (Le et al., 2018).

Finally, scholars have focused on whether sexual motivations are self-inspired or a result of external pressure. In other words, are people engaging in sexual activity on account of intrinsic, autonomous reasons ("I want to have sex"), or are they engaging in sex for extrinsic, non-autonomous reasons ("I'm supposed to have sex," "Other people think I should have sex")? Highlighting this distinction is important because as much as we might hope people engage in sex freely and of their own volition, people can feel obligated to engage in sexual activity or experience pressure to do so (Garcia & Reiber, 2008). To the extent that people pursue sex for intrinsic, autonomous reasons, they tend to experience more satisfying sex lives and maintain more positive feelings about sex (Gravel et al., 2020). People endorsing autonomous motives for sex may tend to engage in more casual sex (Townsend et al., 2020), and for women, intrinsic motives predict experiencing better sex (more likely to orgasm) in casual contexts (Wongsomboon et al., 2022). Intrinsic and extrinsic motivations appear to operate similarly in monogamous and consensually non-monogamous partners, with more intrinsic motivation consistently predicting more satisfying sex lives and higher relationship satisfaction, possibly because intrinsic motives support sexual need fulfillment (Wood et al., 2018). When people pursue sexual activity for non-autonomous reasons, such behavior is linked to poorer sexual health (e.g., pain, function) and more sexual distress (Gravel et al., 2016). Engaging in sex on account of non-autonomous reasons is linked to lower self-esteem, and – for women – more sexual victimization and depression (Townsend et al., 2020). Of course, people can endorse multiple motives for sex (see the *Article Spotlight*), and this can include a mix of autonomous and non-autonomous reasons. Still, those who tend to endorse mostly, if not all, non-autonomous reasons tend to report less satisfying sex lives, less harmony with their sexual partners, and more negative feelings than people who endorse mixed motives or nearly all (or all) highly autonomous reasons (Tóth-Király et al., 2019).

ARTICLE SPOTLIGHT

Latent Profile Analysis: Understanding Variation in Sexual Motives

When we ask someone the question, "Why do you have sex?" one answer alone may not be accurate. Sure, the rare person might say, "100 percent pure love," but chances are, most people endorse multiple reasons for pursuing sex, often simultaneously. For any given person, multiple sexual motivations may concurrently shape their sexual behaviors. With this complexity in mind, Tóth-Király, Vallerand, Bőthe, Rigó, and Orosz (2019) were the first to apply **latent profile analysis** (LPA) to the study of why people engage in sexual activity. LPA, a person-centered approach to modeling data, is gaining in popularity, and is particularly useful for understanding human motivations (Pastor et al., 2007).

To appreciate this approach, first consider the more familiar and common method to analyzing data, regression, which focuses on specific variables and how they relate. Regression allows us to learn, for example, how predictor variables, like separate sexual motives (e.g., intrinsic, extrinsic), are associated with outcome variables, such as people's emotional responses to a hookup. Using LPA changes the focus; instead of looking at the data at the variable level, LPA is person centered, its analysis focuses on types of people. By clustering participants together based on similarities, LPA reveals different "profiles" that characterize smaller groups within the broader sample (Marsh et al., 2009; Pastor et al., 2007). In other words, LPA assumes that the participant sample is diverse, comprised of groups representing different populations that have specific motivational profiles. LPA's purpose is to reveal these latent, or "hidden," groups, and statistical criteria are used to determine how many groups best represent the data. Once discovered, these groups can be described by the profile of characteristics associated with them and can be compared to other groups, both qualitatively and by their associated outcomes. For the study of sexual motivations, LPA provides an exciting opportunity to recognize the complexity of why people have sex and to see how people who share similar motive profiles experience sexual activity.

Tóth-Király and colleagues (2019) applied LPA to examine the multiple intrinsic and extrinsic motivations that people have for engaging in sexual activity. Following from self-determination theory (Deci & Ryan, 1991; Ryan & Deci, 2017), they measured the sexual motivations of Hungarian adults ($n = 687$ in Study 1; 632 in Study 2) along an intrinsic-extrinsic continuum and also assessed amotivation, a lack of autonomy and agency regarding sexual activity (see Table 11.2 for measured motives and their definitions).

Results from LPA revealed four distinct profiles (Tóth-Király et al., 2019), as shown in Table 11.2. The "highly self-determined" profile captured the multiple motivations of approximately one-third of the sample. This group feel empowered in their sexual decisions and pursue sex for their own, not for others', expectations. Approximately another third of participants, the "moderately self-determined," represented a population also unlikely to see their sexual behavior resulting from external control, yet showing relatively lower (average level) inclination to pursue sex for its own sake. A third profile, the "moderately non-self-determined" group, may sometimes engage in sex for autonomous reasons, while other times pursuing sex in response to external pressures. The final profile ("highly non-self-determined"), representing about 11 percent of the sample, demonstrates minimal self-directed agency when engaging in sexual activity.

Not only do profiles differ qualitatively, helping us see the complexity of sexual motivations, but they also differ from one another in their correlates. Of note, for example, people within the more autonomous profiles are happier with their sex lives and more satisfied with life in general compared to groups defined by more non-autonomous profiles (Tóth-Király et al., 2019). Latent profile analysis offers a contemporary approach to data analysis that helps respect the different configurations of sexual motivation, highlighting how people might simultaneously experience multiple, even conflicting, motivations. What other areas of relationship science might benefit from using LPA?

Table 11.2 Profiles of sexual motivations

| Profile | % of sample | Most intrinsic | | | | Most extrinsic | |
		Intrinsic motivation (sex for its own sake)	Integrated motivation (sex is tied to one's identity)	Identified motivation (sex is important and tied to personal goals)	Introjected motivation (sex reduces negative feelings in response to internalized pressures)	External motivation (sex produces outside rewards or avoids outside costs)	Amotivational (no motivation; external forces determine sexual activity)
Highly self-determined	37%	High	High	High	Average	Low	Low
Moderately self-determined	29%	Average	Low	Low	Low	Low	Low
Moderately non-self-determined	22%	Average	Average	Average	High	tableHigh	Average
Highly non-self-determined	11%	Low	Low	Low	Low	High	High

Results from Study 1, which replicated in Study 2, showed four profiles of sexual motivations. Which best describes your motivations for sexual activity?
Source: Drawn based on data from Tóth-Király et al. (2019).

The extent to which an individual's motives for sex will actually translate into outcomes (e.g., Will I have sex tonight? Tomorrow? Ever?) depends on relationship context, and critically, individuals' motives operate in light of, and in combination with, their partners' motives (Cooper et al., 2015). In other words, it's not just about what you want. Women's motives appear especially influential in determining whether people in different-sex relationships have sex: in these relationships, men's sexual activity is more a function of their partner's motives than their own (Cooper et al., 2015).

Sexual Behaviors

Sexual motives may set the stage for sexual behavior. When might you, or did you, have your sexual debut? This first sexual experience is considered a critical developmental milestone across sexual orientations (Barnett & Moore, 2017; Gillespie et al., 2021) and it commonly occurs in adolescence or emerging adulthood, periods that are characterized by identity exploration and relationship instability (Halpern & Kaestle, 2013; Olmstead & Anders, 2021). Typically, sexual behavior begins with romantic behaviors (e.g., hand holding, kissing) and moves to more intimate behaviors (e.g., touching) and to sex (De Graaf et al., 2009; O'Sullivan et al., 2007). This progression, which captures over 70 percent of individuals' trajectories, may be healthier, that is, characterized by more agency (e.g., contraceptive use), than non-linear patterns (De Graaf et al., 2009).

To understand sexual behaviors, remember that at any time, the current gender of a person's sexual partners may or may not align with that person's past, current, or future sexual orientation. Also make note that when scholars talk about sex, they are often defining sex as penetrative penile-vaginal intercourse, consistent with survey results asking what constitutes sex and what different-sex partners typically say they did when they last "had sex" (Pitts & Rahman, 2001; Sanders & Reinisch, 1999; Laumann et al., 2000). This definition overlooks anal sex, which most people agree constitutes sex (Horowitz & Spicer, 2013), excludes behaviors that some people would constitute as sex (e.g., "is oral sex, sex?"), and, critically, prioritizes different-sex partner combinations. While men who engage in sexual activity with other men can also use a penetrative definition of sex (i.e., penile-anal sex), there is less consensus on what sex is among women with same-sex partners. Definitions of "having sex" might include giving and/or receiving genital stimulation, oral sex, or both (Dion & Boislard, 2020). Interestingly, these behaviors do not necessarily translate to "having sex" when partners include at least one male. In other words, context and individuals' own subjective judgments matter when we try to understand the significance of various forms of sexual activity.

In the United States, young people today seem to be having their sexual debuts later than previous generations. As shown in Figure 11.9, fewer students between the ages of approximately 14 and 18 report having had sexual intercourse compared to the previous generation (CDC, 2019). These averages, of course, obscure considerable variation, but nonetheless matter.

When precisely people have their sexual debut depends on a variety of factors. It could, for example, be one aspect of a broader reproductive strategy that makes sense given the particular environment in which an individual was raised. According to life history theory (see Chapter 2), people whose childhood environments were gentle and predictable might

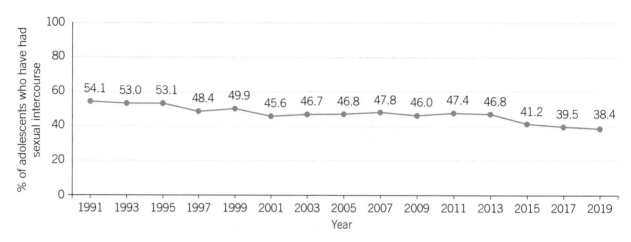

Figure 11.9 Fewer adolescents (approximately aged 14–18) have had sexual intercourse today than age-matched cohorts a few decades ago. Why might this be? (Source: Centers for Disease Control and Prevention (CDC). 1991–2019 High School Youth Risk Behavior Survey Data. Available at http://yrbs-explorer.services.cdc.gov/. Accessed on August 11, 2022)

adopt slow strategies and delay sex, whereas people who were raised in harsh and/or unpredictable environments might be better served with fast strategies (Ellis et al., 2009; Kaplan & Gangestad, 2005). Consistent with this idea, meta-analysis shows that having a harsher early childhood, which in modern days often translates to having access to fewer resources, that is, lower SES, is associated with having sex earlier in life (Xu et al., 2018). When people retrospectively reflect on whether they had their sexual debut at the "right time," their answers are less linked to age and more associated with simply whether they wanted the sex experience (Sprecher et al., 2021). Women and men both report more pleasure and less guilt about their sexual debuts when they view its timing as optimal. That said, women also tend to report more positive reactions to their sexual debuts when they have them at an older age (Sprecher et al., 2021).

 IS THIS TRUE FOR YOU?

Hookup behavior

Casual sex comes in many forms (e.g., friends-with-benefits relationships, booty-call relationships), yet hookups are especially prominent, particularly among emerging adults. By some estimates, between 60 and 80 percent of college students have had a hookup (Garcia et al., 2012), defined as a casual and consensual sexual encounter in which partners participate with no assumption of a future relationship (Fielder & Carey, 2010; Lewis et al., 2013; Owen et al., 2011). As we consider hookups and sexual firsts, note that hookup research has focused on White, cisgender, higher SES, college-attending emerging adults participating in dyadic different-sex hookups. The field recognizes the need to address the problem of minimal attention to diversity or intersectionality within hookup literature (Watson et al., 2017).

What precisely do partners do when hooking up? It varies. Indeed, the term "hooking up" is a catchall that covers a wide range of possible sexual behaviors (Figure 11.10). Among different-sex partners, some evidence suggests that nearly all hookups include kissing, but only about half involve penetrative sex (Fielder & Carey, 2010; Garcia & Reiber, 2008; Owen et al., 2011; Weitbrecht & Whitton, 2020). Does this ring true to you? Whether a hookup between different-sex partners means sex to you may depend on aspects of yourself

Figure 11.10 Hookup behaviors can vary. What are the pros and cons to having hookup sex? (Photo: Thomas Barwick / DigitalVision / Getty Images)

and any hookup experiences you have had. People who engage in hookup sex tend to have more liberal attitudes about sex, consume more pornography, and have less dating anxiety (e.g., less stress about initiating relationships) than people who constrain their hookup behaviors to kissing and/or touching (Paul, 2021). People who have hookup sex also tend to have more previous sexual partners and report more sexual attraction to their partners (Paul, 2021). Once people engage in sex during hook-ups, they may be more likely to do so again. Indeed, some evidence suggests 600 percent more likely (that's not a typo!; Owen et al., 2011).

Given the prevalence of hookups, some people (though not a majority) have their sexual debuts in the context of a hookup (Higgins et al., 2010). Sexual debuts in these less serious relationship contexts are typically experienced less positively than sexual debuts in the context of a committed relationship (Higgins et al., 2010; Schwartz & Coffield, 2020). However, this finding has been observed more consistently for women than men and was studied exclusively in different-sex pairings. Less insight is available for how relationship context might shape the sexual debuts of sexual and gender minorities. In general, same-sex pairings, particularly women, may experience uncertainty on whether/if they have had sex for the first time, with the idea of virginity often judged as heteronormative and inapplicable to many sexual minorities (Gillespie et al., 2021).

Beyond its debut, sexual behavior continues to be an important part of many individuals' lives. In a nationally representative sample, Americans report engaging in a wide array of sexual behaviors across the lifespan, with penile-vaginal sex particularly common among emerging adults and middle-aged individuals (Herbenick et al., 2010). In different-sex relationships, genital touching may be especially important for enhancing women's sexual pleasure, with less than a fifth of women in these relationships reporting they orgasm from penile-vaginal sex alone (Herbenick et al., 2018). Among female same-gender partners, genital touching and oral sex are common behaviors, the use of sex toys less common, and anal stimulation/penetration least common (Scott et al., 2018). Anal sex is also less likely to have occurred during the last male sexual encounter had by self-identified gay and bisexual men as compared to oral sex or partnered masturbation (Rosenberger et al., 2011). Indeed, in a nationally representative US sample, more than half of mid-life women, and about a third of men, regularly give oral sex, with these numbers declining into older age, and with anal sex a less frequent but not uncommon experience across the lifespan (Herbenick et al., 2010). Kissing during sexual encounters is common across relationship structures and age groups, a behavior that predicts sexual pleasure, but might also be used to regulate intimacy (Busby et al., 2020; Frederick et al., 2021; Herbenick et al., 2019; Townes et al., 2021). While some people do not kiss because they or their partner does not like kissing, others refrain from kissing to limit feelings of emotional closeness (Busby et al., 2020; Herbenick et al., 2019). Finally, people's sexual repertoires can also include **sexting**, the sharing of sexually explicit messages, photos, or videos. Sexting is more common among younger than older people, with approximately 40 percent of emerging adults having sent or received sexts, with closer to 50 percent having engaged in reciprocal sexting (Galovan et al., 2018; Mori et al., 2020).

As an additional consideration, the behaviors that people find pleasurable during sex can be gentle (e.g., caresses, massage), or rough. Biting, spanking, and hair-pulling, for instance, are sometimes considered aspects of consensual sex, and choking/strangulation, its dangers notwithstanding, is potentially engaged in more frequently today during consensual sex than previous generations and possibly more frequently among sexual minorities (Burch & Salmon, 2019; Herbenick et al., 2020, 2021). Pornography consumption, which informs people's sexual scripts (Wright, 2011), is linked to engaging in rougher and more dominant sexual behaviors (Herbenick et al., 2020; Wright, 2011; Wright et al., 2021). BDSM, which includes bondage and discipline, domination and submission, and/or sadomasochism, constitutes another set of sexual behaviors that people can endorse. A recent review suggests that 40 to 70 percent of people fantasize about BDSM, with approximately 20 percent of people engaging in these behaviors (Brown et al., 2020).

Despite people's diverse sexual repertoires and their general interest in sex across the lifespan (Herbenick et al., 2010), people across the globe are engaging in less sex than previous generations. Americans' **sexual frequency**, for example, has markedly decreased from the early 2000s to the end of the last decade (Ueda et al., 2020). This can be seen in Figure 11.11, which shows responses from people aged 18–44, from the nationally representative General Social Survey to the question "About how often did you have sex during the last 12 months?" More people between the ages of 18 to 34 are not having sex and fewer people are having sex at least once a week than about twenty years ago (except for unmarried women, whose rates have not changed). This difference is largely driven by younger men. Nearly a third of young men between 18 and 34 (30.9 percent) indicated they had not had sex in the recent survey when polled in 2016–2018, a 12 percent increase from 2000–2002 (18.9 percent). Along the same lines, men aged 25 to 34 were twice as likely to report they had not had sex in the recent survey (14.1 percent) compared to the early 2000s (7 percent). Among slightly older men, aged 35 to 44, changes were more modest, but still trending down. Meanwhile, women's rates of declining sexual activity were less pronounced than men's, but still evident among younger women (Ueda et al., 2020). Mid-life women (ages 35 to 44), however, showed a slight numerical trend toward having more (not less) sex.

Other patterns have stayed consistent over time. For instance, married people might be having less sex, but they continue to have sex more frequently than unmarried individuals

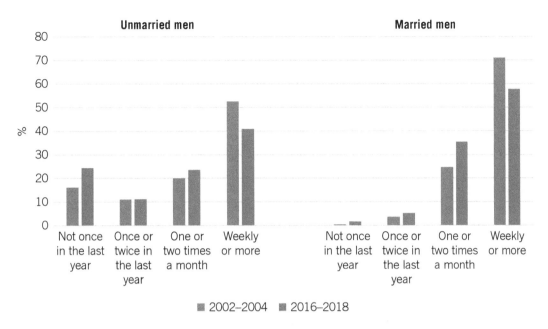

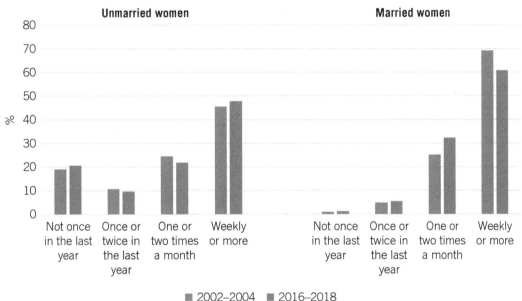

Figure 11.11 Survey data from 18–44 year olds suggest that more people are having less sex now than twenty years ago (Ueda et al., 2020). Why? While we do not know for sure, delayed adulthood and the growing prevalence of the Internet and social media provide two possible explanations (Twenge, 2020). Can you think of possible personal and/or relational consequences of less sexual behavior? (Source: Drawn based on data from Ueda et al. [2020])

(Ueda et al., 2020). As shown in Figure 11.11, about 60 percent of married adults (ages 18–44) today report having sex at least once a week (compared to about 40 to 47 percent of unmarried adults), with a little more than 30 percent reporting they have sex one to three times per month (compared to about 30 percent of unmarried adults). Only a small minority of married individuals report not having had sex in the last year compared to about one-fifth of unmarried individuals.

What about cross-culturally? British men and women have recently experienced declines in sexual frequency parallel to those experienced in the U.S. Compared to 2001, data from the 2012 National Surveys of Sexual Attitudes and Lifestyles showed that more women (from 23 to 29.3 percent) and more men (from 26 to 29.2 percent) reported no sex in the last month, and fewer women (from 20.6 to 13.2 percent) and fewer men (from 20.2 to 14.4 percent) reported having sex ten or more times in the last month (Wellings et al., 2019). Like Americans, married British men (50.2 percent) and married British women (48.3 percent) have more frequent sex (i.e., at least once a week) than single men (31.3 percent) and single women (32.1 percent). These married–unmarried differences may be more pronounced in countries with less accepting attitudes toward sex outside of marriage. For example, the vast majority of people in Muslim countries view pre-marital sex as highly unacceptable and correspondingly fewer unmarried women are engaging in sex (Ueffing et al., 2020). Further, marriage does not necessarily translate into sexual activity. When most married women in a given country report not having had sex in the last month (or year, such as in areas of Western Africa), their experiences may reflect diverse factors such as seasonal migration, cultural norms requiring extended postpartum abstinence, the "grandmother rule" (no sex after becoming a grandmother), or polygamous marital arrangements (Ueffing et al., 2020). Such variations in sexual frequency remind us that sex might have biological roots, but it is also strongly shaped by cultural forces.

Sexual orientation may have some bearing on sexual frequency. Week by week, women in same-sex relationships tend to have sex less frequently than men in same-sex relationships and women and men in different-sex relationships; however, when they do have sex, they engage in sexual activity for a comparatively longer duration (Blair & Pukall, 2014; Frederick et al., 2021). Whereas the median length for sex is about 15 to 30 minutes for other pairings, the median length for women engaging in same-sex sex is between 30 and 45 minutes (Blair & Pukall, 2014).

Sexuality in Relationship Development and Maintenance

The desires, attitudes, motives, and behaviors that define sexuality help us appreciate its complexity and diversity. The importance of sex, however, truly comes alive when we consider it within the context of a relationship's trajectory (and possible maintenance). As shown in Figure 11.12, the sexual system contributes to all time-points in the trajectory of both casual and committed relationships.

Attraction and Partner Selection

From the very outset, that is, the experience of attraction, people's sexuality operates as an internal compass, guiding their thoughts and behaviors. For instance, their sex drives help direct their interest toward same- or different-gender partners, and their sociosexuality can bias them toward short-term or long-term relationships (Hallam et al., 2018; Lippa, 2007b). Even if it happens implicitly, when sexuality shapes early attraction, it can help us achieve specific goals. Consider the goal of finding a long-term partner. Securely attached individuals tend to be more interested in having sex with highly responsive new acquaintances than new acquaintances who show less responsiveness (Birnbaum & Reis, 2012); in this case, feeling

Sexuality across the life of a relationship

Attraction:
Sexuality shapes romantic motives (short-term and long-term)

Partner selection:
Sexuality helps identify suitable partners

Initiation:
Sexuality encourages behaviors that can help people connect with desired partners

Development:
Sexuality facilitates closeness, trust, and commitment

Assessment:
Sexuality is an ongoing assessment of compatibility

Stability:
Sexuality triggers responses to conflicts of interdependence, promoting stay or leave behaviors

Figure 11.12 How have aspects of your sexuality (including desires, attitudes, beliefs, and behaviors) shaped your relationship experiences? Based on Birnbaum (2013), this developmental model of sexuality points to its role in each stage of a relationship's life course. (Photo: Leontura / Getty Images)

sexually attracted to someone could be an early, sensitive metric of a potential partner's ability to be a good partner. Sexual desire can thus be a "visceral gauge of romantic compatibility," instigating efforts to encourage an attachment (Birnbaum & Finkel, 2015).

Initiation and Assessment of Compatibility

Whether and how you approach a casual or possible long-term partner is also tied to the sexual behavioral system. When people are focused on sex, they engage in more initiation behaviors (e.g., smiling, eye contact, proximity seeking); they synchronize more with their desired partner; they self-disclose more, offer more help, and are more responsive to a desired partner (relationship-promoting behaviors; Birnbaum et al., 2017, 2019). People also judge desired partners as more attractive and they think potential partners are romantically interested in them, when they themselves are focused on sex (Birnbaum, Iluz, Plotkin et al., 2020). Sexual activation may even lead people to be deceptive when they believe it could make them appear as more desirable (Birnbaum, Iluz, & Reis, 2020).

Once contact is made, sexuality provides further assessment of partner suitability and works to enhance pair-bonds. How important is a "good" first kiss to you? Early on, people often judge "good kissers" as more attractive, desirable partners (Wlodarski & Dunbar, 2014). In particular, people with high mate value, unrestricted sociosexuality, and women (more than men) emphasize the importance of a "good" first kiss (Wlodarski & Dunbar, 2013). This partner-assessment function of kissing may be biologically based: mouth-to-mouth kissing can provide biomarkers of fitness or immune system compatibility (Wlodarski & Dunbar, 2013). Beyond kissing, being "good in bed" is a desired partner quality early on, and people sometimes judge "bad" sex as a dealbreaker (Jonason et al., 2015). Thus, human sexuality not only orients us toward some partners (and away from others), but also informs early judgments about whether we want to see someone again, possibly encouraging a transition from attraction to attachment.

Stability

Despite being a pervasive and signature feature of ongoing relationships, historically, sexuality has often been missing from discussions of relationship maintenance (Impett, Muise et al., 2020). A new wave of recent research is attending to this oversight, and the field is developing a much stronger understanding of sexuality's purpose in both developing and ongoing relationships. For instance, scholars now know that make-up sex can briefly buffer the adverse effects of conflict on daily relationship satisfaction (Maxwell & Meltzer, 2020). Emerging findings such as this underscore sex's role in relationship maintenance, and accompany growing evidence of the importance of both the quantity (frequency) and quality of people's sex lives in relationship stability.

Sexual Frequency

The notion that "more sex is better," which might be emphasized in some cultures, is not necessarily accurate. On the one hand, sexual frequency links to implicit partner evaluations, with more frequent sex associated with more automatic positive partner evaluations (Costa & Brody, 2012; Hicks et al., 2016). Further, people in committed relationships who have more sex also report greater personal well-being and greater relationship satisfaction . . ., but, on the other hand, this appears only to a point (Muise, Schimmack et al., 2016). Having sex more frequently provides gains up to a once-a-week frequency. Beyond once a week, more frequent sex no longer predicts personal or relationship well-being, a curvilinear relation that is depicted in Figure 11.13. This suggests that more sex is not always better. Relatedly, sometimes no sex is

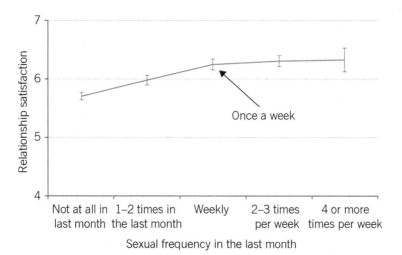

Figure 11.13 Having sex more frequently up to once a week predicts greater relationship satisfaction, after which, additional sexual encounters do not predict relationship satisfaction. How does this align with your previous understanding of sexual frequency? (Source: Muise, Schimmack et al. [2016])

the best sex. For instance, when new fathers in different-sex relationships understand the needs of their wives to not have sex and are committed to meeting those needs, these couples tend to report more satisfying sex lives and more relationship satisfaction (Muise, Kim et al., 2017).

Longitudinal evidence also shows that sexual frequency is bidirectionally associated with sexual satisfaction (McNulty et al., 2016). Sexual satisfaction refers to the extent to which people hold favorable judgments of their sex lives, or, in other words, the extent to which people perceive more rewards than costs in their sexual relationships (Lawrance & Byers, 1995). Over time, the more often partners have sex, the higher their sexual satisfaction tends to be, and higher sexual satisfaction predicts future relationship satisfaction (McNulty et al., 2016).

Perhaps frequent sex supports sexual satisfaction not just because of the encounter itself, but because of what happens after sex. Indeed, when sex ends, partners find themselves in a unique moment of heightened intimacy. This post-sex period, that is, the time interval after sex and before partners fall asleep, shift their attention, or go their separate ways, has the potential to enhance bonding and sexual satisfaction. In the post-sex period, people often engage in intimate post-sex conversation ("pillow talk") and engage in relationship maintenance behaviors, such as reassurance (Denes, 2012; Denes, Dhillon, & Speer, 2017, 2020). The emotional vulnerability and intimacy potential of the post-sex period may explain why people in booty-call relationships leave immediately after sex, whereas this is less common within serious relationships (Jonason et al., 2011): they may want to keep the relationship casual. Post-sex touch is also important. Partners who engage in more satisfying post-sex affection (e.g., cuddling, touching) report subsequently higher sexual satisfaction and relationship satisfaction (Muise et al., 2014). Whether because of the act itself or the intimate post-sex period, having sex may serve as a relationship-enhancing function by producing an "afterglow" of sexual satisfaction that lingers for approximately 48 hours after people have sex (Meltzer et al., 2017). This sexual satisfaction additionally appears to be a central dimension of healthy romantic relationships.

Sexual Satisfaction

How happy are you with your sex life? Defining sexual satisfaction as we did a moment ago, as a global judgment of perceived sexual rewards relative to sexual costs, focuses on broad perceptions rather than anchoring sexual satisfaction to specific sexual encounters. This definition is consistent with the interpersonal exchange model of sexual satisfaction (IEMSS; Lawrance & Byers, 1995), one of the most influential models of sexual satisfaction. As a relational model, the IEMSS considers, for example, how comfortable people are being vulnerable with their partners, how affectionate people perceive their partners to be during and after sexual activity, and how emotionally intimate and secure people feel with their partners. No one specific encounter determines sexual satisfaction (see Figure 11.14). Instead, this model contends

Figure 11.14 Sexual satisfaction is derived from a comparison of sexual rewards with sexual costs and is not linked to any one sexual encounter. How might this be especially important for long-distance partners, new parents, and partners as they age? (Photo: MoMo Productions / DigitalVision / Getty Images)

that the rewards and costs of ongoing sexual exchanges form the building blocks that give rise to an individual's overall judgment of sexual satisfaction.

In ongoing relationships, sexual satisfaction tends to correspond with people's overall relationship satisfaction. This link appears among monogamous and consensually non-monogamous partners, cross-culturally for same-sex partners and different-sex partners, and for gender minority partners in same- or different-sex relationships (Calvillo et al., 2020; Conley et al., 2018; del Mar Sánchez-Fuentes & Sierra, 2015; Dyar et al., 2020; Fisher et al., 2015; Holmberg et al., 2010). Among older adults a similar pattern emerges, with sexual satisfaction and relationship satisfaction linked across cultures and among same-sex and different-sex older partners (Fleishman et al., 2020; Heiman et al., 2011; Santos-Iglesias & Byers, 2021). Indeed, machine learning points to relationship satisfaction as the single strongest predictor of sexual satisfaction (Vowels et al., 2022).

The strong body of evidence linking sexual satisfaction and relationship satisfaction begs the question: which causes which? Does sex make for better relationships, or vice versa? Likely, both! Longitudinal work persuasively demonstrates both pathways (Figure 11.15): sexual satisfaction begets more satisfying relationships, and in turn, people in more satisfying relationships have more sexual satisfaction (Fallis et al., 2016; McNulty et al., 2016; Yeh et al., 2006). Consistent with this work, research following nearly 1,500 American married individuals for twenty years has revealed a strong tie between sexual satisfaction and relationship satisfaction, such that when one increases or decreases over time, the other tends to do the same, supporting their bidirectional influence (Quinn-Nilas, 2020). What might be the cause of this cycle? One possibility is that satisfying sexual encounters produce positive affect, rendering pro-relationship effects; on the other side, being in a satisfying relationship may introduce positive affect into sexual activity, making those encounters more satisfying (Maxwell & McNulty, 2019).

Beyond relationship satisfaction and reflecting its interpersonal nature, partners who engage in **sexual communication** tend to report higher sexual satisfaction (Cupach & Comstock, 1990; Frederick et al., 2017; Montesi et al., 2011). This may be particularly important for men (Vowels et al., 2022). Sexual communication can be verbal or non-verbal and often involves self-disclosures (ideally to a responsive partner) about one's sexual preferences or fantasies, comforts, values, and needs (MacNeil & Byers, 2009). More than the frequency of either sexual communication or sexual disclosures, meta-analysis suggests the quality of sexual communication is a stronger predictor of sexual satisfaction (Mallory, 2022). Indeed, partners who talk about sex may be setting themselves up for success in the bedroom (e.g., better arousal, desire, function, and pleasure; Mallory et al., 2019), while the costs of neglecting to talk about sex may be steep. Inhibited sexual communication, for example, helps explain why individuals with insecure attachment often experience lower sexual satisfaction (Davis et al., 2006). Despite its benefits, sexual communication is commonly experienced as anxiety-inducing (Rehman et al., 2017), possibly explaining why many partners avoid engaging in sexual communication (Byers, 2011).

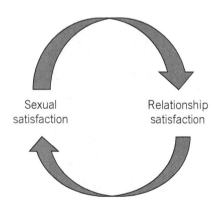

Sexual satisfaction

Relationship satisfaction

Figure 11.15 The bi-directional links between sexual satisfaction and relationship satisfaction underscore the need to maintain healthy cycles and break unhealthy cycles in order to optimize relationships.

Some people may be more adept at nurturing sexual satisfaction, such as individuals with higher sexual communal strength, a partner-oriented focus on caring for and trying to respond to the sexual needs of a partner, with no strings attached (Impett, Kim et al., 2020). Individuals higher in sexual communal strength tend to have partners who report higher sexual satisfaction and relationship satisfaction and who report that their needs are, in fact, better met (Day et al., 2015; Muise & Impett, 2015). To meet a partner's needs does not mean neglecting your own; such neglect does not support relationship well-being, whereas sexual communal strength does (Impett et al., 2019). Other traits may make it particularly challenging to maintain sexual satisfaction. Meta-analysis, for example, suggests neuroticism and negative emotions are adversely associated with sexual satisfaction (Allen & Walter, 2018). Among newlyweds, longitudinal work has also shown that facets of narcissism (e.g., sexual exploitation, a lack of sexual empathy, sexual entitlement) predict lower sexual satisfaction (McNulty & Widman, 2013).

The global nature of how people judge their sex lives makes it no surprise that many other factors, beyond those just discussed, have been identified to predict higher sexual satisfaction within established relationships. These include situational factors, like having a live-in partner; personal factors, like physical health, mental health, identity pride (for sexual minorities), body image positivity, sexual functioning, and low sexual anxiety; and relationship factors like commitment, emotional intimacy, and acts of affection (Buczak-Stec et al., 2021; Dyar et al., 2020; Fisher et al., 2015; Mark et al., 2015; Pujols et al., 2010; Shepler et al., 2018). Relationship factors beyond satisfaction, like love and dyadic desire, may be especially conducive of satisfying sex lives (Vowels et al., 2022). Partnering with individuals who are sexually compatible, meaning they share your sexual preferences and needs, may also support sexual satisfaction and relationship satisfaction (Mark et al., 2013).

Remember that from the sexual exchange perspective, sexual encounters alone do not determine sexual satisfaction. As an example of how the broader relational context can shape sexual satisfaction, among lesbian, bisexual, and heterosexual women, receiving social support from a partner is a top predictor of sexual satisfaction (Henderson et al., 2009). Support from partners is also critically important in non-binary and transgender individuals' experience of a satisfying sex life (Lindley et al., 2021). Along with providing universal rewards like emotional intimacy and satisfying sex, partners who offer gender affirmation, respect boundaries, and show that they are sexually attracted to their gender minority partner support their partner's experience of sexual satisfaction.

Sexual satisfaction certainly contributes to the stability of ongoing relationships, but sexual satisfaction operates more broadly – outside the confines of an established relationship – as well. In fact, women higher in sociosexuality tend to experience lower sexual satisfaction in committed compared to casual relationship contexts (the opposite appears for women with more restricted sociosexuality; Wongsomboon et al., 2020). Sexual satisfaction may play an important role in the relationship decisions of single individuals. Single people who report higher sexual satisfaction tend to be more satisfied with singlehood and less interested in finding a stable partner or getting married (Park, Impett, & MacDonald, 2021). For both partnered and single individuals alike, sexual satisfaction appears to map onto overall judgments about how individuals are navigating their relationships.

RESEARCHER SPOTLIGHT: Allen Mallory, PhD

Figure 11.16 Dr. Allen Mallory is an assistant professor in the Department of Human Sciences at The Ohio State University. (Photo courtesy of Allen Mallory, PhD.)

How did you come to study sexual communication?

I have always been intrigued by the tension between the universality of sexuality in the human experience and it being culturally restricted and taboo. Initially, I was interested in family sexual communication, but there were no research opportunities to study it in my undergraduate program. However, my experience in labs focused on dyadic communication led me to pursue a master's in couple and family therapy. My master's thesis examined the association between young adults' sexual communication with their parents and sexual communication in their relationships.

I shifted to couples' sexual communication during my PhD to get a grasp on the variety of measures for couples' sexual communication I noticed while completing my master's thesis.

Meta-analyses are major undertakings; what has been challenging for you in this work? What is most rewarding?

The most challenging parts of doing meta-analyses are determining their scope and coding the articles. The scope depends on your research question, and a topic like couples' sexual communication can be very broad, which was why I ended up doing two meta-analyses on the topic. Regarding article coding, training research assistants to code reliably and the iterative nature of coding can be a long process. The reward for completing a meta-analysis is a solid grasp of a particular field of study – when they are done well, meta-analyses capture the state of the field, answer questions a single study could not, and highlight new directions in the field.

What's next in sexual communication research?

Historically, research on sexual communication has focused on sexual risk, but I am excited to see more research focusing on sexual communication about pleasure and desire. Recent studies are also incorporating observational, dyadic, and longitudinal designs, which will provide a more nuanced understanding of how sexual communication benefits relationships. I hope to see research on sexual communication within consensual non-monogamy (CNM). We know from qualitative research that healthy CNM relationships require intentional direct communication to manage relationship expectations and sexual activity. However, I have not yet seen any quantitative studies examining sexual communication in CNM relationships.

Making It Happen: Initiating Sex

How people initiate sex depends on context, among other factors. While "Quick! Honey! The baby's asleep – this is our chance!" might work for some committed partners, casual sexual partners and other established partners move toward sexual activity through other, often more subtle, negotiations.

Initiating Sexual Activity in Casual Contexts

The first step to initiating casual sexual activity is to find a desirable willing partner. Usually these partners are friends or casual acquaintances, rather than strangers (Lewis et al., 2012; Weitbrecht & Whitton, 2020). People meet their casual sexual partners at institutional settings (e.g., work, school) and social places (e.g., bars, parties) about 60 percent of the time, but people also meet casual partners in public, in living spaces (e.g., apartments, dormitories), through friends, and on the Internet (Kuperberg & Padgett, 2015). Women hooking up with other women connect less often at bars and may be especially likely to initiate their casual encounters in social gatherings (Watson et al., 2019). For men interested in same-sex partners, social media appears especially helpful in facilitating casual sexual activity (Chow et al., 2016; Kuperberg & Padgett, 2015). Once connected, the progression to sexual activity is an interdependent process in which one partner's advances, whether stated or non-verbal, are either accepted or rejected.

Because people often communicate their sexual interest subtly (e.g., to avoid direct rejection), the process of detecting sexual interest may come with mistakes. Both men and women admit to having misinterpreted others' friendliness as suggesting sexual interest, but this is more common among men (Abbey, 1987). In general, men tend to perceive others' behaviors as more sexually charged than women do, and tend to inflate the degree to which women are sexually interested in them (Abbey, 1982; La France et al., 2009; Fletcher et al., 2014). This **sexual overperception bias** means that women, especially women with the most desirable traits, tend to remember more instances when men falsely believed they (the women) were sexually interested in them (the men) than instances when men under-perceived their actual interest (Haselton, 2003). Among men, individuating factors (e.g., sensation seeking, hostile masculinity, narcissism via hostile masculinity) and contextual factors (e.g., drinking, a casual sex context) predict the frequency of these overperceptions of interest (Jacques-Tiura et al., 2007; Perilloux et al., 2012; Wegner & Abbey, 2016). Research replicating the sexual overestimation bias suggests that cultural factors, like the gender equity within a particular society, have little to do with the effect (Bendixen, 2014). From an evolutionary standpoint, men's sexual overperception bias may be a quirk in the modern brain that evolved over time to favor their reproductive success (Haselton, 2003; Haselton & Buss, 2000). A biased perceptual system that generates more false positives (i.e., seeing interest that does not exist) compared to false negatives (i.e., not recognizing existing interest) may have helped ancestral men by reducing missed opportunities to procreate. More recent research suggests that sexual overperception bias may reflect projection of one's own interest, and a tendency for men to have higher sociosexuality – and thus more interest in sex – than women (Lee et al., 2020; Roth et al., 2021; Samara et al., 2021). Sexual interest, once inferred, can lay the foundation for a sexual advance.

If you are interested in sexual activity, and you think your potential partner is as well, how likely are you to make the first sexual move? Scholars turn to **sexual scripts** in order to understand how people enact sexual behaviors (Simon & Gagnon, 1969, 1986). Like the dating scripts described in Chapter 5, sexual scripts are mental templates that help people know how sex is done, and they help individuals decide how to behave in sexual situations so that the interactions proceed smoothly. Because sexual scripts are known and shared, they provide the "if you do this, I do that" framework that allows strangers to negotiate sexual exchanges. Accordingly, people generally agree on the sequence of steps involved in transitioning from noticing someone at a party to "going some place else" for sexual activity (Edgar & Fitzpatrick, 1993). (In case you're wondering, this typically involves, noticing, approaching, buying/accepting a drink, light conversation, confirming they are there alone, dancing, non-intimate to more intimate touching, and kissing; then asking to go somewhere private.) Similarly, people also agree on a general set of behaviors that people enact when they arrive in private spaces, like an apartment, to transition to sexual activity. The further along these scripts that people progress, people perceive a greater likelihood that they will have sex (La France, 2010).

Sexual scripts cover a wide array of potentially sexual situations, shaping how people interpret others' behaviors and guiding their own. Along with hookup scripts, people hold sexual scripts for negotiating condom and/or birth control use, for offering and confirming consent (see *In the News* box), for initiating a threesome, and for delaying or refraining from having sex (Broaddus et al., 2010; Coffelt, 2018; Hust et al., 2017; Thompson & Byers, 2021). Not everyone knows how to have these conversations. Talking about topics related to sex (e.g., preferences, STIs, condom use, birth control) can feel confusing, awkward, and unscripted (La France, 2020). If uncertainty means avoiding a conversation, this could be problematic. Communication helps facilitate health behaviors, like using condoms (Noar et al., 2006; Widman et al., 2014), and even if people want to engage in safer sex or have their preferences expressed, not knowing how to have those conversations can present a considerable obstacle.

Sexual scripts are strongly gendered in different-sex encounters. This theme emerges again and again, even with greater gender equity in other contexts. Traditional gender roles in sex tend to emphasize men's dominance, initiative, and agency, and women's submissiveness and gate-keeping (Jozkowski & Peterson, 2013). These scripts are dominant even as they are a point of critique, particularly among individuals engaging in same-sex hookups. Initial evidence suggests that people in same-sex casual encounters relish the chance to redefine hookup scripts to emphasize communication, consent, and equity, but nonetheless, often replicate aspects of the gendered scripts that they eschew (Lamont et al., 2018). Meanwhile, women in different-sex contexts who attempt to deviate from a submissive role and engage in sexually assertive behaviors are punished with negative judgments (Klein et al., 2019). These negative reactions operate as sanctions to reinforce gender roles – gender roles that permeate people's cultural-level sexual scripts (Masters et al., 2013). Qualitative work suggests most people integrate the traditional gender roles perceived at the cultural level into their own behaviors and personal ideas about sex, even if they feel constrained by these roles. Other times, however, they may bend the "gender rules" and deviate a bit or endorse a non-traditional approach (Masters et al., 2013). Traditional gender roles are acknowledged and enacted, but they are also perceived as less desired ways of negotiating sex (Morrison et al., 2015), possibly suggesting that norms are changing. This possibility is reflected in the preferences of men who, even if they practice traditional gendered scripts, often want a more egalitarian script that empowers women to initiate, they want to "be desired" not just "to desire," and their masculine notions of sex include not only a "player" mentality but also pro-women ideas about sex (Dworkin & O'Sullivan, 2005; Morrison et al., 2015; Murray & Brotto, 2021). This is good news. More egalitarian sexual scripts that give freedom to men and women to initiate sex may support more satisfying sex lives, not only for women, but for men as well (Sanchez et al., 2012). Both within cultures over time and from a cross-cultural standpoint, variation in egalitarianism may thus have implications for people's sexual experiences. Egalitarian views may support communication and **sexual self-efficacy**, the capacity to advocate for one's self sexually, which may in turn enhance people's sex lives (Carlson & Soller, 2019).

 IN THE NEWS

Consent in the Era of #MeToo

In 2006, Tarana Burke, a survivor of sexual assault, founded the "Me Too" Movement as a way to provide support for people who have experienced sexual violence and harassment (MeTooMvmt.Org, 2022). She likely never anticipated the cultural impact her vision would ultimately inspire. Jump forward to 2017, when a wave of sexual assault allegations emerged against prominent film producer, Harvey Weinstein. Amid these allegations, on October 15 of that year, actress Alyssa Milano posted a simple request on Twitter (Slawson, 2017). Following a suggestion from a friend, she asked women who have been harassed and/or assaulted to tweet, "Me Too," and help expose the prevalence of violence against women. It worked, dramatically. #MeToo went viral, sparking a cultural reckoning demanding change and an end to power-based victimization of women (Khomami, 2017). Today, the #MeToo hashtag is well entrenched in public consciousness, new allegations continue to emerge, and advocacy organizations like "Time's Up" work to address gender discrimination and support victims of sexual misconduct (TimesUpNow.Org, 2022).

Much of the #MeToo movement focuses on sexual abuse in contexts that are not romantic and when abusers are not potential or current partners, yet the Movement also gives voice to survivors of assault within casual or committed romantic contexts. One critical issue energized by the "Me Too" Movement is how partners communicate consent, with non-consensual sexual activity a defining feature of sexual assault. **Consent** refers to agreeing, freely without coercion, to participate in sexual activity (Beres, 2007). More complex than it might initially seem (e.g., Is consent a behavior? An internal state? An explicit statement?; Muehlenhard et al., 2016), ideas about how best to operationalize consent are changing. For instance, educational programs and legal policies that once emphasized "no means no" have transitioned to a "yes means yes" criterion for consent. The move to **affirmative consent** prevents silence from being interpreted as tacit consent and supports an ongoing check-in with a partner to confirm their willingness (Halley, 2016; Jozkowski, 2015). Yet this approach too has shortcomings as affirmative consent can feel awkward in practice: people might recognize the benefits of obtaining clear verbal consent, but might prefer an indirect approach in which they interpret their partners' non-verbal behaviors as consent (Jozkowski et al., 2014; Shumlich & Fisher, 2020). This becomes problematic given that people can engage in external signals of consent (e.g., removing clothes) while not wanting to engage in sexual activity, that is, not offering internal consent (Jozkowski & Peterson, 2014). At the same time, people can engage in sex consensually without having verbally spoken their consent, which may be less likely in casual sex contexts than in established relationships (Marcantonio et al., 2018). Sexual scripts can guide interpretations, but not necessarily produce accurate inferences: for instance, people might interpret someone's agreeing to go up to a person's apartment as consent for sex (Groggel et al., 2021), even if no such consent was intended. Understanding how to support sexual communication and normalizing unambiguous consent processes could encourage safer, healthier sexual encounters. Sexual minority men and women are at an especially high risk for sexual victimization, as shown in Figure 11.17 (Anderson et al., 2021; Balsam et al., 2005; López & Yeater, 2021), a reminder that different relational contexts may demand different ways of ensuring that all parties involved desire and consent to any engaged-in sexual activity.

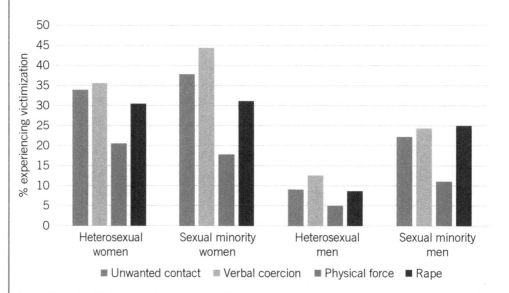

Figure 11.17 Identity factors explain some variability in sexual victimization, as measured by the Sexual Experience Survey. (Source: Drawn based on data from Anderson et al. [2021])

Initiating Sexual Activity in Committed Relationships

Within committed relationships, initiating sexual activity may, at first look, seem significantly easier. With a desirable partner already selected and available, one needs only to communicate interest, right? Not quite. Sex is an interdependent experience, making it a "breeding ground" (pun intended) for **sexual interdependence dilemmas** (Day et al., 2015), situations in which partners' sexual needs and desires are opposed, rather than aligned. Although receiving an invitation for sex from a partner is highly rewarding (boosting the receiver's positive feelings about their sex lives for up to 72 hours; Dobson et al., 2020), invitations for sex are not always successful. Early research suggests that a little over a quarter of sexual advances occurring within married and cohabiting different-sex couples are denied (Byers & Heinlein, 1989).

Accordingly, sex is a frequent source of conflict, even in CNM relationships, where there is greater flexibility for sexual fulfillment through multiple relationships (Balzarini et al., 2019; Conley & Moors, 2014). Conflicts and disappointments pertaining to sex can center on myriad issues (e.g., boredom in the bedroom, specific sexual acts, low-quality sex), with discrepancies between partners' sexual desire a particularly common problem (Davies et al., 1999; Willoughby et al., 2014). Sexual desire discrepancies fluctuate for couples (as sexual desire also fluctuates; Vowels et al., 2018), perhaps being especially salient during stressful times, illnesses, or major changes, such as when partners enter parenthood, or when one partner is transitioning genders (Muise, Kim et al., 2017; Rosen et al., 2018; Rubinsky, 2021). Among both same-sex and different-sex partners, experiencing sexual desire discrepancies predicts next-day sexual distress, a pattern that emphasizes how sensitive people are to their own and their partner's interest in sex (Jodouin et al., 2021). Emerging evidence suggests partner mismatch in sexual desire may be less problematic than chronically low sex drives (Kim et al., 2021), yet the interpersonal nature of sexual desire is clear: when one partner's sex drive declines, relationship functioning for both partners appears to suffer (McNulty et al., 2019). When a partner denies a sexual advance, the initiator can suffer from negative feelings about their sex life that linger for up to two days (Dobson et al., 2020).

Is there a way to reject sex without damaging the relationship or upsetting the initiator? As shown in the left-hand column of Table 11.3, people reject their partners' advances in ways that vary in positivity and directness (Kim et al., 2020). Some people, such as individuals higher in **sexual communal strength** (i.e., people strongly motivated to meet their partner's

Table 11.3 Ways of rejecting a partner's advance

How do people reject a partner's advance?	1 (never) – 5 (very frequently)				
With reassurance					
I reassure my partner that I love them	1	2	3	4	5
I offer to make it up with my partner in the future	1	2	3	4	5
With hostility					
I am short or curt with my partner	1	2	3	4	5
I give my partner the silent treatment	1	2	3	4	5
Assertively					
I am clear and direct about why I don't want to have sex	1	2	3	4	5
I say "no" in a direct manner	1	2	3	4	5
With deflection					
I don't reciprocate my partner's affection	1	2	3	4	5
I pretend to sleep	1	2	3	4	5

People can reject their partners' sexual advances in ways that show or do not show responsiveness; initiators can then experience reactions varying from understanding to insecurity. The statements on the left are sampled from the twenty-item Sexual Rejection Scale. How is rejection different within committed relationships compared to casual relationships?
Source: Kim et al. (2020).

sexual needs) and people lower in attachment avoidance, tend to reject in a reassuring manner, an approach linked to favorable relationship judgments. Sexual communal strength and low attachment avoidance also predict less reliance on deflection and hostile rejection, strategies that are associated with low relationship quality (Kim et al., 2020). What about simply having sex rather than rejecting a partner, with the goal of preventing a beloved from the insult and hurt that might follow from a rejection? This might seem like a viable short-term solution, and indeed, it might temporarily predict more satisfying sex lives (Kim, Muise, & Impett, 2018), but it is ill-advised. Pursuing sex for avoidance goals is linked to worse relationship functioning over time than offering rejections, provided they are positive, reassuring rejections (Kim, Muise, & Impett, 2018). In other words, kind rejections trump having sex to avoid displeasing a partner.

After being rejected, in the dyadic back-and-forth of sexual negotiations, the initiator has a chance to react to the rejection (Kim et al., 2019). Do they storm away in a huff? Start questioning the fate of the relationship? Whether initiators respond with understanding, resentment, renewed attempts at seduction, or insecurity is linked to aspects of their personality (e.g., narcissism, aggressiveness), their attachment anxiety, and their sexual communal strength.

Of course, perceiving rejection does not necessarily mean a person has been rejected. Like so many of our relationship experiences, making sense of our partner's behaviors and presumed intentions includes subjectivity. On the one hand, people do show tracking accuracy with their judgments of rejection, but on the other hand, they consistently infuse bias into their evaluations, such that they perceive stronger and more frequent sexual rejection than their partners offer (Dobson et al., 2022). Think about this for a moment: people believe that their partners are rejecting them more often than they are, which suggests unnecessary hurt, as well as missed opportunities to engage in sex and indulge in its related benefits to intimacy and closeness. Other misperceptions also shape the sexual initiation game. For example, in direct contrast to what we see in casual contexts, if men in committed different-sex relationships make a mistake, they tend to under-perceive, rather than over-perceive, their partner's desire for sex (Dobson et al., 2018; Muise, Stanton et al., 2016). This bias means that men may be missing out on welcomed opportunities for sexual encounters. Meanwhile, women in committed relationships are apt to err on the side of over-perceiving their partner's interest (Dobson et al., 2018). As you can see, even in highly committed contexts, people do not necessarily know what the other is thinking when it comes to sexual advances and rejections. As emotionally risky as they might feel at times, attempts to initiate sex happen frequently within both committed relationships and casual contexts. How frequently is an empirical question, one that has long attracted the attention of relationship scientists.

Conclusion

When Willow Smith speaks of polyamory and her own feelings toward sex, she broaches a subject that people often experience as private, even as their curiosities about the who, what, when, and how of sex are peaked. Indeed, as fundamental as sexuality is to the human experience, many people have an understanding of sexuality that is clouded by misconceptions. We hope this chapter answered many of your questions about sexuality, its basic features, and its role in casual and committed relationships. As we learned in this chapter, people pursue sex for diverse reasons and with different frequencies, and within ongoing relationships, sexuality is inextricably intertwined with relationship quality. This link with relationship quality becomes especially interesting as we move away from relationship maintenance to consider the final stage in a relationship's life cycle: relationship dissolution. Spoiler alert! As much as sex can provide an opportunity to build intimacy and connection, it can also fuel relationship distress, sometimes serving as the catalyst for a break-up. With a solid understanding of sexuality in casual and ongoing relationships, along with your knowledge of ways that partners prevent and respond to relationship threats, we can now examine why people end their relationships.

Major Take-Aways

- Sexuality is a multidimensional construct (i.e., it includes desires, attitudes, motives, and behaviors) that is shaped by biological and social forces. While common patterns emerge, people experience and approach their sex lives in diverse ways, often as a function of life stage, relationship structure, and relationship context (e.g., short-term versus long-term).
- More sex is generally beneficial, but only to a point. Critically, how often people have sex may be less revealing about the quality of a person's sex life than their overall judgment of sexual satisfaction, which is not tied to one sexual encounter, but is closely linked (in ongoing relationships) to relationship satisfaction.
- People can initiate sex indirectly or directly, but whether occurring in casual or committed relationships, the highly interdependent experience of initiation can be tricky to navigate successfully.

Further Readings

If you're interested in ...

... the first sexual experiences of LGB+ individuals, read:
Gillespie, I. J., Armstrong, H. L., & Ingham, R. (2022). Exploring reflections, motivations, and experiential outcomes of first same-sex/gender sexual experiences among Lesbian, Gay, Bisexual, and other sexual minority individuals. *Journal of Sex Research*, *59*(1), 26–38.

... an accessible review of how sexual processes shape relationships, read:
Maxwell, J. A., & McNulty, J. K. (2019). No longer in a dry spell: The developing understanding of how sex influences romantic relationships. *Current Directions in Psychological Science*, *28*(1), 102–107.

... consensual non-monogamy, read:
Scoats, R., & Campbell, C. (2022). What do we know about consensual non-monogamy?. *Current Opinion in Psychology*, 101468.

. . . the diverse reasons people pursue short-term sexual encounters, read:
Thorpe, S., & Kuperberg, A. (2021). Social motivations for college hookups. *Sexuality & Culture*, *25*(2), 623–645.

. . . human sexual behaviors and sexuality research on under-represented populations, read:

Townes, A., Thorpe, S., Parmer, T., Wright, B., & Herbenick, D. (2021). Partnered sexual behaviors, pleasure, and orgasms at last sexual encounter: Findings from a US probability sample of black women ages 18 to 92 years. *Journal of Sex & Marital Therapy*, *47*(4), 353–367.

PART IV

DISSOLUTION AND INTERVENTIONS

12 RELATIONSHIP DISSOLUTION

Different People, Different Relationships, Different Endings

Recalling their first date – which also would be their last date – Ben remembers an unexpected chemistry with Robbie (Figure 12.1a). In his mind's eye, he sees them laughing, sharing personal stories, and playfully conversing. A brilliant evening, a startlingly good date. These memories resurface in an episode of *Modern Love*, an anthology series that highlights a wide range of relationship beginnings, middles, and ends. This particular episode transpires during the brief moment that Ben and Robbie walk past each other on the streets of New York, a year after their first/last date. They see each other and remember the evening when their easy rapport and mutual attraction carried them from sharing a meal at a restaurant to dancing at a club to sexual intimacy at Ben's place. Later that same night, Ben learns his father has been hospitalized. In the stress of the moment, he asks Robbie to leave and shuts down Robbie's protests. The relationship is over.

(a)   (b)

Figure 12.1 The show *Modern Love* depicts relationships that end after little commitment (Ben and Robbie [a]) and after significant commitment (Kenji and Margot [b]), in varied ways, with varied emotions, and with varied consequences. Why do you think romantic endings are so often the plot of the media we consume? (Photo: © Jamie McCarthy / Getty Images Entertainment [a] and Album / Alamy Stock Photo [b])

In a different episode, viewers meet Margot, an older woman, energetic and reflective, preparing to attend the funeral of her husband, Kenji (Figure 12.1b). As she readies herself, Margot recollects the tender early days of their relationship, when they bonded over a shared interest in running. This late-in-life love unfolded slowly at first, as Kenji mourned the loss of his (first) wife six years prior, and then accelerated with vigor, as they discovered how much they needed and enjoyed each other. Here, viewers see heartache of a different kind than Ben and Robbie's, one defined by a loss of an intimately known, deeply cherished life partner. Are there similarities? Perhaps. Are there differences? Surely. Even so, as varied as these two relationship endings are, neither is likely the scenario that comes to mind when you first think of a relationship ending. The prototypical relationship ending – a decision-based **breakup** of an ongoing, established romantic relationship – is only one way relationships end. Indeed, relationship endings are as varied as the people that experience them.

Romantic relationships end. This fact is universal. If not by choice or circumstance, relationships end because humans are unavoidably mortal (sorry for this downer!). In no way, however, does universality make the experience of relationship dissolution any easier; nor does universality suggest that all relationships end in the same way, with the same causes, processes, or consequences. The variability we see in shows like *Modern Love* is a mere reflection of the diverse ways relationships end in real life. Relationship scientists value this diversity as they explore central questions of relationship dissolution: Why and how do people voluntarily break up? What are the consequences of a close relationship ending? How do people recover and move on from difficult relationship endings? As you read this chapter, your goal is to keep in mind the diversity that characterizes relationship endings while gaining insight into typical precursors, processes, and consequences.

 GUIDING QUESTIONS

Consider these questions as you read this chapter:
- What individual characteristics and behaviors, relational processes (i.e., changes to intimacy, and interdependence, and commitment), and situational contexts predict relationship dissolution?
- What is the process of a breakup, and what strategies do people use to voluntarily end their relationships?
- How do people experience relationship endings, and what factors explain the diversity of their experiences?
- How do people navigate relationships with their exes, changes to their self-concepts, and new romantic relationships after a relationship ends?

How Common Is Relationship Dissolution?

Relationship scientists struggle to pin down exactly how often people's relationships dissolve. This is tricky business even if we focus only on romantic breakups (and not on the ends of friendships or relationships with colleagues, neighbors, or family). Why is this so challenging? For one reason, people have diverse relationship statuses that complicate the tallying process (does the end of a friends-with-benefits relationship represent a breakup? Should "legally separated" be included in a divorce rate?). Another problem is access to data. Scientists often use surveys or, when possible, vital statistics (data collected nationally, which include births, deaths, marriages, and divorces) as the basis for their analysis. As ideal as national data might seem, vital statistics can be incomplete: in the United States, for example, funding issues have periodically prevented some states from submitting their data (Amato, 2010b). Still, these data, even if incomplete, provide a helpful basis for the next challenge: how should we calculate an estimate of dissolution rates?

The most often measured dissolution rate is that for divorce, which, as shown in Table 12.1, can be calculated in multiple ways. As you consider these approaches, keep in mind that divorce rates require not only proper interpretation, but a critical eye so we know which conclusions are appropriate to make about the state of relationship stability. For example, divorce rates ignore the endings of long-term partnerships or cohabitating relationships that operate similarly to marriages without the legal designation. Unless specified, they also generally fail to differentiate first divorces from second, third, etc. divorces. Other caveats, specific to the method used, are also worth noting. The crude divorce rate, for example, though highly popular, skews our perception of divorce frequency by relying on the number of divorces per 1,000 people, with no adjustments for the population's age distribution nor its proportion of married individuals. In other words, the "1,000 people" used in the denominator of this equation includes children and unmarried adults, none of whom is at risk of divorce. Accordingly, scholars often prefer the refined divorce rate, which uses a more precise denominator: 1,000 *married women*, not 1,000 *people*. The refined divorce rate lets you estimate the percentage of women who

Table 12.1 Different ways to compute divorce rates

Method	Definition
Crude divorce rate	Number of divorces per 1000 people in a given year
Refined divorce rate	Number of divorces per 1000 married women in a given year
Cohort approach	The lifetime probability of marriages to end in divorce for a given cohort of individuals

Divorce rates can be computed in different ways. Which do you find most informative?
Source: Developed based on data from Amato (2010b).

divorce per year (a rate of 15/1,000 would mean 1.5 percent of women), but it excludes the divorces of same-sex male marriages. In practice, whether scientists report the crude rate or the refined rate may make little difference provided you know how to interpret them: evidence suggests they are highly correlated (i.e., above 0.90; Amato, 2010b). Neither rate, however, will offer insight into how probable divorce might be for a given group of people. For that, we need to take a **cohort approach** (Amato, 2010b). The cohort approach allows scientists, for example, to count divorces among people married in the year 2000 and then estimate the likelihood that anyone married in 2000 will eventually divorce. Like its alternatives, it can rely on incomplete data, but also – like its alternatives – with proper interpretation, it provides much-needed insight into the experience of relationship dissolution.

Marital Dissolution

Knowing what we now know about divorce rates, how often do people experience marital dissolution? In the United States, the crude divorce rate was estimated at 2.3 in 2020, meaning that an estimated 2.3 people divorced per 1,000 people that year (CDC, 2020). For that same year, the refined divorce rate has been estimated at 14 women per 1,000 women 15 or older (Westrick-Payne, 2022). If we take the cohort approach, we can project that 43 to 46 percent of marriages between 2005 and 2010 will end in divorce (Smock & Schwartz, 2020). Divorce rates are similar among same-sex partners (Rosenfeld, 2014). Historically, the divorce rate rose precipitously in the United States after no-fault divorce laws were enacted in the 1970s, peaking in 1979 (NCHS, 1980; Nakonezny et al., 1995). The divorce rate has shown a fairly steady decline since then, even in the last decade or so (see Figure 12.2), a trend that also appears cross-culturally. These declines in divorce likely follow from cultural movements away from marriage, including delayed marriage and higher rates of cohabitation (Cohen, 2019; Raley & Sweeney, 2020). Projections

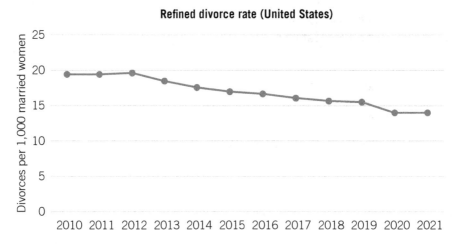

Figure 12.2 Divorce rates are generally declining, even as they remain high. In what ways might divorce be problematic, and in what ways does it support personal and relational well-being? (Source: Drawn based on data from American Community Survey, women 15 or older; US Census Bureau [2021])

suggest divorce rates will continue to fall; these models anticipate that while fewer people will enter marriage in the years to come, their marriages will likely be more stable (Cohen, 2019). Today, in the United States, divorce rates tend to be higher among individuals who are Black, Native American, or US-born Hispanic compared to White Americans, among individuals who are less educated, and among partners in a re-marriage rather than a first-time marriage (Cohen, 2019; Raley & Sweeney, 2020; Reynolds, 2021). Older adults are also at higher risk of divorce, with rates steady or accelerating, countering general declining trends (Brown & Lin, 2012; Cohen, 2019; Kennedy & Ruggles, 2014). Adults over 65 – who make up only about 20 percent of the general adult population – also account for about 70 percent of people who enter widowhood each year (Gurrentz & Mayol-Garcia, 2021). These estimates would likely rise by including older adults with unmarried partners, underscoring the importance of age as a vulnerability factor for relationship dissolution.

 DIVERSITY AND INCLUSION

The Rise of the Grey Divorce

Before the 1990s, marriages among older adults typically ended with the death of a spouse, with divorce primarily something that younger people did (Brown & Lin, 2022; Carr & Utz, 2020). Such is not the case today. In fact, even as overall rates of divorce have declined, the rates of **grey divorce**, divorces among people over 50, have *accelerated* in the United States over the last few decades. Back in 1990, fewer than one in ten older adults divorced, but, as shown in Figure 12.3, this number skyrocketed to one in four older adults in a matter of twenty years, doubling the divorce rate and inspiring scholars to dub this period as the "grey divorce revolution" (Brown & Lin, 2012). Today, grey divorce accounts for 36 percent of all divorces in the United States, with about 25 percent of older women's marriages and over 50 percent of older men's marriages ending in divorce (Brown et al., 2018; Brown & Lin, 2022). These statistics show the critical need to study divorce among older adults, for whom widowhood is no longer the assumed path toward relationship dissolution. Recent estimates suggest that the divorce rate is holding high and somewhat steady for people who are 50 to 65, but the divorce rate among people 65 and older continues to rise (Brown & Lin, 2022). In a world where overall divorce rates are declining, why are they high and climbing for older adults?

Many **social gerontologists**, scientists who apply a social perspective to the study of ageing (Phillips et al., 2012), anticipated the uptick in grey divorces (Cain, 1988; Uhlenberg & Myers, 1981). Central to their forecast was that older adults increasingly represent baby boomers, and baby boomers generally have a more open attitude toward divorce than prior older-adult cohorts (Brown & Wright, 2019). This cultural shift was accompanied by an experience shift: more older adults today enter their sunset years in a remarriage, and remarriages are more likely to dissolve than first marriages (Amato, 2010a; Brown & Lin, 2012). As another cultural change, more older women today have participated in the work force and have the resources to leave unsatisfying marriages than older women of previous

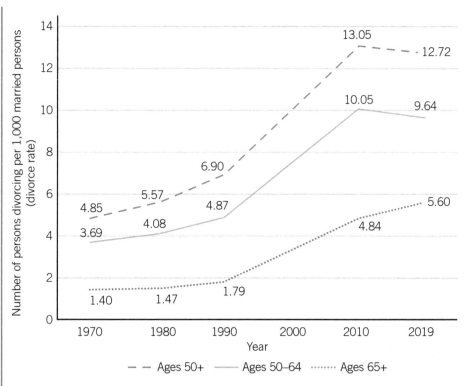

Figure 12.3 Grey divorces in the United States are steady and high for ages 50+ and 50–64, but are accelerating for people over age 65. How might older adults' divorces affect their broader family structure? (Source: Brown, S. and Lin, I-Fen [2022], The graying of divorce: A half-century of change. *The Journals of Gerontology: Series B, 77*(9), 1710–1720, https://doi.org/10.1093/geronb/gbac057. Translated and reproduced by permission of Oxford University Press on behalf of The Gerontological Society of America.)

generations (Lin & Brown, 2021; Schoen et al., 2002). Further, increases in life expectancy reduce the likelihood of early spousal death, while offering more opportunity for voluntary separations and divorces. Thus, older age today operates with a backdrop that is more amenable to divorce than in previous generations.

Why are older adults divorcing? This question led scholars to consider age-related turning points that theoretically might increase divorce risk, such as retirement, health problems, or becoming empty nesters; however, longitudinal data do not support the idea that these life events precipitate divorce (Lin et al., 2018). Instead, factors predicting grey divorce tend to mirror factors predicting divorce for younger adults, with similar social and economic factors introducing vulnerabilities, such as unemployment or having a marginalized racial or ethnic identity (Brown & Lin, 2022; Lin et al., 2018). Emerging cross-cultural evidence does suggest, however, one age-related event that reduces divorce likelihood: data suggest that becoming grandparents protects couples against marital dissolution (Alderotti et al., 2022; Brown, Lin et al., 2021).

Nonmarital Relationship Dissolution

Marriage, with its legal contracts and "until death do us part" vows, is considered a protective factor against breaking up (Rosenfeld, 2018), so if divorce rates are high, what about non-marital breakups? In one sample of American university students, 68 percent reported having ever experienced a breakup, with an average of 2.5 prior breakups (Field et al., 2009). A different sample of emerging adults (mean age about 25) reported an average of 3.3 prior relationships (Beckmeyer & Jamison, 2020). Another study, which tracked a Canadian sample's romantic involvement from age 16 to 24, found considerable variability, with subgroups averaging about one partner across those eight years, others around three partners, still others around seven partners, and one group around twelve partners (Boisvert & Poulin, 2017). These estimates likely ignore the dissolution of casual relationships and predominantly sexual relationships (e.g., friends-with-benefits); further, as people age and accrue more life experiences, these numbers likely rise. In other words, non-marital romantic breakups may not be universal, but they are certainly normative, and some people experience more breakups than others.

RESEARCHER SPOTLIGHT: Philip N. Cohen, PhD

How did you come to be a sociologist and a demographer?
I entered graduate school in sociology after an undergraduate degree in American Studies. I wanted to be more practical, and scientific, in my career, and sociology was a good way to do that. As I got involved in empirical sociology – with an interest in families and the intersections of different kinds of inequality – demography was a natural fit for my development.

What do you hope students will hold on to as they learn about recent divorce trends?
One thing people often forget when they look at divorce trends is that some divorce is good, even essential. If no one ever divorced, that would probably mean people weren't really freely married in the first place. Of course, most people who get married hope they will never get divorced, but we shouldn't assume less divorce is always better. In addition, it's generally true that happier, more privileged people are less likely to get divorced whereas, for

Figure 12.4 Dr. Philip N. Cohen is a professor of sociology and a demographer at the University of Maryland, College Park. (Photo courtesy of Philip N. Cohen, PhD.)

people who are having a hard time, divorce is definitely more likely. So, finding ways to reduce divorce (without restricting people's freedoms) may be a way to help people lead happier, more fulfilling lives. It's complicated!

What are some frontiers in research on relationship dissolution?
We still don't know nearly enough about same-sex couples, about non-marital relationships (like cohabitation and living apart together), or about relationships that don't include sex and reproduction (but are still "like

family"). We need better data, better theorizing, more exploration and study on these topics. I'm excited to see what the next generation of researchers will be able to do.

What do you enjoy most about your work?
I love that I learn new things every single day, and that the students and scholars and other people I meet challenge me with new experiences and ideas. Being a scholar – a teacher, a writer, a researcher – is a great privilege.

Predictors of Relationship Dissolution

Why do people work to build and maintain a relationship with another person, only to change directions and move out of that romantic relationship? Consistent with the SABI model of social interactions (described in Chapter 2), the precursors to breaking up may be anchored to critical interaction problems derived from aspects of "me," "you," and "us." As we will see, the individual differences that define "me" and "you" may only become problematic when these personal traits or habits start threatening the "us," that is, when they introduce problematic dependency structures that compromise healthy relationship factors like intimacy, interdependence, and commitment. Additionally, no relationship occurs in isolation: the holiday love affair, so easy to maintain in sunny, stress-free, all-inclusive-vacation-fun land, might crumble once you're back at home. As shown in Figure 12.5, along with problems with "me," "you," and "us," problems with context can weaken relationship stability.

Problems with "Me" or "You"

"It's not you … it's me." Have you ever uttered these words? Did you mean them? Sometimes people genuinely identify aspects of themselves as the reason to end a relationship. Other times, this phrase is a polite way of saying, "Babe, you're 100 percent the reason we're over." What is it about "me" or "you" that might alter an ongoing relationship's trajectory?

Personality Traits
In general, personality is a robust predictor of relationship events, including breakups. Meta-analytic work on the Big Five, for example, points strongly to neuroticism predicting a higher likelihood of subsequent divorce and conscientiousness and agreeableness each predicting a lower likelihood of subsequent divorce (Roberts et al., 2007). The role of extraversion and openness in predicting breakups is less consistent, with some data suggesting higher levels of each could be a risk factor for divorce (Schwaba et al., 2019; Solomon & Jackson, 2014; Spikic & Mortelmans, 2021).

Of the Big Five traits, neuroticism, with its signature feature of negativity (Watson & Clark, 1984), stands apart as a particularly potent vulnerability for low relationship quality and romantic breakups (Dyrenforth et al., 2010; Karney & Bradbury, 1995, 1997; O'Meara & South, 2019; Solomon & Jackson, 2014). If you think about it, neuroticism introduces

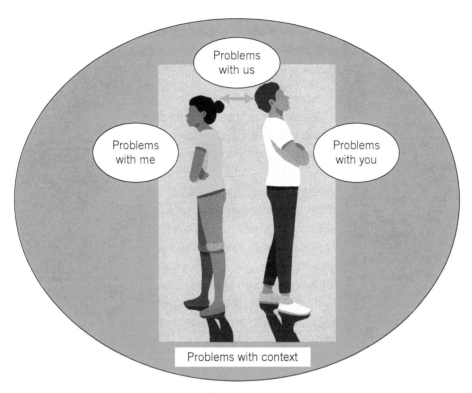

Figure 12.5 What predicts relationship dissolution? Individual differences, relationship factors, and the broader context all play their role in keeping relationships intact and prompting their breakup. (Photo: adapted from gmast3r)

challenges from cognitive, behavioral, and emotional angles. Cognitively, people higher in neuroticism perceive and interpret interactions with their partner more negatively than people lower in neuroticism, engaging in more hostile attributions (Finn et al., 2013; Kreuzer & Gollwitzer, 2022; McNulty, 2008b). Behaviorally, neuroticism is linked to passive-aggressive behaviors, less willingness to forgive, withdrawal, and less adaptive coping approaches, as well as a tendency to elicit negative behaviors from romantic partners (Braithwaite, Mitchell et al., 2016; Kreuzer & Gollwitzer, 2022; McNulty, 2008b). Emotionally, people with higher neuroticism experience a high degree of negative affect. This is problematic given the role of positive emotions in supporting relationships (see Chapter 10). Underscoring the stability of personality over time, adults who divorce are less likely to have, as adolescents, smiled intensely in photographs (Hertenstein et al., 2009).

Each Dark Triad trait – narcissism, Machiavellianism, and psychopathy – also reflects an inclination toward thoughts, emotions, and behaviors that could be hazardous for relationship stability. Consider narcissism, with its strong sense of entitlement, vanity, and inflated self-esteem. Highly narcissistic individuals tend to be commitment-averse, and if they do enter a relationship, they are more likely to engage in infidelity, which helps in part to explain their general greater risk for divorce (Campbell & Foster, 2002; Meltzer et al., 2014; Wetzel et al., 2020). Likewise, Machiavellianism (i.e., a manipulative, calculated style) and psychopathy (with its pervasive negativity) each appear to predict less stable relationships in Western and Eastern societies (Weiss et al., 2018; Yu et al., 2020). The Dark Triad traits may predict relationship instability for many reasons, including the tendency of people higher in these traits to engage in more hostile and destructive behaviors and to rely more heavily on the "Four Horsemen" (contempt, criticism, defensiveness, and stonewalling) during conflict (Campbell & Foster, 2002; Horan et al., 2015; Jonason et al., 2010).

Individual Differences in Attachment Orientation

Attachment orientation is another factor that should theoretically predict relationship dissolution. Consider the easy coordination and consistent responsiveness and support that might characterize a healthy romantic attachment. Introduce attachment insecurity and this healthy pattern can give way to a more tenuous dynamic. Indeed, greater attachment insecurity is associated with less closeness, worse support, and more conflict (Li & Chan, 2012), which may explain why attachment insecurity is associated with poorer relationship quality (Candel & Turliuc, 2019; Li & Chan, 2012) and may contribute to relationship instability as well. How directly attachment predicts patterns of relationship dissolution is an underdeveloped area of research, but available evidence aligns with theoretical expectations. People in unhappy-but-stable relationships are more likely to have insecure attachments than secure orientations, and having an anxious or avoidant attachment orientation is associated with individuals' histories of divorce, as well as current status as a single person (Davila & Bradbury, 2001; McNelis & Segrin, 2019).

Habits and Behaviors

Sometimes, the most salient reasons for why we end relationships are anchored to aspects of "me" or "you," but are not specifically related to personality or attachment. For instance, sometimes people identify their own desire for more excitement as a reason to leave, or they consider leaving because they feel like they do not have time for the relationship (Joel, MacDonald, & Page-Gould, 2018). Such self-oriented reasons are important. Indeed, believing that your personal needs for self-growth, independence, or adventure are not being met is a leading reason people break up (Drigotas & Rusbult, 1992; Machia & Ogolsky, 2021). These authentic "it's not you, it's me" scenarios are joined by breakup motivations pointed directly at the partner (Joel, MacDonald, & Page-Gould, 2018). Retrospectively, people tend to blame their partners for a divorce more than themselves (Amato & Previti, 2004). They perceive their partners to have unfavorable qualities, like being uncaring, insecure, or undependable (Felmlee, 1995), or might judge them as "immature," a sometimes-cited reason for divorce (Amato & Previti, 2004).

Other commonly cited motives for dissolution include partner behaviors, such as partners working too much or not doing their share of household work (Amato & Previti, 2004). Indeed, in one Dutch sample of divorced individuals, over 20 percent reported that unsatisfying division of household chores was a motivator for divorce (De Graaf & Kalmijn, 2006). Partners can also exhibit significant personal problems that might jeopardize their relationship's stability, such as addiction, mental health challenges, or legal issues (Joel, MacDonald, & Page-Gould, 2018). Data from Greece suggest that people believe having a "harmful spouse," someone who is abusive, aggressive, or engaging in risky behavior (e.g., substance use, gambling), would be a reason to divorce (Apostolou, Constantinou et al., 2019). Domestic violence, mental health challenges, and substance use can serve as the "last straw" that precipitates the end of relationships (Scott et al., 2013, 2021).

Problems with "Us"

Maybe instead of, "it's not you, it's me," people should say, "it's not just you or just me ... it's *us*." This reflects a central notion in the SABI model: that individuals create a dependency structure (the unique and influential entity called "us") that must be considered to understand their relationship and their relationship dissolution, or breakup. Indeed, why do you think we use the phrase "break up"? What exactly "breaks" or is damaged when people break up? If you think of breakups as the disentangling or deconstruction of a close relationship, it is sensible that breakups target the three signature features of close relationships: intimacy, interdependence, and commitment. When partners break up, they cease building emotional and informational closeness (intimacy), they sever their reliance on each other to form separate lives (interdependence), and they choose to stop their relationship (commitment). In other words, to break up is to break – slowly or suddenly – the core components of "us": intimacy, interdependence, and commitment. Perhaps unsurprisingly, breakdowns in each of these domains also tend to precede the final breakup decision and communication that "it's over."

Breaking Intimacy

"I don't even know you anymore." How often have you heard this phrase in fictional depictions of breakups? How about in real-life breakups? The loss of intimacy – reflecting intimate knowledge, connection, and feelings of closeness – is central to relationship dissolution. Feeling close with someone is inherently rewarding (Krach et al., 2010) and prospective research suggests that couples who experience fewer intimacy-related rewards are at greater risk of subsequent breakup (Park, Impett, & Spielmann, 2021). Emotional intimacy and emotional investment are strong reasons people feel compelled to stay in their relationships, with a lack of relational need fulfillment a key reason people consider leaving (Joel, MacDonald, & Page-Gould, 2018; Machia & Ogolsky, 2021). Low emotional intimacy and waning love not only can motivate people to seek counseling but also can compel them to terminate their relationships (Doss et al., 2004; Strizzi et al., 2020).

Intimacy can die a slow death. According to social penetration theory, as much as relationships build through vulnerable self-disclosures, the "depenetration" process involves increasingly more shallow and superficial conversations (Altman & Taylor, 1973). Partners who were once so very close can gradually become distant, emotionally detached, and indifferent toward each other (Barry et al., 2008). This new state, referred to as disaffection (or synonymously, as romantic disengagement), is marked by neutral feelings where positive feelings once were, and apathy in lieu of love (Kayser, 1993; Kayser & Rao, 2013). Disaffection represents a significant move toward dissolution (Kayser, 1993). Critically, romantic disengagement is not marked by anger or conflict; instead, partners stand by as their bond erodes and they (not surprisingly) experience decreasing relationship satisfaction and commitment (Barry et al., 2008).

A loss of closeness, affection, and love, feelings of disappointment, and a lack of faith in one's partner and relationship can also reflect the toxic state of relationship disillusionment (Huston, 1994; Huston et al., 2001). In the same way that lacking positive illusions places non-marital partners at risk of breakup, disillusionment predicts divorce likelihood for married partners and is an even stronger predictor of relationship dissolution for cohabitating partners who have fewer commitment constraints (Huston et al., 2001; Le et al., 2010; Niehuis et al., 2015). Highly passionate dating relationships, when they transition to the pedestrian routines of day-to-day married life, may be especially at risk of perceived losses in affectionate behaviors and accompanying disillusionment (Niehuis et al., 2016). Once-in-love-now-not partners can end up living parallel – not intersecting – lives; they might go about their days without interest in each other's affairs, intentionally limiting interactions with each other. According to early models of divorce, this type of romantic disengagement constitutes emotional divorce, a key dimension of marital breakdown (Bohannan, 1970).

From a cognitive perspective, closeness reflects interdependent mental representations of self and other, and *not* including the other in the self may create a dissolution risk. Lower levels of inclusion of other in the self is associated with less commitment, greater susceptibility to infidelity, and a greater likelihood of breaking up (Agnew et al., 1998; Le et al., 2010; Lewandowski & Ackerman, 2010; McIntyre et al., 2015). People who experience a lack of self-expansion in their relationships (a key facilitator of continued self-expansion) also think about breaking up more frequently, more readily consider alternatives, and – over time – are less likely to stay together (Mattingly et al., 2019). The emotional closeness that tethers partners together can thus be conceptualized in multiple ways. When closeness falters, it could be a cause or a symptom of other challenges, including the breaking of interdependence.

Breaking Interdependence

Another part of the relationship that often begins "breaking" prior to a breakup is related to partners' interdependence. Specifically, relationship stability is threatened when partners experience incompatibility, repeatedly misaligned interests that make interdependence challenging ("I know you want to do that, but I want to do this"; see Chapter 8). When partners' interests frequently conflict, they can experience immediate, reactive reductions in trust and then suffer lingering effects, including lower commitment (the intention to remain in the relationship) a week later (Balliet et al., 2022; Columbus et al., 2021). Nearly 20 percent of divorced individuals indicate incompatibility as a reason their relationship dissolved (Previti & Amato, 2004), and people often consider ending ongoing relationships when they see a high degree of incompatibility (Joel, MacDonald, & Page-Gould, 2018).

Given the challenges of incompatibility, not surprisingly, many people pre-emptively limit conflicting interests, habits, or perspectives by entering relationships with similar others (see Chapter 4). Although this helps (Moore et al., 2017), even similar partners encounter unfamiliar situations, take on new goals, and experience unforeseen challenges that can provide opportunities for conflicts of interest to develop. People regularly endorse conflict as a negative turning point in an ongoing relationship and see "too many" conflicts as a reason to leave (Joel, MacDonald, & Page-Gould, 2018; Machia & Ogolsky, 2021). Evidence from both different-sex relationships and recent work on female same-gender relationships suggests that perceiving "too much" fighting, arguing, and conflict is a leading reason underlying breakup decisions (Scott et al., 2013, 2021). However, compared to other predictors of non-marital relationship dissolution, meta-analysis suggests conflict is a relatively weak predictor of breakups (Le et al., 2010). Conflict may be part of the story, but for many partners, other factors may be more salient explanations for why relationships end.

Breaking Commitment

A breakup is also typically precipitated by a decline in commitment, the decision, or glue, that keeps a relationship together (Sternberg, 1986). As commitment breaks down, the likelihood of breakup increases. Therefore, appreciating commitment's precursors can help provide a more complete picture of why some relationships dissolve. Recall from the investment model of commitment (see Chapter 2) that people stay committed to their relationships when they have high investment and satisfaction and have fewer alternatives (Rusbult, 1980; Tran et al., 2019). Inversely, then, dissolution is more likely when people have low investment, low satisfaction (perhaps due to the partner characteristics and behaviors described above), and notice more (or more desirable) alternatives (e.g., Tran et al., 2019). Critically, the Investment Model predictors contribute to commitment and stay-leave behavior in concert. Although low relationship satisfaction inspires people to think about leaving their relationships and is a strong predictor of relationship dissolution, in general (Joel, MacDonald, & Page-Gould, 2018; Røsand et al., 2014), low satisfaction does not automatically translate into a breakup. Sometimes relationship satisfaction might take a backseat in the presence of considerable investments (e.g., children, resources), no perceivable alternative partners, or a fear of being single (George et al., 2020; Slotter & Finkel, 2009; Spielmann et al., 2013).

Relationship dissolution can also be precipitated by a partner's unilateral choice to change (or break) the nature of their commitment by engaging in infidelity: a secret sexual and/or emotional betrayal. Infidelity is considered a serious relational transgression, one that violates cardinal rules in monogamous relationships (Jones et al., 2004). As such, infidelity is a robust predictor of relationship dissolution across at least 160 countries and is a concern among same-sex and different-sex committed partners (Amato & Previti, 2004; Betzig, 1989; Hoy et al., 2022; Jankowiak & Nell, 2002). Among female same-sex couples, for example, infidelity is the most commonly endorsed "final straw" that leads to a relationship ending (Scott et al., 2021). Trajectory research shows that attention to romantic alternatives upticks in the time preceding infidelity and also before relationships end (Ritchie et al., 2021). In other words, weakening commitment can trigger attention to alternatives, and this alternative monitoring can promote behaviors or conditions that create further relational instability.

Despite its toxic effect on relationships, potentially increasing the odds of breakup by 363 percent (that's right … 363 percent! Balsam et al., 2017), infidelity is surprisingly common. According to the Global Social Survey, about 17 percent of married individuals have had a sexual encounter with someone who is not their spouse at least once over the course of their relationship, with some suggestion that sexual infidelity occurs within 1 to 6 percent of marriages each year (Davern et al., 2021; Whisman et al., 2007; Whisman & Snyder, 2007). Compared to marriages, cohabiting relationships suffer a higher risk of infidelity, but not as high as dating relationships, which are even more vulnerable (Adamopoulou, 2013; Wagner, 2019). Indeed, approximately 65 percent of university students report having once cheated on a non-marital romantic partner (Shackelford et al., 2000). Past infidelity may pave the way for more: people unfaithful in previous relationships are more likely to be unfaithful in subsequent relationships, and likewise, those who have been victims of infidelity in the past are more likely to be victims in future relationships (Adamopoulou, 2013; Knopp et al., 2017).

Figure 12.6 Infidelity often has deleterious effects on individuals and their relationships. In *Saints of Newark*, the prequel to the *Sopranos* series, Dickie Moltisanti (left) is married to Joanne (left), but has an ongoing affair with Giuseppina (right). Enacting an impressive double standard, Dickie murders Giuseppina when he learns that she slept with another man. Most men do not physically hurt their partners after learning of their unfaithfulness, but spousal killings are disproportionally explained by suspected or known infidelity, and homicidal thoughts in response to a partner's infidelity are more common among men than women (Daly et al., 1982; Shackelford et al., 2000). How might evolutionary theories, attachment theory, or interdependence theory explain intense reactions to infidelity? (Photo: Entertainment Pictures / Alamy Stock Photo)

Figure 12.7 Married in 1975, Hillary and Bill Clinton's relationship has endured decade upon decade, surviving public scrutiny in response to Bill's infidelity, most notoriously his affair with Monica Lewinsky in the late 1990s. Why do some monogamous couples persist and others break up when someone cheats? (Photo: Eduardo Munoz Alvarez / AFP / Getty Images)

Unfaithful partners adopt multiple strategies to hide their infidelity, including being discreet, eliminating digital evidence, and keeping routines and habits consistent so as to avoid detection (Apostolou, 2022). Unfaithful partners might also ask their friends to cover for them, introduce their extradyadic partner as a friend/colleague, or shower additional attention on their primary partner to dodge suspicion. These efforts may reflect anticipated relationship and partner harm as well as the moral taint of infidelity. Indeed, most people across the globe (a median of 78 percent) believe sexual infidelity is immoral (Poushter, 2014). The United States holds an especially strong moral stance (with between 84 and 89 percent condemning infidelity), stronger than Canada (76 percent) and most of Europe (e.g., Britain, 76 percent; especially France, 42 percent; Brenan, 2019; Poushter, 2014; Wike, 2014). Yet, as suggested by Figure 12.6, not everyone in monogamous relationships is held to the same standards.

Would you end your relationship if your partner cheated? Most people in same-sex and different-sex relationships see infidelity as unforgiveable and a reason to break up (Hoy et al., 2022; Jones, 2008; Scott et al., 2013, 2021). Still, people's responses vary and some people forgive (see Figure 12.7; Hall & Fincham, 2006). People are more likely to forgive an unfaithful partner when they have children together, when their unfaithful partner assures them of their love and future faithfulness, and when they are highly dependent on the partner (Apostolou & Demosthenous, 2021). They are also more prone to forgiveness if they themselves have cheated on their partner, or they plan to cheat on their partner. Similarly, past cheating in other relationships is also associated with staying in relationships after a partner's infidelity (Apostolou, Aristidou et al., 2019), perhaps because it facilitates empathy which allows for forgiveness (Riek & Mania, 2012).

Would the reason your partner cheated influence your decision to forgive them or break up? Review the reasons in Table 12.2 (Selterman et al., 2019), and imagine your reaction if your partner offered these explanations for their infidelity.

Table 12.2 Why do people cheat?

Reasons people engage in extradyadic relationships	
Motivation category	*Sample explanation*
1. Anger	"I wanted to 'get back at' my primary partner for something they did."
2. Sexual desire	"My primary partner was not interested in sexual activities that I find exciting."
3. Lack of love	"I had 'fallen out of love' with my primary partner."
4. Neglect	"My primary partner was emotionally distant."
5. Lack of commitment	"I thought my relationship with my primary partner was in trouble."
6. Situational reasons	"I was drunk/intoxicated and I was not thinking clearly."
7. Self-esteem	"I wanted to boost my self-esteem/feel better about myself."
8. Variety	"I knew there would come a time when I would be married; I wanted to take advantage of all opportunities when still 'single.'"

Reasons vary: which would end your relationship?
Source: 1–5 – sample items sourced from Barta & Kiene (2005); 6–8 – Selterman, D., Garcia, J. R., & Tsapelas, I. (2019). Motivations for extradyadic infidelity revisited. *Journal of Sex Research*, *56*(3), 273–286; Taylor & Francis Ltd, www.tandfonline.com, reproduced with permission.

The research shows that when people pursue infidelity for relationship-based reasons, like lack of love, neglect, low commitment, or anger at one's partner, their relationships are more likely to end, whereas situationally driven affairs tend to be short-term and less likely to lead to relationship dissolution (Selterman et al., 2020). In other words, infidelity is especially toxic when it follows deliberately from dissatisfaction or a desire to hurt one's partner or the relationship. The idea that not all infidelity is premeditated is underscored in the yearly seasonal patterns that show infidelity peaks in summer, when people might find themselves in circumstances (e.g., intoxicated, on vacation) that encourage infidelity (Adamopoulou, 2013). Situational stressors, such as work stress or stress from global events like a pandemic or war, can also make it more likely for people to engage in infidelity (Coop Gordon & Mitchell, 2020).

The characteristics of an extradyadic partner can also affect a relationship's stability. People in different-sex relationships tend to take more offense when their partner's extra-dyadic partner is of their own gender (e.g., a man married to a woman cheats with another woman) than a same-gender extradyadic partner; at the same time, men tolerate their partner's same-gender infidelity more than women (Confer & Cloud, 2011; Denes et al., 2015; Sagarin et al., 2003; Wang & Apostolou, 2019). Further, marriages are more likely to end when a spouse's extradyadic partner is a close personal friend than, say, a stranger (Labrecque & Whisman, 2020). If cheating partners confess their unfaithfulness, they are more likely to be forgiven, perhaps because their unsolicited disclosures suggest their future intentions (Afifi et al., 2001). These relationships dissolve at a 44 percent rate, as compared to solicited partner disclosures (86 percent), finding out from friends or gossip (68 percent), or catching a partner "red-handed" (83 percent).

Whether infidelity means the end of a relationship may also depend on whether the infidelity was emotional or sexual. Women in different-sex relationships experience particular distress in response to their partner's emotional infidelity, whereas men find women's sexual infidelity more upsetting and especially hard to forgive (Buss, 2018; Buss et al., 1992, 1999). Both women and men tend to engage in more abandonment behaviors as a function of infidelity type (more for emotional infidelity for women, sexual infidelity for men; Walsh et al., 2019). For sexual minorities, infidelity is still threatening, but these gender differences tend to fall away (Frederick & Fales, 2016).

Problems with Context

Why do so many cruise-ship, holiday, and study-abroad romances fail to last? Despite Hollywood's various attempts to suggest otherwise, relationships founded in isolation from the very many stressors, obligations, and expectations that characterize everyday life often struggle when partners step back into reality. In other words, well-matched partners are not immune to relationship dissolution. Here, we are reminded that relationships operate within situational contexts that affect their success.

Some romantic relationships exist in highly stressful contexts. As you know, external stressors come in many forms, and if they exceed partners' capacities to cope, these stressors can derail partners' abilities to offer the social support and engage in the adaptive processes that encourage relationship stability (Karney & Bradbury, 1995; Neff et al., 2021; Schiltz & Van Hecke, 2021). In other words, circumstances beyond partners' control can place them at risk for low marital quality or dissolution. Divorced couples may not retrospectively attribute their divorce to their general stress, but they do recognize the accumulation of chronic everyday stressors as underlying their divorce decisions (Bodenmann, Charvoz et al., 2007). Along those lines, women's persistent strain can predict relationship dissolution among new parents (Røsand et al., 2014).

Financial Stress and Incarceration

Living with low income exemplifies a stressful context ripe for relationship instability. In fact, low-income partners of diverse ethnicities tend to identify situational challenges, like money management, when asked about the most salient problems within their relationships, with internal problems, such as communication issues, less pressing (Jackson et al., 2016). Highlighting the problem of financial insecurity, socioeconomically disadvantaged marriages dissolve more quickly and at higher rates than affluent relationships (Rosenfeld & Roesler, 2019). Financial problems and work-related pressures, even working the night shift or having an inconsistent work schedule, tend to increase odds for divorce (Poortman, 2005; Presser, 2000).

For some partners, financial stress is tied to incarceration, another well-documented risk factor for relationship dissolution (Apel, 2016; Western et al., 2004). Incarceration disrupts work life and earning opportunities, involves legal fees and hefty visitation and phone call expenses, and, in its aftermath, confers wage penalties and access restrictions to housing, resources, and government assistance (Adams, 2018; Western et al., 2001). Along with these economic-related stressors, long periods of separation tend to harm relationship stability (Massoglia et al., 2011). Partners can feel lonely, insecure, and isolated, even as they may draw strength from their special connection or commitment (De Claire et al., 2020). The partners of incarcerated individuals can also feel stigmatized and feel pressure from friends and family to leave (Tadros et al., 2022). By some estimates, only 30 percent of relationships persist through the duration of an incarceration (Dwyer Emory, 2022). The risk of dissolution during incarceration is especially high for Black, relative to White or Hispanic, partners, perhaps because Black individuals are less likely to have the protective factors of being married (e.g., versus cohabitating), being in a longer pre-incarceration relationship, having shorter sentences, and having full-time employment post-release (Widdowson et al., 2020).

Parenting Challenges

Another significant stressor uniquely poised to harm romantic relationship stability is infertility. Approximately 20 percent of American women experience primary (first-child) infertility, meaning they do not become pregnant after one year of trying; with fewer (6 percent) experiencing secondary (second-child) infertility (CDC, 2022). Infertility is more prevalent in lower socioeconomic countries, but is rising globally (Sun et al., 2019), and is associated with anxiety, stigmatization, social isolation, and relationship problems. Emerging evidence within Muslim and African nations suggests women's infertility can encourage conflict, intimate partner violence, and divorce (Amiri et al., 2015; Fledderjohann, 2012; Naab et al., 2019; Onat & Beji, 2012; Wang et al., 2022). Initial evidence in Western cultures also suggests higher breakup odds for marital or cohabitating relationships among women whose infertility results in childlessness compared to women who have children (Kjaer et al., 2014). However, some partners move through unsuccessful fertility treatments with stable and healthy relationship satisfaction (Sydsjö et al., 2005). Reconciling these findings, evidence shows that partners who separate during treatment reported more baseline infertility stress at the start of treatment (Martins et al., 2014). In other words, infertility may lead lower-quality relationships to dissolve, but may pose a less serious threat for high-quality relationships.

If romantic partners do have a child, what happens if the child faces significant health or developmental challenges? Parents of children with cerebral palsy, HIV or AIDS, spina bifida, and cancer, for example, report significantly more parental stress than other parents (Davis et al., 2010; Pinquart, 2018), as do parents of children with Autism Spectrum Disorder (Schiltz & Van Hecke, 2021). The social and emotional hardships of experiencing difficult diagnoses, the associated financial strain, and the added day-to-day demands can create a stressful context for parents' relationships. Critically, no one story captures the impact of these contexts on individuals' relationships. Parents of children with significant challenges might report strained intimacy or other relationship challenges, and some might consider separating, but others do well, with some parents suggesting their relationship is all the stronger (Silva-Rodrigues et al., 2016; Singh, 2003; Wiener et al., 2017). For instance, though early evidence sounded the alarm and hinted at a strong risk of divorce for parents of children with Autism Spectrum Disorder (ASD), this link was likely overstated (Hartley et al., 2010; Saini et al., 2015). We now know that some parents are able to engage in positive communication, even on days when their child experiences intense ASD-related behavioral challenges (Hartley et al., 2016). Even for the unthinkable – the death of a child – the picture is powerfully diverse: whereas some partners' relationships deteriorate, many bereaved parents maintain healthy bonds (Albuquerque et al., 2016; Finnäs et al., 2018). The compass clearly points to a need for additional research on the vulnerabilities and strengths that help differentiate relationships that can be resilient and those at risk on account of their children's well-being (Schiltz & Van Hecke, 2021).

Relationships with Other Network-Members

Beyond children, consider the role of partners' social network, the people who can make it easier, or harder, for partners to stay together (Sprecher, 2011; Sprecher, Felmlee et al., 2013; Sprecher & Felmlee, 1992). How much do you like your partner's buddies? For newlyweds, especially men, holding stronger negative perceptions of a partner's friends is a risk factor for divorce (Fiori et al., 2018). Similarly, tensions about a partner's friends, or believing those friends are interfering, predicts worse relationship quality (Murphy et al., 2020). In general, people who believe their friends and family approve of and support their relationship tend to report more satisfaction and stronger relationship functioning (Blair & Holmberg, 2008; Etcheverry et al., 2008). Although our friends' supportive behaviors can encourage our relationship stability (Sprecher, 2011), our friends' breakups can put our relationship at risk. Evidence suggests that divorces occur in social clusters, with divorced friends influencing their friends and then friends-of-friends, perhaps serving as successful models and supports for divorce (McDermott et al., 2013).

Social networks can also weaken a person's relationship stability to the extent that the social network rejects that person's relationship based on demographic or situational factors. The feeling of stigmatization or marginalization, especially by one's social network, tends to erode relationship well-being (Doyle & Molix, 2015; Lehmiller & Agnew, 2006, 2007). Interracial, intercultural, same-sex, age-gap, and non-monogamous relationships, among others, face prejudice and discrimination detrimental to relationship health (Lehmiller & Ioerger, 2014; Yampolsky et al., 2020). Thus, as much as these forces might be overlooked, a relationship's success is critically connected to its situation. Whether partners stay together or break up depends in part on situational forces from within a socioeconomic sphere, within the family, within a social network, and even within a broader historical and sociocultural context.

 IS THIS TRUE FOR YOU?

Long Distance Love: What Is the Role of Your Social Network?

Long-distance dating is common. By some estimates, over one-third of college dating relationships are long-distance, with over 7 percent of college students reporting they have been in at least one long-distance relationship (Beckmeyer et al., 2021; Belus et al., 2019). Of course, college students are not the only people in LDRs. Adults maintain long-distance romantic relationships for a variety of reasons, such as work, family obligations, or having met online. In general, people in LDRs are no more or less likely to break up or endure infidelity than individuals in geographically close relationships; in fact, they tend to report comparable (if not higher!) levels of intimacy, commitment, and sexual and relationship satisfaction (Dargie et al., 2015; Goldsmith & Sandra Byers, 2018; Kelmer et al., 2013). Yet, some people, consistent with the media's typical portrayal of LDRs, hold negative views of long-distance relationships (Goldsmith & Sandra Byers, 2018; Schmall, 2018). They might believe that LDRs are unsatisfying, prone to infidelity, and cannot last. Many a sitcom episode is based on this premise!

For some LDR partners, these pessimistic views are not abstract stereotypes; they are beliefs actively held by their social networks (see Figure 12.8; Johnson & Hall, 2021). In interviews, over half of people in LDRs confessed to having friends who offer non-supportive comments about their relationships (Johnson & Hall, 2021). Friends might say their relationship is doomed or that long-distance relationships never work. Such negative comments can lead people in LDRs to stop talking about their relationship or to disclose their long-distance status only selectively.

Figure 12.8 Technology makes it easy to see long-distance romantic partners, even introduce them to your friends. What happens if your friends disapprove of long-distance relationships? (Photo: FG Trade / iStock / Getty Images Plus)

Not surprisingly, people in LDRs feel less supported by their friends than people in geographically close relationships (Johnson & Hall, 2021). If you have been in a LDR, is this true for you?

If so, of concern is whether friends' pessimism about LDRs creates a toxic social context that might adversely affect the stability of LDRs. Interestingly, although social (dis)approval appears to predict relationship well-being for people in geographically close relationships, initial evidence suggests it does *not* predict relationship well-being for people in LDRs (Johnson & Hall, 2021). How can we explain this? Perhaps, as suggested by the interview data, people in LDRs believe others are misinformed and do not understand long-distance relationships; people in LDRs might also see their own experience as an exception to the rule ("sure, some LDRs are like that, but not us!"). Such pro-relational interpretations may protect individuals' relationships from an otherwise harmful context. Additional research is necessary to build on these initial findings.

The Experience of Relationship Dissolution

The poignancy of relationship dissolution makes it a common theme not only in the mini-series *Modern Love*, but in many forms of human expression, including movies, novels, dance, art, photography, and music. From the casual end of a one-night stand to the

Figure 12.9 What's your favorite breakup song? How do the themes in this song connect to major theories in relationship science, like attachment and evolutionary theories, and interdependence theory? (Photo: Westend61 / Getty Images)

heartbreaking death of a long-term partner, people's relationship stories capture our attention. Think about how easy it is to find a breakup song on the radio! The rich variety of relationship endings in music and media reveals profound diversity in relationship dissolution (Figure 12.9). With each unique end comes a unique reaction: people are crying, mourning, yelling, feeling betrayed and hurt, breathing for the first time, dancing with strangers, and scraping their keys along the side of their partner's four-wheel drives. They are also (dare we say it) moving on.

How Relationships End

Recalling "the day we broke up" makes breakups feel like singular events, but rarely do relationships end in a sudden, discrete fashion (Coleman et al., 2018). Rather, relationships typically dissolve over time, with one or more problems simmering, erosively, until bubbling over. This process view of how relationships end aligns with the **divorce-stress-adjustment perspective** on marital dissolution, which argues that un-partnering begins when partners are very much together, continues as they separate, and includes an adjustment period after the separation (Amato, 2000). People can begin to experience **commitment uncertainty**: they question whether they wish to remain in their current relationship (Owen et al., 2014). They may feel conflicted, caught in the ambiguous space of wanting to stay, but also wanting to leave (Joel, MacDonald, & Page-Gould, 2018). Along with commitment uncertainty, people start engaging in **dissolution consideration** (often called **divorce ideation** for married people), when they actively contemplate ending their relationship (VanderDrift et al., 2009).

The Process of Breaking Up

Contemplating leaving is an essential part of ending a relationship. Even relationships marked by low commitment are likely to stay intact in the absence of active dissolution consideration (VanderDrift et al., 2009). We see this, for example, when people let their relationships "slide," from cohabitation to marriage (Stanley et al., 2006). At the same time, dissolution consideration is common and does not automatically mean the end of a relationship. For example, in a nationally representative US sample of over 2,250 currently married individuals, 28 percent said they had at one time, but not recently, considered divorce (88 percent of whom were glad they stayed married), while another quarter of respondents said they recently engaged in divorce ideation (Hawkins, Galovan et al., 2017). Together, this suggests over 50 percent of people in intact marriages have at one time considered divorce. Emerging evidence suggests similar trends among sexual minorities. A small qualitative study found that about 43 percent of the sample of married gay men and lesbian women reported some level of divorce ideation (Hoy et al., 2022). Perhaps fleeting thoughts, perhaps serious debate, commitment uncertainty and dissolution considerations among married and non-marital partners are not stable. They can fluctuate day to day, even as a function of the day's relationship experiences, and the more people feel stay-or-leave ambivalence, the greater the fluctuations (Allen et al., 2022; Joel et al., 2021).

Dissolution consideration occurs early in the disengagement process, according to a phase model of relationship dissolution (Duck, 1982, 2005; Rollie & Duck, 2006). This model suggests that breakups (1) begin inside the mind of one person before (2) moving to an interpersonal space as they share their discontent with their partner. Next, the breakup is (3) shared with the partners' social network before (4) individuals, now no longer in the relationship, engage in meaning making and (5) prepare for future relationships (Rollie & Duck, 2006). Communication patterns and communication topics are expected to change as time progresses and people move through their uncertainty in the early phases of dissolution. Shifts in thought and leaps from internal notions to interpersonal discussion are not expected to occur suddenly. Instead, as shown in the *Article Spotlight*, people transition gradually from "we" to "me."

 ARTICLE SPOTLIGHT

From "We" to "Me": Changes in Online Language Use Reveal the Breakup Process

Do people's word choices provide insight into their breakup experiences? An innovative study of archived social media data suggests yes. Researchers Seraj, Blackburn, and Pennebaker (2021) applied linguistic analysis to online posts and discovered fascinating changes in how people communicate leading up to and after their romantic breakups. These language changes appear to track the mental and emotional work of navigating uncertainty and disentangling one's self from one's partner. As such, this work provides a remarkable illustration of the all-encompassing cognitive impact of relationship endings.

To understand this research, we need to appreciate how word patterns link to varied ways of thinking. As the authors review, people's language can confer different thinking modes, including analytic thinking and cognitive processing. Analytic thinking refers to logical or non-emotional reasoning and comes across in a formal, impersonal way of speaking. It relies heavily on function words (e.g., articles, prepositions). Cognitive processing, meanwhile, refers to the mental effort used to comprehend a difficult idea. It appears as words that convey insight or causality or in words that convey meaning (Seraj et al., 2021). Language can also vary to the extent that it is self-focused (e.g., words like "I" and "me,") or collective-focused (e.g., words like "we" or "us").

To assess whether and how language use changes surrounding a breakup, Seraj and team (2021) obtained the complete posting histories of 6,803 Reddit users, all of whom described a romantic breakup on the forum r/BreakUps. The researchers established users' baseline language patterns by looking at data four months before users' breakups, and then observed linguistic patterns leading up to, during, and after users' breakup disclosures. Over 1 million posts were analyzed, including users' posts on forums unrelated to breaking up (e.g., cooking, sports, news forums). In this case, analyzing posts involved using a specialized software to categorize words and obtain estimates of analytical thinking, cognitive processing, self-focus, and collective-focus over time.

Much as the researchers hypothesized, language patterns on Reddit track the complicated, difficult experience of breaking up (Figure 12.10). Beginning approximately three months prior to their breakup disclosures (i.e., "−12 weeks" on Figure 12.10), Reddit users entered a pre-breakup phase in which their language shifted to manifest the internal struggle that precedes a breakup decision (Rollie & Duck, 2006). Analytic reasoning fell, as people made more emotional and less logical statements like, "how do you stop associating everything with her? I can't seem to do anything without triggering memories, how do I make it stop?" Meanwhile, language reflecting cognitive processing and meaning-making increased, such as: "I'm undecided whether or not to share my story. I need some help because I feel lost but my story is long and not sure whether it's worth sharing" (Seraj et al., 2021, Appendix). Fascinatingly, changes in these linguistic patterns were not limited to breakup-related posts; rather, they appeared even in communication that had nothing to do with breakups. Also shown in Figure 12.10, both self-focused and collective-focused language rose sharply at the time of breakup disclosure. Language markers for cognitive disruption were observed up to six months post-breakup. This work underscores the pervasive cognitive impact of a romantic breakup, and shows one way in which the mental work required for dissolution permeates everyday behavior.

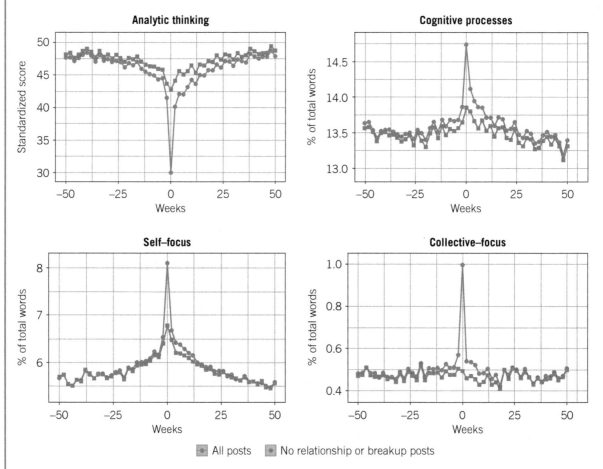

Figure 12.10 The mental work of breaking up leaks into how we communicate across varied domains. These figures show changes in the use of words reflecting analytic thinking and cognitive process, as well as self-focused and collective-focused words, leading up to breakup disclosures (marked as time "0") and after the breakup disclosure. Red lines include all posts; green lines include only posts in forums unrelated to breakups. Data points are averages across participants and represent two-week intervals. (Source: Seraj et al. [2021], printed with permission)

It's Really Over: Strategies for Ending Relationships

Even after people decide to end their relationships, pulling the proverbial plug can be a challenge (Beckmeyer & Jamison, 2020). In non-marital different-sex relationships, men and women tend to initiate breakups at the same rate, with people reporting their breakups were "mutual" only about 20 to 25 percent of the time (Carter et al., 2018; Saini et al., 2015). Women tend to desire and initiate the majority of different-sex divorces, however, a pattern that is consistent cross-culturally (Charvoz et al., 2009; Sayer et al., 2011). Indeed, over two-thirds of divorces are initiated by women (Rosenfeld, 2018). This is despite the substantial economic impact that divorce disproportionally has on women, introducing chronic and long-lasting financial challenges and typically including the bulk of childcare responsibilities (Drewianka & Meder, 2020; Mortelmans, 2020). For women more than men, the benefits of leaving a marriage may more readily outweigh the costs of staying (Brinig & Allen, 2000; Louzek, 2022).

So, what exactly do people *do* to end a relationship? Whereas one-time sexual encounters often end in formal, business-like ways (e.g., mentioning having to work the next day, thanking someone and leaving; Cox, Currin et al., 2021), breaking up long-standing relationships can be more involved. Empirical work extends and integrates earlier taxonomies to suggest seven unique **breakup strategies** (Collins & Gillath, 2012). Take a look at Table 12.3. Which would you use, and which would you like used if someone were to break up with you?

Table 12.3 Breakup strategies

Breakup strategy	Example Items
Avoidance/ withdrawal	"I disclosed little about my personal activities and interests." "I kept our conversations brief."
Positive tone/self-blame	"I avoided hurting my partner's feelings at all costs." "I told my partner that I did not regret the time we had spent together."
Open confrontation	"I explained to my partner my reasons for desiring the breakup." "I honestly conveyed my wishes to my partner."
Cost escalation	"I picked an argument with my partner as an excuse to break up." "I became unpleasant to my partner in the hopes that they would make the first move."
Manipulation	"I gave hints of my desire to break up to people who know the other person." "I started dating someone else in the hopes my partner would learn about my desire to break up through my actions."
Distant/mediated communication	"I ended the relationship indirectly, for example, through text." "I ended the relationship without letting my partner know about it directly."
De-escalation	"I procrastinated in doing anything in the hopes that things would improve." "I 'waited it out' until it was a good time to break up."

Source: Reprinted from *Journal of Research in Personality, 46*(2), Collins, T. J., & Gillath, O, Attachment, breakup strategies, and associated outcomes: The effects of security enhancement on the selection of breakup strategies, Copyright (2012), with permission from Elsevier.

Many people consider an open, honest conversation (e.g., "open confrontation") to be the "ideal" breakup strategy, one that is compassionate, limits anger, and is linked to intimacy prior to the breakup (Collins & Gillath, 2012; Hoffman, 2020; Sprecher et al., 2010). This likely assumes a respectful tone; hostile, berating fights are not going to win "best breakup" awards. Using a positive tone/self-blame strategy may seem kind, but has mixed results. On the one hand, taking pains not to hurt a partner and recalling positive times together is seen as compassionate, but on the other hand, such a tone during a breakup can come across as insincere ("If we are so great together, why are we breaking up?"; Collins & Gillath, 2012; Lambert & Hughes, 2010; Sprecher et al., 2010). Initiators who use a positive tone may remain friends with their ex, and may even get back together (Collins & Gillath, 2012). Positive tone during a breakup, however, is not a prerequisite for subsequent relationship renewals: partners in on-again off-again relationships break up in diverse ways and still get back together (Dailey et al., 2013).

Instead of taking a direct approach, initiators can choose to disengage indirectly, such as through avoidance or withdrawal. For example, imagine that one day you and your partner are happily together, the next day whoosh ... your partner vanishes. Sound familiar? People have been performing disappearing acts for as long as people have had relationships, but ghosting has new meaning in today's technological age, with some estimates suggesting that 60 to 70 percent of emerging adults have tried this breakup strategy (LeFebvre et al., 2019; Timmermans et al., 2020). Ghosting occurs when one partner suddenly or gradually ceases all communication, ignores any contact attempts, and their digital presence vanishes (LeFebvre, 2017; LeFebvre et al., 2019; Timmermans et al., 2020). Ghosting is used more often, and is viewed as more appropriate, when terminating less-committed, shorter relationships than highly committed, long-term relationships, and tends to benefit the ghoster more than the ghostee (Jonason et al., 2021; Koessler et al., 2019; LeFebvre, 2017; LeFebvre et al., 2019). Ghosters might take a reputational hit, but the strategy provides a convenient, easy way to break up, one that lets them avoid awkward conversations and circumvent responsibility for managing a partner's sadness, anger, or hurt. However, as callous as it may seem, not all ghosting is cowardly, shameless, or uncaring: some people ghost out of legitimate safety concerns or because they learn new negative information that suggests they should cut ties quickly (LeFebvre et al., 2019; Timmermans et al., 2020).

Ghostees take a self-esteem hit and typically feel confused and uncertain; they lack closure, are hurt and angry, and may even feel worried about the ghoster (Collins & Gillath, 2012; LeFebvre & Fan, 2020; Pancani et al., 2021; Timmermans et al., 2020). A milder variant of ghosting, called orbiting, which has all the features of ghosting without the complete digital disappearance, is experienced like ghosting as a form of social ostracism (Pancani et al., 2021; Pancani & Aureli, 2022). Interestingly, however, the way that orbiters linger in the digital periphery, liking social media posts and sharing content, may soften the blow of their disappearance. Orbiting is associated with better breakup outcomes (e.g., less anger) than ghosting, both of which have worse effects than direct rejection (Pancani & Aureli, 2022).

Keep in mind that breakup strategies are, well ... strategic. As goal-directed behaviors, they are chosen by initiators to accomplish specific tasks. Initiators may want to terminate relationships permanently, remain friends, or eventually reunite; they may want to limit their own costs or ease their now-ex-partner's suffering; they may hold specific priorities outside of the relationship, such as protecting the well-being of children or managing impressions with friends or family. How they break up likely reflects motivations beyond the desire to end a relationship and while – as mentioned – methods may predict certain post-dissolution reactions, these differences are relative. The end of a relationship, whether voluntarily initiated or on account of a partner's death, introduces an array of negative consequences.

Consequences of Relationship Dissolution

For Kenji and Margot in *Modern Love* (and for many of us), unwanted relationship dissolution comes at a considerable emotional, psychological, and physical cost. Mentioned briefly earlier in this chapter, the divorce-stress-adjustment (DSA) perspective provides a framework for understanding the long-term outcomes of divorce, one that can be applied to non-marital relationships and widowhood as well (Amato, 2000; Lin & Brown, 2020). This perspective suggests that the negative outcomes linked to divorce begin while partners are together and conclude well after the divorce. The consequences of dissolution unfold during the entire turbulent process of a breakup as people experience a series of separation-related stressors. Considering all of the decisions and struggles that accompany relationship endings, especially for divorce and widowhood, the burden can be quite overwhelming. Before reading through the specific consequences of relationship dissolution, know this: most (though not all) people show considerable resilience and recover well from non-marital breakups, divorce, and even the death of a spouse (Lin & Brown, 2020; Mancini et al., 2011; Sbarra & Emery, 2005).

Immediate, Short-Term, Consequences

Whether they occur after thirty weeks or thirty years, breakups can generate considerable distress. This makes sense when we consider that romantic partners often serve as adults' primary attachment figures. In the same way that children protest separation from their primary caregivers, adults who lose a desired relationship can experience dysregulation, grief, and despair (Bowlby, 1980; LeRoy et al., 2019; Mikulincer & Shaver, 2022). These responses reflect an intense surge of an attachment behavior system that is designed to promote proximity, yet is being denied access to the one person who can render a calming effect. As you may know from experience, romantic breakups can trigger an array of negative emotions, including sadness, regret, anxiety, confusion, fear, and vengefulness, and perhaps (particularly for initiators) some positive emotions as well, such as happiness or relief (Perilloux & Buss, 2008; Sbarra & Emery, 2005).

The intensity of breakup distress tends to be associated with the degree of interdependence and commitment in the relationship prior to dissolution. Specifically, non-marital breakups are often less disruptive than divorce or widowhood, though unmarried individuals who are cohabiting or engaged can face comparable distress to married individuals during a breakup (Rhoades et al., 2011). Cohabitating and engaged partners, like married partners, not only live or plan to live together, they often share finances, family, and friends, and they might co-parent or co-own pets. With lives intertwined, they are part of each other's pasts, day-to-day present, and future goals and plans (Cupach & Metts, 1986; Finkel et al., 2014). Relationship dissolution disrupts this entanglement and people feel it. Over 95 percent of people who divorce consider the experience somewhat or extremely distressing, while the death of a partner is identified as one of the most stressful possible life experiences (Hetherington, 2003; Scully et al., 2000). More than the disruption of most non-marital relationships, both divorce and widowhood create upheaval for individuals and their families (Raley & Sweeney, 2020; Scully et al., 2000).

Relationship endings can take a significant toll on mental health. We see this for non-marital relationships among emerging adults, where breakups can be a catalyst for major depressive disorder, lower self-esteem, rumination, sleep disturbance, intrusive thoughts, and suicide risk (Carter et al., 2018; Ebert et al., 2019; Field, 2011; Perilloux & Buss, 2008; Rhoades et al., 2011). Even as initiators tend to fare better than their partners, they can still suffer regret and guilt, can be subject to reputational damage, and – particularly if they have lower self-compassion and less self-forgiveness – they can also be at risk of developing depression (Akbari et al., 2022; Perilloux & Buss, 2008). People navigating a divorce are also at heightened risk of developing a psychiatric disorder, and commonly experience disruptions to their social support network and finances that can further harm their mental well-being (Amato, 2000; Mortelmans, 2020; Sbarra & Borelli, 2019; Sbarra & Whisman, 2022; Whisman et al., 2022). The death of a partner has the potential to be similarly, if not more, hazardous (Mikulincer & Shaver, 2022; Sbarra & Borelli, 2019). Along with the complex emotions of grief, losing a life partner can elevate the risk of depression and anxiety disorders, accelerate declines in cognitive functioning, and adversely impact physical well-being (Blanner Kristiansen et al., 2019; Ennis & Majid, 2021; Onrust & Cuijpers, 2006; Shin et al., 2018). In fact, both widowhood and divorce predict worse health, including chronic conditions and mobility issues (Hughes & Waite, 2009).

Perhaps even more alarming, robust evidence points to the potential for relationship disruption to increase mortality risk (Ennis & Majid, 2021; Holt-Lunstad et al., 2010; Moon et al., 2011; Sbarra et al., 2011). Cross-cultural meta-analytic work that included over 600 million people documented a 3 percent greater risk of early death among divorced or separated individuals compared to married people (Shor et al., 2012). Meanwhile, so detrimental to physical health is the death of a spouse that it has its own term, the **widowhood effect**, which refers to a precipitous increase in mortality for adults who lose their partners (Elwert & Christakis, 2008; Ennis & Majid, 2021; Moon et al., 2011). Maybe you have heard of long-time spouses who die in close temporal proximity to each other. The widowhood effect is especially strong in the first few months after a partner's passing, is especially hazardous for men, and may vary by race (Elwert & Christakis, 2006; Liu, Umberson, & Xu, 2020; Moon et al., 2014).

Longer-Term Consequences
The divorce-stress-adjustment perspective posits two competing perspectives on the trajectory of distress and well-being costs after a relationship ends (Amato, 2000, 2010a). The **crisis model** suggests that relationship dissolution produces acute negative outcomes, but with time, people adjust; the adverse effects are temporary. In contrast, the **chronic strain model**, sometimes called the resource perspective, contends that relationship dissolution creates resource deficits (e.g., money, social support) and accompanying hardships (e.g., psychological, health) that extend indefinitely; in some sense, the adverse effects are permanent.

Aligned with the crisis model, there is evidence that relationship endings are generally accompanied by a surge of distress, but over time, this distress lessens. For example, when non-marital relationships end, people feel significantly less satisfied with their lives and suffer worse mental health, but within a year, people return to their baseline levels, a process that tends to be longer and harder for men than women (Preetz, 2022). Much of these improvements can occur rapidly; within the first couple of weeks of a breakup, people experience substantial decreases in love, sadness, and anger (Sbarra & Emery, 2005).

Similarly, people who divorce do not typically stay psychologically distressed, they do not perpetually report depression, anxiety, or poor quality of life; their well-being recovers (Hald et al., 2020; Hope et al., 1999; Luhmann et al., 2012; Sander et al., 2020). For instance, life satisfaction tends to decline in the years leading up to divorce, plummet precipitously during the year of a divorce, and then increase in subsequent years (van Scheppingen & Leopold, 2020). Mental health challenges, such as depressive symptoms, follow the opposite pattern: they increase leading up to divorce, spike proximally to the divorce, but then return to baseline level (Tosi & van den Broek, 2020). In general, as predicted by the crisis model, most people experience divorce as a difficult time, but two years after the divorce are considerably less distressed, and by six years out, are well-adjusted by many accounts (Hetherington, 2003).

Compared to divorce, widowhood triggers stronger and longer-lasting depression (Lin et al., 2019), but can follow a similar time-course. Meta-analyses show that the challenges of losing a spouse can begin before death: anticipatory grief is strong in magnitude for caregivers when their loved one, for example, has a life-threatening illness (Kustanti et al., 2022). With the loss of their partner, individuals struggle with day-to-day living, loneliness, depression, and waves of intense grief (Maccallum et al., 2015; Naef et al., 2013). With time, however, most people recalibrate and return to baseline level of well-being (Bonanno et al., 2002; Maccallum et al., 2015; Powers et al., 2014). The widowhood effect also tends to spike close to their partner's death, but is tempered over time (Moon et al., 2011). From a relational standpoint, time since partner loss predicts less frequent conversations with a deceased partner, less frequent anniversary reactions, and feeling less upset after thinking about a partner (Carnelley et al., 2006). In other words, most people acclimate to life without their partner. After a while, they can remember their deceased partner without pain or anguish and the throbbing intensity of grief transforms to something manageable. They can find joy in the next phase of their lives.

But not everyone recovers. Consistent with the chronic strain model, some people still suffer from relationship dissolutions that happened years ago (Lorenz et al., 2006; Maccallum et al., 2015). For some people, psychological stress continues and life satisfaction never quite recovers following a divorce (Johnson & Wu, 2002; Lucas, 2005). Although *most* people recover well, some people – by some estimates about 20 percent of people in response to divorce (Mancini et al., 2011; Perrig-Chiello et al., 2015) – suffer intensely for a prolonged period. Prolonged suffering is different from fluctuations in well-being that we might expect in the post-dissolution period. Like any grieving process, the recovery process is not linear.

Also aligned with the chronic strain model, the effects of widowhood have the potential to linger. Rates of depression might be especially high in the immediate aftermath of losing a spouse, but even as they decrease, they are still high five years after a spouse's death

(Kristiansen et al., 2019). Among older adults, the effect of widowhood on cognitive decline is also noticeable both cross-sectionally (i.e., compared to married individuals) and longitudinally, with longer widowhood associated with stronger declines over time (Singham et al., 2021). A minority of spouses who cared for their partner before they died struggle to cope during their bereavement and disproportionally suffer worse anxiety, depression, and poorer health (Miller et al., 2020).

Thinking about the crisis model and the chronic strain model may remind you of the overarching story of relationship dissolution: seemingly contradictory findings can often be reconciled by attending to diversity. Heterogeneity is the name of the game! Whereas most people adjust well to the ends of their relationships, and some especially well, a subset of these populations are especially vulnerable: they struggle with low levels of life satisfaction, poor subjective health, hopelessness, mourning, and depression (Knöpfli et al., 2016; Spahni et al., 2015). What might predict these different outcomes?

Explaining Diverse Post-Dissolution Outcomes

Efforts to understand diversity in post-dissolution experiences anchor to several intrapersonal and relationship factors. On the intrapersonal side, pre-existing vulnerabilities may predispose individuals for difficult adjustments. For instance, people are more likely to experience a major depressive episode following a divorce if they have previously experienced depression symptoms (Sbarra et al., 2014). People with higher attachment anxiety are also at risk of more distress in response to divorce and more prolonged grief symptoms after a partner's death (Birnbaum et al., 1997; Halford & Sweeper, 2013; Maccallum & Bryant, 2018). They tend to perseverate over their lost relationships, desire to reconnect in a seemingly desperate manner, and report intense anger and distraction (Davis et al., 2003). These responses are consistent with hyperactivation of the attachment behavioral system, the hallmark of attachment anxiety (Mikulincer & Shaver, 2018). If hyperactivation involves prolonged rumination, this can weaken immune system functioning, a potential pathway toward worse health outcomes post-divorce (Kiecolt-Glaser, 2018; Kiecolt-Glaser et al., 1987). With widowhood, this hyperactivation can generate complicated or prolonged grief as well as coping challenges (Currier et al., 2015; Field & Sundin, 2001; Maccallum & Bryant, 2018).

Personality factors can also help predict diverse outcomes following relationship dissolution. When it comes to divorce, poorer outcomes are tied to higher levels of neuroticism, lower extraversion, and lower openness (Clark & Georgellis, 2013; Perrig-Chiello et al., 2015). Higher neuroticism also corresponds with more difficulty coping following a partner's death (West et al., 2021). Likewise, different trajectories could reflect different levels of resilience. After non-marital breakups, trait resilience may protect individuals against depression and rumination, buffer the effects of grief and loss after divorce, and promote stronger post-divorce psychological well-being, particularly for non-initiators (Kołodziej-Zaleska & Przybyła-Basista, 2020; O'Sullivan et al., 2019). Similarly, trait resilience is associated with resilience in the face of a partner's death, and may be particularly important for men as they face the loss of a spouse (King et al., 2019; West et al., 2021).

What about gender? In different-sex relationships, gender may help explain some variation in outcomes after relationship dissolution. Men generally experience a worse short-term adjustment to divorce, including heightened risk of death following divorce, but then they recover well; whereas women (who initiate most divorces) respond better initially, but have relatively worse outcomes over the long run (Leopold, 2018; Sbarra et al., 2011). This may be because of disproportional childcare responsibilities and greater sustained economic disadvantages from the divorce. In general, divorced individuals suffer financially relative to people who stay married (Kapelle, 2022), but women are especially vulnerable to lasting financial problems following either a divorce or a spouse's death (Lichtenstein et al., 2022; Raley & Sweeney, 2020). Outside of finances, widowhood appears to be especially toxic for men's well-being (Moon et al., 2011).

Beyond these intrapersonal factors, the quality of a relationship prior to its dissolution may also shape people's adjustment experiences. For example, although romantic endings typically threaten subjective well-being, leaving low-quality relationships, such as high-conflict marriages, can lead to increases in happiness and life satisfaction (Amato & Hohmann-Marriott, 2007; Bourassa et al., 2015; Symoens et al., 2014). Similarly, leaving a marriage that included an on-again/off-again period prior to a divorce, a marker of a low-quality relationship (Dailey, Pfiester et al., 2009), can have divergent effects. When these low-quality relationships end, women tend to experience less distress than when non-cyclical marriages end (Monk, Kanter et al., 2022). Meanwhile, the death of a long-term partner can be devastating, but prior relationship quality can influence whether their passing is ultimately a source of stress, or possibly a source of relief from stress (Ennis & Majid, 2020). Widowhood is more challenging when people lose a high-quality relationship. Widowed individuals report higher depression and yearn for their partners more to the extent that their relationship was higher quality, marked by greater closeness and dependence (Carr et al., 2000; Schaan, 2013). These findings support the premise that the loss of a close attachment figure is particularly difficult.

 IN THE NEWS

Are Children of Divorced Parents More Likely to Divorce?

News outlets regularly address how parental separations might affect children, tackling such concerns as how to make divorce less stressful for children (Duffy, 2021) and weighing the pros and cons of "birdnesting," that is, when children stay in one home while parents rotate in and out (Savage, 2021). Recognizing that many children of separated parents are now adults themselves, the press also investigates questions targeted to this adult population. For example, how do parents' separations affect the quality of adult children's romantic relationships? In other words, is relational instability transmitted intergenerationally?

Consistent with media reports (Pinsker, 2019), adult children of divorce are indeed more likely to experience relationship dissolution themselves, compared to adult children whose parents remained together (Amato & Patterson, 2017). Why might this be? Consider Figure 12.11, which outlines potential parent-to-child relational transmission pathways (Amato & Patterson, 2017). At the crux of this model is the notion that children learn ideas about love, intimacy, and romantic relationships by observing their parents. Intentionally or otherwise, adult children of divorce or dissolution (ACD) may use their parents' relationship as a template for how to conduct and structure their own relationships (Sassler, Cunningham, & Lichter, 2009). Perhaps because they learn fewer or poorer relational skills, have more relational insecurities, or endure more cumulative stress, ACD tend to have romantic relationships marked by lower satisfaction and more distress compared to adult children of intact relationships (ACI; Roper et al., 2020). Interestingly, however, relationship quality can be comparatively worse (e.g., lower commitment, poorer communication, more aggression) among an often unstudied group, adults whose parents never married (and generally never lived together) versus ACD or ACI (Rhoades, Stanley, Markman, & Ragan, 2012b).

ACD also have more positive views of divorce than ACI (Amato & Booth, 1991; Sassler, Cunningham, & Lichter, 2009), perhaps making them more willing to consider divorce as a real possibility. These more positive views of divorce could be due to witnessing their parents' strained relationships or due to shared race/ethnicity, religious, and socioeconomic characteristics between parents and their adult children. For instance, parents who did not experience religious or socioeconomic obstacles to divorce may have adult children who similarly lack these obstacles.

Following the map in Figure 12.11, the story of intergenerational transmission of relationships may extend beyond divorce to dating habits, relational churning, and romantic quality. For example, adults are at greater risk for experiencing their own on-again/off-again relationships when their parents have had their own cyclical relationships (Charvat et al., 2022; Kamp Dush et al., 2018). All told, the story of intergenerational transmission is another story of diverse relationships and diverse outcomes. Some parents maintain marriages fraught with conflict, while some divorced parents maintain healthy, cordial, and respectful, albeit non-marital, relationships. When intact parental marriages are characterized by high conflict, adult children tend to show less stability and lower satisfaction in their own romantic relationships, but when high-conflict parental marriages end in divorce, this divorce breaks the link between high-conflict parenting relationships and adult children's romantic outcomes (Braithwaite, Doxey et al., 2016).

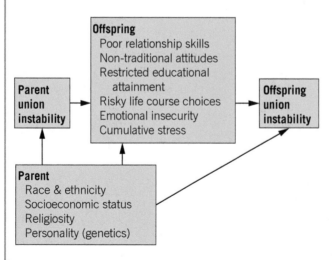

Figure 12.11 Parents' divorce may be a less interesting predictor of adult children's romantic relationships than the *quality* of parents' relationships. What other factors might you add to this model? How might variation in parents' repartnering experiences shape adult children's experiences? (Source: Used with permission of Blackwell Publishing, John Wiley & Sons, from Amato, P. R., & Patterson, S. E. [2017], The intergenerational transmission of union instability in early adulthood, *Journal of Marriage and Family, 79*[3], 723–738; permission conveyed through Copyright Clearance Center, Inc.)

Life after Relationship Dissolution

The end of a relationship, including saying goodbye to all the hopes and expectations tied to that relationship, comes with myriad challenges, many of which we have discussed. What remains is a critical question: how do people navigate post-dissolution relationships? When life moves forward, so too do people's relationships. This future can include establishing a new way of interacting with an ex-partner; it could mean figuring out who they are without their partner; and it could involve preparing for and entering new romantic relationships.

Post-Dissolution Relationships with Ex-Partners

Do you tend to stay in contact with ex-partners? Should you? In general, contact with an ex-partner can be distressing, particularly for people who have not yet accepted the end of their relationship (Mason, Sbarra et al., 2012; O'Hara et al., 2020; Sbarra & Emery, 2005). Limiting contact may support post-dissolution adjustment. And yet, by some estimates, about 60 percent of people stay friends with an ex-romantic partner, a practice that is especially common within the LGBTQ community (Griffith et al., 2017). Post-dissolution friendships are more common when people were friends with their ex first, prior to entering a romantic relationship (Metts et al., 1989). They also tend to be of higher quality (e.g., greater closeness, more maintenance behaviors) when partners judge their former romantic relationship as more satisfying and more committed (Bullock et al., 2011; Tan et al., 2014).

Of course, motivations for retaining post-dissolution friendships vary. Some ex-partners establish a post-dissolution friendship for practical purposes (e.g., to coordinate parenting responsibilities). Competent and cooperative co-parenting helps protect children from negative effects of their parents' separation (Kelly & Emery, 2003) and facilitates optimal family functioning (Lamela et al., 2016). Others feel safe with their ex-partner, and their post-dissolution friendship reflects an attachment (Griffith et al., 2017). More problematic for "moving on" are post-dissolution friendships driven by lingering romantic feelings (Griffith et al., 2017). Lingering romantic feelings, and more frequent communication with an ex-partner, are associated with worse post-breakup adjustment (Rodriguez et al., 2016).

For some exes, especially men, maintaining post-dissolution friendships are a way to access sex (Mogilski & Welling, 2017). **Breakup sex** may seem like risky behavior for people who are trying to separate from each other. Along these lines, breakup sex is pursued more often by people with lingering attachments and can be linked to getting back together (Dailey, Zhang et al., 2020; Spielmann et al., 2019). In the absence of a reunion, however, breakup sex does not slow post-dissolution recovery (Spielmann et al., 2019). If anything, when people are struggling to accept their relationship's end, breakup sex predicts better (not worse) adjustment, with men feeling better about themselves, and women feeling better about their relationship (Mason, Sbarra et al., 2012; Moran et al., 2020).

Sometimes the post-dissolution period is marred by **unwanted pursuit behaviors**, contact attempts that are not desired or welcomed by one partner (Langhinrichsen-Rohling et al., 2000). Such contact attempts fall on a continuum, ranging from benign to serious (Dutton & Winstead, 2006). On one end, unwanted pursuit behaviors refer to aggravating (e.g., unwanted gifts) or annoying behaviors (e.g., frequent text messages); on the other end is **stalking**, a legal term describing behaviors, like threats or physical violence, designed to invoke fear. Mild unwanted pursuit behaviors are fairly common among different-sex and same-sex ex-partners, yet same-sex partners may be at a higher risk for the full spectrum of such behaviors, including stalking (De Smet et al., 2012; Derlega et al., 2011; Edwards et al., 2015). Meta-analysis shows that half of stalking cases involve ex-romantic partners, women are most often the victims, and stalking lasts on average about two years (Spitzberg & Cupach, 2007).

In addition to in-person unwanted pursuit behaviors, online monitoring or tracking can also inappropriately invade an ex-partner's privacy. Whereas most people adopt a "clean break" style online, in which they passively ignore but do not actively delete or unfollow their ex-partner, people with poorer post-dissolution adjustment might use social media to monitor their ex-partner, interact with people linked to their ex, and ritually or impulsively delete their online history (McDaniel, Drouin et al., 2021). If casual curiosity transitions to obsessive tracking, the behavior could become cyberstalking, an online form of traditional stalking whose victims tend to suffer feelings of threat, anxiety, and depression (Kaur et al., 2021; Worsley et al., 2017). As costly as it is for its victims, from an evolutionary perspective, unwanted pursuit behaviors may persist as post-dissolution tactics because of their adaptive potential to restore access to a lost relationship (Duntley & Buss, 2012; Perilloux & Buss, 2008). Post-dissolution pursuit behaviors can signal a perpetrator's commitment, investment, and effort; secure a victim's attention; and interfere with a victim's potential to start a new relationship (Duntley & Buss, 2012). Still, as a strategy, the success rate is low, especially in extreme forms, and the costs are high, making engaging in unwanted pursuit behaviors a problematic and maladaptive post-dissolution tactic. There are, however, healthier attempts to renew a relationship following dissolution. People might have open, lengthy discussions about whether they should try again; or, they might resume spending time together and, either implicitly or after a conversation, find themselves together again (Dailey et al., 2012).

Relationships that end and then renew, that is, churning, cyclical, or on-again/off-again relationships, are common, experienced by over 60 percent of people with rates similar among same-sex and different-sex partners (Dailey, 2020; Dailey, Pfiester et al., 2009; Monk et al., 2018). During the post-dissolution period, people can experience ambivalence about their breakup; they might desire to rekindle their romance because of lingering feelings, companionship desires, and the familiarity of their old relationship (Dailey et al., 2011; Dailey, Zhong et al., 2020). They might think their ex-partner is "the one," believe this time will be different, or feel unsure of themselves without their ex-partner (Cope & Mattingly, 2021; Dailey et al., 2011). When ex-partners discover that they are communicating better and they see positive changes in their partner or themselves, these observations can also encourage a relationship renewal (Dailey, Rossetto et al., 2009). Still, people describe on-again/off-again relationships as emotional rollercoasters, fraught with uncertainty, frustrations, and doubts (Dailey et al., 2011). When "on," these relationships boast fewer positives and more negatives, including more violence and abuse, than non-cyclical relationships, with a history of more on-off cycles associated with worse relationship quality (Dailey, Pfiester et al., 2009; Halpern-Meekin et al., 2013). For both same-sex and different-sex partners, relationship instability aligns with psychological distress, and over time, more frequent on-off cycles correspond with greater distress (Monk et al., 2018; Monk, Ogolsky et al., 2022).

Forging a New Self Separate from an Ex-Partner

"I'm lost." "I don't even know who I am anymore." Have you heard versions of these statements, as friends struggle after losing a partner? Why might this be? Recall how, in the building of relationships, people integrate their romantic partner into their own mental representation of self (a form of self-expansion; Mattingly et al., 2020). This is a healthy form of closeness for an ongoing relationship, but can make endings more difficult: the more people include ex-partners or deceased partners into their own self-concepts, the more breakup grief they experience and the more vulnerable they are to prolonged grief disorder (Boelen & van den Hout, 2010; Harrison et al., 2021). From a cognitive interdependence standpoint, when relationships end, people move forward alone. To know who they are alone, they often must disentangle their own self-concept from their mental representation of their former partner. This is not an easy task. In the process of breaking cognitive interdependence, people's self-concepts tend to shrink, and people often experience a lack of self-concept clarity (Lewandowski et al., 2006; Slotter et al., 2010). Anxiously attached individuals and people whose relationships were especially rich with self-expansion opportunities often struggle the most with low self-concept clarity and a loss of a sense of self after their relationship ends (Lewandowski et al., 2006; Slotter & Gardner, 2012b). On the flip side, losing a low-quality, low-self-expanding relationship can predict self-rediscovery, positive emotions, and self-growth (see Figure 12.12; Lewandowski & Bizzoco, 2007). Different relationships, different losses, different effects on the self. In general, the time-course for rebuilding the self is not fully understood, but self-concept repair may precede emotional recovery (Emery & Gardner, 2020; Mason, Law et al., 2012).

As people work to redefine and restore their self-concepts, they often keep some self-aspects that they acquired from their former partner. People tend to retain the partner-influenced skills, hobbies, or interests that they themselves exerted effort to develop as their own (Slotter et al., 2014). Maybe your partner helped you both become avid spelunkers; upon dissolution, you would retain your cave-exploring knowledge, maybe debate how much spelunking was your versus your former partner's passion – but perhaps usurp the hobby as your own, even as you drop other partner-influenced aspects of yourself. Over time, with each relationship, people experience a net gain in self-concept content. In other words, people grow through relationships. They retain some **self-expansion residue** (thank you!), even as they move on (next!; Carpenter & Spottswood, 2013).

Figure 12.12 Dissolution can afford people the chance to renew lost hobbies, reclaim forgotten aspects of themselves, or focus on long-ignored needs; such self-rediscovery can correspond with feeling energized, wise, strong, and happy (Lewandowski & Bizzoco, 2007). What other silver linings might be tied to relationship dissolution? (Photo: Kelvin Murray / Stone / Getty Images)

These gains point to benefits from having had, and lost, a relationship, but there are other gains as well. From the **stress-related growth** perspective, a relationship's end offers a unique opportunity for self-growth (Park et al., 1996; Tedeschi et al., 2018). Bereaved spouses, for instance, might discover new confidence, independence, or greater appreciation for friends and family (Michael & Cooper, 2013). Likewise, the distress of divorce may accompany hope and personal thriving, with positive outcomes occurring as frequently as negative outcomes (Tashiro et al., 2013). In general, women tend to report more post-dissolution growth than men and social support is often part of the growth process (Tashiro et al., 2013; Tashiro & Frazier, 2003). Post dissolution, people often retrospectively note having experienced positive personal gains, such as discovering strength or confidence; they report having learned what they want (or don't want) in a future partner; they recognize having acquired relationship skills; and they report valuing their friends more (Tashiro & Frazier, 2003). Work that shifts away from reliance on retrospection suggests that beliefs about post-dissolution growth could reflect positive reappraisal more than actual growth (Owenz & Fowers, 2019); however, people's beliefs may be important in-and-of-themselves. Perceiving self-improvements may help prepare people for seeking out their next relationship.

New Romantic Relationships

In the aftermath of a breakup, some people enter new relationships … quickly. New relationships are considered **rebound relationships** when they begin before a person has recovered from a recent relationship loss, when they still have lingering feelings for their former partner (Brumbaugh & Fraley, 2015). Rebound relationships are different from **rebound sex**, which tends to refer to casual post-dissolution sex with a stranger (Barber & Cooper, 2014). Some of the driving motivations are the same – for example, coping with breakup distress or deflated self-esteem, or wanting to enact revenge on an ex-partner – but unlike rebound sex, rebound relationships are a new attempt at pair-bonding. Accordingly, people might assume that rebound relationships are categorically unhealthy, that they "use" a new partner, or that they are destined to fail. Such is not always the case. Controlling for prior psychological health, people who jump into new relationships with little time being single tend to report greater well-being and greater self-esteem (Brumbaugh & Fraley, 2015). Even if enacted out of revenge, participation in a rebound relationship may help people "move on" from their prior relationship. They serve as a distraction from lingering attachments to an ex, as a source for social support, and as a way to rebuild the self-concept (Branand et al., 2019; Shimek & Bello, 2014). For anxiously attached individuals, who are more likely to enter rebound relationships, attending to a new partner helps them "get over" an ex-partner (Marshall, Bejanyan, & Ferenczi, 2013; Spielmann et al., 2009). Critically, no evidence suggests that entering a new relationship quickly sentences the relationship to failure. For example, the stability of new post-divorce relationships is not linked to how long – between divorce and the new relationship – people are single (Wolfinger, 2007).

Finding a new partner can be an intimidating, but exciting, prospect after relationship dissolution. Along with the possibility for new love, passion, intimacy, and commitment, re-partnering can provide a catalyst for new self-growth and offer a new support system for future goals (Aron et al., 2013; Gomillion et al., 2015). New relationships can provide some very practical benefits too. When relevant, re-partnering can reverse declines in standard of living brought about by relationship disruption, which can be especially beneficial to women (Brown et al., 2018, 2019; Lin & Brown, 2021). Still, men tend to re-partner after divorce or widowhood more than women, perhaps because women tend to assume more parenting responsibilities, and parenting children tends to reduce likelihood of re-partnering (Di Nallo, 2019; Raley & Sweeney, 2020). Among older adults, women may prioritize their autonomy and freedom over the caretaking responsibilities that may be disproportionally assigned to women in different-sex relationships. When people do enter new relationships, they step into an upward trajectory in life satisfaction not present among those who remain unpartnered (Gloor et al., 2021).

Conclusion

In this chapter, you learned that relationship dissolution occurs for different reasons and in different ways, and likewise has diverse consequences. Relationship dissolution is common, and ultimately inevitable, with widowhood associated with some of the strongest post-dissolution challenges. You read about the intrapersonal, interpersonal, and situational precursors of voluntary breakups, the important role of dissolution consideration, and the strategies people use to end their relationships (e.g., ghosting). We also reviewed more immediate and longer-term consequences associated with the loss of a relationship. Finally, we discussed the post-dissolution experience, including navigating relationships with an ex-partner, changes to the self, and forming new relationships. While many relationships end (and many should), others teeter on the edge of relationship dissolution but find their way back to stability, finding new ways to thrive. How? Chapter 13 examines contemporary relationship interventions and their potential to support distressed relationships.

Major Take-Aways

- Aspects of people's personalities (e.g., neuroticism) can predict breakups, but we tend to blame breakups on our partners more than ourselves.
- Closeness can dissipate, incompatibility is a key predictor of divorce, and issues of commitment (especially infidelity) can jeopardize relationship stability.
- Low income and incarceration are key situational factors predicting dissolution.
- People can adopt myriad strategies to end their relationships, and the strategies they choose reflect their own attributes and influence the intensity of the breakup experience.

- The loss of a relationship is associated with psychological distress and poorer physical health, and while some people experience the strain of dissolution in an acute crisis fashion, others experience chronic challenges tied to the loss of their relationship.
- Forming friendships with an ex-partner is common and perhaps especially important in some contexts. The self-concept shrinks in the aftermath of a relationship dissolution and requires rebuilding; people who re-partner tend to have better outcomes than those who do not.

Further Readings

If you're interested in ...

... the ways people manage infidelity, read:
Apostolou, M. (2022). Catch me if you can: Strategies for hiding infidelity. *Personality and Individual Differences*, *189*, 111494.

... divorce among older adults, read:
Brown, S. L., & Lin, I. F. (2022). The graying of divorce: A half century of change. *Journals of Gerontology: Series B*, *77*(9), 1710–1720.

... why people return to ex-partners and the latest research on cyclical relationships, read:
Dailey, R. E. (2022). *On-again / off-again dating relationships*. Taylor & Francis.

... how the self changes when people experience romantic breakups, read:
Mattingly, B. A., McIntyre, K. P., & Lewandowski, G. W. (2020). Relationship dissolution and self-concept change. In B. A. Mattingly, K. P. McIntyre, & G. W. Lewandowski, Jr. (Eds.), *Interpersonal relationships and the self-concept* (pp. 145–161). Springer International Publishing.

... the importance of closeness in fostering relationship stability, read:
Park, Y., Impett, E. A., Spielmann, S. S., Joel, S., & MacDonald, G. (2021). Lack of intimacy prospectively predicts breakup. *Social Psychological and Personality Science*, *12*(4), 442–451.

INTERVENTIONS TO REPAIR AND STRENGTHEN RELATIONSHIPS

Listening in on Couple Therapy

"What you are about to hear is an unscripted one-time couples coun-seling session. It contains mature themes and listener discretion is advised. For the purposes of maintaining confidentiality, names and some identifiable characteristics have been removed, but their voices and their stories are real." This is the introduction to the popular podcast series, *Where Should We Begin? With Esther Perel*. In each episode, Esther Perel – a psychotherapist, bestselling author, and renowned speaker – meets with one couple to discuss an ongoing issue in their relationship and to offer insight and strategies to help them to move forward. Listeners are a fly on the wall as couples share their stories of infidelity, unmet expectations, sexual and emo-tional disconnection, overwhelming anger and resentment, and family disapproval (to name just a few). As the sessions unfold, Esther guides each partner through sharing their own experience, as well as understanding and validating their partner's (often quite different) experience. With her help, some partners are able to hear each other for the first time in a long time. Other partners come to under-stand how their current issues connect to their past personal histories (e.g., trauma or neglect), creating space for compassion and reconnection. In describing what drew her to this work, Esther stated, "You could actually see the change happening in front of you if you helped people to connect or to open up or to be vulnerable with each other or to speak truth to each other or to apologize to each other. I thought, this is a full human theater. It's the best theater in the world" (Perel, 2020). It seems that Esther Perel's many loyal podcast listeners agree.

Figure 13.1 Esther Perel is the host of the popular podcast, *Where Should We Begin?* In this podcast, audiences witness how therapeutic interventions can help partners repair distressed relationships and can learn strategies to prevent similar problems in their own relationships. Perel was born in Belgium, is fluent in nine languages, and practices psychotherapy in New York City. She is *The New York Times* bestselling author of *The State of Affairs* and *Mating in Captivity*. (Photo: Michael Loccisano / Getty Images Entertainment)

In this chapter, you will learn about therapeutic interventions that can repair distressed relationships and about educational interventions that can strengthen relationships and keep them from becoming distressed. The interventions presented in this chapter are research-based, meaning that (1) they are informed by the theories and empirical findings presented in the previous chapters and (2) their efficacy has been tested. Your goal in this chapter is to learn how the presented interventions work, evaluate the available evidence supporting their effectiveness, and recognize ways they can be improved.

 GUIDING QUESTIONS

Consider these questions as you read this chapter:
- How do the dominant therapeutic interventions differ in their approaches to improving distressed relationships?
- What are the short-term and long-term consequences of therapeutic interventions for partners' relationships?
- What do people learn through relationship education interventions that helps them to protect their relationships from becoming distressed?
- What can be done to increase the impact of relationship interventions, including both the effectiveness of the interventions and their reach?

Therapeutic Interventions to Reduce Distress

In the United States, at any given time, approximately 20 percent of early-stage marriages (those between one and three years in length) and approximately 30 percent of all marriages have poor enough functioning to be characterized as clinically distressed (Beach et al., 2005; Lebow et al., 2012; Whisman et al., 2008). Relationship distress increases the risk of relationship dissolution (remember, over 40 percent of first marriages are expected to eventually end in divorce) and makes people vulnerable to the associated psychological and physical consequences that accompany many breakups (see Chapter 12). Even in the absence of a breakup, being involved in a distressed relationship is associated with poor physical health and poor psychological well-being (e.g., Proulx et al., 2007; Robles et al., 2014; Whisman & Uebelacker, 2006). Indeed, people in dissatisfying romantic relationships report greater depression, anxiety, substance use, and cardiovascular health problems than people in satisfying relationships. Being involved in an unstable marriage (i.e., seriously considering divorce or separation) is also associated with increases in anxiety and loneliness, which contribute to subsequent physical and mental health problems (Lee et al., 2021; Wickrama & O'Neal, 2021). Relationship distress is clearly best avoided, but when a relationship becomes distressed, what are we to do? The best research-backed intervention is **couple therapy** (also called couples therapy or couples counseling; note this type of therapy is also available for relationships comprised of more than two people).

Who Seeks Couple Therapy?

Not all distressed partners seek therapy (Figure 13.2; Doss et al., 2009b; Gottman et al., 2020). One large statewide sample of Oklahomans suggested that only about 35 percent of divorced individuals try couple therapy before divorcing (Johnson et al., 2002). Partners with lower socioeconomic status are particularly unlikely to access relationship interventions (Halford et al., 2006; Sullivan & Bradbury, 1997), with only about 30 percent of low-income partners who consider couple therapy receiving treatment (Williamson, Karney et al., 2019). These partners most commonly cite structural barriers, such as costs (approximately 40 percent) or not knowing where to go for help (approximately 35 percent), as obstacles to accessing treatment. As a different type of treatment obstacle, women in

Figure 13.2 "Maybe we should try couple therapy." Although hearing these words may be distressing, couple therapy is the best research-backed intervention for people in distressed relationships. (Photo: FatCamera / E+ / Getty Images)

different-sex relationships (approximately 35 percent) also frequently complain of their partner's unwillingness to attend couple therapy (Williamson, Karney et al., 2019). Partner's unwillingness is typically not an obstacle cited by men (mentioned by fewer than 15 percent of men). This gendered pattern aligns with evidence that it is the woman's dissatisfaction that typically serves as the impetus for seeking therapy (Eubanks Fleming & Córdova, 2012) and that women are more likely to initiate divorce (e.g., Parker et al., 2022).

Partners who do choose to attend therapy often wait several years after problems arise before seeking help, meaning that they tend to be quite distressed by the time they start therapy (Gottman et al., 2020; Gottman & Gottman, 1999). However, just like not all partners who are distressed attend therapy, not all partners who attend therapy are distressed (see Figure 13.3).

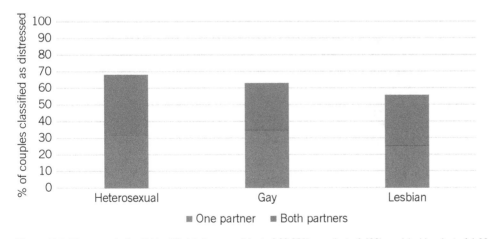

Figure 13.3 The percent of self-identified heterosexual (out of 39,251), gay (out of 438), and lesbian (out of 1,022) partners in which one or both partners scored below the distressed cutoff on the global happiness scale (e.g., "I think my partner really cares about me") prior to starting couple therapy. Why do you think people wait to pursue couple therapy? (Source: Drawn based on data from Gottman et al. [2020])

Figure 13.3 shows data on the percent of heterosexual, gay, and lesbian couples in which one or both partners were categorized as clinically distressed based on low relationship satisfaction when they enrolled in couple therapy (Gottman et al., 2020). As you can see, among heterosexual couples, approximately one-third begin therapy with both partners distressed, approximately one-third begin therapy with only one partner distressed, and approximately one-third begin therapy with neither partner distressed. This distribution appears similar among gay and lesbian couples, though a greater proportion of sexual-minority couples begin couple therapy with neither partner experiencing relationship distress.

Although not all partners report clinical relationship distress during their therapy intake, some specific relationship problems appear among nearly all partners. For instance, partners regularly report a high incidence of problematic communication patterns and a lack of intimacy in their intake forms (see Figure 13.4). They also cite **flooding** during conflict (i.e., feeling overwhelmed and in fight-or-flight mode while communicating about disagreements), an experience reported by at least one partner in over 97 percent of heterosexual, gay, and lesbian couples and by *both* partners in over 87 percent of heterosexual, gay, and lesbian couples. Romance problems (i.e., dissatisfaction with romance, passion, and the quality of sex) are also typical, cited by at least one partner in the majority of heterosexual (83 percent), gay (80 percent), and lesbian (78 percent) couples. These findings are consistent with other research showing that trouble with communication and a lack of intimacy often precipitate couple therapy (Doss et al., 2004, 2009b).

Figure 13.4 also shows how frequently several other specific problem areas are endorsed during intake for couple therapy (Gottman et al., 2020). Of note, at least one partner generally reports problems handling stress, problems with relatives and extended family, differing values and goals, financial issues, and/or problems having fun together in the majority of treatment-seeking couples.

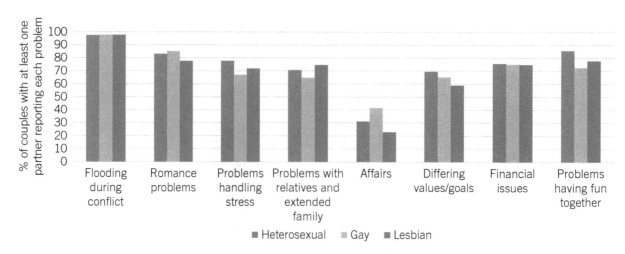

Figure 13.4 The percent of couples in which *at least one partner* identified each topic as problematic in their relationship during intake to couple therapy. What problems would spur you to seek couple therapy? (Source: Drawn based on data from Gottman et al. [2020])

(a)　　　　　　　　　　　　　　　　　　　　(b)

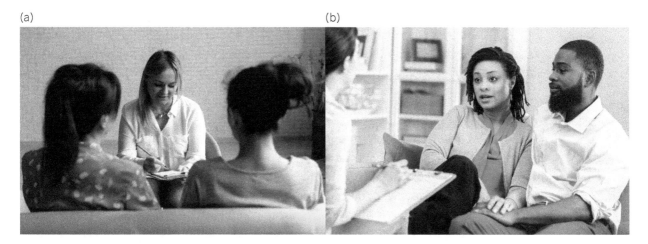

Figure 13.5 What do you believe happens in couple therapy? Read on to move beyond the image of a couple therapy room setup to learn the practical "nuts and bolts" of the intervention approaches that constitute couple therapy. (Photo: Fiordaliso / Moment / Getty Images [a] and SDI Productions / E+ / Getty Images [b])

Therapeutic Approaches

When you hear the term "couple therapy," you probably picture two partners sitting next to each other on a sofa, while a therapist sits across from them (Figure 13.5). Beyond the setup of the room – and perhaps some sharing of problems, some precise questions, and some nods of encouragement – what happens in couple therapy? And how well does couple therapy work?

Two evidence-based approaches to treating relationship distress dominate the field: **behavioral couple therapy** (plus its newer adaptations) and **emotionally focused couple therapy**. These two approaches (1) were developed from relationship theory and empirical research, (2) have been manualized, meaning the field has established systematic ways to implement these treatments, and (3) have been meta-analytically supported, meaning that they have been shown to be more effective than no intervention across multiple studies. Other distinct interventions, many of which are effective, can also be provided in the context of couple therapy, but today behavioral couple therapy and emotionally focused couple therapy are the most prominent (Gurman, 2015).

Behavioral Couple Therapy

Behavioral couple therapy was originally developed in the 1960s on the foundation of social exchange theory (Baucom, Epstein et al., 2015; Jacobson & Margolin, 1979), though it has been adapted more recently to incorporate additional theoretical perspectives. Recall from Chapter 2 that social exchange theory emphasizes the balance of relationship rewards and costs in determining partners' outcomes. Specifically, social exchange theory posits that people will have better experiences in their relationships and more relationship satisfaction when they experience greater rewards (positive exchanges) and fewer costs (negative exchanges; Thibaut & Kelley, 1959). As an extension of this theory, relationship distress results when people experience too few positive exchanges (insufficient rewards) and too many negative exchanges (excessive costs). This conceptualization of the causes of distress is supported by work showing that difficult personality traits, annoying habits and behaviors, incompatible interests and goals, and transgressions such as infidelity (all negative exchanges or causes of negative exchanges) predict breakup (see Chapter 12). As we review each of the following behavioral therapies (traditional, cognitive-behavioral, and integrative), notice how rewards/costs are seen as sources of, and thereby possible solutions for, relationship distress.

Traditional Behavioral Couple Therapy

Traditional behavioral couple therapy (TBCT) involves improving the balance of positive and negative exchanges through targeted behavior change (Baucom, Epstein et al., 2015; Christensen et al., 2004, 2015). After a few sessions where the therapist can learn about the partners and their relationship, the partners receive feedback about their strengths and about specific areas in which they could improve their communication and problem-solving skills. Then, the therapist will work with the partners to identify ways to increase positive exchanges in the relationship (called "**behavioral exchange**"). For instance, partners could each make a list of kind deeds they could do for each other and practice adding those kind deeds into their daily lives. By increasing the occurrence of positive exchanges (i.e., rewards), the balance of positive and negative interactions can improve. In addition to behavioral exchange, the second major intervention used in traditional behavioral couple therapy is direct **skills training** intended to lessen negative interactions (Christensen et al., 2004). Therapists teach communication and problem-solving skills, provide opportunities for partners to practice the skills in session, and encourage partners to incorporate their new skills into their interactions outside of session.

One skill that partners tend to find particularly useful is the **speaker-listener technique** (Markman, Stanley, & Blumberg, 2010). This technique provides a structure – an agreed-upon set of steps – for partners to use when they are sharing sensitive thoughts and emotions or when they are experiencing a contentious conflict (Stanley et al., 1997). As the name implies, the speaker-listener technique involves partners taking the roles of "speaker" and "listener." One partner starts first as "speaker," meaning that they "have the floor" first. To make roles clear, partners are encouraged to use an object to signify speaker status. The originators of this approach actually gave speakers a piece of linoleum flooring: the speaker literally had the floor (Markman, Stanley, & Blumberg, 2010). In practice, any object (e.g., a ball, a hat) can be used. After the speaker talks, they hand the object to their partner, and the roles are switched (the speaker becomes the listener).

When using the speaker-listener technique, partners are not supposed to try to resolve their problems or come up with solutions. The only goal is for each partner to share their thoughts and feelings and to try to understand each other's experience. To achieve this goal, speakers are encouraged to use "I" statements (Markman, Stanley, & Blumberg, 2010; Stanley et al., 1997). Using "I" statements means speaking for yourself, not trying to mind-read a partner's perspective, and not trying to describe the objective truth of the situation (one's partner likely would see a different "objective" truth anyway).

Which of the following do you think are "I" statements?

A. "I feel overwhelmed when I get home from work and the sink is full of dishes. I'm already exhausted from the day and the commute, and the dishes are just too much for me in that moment."

B. "I think you just want me to be responsible for the household tasks."

C. "I felt unimportant when you didn't make any plans for my birthday."

D. "I feel like anyone could see that you don't prioritize me."

If you guessed A and C, you are accurate. Both statements A and C describe the speaker's own feelings, whereas statements B and D do not. In statement B, the speaker presumes to know the listener's thoughts and feelings (mind-reading), and in statement D, the speaker starts the sentence with an "I," but speaks to an assumed objective reality (anyone would agree, so it is objectively true).

In addition to using "I" statements, the speaker's other primary job is to give up the speaker role. While it can be tempting to hold the floor continuously, delivering a never-ending monologue is unproductive because it interferes with the listener's primary task: reflecting back what they heard. Reflecting back is simply paraphrasing – or repeating back – what you heard your partner say, in your own words. Reflecting back is a powerful tool because it (1) requires the speaker to pause and take a moment to process what the speaker said, (2) can demonstrate the listener's understanding (a key component of perceived partner responsiveness), and (3) can provide an opportunity for misunderstandings to be corrected. Reread statement A above, and try to reflect back what the speaker said. How could you paraphrase that statement?

Try, "Dishes in the sink after work feels like too much to you after a long day – did I get that right?" The listener does not have to perfectly understand for reflecting back to be effective. In fact, a lot of progress is made when the listener misunderstands and gives the speaker an opportunity to clarify. Imagine that the listener paraphrased, "So ... after a long day, you can't take on anything else for a while: the dishes, the chores, the kids ... you just need a break from it all." In this example, the listener – perhaps without even knowing it – extrapolated beyond the speaker's point about the dishes to other issues that the speaker might (or might not) find overwhelming. By reflecting this back, they give the speaker an opportunity to say "Yes, that's right" or "Actually, no. I want to connect with the kids. It's the dishes that set me off, partially because they prevent me from playing with the kids."

Although the listener's role may sound simple (most of us can repeat back what we just heard, right?), it actually can be quite difficult. Imagine your partner says, "When you get home after midnight, I feel lonely and abandoned, like I'm not worth coming home to." Many of us might immediately jump into a rebuttal. "That almost never happens!" or "I work late to support our family! How could you think that I don't care about you?" The listener's job is simply to hear and to understand the truth of another person's experience. Whether the experience seems reasonable or justified is not the point. In one episode of Esther Perel's podcast (Perel, 2017b), a woman rejected her partner's claim that he felt abandoned by her when she focused her attention on their young children. As the woman disagreed and tried to rebut his feelings, Perel interjected, "[Do] you want to hear, or [do] you want to be right?" When the woman acknowledged that she wanted to hear, Perel continued, "Then you're going to have to, maybe, not be so right." See Table 13.1 for a summary of the skills that therapists teach partners to use while communicating about their thoughts and feelings (Baucom, Epstein et al., 2015).

Along with the speaker-listener technique, therapists can also teach partners how to problem solve effectively. Behavior-based strategies for partner problem solving incorporate

Table 13.1 Behavior-based strategies for communicating more effectively

How to *communicate* effectively with your partner	
While you're sharing your thoughts and emotions (speaker role):	**While your partner is sharing (listener role):**
1. Describe only your own experience of the situation, not an objective reality, or what you imagine is your partner's experience. Try saying "I think …," "I feel …," or "It feels to me like …," but be careful not to say "I think you …" 2. Make specific statements rather than generalizations. 3. It can be easy to get caught up in sharing what you think, but don't forget to also share what you feel. 4. Try to balance the negative with some positive. If you're sharing negative thoughts or feelings about your partner, sharing positive things as well will make it easier for them to listen without becoming defensive. 5. Remember to give your partner chances to respond after you have explained each main point.	1. Use your non-verbals (eye contact, posture) to show that you are attentive. 2. Take your partner's perspective. Try to understand how your partner is thinking and feeling based on their experience of the situation. 3. Even if you do not agree with your partner's thoughts or feelings, remind yourself that your partner has the right to have those thoughts and feelings. 4. When your partner is finished speaking, reflect back the most important information your partner shared. By summarizing what you heard, you can ensure you understood and give your partner a chance to clarify. 5. Avoid immediately expressing your own opinion, offering advice, or trying to reinterpret your partner's experience ("maybe you actually feel …"). Just focus on hearing and understanding what they are sharing.

How easily could you use these strategies?
Source: Based on data from Baucom, Epstein et al. (2015).

step-by-step individual problem-solving strategies with effective communication strategies that allow partners to problem solve jointly (Baucom, Epstein et al., 2015). See Table 13.2 for these steps. Therapists teach partners that before they can discuss possible solutions (step 3), they need to be sure they are discussing the same specific issue (step 1), and they need to take the time to understand each other's perspectives and needs (perhaps using the speaker-listener technique, step 2). When partners take the time to align themselves on the issue at hand (i.e., jointly define and state the problem), they can keep their discussion focused and productive. Understanding each other's needs is also imperative because any effective solution must satisfy both partners' needs. Partners who understand each other's perspectives can offer mutually satisfying suggestions rather than ping-ponging solutions that meet only one or the other's needs. Offering a solution that meets both partners' needs not only saves time, but more importantly, it communicates understanding, validating, and care (perceived partner responsiveness again!). The final steps (4 and 5) involve selecting a

Table 13.2 Behavior-based strategies for problem solving more effectively

Steps for *problem solving* effectively with your partner
1. Start by stating the specific issue. What needs to be decided? Or what is occurring or not occurring that is problematic? If the issue is broad or involved, select a specific part of the issue to start with and state that issue clearly.
2. Describe your perspective. Why is this issue important to you? What needs do you have that will need to be considered in any eventual solution? (Do not propose a solution just yet.) Then, let your partner describe their perspective in the same way. The skills for communicating effectively when sharing and listening apply at this step (see Table 13.1). Reflecting back can ensure you and your partner understand each other's perspective before moving to the next step.
3. Now, discuss possible solutions that would meet both your own and your partner's needs. Your goal now is to stay solution-focused, so avoid talking about the past. Solutions can only be enacted in the present and the future. If there is no solution that would meet both your and your partner's needs, try to identify a compromise.
4. Select one solution to try first, and state it clearly. Ensure that both partners are willing to go forward with it and are happy (enough) with it (e.g., not feeling angry or resentful about this plan).
5. Decide on a time frame that will provide several opportunities to try out the solution (one week, one month, etc.). Try carrying out the solution. At the end of the planned time frame, check in about how it is working, and revise the solution if necessary.

Why is each step important?
Source: Based on data from Baucom, Epstein et al. (2015).

solution that partners both see as tenable and to check in at a planned later time (after partners both have an opportunity to evaluate the solution) to discuss whether the solution is working and revise or try a new solution, if necessary.

Traditional behavioral couple therapy is a precise intervention aimed at improving the quality of interactions between partners. If partners can learn to use the prescribed communication and problem-solving skills and can commit to increasing positive interactions through behavioral exchange, they can expect to experience more rewards and fewer costs in their relationship. In social exchange theory lingo, they can expect their "outcomes" to improve. Evidence suggests that TBCT does improve couples' communication; objective raters observed less negativity and withdrawal in partners' conversations following the intervention than before it (Baucom et al., 2011). But *think* about it, is behavior change enough to alleviate distress? No really, *think* about it. What else – besides problematic behaviors – might contribute to and sustain distress? What do you *think*? The answer, as you might have guessed, is thinking itself.

Cognitive Behavioral Couple Therapy

The way that partners think about (i.e., interpret or make sense of) the interactions they have together and their relationships in general (e.g., the expectations and standards they hold) can contribute to and maintain their distress (Baucom, Epstein et al., 2015). Accordingly, as clinicians increasingly recognized the importance of cognition to relationship functioning, traditional behavioral couple therapy was adapted to include interventions that address problematic thoughts (Epstein & Zheng, 2017). The resulting cognitive behavioral couple therapy (CBCT) incorporates the behavioral interventions described above (i.e., behavioral exchange, skills training), as well as cognitive restructuring interventions intended to help partners identify and correct distorted or unhelpful thought patterns (Baucom, Epstein et al., 2015; Epstein & Zheng, 2017; Halford & Pepping, 2019). Therapists primarily focus on five types of thought processes that can contribute to relationship distress (see Table 13.3). These are all normal thought processes that are not necessarily harmful, but can become problematic when they are left unchecked – taken as objective reality rather than identified as thoughts.

For instance, when people inadvertently attend to only certain kinds of information (e.g., selective attention to negative interactions), they can fail to realize that their perception is distorted, leading them to base their judgments on incomplete information. Similarly, the automatic attributions people make for their partners' behaviors (discussed in detail in Chapter 7) can be damaging, particularly when negative internal explanations are taken as

Table 13.3 Types of cognitions that can contribute to relationship distress

Types of cognitions	Examples of how they might contribute to relationship distress if left unchecked
Selective attention: Noticing some things and overlooking others	• Noticing the partner's flaws, but not their good characteristics and habits • Noticing the uncomfortable moments of a date and ignoring the connected moments
Attributions: Inferences about the causes of events (e.g., relationship events, a partner's behavior)	• Thinking that a partner's distraction during a conversation is due to a lack of interest or care • Thinking that a partner only gave a gift because they are trying to make up for some misdeed
Expectancies: Predictions about what will happen in the future (e.g., beliefs about the likelihood that a partner will behave in a particular way)	• Thinking that asking for help will lead a partner to criticize or blame • Thinking that reaching for the partner's hand will lead a partner to pull away
Assumptions: Beliefs about the way things are (e.g., beliefs about the nature of relationships)	• Thinking that relationships are either effortless or are destined to end • Thinking that relationships are fragile and require perfection on the part of both partners
Standards: Beliefs about how things "should" be (e.g., beliefs about what a good relationship should be like)	• Thinking that partners should be "on the same page" in every way • Thinking that a good partner should be able to guess how you're feeling without asking

Source: Based on data from Baucom, Epstein et al. (2015); Epstein & Zheng (2017).

objective truth. For instance, a person who is dissatisfied with the lack of sexual intimacy in their relationship may falsely infer that their partner is disinterested in being intimate (an internal attribution) rather than acknowledging situational constraints that limit sexual intimacy (an external attribution). Such internal attributions are likely to produce more hurt feelings and encourage more destructive behavior (e.g., withdrawal, looking elsewhere for affection) than an external attribution. Partners who can acknowledge that their attribution is a thought rather than reality can question their attribution before reacting.

Unacknowledged and unexamined expectancies can also get people – and their relationships – into trouble. Consider how the sexually dissatisfied person just discussed may be unwilling to initiate sex with their partner because they expect rejection. As Esther Perel said in one episode of her podcast, "Do you ask him, or do you suppose?" (Perel, 2017b). When people suppose and presume rather than test their expectancies, their expectancies can become anchors that keep partners stuck in the same dissatisfying pattern. When partners can instead learn to identify their expectancies as just thoughts, they can question the accuracy of their expectations, try something new, and perhaps receive an unexpected response.

Unlike selective attention, attributions, and expectancies, which tend to pop up in the ongoing stream of consciousness as people are thinking about their relationships, assumptions and standards are more static belief systems about relationships in general. Assumptions are the beliefs people have about the nature of relationships. These might include assumptions about the effort or maintenance that relationships require (e.g., "Good relationships work without effort" or "All relationships require continual effort"), assumptions about the fragility of relationships in the face of threats ("Relationships are easily damaged" or "Relationships are resilient"), or assumptions about how relationships change over time ("Relationships get worse over time" or "Relationships don't change"). These assumptions can influence how people evaluate their relationships. For example, a person who believes that "Partners are either compatible or they're not" (assumption) may determine that their relationship is "not meant to be" if they have to work hard to understand their partner or problem solve with them (see the *Is This True for You?* box for more on this assumption).

 IS THIS TRUE FOR YOU?

Do You Believe in Destiny?

Do you believe that a successful relationship comes down to finding the "right" partner? Does a rocky start foretell of a relationship's inevitable failure? These questions target destiny beliefs, beliefs that partners are either compatible or not, and that this compatibility is the primary factor in relationship success (Knee et al., 2003). People who strongly endorse destiny beliefs have poorer relationship outcomes when they face relationship challenges (such as conflict) than people who do not believe in relationship destiny (e.g., Franiuk et al., 2004; Knee et al., 2003, 2004). For people who believe in relationship destiny, conflict signifies that they have not found their "soulmate." Perhaps this is why people with high destiny beliefs are prone to ghosting (severing all contact as a way to end a relationship; Freedman et al., 2019). Once a destiny believer has determined that this

Figure 13.6 Do you believe that having a successful relationship requires finding your soulmate(s), the partner(s) who is effortlessly compatible with you? (Photo: malerapaso / E+ / Getty Images)

relationship is not meant to be, poof, they might as well disappear because the relationship is doomed. Is this true for you (Figure 13.6)?

An alternative assumption is that relationships need to be cultivated, that "with enough effort, almost any relationship can work," and that "challenges and obstacles in a relationship can bring partners closer together" (Knee et al., 2003, p. 43). People who endorse these statements have strong **growth beliefs**, beliefs that relationship challenges are par for the course and can be overcome to build a satisfying relationship (Knee et al., 2003). People with greater growth beliefs maintain their commitment in the face of conflicts and sustain their positive relationship perceptions even when they evaluate their partner's behavior negatively (Knee et al., 2004). The assumption that conflict is inevitable makes partners more resilient to relationship challenges and more willing to work to strengthen their relationships. Can you see how destiny and growth beliefs might shape people's willingness to seek couple therapy, engage during sessions, and do the work required to heal a distressed relationship?

Whereas relationship assumptions capture people's beliefs about relationship effort, resilience, and change over time, relationship standards reflect beliefs about how relationships "should" be. For instance, some people believe that dyadic romantic partners should meet the majority of each other's psychological needs (e.g., needs for intimacy, companionship, sexual contact), whereas others believe people should distribute need fulfillment across multiple romantic partners or rely on friendships and family to meet most of their needs (Finkel et al., 2014; Moors et al., 2017). As another example, some people may believe that partners should always be "on the same page," whereas others may believe that partners should challenge each other through healthy disagreements. A strong body of work shows that some assumptions and standards are dysfunctional and unrealistic (Eidelson & Epstein, 1982). Therapists commonly report that the following five assumptions (#1–3) and standards (#4–5) are problematic.

1. Disagreement is destructive to a relationship.
2. Partners cannot change.
3. Women and men have fundamentally different personalities. (This assumption is relevant for partners in different-sex relationships.)
4. People who care about us should be able to sense what we need without being told.
5. One should be a perfect sexual partner, always performing well and completely satisfying their partner.

Couple therapists help partners to question their problematic thought processes through a process of guided discovery (Baucom, Epstein et al., 2015). For instance, partners may be asked to share their attributions for each other's behavior ("I assume you looked away right then because you think this conversation is a waste of time") or to describe their expectancies ("I figured if I texted during the workday, that would annoy you) to provide an opportunity for misunderstandings to be corrected. Therapists may also guide partners in identifying and then sharing their implicit assumptions and standards about relationships in order to reach decisions about which assumptions and standards are useful for them to maintain in their relationship. These cognition-focused interventions supplement traditional behavioral interventions in CBCT.

Integrative Behavioral Couple Therapy

Your partner's frustration when you make spur-of-the-moment plans, their spending habits which are so different from yours, their desire for children when you are not interested ... will these break your relationship? One adaptation of traditional behavioral couple therapy that has gained prominence and addresses issues like these (and many more) is integrative behavioral couple therapy. This approach supplements TBCT's change-focused interventions with new acceptance-focused interventions, placing more emphasis on the latter than the former (Christensen et al., 2004, 2015; Christensen & Doss, 2017). In this framework, acceptance means acknowledging a partner's differences and maintaining a positive connection despite them (Christensen et al., 2015). Critically, acceptance is not synonymous with resignation ("well, I guess I have to put up with this"); acceptance is a true willingness to allow differences to exist as they are and perhaps even to embrace them. Before we dive deeper, note this important caveat about acceptance: IBCT does not encourage partners to accept problematic behaviors or differences that are truly unacceptable to them. For instance, a therapist providing IBCT would never encourage someone to accept a partner's abusive behavior. Some behaviors and some differences are indeed important enough to end the relationship. Deciding whether the difference is acceptable or not can be part of the conversation in integrative behavioral couple therapy (and all couple therapies).

Partners' differences – in personality, interests, goals, and so on – are of fundamental importance in IBCT because they can be the source for problematic behaviors and negative exchanges. Whereas traditional behavioral couple therapy would attempt to directly change the problematic behaviors and negative exchanges, integrative behavioral couple therapy focuses on the deeper fundamental differences and responses to those differences. Specifically, IBCT aims to have partners understand and accept their core differences, which can weaken negative reactions to "problematic" behaviors and perhaps indirectly reduce the frequency and intensity of negative exchanges. Two common differences that come up in couple therapy are the artist versus scientist theme (one partner values spontaneity and excitement, while the other prioritizes predictability and practicality) and the closeness versus distance theme (one partner values independence and autonomy, while the other prioritizes connection and closeness; Christensen et al., 2015). Why might these themes create problems for partners?

From the perspective of IBCT, differences need not be contentious and likely did not start that way. Differences only become fraught over time through a series of common, but

Figure 13.7 Empathic joining enables partners to understand and accept each other as they are. When partners share their own fears and vulnerabilities, their natural empathy for each other can soften their negative reactions to their differences. (Photo: FG Trade / E+ / Getty Images)

destructive, relationship patterns (Christensen et al., 2015). Differences might start as a source of attraction ("It's fun to be spontaneous with you"), but partners often try to change each other as the relationship progresses ("Can we *please* have a plan just this once?") If initial change attempts are not effective, change attempts may become more and more destructive as partners turn to criticism, demands, or sulking to affect change. As more time progresses and the differences become more upsetting, partners can begin to see each other not as different, but as deficient ("There is something wrong with you for being this way"). This might lead partners to become polarized in their views and behaviors and could lead differences – and negative reactions to differences – to intensify.

Couple therapists who provide IBCT work with partners to identify the broad differences that underlie many of their specific disagreements. Therapists then use three strategies to deconstruct the toxic patterns partners have built around their differences and to instead facilitate acceptance of these differences (see Christensen et al., 2015 for a review). First, in empathic joining, the therapist encourages partners to share their emotional reactions to their differences, including the fears and vulnerabilities that make these differences so upsetting (Figure 13.7). For example, in a couple with different spending versus saving financial preferences, one partner might share their experiences of feeling stifled by penny-pinching, whereas the other partner might explain how excessive spending triggers memories of negative bank balances and concerns about returning to financial insecurity. In IBCT, the therapist would not instruct partners to respond in any particular way; there is no skills training involved in this approach. Instead, the therapist would model empathy and compassion and allow partners to access their own empathy and compassion for each other more naturally. When partners can understand the deeper fears and vulnerabilities that underlie each other's behaviors, the behaviors that initially seemed wrong or deficient ("you spend too much") can seem more understandable and reasonable ("you spend more than I do, and I can see why that's important to you"). Rather than changing the behavior, this intervention can encourage partners to be more accepting of each other than they already are.

Second, with unified detachment, the therapist helps partners to "take a step back" and view their difference or specific problem with more objectivity. Partners are encouraged to describe – rather than evaluate – the difference between themselves and how it shapes their interactions (e.g., triggers, emotional and behavioral reactions). Therapists often ask partners to come up with a descriptive (or even humorous) name for their problem (e.g., "The Cash Flow Foe") or even to picture their problem sitting in another chair in the room with them. These strategies externalize the problem, allowing partners to begin thinking of it as separate from who they are as a couple and to unite as allies against the problem, a common enemy.

In addition to these two acceptance-focused interventions, IBCT includes a variety of tolerance-building interventions. These interventions help partners to become better able to tolerate their differences rather than trying to change each other. First, therapists may help partners to identify a positive function of their difference. Their differences might, for example, help balance them ("If we were both like me, we would be broke; if we were both like you, we would be rich in cash but poor in experiences. Our difference serves us.") Second, therapists can facilitate tolerance building by asking partners to practice negative behaviors in therapy or to fake negative behaviors at home so that they can desensitize themselves to these behaviors and reduce the intensity of their responses to them. By engaging in these frustrating behaviors when they are not actually invested or upset, partners may see the absurdity in some of their behaviors.

Acceptance and tolerance building is also particularly useful for insoluble problems – problems where behavior change is impractical or impossible. For instance, imagine that Deepti wants to have a child, while her partner, Shawna, wants to remain childfree. This disagreement is unlikely to be resolved solely through behavioral strategies, such as problem-solving discussions, because no compromise would satisfy both partners. Cognitive restructuring by making more generous attributions (e.g., maybe it's not a lack of commitment that holds Shawna back, but a desire instead to give Deepti 100 percent of their attention) could help somewhat, but still would not resolve the disagreement. When partners face insoluble problems, acceptance can allow them to stop trying to change each other and make a plan to move forward in spite of their difference.

Even when behavior change is possible, a focus on change is not always wise. For instance, imagine that Kamal is continuously irked by Anne's disregard for household cleaning tasks. Even after Kamal expresses his irritation, Anne still lets the laundry pile up on the floor, leaves the toothpaste cap off, and lets dirty dishes turn into science projects. This is not an insoluble problem: Anne could change. But if she will not, and if Kamal wants to maintain the relationship, his best option is to try to accept Anne's messiness and manage his negative reaction to it. Indeed, how people react to a problematic behavior can be more damaging to the relationship than the original behavior itself (Christensen et al., 2015). For instance, if Kamal becomes enraged at the sight of an uncapped toothpaste and unleashes a torrent of criticisms and contemptuous name-calling, an acceptance intervention that helps soften Kamal's reaction may be more beneficial to the relationship than an intervention to increase Anne's tidying. Acceptance-based interactions can, paradoxically, bring about the desired behavior change. If Anne's messiness has become a major source of conflict in the relationship, continual pressure to change may actually undermine her willingness to do so. Remember how differences can become polarized? Anne may be even messier than she prefers, but will stubbornly persist as part of the polarized power struggle. If Kamal accepts Anne as she is, the power struggle ends, and Anne may choose to become a bit neater (Christensen et al., 2015).

ARTICLE SPOTLIGHT

A Qualitative Investigation of IBCT in Intercultural Partners

Intercultural partners – those partners who do not share traditions, beliefs, history or experiences, either based on their racial group or another distinguishable group membership – are at particular risk for relationship distress resulting from broad, thematic differences (Bustamante et al., 2011). When partners' culturally-rooted beliefs and practices conflict, their differences may be insoluble, as neither partner may be willing to change. As such, interracial partners may be especially well-suited for integrative behavioral couple therapy.

Kalai and Eldridge (2021) assessed the utility of IBCT for intercultural couples, using a **qualitative** study that involved the survey responses of three experienced IBCT couple therapists. Each therapist was asked to complete the survey thinking of one intercultural couple they had treated. They answered open-ended questions about the culture-specific differences the couple faced, the specific interventions the therapist used, and the changes the therapist observed over the course of treatment. Each therapist also answered questions about their overall impressions of using IBCT with intercultural couples (versus couples navigating other differences). Once data were collected, the therapists' responses formed separate "case studies" and the researchers used a method called **cross-case analysis** to identify similarities and differences between the three therapists' responses (Mathison, 2011). Cross-case analysis allows researchers to garner new insight beyond the insight obtained within the separate case studies themselves.

The case studies themselves provided rich information (Figure 13.8). One therapist described a couple in which one partner (an African American female) reported experiencing systemic racism that her spouse (a White male) interpreted as simple miscommunications (she was "too sensitive"). The therapist recognized that entrenched systems of privilege, power, and inequality were underlying differences in the couple's experiences and perspectives; their cultural differences were impeding their ability to connect. The therapist used empathic joining to help the male partner express his helplessness in response to the racism his spouse faced, allowing the female partner to be more open and accepting. Another therapist reported on a couple in which a Hispanic American Catholic female had persistent conflicts with her Caucasian Agnostic male partner over interactions with extended family. The female partner's heavy involvement with her extended family caused conflicts with her partner who was distant from his own family. Noticing this culturally rooted problem, the therapist instructed partners to role-play negative behaviors (e.g., the female pretended to ask a family member for help regarding a trivial issue; the male partner reacted with hostility) to help each partner build tolerance. The third therapist reported on a couple in which the male partner was raised in a Mexican American family where it was not acceptable for women to socialize with men other than

Figure 13.8 Qualitative researchers typically collect open-ended responses, which they then interpret and synthesize. In what important ways does qualitative research add to other methods we have reviewed in this book? (Photo: Nora Carol Photography / Moment / Getty Images)

their husband, whereas the female partner was raised in a White family where cross-sex socialization was common and expected. The therapist identified cultural expectations as a source of their problems and used unified detachment to help each partner view the cultural difference as an external problem that they could jointly work to overcome.

Based on the therapists' responses, Kalai and Eldridge (2021) determined that IBCT in its standard form is well-suited for intercultural couples. Kalai and Eldridge also identified an important commonality in how the three therapists provided IBCT to intercultural couples: they each invited culture into the treatment. Even as they differed in the extent they incorporated culture into their acceptance-based approaches, they each identified and then promptly communicated the potential relevance of cultural differences in their conceptualization of the couple's problem.

Qualitative researchers play an essential role in their work, actively interpreting and synthesizing data. What they choose to focus on matters. Because qualitative researchers take this active role, their own biases and perspectives may influence their findings. Therefore, qualitative researchers often provide **positionality statements** – statements describing their own identities – so that readers can consider how the researchers' identities might influence their conclusions. For instance, Kalai described herself as "a cisgender Middle-Eastern, Jewish, heterosexual female" and Eldridge described herself as "a cis-gender European American, Christian, heterosexual female" (Kalai & Eldridge, 2021, p. 263). Both authors also shared their status as clinical psychology doctoral students at the time of the study, and that they "believed that IBCT was a good fit for inter-cultural couples" (Kalai & Eldridge, 2021, p. 263). Understanding the authors' identities and beliefs provides context when considering which questions they asked, the themes they identified, and their broad interpretations (Darwin Holmes, 2020).

IBCT is unique from its precursors (TBCT and CBCT) not only in what interventions are used, but also in how the interventions are implemented. In earlier behavioral couple therapies, the therapist teaches partners rules and protocols designed to change their behaviors and reframe their thoughts. In IBCT, therapists do not provide partners with explicit instructions to change their behavior or their thoughts; therapists also do not instruct partners to be more accepting or tolerant. Instead, the therapist actively models the strategies (e.g., empathizing with one partner's experience, describing the problem as its own entity), which provides an opportunity for partners to naturally become more accepting and tolerant. The acceptance-focused strategies modeled by the therapist can then foster a motivation for partners to behave more constructively and less destructively in their interactions. IBCT does incorporate some behavioral interventions (e.g., behavioral exchange), but the bulk of behavior change is intended to occur naturally as partners deconstruct polarized patterns and are able to authentically and spontaneously work to improve their relationship (Christensen et al., 2015). IBCT assumes that partners already have many relationship skills; they just need the motivation to use them. Consistent with this perspective, evidence suggests that IBCT improves couples' observed communication as effectively as a TBCT intervention, despite less emphasis on skills training (Baucom et al., 2011).

Emotionally Focused Couple Therapy

Emotionally focused couple therapy (EFCT) is grounded in another key theoretical perspective, attachment theory (Johnson, 2015, 2019b). From the perspective of EFCT, distressed partners primarily suffer from emotional disconnection and attachment insecurity (Johnson, 2019a). These are considered the central problems – the underlying "viruses" – that manifest in specific behavioral "symptoms" such as conflict, resentment, anger, and irreconcilable differences (Johnson, 2019a, p. 101). In other words, destructive behavioral patterns – viewed as primary causes of distress in behavioral frameworks – are viewed as merely expressions of an insecure attachment bond in EFCT. Accordingly, EFCT aims to alleviate symptoms of insecurity by repairing the underlying attachment bond.

In attachment theory, as you might recall, people's beliefs about themselves and others reflect how well their attachment figures meet their proximity bids and offer a safe haven and secure base. From the perspective of emotionally focused couple therapy, problems arise within romantic relationships when partners do not meet each other's attachment needs (needs for safety, security, and emotional connection). A perceived abandonment or betrayal (e.g., infidelity), for example, may suddenly derail trust, or a partner's persistent unavailability, inattentiveness, or unresponsiveness may gradually undermine the partner's role as a supportive attachment figure (Johnson, 2015, 2019b). When an attachment relationship is threatened in some way, partners generally turn to maladaptive strategies (i.e., angry protest, followed by clinging, and ultimately detachment) to have their needs met the best they can (Beasley & Ager, 2019; Johnson, 2015). These strategies, however, inadvertently maintain distance and undermine security. For instance, the common demand-withdraw pattern, described in Chapter 8, can be understood as two partners using different insecure strategies to meet their needs. One partner's demanding behavior serves as an any-means-necessary strategy to connect with an inaccessible (withdrawing) partner. The other partner's withdrawing behavior serves to protect them in the face of perceived criticism or rejection (of a partner's fervent demands). Although these behaviors make sense in the couple's interactional system, both partners reinforce each other's insecurity, though both partners see their behavior as the necessary response in the context of their partner's behavior.

Emotionally focused couple therapy involves systematically de-escalating the entrenched cycles that maintain distress, identifying the unmet attachment needs that are the real foundational relational problem, and finding ways to have those needs met more effectively moving forward. Although this may sound like a tall order, EFCT generally includes ten to twenty therapy sessions across three "stages" of treatment (Johnson, 2015, 2019b).

In Stage 1, **cycle de-escalation**, the therapist helps partners to recognize the negative interaction cycle (also called a vicious cycle) that they repeatedly experience (see Table 13.4). Partners can learn to identify how they take the same roles (e.g., as demander and withdrawer) in many seemingly unique situations (e.g., an argument about laundry, a fight about in-laws). Recognizing the cycle is, however, not the primary means to de-escalate it. Instead, partners need to understand the **vulnerable emotions** (e.g., fear/anxiety, shame, sadness/grief) that drive each person's behavior in the cycle. Partners typically express anger, aggression, frustration, numbness, or other secondary emotions as they bicker over myriad surface issues, while the core vulnerable emotions that drive their cycles go unexpressed and unacknowledged. A key goal in cycle de-escalation is thus for the therapist to help each partner to identify their own unacknowledged vulnerable emotions, which therapists achieve by asking partners to reflect on their experiences (e.g., "What is it like for you when …") and by asking targeted questions that encourage partners to consider whether vulnerable emotions apply to their situation (e.g., "I wonder, might you also be feeling fear in those moments?").

Table 13.4 The five basic "moves" of emotion-focused couple therapy

Strategy	Example therapist statement
1. **Reflect patterns of emotional processing and interpersonal responses:** Therapist notices and clarifies cycles of interactions	"You sound angry but then lapse into 'lonely' tears, but he only hears the anger and then he withdraws, priming your sense of loss and anger." (Johnson, 2019a, p. 103)
2. **Affect assembly and deepening**: Therapist works collaboratively with each partner to identify the vulnerable emotions underlying their behavior in the cycle	"Underneath the anger there is this 'desperation' and sense of not mattering." (Johnson, 2019a, p. 103)
3. **Choreographing engaged encounters**: Therapist guides the couple through a new choreographed conversation to create a new behavioral pattern for the future	"Can you tell him, 'I get so scared that I don't matter to you – you can just shut me out – that I yell to try to reach you.'" (Johnson, 2019a, p. 103)
4. **Processing the encounter**: Therapist helps the couple to process and troubleshoot the new way of interacting	"How does it feel to say this?" – "How does it feel to hear this?" – "Can you let that in – help her with this feeling?" (Johnson, 2019a, p. 103)
5. **Integrating and validating**: Therapist validates the partners' efforts and reinforces their growth	"Look how well you did. You risked and reached, put your emotions together in a new way, responded to each other. You can do this. You can make sense of your relationships and find a way home." (Johnson, 2019a, p. 103)

Source: Based on data from Johnson (2019a), (2019b).

A second goal in cycle de-escalation is for partners to begin expressing their vulnerable emotions to each other. As Esther Perel says, "You can both tell me all kinds of things, and I can listen to each of you. I'm married to none of you, so it's very easy … you need to reach each other" (Perel, 2017b). After an EFCT therapist helps one partner to explore their vulnerable emotion, the therapist typically provides an opportunity for the partner to share the emotional experience with their partner. For instance, a therapist might say, "When you hear criticism, you feel vulnerable and overwhelmed. Can you tell her? Say it to her in your own words." In this first stage of the EFCT intervention (which takes approximately five to six sessions), partners learn to reframe their problem as a cycle that they each contribute to and suffer from. Partners can then move forward, working together to change the cycle.

In Stage 2, **changing interactional positions** (or "restructuring attachment"), partners dive deeper. With the therapist's help, they work to identify how the vulnerable emotions they experience result from underlying attachment-related concerns or insecurities (e.g., fear of abandonment, a lack of trust in a partner's responsiveness). Moreover, partners acknowledge their own attachment needs (e.g., reassurance, intimacy, affection) and develop empathy for each other's attachment needs. In this stage, partners practice expressing their needs and wants in a softer, more vulnerable way.

Finally, Stage 3, consolidation and integration, involves creating a coherent narrative for partners to understand how their relationship became distressed and how they were able to reconnect. Additionally, in this final phase, partners work on actively resolving any ongoing relationship problems from their newfound position of clarity and connection.

Across all three stages, EFT intervention includes five strategies (see Table 13.4). Therapists often liken EFCT to a "tango," and the five strategies make up the basic "moves" (Johnson, 2019b, 2019a). Evidence suggests that EFCT effectively improves the attachment bond between partners (Johnson, 2019a). Specifically, people who complete the intervention show increases in attachment security, increases in secure base use, and increases in responsive support provision from before to after the intervention (Burgess Moser et al., 2016, 2018; Wiebe et al., 2017).

How Effective Are Therapeutic Interventions to Reduce Distress?

How well do these interventions work? One way to assess the efficacy of couple therapy interventions is to evaluate how often distressed partners improve (i.e., their relationship satisfaction increases, but some degree of distress remains) or even experience a full recovery (i.e., they are no longer clinically distressed) following couple therapy. This approach involves comparing a person's relationship distress before and after the intervention. Figure 13.9 shows the proportion of participants who recover, improve, have no change, or worsen immediately following a therapeutic intervention ("post-treatment"), two years after the intervention, and five years after the intervention (Christensen et al., 2004; Wiebe et al., 2017). As shown in the dark green (recovered) and light green (improved) portions of the

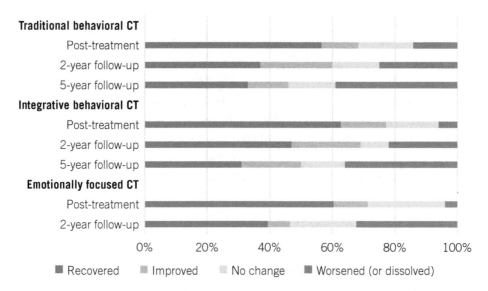

Figure 13.9 Post-therapy relationship well-being immediately after, two years after, and five years after (TBCT and IBCT only) treatment. What do these data reveal about couple therapy's effectiveness? (Source: Drawn based on data from Christensen et al. [2004], [2010]; Wiebe et al. [2017])

bars, most partners benefit from couple therapy. Estimates suggest that approximately 60 to 72 percent of partners who complete TBCT, IBCT, or EFCT will experience reliable increases in relationship satisfaction (Bradbury & Bodenmann, 2020). For many couples (approximately 60 percent), these gains persist two years after completing treatment, as they continue to be classified as "recovered" or "improved" (Christensen et al., 2004; Dalgleish et al., 2015; Wiebe et al., 2017). Longer maintenance is less common: for example, only about one-half of couples who receive TBCT or IBCT maintain their improvement or recovery over five years (Christensen et al., 2010); no comparable five-year follow-up data are available for EFCT.

Although it may be tempting to use the data from Figure 13.9 to compare the relative effectiveness of TBCT, IBCT, and EFCT, the only comparison that is appropriate is between TBCT and IBCT because researchers assessed these two interventions in the same study (Christensen et al., 2004, 2010). By randomly assigning couples to receive TBCT or IBCT, researchers could compare TBCT and IBCT "head-to-head" and assess whether the acceptance-focused interventions included in IBCT offer any benefit above and beyond the skills-based behavioral interventions provided in TBCT (Christensen et al., 2004, 2010). Their work showed that the rate of change differs (TBCT, with its immediate emphasis on increasing positive exchanges, produces faster results than the gradual theme-revealing approach of IBCT), but by the end of the treatment (approximately twenty-two sessions across thirty-six weeks), TBCT and IBCT did not produce different results. Follow-ups similarly suggest that both interventions are effective, but neither more than the other (Christensen et al., 2004, 2010). Interestingly, partners who have been together longer appear to benefit more from either intervention than couples who are less established, regardless of their initial distress (Baucom, Atkins et al., 2015; Baucom et al., 2009). The greater investment of more established couples may provide partners with either encouraging confidence (they can overcome this period of distress) or critical motivation to engage with the intervention (they have more to lose if their relationship were to end).

As much as these data are useful, as it turns out, some partners recover even without any therapeutic intervention (Barton et al., 2021; Roddy et al., 2020). Partners typically seek therapy at a low point in their relationship (a period of particularly high relationship distress), so partners can expect some natural improvement simply by returning to their normal level of functioning when the crisis passes. Therefore, to be considered effective, a therapeutic intervention must also produce relationship improvements that are measurably larger than any improvements that occur naturally without intervention.

Randomized controlled trials (RCTs), a type of experiment in which the independent variable is a clinical treatment condition (Donnon, 2012), provide the most rigorous evidence supporting the efficacy of therapeutic couple interventions. In RCTs, researchers randomly assign participants to receive a clinical treatment (in this case, a specific form of couple therapy), an alternative clinical treatment (active control), or no treatment (passive control). A common passive control is a "waitlist control" in which researchers assign some participants to a legitimate waitlist to receive the clinical treatment later. In the meantime, they receive no intervention, allowing researchers to compare their experiences with those of the participants who receive the clinical treatment.

Many randomized controlled trials have supported the efficacy of couple therapy to improve relationship satisfaction, and meta-analytic summaries of these RCTs indicate that behavioral and emotionally focused couple therapies produce comparable gains in relationship satisfaction (Beasley & Ager, 2019; Doss et al., 2022; Rathgeber et al., 2019; Shadish & Baldwin, 2003, 2005). For both behavioral and emotionally focused therapies, the overall effect size of the treatment (compared to a control) is considered moderate and relatively short-lived. Specifically, data suggest almost three-quarters of participants who complete either a behavioral or emotionally focused couple therapy intervention benefit more (i.e., report higher relationships satisfaction) than partners who experience no intervention (Rathgeber et al., 2019). After six months, the effect of the therapeutic intervention is largely maintained, with about two-thirds retaining their benefit over no intervention. Critically, after twelve months, the therapeutic interventions no longer produce any benefit relative to controls (Rathgeber et al., 2019). This last finding may seem at odds with the evidence reported earlier – that approximately 60 percent of couples who complete one of these treatments are still classified as "recovered" or "improved" two years after completing treatment. Recall, however, the differences in these approaches. Many couples improve after completing couple therapy, but many couples also improve without therapy.

Several caveats are warranted as we evaluate the effectiveness of couple therapy interventions. First, although couple therapy interventions may be effective (at least in the short term), their effects are likely weaker than efficacy trials in research settings suggest. In research settings, participants are compensated based on completing the treatment and are therefore incentivized to complete all components of the intervention (or their data are not included in assessments of the intervention). In the "real world," however, only about 50 percent of partners complete the therapy they begin (Roesler, 2020). Initial studies assessing "real-world" effectiveness suggest that 40 to 50 percent of partners show improvements in relationship quality, compared to their pre-therapy assessments (Roesler, 2020), a number that is more conservative than estimates based on efficacy trials (Bradbury & Bodenmann, 2020).

A second caveat touches on the generalizability of findings. Efficacy research tends to focus on different-sex monogamous couples, creating concerns about the generalizability of therapy's effectiveness for sexual minority and consensually non-monogamous partners. In one recent review, only 4.6 percent of participants (out of over 100,000 participants in 111 intervention studies) were seeking treatment for a same-sex relationship (Spengler et al., 2020). Although initial evidence suggests that couple therapy interventions are effective for sexual minority partners (Pentel et al., 2021), and practitioners are working to develop guidelines for providing effective therapy for CNM partners (Addison & Clason, 2021; Gebel et al., 2022; Kolmes & Witherspoon, 2017), more work is needed in these areas.

Finally, to evaluate the efficacy of couple therapy, we need to grapple with what makes a relationship intervention effective. Rather than assuming relationship repair is the only potential benefit of therapy, perhaps partners benefit by recognizing that their paths are best diverging. With this broader conceptualization of effectiveness, relationship dissolution after a therapeutic intervention does not necessarily suggest a failed intervention. Therapists must leave room for this possibility. As Esther Perel said, "I think the most important thing for any couples therapist is to accept the choices that people make ... not to be the defendant of marriage at all cost or the advocate of divorce at all cost. Life is complicated and so are people's choices" (Perel, 2017a).

Educational Interventions to Prevent Distress

What if partners knew – early on – the strategies we have just discussed? Could they circumvent years of relationship distress and avoid needing therapy? Relationship researchers and clinicians have asked this question, and today, we have an array of preventative psychoeducational interventions that teach partners many of the same communications skills and acceptance-focused skills that are used to relieve distress in couple therapy. These couple relationship education (CRE) programs (which also have potential for consensually non-monogamous partners) target romantic partners who are relatively satisfied, that is, not distressed or only moderately distressed (Halford et al., 2015; Halford & Bodenmann, 2013; Pepping et al., 2020; Snyder & Halford, 2012). These well-functioning partners may find ways to enhance their existing relationship and potentially make adjustments that can benefit their relationship over the long-haul.

Figure 13.10 Couple relationship education programs include a structured curriculum, hands-on exercises, and homework assignments that allow partners to try out new relationship skills. What are some pros and cons of these one-size-fits-all interventions? (Photo: FreshSplash / E+ / Getty Images)

Participating in a CRE program is like taking a class: the instructor covers a structured curriculum of relationship-related topics, and "student" partners first practice the concepts during class and then try to apply the concepts outside of class through homework assignments. Courses typically incorporate much of what is known about successful relationships to strengthen couples' relationships (akin to a kitchen-sink approach to a relationship intervention; see Figure 13.10). Specifically, these educational interventions tend to include information and strategies related to (1) managing inevitable conflicts, (2) enhancing positive aspects of one's relationship (e.g., friendship, fun, sensuality), and (3) strengthening commitment (Stanley et al., 2020). These sessions typically occur in-person, though recent changes include shifting CRE programs online to increase their accessibility (Megale et al., 2021). They also tend to be brief, especially when compared to couple therapy. Evidence-based CRE programs typically include 12 to 18 hours of curriculum delivered over a few weekly sessions or a one-weekend-long seminar, compared to months-long couple therapy interventions (Bradbury & Bodenmann, 2020; Halford & Bodenmann, 2013). CRE programs also differ from therapy interventions in that they are delivered to a group rather than to an individual couple, meaning that the intervention is not tailored to a couple's specific challenges or strengths. In some cases, however, CRE programs do incorporate additional individualized coaching and feedback for participant partners, to help partners apply the psychoeducational intervention to their own relationships and increase the impact of the intervention (Baker & Terrill, 2017).

Research-Based Couple Relationship Education Programs

CRE programs come in many forms, with the Prevention and Relationship Enhancement Program (PREP) the most commonly used and the most empirically tested (e.g., Markman

Table 13.5 Selected modules from PREP

Topic	Brief description
Communication Danger Signs	Partners learn to identify and stop destructive behaviors and interpretations that undermine their communication effectiveness. Partners learn to use a "time out" to pause conversations that are escalating and to return to the conversation after refocusing.
Honey, Let's Talk (Good Communication)	The PREP leader explains the speaker-listener technique and shows video examples of the technique. Participants practice this technique throughout the program.
Fun and Friendship	Partners learn about the importance of fun and friendship in their relationships and learn strategies to help them have fun together and build their friendship.
You, Me, and Us	Partners complete personality quizzes and learn to recognize each partner's strengths and weaknesses. Partners consider how their personalities impact their relationship.
Stress and Relaxation	Partners learn about the effects of stress and ways to reduce stress.
Supporting Each Other	Partners learn about the many types of social support, and partners are encouraged to discuss the types of support they most prefer with each other.
The Sensual/Sexual Relationship	Partners learn about the roles of affection and sexuality in relationship, and the leader explains ways to preserve sensuality and sexuality in ongoing relationships.

Source: Based on data from Tonelli et al. (2016).

et al., 2022; Stanley et al., 2020). PREP focuses heavily on communication skills training, with a particular emphasis on teaching behavioral strategies such as the speaker-listener technique, to enable partners to navigate conflicts successfully (Markman, Stanley, & Blumberg, 2010; Tonelli et al., 2016). PREP has appropriately evolved over time, with curriculum revisions mirroring the field's shift from a focus on negative to positive relationship processes. For instance, recent versions of PREP focus less on avoiding destructive conflict behaviors and more on behaving constructively, spending shared positive time, and behaving affectionately (see Table 13.5 for an explanation of some components of the PREP curriculum). PREP's curriculum focuses on behaviors as well as interpretations and expectations that foster relationship success, consistent with the theoretical approach used in cognitive-behavioral couple therapy (Tonelli et al., 2016).

The **Couple Commitment and Relationship Enhancement (CARE) program**, the second-most tested CRE program over the last decade, covers many of the same skills as PREP, but has a unique focus on self-regulation and self-reflection (Halford et al., 2004). In this program, partners first learn about self-change (e.g., how to evaluate their relationship and set goals to improve their relationship) and then complete modules on five relationship-related topics: effective communication, intimacy and caring, managing conflict, sexuality, and adapting to change/stress (Halford et al., 2004). As partners learn about each topic, they are encouraged to reflect on and evaluate their own behavior and develop a self-change plan to improve their behavior related to that domain. For example, during the "adapting to change" section of the program, partners self-reflect on the types of changes they expect to occur over the next year (e.g., transition to parenthood, career changes) and self-reflect on their goals for managing that change, based on the educational content provided in the section (Halford et al., 2004).

Another CRE program, the **Couple Coping Enhancement Training (CCET) program**, likewise, has a unique focus: this program prioritizes teaching skills that make a relationship resilient to stress (Bodenmann & Shantinath, 2004). Therefore, in addition to teaching the speaker-listener technique and other general communication and problem-solving skills, the CCET program focuses on coping-related skills. Partners learn to understand and communicate about their stressors, support each other emotionally, and work together to manage external stressors by completing several unique modules (Bodenmann & Shantinath, 2004). For instance, partners complete a module called "Knowledge of stress and coping" (2.5 hours) that explains what stress is and how it is shaped by primary and secondary appraisals. In another module, called "Improvement of individual coping" (3 hours), partners learn how to prepare for, counter, and reduce their stress using individual coping strategies (e.g., relaxation methods). The longest module in this program, "Enhancement of dyadic coping" (5 hours), includes lectures on how to communicate about stress with one's partner, how to provide effective social support (e.g., practical assistance, encouragement, joint problem solving), and how to avoid negative interactions during stress (e.g., distancing, mocking, insincere support). Partners role-play to practice the techniques they learn, with the goal of building relationship resilience (Bodenmann & Shantinath, 2004).

 IN THE NEWS

Mindfulness as a Relationship Intervention

Mindfulness is a ubiquitous wellness buzzword and the "fastest growing health trend in America" (Tlalka, 2018). Although mindfulness initially gained popular appeal for its personal benefits (e.g., lower depression, stress, substance use; Goldberg et al., 2022; Khoury et al., 2015), more recent media buzz has centered on the rapidly accumulating evidence that mindfulness can confer relationship benefits (Cuncic, 2020; Ellwood, 2021; Lee, 2015; Moldovan, 2019). For instance, ABC News published the article: "You probably knew mindfulness could help you with stress. But did you know it could save your marriage?" While the empirical evidence has not quite established mindfulness as a relationship savior, mindfulness-based relationship interventions do show some exciting promise (e.g., Carson et al., 2006; Kappen et al., 2019; Karremans et al., 2017; Khaddouma et al., 2017; Leavitt et al., 2022; Winter et al., 2021).

Mindfulness refers to a state of being in which one focuses their attention on the present moment (sometimes called "present moment awareness") and acknowledges their experience with openness and without judgment (sometimes called "acceptance"). Stated differently, a person experiences mindfulness when they (1) focus on the here-and-now without becoming lost in thought and (2) accept the present moment just as it is, not seeking to change it, grasp onto it, avoid it, or judge it (e.g., Kabat-Zinn, 2015). Mindfulness is a skill, which means that people can learn mindfulness even as they might vary in natural ability.

Mindfulness practice involves (1) intentionally focusing one's attention on a particular internal experience (e.g., sensations, thoughts, emotions) or external experience (e.g., sounds, objects in the environment) and (2) repeatedly noticing when the mind wanders, observing the passing thoughts, and bringing attention back to the intended focus. Critically, mindfulness practice includes a non-judgmental, accepting attitude. For example, a person might practice mindfulness by focusing their attention on their breath (in, out, in, out) for 5 minutes. Thoughts about the past ("Why did my sister say that?"), worries about the future ("When will they deposit my paycheck?"), and all sorts of other thoughts ("Oh, a bug," "What are jeans made out of," "I wonder if you could fry pizza") will naturally arise. The goal is to notice these thoughts without getting carried away by them, pushing them away, or judging yourself for having them. After noticing, the next step is to kindly return attention to the intended focus ("Interesting thoughts. Now back to my breath."). People can practice mindfulness formally, such as engaging in a guided mindfulness meditation (e.g., body scan, awareness of breath; Figure 13.11), or informally, such as focusing attention on washing the dishes, driving, taking a shower, or having a conversation.

A review of sixteen mindfulness-based couple intervention studies showed that these interventions can increase relationship quality (Winter et al., 2021). Preliminary evidence also suggests that one partner completing an individual mindfulness intervention improves relationship quality for them and their non-participating partner (Khaddouma et al., 2017; May et al., 2020). In one cleverly designed study, researchers assigned participants to engage in a mindfulness meditation practice on and off for two-week periods over an eight-week study (e.g., two weeks on, two weeks off, etc.) while their partner was not meditating (May et al., 2020). Participants reported greater positive affect and lower negative affect during the weeks when they meditated, and their romantic partners similarly experienced lower negative affect during the meditation phases.

Figure 13.11 Mindfulness practice can help people to develop non-judgmental present moment awareness. How might staying in the present moment and adopting a non-judgmental attitude impact relationship functioning? (Photo: NickyLloyd / E+ / Getty Images)

How exactly does mindfulness enable satisfying relationships? More mindful partners are more accepting of their partners, perceive their partners as more responsive, and are rated as more responsive by their partners (Adair et al., 2018; Kappen et al., 2018). More mindful partners also experience more gratitude and willingness to forgive, and engage in more constructive conflict (use more positive problem solving and less withdrawal) than people who are less mindful, and these links partially explain the relationship between mindfulness and both partners' relationship satisfaction (Eyring et al., 2021; Gesell et al., 2020; Johns et al., 2015; Mirnics et al., 2022). Finally, people who are more mindful are better able to regulate their own emotions and have less extreme physiological reactions to relationship stress, which improves relationship functioning (Fincham, 2022; Kimmes, 2018; Wachs & Cordova, 2007).

How Effective Are Relationship Education Interventions?

Stable and satisfying relationships can still improve. Meta-analytic evidence suggests that couple relationship education interventions do benefit non-distressed partners, at least in the short term (e.g., Arnold & Beelmann, 2019; Fawcett et al., 2010; Hawkins et al., 2008). Evidence of CRE programs' effectiveness comes from several countries, including Australia, Germany, the Netherlands, Norway, and Iran, though most studies rely on samples from the United States (Fallahchai et al., 2017; Markman et al., 2022; Van Widenfelt et al., 1996). This evidence shows that partners report moderately higher relationship quality and moderately better communication following participation in a CRE program relative to non-participating controls (Hawkins et al., 2008). Those who complete longer programs (9 to 20 hours of intervention) show greater improvements than partners who complete programs of a shorter duration (1 to 8 hours), suggesting that more intensive educational interventions produce stronger benefits (Hawkins et al., 2008).

Short-term improvements are great, but what about long-term gains? After all, a central goal of CRE programs is to prevent future relationship distress. Happily, the data are promising. One review of the literature showed that in most studies (fourteen out of seventeen), partners who completed CRE programs maintain their high relationship satisfaction over at least one year (Halford & Bodenmann, 2013). CRE programs may also reduce partners' future risk of divorce; for instance, military couples who completed a version of the PREP program were less likely to be divorced two years after the intervention than military couples who were randomly assigned to an untreated control condition (Stanley et al., 2014).

Assessments of CRE intervention effectiveness have consistently revealed one (perhaps unsurprising) finding: CRE programs are more effective among partners who are at greater risk of distress (e.g., Bradbury & Bodenmann, 2020; Halford et al., 2015, 2017; Halford & Bodenmann, 2013; Williamson et al., 2015). Risk of distress is conceptualized as low (though not clinically low) relationship satisfaction. People with lower relationship satisfaction prior to a CRE intervention report greater increases in relationship satisfaction from before to after the intervention than people who report more relationship satisfaction initially, and these relatively stronger effects of the treatment continue to be observed six months after the intervention (e.g., Halford et al., 2015, 2017). Perhaps this reflects a ceiling effect among more satisfied participants; people with lower relationship satisfaction have more room to improve than people who are already very satisfied with their relationships.

In general, CRE programs offer a promising intervention, though the minimal effect sizes suggest that it is necessary to adapt these interventions to maximize their benefits, as described next.

 DIVERSITY AND INCLUSION

Relationship Education Interventions for Low-Income Couples

Economic disadvantage introduces stressors and vulnerabilities that can increase partners' risk of divorce and distress. Accordingly, researchers have prioritized assessing whether CRE programs can benefit partners whose relationships are at risk due to economic disadvantage (e.g., Liu, Wheeler et al., 2020; Markman et al., 2022; Williamson et al., 2016). In one study of over 1,000 low-income couples, partners who completed a CRE intervention reported greater relationship satisfaction at follow-up (thirty months after the intervention) than couples who were randomly assigned to a no-treatment control condition (Williamson et al., 2016). Meta-analyses similarly show that CRE programs benefit low SES couples; however, the effect sizes are quite small. Participants in a CRE program reported higher relationship satisfaction and communication skills than only approximately 5 percent of control partners, a smaller effect than is typically observed in studies that are not restricted to low-income individuals (Arnold & Beelmann, 2019; Hawkins & Erickson, 2015). Despite minimal improvements, evidence suggests that CRE interventions provide low SES couples with hope that the relationship will succeed, an important benefit in itself (Hawkins, Allen et al., 2017).

The US Administration for Children and Families (ACF) has invested over a billion dollars in public CRE programs since 2006 in an effort to strengthen the relationships of lower-income American couples (Hawkins et al., 2022). This social policy program – called the Healthy Marriage and Relationship Education Initiative (HMREI) – continues to be federally funded; approximately $75 million was allocated for this program in 2021 (US Congress Joint Economic Committee, 2022). Of the approximately 2.5 million people who have participated in these CRE programs, the majority (56 percent) had incomes below the federal poverty line, and the majority were African American (30 percent) or Hispanic (30 percent; Hawkins et al., 2022). A meta-analysis of all of the federally funded HMREI interventions showed that these programs have small effects on relationship quality and relationship skills, but no observable effect on the likelihood of divorce (Hawkins et al., 2022). Critics of these interventions argue that the "soft skills" provided by CRE programs are no match for the hardships that partners with low SES face (e.g., Johnson, 2012; Karney et al., 2018; Lavner et al., 2015). These critics argue that the high cost of federally funded CRE programs (in some cases, close to $10,000 per couple) could be put to better use in programs that address partners' financial difficulties and the associated stressors directly rather than in helping partners to communicate about and problem solve issues related to their financial difficulties (Karney et al., 2018).

Enhancing Interventions for Partners

The researchers and clinicians who design relationship interventions continuously work to improve the interventions to be more effective and to reach more partners in need. While many different efforts have strengthened existing interventions, we focus on two recent trends: (1) increasing the accessibility of interventions; and (2) adapting interventions for same-sex partners (Pentel & Baucom, 2022). Both of these trends are forward-looking, with the potential to have a substantial impact on the next generation of relationship interventions.

Increasing Accessibility of Relationship Interventions

Could you and your partner easily drive to a therapy appointment once a week, in the middle of the workday? Unfortunately, partners who need interventions the most often find them highly inaccessible (Markman et al., 2022; Stanley et al., 2020; Williamson, Karney et al., 2019). This is a key limitation of couple interventions. External challenges – which likely contribute to relationship distress or put partners at high risk for future distress – limit the time and financial resources that partners have available to attend and sustain a therapeutic or educational intervention (Williamson, Karney et al., 2019). If you are working for wages or under immense pressure at work, if you are caring for children or rely on public transportation, or if you are overwhelmed by the prospect of another expense, accessing a relationship intervention may not be feasible.

Briefer, less intensive interventions offer a potential solution; partners are more likely to agree to attend brief interventions than more intensive ones (Busby et al., 2015). The Relationship Checkup – one empirically supported brief intervention – involves only two 90-minute sessions, during which a trained facilitator evaluates partners' strengths and concerns and then provides feedback, including suggestions and a proposed action plan (e.g., Cordova et al., 2014). This approach does not include any skills training, and it is up to the couple to decide how to implement any recommendations. Despite its minimalism, the Relationship Checkup is effective at increasing relationship satisfaction, and partners often maintain these increases over two years (Coop Gordon et al., 2019; Fentz & Trillingsgaard, 2017; Trillingsgaard et al., 2016). The Relationship Checkup is designed for partners to use repeatedly, akin to a yearly physical or a routine automotive inspection. Regular relationship maintenance can help satisfied and moderately distressed couples to identify small problems and intervene before they become big problems (Morrill et al., 2011). The Relationship Checkup is also suitable for couples who are already distressed; in one study, 46 percent of participants who were considered clinically distressed at baseline experienced large enough increases to be classified as non-distressed one month after the Relationship Checkup intervention (Coop Gordon et al., 2019).

Another solution to improve accessibility of couple interventions has been to move interventions online. Online couple relationship education interventions are indeed effective at increasing relationship satisfaction, communication skills, commitment, and relationship confidence, as shown in recent meta-analyses (Megale et al., 2021; Spencer & Anderson, 2021). Moreover, initial evidence suggests that online CRE programs are even more effective than in-person CRE programs to improve relationship outcomes, even though online

Figure 13.12 Online relationship education courses offer accessibility for busy partners and for partners who lack transportation or childcare. Online classes can also be provided on-demand, meaning that couples can start as soon as they like rather than waiting for the start of the next course or adding their name to a waitlist. What other benefits or drawbacks do you see of online relationship education courses? (Photo: AzmanL / E+ / Getty Images)

programs tend to be less time-intensive (Doss et al., 2020; Hawkins et al., 2022). Think about it: if participants can more easily attend online interventions, they may benefit more from a briefer online treatment (one that they actually attend) than a more intensive in-person treatment that they regularly have to miss (Figure 13.12). Some online CRE programs include brief support calls or regular online skills coaching with a relationship coach or trainer (Markman et al., 2022). This extra support can indirectly benefit partners: partners who engage online with a coach or trainer are more likely to complete the program than partners who complete online CRE programs on their own (Busby et al., 2015).

The two most common online CRE interventions are **ePREP**, a 6-hour version of traditional PREP adapted for online training (e.g., Braithwaite & Fincham, 2007, 2011), and **OurRelationship**, an 8-hour program based on Integrative Behavioral Couple Therapy (e.g., Doss et al., 2013, 2016, 2019, 2020). The OurRelationship curriculum guides partners through activities separately and together, and like ePREP, can be completed without a therapist, coach, or trainer (Doss et al., 2013). First, partners individually complete relationship assessments that help them to identify core problems in their relationship, after which partners discuss and jointly select one (or perhaps two) issues to focus on in the program. Second, partners individually read prepared content, watch videos, and complete activities designed to help them understand how their problem results from intensified fundamental differences, after which they share their understanding with each other. Finally, partners learn to use both acceptance strategies and behavioral changes together to resolve their core problem(s).

Although ePREP and OurRelationship differ in their focus, their benefits are comparable (Doss et al., 2020; Megale et al., 2021; Roddy et al., 2021). For instance, one randomized controlled trial compared the effects of ePREP, OurRelationship, and a waitlist control for low-income couples, most of whom were clinically distressed (Doss et al., 2020). Participants who were assigned to either of the CRE programs reported greater increases in relationship satisfaction and greater decreases in breakup potential (i.e., their perceived likelihood of breakup) and conflict than participants assigned to the control (see Figure 13.13), and these improvements were maintained at a four-month follow-up (Doss et al., 2020) and a one-year follow-up (Roddy et al., 2021). No differences between ePREP and OurRelationship were observed following the intervention or after one year (Doss et al., 2020; Roddy et al., 2021).

Interventions for Sexual Minority Partners

As you have learned throughout this book, relationships evince a great deal of commonality, despite their diverse structures. Sexual minority partners experience relationship distress in much the same way as different-sex partners: they experience comparable levels of distress,

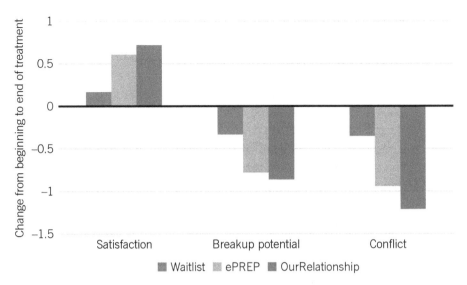

Figure 13.13 Online couple relationship interventions (ePREP and OurRelationship) improve relationships relative to a waitlist control. These data show the size of changes in satisfaction, breakup potential, and conflict (Cohen's d effect sizes) for 742 couples who were randomly assigned to complete ePREP, OurRelationship, or a waitlist. Which intervention appeals to you? (Source: Doss et al. [2020]; Copyright © 2020 by American Psychological Association, reproduced and adapted with permission. The official citation that should be used in referencing this material is Doss, B. D., Knopp, K., Roddy, M. K., Rothman, K., Hatch, S. G., & Rhoades, G. K. (2020). Online programs improve relationship functioning for distressed low-income couples: Results from a nationwide randomized controlled trial. *Journal of Consulting and Clinical Psychology, 88*[4], 283–294. https://doi.org/10 .1037/ccp0000479. No further reproduction or distribution is permitted without written permission from the American Psychological Association.)

become distressed for the same reasons, and often report seeking therapy to discuss issues that are considered "universal," common to different-sex and sexual minority romantic relationships (e.g., communication challenges; Pentel et al., 2021). Because of these similarities, same-sex couples may benefit from the same interventions to repair and strengthen their relationships as different-sex couples (Pentel & Baucom, 2022). Nonetheless, the vast majority of sexual minority partners (approximately 87 percent) report wanting to receive interventions that are tailored to their identity (Pepping et al., 2017).

To tailor existing treatments, clinicians provide the typical interventions (e.g., communication skills training), but modify their approach to be sensitive to the unique stressors and challenges faced by sexual minority partners (Pentel et al., 2021). For instance, in couple therapy, the therapist may facilitate conversations related to experiences of discrimination and decisions about disclosing the relationship, or a therapist may help partners problem solve in the absence of relationship scripts to follow (e.g., gendered division of labor scripts). As therapists focus on accessing vulnerable emotions with sexual minority partners, they may also probe for experiences of internalized homonegativity or bi-negativity that foster relationship insecurities. One initial efficacy study suggests that systematically tailoring a cognitive-behavioral couple therapy intervention to treat sexual minority partners is effective (i.e., it produced decreases in distress from pre-treatment to post-treatment) and is well-received (i.e., treated partners were satisfied with the intervention; Pentel et al., 2021).

Relationship education programs have similarly been adapted for sexual minority partners (e.g., Pepping et al., 2020; Whitton et al., 2016, 2017; Whitton & Buzzella, 2012; Whitton, Scott, & Weitbrecht, 2018). Based on feedback from sexual minority partners and therapists who treat sexual minority partners, for example, developers modified existing relationship education programs in a few notable ways, such as eliminating heteronormative biases (e.g., in language, in examples) and focusing on the unique challenges that sexual minority partners are likely to face (Scott et al., 2019; Scott & Rhoades, 2014; Whitton, Scott, & Weitbrecht, 2018). For instance, an adaptation of the CoupleCare relationship education program for sexual minority partners (a program rebranded as "Rainbow CoupleCare") now includes topics related to internalized stigma, discrimination and prejudice, and decisions about disclosing a relationship to others (Pepping et al., 2020). Participants who complete the Better Together Program – another tailored relationship education program for sexual minority partners – report a preference for the tailored approach and appear to benefit from the intervention; they report improvements in satisfaction and communication effectiveness from pre- to post-program (Whitton et al., 2017; Whitton, Scott, & Weitbrecht, 2018). Non-tailored ePREP and OurRelationship interventions improve relationship well-being for same-gender couples, but the benefits of these non-tailored programs are weaker for same-gender than different-gender couples (Hatch et al., 2021). The differential consequences of these interventions (shown in Figure 13.14) support the importance of tailoring to maximize benefits of CRE interventions for sexual minority participants.

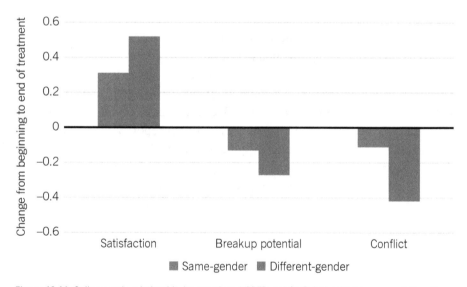

Figure 13.14 Online couple relationship interventions (ePREP and OurRelationship) improve relationships more for different-gender couples than same-gender couples, suggesting that tailoring interventions for same-gender couples may be needed to maximize benefits. These data show the size of changes in satisfaction, breakup potential, and conflict (Cohen's d effect sizes) for forty-nine same-gender couples and group of matched different-gender couples with a similar background. (Source: Copyright © 2021, John Wiley & Sons, adapted and reprinted with permission from John Wiley & Sons. Hatch, S. G., Rothman, K., Roddy, M. K., Dominguez, R. M., Le, Y., & Doss, B. D. [2021]. Heteronormative relationship education for same-gender couples. *Family Process, 60*, 119–133.)

RESEARCHER SPOTLIGHT: Sarah Whitton, PhD

How did you come to study relationship interventions?

My career path – like that of many researchers I know – has been pretty curvy! In undergrad, I was interested in child psychology, but no faculty studying children were taking on students. So, I did my honors thesis with a social psychologist who studied romantic relationships. I really enjoyed that, but wanted to do interventions, so I went to grad school in clinical psychology in a lab that evaluated the effectiveness of relationship education (PREP). I was in Boston as a post-doc, when same-sex marriage was legalized, and I wanted to provide relationship education to sexual and gender minority (SGM) couples. I quickly realized, however, that existing programs needed to be adapted for SGM to remove heteronormativity and address the stigma-based stressors they face. So, a grad student (Brian Buzzella) and I created and tested an initial adapted program for his dissertation. This launched my work on what is now the Better Together program and inspired my basic science studies focused on young SGM and their romantic relationships.

Figure 13.15 Dr. Sarah Whitton is a professor of clinical psychology at the University of Cincinnati. (Photo courtesy of Sarah Whitton, PhD.)

What challenges have you faced in your work?

There are so many challenges, but I'll comment on two. First, recruiting couples can be difficult and slow, which at times feels frustrating because we're offering them free access to our programs. A second challenge is obtaining research funding. There is funding for relationship interventions aimed at treating mental or physical health issues, but I think SGM deserve programs specifically focused on their relationships, which have been historically denied and pathologized.

What do you enjoy about your work?

To me, my work is the perfect combination of intellectual challenge and making a difference in the world. I enjoy challenging my brain as I conduct science, learn and apply new methodologies and statistical approaches, and grapple with thorny theoretical issues. But what makes it really great is when my work can help people, especially those who face significant challenges. I also love mentoring students – seeing them catch the research bug and get excited about relationship science is so rewarding!

Conclusion

In this chapter, you learned about the therapeutic interventions that help to repair distressed relationships and about the educational interventions that aim to strengthen relationships and prevent distress. We reviewed the characteristics of partners who seek (and do not seek) couple therapy, behavioral and emotionally focused approaches to treatment, and the efficacy of these treatments to repair relationships. We also reviewed the format, content, and effectiveness of couple relationship education interventions, including a discussion of the effectiveness for partners who are at-risk of relationship distress because of their low relationship satisfaction or low socioeconomic status. Finally, we reviewed efforts to improve the effectiveness of couple interventions by making these interventions more accessible and by tailoring these interventions to meet couples' unique circumstances.

Major Take-Aways

- Each prominent therapeutic intervention has a unique focus. Traditional behavioral couple therapy focuses on behavior change; cognitive behavioral couple therapy incorporates behavior change and cognitive restructuring; integrative behavioral couple therapy emphasizes acceptance; and emotionally focused couple therapy prioritizes fostering connection and increasing attachment security.
- Therapeutic interventions produce moderate, though relatively short-lived, improvements in relationship satisfaction. The majority of partners who complete a therapeutic intervention benefit, but differences between treated and untreated partners typically dissipate a year after the intervention.
- Couple relationship education interventions cover many of the same strategies that are incorporated in therapeutic interventions (e.g., the speaker-listener technique, problem solving, acceptance). However, these interventions are typically briefer and are provided in the form of a structure curriculum that is not adapted to any couple's individual needs. CRE interventions increase relationship satisfaction, particularly for people with lower satisfaction prior to the intervention, and there is some evidence that they are effective to prevent subsequent distress. Large-scale efforts to deliver CRE to low-SES partners produce reliable but small improvements in relationship satisfaction and communication skills.
- Many partners cite inaccessibility as a reason that they do not take advantage of relationship interventions. Efforts to increase accessibility through briefer interventions and online interventions have been successful, highlighting the importance of additional efforts to increase accessibility. Additionally, sexual minority partners report preferring, and benefiting from, interventions that are tailored to their unique relationship circumstances.

Further Readings

If you're interested in ...

... the process and consequences of behavioral couple therapies, read:
Christensen, A., Atkins, D. C., Baucom, B., & Yi, J. (2010). Marital status and satisfaction five years following a randomized clinical trial comparing traditional versus integrative behavioral couple therapy. *Journal of Consulting and Clinical Psychology, 78*(2), 225–235.

... the unique challenges and opportunities in intervening with low-income couples, read:
Karney, B. R., Bradbury, T. N., & Lavner, J. A. (2018). Supporting healthy relationships in low-income couples: Lessons learned and

policy implications. *Policy Insights from the Behavioral and Brain Sciences*, *5*(1), 33–39.

... how couple therapies are adapted for sexual minority relationships, read:
Pentel, K. Z., & Baucom, D. H. (2022). A clinical framework for sexual minority couple therapy. *Couple and Family Psychology: Research and Practice*, *11*(2), 177–191.

... learning more about what makes relationship education work, read:
Stanley, S. M., Carlson, R. G., Rhoades, G. K., Markman, H. J., Ritchie, L. L., & Hawkins, A. J. (2020). Best practices in relationship education focused on intimate relationships. *Family Relations*, *69*(3), 497–519.

... the process and consequences of emotionally focused couples therapy, read:
Wiebe, S. A., Johnson, S. M., Lafontaine, M. F., Burgess Moser, M., Dalgleish, T. L., & Tasca, G. A. (2017). Two-year follow-up outcomes in emotionally focused couple therapy: An investigation of relationship and attachment trajectories. *Journal of Marital and Family Therapy*, *43*(2), 227–244.

GLOSSARY

Accelerated-arrested trajectory A relationship trajectory that starts strong and then stalls

Accelerated trajectory A relationship trajectory that shows a steep and steady ascent in interdependence

Acceptance A willingness to acknowledge a partner's differences, allow these differences to exist, and perhaps even embrace these differences

Access (to potential partners) The availability of potential romantic partners

Accommodation Behaviors flowing from a relationship-protective motivation

Active-constructive responses In response to capitalization attempts, responders pay attention and actively convey enthusiasm and excitement

Active-destructive responses In response to capitalization attempts, responders actively undercut the discloser's success and downgrade its worthiness of celebration

Active strategies An approach to information seeking that involves finding ways to observe a person of interest's behavior or asking others about a person of interest

Adaptation Over time, individuals develop habitual responses to certain interdependent structures

Adverse contexts Situations that are threatening and require coping

Affection Feeling love for, fondness of, or closeness toward someone

Affection deprivation Receiving less affection than one desires

Affection exchange theory The idea that people have an inborn need and capacity to express and to receive affection

Affectionate communication The words, gestures, or other expressions we use to convey our feelings of love, closeness, and fondness for others

Affectionate touch Behaviors, such as kissing or hugging, that exemplify non-verbal affection

Affective valence The positivity or negativity of an emotion

Affiliate To be near and to interact with others

Affirmative consent A "yes means yes" criterion for engaging in sex

Alternative-devaluation Perceiving potential alternative partners unrealistically negatively

Ambivalence A co-occurrence of strong positivity and strong negativity

Angry withdrawal When one partner actively ignores another partner, for example, using a stony silence or averted gaze

Anonymity When the identity of participants is not revealed or known

Anxious attachment An attachment style in which the self is viewed as unworthy of love and attachment figures are inconsistently available and/or responsive

Apology An attempt to repair the damage of one's transgression by admitting responsibility, conveying remorse, and communicating an intention not to transgress in the same way again

Appetitive system A drive toward seeking rewarding experiences

Applied research Research designed to inform an intervention or in other ways directly affect the lives of others

Approach motives Enacting a behavior in order to obtain a benefit

Approach relationship goals A strong motivation to achieve positive relationship outcomes, such as growth and intimacy

Arranged marriages Marriages orchestrated by a third party, often parents

Asexuality Experiencing no sexual attraction toward others

Assortative mating People connect with others who are like them on a host of traits, behavioral tendencies, attitudes, and demographics

Assumptions The set of beliefs people have about the nature of relationships

Attachment anxiety Pervasive concerns about not being loved and fears about being abandoned

Attachment avoidance Discomfort with intimacy and a preference for independence

Attachment behavioral system An evolved human system that includes all the actions that govern how people naturally approach their primary relationships in order to achieve felt security

Attachment figure A person who receives another's proximity bids, serves as their safe haven and secure base, and is the focus of their separation distress

Attachment love A type of love between people that compels them toward each other for support seeking, safety, security, and fulfilling attachment functions

Attachment styles Chronic patterns of thought, emotion, and behavior which reflect underlying working models of self and other and are derived from individuals' attachment history

Attachment theory A theory that explains human thought, emotion, and behavior as solving the problem of maintaining support from close others

Attention checks Items that participants are instructed to answer in a particular way to demonstrate that they are reading carefully

Attributions Explanations or interpretations of someone else's behaviors

Attrition When participants begin, but do not finish, a study

Availability Being ready, able, and willing to provide help

Avoidance motives Enacting a behavior in order to avoid a negative consequence

Avoidance relationship goals A strong motivation to avoid negative relationship outcomes, such as rejection or conflict

Avoidant attachment An attachment style in which attachment figures are viewed as untrustworthy and unresponsive

Basic research Research conducted for the sake of understanding

Behavioral couple therapy A type of couple therapy based on social exchange theory, which conceptualizes distress as experiencing more costs than rewards to their relationship

Behavioral exchange Behaviors that partners engage in within their relationship

Behavioral synchrony Coordinated movements and gestures

Behavioral uncertainty When people do not know or are not confident about how they should behave or what their interaction partner will do next

Belongingness hypothesis The innate, fundamental human motivation to form, maintain, and keep close interpersonal connections

Benevolence A dispositional orientation toward kindness, generosity, and goodwill

Better-than-average effect A tendency for people to rate themselves higher than most people on socially desirable traits

Better Together Program An example of a relationship education program tailored for sexual minority partners

Between-subjects experimental design Experimental design in which participants are assigned to experience only one of the conditions

Big data Massive data sets typically pulled from websites, apps, and mobile sensors

Biological sex A designation assigned to individuals based on their physical bodies, specifically their genitals and reproductive organs

Bisexuality Attraction to both men and women

Blaming Criticism or implying fault

Booty-call relationship Low commitment, primarily sexual relationship that includes an ongoing emotional component

Breakup A decision-based end of an ongoing established romantic relationship

Breakup sex Engaging in sex with an ex-partner

Breakup strategies Goal-oriented approaches to ending relationships

Bumbling Awkward, uncomfortable, or intrusive behaviors

Capitalization The process by which one person shares personal good news with another person and this other person responds in a way that the discloser's positive emotion is amplified

Cardiovascular reactivity When the cardiovascular system responds to a perceived demand in the environment by working harder and faster

Caregiving behavioral system An innate motivational system designed toward offering responsiveness and support

Catfishing Creating a false identity or impersonating someone else and then initiating an online relationship with an unsuspecting person

Ceiling effect When scores are clustered on the high end of a numeric scale

Changing interactional positions Stage two of emotionally focused couple therapy; partners identify how their vulnerable emotions are connected to underlying attachment-related concerns

Chemistry A unique relationship-level connection that can emerge between people and cannot be predicted by individual characteristics alone

Childfree People who are childless by choice

Chronic strain model A model of relationship dissolution that suggests dissolution creates resource deficits and related hardships that have long-term, possibly permanent, adverse outcomes

Chronosystem The temporal context underlying other environmental forces shaping people's relationship experiences

Cisgender Individuals who experience a match between their biological sex and psychological gender (i.e., male – man; female – woman)

Close relationships Intimate, or personal, relationships characterized by interdependence, intimacy, and personal knowledge

Co-experience positive affect To share together an experience of positive emotions

Cognitive behavioral couple therapy An intervention approach that incorporates behavioral interventions and cognitive restructuring interventions

Cognitive interdependence Integrated mental representations of self and other; a collective sense of self

Cognitive restructuring A type of intervention that helps partners identify and correct distorted or unhelpful thought patterns

Cognitive uncertainty When people do not know or are not confident about their own or others' attitudes

Cohabitate Romantic partners who live together and are not married

Cohabitation effect The idea that pre-marital cohabitation leads to long-term marital instability, low relationship quality, and a higher likelihood of divorce

Cohort approach A method for estimating divorce that projects the likelihood a given cohort (e.g., people married in 2020) will eventually divorce

Collectivist orientation An orientation that values group harmony, connection, reliance on others, and fitting in (i.e., generally individuals in Eastern cultures)

Colorism Use of skin tone to discriminate among people of color, privileging lighter-skinned individuals over darker-skinned individuals

Commitment An intention to remain in a relationship now and into the future

Commitment readiness A holistic sense that someone is prepared for entering a potentially long-term romantic relationship

Commitment uncertainty When a person questions if they wish to remain in their current relationship

Communal sexual motives Desire and effort to respond to and meet the sexual needs of a partner

Companionate love A type of love characterized by affection toward close others

Comparison level (CL) The outcomes people expect to experience in close relationships

Comparison level alternatives (CL_{alt}) The extent to which people's alternatives to their current relationship are appealing

Compassionate love A type of love defined by a tender concern for another person and selfless acts of sacrifice and support

Competition for resources Within (or between) species competition to secure what is needed to survive and reproduce

Concealed ovulation When the exact moment of ovulation (i.e., egg release) is not obvious, even to the woman herself

Concrete outcomes The immediate satisfying or dissatisfying experience of a situation

Confederates People who appear as participants or bystanders, but are actually research assistants following predetermined behavioral scripts

Confirmatory analyses Analyses used to test planned hypotheses

Conflict A social interaction in which people have opposing interests, incompatible goals, or disparate views

Conflict avoidance Withdrawal to avoid the conflict, can involve changing the subject, joking, or finding a distraction

Conflict of interest A situation in which one person's best outcome corresponds to a non-optimal outcome for another person

Confound An unmeasured variable that provides an alternative explanation for a study's findings

Consensually non-monogamous relationships Romantic relationships that include more than two people

Consent Agreeing, freely without coercion, to participate in sexual activity

Consolidation and integration Stage three of emotionally focused couple therapy; involves creating a coherent narrative for partners to understand how their relationship became distressed and how they were able to reconnect

Conspicuous conservation Showing one's interest in caring for the environment

Conspicuous consumption Showy spending

Construct validity Whether a measurement strategy actually captures the construct researchers are intending to measure

Constructive Likely to produce positive personal and relationship consequences

Contempt Purposeful attempts to belittle, hurt, or humiliate a partner

Context The setting, framework, or environment in which something occurs

Control condition A neutral or comparison condition used in experimental designs

Convenience sampling Recruiting participants who are easy to access and readily available to participate

Cooperative courtship When friends (e.g., "wingmen") help each other avoid undesirable potential partners and gain access to desirable potential partners

Correlational design A research design in which researchers measure two variables and test for their association

Costly signaling theory A theory that suggests behaviors that require sacrifice (i.e., are costly) are reliable signals of underlying qualities

Costs Any "con" or aspect of a relationship that adds negative value

Counterbalancing Randomly assigning participants in an experiment/study to experience the conditions in different orders

Couple Commitment and Relationship Enhancement (CCRE) program The second-most tested CRE program that includes a unique focus on self-regulation and self-reflection

Couple Coping Enhancement Training (CCET) program A type of Couple Relationship Education program focused on teaching skills that make a relationship resilient to stress

Couple therapy A research-backed intervention designed to support distressed partners; also called couples therapy and couples counseling

Covariation Across people, higher and lower values correspond in a consistent way with variation in another variable

Crisis model A model of relationship dissolution that suggests the acute negative outcomes linked to a relationship's end are temporary

Criticism An attack on someone's character (not necessarily intentionally malicious)

Cross-case analysis An approach to understanding qualitative data that relies on identifying similarities and differences between respondents (i.e., "cases")

Crossover When one partner's stress leads the other partner to feel negatively

Cross-sectional study A study in which researchers collect descriptive data at one moment in time

Crude divorce rate An estimate for divorce based on the ratio of divorces per 1,000 people in a given year

Culture The vast and dynamic set of norms, practices, institutions, and artifacts that surround us and respond to us

Cyberstalking An online form of traditional stalking

Cycle de-escalation Stage one of emotionally focused couple therapy; partners learn to recognize the negative interaction cycle that they repeatedly experience

Dad bod A soft, not-overweight-but-not-particularly-fit body type stereotypically common among middle-aged married (American) men

Daily-diary method An interval-contingent approach to longitudinal data collection in which participants complete assessments once per day

Daily hassles Small, but still impactful, everyday difficulties

Dark Triad A personality defined by high levels of narcissism, psychopathy, and Machiavellianism

Dating pool The accessible people who could be potential romantic partners

Dating scripts Mental representations of the sequence of events and expectations characterizing early relationship experiences

Deactivation A secondary attachment strategy that involves a defensive, protective down-regulation of the attachment behavioral system

Dealbreakers Traits that people perceive as not desirable, toxic, risky, or costly in potential romantic partners

Defensiveness Attempts to refuse or deny responsibility, sometimes includes a counter-attack

Demand-withdraw pattern When one partner makes demands (e.g., complains), prompting the other partner to withdraw

Demands-rewards perspective A perspective applied to parenthood that recognizes an influx of both demands and rewards

Dependency The extent to which we rely on, and therefore need to stay in, a relationship

Dependency paradox The notion that in order for people to be truly independent, they must be able to depend on others

Dependent variable (DV) Outcome variable that is measured and the independent variable is meant to change or impact

Depression A clinical condition defined by distorted negative self-views, sadness, lack of interest in previously enjoyed activities, an inability to experience pleasure, and feelings of worthlessness, hopelessness, and inadequacy

Destiny beliefs The idea that romantic partners are either compatible or they are not, and this compatibility determines the relationship's success

Destructive Likely to produce negative personal and relationship consequences

Diagnostic situations Conflicts of interest situations in which one partner's underlying thoughts and motivations are made evident

Differential parental investment Sex-based asymmetry in minimum required effort, energy, and commitment of resources to successfully pass along one's genes

Directional Prediction that describes the direction we expect the observed association to take

Disaffection A state in which neutral feelings and apathy have replaced love; also called romantic disengagement

Disillusionment A toxic relationship state characterized by a loss of closeness, affection, and love, feelings of disappointment, and a lack of interest in one's partner

Dissolution consideration When people contemplate ending their relationship

Distancing Behavioral or emotional disengagement

Distress Describes quieter negative emotions and milder negative behaviors

Divorce ideation When married people contemplate pursuing a divorce

Divorce-stress-adjustment perspective The viewpoint that relationship endings begin with partners who are together and end after they have parted

Domain-general rewards Broad rewards that motivate human thought, emotion, and behavior, such as self-esteem or pleasure

Domain-specific evolutionary goals Goals that advance individuals toward survival and reproduction

Dopamine A neurotransmitter implicated in rewarding experiences

Dual staircase model A model for how relationships escalate during formation and de-escalate during dissolution

Dyadic relationships Relationships between two people

Ecological systems theory A social ecological theory that posits people (and their relationships) operate within nested layers of environmental influence

Effect size The strength of an effect or relation

Emotional capital The positive moments a person has experienced in a particular relationship

Emotional divorce A dimension of marital breakdown characterized by romantic disengagement

Emotionally focused couple therapy A type of couple therapy based on attachment theory, which conceptualizes distress as a result of emotional disconnection and attachment insecurity

Empathetic accuracy Accurate detection of another person's emotional experiences

Empathetic joining When partners share their emotional reactions to their differences and come to understand the deeper fears and vulnerabilities that underlie each other's behaviors

Empathy Being able to feel what another person is feeling

Empiricism Making many careful observations and integrating these observations in order to understand general trends

Enacted/received support Support actions that people provide with the intention of benefiting another's ability to cope with stress

Encouragement Conveying excitement and enthusiasm about an opportunity or goal and expressing confidence that an exploration will be successful

Engagement When partners enter into an agreement to marry

ePREP A 6-hour version of the traditional Prevention and Relationship Enhancement program adapted for online training

Evolutionary-mismatch theory When evolved needs or drives do not correspond well with modern life

Evolutionary theories Theories that explain human thought, emotion, and behavior as adaptations that help solve survival and reproduction problems

Excessive affection Receiving more affection than one deserves

Exosystem The structures and institutions in which people's immediate environments reside

Expectancies What people expect, including how they expect an interaction partner to behave

Experience sampling An intensive type of longitudinal study commonly used by relationship scientists, in which participants complete many assessments throughout their daily lives

Experimental designs Research designs in which researchers manipulate one or more variables and assess changes in another variable

Exploratory analyses After-the-fact exploration of the data for any interesting patterns

Exploratory behavioral system An innate motivational system oriented toward exploration and discovery

External validity How well study results generalize to other situations, people, or studies

Extractive strategies A form of information seeking that involves online searches about a person of interest

Extradyadically Outside of a monogamous dyadic relationship

Facial adiposity Perceived weight in a person's face

Facial averageness The extent to which facial features and shapes are typical or average, rather than distinctive

Facial sexual dimorphism The perceived femininity of female faces and masculinity of male faces

Facial symmetry A match between each side of one's face

Falling in love A transitional period, a move from a state of "not in love" to a state of "in love"

Familiarity How well someone knows another person

Fatal attractions Traits that draw people toward a partner which later become the very traits that undermine their relationship

Felt security A state of well-being that results from feeling safe, protected, and loved

Five Factor Model A five-trait model of personality featuring extraversion, conscientiousness, neuroticism, openness to new experiences, and agreeableness

Flexible ideal standards Adjusting ideal partner standards to correspond with a partner's actual qualities

Flirtation The art of displaying your own desirable qualities while subtly assessing another's interest

Flooding Feeling overwhelmed and in fight-or-flight mode when communicating during disagreements

Forgiveness A constructive response to a partner's transgression that involves shifting away from revenge-seeking or avoidance and toward an abatement of negative feelings

Four horsemen of the apocalypse The four conflict behaviors (contempt, criticism, defensiveness, and stonewalling) that Gottman identifies as the most destructive for relationships

Gender The psychological experience and expression of masculinity and femininity

Gender minority Individuals whose gender identification does not fall into the traditional men/women categories (e.g., non-binary individuals), which may be similar to or different from those who identify as men or women

Gender roles Culturally endorsed and reinforced behaviors linked to specific genders

Ghosting When one partner suddenly or gradually ceases all communication and "disappears"

Goal conflict When a partner's goals are incompatible with one's own goals

Golden ratio The notion that when the geometric layout of facial features is proportionally closer to Phi (1.618), faces are perceived as more beautiful

Gratitude A positive emotion that someone feels toward another when they recognize that the other's actions have benefited them

Grey divorce Divorce among people who are over 50

Growth beliefs The idea that relationship challenges can be expected and can be overcome to build a satisfying relationship

Harshness Scarcity of resources and a lower life expectancy

Hedge An uncertainty reduction strategy in which people attempt to gain information without giving away too much information or assuming too much

Heterosexuality Attraction to a different gender

High openers People who bring out others' disclosures by displaying attentiveness and by asking questions

Homosexuality Attraction to the same gender, for example, gay (men attracted to men); lesbian (women attracted to women)

Hostile sexism The attitude that women are trying to control men

Hostility Negative behaviors that are displayed with a high level of energy

Hyperactivation A secondary attachment strategy that involves a revving up of the attachment behavioral system

Hypothalamus-Pituitary-Adrenal (HPA) axis A slow-acting, long-lasting stress response that helps the body fight or flee

Hypothesis Prediction that follows logically from the theory being tested

"I" statements Sentences that are about one's self

Ideal partner preferences Traits and characteristics that comprise people's mental representations of a hypothetical, hoped-for romantic partner

Implicit measures Measures that assess attitudes indirectly (e.g., by observing reaction time or task accuracy)

Implicit support Spending time with others, without disclosing a stressor or divulging one's distress

Incompatibility Misaligned interests that make interdependence challenging

Independent variable (IV) Predictor variable that is manipulated in an experimental design

Individualistic orientation A cultural orientation that prioritizes separateness, self-reliance, uniqueness, and standing up for oneself (i.e., generally individuals in Western cultures)

Inertia effect When people "slide" rather than "decide" into greater commitment (e.g., marriage)

Infidelity A relational transgression that involves sexual or emotional unfaithfulness

Information seeking An uncertainty-reduction strategy in which people attempt to gain information

Inhibitory system A drive toward avoiding aversive experiences

Insecure attachments Attachment styles derived from inconsistently available/responsive attachment figures (e.g., anxious attachment) or reliably unavailable/unresponsive attachment figures (e.g., avoidant attachment)

Insoluble problems Problems where behavior change is impractical or impossible

Instrumentality Having the ability to help us make progress toward important goals

Integrative behavioral couple therapy An adaptation of traditional behavioral couple therapy that includes acceptance-focused interventions

Intensified affection When people express affection without feeling it

Intensity The extent to which behaviors (or thoughts or emotions) are active and forceful versus passive and gentle

Interactive strategies A form of information seeking that involves directly communicating with a person of interest

Interdependence A state of mutual influence; changes experienced by each person affect the other person

Interdependence structure The nature of influence underlying a specific interaction

Interdependence theory A theory that explains people's thoughts, emotions, and behaviors as solving situation-based problems

Intermediate trajectory A relationship trajectory that describes a steady acceleration toward interdependence that is less strong than the accelerated trajectory

Internal validity Ability to know if one variable is actually causing a change in the other variable

Internal working models Mental representations of self and other that are built on past interactions and allow for predictions of future relationship interactions

Interpersonal attraction The subjective appeal of another person, a positive evaluation that can be accompanied by a desire for greater closeness to that person

Interpersonal coordination The behavioral, physiological, emotional, or cognitive harmony that occurs between two interaction partners

Interpersonal exchange model of sexual satisfaction (IEMSS) A model of sexual satisfaction that considers rewards and costs and suggests that satisfaction is not tied to one sexual encounter

Interpersonal process model of intimacy (IPM) A model that suggests intimacy emerges from a dynamic process in which one partner offers a self-disclosure and the other, in turn, offers responsiveness

Interpersonal synchrony A subdivision of interpersonal coordination which focuses on coordinated timing of similar or complementary behaviors

Interracial marriages Marriages between individuals who identify as different races

Intersectionality Consideration of multiple dimensions of people's identities (e.g., race, sexual orientation, gender) and their related social consequences of oppression or privilege (e.g., racism, homophobia, sexism) simultaneously and in light of system-level forces

Intersexual selection Between sexes; occurs when certain traits become more important for reproductive success because the other sex preferentially chooses partners with those traits

Intimacy In conflict, a meta-category that describes positive, high-intensity behaviors

Intimate knowledge The personal details that people know about each other which strangers or mere acquaintances might not know

Intrasexual selection Within sex; occurs when a trait or characteristic helps animals out-compete their same-sex rivals for access to sexual partners

Investment How much one would lose if a relationship were to end

Investment model of commitment An extension of social exchange theory that suggests people's relationship commitment (and relationship stability) follows from the joint influence of satisfaction, investments, and the (low) appeal of relationship alternatives

Invisible support Support that is either not noticed or noticed but not interpreted as help

Latent profile analysis (LPA) A person-centered approach to modeling data which involves clustering participants based on similarities

Level of abstraction The extent to which a trait or quality is concrete or abstract

Life history theory A theory that explains people's fast or slow reproductive strategies as rational responses to childhoods marked as being harsh and unpredictable, or gentle and predictable, childhoods

Limbal rings The dark outline surrounding the iris of the eye

Living apart together (LAT) When romantic partners maintain separate residences, but generally live within an easy drive from each other

Loneliness An unpleasant, distressing feeling tied to a perceived deficit in the quality of one's social connections

Longitudinal study A research study in which variables are measured more than once over time

Love A cross-cultural experience that often includes sexual attraction, altruistic self-sacrifice, preoccupying thoughts, partner well-being, and happiness

Love-the-emotion People experience their love and affection for each other in moments when their emotions, behaviors, and physiology are synchronized

Machiavellianism A Dark Triad trait defined by a tendency to manipulate others

Macrosystem Overarching cultural ideologies that shape people's environments and relationships

Magic ratio The 5 to 1 ratio of positive to negative conflict interactions, identified by John Gottman, which he proposes protects a relationship

Marriage bar The prerequisites that people believe they need to meet before getting married

Marriage effect The idea that marriage may provide a protective benefit against psychological distress and physical disease

Matching hypothesis The idea that people "match" with others along dimensions of social desirability

Mate-copying Considering another person's romantic interest in a target as an indicator of the target's value as a potential partner

Mate poaching Stealing someone away from an existing relationship for a short-term or long-term relationship

Mate preferences The qualities that people desire in a short-term or long-term partner

Mating motives Goals regarding the type of relationships people desire (e.g., short-term, long-term)

Mating strategies The goal-oriented strategies people use to acquire and retain their desired relationships

Mating tactics The behaviors that people enact in order to initiate relationships

Mean Mathematical average

Mean-level bias A tendency to over-perceive (or under-perceive) a particular trait

Mediation Indirect effects; a mediator explains the relation between two variables

Mere-repeated-exposure effect The more frequently people are seen by others, the more those people tend to be liked by them

Mesosystem Interrelations among people's immediate environments

Meta-analysis An approach in which researchers quantitatively integrate the results of multiple studies to estimate the overall effect across studies

Meta-labels Overarching descriptions

Michelangelo phenomenon A congenial process by which perceptual and behavioral affirmation support a person's movement toward their ideal self

Microsystem People's immediate environments

Mimicry A subdivision of interpersonal coordination which reflects a non-conscious mirroring of behavior, language, emotion, or facial expression

Mindfulness A state of being in which a person focuses their attention on the present moment and acknowledges their experience with openness and without judgment

Minimizing Forcing optimism or downplaying concerns

Minority stress The stress that individuals experience specifically because of their identification with a minority group

Misattribution theory People misinterpret physiological arousal caused by a different source as an indicator of romantic attraction

Mobile data donations Data obtained from participants who voluntarily share their mobile data

Moderator A variable that changes the pattern of results

Monogamy Maintaining only one romantic partner at any given time

Motivated cognition The tendency for people to think in ways that are consistent with their goals

Narcissism An individual difference variable that captures an inflated sense of self, low empathy, high confidence, a strong sense of entitlement, and a tendency toward exploiting others

Natural selection The process by which whatever helps a species survive and reproduce becomes standard within that species

Neuroimaging Physiological measurement technique that records images of the brain

Non-adverse contexts Situations that are not threatening and allow for exploration and growth

Non-experimental designs Research designs consisting of observations of naturally occurring patterns that can reveal associations between variables

Non-interference A passive waiting role that supports the effectiveness of availability

Non-verbal affection Showing affection through such behaviors as gestures, proximity, facial expressions, and affectionate touch

Nubility Sexual maturity without prior pregnancy

Objective stressors Situations that are presumed to be disruptive, impacting everyone

Observational coders Neutral third-party observers who quantify behaviors of interest using a coding system

Observational measures Measures that involve observing behaviors

On-again/off-again relationships Relationships defined by a trajectory that includes a series of separations and reunions, also called cyclical or churning relationships

Open relationships Engaging in primarily sexual, not usually romantic, relationships with people other than one's primary partner

Opening gambits A direct overture strategy; also known as pick-up lines

Operationalize How researchers manipulate, measure, or observe variables of interest

Optimal matching model of stress and social support The idea that enacted support is most beneficial when it matches the needs of the support recipient

Orbiting Like ghosting, but without a complete disappearance; orbiters linger in the digital periphery

OurRelationship An 8-hour online Couple Relationship Education program based on Integrative Behavioral Couple Therapy

Outcome matrix Conceptual representation of dependency structures underlying social interactions

Ovulatory-shift hypothesis The idea that women would have an adaptive advantage by preferring "good genes" men during peak fertility and "good partner" men when pregnancy is less likely

Oxytocin A neuropeptide implicated in affiliative drive that promotes proximity and closeness behaviors

Pair-bonds Lifelong romantic attachments

Pansexuality Attraction to all genders

Paradox of choice Where more options make for a worse rather than a better experience

Parasocial relationships One-sided relationships with non-humans, fictional characters, or celebrities, or imagined relationships with strangers or people with whom individuals do not have an actual relationship

Parental investment A parent's commitment of energy, resources, time, etc. to one offspring, which limits their ability to invest in other offspring

Parental investment theory A theory that explains sex-based differences in human mating as resulting from biologically based differences in the minimum parental investment required to successfully pass along one's genes

Partner-enhancement A motivated tendency to view one's partner(s) unrealistically favorably

Partner shortage Little access or opportunity to interact with potential partners

Partner-specific attachment anxiety The normative experience of uncertainty, anxiety, or preoccupation with a new romantic partner

Partner surplus Abundant access and opportunity to interact with potential partners

Passionate love A type of love that is exciting and physically arousing and includes intense feelings of longing

Passive strategy Gathering information about a prospective romantic partner by passively observing their social media

Passive-constructive responses In response to capitalization attempts, responders react positively, but without elaboration and less energy than active-constructive responses

Passive-destructive responses In response to capitalization attempts, responders show disinterest and minimal, if any, acknowledgement of the positive event

Perceived partner responsiveness Feeling understood, feeling validated, and feeling cared for

Perceived relationship superiority The tendency to view one's own relationship as better than others' relationships

Perceived support availability A subjective belief that others would provide appropriate assistance if needed

Permissiveness A free and casual approach to sex

Personal self-expansion Learning, growth, and excitement that a person experiences independently or with other individuals as opposed to with a partner

Personality Individual difference variables that describe typical patterns in thought, emotion, and behavior that endure over time

Phase model of relationship dissolution A model of a relationship breakup that begins with one person's thoughts, progresses toward sharing those thoughts, leads to a breakup and meaning making, and ends when individuals prepare for future relationships

Phubbing When people snub, or ignore, someone in favor of attending to their phone

Physical attractiveness The aesthetic appeal of a person's outward appearance, especially their face and body

Physiological measures Measures that assess bodily functions (e.g., heart rate, sweating)

Physiological synchrony A link in people's biological responses, such as their physiological activity (e.g., heart rate)

Planning An uncertainty-reduction strategy in which people plot out how they will behave in an anticipated future interaction

Play Activities that are enjoyable, approached in a non-serious way, interactive, and enacted for the purpose of amusement or fun, rather than an end-goal

Playfulness A personality trait describing a propensity toward play

Playing hard-to-get A strategic attempt to increase one's own desirability by creating the impression of unavailability

Polyamory Maintaining ongoing romantic and sexual relationships with multiple partners

Population change When unique adaptations, because they confer survival and reproduction advantages, become common in the population over time

Positionality statements Statements in which researchers describe their own identities to disclose potential biases

Positive illusions False positive beliefs about a partner

Positive interpersonal processes Interactions between people that actively enhance their close relationship

Positivity resonance The co-experience of positive affect, behavioral synchrony, and physiological synchrony

Post-sex period The time interval after sex and before partners fall asleep, shift their attention, or go their separate ways

Power The ability to control or influence another person's outcomes

Practice flirting When people flirt without romantic motives, for fun or skill building

Predicted outcome value theory A theory that suggests people engage in uncertainty-reduction behaviors to help them better predict future costs and rewards tied to a specific relationship

Pre-marital dyadic formation model A model of relationship building that considers how social and situational forces might encourage or discourage relationship formation

Pre-registration A clear and comprehensive plan for a research study that is set in a permanent, inalterable form prior to implementation and made accessible to others

Prevention and Relationship Enhancement Program The most commonly used and empirically tested Couple Relationship Education program

Primary appraisal An initial assessment of the demand that a stressor imposes and the extent of harm or disruption the stressor can cause

Principle of least interest The idea that, in relationships, the balance of power is usually in favor of the partner who is less committed to the relationship

Problem solving Constructive communication that is low in intensity

Prolonged trajectory A relationship trajectory that describes an extended, lengthy courtship

Prospective research designs Longitudinal designs that allow researchers to see how initial observations predict later observations

Proximate explanations Low-level explanations for how psychological mechanisms work

Proximity Propinquity; the simple geographic nearness between people

Psychological stress A subjective judgment in a perceived disruptive or demanding situation characterized by feeling overwhelmed, anxious, or agitated

Psychopathy A Dark Triad trait defined by impulsivity, low empathy, and thrill seeking

Qualitative A type of research study that gathers word-based responses (e.g., interviews) rather than number-based responses (e.g., survey responses)

Rainbow CoupleCare A relationship education program that includes topics like internalized stigma, discrimination, prejudice, and relationship disclosure decisions

Random assignment The practice of assigning participants to experimental conditions by relying on chance to ensure that groups do not differ at the outset

Randomized controlled trials A type of experiment in which the independent variable is a clinical treatment condition

Rapport A satisfying harmony and easy synchrony within a social interaction

Realistic accuracy model A model of person perception that suggests accuracy depends on the target exhibiting relevant behaviors that are available to the observer and on the observer detecting and using those behaviors to inform perceptions

Rebound relationships A new attempt at pair-bonding that begins before a person has adjusted to a recent relationship loss

Rebound sex Casual post-dissolution sex, often with a stranger

Reciprocity effect of attraction Tendency for expressed attraction to breed attraction

Refined divorce rate An estimate for divorce based on the ratio of divorces per 1,000 married women in a given year

Reflecting back Paraphrasing (or repeating back) what you hear someone else say in your own words

Relational regulation theory The idea that spending ordinary time with close others enhances relationships and provides personal benefits

Relational turbulence model The idea that major relationship transitions create challenges by introducing uncertainty and causing disruptions in existing patterns of interdependence

Relationship A mutually recognized interpersonal context in which two (or more) people engage in multiple social interactions and anticipate future social interactions

Relationship Checkup An empirically supported relationship intervention that is briefer than traditional interventions

Relationship coordination and strategic timing (RECAST) model A model of relationship trajectories that suggests that short-term and long-term relationships are indistinguishable early on, until short-term relationships end

Relationship dissolution The end of a relationship, typically a process that unfolds over time

Relationship-guarding behaviors Actions designed to protect a relationship against threatening rivals

Relationship identification How much a person has internalized their partner and relationship as part of their self

Relationship initiation The process by which people come to mutually identify themselves as in a relationship

Relationship maintenance The various strategies that individuals and partners use to preserve their relationships

Relationship maintenance strategies Active and passive strategies that partners use to help maintain commitment

Relationship quality A subjective overall judgment about one's relationship

Relationship receptivity theory A theory suggesting that timing is a critical contextual factor in relationship initiation

Relationship science An interdisciplinary field devoted to understanding all aspects of human relationships

Relationship status A designation of whether someone is in a romantic relationship, and if they are in a relationship, which type of relationship they are in, presumably a proxy for commitment

Relationship talk When partners talk specifically about their relationship

Relationship trajectories framework A meta-theoretical approach to structuring how relationships change over time

Relationship trajectory An arc, or path, that plots how romantic evaluations change over time

Repeatable Able to be obtained again by the same researchers using the same study design

Replicable Able to be obtained again by different researchers using the same study design

Representative sample A sample that is roughly similar to the population of interest in meaningful ways

Reproducible Able to be obtained again by different researchers using a different study design

Research process Series of steps to obtain and interpret evidence

Restricted sociosexual orientations Maintaining a high threshold (e.g., commitment, closeness) for sexual activity

Reverse-causal relationship When the presumed outcome variable is actually the causal variable (or the variables have an unexpected bidirectional relation)

Reverse-scoring When items in a measure are worded oppositely of other items and higher (lower) scores are recoded to lower (higher) scores

Rewards Any "pro" or aspect of a relationship that benefits an individual

Romantic jealousy The emotional, cognitive, and behavioral response to the presence of a potential rival

Romantic relationships Close relationships that often include a sexual aspect and commitment; usually adults' closest relationship

Romeo and Juliet effect The (unsupported) idea that family interference can intensify love and commitment

SABI model A model of social interaction that suggests any social interaction is a function of the situation and each individual person

Sacrifice Prioritizing one's partner's needs, desires, or motives over one's own at a cost to the self

Safe haven An interpersonal space of refuge, relief, and protection

Secondary appraisal An evaluation of the extent to which a person has the ability and resources to cope with a specific stressor

Secure attachment An attachment style in which the self is viewed as valued and trustworthy, and close others as available, reliable, and trustworthy

Secure base An available source of support that enables exploration

Secure base script A set of expectations developed from past experiences that includes beliefs of an attachment figure's availability and responsiveness

Selective attention Noticing some things and overlooking others

Self-adulteration An increase in negative self-concept content

Self-concept "The self"; refers to a dynamic set of traits, attitudes, beliefs, and behaviors that we maintain, which comprises our identity and interacts with our context to guide our behavior

Self-contraction A decrease in positive self-concept content

Self-disclosure The intentional sharing of personal information with other people (e.g., feelings, preferences, motivations, goals)

Self-enhancement A motivated tendency to view oneself unrealistically favorably

Self-esteem People's general feeling of self-worth

Self-expanding activities Activities that partners can engage in together that allow them to experience self-expansion

Self-expansion An increase in positive self-concept content

Self-expansion residue The growth a person achieves through a relationship which stays with them, after the relationship ends

Self-fulfilling prophesies When people hold a belief or expectation, they may behave in ways that make that expectation a reality

Self-pruning A decrease in negative self-concept content

Self-report When people report on their own thoughts, emotions, or behaviors

Self-verification A motivation to be seen by others as one sees oneself

Serial cohabitation The practice of sequentially living with dating partners

Sexting Sharing sexually explicit messages, photos, or videos

Sexual arousal An excitatory phase that includes both a physiological response that helps prepare people for sex and heightened thoughts and motivations toward sex

Sexual attitudes People's beliefs, perspectives, and values pertaining to sex

Sexual behavioral system An innate motivation system that promotes intercourse and reproduction

Sexual communal strength A strong motivation to meet a partner's sexual needs

Sexual communication Verbal or non-verbal communication that often involves self-disclosure about one's sexual preferences, fantasies, comforts, values, and needs

Sexual debut A person's first sexual experience

Sexual desire All that propels people toward engaging in sexual activity, often referred to by the narrower term sex drive

Sexual frequency How often people engage in sex

Sexual inhibition A counterpoint to sexual arousal that lowers or inhibits sexual desire

Sexual interdependence dilemmas Situations in which partners' sexual needs and desires are opposed

Sexual motivations People's reasons for engaging in sexual activity

Sexual orientation The direction of individuals' romantic and sexual interests, either toward members of the same gender or toward others

Sexual overperception bias Women tend to remember more instances when men falsely believed they (the women) were sexually interested in them (the men) than instances when men under-perceived their actual interest

Sexual satisfaction The extent to which people hold favorable judgments of their sex lives, perceiving more rewards than costs in their sexual relationships

Sexual scripts Mental templates that help people know how to engage in sex and how to behave in sexual situations

Sexual selection theory A theory that looks at the mating game through an evolutionary lens, suggesting that adaptations retained over generations are retained because they help with reproductive success

Sexual self-efficacy The capacity to advocate for one's self sexually

Sexual strategies theory A theory that proposed that modern men and women navigate the sex-specific challenges put in place by differential parental investment by drawing on an evolved set of psychological adaptations and mating strategies

Sexuality A multidimensional term that includes all aspects of human sex, including sexual desire and drive, attitudes and beliefs about sex, sexual behaviors, and sexual motives

Sexually compatible People who share similar sexual preferences and needs

Shared leisure When partners spend time together playing games, exercising, socializing, or attending events

Situationship An ongoing romantic or sexual relationship that has no formal relationship status

Shyness A personality trait characterized by reserve and inhibition in the presence of unknown others

Single parents by choice Unpartnered people who choose to become parents

Skills training When therapists teach individuals ways to lessen negative interactions, such as communication skills or problem-solving skills

Skin-tone trauma The serious negative consequences endured by people of color on account of distorted beauty ideals that favor Western, European standards

Social acceptance The inherently rewarding experience of belonging

Social affiliation model A model that suggests that people regulate their own need for social contact

Social anxiety An intense concern about others' impressions and a strong fear of negative evaluation

Social baseline theory The idea that the human brain's default expectation is social integration

Social ecological theories Theories that attend to the person–environment interaction

Social exchange theory A situation-based theory that explains social interactions as a calculated give-and-take, a reciprocal exchange of tangible and intangible offerings, which vary in their benefits and costs

Social exclusion A state of emotional or physical separation from others which is perceived as intentional and punitive

Social gerontologists Scientists who apply a social perspective to the study of ageing

Social homeostasis A personal balance point at which people have not too much, and not too little, social interaction

Social integration Participating in a broad range of social relationships; having a strong social network

Social network effect The idea that relationships benefit from their social network's approval

Social network perspective A perspective in relationship science that highlights the role of social context in shaping relationship experiences

Social ostracism A form of social exclusion that involves actively or passively ignoring someone

Social penetration theory A theory that emphasizes the role of self-disclosure in moving people toward progressively more intimate connections

Social rejection A form of social exclusion that involves direct negative attention

Social status A person's relative standing on socially valued traits like wealth, athletics, or power

Social support Help from others; can be emotional, instrumental, or informational

Social surrogates Substitutes that people use for actual human interaction partners

Socially desirable responding When participants respond to survey questions so that they present themselves in the best possible light

Socioeconomic status (SES) An individual's social power, wealth, and educational opportunities, as well as perceptions of their social class

Sociometer theory A theory that connects social relationships to self-esteem

Sociosexual attitudes How people evaluate casual sex

Sociosexual behaviors Engaging in sexual activity outside of a committed relationship

Sociosexual desire The degree to which people are motivated to pursue uncommitted sex

Sociosexuality How much relationship investment individuals require before engaging in sexual activity with another person

Solitary confinement A form of social exclusion that involves separating an inmate from the general prison population for 22 to 24 hours a day for at least fifteen consecutive days

Speaker-listener technique An intervention technique that includes an agreed-upon communication structure that includes a speaker and a listener role

Spillover When experiencing stress in one domain can lead a person to feel negatively in a different, separate domain

Stalking A legal term describing behaviors (e.g., threats, physical violence) designed to invoke fear

Standards Beliefs about how things "should" be

Stonewalling An intentional lack of engagement in a conflict

Strategic pluralism theory A theory that explains diverse mating strategies by recognizing that people flexibly use the mating approach that produces the best outcome for them

Stress exposure The extent of objective stressors a person has experienced

Stress inoculating hypothesis The idea that a modest degree of stress early in a relationship allows for skill building that helps partners manage larger stressors later in their relationship

Stress-related growth A perspective that difficult, challenging times offer a unique opportunity for growth

Stress response A physiological reaction to stress that includes the Sympathetic-Adreno-Medullar system and the Hypothalamus-Pituitary-Adrenal axis

Strong ties Close relationships that define the center of individuals' social networks

Supportive affection Behaviors, such as offering social support or acknowledging accomplishments, that communicate affection and are enacted to convey affection

Survival of the fittest Animals that have adaptations that enhance survival are more likely to live longer and reproduce (i.e., pass along their genes)

Swinging Engaging in sexual relationships as partners with other partners

Symbolic outcomes Positive or negative consequences based on a situation's broader implications

Sympathetic-Adreno-Medullar (SAM) system A fast-acting component of the stress response that helps the body fight or flee

Technoference Ways technology intrudes upon, interrupts, or otherwise alters the quality of partners' interactions when they are together

Temporal order An inference of which variables precede others in time, allowed in longitudinal studies

Testable Capable of being supported or not supported by evidence

Theories Logical statements that explain how and why a set of two or more constructs are related

Third variable A variable that could be the cause of a correlation between two other variables

Tolerance building An intervention type that focuses on helping partners become better able to tolerate their differences rather than to try to change each other

Tracking accuracy A correlation between objective ratings and partner ratings

Traditional behavioral couple therapy An intervention that focuses on improving the balance of positive and negative exchanges through targeted behavioral change

Trait affection level The extent to which you easily and comfortably express affection

Transactional stress model A model that helps explain how people appraise an objective stressor

Transactive goal dynamics The theory that when people are interdependent, share common goals, and are coordinated in their goals, each person's experience is enhanced

Transformation of motivation A motivation toward the "effective" situation, one that reflects partner concern, long-term goals and strategies, and other broader considerations

Transgender Individuals who identify as a gender different from their assigned biological sex

Transgressions Actions that intentionally or unintentionally hurt someone

Transition A period of instability when current modes of operating no longer work and adjustments must be made

Triangular theory of love A schematic that partitions love into three components: passion, intimacy, and commitment

Tripartite model of affectionate communication The idea that people typically express their affection for one another either verbally, through non-verbal gestures, or through supportive behaviors

Turning points Distinct moments that change the trajectory of a relationship

Two-dimensional model of attraction The idea that people are attracted to others whom they evaluate as being able to support their goals and needs and as willing to do so

Two-dimensional model of self-change A model of relationship-based self-concept change that describes increases or decreases in positive or negative quality self-content

Ultimate explanations High-level explanations for why humans are as they are

Uncertainty reduction theory A theory that suggests that a primary purpose of communication in ambiguous situations is to add clarity, confidence, and predictability

Unified detachment Partners are encouraged to step back and view their differences or problems with more objectivity

Unpredictability Erratic changes to the family environment, such as moving, divorces, remarriages, and parents' job changes

Unrequited love Loving someone who does not return your affection

Unrestricted sociosexual orientations Having a low threshold (few, if any commitment or closeness prerequisites) for sexual activity

Unwanted pursuit behaviors Unwelcomed and undesired contact attempts

Vasopressin A neuropeptide implicated in aggressive and protective behaviors

Verbal affection When people express their affection verbally, by speaking or writing

Vital statistics Nationally collected data that include estimates of births, deaths, marriages, and divorces

Vulnerability-stress-adaptation model Model that views relationship outcomes as a function of (1) the external stressors imposed on a relationship, (2) the pre-existing vulnerabilities that shape how partners interpret and react to those stressors, and (3) the adaptive processes that partners enact to cope with those stressors

Vulnerable emotions The underlying emotions (e.g., fear, anxiety, sadness) that are recognized as driving individuals' behaviors in emotionally focused couple therapy

Waist-to-hip ratio A mathematical ratio of waist circumference to hip circumference

Weak ties Relationships characterized by minimal intimacy, low emotional involvement, and irregular or infrequent interaction

What is beautiful is good A maxim that captures the idea that people over-ascribe positive attributes to beautiful people

Widowhood effect The increased risk of mortality in the aftermath of a partner's death

Withdrawal Disengagement from a discussion

Withheld affection When people experience affection, but do not express it

Within-subjects experimental design Experimental design in which every participant experiences all conditions and reports their experience in all conditions

REFERENCES

Abajobir, A. A., Maravilla, J. C., Alati, R. et al. (2016). A systematic review and meta-analysis of the association between unintended pregnancy and perinatal depression. *Journal of Affective Disorders*, *192*, 56–63.

Abbey, A. (1982). Sex differences in attributions for friendly behavior: Do males misperceive females' friendliness? *Journal of Personality and Social Psychology*, *42*(5), 830–838.

Abbey, A. (1987). Misperceptions of friendly behavior as sexual interest: A survey of naturally occurring incidents. *Psychology of Women Quarterly*, *11*(2), 173–194.

Abraham, R. (2019, June 19). What's with the gender inequality? Dutee Chand talks about the tests female athletes face before competing. *The Economic Times*. https://economictimes.indiatimes.com/magazines/panache/whats-with-the-gender-inequality-dutee-chand-talks-about-the-tests-female-athletes-face-before-competing/articleshow/69851149.cms

Abramova, O., Baumann, A., Krasnova, H. et al. (2016). *Gender differences in online dating: What do we know so far? A systematic literature review*. Paper presented at the Proceedings of the Annual Hawaii International Conference on System Sciences, 2016-March.

Abu-Raiya, H., & Ayten, A. (2020). Religious involvement, interpersonal forgiveness and mental health and well-being among a multinational sample of Muslims. *Journal of Happiness Studies*, *21*(8), 3051–3067.

Acevedo, B. P., & Aron, A. (2009). Does a long-term relationship kill romantic love? *Review of General Psychology*, *13*(1), 59–65.

Ackerman, J. M., Griskevicius, V., & Li, N. P. (2011). Let's get serious: Communicating commitment in romantic relationships. *Journal of Personality and Social Psychology*, *100*(6), 1079–1094.

Ackerman, J. M., & Kenrick, D. T. (2009). Cooperative courtship: Helping friends raise and raze relationship barriers. *Personality and Social Psychology Bulletin*, *35*(10), 1285–1300.

Adair, K. C., Boulton, A. J., & Algoe, S. B. (2018). The effect of mindfulness on relationship satisfaction via perceived responsiveness: Findings from a dyadic study of heterosexual romantic partners. *Mindfulness*, *9*(2), 597–609.

Adam, A. (2021). Beauty is in the eye of the beautiful: Enhanced eyelashes increase perceived health and attractiveness. *Evolutionary Behavioral Sciences*, *15*(4), 356–367.

Adamopoulou, E. (2013). New facts on infidelity. *Economics Letters*, *121*(3), 458–462.

Adams, B. L. (2018). Paternal incarceration and the family: Fifteen years in review. *Sociology Compass*, *12*(3), e12567.

Addison, S. M., & Clason, N. (2021). "I will always come home to you." In R. Harvey, M. J. Murphy, J. J. Bigner, & J. L. Wetchler, *Handbook of LGBTQ-affirmative couple and family therapy* (2nd ed., pp. 297–323). Routledge.

Addo, F. R. (2014). Debt, cohabitation, and marriage in young adulthood. *Demography*, *51*(5), 1677–1701.

Afifi, W. A., Falato, W. L., & Weiner, J. L. (2001). Identity concerns following a severe relational transgression: The role of discovery method for the relational outcomes of infidelity. *Journal of Social and Personal Relationships*, *18*(2), 291–308.

Afifi, W. A., & Faulkner, S. L. (2000). On being "just friends": The frequency and impact of sexual activity in cross-sex friendships. *Journal of Social and Personal Relationships*, *17*(2), 205–222.

Agnew, C. R., Hadden, B. W., & Tan, K. (2019). It's about time: Readiness, commitment, and stability in close relationships. *Social Psychological and Personality Science*, *10*(8), 1046–1055.

Agnew, C. R., Hadden, B. W., & Tan, K. (2020). Relationship receptivity theory: Timing and interdependent relationships. In L. V. Machia, C. R. Agnew, & X. B. Arriaga (Eds.), *Interdependence, interaction, and close relationships* (pp. 269–292). Cambridge University Press.

Agnew, C. R., Rusbult, C. E., Van Lange, P. A. M. et al. (1998). Cognitive interdependence: Commitment and the mental representation of close relationships. *Journal of Personality and Social Psychology*, *74*(4), 939–954.

Aharon, I., Etcoff, N., Ariely, D. et al. (2001). Beautiful faces have variable reward value: FMRI and behavioral evidence. *Neuron*, *32*(3), 537–551.

Ahern, K., & Le Brocque, R. (2005). Methodological issues in the effects of attrition: Simple solutions for social scientists. *Field Methods*, *17*(1), 53–69.

Ainsworth, C. (2015). Sex redefined. *Nature*, *518*, 288–291.

Ainsworth, M. (1967). *Infancy in Uganda: Infant care and the growth of love*. Johns Hopkins Press.

Ainsworth, M., Blehar, M., Waters, E. et al. (1978). *Patterns of attachment: A psychological study of the strange situation*. Lawrence Erlbaum.

Ainsworth, M. D. S. (1993). Attachments and other affectional bonds across the life cycle. In C. M. Parker, J. Stevenson-

Hinde, & P. Marris (Eds.), *Attachment across the life cycle* (pp. 33–51). Routledge.

Ainsworth, S. E., & Maner, J. K. (2019). Pathogen avoidance mechanisms affect women's preference for symmetrical male faces. *Evolutionary Behavioral Sciences*, *13*(3), 265–271.

Akbari, M., Kim, J. J., Seydavi, M. et al. (2022). Neglected side of romantic relationships among college students: Breakup initiators are at risk for depression. *Family Relations*, *71*, 1698–1712.

Akbulut, V., & Weger, H. (2016). Predicting responses to bids for sexual and romantic escalation in cross-sex friendships. *Journal of Social Psychology*, *156*(1), 98–114.

Akinro, N., & Mbunyuza-Memani, L. (2019). Black is not beautiful: Persistent messages and the globalization of "white" beauty in African women's magazines. *Journal of International and Intercultural Communication*, *12*(4), 308–324.

Albuquerque, S., Pereira, M., & Narciso, I. (2016). Couple's relationship after the death of a child: A systematic review. *Journal of Child and Family Studies*, *25*(1), 30–53.

Alderotti, G., Tomassini, C., & Vignoli, D. (2022). "Silver splits" in Europe: The role of grandchildren and other correlates. *Demographic Research*, *46*, 619–652.

Alexander, M. G., & Fisher, T. D. (2003). Truth and consequences: Using the bogus pipeline to examine sex differences in self-reported sexuality. *Journal of Sex Research*, *40*(1), 27–35.

Algoe, S. B. (2012). Find, remind, and bind: The functions of gratitude in everyday relationships. *Social and Personality Psychology Compass*, *6*(6), 455–469.

Algoe, S. B. (2019). Positive interpersonal processes. *Current Directions in Psychological Science*, *28*(2), 183–188.

Algoe, S. B., Fredrickson, B. L., & Gable, S. L. (2013). The social functions of the emotion of gratitude via expression. *Emotion*, *13*(4), 605–609.

Algoe, S. B., Gable, S. L., & Maisel, N. C. (2010). It's the little things: Everyday gratitude as a booster shot for romantic relationships. *Personal Relationships*, *17*(2), 217–233.

Algoe, S. B., & Haidt, J. (2009). Witnessing excellence in action: The 'other-praising' emotions of elevation, gratitude, and admiration. *The Journal of Positive Psychology*, *4*(2), 105–127.

Algoe, S. B., Haidt, J., & Gable, S. L. (2008). Beyond reciprocity: Gratitude and relationships in everyday life. *Emotion*, *8*(3), 425–429.

Algoe, S. B., & Zhaoyang, R. (2016). Positive psychology in context: Effects of expressing gratitude in ongoing relationships depend on perceptions of enactor responsiveness. *Journal of Positive Psychology*, *11*(4), 399–415.

Alhola, P., & Polo-Kantola, P. (2007). Sleep deprivation: Impact on cognitive performance. *Neuropsychiatric Disease and Treatment*, *3*(5), 553–567.

Alicke, M. D., & Govorun, O. (2005). The better-than-average effect. In M. D. Alicke, D. A. Dunning, & J. I. Krueger (Eds.), *The self in social judgment* (pp. 85–106). Psychology Press.

Allen, J. S., & Bailey, K. G. (2007). Are mating strategies and mating tactics independent constructs? *Journal of Sex Research*, *44*(3), 225–232.

Allen, K. (2002). Cardiovascular reactivity and the presence of pets, friends, and spouses: The truth about cats and dogs. *Psychosomatic Medicine*, *64*(5), 727–739.

Allen, K., Blascovich, J., Tomaka, J. et al. (1991). Presence of human friends and pet dogs as moderators of autonomic responses to stress in women. *Journal of Personality and Social Psychology*, *61*, 582–589.

Allen, M. S., & Walter, E. E. (2018). Linking big five personality traits to sexuality and sexual health: A meta-analytic review. *Psychological Bulletin*, *144*(10), 1081–1110.

Allen, S., Hawkins, A. J., Harris, S. M. et al. (2022). Day-to-day changes and longer-term adjustments to divorce ideation: Marital commitment uncertainty processes over time. *Family Relations*, *71*(2), 611–629.

Alley, J. C., & Diamond, L. M. (2020). Oxytocin and human sexuality: Recent developments. *Current Sexual Health Reports*, *12*(3), 182–185.

Allport, G. (1937). *Personality: A psychological interpretation.* Holt.

Alterovitz, S. S. R., & Mendelsohn, G. A. (2009). Partner preferences across the life span: Online dating by older adults. *Psychology and Aging*, *24*(2), 513–517.

Altman, I., & Taylor, D. A. (1973). *Social penetration: The development of interpersonal relationships.* Holt, Rinehart, & Winston.

Amato, P. R. (2000). The consequences of divorce for adults and children. *Journal of Marriage and Family*, *62*(4), 1269–1287.

Amato, P. R. (2010a). Research on divorce: Continuing trends and new developments. *Journal of Marriage and Family*, *72*(3), 650–666.

Amato, P. R. (2010b). *Interpreting divorce rates, marriage rates, and data on the percentage of children with single parents.* Research Brief. National Healthy Marriage Resource Center. Available from www.healthymarriageinfo.org/resource-detail/index.aspx?rid=3284

Amato, P. R., & Booth, A. (1991). The consequences of divorce for attitudes toward divorce and gender roles. *Journal of Family Issues*, *12*(3), 306–322.

Amato, P. R., & Hohmann-Marriott, B. (2007). A comparison of high- and low-distress marriages that end in divorce. *Journal of Marriage and Family*, *69*(3), 621–638.

Amato, P. R., & Patterson, S. E. (2017). The intergenerational transmission of union instability in early adulthood. *Journal of Marriage and Family*, *79*(3), 723–738.

Amato, P. R., & Previti, D. (2004). People's reasons for divorcing: Gender, social class, the life course, and adjustment. *Journal of Family Issues*, *24*(5), 602–626.

American Psychological Association. (2013). *Diagnostic and statistical manual of mental disorders* (5th ed.).

American Psychological Association, APA Working Group on Stress and Health Disparities. (2017). *Stress and health disparities: Contexts, mechanisms, and interventions among racial/ethnic minority and low-socioeconomic status populations*. Retrieved from www.apa.org/pi/health-equity/resources/stress-report.aspx

Amiri, M., Khosravi, A., Chaman, R. et al. (2015). Social consequences of infertility on families in Iran. *Global Journal of Health Science*, *8*(5), 89–95.

Amodio, D. M., & Showers, C. J. (2005). "Similarity breeds liking" revisited: The moderating role of commitment. *Journal of Social and Personal Relationships*, *22*(6), 817–836.

Andersen, P. A. (2011). Tactile traditions: Culture differences and similarities in haptic communication. In M. J. Hertenstein & S. Weiss (Eds.), *The handbook of touch: Neuroscience, behavioral, and health perspectives* (pp. 351–369). Springer.

Andersen, P. A., Eloy, S. V., Guerrero, L. K. et al. (1995). Romantic jealousy and relational satisfaction: A look at the impact of jealousy experiences and expression. *Communication Reports*, *8*(2), 77–85.

Anderson, G. O. (2010, September). *Loneliness among older adults: A national survey of Adults 45 +* . AARP Research. www.aarp.org/research/topics/life/info-2014/loneliness_2010.html

Anderson, M., & Jiang, J. (2018). *Teens, social media & technology 2018*. Pew Research Center. www.pewresearch.org/internet/2018/05/31/teens-social-media-technology-2018/

Anderson, M., Vogels, E., & Turner, E. (2020). *The virtues and downsides of online dating*. Pew Research Center. www.pewresearch.org/internet/2020/02/06/the-virtues-and-downsides-of-online-dating/

Anderson, R. A. E., Carstens Namie, E. M., & Goodman, E. L. (2021). Valid for who? A preliminary investigation of the validity of two sexual victimization questionnaires in men and sexual minorities. *American Journal of Criminal Justice*, *46*(1), 168–185.

Anderson, R. C., & Surbey, M. K. (2018). Human mate copying as a form of nonindependent mate selection: Findings and considerations. *Evolutionary Behavioral Sciences*, *14*(2), 173–196.

Andrighetto, L., Riva, P., & Gabbiadini, A. (2019). Lonely hearts and angry minds: Online dating rejection increases male (but not female) hostility. *Aggressive Behavior*, *45*(5), 571–581.

Anicich, E. M., Lee, A. J., & Liu, S. (2021). Thanks, but no thanks: Unpacking the relationship between relative power and gratitude. *Personality and Social Psychology Bulletin*, *48*(7), 1005–1023.

Antfolk, J. (2017). Age limits: Men's and women's youngest and oldest considered and actual sex partners. *Evolutionary Psychology*, *15*(1).

Anukriti, S., & Dasgupta, S. (2017). Marriage markets in developing countries. In S. L. Averett, L. M. Argys, & S. D. Hoffman (Eds.), *The Oxford handbook of women and the economy* (pp. 97–120). Oxford University Press.

Apel, R. (2016). The effects of jail and prison confinement on cohabitation and marriage. *Annals of the American Academy of Political and Social Science*, *665*(1), 103–126.

Apostolou, M. (2017). Why people stay single: An evolutionary perspective. *Personality and Individual Differences*, *111*, 263–271.

Apostolou, M. (2021a). Involuntary singlehood and its causes: The effects of flirting capacity, mating effort, choosiness and capacity to perceive signals of interest. *Personality and Individual Differences*, *176*, 110782.

Apostolou, M. (2021b). Plurality in mating: Exploring the occurrence and contingencies of mating strategies. *Personality and Individual Differences*, *175*, 110689.

Apostolou, M. (2022). Catch me if you can: Strategies for hiding infidelity. *Personality and Individual Differences*, *189*, 111494.

Apostolou, M., Aristidou, A., & Eraclide, C. (2019). Reactions to and forgiveness of infidelity: Exploring severity, length of relationship, sex, and previous experience effects. *Adaptive Human Behavior and Physiology*, *5*(4), 317–330.

Apostolou, M., & Christoforou, C. (2020). The art of flirting: What are the traits that make it effective? *Personality and Individual Differences*, *158*, 109866.

Apostolou, M., & Christoforou, C. (2022). What makes single life attractive: An explorative examination of the advantages of singlehood. *Evolutionary Psychological Science*, *8*, 403–412.

Apostolou, M., Constantinou, C., & Anagnostopoulos, S. (2019). Reasons that could lead people to divorce in an evolutionary perspective: Evidence from Cyprus. *Journal of Divorce and Remarriage*, *60*(1), 27–46.

Apostolou, M., & Demosthenous, A. (2021). Why people forgive their intimate partners' infidelity: A taxonomy of reasons. *Adaptive Human Behavior and Physiology*, *7*(1), 54–71.

Apostolou, M., Jiaqing, O., & Esposito, G. (2020). Singles' reasons for being single: Empirical evidence from an evolutionary perspective. *Frontiers in Psychology*, *11*, 746.

Apostolou, M., Papadopoulou, I., Christofi, M., & Vrontis, D. (2019). Mating performance: Assessing flirting skills, mate signal-detection ability, and shyness effects. *Evolutionary Psychology*, *17*(3).

Apostolou, M., Papadopoulou, I., & Georgiadou, P. (2019). Are people single by choice? Involuntary singlehood in an evolutionary perspective. *Evolutionary Psychological Science*, *5*(1), 98–103.

Apostolou, M., Shialos, M., Kyrou, E. et al. (2018). The challenge of starting and keeping a relationship: Prevalence rates and predictors of poor mating performance. *Personality and Individual Differences*, *122*, 19–28.

Archer, J. (2019). The reality and evolutionary significance of human psychological sex differences. *Biological Reviews*, *94*(4), 1381–1415.

Argyle, M., & Henderson, M. (1984). The rules of friendship. *Journal of Social and Personal Relationships*, *1*(2), 211–237.

Arikewuyo, A. O., Eluwole, K. K., & Özad, B. (2021). Influence of lack of trust on romantic relationship problems: The mediating role of partner cell phone snooping. *Psychological Reports*, *124*(1), 348–365.

Arístegui, I., Castro Solano, A., & Buunk, A. P. (2018). Mate preferences in Argentinean transgender people: An evolutionary perspective. *Personal Relationships*, *25*(3), 330–350.

Armstrong, B. F., & Kammrath, L. K. (2015). Depth and breadth tactics in support seeking. *Social Psychological and Personality Science*, *6*(1), 39–46.

Armstrong, H. L., & Reissing, E. D. (2015). Women's motivations to have sex in casual and committed relationships with male and female partners. *Archives of Sexual Behavior*, *44*(4), 921–934.

Arnett, J. J. (2008). The neglected 95%: Why American psychology needs to become less American. *American Psychologist*, *63*(7), 602–614.

Arnold, L. S., & Beelmann, A. (2019). The effects of relationship education in low-income couples: A meta-analysis of randomized-controlled evaluation studies. *Family Relations*, *68*(1), 22–38.

Aron, A., & Aron, E. (1986). *Love and the expansion of self: Understanding attraction and satisfaction*. Hemisphere Publishing Corp./Harper & Row Publishers.

Aron, A., & Aron, E. N. (1991). Love and sexuality. In K. McKinney & S. Sprecher (Eds.), *Sexuality in close relationships* (pp. 25–48). Lawrence Erlbaum.

Aron, A., Aron, E. N., & Smollan, D. (1992). Inclusion of other in the self scale and the structure of interpersonal closeness. *Journal of Personality and Social Psychology*, *63*(4), 596–612.

Aron, A., Aron, E. N., Tudor, M. et al. (1991). Close relationships as including other in the self. *Journal of Personality and Social Psychology*, *60*(2), 241–253.

Aron, A., Fisher, H., Mashek, D. J. et al. (2005). Reward, motivation, and emotion systems associated with early-stage intense romantic love. *Journal of Neurophysiology*, *94*(1), 327–337.

Aron, A., Fisher, H., Strong, G. et al. (2008). Falling in love. In S. Sprecher, A. Wenzel, & J. Harvey (Eds.), *The handbook of relationship initiation* (pp. 315–336). Psychology Press.

Aron, A., Lewandowski, G. W. Jr., Mashek, D. J. et al. (2013). The self-expansion model of motivation and cognition in close relationships. In J. A. Simpson & L. Campbell (Eds.), *The Oxford Handbook of close relationships* (pp. 90–115). Oxford University Press.

Aron, A., Mashek, D., McLaughlin-Volpe, T. et al. (2005). Including close others in the cognitive structure of the self. In M. W. Baldwin (Ed.), *Interpersonal cognition* (pp. 206–232). Guilford Press.

Aron, A., Melinat, E., Aron, E. N. et al. (1997). The experimental generation of interpersonal closeness: A procedure and some preliminary findings. *Personality and Social Psychology Bulletin*, *23*(4), 363–377.

Aron, A., Norman, C., Aron, E. et al. (2000). Couples' shared participation in novel and arousing activities and experienced relationship quality. *Journal of Personality and Social Psychology*, *78*, 273–284.

Aron, A., Paris, M., & Aron, E. N. (1995). Falling in love: Prospective studies of self-concept change. *Journal of Personality and Social Psychology*, *69*(6), 1102–1112.

Aron, E. N., & Aron, A. (1996). Love and expansion of the self: The state of the model. *Personal Relationships*, *3*(1), 45–58.

Aronson, E., & Worchel, P. (1966). Similarity versus liking as determinants of interpersonal attractiveness. *Psychonomic Science*, *5*(4), 157–158.

Arriaga, X. B. (2013). An interdependence theory analysis of close relationships. In J. A. Simpson & L. Campbell (Eds.), *The Oxford Handbook of close relationships* (pp. 39–65). Oxford University Press.

Arriaga, X. B., & Agnew, C. R. (2001). Being committed: Affective, cognitive, and conative components of relationship commitment. *Personality and Social Psychology Bulletin*, *27*(9), 1190–1203.

Arslan, R. C., Schilling, K. M., Gerlach, T. M. et al. (2018). Using 26,000 diary entries to show ovulatory changes in sexual desire and behavior. *Journal of Personality and Social Psychology, 121*(2), 410–431.

Asendorpf, J. B. (2000). Shyness and adaptation to the social world of university. In W. R. Crozier (Ed.), *Shyness: Development, consolidation, and change* (pp. 119–136). Routledge.

Ashokkumar, A., & Swann, W. B. (2020). The saboteur within: Self-verification strivings can make praise toxic. In E. Brummelman (Ed.), *Psychological perspectives on praise* (pp. 11–18). Routledge.

Atari, M., Chaudhary, N., & Al-Shawaf, L. (2020). Mate preferences in three Muslim-majority countries: Sex differences and personality correlates. *Social Psychological and Personality Science, 11*(4), 533–545.

Attridge, M. (2013). Jealousy and relationship closeness: Exploring the good (reactive) and bad (suspicious) sides of romantic jealousy. *SAGE Open, 3*(1), 2158244013476054.

Auger, E., Hurley, S., & Lydon, J. E. (2016). Compensatory relationship enhancement: An identity motivated response to relationship threat. *Social Psychological and Personality Science, 7*(3), 223–231.

Austin, H. (2021, July 30). What are the "twisties?" Simone Biles explains gymnastics struggle at Tokyo Olympics. *NBC News.* www.nbcnews.com/news/olympics/what-are-twisties-simone-biles-explains-gymnastics-struggle-tokyo-olympics-n1275460

Axinn, W. G., & Thornton, A. (1992). The relationship between cohabitation and divorce: Selectivity or causal influence? *Demography, 29*(3), 357–374.

Aydin, N., Krueger, J. I., Fischer, J. et al. (2012). "Man's best friend": How the presence of a dog reduces mental distress after social exclusion. *Journal of Experimental Social Psychology, 48*(1), 446–449.

Ayuso, L. (2019). What future awaits couples Living Apart Together (LAT)? *Sociological Review, 67*(1), 226–244.

Backman, C. W., & Secord, P. F. (1959). The effect of perceived liking on interpersonal attraction. *Human Relations, 12*(4), 379–384.

Bäckström, C., Kåreholt, I., Thorstensson, S. et al. (2018). Quality of couple relationship among first-time mothers and partners, during pregnancy and the first six months of parenthood. *Sexual and Reproductive Healthcare, 17*, 56–64.

Bagley, L. A., Kimberly, C., Marino, A. et al. (2020). Beliefs about premarital cohabitation: Do individuals believe living together helps divorce-proof marriage? *Contemporary Family Therapy, 42*(3), 284–290.

Baker, L. R., & McNulty, J. K. (2020). The Relationship Problem Solving (RePS) Model: How partners influence one another to resolve relationship problems. *Personality and Social Psychology Review, 24*(1), 53–77.

Baker, L. R., McNulty, J. K., & VanderDrift, L. E. (2017). Expectations for future relationship satisfaction: Unique sources and critical implications for commitment. *Journal of Experimental Psychology: General, 146*(5), 700–721.

Baker, M., & Elizabeth, V. (2013). "Did you just ask me to marry you?": The gendered nature of heterosexual relationship progressions. *Women's Studies Journal, 27*(2), 32–43.

Baker, R. E., & Terrill, J. L. (2017). Marriage enrichment. In J. Carson & S. B. Dermer (Eds.), *The Sage encyclopedia of marriage, family, and couples counseling* (pp. 1028–1034). Sage Publications.

Balliet, D., Molho, C., Columbus, S. et al. (2022). Prosocial and punishment behaviors in everyday life. *Current Opinion in Psychology, 43*, 278–283.

Balsam, K. F., Rothblum, E. D., & Beauchaine, T. P. (2005). Victimization over the life span: A comparison of lesbian, gay, bisexual, and heterosexual siblings. *Journal of Consulting and Clinical Psychology, 73*(3), 477–487.

Balsam, K. F., Rothblum, E. D., & Wickham, R. E. (2017). Longitudinal predictors of relationship dissolution among same-sex and heterosexual couples. *Couple and Family Psychology: Research and Practice, 6*(4), 247–257.

Balzarini, R. N., Campbell, L., Kohut, T. et al. (2017). Perceptions of primary and secondary relationships in polyamory. *PLOS One, 12*(5), e0177841.

Balzarini, R. N., Dharma, C., Muise, A. et al. (2019). Eroticism versus nurturance: How eroticism and nurturance differs in polyamorous and monogamous relationships. *Social Psychology, 50*(3), 185–200.

Balzarini, R. N., Dobson, K., Kohut, T. et al. (2018). *The role of relationship acceptance and romantic secrecy in commitment processes and proportion of time spent on sex.* Manuscript in preparation.

Banerjee, S. (2020, February 4). Dutee Chand is helping a new India sprint to the finish line. *OlympicChannel.Com.* www.olympicchannel.com/en/stories/features/detail/dutee-chand-running-india-tokyo-2020-olympics/

Baranowski, A. M., & Hecht, H. (2015). Gender differences and similarities in receptivity to sexual invitations: Effects of location and risk perception. *Archives of Sexual Behavior, 44*(8), 2257–2265.

Barbaro, N., Sela, Y., Atari, M. et al. (2019). Romantic attachment and mate retention behavior: The mediating role of perceived risk of partner infidelity. *Journal of Social and Personal Relationships, 36*(3), 940–956.

Barber, L. L., & Cooper, M. L. (2014). Rebound sex: Sexual motives and behaviors following a relationship breakup. *Archives of Sexual Behavior*, *43*(2), 251–265.

Barclay, P. (2010). Altruism as a courtship display: Some effects of third-party generosity on audience perceptions. *British Journal of Psychology*, *101*(1), 123–135.

Barelds, D. P. H., & Dijkstra, P. (2009). Positive illusions about a partner's physical attractiveness and relationship quality. *Journal of Research in Personality*, *16*, 263–283.

Barelds, D. P. H., & Dijkstra, P. (2011). Positive illusions about a partner's personality and relationship quality. *Journal of Research in Personality*, *45*(1), 37–43.

Barelds, D. P. H., Dijkstra, P., Koudenburg, N. et al. (2011). An assessment of positive illusions of the physical attractiveness of romantic partners. *Journal of Social and Personal Relationships*, *28*(5), 706–719.

Bar-Kalifa, E., Pshedetzky-Shochat, R., Rafaeli, E. et al. (2017). Daily support equity in romantic couples. *Social Psychological and Personality Science*, *9*(7), 790–801.

Bar-Kalifa, E., & Rafaeli, E. (2014). Above and below baselines: The nonmonotonic effects of dyadic emotional support in daily life. *Journal of Social and Personal Relationships*, *32*(2), 161–179.

Barnett, M., Maciel, I., & Moore, J. (2021). "Coming out" as a virgin (or not): The disclosure of virginity status scale. *Sexuality and Culture*, *25*(6), 2142–2157.

Barnett, M. D., & Moore, J. M. (2017). The construct validity of the First Coital Affective Reaction Scale and Virginity Beliefs Scale. *Personality and Individual Differences*, *109*, 102–110.

Barrera, M., Sandler, I. N., & Ramsay, T. B. (1981). Preliminary development of a scale of social support: Studies on college students. *American Journal of Community Psychology*, *9*(4), 435–447.

Barrios, R. J., & Lundquist, J. H. (2012). Boys just want to have fun? Masculinity, sexual behaviors, and romantic intentions of gay and straight males in college. *Journal of LGBT Youth*, *9*(4), 271–296.

Barry, R. A., Lawrence, E., & Langer, A. (2008). Conceptualization and assessment of disengagement in romantic relationships. *Personal Relationships*, *15*(3), 297–315.

Barta, W. D., & Kiene, S. M. (2005). Motivations for infidelity in heterosexual dating couples: The roles of gender, personality differences, and sociosexual orientation. *Journal of Social and Personal Relationships*, *22*(3), 339–360.

Bartholomew, K. (1990). Avoidance of intimacy: An attachment perspective. *Journal of Social and Personal Relationships*, *7*(2), 147–178.

Bartholomew, K., & Horowitz, L. M. (1991). Attachment styles among young adults: A test of a four-category model of childhood attachment and internal models. *Journal of Personality and Social Psychology*, *61*(2), 226–244.

Bartoli, A. M., & Clark, M. D. (2006). The dating game: Similarities and differences in dating scripts among college students. *Sexuality and Culture*, *10*(4), 54–80.

Barton, A. W., Beach, S. R. H., Bryant, C. M. et al. (2018). Stress spillover, African Americans' couple and health outcomes, and the stress-buffering effect of family-centered prevention. *Journal of Family Psychology*, *32*(2), 186–196.

Barton, A. W., & Bryant, C. M. (2016). Financial strain, trajectories of marital processes, and African American Newlyweds' Marital Instability. *Journal of Family Psychology*, *30*(6), 657–664.

Barton, A. W., Futris, T. G., & Nielsen, R. B. (2015). Linking financial distress to marital quality: The intermediary roles of demand/withdraw and spousal gratitude expressions. *Personal Relationships*, *22*(3), 536–549.

Barton, A. W., Lavner, J. A., Hawrilenko, M. J. et al. (2021). Trajectories of relationship and individual functioning among waitlisted couples for an online relationship intervention. *Family Process*, *60*(4), 1233–1248.

Barton, A. W., Lavner, J. A., Stanley, S. M. et al. (2020). "Will you complete this survey too?" Differences between individual versus dyadic samples in relationship research. *Journal of Family Psychology*, *34*(2), 196–203.

Bateman, A. J. (1948). Intra-sexual selection in Drosophila. *Heredity*, *2*(3), 349–368.

Baucom, B. R., Atkins, D. C., Rowe, L. S. et al. (2015). Prediction of treatment response at 5-year follow-up in a randomized clinical trial of behaviorally based couple therapies. *Journal of Consulting and Clinical Psychology*, *83*(1), 103–114.

Baucom, B. R., Dickenson, J. A., Atkins, D. C. et al. (2015). The interpersonal process model of demand/withdraw behavior. *Journal of Family Psychology*, *29*(1), 80–90.

Baucom, B. R., Simpson, L. E., Atkins, D. C. et al. (2009). Prediction of response to treatment in a randomized clinical trial of couple therapy: A 2-year follow up. *Journal of Consulting and Clinical Psychology*, *77*(1), 160–173.

Baucom, D. H., Epstein, N. B., Kirby, J. S. et al. (2015). Cognitive-behavioral couple therapy. In A. S. Gurman, J. L. Lebow, & D. K. Snyder (Eds.), *Clinical handbook of couple therapy* (5th ed., pp. 23–60). Guilford Press.

Baucom, K. J. W., Sevier, M., Eldridge, K. A. et al. (2011). Observed communication in couples 2 years after Integrative and Traditional Behavioral Couple Therapy: Outcome and link with 5-year follow-up. *Journal of Consulting and Clinical Psychology*, *79*(5), 565–576.

Baughman, H. M., Jonason, P. K., Veselka, L. et al. (2014). Four shades of sexual fantasies linked to the Dark Triad. *Personality and Individual Differences*, *67*, 47–51.

Baumeister, R. F. (2000). Gender differences in erotic plasticity: The female sex drive as socially flexible and responsive. *Psychological Bulletin, 126*(3), 347–374.

Baumeister, R. F., & Bratslavsky, E. (1999). Passion, intimacy, and time: Passionate love as a function of change in intimacy. *Personality and Social Psychology Review, 3*(1), 49–67.

Baumeister, R. F., Catanese, K. R., & Vohs, K. D. (2001). Is there a gender difference in strength of sex drive? Theoretical views, conceptual distinctions, and a review of relevant evidence. *Personality and Social Psychology Review, 5*(3), 242–272.

Baumeister, R. F., & Dhavale, D. (2012). Two sides of romantic rejection. In M. Leary (Ed.), *Interpersonal rejection* (pp. 55–71). Oxford University Press.

Baumeister, R. F., & Leary, M. R. (1995). The need to belong: Desire for interpersonal attachments as a fundamental human motivation. *Psychological Bulletin, 117*, 497–529.

Baumeister, R. F., & Tice, D. M. (1990). Anxiety and social exclusion. *Journal of Social and Clinical Psychology, 9*(2), 165–195.

Baumeister, R. F., & Twenge, J. M. (2002). Effects of social exclusion on cognitive processes: Anticipated aloneness reduces intelligent thought. *Journal of Personality and Social Psychology, 83*(4), 817–827.

Baumeister, R. F., Wotman, S. R., & Stillwell, A. (1993). Unrequited love: On heartbreak, anger, guilt, scriptlessness, and humiliation. *Journal of Personality and Social Psychology, 64*, 377–394.

Baxter, L. A., & Bullis, C. (1986). Turning points in developing relationships. *Human Communication Research, 12*(4), 469–493.

Baxter, L. A., Dun, T., & Sahistein, E. (2001). Rules for relating communicated among social network members. *Journal of Social and Personal Relationships, 18*(2), 173–199.

Baxter, L. A., & Montgomery, B. (1996). *Relating: Dialogues and dialectics*. Guilford Press.

Baxter, L. A., & Widenmann, S. (1993). Revealing and not revealing the status of romantic relationships to social networks. *Journal of Social and Personal Relationships, 10*(3), 321–337.

Bazzini, D. G., & Shaffer, D. R. (1999). Resisting temptation revisited: Devaluation versus enhancement of an attractive suitor by exclusive and nonexclusive daters. *Personality and Social Psychology Bulletin, 25*(2), 162–176.

BBC. (2019, May 19). Dutee Chand becomes first openly gay Indian athlete. *BBC.Com*. www.bbc.com/news/world-asia-india-48327918

Beach, S. R. H., Amir, N., Fincham, F. D. et al. (2005). The taxometrics of marriage: Is marital discord categorical? *Journal of Family Psychology, 19*(2), 276–285.

Beals, K. P., Impett, E. A., & Peplau, L. A. (2002). Lesbians in love: Why some relationships endure and others end. *Journal of Lesbian Studies, 6*(1), 53–63.

Beasley, C. C., & Ager, R. (2019). Emotionally focused couples therapy: A systematic review of its effectiveness over the past 19 years. *Journal of Evidence-Based Social Work, 16*(2), 144–159.

Beck, L. (2021, April 28). Willow Smith says she's not polyamorous for sex: "I have the least sex." *BestLifeOnline.Com*. https://bestlifeonline.com/news-willow-smith-polyamorous/

Beckes, L., & Coan, J. A. (2011). Social baseline theory: The role of social proximity in emotion and economy of action. *Social and Personality Psychology Compass, 5*, 976–988.

Beckes, L., & Coan, J. A. (2015). The distress-relief dynamic in attachment bonding. In V. Zayas & C. Hazan (Eds.), *Bases of adult attachment* (pp. 11–33). Springer Science and Business Media LLC.

Beckes, L., & Sbarra, D. A. (2022). Social baseline theory: State of the science and new directions. *Current Opinion in Psychology, 43*, 36–41.

Beckmeyer, J. J., Herbenick, D., & Eastman-Mueller, H. (2021). Long-distance romantic relationships among college students: Prevalence, correlates, and dynamics in a campus probability survey. *Journal of American College Health*. Advance online publication. https://doi.org/10.1080/07448481.2021.1978464

Beckmeyer, J. J., & Jamison, T. B. (2020). Is breaking up hard to do? Exploring emerging adults' perceived abilities to end romantic relationships. *Family Relations, 69*(5), 1028–1040.

Bell, C. A., Kamble, S. V., & Fincham, F. D. (2018). Forgiveness, attributions, and marital quality in U.S. and Indian marriages. *Journal of Couple and Relationship Therapy, 17*(4), 276–293.

Belus, J. M., Pentel, K. Z., Cohen, M. J. et al. (2019). Staying connected: An examination of relationship maintenance behaviors in long-distance relationships. *Marriage and Family Review, 55*(1), 78–98.

Bendixen, M. (2014). Evidence of systematic bias in sexual over- and underperception of naturally occurring events: A direct replication of Haselton (2003) in a more gender-equal culture. *Evolutionary Psychology, 12*(5), 1004–1021.

Benjamin, L., Ni, X., & Wang, S. (2021). Implicit support differs across five groups in the US, Taiwan, and Mexico. *Cultural Diversity and Ethnic Minority Psychology, 27*(4), 675–683.

Bennett, M., & Denes, A. (2019). Lying in bed: An analysis of deceptive affectionate messages during sexual activity in young adults' romantic relationships. *Communication Quarterly, 67*, 140–157.

Bennett, M., LoPresti, B. J., & Denes, A. (2019). Exploring trait affectionate communication and post sex communication as mediators of the association between attachment and sexual satisfaction. *Personality and Individual Differences*, *151*, 109505.

Bereczkei, T., & Mesko, N. (2006). Hair length, facial attractiveness, personality attribution: A multiple fitness model of hairdressing. *Review of Psychology*, *13*(1), 35–42.

Beres, M. A. (2007). "Spontaneous" sexual consent: An analysis of sexual consent literature. *Feminism and Psychology*, *17*(1), 93–108.

Berg, E., Trost, M., Schneider, I. E. et al. (2001). Dyadic exploration of the relationship of leisure satisfaction, leisure time, and gender to relationship satisfaction. *Leisure Sciences*, *23*(1), 35–46.

Berger, C. R. (1997). Producing messages under uncertainty. In J. Greene (Ed.), *Message Production: Advances in communication theory* (pp. 221–244). Lawrence Erlbaum.

Berger, C. R., & Bradac, J. (1982). *Language and social knowledge: Uncertainty in interpersonal relations*. Edward Arnold.

Berger, C. R., & Calabrese, R. J. (1975). Some explorations in initial interaction and beyond: Toward a developmental theory of interpersonal communication. *Human Communication Research*, *1*(2), 99–112.

Berinsky, A. J., Huber, G. A., & Lenz, G. S. (2012). Evaluating online labor markets for experimental research: Amazon.com's Mechanical Turk. *Political Analysis*, *20*(3), 351–368.

Berinsky, A. J., Margolis, M. F., & Sances, M. W. (2014). Separating the shirkers from the workers? Making sure respondents pay attention on self-administered surveys. *American Journal of Political Science*, *58*(3), 739–753.

Berkman, L. F., & Syme, S. L. (1979). Social networks, host resistance, and mortality: A nine-year follow-up study of Alameda County residents. *Social Networks*, *109*, 186–204.

Bernieri, F. J., & Rosenthal, R. (1991). Interpersonal coordination: Behavior matching and interactional synchrony. In R. S. Feldman & B. Rimé (Eds.), *Fundamentals of nonverbal behavior* (pp. 401–432). Cambridge University Press.

Bernstein, M. J., Young, S. G., Brown, C. M. et al. (2008). Adaptive responses to social exclusion: Social rejection improves detection of real and fake smiles. *Psychological Science*, *19*(10), 981–983.

Berscheid, E. (2006). Searching for the meaning of "love." In R. J. Sternberg & K. Weis (Eds.), *The new psychology of love* (pp. 171–183). Yale University Press.

Berscheid, E. (2010). Love in the fourth dimension. *Annual Review of Psychology*, *61*, 1–25.

Berscheid, E., Dion, K., Walster, E. et al. (1971). Physical attractiveness and dating choice: A test of the matching hypothesis. *Journal of Experimental Social Psychology*, *7*(2), 173–189.

Berscheid, E., & Hatfield, E. (1969). *Interpersonal attraction*. Addison-Wesley.

Berscheid, E., & Walster, E. (1978). *Interpersonal attraction* (2nd ed.). Addison-Wesley.

Bertsch, L., Choinski, W., Kempf, K., Baldwin, J., Clarke, H., Lampert, B., ... & Zoghi, A. (2020). *Time-in-cell 2019: A snapshot of restrictive housing based on a nationwide survey of US prison systems*. The Liman Center at Yale Law School. http://dx.doi.org/10.2139/ssrn.3694548

Betz, D. E., & DiDonato, T. E. (2020). Is it sexy to be sexist? How stereotyped humor affects romantic attraction. *Personal Relationships*, *27*(4), 732–759.

Betzig, L. (1989). Causes of conjugal dissolution: A cross-cultural study. *Current Anthropology*, *30*(5), 654–676.

Bevan, J. L., Hefner, V., & Love, A. (2014). An exploration of topics, conflict styles, and rumination in romantic non-serial and serial arguments. *Southern Communication Journal*, *79*(4), 347–360.

Bhogal, M. S., & Bartlett, J. E. (2021). Further support for the role of heroism in human mate choice. *Evolutionary Behavioral Sciences*, *15*(3), 299–304.

Bhogal, M. S., Farrelly, D., Galbraith, N. et al. (2020). The role of altruistic costs in human mate choice. *Personality and Individual Differences*, *160*, 109939.

Biehle, S. N., & Mickelson, K. D. (2012). Provision and receipt of emotional spousal support: The impact of visibility on well-being. *Couple and Family Psychology: Research and Practice*, *1*(3), 244–251.

Birditt, K. S., Brown, E., Orbuch, T. L. et al. (2010). Marital conflict behaviors and implications for divorce over 16 years. *Journal of Marriage and Family*, *72*(5), 1188–1204.

Birditt, K. S., Hope, S., Brown, E. et al. (2012). Developmental trajectories of marital happiness over 16 years. *Research in Human Development*, *9*(2), 126–144.

Birditt, K. S., Wan, W. H., Orbuch, T. L., & Antonucci, T. C. (2017). The development of marital tension: Implications for divorce among married couples. *Developmental Psychology*, *53*(10), 1995–2006.

Birmingham, W. C., Wadsworth, L. L., Hung, M. et al. (2019). Ambivalence in the early years of marriage: Impact on ambulatory blood pressure and relationship processes. *Annals of Behavioral Medicine*, *53*, 1069–1080.

Birnbaum, G. E. (2013). Sexy building blocks: The contribution of the sexual system to attachment formation and maintenance. In M. Mikulincer & P. R. Shaver (Eds.), *Mechanisms of social connection: From brain to group* (pp. 315–332). American Psychological Association.

Birnbaum, G. E. (2015). On the convergence of sexual urges and emotional bonds. In J. A. Simpson & W. S. Rholes (Eds.), *Attachment theory and research: New directions and emerging themes* (pp. 170–194). Guilford Press.

Birnbaum, G. E., & Finkel, E. J. (2015). The magnetism that holds us together: Sexuality and relationship maintenance across relationship development. *Current Opinion in Psychology*, *1*, 29–33.

Birnbaum, G. E., Idit, O., Mikulincer, M. et al. (1997). When marriage breaks up: Does attachment style contribute to coping and mental health? *Journal of Social and Personal Relationships*, *14*(5), 643–654.

Birnbaum, G. E., Iluz, M., Plotkin, E. et al. (2020). Seeing what you want to see: Sexual activation makes potential partners seem more appealing and romantically interested. *Journal of Social and Personal Relationships*, *37*(12), 3051–3069.

Birnbaum, G. E., Iluz, M., & Reis, H. T. (2020). Making the right first impression: Sexual priming encourages attitude change and self-presentation lies during encounters with potential partners. *Journal of Experimental Social Psychology*, *86*, 103904.

Birnbaum, G. E., Kanat-Maymon, Y., Mizrahi, M. et al. (2018). Are you into me? Uncertainty and sexual desire in online encounters and established relationships. *Computers in Human Behavior*, *85*, 372–384.

Birnbaum, G. E., Mizrahi, M., Kaplan, A. et al. (2017). Sex unleashes your tongue: Sexual priming motivates self-disclosure to a new acquaintance and interest in future interactions. *Personality and Social Psychology Bulletin*, *43*(5), 706–715.

Birnbaum, G. E., Mizrahi, M., & Reis, H. T. (2019). Fueled by desire: Sexual activation facilitates the enactment of relationship-initiating behaviors. *Journal of Social and Personal Relationships*, *36*(10), 3057–3074.

Birnbaum, G. E., & Reis, H. T. (2012). When does responsiveness pique sexual interest? Attachment and sexual desire in initial acquaintanceships. *Personality and Social Psychology Bulletin*, *38*(7), 946–958.

Bisson, M. A., & Levine, T. R. (2009). Negotiating a friends with benefits relationship. *Archives of Sexual Behavior*, *38*(1), 66–73.

Bittman, M., & Wajcman, J. (2000). The rush hour: The character of leisure time and gender equity. *Social Forces*, *79*(1), 165–189.

Bjorklund, D. F., & Shackelford, T. K. (1999). Differences in parental investment contribute to important differences between men and women. *Current Directions in Psychological Science*, *8*(3), 86–89.

Blackhart, G. C., Nelson, B. C., Knowles, M. L. et al. (2009). Rejection elicits emotional reactions but neither causes immediate distress nor lowers self-esteem: A meta-analytic review of 192 studies on social exclusion. *Personality and Social Psychology Review*, *13*(3), 269–309.

Blackstone, A., & Stewart, M. D. (2012). Choosing to be child-free: Research on the decision not to parent. *Sociology Compass*, *6*(9), 718–727.

Blair, K. L., & Holmberg, D. (2008). Perceived social network support and well-being in same-sex versus mixed-sex romantic relationships. *Journal of Social and Personal Relationships*, *25*(5), 769–791.

Blair, K. L., Holmberg, D., & Pukall, C. F. (2018). Support processes in same- and mixed-sex relationships: Type and source matters. *Personal Relationships*, *25*(3), 374–393.

Blair, K. L., & Hoskin, R. A. (2019). Transgender exclusion from the world of dating: Patterns of acceptance and rejection of hypothetical trans dating partners as a function of sexual and gender identity. *Journal of Social and Personal Relationships*, *36*(7), 2074–2095.

Blair, K. L., & Pukall, C. F. (2014). Can less be more? Comparing duration vs. Frequency of sexual encounters in same-sex and mixed-sex relationships. *Canadian Journal of Human Sexuality*, *23*(2), 123–136.

Blair, K. L., & Pukall, C. F. (2015). Family matters, but sometimes chosen family matters more: Perceived social network influence in the dating decisions of same- and mixed-sex couples. *Canadian Journal of Human Sexuality*, *24*(3), 257–270.

Blanner Kristiansen, C., Kjær, J. N., Hjorth, P. et al. (2019). Prevalence of common mental disorders in widowhood: A systematic review and meta-analysis. *Journal of Affective Disorders*, *245*, 1016–1023.

Blascovich, J., & Tomaka, J. (1996). The biopsychosocial model of arousal regulation. In M. P. Zanna (Ed.), *Advances in experimental social psychology* (pp. 1–46). Academic Press.

Blau, P. (1964). *Social exchange theory*. John Wiley & Sons.

Bleske-Rechek, A., Somers, E., Micke, C. et al. (2012). Benefit or burden? Attraction in cross-sex friendship. *Journal of Social and Personal Relationships*, *29*(5), 569–596.

Bode, A., & Kushnick, G. (2021). Proximate and ultimate perspectives on romantic love. *Frontiers in Psychology*, *12*, 573123.

Bodenmann, G., Charvoz, L., Bradbury, T. N. et al. (2007). The role of stress in divorce: A three-nation retrospective study. *Journal of Social and Personal Relationships*, *24*(5), 707–728.

Bodenmann, G., Ledermann, T., & Bradbury, T. N. (2007). Stress, sex, and satisfaction in marriage. *Personal Relationships*, *14*(4), 551–569.

Bodenmann, G., Meuwly, N., Germann, J. et al. (2015). Effects of stress on the social support provided by men and women in intimate relationships. *Psychological Science, 26* (10), 1584–1594.

Bodenmann, G., & Shantinath, S. D. (2004). The Couples Coping Enhancement Training (CCET): A new approach to prevention of marital distress based upon stress and coping. *Family Relations, 53*(5), 477–484.

Boelen, P. A., & van den Hout, M. A. (2010). Inclusion of other in the self and breakup-related grief following relationship dissolution. *Journal of Loss and Trauma, 15*(6), 534–547.

Bogaert, A. F. (2004). Asexuality: Prevalence and associated factors in a national probability sample. *Journal of Sex Research, 41*(3), 279–287.

Bogaert, A. F. (2015). Asexuality: What it is and why it matters. *Journal of Sex Research, 52*(4), 362–379.

Bohannan, P. (1970). Divorce chains, households of remarriage, and multiple divorcers. In P. Bohannan (Ed.), *Divorce and after* (pp. 128–139). Anchor.

Boiger, M. (2019). A cultural psychological perspective on close relationships. In D. Schoebi & B. Campos (Eds.), *New directions in the psychology of close relationships* (pp. 83–99). Routledge.

Boisvert, S., & Poulin, F. (2017). Navigating in and out of romantic relationships from adolescence to emerging adulthood: Distinct patterns and their correlates at age 25. *Emerging Adulthood, 5*(3), 216–223.

Bolger, N., & Amarel, D. (2007). Effects of social support visibility on adjustment to stress: Experimental evidence. *Journal of Personality and Social Psychology, 92*(3), 458–475.

Bolger, N., & Laurenceau, J. P. (2012). *Intensive longitudinal methods: An introduction to diary and experience sampling research.* Guilford Press.

Bolger, N., Zuckerman, A., & Kessler, R. C. (2000). Invisible support and adjustment to stress. *Journal of Personality and Social Psychology, 79*(6), 953–961.

Bonam, C. M., & Shih, M. (2009). Exploring multiracial individuals' comfort with intimate interracial relationships. *Journal of Social Issues, 65*(1), 87–103.

Bonanno, G. A., Wortman, C. B., Lehman, D. R. et al. (2002). Resilience to loss and chronic grief: A prospective study from preloss to 18-months postloss. *Journal of Personality and Social Psychology, 83*(5), 1150–1164.

Borau, S., Elgaaied-Gambier, L., & Barbarossa, C. (2021). The green mate appeal: Men's pro-environmental consumption is an honest signal of commitment to their partner. *Psychology and Marketing, 38*, 266–285.

Borbely, A., Bauman, F., Bradeis, D. et al. (1981). Sleep deprivation: Effect on sleep stages and EEG power density in man. *Electroencephalography and Clinical Neurophysiology, 51*(5), 483–493.

Borelli, J., & Prinstein, M. (2006). Reciprocal, longitudinal associations among adolescents' negative feedback-seeking, depressive symptoms, and peer relations. *Journal of Abnormal Child Psychology, 34*, 159–169.

Bossard, J. (1932). Residential propinquity as a factor in marriage selection. *American Journal of Sociology, 38*(2), 219–224.

Bourassa, K. J., Sbarra, D. A., & Whisman, M. A. (2015). Women in very low quality marriages gain life satisfaction following divorce. *Journal of Family Psychology, 29*(3), 490–499.

Bouza, J., Camacho-Thompson, D. E., Carlo, G. et al. (2018, June 21). *The science is clear: Separating families has long-term damaging psychological and health consequences for children, families, and communities.* The Chronical of Evidence-Based Mentoring. www.evidencebasedmentoring .org/the-science-is-clear-separating-families-has-long-term-damaging-psychological-and-health-consequences-for-chil dren-families-and-communities/

Bovet, J. (2019). Evolutionary theories and men's preferences for women's waist-to-hip ratio: Which hypotheses remain? A systematic review. *Frontiers in Psychology, 10*, 1221.

Bowdring, M. A., & Sayette, M. A. (2018). Perception of physical attractiveness when consuming and not consuming alcohol: A meta-analysis. *Addiction, 113*(9), 1585–1597.

Bowlby, J. (1973). *Attachment and loss,* Vol. 2: *Separation: Anxiety and anger.* Basic Books.

Bowlby, J. (1980). *Attachment and loss,* Vol. 3: *Sadness and depression.* Basic Books.

Bowlby, J. (1982). *Attachment and loss,* Vol. 1: *Attachment* (2nd ed.). Basic Books.

Bowlby, J. (1988). *A secure base: Parent–child attachment and healthy human development.* Basic Books.

Bowman, J. L., & Dollahite, D. C. (2013). "Why would such a person dream about Heaven?" Family, faith, and happiness in arranged marriages in India. *Journal of Comparative Family Studies, 44*(2), 207–226.

Boyd, B., Stephens, D. P., Eaton, A. et al. (2020). Exploring partner scarcity: Highly educated Black women and dating compromise. *Sexuality Research and Social Policy, 18*, 702–714.

Boyes, A. D., & Fletcher, G. J. O. (2007). Metaperceptions of bias in intimate relationships. *Journal of Personality and Social Psychology, 92*(2), 286–306.

Boysen, G. A., Morton, J., & Nieves, T. (2019). Mental illness as a relationship dealbreaker. *Stigma and Health, 4*(4), 421–428.

Bradbury, T. N., & Bodenmann, G. (2020). Interventions for couples. *Annual Review of Clinical Psychology, 16*, 99–123.

Bradbury, T. N., & Fincham, F. D. (1990). Attributions in marriage: Review and critique. *Psychological Bulletin, 107*(1), 3–33.

Bradford, N. J., & Catalpa, J. M. (2019). Social and psychological heterogeneity among binary transgender, non-binary transgender and cisgender individuals. *Psychology and Sexuality, 10*(1), 69–82.

Brady, A., Baker, L. R., & Miller, R. S. (2020). Look but don't touch? Self-regulation determines whether noticing attractive alternatives increases infidelity. *Journal of Family Psychology, 34*(2), 135–144.

Brady, A., Baker, L. R., Muise, A. et al. (2021). Gratitude increases the motivation to fulfill a partner's sexual needs. *Social Psychological and Personality Science, 12*(2), 273–281.

Braithwaite, S., & Holt-Lunstad, J. (2017). Romantic relationships and mental health. *Current Opinion in Psychology, 13*, 120–125.

Braithwaite, S. R., Delevi, R., & Fincham, F. D. (2010). Romantic relationships and the physical and mental health of college students. *Personal Relationships, 17*(1), 1–12.

Braithwaite, S. R., Doxey, R. A., Dowdle, K. K. et al. (2016). The unique influences of parental divorce and parental conflict on emerging adults in romantic relationships. *Journal of Adult Development, 23*(4), 214–225.

Braithwaite, S. R., & Fincham, F. D. (2007). ePREP: Computer based prevention of relationship dysfunction, depression and anxiety. *Journal of Social and Clinical Psychology, 26*(5), 609–622.

Braithwaite, S. R., & Fincham, F. D. (2011). Computer-based dissemination: A randomized clinical trial of ePREP using the actor partner interdependence model. *Behaviour Research and Therapy, 49*(2), 126–131.

Braithwaite, S. R., Mitchell, C. M., Selby, E. A. et al. (2016). Trait forgiveness and enduring vulnerabilities: Neuroticism and catastrophizing influence relationship satisfaction via less forgiveness. *Personality and Individual Differences, 94*, 237–246.

Branand, B., Mashek, D., & Aron, A. (2019). Pair-bonding as inclusion of other in the self: A literature review. *Frontiers in Psychology, 10*(OCT), 2399.

Bratter, J. L., & King, R. B. (2008). "But will it last?": Marital instability among interracial and same-race couples. *Family Relations, 57*(2), 160–171.

Brauer, K., Proyer, R. T., & Chick, G. (2021). Adult playfulness: An update on an understudied individual differences variable and its role in romantic life. *Social and Personality Psychology Compass, 15*(4), e12589.

Bredow, C. A., Cate, R. M., & Huston, T. L. (2008). Have we met before? A conceptual model of first romantic encounters. In S. Sprecher, A. Wenzel, & J. Harvey (Eds.), *Handbook of relationship initiation* (pp. 2–28). Psychology Press.

Brenan, M. (2019, May 29). *Birth control still tops list of morally acceptable issues*. Gallup Poll. https://news.gallup.com/poll/257858/birth-control-tops-list-morally-acceptable-issues.aspx

Brennan, K. A., Clark, C. L., & Shaver, P. R. (1998). Self-report measurement of adult attachment: An integrative overview. In J. A. Simpson & W. S. Rholes (Eds.), *Attachment theory and close relationships* (pp. 46–76). Guilford Press.

Brennan, K. A., Wu, S., & Loev, J. (1998). Adult romantic attachment and individual differences in attitudes toward physical contact in the context of adult romantic relationships. In J. A. Simpson & W. S. Rholes (Eds.), *Attachment theory and close relationships* (pp. 394–428). Guilford Press.

Bretherton, I. (1985). Attachment theory: Retrospect and prospect. *Monographs of the Society for Research in Child Development, 50*, 3–35.

Bretherton, I. (1987). New perspectives on attachment relations: Security, communication, and internal working models. In J. Osofsky (Ed.), *Handbook of infant development* (pp. 1061–1100). John Wiley & Sons.

Bretherton, I. (2010). Fathers in attachment theory and research: A review. *Early Child Development and Care, 180*(1–2), 9–23.

Brewer, M. B., & Gardner, W. (1996). Who is this "we"? Levels of collective identity and self representations. *Journal of Personality and Social Psychology, 71*(1), 83–93.

Brinberg, M., Vanderbilt, R. R., Solomon, D. H., Brinberg, D., & Ram, N. (2021). Using technology to unobtrusively observe relationship development. *Journal of Social and Personal Relationships, 38*(12), 3429–3450.

Bringle, R. G., Winnick, T., & Rydell, R. J. (2013). The prevalence and nature of unrequited love. *SAGE Open, 3*(2), 1–15.

Brinig, M. F., & Allen, D. W. (2000). "These boots are made for walking": Why most divorce filers are women. *American Law and Economics Review, 2*, 126–169.

Broaddus, M. R., Morris, H., & Bryan, A. D. (2010). "It's not what you said, it's how you said it": Perceptions of condom proposers by gender and strategy. *Sex Roles, 62*(9), 603–614.

Brock, R. L., & Lawrence, E. (2014). Intrapersonal, interpersonal, and contextual risk factors for overprovision of partner support in marriage. *Journal of Family Psychology, 28*(1), 54–64.

Bronfenbrenner, U. (1977). Toward an experimental ecology of human development. *American Psychologist, 32*(7), 513–531.

Bronfenbrenner, U. (1979). *The ecology of human development: Experiments by nature and design.* Harvard University Press.

Bronfenbrenner, U., Arastah, J., Hetherington, M. et al. (1986). Ecology of the family as a context for human development: Research perspectives. *Developmental Psychology, 22*(6), 723–742.

Bronfenbrenner, U., & Morris, P. A. (1998). The ecology of developmental processes. In W. Damon & R. M. Lerner (Eds.), *Handbook of child psychology: Theoretical models of human development* (pp. 993–1028). John Wiley & Sons.

Brotto, L., Atallah, S., Johnson-Agbakwu, C. et al. (2016). Psychological and interpersonal dimensions of sexual function and dysfunction. *Journal of Sexual Medicine, 13*(4), 538–571.

Brotto, L. A., & Yule, M. (2017). Asexuality: Sexual orientation, paraphilia, sexual dysfunction, or none of the above? *Archives of Sexual Behavior, 46,* 619–627.

Brown, A., Barker, E. D., & Rahman, Q. (2020). A systematic scoping review of the prevalence, etiological, psychological, and interpersonal factors associated with BDSM. *Journal of Sex Research, 57*(6), 781–811.

Brown, C. L., Chen, K.-H., Wells, J. L. et al. (2021). Shared emotions in shared lives: Moments of co-experienced affect, more than individually experienced affect, linked to relationship quality. *Emotion, 22*(6), 1387–1393.

Brown, C. L., & Fredrickson, B. L. (2021). Characteristics and consequences of co-experienced positive affect: Understanding the origins of social skills, social bonds, and caring, healthy communities. *Current Opinion in Behavioral Sciences, 39,* 58–63.

Brown, M., Keefer, L., Sacco, D. et al. (2021). Demonstrate values: Behavioral displays of moral outrage as a cue to long-term mate potential. *Emotion, 22*(6), 1239–1254.

Brown, M., & Sacco, D. F. (2018). Put a (limbal) ring on it: Women perceive men's limbal rings as a health cue in short-term mating domains. *Personality and Social Psychology Bulletin, 44*(1), 80–91.

Brown, M., & Sacco, D. F. (2019). Is pulling the lever sexy? Deontology as a downstream cue to long-term mate quality. *Journal of Social and Personal Relationships, 36*(3), 957–976.

Brown, M., Sacco, D. F., & Medlin, M. M. (2019). Women's short-term mating goals elicit avoidance of faces whose eyes lack limbal rings. *Evolutionary Behavioral Sciences, 13*(3), 278–285.

Brown, S. L., Bulanda, J. R., & Lee, G. R. (2012). Transitions into and out of cohabitation in later life. *Journal of Marriage and Family, 74*(4), 774–793.

Brown, S. L., & Lin, I.-F. (2012). The gray divorce revolution: Rising divorce among middle-aged and older adults,

1990–2010. *Journals of Gerontology: Series B, 67*(6), 731–741.

Brown, S. L., & Lin, I.-F. (2022). The graying of divorce: A half century of change. *Journals of Gerontology: Series B, 77*(9), 1710–1720.

Brown, S. L., Lin, I. F., Hammersmith, A. M. et al. (2018). Later life marital dissolution and repartnership status: A national portrait. *Journals of Gerontology – Series B, 73*(6), 1032–1042.

Brown, S. L., Lin, I.-F., Hammersmith, A. M. et al. (2019). Repartnering following gray divorce: The roles of resources and constraints for women and men. *Demography, 56*(2), 503–523.

Brown, S. L., Lin, I.-F., & Mellencamp, K. A. (2021). Does the transition to grandparenthood deter gray divorce? A test of the braking hypothesis. *Social Forces, 99*(3), 1209–1232.

Brown, S. L., Manning, W. D., & Payne, K. K. (2017). Relationship quality among cohabiting versus married couples. *Journal of Family Issues, 38*(12), 1730–1753.

Brown, S. L., & Wright, M. R. (2019). Divorce attitudes among older adults: Two decades of change. *Journal of Family Issues, 40*(8), 1018–1037.

Browning, J. R., Hatfield, E., Kessler, D. et al. (2000). Sexual motives, gender, and sexual behavior. *Archives of Sexual Behavior, 29*(2), 135–153.

Brumbaugh, C. C., & Fraley, R. C. (2015). Too fast, too soon? An empirical investigation into rebound relationships. *Journal of Social and Personal Relationships, 32*(1), 99–118.

Brumbaugh, C. C., & Wood, D. (2013). Mate preferences across life and across the world. *Social Psychological and Personality Science, 4*(1), 100–107.

Bryant, C. M., Wickrama, K. A. S., Bolland, J. et al. (2010). Race matters, even in marriage: Identifying factors linked to marital outcomes for African Americans. *Journal of Family Theory & Review, 2*(3), 157–174.

Buck, A., Lange, K., Sackett, K. et al. (2019). Reactions to homosexual, transgender, and heterosexual public displays of affection. *Journal of Positive Sexuality, 5*(2), 34–47.

Buck, A. A., & Neff, L. A. (2012). Stress spillover in early marriage: The role of self-regulatory depletion. *Journal of Family Psychology, 26*(5), 698–708.

Buczak-Stec, E., König, H. H., & Hajek, A. (2021). Sexual satisfaction of middle-aged and older adults: Longitudinal findings from a nationally representative sample. *Age and Ageing, 50*(2), 559–564.

Buecker, S., Maes, M., Denissen, J. J. A. et al. (2020). Loneliness and the big five personality traits: A meta-analysis. *European Journal of Personality, 34,* 8–28.

Bui, Q., & Miller, C. C. (2018, August 4). The age that women have babies: how a gap divides America. *The New York*

Times. www.nytimes.com/interactive/2018/08/04/upshot/up-birth-age-gap.html

Bulanda, J. R., & Brown, S. L. (2007). Race-ethnic differences in marital quality and divorce. *Social Science Research, 36*(3), 945–967.

Bullis, C., Clark, C., & Sline, R. (1993). From passion to commitment: Turning points in romantic relationships. In P. J. Kalbfleisch (Ed.), *Interpersonal communication: Evolving interpersonal relationships* (pp. 213–236). Lawrence Erlbaum.

Bullock, M., Hackathorn, J., Clark, E. M. et al. (2011). Can we be (and stay) friends? Remaining friends after dissolution of a romantic relationship. *Journal of Social Psychology, 151*(5), 662–666.

Bunt, S., & Hazelwood, Z. J. (2017). Walking the walk, talking the talk: Love languages, self-regulation, and relationship satisfaction. *Personal Relationships, 24*(2), 280–290.

Burch, R. L., & Salmon, C. (2019). The rough stuff: Understanding aggressive consensual sex. *Evolutionary Psychological Science, 5*(4), 383–393.

Burgess Moser, M., Johnson, S. M., Dalgleish, T. L. et al. (2016). Changes in relationship-specific attachment in emotionally focused couple therapy. *Journal of Marital and Family Therapy, 42*(2), 231–245.

Burgess Moser, M., Johnson, S. M., Dalgleish, T. L. et al. (2018). The impact of blamer-softening on romantic attachment in emotionally focused couples therapy. *Journal of Marital and Family Therapy, 44*(4), 640–654.

Burleson, M. H., Roberts, N. A., Coon, D. W. et al. (2019). Perceived cultural acceptability and comfort with affectionate touch: Differences between Mexican Americans and European Americans. *Journal of Social and Personal Relationships, 36*(3), 1000–1022.

Burleson, M. H., Trevathan, W. R., & Todd, M. (2007). In the mood for love or vice versa? Exploring the relations among sexual activity, physical affection, affect, and stress in the daily lives of mid-aged women. *Archives of Sexual Behavior, 36*(3), 357–368.

Burnette, J. L., Davisson, E. K., Finkel, E. J. et al. (2014). Self-control and forgiveness: A meta-analytic review. *Social Psychological and Personality Science, 5*(4), 443–450.

Burns, T. (1973). A structural theory of social exchange. *Acta Sociologica, 16*(3), 188–208.

Busby, D. M., Boden, J., Niehuis, S. et al. (2017). Predicting partner enhancement in marital relationships: The family of origin, attachment, and social network approval. *Journal of Family Issues, 38*(15), 2178–2199.

Busby, D. M., Hanna-Walker, V., & Leavitt, C. E. (2020). A kiss is not just a kiss: Kissing frequency, sexual quality, attachment, and sexual and relationship satisfaction. *Sexual and Relationship Therapy*. Online publication. https://doi.org/10.1080/14681994.2020.1717460.

Busby, D. M., Larson, J. H., Holman, T. B. et al. (2015). Flexible delivery approaches to couple relationship education: Predictors of initial engagement and retention of couples. *Journal of Child and Family Studies, 24*(10), 3018–3029.

Busby, D. M., Willoughby, B. J., & Carroll, J. S. (2013). Sowing wild oats: Valuable experience or a field full of weeds? *Personal Relationships, 20*(4), 706–718.

Busby, D. M., Willoughby, B. J., & McDonald, M. L. (2019). Is it the sex, the romance, or the living together? The differential impact of past sexual, romantic, and cohabitation histories on current relationship functioning. *Couple and Family Psychology: Research and Practice, 8*(2), 90–104.

Buss, D. M. (1988a). Love acts: The evolutionary biology of love. In R. J. Sternberg & M. Barnes (Eds.), *The psychology of love* (pp. 100–118). Yale University Press.

Buss, D. M. (1988b). From vigilance to violence. *Ethology and Sociobiology, 9*(5), 291–317.

Buss, D. M. (1989). Sex differences in human mate preferences: Evolutionary hypotheses tested in 37 cultures. *Behavioral and Brain Sciences, 12*(1), 1–14.

Buss, D. M. (2016). *The evolution of desire*. Basic Books.

Buss, D. M. (2018). Sexual and emotional infidelity: Evolved gender differences in jealousy prove robust and replicable. *Perspectives on Psychological Science, 13*(2), 155–160.

Buss, D. M. (2019). The evolution of love in humans. In R. J. Sternberg & K. Sternberg (Eds.), *The new psychology of love* (2nd ed., pp. 42–63). Cambridge University Press.

Buss, D. M. (2020). Evolutionary psychology is a scientific revolution. *Evolutionary Behavioral Sciences, 14*(4), 316–323.

Buss, D. M., & Barnes, M. (1986). Preferences in human mate selection. *Journal of Personality and Social Psychology, 50*(3), 559–570.

Buss, D. M., & Haselton, M. (2005). The evolution of jealousy. *Trends in Cognitive Sciences, 9*(11), 506–507.

Buss, D. M., Larsen, R. J., Westen, D. et al. (1992). Sex differences in jealousy: Evolution, physiology, and psychology. *Psychological Science, 3*(4), 251–255.

Buss, D. M., & Schmitt, D. P. (1993). Sexual strategies theory: An evolutionary perspective on human mating. *Psychological Review, 100*(2), 204–232.

Buss, D. M., & Schmitt, D. P. (2019). Mate preferences and their behavioral manifestations. *Annual Review of Psychology, 70*(1), 77–110.

Buss, D. M., & Shackelford, T. K. (1997). From vigilance to violence: Mate retention tactics in married couples. *Journal of Personality and Social Psychology, 72*(2), 346–361.

Buss, D. M., Shackelford, T. K., Kirkpatrick, L. A. et al. (1999). Jealousy and the nature of beliefs about infidelity: Tests of competing hypotheses about sex differences in the United States, Korea, and Japan. *Personal Relationships*, 6(1), 125–150.

Buss, D. M., Shackelford, T. K., Kirkpatrick, L. A. et al. (2001). A half century of mate preferences: The cultural evolution of values. *Journal of Marriage and Family*, 63(2), 491–503.

Buss, D. M., Shackelford, T. K., & McKibbin, W. F. (2008). The Mate Retention Inventory-Short Form (MRI-SF). *Personality and Individual Differences*, 44(1), 322–334.

Bustamante, R. M., Nelson, J. A., Henriksen, R. C. et al. (2011). Intercultural couples: Coping with culture-related stressors. *Family Journal*, 19(2), 154–164.

Butler, E. A., & Randall, A. K. (2013). Emotional coregulation in close relationships. *Emotion Review*, 5(2), 202–210.

Buunk, A. P., & Fisher, M. (2009). Individual differences in intrasexual competition. *Journal of Evolutionary Psychology*, 7(1), 37–48.

Buunk, B. P. (2001). Perceived superiority of one's own relationship and perceived prevalence of happy and unhappy relationships. *British Journal of Social Psychology*, 40(4), 565–574.

Buunk, B. P., Dijkstra, P., Fetchenhauer, D. et al. (2002). Age and gender differences in mate selection criteria for various involvement levels. *Personal Relationships*, 9(3), 271–278.

Buunk, B. P., Dijkstra, P., Kenrick, D. T., & Warntjes, A. (2001). Age preferences for mates as related to gender, own age, and involvement level. *Evolution and Human Behavior*, 22(4), 241–250.

Buunk, B. P., & van der Eijnden, R. J. J. M. (1997). Perceived prevalence, perceived superiority, and relationship satisfaction: Most relationships are good, but ours is the best. *Personality and Social Psychology Bulletin*, 23(3), 219–228.

Byers, E. S. (2011). Beyond the birds and the bees and was it good for you? Thirty years of research on sexual communication. *Canadian Psychology*, 52(1), 20–28.

Byers, E. S., & Heinlein, L. H. (1989). Predicting initiations and refusals of sexual activities in married and cohabiting heterosexual couples. *Journal of Sex Research*, 26(2), 210–231.

Byrne, D. (1961). Interpersonal attraction and attitude similarity. *Journal of Abnormal and Social Psychology*, 62(3), 713–715.

Cacioppo, J. T., Fowler, J. H., & Christakis, N. A. (2009). Alone in the crowd: The structure and spread of loneliness in a large social network. *Journal of Personality and Social Psychology*, 97(6), 977–991.

Cacioppo, J. T., Gardner, W. L., & Berntson, G. G. (1997). Beyond bipolar conceptualizations and measures: The case of attitudes and evaluative space. *Personality and Social Psychology Review*, 1, 3–25.

Cacioppo, J. T., & Hawkley, L. C. (2009). Perceived social isolation and cognition. *Trends in Cognitive Sciences*, 13(10), 447–454.

Cain, B. S. (1988). Divorce among elderly women: A growing social phenomenon. *Social Casework*, 69(9), 563–568.

Calabrò, R. S., Cacciola, A., Bruschetta, D. et al. (2019). Neuroanatomy and function of human sexual behavior: A neglected or unknown issue? *Brain and Behavior*, 9(12), e01389.

Caldwell-Harris, C., Kronrod, A., & Yang, J. (2013). Do more, say less: Saying "I love you" in Chinese and American cultures. *Intercultural Pragmatics*, 10(1), 41–69.

Calvillo, C., del Mar Sánchez-Fuentes, M., Parrón-Carreño, T. et al. (2020). Validation of the Interpersonal Exchange Model of Sexual Satisfaction Questionnaire in adults with a same-sex partner. *International Journal of Clinical and Health Psychology*, 20(2), 140–150.

Cameron, J. J., & Curry, E. (2020). Gender roles and date context in hypothetical scripts for a woman and a man on a first date in the twenty-first century. *Sex Roles*, 82(5–6), 345–362.

Cameron, J. J., Stinson, D. A., Gaetz, R. et al. (2010). Acceptance is in the eye of the beholder: Self-esteem and motivated perceptions of acceptance from the opposite sex. *Journal of Personality and Social Psychology*, 99(3), 513–529.

Campa, M. I., Hazan, C., & Wolfe, J. E. (2009). The form and function of attachment behavior in the daily lives of young adults. *Social Development*, 18(2), 288–304.

Campbell, K., Nelson, J., Parker, M. L. et al. (2018). Interpersonal chemistry in friendships and romantic relationships. *Interpersona: An International Journal on Personal Relationships*, 12(1), 34–50.

Campbell, K., & Parker, M. L. (2022). Catfish: Exploring the individual predictors and interpersonal characteristics of deceptive online romantic relationships. *Contemporary Family Therapy*, 44, 422–435.

Campbell, L., Lackenbauer, S. D., & Muise, A. (2006). When is being known or adored by romantic partners most beneficial? Self-perceptions, relationship length, and responses to partner's verifying and enhancing appraisals. *Personality and Social Psychology Bulletin*, 32(10), 1283–1294.

Campbell, W. K., & Foster, C. A. (2002). Narcissism and commitment in romantic relationships: An investment model analysis. *Personality and Social Psychology Bulletin*, 28(4), 484–495.

Candel, O. S., & Turliuc, M. N. (2019). Insecure attachment and relationship satisfaction: A meta-analysis of actor and partner associations. *Personality and Individual Differences*, *147*, 190–199.

Cao, H., Zhou, N., Fine, M. et al. (2017). Sexual minority stress and same-sex relationship well-being: A meta-analysis of research prior to the U.S. nationwide legalization of same-sex marriage. *Journal of Marriage and Family*, *79*(5), 1258–1277.

Capozzi, F., Human, L. J., & Ristic, J. (2020). Attention promotes accurate impression formation. *Journal of Personality*, *88*(3), 544–554.

Carli, L. L., Anzelmo, E., Pozzi, S. et al. (2019). Attachment networks in committed couples. *Frontiers in Psychology*, *10*(MAY), 1105.

Carlson, D. L., & Soller, B. (2019). Sharing's more fun for everyone? Gender attitudes, sexual self-efficacy, and sexual frequency. *Journal of Marriage and Family*, *81*(1), 24–41.

Carmichael, C. L., Goldberg, M. H., & Coyle, M. A. (2021). Security-based differences in touch behavior and its relational benefits. *Social Psychological and Personality Science*, *12*(4), 550–560.

Carmichael, G. A., & Whittaker, A. (2007). Choice and circumstance: Qualitative insights into contemporary childlessness in Australia. *European Journal of Population / Revue Européenne de Démographie*, *23*(2), 111–143.

Carnelley, K. B., & Ruscher, J. B. (2000). Adult attachment and exploratory behavior in leisure. *Journal of Social Behavior and Personality*, *15*(2), 153–165.

Carnelley, K. B., Wortman, C. B., Bolger, N. et al. (2006). The time course of grief reactions to spousal loss: Evidence from a national probability sample. *Journal of Personality and Social Psychology*, *91*(3), 476–492.

Carone, N., Baiocco, R., & Lingiardi, V. (2017). Single fathers by choice using surrogacy: Why men decide to have a child as a single parent. *Human Reproduction*, *32*(9), 1871–1879.

Carpenter, C. J., & Spottswood, E. L. (2013). Exploring romantic relationships on social networking sites using the self-expansion model. *Computers in Human Behavior*, *29*(4), 1531–1537.

Carr, C. T., & Walther, J. B. (2014). Increasing attributional certainty via social media: Learning about others one bit at a time. *Journal of Computer-Mediated Communication*, *19*(4), 922–937.

Carr, D., & Boerner, K. (2013). Dating after late-life spousal loss: Does it compromise relationships with adult children? *Journal of Aging Studies*, *27*(4), 487–498.

Carr, D., House, J. S., Kessler, R. C. et al. (2000). Marital quality and psychological adjustment to widowhood among older adults: A longitudinal analysis. *Journals of Gerontology: Series B*, *55*(4), S197–207.

Carr, D., & Utz, R. L. (2020). Families in later life: A decade in review. *Journal of Marriage and Family*, *82*(1), 346–363.

Carrasco, M. (2021, November 12). *Rooming with rabbits (and other nonhumans)*. Inside Higher Ed. www.insidehighered.com/news/2021/11/12/more-students-bring-pets-campus-emotional-support

Carrère, S., & Gottman, J. M. (1999). Predicting divorce among newlyweds from the first three minutes of a marital conflict discussion. *Family Process*, *38*(3), 293–301.

Carson, J. W., Carson, K. M., Gil, K. M. et al. (2006). Mindfulness-based relationship enhancement (MBRE) in couples. In R. A. Baer (Ed.), *Mindfulness based treatment approaches: Clinician's guide to evidence base and applications* (pp. 309–331). Elsevier.

Carswell, K. L., & Impett, E. A. (2021). What fuels passion? An integrative review of competing theories of romantic passion. *Social and Personality Psychology Compass*, *15*(8), e12629.

Carswell, K. L., Muise, A., Harasymchuk, C. et al. (2021). Growing desire or growing apart? Consequences of personal self-expansion for romantic passion. *Journal of Personality and Social Psychology*, *121*(2), 354–377.

Carter, K. R., Knox, D., & Hall, S. S. (2018). Romantic breakup: Difficult loss for some but not for others. *Journal of Loss and Trauma*, *23*(8), 698–714.

Carton, S. T., & Horan, S. M. (2014). A diary examination of romantic and sexual partners withholding affectionate messages. *Journal of Social and Personal Relationships*, *31*(2), 221–246.

Carver, C. S. (2007). Stress, coping, and health. In H. S. Friedman & R. C. Silver (Eds.), *Foundations of health psychology* (pp. 117–144). Oxford University Press.

Castellano, J. (2021, July 6). Pet therapy is a nearly cost-free anxiety reducer on college campuses. *Forbes*. www.forbes.com/sites/jillcastellano/2015/07/06/pet-therapy-is-a-nearly-cost-free-anxiety-reducer-on-college-campuses/

Caughlin, J. P., & Huston, T. L. (2002). A contextual analysis of the association between demand/withdraw and marital satisfaction. *Personal Relationships*, *9*(1), 95–119.

Caughlin, J. P., Vangelisti, A. L., & Mikucki-Enyart, S. L. (2013). Conflict in dating and marital relationships. In J. G. Oetzel & S. Ting-Toomey (Eds.), *The SAGE Handbook of conflict communications: Integrating theory, research, and practice* (pp. 161–186). Sage Publications.

Cavallo, J. V., & Hirniak, A. (2019). No assistance desired: How perceptions of others' self-esteem affect support-seeking. *Social Psychological and Personality Science*, *10*(2), 193–200.

Cavanagh, S. E., & Fomby, P. (2019). Family instability in the lives of American children. *Annual Review of Sociology, 45*(1), 493–513.

Cazzell, A. R., Rivers, A. S., Sanford, K. et al. (2022). Positive exchanges buffer negative exchanges: Associations with marital satisfaction among US mixed-sex couples. *Journal of Family Psychology, 36*(7), 1050–1060.

CDC. (2019). *Youth risk behavior survey questionnaire.* Center for Disease Control. www.cdc.gov/yrbs

CDC. (2020). *National marriage and divorce rate trends, 2000–2020.* Center for Disease Control. www.cdc.gov/nchs/data/dvs/national-marriage-divorce-rates-00-20.pdf

CDC. (2022). *Reproductive health: Infertility FAQs.* Center for Disease Control www.cdc.gov/reproductivehealth/infertility/index.htm

Census.gov. (2020). *Historical marriage status tables.* www.census.gov/data/tables/time-series/demo/families/marital.html

Chakravorty, S., Goli, S., & James, K. S. (2021). Family demography in India: Emerging patterns and its challenges. *SAGE Open, 11*(2), 215824402110081.

Chan, C. D., & Erby, A. N. (2018). A critical analysis and applied intersectionality framework with intercultural queer couples. *Journal of Homosexuality, 65*(9), 1249–1274.

Chan, T., Reese, Z. A., & Ybarra, O. (2021). Better to brag: Underestimating the risks of avoiding positive self-disclosures in close relationships. *Journal of Personality, 89*(5), 1044–1061.

Chandler, J., & Shapiro, D. (2016). Conducting clinical research using crowdsourced convenience samples. *Annual Review of Clinical Psychology, 12*(1), 53–81.

Chapman, B., & Guven, C. (2016). Revisiting the relationship between marriage and wellbeing: Does marriage quality matter? *Journal of Happiness Studies, 17*(2), 533–551.

Chapman, G. (2009). *The five love languages: How to express heartfelt commitment to your mate.* Moody Publishers.

Chartrand, T. L., & Bargh, J. A. (1999). The chameleon effect: The perception-behavior link and social interaction. *Journal of Personality and Social Psychology, 76*(6), 893–910.

Chartrand, T. L., & Van Baaren, R. (2009). Human mimicry. *Advances in Experimental Social Psychology, 41*, 219–274.

Charvat, E. J., Garneau-Rosner, C. L., Monk, J. K. et al. (2022). The intergenerational transmission of relationship instability: A focus on emerging adult on-off relationships. *Family Process.* Advance online publication. https://doi.org/10.1111/famp.12765

Charvoz, L., Bodenmann, G., Bertoni, A. et al. (2009). Is the partner who decides to divorce more attractive? A comparison between initiators and noninitiators. *Journal of Divorce and Remarriage, 50*(1), 22–37.

Cheek, J., & Buss, A. (1981). Shyness and sociability. *Journal of Personality and Social Psychology, 41*, 330–339.

Chen, H., Cohen, P., Kasen, S. et al. (2006). Predicting conflict within romantic relationships during the transition to adulthood. *Personal Relationships, 13*(4), 411–427.

Chen, K.-H., Brown, C. L., Wells, J. L. et al. (2021). Physiological linkage during shared positive and shared negative emotion. *Journal of Personality and Social Psychology, 121*(5), 1029–1056.

Chen, Z., Poon, K. T., DeWall, C. N. et al. (2020). Life lacks meaning without acceptance: Ostracism triggers suicidal thoughts. *Journal of Personality and Social Psychology, 119*(6), 1423–1443.

Choi, H., Oishi, S., Shin, J. et al. (2019). Do happy events love company? Cultural variations in sharing positive events with others. *Personality and Social Psychology Bulletin, 45*(4), 528–540.

Chopik, W. J., Edelstein, R. S. R., van Anders, S. M. et al. (2014). Too close for comfort? Adult attachment and cuddling in romantic and parent–child relationships. *Personality and Individual Differences, 69*, 212–216.

Chopik, W. J., Moors, A. C., & Edelstein, R. S. (2014). Maternal nurturance predicts decreases in attachment avoidance in emerging adulthood. *Journal of Research in Personality, 53*, 47–53.

Chow, E. P. F., Cornelisse, V. J., Read, T. R. H. et al. (2016). Risk practices in the era of smartphone apps for meeting partners: A cross-sectional study among men who have sex with men in Melbourne, Australia. *AIDS Patient Care and STDs, 30*(4), 151–154.

Chow, R. M., Tiedens, L. Z., & Govan, C. L. (2007). Excluded emotions: The role of anger in antisocial responses to ostracism. *Journal of Experimental Social Psychology, 44*(3), 896–903.

Christensen, A., Atkins, D. C., Baucom, B. et al. (2010). Marital status and satisfaction five years following a randomized clinical trial comparing traditional versus integrative behavioral couple therapy. *Journal of Consulting and Clinical Psychology, 78*(2), 225–235.

Christensen, A., Atkins, D. C., Berns, S. et al. (2004). Traditional versus integrative behavioral couple therapy for significantly and chronically distressed married couples. *Journal of Consulting and Clinical Psychology, 72*, 176–191.

Christensen, A., Dimidjian, S., & Martell, C. R. (2015). Integrative behavioral couple therapy. In A. S. Gurman, J. L. Lebow, & D. K. Snyder (Eds.), *Clinical handbook of couple therapy* (5th ed., pp. 61–96). Guilford Press.

Christensen, A., & Doss, B. D. (2017). Integrative behavioral couple therapy. *Current Opinion in Psychology*, *13*, 111–114.

Chuang, R., Wilkins, C., Tan, M. et al. (2021). Racial minorities' attitudes toward interracial couples: An intersection of race and gender. *Group Processes and Intergroup Relations*, *24*(3), 453–467.

Chuan-Peng, H., Huang, Y., Eickhoff, S. B. et al. (2020). Seeking the "beauty center" in the brain: A meta-analysis of fMRI studies of beautiful human faces and visual art. *Cognitive, Affective, & Behavioral Neuroscience*, *20*(6), 1200–1215.

Chung, M., & Harris, C. R. (2018). Jealousy as a specific emotion: The dynamic functional model. *Emotion Review*, *10*(4), 272–287.

Cicirelli, V. G. (2010). Attachment relationships in old age. *Journal of Social and Personal Relationships*, *27*(2), 191–199.

Clark, A. E., & Georgellis, Y. (2013). Back to baseline in Britain: Adaptation in the British household panel survey. *Economica*, *80*(319), 496–512.

Clark, C. L., Shaver, P. R., & Abrahams, M. F. (1999). Strategic behaviors in romantic relationship initiation. *Personality and Social Psychology Bulletin*, *25*(6), 707–720.

Clark, R. D. (1990). The impact of AIDS on gender differences in willingness to engage in casual sex. *Journal of Applied Social Psychology*, *20*(9), 771–782.

Clark, R. D., & Hatfield, E. (1989). Gender differences in receptivity to sexual offers. *Journal of Psychology and Human Sexuality*, *2*(1), 39–55.

Clavél, F. D., Cutrona, C. E., & Russell, D. W. (2017). United and divided by stress: How stressors differentially influence social support in African American couples over time. *Personality and Social Psychology Bulletin*, *43*(7), 1050–1064.

Claxton, A., & Perry-Jenkins, M. (2008). No fun anymore: Leisure and marital quality across the transition to parenthood. *Journal of Marriage and Family*, *70*(1), 28–43.

Cloutier, J., Heatherton, T. F., Whalen, P. J. et al. (2008). Are attractive people rewarding? Sex differences in the neural substrates of facial attractiveness. *Journal of Cognitive Neuroscience*, *20*(6), 941–951.

Coan, J. A., Beckes, L., Gonzalez, M. Z. et al. (2017). Relationship status and perceived support in the social regulation of neural responses to threat. *Social Cognitive and Affective Neuroscience*, *12*, 1574–1583.

Coan, J. A., & Gottman, J. M. (2007). The Specific Affect Coding System (SPAFF). In J. Coan & J. Allen (Eds.), *Handbook of emotion elicitation and assessment* (pp. 267–285). Oxford University Press.

Coan, J. A., & Sbarra, D. A. (2015). Social baseline theory: The social regulation of risk and effort. *Current Opinion in Psychology*, *1*, 87–91.

Coan, J. A., Schaefer, H. S., & Davidson, R. J. (2006). Lending a hand: Social regulation of the neural response to threat. *Psychological Science*, *17*, 1032–1039.

Coduto, K. D., & Eveland Jr, W. P. (2022). Listening and being listened to as affection exchange in marital discussions about the #MeToo movement. *Journal of Social and Personal Relationships*, *39*(5), 1460–1481.

Coetzee, V., Greeff, J. M., Stephen, I. D. et al. (2014). Cross-cultural agreement in facial attractiveness preferences: The role of ethnicity and gender. *PLOS One*, *9*(7), e99629.

Coetzee, V., Perrett, D. I., & Stephen, I. D. (2009). Facial adiposity: A cue to health? *Perception*, *38*(11), 1700–1711.

Coffelt, T. A. (2018). Sexual goals, plans, and actions: Toward a sexual script emerging adults use to delay or abstain from sexual intercourse. *Western Journal of Communication*, *82*(4), 416–438.

Cohen, P. N. (2019). The coming divorce decline. *Socius: Sociological Research for a Dynamic World*, *5*, 237802311987349.

Cohen, S. (1991). Social supports and physical health: Symptoms, health behaviors, and infectious disease. In M. Cummings, A. L., Greene, & K. H. Karraker (Eds.), *Life-span developmental psychology: Perspectives on stress and coping* (pp. 213–234). Lawrence Erlbaum.

Cohen, S. (2004). Social relationships and health. *American Psychologist*, *59*, 676–684.

Cohen, S., Gianaros, P. J., & Manuck, S. B. (2016). A stage model of stress and disease. *Perspectives on Psychological Science*, *11*, 456–463.

Cohen, S., & Janicki-Deverts, D. (2009). Can we improve our physical health by altering our social networks? *Perspectives on Psychological Science*, *4*(4), 375–378.

Cohen, S., Janicki-Deverts, D., & Miller, G. E. (2007). Psychological stress and disease. *JAMA: The Journal of the American Medical Association*, *298*(14), 1685–1687.

Cohen, S., Janicki-Deverts, D., Turner, R. B. et al. (2015). Does hugging provide stress-buffering social support? A study of susceptibility to upper respiratory infection and illness. *Psychological Science*, *26*(2), 135–147.

Cohen, S., Kamarck, T., & Mermelstein, R. (1983). A global measure of perceived stress. *Journal of Health and Social Behavior*, *24*, 385–396.

Cohen, S., Kessler, R. C., & Gordon, L.U. (1997). Strategies for measuring stress in studies of psychiatric and physical disorders. In S. Cohen, R. C. Kessler, & L. U. Gordon (Eds.), *Measuring stress: A guide for health and social scientists* (pp. 3–28). Oxford University Press.

Cohen, S., Mermelstein, R., & Hoberman, H. (1985). Measuring the functional components of social support. In I. G. Sarason & B. Sarason (Eds.), *Social support: Theory, research, and application* (pp. 73–94). Martinus Nijhoff.

Cohen, S., Murphy, M. L. M., & Prather, A. A. (2019). Ten surprising facts about stressful life events and disease risk. *Annual Review of Psychology, 70*(1), 577–597.

Cohen, S., & Wills, T. A. (1985). Stress, social support, and the buffering hypothesis. *Psychological Bulletin, 98*, 310–357.

Cole, S., Trope, Y., & Balcetis, E. (2016). In the eye of the betrothed: Perceptual downgrading of attractive alternative romantic partners. *Personality and Social Psychology Bulletin, 42*(7), 879–892.

Coleman, D. (2004). Why we don't have to believe without doubting in the "Second Demographic Transition": Some agnostic comments. *Vienna Yearbook of Population Research*, 11–24.

Coleman, M., Ganong, L., & Mitchell, S. N. (2018). Divorce and postdivorce relationships. In A. L. Vangelisti & D. Perlman (Eds.), *The Cambridge handbook of personal relationships* (2nd ed., pp. 106–116). Cambridge University Press.

Collins, N. L. (1996). Working models of attachment: Implications for explanation, emotion and behavior. *Journal of Personality and Social Psychology, 71*(4), 810–832.

Collins, N. L., Clark, C., & Shaver, P. (1996). Attachment styles and internal working models of self and relationship partners. In G. J. O. Fletcher & J. Fitness (Eds.), *Knowledge structures in close relationships: A social psychological approach* (pp. 25–61). Lawrence Erlbaum.

Collins, N. L., & Feeney, B. C. (2000). A safe haven: An attachment theory perspective on support seeking and caregiving in intimate relationships. *Journal of Personality and Social Psychology, 78*(6), 1053–1073.

Collins, N. L., & Feeney, B. C. (2004). Working models of attachment shape perceptions of social support: Evidence from experimental and observational studies. *Journal of Personality and Social Psychology, 87*, 363–383.

Collins, N. L., & Feeney, B. C. (2010). An attachment theoretical perspective on social support dynamics in couples: Normative processes and individual differences. In K. Sullivan & J. Davila (Eds.), *Support processes in intimate relationships* (pp. 89–120). Oxford University Press.

Collins, N. L., & Ford, M. B. (2010). Responding to the needs of others: The caregiving behavioral system in intimate relationships. *Journal of Social and Personal Relationships, 27*(2), 235–244.

Collins, N. L., Ford, M. B., Guichard, A. C. et al. (2006). Working models of attachment and attribution processes in intimate relationships. *Personality and Social Psychology Bulletin, 32*(2), 201–219.

Collins, N. L., Ford, M. B., Guichard, A. C. et al. (2009). Responding to need in intimate relationships: Social support and caregiving processes in couples. In M. Mikulincer & P. R. Shaver (Eds.), *Prosocial motives, emotions, and behavior* (pp. 367–389). American Psychological Association.

Collins, N. L., & Miller, L. C. (1994). Self-disclosure and liking: A meta-analytic review. *Psychological Bulletin, 116*(3), 457–475.

Collins, N. L., & Read, S. J. (1990). Adult attachment, working models, and relationship quality in dating couples. *Journal of Personality and Social Psychology, 58*(4), 644–663.

Collins, P., & Bilge, S. (2016). *Intersectionality.* Polity.

Collins, T. J., & Gillath, O. (2012). Attachment, breakup strategies, and associated outcomes: The effects of security enhancement on the selection of breakup strategies. *Journal of Research in Personality, 46*(2), 210–222.

Collins, T. J., & Horn, T. L. (2019). "I'll call you …" Communication frequency as a regulator of satisfaction and commitment across committed and casual sexual relationship types. *Journal of Social and Personal Relationships, 36*(4), 1123–1145.

Columbus, S., Molho, C., Righetti, F. et al. (2021). Interdependence and cooperation in daily life. *Journal of Personality and Social Psychology, 120*(3), 626–650.

Confer, J. C., & Cloud, M. D. (2011). Sex differences in response to imagining a partner's heterosexual or homosexual affair. *Personality and Individual Differences, 50*(2), 129–134.

Conger, R. D., Elder, G. H., Lorenz, F. O. et al. (1990). Linking economic hardship to marital quality and instability. *Journal of Marriage and the Family, 52*(3), 643–656.

Conley, T. D., & Moors, A. C. (2014). More oxygen please! How polyamorous relationship strategies might oxygenate marriage. *Psychological Inquiry, 25*(1), 56–63.

Conley, T. D., Moors, A. C., Matsick, J. L. et al. (2011). Women, men, and the bedroom: Methodological and conceptual insights that narrow, reframe, and eliminate gender differences in sexuality. *Current Directions in Psychological Science, 20*(5), 296–300.

Conley, T. D., Moors, A. C., Matsick, J. L. et al. (2013). The fewer the merrier? Assessing stigma surrounding consensually non-monogamous romantic relationships. *Analyses of Social Issues and Public Policy, 13*(1), 1–30.

Conley, T. D., Piemonte, J. L., Gusakova, S. et al. (2018). Sexual satisfaction among individuals in monogamous and consensually non-monogamous relationships. *Journal of Social and Personal Relationships, 35*(4), 509–531.

Conley, T. D., Roesch, S. C., Peplau, L. A. et al. (2009). A test of positive illusions versus shared reality models of relationship satisfaction among gay, lesbian, and heterosexual couples. *Journal of Applied Social Psychology, 39*(6), 1417–1431.

Conoley, C. W., Vasquez, E., Del, B. et al. (2015). Celebrating the accomplishments of others: Mutual benefits of capitalization. *Counseling Psychology*, 1–18.

Conradi, H. J., Noordhof, A., & Arntz, A. (2020). Improvement of conflict handling: Hand-holding during and after conflict discussions affects heart rate, mood, and observed communication behavior in romantic partners. *Journal of Sex and Marital Therapy, 46*(5), 419–434.

Conroy-Beam, D., & Buss, D. M. (2016). Do mate preferences influence actual mating decisions? Evidence from computer simulations and three studies of mated couples. *Journal of Personality and Social Psychology, 111*(1), 53–66.

Conroy-Beam, D., & Buss, D. M. (2018). Why is age so importance in human mating? Evolved age preferences and their influences on multiple mating behaviors. *Evolutionary Behavioral Sciences, 13*(2), 127–157.

Conroy-Beam, D., Buss, D. M., Pham, M. N. et al. (2015). How sexually dimorphic are human mate preferences? *Personality and Social Psychology Bulletin, 41*(8), 1082–1093.

Coop Gordon, K., Cordova, J. V., Roberson, P. N. E. et al. (2019). An implementation study of relationship checkups as home visitations for low-income at-risk couples. *Family Process, 58*(1), 247–265.

Coop Gordon, K., & Mitchell, E. A. (2020). Infidelity in the time of COVID-19. *Family Process, 59*(3), 956–966.

Cooper, A. N., Tao, C., Totenhagen, C. J. et al. (2020). Daily stress spillover and crossover: Moderating effects of difficulties in emotion regulation in same-sex couples. *Journal of Social and Personal Relationships, 37*(4), 1245–1267.

Cooper, M. L., Barber, L. L., Zhaoyang, R. et al. (2011). Motivational pursuits in the context of human sexual relationships. *Journal of Personality, 79*(6), 1333–1368.

Cooper, M. L., Pioli, M., Levitt, A. et al. (2006). Attachment styles, sex motives, and sexual behaviour: Evidence for gender-specific expressions of attachment dynamics. In M. Mikulincer & G. S. Goodman (Eds.), *Dynamics of romantic love: Attachment, caregiving, and sex* (pp. 243–274). Guilford.

Cooper, M. L., Shapiro, C. M., & Powers, A. M. (1998). Motivations for sex and risky sexual behavior among adolescents and young adults: A functional perspective. *Journal of Personality and Social Psychology, 75*(6), 1528–1558.

Cooper, M. L., Talley, A. E., Sheldon, M. S. et al. (2015). A dyadic perspective on approach and avoidance motives for sexual behavior. In A. J. Elliot (Ed.), *Handbook of approach and avoidance motivation* (pp. 615–632). Psychology Press.

Cope, M. A., & Mattingly, B. A. (2021). Putting me back together by getting back together: Post-dissolution self-concept confusion predicts rekindling desire among anxiously attached individuals. *Journal of Social and Personal Relationships, 38*(1), 384–392.

Copen, C. E., Daniels, K., Butner, J. et al. (2012). First Marriages in the United States: Data from the 2006–2010. *National Survey of Family Growth, 49*(1), 1–22.

Cordova, J. V., Eubanks Fleming, C. J., Ippolito Morrill, M. et al. (2014). The marriage checkup: A randomized controlled trial of annual relationship health checkups. *Journal of Consulting and Clinical Psychology, 82*(4), 592–604.

Cornwell, E. Y., & Waite, L. J. (2009). Social disconnectedness, perceived isolation, and health among older adults. *Journal of Health and Social Behavior, 50*(1), 31–48.

Cortes, K., Britton, E., Holmes, J. G. et al. (2020). Our adventures make me feel secure: Novel activities boost relationship satisfaction through felt security. *Journal of Experimental Social Psychology, 89*, 103992.

Costa, R. M., & Brody, S. (2012). Sexual satisfaction, relationship satisfaction, and health are associated with greater frequency of penile-vaginal intercourse. *Archives of Sexual Behavior, 41*(1), 9–10.

Coulter, K., & Malouff, J. M. (2013). Effects of an intervention designed to enhance romantic relationship excitement: A randomized-control trial. *Couple and Family Psychology: Research and Practice, 2*(1), 34–44.

Courtney, A. L., & Meyer, M. L. (2020). Self-other representation in the social brain reflects social connection. *Journal of Neuroscience, 40*(29), 5616–5627.

Cox, D. W., Fleckenstein, J. R., & Sims-Cox, L. R. (2021). Comparing the self-reported health, happiness, and marital happiness of a multinational sample of consensually non-monogamous adults with those of the U.S. general population: Additional comparisons by gender, number of sexual partners, frequency of sex, and marital status. *Archives of Sexual Behavior, 50*(4), 1287–1309.

Cox, K., Currin, J. M., Garos, S. et al. (2021). "That was fun, I gotta run": Comparing exit strategies of a one-time sexual encounter to buyer–seller relationship dissolution. *Sexuality and Culture, 25*(5), 1771–1788.

Craig, L., & Brown, J. E. (2014). Weekend work and leisure time with family and friends: Who misses out? *Journal of Marriage and Family, 76*(4), 710–727.

Crasta, D., Rogge, R. D., Maniaci, M. R. et al. (2021). Toward an optimized measure of perceived partner responsiveness: Development and validation of the perceived responsiveness and insensitivity scale. *Psychological Assessment*, *33*(4), 338–355.

Crawford, D. W., Houts, R. M., Huston, T. L. et al. (2002). Compatibility, leisure, and satisfaction in marital relationships. *Journal of Marriage and Family*, *64*(2), 433–449.

Crenshaw, A. O., Leo, K., Christensen, A. et al. (2021). Relative importance of conflict topics for within-couple tests: The case of demand/withdraw interaction. *Journal of Family Psychology*, *35*(3), 377–387.

Crenshaw, K. (1989). Demarginalizing the intersection of race and sex: A black feminist critique of antidiscrimination doctrine, feminist theory, and antiracist politics. In K. Bartlett (Ed.), *Feminist legal theory: Readings in law and gender* (pp. 57–80). Routledge.

Crockett, E. E., Morrow, Q. J., & Muyshondt, A. C. (2017). Circumnavigating the cost of support. *Journal of Social and Personal Relationships*, *34*(4), 578–593.

Crohan, S. E. (1996). Marital quality and conflict across the transition to parenthood in African American and White Couples. *Journal of Marriage and Family*, *58*(4), 933–944.

Cross, E. J., Overall, N. C., Low, R. S. T. et al. (2019). An interdependence account of sexism and power: Men's hostile sexism, biased perceptions of low power, and relationship aggression. *Journal of Personality and Social Psychology*, *117*(2), 338–363.

CRS. (2019, February 2). *The Trump administration's "zero tolerance" immigration enforcement policy*. Congressional Research Service.

Csajbók, Z., & Berkics, M. (2017). Factor, factor, on the whole, who's the best fitting of all? Factors of mate preferences in a large sample. *Personality and Individual Differences*, *114*, 92–102.

Cuenca-Montesino, M. L., Graña, J. L., & O'Leary, K. D. (2015). Intensity of love in a community sample of Spanish couples in the region of Madrid. *Spanish Journal of Psychology*, *18*, E79.

Cumming, G. (2014). The new statistics: Why and how. *Psychological Science*, *25*(1), 7–29.

Cuncic, A. (2020, October 21). *Understanding mindfulness-based relationship enhancement*. Verywell Mind. www .verywellmind.com/understanding-mindfulness-based-relationship-enhancement-4685242

Cunningham, M. R. (1986). Measuring the physical in physical attractiveness: Quasi-experiments on the sociobiology of female facial beauty. *Journal of Personality and Social Psychology*, *50*(5), 925–935.

Cunningham, M. R. (1989). Reactions to heterosexual opening gambits. *Personality and Social Psychology Bulletin*, *15*(1), 27–41.

Cunningham, M. R., & Barbee, A. (2008). Prelude to a kiss: Nonverbal flirting, opening gambits, and other communication dynamics in the initiation of romantic relationships. In S. Sprecher, A. Wenzel, & J. Harvey (Eds.), *Handbook of relationship initiation* (pp. 97–120). Psychology Press.

Cupach, W. R., & Comstock, J. (1990). Satisfaction with sexual communication in marriage: Links to sexual satisfaction and dyadic adjustment. *Journal of Social and Personal Relationships*, *7*(2), 179–186.

Cupach, W. R., & Metts, S. (1986). Accounts of relational dissolution: A comparison of marital and non-marital relationships. *Communication Monographs*, *53*(4), 311–334.

Currier, J. M., Irish, J. E. F., Neimeyer, R. A. et al. (2015). Attachment, continuing bonds, and complicated grief following violent loss: Testing a moderated model. *Death Studies*, *39*(4), 201–210.

Curtis, R. C., & Miller, K. (1986). Believing another likes or dislikes you: Behaviors making the beliefs come true. *Journal of Personality and Social Psychology*, *51*(2), 284–290.

Custer, L., Holmberg, D., Blair, K. et al. (2008). "So how did you two meet?": Narratives of relationship initiation. In S. Sprecher, A. Wenzel, & J. Harvey (Eds.), *Handbook of relationship initiation* (pp. 453–470). Psychology Press.

Cutrona, C. E. (1990). Stress and social support – in search of optimal matching. *Journal of Social and Clinical Psychology*, *9*(1), 3–14.

Cutrona, C. E., Cohen, B. B., & Igram, S. (1990). Contextual determinants of the perceived supportiveness of helping behaviors. *Journal of Social and Personal Relationships*, *7*(4), 553–562.

Cutrona, C. E., & Russell, D. W. (1990). Type of social support and specific stress: Toward a theory of optimal matching. In B. R. Sarason, I. G. Sarason, & G. R. Pierce (Eds.), *Social support: An interactional view* (pp. 319–366). John Wiley & Sons.

Cutrona, C. E., Russell, D. W., Abraham, W. T. et al. (2003). Neighborhood context and financial strain as predictors of marital interaction and marital quality in African American couples. *Personal Relationships*, *10*(3), 389–409.

Cutrona, C. E., Russell, D. W., & Gardner, K. A. (2005). The relationship enhancement model of social support. In T. A. Revenson, K. Kayser, & G. Bodenmann (Eds.), *Couples coping with stress: Emerging perspectives on dyadic coping* (pp. 73–95). American Psychological Association.

Cutrona, C. E., Shaffer, P. A., Wesner, K. A. et al. (2007). Optimally matching support and perceived spousal sensitivity. *Journal of Family Psychology*, *21*(4), 754–758.

Dai, X., Dong, P., & Jia, J. S. (2014). When does playing hard to get increase romantic attraction? *Journal of Experimental Psychology: General*, *143*(2), 521–526.

Dailey, R. M. (2020). *On-again, off-again relationships navigating (in) stability in romantic relationships*. Cambridge University Press.

Dailey, R. M., Brody, N., LeFebvre, L. et al. (2013). Charting changes in commitment: Trajectories of on-again/off-again relationships. *Journal of Social and Personal Relationships*, *30*(8), 1020–1044.

Dailey, R. M., Jin, B., Pfiester, A. et al. (2011). On-again/off-again dating relationships: What keeps partners coming back? *Journal of Social Psychology*, *151*(4), 417–440.

Dailey, R. M., Pfiester, A., Jin, B. et al. (2009). On-again/off-again dating relationships: How are they different from other dating relationships? *Personal Relationships*, *16*(1), 23–47.

Dailey, R. M., Rossetto, K. R., McCracken, A. A. et al. (2012). Negotiating breakups and renewals in on-again/off-again dating relationships: Traversing the transitions. *Communication Quarterly*, *60*(2), 165–189.

Dailey, R. M., Rossetto, K. R., Pfiester, A. et al. (2009). A qualitative analysis of on-again/off-again romantic relationships: "It's up and down, all around." *Journal of Social and Personal Relationships*, *26*(4), 443–466.

Dailey, R. M., Zhang, Z., & Kearns, K. (2020). Exploring the role of sexual experiences in on-again/off-again dating relationships. *Personal Relationships*, *27*(2), 460–483.

Dailey, R. M., Zhong, L., Pett, R. et al. (2020). Post-dissolution ambivalence, breakup adjustment, and relationship reconciliation. *Journal of Social and Personal Relationships*, *37*(5), 1604–1625.

Daily Mail Online. (2015, June 4). Jada Pinkett-Smith talks about "open relationship" with husband Will. *Daily Mail*. www.dailymail.co.uk/tvshowbiz/article-3109793/Jada-Pinkett-Smith-talks-open-relationship-husband-admits-s-advised-children-AGAINST-getting-married.html

Dalgleish, T. L., Johnson, S. M., Burgess Moser, M. et al. (2015). Predicting change in marital satisfaction throughout emotionally focused couple therapy. *Journal of Marital and Family Therapy*, *41*(3), 276–291.

Daly, M., Wilson, M., & Weghorst, S. J. (1982). Male sexual jealousy. *Ethology and Sociobiology*, *3*(1), 11–27.

D'Angelo, J. D., & Toma, C. L. (2017). There are plenty of fish in the sea: The effects of choice overload and reversibility on online daters' satisfaction with selected partners. *Media Psychology*, *20*(1), 1–27.

Daniels, G. (Writer/Director), Gervais, R. (Writer), & Merchant, S. (Writer) (2007, September 27). Fun run (Season 4 Episode 1). [TV series episode]. In G. Daniels (Executive Producer), The Office. Deedle-Dee Productions; Revelle Productions; Universal Media Studios.

Darghouth, S., Brody, L., & Alegría, M. (2015). Does marriage matter? Marital status, family processes, and psychological distress among Latino men and women. *Hispanic Journal of Behavioral Sciences*, *37*(4), 482–502.

Dargie, E., Blair, K. L., Goldfinger, C. et al. (2015). Go long! Predictors of positive relationship outcomes in long-distance dating relationships. *Journal of Sex and Marital Therapy*, *41*(2), 181–202.

Darwin, C. (1859). *On the origin of species by means of natural selection, or preservation of favoured races in the struggle for life*. John Murray.

Darwin, C. (1871). *The descent of man and selection in relation to sex*. John Murray.

Darwin Holmes, A. G. (2020). Researcher positionality – a consideration of its influence and place in qualitative research – a new researcher guide. *Shanlax International Journal of Education*, *8*(4), 1–10.

Davenport, L. (2020). The fluidity of racial classifications. *Annual Review of Political Science*, *23*, 221–240.

Davern, M., Bautista, R., Freese, J., Morgan, S. L., & Smith, T. W. (2021). General Social Surveys, 1972–2021 Cross-section [machine-readable data file, 68,846 cases]. Principal Investigator, Michael Davern; Co-Principal Investigators, Rene Bautista, Jeremy Freese, Stephen L. Morgan, and Tom W. Smith; Sponsored by National Science Foundation. – NORC ed. – Chicago: NORC: NORC at the University of Chicago [producer and distributor]. Data accessed from the GSS Data Explorer website at gssdataexplorer.norc.org

Davey, A., Fincham, F. D., Beach, S. R. H. et al. (2001). Attributions in marriage: Examining the entailment model in dyadic context. *Journal of Family Psychology*, *15*, 721–734.

Davie, M. R., & Reeves, R. J. (1939). Propinquity of residence before marriage. *American Journal of Sociology*, *44*(4), 510–517.

Davies, A. P. C., Shackelford, T. K., & Hass, R. G. (2007). When a "poach" is not a poach: Re-defining human mate poaching and re-estimating its frequency. *Archives of Sexual Behavior*, *36*(5), 702–716.

Davies, A. P. C., Tratner, A. E., & Shackelford, T. K. (2019). Not clearly defined, not reliably measured, and not replicable: Revisiting the definition and measurement of human mate poaching. *Personality and Individual Differences*, *145*, 103–105.

Davies, S., Katz, J., & Jackson, J. L. (1999). Sexual desire discrepancies: Effects on sexual and relationship satisfaction in heterosexual dating couples. *Archives of Sexual Behavior*, *28*(6), 553–567.

Davila, J., & Bradbury, T. N. (2001). Attachment insecurity and the distinction between unhappy spouses who do and do not divorce. *Journal of Family Psychology*, *15*(3), 371–393.

Davis, A. C., Dufort, C., Desrochers, J. et al. (2018). Gossip as an intrasexual competition strategy: Sex differences in gossip frequency, content, and attitudes. *Evolutionary Psychological Science*, 4(2), 141–153.

Davis, D., Shaver, P. R., & Vernon, M. L. (2003). Physical, emotional, and behavioral reactions to breaking up: The roles of gender, age, emotional involvement, and attachment style. *Personality and Social Psychology Bulletin*, 29(7), 871–884.

Davis, D., Shaver, P. R., & Vernon, M. L. (2004). Attachment style and subjective motivations for sex. *Personality and Social Psychology Bulletin*, 30(8), 1076–1090.

Davis, D., Shaver, P. R., Widaman, K. F. et al. (2006). "I can't get no satisfaction": Insecure attachment, inhibited sexual communication, and sexual dissatisfaction. *Personal Relationships*, 13(4), 465–483.

Davis, E., Shelly, A., Waters, E. et al. (2010). The impact of caring for a child with cerebral palsy: Quality of life for mothers and fathers. *Child: Care, Health and Development*, 36(1), 63–73.

Dawson, S. J., & Chivers, M. L. (2014). Gender differences and similarities in sexual desire. *Current Sexual Health Reports*, 6(4), 211–219.

Day, L. C., Muise, A., Joel, S. et al. (2015). To do it or not to do it? How communally motivated people navigate sexual interdependence dilemmas. *Personality and Social Psychology Bulletin*, 41(6), 791–804.

De Becker, G. (1997). *The gift of fear*. Little, Brown.

De Claire, K., Dixon, L., & Larkin, M. (2020). How prisoners and their partners experience the maintenance of their relationship during a prison sentence. *Journal of Community and Applied Social Psychology*, 30(3), 293–306.

De Graaf, H., Vanwesenbeeck, I., Meijer, S. et al. (2009). Sexual trajectories during adolescence: Relation to demographic characteristics and sexual risk. *Archives of Sexual Behavior*, 38(2), 276–282.

De Graaf, P. M., & Kalmijn, M. (2006). Divorce motives in a period of rising divorce: Evidence from a Dutch life-history survey. *Journal of Family Issues*, 27(4), 483–505.

de Jager, S., Coetzee, N., & Coetzee, V. (2018). Facial adiposity, attractiveness, and health: A review. *Frontiers in Psychology*, 9, 2562.

De La Ronde, C., & Swann, W. B. (1998). Partner verification: Restoring shattered images of our intimates. *Journal of Personality and Social Psychology*, 75(2), 374–382.

de Menezes Gomes, R., de Araújo Lopes, F., & Castro, F. N. (2021). Influence of sexual genotype and gender self-perception on sociosexuality and self-esteem among transgender people. *Human Nature*, 31(4), 483–496.

de Munck, V. C., Korotayev, A., de Munck, J. et al. (2011). Cross-cultural analysis of models of romantic love among U.S. residents, Russians, and Lithuanians. *Cross-Cultural Research*, 45(2), 128–154.

de Oliveira, L., Carvalho, J., Sarikaya, S. et al. (2021). Patterns of sexual behavior and psychological processes in asexual persons: A systematic review. *International Journal of Impotence Research*, 33(6), 641–651.

De Smet, O., Loeys, T., & Buysse, A. (2012). Post-breakup unwanted pursuit: A refined analysis of the role of romantic relationship characteristics. *Journal of Family Violence*, 27(5), 437–452.

Debrot, A., Meuwly, N., Muise, A. et al. (2017). More than just sex: Affection mediates the association between sexual activity and well-being. *Personality and Social Psychology Bulletin*, 43, 287–299.

Debrot, A., Schoebi, D., Perrez, M. et al. (2013). Touch as an interpersonal emotion regulation process in couples' daily lives: The mediating role of psychological intimacy. *Personality and Social Psychology Bulletin*, 39, 1373–1385.

Debrot, A., Stellar, J. E., MacDonald, G. et al. (2020). Is touch in romantic relationships universally beneficial for psychological well-being? The role of attachment avoidance. *Personality and Social Psychology Bulletin*, 47, 1495–1509.

DeBruine, L. (2016). *Young adult composite faces*. Figshare. Figure. https://figshare.com/articles/figure/Young_adult_composite_faces/4055130/1

DeBruine, L., Jones, B. C., Frederick, D. A. et al. (2010). Evidence for menstrual cycle shifts in women's preferences for masculinity: A response to Harris (in press) "Menstrual cycle and facial preferences reconsidered." *Evolutionary Psychology*, 8(4), 768–775.

DeBruine, L. M., Jones, B. C., Crawford, J. R. et al. (2010). The health of a nation predicts their mate preferences: Cross-cultural variation in women's preferences for masculinized male faces. *Proceedings of the Royal Society B: Biological Sciences*, 277(1692), 2405–2410.

Deci, E. L., & Ryan, R. M. (1991). A motivational approach to self: Integration in personality. In R. A. Dienstbier (Ed.), *Nebraska Symposium on Motivation, 1990: Perspectives on motivation* (Vol. 38, pp. 237–288). University of Nebraska Press.

Deci, E., & Ryan, R. (2000). The "what" and "why" of goal pursuits: Human needs and the self-determination of behavior. *Psychological Inquiry*, 11(4), 227–268.

Del Guidice, M., Gangestad, S. W., & Kaplan, H. (2016). Life history theory and evolutionary psychology. In D. M. Buss (Ed.), *Handbook of evolutionary psychology* (2nd ed., pp. 88–114). John Wiley & Sons.

del Mar Sánchez-Fuentes, M., & Sierra, J. C. (2015). Sexual satisfaction in a heterosexual and homosexual Spanish sample: The role of socio-demographic characteristics, health indicators, and relational factors. *Sexual and Relationship Therapy*, *30*(2), 226–242.

Delicate, A., Ayers, S., & McMullen, S. (2018). A systematic review and meta-synthesis of the impact of becoming parents on the couple relationship. *Midwifery*, *61*, 88–96.

DeLamater, J. D., & Sill, M. (2005). Sexual desire in later life. *Journal of Sex Research*, *42*(2), 138–149.

DeMaris, A. (2018). Marriage advantage in subjective well-being: Causal effect or unmeasured heterogeneity? *Marriage and Family Review*, *54*(4), 335–350.

Demir, M., & Özdemir, M. (2010). Friendship, need satisfaction and happiness. *Journal of Happiness Studies*, *11*(2), 243–259.

Denes, A. (2012). Pillow talk: Exploring disclosures after sexual activity. *Western Journal of Communication*, *76*(2), 91–108.

Denes, A., Bennett, M., & Winkler, K. L. (2017). Exploring the benefits of affectionate communication: Implications for interpersonal acceptance–rejection theory. *Journal of Family Theory & Review*, *9*(4), 491–506.

Denes, A., Crowley, J. P., Winkler, K. L. et al. (2020). Exploring the effects of pillow talk on relationship satisfaction and physiological stress responses to couples' difficult conversations. *Communication Monographs*, *87*(3), 267–290.

Denes, A., Dhillon, A., & Speer, A. C. (2017). Relational maintenance strategies during the post sex time interval. *Communication Quarterly*, *65*(3), 307–332.

Denes, A., Lannutti, P. J., & Bevan, J. L. (2015). Same-sex infidelity in heterosexual romantic relationships: Investigating emotional, relational, and communicative responses. *Personal Relationships*, *22*(3), 414–430.

DePaulo, B. M., & Morris, W. L. (2005). Singles in society and in science. *Psychological Inquiry*, *16*(2–3), 57–83.

Derby, K., Knox, D., & Easterling, B. (2012). Snooping in romantic relationships. *College Student Journal*, *46*(2), 333–343.

Derlega, V. J., Winstead, B. A., Mathews, A. et al. (2008). Why does someone reveal highly personal information? Attributions for and against self-disclosure in close relationships. *Communication Research Reports*, *25*(2), 115–130.

Derlega, V. J., Winstead, B. A., Pearson, M. R. et al. (2011). Unwanted pursuit in same-sex relationships: Effects of attachment styles, investment model variables, and sexual minority stressors. *Partner Abuse*, *2*(3), 300–322.

Derrick, J. L., Gabriel, S., & Hugenberg, K. (2009). Social surrogacy: How favored television programs provide the experience of belonging. *Journal of Experimental Social Psychology*, *45*(2), 352–362.

DeSteno, D., Valdesolo, P., & Bartlett, M. (2006). Jealousy and the threatened self: Getting to the heart of the green-eyed monster. *Journal of Personality and Social Psychology*, *91*, 626–641.

Dew, J. (2009). Has the marital time cost of parenting changed over time? *Social Forces*, *88*(2), 519–542.

Dew, J. P., & Stewart, R. (2012). A financial issue, a relationship issue, or both? Examining the predictors of marital financial conflict. *Journal of Financial Therapy*, *3*(1), 43–61.

Dewall, C. N., & Baumeister, R. F. (2006). Alone but feeling no pain: Effects of social exclusion on physical pain tolerance and pain threshold, affective forecasting, and interpersonal empathy. *Journal of Personality and Social Psychology*, *91*, 1–15.

DeWall, C. N., & Bushman, B. J. (2011). Social acceptance and rejection: The sweet and the bitter. *Current Directions in Psychological Science*, *20*(4), 256–260.

DeWall, C. N., Lambert, N. M., Slotter, E. B. et al. (2011). So far away from one's partner, yet so close to romantic alternatives: Avoidant attachment, interest in alternatives, and infidelity. *Journal of Personality and Social Psychology*, *101*(6), 1302–1316.

DeWall, C. N., MacDonald, G., Webster, G. D. et al. (2010). Acetaminophen reduces social pain: Behavioral and neural evidence. *Psychological Science*, *21*(7), 931–937.

Dewall, C. N., Maner, J. K., & Rouby, D. A. (2009). Social exclusion and early-stage interpersonal perception: Selective attention to signs of acceptance. *Journal of Personality and Social Psychology*, *96*(4), 729–741.

Dewitte, M., De Houwer, J., Buysse, A. et al. (2008). Proximity seeking in adult attachment: Examining the role of automatic approach-avoidance tendencies. *British Journal of Social Psychology*, *47*(4), 557–573.

Dhillon, A. (2019, June 4). "It's humiliating for us": Village disowns Dutee Chand, India's first openly gay athlete. *The Guardian*. www.theguardian.com/world/2019/jun/05/dutee-chand-india-athlete-coming-out?fbclid = IwAR0VhQvIjNCRBNDWazt24ckf7kYQCtcS92WrMJmu4bRHk7d8aX7ZMDW72i0

Di Giulio, P., Impicciatore, R., & Sironi, M. (2019). The changing pattern of cohabitation: A sequence analysis approach. *Demographic Research*, *40*, 1211–1248.

Di Nallo, A. (2019). Gender gap in repartnering: The role of parental status and custodial arrangements. *Journal of Marriage and Family*, *81*(1), 59–78.

Diamond, L. M. (2003). What does sexual orientation orient? A biobehavioral model distinguishing romantic love and sexual desire. *Psychological Review*, *110*(1), 173–192.

Diamond, L. M. (2004). Emerging perspectives on distinctions between romantic love and sexual desire. *Current Directions in Psychological Science*, *13*(3), 116–119.

Diamond, L. M. (2008). *Sexual fluidity: Understanding women's love and desire.* Harvard University Press.

Diamond, L. M. (2013). Links and distinctions between love and desire. In C. Hazan & M. Campa (Eds.), *Human bonding: The science of affectional ties* (pp. 226–250). Guilford Press.

Diamond, L. M. (2019). Love, desire, and sexual fluidity. In R. J. Sternberg & K. Sternberg (Eds.), *The new psychology of love* (2nd ed., pp. 138–153). Cambridge University Press.

Diamond, L. M., & Butterworth, M. (2008). Questioning gender and sexual identity: Dynamic links over time. *Sex Roles, 59* (5–6), 365–376.

Diamond, L. M., Dickenson, J. A., & Blair, K. L. (2017). Stability of sexual attractions across different timescales: The roles of bisexuality and gender. *Archives of Sexual Behavior, 46*(1), 193–204.

Dibiase, R., & Gunnoe, J. (2004). Gender and culture differences in touching behavior. *Journal of Social Psychology, 144*(1), 49–62.

Dickerson, S. S. (2011). Physiological responses to experiences of social pain. In G. MacDonald & L. A. Jensen-Campbell (Eds.), *Social pain: Neuropsychological and health implications of loss and exclusion* (pp. 79–94). American Psychological Association.

DiDonato, T. E. (2020). Self-authenticity and the Michelangelo phenomenon. In B. A. Mattingly, K. P. McIntyre, & G. W. Lewnadowski (Eds.), *Interpersonal relationships and the self-concept* (pp. 105–123). Springer International Publishing.

DiDonato, T. E., Bedminster, M. C., & Machel, J. J. (2013). My funny valentine: How humor styles affect romantic interest. *Personal Relationships, 20*(2), 374–390.

DiDonato, T. E., & Jakubiak, B. K. (2016a). Strategically funny: Romantic motives affect humor style in relationship initiation. *Europe's Journal of Psychology, 12*(3), 390–405.

DiDonato, T. E., & Jakubiak, B. K. (2016b). Sustainable decisions signal sustainable relationships: How purchasing decisions affect perceptions and romantic attraction. *Journal of Social Psychology, 156*(1), 8–27.

DiDonato, T. E., & Krueger, J. I. (2010). Interpersonal affirmation and self-authenticity: A test of Rogers's self-growth hypothesis. *Self and Identity, 9*(3), 322–336.

Diliman, E. M. (2011). Unrequited love among young Filipino gay men: Subjective experiences of unreciprocated lovers. *Social Science Diliman, 7*(1), 63–81.

Dillard, J. P. (2013). Explicating the goal construct: Tools for theorists. In J. O. Greene (Ed.), *Message Production: Advances in communication theory* (pp. 47–69). Lawrence Erlbaum.

Dillon, L. M., Nowak, N., Weisfeld, G. E. et al. (2015). Sources of marital conflict in five cultures. *Evolutionary Psychology, 13*(1), 147470491501300100.

Dion, K., Berscheid, E., & Walster, E. (1972). What is beautiful is good. *Journal of Personality and Social Psychology, 24* (3), 285–290.

Dion, L., & Boislard, M. A. (2020). "Of course we had sex!": A qualitative exploration of first sex among women who have sex with women. *Canadian Journal of Human Sexuality, 29*(2), 249–261.

Ditzen, B., Neumann, I. D., Bodenmann, G. et al. (2007). Effects of different kinds of couple interaction on cortisol and heart rate responses to stress in women. *Psychoneuroendocrinology, 32*(5), 565–574.

Dixon, H., Reynolds, L. M., & Consedine, N. S. (2022). Will I have sex to please you? Evaluating whether mindfulness buffers links between attachment and sexual motivations in daily life. *Journal of Sex & Marital Therapy, 48*(2), 392–414.

Dobson, K., Campbell, L., & Stanton, S. C. E. (2018). Are you coming on to me? Bias and accuracy in couples' perceptions of sexual advances. *Journal of Social and Personal Relationships, 35*(4), 460–484.

Dobson, K., Kim, J., & Impett, E. A. (2022). Perceptual accuracy for sexual rejection in romantic relationships. *Archives of Sexual Behavior, 51*, 491–503.

Dobson, K., & Ogolsky, B. (2022). The role of social context in the association between leisure activities and romantic relationship quality. *Journal of Social and Personal Relationships, 39*(2), 221–244.

Dobson, K., Zhu, J., Balzarini, R. N. et al. (2020). Responses to sexual advances and satisfaction in romantic relationships: Is yes good and no bad? *Social Psychological and Personality Science, 11*(6), 801–811.

Doherty, N. A., & Feeney, J. A. (2004). The composition of attachment networks throughout the adult years. *Personal Relationships, 11*(4), 469–488.

Don, B. P., Fredrickson, B. L., & Algoe, S. B. (2020). Enjoying the sweet moments: Does approach motivation upwardly enhance reactivity to positive interpersonal processes. *Journal of Personality and Social Psychology, 122*(6), 1022–1055.

Don, B. P., Girme, Y. U., & Hammond, M. D. (2019). Low self-esteem predicts indirect support seeking and its relationship consequences in intimate relationships. *Personality and Social Psychology Bulletin, 45*(7), 1028–1041.

Don, B. P., Mickelson, K. D., & Barbee, A. P. (2013). Indirect support seeking and perceptions of spousal support: An examination of a reciprocal relationship. *Personal Relationships, 20*(4), 655–668.

Donato, S., Pagani, A., Parise, M. et al. (2014). The capitalization process in stable couple relationships: Intrapersonal and interpersonal benefits. *Procedia – Social and Behavioral Sciences, 140*, 207–211.

Donnon, T. (2012). Experimental or RCT research designs: A crisis of nomenclature in medical education. *Canadian Medical Education Journal*, *3*(2), e82–e84.

Donovan, L. A. N., & Priester, J. R. (2017). Exploring the psychological processes underlying interpersonal forgiveness: The superiority of motivated reasoning over empathy. *Journal of Experimental Social Psychology, 71*, 16–30.

Dooley, M. K., Sweeny, K., Howell, J. L. et al. (2018). Perceptions of romantic partners' responsiveness during a period of stressful uncertainty. *Journal of Personality and Social Psychology, 115*, 677–687.

Doss, B. D., Benson, L. A., Georgia, E. J. et al. (2013). Translation of integrative behavioral couple therapy to a web-based intervention. *Family Process, 52*(1), 139–153.

Doss, B. D., Cicila, L. N., Georgia, E. J. et al. (2016). A randomized controlled trial of the web-based OurRelationship program: Effects on relationship and individual functioning. *Journal of Consulting and Clinical Psychology, 84*(4), 285–296.

Doss, B. D., Knopp, K., Roddy, M. K. et al. (2020). Online programs improve relationship functioning for distressed low-income couples: Results from a nationwide randomized controlled trial. *Journal of Consulting and Clinical Psychology, 88*(4), 283–294.

Doss, B. D., & Rhoades, G. K. (2017). The transition to parenthood: Impact on couples' romantic relationships. *Current Opinion in Psychology, 13*, 25–28.

Doss, B. D., Rhoades, G. K., Stanley, S. M. et al. (2009a). The effect of the transition to parenthood on relationship quality: An 8-year prospective study. *Journal of Personality and Social Psychology, 96*(3), 601–619.

Doss, B. D., Rhoades, G. K., Stanley, S. M. et al. (2009b). Marital therapy, retreats, and books: The who, what, when, and why of relationship help-seeking. *Journal of Marital and Family Therapy, 35*(1), 18–29.

Doss, B. D., Roddy, M. K., Nowlan, K. M. et al. (2019). Maintenance of gains in relationship and individual functioning following the online OurRelationship program. *Behavior Therapy, 50*(1), 73–86.

Doss, B. D., Roddy, M. K., Wiebe, S. A. et al. (2022). A review of the research during 2010–2019 on evidence-based treatments for couple relationship distress. *Journal of Marital and Family Therapy, 48*(1), 283–306.

Doss, B. D., Simpson, L. E., & Christensen, A. (2004). Why do couples seek marital therapy? *Professional Psychology: Research and Practice, 35*(6), 608–614.

Doyle, D. M., & Molix, L. (2015). Social stigma and sexual minorities' romantic relationship functioning: A meta-analytic review. *Personality and Social Psychology Bulletin, 41*(10), 1363–1381.

Drewianka, S., & Meder, M. E. (2020). Simultaneity and selection in financial hardship and divorce. *Review of Economics of the Household, 18*(4), 1245–1265.

Drigotas, S. M., & Rusbult, C. E. (1992). Should I stay or should I go? A dependence model of breakups. *Journal of Personality and Social Psychology, 62*(1), 62–87.

Drigotas, S. M., Rusbult, C. E., Wieselquist, J. et al. (1999). Close partner as sculptor of the ideal self: Behavioral affirmation and the Michelangelo phenomenon. *Journal of Personality and Social Psychology, 77*(2), 293–323.

Driscoll, R., Davis, K. E., & Lipetz, M. E. (1972). Parental interference and romantic love: The Romeo and Juliet effect. *Journal of Personality and Social Psychology, 24*(1), 1–10.

Driver, J. L., & Gottman, J. M. (2004). Daily marital interactions and positive affect during marital conflict among newlywed couples. *Family Process, 43*(3), 301–314.

Duck, S. (1982). A topography of relationship disengagement and dissolution. In S. Duck (Ed.), *Personal relationships*, Volume 4: *Dissolving personal relationships* (pp. 1–30). Academic Press.

Duck, S. (2005). How do you tell someone you're letting go? *Psychologist, 18*(4), 210–213.

Duffy, J. (2021, June 14). Creating a stress-free divorce for your kid – or getting as close as you can. *CNN*. www.cnn.com/2021/06/13/health/good-divorce-wellness/index.html

Duffy, K. A., & Chartrand, T. L. (2015). Mimicry: Causes and consequences. *Current Opinion in Behavioral Sciences, 3*, 112–116.

Duncan, S. (2015). Women's agency in living apart together: Constraint, strategy and vulnerability. *Sociological Review, 63*(3), 589–607.

Duncan, S., Phillips, M., Carter, J. et al. (2014). Practices and perceptions of living apart together. *Family Science, 5*(1), 1–10.

Dunkle, R. E., Feld, S., Lehning, A. J. et al. (2014). Does becoming an ADL spousal caregiver increase the caregiver's depressive symptoms? *Research on Aging, 36*(6), 655–682.

Dunlop, W. L., Karan, A., Wilkinson, D. et al. (2020). Love in the first degree: Individual differences in first-person pronoun use and adult romantic attachment styles. *Social Psychological and Personality Science, 11*(2), 254–265.

Dunn, J. (2021, May 19). Why you should give your partner the gift of time apart. *The New York Times*. www.nytimes.com/2021/05/19/well/family/alone-time.html

Duntley, J. D., & Buss, D. M. (2012). The evolution of stalking. *Sex Roles, 66*(5–6), 311–327.

Duran, R. L., & Kelly, L. (1989). The cycle of shyness: A study of self-perceptions of communication performance. *Communication Reports, 2*(1), 30–38.

Durante, K. M., Li, N. P., & Haselton, M. G. (2008). Changes in women's choice of dress across the ovulatory cycle: Naturalistic and laboratory task-based evidence. *Personality and Social Psychology Bulletin*, *34*(11), 1451–1460.

Durkheim, E. (1951). *Suicide: A study in sociology* (J. A. Spaulding & G. Simpson, trans.). Free Press (original work published 1897).

Durtschi, J. A., Fincham, F. D., Cui, M. et al. (2011). Dyadic processes in early marriage: Attributions, behavior, and marital quality. *Family Relations*, *60*(4), 421–434.

Dush, C. M. K., Cohan, C. L., & Amato, P. R. (2003). The relationship between cohabitation and marital quality and stability: Change across cohorts? *Journal of Marriage and Family*, *65*(3), 539–549.

Dutton, D. G., & Aron, A. P. (1974). Some evidence for heightened sexual attraction under conditions of high anxiety. *Journal of Personality and Social Psychology*, *30*(4), 510–517.

Dutton, L. B., & Winstead, B. A. (2006). Predicting unwanted pursuit: Attachment, relationship satisfaction, relationship alternatives, and break-up distress. *Journal of Social and Personal Relationships*, *23*(4), 565–586.

Dworkin, S. L., & O'Sullivan, L. (2005). Actual versus desired initiation patterns among a sample of college men: Tapping disjunctures within traditional male sexual scripts. *Journal of Sex Research*, *42*(2), 150–158.

Dwyer Emory, A. (2022). To stay or go: Relationship dissolution and repartnering after paternal incarceration. *Family Relations*. Advance online publication. https://doi.org/10.1111/fare.12657

Dyar, C., Newcomb, M. E., Mustanski, B. et al. (2020). A structural equation model of sexual satisfaction and relationship functioning among sexual and gender minority individuals assigned female at birth in diverse relationships. *Archives of Sexual Behavior*, *49*(2), 693–710.

Dyrenforth, P. S., Kashy, D. A., Donnellan, M. B. et al. (2010). Predicting relationship and life satisfaction from personality in nationally representative samples from three countries: The relative importance of actor, partner, and similarity effects. *Journal of Personality and Social Psychology*, *99*(4), 690–702.

Eagly, A. H., Ashmore, R. D., Makhijani, M. G. et al. (1991). What is beautiful is good, but . . .: A meta-analytic review of research on the physical attractiveness stereotype. *Psychological Bulletin*, *110*(1), 109–128.

Eagly, A. H., & Wood, W. (1999). The origins of sex differences in human behavior evolved dispositions versus social roles. *American Psychologist*, *54*(6), 408–423.

Eastwick, P. W. (2016). The emerging integration of close relationships research and evolutionary psychology. *Current Directions in Psychological Science*, *25*(3), 183–190.

Eastwick, P. W., Eagly, A. H., Finkel, E. J. et al. (2011). Implicit and explicit preferences for physical attractiveness in a romantic partner: A double dissociation in predictive validity. *Journal of Personality and Social Psychology*, *101*(5), 993–1011.

Eastwick, P. W., Eagly, A. H., Glick, P. et al. (2006). Is traditional gender ideology associated with sex-typed mate preferences? A test in nine nations. *Sex Roles*, *54*(9–10), 603–614.

Eastwick, P. W., & Finkel, E. J. (2008a). The attachment system in fledgling relationships: An activating role for attachment anxiety. *Journal of Personality and Social Psychology*, *95*(3), 628–647.

Eastwick, P. W., & Finkel, E. J. (2008b). Sex differences in mate preferences revisited: Do people know what they initially desire in a romantic partner? *Journal of Personality and Social Psychology*, *94*(2), 245–264.

Eastwick, P. W., Finkel, E. J., Mochon, D. et al. (2007). Selective versus unselective romantic desire: Not all reciprocity is created equal. *Psychological Science*, *18*(4), 317–319.

Eastwick, P. W., Finkel, E. J., & Simpson, J. A. (2019). The relationship trajectories framework: Elaboration and expansion. *Psychological Inquiry*, *30*(1), 48–57.

Eastwick, P. W., Joel, S., Carswell, K. L., Molden, D. C., Finkel, E., & Blozis, S. A. (2022). Predicting romantic interest during early relationship development: A preregistered investigation using machine learning. *European Journal of Personality*, *37*(3), 276–312.

Eastwick, P. W., Keneski, E., Morgan, T. A. et al. (2018). What do short-term and long-term relationships look like? Building the relationship coordination and strategic timing (ReCAST) model. *Journal of Experimental Psychology: General*, *147*(5), 747–781.

Eastwick, P. W., Luchies, L. B., Finkel, E. J. et al. (2014). The predictive validity of ideal partner preferences: A review and meta-analysis. *Psychological Bulletin*, *140*(3), 623–665.

Eaton, A. A., Rose, S. M., Interligi, C. et al. (2016). Gender and ethnicity in dating, hanging out, and hooking up: Sexual scripts among Hispanic and White young adults. *Journal of Sex Research*, *53*(7), 788–804.

Ebbesen, E. B., Kjos, G. L., & Konečni, V. J. (1976). Spatial ecology: Its effects on the choice of friends and enemies. *Journal of Experimental Social Psychology*, *12*(6), 505–518.

Ebert, D. D., Buntrock, C., Mortier, P. et al. (2019). Prediction of major depressive disorder onset in college students. *Depression and Anxiety*, *36*(4), 294–304.

Edgar, T., & Fitzpatrick, M. A. (1993). Expectations for sexual interaction: A cognitive test of the sequencing of sexual communication behaviors. *Health Communication, 5*(4), 239–261.

Edlund, J. E., Clark, D. Q., Kalmus, A. M. et al. (2021). Receptivity to casual sexual requests. *Journal of Social Psychology, 161*(6), 779–784.

Edwards, K., Carter-Tellison, K., & Herring, C. (2004). For richer, for poorer, whether dark or light: Skin tone, marital status, and spouse's earnings. In C. Herring, V. Keith, & H. Horton (Eds.), *Skin deep: How race and complexion matter in the "color-blind" era*. University of Illinois Press.

Edwards, K. M., Sylaska, K. M., Barry, J. E. et al. (2015). Physical dating violence, sexual violence, and unwanted pursuit victimization: A comparison of incidence rates among sexual-minority and heterosexual college students. *Journal of Interpersonal Violence, 30*(4), 580–600.

Egbert, N., & Polk, D. (2006). Speaking the language of relational maintenance: A validity test of Chapman's (1992) five love languages. *Communication Research Reports, 23*(1), 19–26.

Ehlebracht, D., Stavrova, O., Fetchenhauer, D. et al. (2018). The synergistic effect of prosociality and physical attractiveness on mate desirability. *British Journal of Psychology, 109*(3), 517–537.

Eickmeyer, K. J., & Manning, W. D. (2018). Serial cohabitation in young adulthood: Baby boomers to millennials. *Journal of Marriage and Family, 80*(4), 826–840.

Eidelson, R. J., & Epstein, N. (1982). Cognition and relationship maladjustment: Development of a measure of dysfunctional relationship beliefs. *Journal of Consulting and Clinical Psychology, 50*(5), 715–720.

Eisenberger, N. I. (2012). The pain of social disconnection: Examining the shared neural underpinnings of physical and social pain. *Nature Reviews Neuroscience, 13*(6), 421–434.

Eisenberger, N. I. (2015). Social pain and the brain: Controversies, questions, and where to go from here. *Annual Review of Psychology, 66*(1), 601–629.

Eisenberger, N. I., Lieberman, M. D., & Williams, K. D. (2003). Does rejection hurt? An fMRI study of social exclusion. *Science, 302*(5643), 290–292.

Eisenberger, N. I., Master, S. L., Inagaki, T. K. et al. (2011). Attachment figures activate a safety signal-related neural region and reduce pain experience. *Proceedings of the National Academy of Sciences, 108*(28), 11721–11726.

Eldridge, K., Sevier, M., Jones, J. et al. (2007). Demand-withdraw communication in severely distressed, moderately distressed, and nondistressed couples: Rigidity and polarity during relationship and personal problem discussions. *Journal of Family Psychology, 21*, 218–226.

Elliot, A. J., & Church, M. A. (1997). A hierarchical model of approach and avoidance achievement motivation. *Journal of Personality and Social Psychology, 72*(1), 218–232.

Elliot, A. J., Gable, S. L., & Mapes, R. R. (2006). Approach and avoidance motivation in the social domain. *Personality and Social Psychology Bulletin, 32*(3), 378–391.

Elliot, A. J., & Reis, H. T. (2003). Attachment and exploration in adulthood. *Journal of Personality and Social Psychology, 85*, 317–331.

Ellis, B. J., Figueredo, A. J., Brumbach, B. H. et al. (2009). Fundamental dimensions of environmental risk: The impact of harsh versus unpredictable environments on the evolution and development of life history strategies. *Human Nature, 20*(2), 204–268.

Ellwood, B. (2021, May 4). Mindfulness can enhance marital relationships by improving one's capacity for forgiveness and gratitude, study suggests. *PsyPost.* www.psypost.org/2021/05/mindfulness-can-enhance-marital-relationships-by-improving-ones-capacity-for-forgiveness-and-gratitude-study-suggests-60661

Elwert, F., & Christakis, N. A. (2006). Widowhood and race. *American Sociological Review, 71*(1), 16–41.

Elwert, F., & Christakis, N. A. (2008). The effect of widowhood on mortality by the causes of death of both spouses. *American Journal of Public Health, 98*(11), 2092–2098.

Emery, L. F., & Gardner, W. L. (2020). Who in the world am I? Self-concept clarity and self-change in relationships. In B. Mattingly, K. McIntyre, & G. Lewandowski, Jr. (Eds.), *Interpersonal relationships and the self-concept* (pp. 89–104). Springer International Publishing.

Emmons, R. (2004). The psychology of gratitude: An introduction. In R. Emmons & M. McCullough (Eds.), *The psychology of gratitude* (pp. 3–16). Oxford University Press.

Endendijk, J. J., van Baar, A. L., & Deković, M. (2020). He is a stud, she is a slut! A meta analysis on the continued existence of sexual double standards. *Personality and Social Psychology Review, 24*(2), 163–190.

Engblom-Deglmann, M., & Brimhall, A. S. (2016). Not even cold in her grave: How postbereavement remarried couples perceive family acceptance. *Journal of Divorce and Remarriage, 57*(3), 224–244.

England, P., Shafer, E. F., & Fogarty, A. C. K. (2008). Hooking up and forming romantic relationships on today's college campuses. In M. Kimmel & A. Aronson (Eds.), *The gendered society reader* (pp. 531–593). Oxford University Press.

Ennis, J., & Majid, U. (2020). The widowhood effect: Explaining the adverse outcomes after spousal loss using physiological stress theories, marital quality, and attachment. *Family Journal, 28*(3), 241–246.

Ennis, J., & Majid, U. (2021). "Death from a broken heart": A systematic review of the relationship between spousal bereavement and physical and physiological health outcomes. *Death Studies*, *45*(7), 538–551.

Epel, E. S., Crosswell, A. D., Mayer, S. E. et al. (2018). More than a feeling: A unified view of stress measurement for population science. *Frontiers in Neuroendocrinology*, *49*, 146–169.

Epstein, N. B., & Zheng, L. (2017). Cognitive-behavioral couple therapy. *Current Opinion in Psychology*, *13*, 142–147.

Ermer, A. E., & Proulx, C. M. (2020). Social support and well-being among older adult married couples: A dyadic perspective. *Journal of Social and Personal Relationships*, *37*(4), 1073–1091.

Etcheverry, P. E., Le, B., & Charania, M. R. (2008). Perceived versus reported social referent approval and romantic relationship commitment and persistence. *Personal Relationships*, *15*(3), 281–295.

Eubanks Fleming, C. J., & Córdova, J. V. (2012). Predicting relationship help seeking prior to a marriage checkup. *Family Relations*, *61*(1), 90–100.

Evans, S. E., Davies, C., & DiLillo, D. (2008). Exposure to domestic violence: A meta-analysis of child and adolescent outcomes. *Aggression and Violent Behavior*, *13*(2), 131–140.

Eyring, J. B., Leavitt, C. E., Allsop, D. B. et al. (2021). Forgiveness and gratitude: Links between couples' mindfulness and sexual and relational satisfaction in new cisgender heterosexual marriages. *Journal of Sex & Marital Therapy*, *47*(2), 147–161.

Falconier, M. K., Nussbeck, F., Bodenmann, G. et al. (2015). Stress from daily hassles in couples: Its effects on intra-dyadic stress, relationship satisfaction, and physical and psychological well-being. *Journal of Marital and Family Therapy*, *41*(2), 221–235.

Fales, M. R., Frederick, D. A., Garcia, J. R. et al. (2016). Mating markets and bargaining hands: Mate preferences for attractiveness and resources in two national U.S. studies. *Personality and Individual Differences*, *88*, 78–87.

Fallahchai, R., Fallahi, M., & Ritchie, L. L. (2017). The impact of PREP training on marital conflicts reduction: A randomized controlled trial with Iranian distressed couples. *Journal of Couple & Relationship Therapy*, *16*(1), 61–76.

Fallis, E. E., Rehman, U. S., Woody, E. Z. et al. (2016). The longitudinal association of relationship satisfaction and sexual satisfaction in long-term relationships. *Journal of Family Psychology*, *30*(7), 822–831.

Farley, S. D. (2014). Nonverbal reactions to an attractive stranger: The role of mimicry in communicating preferred social distance. *Journal of Nonverbal Behavior*, *38*(2), 195–208.

Farr, C. (2018, August 1). Facebook and Instagram roll out new features to help us realize when we're wasting time on the apps. *CNBC*. www.cnbc.com/2018/08/01/facebook-and-instagram-time-well-spent-features.html

Farrelly, D. (2013). Altruism as an indicator of good parenting quality in long-term relationships: Further investigations using the mate preferences towards altruistic traits scale. *Journal of Social Psychology*, *153*(4), 395–398.

Farrelly, D., Clemson, P., & Guthrie, M. (2016). Are women's mate preferences for altruism also influenced by physical attractiveness? *Evolutionary Psychology*, *14*(1), 1–6.

Fast, N. J., & Chen, S. (2009). When the boss feels inadequate: Power, incompetence, and aggression. *Psychological Science*, *20*(11), 1406–1413.

Faure, R., McNulty, J. K., Hicks, L. L. et al. (2020). The case for studying implicit social cognition in close relationships. *Social Cognition*, *38*(Supplement), s98–s114.

Fawcett, E. B., Hawkins, A. J., Blanchard, V. L. et al. (2010). Do premarital education programs really work? A meta-analytic study. *Family Relations*, *59*(3), 232–239.

Feeney, B. C. (2004). A secure base: Responsive support of goal strivings and exploration in adult intimate relationships. *Journal of Personality and Social Psychology*, *87*, 631–648.

Feeney, B. C. (2007). The dependency paradox in close relationships: Accepting dependence promotes independence. *Journal of Personality and Social Psychology*, *92*, 268–285.

Feeney, B. C., & Collins, N. L. (2001). Predictors of caregiving in adult intimate relationships: An attachment theoretical perspective. *Journal of Personality and Social Psychology*, *80*(6), 972–994.

Feeney, B. C., & Collins, N. L. (2003). Motivations for caregiving in adult intimate relationships: Influences on caregiving behavior and relationship functioning. *Personality and Social Psychology Bulletin*, *29*(8), 950–968.

Feeney, B. C., & Collins, N. L. (2014). Much "I do" about nothing? Ascending Mount Maslow with an oxygenated marriage. *Psychological Inquiry*, *25*(1), 69–79.

Feeney, B. C., & Collins, N. L. (2015a). A new look at social support: A theoretical perspective on thriving through relationships. *Personality and Social Psychology Review*, *19*, 113–147.

Feeney, B. C., & Collins, N. L. (2015b). Thriving through relationships. *Current Opinion in Psychology*, *1*, 22–28.

Feeney, B. C., & Collins, N. L. (2018). Social support in close relationships. In A. L. Vangelisti & D. Perlman (Eds.), *Cambridge handbook of personal relationships* (2nd ed., pp. 282–296). Cambridge University Press.

Feeney, B. C., & Collins, N. L. (2019). The importance of relational support for attachment and exploration needs. *Current Opinion in Psychology*, *25*, 182–186.

Feeney, B. C., & Kirkpatrick, L. (1996). Effects of adult attachment and presence of romantic partners on physiological responses to stress. *Journal of Personality and Social Psychology*, *70*, 255–270.

Feeney, B. C., & Lemay, E. P. (2012). Surviving relationship threats: The role of emotional capital. *Personality & Social Psychology Bulletin*, *38*(8), 1004–1017.

Feeney, B. C., & Thrush, R. L. (2010). Relationship influences on exploration in adulthood: The characteristics and function of a secure base. *Journal of Personality and Social Psychology*, *98*(1), 57–76.

Feeney, B. C., Van Vleet, M., Jakubiak, B. K. et al. (2017). Predicting the pursuit and support of challenging life opportunities. *Personality and Social Psychology Bulletin*, *43*(8), 1171–1187.

Feeney, J. A., & Karantzas, G. C. (2017). Couple conflict: Insights from an attachment perspective. *Current Opinion in Psychology*, *13*, 60–64.

Feeney, J. A., & Noller, P. (1990). Attachment style as a predictor of adult romantic relationships. *Journal of Personality and Social Psychology*, *58*(2), 281–291.

Fehr, B. (1994). Prototype-based assessment of laypeople's views of love. *Personal Relationships*, *1*(4), 309–331.

Fehr, B., Harasymchuk, C., & Sprecher, S. (2014). Compassionate love in romantic relationships: A review and some new findings. *Journal of Social and Personal Relationships*, *31*(5), 575–600.

Fehr, R., Gelfand, M. J., & Nag, M. (2010). The road to forgiveness: A meta-analytic synthesis of its situational and dispositional correlates. *Psychological Bulletin*, *136*(5), 894–914.

Feingold, A. (1992). Good-looking people are not what we think. *Psychological Bulletin*, *111*(2), 304–341.

Feinstein, B. A., Petruzzella, A., Davila, J. et al. (2020). Sharing positive experiences related to one's sexual orientation: Examining the capitalization process in a sample of gay men. *Psychology of Sexual Orientation and Gender Diversity*, *7*(1), 40–45.

Feldman, R., & Bakermans-Kranenburg, M. J. (2017). Oxytocin: A parenting hormone. *Current Opinion in Psychology*, *15*, 13–18.

Feldman, R., Singer, M., & Zagoory, O. (2010). Touch attenuates infants' physiological reactivity to stress. *Developmental Science*, *13*(2), 271–278.

Feldman Barrett, L. (2015, September). Psychology is not in crisis. *The New York Times*. www.nytimes.com/2015/09/01/opinion/psychology-is-not-in-crisis.html

Felmlee, D. H. (1995). Fatal attractions: Affection and disaffection in intimate relationships. *Journal of Social and Personal Relationships*, *12*(2), 295–311.

Felmlee, D. H. (1998). "Be careful what you wish for …": A quantitative and qualitative investigation of "fatal attractions." *Personal Relationships*, *5*(3), 235–253.

Felmlee, D. H. (2001). From appealing to appalling: Disenchantment with a romantic partner. *Sociological Perspectives*, *44*(3), 263–280.

Felmlee, D. H., & Sinclair, H. C. (2018). Social networks and personal relationships. In A. L. Vangelisti & D. Perlman (Eds.), *The Cambridge handbook of personal relationships* (pp. 467–480). Cambridge University Press.

Fentz, H. N., & Trillingsgaard, T. (2017). Checking up on couples: A meta-analysis of the effect of assessment and feedback on marital functioning and individual mental health in couples. *Journal of Marital and Family Therapy*, *43*(1), 31–50.

Ferris, L. J., Jetten, J., Hornsey, M. J. et al. (2019). Feeling hurt: Revisiting the relationship between social and physical pain. *Review of General Psychology*, *23*(3), 320–335.

Feybesse, C., & Hatfield, E. (2019). Passionate love. In R. J. Sternberg & K. Sternberg (Eds.), *The new psychology of love* (pp. 183–207). Cambridge University Press.

Field, N. P., & Sundin, E. C. (2001). Attachment style in adjustment to conjugal bereavement. *Journal of Social and Personal Relationships*, *18*(3), 347–361.

Field, T. (2010). Touch for socioemotional and physical well-being: A review. *Developmental Review*, *30*(4), 367–383.

Field, T. (2011). Romantic breakups, heartbreak and bereavement: Romantic breakups. *Psychology*, *2*(4), 382–387.

Field, T., Diego, M., Pelaez, M. et al. (2009). Breakup distress in university students. *Adolescence*, *44*(176), 705–727.

Fielder, R. L., & Carey, M. P. (2010). Prevalence and characteristics of sexual hookups among first-semester female college students. *Journal of Sex and Marital Therapy*, *36*(4), 346–359.

Fincham, F. D. (2010). Forgiveness: Integral to a science of close relationships? In M. Mikulincer & P. R. Shaver (Eds.), *Prosocial motives, emotions, and behavior: The better angels of our nature* (pp. 347–365). American Psychological Association.

Fincham, F. D. (2022). Trait mindfulness and relationship mindfulness are indirectly related to sexual quality over time in dating relationships among emerging adults. *Journal of Social and Personal Relationships*, *39*(6), 1885–1898.

Fincham, F. D., & Beach, S. R. (2013). Gratitude and forgiveness in relationships. In J. A. Simpson & L. Campbell (Eds.), *The Oxford handbook of close relationships* (pp. 638–663). Oxford University Press.

Fincham, F. D., & Bradbury, T. N. (1992). Assessing attributions in marriage: The Relationship Attribution Measure. *Journal of Personality and Social Psychology, 62*(3), 457–468.

Fincham, F. D., Hall, J., & Beach, S. R. H. (2006). Forgiveness in marriage: Current status and future directions. *Family Relations, 55*(4), 415–427.

Fincham, F. D., & May, R. W. (2021). Divine forgiveness and interpersonal forgiveness: Which comes first? *Psychology of Religion and Spirituality.* Advance online publication. https://doi.org/10.1037/rel0000418

Finer, L. B., & Zolna, M. R. (2016). Declines in unintended pregnancy in the United States, 2008–2011. *Obstetrical & Gynecological Survey, 71*(7), 408–409.

Fink, B., Neave, N., Manning, J. T. et al. (2006). Facial symmetry and judgements of attractiveness, health and personality. *Personality and Individual Differences, 41*(3), 491–499.

Fink, G. (2017). *Stress: Neuroendocrinology and neurobiology.* Elsevier.

Finkel, E. J., & Baumeister, R. F. (2019). Attraction and rejection. In R. F. Baumeister & E. J. Finkel (Eds.), *Advanced social psychology: The state of the science* (2nd ed., pp. 201–226). Oxford University Press.

Finkel, E. J., & Campbell, W. (2001). Self-control and accommodation in close relationships: An interdependence analysis. *Journal of Personality and Social Psychology, 81*(2), 263–277.

Finkel, E. J., & Eastwick, P. W. (2008). Speed-dating. *Current Directions in Psychological Science, 17*(3), 193–197.

Finkel, E. J., & Eastwick, P. W. (2009). Arbitrary social norms influence sex differences in romantic selectivity. *Psychological Science, 20*(10), 1290–1295.

Finkel, E. J., & Eastwick, P. W. (2015). Interpersonal attraction: In search of a theoretical Rosetta Stone. In M. Mikulincer, P. R. Shaver, J. A. Simpson, & J. F. Dovidio (Eds.), *APA handbook of personality and social psychology*, Volume 3: *Interpersonal relations* (pp. 179–210). American Psychological Association.

Finkel, E. J., Eastwick, P. W., Karney, B. R. et al. (2012). Online dating: A critical analysis from the perspective of psychological science. *Psychological Science in the Public Interest, Supplement, 13*(1), 3–66.

Finkel, E. J., Eastwick, P. W., & Matthews, J. (2007). Speed-dating as an invaluable tool for studying romantic attraction: A methodological primer. *Personal Relationships, 14*(1), 149–166.

Finkel, E. J., Eastwick, P. W., & Reis, H. T. (2015). Best research practices in psychology: Illustrating epistemological and pragmatic considerations with the case of relationship science. *Journal of Personality and Social Psychology, 108*(2), 275–297.

Finkel, E. J., Hui, C. M., Carswell, K. L. et al. (2014). The suffocation of marriage: Climbing Mount Maslow without enough oxygen. *Psychological Inquiry, 25*, 1–41.

Finkel, E. J., Norton, M. I., Reis, H. T. et al. (2015). When does familiarity promote versus undermine interpersonal attraction? A proposed integrative model from erstwhile adversaries. *Perspectives on Psychological Science, 10*(1), 3–19.

Finkel, E. J., Rusbult, C. E., Kumashiro, M. et al. (2002). Dealing with betrayal in close relationships: Does commitment promote forgiveness? *Journal of Personality and Social Psychology, 82*(6), 956–974.

Finkel, E. J., Simpson, J. A., & Eastwick, P. W. (2017). The psychology of close relationships: Fourteen core principles. *Annual Review of Psychology, 68*(1), 383–411.

Finkenauer, C., Meij, L. W.-D., Reis, H. T. et al. (2010). The importance of seeing what is not there: A quasi-signal detection analysis of positive and negative behavior in newlywed couples. *Personal Relationships, 17*(4), 615–633.

Finn, C., Mitte, K., & Neyer, F. J. (2013). The relationship-specific interpretation bias mediates the link between neuroticism and satisfaction in couples. *European Journal of Personality, 27*(2), 200–212.

Finnäs, F., Rostila, M., & Saarela, J. (2018). Divorce and parity progression following the death of a child: A register-based study from Finland. *Population Studies, 72*(1), 41–51.

Fiori, K. L., Rauer, A. J., Birditt, K. S. et al. (2018). "I love you, not your friends": Links between partners' early disapproval of friends and divorce across 16 years. *Journal of Social and Personal Relationships, 35*(9), 1230–1250.

Fisher, H., Aron, A., & Brown, L. L. (2005). Romantic love: An fMRI study of a neural mechanism for mate choice. *Journal of Comparative Neurology, 493*(1), 58–62.

Fisher, H., & Thomson, J. A. (2007). Lust, romance, attraction, attachment: Do the side effects of serotonin-enhancing antidepressants jeopardize romantic love, marriage and fertility? In S. M. Platek, J. P. Keenan, & T. K. Shackelford (Eds.), *Evolutionary cognitive neuroscience* (pp. 245–283). MIT Press.

Fisher, H. E. (1998). Lust, attraction, and attachment in mammalian reproduction. *Human Nature, 9*(1), 23–52.

Fisher, H. E. (2000). Lust, attraction, attachment: Biology and evolution of the three primary emotion systems for mating, reproduction, and parenting. *Journal of Sex Education and Therapy, 25*(1), 96–104.

Fisher, H. E. (2005). *Why we love: The nature and chemistry of romantic love.* Holt.

Fisher, H. E., Aron, A., Mashek, D. et al. (2002). Defining the brain systems of lust, romantic attraction, and attachment. *Archives of Sexual Behavior*, *31*(5), 413–419.

Fisher, H. E., Brown, L. L., Aron, A. et al. (2010). Reward, addiction, and emotion regulation systems associated with rejection in love. *Journal of Neurophysiology*, *104*(1), 51–60.

Fisher, H. E., Xu, X., Aron, A. et al. (2016). Intense, passionate, romantic love: A natural addiction? How the fields that investigate romance and substance abuse can inform each other. *Frontiers in Psychology*, *7*, 687.

Fisher, M., & Cox, A. (2011). Four strategies used during intrasexual competition for mates. *Personal Relationships*, *18*(1), 20–38.

Fisher, M. L., Coughlin, S., & Wade, T. J. (2020). Can I have your number? Men's perceived effectiveness of pick-up lines used by women. *Personality and Individual Differences*, *153*, 109664.

Fisher, T. D., Moore, Z. T., & Pittenger, M. J. (2012). Sex on the brain? An examination of frequency of sexual cognitions as a function of gender, erotophilia, and social desirability. *Journal of Sex Research*, *49*(1), 69–77.

Fisher, W. A., Donahue, K. L., Long, J. S. et al. (2015). Individual and partner correlates of sexual satisfaction and relationship happiness in midlife couples: Dyadic analysis of the international survey of relationships. *Archives of Sexual Behavior*, *44*(6), 1609–1620.

Fitzsimons, G. M., & Anderson, J. E. (2013). Interpersonal cognition: seeking, understanding, and maintaining relationships. In D. Carlston (Ed.), *The Oxford handbook of social cognition* (pp. 590–615). Oxford University Press.

Fitzsimons, G. M., & Finkel, E. J. (2018). Transactive-goal-dynamics theory: A discipline-wide perspective. *Current Directions in Psychological Science*, *27*(5), 332–338.

Fitzsimons, G. M., Finkel, E. J., & Vandellen, M. R. (2015). Transactive goal dynamics. *Psychological Review*, *122*(4), 648–673.

Fivecoat, H. C., Tomlinson, J. M., Aron, A. et al. (2015). Partner support for individual self-expansion opportunities: Effects on relationship satisfaction in long-term couples. *Journal of Social and Personal Relationships*, *32*(3), 368–385.

Fledderjohann, J. J. (2012). "Zero is not good for me": Implications of infertility in Ghana. *Human Reproduction*, *27*(5), 1383–1390.

Fleishman, J., Crane, B., & Koch, P. B. (2020). Correlates and predictors of sexual satisfaction for older adults in same-sex relationships. *Journal of Homosexuality*, *67*(14), 1974–1998.

Fletcher, G. J. O., & Kerr, P. S. G. (2010). Through the eyes of love: Reality and illusion in intimate relationships. *Psychological Bulletin*, *136*(4), 627–658.

Fletcher, G. J. O., Kerr, P. S., Li, N. P. et al. (2014). Predicting romantic interest and decisions in the very early stages of mate selection: Standards, accuracy, and sex differences. *Personality and Social Psychology Bulletin*, *40*(4), 540–550.

Fletcher, G. J. O., Simpson, J. A., Campbell, L. et al. (2015). Pair-bonding, romantic love, and evolution: The curious case of homo sapiens. *Perspectives on Psychological Science*, *10*(1), 20–36.

Fletcher, G. J. O., Simpson, J. A., & Thomas, G. (2000). Ideals, perceptions, and evaluations in early relationship development. *Journal of Personality and Social Psychology*, *79*(6), 933–940.

Fletcher, G. J. O., Thomas, G., Giles, L. et al. (1999). Ideals in intimate relationships. *Journal of Personality and Social Psychology*, *76*(1), 72–89.

Fletcher, G. J. O., Tither, J. M., O'loughlin, C. et al. (2004). Warm and homely or cold and beautiful? Sex differences in trading off traits in mate selection. *Personality and Social Psychology Bulletin*, *30*(6), 659–672.

Flood, S. M., & Genadek, K. R. (2016). Time for each other: Work and family constraints among couples. *Journal of Marriage and Family*, *78*(1), 142–164.

Flood, S., Meier, A., & Musick, K. (2020). Reassessing parents' leisure quality with direct measures of well-being: Do children detract from parents' down time? *Journal of Marriage and Family*, *82*(4), 1326–1339.

Floyd, K. (2002). Human affection exchange: V. Attributes of the highly affectionate. *Communication Quarterly*, *50*(2), 135–152.

Floyd, K. (2006). *Communicating affection: Interpersonal behavior and social context*. Cambridge University Press.

Floyd, K. (2014). Relational and health correlates of affection deprivation. *Western Journal of Communication*, *78*(4), 383–403.

Floyd, K. (2016). Affection deprivation is associated with physical pain and poor sleep quality. *Communication Studies*, *67*(4), 379–398.

Floyd, K. (2019). *Affectionate communication in close relationships*. Cambridge University Press.

Floyd, K., Boren, J. P., Hannawa, A. F. et al. (2009). Kissing in marital and cohabiting relationships: Effects on blood lipids, stress, and relationship satisfaction. *Western Journal of Communication*, *73*, 113–133.

Floyd, K., & Hesse, C. (2017). Affection deprivation is conceptually and empirically distinct from loneliness. *Western Journal of Communication*, *81*(4), 446–465.

Floyd, K., & Morman, M. (1998). The measurement of affectionate communication. *Communication Quarterly*, *46*, 144–162.

Floyd, K., Morman, M. T., Maré, J. et al. (2021). How Americans communicate affection: Findings from a representative national sample. *Communication Quarterly*, *69*(4), 383–409.

Floyd, K., & Morr, M. C. (2003). Human affection exchange: VII. Affectionate communication in the sibling/spouse/sibling-in-law triad. *Communication Quarterly*, *51*(3), 247–261.

Floyd, K., & Pauley, P. M. (2011). Affectionate communication is good, except when it isn't: On the dark side of expressing affection. In W. R. Cupach & B. H. Spitzberg (Eds.), *The dark side of close relationships* (pp. 145–174). Routledge.

Floyd, K., Woo, N. T., & Custer, B. E. (2020). The biology of affectionate communication. In K. Floyd & R. Weber (Eds.), *The handbook of communication science and biology* (1st ed., pp. 308–318). Routledge.

Floyd, K., York, C., & Ray, C. D. (2020). Heritability of affectionate communication: A twins study. *Communication Monographs*, *87*(4), 405–424.

Folkes, V. S. (1982). Communicating the reasons for social rejection. *Journal of Experimental Social Psychology*, *18*(3), 235–252.

Folkman, S., Lazarus, R., Schetter, C. et al. (1986). Dynamics of a stressful encounter: Cognitive appraisal, coping, and encounter outcomes. *Journal of Personality and Social Psychology*, *50*, 992–1003.

Foo, Y. Z., Simmons, L. W., Perrett, D. I. et al. (2020). Immune function during early adolescence positively predicts adult facial sexual dimorphism in both men and women. *Evolution and Human Behavior*, *41*(3), 199–209.

Forest, A. L., Walsh, R. M., & Krueger, K. L. (2021). Facilitating and motivating support: How support-seekers can affect the support they receive in times of distress. *Social and Personality Psychology Compass*, *15*(6), e12600.

Formby, E. (2022). LGBT "communities" and the (self-)regulation and shaping of intimacy. *Sociological Research Online*, *27*(1), 8–26.

Foster, C., Witcher, B., Campbell, W. K. et al. (1998). Arousal and attraction: Evidence for automatic and controlled processes. *Journal of Personality and Social Psychology*, *74*(1), 86–101.

Foster, J. D., & Brunell, A. B. (2018). Narcissism and romantic relationships. In A. D. Hermann, A. B. Brunell, & J. D. Foster (Eds.), *The handbook of trait narcissism: Key advances, research methods, and controversies* (pp. 317–326). Springer.

Fowers, B. J., Lyons, E. M., & Montel, K. H. (1996). Positive marital illusions: Self-enhancement or relationship enhancement? *Journal of Family Psychology*, *10*(2), 192–208.

Fowers, B. J., Lyons, E., Montel, K. H. et al. (2001). Positive illusions about marriage among married and single individuals. *Journal of Family Psychology*, *15*(1), 95–109.

Fowers, B. J., & Olson, D. H. (1993). ENRICH Marital Satisfaction Scale: A brief research and clinical tool. *Journal of Family Psychology*, *7*(2), 176–185.

Fowers, B. J., Veingrad, M. R., & Dominicis, C. (2002). The unbearable lightness of positive illusions: Engaged individuals' explanations of unrealistically positive relationship perceptions. *Journal of Marriage and Family*, *64*(2), 450–460.

Fox, J., & Anderegg, C. (2014). Romantic relationship stages and social networking sites: Uncertainty reduction strategies and perceived relational norms on Facebook. *Cyberpsychology, Behavior, and Social Networking*, *17*(11), 685–691.

Fox, J., & Warber, K. M. (2014). Social networking sites in romantic relationships: Attachment, uncertainty, and partner surveillance on Facebook. *Cyberpsychology, Behavior, and Social Networking*, *17*(1), 3–7.

Fraley, R. C. (2002). Attachment stability from infancy to adulthood: Meta-analysis and dynamic modeling of developmental mechanisms. *Personality and Social Psychology Review*, *6*(2), 123–151.

Fraley, R. C. (2019). Attachment in adulthood: Recent developments, emerging debates, and future directions. *Annual Review of Psychology*, *70*(1), 401–422.

Fraley, R. C., & Davis, K. (1997). Attachment formation and transfer in young adults' close friendships and romantic relationships. *Personal Relationships*, *4*(2), 131–144.

Fraley, R. C., & Roisman, G. I. (2019). The development of adult attachment styles: Four lessons. *Current Opinion in Psychology*, *25*, 26–30.

Fraley, R. C., Roisman, G. I., Booth-LaForce, C. et al. (2013). Interpersonal and genetic origins of adult attachment styles: A longitudinal study from infancy to early adulthood. *Journal of Personality and Social Psychology*, *104*(5), 817–838.

Fraley, R. C., & Shaver, P. R. (1998). Airport separations: A naturalistic study of adult attachment dynamics in separating couples. *Journal of Personality and Social Psychology*, *75*(5), 1198–1212.

Francis, Z., Sieber, V., & Job, V. (2019). You seem tired, but so am I: Willpower theories and intention to provide support in romantic relationships. *Journal of Social and Personal Relationships*, *37*(3), 738–757.

Franiuk, R., Pomerantz, E. M., & Cohen, D. (2004). The causal role of theories of relationships: Consequences for satisfaction and cognitive strategies. *Personality and Social Psychology Bulletin*, *30*(11), 1494–1507.

Frascella, J., Potenza, M. N., Brown, L. L. et al. (2010). Shared brain vulnerabilities open the way for nonsubstance addictions: Carving addiction at a new joint. *Annals of the New York Academy of Sciences*, *1187*, 294–315.

Frederick, D. A., & Fales, M. R. (2016). Upset over sexual versus emotional infidelity among gay, lesbian, bisexual, and heterosexual adults. *Archives of Sexual Behavior, 45* (1), 175–191.

Frederick, D. A., Gillespie, B. J., Lever, J. et al. (2021). Debunking lesbian bed death: Using coarsened exact matching to compare sexual practices and satisfaction of lesbian and heterosexual women. *Archives of Sexual Behavior, 50*(8), 3601–3619.

Frederick, D. A., Lever, J., Gillespie, B. J. et al. (2017). What keeps passion alive? Sexual satisfaction is associated with sexual communication, mood setting, sexual variety, oral sex, orgasm, and sex frequency in a national U.S. study. *Journal of Sex Research, 54*(2), 186–201.

Fredrickson, B. L. (2016). Love: Positivity resonance as a fresh, evidence-based perspective on an age-old topic. In L. Barett, M. Lewis, & J. M. Haviland-Jones (Eds.), *Handbook of emotions* (4th ed., p. 847–858). Guilford Press.

Freedman, G., Powell, D. N., Le, B. et al. (2019). Ghosting and destiny: Implicit theories of relationships predict beliefs about ghosting. *Journal of Social and Personal Relationships, 36*(3), 905–924.

Freeman, H., & Simons, J. (2018). Attachment network structure as a predictor of romantic attachment formation and insecurity. *Social Development, 27*(1), 201–220.

Frost, D. M., & Forrester, C. (2013). Closeness discrepancies in romantic relationships: Implications for relational well-being, stability, and mental health. *Personality and Social Psychology Bulletin, 39*(4), 456–469.

Frost, D. M., LeBlanc, A. J., de Vries, B. et al. (2017). Couple-level minority stress: An examination of same-sex couples' unique experiences. *Journal of Health and Social Behavior, 58*(4), 455–472.

Frye, N. E., & Karney, B. R. (2002). Being better or getting better? Social and temporal comparisons as coping mechanisms in close relationships. *Personality and Social Psychology Bulletin, 28*(9), 1287–1299.

Frye, N. E., & Karney, B. R. (2004). Revision in memories of relationship development: Do biases persist over time? *Personal Relationships, 11*(1), 79–98.

Fu, T.-C., Herbenick, D., Dodge, B. et al. (2019). Relationships among sexual identity, sexual attraction, and sexual behavior: Results from a nationally representative probability sample of adults in the United States. *Archives of Sexual Behavior, 48*(5), 1483–1493.

Funder, D. C. (1995). On the accuracy of personality judgment: A realistic approach. *Psychological Review, 102*(4), 652–670.

Funk, J. L., & Rogge, R. D. (2007). Testing the ruler with item response theory: Increasing precision of measurement for relationship satisfaction with the Couples Satisfaction Index. *Journal of Family Psychology, 21*(4), 572–583.

Furnham, A., Tan, T., & McManus, C. (1997). Waist-to-hip ratio and preferences for body shape: A replication and extension. *Personality and Individual Differences, 22*(4), 539–549.

Gabb, J., & Singh, R. (2015). Reflections on the challenges of understanding racial, cultural and sexual differences in couple relationship research. *Journal of Family Therapy, 37*(2), 210–227.

Gable, S. L. (2006). Approach and avoidance social motives and goals. *Journal of Personality, 74*(1), 175–220.

Gable, S. L. (2019). Close relationships. In E. J. Finkel & R. F. Baumeister (Eds.), *Advanced social psychology: The state of the science* (2nd ed.). Oxford University Press.

Gable, S. L., Gonzaga, G. C., & Strachman, A. (2006). Will you be there for me when things go right? Supportive responses to positive event disclosures. *Journal of Personality and Social Psychology, 91*(5), 904–917.

Gable, S. L., & Gosnell, C. L. (2011). The positive side of close relationships. In K. M. Sheldon, T. B. Kashdan, & M. F. Steger (Eds.), *Designing positive psychology: Taking stock and moving forward* (pp. 1–28). Oxford University Press.

Gable, S. L., Gosnell, C. L., Maisel, N. C. et al. (2012). Safely testing the alarm: Close others' responses to personal positive events. *Journal of Personality and Social Psychology, 103*, 963–981.

Gable, S. L., & Impett, E. A. (2012). Approach and avoidance motives and close relationships. *Social and Personality Psychology Compass, 6*(1), 95–108.

Gable, S. L., & Reis, H. T. (2010). Good news! Capitalizing on positive events in an interpersonal context. In M. P. Zanna (Ed.), *Advances in experimental social psychology* (Vol. 42, pp. 195–257). Academic Press.

Gable, S. L., Reis, H. T., Impett, E. A. et al. (2004). What do you do when things go right? The intrapersonal and interpersonal benefits of sharing positive events. *Journal of Personality and Social Psychology, 87*(2), 228–245.

Gabriel, S., Valenti, J., & Young, A. F. (2016). Social surrogates, social motivations, and everyday activities: The case for a strong, subtle, and sneaky social self. *Advances in Experimental Social Psychology, 53*, 189–243.

Gächter, S., Starmer, C., & Tufano, F. (2015). Measuring the closeness of relationships: A comprehensive evaluation of the "inclusion of the other in the self" scale. *PLOS One, 10* (6), e0129478.

Gadassi, R., Bar-Nahum, L. E., Newhouse, S. et al. (2016). Perceived partner responsiveness mediates the association between sexual and marital satisfaction: A daily diary study in newlywed couples. *Archives of Sexual Behavior, 45*, 109–120.

Gaines, S. O., Clark, E. M., & Afful, S. E. (2015). Interethnic marriage in the United States: An introduction. *Journal of Social Issues*, *71*(4), 647–658.

Galbally, M., Lewis, A. J., Van Ijzendoorn, M. et al. (2011). The role of oxytocin in mother–infant relations: A systematic review of human studies. *Harvard Review of Psychiatry*, *19*(1), 1–14.

Gallace, A., & Spence, C. (2010). The science of interpersonal touch: An overview. *Neuroscience and Biobehavioral Reviews*, *34*(2), 246–259.

Gallo, L. C., & Smith, T. W. (2001). Attachment style in marriage: Adjustment and responses to interaction. *Journal of Social and Personal Relationships*, *18*(2), 263–289.

Galloway, S. (2017, September 6). At home with George Clooney in Italy: Amal, the twins, politics, and an incendiary new movie. *The Hollywood Reporter*. www.hollywoodreporter.com/movies/movie-features/at-home-george-clooney-italy-amal-twins-politics-an-incendiary-new-movie-1035363/

Galovan, A. M., Drouin, M., & McDaniel, B. T. (2018). Sexting profiles in the United States and Canada: Implications for individual and relationship well-being. *Computers in Human Behavior*, *79*, 19–29.

Gamarel, K. E., Sevelius, J. M., Reisner, S. L. et al. (2019). Commitment, interpersonal stigma, and mental health in romantic relationships between transgender women and cisgender male partners. *Journal of Social and Personal Relationships*, *36*(7), 2180–2201.

Gangestad, S. W., & Haselton, M. G. (2015). Human estrus: Implications for relationship science. *Current Opinion in Psychology*, *1*, 45–51.

Gangestad, S. W., Haselton, M. G., & Buss, D. M. (2006). Evolutionary foundations of cultural variation: Evoked culture and mate preferences. *Psychological Inquiry*, *17*(2), 75–95.

Gangestad, S. W., Haselton, M. G., Welling, L. L. M. et al. (2016). How valid are assessments of conception probability in ovulatory cycle research? Evaluations, recommendations, and theoretical implications. *Evolution and Human Behavior*, *37*(2), 85–96.

Gangestad, S. W., & Simpson, J. A. (1990). Toward an evolutionary history of female sociosexual variation. *Journal of Personality*, *58*(1), 69–96.

Gangestad, S. W., & Simpson, J. A. (2000). The evolution of human mating: Trade-offs and strategic pluralism. *Behavioral and Brain Sciences*, *23*(4), 573–587.

Gangestad, S. W., & Thornhill, R. (1998). Menstrual cycle variation in women's preferences for the scent of symmetrical men. *Proceedings of the Royal Society B: Biological Sciences*, *265*(1399), 927–933.

Gangestad, S. W., & Thornhill, R. (2008). Human oestrus. *Proceedings of the Royal Society B: Biological Sciences*, *275*(1638), 991–1000.

Garcia, J., & Reiber, C. (2008). Hook-up behavior: A biopsychosocial perspective. *Journal of Social, Evolutionary, and Cultural Psychology*, *2*(4), 192–208.

Garcia, J. R., Reiber, C., Massey, S. G. et al. (2012). Sexual hookup culture: A review. *Review of General Psychology*, *16*(2), 161–176.

Gardner, W. L., Pickett, C. L., & Brewer, M. B. (2000). Social exclusion and selective memory: How the need to belong influences memory for social events. *Personality and Social Psychology Bulletin*, *26*(4), 486–496.

Garfield, C. F., Duncan, G., Gutina, A. et al. (2016). Longitudinal study of body mass index in young males and the transition to fatherhood. *American Journal of Men's Health*, *10*(6), NP158–NP167.

Gebel, G., Griggs, M., & Washington, K. (2022). Evaluating structural therapy from a consensual nonmonogamy lens. *Family Journal*, *31*(1), 10664807221104116.

Genadek, K. R., Flood, S. M., & Roman, J. G. (2016). Trends in spouses' shared time in the United States, 1965–2012. *Demography*, *53*(6), 1801–1820.

Genadek, K. R., Flood, S. M., & Roman, J. G. (2020). Same-sex couples' shared time in the United States. *Demography*, *57*(2), 475–500.

George, T., Hart, J., & Rholes, W. S. (2020). Remaining in unhappy relationships: The roles of attachment anxiety and fear of change. *Journal of Social and Personal Relationships*, *37*(5), 1626–1633.

Gerber, J., & Wheeler, L. (2009). On being rejected: A meta-analysis of experimental research on rejection. *Perspectives on Psychological Science*, *4*(5), 468–488.

Gere, J., & Impett, E. A. (2018). Shifting priorities: Effects of partners' goal conflict on goal adjustment processes and relationship quality in developing romantic relationships. *Journal of Social and Personal Relationships*, *35*(6), 793–810.

Gere, J., & Schimmack, U. (2013). When romantic partners' goals conflict: Effects on relationship quality and subjective well-being. *Journal of Happiness Studies*, *14*(1), 37–49.

Gerin, W., Goyal, T. M., Mostofsky, E. et al. (2008). The measurement of blood pressure in cardiovascular research. In L. J. Luecken & L. Gallo (Eds.), *Handbook of physiological research methods in health psychology* (pp. 115–132). Sage Publications.

Gerlach, T. M., Arslan, R. C., Schultze, T. et al. (2019). Predictive validity and adjustment of ideal partner preferences across the transition into romantic relationships.

Journal of Personality and Social Psychology, 116(2), 313–330.

Germine, L., Russell, R., Bronstad, P. M. et al. (2015). Individual aesthetic preferences for faces are shaped mostly by environments, not genes. *Current Biology, 25* (20), 2684–2689.

Gerpott, F. H., Balliet, D., Columbus, S. et al. (2018). How do people think about interdependence? A multidimensional model of subjective outcome interdependence. *Journal of Personality and Social Psychology, 115*(4), 716–742.

Gesell, N., Niklas, F., Schmiedeler, S. et al. (2020). Mindfulness and romantic relationship outcomes: The mediating role of conflict resolution styles and closeness. *Mindfulness, 11* (10), 2314–2324.

Gesselman, A. N., Webster, G. D., & Garcia, J. R. (2017). Has virginity lost its virtue? Relationship stigma associated with being a sexually inexperienced adult. *Journal of Sex Research, 54*(2), 202–213.

Gewirtz-Meydan, A. (2017). Why do narcissistic individuals engage in sex? Exploring sexual motives as a mediator for sexual satisfaction and function. *Personality and Individual Differences, 105*, 7–13.

Gewirtz-Meydan, A., & Ayalon, L. (2019). Why do older adults have sex? Approach and avoidance sexual motives among older women and men. *Journal of Sex Research, 56*(7), 870–881.

Gibson-Davis, C. M., Edin, K., & McLanahan, S. (2005). High hopes but even higher expectations: The retreat from marriage among low-income couples. *Journal of Marriage and Family, 67*(5), 1301–1312.

Gibson-Davis, C. M., Gassman-Pines, A., & Lehrman, R. (2018). "His" and "hers": Meeting the economic bar to marriage. *Demography, 55*(6), 2321–2343.

Giesler, R. B., Josephs, R. A., & Swann, W. B. (1996). Self-verification in clinical depression: The desire for negative evaluation. *Journal of Abnormal Psychology, 105*(3), 358–368.

Gignac, G. E., & Starbuck, C. L. (2019). Exceptional intelligence and easygoingness may hurt your prospects: Threshold effects for rated mate characteristics. *British Journal of Psychology, 110*(1), 151–172.

Gildersleeve, K., Haselton, M. G., & Fales, M. R. (2014a). Do women's mate preferences change across the ovulatory cycle? A meta-analytic review. *Psychological Bulletin, 140* (5), 1205–1259.

Gildersleeve, K., Haselton, M. G., & Fales, M. R. (2014b). Meta-analyses and p-curves support robust cycle shifts in women's mate preferences: Reply to Wood and Carden (2014) and Harris, Pashler, and Mickes (2014). *Psychological Bulletin, 140*(5), 1272–1280.

Gillespie, I. J., Armstrong, H. L., & Ingham, R. (2021). Exploring reflections, motivations, and experiential outcomes of first same-sex/gender sexual experiences among lesbian, gay, bisexual, and other sexual minority individuals. *Journal of Sex Research, 59*, 26–38.

Girardi, A., Curran, M. S., & Snyder, B. L. (2020). Healthy intimate relationships and the adult with autism. *Journal of the American Psychiatric Nurses Association, 27*(5), 405–414.

Girme, Y. U., Maniaci, M. R., Reis, H. T. et al. (2018). Does support need to be seen? Daily invisible support promotes next day relationship well-being. *Journal of Family Psychology, 32*(7), 882–893.

Girme, Y. U., Overall, N. C., & Faingataa, S. (2014). "Date nights" take two: The maintenance function of shared relationship activities. *Personal Relationships, 21*(1), 125–149.

Girme, Y. U., Overall, N. C., & Simpson, J. A. (2013). When visibility matters: Short-term versus long-term costs and benefits of visible and invisible support. *Personality & Social Psychology Bulletin, 39*, 1441–1454.

Gleason, M. E. J., Iida, M., Bolger, N. et al. (2003). Daily supportive equity in close relationships. *Personality and Social Psychology Bulletin, 29*(8), 1036–1045.

Gleason, M. E. J., Iida, M., Shrout, P. E. et al. (2008). Receiving support as a mixed blessing: Evidence for dual effects of support on psychological outcomes. *Journal of Personality and Social Psychology, 94*(5), 824–838.

Glick, P., & Fiske, S. T. (1996). The Ambivalent Sexism Inventory: Differentiating hostile and benevolent sexism. *Journal of Personality and Social Psychology, 70*(3), 491–512.

Gloor, S., Gonin, S., Hansjö, S. et al. (2021). Repartnering and trajectories of life satisfaction after separation and divorce in middle and later life. *Journal of Social and Personal Relationships, 38*(7), 2205–2224.

Godoy, L. D., Rossignoli, M. T., Delfino-Pereira, P. et al. (2018). A comprehensive overview on stress neurobiology: Basic concepts and clinical implications. *Frontiers in Behavioral Neuroscience, 12*, 127.

Goffman, E. (1959). *The presentation of self in everyday life.* Bantam Doubleday Dell Publishing Group.

Goldberg, A. E., Smith, J. A. Z., & Kashy, D. A. (2010). Preadoptive factors predicting lesbian, gay, and heterosexual couples' relationship quality across the transition to adoptive parenthood. *Journal of Family Psychology, 24* (3), 221–232.

Goldberg, S. B., Riordan, K. M., Sun, S. et al. (2022). The empirical status of mindfulness-based interventions: A systematic review of 44 meta-analyses of randomized controlled trials. *Perspectives on Psychological Science, 17* (1), 108–130.

Goldsmith, K. M., & Sandra Byers, E. (2018). Perceived and reported romantic and sexual outcomes in long-distance and geographically close relationships. *Canadian Journal of Human Sexuality*, *27*(2), 144–156.

Gomillion, S., Murray, S. L., & Lamarche, V. M. (2015). Losing the wind beneath your wings: The prospective influence of romantic breakup on goal progress. *Social Psychological and Personality Science*, *6*(5), 513–520.

Gonzaga, G. C., Carter, S., & Galen Buckwalter, J. (2010). Assortative mating, convergence, and satisfaction in married couples. *Personal Relationships*, *17*(4), 634–644.

Gonzaga, G. C., Haselton, M. G., Smurda, J. et al. (2008). Love, desire, and the suppression of thoughts of romantic alternatives. *Evolution and Human Behavior*, *29*(2), 119–126.

Goodboy, A. K., & Bolkan, S. (2011). Attachment and the use of negative relational maintenance behaviors in romantic relationships. *Communication Research Reports*, *28*(4), 327–336.

Goodboy, A. K., Bolkan, S., Sharabi, L. L. et al. (2020). The relational turbulence model: A meta-analytic review. *Human Communication Research*, *46*(2–3), 222–249.

Goodboy, A. K., & Brann, M. (2010). Flirtation rejection strategies: Toward an understanding of communicative disinterest in flirting. *Qualitative Report*, *15*(2), 268–278.

Gordon, A. M., Cross, E., Ascigil, E. et al. (2022). Feeling appreciated buffers against the negative effects of unequal division of household labor on relationship satisfaction. *Psychological Science*, *33*(8), 1313–1327.

Gordon, A. M., Impett, E. A., Kogan, A. et al. (2012). To have and to hold: Gratitude promotes relationship maintenance in intimate bonds. *Journal of Personality and Social Psychology*, *103*(2), 257–274.

Gordon, C. L., Arnette, R. A. M., & Smith, R. E. (2011). Have you thanked your spouse today? Felt and expressed gratitude among married couples. *Personality and Individual Differences*, *50*(3), 339–343.

Gosling, S. D., & Mason, W. (2015). Internet research in psychology. *Annual Review of Psychology*, *66*(1), 877–902.

Gosling, S. D., Vazire, S., Srivastava, S. et al. (2004). Should we trust web-based studies? A comparative analysis of six preconceptions about internet questionnaires. *American Psychologist*, *59*(2), 93–104.

Gosnell, C. L., & Gable, S. L. (2013). Attachment and capitalizing on positive events. *Attachment & Human Development*, *15*(3), 281–302.

Gosnell, C. L., & Gable, S. L. (2015). Providing partner support in good times and bad: Providers' outcomes. *Family Science*, *6*(1), 150–159.

Gosnell, C. L., & Gable, S. L. (2017). You deplete me: Impacts of providing positive and negative event support on self-control. *Personal Relationships*, *24*(3), 598–622.

Gottman, J. M., Coan, J., Carrere, S. et al. (1998). Predicting marital happiness and stability from newlywed interactions. *Journal of Marriage and Family*, *60*(1), 5–22.

Gottman, J. M., & Gottman, J. S. (1999). The marriage survival kit. In R. Berger & M. T. Hannah (Eds.), *Preventative approaches in couples therapy* (pp. 304–330). Brunner/Mazel Publishers.

Gottman, J. M., Gottman, J. S., Cole, C. et al. (2020). Gay, lesbian, and heterosexual couples about to begin couples therapy: An online relationship assessment of 40,681 couples. *Journal of Marital and Family Therapy*, *46*(2), 218–239.

Gottman, J. M., & Levenson, R. W. (1992). Marital processes predictive of later dissolution: Behavior, physiology, and health. *Journal of Personality and Social Psychology*, *63*(2), 221–233.

Gottman, J. M., Levenson, R. W., Swanson, C. et al. (2003). Observing gay, lesbian and heterosexual couples' relationships: Mathematical modeling of conflict interaction. *Journal of Homosexuality*, *45*(1), 65–91.

Gottman, J. M., McCoy, K., Coan, J. et al. (1995). *The Specific Affect Coding System (SPAFF) for observing emotional communication in marital and family interaction.* Lawrence Erlbaum.

Gottman, J. M., & Notarius, C. I. (2000). Decade review: Observing marital interaction. *Journal of Marriage and Family*, *62*(4), 927–947.

Gouda-Vossos, A., Nakagawa, S., Dixson, B. J., & Brooks, R. C. (2018). Mate choice copying in humans: a systematic review and meta-analysis. *Adaptive Human Behavior and Physiology*, *4*(4), 364–386.

Goyal, T. M., Shimbo, D., Mostofsky, E. et al. (2008). Cardiovascular stress reactivity. In L. J. Luecken & L. C. Gallo (Eds.), *Handbook of physiological research methods in health psychology* (pp. 133–158). Sage Publications.

Graham, E. E. (2009). Affectionate Communication Index (ACI). In R. B. Rubin, A. M. Rubin, E. M. Graham, & D. S. Perse (Eds.), *Communication research measures II: A sourcebook* (pp. 107–111). Routledge.

Graham, J. M. (2011). Measuring love in romantic relationships: A meta-analysis. *Journal of Social and Personal Relationships*, *28*(6), 748–771.

Grahe, J. E., & Bernieri, F. J. (1999). The importance of nonverbal cues in judging rapport. *Journal of Nonverbal Behavior*, *23*(4), 253–269.

Granger, D. A., Kivlighan, K. T., El-Sheikh, M. et al. (2008). Assessment of salivary alpha amylase in biobehavioral research. In L. J. Leucken & L. C. Gallo (Eds.), *Handbook of physiological research methods in health psychology* (pp. 95–114). Sage Publications.

Gravel, E. E., Pelletier, L. G., & Reissing, E. D. (2016). "Doing it" for the right reasons: Validation of a measurement of intrinsic motivation, extrinsic motivation, and amotivation for sexual relationships. *Personality and Individual Differences*, *92*, 164–173.

Gravel, E. E., Reissing, E. D., & Pelletier, L. G. (2020). The ebb and flow of sexual well-being: The contributions of basic psychological needs and autonomous and controlled sexual motivation to daily variations in sexual well-being. *Journal of Social and Personal Relationships*, *37*(7), 2286–2306.

Grebe, N. M., Sarafin, R. E., Strenth, C. R. et al. (2019). Pair-bonding, fatherhood, and the role of testosterone: A meta-analytic review. *Neuroscience and Biobehavioral Reviews*, *98*, 221–233.

Green, J. D., & Campbell, W. K. (2000). Attachment and exploration in adults: Chronic and contextual accessibility. *Personality and Social Psychology Bulletin*, *26*, 452–461.

Greene, D. C., & Britton, P. J. (2015). Predicting relationship commitment in gay men: Contributions of vicarious shame and internalized homophobia to the investment model. *Psychology of Men & Masculinity*, *16*(1), 78–87.

Greengross, G., & Miller, G. (2011). Humor ability reveals intelligence, predicts mating success, and is higher in males. *Intelligence*, *39*(4), 188–192.

Greer, A. E., & Buss, D. M. (1994). Tactics for promoting sexual encounters. *Journal of Sex Research*, *31*(3), 185–201.

Griffith, R. L., Gillath, O., Zhao, X. et al. (2017). Staying friends with ex-romantic partners: Predictors, reasons, and outcomes. *Personal Relationships*, *24*(3), 550–584.

Griskevicius, V., Ackerman, J. M., Cantú, S. M. et al. (2013). When the economy falters, do people spend or save? Responses to resource scarcity depend on childhood environments. *Psychological Science*, *24*(2), 197–205.

Griskevicius, V., Tybur, J. M., Sundie, J. M. et al. (2007). Blatant benevolence and conspicuous consumption: When romantic motives elicit strategic costly signals. *Journal of Personality and Social Psychology*, *93*(1), 85–102.

Griskevicius, V., Tybur, J. M., & Van den Bergh, B. (2010). Going green to be seen: Status, reputation, and conspicuous conservation. *Journal of Personality and Social Psychology*, *98*(3), 392–404.

Groggel, A., Burdick, M., & Barraza, A. (2021). She left the party: College students' meanings of sexual consent. *Violence Against Women*, *27*(6–7), 766–789.

Grossbart, S. (2021, July 27). Why Megan Rapinoe and Sue Bird are happy to be everyone's #CoupleGoals. *ENews*. www.eonline.com/news/1250397/why-megan-rapinoe-and-sue-bird-are-happy-to-be-everyones-couplegoals

Grover, S., & Helliwell, J. F. (2019). How's life at home? New evidence on marriage and the set point for happiness. *Journal of Happiness Studies*, *20*(2), 373–390.

Gudmunson, C. G., Beutler, I. F., Israelsen, C. L. et al. (2007). Linking financial strain to marital instability: Examining the roles of emotional distress and marital interaction. *Journal of Family and Economic Issues*, *28*(3), 357–376.

Guéguen, N., Lourel, M., Charron, C. et al. (2009). A web replication of Snyder, Decker, and Bersheid's (1977) experiment on the self-fulfilling nature of social stereotypes. *Journal of Social Psychology*, *149*(5), 600–602.

Guerrero, L. K., & Andersen, P. A. (2000). Emotion in close relationships. In C. Hendrick & S. Hendrick (Eds.), *Close relationships: A sourcebook* (pp. 171–183). Sage Publications.

Guerrero, L. K., & Chavez, A. M. (2005). Relational maintenance in cross-sex friendships characterized by different types of romantic intent: An exploratory study. *Western Journal of Communication*, *69*(4), 339–358.

Gulledge, A. K., Gulledge, M. H., & Stahmann, R. F. (2003). Romantic physical affection types and relationship satisfaction. *American Journal of Family Therapy*, *31*(4), 233–242.

Gurman, A. S. (2015). The theory and practice of couple therapy: History, contemporary models, and a framework for comparative analysis. In A. S. Gurman, J. L. Lebow, & D. K. Snyder (Eds.), *Clinical handbook of couple therapy* (5th ed., pp. 1–22). Guilford Press.

Gurrentz, B., & Mayol-Garcia, Y. (2021). *Marriage, divorce, widowhood remain prevalent among older populations*. United States Census Bureau. www.census.gov/library/stories/2021/04/love-and-loss-among-older-adults.html

Ha, T., Van Den Berg, J. E. M., Engels, R. C. M. E. et al. (2012). Effects of attractiveness and status in dating desire in homosexual and heterosexual men and women. *Archives of Sexual Behavior*, *41*(3), 673–682.

Haas, S. M., & Lannutti, P. J. (2021). The impact of minority stress and social support on positive relationship functioning in same-sex relationships. *Health Communication*, *36*(3), 315–323.

Hadden, B. W., & Agnew, C. R. (2020). Commitment readiness: Timing, the self, and close relationships. In B. A. Mattingly, K. P. McIntyre, & G. W. Lewandowski (Eds.), *Interpersonal relationships and the self-concept* (pp. 53–67). Springer International Publishing.

Hadden, B. W., Agnew, C. R., & Tan, K. (2018). Commitment readiness and relationship formation. *Personality and Social Psychology Bulletin*, *44*(8), 1242–1257.

Haj-Mohamadi, P., Gillath, O., & Rosenberg, E. L. (2021). Identifying a facial expression of flirtation and its effect on men. *Journal of Sex Research*, *58*(2), 137–145.

Halatsis, P., & Christakis, N. (2009). The challenge of sexual attraction within heterosexuals' cross-sex friendship. *Journal of Social and Personal Relationships*, *26*(6–7), 919–937.

Hald, G. M., Ciprić, A., Sander, S. et al. (2020). Anxiety, depression and associated factors among recently divorced individuals. *Journal of Mental Health*, *31*(4), 462–470.

Halford, W. K., & Bodenmann, G. (2013). Effects of relationship education on maintenance of couple relationship satisfaction. *Clinical Psychology Review*, *33*, 512–525.

Halford, W. K., Moore, E., Wilson, K. L. et al. (2004). Benefits of flexible delivery relationship education: An evaluation of the couple CARE program. *Family Relations*, *53*(5), 469–476.

Halford, W. K., O'Donnell, C., Lizzio, A. et al. (2006). Do couples at high risk of relationship problems attend pre-marriage education? *Journal of Family Psychology*, *20*(1), 160–163.

Halford, W. K., & Pepping, C. A. (2019). What every therapist needs to know about couple therapy. *Behaviour Change*, *36*(3), 121–142.

Halford, W. K., Pepping, C. A., Hilbert, P. et al. (2015). Immediate effect of couple relationship education on low-satisfaction couples: A randomized clinical trial plus an uncontrolled trial replication. *Behavior Therapy*, *46*(1), 409–421.

Halford, W. K., Rahimullah, R. H., Wilson, K. L. et al. (2017). Four year effects of couple relationship education on low and high satisfaction couples: A randomized clinical trial. *Journal of Consulting and Clinical Psychology*, *85*(5), 495–507.

Halford, W. K., & Sweeper, S. (2013). Trajectories of adjustment to couple relationship separation. *Family Process*, *52*(2), 228–243.

Hall, J. A. (2017). The regulation of social interaction in everyday life: A replication and extension of O'Connor and Rosenblood (1996). *Journal of Social and Personal Relationships*, *34*(5), 699–716.

Hall, J. A., Carter, S., Cody, M. J. et al. (2010). Individual differences in the communication of romantic interest: Development of the flirting styles inventory. *Communication Quarterly*, *58*(4), 365–393.

Hall, J. H., & Fincham, F. D. (2006). Relationship dissolution following infidelity: The roles of attributions and forgiveness. *Journal of Social and Clinical Psychology*, *25*(5), 508–522.

Hallam, L., De Backer, C. J. S., Fisher, M. L. et al. (2018). Are sex differences in mating strategies overrated? Sociosexual orientation as a dominant predictor in online dating strategies. *Evolutionary Psychological Science*, *4*(4), 456–465.

Halley, J. (2016). The move to affirmative consent. *Signs: Journal of Women in Culture and Society*, *42*(1), 257–279.

Halpern, C. T., & Kaestle, C. E. (2013). Sexuality in emerging adulthood. In D. L. Tolman, L. M. Diamond, J. A. Baumeister, W. H. George, J. G. Pfaus, & L. M. Ward (Eds.), *APA handbook of sexuality and psychology*, Vol. 1: *Person-based approaches* (pp. 487–522). American Psychological Association.

Halpern, D., & Katz, J. E. (2017). Texting's consequences for romantic relationships: A cross-lagged analysis highlights its risks. *Computers in Human Behavior*, *71*, 386–394.

Halpern-Meekin, S., Manning, W. D., Giordano, P. C. et al. (2013). Relationship churning, physical violence, and verbal abuse in young adult relationships. *Journal of Marriage and Family*, *75*(1), 2–12.

Hames, J. L., Hagan, C. R., & Joiner, T. E. (2013). Interpersonal processes in depression. *Annual Review of Clinical Psychology*, *9*, 355–377.

Hamilton, D., & Carlston, D. (2013). The emergence of social cognition. In D. E. Carlston (Ed.), *The Oxford handbook of social cognition* (pp. 16–32). Oxford University Press.

Hamilton, D., Goldsmith, A. H., & Darity, W. (2009). Shedding "light" on marriage: The influence of skin shade on marriage for black females. *Journal of Economic Behavior and Organization*, *72*(1), 30–50.

Hampton, A. J., Fisher Boyd, A. N., & Sprecher, S. (2019). You're like me and I like you: Mediators of the similarity-liking link assessed before and after a getting-acquainted social interaction. *Journal of Social and Personal Relationships*, *36*(7), 2221–2244.

Han, S. C., Schacter, H. L., Timmons, A. C. et al. (2021). Romantic partner presence and physiological responses in daily life: Attachment style as a moderator. *Biological Psychology*, *161*, 108082.

Hancock, G., Stokes, M. A., & Mesibov, G. (2020). Differences in romantic relationship experiences for individuals with an Autism Spectrum Disorder. *Sexuality and Disability*, *38*(2), 231–245.

Hansen, T. (2012). Parenthood and happiness: A review of folk theories versus empirical evidence. *Social Indicators Research*, *108*(1), 29–64.

Harari, G. M., Lane, N. D., Wang, R. et al. (2016). Using smartphones to collect behavioral data in psychological science: Opportunities, practical considerations, and challenges. *Perspectives on Psychological Science*, *11*(6), 838–854.

Harasymchuk, C., Muise, A., Bacev-Giles, C. et al. (2020). Broadening your horizon one day at a time: Relationship goals and exciting activities as daily antecedents of relational self-expansion. *Journal of Social and Personal Relationships*, *37*(6), 1910–1926.

Harasymchuk, C., Walker, D. L., Muise, A. et al. (2021). Planning date nights that promote closeness: The roles of relationship goals and self-expansion. *Journal of Social and Personal Relationships*, *38*(5), 1692–1709.

Harding, D. J., & Jencks, C. (2003). Changing attitudes toward premarital sex: Cohort, period, and aging effects. *Public Opinion Quarterly, 67*(2), 211–226.

Harper, G. W., Cannon, C., Watson, S. E. et al. (2004). The role of close friends in African American adolescents' dating and sexual behavior. *Journal of Sex Research, 41*(4), 351–362.

Harpo Productions. (2021). *Oprah with Meghan and Harry.* CBS.

Harrar, H., Myers, S., & Ghanem, A. M. (2018). Art or science? An evidence-based approach to human facial beauty a quantitative analysis towards an informed clinical aesthetic practice. *Aesthetic Plastic Surgery, 42*(1), 137–146.

Harris, C. R., Pashler, H., & Mickes, L. (2014). Elastic analysis procedures: An incurable (but preventable) problem in the fertility effect literature: Comment on Gildersleeve, Haselton, and Fales (2014). *Psychological Bulletin, 140*(5), 1260–1264.

Harris, L. E. (2020). Committing before cohabiting: Pathways to marriage among middle-class couples. *Journal of Family Issues, 42*(8), 1762–1768.

Harrison, O., Windmann, S., Rosner, R. et al. (2021). Inclusion of the other in the self as a potential risk factor for prolonged grief disorder: A comparison of patients with matched bereaved healthy controls. *Clinical Psychology and Psychotherapy, 29*(3), 1101–1112.

Hartley, S. L., Barker, E. T., Seltzer, M. M. et al. (2010). The relative risk and timing of divorce in families of children with an autism spectrum disorder. *Journal of Family Psychology, 24*(4), 449–457.

Hartley, S. L., Papp, L. M., Blumenstock, S. M. et al. (2016). The effect of daily challenges in children with autism on parents' couple problem-solving interactions. *Journal of Family Psychology, 30*(6), 732–742.

Haselton, M. G. (2003). The sexual overperception bias: Evidence of a systematic bias in men from a survey of naturally occurring events. *Journal of Research in Personality, 37*(1), 34–47.

Haselton, M. G., & Buss, D. M. (2000). Error management theory: A new perspective on biases in cross-sex mind reading. *Journal of Personality and Social Psychology, 78*(1), 81–91.

Haselton, M. G., & Gildersleeve, K. (2016). Human ovulation cues. *Current Opinion in Psychology, 7*, 120–125.

Haselton, M. G., Mortezaie, M., Pillsworth, E. G. et al. (2007). Ovulatory shifts in human female ornamentation: Near ovulation, women dress to impress. *Hormones and Behavior, 51*(1), 40–45.

Hatch, A. (2017). Saying "I don't" to matrimony: An investigation of why long-term heterosexual cohabitors choose not to marry. *Journal of Family Issues, 38*(12), 1651–1674.

Hatch, L. R., & Bulcroft, K. (2004). Does long-term marriage bring less frequent disagreements? Five explanatory frameworks. *Journal of Family Issues, 25*(4), 465–495.

Hatch, S. G., Rothman, K., Roddy, M. K. et al. (2021). Heteronormative relationship education for same-gender couples. *Family Process, 60*(1), 119–133.

Hatfield, E. (2006). The golden fleece award: Love's labours almost lost. *APS Observer, 19*(6), 16–17.

Hatfield, E., Luckhurst, C., & Rapson, R. L. (2012). A brief history of attempts to measure sexual motives. *Interpersona: An International Journal on Personal Relationships, 6*(2), 138–154.

Hatfield, E., & Rapson, R. L. (2008). Passionate love and sexual desire: Multidisciplinary perspectives. In J. P. Forgas & J. Fitness (Eds.), *Social relationships: Cognitive, affective, and motivational processes* (pp. 21–37). Psychology Press.

Hatfield, E., & Sprecher, S. (1986). Measuring passionate love in intimate relationships. *Journal of Adolescence, 9*(4), 383–410.

Hatzenbuehler, M. L., Keyes, K. M., & Hasin, D. S. (2009). State-level policies and psychiatric morbidity in lesbian, gay, and bisexual populations. *American Journal of Public Health, 99*(12), 2275–2281.

Hatzenbuehler, M. L., Phelan, J. C., & Link, B. G. (2013). Stigma as a fundamental cause of population health inequalities. *American Journal of Public Health, 103*(5), 813–821.

Haupert, M. L., Gesselman, A. N., Moors, A. C. et al. (2017). Prevalence of experiences with consensual nonmonogamous relationships: Findings from two national samples of single Americans. *Journal of Sex and Marital Therapy, 43*(5), 424–440.

Havlíček, J., Třebický, V., Valentova, J. V. et al. (2017). Men's preferences for women's breast size and shape in four cultures. *Evolution and Human Behavior, 38*(2), 217–226.

Hawkins, A. J., Allen, S. E., & Yang, C. (2017). How does couple and relationship education affect relationship hope? An intervention-process study with lower income couples. *Family Relations, 66*(3), 441–452.

Hawkins, A. J., Blanchard, V. L., Baldwin, S. A. et al. (2008). Does marriage and relationship education work? A meta-analytic study. *Journal of Consulting and Clinical Psychology, 76*(5), 723–734.

Hawkins, A. J., & Erickson, S. E. (2015). Is couple and relationship education effective for lower income participants? A meta-analytic study. *Journal of Family Psychology, 29*(1), 59–68.

Hawkins, A. J., Galovan, A. M., Harris, S. M. et al. (2017). What are they thinking? A national study of stability and change in divorce ideation. *Family Process, 56*(4), 852–868.

Hawkins, A. J., Hokanson, S., Loveridge, E. et al. (2022). How effective are ACF-funded couple relationship education programs? A meta-analytic study. *Family Process*, *61*(3), 970–985.

Hawkley, L. C., Hughes, M. E., Waite, L. J. et al. (2008). From social structural factors to perceptions of relationship quality and loneliness: The Chicago Health, Aging, and Social Relations Study. *Journals of Gerontology – Series B Psychological Sciences and Social Sciences*, *63*(6), S375–S386.

Haydon, K. C., Jonestrask, C., Guhn-Knight, H. et al. (2017). The dyadic construction of romantic conflict recovery sabotage. *Journal of Social and Personal Relationships*, *34*(6), 915–935.

Hayes, A. F. (2009). Beyond Baron and Kenny: Statistical mediation analysis in the new millennium. *Communication Monographs*, *76*(4), 408–420.

Hayes, A. F. (2018). Introduction to mediation, moderation and conditional process analysis, *2nd ed.*: A regression-based approach. Guilford Press.

Hazan, C., & Shaver, P. (1987). Romantic love conceptualized as an attachment process. *Journal of Personality and Social Psychology*, *52*(3), 511–524.

Hazan, C., & Shaver, P. R. (1990). Love and work: An attachment-theoretical perspective. *Journal of Personality and Social Psychology*, *59*(2), 270–280.

Hazan, C., & Shaver, P. R. (1994). Attachment as an organizational framework for research on close relationships. *Psychological Inquiry*, *5*(1), 1–22.

Hazan, C., & Zeifman, D. (1994). Sex and the psychological tether. In K. Bartholomew & D. Perlman (Eds.), *Attachment processes in adulthood* (pp. 151–178). Jessica Kingsley Publishers.

Heaton, T. B., & Albrecht, S. L. (1991). Stable unhappy marriages. *Journal of Marriage and Family*, *53*(3), 747–758.

Heavey, C. L., Christensen, A., & Malamuth, N. M. (1995). The longitudinal impact of demand and withdrawal during marital conflict. *Journal of Consulting and Clinical Psychology*, *63*(5), 797–801.

Heavey, C. L., Layne, C., & Christensen, A. (1993). Gender and conflict structure in marital interaction: A replication and extension. *Journal of Consulting and Clinical Psychology*, *61*(1), 16–27.

Heerey, E. A., & Kring, A. M. (2007). Interpersonal consequences of social anxiety. *Journal of Abnormal Psychology*, *116*(1), 125–134.

Heim, C., & Nemeroff, C. B. (2001). The role of childhood trauma in the neurobiology of mood and anxiety disorders: Preclinical and clinical studies. *Biological Psychiatry*, *49*(12), 1023–1039.

Heiman, J. R., Long, J. S., Smith, S. N. et al. (2011). Sexual satisfaction and relationship happiness in midlife and older couples in five countries. *Archives of Sexual Behavior*, *40*(4), 741–753.

Heine, S. J., Foster, J. A. B., & Spina, R. (2009). Do birds of a feather universally flock together? Cultural variation in the similarity-attraction effect. *Asian Journal of Social Psychology*, *12*(4), 247–258.

Helgeson, V. S., & Mascatelli, K. (2018). Gender and relationships. In A. L. Vangelisti & D. Perlman (Eds.), *The Cambridge handbook of personal relationships* (2nd ed., pp. 186–198). Cambridge University Press.

HelloGiggles Team. (2019, February 14). *We asked all the longtime married couples we know to share their advice for a healthy, lasting relationship.* https://hellogiggles.com/love-sex/healthy-relationship-advice-from-long-married-couples/

Henderson, A. W., Lehavot, K., & Simoni, J. M. (2009). Ecological models of sexual satisfaction among lesbian/bisexual and heterosexual women. *Archives of Sexual Behavior*, *38*(1), 50–65.

Hendrick, C., Hendrick, S. S., & Reich, D. A. (2006). The Brief Sexual Attitudes Scale. *Journal of Sex Research*, *43*(1), 76–86.

Hendrie, C., Chapman, R., & Gill, C. (2020). Women's strategic use of clothing and make-up. *Human Ethology*, *35*(1), 16–26.

Hennighausen, C., Hudders, L., Lange, B. P. et al. (2016). What if the rival drives a porsche? Luxury car spending as a costly signal in male intrasexual competition. *Evolutionary Psychology*, *14*(4), 1–13.

Henningsen, D. D. (2004). Flirting with meaning: An examination of miscommunication in flirting interactions. *Sex Roles*, *50*(7–8), 481–489.

Henrich, J., Heine, S. J., & Norenzayan, A. (2010). The weirdest people in the world? *Behavioral and Brain Sciences*, *33*(2–3), 61–83.

Herbenick, D., Fu, T. C., Arter, J. et al. (2018). Women's experiences with genital touching, sexual pleasure, and orgasm: Results from a U.S. probability sample of women ages 18 to 94. *Journal of Sex and Marital Therapy*, *44*(2), 201–212.

Herbenick, D., Fu, T. C., Owens, C. et al. (2019). Kissing, cuddling, and massage at most recent sexual event: Findings from a U.S. nationally representative probability sample. *Journal of Sex and Marital Therapy*, *45*(2), 159–172.

Herbenick, D., Fu, T. C., Patterson, C. et al. (2021). Prevalence and characteristics of choking/strangulation during sex: Findings from a probability survey of undergraduate students. *Journal of American College Health*. Advance online publication. https://doi.org/10.1080/07448481.2021.1920599

Herbenick, D., Fu, T. C., Wright, P. et al. (2020). Diverse sexual behaviors and pornography use: Findings from a nationally representative probability survey of Americans aged 18 to 60 years. *Journal of Sexual Medicine*, *17*(4), 623–633.

Herbenick, D., Reece, M., Schick, V. et al. (2010). Sexual behavior in the United States: Results from a national probability sample of men and women ages 14–94. *Journal of Sexual Medicine*, *7*(Suppl. 5), 255–265.

Hertenstein, M. J., Hansel, C. A., Butts, A. M. et al. (2009). Smile intensity in photographs predicts divorce later in life. *Motivation and Emotion*, *33*(2), 99–105.

Hertlein, K. M., & van Dyck, L. E. (2020). Predicting engagement in electronic surveillance in romantic relationships. *Cyberpsychology, Behavior, and Social Networking*, *23*(9), 604–610.

Hertz, R. (2006). *Single by chance, mothers by choice: How women are choosing parenthood without marriage and creating the new American family*. Oxford University Press.

Hesse, C., Floyd, K., Rains, S. A. et al. (2021). Affectionate communication and health: A meta-analysis. *Communication Monographs*, *88*(2), 194–218.

Hesse, C., & Mikkelson, A. (2021). Relational and health correlates of excessive affection. *Communication Quarterly*, *69*(3), 320–340.

Hesse, C., Mikkelson, A., & Tian, X. (2021). Affection deprivation during the COVID-19 pandemic: A panel study. *Journal of Social and Personal Relationships*, *38*(10), 2965–2984.

Hesse, C., & Mikkelson, A. C. (2017). Affection deprivation in romantic relationships. *Communication Quarterly*, *65*(1), 20–38.

Hesse, C., Mikkelson, A. C., & Saracco, S. (2018). Parent–child affection and helicopter parenting: Exploring the concept of excessive affection. *Western Journal of Communication*, *82*(4), 457–474.

Hesse, C., & Tian, X. (2020). Affection deprivation in marital relationships: An actor–partner interdependence mediation analysis. *Journal of Social and Personal Relationships*, *37*(3), 965–985.

Hesse, C., & Trask, S. L. (2014). Trait affection and adult attachment styles: Analyzing relationships and group differences. *Communication Research Reports*, *31*(1), 53–61.

Hetherington, E. M. (2003). Intimate pathways: Changing patterns in close personal relationships across time. *Family Relations*, *52*(4), 318–331.

Heyman, R. E. (2004). Rapid marital interaction coding system (RMICS). In P. Kerig & D. H. Baucom (Eds.), *Couple observational coding systems* (pp. 67–93). Lawrence Erlbaum.

Heyman, R. E., & Slep, A. M. S. (2001). The hazards of predicting divorce without crossvalidation. *Journal of Marriage and Family*, *63*(2), 473–479.

Heyman, R. E., Weiss, R. L., & Eddy, J. M. (1995). Marital interaction coding system: Revision and empirical evaluation. *Behaviour Research and Therapy*, *33*(6), 737–746.

Hicks, A. M., & Diamond, L. M. (2008). How was your day? Couples' affect when telling and hearing daily events. *Personal Relationships*, *15*(2), 205–228.

Hicks, L. L., McNulty, J. K., Meltzer, A. L. et al. (2016). Capturing the interpersonal implications of evolved preferences? Frequency of sex shapes automatic, but not explicit, partner evaluations. *Psychological Science*, *27*(6), 836–847.

Hicks, T. V., & Leitenberg, H. (2001). Sexual fantasies about one's partner versus someone else: Gender differences in incidence and frequency. *Journal of Sex Research*, *38*(1), 43–50.

Hiew, D., Halford, W., Van de Vijver, F. et al. (2015). Communication and relationship satisfaction in Chinese, western, and intercultural Chinese-Western couples. *Journal of Family Psychology*, *30*(2), 193–202.

Higgins, E. T. (1998). Promotion and prevention: Regulatory focus as a motivational principle. *Advances in Experimental Social Psychology*, *30*, 1–46.

Higgins, E. T., & Bargh, J. A. (1987). Social cognition and social perception. *Annual Review of Psychology*, *38*, 369–425.

Higgins, J. A., Trussell, J., Moore, N. B. et al. (2010). Virginity lost, satisfaction gained? Physiological and psychological sexual satisfaction at heterosexual debut. *Journal of Sex Research*, *47*(4), 384–394.

Hildyard, K. L., & Wolfe, D. A. (2002). Child neglect: Developmental issues and outcomes. *Child Abuse and Neglect*, *26*(6–7), 679–695.

Hill, C. A., & Preston, L. K. (1996). Individual differences in the experience of sexual motivation: Theory and measurement of dispositional sexual motives. *Journal of Sex Research*, *33*(1), 27–45.

Hill, M. E. (2002). Skin color and the perception of attractiveness among African Americans: Does gender make a difference? *Social Psychology Quarterly*, *65*(1), 77–91.

Hill, M. S. (1988). Marital stability and spouses' shared time: A multidisciplinary hypothesis. *Journal of Family Issues*, *9*(4), 427–451.

Hill, S. E., & Buss, D. M. (2008). The mere presence of opposite-sex others on judgments of sexual and romantic desirability: Opposite effects for men and women. *Personality and Social Psychology Bulletin*, *34*(5), 635–647.

Hilpert, P., Xu, F., Milek, A. et al. (2018). Couples coping with stress: Between-person differences and within-person processes. *Journal of Family Psychology*, *32*(3), 366–374.

Hinde, R. (1979). *Towards understanding relationships*. Academic Press.

Hirsch, J. L., & Clark, M. S. (2019). Multiple paths to belonging that we should study together. *Perspectives on Psychological Science, 14*(2), 238–255.

Hirst, M. (2005). Carer distress: A prospective, population-based study. *Social Science & Medicine, 61*(3), 697–708.

Hocker, L., Kline, K., Totenhagen, C. J. et al. (2021). Hold my hand: Associations between minority stress, commitment, and PDA for same-gender couples. *Journal of Social and Personal Relationships, 38*(9), 2742–2750.

Hoffman, W. (2020). Communication modes during romantic dissolution: The impact of attachment and intimacy on initiator breakup strategies. *Interpersona: An International Journal on Personal Relationships, 14*(2), 87–103.

Holland, E. (2008). Marquardt's phi mask: Pitfalls of relying on fashion models and the golden ratio to describe a beautiful face. *Aesthetic Plastic Surgery, 32*(2), 200–208.

Holley, S. R., Haase, C. M., & Levenson, R. W. (2013). Age-related changes in demand-withdraw communication behaviors. *Journal of Marriage and Family, 75*(4), 822–836.

Holmberg, D., & Blair, K. L. (2016). Dynamics of perceived social network support for same-sex versus mixed-sex relationships. *Personal Relationships, 23*(1), 62–83.

Holmberg, D., Blair, K. L., & Phillips, M. (2010). Women's sexual satisfaction as a predictor of well-being in same-sex versus mixed-sex relationships. *Journal of Sex Research, 47*(1), 1–11.

Holmes, J. G. (2002). Interpersonal expectations as the building blocks of social cognition: An interdependence theory perspective. *Personal Relationships, 9*(1), 1–26.

Holmes, T. H., & Rahe, R. H. (1967). The social readjustment rating scale. *Journal of Psychosomatic Research, 11*(2), 213–218.

Holt-Lunstad, J. (2018). Relationships and physical health. In A. L. Vangelisti & D. Perlman (Eds.), *The Cambridge handbook of personal relationships* (pp. 449–464). Cambridge University Press.

Holt-Lunstad, J., Birmingham, W. A., & Light, K. C. (2008). Influence of a "warm touch" support enhancement intervention among married couples on ambulatory blood pressure, oxytocin, alpha amylase, and cortisol. *Psychosomatic Medicine, 70*(9), 976–985.

Holt-Lunstad, J., Birmingham, W. C., & Light, K. C. (2015). Relationship quality and oxytocin: Influence of stable and modifiable aspects of relationships. *Journal of Social and Personal Relationships, 32*(4), 472–490.

Holt-Lunstad, J., Robles, T. F., & Sbarra, D. A. (2017). Advancing social connection as a public health priority in the United States. *American Psychologist, 72*(6), 517–530.

Holt-Lunstad, J., Smith, T. B., & Layton, J. B. (2010). Social relationships and mortality risk: A meta-analytic review. *PLoS Medicine, 7*(7), e1000316.

Holt-Lunstad, J., & Uchino, B. N. (2019). Social ambivalence and disease (SAD): A theoretical model aimed at understanding the health implications of ambivalent relationships. *Perspectives on Psychological Science, 14*(6), 941–966.

Homans, G. C. (1961). *Social interaction in its elementary forms*. Harcourt, Brace, & World.

Hönekopp, J. (2006). Once more: Is beauty in the eye of the beholder? Relative contributions of private and shared taste to judgments of facial attractiveness. *Journal of Experimental Psychology: Human Perception and Performance, 32*(2), 199–209.

Hope, S., Rodgers, B., & Power, C. (1999). Marital status transitions and psychological distress: Longitudinal evidence from a national population sample. *Psychological Medicine, 29*(2), 381–389.

Horan, S. M., & Booth-Butterfield, M. (2019). Understanding the routine expression of deceptive affection in romantic relationships. *Communication Quarterly, 61*, 195–216.

Horan, S. M., Guinn, T. D., & Banghart, S. (2015). Understanding relationships among the dark triad personality profile and romantic partners' conflict communication. *Communication Quarterly, 63*(2), 156–170.

Horowitz, A. D., & Spicer, L. (2013). "Having sex" as a graded and hierarchical construct: A comparison of sexual definitions among heterosexual and Lesbian emerging adults in the U.K. *Journal of Sex Research, 50*(2), 139–150.

Horowitz, J. M., Graf, N., & Livingston, G. (2019, November 6). *Marriage and cohabitation in the United States*. Pew Research Center. www.pewresearch.org/social-trends/2019/11/06/the-landscape-of-marriage-and-cohabitation-in-the-u-s/

House, J. S., Landis, K. R., & Umberson, D. (1988). Social relationships and health. *Science, 241*, 540–545.

Houts, C. R., & Horne, S. G. (2008). The role of relationship attributions in relationship satisfaction among cohabiting gay men. *Family Journal, 16*(3), 240–248.

Hove, M. J., & Risen, J. L. (2009). It's all in the timing: Interpersonal synchrony increases affiliation. *Social Cognition, 27*(6), 949–960.

Howard, R. M., & Perilloux, C. (2017). Is mating psychology most closely tied to biological sex or preferred partner's sex? *Personality and Individual Differences, 115*, 83–89.

Howland, M., & Simpson, J. A. (2010). Getting in under the radar: A dyadic view of invisible support. *Psychological Science, 21*(12), 1878–1885.

Hoy, A., Diiriye, A., & Gunderson, E. (2022). Divorce ideation and "deal breakers" among married gay men and lesbians:

A qualitative exploration. *Journal of Family Issues*, *43*(1), 164–185.

Huang, S. A., Ledgerwood, A., & Eastwick, P. W. (2020). How do ideal friend preferences and interaction context affect friendship formation? Evidence for a domain-general relationship initiation process. *Social Psychological and Personality Science*, *11*(2), 226–235.

Hudson, N. W., Lucas, R. E., & Donnellan, M. B. (2020). The highs and lows of love: Romantic relationship quality moderates whether spending time with one's partner predicts gains or losses in well-being. *Personality and Social Psychology Bulletin*, *46*(4), 572–589.

Hughes, E. K., Slotter, E. B., & Lewandowski, G. W. (2020). Expanding who I am: Validating the Self-Expansion Preference Scale. *Journal of Personality Assessment*, *102*(6), 792–803.

Hughes, M. E., & Waite, L. J. (2009). Marital biography and health at mid-life. *Journal of Health and Social Behavior*, *50*(3), 344–358.

Hull, E. M., Muschamp, J. W., & Sato, S. (2004). Dopamine and serotonin: Influences on male sexual behavior. *Physiology and Behavior*, *83*(2), 291–307.

Hunter, M. L. (2007). The persistent problem of colorism: Skin tone, status, and inequality. *Sociology Compass*, *1*(1), 237–254.

Hunter, M. L. (2013). *Race, gender, and the politics of skin tone*. Routledge.

Huss, B., & Pollmann-Schult, M. (2020). Relationship satisfaction across the transition to parenthood: The impact of conflict behavior. *Journal of Family Issues*, *41*(3), 383–411.

Hust, S. J. T., Rodgers, K. B., & Bayly, B. (2017). Scripting sexual consent: Internalized traditional sexual scripts and sexual consent expectancies among college students. *Family Relations*, *66*(1), 197–210.

Huston, T. L. (1994). Courtship antecedents of marital satisfaction and love. In R. Erber & R. Gilmour (Eds.), *Theoretical frameworks for personal relationships* (pp. 43–65). Psychological Press.

Huston, T. L., Houts, R. M., Caughlin, J. P. et al. (2001). The connubial crucible: Newlywed years as predictors of marital delight, distress, and divorce. *Journal of Personality and Social Psychology*, *80*(2), 237–252.

Ickes, W. (1993). Empathic accuracy. *Journal of Personality*, *61*(4), 587–610.

Ickes, W., & Hodges, S. (2013). Empathic accuracy in close relationships. In J. A. Simpson & L. Campbell (Eds.), *Handbook of close relationships* (pp. 348–373). Oxford University Press.

Iida, M., Seidman, G., Shrout, P. E. et al. (2008). Modeling support provision in intimate relationships. *Journal of Personality and Social Psychology*, *94*(3), 460–478.

Impett, E. A., Beals, K. P., & Peplau, L. A. (2001). Testing the investment model of relationship commitment and stability in a longitudinal study of married couples. *Current Psychology*, *4*(20), 312–326.

Impett, E. A., Gable, S., & Peplau, L. (2005). Giving up and giving in: The costs and benefits of daily sacrifice in intimate relationships. *Journal of Personality and Social Psychology*, *89*, 327–344.

Impett, E. A., Gere, J., Kogan, A. et al. (2014). How sacrifice impacts the giver and the recipient: Insights from approach-avoidance motivational theory. *Journal of Personality*, *82*(5), 390–401.

Impett, E. A., & Gordon, A. M. (2010). Why do people sacrifice to approach rewards versus to avoid costs? Insights from attachment theory. *Personal Relationships*, *17*(2), 299–315.

Impett, E. A., Gordon, A. M., & Strachman, A. (2008). Attachment and daily sexual goals: A study of dating couples. *Personal Relationships*, *15*(3), 375–390.

Impett, E. A., Kim, J. J., & Muise, A. (2020). A communal approach to sexual need responsiveness in romantic relationships. *European Review of Social Psychology*, *31*(1), 287–318.

Impett, E. A., Muise, A., & Harasymchuk, C. (2019). Giving in the bedroom: The costs and benefits of responding to a partner's sexual needs in daily life. *Journal of Social and Personal Relationships*, *36*(8), 2455–2473.

Impett, E. A., Muise, A., & Rosen, N. O. (2020). Sex as relationship maintenance. In B. G. Ogolsky & J. K. Monk (Eds.), *Relationship maintenance: Theory, process, and context* (pp. 215–239). Cambridge University Press.

Impett, E. A., Peplau, L. A., & Gable, S. L. (2005). Approach and avoidance sexual motives: Implications for personal and interpersonal well-being. *Personal Relationships*, *12*(4), 465–482.

Impett, E. A., Strachman, A., Finkel, E. J. et al. (2008). Maintaining sexual desire in intimate relationships: The importance of approach goals. *Journal of Personality and Social Psychology*, *94*(5), 808–823.

Inagaki, T. K., & Eisenberger, N. I. (2012). Neural correlates of giving support to a loved one. *Psychosomatic Medicine*, *74*(1), 3–7.

Inagaki, T. K., & Eisenberger, N. I. (2016). Giving support to others reduces sympathetic nervous system-related responses to stress. *Psychophysiology*, *53*, 427–435.

Inagaki, T. K., Haltom, K. E. B., Suzuki, S. et al. (2016). The neurobiology of giving versus receiving support: The role of stress-related and social reward-related neural activity. *Psychosomatic Medicine*, *78*(4), 443–453.

Inagaki, T. K., & Orehek, E. (2017). On the benefits of giving social support: When, why, and how support providers gain by caring for others. *Current Directions in Psychological Science, 26*, 109–113.

Ingersoll-Dayton, B., Campbell, R., Kurokawa, Y. et al. (1996). Separateness and togetherness: Interdependence over the life course in Japanese and American marriages. *Journal of Social and Personal Relationships, 13*(3), 385–398.

Ingram, K. M., Betz, N. E., Mindes, E. J. et al. (2001). Unsupportive responses from others concerning a stressful life event: Development of the Unsupportive Social Interactions Inventory. *Journal of Social and Clinical Psychology, 20*(2), 173–207.

Ioannidis, J. P. A. (2005). Why most published research findings are false. *PLoS Medicine, 2*(8), 696–701.

Ireland, M. E., Slatcher, R. B., Eastwick, P. W. et al. (2011). Language style matching predicts relationship initiation and stability. *Psychological Science, 22*(1), 39–44.

Iyengar, S. S., & Lepper, M. R. (2000). When choice is demotivating: Can one desire too much of a good thing? *Journal of Personality and Social Psychology, 79*(6), 995–1006.

Jackson, G. L., Trail, T. E., Kennedy, D. P. et al. (2016). The salience and severity of relationship problems among low-income couples. *Journal of Family Psychology, 30*(1), 2–11.

Jackson, P. B., Kleiner, S., Geist, C. et al. (2011). Conventions of courtship: Gender and race differences in the significance of dating rituals. *Journal of Family Issues, 32*(5), 629–652.

Jacobson, N. S., & Margolin, G. (1979). *Marital therapy: Strategies based on social learning and behavior exchange principles*. Brunner/Mazel Publishers.

Jacques-Tiura, A. J., Abbey, A., Parkhill, M. R. et al. (2007). Why do some men misperceive women's sexual intentions more frequently than others do? An application of the confluence model. *Personality and Social Psychology Bulletin, 33*(11), 1467–1480.

Jadva, V., Badger, S., Morrissette, M. et al. (2009). "Mom by choice, single by life's circumstance . . ." Findings from a large scale survey of the experiences of single mothers by choice. *Human Fertility, 12*(4), 175–184.

Jakubiak, B. K. (2021). Providing support is easier done than said: Support providers' perceptions of touch and verbal support provision requests. *Journal of Experimental Social Psychology, 96*, 104168.

Jakubiak, B. K. (2022). Affectionate touch in satisfying and dissatisfying relationships. *Journal of Social and Personal Relationships, 39*(8), 2287–2315.

Jakubiak, B. K., Debrot, A., Kim, J. et al. (2021). Approach and avoidance motives for touch are predicted by attachment and predict daily relationship well-being. *Journal of Social and Personal Relationships, 38*(1), 256–278.

Jakubiak, B. K., & Feeney, B. C. (2016a). A sense of security: Touch promotes state attachment security. *Social Psychological and Personality Science, 7*, 745–753.

Jakubiak, B. K., & Feeney, B. C. (2016b). Daily goal progress is facilitated by spousal support and promotes psychological, physical, and relational well-being throughout adulthood. *Journal of Personality and Social Psychology, 111*, 317–340.

Jakubiak, B. K., & Feeney, B. C. (2016c). Keep in touch: The effects of imagined touch support on stress and exploration. *Journal of Experimental Social Psychology, 65*, 59–67.

Jakubiak, B. K., & Feeney, B. C. (2017). Affectionate touch to promote relational, psychological, and physical well-being in adulthood: A theoretical model and review of the research. *Personality and Social Psychology Review, 21*, 228–252.

Jakubiak, B. K., & Feeney, B. C. (2018). Interpersonal touch as a resource to facilitate positive personal and relational outcomes during stress discussions. *Journal of Social and Personal Relationships, 36*(9), 2918–2936.

Jakubiak, B. K., & Feeney, B. C. (2019). Hand-in-hand combat: Affectionate touch promotes relational well-being and buffers stress during conflict. *Personality and Social Psychology Bulletin, 45*, 431–446.

Jakubiak, B. K., Feeney, B. C., & Ferrer, R. A. (2020). Benefits of daily support visibility versus invisibility across the adult life span. *Journal of Personality and Social Psychology, 118*(5), 1018–1043.

Jakubiak, B. K., Fuentes, J. D., & Feeney, B. C. (2021). Individual and relational differences in desire for touch in romantic relationships. *Journal of Social and Personal Relationships, 38*(7), 2029–2052.

Jakubiak, B. K., Fuentes, J. D., & Feeney, B. C. (2022). Affectionate touch promotes shared positive activities. *Personality and Social Psychology Bulletin*. Advance online publication. https://doi.org/10.1177/01461672221083764

Jakubiak, B. K., & Tomlinson, J. M. (2020). The role of social support in promoting self-development. In B. A. Mattingly, K. P. McIntyre, & G. W. Lewandowski (Eds.), *Interpersonal relationships and the self-concept* (pp. 125–143). Springer International Publishing .

Jankowiak, W. R., & Fischer, E. F. (1992). A cross-cultural perspective on romantic love. *Ethnology, 31*(2), 149–155.

Jankowiak, W. R., & Nell, M. (2002). Managing infidelity: A cross-cultural perspective. *Ethnology, 41*(1), 85–101.

Jaremka, L. M., Lebed, O., & Sunami, N. (2018). Threats to belonging, immune function, and eating behavior: An examination of sex and gender differences. *Current Psychiatry Reports, 20*(9), 71.

Jaspal, R. (2014). Arranged marriage, identity, and well-being among British Asian gay men. *Journal of GLBT Family Studies*, *10*(5), 425–448.

Jaswal, V. K., & Akhtar, N. (2018). Being vs. appearing socially uninterested: Challenging assumptions about social motivation in Autism. *Behavioral and Brain Sciences*, *42*, 1–84.

Jiang, L., Drolet, A., & Kim, H. S. (2018). Age and social support seeking: Understanding the role of perceived social costs to others. *Personality and Social Psychology Bulletin*, *44*(7), 1104–1116.

Jodouin, J. F., Rosen, N. O., Merwin, K. et al. (2021). Discrepancy in dyadic sexual desire predicts sexual distress over time in a community sample of committed couples: A daily diary and longitudinal study. *Archives of Sexual Behavior*, *50*(8), 3637–3649.

Joel, S., Eastwick, P. W., & Finkel, E. J. (2017). Is romantic desire predictable? Machine learning applied to initial romantic attraction. *Psychological Science*, *28*(10), 1478–1489.

Joel, S., Impett, E. A., Spielmann, S. S. et al. (2018). How interdependent are stay/leave decisions? On staying in the relationship for the sake of the romantic partner. *Journal of Personality and Social Psychology*, *115*(5), 805–824.

Joel, S., & MacDonald, G. (2021). We're not that choosy: Emerging evidence of a progression bias in romantic relationships. *Personality and Social Psychology Review*, *25*(4), 317–343.

Joel, S., MacDonald, G., & Page-Gould, E. (2018). Wanting to stay and wanting to go: Unpacking the content and structure of relationship stay/leave decision processes. *Social Psychological and Personality Science*, *9*(6), 631–644.

Joel, S., Stanton, S. C. E., Page-Gould, E. et al. (2021). One foot out the door: Stay/leave ambivalence predicts day-to-day fluctuations in commitment and intentions to end the relationship. *European Journal of Social Psychology*, *51*(2), 294–312.

Joel, S., Teper, R., & MacDonald, G. (2014). People overestimate their willingness to reject potential romantic partners by overlooking their concern for other people. *Psychological Science*, *25*(12), 2233–2240.

John, E. (2019). Elton John: "They wanted to tone down the sex and drugs. But I haven't led a PG-13 life." *The Guardian*. www.theguardian.com/global/2019/may/26/elton-john-in-my-own-words-exclusive-my-life-and-making-rocketman

Johns, K. N., Allen, E. S., & Gordon, K. C. (2015, May 26). The relationship between mindfulness and forgiveness of infidelity. *Mindfulness*, *6*, 1462–1471.

Johnson, C. A., Stanley, S. M., Glenn, N. D. et al. (2002). *Marriage in Oklahoma: 2001 baseline statewide survey on marriage and divorce (S02096 OKDHS)*. Oklahoma Department of Human Services.

Johnson, D. J., & Rusbult, C. E. (1989). Resisting temptation: Devaluation of alternative partners as a means of maintaining commitment in close relationships. *Journal of Personality and Social Psychology*, *57*(6), 967–980.

Johnson, D. R., & Wu, J. (2002). An empirical test of crisis, social selection, and role explanations of the relationship between marital disruption and psychological distress: A pooled time-series analysis of four-wave panel data. *Journal of Marriage and Family*, *64*(1), 211–224.

Johnson, H. A., Zabriskie, R. B., & Hill, B. (2006). The contribution of couple leisure involvement, leisure time, and leisure satisfaction to marital satisfaction. *Marriage & Family Review*, *40*(1), 69–91.

Johnson, M. D. (2012). Healthy marriage initiatives: On the need for empiricism in policy implementation. *American Psychologist*, *67*(4), 296–308.

Johnson M. D., & Anderson J. R. (2013). The longitudinal association of marital confidence, time spent together, and marital satisfaction. *Family Process*, *52*(2), 244–256.

Johnson, M. D., Horne, R. M., Hardy, N. R. et al. (2018). Temporality of couple conflict and relationship perceptions. *Journal of Family Psychology*, *32*(4), 445–455.

Johnson, N. J., Backlund, E., Sorlie, P. D. et al. (2000). Marital status and mortality: The national longitudinal mortality study. *Annals of Epidemiology*, *10*(4), 224–238.

Johnson, R. M., & Hall, J. A. (2021). The discourses surrounding long-distance romantic relationships and perceived network support: A mixed methods investigation. *Journal of Social and Personal Relationships*, *38*(9), 2525–2544.

Johnson, S. M. (2015). Emotionally focused couple therapy. In A. S. Gurman, J. L. Lebow, & D. K. Snyder (Eds.), *Clinical handbook of couple therapy* (5th ed., pp. 97–128). Guilford Press.

Johnson, S. M. (2019a). Attachment in action: Changing the face of 21st century couple therapy. *Current Opinion in Psychology*, *25*, 101–104.

Johnson, S. M. (2019b). *The practice of emotionally focused couple therapy: Creating connection* (3rd ed.). Routledge.

Joiner, T. (2007). *Why people die by suicide*. Harvard University Press.

Joiner, T. E. (1995). The price of soliciting and receiving negative feedback: Self-verification theory as a vulnerability to depression theory. *Journal of Abnormal Psychology*, *104*(2), 364–372.

Joiner, T. E. (2000). Depression's vicious scree: Self-propagating and erosive processes in depression chronicity. *Clinical Psychology: Science and Practice*, *7*(2), 203–218.

Jolink, T. A., Chang, Y.-P., & Algoe, S. B. (2021). Perceived partner responsiveness forecasts behavioral intimacy as measured by affectionate touch. *Personality and Social Psychology Bulletin*, 0146167221993349.

Jonason, P. K., & Antoon, C. N. (2019). Mate preferences for educated partners: Similarities and differences in the sexes depend on mating context. *Personality and Individual Differences*, *148*, 57–61.

Jonason, P. K., Betes, S. L., & Li, N. P. (2020). Solving mate shortages: Lowering standards, searching farther, and abstaining. *Evolutionary Behavioral Sciences*, *14*(2), 160–172.

Jonason, P. K., Garcia, J. R., Webster, G. D. et al. (2015). Relationship dealbreakers: Traits people avoid in potential mates. *Personality and Social Psychology Bulletin*, *41*(12), 1697–1711.

Jonason, P. K., Kaźmierczak, I., Campos, A. C. et al. (2021). Leaving without a word: Ghosting and the Dark Triad traits. *Acta Psychologica*, *220*, 103425.

Jonason, P. K., & Li, N. P. (2013). Playing hard-to-get: Manipulating one's perceived availability as a mate. *European Journal of Personality*, *27*(5), 458–469.

Jonason, P. K., Li, N. P., & Buss, D. M. (2010). The costs and benefits of the Dark Triad: Implications for mate poaching and mate retention tactics. *Personality and Individual Differences*, *48*(4), 373–378.

Jonason, P. K., Li, N. P., & Cason, M. J. (2009). The "booty call": A compromise between men's and women's ideal mating strategies. *Journal of Sex Research*, *46*(5), 460–470.

Jonason, P. K., Li, N. P., & Richardson, J. (2011). Positioning the booty-call relationship on the spectrum of relationships: Sexual but more emotional than one-night stands. *Journal of Sex Research*, *48*(5), 486–495.

Jonason, P. K., Li, N. P., Webster, G. D. et al. (2009). The Dark Triad: Facilitating a short-term mating strategy in men. *European Journal of Personality*, *23*(1), 5–18.

Jonason, P. K., Luevano, V. X., & Adams, H. M. (2012). How the Dark Triad traits predict relationship choices. *Personality and Individual Differences*, *53*(3), 180–184.

Jonason, P. K., Marsh, K., Dib, O. et al. (2019). Is smart sexy? Examining the role of relative intelligence in mate preferences. *Personality and Individual Differences*, *139*, 53–59.

Jonason, P. K., & Schmitt, D. P. (2016). Quantifying common criticisms of evolutionary psychology. *Evolutionary Psychological Science*, *2*(3), 177–188.

Jonason, P. K., White, K. P., & Al-Shawaf, L. (2020). Should I stay or should I go: Individual differences in response to romantic dealmakers and dealbreakers. *Personality and Individual Differences*, *164*, 110120.

Jones, B. C., DeBruine, L. M., Perrett, D. I. et al. (2008). Effects of menstrual cycle phase on face preferences. *Archives of Sexual Behavior*, *37*(1), 78–84.

Jones, B. C., Hahn, A. C., & Debruine, L. M. (2019). Ovulation, sex hormones, and women's mating psychology. *Trends in Cognitive Sciences*, *23*(1), 51–62.

Jones, B. C., Hahn, A. C., Fisher, C. I. et al. (2018). No compelling evidence that preferences for facial masculinity track changes in women's hormonal status. *Psychological Science*, *29*(6), 996–1005.

Jones, J. (2008, March 25). *Most Americans not willing to forgive unfaithful spouse*. Gallop Poll. https://news.gallup.com/poll/105682/most-americans-willing-forgive-unfaithful-spouse.aspx

Jones, M. (1998). Sociosexuality and motivations for romantic involvement. *Journal of Research in Personality*, *32*(2), 173–182.

Jones, W. H., Moore, D. S., Schratter, A. et al. (2004). Interpersonal transgressions and betrayals. In R. M. Kowalski (Ed.), *Behaving badly: Aversive behaviors in interpersonal relationships* (pp. 233–256). American Psychological Association.

Jose, A., Daniel O'Leary, K., & Moyer, A. (2010). Does premarital cohabitation predict subsequent marital stability and marital quality? A meta-analysis. *Journal of Marriage and Family*, *72*(1), 105–116.

Jowett, A., & Peel, E. (2019). Reshaping relational scripts? Marriage and civil partnership proposals among same-gender couples. *Psychology and Sexuality*, *10*(4), 325–337.

Jozkowski, K. N. (2015). "Yes means yes"? Sexual consent policy and college students. *Change: The Magazine of Higher Learning*, *47*(2), 16–23.

Jozkowski, K. N., & Peterson, Z. D. (2013). College students and sexual consent: Unique insights. *Journal of Sex Research*, *50*(6), 517–523.

Jozkowski, K. N., & Peterson, Z. D. (2014). Assessing the validity and reliability of the perceptions of the consent to sex scale. *Journal of Sex Research*, *51*(6), 632–645.

Jozkowski, K. N., Peterson, Z. D., Sanders, S. A. et al. (2014). Gender differences in heterosexual college students' conceptualizations and indicators of sexual consent: Implications for contemporary sexual assault prevention education. *Journal of Sex Research*, *51*(8), 904–916.

Juneau, J. (2019, October 22). Mark Zuckerberg opens up about how he manages screen time for his young daughters. *People*. https://people.com/parents/mark-zuckerberg-daughters-screen-time-facebook-portal-priscilla-chan/

Juneau, J. (2021). OITNB's Samira Wiley, Lauren Morelli welcome baby girl George Elizabeth: "Best first Mother's

Day." *People*. https://people.com/parents/samira-wiley-lauren-morelli-welcome-daughter-george-elizabeth/

Kabat-Zinn, J. (2015). Mindfulness. *Mindfulness*, *6*(6), 1481–1483.

Kalai, C., & Eldridge, K. (2021). Integrative behavioral couple therapy for intercultural couples: Helping couples navigate cultural differences. *Contemporary Family Therapy*, *43*, 259–275.

Kamarck, T. W., Manuck, S. B., & Jennings, J. R. (1990). Social support reduces cardiovascular reactivity to psychological challenge: A laboratory model. *Psychosomatic Medicine*, *52*(1), 42–58.

Kammrath, L. K., Armstrong, B. F., Lane, S. P. et al. (2020). What predicts who we approach for social support? Tests of the attachment figure and strong ties hypotheses. *Journal of Personality and Social Psychology*, *118*(3), 481–500.

Kamp Dush, C. M., & Amato, P. R. (2005). Consequences of relationship status and quality for subjective well-being. *Journal of Social and Personal Relationships*, *22*(5), 607–627.

Kamp Dush, C. M., Arocho, R., Mernitz, S. et al. (2018). The intergenerational transmission of partnering. *PLOS One*, *13*(11), e0205732.

Kamp Dush, C. M., & Taylor, M. G. (2012). Trajectories of marital conflict across the life course: Predictors and interactions with marital happiness trajectories. *Journal of Family Issues*, *33*(3), 341–368.

Kane, H. S., McCall, C., Collins, N. L. et al. (2012). Mere presence is not enough: Responsive support in a virtual world. *Journal of Experimental Social Psychology*, *48*, 37–44.

Kapelle, N. (2022). Time cannot heal all wounds: Wealth trajectories of divorcees and the married. *Journal of Marriage and Family*, *84*(2), 592–611.

Kaplan, H., & Gangestad, S. W. (2005). Life history theory and evolutionary psychology. In D. M. Buss (Ed.), *The handbook of evolutionary psychology* (pp. 68–95). John Wiley & Sons.

Kappen, G., Karremans, J. C., Burk, W. J. et al. (2018). On the association between mindfulness and romantic relationship satisfaction: The role of partner acceptance. *Mindfulness*, *9*, 1543–1556.

Kappen, G., Karremans, J. C., & Burk, W. J. (2019). Effects of a short online mindfulness intervention on relationship satisfaction and partner acceptance: The moderating role of trait mindfulness. *Mindfulness*, *10*, 2186–2199.

Karney, B. R. (February 2010). Keeping marriages healthy, and why it's so difficult. *Psychological Science Agenda*, 1–3. www.apa.org/science/about/psa/2010/02/sci-brief

Karney, B. R. (2021). Socioeconomic status and intimate relationships. *Annual Review of Psychology*, *72*, 391–414.

Karney, B. R., & Bradbury, T. N. (1995). The longitudinal course of marital quality and stability: A review of theory, method, and research. *Psychological Bulletin*, *118*(1), 3–34.

Karney, B. R., & Bradbury, T. N. (1997). Neuroticism, marital interaction, and the trajectory of marital satisfaction. *Journal of Personality and Social Psychology*, *72*(5), 1075–1092.

Karney, B. R., & Bradbury, T. N. (2005). Contextual influences on marriage. *Current Directions in Psychological Science*, *14*(4), 171–174.

Karney, B. R., Bradbury, T. N., & Lavner, J. A. (2018). Supporting healthy relationships in low-income couples: Lessons learned and policy implications. *Policy Insights from the Behavioral and Brain Sciences*, *5*, 33–39.

Karney, B. R., & Coombs, R. H. (2000). Memory bias in long-term close relationships: Consistency or improvement? *Personality and Social Psychology Bulletin*, *26*(8), 959–970.

Karney, B. R., & Frye, N. E. (2002). "But we've been getting better lately": Comparing prospective and retrospective views of relationship development. *Journal of Personality and Social Psychology*, *82*(2), 222–238.

Karney, B. R., & Neff, L. A. (2013). Couples and stress: How demands outside a relationship affect intimacy within the relationship. In J. A. Simpson & L. Campbell (Eds.), *The Oxford handbook of close relationships* (pp. 664–684). Oxford University Press.

Karremans, J. C., Dotsch, R., & Corneille, O. (2011). Romantic relationship status biases memory of faces of attractive opposite-sex others: Evidence from a reverse-correlation paradigm. *Cognition*, *121*(3), 422–426.

Karremans, J. C., Schellekens, M. P. J., & Kappen, G. (2017). Bridging the sciences of mindfulness and romantic relationships. *Personality and Social Psychology Review*, *21*(1), 29–49.

Karremans, J. C., & Verwijmeren, T. (2008). Mimicking attractive opposite-sex others: The role of romantic relationship status. *Personality and Social Psychology Bulletin*, *34*(7), 939–950.

Kashdan, T. B., Goodman, F. R., Stiksma, M. et al. (2018). Sexuality leads to boosts in mood and meaning in life with no evidence for the reverse direction: A daily diary investigation. *Emotion*, *18*(4), 563–576.

Kasser, T., & Sharma, Y. S. (1999). Reproductive freedom, educational equality, and females' preference for resource-acquisition characteristics in mates. *Psychological Science*, *10*(4), 374–377.

Katz, J., & Schneider, M. E. (2013). Casual hook up sex during the first year of college: Prospective associations with attitudes about sex and love relationships. *Archives of Sexual Behavior*, *42*(8), 1451–1462.

Kaur, P., Dhir, A., Tandon, A. et al. (2021). A systematic literature review on cyberstalking. An analysis of past achievements and future promises. *Technological Forecasting and Social Change*, *163*, 120426.

Kayser, K. (1993). *When love dies: The process of marital disaffection*. Guilford Press.

Kayser, K., & Rao, S. S. (2013). Process of disaffection in relationship breakdown. In M. A. Fine & J. H. Harvey (Eds.), *Handbook of divorce and relationship dissolution* (pp. 201–221). Lawrence Erlbaum.

Keefer, L. A., Landau, M. J., & Sullivan, D. (2014). Non-human support: Broadening the scope of attachment theory. *Social and Personality Psychology Compass*, *8*(9), 524–535.

Kelberga, A., & Martinsone, B. (2021). Differences in motivation to engage in sexual activity between people in monogamous and non-monogamous committed relationships. *Frontiers in Psychology*, *12*, 753460.

Keller, H. (2016). Attachment: A pancultural need but a cultural construct. *Current Opinion in Psychology*, *8*, 59–63.

Kelley, H. H. (1983). The situational origins of human tendencies: A further reason for the formal analysis of structures. *Personality and Social Psychology Bulletin*, *9*, 8–30.

Kelley, H. H. (1984). Interdependence theory and its future. *Representative Research in Social Psychology*, *14*(2), 2–15.

Kelley, H. H., Holmes, J. G., Kerr, N. L. et al. (2003). *An atlas of interpersonal situations*. Cambridge University Press.

Kelley, H. H., & Thibaut, J. (1978). *Interpersonal relations: A theory of interdependence*. John Wiley & Sons.

Kelly, A. J., Dubbs, S. L., & Barlow, F. K. (2015). Social dominance orientation predicts heterosexual men's adverse reactions to romantic rejection. *Archives of Sexual Behavior*, *44*(4), 903–919.

Kelly, J. B., & Emery, R. E. (2003). Children's adjustment following divorce: Risk and resilience perspectives. *Family Relations*, *52*(4), 352–362.

Kelmer, G., Rhoades, G. K., Stanley, S. et al. (2013). Relationship quality, commitment, and stability in long-distance relationships. *Family Process*, *52*(2), 257–270.

Kemeny, M. E. (2011). Psychoneuroimmunology. In H. S. Friedman (Ed.), *The Oxford handbook of health psychology* (pp. 138–161). Oxford University Press.

Keneski, E., & Loving, T. J. (2014). Network perceptions of daters' romances. In C. R. Agnew (Ed.), *Social influences on romantic relationships: Beyond the dyad* (pp. 126–147). Cambridge University Press.

Kennedy, S., & Ruggles, S. (2014). Breaking up is hard to count: The rise of divorce in the United States, 1980–2010. *Demography*, *51*(2), 587–598.

Kenney, S. R., Lac, A., Hummer, J. F. et al. (2014). Development and validation of the hookup motives questionnaire (HMQ). *Psychological Assessment*, *26*(4), 1127–1137.

Kenny, D. A., Kashy, D. A., & Cook, W. L. (2006). *Dyadic data analysis*. Guilford Press.

Kenrick, D. T., & Keefe, R. C. (1992). Age preferences in mates reflect sex differences in human reproductive strategies. *Behavioral and Brain Sciences*, *15*(1), 75–91.

Kenrick, D. T., Sadalla, E. K., Groth, G. et al. (1990). Evolution, traits, and the stages of human courtship: Qualifying the parental investment model. *Journal of Personality*, *58*(1), 97–116.

Kent, E., & El-Alayli, A. (2011). Public and private physical affection differences between same-sex and different-sex couples: The role of perceived marginalization. *Interpersona: An International Journal on Personal Relationships*, *5*(2), 149–167.

Kerner, I. (2013, January 10). Your smartphone may be powering down your relationship. *CNN Health*. www.cnn.com/2013/01/10/health/kerner-social-relationship/index.html

Khaddouma, A., Coop Gordon, K., & Strand, E. B. (2017). Mindful mates: A pilot study of the relational effects of mindfulness-based stress reduction on participants and their partners. *Family Process*, *56*(3), 636–651.

Khomami, N. (2017, October 20). #MeToo: How a hashtag became a rallying cry against sexual harassment. *The Guardian*. www.theguardian.com/world/2017/oct/20/women-worldwide-use-hashtag-metoo-against-sexual-harassment

Khoury, B., Sharma, M., Rush, S. E. et al. (2015). Mindfulness-based stress reduction for healthy individuals: A meta-analysis. *Journal of Psychosomatic Research*, *78*(6), 519–528.

Kiecolt-Glaser, J. K. (2018). Marriage, divorce, and the immune system. *American Psychologist*, *73*(9), 1098–1108.

Kiecolt-Glaser, J. K., Glaser, R., Shuttleworth, E. C. et al. (1987). Marital quality, marital disruption, and immune function. *Psychosomatic Medicine*, *49*(1), 13–34.

Kiecolt-Glaser, J. K., Loving, T. J., Stowell, J. R. et al. (2005). Hostile marital interactions, proinflammatory cytokine production, and wound healing. *Archives of General Psychiatry*, *62*(12), 1377–1384.

Kiecolt-Glaser, J. K., Malarkey, W. B., Chee, M. et al. (1993). Negative behavior during marital conflict is associated with immunological down-regulation. *Psychosomatic Medicine*, *55*(5), 395–409.

Kiecolt-Glaser, J. K., & Newton, T. L. (2001). Marriage and health: His and hers. *Psychological Bulletin*, *127*(4), 472–503.

Kiecolt-Glaser, J. K., & Wilson, S. J. (2017). Lovesick: How couples' relationships influence health. *Annual Review of Clinical Psychology*, *13*, 421–443.

Killgore, W. D. S., Kahn-Greene, E. T., Lipizzi, E. L. et al. (2008). Sleep deprivation reduces perceived emotional intelligence and constructive thinking skills. *Sleep Medicine*, *9*(5), 517–526.

Kim, H. S., Sherman, D. K., Ko, D. et al. (2006). Pursuit of comfort and pursuit of harmony: Culture, relationships, and social support seeking. *Personality and Social Psychology Bulletin*, *32*(12), 1595–1607.

Kim, H. S., Sherman, D. K., & Taylor, S. E. (2008). Culture and social support. *American Psychologist*, *63*(6), 518–526.

Kim, J. J., Horne, R. M., Muise, A. et al. (2019). Development and validation of the responses to sexual rejection scale. *Personality and Individual Differences*, *144*, 88–93.

Kim, J. J., Muise, A., Barranti, M. et al. (2021). Are couples more satisfied when they match in sexual desire? New insights from response surface analyses. *Social Psychological and Personality Science*, *12*(4), 487–496.

Kim, J. J., Muise, A., & Impett, E. A. (2018). The relationship implications of rejecting a partner for sex kindly versus having sex reluctantly. *Journal of Social and Personal Relationships*, *35*(4), 485–508.

Kim, J. J., Muise, A., Sakaluk, J. K., Rosen, N. O., & Impet, E. A. (2020). When tonight is not the night: Sexual rejection behaviors and satisfaction in romantic relationships. *Personality and Social Psychology Bulletin*, *46*(10), 1476–1490.

Kim, K. J., Feeney, B. C., & Jakubiak, B. K. (2018). Touch reduces romantic jealousy in the anxiously attached. *Journal of Social and Personal Relationships*, *35*, 1019–1041.

Kimble, L. (2017, March 23). Elton John on fatherhood and turning 70 "Life is fabulous." *People*. https://people.com/parents/elton-john-beats-1-on-fatherhood-turning-70/

Kimmes, J. G. (2018). The association between trait mindfulness and cardiovascular reactivity during marital conflict. *Mindfulness*, *9*, 1160–1169.

King, B. M., Carr, D. C., Taylor, M. G. et al. (2019). Depressive symptoms and the buffering effect of resilience on widowhood by gender. *Gerontologist*, *59*(6), 1122–1130.

King, K. B., & Reis, H. T. (2012). Marriage and long-term survival after coronary artery bypass grafting. *Health Psychology*, *31*(1), 55–62.

Kinsey, A. C., Pomeroy, W. B., & Martin, C. E. (1948). *Sexual behavior in the human male*. American Public Health Association.

Kjaer, T., Albieri, V., Jensen, A. et al. (2014). Divorce or end of cohabitation among Danish women evaluated for fertility problems. *Acta Obstetricia et Gynecologica Scandinavica*, *93*(3), 269–276.

Klein, V., Imhoff, R., Reininger, K. M. et al. (2019). Perceptions of sexual script deviation in women and men. *Archives of Sexual Behavior*, *48*(2), 631–644.

Kleinke, C. L., Meeker, F. B., & Staneski, R. A. (1986). Preference for opening lines: Comparing ratings by men and women. *Sex Roles*, *15*(11–12), 585–600.

Klettner, A. M., Luo, S., & Tine, J. (2020). Cognitive, emotional, and behavioral reactions to snooping: The role of attachment characteristics. *Psychological Reports*, *123*(6), 2147–2172.

Kline, G. H., Stanley, S. M., Markman, H. J. et al. (2004). Timing is everything: Pre-engagement cohabitation and increased risk for poor marital outcomes. *Journal of Family Psychology*, *18*(2), 311–318.

Klinkenberg, D., & Rose, S. (1994). Dating scripts of gay men and lesbians. *Journal of Homosexuality*, *26*(4), 23–35.

Klusmann, D. (2002). Sexual motivation and the duration of partnership. *Archives of Sexual Behavior*, *31*(3), 275–287.

Kluwer, E. S., & Johnson, M. D. (2007). Conflict frequency and relationship quality across the transition to parenthood. *Journal of Marriage and Family*, *69*(5), 1089–1106.

Knapp, M. L. (1978). *Social intercourse: From greeting to goodbye*. Allyn & Bacon.

Knapp, M. L., Vangelisti, A., & Caughlin, J. (2013). *Interpersonal communication and human relationships* (7th ed.). Pearson.

Knee, C. R., Patrick, H., & Lonsbary, C. (2003). Implicit theories of relationships: Orientations toward evaluation and cultivation. *Personality and Social Psychology Review*, *7*(1), 41–55.

Knee, C. R., Patrick, H., Vietor, N. A. et al. (2004). Implicit theories of relationships: Moderators of the link between conflict and commitment. *Personality and Social Psychology Bulletin*, *30*(5), 617–628.

Knobloch, L. K., & Miller, L. E. (2008). Uncertainty and relationship initiation. In S. Sprecher, A. Wenzel, & J. Harvey (Eds.), *Handbook of relationship initiation* (pp. 121–134). Psychology Press.

Knobloch, L. K., & Solomon, D. H. (2002). Information seeking beyond initial interaction: Negotiating relational uncertainty within close relationships. *Human Communication Research*, *28*(2), 243–257.

Knobloch, L. K., & Solomon, D. H. (2004). Interference and facilitation from partners in the development of interdependence within romantic relationships. *Personal Relationships*, *11*(1), 115–130.

Knobloch, L. K., & Theiss, J. A. (2011). Relational uncertainty and relationship talk within courtship: A longitudinal actor–partner interdependence model. *Communication Monographs*, *78*(1), 3–26.

Knöpfli, B., Morselli, D., & Perrig-Chiello, P. (2016). Trajectories of psychological adaptation to marital breakup after a long-term marriage. *Gerontology*, *62*(5), 541–552.

Knopp, K., Rhoades, G. K., Stanley, S. M. et al. (2020). "Defining the relationship" in adolescent and young adult romantic relationships. *Journal of Social and Personal Relationships*, *37*(7), 2078–2097.

Knopp, K., Scott, S., Ritchie, L. et al. (2017). Once a cheater, always a cheater? Serial infidelity across subsequent relationships. *Archives of Sexual Behavior*, *46*(8), 2301–2311.

Koessler, R. B., Kohut, T., & Campbell, L. (2019). When your boo becomes a ghost: The association between breakup strategy and breakup role in experiences of relationship dissolution. *Collabra: Psychology*, *5*(1) Article 29.

Koladich, S. J., & Atkinson, B. E. (2016). The Dark Triad and relationship preferences: A replication and extension. *Personality and Individual Differences*, *94*, 253–255.

Kolmes, K., & Witherspoon, R. G. (2017). Therapy with a consensually nonmonogamous couple. *Journal of Clinical Psychology*, *73*(8), 954–964.

Kolodziejczak, K., Drewelies, J., Pauly, T. et al. (2022). Physical intimacy in older couples' everyday lives: Its frequency and links with affect and salivary cortisol. *Journals of Gerontology: Series B*, *77*(8), 1416–1430.

Kołodziej-Zaleska, A., & Przybyła-Basista, H. (2020). The role of ego-resiliency in maintaining post-divorce well-being in initiators and non-initiators of divorce. *Journal of Divorce and Remarriage*, *61*(5), 366–383.

Kornblith, E., Green, R.-J., Casey, S. et al. (2016). Marital status, social support, and depressive symptoms among lesbian and heterosexual women. *Journal of Lesbian Studies*, *20*(1), 157–173.

Kościński, K. (2019). Breast firmness is of greater importance for women's attractiveness than breast size. *American Journal of Human Biology*, *31*(5), e23287.

Kosfeld, M., Heinrichs, M., Zak, P. J. et al. (2005). Oxytocin increases trust in humans. *Nature*, *435*(7042), 673–676.

Koshi, N. (2019, May 26). First thought world won't allow a girl to be with a girl. But she said, if we want we can make it work: Dutee Chand. *The Indian Express*. https://indianexpress.com/article/sports/sport-others/dutee-chand-same-sex-relationship-indian-sportsperson-5748525/

Kosinski, M. (2019). Computational psychology. In E. J. Finkel & R. F. Baumeister (Eds.), *Advanced social psychology: The state of the science* (2nd ed., pp. 499–524). Oxford University Press.

Kposowa, A. J., Ezzat, D. A., & Breault, K. D. (2020). Marital status, sex, and suicide: New longitudinal findings and Durkheim's marital status propositions. *Sociological Spectrum*, *40*(2), 81–98.

Krach, S., Paulus, F. M., Bodden, M. et al. (2010). The rewarding nature of social interactions. *Frontiers in Behavioral Neuroscience*, *4*, 22.

Kreuzer, M., & Gollwitzer, M. (2022). Neuroticism and satisfaction in romantic relationships: A systematic investigation of intra- and interpersonal processes with a longitudinal approach. *European Journal of Personality*, *36*(2), 149–179.

Kristiansen, C. B., Kjær, J. N., Hjorth, P. et al. (2019). The association of time since spousal loss and depression in widowhood: A systematic review and meta-analysis. *Social Psychiatry and Psychiatric Epidemiology*, *54*(7), 781–792.

Kross, E., Berman, M. G., Mischel, W. et al. (2011). Social rejection shares somatosensory representations with physical pain. *Proceedings of the National Academy of Sciences*, *108*(15), 6270–6275.

Kubacka, K. E., Finkenauer, C., Rusbult, C. E. et al. (2011). Maintaining close relationships: Gratitude as a motivator and a detector of maintenance behavior. *Personality and Social Psychology Bulletin*, *37*(10), 1362–1375.

Kuperberg, A. (2019). Premarital cohabitation and direct marriage in the United States: 1956–2015. *Marriage and Family Review*, *55*(5), 447–475.

Kuperberg, A., & Padgett, J. E. (2015). Dating and hooking up in college: Meeting contexts, sex, and variation by gender, partner's gender, and class standing. *Journal of Sex Research*, *52*(5), 517–531.

Kurdek, L. A. (1994a). Areas of conflict for gay, lesbian, and heterosexual couples: What couples argue about influences relationship satisfaction. *Journal of Marriage and Family*, *56*(4), 923–934.

Kurdek, L. A. (1994b). Conflict resolution styles in gay, lesbian, heterosexual nonparent, and heterosexual parent couples. *Journal of Marriage and Family*, *56*(3), 705–722.

Kurtz, J. L., Wilson, T. D., & Gilbert, D. T. (2007). Quantity versus uncertainty: When winning one prize is better than winning two. *Journal of Experimental Social Psychology*, *43*(6), 979–985.

Kurtz, L. E., & Algoe, S. B. (2015). Putting laughter in context: Shared laughter as behavioral indicator of relationship well-being. *Personal Relationships*, *22*(4), 573–590.

Kurtz, L. E., & Algoe, S. B. (2017). When sharing a laugh means sharing more: Testing the role of shared laughter on short-term interpersonal consequences. *Journal of Nonverbal Behavior*, *41*(1), 45–65.

Kustanti, C. Y., Chu, H., Kang, X. L. et al. (2022). Anticipatory grief prevalence among caregivers of persons with a life-threatening illness: A meta-analysis. *BMJ Supportive & Palliative Care*, bmjspcare-2021-003338.

Kuyper, L., & Fokkema, T. (2010). Loneliness among older lesbian, gay, and bisexual adults: The role of minority stress. *Archives of Sexual Behavior*, *39*(5), 1171–1180.

Kwang, T., & Swann, W. B. (2010). Do people embrace praise even when they feel unworthy? A review of critical tests of self-enhancement versus self-verification. *Personality and Social Psychology Review*, *14*(3), 263–280.

La France, B. H. (2010). What verbal and nonverbal communication cues lead to sex? An analysis of the traditional sexual script. *Communication Quarterly*, *58*(3), 297–318.

La France, B. H. (2020). Sexual interactions (un)scripted: An exploration of consequential unscripted sexual interactions. *Communication Quarterly*, *68*(4), 355–374.

La France, B. H., Henningsen, D. D., Oates, A. et al. (2009). Social-sexual interactions? Meta-analyses of sex differences in perceptions of flirtatiousness, seductiveness, and promiscuousness. *Communication Monographs*, *76*(3), 263–285.

Labrecque, L. T., & Whisman, M. A. (2020). Extramarital sex and marital dissolution: Does identity of the extramarital partner matter? *Family Process*, *59*(3), 1308–1318.

Lackenbauer, S. D., Campbell, L., Rubin, H. et al. (2010). The unique and combined benefits of accuracy and positive bias in relationships. *Personal Relationships*, *17*(3), 475–493.

Lakey, B. (2013). Social support processes in relationships. In J. A. Simpson & L. Campbell (Eds.), *The Oxford handbook of close relationships* (pp. 711–728). Oxford University Press.

Lakey, B., & Orehek, E. (2011). Relational regulation theory: A new approach to explain the link between perceived social support and mental health. *Psychological Review*, *118*, 482–495.

Lakin, J. L., & Chartrand, T. L. (2003). Using nonconscious behavioral mimicry to create affiliation and rapport. *Psychological Science*, *14*(4), 334–339.

Lamarche, V. M., & Murray, S. L. (2014). Selectively myopic? Self-esteem and attentional bias in response to potential relationship threats. *Social Psychological and Personality Science*, *5*(7), 786–795.

Lambert, A. N., & Hughes, P. C. (2010). The influence of goodwill, secure attachment, and positively toned disengagement strategy on reports of communication satisfaction in non-marital post-dissolution relationships. *Communication Research Reports*, *27*(2), 171–183.

Lambert, N. M., Clark, M. S., Durtschi, J. et al. (2010). Benefits of expressing gratitude: Expressing gratitude to a partner changes one's view of the relationship. *Psychological Science*, *21*(4), 574–580.

Lambert, N. M., & Fincham, F. D. (2011). Expressing gratitude to a partner leads to more relationship maintenance behavior. *Emotion*, *11*(1), 52–60.

Lambert, N. M., Gwinn, A. M., Baumeister, R. F. et al. (2013). A boost of positive affect: The perks of sharing positive experiences. *Journal of Social and Personal Relationships*, *30*(1), 24–43.

Lamela, D., Figueiredo, B., Bastos, A. et al. (2016). Typologies of post-divorce coparenting and parental well-being, parenting quality and children's psychological adjustment. *Child Psychiatry and Human Development*, *47*(5), 716–728.

Lamont, E. (2014). Negotiating courtship: Reconciling egalitarian ideals with traditional gender norms. *Gender and Society*, *28*(2), 189–211.

Lamont, E. (2017). "We can write the scripts ourselves": Queer challenges to heteronormative courtship practices. *Gender and Society*, *31*(5), 624–646.

Lamont, E., Roach, T., & Kahn, S. (2018, December). Navigating campus hookup culture: LGBTQ students and college hookups. *Sociological Forum*, *33*(4), 1000–1022.

Lamphier, J. (2016, December 29). The love portfolio: Samira Wiley + Lauren Morelli. *Out*. www.out.com/love-issue/2016/12/29/love-portfolio-samira-wiley-lauren-morelli

Landor, A., & Smith, S. M. (2019). Skin-tone trauma: Historical and contemporary influences on the health and interpersonal outcomes of African Americans. *Perspectives on Psychological Science*, *14*(5), 797–815.

Lane, A., Luminet, O., Nave, G. et al. (2016). Is there a publication bias in behavioural intranasal oxytocin research on humans? Opening the file drawer of one laboratory. *Journal of Neuroendocrinology*, *28*(4).

Laner, M. R., & Ventrone, N. A. (2000). Dating scripts revisited. *Journal of Family Issues*, *21*(4), 488–500.

Langhinrichsen-Rohling, J., Palarea, R. E., Cohen, J. et al. (2000). Breaking up is hard to do: Unwanted pursuit behaviors following the dissolution of a romantic relationship. *Violence and Victims*, *15*(1), 73–90.

Langlois, J. H., Kalakanis, L., Rubenstein, A. J. et al. (2000). Maxims or myths of beauty? A meta-analytic and theoretical review. *Psychological Bulletin*, *126*(3), 390–423.

Langlois, J. H., & Roggman, L. A. (1990). Attractive faces are only average. *Psychological Science*, *1*(2), 115–121.

Langlois, J. H., Roggman, L. A., Casey, R. J. et al. (1987). Infant preferences for attractive faces: Rudiments of a stereotype? *Developmental Psychology*, *23*(3), 363–369.

Langston, C. A. (1994). Capitalizing on and coping with daily-life events: Expressive responses to positive events. *Journal of Personality and Social Psychology*, *67*(6), 1112–1125.

Larson, R. W., & Almeida, D. M. (1999). Emotional transmission in the daily lives of families: A new paradigm for studying family process. *Journal of Marriage and Family*, *61*(1), 5–20.

Lassek, W. D., & Gaulin, S. J. C. (2018). Do the low WHRs and BMIs judged most attractive indicate higher fertility? *Evolutionary Psychology*, *16*(4), 1474704918800063.

Lassek, W. D., & Gaulin, S. J. C. (2019). Evidence supporting nubility and reproductive value as the key to human female physical attractiveness. *Evolution and Human Behavior, 40*(5), 408–419.

Laumann, E. O., Gagnon, J. H., Michael, R. T. et al. (2000). *The social organization of sexuality: Sexual practices in the United States.* University of Chicago Press.

Laurenceau, J. P., Barrett, L. F., & Pietromonaco, P. R. (1998). Intimacy as an interpersonal process: The importance of self-disclosure, partner disclosure, and perceived partner responsiveness in interpersonal exchanges. *Journal of Personality and Social Psychology, 74*(5), 1238–1251.

Laurenceau, J. P., Barrett, L. F., & Rovine, M. J. (2005). The interpersonal process model of intimacy in marriage: A daily-diary and multilevel modeling approach. *Journal of Family Psychology, 19*(2), 314–323.

Laurent, H., & Powers, S. (2007). Emotion regulation in emerging adult couples: Temperament, attachment, and HPA response to conflict. *Biological Psychology, 76*(1–2), 61–71.

Lavner, J. A., Karney, B. R., & Bradbury, T. N. (2013). Newlyweds' optimistic forecasts of their marriage: For better or for worse? *Journal of Family Psychology, 27*(4), 531–540.

Lavner, J. A., Karney, B. R., & Bradbury, T. N. (2015). New directions for policies aimed at strengthening low-income couples. *Behavioral Science & Policy, 1*(2), 13–24.

Lawrance, K., & Byers, E. S. (1995). Sexual satisfaction in long-term heterosexual relationships: The interpersonal exchange model of sexual satisfaction. *Personal Relationships, 2*(4), 267–285.

Lawrence, E. M., Rogers, R. G., Zajacova, A. et al. (2019). Marital happiness, marital status, health, and longevity. *Journal of Happiness Studies, 20*(5), 1539–1561.

Lazarus, R. S., & Folkman, S. (1984). *Stress, appraisal, and coping.* Springer.

Le, B., Dove, N. L., Agnew, C. R. et al. (2010). Predicting nonmarital romantic relationship dissolution: A meta-analytic synthesis. *Personal Relationships, 17*(3), 377–390.

Le, B. M., Impett, E. A., Lemay, E. P. et al. (2018). Communal motivation and well-being in interpersonal relationships: An integrative review and meta-analysis. *Psychological Bulletin, 144*(1), 1–25.

Le, Y., Fredman, S. J., Marshall, A. D. et al. (2022). Relational impacts of capitalization in early parenthood. *Journal of Family Psychology, 36*(1), 69–79.

Leary, M. R. (2007). Motivational and emotional aspects of the self. *Annual Review of Psychology, 58*(1), 317–344.

Leary, M. R. (2010). Affiliation, acceptance, and belonging: The pursuit of interpersonal connection. In S. T. Fiske, D.

T. Gilbert, & G. Lindzey (Eds.), *Handbook of social psychology* (pp. 864–897). John Wiley & Sons.

Leary, M. R., & Baumeister, R. F. (2000). The nature and function of self-esteem: Sociometer theory. *Advances in Experimental Social Psychology, 32*, 1–62.

Leary, M. R., & Jongman-Sereno, K. P. (2014). Social anxiety as an early warning system: A refinement and extension of the self-presentation theory of social anxiety. In S. G. Hofmann & P. M. DiBartolo (Eds.), *Social anxiety: Clinical, developmental, and social perspectives* (3rd ed., pp. 579–597).

Leary, M. R., Kowalski, R. M., Smith, L. et al. (2003). Teasing, rejection, and violence: Case studies of the school shootings. *Aggressive Behavior, 29*(3), 202–214.

Leavitt, C. E., Allsop, D. B., Gurr, J. et al. (2022). A couples' relationship education intervention examining sexual mindfulness and trait mindfulness. *Sexual and Relationship Therapy.* https://doi.org/10.1080/14681994.2021.2024802

LeBlanc, A. J., Frost, D. M., & Wight, R. G. (2015). Minority stress and stress proliferation among same-sex and other marginalized couples. *Journal of Marriage and Family, 77*(1), 40–59.

Lebow, J. L., Chambers, A. L., Christensen, A. et al. (2012). Research on the treatment of couple distress. *Journal of Marital and Family Therapy, 38*(1), 145–168.

Lee, A. J., Sidari, M. J., Murphy, S. C. et al. (2020). Sex differences in misperceptions of sexual interest can be explained by sociosexual orientation and men projecting their own interest onto women. *Psychological Science, 31*(2), 184–192.

Lee, D. S., Ybarra, O., Gonzalez, R., & Ellsworth, P. (2018). I-through-we: How supportive social relationships facilitate personal growth. *Personality and Social Psychology Bulletin, 44*(1), 37–48.

Lee, J. (2015, September 21). How meditation can improve your marriage. *Huffington Post.* www.huffpost.com/entry/how-meditation-can-improv_b_8156128

Lee, K. H., & Zvonkovic, A. M. (2014). Journeys to remain childless: A grounded theory examination of decision-making processes among voluntarily childless couples. *Journal of Social and Personal Relationships, 31*(4), 535–553.

Lee, S., Rogge, R. D., & Reis, H. T. (2010). Assessing the seeds of relationship decay: Using implicit evaluations to detect the early stages of disillusionment. *Psychological Science, 21*(6), 857–864.

Lee, S., Wickrama, K. K. A. S., Lee, T. K. et al. (2021). Long-term physical health consequences of financial and marital stress in middle-aged couples. *Journal of Marriage and Family, 83*(4), 1212–1226.

Lee, W.-Y., Nakamura S.-I., Chung M. J. et al. (2013). Asian couples in negotiation: A mixed-method observational study of cultural variations across given Asian regions. *Family Process, 52*(3), 499–518.

LeFebvre, L. E. (2017). Ghosting as a relationship dissolution strategy in the technological age. In N. Punyanunt-Carter & J. S. Wrench (Eds.), *The impact of social media in modern romantic relationships* (pp. 219–235). Rowman & Littlefield.

LeFebvre, L. E., Allen, M., Rasner, R. D. et al. (2019). Ghosting in emerging adults' romantic relationships: The digital dissolution disappearance strategy. *Imagination, Cognition and Personality, 39*(2), 125–150.

LeFebvre, L. E., & Fan, X. (2020). Ghosted? Navigating strategies for reducing uncertainty and implications surrounding ambiguous loss. *Personal Relationships, 27*(2), 433–459.

Lehmann, V., Tuinman, M. A., Braeken, J. et al. (2015). Satisfaction with relationship status: Development of a new scale and the role in predicting well-being. *Journal of Happiness Studies, 16*(1), 169–184.

Lehmiller, J. J. (2009). Secret romantic relationships: Consequences for personal and relational well-being. *Personality and Social Psychology Bulletin, 35*(11), 1452–1466.

Lehmiller, J. J. (2010). Differences in relationship investments between gay and heterosexual men. *Personal Relationships, 17*(1), 81–96.

Lehmiller, J. J., & Agnew, C. R. (2006). Marginalized relationships: The impact of social disapproval on romantic relationship commitment. *Personality and Social Psychology Bulletin, 32*(1), 40–51.

Lehmiller, J. J., & Agnew, C. R. (2007). Perceived marginalization and the prediction of romantic relationship stability. *Journal of Marriage and Family, 69*(4), 1036–1049.

Lehmiller, J. J., & Ioerger, M. (2014). Prejudice and stigma in intimate relationships: Implications for relational and personal health outcomes. In C. R. Agnew (Ed.), *Social influences on romantic relationships: Beyond the dyad* (pp. 83–102). Cambridge University Press.

Lehrer, E. L. (1996). Religion as a determinant of marital fertility. *Journal of Population Economics, 9*(2), 173–196.

Lehrer, E. L. (2000). Religion as a determinant of entry into cohabitation and marriage. In L. J. Waite, C. Bachrach, M., Hindin, E. Thomson, & A. Thornton (Eds.), *The ties that bind: Perspectives on marriage and cohabitation* (pp. 227–252). Aldine de Gruyter.

Leigh, B. C. (1989). Reasons for having and avoiding sex: Gender, sexual orientation, and relationship to sexual behavior. *Journal of Sex Research, 26*(2), 199–209.

Lemay, E. P., Lin, J. L., & Muir, H. J. (2015). Daily Affective and behavioral forecasts in romantic relationships: Seeing tomorrow through the lens of today. *Personality and Social Psychology Bulletin, 41*(7), 1005–1019.

Lemay, E. P., & Venaglia, R. B. (2016). Relationship expectations and relationship quality. *Review of General Psychology, 20*(1), 57–70.

Lemay, E. P., & Wolf, N. R. (2016). Human mate poaching tactics are effective: Evidence from a dyadic prospective study on opposite-sex "friendships." *Social Psychological and Personality Science, 7*(4), 374–380.

Lemay Jr., E. P., & Razzak, S. (2016). Perceived acceptance from outsiders shapes security in romantic relationships: The overgeneralization of extradyadic experiences. *Personality and Social Psychology Bulletin, 42*(5), 632–644.

Lenton-Brym, A. P., Monson, C. M., & Antony, M. M. (2020). Responses to perceived intimate partner rejection among individuals with social anxiety disorder and healthy controls. *Journal of Anxiety Disorders, 75*, 102281.

Leong, J. L. T., Chen, S. X., Fung, H. H. L. et al. (2020). Is gratitude always beneficial to interpersonal relationships? The interplay of grateful disposition, grateful mood, and grateful expression among married couples. *Personality and Social Psychology Bulletin, 46*(1), 64–78.

Leonhardt, N. D., Rosen, N. O., Dawson, S. J. et al. (2022). Relationship satisfaction and commitment in the transition to parenthood: A couple-centered approach. *Journal of Marriage and Family, 84*, 80–100.

Leopold, T. (2018). Gender differences in the consequences of divorce: A study of multiple outcomes. *Demography, 55*(3), 769–797.

Lepore, S., Allen, K., & Evans, G. (1993). Social support lowers cardiovascular reactivity to an acute stressor. *Psychosomatic Medicine, 55*, 518–524.

Leri, G., & DelPriore, D. J. (2021). Understanding variation in women's sexual attitudes and behavior across sexual orientations: Evaluating three hypotheses. *Personality and Individual Differences, 173*, 110629.

LeRoy, A. S., Knee, C. R., Derrick, J. L. et al. (2019). Implications for reward processing in differential responses to loss: Impacts on attachment hierarchy reorganization. *Personality and Social Psychology Review, 23*(4), 391–405.

Lesthaeghe, R. J. (2020). The second demographic transition: Cohabitation. In W. K. Halford & F. van de Vijver (Eds.), *Cross-cultural family research and practice* (pp. 103–141). Academic Press.

Letzring, T. D., & Funder, D. C. (2019). The realistic accuracy model. In T. D. Letzring & J. S. Spain (Eds.), *The Oxford handbook of accurate personality judgment* (pp. 9–22). Oxford University Press.

Lever, J., Frederick, D. A., & Hertz, R. (2015). Who pays for dates? Following versus challenging gender norms. *SAGE Open*, 5(4), 1–14.

Lévesque, S., Bisson, V., Charton, L. et al. (2020). Parenting and relational well-being during the transition to parenthood: Challenges for first-time parents. *Journal of Child and Family Studies*, 29(7), 1938–1956.

Levin, I. (2004). Living apart together: A new family form. *Current Sociology*, 52(2), 223–240.

Levin, I., & Trost, J. (1999). Living apart together. *Community, Work & Family*, 2(3), 279–294.

Lewandowski, G. W., & Ackerman, R. A. (2010). Something's missing: Need fulfillment and self-expansion as predictors of susceptibility to infidelity. *Journal of Social Psychology*, 146(4), 389–403.

Lewandowski, G. W., & Aron, A. (2002). *The Self Expansion Scale: Construction and validation* [paper]. Annual Meeting of the Society of Personality and Social Psychology, Savannah, GA.

Lewandowski, G. W., Aron, A., Bassis, S. et al. (2006). Losing a self-expanding relationship: Implications for the self-concept. *Personal Relationships*, 13(3), 317–331.

Lewandowski, G. W., Aron, A., & Gee, J. (2007). Personality goes a long way: The malleability of opposite-sex physical attractiveness. *Personal Relationships*, 14(4), 571–585.

Lewandowski, G. W., & Bizzoco, N. M. (2007). Addition through subtraction: Growth following the dissolution of a low quality relationship. *Journal of Positive Psychology*, 2(1), 40–54.

Lewin, A. C. (2018). Intentions to live together among couples living apart: Differences by age and gender. *European Journal of Population*, 34(5), 721–743.

Lewis, D. M. G., Conroy-Beam, D., Al-Shawaf, L. et al. (2011). Friends with benefits: The evolved psychology of same- and opposite-sex friendship. *Evolutionary Psychology*, 9(4), 543–563.

Lewis, J. T., Parra, G. R., & Cohen, R. (2015). Apologies in close relationships: A review of theory and research. *Journal of Family Theory & Review*, 7(1), 47–61.

Lewis, M. A., Atkins, D. C., Blayney, J. A. et al. (2013). What is hooking up? Examining definitions of hooking up in relation to behavior and normative perceptions. *Journal of Sex Research*, 50(8), 757–766.

Lewis, M. A., Granato, H., Blayney, J. A. et al. (2012). Predictors of hooking up sexual behaviors and emotional reactions among U.S. college students. *Archives of Sexual Behavior*, 41(5), 1219–1229.

Lewis, R. A. (1972). A developmental framework for the analysis of premarital dyadic formation. *Family Process*, 11(1), 17–48.

Lewis, R. A. (1973). A longitudinal test of a developmental framework for premarital dyadic formation. *Journal of Marriage and the Family*, 35(1), 16–25.

Li, N. P., & Kenrick, D. T. (2006). Sex similarities and differences in preferences for short-term mates: What, whether, and why. *Journal of Personality and Social Psychology*, 90(3), 468–489.

Li, N. P., Kenrick, D. T., Bailey, J. M. et al. (2002). The necessities and luxuries of mate preferences: Testing the tradeoffs. *Journal of Personality and Social Psychology*, 82(6), 947–955.

Li, N. P., & Meltzer, A. L. (2015). The validity of sex-differentiated mate preferences: Reconciling the seemingly conflicting evidence. *Evolutionary Behavioral Sciences*, 9(2), 89–106.

Li, N. P., Valentine, K. A., & Patel, L. (2011). Mate preferences in the US and Singapore: A cross-cultural test of the mate preference priority model. *Personality and Individual Differences*, 50(2), 291–294.

Li, N. P., Yong, J. C., Tov, W. et al. (2013). Mate preferences do predict attraction and choices in the early stages of mate selection. *Journal of Personality and Social Psychology*, 105(5), 757–776.

Li, N. P., Yong, J. C., Tsai, M. H. et al. (2020). Confidence is sexy and it can be trained: Examining male social confidence in initial, opposite-sex interactions. *Journal of Personality*, 88(6), 1235–1251.

Li, T., & Chan, D. K. S. (2012). How anxious and avoidant attachment affect romantic relationship quality differently: A meta-analytic review. *European Journal of Social Psychology*, 42(4), 406–419.

Li, X., Curran, M., Paschall, K. et al. (2019). Pregnancy intentions and family functioning among low-income, unmarried couples: Person-centered analyses. *Journal of Family Psychology*, 33(7), 830–840.

Lichtenstein, B., Lucke, J., & Loxton, D. (2022). Women and divorce: Financial coping from midlife to older age. *Journal of Women & Aging*, 34(3), 323–340.

Lichter, D. T., Sassler, S., & Turner, R. N. (2014). Cohabitation, post-conception unions, and the rise in nonmarital fertility. *Social Science Research*, 47, 134–147.

Lichter, D. T., Turner, R. N., & Sassler, S. (2010). National estimates of the rise in serial cohabitation. *Social Science Research*, 39(5), 754–765.

Lick, D. J., Durso, L. E., & Johnson, K. L. (2013). Minority stress and physical health among sexual minorities. *Perspectives on Psychological Science*, 8(5), 521–548.

Lidborg, L. H., Cross, C. P., & Boothroyd, L. G. (2022). A meta-analysis of the association between male dimorphism and fitness outcomes in humans. *Elife*, 11, e65031.

Liebler, C. A., Porter, S. R., Fernandez, L. E. et al. (2017). America's churning races: Race and ethnicity response changes between census 2000 and the 2010 census. *Demography*, *54*(1), 259–284.

Liefbroer, A. C., Poortman, A. R., & Seltzer, J. A. (2015). Why do intimate partners live apart? Evidence on LAT relationships across Europe. *Demographic Research*, *32*(1), 251–286.

Lim, E. (2020, Feburary 10). Old couples explain how they've stayed together so long. *Vice*. www.vice.com/en/article/y3mbgj/old-couples-explain-how-theyve-stayed-together-so-long

Lin, I.-F., & Brown, S. L. (2020). Consequences of later-life divorce and widowhood for adult well-being: A call for the convalescence model. *Journal of Family Theory and Review*, *12*(2), 264–277.

Lin, I.-F., & Brown, S. L. (2021). The economic consequences of gray divorce for women and men. *Journals of Gerontology: Series B*, *76*(10), 2073–2085.

Lin, I.-F., Brown, S. L., Wright, M. R. et al. (2018). Antecedents of gray divorce: A life course perspective. *Journals of Gerontology: Series B*, *73*(6), 1022–1031.

Lin, I.-F., Brown, S. L., Wright, M. R. et al. (2019). Depressive symptoms following later-life marital dissolution and subsequent repartnering. *Journal of Health and Social Behavior*, *60*(2), 153–168.

Linardatos, L., & Lydon, J. E. (2011). Relationship-specific identification and spontaneous relationship maintenance processes. *Journal of Personality and Social Psychology*, *101*(4), 737–753.

Lincoln, K. D. (2000). Social support, negative social interactions, and psychological well-being. *Social Service Review*, *74*(2), 231–252.

Lindley, L., Anzani, A., Prunas, A. et al. (2021). Sexual satisfaction in trans masculine and nonbinary individuals: A qualitative investigation. *Journal of Sex Research*, *58*(2), 222–234.

Lippa, R. A. (2007a). The preferred traits of mates in a cross-national study of heterosexual and homosexual men and women: An examination of biological and cultural influences. *Archives of Sexual Behavior*, *36*(2), 193–208.

Lippa, R. A. (2007b). The relation between sex drive and sexual attraction to men and women: A cross-national study of heterosexual, bisexual, and homosexual men and women. *Archives of Sexual Behavior*, *36*(2), 209–222.

Lippa, R. A. (2009). Sex differences in sex drive, sociosexuality, and height across 53 nations: Testing evolutionary and social structural theories. *Archives of Sexual Behavior*, *38*, 631–651.

Little, A. C., Apicella, C. L., & Marlowe, F. W. (2007). Preferences for symmetry in human faces in two cultures: Data from the UK and the Hadza, an isolated group of hunter-gatherers. *Proceedings of the Royal Society B: Biological Sciences*, *274*(1629), 3113–3117.

Littlewood, D. L., Kyle, S. D., Carter, L.-A. et al. (2018). Short sleep duration and poor sleep quality predict next-day suicidal ideation: An ecological momentary assessment study. *Psychological Medicine*, *49*, 403–411.

Liu, H., Umberson, D., & Xu, M. (2020). Widowhood and mortality: Gender, race/ethnicity, and the role of economic resources. *Annals of Epidemiology*, *45*, 69–75.

Liu, H., & Umberson, D. J. (2008). The times they are a changin': Marital status and health differentials from 1972 to 2003. *Journal of Health and Social Behavior*, *49*(3), 239–253.

Liu, X., Wheeler, N. J., Broda, M. D. et al. (2020). Relationship satisfaction trajectories among low-income ethnic minority couples before and after a relationship education intervention. *Journal of Social and Personal Relationships*, *37*(7), 2053–2077.

Livingston, G., & Brown, A. (2017). *Intermarriage in the U.S. 50 years after Loving v. Virginia: One-in-six newlyweds are married to someone of a different race or ethnicity*. Pew Research Center. www.pewresearch.org/social-trends/2017/05/18/intermarriage-in-the-u-s-50-years-after-loving-v-virginia/

Logan, J. M., & Cobb, R. J. (2013). Trajectories of relationship satisfaction: Independent contributions of capitalization and support perceptions. *Personal Relationships*, *20*(2), 277–293.

Loken, E. (2019, April). The replication crisis is good for science. *The Associated Press*. https://apnews.com/article/f12fb6f0e3c462d8e6d025b9f47daf15

López, G., & Yeater, E. A. (2021). Comparisons of sexual victimization experiences among sexual minority and heterosexual women. *Journal of Interpersonal Violence*, *36*(8), 4250–4270.

Lorenz, F. O., Wickrama, K. A. S., Conger, R. D. et al. (2006). The short-term and decade-long effects of divorce on women's midlife health. *Journal of Health and Social Behavior*, *47*(2), 111–125.

Louzek, M. (2022). An economic approach to marriage. *Journal of Applied Economics*, *25*(1), 299–314.

Lucas, M., Koff, E., Grossmith, S. et al. (2011). Sexual orientation and shifts in preferences for a partner's body attributes in short-term versus long-term mating contexts. *Psychological Reports*, *108*(3), 699–710.

Lucas, R. E. (2005). Time does not heal all wounds: A longitudinal study of reaction and adaptation to divorce. *Psychological Science*, *16*(12), 945–950.

Luchies, L. B., Finkel, E. J., Coy, A. E. et al. (2019). People feel worse about their forgiveness when mismatches between forgiveness and amends create adaptation risks. *Journal of Social and Personal Relationships, 36*(2), 681–705.

Luchies, L. B., Finkel, E. J., McNulty, J. K. et al. (2010). The doormat effect: When forgiving erodes self-respect and self-concept clarity. *Journal of Personality and Social Psychology, 98*(5), 734–749.

Luerssen, A., Jhita, G. J., & Ayduk, O. (2017). Putting yourself on the line: Self-esteem and expressing affection in romantic relationships. *Personality and Social Psychology Bulletin, 43*(7), 940–956.

Luhmann, M., Hofmann, W., Eid, M., & Lucas, R. E. (2012). Subjective well-being and adaptation to life events: A meta-analysis. *Journal of Personality and Social Psychology, 102*(3), 592–615.

Lukas, D., & Clutton-Brock, T. H. (2013). The evolution of social monogamy in mammals. *Science, 341*(6145), 526–530.

Lundberg, S., Pollak, R. A., & Stearns, J. (2016). Family inequality: Diverging patterns in marriage, cohabitation, and childbearing. *Journal of Economic Perspectives, 30*(2), 79–102.

Luo, S. (2017). Assortative mating and couple similarity: Patterns, mechanisms, and consequences. *Social and Personality Psychology Compass, 11*(8), 1–14.

Luo, S., & Zhang, G. (2009). What leads to romantic attraction: Similarity, reciprocity, security, or beauty? Evidence from a speed-dating study. *Journal of Personality, 77*(4), 933–964.

Lydon, J. E., Fitzsimons, G. M., & Naidoo, L. (2003). Devaluation versus enhancement of attractive alternatives: A critical test using the calibration paradigm. *Personality and Social Psychology Bulletin, 29*(3), 349–359.

Lydon, J. E., Meana, M., Sepinwall, D. et al. (1999). The commitment calibration hypothesis: When do people devalue attractive alternatives? *Personality and Social Psychology Bulletin, 25*(2), 152–161.

Lynn, B. K., López, J. D., Miller, C. et al. (2019). The relationship between marijuana use prior to sex and sexual function in women. *Sexual Medicine, 7*(2), 192–197.

Lyons, H., Manning, W., Giordano, P. et al. (2013). Predictors of heterosexual casual sex among young adults. *Archives of Sexual Behavior, 42*(4), 585–593.

Ma, Y., Xue, W., & Tu, S. (2019a). Automatic inattention to attractive alternative partners helps male heterosexual Chinese college students maintain romantic relationships. *Frontiers in Psychology, 10*, 1–9.

Ma, Y., Xue, W., Zhao, G. et al. (2019). Romantic love and attentional biases toward attractive alternatives and rivals: Long-term relationship maintenance among female Chinese college students. *Evolutionary Psychology, 17*(4), 1–14.

Ma, Y., Zhao, G., Tu, S. et al. (2015). Attentional biases toward attractive alternatives and rivals: Mechanisms involved in relationship maintenance among Chinese women. *PLOS One, 10*(8), e0136662.

Maccallum, F., & Bryant, R. A. (2018). Prolonged grief and attachment security: A latent class analysis. *Psychiatry Research, 268*, 297–302.

Maccallum, F., Galatzer-Levy, I. R., & Bonanno, G. A. (2015). Trajectories of depression following spousal and child bereavement: A comparison of the heterogeneity in outcomes. *Journal of Psychiatric Research, 69*, 72–79.

MacDonald, G., & Leary, M. R. (2005). Why does social exclusion hurt? The relationship between social and physical pain. *Psychological Bulletin, 131*(2), 202–223.

MacDonald, G., & Park, Y. (2022). Associations of attachment avoidance and anxiety with life satisfaction, satisfaction with singlehood, and desire for a romantic partner. *Personal Relationships, 29*(1), 163–176.

MacGregor, J. C. D., & Cavallo, J. V. (2011). Breaking the rules: Personal control increases women's direct relationship initiation. *Journal of Social and Personal Relationships, 28*(6), 848–867.

MacGregor, J. C. D., Fitzsimons, G. M., & Holmes, J. G. (2013). Perceiving low self-esteem in close others impedes capitalization and undermines the relationship. *Personal Relationships, 20*(4), 690–705.

Machia, L. V., & Ogolsky, B. G. (2021). The reasons people think about staying and leaving their romantic relationships: A mixed-method analysis. *Personality and Social Psychology Bulletin, 47*(8), 1279–1293.

Machia, L. V., & Proulx, M. L. (2020). The diverging effects of need fulfillment obtained from within and outside of a romantic relationship. *Personality and Social Psychology Bulletin, 46*(5), 781–793.

Mackey, R., Diemer, M., & O'Brien, B. (2000). Psychological intimacy in the lasting relationships of heterosexual and same-gender couples. *Sex Roles, 43*(617), 201–227.

MacNeil, S., & Byers, E. S. (2009). Role of sexual self-disclosure in the sexual satisfaction of long-term heterosexual couples. *Journal of Sex Research, 46*(1), 3–14.

MacNiel-Kelly, T. (2020). Exploring conflict within interracial dating dyads. In T. MacNiel-Kelly (Ed.), *The role of conflict on the individual and society* (pp. 53–70). Lexington Books.

Macur, J. (2017). What qualifies a woman to compete as a woman? An ugly fight resumes. *The New York Times.* www.nytimes.com/2017/08/04/sports/olympics/gender-dutee-chand-india.html

Maisel, N. C., & Gable, S. L. (2009). The paradox of received social support: The importance of responsiveness. *Psychological Science*, *20*(8), 928–932.

Malarkey, W. B., Kiecolt-glaser, J. K., Pearl, D. et al. (1994). Hostile behavior during marital conflict alters pituitary and adrenal hormones. *Psychosomatic Medicine*, *56*(1), 41–51.

Mallory, A. B. (2022). Dimensions of couples' sexual communication, relationship satisfaction, and sexual satisfaction: A meta-analysis. *Journal of Family Psychology*, *36*(3), 358–371.

Mallory, A. B., Stanton, A. M., & Handy, A. B. (2019). Couples' sexual communication and dimensions of sexual function: A meta-analysis. *Journal of Sex Research*, *56*(7), 882–898.

Mancini, A. D., Bonanno, G. A., & Clark, A. E. (2011). Stepping off the hedonic treadmill: Individual differences in response to major life events. *Journal of Individual Differences*, *32*(3), 144–152.

Maner, J. K., Dewall, C. N., Baumeister, R. F. et al. (2007). Does social exclusion motivate interpersonal reconnection? Resolving the "porcupine problem." *Journal of Personality and Social Psychology*, *92*(1), 42–55.

Maner, J. K., Gailliot, M. T., & Miller, S. L. (2009). The implicit cognition of relationship maintenance: Inattention to attractive alternatives. *Journal of Experimental Social Psychology*, *45*(1), 174–179.

Maner, J. K., Gailliot, M. T., Rouby, D. A. et al. (2007). Can't take my eyes off you: Attentional adhesion to mates and rivals. *Journal of Personality and Social Psychology*, *93*(3), 389–401.

Maner, J. K., Kenrick, D. T., Becker, D. V. et al. (2003). Sexually selective cognition: Beauty captures the mind of the beholder. *Journal of Personality and Social Psychology*, *85*(6), 1107–1120.

Maner, J. K., Rouby, D. A., & Gonzaga, G. C. (2008). Automatic inattention to attractive alternatives: The evolved psychology of relationship maintenance. *Evolution and Human Behavior*, *29*(5), 343–349.

Maner, J. K., & Shackelford, T. K. (2008). The basic cognition of jealousy: An evolutionary perspective. *European Journal of Personality*, *22*(1), 31–36.

Maniam, J., Antoniadis, C., & Morris, M. J. (2014). Early-life stress, HPA axis adaptation, and mechanisms contributing to later health outcomes. *Frontiers in Endocrinology*, *5*, 73.

Manning, W. D. (2020). *Thirty years of changing cohabitation experience in the US, 1987–2017*. Family Profiles, FP-20-27. National Center for Family & Marriage Research.

Manning, W. D., Giordano, P. C., Longmore, M. A. et al. (2010). *Romantic relationships and academic/career trajectories in emerging adulthood*. Romantic Relationships in Emerging Adulthood Working Paper Series (pp. 317–334).

Manning, W. D., Smock, P. J., & Fettro, M. N. (2019). Cohabitation and marital expectations among single millennials in the U.S. *Population Research and Policy Review*, *38*(3), 327–346.

Manning, W. D., Smock, P. J., & Kuperberg, A. (2021). Cohabitation and marital dissolution: A comment on Rosenfeld and Roesler (2019). *Journal of Marriage and Family*, *83*(1), 260–267.

Mansson, D. H., Floyd, K., & Soliz, J. (2017). Affectionate communication is associated with emotional and relational resources in the grandparent–grandchild relationship. *Journal of Intergenerational Relationships*, *15*(2), 85–103.

Mansson, D. H., Marko, F., Bachratá, K. et al. (2016). Young adults' trait affection given and received as functions of Hofstede's dimensions of cultures and national origin. *Journal of Intercultural Communication Research*, *45*(5), 404–418.

Mansson, D. H., & Sigurðardóttir, A. G. (2017). Trait affection given and received: A test of Hofstede's theoretical framework. *Journal of Intercultural Communication Research*, *46*(2), 161–172.

Mantelakis, A., Iosifidis, M., Al-Bitar, Z. B. et al. (2018). Proportions of the aesthetic African-Caribbean face: Idealized ratios, comparison with the golden proportion and perceptions of attractiveness. *Maxillofacial Plastic and Reconstructive Surgery*, *40*(1), 20.

Marazziti, D., Akiskal, H. S., Rossi, A. et al. (1999). Alteration of the platelet serotonin transporter in romantic love. *Psychological Medicine*, *29*, 741–745.

Marazziti, D., & Baroni, S. (2012). Romantic love: The mystery of its biological roots. *Clinical Neuropsychiatry*, *9*(1), 14–19.

Marazziti, D., & Canale, D. (2004). Hormonal changes when falling in love. *Psychoneuroendocrinology*, *29*(7), 931–936.

Marcantonio, T., Jozkowski, K. N., & Wiersma-Mosley, J. (2018). The influence of partner status and sexual behavior on college women's consent communication and feelings. *Journal of Sex and Marital Therapy*, *44*(8), 776–786.

March, E., Van Doorn, G., & Grieve, R. (2018). Netflix and chill? What sex differences can tell us about mate preferences in (hypothetical) booty-call relationships. *Evolutionary Psychology*, *16*(4), 1474704918812138.

March, P. (2020, December 26). Couple goals could harm our relationships, here's how. *Cosmopolitan*. www.cosmopolitan.com/uk/love-sex/relationships/a34782472/couple-goals/

Marches, J. R., & Turbeville, G. (1953). The effect of residential propinquity on marriage selection. *American Journal of Sociology*, *58*(6), 592–595.

Margana, L., Bhogal, M. S., Bartlett, J. E. et al. (2019). The roles of altruism, heroism, and physical attractiveness in female mate choice. *Personality and Individual Differences*, *137*, 126–130.

Mark, K. P., Garcia, J. R., & Fisher, H. E. (2015). Perceived emotional and sexual satisfaction across sexual relationship contexts: Gender and sexual orientation differences and similarities. *Canadian Journal of Human Sexuality*, *24*(2), 120–130.

Mark, K. P., Milhausen, R. R., & Maitland, S. B. (2013). The impact of sexual compatibility on sexual and relationship satisfaction in a sample of young adult heterosexual couples. *Sexual and Relationship Therapy*, *28*(3), 201–214.

Markman, H. J., Hawkins, A. J., Stanley, S. M. et al. (2022). Helping couples achieve relationship success: A decade of progress in couple relationship education research and practice, 2010-2019. *Journal of Marital and Family Therapy*, *48*(1), 251–282.

Markman, H. J., Rhoades, G. K., Stanley, S. M. et al. (2010). The premarital communication roots of marital distress and divorce: The first five years of marriage. *Journal of Family Psychology*, *24*(3), 289–298.

Markman, H. J., Stanley, S. M., & Blumberg, S. (2010). *Fighting for your marriage* (3rd ed.). Jossey-Bass.

Marks, L., Nesteruk, O., Hopkins-Williams, K. et al. (2006). Stressors in African American marriages and families: A qualitative exploration. *Stress, Trauma and Crisis*, *9*, 203–225.

Markus, H. R., & Kitayama, S. (1991). Culture and the self: Implications for cognition, emotion, and motivation. *Psychological Review*, *98*(2), 224–253.

Markus, H. R., & Kitayama, S. (2003). Culture, self, and the reality of the social. *Psychological Inquiry*, *14*(3–4), 277–283.

Markus, H. R., & Kitayama, S. (2010). Cultures and selves: A cycle of mutual constitution. *Perspectives on Psychological Science*, *5*(4), 420–430.

Marsh, H. W., Lüdtke, O., Trautwein, U. et al. (2009). Classical latent profile analysis of academic self-concept dimensions: Synergy of person- and variable-centered approaches to theoretical models of self-concept. *Structural Equation Modeling*, *16*(2), 191–225.

Marshall, T. C. (2008). Cultural differences in intimacy: The influence of gender-role ideology and individualism-collectivism. *Journal of Social and Personal Relationships*, *25*(1), 143–168.

Marshall, T. C., Bejanyan, K., Castro, G. D. et al. (2013). Attachment styles as predictors of Facebook-related jealousy and surveillance in romantic relationships. *Personal Relationships*, *20*(1), 1–22.

Marshall, T. C., Bejanyan, K., & Ferenczi, N. (2013). Attachment styles and personal growth following romantic breakups: The mediating roles of distress, rumination, and tendency to rebound. *PLOS One*, *8*(9), e75161.

Martin, J. A., Hamilton, B. E., Osterman, M. J. K. et al. (2021). Births: Final data for 2019. *National Vital Statistics Reports*, *70*(2), 1–51.

Martins, M. V., Costa, P., Peterson, B. D. et al. (2014). Marital stability and repartnering: Infertility-related stress trajectories of unsuccessful fertility treatment. *Fertility and Sterility*, *102*(6), 1716–1722.

Marzoli, D., Moretto, F., Monti, A. et al. (2013). Environmental influences on mate preferences as assessed by a scenario manipulation experiment. *PLOS One*, *8*(9), e74282.

Masarik, A. S., Martin, M. J., Ferrer, E. et al. (2016). Couple resilience to economic pressure over time and across generations. *Journal of Marriage and the Family*, *78*(2), 326–345.

Mashek, D. J., Aron, A., & Boncimino, M. (2003). Confusions of self with close others. *Personality and Social Psychology Bulletin*, *29*(3), 382–392.

Mashek, D., Oriña, M., & Ickes, W. (2018). Navigating methodological trade-offs in close relationships research. In A. L. Vangelisti & D. Perlman (Eds.), *The Cambridge handbook of personal relationships*. Cambridge University Press.

Maslow, A. H. (1943). A theory of human motivation. *Psychological Review*, *50*(4), 370–396.

Mason, A. E., Law, R. W., Bryan, A. E. B. et al. (2012). Facing a breakup: Electromyographic responses moderate self-concept recovery following a romantic separation. *Personal Relationships*, *19*(3), 551–568.

Mason, A. E., Sbarra, D. A., Bryan, A. E. B. et al. (2012). Staying connected when coming apart: The psychological correlates of contact and sex with an ex-partner. *Journal of Social and Clinical Psychology*, *31*(5), 488–507.

Massoglia, M., Remster, B., & King, R. D. (2011). Stigma or separation? Understanding the incarceration-divorce relationship. *Social Forces*, *90*(1), 133–155.

Master, S. L., Eisenberger, N. I., Taylor, S. E. et al. (2009). A picture's worth: Partner photographs reduce experimentally induced pain. *Psychological Science*, *20*(11), 1316–1318.

Masters, N. T., Casey, E., Wells, E. A. et al. (2013). Sexual scripts among young heterosexually active men and women: Continuity and change. *Journal of Sex Research*, *50*(5), 409–420.

Mathison, S. (2011). Cross-case analysis. In S. Matthison (Ed.), *Encyclopedia of evaluation* (p. 96). Sage Publications.

Matsick, J. L., Kruk, M., Conley, T. D. et al. (2021). Gender similarities and differences in casual sex acceptance among lesbian women and gay men. *Archives of Sexual Behavior*, *50*, 1151–1166a.

Matthews, L. S., Wickrama, K. A. S., & Conger, R. D. (1996). Predicting marital instability from spouse and observer reports of marital interaction. *Journal of Marriage and Family*, *58*(3), 641–655.

Mattingly, B. A., & Lewandowski, G. W. (2013). An expanded self is a more capable self: The association between self-concept size and self-efficacy. *Self and Identity*, *12*(6), 621–634.

Mattingly, B. A., Lewandowski, G. W., & McIntyre, K. P. (2014). "You make me a better/worse person": A two-dimensional model of relationship self-change. *Personal Relationships*, *21*(1), 176–190.

Mattingly, B. A., McIntyre, K. P., Knee, C. R. et al. (2019). Implicit theories of relationships and self-expansion: Implications for relationship functioning. *Journal of Social and Personal Relationships*, *36*(6), 1579–1599.

Mattingly, B. A., McIntyre, K. P., & Lewandowski Jr., G. W. (2012). Approach motivation and the expansion of self in close relationships. *Personal Relationships*, *19*(1), 113–127.

Mattingly, B. A., McIntyre, K. P., & Lewandowski, G. W. (2020). Relationship dissolution and self-concept change. In B. A. Mattingly, K. P. McIntyre, & G. W. Lewandowski (Eds.), *Interpersonal relationships and the self-concept* (pp. 145–161). Springer International Publishing.

Mattingly, B., Tomlinson, J. M., & McIntyre, K. (2020). Advances in self-expansion. In L. VanderDrift, C. R. Agnew, & X. B. Arriaga (Eds.), *Advances in personal relationships* (pp. 225–245). Cambridge University Press.

Maxwell, J. A., & McNulty, J. K. (2019). No longer in a dry spell: The developing understanding of how sex influences romantic relationships. *Current Directions in Psychological Science*, *28*(1), 102–107.

Maxwell, J. A., & Meltzer, A. L. (2020). Kiss and makeup? Examining the co-occurrence of conflict and sex. *Archives of Sexual Behavior*, *49*(8), 2883–2892.

May, C. J., Ostafin, B. D., & Snippe, E. (2020). Mindfulness meditation is associated with decreases in partner negative affect in daily life. *European Journal of Social Psychology*, *50*(1), 35–45.

Mayo, O., & Gordon, I. (2020). In and out of synchrony: Behavioral and physiological dynamics of dyadic interpersonal coordination. *Psychophysiology*, *57*(6), e13574.

McCarty, M. K., & Kelly, J. R. (2015). Perceptions of dating behavior: The role of ambivalent sexism. *Sex Roles*, *72*(5–6), 237–251.

McClure, M. J., Xu, J. H., Craw, J. P. et al. (2014). Understanding the costs of support transactions in daily life. *Journal of Personality*, *82*(6), 563–574.

McCrae, R. R., & Costa, P. T. (1997). Personality trait structure as a human universal. *American Psychologist*, *52*(5), 509–516.

McDaniel, B. T, & Coyne, S. M. (2016). "Technoference": The interference of technology in couple relationships and implications for women's personal and relational well-being. *Psychology of Popular Media Culture*, *5*(1), 85–98.

McDaniel, B. T., Drouin, M., Dibble, J. et al. (2021). Are you going to delete me? Latent profiles of post-relationship breakup social media use and emotional distress. *Cyberpsychology, Behavior, and Social Networking*, *24*(7), 464–472.

McDaniel, B. T., Galovan, A. M., & Drouin, M. (2021). Daily technoference, technology use during couple leisure time, and relationship quality. *Media Psychology*, *24*, 637–665.

McDermott, R., Fowler, J. H., & Christakis, N. A. (2013). Breaking up is hard to do, unless everyone else is doing it too: Social network effects on divorce in a longitudinal sample. *Social Forces*, *92*(2), 491–519.

McGonagle, K. A., Kessler, R. C., & A. Schilling, E. (1992). The frequency and determinants of marital disagreements in a community sample. *Journal of Social and Personal Relationships*, *9*(4), 507–524.

McIntyre, K. P., Mattingly, B. A., & Lewandowski, G. W. (2015). When "we" changes "me": The two-dimensional model of relational self-change and relationship outcomes. *Journal of Social and Personal Relationships*, *32*(7), 857–878.

McNamara, J. R., & Grossman, K. (1991). Initiation of dates and anxiety among college men and women. *Psychological Reports*, *69*(1), 252–254.

McNelis, M., & Segrin, C. (2019). Insecure attachment predicts history of divorce, marriage, and current relationship status. *Journal of Divorce and Remarriage*, *60*(5), 404–417.

McNulty, J. K. (2008a). Forgiveness in marriage: Putting the benefits into context. *Journal of Family Psychology*, *22*(1), 171–175.

McNulty, J. K. (2008b). Neuroticism and interpersonal negativity: The independent contributions of perceptions and behaviors. *Personality and Social Psychology Bulletin*, *34*(11), 1439–1450.

McNulty, J. K. (2010). When positive processes hurt relationships. *Current Directions in Psychological Science*, *19*(3), 167–171.

McNulty, J. K. (2013). Personality and relationships. In J. A. Simpson & L. Campbell (Eds.), *The Oxford handbook of close relationships* (pp. 535–552). Oxford University Press.

McNulty, J. K., & Fincham, F. D. (2012). Beyond positive psychology? *American Psychologist, 67*(2), 101–110.

McNulty, J. K., & Karney, B. R. (2004). Positive expectations in the early years of marriage: Should couples expect the best or brace for the worst? *Journal of Personality and Social Psychology, 86*(5), 729–743.

McNulty, J. K., Maxwell, J. A., Meltzer, A. L. et al. (2019). Sex-differentiated changes in sexual desire predict marital dissatisfaction. *Archives of Sexual Behavior, 48*(8), 2473–2489.

McNulty, J. K., Meltzer, A. L., Makhanova, A. et al. (2018). Attentional and evaluative biases help people maintain relationships by avoiding infidelity. *Journal of Personality and Social Psychology, 115*(1), 76–95.

McNulty, J. K., Meltzer, A. L., Neff, L. A. et al. (2021). How both partners' individual differences, stress, and behavior predict change in relationship satisfaction: Extending the VSA model. *Proceedings of the National Academy of Sciences, 118*(27), e2101402118.

McNulty, J. K., Olson, M. A., Meltzer, A. L. et al. (2013). Though they may be unaware, newlyweds implicitly know whether their marriage will be satisfying. *Science, 342*(6162), 1119–1120.

McNulty, J. K., O'Mara, E. M., & Karney, B. R. (2008). Benevolent cognitions as a strategy of relationship maintenance: "Don't sweat the small stuff" … But it is not all small stuff. *Journal of Personality and Social Psychology, 94*(4), 631–646.

McNulty, J. K., & Russell, V. M. (2010). When "negative" behaviors are positive: A contexutal analysis of the long-term effects of problem-solving behaviors on changes in relationship satisfaction. *Journal of Personality and Social Psychology, 98*(4), 587–604.

McNulty, J. K., & Russell, V. M. (2016). Forgive and forget, or forgive and regret? Whether forgiveness leads to less or more offending depends on offender agreeableness. *Personality and Social Psychology Bulletin, 42*(5), 616–631.

McNulty, J. K., Wenner, C. A., & Fisher, T. D. (2016). Longitudinal associations among relationship satisfaction, sexual satisfaction, and frequency of sex in early marriage. *Archives of Sexual Behavior, 45*(1), 85–97.

McNulty, J. K., & Widman, L. (2013). The implications of sexual narcissism for sexual and marital satisfaction. *Archives of Sexual Behavior, 42*(6), 1021–1032.

McWilliams, S., & Barrett, A. E. (2014). Online dating in middle and later life: Gendered expectations and experiences. *Journal of Family Issues, 35*(3), 411–436.

Medin, D. L. (2017). Psychological science as a complex system: Report card. *Perspectives on Psychological Science, 12*(4), 669–674.

Medlin, M. M., Brown, M., & Sacco, D. F. (2018). That's what she said! Perceived mate value of clean and dirty humor displays. *Personality and Individual Differences, 135,* 192–200.

Megale, A., Peterson, E., & Friedlander, M. L. (2021). How effective is online couple relationship education? A systematic meta-content review. *Contemporary Family Therapy: An Interntational Journal.* Advance online publication.

Meier, S. C., Sharp, C., Michonski, J. et al. (2013). Romantic relationships of female-to-male trans men: A descriptive study. *International Journal of Transgenderism, 14*(2), 75–85.

Meijer, W. M., Van IJzendoorn, M. H., & Bakermans - Kranenburg, M. J. (2019). Challenging the challenge hypothesis on testosterone in fathers: Limited meta-analytic support. *Psychoneuroendocrinology, 110,* 104435

Melis, M. R., & Argiolas, A. (1995). Dopamine and sexual behavior. *Neuroscience and Biobehavioral Reviews, 19*(1), 19–38.

Meltzer, A. L., Makhanova, A., Hicks, L. L. et al. (2017). Quantifying the sexual afterglow: The lingering benefits of sex and their implications for pair-bonded relationships. *Psychological Science, 28*(5), 587–598.

Meltzer, A. L., & McNulty, J. K. (2019). Relationship formation and early romantic relationships. In D. Schoebi & B. Campos (Eds.), *New directions in the psychology of close relationships* (pp. 9–27). Routledge.

Meltzer, A. L., McNulty, J. K., Jackson, G. L. et al. (2014). Sex differences in the implications of partner physical attract-iveness for the trajectory of marital satisfaction. *Journal of Personality and Social Psychology, 106*(3), 418–428.

Merino, M. D., & Privado, J. (2020). Is love triarchic or monarchical-hierarchical? A proposal of a general factor of love and a scale to measure it. *Spanish Journal of Psychology, 23,* e10.

Mesko, N., & Bereczkei, T. (2004). Hairstyle as an adaptive means of displaying phenotypic quality. *Human Nature, 15*(3), 251–270.

Mesman, J., Van Ijzendoorn, M. H., & Sagi-Schwartz, A. (2016). Cross-cultural patterns of attachment. In J. Cassidy & P. R. Shaver (Eds.), *Handbook of attachment: Theory, research, and clinical applications* (3rd ed., pp. 852–877). Guilford Press.

Meston, C. M., & Buss, D. M. (2007). Why humans have sex. *Archives of Sexual Behavior, 36*(4), 477–507.

Meston, C. M., Hamilton, L. D., & Harte, C. B. (2009). Sexual motivation in women as a function of age. *Journal of Sexual Medicine, 6*(12), 3305–3319.

Meston, C. M., Kilimnik, C. D., Freihart, B. K. et al. (2020). Why humans have sex: Development and psychometric assessment of a short-form version of the Ysex? Instrument. *Journal of Sex and Marital Therapy*, *46*(2), 141–159.

MeTooMvmt.org. (2022). https://Metoomvmt.Org/

Metts, S., Cupach, W. R., & Bejlovec, R. A. (1989). "I love you too much to ever start liking you": Redefining romantic relationships. *Journal of Social and Personal Relationships*, *6*(3), 259–274.

Meyer, D., & Sledge, R. (2022). The relationship between conflict topics and romantic relationship dynamics. *Journal of Family Issues*, *43*(2), 306–323.

Meyer, I. H. (2003). Prejudice, social stress, and mental health in lesbian, gay, and bisexual populations: Conceptual issues and research evidence. *Psychological Bulletin*, *129*(5), 674–697.

Michael, C., & Cooper, M. (2013). Post-traumatic growth following bereavement: A systematic review of the literature. *Counselling Psychology Review*, *28*(4), 18–33.

Mickelson, K. D., Kessler, R. C., & Shaver, P. R. (1997). Adult attachment in a nationally representative sample. *Journal of Personality and Social Psychology*, *73*(5), 1092–1106.

Mierop, A., Mikolajczak, M., Stahl, C. et al. (2020). How can intranasal oxytocin research be trusted? A systematic review of the interactive effects of intranasal oxytocin on psychosocial outcomes. *Perspectives in Psychological Science*, *15*(5), 1228–1242.

Mikulincer, M., & Erev, I. (1991). Attachment style and the structure of romantic love. *British Journal of Social Psychology*, *30*(4), 273–291.

Mikulincer, M., Gillath, O., & Shaver, P. R. (2002). Activation of the attachment system in adulthood: Threat-related primes increase the accessibility of mental representations of attachment figures. *Journal of Personality and Social Psychology*, *83*(4), 881–895.

Mikulincer, M., & Shaver, P. R. (2003). The attachment behavioral system in adulthood: Activation, psychodynamics, and interpersonal processes. *Advances in Experimental Social Psychology*, *35*, 53–152.

Mikulincer, M., & Shaver, P. R. (2004). Security-based self-representations in adulthood: Contents and processes. In N. S. Rholes, & J. A. Simpson (Eds), *Adult attachment: Theory, research, and clinical implications* (pp. 159–195). Guilford Press.

Mikulincer, M., & Shaver, P. R. (2007). Boosting attachment security to promote mental health, prosocial values, and inter-group tolerance. *Psychological Inquiry*, *18*, 139–156.

Mikulincer, M., & Shaver, P. R. (2009). An attachment and behavioral systems perspective on social support. *Journal of Social and Personal Relationships*, *26*(1), 7–19.

Mikulincer, M., & Shaver, P. R. (2013). The role of attachment security in adolescent and adult close relationships. In J. A. Simpson & L. Campbell (Eds.), *The Oxford handbook of close relationships* (pp. 66–89). Oxford University Press.

Mikulincer, M., & Shaver, P. R. (2016). *Attachment theory in adulthood: Structure, dynamics, and change* (2nd ed.). Guilford Press.

Mikulincer, M., & Shaver, P. (2018). Attachment theory as a framework for studying relationship dynamics and functioning. In A. L. Vangelisti & D. Perlman (Eds.), *The Cambridge handbook of personal relationships* (pp. 175–185). Cambridge University Press.

Mikulincer, M., & Shaver, P. R. (2020). Broaden-and-build effects of contextually boosting the sense of attachment security in adulthood. *Current Directions in Psychological Science*, *29*, 22–26.

Mikulincer, M., & Shaver, P. R. (2022). An attachment perspective on loss and grief. *Current Opinion in Psychology*, *45*, 101283.

Mikulincer, M., Shaver, P. R., & Pereg, D. (2003). Attachment theory and affect regulation: The dynamics, development, and cognitive consequences of attachment-related strategies. *Motivation and Emotion*, *27*(2), 77–102.

Mikulincer, M., Shaver, P., Sahdra, B. K. et al. (2013). Can security-enhancing interventions overcome psychological barriers to responsiveness in couple relationships? *Attachment & Human Development*, *15*(3), 246–260.

Milek, A., Butler, E. A., & Bodenmann, G. (2015). The interplay of couple's shared time, women's intimacy, and intra-dyadic stress. *Journal of Family Psychology*, *29*(6), 831–842.

Miller, B., Catalina, S., Rocks, S., & Tillman, K. (2022). It is your decision to date interracially: The influence of family approval on the likelihood of interracial/interethnic dating. *Journal of Family Issues*, *43*(2), 443–466.

Miller, G. (2000). Sexual selection for indicators of intelligence. *Novartis Foundation Symposium*, *233*, 260–270.

Miller, G., Chen, E., & Cole, S. W. (2009). Health psychology: Developing biologically plausible models linking the social world and physical health. *Annual Review of Psychology*, *60*(1), 501–524.

Miller, G., Tybur, J. M., & Jordan, B. D. (2007). Ovulatory cycle effects on tip earnings by lap dancers: Economic evidence for human estrus? *Evolution and Human Behavior*, *28*(6), 375–381.

Miller, G. F. (2007). Sexual selection for moral virtues. *Quarterly Review of Biology*, *82*(2), 97–125.

Miller, L. C., & Berg, J. H. (1984). Selectivity and urgency in interpersonal exchange. In V. J. Derlega (Ed.), *Communication, intimacy, and close relationships* (pp. 161–206). Academic Press.

Miller, L. C., Berg, J. H., & Archer, R. L. (1983). Openers: Individuals who elicit intimate self-disclosure. *Journal of Personality and Social Psychology*, *44*(6), 1234–1244.

Miller, L. M., Utz, R. L., Supiano, K. et al. (2020). Health profiles of spouse caregivers: The role of active coping and the risk for developing prolonged grief symptoms. *Social Science & Medicine*, *266*, 113455.

Miller, P. J. E., Niehuis, S., & Huston, T. L. (2006). Positive illusions in marital relationships: A 13-year longitudinal study. *Personality and Social Psychology Bulletin*, *32*(12), 1579–1594.

Miller, P. J. E., & Rempel, J. K. (2004). Trust and partner-enhancing attributions in close relationships. *Personality and Social Psychology Bulletin*, *30*, 695–705.

Miller, R. S. (1995). On the Nature of embarrassabllity: Shyness, social evaluation, and social skill. *Journal of Personality*, *63*(2), 315–339.

Miller, R. S. (1997). Inattentive and contented: Relationship commitment and attention to alternatives. *Journal of Personality and Social Psychology*, *73*, 758–766.

Mirnics, Z., Hittner, J. B., Swickert, R. et al. (2022). Gratitude and social support mediate the association between mindfulness and mood: A cross-cultural replication study. *Journal of Health Psychology*, *27*(1), 246–252.

Mitchell, M. E., Bartholomew, K., & Cobb, R. J. (2014). Need fulfillment in polyamorous relationships. *Journal of Sex Research*, *51*(3), 329–339.

Mitchell, V. E., Mogilski, J. K., Donaldson, S. H. et al. (2020). Sexual motivation and satisfaction among consensually non-monogamous and monogamous individuals. *Journal of Sexual Medicine*, *17*(6), 1072–1085.

Mitnick, D. M., Heyman, R. E., & Smith Slep, A. M. (2009). Changes in relationship satisfaction across the transition to parenthood: A meta-analysis. *Journal of Family Psychology*, *23*(6), 848–852.

Mogan, R., Fischer, R., & Bulbulia, J. A. (2017). To be in synchrony or not? A meta-analysis of synchrony's effects on behavior, perception, cognition and affect. *Journal of Experimental Social Psychology*, *72*, 13–20.

Mogilski, J. K., Memering, S. L., Welling, L. L. M. et al. (2017). Monogamy versus consensual non-monogamy: Alternative approaches to pursuing a strategically pluralistic mating strategy. *Archives of Sexual Behavior*, *46*(2), 407–417.

Mogilski, J. K., Reeve, S. D., Nicolas, S. C. A. et al. (2019). Jealousy, consent, and compersion within monogamous and consensually non-monogamous romantic relationships. *Archives of Sexual Behavior*, *48*(6), 1811–1828.

Mogilski, J. K., & Wade, T. J. (2013). Friendship as a relationship infiltration tactic during human mate poaching. *Evolutionary Psychology*, *11*(4), 926–943.

Mogilski, J. K., & Welling, L. L. M. (2017). Staying friends with an ex: Sex and dark personality traits predict motivations for post-relationship friendship. *Personality and Individual Differences*, *115*, 114–119.

Mohr, J. J., & Daly, C. A. (2008). Sexual minority stress and changes in relationship quality in same-sex couples. *Journal of Social and Personal Relationships*, *25*(6), 989–1007.

Moldovan, A. (2019, December 14). You probably knew mindfulness could help you with stress. But did you know it could save your marriage? *ABC News.* www.abc.net.au/news/2019-12-15/dr-eng-kong-tan-says-mindfulness-can-save-your-marriage/11719332

Møller, A. P., & Thornhill, R. (1998). Bilateral symmetry and sexual selection: A meta-analysis. *American Naturalist*, *151*(2), 174–192.

Monfort, S. S., Kaczmarek, L. D., Kashdan, T. B. et al. (2014). Capitalizing on the success of romantic partners: A laboratory investigation on subjective, facial, and physiological emotional processing. *Personality and Individual Differences*, *68*, 149–153.

Mongeau, P. A. (2008). Stage theories of relationship development. In L. A. Baxter & D. O. Braithwaite (Eds.), *Engaging theories in interpersonal communication, multiple perspectives* (pp. 363–375). Routledge.

Monk, J. K., Kanter, J. B., & Ogan, M. A. (2022). Prior on–off relationship instability and distress in the separation and divorce transition. *Family Process*, *61*(1), 246–258.

Monk, J. K., Ogolsky, B. G., & Maniotes, C. (2022). On–off relationship instability and distress over time in same- and different-sex relationships. *Family Relations*, *71*(2), 630–643.

Monk, J. K., Ogolsky, B. G., & Oswald, R. F. (2018). Coming out and getting back in: Relationship cycling and distress in same- and different-sex relationships. *Family Relations*, *67*(4), 523–538.

Monroe, S. M., Rohde, P., Seeley, J. R. et al. (1999). Life events and depression in adolescence: Relationship loss as a prospective risk factor for first onset of major depressive disorder. *Journal of Abnormal Psychology*, *108*(4), 606–614.

Monroe, S. M., & Slavich, G. M. (2020). Major life events: A review of conceptual, definitional, measurement issues, and practices. In K. L. Harkness & E. P. Hayden (Eds.), *The Oxford handbook of stress and mental health* (pp. 6–26). Oxford University Press.

Montesi, J. L., Fauber, R. L., Gordon, E. A. et al. (2011). The specific importance of communicating about sex to couples' sexual and overall relationship satisfaction. *Journal of Social and Personal Relationships*, *28*(5), 591–609.

Montoya, R. M. (2008). I'm hot, so I'd say you're not: The influence of objective physical attractiveness on mate selection. *Personality and Social Psychology Bulletin, 34* (10), 1315–1331.

Montoya, R. M., Faiella, C. M., Lynch, B. P. et al. (2015). Further exploring the relation between uncertainty and attraction. *Psychologia, 58*(2), 84–97.

Montoya, R. M., & Horton, R. S. (2012). The reciprocity of liking effect. In M. Paludi (Ed.), *The psychology of love* (pp. 39–57). Praeger.

Montoya, R. M., & Horton, R. S. (2013). A meta-analytic investigation of the processes underlying the similarity-attraction effect. *Journal of Social and Personal Relationships, 30*(1), 64–94.

Montoya, R. M., & Horton, R. S. (2014). A two-dimensional model for the study of interpersonal attraction. *Personality and Social Psychology Review, 18*(1), 59–86.

Montoya, R. M., & Horton, R. S. (2020). Understanding the attraction process. *Social and Personality Psychology Compass, 14*(4), e12526.

Montoya, R. M., Horton, R. S., & Kirchner, J. (2008). Is actual similarity necessary for attraction? A meta-analysis of actual and perceived similarity. *Journal of Social and Personal Relationships, 25*(6), 889–922.

Montoya, R. M., & Insko, C. A. (2008). Toward a more complete understanding of the reciprocity of liking effect. *Wiley Online Library, 38*(3), 477–498.

Montoya, R. M., Kershaw, C., & Prosser, J. L. (2018). A meta-analytic investigation of the relation between interpersonal attraction and enacted behavior. *Psychological Bulletin, 144*(7), 673–709.

Montoya, R. M., & Sloat, N. T. (2019). People do not always act as positively as they feel: Evidence of affiliation suppression. *International Review of Social Psychology, 32*(1), Article 9.

Moon, J. R., Glymour, M. M., Vable, A. M. et al. (2014). Short- and long-term associations between widowhood and mortality in the United States: Longitudinal analyses. *Journal of Public Health (United Kingdom), 36*(3), 382–389.

Moon, J. R., Kondo, N., Glymour, M. M. et al. (2011). Widowhood and mortality: A meta-analysis. *PLOS One, 6* (8), e23465.

Moore, A. C., & Henderson, K. A. (2018). "Like precious gold": Recreation in the lives of low-income committed couples. *Journal of Leisure Research, 49*(1), 46–69.

Moore, D., Wigby, S., English, S. et al. (2013). Selflessness is sexy: Reported helping behaviour increases desirability of men and women as long-term sexual partners. *BMC Evolutionary Biology, 13*(1), 182.

Moore, J., Kienzle, J., Flood Grady, E. et al. (2015). Discursive struggles of tradition and nontradition in the retrospective accounts of married couples who cohabited before engagement. *Journal of Family Communication, 15*(2), 95–112.

Moore, M. M. (1985). Nonverbal courtship patterns in women: Context and consequences. *Ethology and Sociobiology, 6* (4), 237–247.

Moore, M. M. (1998). Nonverbal courtship patterns in women: Rejection signaling – an empirical investigation. *Semiotica, 118*(3-4), 201–214.

Moore, M. M. (2010). Human nonverbal courtship behavior: A brief historical review. *Journal of Sex Research, 47*(2–3), 171–180.

Moore, S., & Diener, E. (2019). Types of subjective well-being and their associations with relationship outcomes. *Journal of Positive Psychology & Wellbeing, 3*(2), 112–118.

Moore, S. M., Uchino, B. N., Baucom, B. R. W. et al. (2017). Attitude similarity and familiarity and their links to mental health: An examination of potential interpersonal mediators. *Journal of Social Psychology, 157*(1), 77–85.

Moors, A. C., Conley, T. D., Edelstein, R. S. et al. (2015). Attached to monogamy? Avoidance predicts willingness to engage (but not actual engagement) in consensual non-monogamy. *Journal of Social and Personal Relationships, 32*(2), 222–240.

Moors, A. C., & Matsick, J. L. (2018, July 3). *Engagement in and benefits of consensually non-monogamous relation-ships*. Discover Society. https://archive.discoversociety .org/2018/07/03/engagement-in-and-benefits-of-consen sually-non-monogamous-relationships/

Moors, A. C., Matsick, J. L., & Schechinger, H. A. (2017). Unique and shared relationship benefits of consensually non-monogamous and monogamous relationships: A review and insights for moving forward. *European Psychologist, 22*(1), 55–71.

Moors, A. C., Ryan, W., & Chopik, W. J. (2019). Multiple loves: The effects of attachment with multiple concurrent romantic partners on relational functioning. *Personality and Individual Differences, 147*, 102–110.

Moors, A. C., Schechinger, H. A., Balzarini, R. et al. (2021). Internalized consensual non-monogamy negativity and relationship quality among people engaged in polyamory, swinging, and open relationships. *Archives of Sexual Behavior, 50*(4), 1389–1400.

Moran, J. B., Salerno, K. J., & Wade, T. J. (2018). Snapchat as a new tool for sexual access: Are there sex differences? *Personality and Individual Differences, 129*, 12–16.

Moran, J. B., Wade, T. J., & Murray, D. R. (2020). The psych-ology of breakup sex: Exploring the motivational factors and affective consequences of post-breakup sexual activ-ity. *Evolutionary Psychology, 18*(3), 1474704920936916.

Moreland, R. L., & Beach, S. R. (1992). Exposure effects in the classroom: The development of affinity among students. *Journal of Experimental Social Psychology, 28,* 255–276.

Moreland, R. L., & Zajonc, R. B. (1982). Exposure effects in person perception: Familiarity, similarity, and attraction. *Journal of Experimental Social Psychology, 18*(5), 395–415.

Morgan, H. J., & Shaver, P. R. (1999). Attachment processes and commitment to romantic relationships. In J. M. Adams & W. H. Jones (Eds.), *Handbook of interpersonal commitment and relationship stability* (pp. 109–124). Springer US.

Mori, C., Cooke, J. E., Temple, J. R. et al. (2020). The prevalence of sexting behaviors among emerging adults: A meta-analysis. *Archives of Sexual Behavior, 49*(4), 1103–1119.

Morman, M. T., & Floyd, K. (1999). Affectionate communication between fathers and young adult sons: Individual-and relational-level correlates. *Communication Studies, 50*(4), 294–309.

Morrill, M. I., Eubanks-Fleming, C., Harp, A. G. et al. (2011). The marriage checkup: Increasing access to marital health care. *Family Process, 50*(4), 471–485.

Morrison, D. M., Masters, N. T., Wells, E. A. et al. (2015). "He enjoys giving her pleasure": Diversity and complexity in young men's sexual scripts. *Archives of Sexual Behavior, 44*(3), 655–668.

Morrison, T. G., Beaulieu, D., Brockman, M. et al. (2013). A comparison of polyamorous and monoamorous persons: Are there differences in indices of relationship well-being and sociosexuality? *Psychology and Sexuality, 4*(1), 75–91.

Morry, M. M., Chee, K. C., Penniston, T. L. et al. (2019). Relationship social comparisons: Comparison interpretations and attributions as predictors of relationship quality. *Journal of Social and Personal Relationships, 36*(4), 1069–1097.

Morry, M. M., & Sucharyna, T. A. (2016). Relationship social comparison interpretations and dating relationship quality, behaviors, and mood. *Personal Relationships, 23*(3), 554–576.

Morry, M. M., & Sucharyna, T. A. (2019). Relationship social comparisons in dating and marital relationships: Adding relationship social comparison interpretations. *Journal of Social Psychology, 159*(4), 398–416.

Morry, M. M., Sucharyna, T. A., & Petty, S. K. (2018). Relationship social comparisons: Your Facebook page affects my relationship and personal well-being. *Computers in Human Behavior, 83,* 140–167.

Mortelmans, D. (2020). Economic consequences of divorce: A review. *Life Course Research and Social Policies, 12,* 23–41.

Mrkva, K., & Van Boven, L. (2020). Salience theory of mere exposure: Relative exposure increases liking, extremity, and emotional intensity. *Journal of Personality and Social Psychology, 118*(6), 1118–1145.

Muehlenhard, C. L., Humphreys, T. P., Jozkowski, K. N. et al. (2016). The complexities of sexual consent among college students: A conceptual and empirical review. *Journal of Sex Research, 53,* 457–487.

Muise, A., Boudreau, G. K., & Rosen, N. O. (2017). Seeking connection versus avoiding disappointment: An experimental manipulation of approach and avoidance sexual goals and the implications for desire and satisfaction. *Journal of Sex Research, 54*(3), 296–307.

Muise, A., Christofides, E., & Desmarais, S. (2009). More information than you ever wanted: Does Facebook bring out the green-eyed monster of jealousy? *CyberPsychology & Behavior, 12*(4), 441–444.

Muise, A., Giang, E., & Impett, E. A. (2014). Post sex affectionate exchanges promote sexual and relationship satisfaction. *Archives of Sexual Behavior, 43*(7), 1391–1402.

Muise, A., Harasymchuk, C., Day, L. C. et al. (2019). Broadening your horizons: Self-expanding activities promote desire and satisfaction in established romantic relationships. *Journal of Personality and Social Psychology, 116*(2), 237–258.

Muise, A., & Impett, E. A. (2015). Good, giving, and game: The relationship benefits of communal sexual motivation. *Social Psychological and Personality Science, 6*(2), 164–172.

Muise, A., & Impett, E. A. (2016). Applying theories of communal motivation to sexuality. *Social and Personality Psychology Compass, 10*(8), 455–467.

Muise, A., Impett, E. A., & Desmarais, S. (2013). Getting it on versus getting it over with: Sexual motivation, desire, and satisfaction in intimate bonds. *Personality and Social Psychology Bulletin, 39*(10), 1320–1332.

Muise, A., Kim, J. J., Impett, E. A. et al. (2017). Understanding when a partner is not in the mood: Sexual communal strength in couples transitioning to parenthood. *Archives of Sexual Behavior, 46*(7), 1993–2006.

Muise, A., Laughton, A. K., Moors, A. et al. (2019). Sexual need fulfillment and satisfaction in consensually nonmonogamous relationships. *Journal of Social and Personal Relationships, 36*(7), 1917–1938.

Muise, A., Schimmack, U., & Impett, E. A. (2016). Sexual frequency predicts greater well-being, but more is not always better. *Social Psychological and Personality Science, 7*(4), 295–302.

Muise, A., Stanton, S. C. E., Kim, J. et al. (2016). Not in the mood? Men under- (not over-) perceive their partner's sexual desire in established intimate relationships. *Journal of Personality and Social Psychology, 110*(5), 725–742.

Murphy, B., Fiori, K., & Stein, J. (2020). Network interference negatively predicts relationship quality and mental health in dating couples. *Journal of Social, Behavioral, and Health Sciences*, *14*(1), 138–152.

Murray, S. H., & Brotto, L. (2021). I want you to want me: A qualitative analysis of heterosexual men's desire to feel desired in intimate relationships. *Journal of Sex and Marital Therapy*, *47*(5), 419–434.

Murray, S. L. (1999). The quest for conviction: Motivated cognition in romantic relationships. *Psychological Inquiry*, *10*(1), 23–34.

Murray, S. L., Griffin, D. W., Derrick, J. L., Harris, B., Aloni, M., & Leder, S. (2011). Tempting fate or inviting happiness? Unrealistic idealization prevents the decline of marital satisfaction. *Psychological Science*, *22*(5), 619–626.

Murray, S. L., & Holmes, J. G. (1997). A leap of faith? Positive illusions in romantic relationships. *Personality and Social Psychology Bulletin*, *23*(6), 586–604.

Murray, S. L., & Holmes, J. G. (1999). The (mental) ties that bind: Cognitive structures that predict relationship resilience. *Journal of Personality and Social Psychology*, *77*(6), 1228–1244.

Murray, S. L., Holmes, J. G., Bellavia, G. et al. (2002). Kindred spirits? The benefits of egocentrism in close relationships. *Journal of Personality and Social Psychology*, *82*(4), 563–581.

Murray, S. L., Holmes, J. G., & Collins, N. L. (2006). Optimizing assurance: The risk regulation system in relationships. *Psychological Bulletin*, *132*(5), 641–666.

Murray, S. L., Holmes, J. G., & Griffin, D. W. (1996a). The benefits of positive illusions: Idealization and the construction of satisfaction in close relationships. *Journal of Personality & Social Psychology*, *70*(1), 381–408.

Murray, S. L., Holmes, J. G., & Griffin, D. W. (1996b). The self-fulfilling nature of positive illusions in romantic relationships: Love is not blind, but prescient. *Journal of Personality and Social Psychology*, *71*(6), 1155–1180.

Murray, S. L., Holmes, J. G., & Griffin, D. W. (2000). Self-esteem and the quest for felt security: How perceived regard regulates attachment processes. *Journal of Personality and Social Psychology*, *78*(3), 478–498.

Murray, S. L., Holmes, J. G., Griffin, D. W. et al. (2001). The mismeasure of love: How self-doubt contaminates relationship beliefs. *Personality and Social Psychology Bulletin*, *27*(4), 423–436.

Muscatell, K. A., Slavich, G. M., Monroe, S. M. et al. (2009). Stressful life events, chronic difficulties, and the symptoms of clinical depression. *Journal of Nervous and Mental Disease*, *197*(3), 154–160.

Musick, K., & Bumpass, L. (2012). Reexamining the case for marriage: Union formation and changes in well-being. *Journal of Marriage and Family*, *74*(1), 1–18.

Musick, K., Meier, A., & Flood, S. (2016). How parents fare: Mothers' and fathers' subjective well-being in time with children. *American Sociological Review*, *81*, 1069–1095.

Musick, K., & Michelmore, K. (2015). Change in the stability of marital and cohabiting unions following the birth of a child. *Demography*, *52*(5), 1463–1485.

Naab, F., Lawali, Y., & Donkor, E. S. (2019). "My mother in-law forced my husband to divorce me": Experiences of women with infertility in Zamfara State of Nigeria. *PLOS One*, *14*(12), e0225149.

Naef, R., Ward, R., Mahrer-Imhof, R. et al. (2013). Characteristics of the bereavement experience of older persons after spousal loss: An integrative review. *International Journal of Nursing Studies*, *50*(8), 1108–1121.

Nakonezny, P. A., Shull, R. D., & Rodgers, J. L. (1995). The effect of no-fault divorce law on the divorce rate across the 50 states and its relation to income, education, and religiosity. *Journal of Marriage and the Family*, *57*(2), 477.

National Center for Health Statistics (NCHS) (1985). *Vital statistics of the United States, Vol. III, Marriage and divorce, Table 2-4*. DHHS Pub. No. (PHS) 851103. Public Health Service. Washington, DC. US Government Printing Office.

NBCnews. (2019, November 12). US held record 69,550 migrant children in custody in 2019: Report. *Al Jazeera*. www.aljazeera.com/news/2019/11/12/us-held-record-69550-migrant-children-in-custody-in-2019-report

Neal, A. M., & Lemay, E. P. (2019). The wandering eye perceives more threats: Projection of attraction to alternative partners predicts anger and negative behavior in romantic relationships. *Journal of Social and Personal Relationships*, *36*(2), 450–468.

Neff, L. A, & Broady, E. F. (2011). Stress resilience in early marriage: Can practice make perfect? *Journal of Personality and Social Psychology*, *101*(5), 1050–1067.

Neff, L. A., & Geers, A. L. (2013). Optimistic expectations in early marriage: A resource or vulnerability for adaptive relationship functioning? *Journal of Personality and Social Psychology*, *105*(1), 38–60.

Neff, L. A., & Karney, B. R. (2002). Judgments of a relationship partner: Specific accuracy but global enhancement. *Journal of Personality*, *70*(6), 1079–1112.

Neff, L. A., & Karney, B. R. (2003). The dynamic structure of relationship perceptions: differential importance as a strategy of relationship maintenance. *Personality and Social Psychology Bulletin*, *29*(11), 1433–1446.

Neff, L. A, & Karney, B. R. (2004). How does context affect intimate relationships? Linking external stress and cognitive processes within marriage. *Personality and Social Psychology Bulletin*, *30*(2), 134–148.

Neff, L. A., & Karney, B. R. (2005). Gender differences in social support: A question of skill or responsiveness? *Journal of Personality and Social Psychology*, *88*(1), 79–90.

Neff, L. A., & Karney, B. R. (2007). Stress crossover in newlywed marriage: A longitudinal and dyadic perspective. *Journal of Marriage and Family*, *69*(3), 594–607.

Neff, L. A., & Karney, B. R. (2017). Acknowledging the elephant in the room: How stressful environmental contexts shape relationship dynamics. *Current Opinion in Psychology*, *13*, 107–110.

Neff, L. A., Nguyen, T. T., & Williamson, H. C. (2021). Too stressed to help? The effects of stress on noticing partner needs and enacting support. *Personality and Social Psychology Bulletin*, *47*, 1565–1579.

Neilson, J., & Stanfors, M. (2018). Time alone or together? Trends and trade-offs among dual-earner couples, Sweden 1990–2010. *Journal of Marriage and Family*, *80*(1), 80–98.

Nelissen, R. M. A., & Meijers, M. H. C. (2011). Social benefits of luxury brands as costly signals of wealth and status. *Evolution and Human Behavior*, *32*(5), 343–355.

Nelson, A. J., & Yon, K. J. (2019). Core and peripheral features of the cross-cultural model of romantic love. *Cross-Cultural Research*, *53*(5), 447–482.

Nelson, S. K., Kushlev, K., English, T. et al. (2013). In defense of parenthood: Children are associated with more joy than misery. *Psychological Science*, *24*(1), 3–10.

Nelson, S. K., Layous, K., Cole, S. W. et al. (2016). Do unto others or treat yourself? The effects of prosocial and self-focused behavior on psychological flourishing. *Emotion*, *16*(6), 850–861.

Nelson-Coffey, S. K., Killingsworth, M., Layous, K. et al. (2019). Parenthood is associated with greater well-being for fathers than mothers. *Personality and Social Psychology Bulletin*, *45*(9), 1378–1390.

Neto, F. L., & Wilks, D. C. (2017). Compassionate love for a romantic partner across the adult life span. *Europe's Journal of Psychology*, *13*(4), 606–617.

Nettle, D. (2010). Dying young and living fast: Variation in life history across English neighborhoods. *Behavioral Ecology*, *21*(2), 387–395.

Newcomb, T. (1961). The acquaintance process as a prototype of human interaction. In T. M. Newcomb (Ed.), *The acquaintance process* (pp. 259–261). Holt, Rinehart & Winston.

Newsbeat. (2021, April 29). Willow Smith opens up about being polyamorous. *BBC.Com*. www.bbc.com/news/newsbeat-56852099

Nguyen, T. P., Karney, B. R., & Bradbury, T. N. (2020). When poor communication does and does not matter: The moderating role of stress. *Journal of Family Psychology*, *34*(6), 676–686.

Nichols, A. L., & Webster, G. D. (2013). The single-item need to belong scale. *Personality and Individual Differences*, *55*(2), 189–192.

Nicolson, N. A. (2008). Measurement of cortisol. In L. J. Luecken & L. C. Gallo (Eds.), *Handbook of physiological research methods in health psychology* (pp. 37–74). Sage Publications.

Niehuis, S., Lee, K.-H., Reifman, A. et al. (2011). Idealization and disillusionment in intimate relationships: A review of theory, method, and research. *Journal of Family Theory & Review*, *3*(4), 273–302.

Niehuis, S., Reifman, A., Feng, D. et al. (2016). Courtship progression rate and declines in expressed affection early in marriage: A test of the disillusionment model. *Journal of Family Issues*, *37*(8), 1074–1100.

Niehuis, S., Reifman, A., & Lee, K. H. (2015). Disillusionment in cohabiting and married couples: A national study. *Journal of Family Issues*, *36*(7), 951–973.

Nilsson, J. P., Söderström, M., Karlsson, A. U. et al. (2005). Less effective executive functioning after one night's sleep deprivation. *Journal of Sleep Research*, *14*(1), 1–6.

Noar, S., Carlyle, K., & Cole, C. (2006). Why communication is crucial: Meta-analysis of the relationship between safer sexual communication and condom use. *Journal of Health Communication*, *11*(4), 365–390.

Nomaguchi, K. M., & Milkie, M. A. (2003). Costs and rewards of children: The effects of becoming a parent on adults' lives. *Journal of Marriage and Family*, *65*(2), 356–374.

Nomaguchi, K. M., & Milkie, M. A. (2020). Parenthood and well-being: A decade in review. *Journal of Marriage and Family*, *82*(1), 198–223.

Norman, I., & Fleming, P. (2019). Perceived attractiveness of two types of altruist. *Current Psychology*, *38*(4), 982–990.

Norton, M. I., Frost, J. H., & Ariely, D. (2007). Less is more: The lure of ambiguity, or why familiarity breeds contempt. *Journal of Personality and Social Psychology*, *92*(1), 97–105.

Nosek, B. A., & Banaji, M. R. (2001). The GO/NO-GO Association Task. *Social Cognition*, *19*(6), 625–664.

Ockenfels, M. C., Porter, L., Smyth, J. et al. (1995). Effect of chronic stress associated with unemployment on salivary cortisol: Overall cortisol levels, diurnal rhythm, and acute stress reactivity. *Psychosomatic Medicine*, *57*(5), 460–467.

O'Connor, S. C., & Rosenblood, L. K. (1996). Affiliation motivation in everyday experience: A theoretical comparison. *Journal of Personality and Social Psychology*, *70*(3), 513–522.

OECD. (2016). *Cohabitation rate and prevalence of other forms of partnership*. Organisation for Economic Co-operation and Development. www.oecd.org/els/family/SF_3-3-Cohabitation-forms-partnership.pdf

OECD. (2020). *Income inequality (indicator)*. Organisation for Economic Co-operation and Development.

Oggins, J. (2003). Topics of marital disagreement among African-American and Euro-American newlyweds. *Psychological Reports, 92*(2), 419–425.

Ognibene, T. C., & Collins, N. L. (1998). Adult attachment styles, perceived social support and coping strategies. *Journal of Social and Personal Relationships, 15*(3), 323–345.

Ogolsky, B. G., Monk, J. K., Rice, T. K. M. et al. (2017). Relationship maintenance: A review of research on romantic relationships. *Journal of Family Theory and Review, 9*(3), 275–306.

O'Hara, K. L., Grinberg, A. M., Tackman, A. M. et al. (2020). Contact with an ex-partner is associated with psychological distress after marital separation. *Clinical Psychological Science, 8*(3), 450–463.

O'Leary, K. D., Acevedo, B. P., Aron, A. et al. (2012). Is long-term love more than a rare phenomenon? If so, what are its correlates? *Social Psychological and Personality Science, 3*(2), 241–249.

Olivier, J. D. A., Esquivel-Franco, D. C., Waldinger, M. D. et al. (2019). Serotonin and sexual behavior. In M. D. Tricklebank & E. Daly (Eds.), *The serotonin system: History, neuropharmacology, and pathology* (pp. 117–132). Academic Press.

Olmstead, S. B., & Anders, K. M. (2021). Sexuality in emerging adulthood: A primer on theory. In E. M. Morgan & M. H. M. van Dulmen (Eds.), *Sexuality in emerging adulthood*. Oxford University Press.

O'Meara, J. D. (1989). Cross-sex friendship: Four basic challenges of an ignored relationship. *Sex Roles, 21*(7–8), 525–543.

O'Meara, M. S., & South, S. C. (2019). Big Five personality domains and relationship satisfaction: Direct effects and correlated change over time. *Journal of Personality, 87*(6), 1206–1220.

Ömür, M., & Büyükşahin-Sunal, A. (2015). Preferred strategies for female and male initiators in romantic relationship initiation: The role of stereotypes related to romantic relationships, rejection sensitivity and relationship anxiety. *Journal of Educational and Social Research, 5*(1), 476–482.

Onat, G., & Beji, N. K. (2012). Marital relationship and quality of life among couples with infertility. *Sexuality and Disability, 30*(1), 39–52.

Onrust, S. A., & Cuijpers, P. (2006). Mood and anxiety disorders in widowhood: A systematic review. *Aging and Mental Health, 10*(4), 327–334.

Orbuch, T. L., Veroff, J., Hassan, H. et al. (2002). Who will divorce: A 14-year longitudinal study of black couples and white couples. *Journal of Social and Personal Relationships, 19*(2), 179–202.

Ortigue, S., Bianchi-Demicheli, F., Hamilton, A. F. D. C. et al. (2007). The neural basis of love as a subliminal prime: An event-related functional magnetic resonance imaging study. *Journal of Cognitive Neuroscience, 19*(7), 1218–1230.

O'Sullivan, L. F., Cheng, M. M., Harris, K. M. et al. (2007). I wanna hold your hand: The progression of social, romantic and sexual events in adolescent relationships. *Perspectives on Sexual and Reproductive Health, 39*(2), 100–107.

O'Sullivan, L. F., Hughes, K., Talbot, F., & Fuller, R. (2019). Plenty of fish in the ocean: How do traits reflecting resiliency moderate adjustment after experiencing a romantic breakup in emerging adulthood? *Journal of Youth and Adolescence, 48*, 949–962.

Otero, M. C., Wells, J. L., Chen, K.-H. et al. (2020). Behavioral indices of positivity resonance associated with long-term marital satisfaction. *Emotion, 20*(7), 1225–1233.

Overall, N. C. (2018). Does partners' negative-direct communication during conflict help sustain perceived commitment and relationship quality across time? *Social Psychological and Personality Science, 9*(4), 481–492.

Overall, N. C. (2020). Behavioral variability reduces the harmful longitudinal effects of partners' negative-direct behavior on relationship problems. *Journal of Personality and Social Psychology, 119*(5), 1057–1085.

Overall, N. C., & Cross, E. (2019). Attachment insecurity and the regulation of power and dependence in intimate relationships. In C. R. Agnew & J. J. Harman (Eds.), *Power in close relationships: Advances in personal relationship* (pp. 28–54). Cambridge University Press.

Overall, N. C., Fletcher, G. J. O., Simpson, J. A. et al. (2009). Regulating partners in intimate relationships: The costs and benefits of different communication strategies. *Journal of Personality and Social Psychology, 96*(3), 620–639.

Overall, N. C., Fletcher, G. J. O., & Simpson, J. A. (2010). Helping each other grow: Romantic partner support, self-improvement, and relationship quality. *Personality & Social Psychology Bulletin, 36*, 1496–1513.

Overall, N. C., Hammond, M. D., McNulty, J. K. et al. (2016). When power shapes interpersonal behavior: Low relationship power predicts men's aggressive responses to low situational power. *Journal of Personality and Social Psychology, 111*(2), 195–217.

Overall, N. C., & McNulty, J. K. (2017). What type of communication during conflict is beneficial for intimate relationships? *Current Opinion in Psychology, 13*, 1–5.

Overall, N. C., Simpson, J. A., & Struthers, H. (2013). Buffering attachment-related avoidance: Softening emotional and behavioral defenses during conflict discussions. *Journal of Personality and Social Psychology*, *104*, 854–871.

Owen, J., Fincham, F. D., & Moore, J. (2011). Short-term prospective study of hooking up among college students. *Archives of Sexual Behavior*, *40*(2), 331–341.

Owen, J., Rhoades, G., Shuck, B. et al. (2014). Commitment uncertainty: A theoretical overview. *Couple and Family Psychology: Research and Practice*, *3*(4), 207–219.

Owenz, M., & Fowers, B. J. (2019). Perceived post-traumatic growth may not reflect actual positive change: A short-term prospective study of relationship dissolution. *Journal of Social and Personal Relationships*, *36*(10), 3098–3116.

Paat, Y. F., & Markham, C. (2021). Digital crime, trauma, and abuse: Internet safety and cyber risks for adolescents and emerging adults in the 21st century. *Social Work in Mental Health*, *19*(1), 18–40.

Pagani, A., Donato, S., Parise, M. et al. (2015). When good things happen: Explicit capitalization attempts of positive events promote intimate partners' daily well-being. *Family Science*, *6*, 119–128.

Pagani, A. F., Parise, M., Donato, S. et al. (2020). If you shared my happiness, you are part of me: Capitalization and the experience of couple identity. *Personality and Social Psychology Bulletin*, *46*(2), 258–269.

Palmer, K. (2016, March). Psychology is in crisis over whether it's in crisis. *Wired*. www.wired.com/2016/03/psychology-crisis-whether-crisis/

Palomo-Vélez, G., Tybur, J. M., & van Vugt, M. (2021). Is green the new sexy? Romantic of conspicuous conservation. *Journal of Environmental Psychology*, *73*, 101530.

Pancani, L., & Aureli, N. (2022). Relationship dissolution strategies: Comparing the psychological consequences of ghosting, orbiting, and rejection. *CyberPsychology*, *16*(2), 87–103.

Pancani, L., Mazzoni, D., Aureli, N. et al. (2021). Ghosting and orbiting: An analysis of victims' experiences. *Journal of Social and Personal Relationships*, *38*(7), 1987–2007.

Papp, L. M. (2018). Topics of marital conflict in the everyday lives of empty nest couples and their implications for conflict resolution. *Journal of Couple & Relationship Therapy*, *17*(1), 7–24.

Papp, L. M., Cummings, E. M., & Goeke-Morey, M. C. (2009). For richer, for poorer: Money as a topic of marital conflict in the home. *Family Relations*, *58*(1), 91–103.

Papp, L. M., Kouros, C. D., & Cummings, E. M. (2009). Demand-withdraw patterns in marital conflict in the home. *Personal Relationships*, *16*(2), 285–300.

Park, C. L., Cohen, L. H., & Murch, R. L. (1996). Assessment and prediction of stress-related growth. *Journal of Personality*, *64*(1), 71–105.

Park, Y., Impett, E. A., & MacDonald, G. (2021). Singles' sexual satisfaction is associated with more satisfaction with singlehood and less interest in marriage. *Personality and Social Psychology Bulletin*, *47*(5), 741–752.

Park, Y., Impett, E. A., MacDonald, G. et al. (2019). Saying "thank you": Partners' expressions of gratitude protect relationship satisfaction and commitment from the harmful effects of attachment insecurity. *Journal of Personality and Social Psychology*, *117*(4), 773–806.

Park, Y., Impett, E. A., Spielmann, S. S. et al. (2021). Lack of intimacy prospectively predicts breakup. *Social Psychological and Personality Science*, *12*(4), 442–451.

Park, Y., Page-Gould, E., & MacDonald, G. (2022). Satisfying singlehood as a function of age and cohort: Satisfaction with being single increases with age after midlife. *Psychology and Aging*, *37*(5), 626–636.

Parker, G., Durante, K. M., Hill, S. E. et al. (2022). Why women choose divorce: An evolutionary perspective. *Current Opinion in Psychology*, *43*, 300–306.

Parsons, J. A., Prager, K. J., Wu, S. et al. (2020). How to kiss and make-up (or not!): Postconflict behavior and affective recovery from conflict. *Journal of Family Psychology*, *34*(1), 35–45.

Pastor, D. A., Barron, K. E., Miller, B. J. et al. (2007). A latent profile analysis of college students' achievement goal orientation. *Contemporary Educational Psychology*, *32*(1), 8–47.

Paul, A. (2021). Making out, going all the way, or risking it: Identifying individual, event, and partner-level predictors of non-penetrative, protected penetrative, and unprotected penetrative hookups. *Personality and Individual Differences*, *174*, 110681.

Paul, E. L. (2013). Beer goggles, catching feelings, and the walk of shame: The myths and realities of the hookup experience. In D. C. Kirkpatrick, S. Duck, & M. K. Foley (Eds.), *Relating difficulty: The processes of constructing and managing difficult interaction* (pp. 141–160). Lawrence Erlbaum.

Paulhus, D. L., & Williams, K. M. (2002). The Dark Triad of personality: Narcissism, Machiavellianism, and psychopathy. *Journal of Research in Personality*, *36*(6), 556–563.

Pazhoohi, F., & Kingstone, A. (2020). The effect of eyelash length on attractiveness: A previously uninvestigated indicator of beauty. *Evolutionary Behavioral Sciences*, *16*(2), 176–180.

Peer, E., Brandimarte, L., Samat, S. et al. (2017). Beyond the Turk: Alternative platforms for crowdsourcing behavioral research. *Journal of Experimental Social Psychology*, *70*, 153–163.

Penke, L., & Asendorpf, J. B. (2008). Beyond global sociosexual orientations: A more differentiated look at sociosexuality and its effects on courtship and romantic relationships. *Journal of Personality and Social Psychology*, *95*(5), 1113–1135.

Pentel, K. Z., & Baucom, D. H. (2022). A clinical framework for sexual minority couple therapy. *Couple and Family Psychology: Research and Practice*, *11*(2), 177–191.

Pentel, K. Z., Baucom, D. H., Weber, D. M. et al. (2021). Cognitive-behavioral couple therapy for same-sex female couples: A pilot study. *Family Process*, *60*(4), 1083–1097.

Pepping, C. A., Halford, W. K., Cronin, T. J. et al. (2020). Couple relationship education for same-sex couples: A preliminary evaluation of Rainbow CoupleCARE. *Journal of Couple and Relationship Therapy*, *19*(3), 230–249.

Pepping, C. A., Lyons, A., Halford, W. K. et al. (2017). Couple interventions for same-sex couples: A consumer survey. *Couple and Family Psychology: Research and Practice*, *6*(4), 258–273.

Pepping, C. A., & MacDonald, G. (2019). Adult attachment and long-term singlehood. *Current Opinion in Behavioral Sciences*, *25*, 105–109.

Pepping, C. A., MacDonald, G., & Davis, P. J. (2018). Toward a psychology of singlehood: An attachment-theory perspective on long-term singlehood. *Current Directions in Psychological Science*, *27*(5), 324–331.

Pereg, D., & Mikulincer, M. (2004). Attachment style and the regulation of negative affect: Exploring individual differences in mood congruency effects on memory and judgment. *Personality and Social Psychology Bulletin*, *30*(1), 67–80.

Perel, E. (2017a). *Impotent is no way to define a man.* https://esther.libsyn.com/ep-5-impotent-is-no-way-to-define-a-man

Perel, E. (2017b). *I've had better.* www.estherperel.com/podcasts/wswb-s1-episode-1

Perel, E. (2020, September). *Esther Perel: How can we develop resilience in our relationships?* [TED Conferences]. www.npr.org/transcripts/911398921

Perilloux, C., & Buss, D. M. (2008). Breaking up romantic relationships: Costs experienced and coping strategies deployed. *Evolutionary Psychology*, *6*(1), 164–181.

Perilloux, C., Easton, J. A., & Buss, D. M. (2012). The misperception of sexual interest. *Psychological Science*, *23*(2), 146–151.

Perlman, D., Duck, S., & Hengstebeck, N. D. (2018). The seven seas of the study of personal relationships research. In A. L. Vangelisti & D. Perlman (Eds.), *The Cambridge handbook of personal relationships* (pp. 9–27). Cambridge University Press.

Perlman, D., & Peplau, L. (1981). Toward a social psychology of loneliness. In S. Duck & R. Gilmour (Eds.), *Personal relationships in disorder* (pp. 31–56). Academic Press.

Perrig-Chiello, P., Hutchison, S., & Morselli, D. (2015). Patterns of psychological adaptation to divorce after a long-term marriage. *Journal of Social and Personal Relationships*, *32*(3), 386–405.

Perunovic, M., & Holmes, J. G. (2008). Automatic accommodation: The role of personality. *Personal Relationships*, *15*(1), 57–70.

Peshek, D., Semmaknejad, N., Hoffman, D. et al. (2011). Preliminary evidence that the limbal ring influences facial attractiveness. *Evolutionary Psychology*, *9*(2), 137–146.

Peters, B. J., Reis, H. T., & Gable, S. L. (2018). Making the good even better: A review and theoretical model of interpersonal capitalization. *Social and Personality Psychology Compass*, *12*(7), e12407.

Petersen, J. L., & Hyde, J. S. (2010). A meta-analytic review of research on gender differences in sexuality, 1993–2007. *Psychological Bulletin*, *136*(1), 21–38.

Pettit, J., & Joiner, T. E. (2001). Negative-feedback seeking leads to depressive symptom increases under conditions of stress. *Journal of Psychopathology and Behavioral Assessment*, *23*(1), 69–74.

Peugh, J., & Belenko, S. (2001). Alcohol, drugs and sexual function: A review. *Journal of Psychoactive Drugs*, *33*(3), 223–232.

Pew Research Center. (2019, May 14). *Changing attitudes on same-sex marriage.* Pew Research Center. www.pewforum.org/fact-sheet/changing-attitudes-on-gay-marriage/

Pfaus, J. G. (2009). Pathways of sexual desire. *Journal of Sexual Medicine*, *6*(6), 1506–1533.

Pfundmair, M. (2019). Ostracism promotes a terroristic mindset. *Behavioral Sciences of Terrorism and Political Aggression*, *11*(2), 134–148.

Phillips, J., Ajrouch, K., & Hillcoat-Nallétamby, S. (2012). *Key concepts in social gerontology.* Sage Publications.

Pickett, C. L., Gardner, W. L., & Knowles, M. (2004). Getting a cue: The need to belong and enhanced sensitivity to social cues. *Personality and Social Psychology Bulletin*, *30*(9), 1095–1107.

Piechota, A., Ali, T., Tomlinson, J. M. et al. (2022). Social participation and marital satisfaction in mid to late life marriage. *Journal of Social and Personal Relationships*, *39*(4), 1175–1188.

Pietromonaco, P. R., & Barrett, L. F. (1997). Working models of attachment and daily social interactions. *Journal of Personality and Social Psychology*, *73*(6), 1409–1423.

Pietromonaco, P. R., Greenwood, D., & Barrett, L. F. (2004). Conflict in adult close relationships: An attachment perspective. In W. S. Rholes & J. A. Simpson (Eds.), *Adult attachment: New directions and emerging issues* (pp. 1–49). Guilford Press.

Pietromonaco, P. R., & Overall, N. C. (2020). Applying relationship science to evaluate how the COVID-19 pandemic may impact couples' relationships. *American Psychologist*, *76*(3), 438–450.

Pietromonaco, P. R., Overall, N. C., Beck, L. A. et al. (2021). Is low power associated with submission during marital conflict? Moderating roles of gender and traditional gender role beliefs. *Social Psychological and Personality Science*, *12*(2), 165–175.

Pilkonis, P. A. (1977). The behavioral consequences of shyness. *Journal of Personality*, *45*(4), 596–611.

Pinquart, M. (2018). Parenting stress in caregivers of children with chronic physical condition: A meta-analysis. *Stress and Health*, *34*(2), 197–207.

Pinquart, M., Feubner, C., & Ahnert, L. (2013). Meta-analytic evidence for stability in attachments from infancy to early adulthood. *Attachment and Human Development*, *15*(2), 189–218.

Pinquart, M., & Sörensen, S. (2001). Gender differences in self-concept and psychological well-being in old age: A meta-analysis. *Journals of Gerontology: Series B*, *56*(4), P195–213.

Pinsker, J. (2019, May 30). How successful are the marriages of people with divorced parents? *The Atlantic*. www.theatlantic.com/family/archive/2019/05/divorced-parents-marriage/590425/

Pistole, C. M. (1994). Adult attachment styles: Some thoughts on closeness-distance struggles. *Family Process*, *33*(2), 147–159.

Pitts, M., & Rahman, Q. (2001). Which behaviors constitute "having sex" among university students in the UK? *Archives of Sexual Behavior*, *30*(2), 169–176.

Plamondon, A., & Lachance-Grzela, M. (2018). What if they are right? Network approval, expectations, and relationship maintenance behaviors. *Personal Relationships*, *25*(2), 190–204.

Plesser, H. E. (2018). Reproducibility vs. replicability: A brief history of a confused terminology. *Frontiers in Neuroinformatics*, *11*, 76.

Polheber, J. P., & Matchock, R. L. (2014). The presence of a dog attenuates cortisol and heart rate in the Trier Social Stress Test compared to human friends. *Journal of Behavioral Medicine*, *37*(5), 860–867.

Polk, D. M. (2013). Speaking the language of love: On whether Chapman's (1992) claims stand up to empirical testing. *Open Communication Journal*, *7*(1), 1–11.

Pollet, T. V., & Saxton, T. K. (2020). Jealousy as a function of rival characteristics: Two large replication studies and meta-analyses support gender differences in reactions to rival attractiveness but not dominance. *Personality and Social Psychology Bulletin*, *46*(10), 1428–1443.

Pollmann-Schult, M. (2014). Parenthood and life satisfaction: Why don't children make people happy? *Journal of Marriage and Family*, *76*, 319–336.

Poortman, A. R. (2005). How work affects divorce: The mediating role of financial and time pressures. *Journal of Family Issues*, *26*(2), 168–195.

Posada, G., Lu, T., Trumbell, J. et al. (2013). Is the secure base phenomenon evident here, there, and anywhere? A cross-cultural study of child behavior and experts' definitions. *Child Development*, *84*(6), 1896–1905.

Poulin, M. J., Brown, S. L., Dillard, A. J. et al. (2013). Giving to others and the association between stress and mortality. *American Journal of Public Health*, *103*(9), 1649–1655.

Poushter, J. (2014, April 15). *What's morally acceptable? It depends on where in the world you live.* Pew Research Center. www.pewresearch.org/fact-tank/2014/04/15/whats-morally-acceptable-it-depends-on-where-in-the-world-you-live/

Powers, S. I., Pietromonaco, P. R., Gunlicks, M. et al. (2006). Dating couples' attachment styles and patterns of cortisol reactivity and recovery in response to a relationship conflict. *Journal of Personality and Social Psychology*, *90*(4), 613–628.

Powers, S. M., Bisconti, T. L., & Bergeman, C. S. (2014). Trajectories of social support and well-being across the first two years of widowhood. *Death Studies*, *38*(8), 499–509.

Prager, K. J., Poucher, J., Shirvani, F. K. et al. (2019). Withdrawal, attachment security, and recovery from conflict in couple relationships. *Journal of Social and Personal Relationships*, *36*(2), 573–598.

Prager, K. J., Shirvani, F., Poucher, J. et al. (2015). Recovery from conflict and revival of intimacy in cohabiting couples. *Personal Relationships*, *22*(2), 308–334.

Prause, N., & Graham, C. A. (2007). Asexuality: Classification and characterization. *Archives of Sexual Behavior*, *36*(3), 341–356.

Preetz, R. (2022). Dissolution of non-cohabiting relationships and changes in life satisfaction and mental health. *Frontiers in Psychology*, *13*, 812831.

Press Trust of India. (2020, July 1). One may fall in love anytime and with anyone: Dutee Chand on her same-sex relationship. *India Today*. www.indiatoday.in/sports/athletics/story/dutee-chand-opens-up-on-her-same-sex-relationship-asks-people-to-be-more-courageous-1695933-2020-07-01

Presser, H. B. (2000). Nonstandard work schedules and marital instability. *Journal of Marriage and Family*, *62*(1), 93–110.

Previti, D., & Amato, P. R. (2004). Is infidelity a cause or a consequence of poor marital quality? *Journal of Social and Personal Relationships*, *21*(2), 217–230.

Prokopakis, E. P., Vlastos, I. M., Picavet, V. et al. (2013). The golden ratio in facial symmetry. *Rhinology, 51*(1), 18–21.

Pronk, T. M., Karremans, J. C., & Wigboldus, D. H. J. (2011). How can you resist? Executive control helps romantically involved individuals to stay faithful. *Journal of Personality and Social Psychology, 100*, 825–837.

Proulx, C. M., Ermer, A. E., & Kanter, J. B. (2017). Group-based trajectory modeling of marital quality: A critical review. *Journal of Family Theory & Review, 9*(3), 307–327.

Proulx, C. M., Helms, H. M., & Buehler, C. (2007). Marital quality and personal well-being: A meta-analysis. *Journal of Marriage and Family, 69*(3), 576–593.

Provost, M. P., Kormos, C., Kosakoski, G. et al. (2006). Sociosexuality in women and preference for facial masculinization and somatotype in men. *Archives of Sexual Behavior, 35*(3), 305–312.

Pruett-Jones, S. (1992). Independent versus nonindependent mate choice: Do females copy each other? *American Naturalist, 140*(6), 1000–1009.

Przybylski, A. K., & Weinstein, N. (2013). Can you connect with me now? How the presence of mobile communication technology influences face-to-face conversation quality. *Journal of Social and Personal Relationships, 30* (3), 237–246.

Pujols, Y., Meston, C. M., & Seal, B. N. (2010). The association between sexual satisfaction and body image in women. *Journal of Sexual Medicine, 7*, 905–916.

Pulice-Farrow, L., Bravo, A., & Galupo, M. P. (2019). "Your gender is valid": Microaffirmations in the romantic relationships of transgender individuals. *Journal of LGBT Issues in Counseling, 13*(1), 45–66.

Puts, D. (2016). Human sexual selection. *Current Opinion in Psychology, 7*, 28–32.

Quinn-Nilas, C. (2020). Relationship and sexual satisfaction: A developmental perspective on bidirectionality. *Journal of Social and Personal Relationships, 37*(2), 624–646.

Rafaeli, E., & Gleason, M. E. J. (2009). Skilled support within intimate relationships. *Journal of Family Theory & Review, 1*, 20–37.

Rahman, Q., Xu, Y., Lippa, R. A. et al. (2020). Prevalence of sexual orientation across 28 nations and its association with gender equality, economic development, and individualism. *Archives of Sexual Behavior, 49*, 595–606.

Raine, L., & Zickuhr, K. (2015, August 26). *Americans' views on mobile etiquette*. Pew Research Center. www .pewresearch.org/internet/2015/08/26/americans-views-on-mobile-etiquette/

Rajanahally, S., Raheem, O., Rogers, M. et al. (2019). The relationship between cannabis and male infertility, sexual health, and neoplasm: A systematic review. *Andrology, 7* (2), 139–147.

Raley, R. K., & Bumpass, L. (2003). The topography of the divorce plateau: Levels and trends in union stability in the United States after 1980. *Demographic Research, 8*, 245–260.

Raley, R. K., & Sweeney, M. M. (2020). Divorce, repartnering, and stepfamilies: A decade in review. *Journal of Marriage and Family, 82*(1), 81–99.

Ramirez, A., Walther, J. B., Burgoon, J. K. et al. (2002). Information-seeking strategies, uncertainty, and computer-mediated communication toward a conceptual model. *Human Communication Research, 28*(2), 213–228.

Randall, A. K., & Bodenmann, G. (2009). The role of stress on close relationships and marital satisfaction. *Clinical Psychology Review, 29*(2), 105–115.

Randall, A. K., & Messerschmitt-Coen, S. (2019). Dyadic coping as relationship maintenance. In B. G. Ogolsky & J. K. Monk (Eds.), *Relationship maintenance* (1st ed., pp. 178–193). Cambridge University Press.

Rantala, M. J., Coetzee, V., Moore, F. R. et al. (2013). Adiposity, compared with masculinity, serves as a more valid cue to immunocompetence in human mate choice. *Proceedings of the Royal Society B: Biological Sciences, 280* (1751), 20122495.

Ranzini, G., & Lutz, C. (2017). Love at first swipe? Explaining Tinder self-presentation and motives. *Mobile Media and Communication, 5*(1), 80–101.

Raposo, S., Rosen, N. O., & Muise, A. (2020). Self-expansion is associated with greater relationship and sexual well-being for couples coping with low sexual desire. *Journal of Social and Personal Relationships, 37*(2), 602–623.

Rathgeber, M., Bürkner, P. C., Schiller, E. M. et al. (2019). The efficacy of emotionally focused couples therapy and behavioral couples therapy: A meta-analysis. *Journal of Marital and Family Therapy, 45*(3), 447–463.

Reback, C. J., & Larkins, S. (2010). Maintaining a heterosexual identity: Sexual meanings among a sample of heterosexually identified men who have sex with men. *Archives of Sexual Behavior, 39*(3), 766–773.

Reczek, C. (2020). Sexual- and gender-minority families: A 2010 to 2020 decade in review. *Wiley Online Library, 82* (1), 300–325.

Reed, L. A., Tolman, R. M., & Safyer, P. (2015). Too close for comfort: Attachment insecurity and electronic intrusion in college students' dating relationships. *Computers in Human Behavior, 50*, 431–438.

Reese-Weber, M., Kahn, J. H., & Nemecek, R. (2015). Topics of conflict in emerging adults' romantic relationships. *Emerging Adulthood, 3*(5), 320–326.

Regan, P. C., Levin, L., Gate, R. et al. (2000). Partner preferences: What characteristics do men and women desire in their short-term sexual and long-term romantic partners? *Journal of Psychology and Human Sexuality, 12*(3), 1–21.

Regan, P. C., Medina, R., & Joshi, A. (2001). Partner preferences among homosexual men and women: What is desirable in a sex partner is not necessarily desirable in a romantic partner. *Social Behavior and Personality, 29*(7), 733–742.

Rehman, U. S., Lizdek, I., Fallis, E. E. et al. (2017). How is sexual communication different from nonsexual communication? A moment-by-moment analysis of discussions between romantic partners. *Archives of Sexual Behavior, 46*(8), 2339–2352.

Reis, H. T. (2012). Perceived partner responsiveness as an organizing theme for the study of relationships and well-being. In L. Campbell & T. J. Loving (Eds.), *Interdisciplinary research on close relationships: The case for integration* (pp. 27–52). American Psychological Association.

Reis, H. T., & Aron, A. (2008). Love: What is it, why does it matter, and how does it operate? *Perspectives on Psychological Science, 3*(1), 80–86.

Reis, H. T., Aron, A., Clark, M. S. et al. (2013). Ellen Berscheid, Elaine Hatfield, and the emergence of relationship science. *Perspectives on Psychological Science, 8*(5) 558–572.

Reis, H. T., Caprariello, P. A., & Velickovic, M. (2011). The relationship superiority effect is moderated by the relationship context. *Journal of Experimental Social Psychology, 47*(2), 481–484.

Reis, H. T., Clark, M. S., & Holmes, J. G. (2004). Perceived partner responsiveness as an organizing construct in the study of intimacy and closeness. In H. T. Reis, M. S. Clark, & J. G. Holmes (Eds.), *Handbook of closeness and intimacy* (pp. 201–225). Lawrence Erlbaum.

Reis, H. T., & Gable, S. L. (2003). Toward a positive psychology of relationships. In C. L. M. Keyes & J. Haidt (Eds.), *Flourishing: Positive psychology and the life well-lived* (pp. 129–159). American Psychological Association.

Reis, H. T., Gable, S. L., & Maniaci, M. R. (2014). Methods for studying everyday experience in its natural context. In H. T. Reis & C. M. Judd (Eds.), *Handbook of research methods in social and personality psychology* (pp. 373–403). Cambridge University Press.

Reis, H. T., Lemay, E. P., & Finkenauer, C. (2017). Toward understanding understanding: The importance of feeling understood in relationships. *Social and Personality Psychology Compass, 11*(3), 1–22.

Reis, H. T., Li, S., Ruan, Y. et al. (2022). Are you happy for me? Responses to sharing good news in North America and East Asia. *Journal of Social and Personal Relationships, 39* (11), 3458–3486.

Reis, H. T., Maniaci, M. R., Caprariello, P. A. et al. (2011). Familiarity does indeed promote attraction in live interaction. *Journal of Personality and Social Psychology, 101* (3), 557–570.

Reis, H. T., & Patrick, B. (1996). Attachment and intimacy: Component processes. In E. T. Higgins & A. W. Kruglanski (Eds.), *Social psychology: Handbook of basic principles* (pp. 523–563). Guilford Press.

Reis, H. T., Regan, A., & Lyubomirsky, S. (2022). Interpersonal chemistry: What is it, how does it emerge, and how does it operate? *Perspectives on Psychological Science, 17*(2), 530–558.

Reis, H. T., & Shaver, P. (1988). Intimacy as an interpersonal process. In S. Duck (Ed.), *Handbook of personal relationships* (pp. 367–389). John Wiley & Sons.

Reis, H. T., Smith, S. M., Carmichael, C. L. et al. (2010). Are you happy for me? How sharing positive events with others provides personal and interpersonal benefits. *Journal of Personality and Social Psychology, 99*(2), 311–329.

Reissman, C., Aron, A., & Bergen, M. R. (1993). Shared activities and marital satisfaction: Causal direction and self-expansion versus boredom. *Journal of Social and Personal Relationships, 10*(2), 243–254.

Reiter, K., Ventura, J., Lovell, D. et al. (2020). Psychological distress in solitary confinement: Symptoms, severity, and prevalence in the United States, 2017–2018. *American Journal of Public Health, 110*(S1), 56–62.

Remland, M. S., Jones, T. S., & Brinkman, H. (1995). Interpersonal distance, body orientation, and touch: Effects of culture, gender, and age. *Journal of Social Psychology, 135*(3), 281–297.

Rendall, M. S., Weden, M. M., Favreault, M. M. et al. (2011). The protective effect of marriage for survival: A review and update. *Demography, 48*(2), 481–506.

Renninger, L. A., Wade, T. J., & Grammer, K. (2004). Getting that female glance: Patterns and consequences of male nonverbal behavior in courtship contexts. *Evolution and Human Behavior, 25*(6), 416–431.

Repetti, R. L. (1989). Effects of daily workload on subsequent behavior during marital interaction: The roles of social withdrawal and spouse support. *Journal of Personality and Social Psychology, 57*, 651–659.

Repetti, R., Wang, S., & Saxbe, D. (2009). Bringing it all back home: How outside stressors shape families' everyday lives. *Current Directions in Psychological Science, 18*(2), 106–111.

Resnik, J., VanCleave, A., Bell, K. et al. (2018). Reforming restrictive housing: The 2018 ASCA-Liman nationwide survey of time-in-cell. *SSRN Electronic Journal*.

Reynolds, L. (2021). *First divorce rate in the U.S., 2019.* Family Profiles, FP-21-10.

Reynolds, T., Baumeister, R. F., & Maner, J. K. (2018). Competitive reputation manipulation: Women strategically transmit social information about romantic rivals. *Journal of Experimental Social Psychology, 78*, 195–209.

Rhoades, G. K., Kamp Dush, C. M., Atkins, D. C. et al. (2011). Breaking up is hard to do: The impact of unmarried relationship dissolution on mental health and life satisfaction. *Journal of Family Psychology*, *25*(3), 366–374.

Rhoades, G. K., Stanley, S. M., & Markman, H. J. (2009a). The pre-engagement cohabitation effect: A replication and extension of previous findings. *Journal of Family Psychology*, *23*(1), 107–111.

Rhoades, G. K., Stanley, S. M., & Markman, H. J. (2009b). Couples' reasons for cohabitation: Associations with individual well-being and relationship quality. *Journal of Family Issues*, *30*(2), 233–258.

Rhoades, G. K., Stanley, S. M., & Markman, H. J. (2012a). The impact of the transition to cohabitation on relationship functioning: Cross-sectional and longitudinal findings. *Journal of Family Psychology*, *26*(3), 348–358.

Rhoades, G. K., Stanley, S. M., Markman, H. J. et al. (2012b). Parents' marital status, conflict, and role modeling: Links with adult romantic relationship quality. *Journal of Divorce and Remarriage*, *53*(5), 348–367.

Rhoades, K. A. (2008). Children's responses to interparental conflict: A meta-analysis of their associations with child adjustment. *Child Development*, *79*(6), 1942–1956.

Rhodes, G. (2006). The evolutionary psychology of facial beauty. *Annual Review of Psychology*, *57*, 199–226.

Rhodes, G., Chan, J., Zebrowitz, L. A. et al. (2003). Does sexual dimorphism in human faces signal health? *Proceedings of the Royal Society B: Biological Sciences*, *270*, S93–S95.

Rhodes, G., Yoshikawa, S., Clark, A. et al. (2001). Attractiveness of facial averageness and symmetry in nonwestern cultures: In search of biologically based standards of beauty. *Perception*, *30*(5), 611–625.

Richman, S. B., Slotter, E. B., Gardner, W. L. et al. (2015). Reaching out by changing what's within: Social exclusion increases self-concept malleability. *Journal of Experimental Social Psychology*, *57*, 64–77.

Ridge, S. R., & Feeney, J. A. (1998). Relationship history and relationship attitudes in gay males and lesbians: Attachment style and gender differences. *Australian and New Zealand Journal of Psychiatry*, *32*(6), 848–859.

Riek, B. M., & Mania, E. W. (2012). The antecedents and consequences of interpersonal forgiveness: A meta-analytic review. *Personal Relationships*, *19*(2), 304–325.

Righetti, F., Gere, J., Hofmann, W. et al. (2016). The burden of empathy: Partners' responses to divergence of interests in daily life. *Emotion*, *16*(5), 684–690.

Righetti, F., & Impett, E. (2017). Sacrifice in close relationships: Motives, emotions, and relationship outcomes. *Social and Personality Psychology Compass*, *11*(10), 1–11.

Righetti, F., Schneider, I., Ferrier, D. et al. (2020). The bittersweet taste of sacrifice: Consequences for ambivalence and mixed reactions. *Journal of Experimental Psychology: General*, *149*(10), 1950–1968.

Ritchie, L. L., Stanley, S. M., Rhoades, G. K. et al. (2021). Romantic alternative monitoring increases ahead of infidelity and break-up. *Journal of Social and Personal Relationships*, *38*(2), 711–724.

Ritter, S. M., Karremans, J. C., & van Schie, H. T. (2010). The role of self-regulation in derogating attractive alternatives. *Journal of Experimental Social Psychology*, *46*(4), 631–637.

Rivers, A. S., & Sanford, K. (2020). When we say "perceived support," what do we mean? Contexts and components of support among people with serious medical conditions. *Journal of Social and Personal Relationships*, *37*, 2758–2778.

Roberts, B. W., Kuncel, N. R., Shiner, R. et al. (2007). The power of personality: The comparative validity of personality traits, socioeconomic status, and cognitive ability for predicting important life outcomes. *Perspectives on Psychological Science*, *2*(4), 313–345.

Roberts, J. A., & David, M. E. (2016). My life has become a major distraction from my cell phone: Partner phubbing and relationship satisfaction among romantic partners. *Computers in Human Behavior*, *54*, 134–141.

Roberts, L. J. (2000). Fire and ice in marital communication: Hostile and distancing behaviors as predictors of marital distress. *Journal of Marriage and Family*, *62*(3), 693–707.

Robles, T. F., & Kiecolt-Glaser, J. K. (2003). The physiology of marriage: Pathways to health. *Physiology and Behavior*, *79*(3), 409–416.

Robles, T. F., Slatcher, R. B., Trombello, J. M. et al. (2014). Marital quality and health: A meta-analytic review. *Psychological Bulletin*, *140*(1), 140–187.

Robnett, R. D., & Leaper, C. (2013). "Girls don't propose! Ew.": A mixed-methods examination of marriage tradition preferences and benevolent sexism in emerging adults. *Journal of Adolescent Research*, *28*(1), 96–121.

Roddy, M. K., Knopp, K., Georgia Salivar, E. et al. (2021). Maintenance of relationship and individual functioning gains following online relationship programs for low-income couples. *Family Process*, *60*(1), 102–118.

Roddy, M. K., Stamatis, C. A., Rothman, K. et al. (2020). Mechanisms of change in a brief, online relationship intervention. *Journal of Family Psychology*, *34*(1), 57–67.

Rodeheffer, C. D., Leyva, R. P. P., & Hill, S. E. (2016). Attractive female romantic partners provide a proxy for unobservable male qualities: The when and why behind human female mate choice copying. *Evolutionary Psychology*, *14*(2), 1–8.

Rodriguez, L., Øverup, C. S., & Wickham, R. E. (2016). Communication with former romantic partners and current relationship outcomes among college students. *Personal Relationships*, 23(3), 409–424.

Roesler, C. (2020). Effectiveness of couple therapy in practice settings and identification of potential predictors for different outcomes. *Family Process*, 59(2), 390–408.

Rogge, R. D., Fincham, F. D., Crasta, D. et al. (2017). Positive and negative evaluation of relationships: Development and Validation of the Positive-Negative Relationship Quality (PN-RQ) scale. *Psychological Assessment*, 29(8), 1028–1043.

Roisman, G., Clausell, E., Holland, A. et al. (2008). Adult romantic relationships as contexts of human development: A multimethod comparison of same-sex couples with opposite-sex dating, engaged, and married dyads. *Developmental Psychology*, 44, 91–101.

Rollie, S. S., & Duck, S. (2006). Divorce and dissolution of romantic relationships: Stage models and their limitations. In S. S. Rollie & S. Duck (Eds.), *Handbook of divorce and relationship dissolution* (pp. 223–240). Psychology Press.

Roman, J. G., Flood, S. M., & Genadek, K. R. (2017). Parents' time with a partner in a cross-national context: A comparison of the United States, Spain, and France. *Demographic Research*, 36, 111–144.

Roper, S. W., Fife, S. T., & Seedall, R. B. (2020). The intergenerational effects of parental divorce on young adult relationships. *Journal of Divorce and Remarriage*, 61(4), 249–266.

Røsand, G. M. B., Slinning, K., Røysamb, E. et al. (2014). Relationship dissatisfaction and other risk factors for future relationship dissolution: A population-based study of 18,523 couples. *Social Psychiatry and Psychiatric Epidemiology*, 49(1), 109–119.

Rose, S., & Frieze, I. H. (1989). Young singles' scripts for a first date. *Gender & Society*, 3(2), 258–268.

Rose, S., & Frieze, I. H. (1993). Young singles' contemporary dating scripts. *Sex Roles*, 28(9–10), 499–509.

Rose, S., & Zand, D. (2002). Lesbian dating and courtship from young adulthood to midlife. *Journal of Lesbian Studies*, 6(1), 85–109.

Rose, S., Zand, D., & Cini, M. A. (1993). Lesbian courtship scripts. In E. D. Rothblum & K. A. Brehony (Eds.), *Boston marriages: Romantic but asexual relationships among contemporary lesbians* (pp. 71–85). University of Massachusetts Press.

Rosen, N. O., Bailey, K., & Muise, A. (2018). Degree and direction of sexual desire discrepancy are linked to sexual and relationship satisfaction in couples transitioning to parenthood. *Journal of Sex Research*, 55(2), 214–225.

Rosen, N. O., Dawson, S. J., Leonhardt, N. D. et al. (2021). Trajectories of sexual well-being among couples in the transition to parenthood. *Journal of Family Psychology*, 35(4), 523–533.

Rosenberger, J. G., Reece, M., Schick, V. et al. (2011). Sexual behaviors and situational characteristics of most recent male-partnered sexual event among gay and bisexually identified men in the United States. *Journal of Sexual Medicine*, 8(11), 3040–3050.

Rosenfeld, M. J. (2014). Couple longevity in the era of same-sex marriage in the United States. *Journal of Marriage and Family*, 76(5), 905–918.

Rosenfeld, M. J. (2018). Who wants the breakup? Gender and breakup in heterosexual couples. In D. F. Alwin, D. Felmlee, & D. Kreager (Eds.), *Social networks and the life course: Integrating the development of human lives and social relational networks* (pp. 221–243). Springer.

Rosenfeld, M. J., & Roesler, K. (2019). Cohabitation experience and cohabitation's association with marital dissolution. *Journal of Marriage and Family*, 81(1), 42–58.

Rosenfeld, M., & Thomas, R. J. (2010). *Meeting online: The rise of the Internet as a social intermediary*. Unpublished manuscript, Department of Sociology, Stanford University, Stanford, CA.

Rosenfeld, M., Thomas, R. J., Hausen, S. et al. (2019). Disintermediating your friends: How online dating in the United States displaces other ways of meeting. *Proceedings of the National Academy of Sciences*, 116(36), 17753–17758.

Rosenthal, L., Deosaran, A., Young, D. S. L. et al. (2019). Relationship stigma and well-being among adults in interracial and same-sex relationships. *Journal of Social and Personal Relationships*, 36(11–12), 3408–3428.

Ross, J. M., Karney, B. R., Nguyen, T. P. et al. (2019). Communication that is maladaptive for middle-class couples is adaptive for socioeconomically disadvantaged couples. *Journal of Personality and Social Psychology*, 116(4), 582–597.

Rostosky, S. S., & Riggle, E. D. B. (2017). Same-sex relationships and minority stress. *Current Opinion in Psychology*, 13, 29–38.

Roth, T. S., Samara, I., & Kret, M. E. (2021). Ultimate and proximate factors underlying sexual overperception bias: A reply to Lee et al. (2020). *Evolution and Human Behavior*, 42(1), 73–75.

Rothbaum, F., Weisz, J., Pott, M. et al. (2000). Attachment and culture: Security in the United States and Japan. *American Psychologist*, 55(10), 1093–1104.

Rothblum, E. D., Krueger, E. A., Kittle, K. R. et al. (2020). Asexual and non-asexual respondents from a U.S.

population-based study of sexual minorities. *Archives of Sexual Behavior*, *49*(2), 757–767.

Roxburgh, S. (2006). "I wish we had more time to spend together...": The distribution and predictors of perceived family time pressures among married men and women in the paid labor force. *Journal of Family Issues*, *27*(4), 529–553.

Ruan, Y., Reis, H. T., Clark, M. S. et al. (2020). Can I tell you how I feel? Perceived partner responsiveness encourages emotional expression. *Emotion*, *20*(3), 329–342.

Rubinsky, V. (2018). Bringing up the green-eyed monster: Conceptualizing and communicating jealousy with a partner who has other partners. *Qualitative Report*, *23*(6), 1441–1455.

Rubinsky, V. (2019). Identity gaps and jealousy as predictors of satisfaction in polyamorous relationships. *Southern Communication Journal*, *84*(1), 17–29.

Rubinsky, V. (2021). Sources and strategies for managing sexual conflict in diverse relationships. *Sexuality & Culture*, *25*, 904–924.

Rubio, G. (2014). *How love conquered marriage: Theory and evidence on the disappearance of arranged marriages*. Unpublished manuscript.

Rusbult, C. E. (1980). Commitment and satisfaction in romantic associations: A test of the investment model. *Journal of Experimental Social Psychology*, *16*(2), 172–186.

Rusbult, C. E., & Arriaga, X. B. (2000). Interdependence in personal relationships. In W. Ickes & S. Duck (Eds.), *The social psychology of personal relationships* (pp. 79–108). John Wiley & Sons.

Rusbult, C. E., Finkel, E. J., & Kumashiro, M. (2009). The Michelangelo phenomenon. *Current Directions in Psychological Science*, *18*(6), 305–309.

Rusbult, C. E., & Martz, J. M. (1995). Remaining in an abusive relationship: An investment model analysis of nonvoluntary dependence. *Personality and Social Psychology Bulletin*, *21*(6), 558–571.

Rusbult, C. E., Martz, J. M., & Agnew, C. R. (1998). The Investment Model Scale: Measuring commitment level, satisfaction level, quality of alternatives, and investment size. *Personal Relationships*, *5*(4), 357–387.

Rusbult, C. E., & Van Lange, P. A. M. (1996). Interdependence processes. In E. T. Higgins & A. W. Kruglanski (Eds.), *Social psychology: Handbook of basic principles* (pp. 564–596). Guilford Press.

Rusbult, C. E., & Van Lange, P. A. M. (2003). Interdependence, interaction, and relationships. *Annual Review of Psychology*, *54*, 351–375.

Rusbult, C. E., & Van Lange, P. A. M. (2008). Why we need interdependence theory. *Social and Personality Psychology Compass*, *2*(5), 2049–2070.

Rusbult, C. E., Van Lange, P. A. M., Wildschut, T. et al. (2000). Perceived superiority in close relationships: Why it exists and persists. *Journal of Personality and Social Psychology*, *79*(4), 521–545.

Rusbult, C. E., Verette, J., Whitney, G. A. et al. (1991). Accommodation processes in close relationships: Theory and preliminary empirical evidence. *Journal of Personality and Social Psychology*, *60*(1), 53–78.

Russell, A. (1997). Individual and family factors contributing to mothers' and fathers' positive parenting. *International Journal of Behavioral Development*, *21*(1), 111–132.

Russell, E. M., Babcock, M. J., Lewis et al. (2018). Why attractive women want gay male friends: A previously undiscovered strategy to prevent mating deception and sexual exploitation. *Personality and Individual Differences*, *120*, 283–287.

Russell, E. M., Ta, V. P., Lewis, D. M. G. et al. (2017). Why (and when) straight women trust gay men: Ulterior mating motives and female competition. *Archives of Sexual Behavior*, *46*(3), 763–773.

Russell, R., Sweda, J. R., Porcheron, A. et al. (2014). Sclera color changes with age and is a cue for perceiving age, health, and beauty. *Psychology and Aging*, *29*(3), 626–635.

Rutter, M., Kumsta, R., Schlotz, W. et al. (2012). Longitudinal studies using a "natural experiment" design: The case of adoptees from Romanian institutions. *Journal of the American Academy of Child and Adolescent Psychiatry*, *51*(8), 762–770.

Ryan, R. M., & Deci, E. L. (2000). Self-determination theory and the facilitation of intrinsic motivation, social development, and well-being. *American Psychologist*, *55*, 68–78.

Ryan, R. M., & Deci, E. L. (2017). *Self-determination theory: Basic psychological needs in motivation, development, and wellness*. Guilford Press.

Ryon, H. S., & Gleason, M. E. J. (2018). Reciprocal support and daily perceived control: Developing a better understanding of daily support transactions across a major life transition. *Journal of Personality and Social Psychology*, *115*(6), 1034–1053.

Sabatelli, R. M., & Cecil-Pigo, E. F. (1985). Relational interdependence and commitment in marriage. *Journal of Marriage and the Family*, *47*(4), 931–937.

Sabathia, C. (2016, March 8). My toughest out. *The Player's Tribune*. www.theplayerstribune.com/articles/cc-sabathia-yankees-alcohol-addiction-recovery

Sabourin, S., Lussier, Y., & Wright, J. (1991). The effects of measurement strategy on attributions for marital problems and behaviors. *Journal of Applied Social Psychology*, *21*(9), 734–746.

Sacco, D. F., Holifield, K., Drea, K. et al. (2020). Dad and mom bods? Inferences of parenting ability from bodily cues. *Evolutionary Psychological Science, 6,* 207–214.

Sackett-Fox, K., Gere, J., & Updegraff, J. (2021). Better together: The impact of exercising with a romantic partner. *Journal of Social and Personal Relationships, 38*(11), 3078–3096.

Sagarin, B. J., Vaughn Becker, D., Guadagno, R. E. et al. (2003). Sex differences (and similarities) in jealousy: The moderating influence of infidelity experience and sexual orientation of the infidelity. *Evolution and Human Behavior, 24*(1), 17–23.

Saini, M., Stoddart, K. P., Gibson, M. et al. (2015). Couple relationships among parents of children and adolescents with Autism Spectrum Disorder: Findings from a scoping review of the literature. *Research in Autism Spectrum Disorders, 17,* 142–157.

Salvatore, J. E., Kuo, S. I.-C., Steele, R. D. et al. (2011). Recovering from conflict in romantic relationships: A developmental perspective. *Psychological Science, 22*(3), 376–383.

Samara, I., Roth, T. S., & Kret, M. E. (2021). The role of emotion projection, sexual desire, and self-rated attractiveness in the sexual overperception bias. *Archives of Sexual Behavior, 50*(6), 2507–2516.

Sanchez, D. T., Fetterolf, J. C., & Rudman, L. A. (2012). Eroticizing inequality in the United States: The consequences and determinants of traditional gender role adherence in intimate relationships. *Journal of Sex Research, 49,* 168–183.

Sander, S., Strizzi, J. M., Øverup, C. S. et al. (2020). When love hurts – mental and physical health among recently divorced Danes. *Frontiers in Psychology, 11,* 578083.

Sanders, S. A., & Reinisch, J. M. (1999). Would you say you "had sex" if . . .? *Journal of the American Medical Association, 281*(3), 275–277.

Sandstrom, G. M., & Dunn, E. W. (2014a). Is efficiency overrated? Minimal social interactions lead to belonging and positive affect. *Social Psychological and Personality Science, 5*(4), 437–442.

Sandstrom, G. M., & Dunn, E. W. (2014b). Social interactions and well-being: The surprising power of weak ties. *Personality and Social Psychology Bulletin, 40*(7), 910–922.

Santos-Iglesias, P., & Byers, E. S. (2021). Sexual satisfaction of older adults: Testing the interpersonal exchange model of sexual satisfaction in the ageing population. *Ageing and Society, 43*(1), 1–23.

Sarno, E. L., Dyar, C., Newcomb, M. E., & Whitton, S. W. (2022). Relationship quality and mental health among sexual and gender minorities. *Journal of Family Psychology, 36*(5), 770–779.

Sasaki, E., & Overall, N. (2021). Partners' withdrawal when actors behave destructively: Implications for perceptions of partners' responsiveness and relationship satisfaction. *Personality and Social Psychology Bulletin, 47*(2), 307–323.

Sassler, S. (2004). The process of entering into cohabiting unions. *Journal of Marriage and Family, 66*(2), 491–505.

Sassler, S., Cunningham, A., & Lichter, D. T. (2009). Intergenerational patterns of union formation and relationship quality. *Journal of Family Issues, 30*(6), 757–786.

Sassler, S., Michelmore, K., & Qian, Z. (2018). Transitions from sexual relationships into cohabitation and beyond. *Demography, 55*(2), 511–534.

Sassler, S., Miller, A., & Favinger, S. M. (2009). Planned parenthood? Fertility intentions and experiences among cohabiting couples. *Journal of Family Issues, 30*(2), 206–232.

Sassler, S., & Miller, A. J. (2011). Class differences in cohabitation processes. *Family Relations, 60*(2), 163–177.

Sassler, S., & Miller, A. J. (2017). *Cohabitation nation: Gender, class, and the remaking of relationships.* University of California Press.

Savage, M. (2021, August 5). Birdnesting: The divorce trend where parents rotate homes. *BBC Worklife.* www.bbc .com/worklife/article/20210804-birdnesting-the-divorce-trend-in-which-parents-rotate-homes

Savin-Williams, R. C. (2016). Sexual orientation: Categories or continuum? Commentary on Bailey et al. (2016). *Psychological Science in the Public Interest, 17*(2), 37–44.

Savin-Williams, R. C., & Vrangalova, Z. (2013). Mostly heterosexual as a distinct sexual orientation group: A systematic review of the empirical evidence. *Developmental Review, 33*(1), 58–88.

Sayer, L. C., England, P., Allison, P. D. et al. (2011). She left, he left: How employment and satisfaction affect women's and men's decisions to leave marriages. *American Journal of Sociology, 116*(6), 1982–2018.

Sbarra, D. A., & Borelli, J. L. (2019). Attachment reorganization following divorce: Normative processes and individual differences. *Current Opinion in Psychology, 25,* 71–75.

Sbarra, D., Bourassa, K., & Manvelian, A. (2019). Marital separation and divorce: Correlates and consequences. In B. H. Fiese, M. Celano, K. Deater-Deckard, E. N. Jouriles, & M. A. Whisman (Eds.), *APA handbook of contemporary family psychology: Foundations, methods, and contemporary issues across the lifespan* (pp. 687–705). American Psychological Association.

Sbarra, D. A., Briskin, J. L., & Slatcher, R. B. (2019). Smartphones and close relationships: The case for an evolutionary mismatch. *Perspectives on Psychological Science, 14*(4), 596–618.

Sbarra, D. A., & Emery, R. E. (2005). The emotional sequelae of nonmarital relationship dissolution: Analysis of change and intraindividual variability over time. *Personal Relationships, 12*(2), 213–232.

Sbarra, D. A., Emery, R. E., Beam, C. R., & Ocker, B. L. (2014). Marital dissolution and major depression in midlife: A propensity score analysis. *Clinical Psychological Science, 2*(3), 249–257.

Sbarra, D. A., Hasselmo, K., & Bourassa, K. J. (2015). Divorce and health: Beyond individual differences. *Current Directions in Psychological Science, 24*(2), 109–113.

Sbarra, D. A., Law, R. W., & Portley, R. M. (2011). Divorce and death: A meta-analysis and research agenda for clinical, social, and health psychology. *Perspectives on Psychological Science, 6*(5), 454–474.

Sbarra, D. A., & Whisman, M. A. (2022). Divorce, health, and socioeconomic status: An agenda for psychological science. *Current Opinion in Psychology, 43*, 75–78.

Schaan, B. (2013). Widowhood and depression among older Europeans: The role of gender, caregiving, marital quality, and regional context. *Journals of Gerontology: Series B, 68*(3), 431–442.

Schachner, D. A., & Shaver, P. R. (2004). Attachment dimensions and sexual motives. *Personal Relationships, 11*(2), 179–195.

Schachner, D. A., Shaver, P. R., & Gillath, O. (2008). Attachment style and long-term singlehood. *Personal Relationships, 15*(4), 479–491.

Schachter, S. (1964). The interaction of cognitive and physiological determinants of emotional state. *Advances in Experimental Social Psychology, 1*, 49–80.

Schachter, S., & Singer, J. (1962). Cognitive, social, and physiological determinants of emotional state. *Psychological Review, 69*(5), 379–399.

Schäfer, K., & Eerola, T. (2017). *Social surrogacy: How music provides a sense of belonging.* Paper presented at the Proceedings of the 10th International Conference of Students of Systematic Musicology (SysMus17). London.

Scheib, J. E., Gangestad, S. W., & Thornhill, R. (1999). Facial attractiveness, symmetry and cues of good genes. *Proceedings of the Royal Society B: Biological Sciences, 266*(1431), 1913–1917.

Scherrer, K. S. (2008). Coming to an asexual identity: Negotiating identity, negotiating desire. *Sexualities, 11*(5), 621–641.

Schiltz, H. K., & Van Hecke, A. V. (2021). Applying the vulnerability stress adaptation model of marriage to couples raising an autistic child: A call for research on adaptive processes. *Clinical Child and Family Psychology Review, 24*(1), 120–140.

Schimmack, U. (2021). Invalid claims about the validity of implicit association tests by prisoners of the implicit social-cognition paradigm. *Perspectives on Psychological Science, 16*(2), 435–442.

Schmall, T. (2018, October 31). Long-distance relationships are more successful than you think. *New York Post.* https:// nypost.com/2018/10/31/long-distance-relationships-are-more-successful-than-you-think/

Schmiedeberg, C., Huyer-May, B., Castiglioni, L. et al. (2017). The more or the better? How sex contributes to life satisfaction. *Archives of Sexual Behavior, 46*(2), 465–473.

Schmitt, D. P. (2004). Patterns and universals of mate poaching across 53 nations: The effects of sex, culture, and personality on romantically attracting another person's partner. *Journal of Personality and Social Psychology, 86*(4), 560–584.

Schmitt, D. P. (2015). The evolution of culturally-variable sex differences: men and women are not always different, but when they are … it appears not to result from patriarchy or sex role socialization. In T. K. Shackelford & R. D. Hansen (Eds.), *The evolution of sexuality* (pp. 221–256). Springer.

Schmitt, D. P., Alcalay, L., Allik, J. et al. (2003). Universal sex differences in the desire for sexual variety: Tests from 52 nations, 6 continents, and 13 islands. *Journal of Personality and Social Psychology, 85*(1), 85–104.

Schmitt, D. P., & Buss, D. M. (1996). Strategic self-promotion and competitor derogation: Sex and context effects on the perceived effectiveness of mate attraction Tactics. *Journal of Personality and Social Psychology, 70*(6), 1185–1204.

Schmitt, D. P., & Buss, D. M. (2001). Human mate poaching: Tactics and temptations for infiltrating existing mateships. *Journal of Personality and Social Psychology, 80*(6), 894–917.

Schmitt, D. P., & Jonason, P. K. (2015). Attachment and sexual permissiveness: Exploring differential associations across sexes, cultures, and facets of short-term mating. *Journal of Cross-Cultural Psychology, 46*(1), 119–133.

Schmitt, D. P., Shackelford, T. K., Duntley, J. et al. (2002). Is there an early-30s peak in female sexual desire? Cross-sectional evidence from the United States and Canada. *Canadian Journal of Human Sexuality, 11*(1), 1–18.

Schnall, S., Harber, K. D., Stefanucci, J. K. et al. (2008). Social support and the perception of geographical slant. *Journal of Experimental Social Psychology, 44*(5), 1246–1255.

Schneiderman, I., Zagoory-Sharon, O., Leckman, J. F. et al. (2012). Oxytocin during the initial stages of romantic attachment: Relations to couples' interactive reciprocity. *Psychoneuroendocrinology, 37*(8), 1277–1285.

Schoebi, D., & Campos, B. (2019). *New directions in the psychology of close relationships*. Routledge.

Schoebi, D., Wang, Z., Ababkov, V. et al. (2010). Affective interdependence in married couples' daily lives: Are there cultural differences in partner effects of anger? Family Science. *Family Science*, *1*, 83–92.

Schoen, R., Astone, N., Kim, Y. et al. (2002). Women's employment, marital happiness, and divorce. *Social Forces*, *81*(2), 643–662.

Schoumaker, B. (2019). Male fertility around the world and over time: How different is it from female fertility? *Population and Development Review*, *45*(3), 459–487.

Schrodt, P., Witt, P. L., & Shimkowski, J. R. (2014). A meta-analytical review of the demand/withdraw pattern of interaction and its associations with individual, relational, and communicative outcomes. *Communication Monographs*, *81*(1), 28–58.

Schulz, R., Beach, S. R., Czaja, S. J. et al. (2020). Family caregiving for older adults. *Annual Review of Psychology*, *71*(1), 635–659.

Schützwohl, A., Fuchs, A., McKibbin, W. F. et al. (2009). How willing are you to accept sexual requests from slightly unattractive to exceptionally attractive imagined requestors? *Human Nature*, *20*(3), 282–293.

Schwaba, T., Robins, R. W., Grijalva, E. et al. (2019). Does openness to experience matter in love and work? Domain, facet, and developmental evidence from a 24-year longitudinal study. *Journal of Personality*, *87*(5), 1074–1092.

Schwartz, B. (2004). *The paradox of choice: Why more is less*. Harper Perennial.

Schwartz, I. M., & Coffield, E. (2020). A two dimension approach to understanding negative and positive affective reactions to first coitus. *Sexuality and Culture*, *24*(5), 1189–1206.

Schwarz, S., & Hassebrauck, M. (2008). Self-perceived and observed variations in women's attractiveness throughout the menstrual cycle – a diary study. *Evolution and Human Behavior*, *29*(4), 282–288.

Schweingruber, D., Anahita, S., & Berns, N. (2004). "Popping the question" when the answer is known: The engagement proposal as performance. *Sociological Focus*, *37*(2), 143–161.

Schweingruber, D., Cast, A. D., & Anahita, S. (2008). "A story and a ring": Audience judgments about engagement proposals. *Sex Roles*, *58*(3–4), 165–178.

Scott, S. B., Garibay, B., & Do, Q. A. (2021). Reasons for relationship dissolution in female same-gender and queer couples. *Couple and Family Psychology: Research and Practice*, *11*(2), 132–140.

Scott, S. B., & Rhoades, G. K. (2014). Relationship education for lesbian couples: Perceived barriers and content considerations. *Journal of Couple & Relationship Therapy*, *13*(4), 339–364.

Scott, S. B., Rhoades, G. K., Stanley, S. M. et al. (2013). Reasons for divorce and recollections of premarital intervention: Implications for improving relationship education. *Couple and Family Psychology: Research and Practice*, *2*(2), 131–145.

Scott, S., Ritchie, L., Knopp, K. et al. (2018). Sexuality within female same-gender couples: Definitions of sex, sexual frequency norms, and factors associated with sexual satisfaction. *Archives of Sexual Behavior*, *47*(3), 681–692.

Scott, S. B., Whitton, S. W., & Buzzella, B. A. (2019). Providing relationship interventions to same-sex couples: Clinical considerations, program adaptations, and continuing education. *Cognitive and Behavioral Practice*, *26*(2), 270–284.

Scully, J. A., Tosi, H., & Banning, K. (2000). Life event checklists: Revisiting the social readjustment rating scale after 30 years. *Educational and Psychological Measurement*, *60*(6), 864–876.

Segal, N., & Fraley, R. C. (2016). Broadening the investment model: An intensive longitudinal study on attachment and perceived partner responsiveness in commitment dynamics. *Journal of Social and Personal Relationships*, *33*(5), 581–599.

Seidman, G. (2012). Positive and negative: Partner derogation and enhancement differentially related to relationship satisfaction. *Personal Relationships*, *19*(1), 51–71.

Seki, K., Matsumoto, D., & Imahori, T. T. (2002). The conceptualization and expression of intimacy in Japan and the United States. *Journal of Cross-Cultural Psychology*, *33*(3), 303–319.

Selcuk, E., & Ong, A. D. (2013). Perceived partner responsiveness moderates the association between received emotional support and all-cause mortality. *Health Psychology*, *32*(2), 231–235.

Selcuk, E., Stanton, S. C. E., Slatcher, R. B. et al. (2017). Perceived partner responsiveness predicts better sleep quality through lower anxiety. *Social Psychological and Personality Science*, *8*(1), 83–92.

Selterman, D. F., Chagnon, E., & Mackinnon, S. P. (2015). Do men and women exhibit different preferences for mates? A replication of Eastwick and Finkel (2008). *SAGE Open*, *5*(3).

Selterman, D. F., Garcia, J. R., & Tsapelas, I. (2019). Motivations for extradyadic infidelity revisited. *Journal of Sex Research*, *56*(3), 273–286.

Selterman, D. F., Garcia, J. R., & Tsapelas, I. (2020). What do people do, say, and feel when they have affairs? Associations between extradyadic infidelity motives with behavioral, emotional, and sexual outcomes. *Journal of Sex and Marital Therapy*, *47*(3), 238–252.

Semenyna, S. W., Belu, C., Vasey, P. L. et al. (2017). Not straight and not straightforward: The relationships between sexual orientation, sociosexuality, and dark triad traits in women. *Evolutionary Psychological Science*, *4*(1), 24–37.

Senko, C., & Fyffe, V. (2010). An evolutionary perspective on effective vs. ineffective pick-up lines. *Journal of Social Psychology*, *150*(6), 648–667.

Seraj, S., Blackburn, K. G., & Pennebaker, J. W. (2021). Language left behind on social media exposes the emotional and cognitive costs of a romantic breakup. *Proceedings of the National Academy of Sciences*, *118*(7), e2017154118.

Serretti, A., & Chiesa, A. (2009). Treatment-emergent sexual dysfunction related to antidepressants: A meta-analysis. *Journal of Clinical Psychopharmacology*, *29*(3), 259–266.

Sevi, B., Aral, T., & Eskenazi, T. (2018). Exploring the hook-up app: Low sexual disgust and high sociosexuality predict motivation to use Tinder for casual sex. *Personality and Individual Differences*, *133*, 17–20.

Sevilla, A., Gimenez-Nadal, J. I., & Gershuny, J. (2012). Leisure inequality in the United States: 1965–2003. *Demography*, *49*(3), 939–964.

Shackelford, T. K., Goetz, A. T., & Buss, D. M. (2005). Mate retention in marriage: Further evidence of the reliability of the Mate Retention Inventory. *Personality and Individual Differences*, *39*(2), 415–425.

Shackelford, T. K., LeBlanc, G. J., & Drass, E. (2000). Emotional reactions to infidelity. *Cognition and Emotion*, *14*(5), 643–659.

Shackelford, T. K., Schmitt, D. P., & Buss, D. M. (2005). Universal dimensions of human mate preferences. *Personality and Individual Differences*, *39*(2), 447–458.

Shadish, W. R., & Baldwin, S. A. (2003). Meta-analysis of MFT interventions. *Journal of Marital and Family Therapy*, *29*(4), 547–570.

Shadish, W. R., & Baldwin, S. A. (2005). Effects of behavioral marital therapy: A meta-analysis of randomized controlled trials. *Journal of Consulting and Clinical Psychology*, *73*(1), 6–14.

Shallcross, S. L., Howland, M., Bemis, J. et al. (2011). Not "capitalizing" on social capitalization interactions: The role of attachment insecurity. *Journal of Family Psychology*, *25*(1), 77–85.

Sharkey, J. A., Feather, J. S., & Goedeke, S. (2022). The current state of relationship science: A cross-disciplines review of key themes, theories, researchers and journals. *Journal of Social and Personal Relationships*, *39*(4), 864–885.

Shaver, P., Hazan, C., & Bradshaw, D. (1988). Love as attachment. In R. Sternberg & M. L. Barnes (Eds.), *The psychology of love* (pp. 68–99). Yale University Press.

Shaver, P. R., & Mikulincer, M. (2019). A behavioral systems approach to romantic love relationships: Attachment, caregiving, and sex. In R. J. Sternberg & K. Sternberg (Eds.), *The new psychology of love* (2nd ed., pp. 259–279). Cambridge University Press.

Shaw Taylor, L., Mendelsohn, G. A., & Cheshire, C. (2011). "Out of my league": A real-world test of the matching hypothesis. *Personality and Social Psychology Bulletin*, *37*(7), 942–954.

Sheets, V. L. (2014). Passion for life: Self-expansion and passionate love across the life span. *Journal of Social and Personal Relationships*, *31*(7), 958–974.

Shepler, D. K., Smendik, J. M., Cusick, K. M. et al. (2018). Predictors of sexual satisfaction for partnered lesbian, gay, and bisexual adults. *Psychology of Sexual Orientation and Gender Diversity*, *5*(1), 25–35.

Shih, H. C., Kuo, M. E., Wu, C. W. et al. (2022). The Neurobiological basis of love: A meta-analysis of human functional neuroimaging studies of maternal and passionate love. *Brain Sciences*, *12*(7), 830.

Shimek, C., & Bello, R. (2014). Coping with break-ups: Rebound relationships and gender socialization. *Social Sciences*, *3*(1), 24–43.

Shimoda, R., Campbell, A., & Barton, R. A. (2018). Women's emotional and sexual attraction to men across the menstrual cycle. *Behavioral Ecology*, *29*(1), 51–59.

Shin, S. H., Kim, G., & Park, S. (2018). Widowhood status as a risk factor for cognitive decline among older adults. *American Journal of Geriatric Psychiatry*, *26*(7), 778–787.

Shonkoff, J. P., Garner, A. S., Siegel, B. S. et al. (2012). The lifelong effects of early childhood adversity and toxic stress. *Pediatrics*, *129*(1), e232–246.

Shor, E., Roelfs, D. J., Bugyi, P. et al. (2012). Meta-analysis of marital dissolution and mortality: Reevaluating the intersection of gender and age. *Social Science and Medicine*, *75*(1), 46–59.

Short, M. A., & Louca, M. (2015). Sleep deprivation leads to mood deficits in healthy adolescents. *Sleep Medicine*, *16*(8), 987–993.

Shreffler, K. M., Gibbs, L., Tiemeyer, S. et al. (2021). Is reproductive orientation associated with sexual satisfaction among partnered U.S. women? *Archives of Sexual Behavior*, *50*(6), 2459–2469.

Shumlich, E. J., & Fisher, W. A. (2020). An exploration of factors that influence enactment of affirmative consent behaviors. *Journal of Sex Research*, *57*(9), 1108–1121.

Sillars, A. L., & Overall, N. C. (2017). Coding observed interaction. In C. A. VanLear & D. J. Canary (Eds.), *Researching interactive communication behavior: A sourcebook of methods and measures* (pp. 199–216). Sage Publications.

Silman, A. (2017, April 4). Samira Wiley's most radical protest. *The Cut.* www.thecut.com/2017/04/samira-wileys-most-radical-protest-is-being-herself.html

Silva-Rodrigues, F. M., Pan, R., Pacciulio Sposito, A. M. et al. (2016). Childhood cancer: Impact on parents' marital dynamics. *European Journal of Oncology Nursing, 23,* 34–42.

Silvestrini, M. (2020). "It's not something I can shake": The effect of racial stereotypes, beauty standards, and sexual racism on interracial attraction. *Sexuality and Culture, 24* (1), 305–325.

Simon, W., & Gagnon, J. H. (1969). Psychosexual development. *Society, 6*(5), 9–17.

Simon, W., & Gagnon, J. H. (1986). Sexual scripts: Permanence and change. *Archives of Sexual Behavior, 15*(2), 97–120.

Simpson, J. A. (1990). Influence of attachment styles on romantic relationships. *Journal of Personality and Social Psychology, 59*(5), 971–980.

Simpson, J. A. (2019). Bringing life history theory into relationship science. *Personal Relationships, 26*(1), 4–20.

Simpson, J. A., Fletcher, G. J. O., & Campbell, L. (2001). The structure and function of ideal standards in close relationships. In G. J. O. Fletcher & M. S. Clark (Eds.), *Blackwell handbook of social psychology: Interpersonal processes* (pp. 86–106). Blackwell Publishing.

Simpson, J. A., & Gangestad, S. W. (1990). Perception of physical attractiveness: Mechanisms involved in the maintenance of romantic relationships. *Journal of Personality and Social Psychology, 59*(6), 1192–1201.

Simpson, J. A., & Gangestad, S. W. (1991). Individual differences in sociosexuality: Evidence for convergent and discriminant validity. *Journal of Personality and Social Psychology, 60*(6), 870–883.

Simpson, J. A., Gangestad, S. W., Christensen, P. N. et al. (1999). Fluctuating asymmetry, sociosexuality, and intrasexual competitive tactics. *Journal of Personality and Social Psychology, 76*(1), 159–172.

Simpson, J. A., Gangestad, S. W., Simpson, J. A. et al. (1990). Perception of physical attractiveness: Mechanisms involved in maintenance of romantic relationships. *Journal of Personality and Social Psychology, 59*(6), 1192–1201.

Simpson, J. A., Griskevicius, V., Szepsenwol, O. et al. (2017). An evolutionary life history perspective on personality and mating strategies. In A. T. Church (Ed.), *The Prager handbook of personality across cultures: Evolutionary, ecological, and cultural contexts of personality* (pp. 1–29). Prager/ABC-CLIO.

Simpson, J. A., Rholes, W. S., & Nelligan, J. S. (1992). Support seeking and support giving within couples in an anxiety-provoking situation: The role of attachment styles. *Journal of Personality and Social Psychology, 62,* 434–446.

Simpson, J. A., Rholes, W. S., & Phillips, D. (1996). Conflict in close relationships: An attachment perspective. *Journal of Personality and Social Psychology, 71,* 899–914.

Simpson, R. (2005, Feburary 8). Will: Ask your wife before you cheat on her. *Daily Mail Online.* www.dailymail.co.uk/tvshowbiz/article-337032/Will-Ask-wife-cheat-her.html

Sinclair, H. C., & Ellithorpe, C. (2014). The new story of Romeo and Juliet. In C. R. Agnew (Ed.), *Social influences on romantic relationships: Beyond the dyad* (pp. 148–170). Cambridge University Press.

Sinclair, H. C., Felmlee, D., Sprecher, S. et al. (2015). Don't tell me who I can't love: A multimethod investigation of social network and reactance effects on romantic relationships. *Social Psychology Quarterly, 78*(1), 77–99.

Sinclair, H. C., Hood, K. B., & Wright, B. L. (2014). Revisiting the Romeo and Juliet effect (Driscoll, Davis, & Lipetz, 1972): Reexamining the links between social network opinions and romantic relationship outcomes. *Social Psychology, 45*(3), 170–178.

Singh, D. (1993). Adaptive significance of female physical attractiveness: Role of waist-to-hip ratio. *Journal of Personality and Social Psychology, 65*(2), 293–307.

Singh, D., Dixson, B. J., Jessop, T. S. et al. (2010). Cross-cultural consensus for waist-hip ratio and women's attractiveness. *Evolution and Human Behavior, 31*(3), 176–181.

Singh, D., & Young, R. K. (1995). Body weight, waist-to-hip ratio, breasts, and hips: Role in judgments of female attractiveness and desirability for relationships. *Ethology and Sociobiology, 16*(6), 483–507.

Singh, D. K. (2003). Families of children with spina bifida: A review. *Journal of Developmental and Physical Disabilities, 15*(1), 37–55.

Singh, P., Vijayan, R., & Mosahebi, A. (2019). The golden ratio and aesthetic surgery. *Aesthetic Surgery Journal, 39*(1), NP4–NP5.

Singh, R., Wegener, D. T., Sankaran, K. et al. (2017). Attitude similarity and attraction: Validation, positive affect, and trust as sequential mediators. *Personal Relationships, 24* (1), 203–222.

Singham, T., Bell, G., Saunders, R. et al. (2021). Widowhood and cognitive decline in adults aged 50 and over: A systematic review and meta-analysis. *Ageing Research Reviews, 71,* 101461.

Skinner, A. L., & Rae, J. R. (2019). A robust bias against interracial couples among white and black respondents, relative to multiracial respondents. *Social Psychological and Personality Science, 10*(6), 823–831.

Slatcher, R. B. (2010). When Harry and Sally met Dick and Jane: Creating closeness between couples. *Personal Relationships, 17*(2), 279–297.

Slavich, G. M., O'Donovan, A., Epel, E. S. et al. (2010). Black sheep get the blues: A psychobiological model of social rejection and depression. *Neuroscience and Biobehavioral Reviews*, *35*(1), 39–45.

Slawson, N. (2017, October 15). #Metoo trend highlights sexual harassment in wake of Weinstein claims. *The Guardian*. www.theguardian.com/uk-news/2017/oct/16/me-too-social-media-trend-highlights-sexual-harassment-of-women

Slotter, E. B., Emery, L. F., & Luchies, L. B. (2014). Me after you: Partner influence and individual effort predict rejection of self-aspects and self-concept clarity after relationship dissolution. *Personality and Social Psychology Bulletin*, *40*(7), 831–844.

Slotter, E. B., & Finkel, E. J. (2009). The strange case of sustained dedication to an unfulfilling relationship: Predicting commitment and breakup from attachment anxiety and need fulfillment within relationships. *Personality and Social Psychology Bulletin*, *35*(1), 85–100.

Slotter, E. B., & Gardner, W. L. (2009). Where do you end and i begin? Evidence for anticipatory, motivated self-other integration between relationship partners. *Journal of Personality and Social Psychology*, *96*(6), 1137–1151.

Slotter, E. B., & Gardner, W. L. (2012a). The dangers of dating the "bad boy" (or girl): When does romantic desire encourage us to take on the negative qualities of potential partners? *Journal of Experimental Social Psychology*, *48*(5), 1173–1178.

Slotter, E. B., & Gardner, W. L. (2012b). How needing you changes me: The influence of attachment anxiety on self-concept malleability in romantic relationships. *Self and Identity*, *11*(3), 386–408.

Slotter, E. B., Gardner, W. L., & Finkel, E. J. (2010). Who am I without you? The influence of romantic breakup on the self-concept. *Personality and Social Psychology Bulletin*, *36*(2), 147–160.

Slotter, E. B., & Kolarova, L. (2020). Making sure you see the real me: The role of self-esteem in spontaneous self-expansion. *Social Psychological and Personality Science*, *11*(1), 46–55.

Smith, E. R., Coats, S., & Walling, D. (1999). Overlapping mental representations of self, in-group, and partner: Further response time evidence and a connectionist model. *Personality and Social Psychology Bulletin*, *25*(7), 873–882.

Smith, T. W., Baron, C., Deits-Lebehn, C. et al. (2020). Is it me or you? Marital conflict behavior and blood pressure reactivity. *Journal of Family Psychology*, *34*(4), 503–508.

Smith, T. W., Ruiz, J. M., & Uchino, B. N. (2004). Mental activation of supportive ties, hostility, and cardiovascular reactivity to laboratory stress in young men and women. *Health Psychology*, *23*(5), 476–485.

Smock, P. J. (2000). Cohabitation in the United States: An appraisal of research themes, findings, and implications. *Annual Review of Sociology*, *26*, 1–20.

Smock, P. J., & Schwartz, C. R. (2020). The demography of families: A review of patterns and change. *Journal of Marriage and Family*, *82*(1), 9–34.

Snapp, S., Lento, R., Ryu, E. et al. (2014). Why do they hook up? Attachment style and motives of college students. *Personal Relationships*, *21*(3), 468–481.

Snyder, D. K., & Halford, W. K. (2012). Evidence-based couple therapy: Current status and future directions. *Journal of Family Therapy*, *34*(3), 229–249.

Snyder, M., Tanke, E. D., & Berscheid, E. (1977). Social perception and interpersonal behavior: On the self-fulfilling nature of social stereotypes. *Journal of Personality and Social Psychology*, *35*(9), 656–666.

Society, E. (2019). *Actor Idris Elba comes to aid of woman having a seizure*. Epilepsy Society.

Solomon, B., & Vazire, S. (2014). You are so beautiful . . . To me: Seeing beyond biases and achieving accuracy in romantic relationships. *Journal of Personality and Social Psychology*, *107*(3), 516–528.

Solomon, B. C., & Jackson, J. J. (2014). Why do personality traits predict divorce? Multiple pathways through satisfaction. *Journal of Personality and Social Psychology*, *106*(6), 978–996.

Solomon, D. H., & Knobloch, L. K. (2001). Relationship uncertainty, partner interference, and intimacy within dating relationships. *Journal of Social and Personal Relationships*, *18*(6), 804–820.

Solomon, D. H., & Knobloch, L. K. (2004). A model of relational turbulence: The role of intimacy, relational uncertainty, and interference from partners in appraisals of irritations. *Journal of Social and Personal Relationships*, *21*(6), 795–816.

Solomon, D. H., Knobloch, L. K., Theiss, J. A. et al. (2016). Relational turbulence theory: Explaining variation in subjective experiences and communication within romantic relationships. *Human Communication Research*, *42*(4), 507–532.

Solomon, D. H., & Roloff, M. E. (2018). Relationship initiation and growth. In A. L. Vangelisti & D. Perlman (Eds.), *The Cambridge handbook of personal relationships* (pp. 79–89). Cambridge University Press.

Solomon, D. H., & Theiss, J. A. (2011). Relational turbulence: What doesn't kill us makes us stronger. In W. R. Cupach & B. H. Spitzberg (Eds.), *The dark side of close relationships II* (pp. 197–216). Routledge.

Solomon, D. H., Weber, K. M., & Steuber, K. R. (2010). Turbulence in relational transitions. In S. W. Smith & S. R. Wilson (Eds.), *New directions in interpersonal communication research* (pp. 115–134). Sage Publications.

Sorokowska, A., Saluja, S., Sorokowski, P. et al. (2021). Affective interpersonal touch in close relationships: A cross-cultural perspective. *Personality and Social Psychology Bulletin, 47*(12), 1705–1721.

Sorokowski, P., Sorokowska, A., Karwowski, M. et al. (2021). Universality of the triangular theory of love: Adaptation and psychometric properties of the triangular love scale in 25 countries. *Journal of Sex Research, 58*(1), 106–115.

Spaeth, A. M., Dinges, D. F., & Goel, N. (2013). Effects of experimental sleep restriction on weight gain, caloric intake, and meal timing in healthy adults. *Sleep, 36*(7), 981–990.

Spahni, S., Morselli, D., Perrig-Chiello, P. et al. (2015). Patterns of psychological adaptation to spousal bereavement in old age. *Gerontology, 61*(5), 456–468.

Sparks, J., Daly, C., Wilkey, B. M. et al. (2020). Negligible evidence that people desire partners who uniquely fit their ideals. *Journal of Experimental Social Psychology, 90,* 103968.

Spencer, C. M., & Anderson, J. R. (2021). Online relationship education programs improve individual and relationship functioning: A meta-analytic review. *Journal of Marital and Family Therapy, 47*(2), 485–500.

Spengler, E. S., DeVore, E. N., Spengler, P. M. et al. (2020). What does "couple" mean in couple therapy outcome research? A systematic review of the implicit and explicit, inclusion and exclusion of gender and sexual minority individuals and identities. *Journal of Marital and Family Therapy, 46*(2), 240–255.

Spielmann, S. S., Joel, S., & Impett, E. A. (2019). Pursuing sex with an ex: Does it hinder breakup recovery? *Archives of Sexual Behavior, 48*(3), 691–702.

Spielmann, S. S., MacDonald, G., Maxwell, J. A. et al. (2013). Settling for less out of fear of being single. *Journal of Personality and Social Psychology, 105*(6), 1049–1073.

Spielmann, S. S., MacDonald, G., & Wilson, A. E. (2009). On the rebound: Focusing on someone new helps anxiously attached individuals let go of ex-partners. *Personality and Social Psychology Bulletin, 35*(10), 1382–1394.

Spikic, S., & Mortelmans, D. (2021). A preliminary meta-analysis of the big five personality traits' effect on marital separation. *Journal of Divorce and Remarriage, 62*(7), 551–571.

Spitzberg, B. H., & Cupach, W. R. (2007). The state of the art of stalking: Taking stock of the emerging literature. *Aggression and Violent Behavior, 12*(1), 64–86.

Spottswood, E. L., & Carpenter, C. J. (2020). Facebook jealousy: A hyperperception perspective. *Communication Quarterly, 68*(4), 397–416.

Sprankles, J. (2021, June 23). 90 This Is Us quotes that'll make you wish you were part of the Pearson fam. *ScaryMommy.* www.scarymommy.com/this-is-us-quotes/

Sprecher, S. (1999). "I love you more today than yesterday": Romantic partners' perceptions of changes in love and related affect over time. *Journal of Personality and Social Psychology, 76*(1), 46–53.

Sprecher, S. (2011). The influence of social networks on romantic relationships: Through the lens of the social network. *Personal Relationships, 18*(4), 630–644.

Sprecher, S. (2014). Effects of actual (manipulated) and perceived similarity on liking in get-acquainted interactions: The role of communication. *Communication Monographs, 81*(1), 4–27.

Sprecher, S. (2019). Beliefs about finding a compatible partner in three settings. *Interpersona, 13*(2), 253–264.

Sprecher, S. (2021). Closeness and other affiliative outcomes generated from the Fast Friends procedure: A comparison with a small-talk task and unstructured self-disclosure and the moderating role of mode of communication. *Journal of Social and Personal Relationships, 38*(5), 1452–1471.

Sprecher, S., Christopher, F. S., Regan, P. et al. (2018). Sexuality in personal relationships. In A. L. Vangelisti & D. Perlman (Eds.), *The Cambridge handbook of personal relationships* (pp. 311–326). Cambridge University Press.

Sprecher, S., Econie, A., & Treger, S. (2019). Mate preferences in emerging adulthood and beyond: Age variations in mate preferences and beliefs about change in mate preferences. *Journal of Social and Personal Relationships, 36* (10), 3139–3158.

Sprecher, S., & Fehr, B. (2005). Compassionate love for close others and humanity. *Journal of Social and Personal Relationships, 22*(5), 629–651.

Sprecher, S., & Felmlee, D. (1992). The influence of parents and friends on the quality and stability of romantic relationships: A three-wave longitudinal investigation. *Journal of Marriage and the Family, 54*(4), 888–900.

Sprecher, S., Felmlee, D., Schmeeckle, M. et al. (2013). No breakup occurs on an island: Social networks and relationship dissolution. In M. A. Fine & J. H. Harvey (Eds.). *Handbook of divorce and relationship dissolution* (pp. 457–478). Routledge.

Sprecher, S., & Hendrick, S. S. (2004). Self-disclosure in intimate relationships: Associations with individual and relationship characteristics over time. *Journal of Social and Clinical Psychology, 23*(6), 857–877.

Sprecher, S., O'Sullivan, L. F., Drouin, M. et al. (2021). Perhaps it was too soon: College students' reflections on the timing of their sexual debut. *Journal of Sex Research, 59*(1), 39–52.

Sprecher, S., & Regan, P. C. (1998). Passionate and companionate love in courting and young married couples. *Sociological Inquiry*, 68(2), 163–185.

Sprecher, S., & Regan, P. C. (2002). Liking some things (in some people) more than others: Partner preferences in romantic relationships and friendships. *Journal of Social and Personal Relationships*, 19(4), 463–481.

Sprecher, S., Treger, S., Hilaire, N. et al. (2013). You validate me, you like me, you're fun, you expand me: "I'm yours!" *Current Research in Social Psychology*, 21(3), 22–34.

Sprecher, S., Zimmerman, C., & Abrahams, E. M. (2010). Choosing compassionate strategies to end a relationship: Effects of compassionate love for partner and the reason for the breakup. *Social Psychology*, 41(2), 66–75.

Sripada, C. (2022). Whether implicit attitudes exist is one question, and whether we can measure individual differences effectively is another. *Wiley Interdisciplinary Reviews: Cognitive Science*. Advance online publication.

Sroufe, L. A., & Waters, E. (1977). Attachment as an organizational construct. *Child Development*, 48(4), 1184–1199.

Stack, S., & Eshleman, J. (1998). Marital status and happiness: A 17-nation study. *Journal of Marriage and Family*, 60, 527–536.

Stammwitz, M., & Wessler, J. (2021). A public context with higher minority stress for LGBTQ* couples decreases the enjoyment of public displays of affection. *PLOS One*, 16(11), e0259102.

Stander, V. A., Hsiung, P. C., & MacDermid, S. (2001). The relationship of attributions to marital distress: A comparison of mainland Chinese and U.S. couples. *Journal of Family Psychology*, 15(1), 124–134.

Stanley, S. M., Bradbury, T. N., & Markman, H. J. (2000). Structural flaws in the bridge from basic research on marriage to interventions for couples. *Journal of Marriage and Family*, 62(1), 256–264.

Stanley, S. M., Carlson, R. G., Rhoades, G. K. et al. (2020). Best practices in relationship education focused on intimate relationships. *Family Relations*, 69(3), 497–519.

Stanley, S. M., & Markman, H. J. (1992). Assessing commitment in personal relationships. *Journal of Marriage and the Family*, 54(3), 595–608.

Stanley, S. M., Markman, H. J., & Blumberg, S. L. (1997). The speaker/listener technique. *Family Journal*, 5(1), 82–83.

Stanley, S. M., Markman, H. J., & Whitton, S. W. (2002). Communication, conflict, and commitment: Insights on the foundations of relationship success from a national survey. *Family Process*, 41(4), 659–675.

Stanley, S. M., Rhoades, G. K., Loew, B. A. et al. (2014). A randomized controlled trial of relationship education in the U.S. army: 2-year outcomes. *Family Relations*, 63(4), 482–495.

Stanley, S. M., Rhoades, G. K., & Markman, H. J. (2006). Sliding versus deciding: Inertia and the premarital cohabitation effect. *Family Relations*, 55(4), 499–509.

Starks, T. J., & Parsons, J. T. (2014). Adult attachment among partnered gay men: Patterns and associations with sexual relationship quality. *Archives of Sexual Behavior*, 43(1), 107–117.

Starr, L. R., & Davila, J. (2015). Social anxiety and romantic relationships. In K. Ranta, A. M. La Greca, L.-J. Garcia-Lopez, & M. Marttunen (Eds.), *Social anxiety and phobia in adolescents: Development, manifestation and intervention strategies* (pp. 183–199). Springer International Publishing.

Statistic Brain Research Institute, publishing as Statistic Brain. (2018). *Arranged / Forced Marriage Statistics – Statistic Brain*. www.statisticbrain.com/arranged-marriage-statistics/

Stavrova, O., & Ehlebracht, D. (2015). A longitudinal analysis of romantic relationship formation: The effect of prosocial behavior. *Social Psychological and Personality Science*, 6(5), 521–527.

Stegen, H., Switsers, L., & De Donder, L. (2020). Life stories of voluntarily childless older people: A retrospective view on their reasons and experiences. *Journal of Family Issues*, 42(7), 1536–1558.

Stein, J. Mongeau, P., Posteher, K., & Veluscek, A. (2019). Netflix and chill? Exploring and refining differing motivations in friends with benefits relationships. *Canadian Journal of Human Sexuality*, 28(3), 317–327.

Stel, M., & Van Knippenberg, A. (2008). The role of facial mimicry in the recognition of affect. *Psychological Science*, 19(10), 984–985.

Stephenson, K. R., & Meston, C. M. (2015). The conditional importance of sex: Exploring the association between sexual well-being and life satisfaction. *Journal of Sex and Marital Therapy*, 41(1), 25–38.

Sternberg, R. J. (1986). A triangular theory of love. *Psychological Review*, 93(2), 119–135.

Sternberg, R. J. (1988). Triangulating love. In R. J. Sternberg & M. L. Barnes (Eds.), *The psychology of love* (pp. 119–138). Yale University Press.

Stewart-Williams, S., Butler, C. A., & Thomas, A. G. (2017). Sexual history and present attractiveness: People want a mate with a bit of a past, but not too much. *Journal of Sex Research*, 54(9), 1097–1105.

Stieger, S., & Swami, V. (2015). Time to let go? No automatic aesthetic preference for the golden ratio in art pictures. *Psychology of Aesthetics, Creativity, and the Arts*, 9(1), 91–100.

Stinson, D. A., Cameron, J. J., & Hoplock, L. B. (2022). The friends-to-lovers pathway to romance: Prevalent, preferred, and overlooked by science. *Social Psychological and Personality Science, 13*(2), 562–571.

Stratmoen, E., Greer, M. M., Martens, A. L. et al. (2018). What, I'm not good enough for you? Individual differences in masculine honor beliefs and the endorsement of aggressive responses to romantic rejection. *Personality and Individual Differences, 123,* 151–162.

Stratmoen, E., Rivera, E. D., & Saucier, D. A. (2020). "Sorry, I already have a boyfriend": Masculine honor beliefs and perceptions of women's use of deceptive rejection behaviors to avert unwanted romantic advances. *Journal of Social and Personal Relationships, 37*(2), 467–490.

Stritzke, W. G. K., Nguyen, A., & Durkin, K. (2004). Shyness and computer-mediated communication: A self-presentational theory perspective. *Media Psychology, 6*(1), 1–22.

Strizzi, J. M., Sander, S., Ciprić, A. et al. (2020). I had not seen Star Wars and other motives for divorce in Denmark. *Journal of Sex & Marital Therapy, 46*(1), 57–66.

Strohm, C. Q., Seltzer, J. A., Cochran, S. D. et al. (2009). "Living apart together" relationships in the United States. *Demographic Research, 21,* 177–214.

Strunz, S., Schermuck, C., Ballerstein, S. et al. (2017). Romantic relationships and relationship satisfaction among adults with Asperger Syndrome and high-functioning Autism. *Journal of Clinical Psychology, 73*(1), 113–125.

Sullivan, K. T., & Bradbury, T. N. (1997). Are premarital prevention programs reaching couples at risk for marital dysfunction? *Journal of Consulting and Clinical Psychology, 65*(1), 24–30.

Sullivan, K. T., Pasch, L. A., Johnson, M. D. et al. (2010). Social support, problem solving, and the longitudinal course of newlywed marriage. *Journal of Personality and Social Psychology, 98*(4), 631–644.

Sümer, N., & Cozzarelli, C. (2004). The impact of adult attachment on partner and self-attributions and relationship quality. *Personal Relationships, 11*(3), 355–371.

Sun, H., Gong, T. T., Jiang, Y. T. et al. (2019). Global, regional, and national prevalence and disability-adjusted life-years for infertility in 195 countries and territories, 1990–2017: Results from a global burden of disease study, 2017. *Aging, 11*(23), 10952–10991.

Sundie, J. M., Kenrick, D. T., Griskevicius, V. et al. (2011). Peacocks, porsches, and thorstein veblen: Conspicuous consumption as a sexual signaling system. *Journal of Personality and Social Psychology, 100*(4), 664–680.

Sunnafrank, M. (1986). Predicted outcome value during initial interactions a reformulation of uncertainty reduction theory. *Human Communication Research, 13*(1), 3–33.

Sunnafrank, M. (1988). Predicted outcome value in initial conversations. *Communication Research Reports, 5*(2), 169–172.

Sunnafrank, M. (1990). Predicted outcome value and uncertainty reduction theories: A test of competing perspectives. *Human Communication Research, 17*(1), 76–103.

Surijah, E. A., Prasetyaningsih, N. M. M., & Supriyadi, S. (2021). Popular psychology versus scientific evidence: Love languages' factor structure and connection to marital satisfaction. *Psympathic: Jurnal Ilmiah Psikologi, 7*(2), 155–168.

Surkalim, D. L., Luo, M., Eres, R. et al. (2022). The prevalence of loneliness across 113 countries: Systematic review and meta-analysis. *British Medical Journal, 376,* e067068.

Surra, C. A. (1985). Courtship types: Variations in interdependence between partners and social networks. *Journal of Personality and Social Psychology, 49*(2), 357–375.

Surra, C. A., & Longstreth, M. (1990). Similarity of outcomes, interdependence, and conflict in dating relationships. *Journal of Personality and Social Psychology, 59*(3), 501–516.

Swami, V., Furnham, A., Chamorro-Premuzic, T. et al. (2010). More than just skin deep? Personality information influences men's ratings of the attractiveness of women's body sizes. *Journal of Social Psychology, 150*(6), 628–647.

Swann, W. B. (2011). Self-verification theory. In P. A. M. Van Lange, A. W. Kruglanski, & E. T. Higgins (Eds.), *Handbook of theories of social psychology* (Vol. 2, pp. 23–42). Sage Publications.

Swann, W. B., Bosson, J. K., & Pelham, B. W. (2002). Different partners, different selves: Strategic verification of circumscribed identities. *Personality and Social Psychology Bulletin, 28*(9), 1215–1228.

Swann, W. B., De La Ronde, C., & Hixon, J. G. (1994). Authenticity and positivity strivings in marriage and courtship. *Journal of Personality and Social Psychology, 66*(5), 857–869.

Swann, W. B., Wenzlaff, R. M., Krull, D. S. et al. (1992). Allure of negative feedback: Self-verification strivings among depressed persons. *Journal of Abnormal Psychology, 101*(2), 293–306.

Swann, W. B., Wenzlaff, R. M., & Tafarodi, R. W. (1992). Depression and the search for negative evaluations: More evidence of the role of self-verification strivings. *Journal of Abnormal Psychology, 101*(2), 314–317.

Sydsjö, G., Ekholm, K., Wadsby, M. et al. (2005). Relationships in couples after failed IVF treatment: A prospective follow-up study. *Human Reproduction, 20*(7), 1952–1957.

Symoens, S., Colman, E., & Bracke, P. (2014). Divorce, conflict, and mental health: How the quality of intimate relationships is linked to post-divorce well-being. *Journal of Applied Social Psychology, 44*(3), 220–233.

Szepsenwol, O., Griskevicius, V., Simpson, J. A. et al. (2017). The effect of predictable early childhood environments on sociosexuality in early adulthood. *Evolutionary Behavioral Sciences, 11*(2), 131–145.

Tadros, E., Presley, S., & Gomez, E. (2022). "Not for the weak": The lived experience of women in romantic relationships with incarcerated individuals. *Crime and Delinquency, 68* (12), 2274–2297.

Takahashi, K., Mizuno, K., Sasaki, A. T. et al. (2015). Imaging the passionate stage of romantic love by dopamine dynamics. *Frontiers in Human Neuroscience, 9*, 191.

Tan, K., Agnew, C. R., VanderDrift, L. E. et al. (2014). Committed to us: Predicting relationship closeness following nonmarital romantic relationship breakup. *Journal of Social and Personal Relationships, 32*(4), 456–471.

Tang, N., Bensman, L., & Hatfield, E. (2012). The impact of culture and gender on sexual motives: Differences between Chinese and North Americans. *International Journal of Intercultural Relations, 36*(2), 286–294.

Tashakkori, A., Teddlie, C., & Sines, M. C. (2012). Utilizing mixed methods in psychological research. In J. A. Schinka, W. F. Velicer, & I. B. Weiner (Eds.), *Handbook of psychology*, Vol. 2: *Research methods in psychology* (2nd ed., pp. 428–450). John Wiley & Sons.

Tashiro, T., & Frazier, P. (2003). "I'll never be in a relationship like that again": Personal growth following romantic relationship breakups. *Personal Relationships, 10*(1), 113–128.

Tashiro, T., Frazier, P., & Berman, M. (2013). Stress-related growth following divorce and relationship dissolution. In M. A. Fine & J. H. Harvey (Eds.), *Handbook of divorce and relationship dissolution* (pp. 361–384). Lawrence Erlbaum.

Taylor, S. E. (1991). Asymmetrical effects of positive and negative events: The mobilization-minimization hypothesis. *Psychological Bulletin, 110*(1), 67–85.

Taylor, S. E. (2012). Social support: A review. In H. S. Friedman (Ed.), *The Oxford handbook of health psychology* (pp. 189–214). Oxford University Press.

Taylor, S. E., Seeman, T. E., Eisenberger, N. I. et al. (2010). Effects of a supportive or unsuportive audience on biological and psychological responses to stress. *Journal of Personality and Social Psychology, 98*(1), 47–56.

Taylor, S. E., Sherman, D. K., Kim, H. S. et al. (2004). Culture and social support: Who seeks it and why? *Journal of Personality and Social Psychology, 87*(3), 354–362.

Taylor, S., & Welch, W. (2007). Cultural differences in the impact of social support on psychological and biological stress responses. *Psychological Science, 18*(9), 831–838.

Teachman, J. (2003). Premarital sex, premarital cohabitation, and the risk of subsequent marital dissolution among women. *Journal of Marriage and Family, 65*(2), 444–455.

Tedeschi, R. G., Shakespeare-Finch, J., Taku, K. et al. (2018). *Posttraumatic growth*. Routledge.

Tennov, D. (1978). *Love and limerence: The experience of being in love*. New Scarborough House.

ter Kuile, H., van der Lippe, T., & Kluwer, E. S. (2021). Relational processes as predictors of relationship satisfaction trajectories across the transition to parenthood. *Family Relations, 70*(4), 1238–1252.

Testa, M., & Hone, L. S. E. (2019). Sociosexuality predicts drinking frequency among first-year college women. *Psychology of Addictive Behaviors, 33*(7), 644–648.

Thai, S., Lockwood, P., & Boksh, R. J. (2020). Committed to succeed: Commitment determines reactions to upward relationship comparisons. *Personal Relationships, 27*(2), 303–335.

The Knot Research & Insights Team. (2021, February 15). *The Knot 2021 real weddings study*. The Knot. www .theknot.com/content/wedding-data-insights/real-wed dings-study

Theiss, J. A., & Nagy, M. E. (2012). A cross-cultural test of the relational turbulence model: Relationship characteristics that predict turmoil and topic avoidance for Koreans and Americans. *Journal of Social and Personal Relationships, 29*(4), 545–565.

Thibaut, J., & Kelley, H. H. (1959). *The social psychology of groups*. John Wiley & Sons.

Thiel, K. J., & Dretsch, M. N. (2011). The basics of the stress response: A historical context and introduction. In C. D. Conrad (Ed.), *The handbook of stress: Neuropsychological effects on the brain* (pp. 3–28). Blackwell Publishing Ltd.

Thomas, A. G., Jonason, P. K., Blackburn, J. D. et al. (2020). Mate preference priorities in the East and West: A cross-cultural test of the mate preference priority model. *Journal of Personality, 88*(3), 606–620.

Thompson, A. E., & Byers, E. S. (2021). An experimental investigation of variations in judgments of hypothetical males and females initiating mixed-gender threesomes: An application of sexual script theory. *Archives of Sexual Behavior, 50*(3), 1129–1142.

Thorne, S. R., Hegarty, P., & Hepper, E. G. (2019). Equality in theory: From a heteronormative to an inclusive psychology of romantic love. *Theory & Psychology, 29*(2), 240–257.

Thornhill, R., & Gangestad, S. W. (1999). Facial attractiveness. *Trends in Cognitive Sciences, 3*(12), 452–460.

Thornhill, R., & Møller, A. P. (1997). Developmental stability, disease and medicine. *Biological Reviews, 72*(4), 497–548.

Thorpe, S., & Kuperberg, A. (2021). Social motivations for college hookups. *Sexuality and Culture, 25*(2), 623–645.

Thorsen, M. L. (2019). Shifting influences of pregnancy on union formation across age and union stability across cohabitation duration. *Journal of Family Issues, 40*(2), 190–214.

Tickle-Degnen, L., & Rosenthal, R. (1990). The nature of rapport and its nonverbal correlates. *Psychological Inquiry, 1*(4), 285–293.

Tidwell, L. C., & Walther, J. B. (2002). Computer-mediated communication effects on disclosure, impressions, and interpersonal evaluations: Getting to know one another a bit at a time. *Human Communication Research, 28*(3), 317–348.

Tidwell, N. D., Eastwick, P. W., & Finkel, E. J. (2013). Perceived, not actual, similarity predicts initial attraction in a live romantic context: Evidence from the speed-dating paradigm. *Personal Relationships, 20*(2), 199–215.

Till, B., Tran, U. S., & Niederkrotenthaler, T. (2017). Relationship satisfaction and risk factors for suicide. *Crisis, 38*(1), 7–16.

TimesUpNow.org. (2022). https://timesupnow.org/

Timmermans, E., Hermans, A.-M., & Opree, S. J. (2020). Gone with the wind: Exploring mobile daters' ghosting experiences. *Journal of Social and Personal Relationships, 38*(2), 783–801.

Timmons, A. C., Baucom, B. R., Han, S. C. et al. (2017). New frontiers in ambulatory assessment: Big data methods for capturing couples' emotions, vocalizations, and physiology in daily life. *Social Psychological and Personality Science, 8*(5), 552–563.

Tissera, H., Kerr, L. G., Carlson, E. N. et al. (2021). Social anxiety and liking: Towards understanding the role of metaperceptions in first impressions. *Journal of Personality and Social Psychology, 121*(4), 948–968.

Tlalka, S. (2018, December 11). Meditation is the fastest growing health trend in America. *Mindful.* www.mindful.org/meditation-is-the-fastest-growing-health-trend-in-america/

Toma, C. L., Hancock, J. T., & Ellison, N. B. (2008). Separating fact from fiction: An examination of deceptive self-presentation in online dating profiles. *Personality and Social Psychology Bulletin, 34*(8), 1023–1036.

Tomlinson, J. M., Aron, A., Carmichael, C. L. et al. (2014). The costs of being put on a pedestal: Effects of feeling over-idealized. *Journal of Social and Personal Relationships, 31*(3), 384–409.

Tomlinson, J. M., Aron, A., & Hatfield, E. (2018). Romantic love. In A. L. Vangelisti & D. Perlman (Eds.), *Personal relationships* (2nd ed., pp. 407–421). Cambridge University Press.

Tomlinson, J. M., Feeney, B. C., & Van Vleet, M. (2015). A longitudinal investigation of relational catalyst support of goal strivings. *Journal of Positive Psychology, 11*, 246–257.

Tomlinson, J. M., Hughes, E. K., Lewandowski, G. W. et al. (2019). Do shared self-expanding activities have to be physically arousing? *Journal of Social and Personal Relationships, 36*(9), 2781–2801.

Tonelli, L. A., Pregulman, M., & Markman, H. J. (2016). The Prevention and Relationship Education Program (PREP) for individuals and couples. In J. J. Ponzetti (Ed.), *Evidence-based approaches to relationship and marriage education* (pp. 180–196). Routledge.

Tong, S. T., & Walther, J. B. (2011). Just say "no thanks": Romantic rejection in computer-mediated communication. *Journal of Social and Personal Relationships, 28*(4), 488–506.

Tosi, M., & van den Broek, T. (2020). Gray divorce and mental health in the United Kingdom. *Social Science and Medicine, 256*, 113030.

Totenhagen, C. J., Randall, A. K., Cooper, A. N. et al. (2017). Stress spillover and crossover in same-sex couples: Concurrent and lagged daily effects. *Journal of GLBT Family Studies, 13*(3), 236–256.

Tóth-Király, I., Vallerand, R. J., Bőthe, B. et al. (2019). Examining sexual motivation profiles and their correlates using latent profile analysis. *Personality and Individual Differences, 146*, 76–86.

Townes, A., Thorpe, S., Parmer, T. et al. (2021). Partnered sexual behaviors, pleasure, and orgasms at last sexual encounter: Findings from a US probability sample of black women ages 18 to 92 years. *Journal of Sex and Marital Therapy, 47*(4), 353–367.

Townsend, J. M., Jonason, P. K., & Wasserman, T. H. (2020). Associations between motives for casual sex, depression, self-esteem, and sexual victimization. *Archives of Sexual Behavior, 49*(4), 1189–1197.

Townsend, J. M., & Wasserman, T. H. (2011). Sexual hookups among college students: Sex differences in emotional reactions. *Archives of Sexual Behavior, 40*(6), 1173–1181.

Tracy, J. L., Shaver, P. R., Albino, A. W. et al. (2003). Attachment styles and adolescent sexuality. In P. Florsheim (Ed.), *Adolescent romantic relations and sexual behavior: Theory, research, and practical implications* (pp. 137–159). Psychology Press.

Trail, T. E., & Karney, B. R. (2012). What's (not) wrong with low-income marriages. *Journal of Marriage and Family, 74*(3), 413–427.

Tran, P., Judge, M., & Kashima, Y. (2019). Commitment in relationships: An updated meta-analysis of the Investment Model. *Personal Relationships, 26*(1), 158–180.

Trask, S. L., Horstman, H. K., & Hesse, C. (2020). Deceptive affection across relational contexts: A group comparison of romantic relationships, cross-sex friendships, and friends with benefits relationships. *Communication Research, 47*(4), 623–643.

Trillingsgaard, T., Baucom, K. J. W., & Heyman, R. E. (2014). Predictors of change in relationship satisfaction during the transition to parenthood. *Family Relations, 63*(5), 667–679.

Trillingsgaard, T., Fentz, H. N., Hawrilenko, M. et al. (2016). A randomized controlled trial of the Marriage Checkup adapted for private practice. *Journal of Consulting and Clinical Psychology, 84*(12), 1145–1152.

Trinke, S. J., & Bartholomew, K. (1997). Hierarchies of attachment relationships in young adulthood. *Journal of Social and Personal Relationships, 14*(5), 603–625.

Trivers, R. L. (1972). Parental investment and sexual selection. In B. Campbell (Ed.), *Sexual selection and the descent of man 1871–1971* (pp. 136–179). Aldine Publishing Company.

Trivers, R. L. (2017). Parental investment and sexual selection. In B. G. Campbell (Ed.), *Sexual selection and the descent of man: The Darwinian pivot* (pp. 136–179). Routledge.

Troisi, J. D., & Gabriel, S. (2011). Chicken soup really is good for the soul: "Comfort food" fulfills the need to belong. *Psychological Science, 22*(6), 747–753.

Trujillo, L. T., Jankowitsch, J. M., & Langlois, J. H. (2014). Beauty is in the ease of the beholding: A neurophysiological test of the averageness theory of facial attractiveness. *Cognitive, Affective and Behavioral Neuroscience, 14*(3), 1061–1076.

Tsai, J., Levenson, R., & McCoy, K. (2006). Cultural and temperamental variation in emotional response. *Emotion, 6*(3), 484–497.

Tsang, J., Mccullough, M. E., & Fincham, F. D. (2006). The longitudinal association between forgiveness and relationship closeness and commitment. *Journal of Social and Clinical Psychology, 25*(4), 448–472.

Tsapelas, I., Beckes, L., & Aron, A. (2020). Manipulation of self-expansion alters responses to attractive alternative partners. *Frontiers in Psychology, 11*, 938.

Tucker, J. (2016, March 9). Does social science have a replication crisis? *The Washington Post.* www.washingtonpost.com/news/monkey-cage/wp/2016/03/09/does-social-science-have-a-replication-crisis/

Turner, A. I., Smyth, N., Hall, S. J. et al. (2020). Psychological stress reactivity and future health and disease outcomes: A systematic review of prospective evidence. *Psychoneuroendocrinology, 114*, 104599.

Twardosz, S., Schwartz, S., Fox, J. et al. (1979). Development and evaluation of a system to measure affectionate behavior. *Behavioral Assessment, 1*, 177–190.

Twenge, J. (2017). *Igen: Why today's super-connected kids are growing up less rebellious, more tolerant, less happy – and completely unprepared for adulthood – and what that means for the rest of us.* Atria Books.

Twenge, J. M. (2020). Possible reasons US adults are not having sex as much as they used to. *JAMA Network Open, 3*(6), e203889.

Twenge, J. M., Baumeister, R. F., Tice, D. M., & Stucke, T. S. (2001). If you can't join them, beat them: Effects of social exclusion on aggressive behavior. *Journal of Personality and Social Psychology, 81*(6), 1058–1069.

Twenge, J. M., & Blake, A. B. (2021). Increased support for same-sex marriage in the US: Disentangling age, period, and cohort effects. *Journal of Homosexuality, 68*(11), 1774–1884.

Twenge, J. M., Campbell, W. K., & Foster, C. A. (2003). Parenthood and marital satisfaction: A meta-analytic review. *Journal of Marriage and Family, 65*(3), 574–583.

Twenge, J. M., Sherman, R. A., & Wells, B. E. (2015). Changes in American adults' sexual behavior and attitudes, 1972–2012. *Archives of Sexual Behavior, 44*(8), 2273–2285.

Twenge, J. M., Sherman, R. A., & Wells, B. E. (2016). Changes in American adults' reported same-sex sexual experiences and attitudes, 1973–2014. *Archives of Sexual Behavior, 45*(7), 1713–1730.

Twenge, J. M., Spitzberg, B. H., & Campbell, W. K. (2019). Less in-person social interaction with peers among U.S. adolescents in the 21st century and links to loneliness. *Journal of Social and Personal Relationships, 36*(6), 1892–1913.

Uchino, B. N. (2009a). Understanding the links between social support and physical health. *Perspectives on Psychological Science, 4*(3), 236–255.

Uchino, B. N. (2009b). What a lifespan approach might tell us about why distinct measures of social support have differential links to physical health. *Journal of Social and Personal Relationships, 26*(1), 53–62.

Uchino, B. N., & Garvey, T. S. (1997). The availability of social support reduces cardiovascular reactivity to acute psychological stress. *Journal of Behavioral Medicine, 20*, 15–27.

Ueda, P., Mercer, C. H., Ghaznavi, C. et al. (2020). Trends in frequency of sexual activity and number of sexual partners among adults aged 18 to 44 years in the US, 2000–2018. *JAMA Network Open, 3*(6), e203833.

Ueffing, P., Dasgupta, A., & Kantorová, V. (2020). Sexual activity by marital status and age: A comparative perspective. *Journal of Biosocial Science, 52*(6), 860–884.

Uhlenberg, P., & Myers, M. (1981). Divorce and the elderly. *The Gerontologist, 21*(3), 276–282.

Umberson, D., Williams, K., Powers, D. A. et al. (2006). You make me sick: Marital quality and health over the life course. *Journal of Health and Social Behavior, 47*(1), 1–16.

Umemura, T., Lacinová, L., Kotrčová, K., & Fraley, R. C. (2018). Similarities and differences regarding changes in attachment preferences and attachment styles in relation to romantic relationship length: longitudinal and concurrent analyses. *Attachment & Human Development, 20*(2), 135–159.

Underwood, L. G. (2002). The human experience of compassionate love: Conceptual mapping and data from selected studies. In S. G. Post, L. G. Underwood, J. P. Schloss, & W. B. Hurlbut (Eds.), *Altruism and altruistic love: Science, philosophy, and religion in dialogue* (pp. 72–88). Oxford University Press.

Underwood, L. G. (2009). Compassionate love: A framework for research. In B. Fehr, S. Sprecher, & L. G. Underwood (Eds.), *The science of compassionate love: Theory, research, and applications* (pp. 3–25). Wiley Blackwell.

UNICEF. (1997). *Children at risk in Central and Eastern Europe: Perils and promises – a summary.* Regional monitoring report No 4. United Nations Children's Fund International Child Development Centre. www.unicef-irc.org/publications/pdf/monee4sume.pdf

US Census Bureau. (2021). *American community survey data.* Retrieved from www.census.gov/programs-surveys/acs/data.html

US Congress Joint Economic Committee. (2022, March 4). *Building a happy home: Marriage education as a tool to strengthen families.* www.jec.senate.gov/public/index.cfm/republicans/2022/3/building-a-happy-home-marriage-education-as-a-tool-to-strengthen-families

Valentine, K. A., Li, N. P., Meltzer, A. L. et al. (2020). Mate preferences for warmth-trustworthiness predict romantic attraction in the early stages of mate selection and satisfaction in ongoing relationships. *Personality and Social Psychology Bulletin, 46*(2), 298–311.

van Anders, S. M., Herbenick, D., Brotto, L. A. et al. (2021). The heteronormativity theory of low sexual desire in women partnered with men. *Archives of Sexual Behavior, 51*, 391–415.

Van Assche, L., Luyten, P., Bruffaerts, R. et al. (2013). Attachment in old age: Theoretical assumptions, empirical findings and implications for clinical practice. *Clinical Psychology Review, 33*(1), 67–81.

van de Vliert, E., & Euwema, M. C. (1994). Agreeableness and activeness as components of conflict behaviors. *Journal of Personality and Social Psychology, 66*(4), 674–687.

van der Meij, L., Buunk, A. P., & Salvador, A. (2010). Contact with attractive women affects the release of cortisol in men. *Hormones and Behavior, 58*(3), 501–505.

van der Meij, L., Demetriou, A., Tulin, M. et al. (2019). Hormones in speed-dating: The role of testosterone and cortisol in attraction. *Hormones and Behavior, 116*, 104555.

Van Gasse, D., & Mortelmans, D. (2020). With or without you – starting single-parent families: A qualitative study on how single parents by choice reorganise their lives to facilitate single parenthood from a life course perspective. *Journal of Family Issues, 41*(11), 2223–2248.

Van IJzendoorn, M. H., & Bakermans-Kranenburg, M. J. (2010). Invariance of adult attachment across gender, age, culture, and socioeconomic status? *Journal of Social and Personal Relationships, 27*(2), 200–208.

Van Ijzendoorn, M. H., & De Wolff, M. S. (1997). In search of the absent father – meta-analyses of infant–father attachment: A rejoinder to our discussants. *Child Development, 68*(4), 604–609.

Van Lange, P. A. M., & Balliet, D. (2015). Interdependence theory. In M. Mikulincer, P. R. Shaver, J. A. Simpson, & J. F. Dovidio (Eds.), *APA handbook of personality and social psychology*, Volume 3: *Interpersonal relations* (pp. 65–92). American Psychological Association.

Van Lange, P. A. M., & Rusbult, C. E. (1995). My relationship is better than – and not as bad as – yours is: The perception of superiority in close relationships. *Personality and Social Psychology Bulletin, 21*(1), 32–44.

Van Lange, P. A. M., & Rusbult, C. E. (2012). Interdependence theory. In P. A. M. Van Lange, A. W. Kruglanski, & E. T. Higgins (Eds.), *Handbook of theories of social psychology* (pp. 251–272). Sage Publications.

Van Lange, P. A. M., Rusbult, C. E., Drigotas, S. M. et al. (1997). Willingness to sacrifice in close relationships. *Journal of Personality and Social Psychology, 72*(6), 1373–1395.

Van Laningham, J., Johnson, D. R., & Amato, P. R. (2001). Marital happiness, marital duration, and the U-shaped curve: Evidence from a five-wave panel study. *Social Forces, 79*(4), 1313–1341.

Van Orden, K. A., Witte, T. K., Cukrowicz, K. C. et al. (2010). The interpersonal theory of suicide. *Psychological Review, 117*(2), 575–600.

Van Raalte, L. J., & Floyd, K. (2022). Examining the moderating influence of relationship satisfaction on affection and trust, closeness, stress, and depression. *Journal of Family Communication, 22*(1), 18–32.

Van Raalte, L. J., Floyd, K., Kloeber, D. et al. (2021). Exploring the associations between unwanted affection, stress, and anxiety. *Journal of Social and Personal Relationships, 38*(2), 524–543.

Van Raalte, L. J., Floyd, K., & Mongeau, P. A. (2021). The effects of cuddling on relational quality for married couples: A longitudinal investigation. *Western Journal of Communication*, *85*(1), 61–82.

van Scheppingen, M. A., & Leopold, T. (2020). Trajectories of life satisfaction before, upon, and after divorce: Evidence from a new matching approach. *Journal of Personality and Social Psychology*, *119*(6), 1444–1458.

Van Vleet, M., & Feeney, B. C. (2015a). Play behavior and playfulness in adulthood. *Social and Personality Psychology Compass*, *9*(11), 630–643.

Van Vleet, M., & Feeney, B. C. (2015b). Young at heart: A perspective for advancing research on play in adulthood. *Perspectives on Psychological Science*, *10*(5), 639–645.

Van Widenfelt, B., Hosman, C., Schaap, C. et al. (1996). The prevention of relationship distress for couples at risk: A controlled evaluation with nine-month and two-year follow-ups. *Family Relations*, *45*(2), 156–165.

Vandenbroele, J., Van Kerckhove, A., & Geuens, M. (2020). If you work it, flaunt it: Conspicuous displays of exercise efforts increase mate value. *Journal of Business Research*, *120*, 586–598.

VanderDrift, L., Agnew, C. R., & Wilson, J. E. (2009). Nonmarital romantic relationship commitment and leave behavior: The mediating role of dissolution consideration. *Personality and Social Psychology Bulletin*, *35*(9), 1220–1232.

Vaquera, E., & Kao, G. (2005). Private and public displays of affection among interracial and intra-racial adolescent couples. *Social Science Quarterly*, *86*(2), 484–508.

Venaglia, R. B., & Lemay, E. P. (2019). Accurate and biased perceptions of partner's conflict behaviors shape emotional experience. *Journal of Social and Personal Relationships*, *36*(10), 3293–3312.

Verhofstadt, L. L., Buysse, A., Ickes, W. et al. (2008). Support provision in marriage: The role of emotional similarity and empathic accuracy. *Emotion*, *8*(6), 792–802.

Verhofstadt, L. L., Ickes, W., & Buysse, A. (2010). "I know what you need right now": Empathic accuracy and support provision in marriage. In K. Sullivan & J. Davila (Eds.), *Support processes in intimate relationships* (pp. 71–88). Oxford University Press.

Vicaria, I. M., & Dickens, L. (2016). Meta-analyses of the intra- and interpersonal outcomes of interpersonal coordination. *Journal of Nonverbal Behavior*, *40*(4), 335–361.

Visserman, M. L., & Karremans, J. C. (2014). Romantic relationship status biases the processing of an attractive alternative's behavior. *Personal Relationships*, *21*(2), 324–334.

Visserman, M. L., Righetti, F., Muise, A. et al. (2021). Taking stock of reality: Biased perceptions of the costs of romantic partners' sacrifices. *Social Psychological and Personality Science*, *12*(1), 54–62.

Vollmann, M., Sprang, S., & Van Den Brink, F. (2019). Adult attachment and relationship satisfaction: The mediating role of gratitude toward the partner. *Journal of Social and Personal Relationships*, *36*(11–12), 3875–3886.

von Soest, T., Luhmann, M., Hansen, T. et al. (2020). Development of loneliness in midlife and old age: Its nature and correlates. *Journal of Personality and Social Psychology*, *118*(2), 388–406.

Voorpostel, M., van der Lippe, T., & Gershuny, J. (2009). Trends in free time with a partner: A transformation of intimacy? *Social Indicators Research*, *93*(1), 165–169.

Voorpostel, M., van der Lippe, T., & Gershuny, J. (2010). Spending time together: Changes over four decades in leisure time spent with a spouse. *Journal of Leisure Research*, *42*(2), 243–265.

Vormbrock, J. K., & Grossberg, J. M. (1988). Cardiovascular effects of human-pet dog interactions. *Journal of Behavioral Medicine*, *11*(5), 509–517.

Vowels, L. M., & Carnelley, K. B. (2022). Partner support and goal outcomes: A multilevel meta-analysis and a methodological critique. *European Journal of Social Psychology*, *52*, 679–694.

Vowels, L. M., Vowels, M. J., & Mark, K. P. (2022). Identifying the strongest self-report predictors of sexual satisfaction using machine learning. *Journal of Social and Personal Relationships*, *39*(5), 1191–1212.

Vowels, M. J., Mark, K. P., Vowels, L. M., & Wood, N. D. (2018). Using spectral and cross-spectral analysis to identify patterns and synchrony in couples' sexual desire. *PLOS One*, *13*(10), e0205330.

Vrangalova, Z., & Savin-Williams, R. C. (2012). Mostly heterosexual and mostly gay/lesbian: Evidence for new sexual orientation identities. *Archives of Sexual Behavior*, *41*(1), 85–101.

Wachs, K., & Cordova, J. V. (2007). Mindful relating: Exploring mindfulness and emotion repertoires in intimate relationships. *Journal of Marital and Family Therapy*, *33*(4), 464–481.

Wade, T. J., Butrie, L. K., & Hoffman, K. M. (2009). Women's direct opening lines are perceived as most effective. *Personality and Individual Differences*, *47*(2), 145–149.

Wade, T. J., & Feldman, A. (2016). Sex and the perceived effectiveness of flirtation techniques. *Human Ethology Bulletin*, *31*(2), 30–44.

Wade, T. J., & Slemp, J. (2015). How to flirt best: The perceived effectiveness of flirtation techniques. *Interpersona: An International Journal on Personal Relationships*, *9*(1), 32–43.

Wagner, B. G. (2019). Marriage, cohabitation, and sexual exclusivity: Unpacking the effect of marriage. *Social Forces*, *97*(3), 1231–1256.

Wagner, J. (2021, May 12). After years in a supporting role, Amber Sabathia is in charge. *The New York Times*. www .nytimes.com/2021/05/10/sports/baseball/amber-sabathia-agent.html

Wagner, K. (2018, August 1). Facebook and Instagram are making it easier to spend less time on Facebook and Instagram. But why? *Vox*. www.vox.com/2018/8/1/17637428/facebook-instagram-time-well-spent-screen-time

Wakeling, S., Stukas, A. A., Wright, B. J. et al. (2020). Negative feedback seeking and excessive reassurance seeking behavior and depression: A meta-analytic review. *Journal of Social and Clinical Psychology*, *39*(9), 788–823.

Wallach, M. A., & Wallach, L. (1983). *Psychology's sanction for selfishness: The error of egoism in theory and therapy*. W. H. Freeman.

Walsh, C. M., & Neff, L. A. (2020). The importance of investing in your relationship: Emotional capital and responses to partner transgressions. *Journal of Social and Personal Relationships*, *37*(2), 581–601.

Walsh, C. M., Neff, L. A., & Gleason, M. E. J. (2017). The role of emotional capital during the early years of marriage: Why everyday moments matter. *Journal of Family Psychology*, *31*(4), 513–519.

Walsh, M., Millar, M., & Westfall, R. S. (2019). Sex differences in responses to emotional and sexual infidelity in dating relationships. *Journal of Individual Differences*, *40*(2), 63–70.

Walster, E., Aronson, V., Abrahams, D. et al. (1966). Importance of physical attractiveness in dating behavior. *Journal of Personality and Social Psychology*, *4*(5), 508–516.

Walter, K. V., Conroy-Beam, D., Buss, D. M. et al. (2020). Sex differences in mate preferences across 45 countries: A large-scale replication. *Psychological Science*, *31*(4), 408–423.

Walters, B., Carter, C., Teta, B., & Estey McLoughlin, H. (Executive Producers). (1997–present). *The View* [TV series]. Lincoln Square Productions.

Wang, C. C. D. C., & Mallinckrodt, B. S. (2006). Differences between Taiwanese and U.S. cultural beliefs about ideal adult attachment. *Journal of Counseling Psychology*, *53*(2), 192–204.

Wang, Y., & Apostolou, M. (2019). Male tolerance to same-sex infidelity: A cross-cultural investigation. *Evolutionary Psychology*, *17*(2), 1474704919843892.

Wang, Y., Fu, Y., Ghazi, P. et al. (2022). Prevalence of intimate partner violence against infertile women in low-income and middle-income countries: A systematic review and meta-analysis. *The Lancet: Global Health*, *10*(6), e820–e830.

Watkins, C., Bovet, J., Fernandez, A. M. et al. (2022). Men say "I love you" before women do: Robust across several countries. *Journal of Social and Personal Relationships*, *39*(7), 2134–2153.

Watson, D., & Clark, L. A. (1984). Negative affectivity: The disposition to experience aversive emotional states. *Psychological Bulletin*, *96*(3), 465–490.

Watson, D., Wiese, D., Vaidya, J. et al. (1999). The two general activation systems of affect: Structural findings, evolutionary considerations, and psychobiological evidence. *Journal of Personality and Social Psychology*, *76*(5), 820–838.

Watson, R. J., Shahin, Y. M., & Arbeit, M. R. (2019). Hookup initiation and emotional outcomes differ across LGB young men and women. *Sexualities*, *22*(5–6), 932–950.

Watson, R. J., Snapp, S., & Wang, S. (2017). What we know and where we go from here: A review of lesbian, gay, and bisexual youth hookup literature. *Sex Roles*, *77*(11–12), 801–811.

Weber, K., Goodboy, A. K., & Cayanus, J. L. (2010). Flirting competence: An experimental study on appropriate and effective opening lines. *Communication Research Reports*, *27*(2), 184–191.

Weeden, J., & Sabini, J. (2005). Physical attractiveness and health in Western societies: A review. *Psychological Bulletin*, *131*(5), 635–653.

Weger, H., & Emmett, M. C. (2009). Romantic intent, relationship uncertainty, and relationship maintenance in young adults' cross-sex friendships. *Journal of Social and Personal Relationships*, *26*(7), 964–988.

Wegner, R., & Abbey, A. (2016). Individual differences in men's misperception of women's sexual intent: Application and extension of the confluence model. *Personality and Individual Differences*, *94*, 16–20.

Weinstock, L. M., & Whisman, M. A. (2004). The self-verification model of depression and interpersonal rejection in heterosexual dating relationships. *Journal of Social and Clinical Psychology*, *23*(2), 240–259.

Weiss, B., Lavner, J. A., & Miller, J. D. (2018). Self- and partner-reported psychopathic traits' relations with couples' communication, marital satisfaction trajectories, and divorce in a longitudinal sample. *Personality Disorders: Theory, Research, and Treatment*, *9*(3), 239–249.

Weitbrecht, E. M., & Whitton, S. W. (2017). Expected, ideal, and actual relational outcomes of emerging adults' "hook ups." *Personal Relationships*, *24*(4), 902–916.

Weitbrecht, E. M., & Whitton, S. W. (2020). College students' motivations for "hooking up": Similarities and differences in motives by gender and partner type. *Couple and Family Psychology: Research and Practice*, *9*(3), 123–143.

Wellings, K., Palmer, M. J., Machiyama, K. et al. (2019). Changes in, and factors associated with, frequency of sex in Britain: Evidence from three National Surveys of Sexual Attitudes and Lifestyles (Natsal). *British Medical Journal*, *365*, 1525.

Wells, J. L., Haase, C. M., Rothwell, E. S. et al. (2022). Positivity resonance in long-term married couples: Multimodal characteristics and consequences for health and longevity. *Journal of Personality and Social Psychology*, *123*(5), 983–1003.

Wenzel, A., & Kashdan, T. B. (2008). Emotional disturbances and the initial stages of relationship development: Processes and consequences of social anxiety and depression. In S. Sprecher, A. Wenzel, & J. Harvey (Eds.), *Handbook of relationship initiation* (pp. 425–450). Psychology Press.

Wesselmann, E. D., Grzybowski, M. R., Steakley-Freeman, D. M. et al. (2016). Social exclusion in everyday life. In P. Riva & J. Eck (Eds.), *Social exclusion: Psychological approaches to understanding and reducing its impact* (pp. 3–23). Springer International Publishing.

West, C. L., Dreeben, S. J., & Busing, K. (2021). The development of the Widowhood Resilience Scale. *Omega: Journal of Death and Dying*, *83*(4), 958–975.

West, T. V., & Kenny, D. A. (2011). The truth and bias model of judgment. *Psychological Review*, *118*(2), 357–378.

Western, B., Kling, J. R., & Weiman, D. F. (2001). The labor market consequences of incarceration. *Crime and Delinquency*, *47*(3), 410–427.

Western, B., Lopoo, L., & McLanahan, S. (2004). Incarceration and the bonds among parents in fragile families. In M. Patillo, D. Weiman, & B. Western (Eds.), *Imprisoning America: The social effects of mass incarceration* (pp. 21–45). Russel Sage Foundation.

Westrick-Payne, K. K. (2022). *Charting marriage & divorce in the U.S.: The adjusted divorce rate, 2008–2020*. Bowling Green, OH: National Center for Family & Marriage Research.

Wethington, E. (2016). Life events scale. In G. Fink (Ed.), *Stress: Concepts, cognition, emotion, and behavior* (pp. 103–108). Academic Press.

Wethington, E., & Kessler, R. C. (1986). Perceived support, received support, and adjustment to stressful life events. *Journal of Health and Social Behavior*, *27*(1), 78–89.

Wetzel, E., Grijalva, E., Robins, R. W. et al. (2020). You're still so vain: Changes in narcissism from young adulthood to middle age. *Journal of Personality and Social Psychology*, *119*(2), 479–496.

Wheeler, L., & Kim, Y. (1997). What is beautiful is culturally good: The physical attractiveness stereotype has different content in collectivistic cultures. *Personality and Social Psychology Bulletin*, *23*(8), 795–800.

Whisman, M. A., Beach, S. R. H., & Snyder, D. K. (2008). Is marital discord taxonic and can taxonic status be assessed reliably? Results from a national, representative sample of married couples. *Journal of Consulting and Clinical Psychology*, *76*(5), 745–755.

Whisman, M. A., Gordon, K. C., & Chatav, Y. (2007). Predicting sexual infidelity in a population-based sample of married individuals. *Journal of Family Psychology*, *21*(2), 320–324.

Whisman, M. A., Salinger, J. M., & Sbarra, D. A. (2022). Relationship dissolution and psychopathology. *Current Opinion in Psychology*, *43*, 199–204.

Whisman, M. A., & Snyder, D. K. (2007). Sexual infidelity in a national survey of American women: Differences in prevalence and correlates as a function of method of assessment. *Journal of Family Psychology*, *21*(2), 147–154.

Whisman, M. A., & Uebelacker, L. A. (2006). Impairment and distress associated with relationship discord in a national sample of married or cohabiting adults. *Journal of Family Psychology*, *20*(3), 369–377.

Whitchurch, E. R., Wilson, T. D., & Gilbert, D. T. (2011). "He loves me, he loves me not …": Uncertainty can increase romantic attraction. *Psychological Science*, *22*(2), 172–175.

White, K. P., Jonason, P. K., & Al-Shawaf, L. (2021). Mating decisions in the absence of physical attraction. *Adaptive Human Behavior and Physiology*, *7*, 43–53.

White, R. W. (1959). Motivation reconsidered: The concept of competence. *Psychological Review*, *66*, 297–333.

Whitton, S. W., & Buzzella, B. A. (2012). Using relationship education programs with same-sex couples: A preliminary evaluation of program utility and needed modifications. *Marriage & Family Review*, *48*(7), 667–688.

Whitton, S. W., James-Kangal, N., Rhoades, G. K. et al. (2018). Understanding couple conflict. In A. L. Vangelisti & D. Perlman (Eds.), *The Cambridge handbook of personal relationships* (pp. 297–310). Cambridge University Press.

Whitton, S. W., & Kuryluk, A. D. (2014). Associations between relationship quality and depressive symptoms in same-sex couples. *Journal of Family Psychology*, *28*(4), 571–576.

Whitton, S. W., Scott, S. B., Dyar, C. et al. (2017). Piloting relationship education for female same-sex couples: Results of a small randomized waitlist-control trial. *Journal of Family Psychology*, *31*(7), 878–888.

Whitton, S. W., Scott, S. B., & Weitbrecht, E. M. (2018). Participant perceptions of relationship education programs adapted for same-sex couples. *Journal of Couple & Relationship Therapy*, *17*(3), 181–208.

Whitton, S. W., Weitbrecht, E. M., Kuryluk, A. D. et al. (2016). A randomized waitlist-controlled trial of culturally sensitive relationship education for male same-sex couples. *Journal of Family Psychology, 30*(6), 763–768.

Whitty, M. T., & Buchanan, T. (2009). Looking for love in so many places: Characteristics of online daters and speed daters. *Interpersona: An International Journal on Personal Relationships, 3*, 63–86.

Whyte, S., Torgler, B., & Harrison, K. L. (2016). What women want in their sperm donor: A study of more than 1000 women's sperm donor selections. *Economics and Human Biology, 23*, 1–9.

Wickrama, K. A. S., & O'Neal, C. W. (2021). Midlife marital and financial stress and the progression of later-life health problems for husbands and wives. *Journal of Aging and Health, 33*(9), 685–697.

Widdowson, A. O., Jacobsen, W. C., Siennick, S. E. et al. (2020). Together despite the odds: Explaining racial and ethnic heterogeneity in union dissolution after incarceration. *Criminology, 58*(1), 129–155.

Widman, L., Noar, S. M., Choukas-Bradley, S. et al. (2014). Adolescent sexual health communication and condom use: A meta-analysis. *Health Psychology, 33*(10), 1113–1124.

Wiebe, S. A., Johnson, S. M., Lafontaine, M.-F. et al. (2017). Two-year follow-up outcomes in emotionally focused couple therapy: An investigation of relationship satisfaction and attachment trajectories. *Journal of Marital and Family Therapy, 43*(2), 227–244.

Wiener, L., Battles, H., Zadeh, S. et al. (2017). The perceived influence of childhood cancer on the parents' relationship. *Psycho-Oncology, 26*(12), 2109–2117.

Wieselquist, J., Rusbult, C. E., Foster, C. A. et al. (1999). Commitment, pro-relationship behavior, and trust in close relationships. *Journal of Personality and Social Psychology, 77*(5), 942–966.

Wight, R. G., LeBlanc, A. J., & Lee Badgett, M. V. (2013). Same-sex legal marriage and psychological well-being: Findings from the California health interview survey. *American Journal of Public Health, 103*(2), 339–346.

Wight, V. R., Raley, S. B., & Bianchi, S. M. (2008). Time for children, one's spouse and oneself among parents who work nonstandard hours. *Social Forces, 87*(1), 243–271.

Wike, R. (2014, January 14). *French more accepting of infidelity than people in other countries*. Pew Research Center. www.pewresearch.org/fact-tank/2014/01/14/french-more-accepting-of-infidelity-than-people-in-other-countries/

Wildsmith, E., Manlove, J., & Cook, E. (2018). *Dramatic increase in the proportion of births outside of marriage in the United States from 1990 to 2016*. Child Trends. www.childtrends.org/publications/dramatic-increase-in-per centage-of-births-outside-marriage-among-whites-hispan ics-and-women-with-higher-education-levels

Williams, K. D., Cheung, C. K. T., & Choi, W. (2000). Cyberostracism: Effects of being ignored over the internet. *Journal of Personality and Social Psychology, 79*(5), 748–762.

Williams, K. D., & Nida, S. A. (2022). Ostracism and social exclusion: Implications for separation, social isolation, and loss. *Current Opinion in Psychology, 47*, 101353. https://doi.org/10.1016/j.copsyc.2022.101353

Williams, S. L., Laduke, S. L., Klik, K. A. et al. (2016). A paradox of support seeking and support response among gays and lesbians. *Personal Relationships, 23*(2), 296–310.

Williamson, H. C., Altman, N., Hsueh, J. A. et al. (2016). Effects of relationship education on couple communication and satisfaction: A randomized controlled trial with low-income couples. *Journal of Consulting and Clinical Psychology, 84*(2), 156–166.

Williamson, H. C., Bornstein, J. X., Cantu, V. et al. (2022). How diverse are the samples used to study intimate relationships? A systematic review. *Journal of Social and Personal Relationships, 39*(4), 1087–1109.

Williamson, H. C., Ju, X., Bradbury, T. N. et al. (2012). Communication behavior and relationship satisfaction among American and Chinese newlywed couples. *Journal of Family Psychology, 26*(3), 308–315.

Williamson, H. C., Karney, B. R., & Bradbury, T. N. (2013). Financial strain and stressful events predict newlyweds' negative communication independent of relationship satisfaction. *Journal of Family Psychology, 27*(1), 65–75.

Williamson, H. C., Karney, B. R., & Bradbury, T. N. (2019). Barriers and facilitators of relationship help-seeking among low-income couples. *Journal of Family Psychology, 33*(2), 234–239.

Williamson, H. C., & Lavner, J. A. (2020). Trajectories of marital satisfaction in diverse newlywed couples. *Social Psychological and Personality Science, 11*(5), 597–604.

Williamson, H. C., Rogge, R. D., Cobb, R. J. et al. (2015). Risk moderates the outcome of relationship education: A randomized controlled trial. *Journal of Consulting and Clinical Psychology, 83*(3), 617–629.

Williamson, J. A., Oliger, C., Wheeler, A. et al. (2019). More social support is associated with more positive mood but excess support is associated with more negative mood. *Journal of Social and Personal Relationships, 36*(11–12), 3588–3610.

Willoughby, B. J., Carroll, J. S., & Busby, D. M. (2012). The different effects of "living together": Determining and comparing types of cohabiting couples. *Journal of Social and Personal Relationships, 29*(3), 397–419.

Willoughby, B. J., Farero, A. M., & Busby, D. M. (2014). Exploring the effects of sexual desire discrepancy among married couples. *Archives of Sexual Behavior*, *43*(3), 551–562.

Wilson, C., & Oswald, A. (2005, May). *How does marriage affect physical and psychological health? A survey of the longitudinal evidence*. Institute for the Study of Labor Discussion Papers. https://docs.iza.org/dp1619.pdf

Wilson, T. D., Centerbar, D. B., Kermer, D. A. et al. (2005). The pleasures of uncertainty: Prolonging positive moods in ways people do not anticipate. *Journal of Personality and Social Psychology*, *88*(1), 5–21.

Winczewski, L. A., Bowen, J. D., & Collins, N. L. (2016). Is empathic accuracy enough to facilitate responsive behavior in dyadic interaction? Distinguishing ability from motivation. *Psychological Science*, *27*(3), 394–404.

Winter, F., Steffan, A., Warth, M. et al. (2021). Mindfulness-based couple interventions: A systematic literature review. *Family Process*, *60*(3), 694–711.

Winterhead, H., & Simpson, J. A. (2018). Personality in close relationships. In A. L. Vangelisti & D. Perlman (Eds.), *The Cambridge handbook of personal relationships* (2nd ed., pp. 163–174). Camrbridge University Press.

Wlodarski, R., & Dunbar, R. I. M. (2013). Examining the possible functions of kissing in romantic relationships. *Archives of Sexual Behavior*, *42*(8), 1415–1423.

Wlodarski, R., & Dunbar, R. I. M. (2014). What's in a kiss? The effect of romantic kissing on mating desirability. *Evolutionary Psychology*, *12*(1), 178–199.

Wolfe, D. A., Crooks, C. V., Lee, V. et al. (2003). The effects of children's exposure to domestic violence: A meta-analysis and critique. *Clinical Child and Family Psychology Review*, *6*(3), 171–187.

Wolfinger, N. H. (2007). Does the rebound effect exist? Time to remarriage and subsequent union stability. *Journal of Divorce and Remarriage*, *46*(3–4), 9–20.

Wongsomboon, V., Burleson, M. H., & Webster, G. D. (2020). Women's orgasm and sexual satisfaction in committed sex and casual sex: Relationship between sociosexuality and sexual outcomes in different sexual contexts. *Journal of Sex Research*, *57*(3), 285–295.

Wongsomboon, V., Webster, G. D., & Burleson, M. H. (2022). It's the "why": Links between (non)autonomous sexual motives, sexual assertiveness, and women's orgasm in casual sex. *Archives of Sexual Behavior*, *51*, 621–632.

Wood, J., Desmarais, S., Burleigh, T. et al. (2018). Reasons for sex and relational outcomes in consensually nonmonogamous and monogamous relationships: A self-determination theory approach. *Journal of Social and Personal Relationships*, *35*(4), 632–654.

Wood, J. R., Milhausen, R. R., & Jeffrey, N. K. (2014). Why have sex? Reasons for having sex among lesbian, bisexual, queer, and questioning women in romantic relationships. *Canadian Journal of Human Sexuality*, *23*(2), 75–88.

Wood, W., Kressel, L., Joshi, P. D. et al. (2014). Meta-analysis of menstrual cycle effects on women's mate preferences. *Emotion Review*, *6*(3), 229–249.

Woodin, E. M. (2011). A two-dimensional approach to relationship conflict: Meta-analytic findings. *Journal of Family Psychology*, *25*(3), 325–335.

Worsley, J. D., Wheatcroft, J. M., Short, E. et al. (2017). Victims' voices: Understanding the emotional impact of cyberstalking and individuals' coping responses. *SAGE Open*, *7*(2).

Wright, A. G. C., Aslinger, E. N., Bellamy, B. et al. (2020). Daily stress and hassles. In K. L. Harkness & E. P. Hayden (Eds.), *The Oxford handbook of stress and mental health* (pp. 26–44). Oxford University Press.

Wright, B. L., & Loving, T. J. (2011). Health implications of conflict in close relationships. *Social and Personality Psychology Compass*, *5*(8), 552–562.

Wright, B. L., & Sinclair, H. C. (2012). Pulling the strings: Effects of friend and parent opinions on dating choices. *Personal Relationships*, *19*(4), 743–758.

Wright, P. J. (2011). Mass media effects on youth sexual behavior assessing the claim for causality. *Annals of the International Communication Association*, *35*(1), 343–385.

Wright, P. J., Herbenick, D., Paul, B. et al. (2021). Exploratory findings on U.S. adolescents' pornography use, dominant behavior, and sexual satisfaction. *International Journal of Sexual Health*, *33*(2), 222–228.

Wu, A. K., Marks, M. J., Young, T. M. et al. (2020). Predictors of bisexual individuals' dating decisions. *Sexuality and Culture*, *24*(3), 596–612.

Wu, H., & Brown, S. L. (2021). Union formation expectations among older adults who live apart together in the USA. *Journal of Family Issues*, *43*(10), 2577–2598.

Wu, K., Chen, C., Greenberger, E. et al. (2020). No need for pedestals: Idealization does not predict better relationships among Asians. *Personal Relationships*, *27*(2), 336–365.

Wu, P. L., & Chiou, W. Bin. (2009). More options lead to more searching and worse choices in finding partners for romantic relationships online: An experimental study. *Cyberpsychology & Behavior*, *12*(3), 315–318.

Wynne, G. (2019, September 7). Megan Rapinoe and Sue Bird's relationship timeline is actual goals. *Elite Daily*. www.elitedaily.com/p/megan-rapinoe-sue-birds-relationship-timeline-is-literally-power-couple-goals-18188374

Wyverkens, E., Dewitte, M., Deschepper, E. et al. (2018). YSEX? A replication study in different age groups. *Journal of Sexual Medicine*, *15*(4), 492–501.

Xu, X., Aron, A., Brown, L. et al. (2011). Reward and motivation systems: A brain mapping study of early-stage intense romantic love in Chinese participants. *Human Brain Mapping*, *32*(2), 249–257.

Xu, Y., Norton, S., & Rahman, Q. (2018). Early life conditions, reproductive and sexuality-related life history outcomes among human males: A systematic review and meta-analysis. *Evolution and Human Behavior*, *39*(1), 40–51.

Yampolsky, M. A., West, A. L., Zhou, B. et al. (2020). Divided together: How marginalization of intercultural relationships is associated with identity integration and relationship quality. *Social Psychological and Personality Science*, *12*(6), 887–897.

Yancey, G. (2009). Crossracial differences in the racial preferences of potential dating partners: A test of the alienation of African Americans and social dominance orientation. *Sociological Quarterly*, *50*(1), 121–143.

Yang, M.-L., & Chiou, W.-B. (2009). Looking online for the best romantic partner reduces decision quality: The moderating role of choice-making strategies. *CyberPsychology & Behavior*, *13*(2), 207–210.

Yeh, H. C., Lorenz, F. O., Wickrama, K. A. S. et al. (2006). Relationships among sexual satisfaction, marital quality, and marital instability at midlife. *Journal of Family Psychology*, *20*(2), 339–343.

Yew, R. Y., Samuel, P., Hooley, M. et al. (2021). A systematic review of romantic relationship initiation and maintenance factors in autism. *Personal Relationships*, *28*(4), 777–802.

Yost, M. R., & Zurbriggen, E. L. (2006). Gender differences in the enactment of sociosexuality: An examination of implicit social motives, sexual fantasies, coercive sexual attitudes, and aggressive sexual behavior. *Journal of Sex Research*, *43*(2), 163–173.

Young, L. J., Wang, Z., & Insel, T. R. (1998). Neuroendocrine bases of monogamy. *Trends in Neurosciences*, *21*(2), 71–75.

Yovetich, N., & Rusbult, C. (1994). Accommodative behavior in close relationships: Exploring transformation of motivation. *Journal of Experimental Social Psychology*, *30*, 138–164.

Yu, Y., Wu, D., Wang, J. M. et al. (2020). Dark personality, marital quality, and marital instability of Chinese couples: An actor–partner interdependence mediation model. *Personality and Individual Differences*, *154*, 109689.

Yule, M. A., Brotto, L. A., & Gorzalka, B. B. (2017). Sexual fantasy and masturbation among asexual individuals: An in-depth exploration. *Archives of Sexual Behavior*, *46*(1), 311–328.

Zagaria, A., Ando', A., & Zennaro, A. (2020). Psychology: A giant with feet of clay. *Integrative Psychological and Behavioral Science Psychology*, *54*, 521–562.

Zahavi, A. (1975). Mate selection: A selection for a handicap. *Journal of Theoretical Biology*, *53*(1), 205–214.

Zahn, R., Lythe, K. E., Gethin, J. A. et al. (2015). The role of self-blame and worthlessness in the psychopathology of major depressive disorder. *Journal of Affective Disorders*, *186*, 337–341.

Zaidi, A. U., & Shuraydi, M. (2002). Perceptions of arranged marriages by young Pakistani Muslim women living in a western society. *Journal of Comparative Family Studies*, *33*(4), 495–514.

Zajonc, R. B. (1968). Attitudinal effects of mere exposure. *Journal of Personality and Social Psychology Monograph Supplement*, *9*(2), 1–27.

Zajonc, R. B. (2001). Mere exposure: A gateway to the subliminal. *Current Directions in Psychological Science*, *10*(6), 224–228.

Zaki, J., Bolger, N., & Ochsner, K. (2008). It takes two: The interpersonal nature of empathic accuracy. *Psychological Science*, *19*(4), 399–404.

Zee, K. S., & Bolger, N. (2019). Visible and invisible social support: How, why, and when. *Current Directions in Psychological Science*, *28*(3), 314–320.

Zee, K. S., Cavallo, J. V., Flores, A. J. et al. (2018). Motivation moderates the effects of social support visibility. *Journal of Personality and Social Psychology*, *114*(5), 735–765.

Zeki, S. (2007). The neurobiology of love. *FEBS Letters*, *581*(14), 2575–2579.

Zeki, S., & Romaya, J. P. (2010). The brain reaction to viewing faces of opposite- and same-sex romantic partners. *PLOS One*, *5*(12), e15802.

Zell, E., Strickhouser, J. E., Sedikides, C. et al. (2020). The better-than-average effect in comparative self-evaluation: A comprehensive review and meta-analysis. *Psychological Bulletin*, *146*(2), 118–149.

Zentner, M., & Eagly, A. H. (2015). A sociocultural framework for understanding partner preferences of women and men: Integration of concepts and evidence. *European Review of Social Psychology*, *26*(1), 328–373.

Zhang, Q., Maner, J. K., Xu, Y. et al. (2017). Relational motives reduce attentional adhesion to attractive alternatives in heterosexual university students in China. *Archives of Sexual Behavior*, *46*(2), 503–511.

Zhang, Q., & Wills, M. (2016). A U.S.–Chinese comparison of affectionate communication in parent–child relationships. *Communication Research Reports*, *33*(4), 317–323.

Zilcha-Mano, S., Mikulincer, M., & Shaver, P. R. (2012). Pets as safe havens and secure bases: The moderating role of pet attachment orientations. *Journal of Research in Personality*, *46*(5), 571–580.

Zsok, F., Haucke, M., De Wit, C. Y. et al. (2017). What kind of love is love at first sight? An empirical investigation. *Personal Relationships*, *24*(4), 869–885.

INDEX

Printed in the USA
CPSIA information can be obtained
at www.ICGtesting.com
LVHW082121250823
756129LV00018B/26